VALUE CLARIFICATION *as Learning Process*

A GUIDEBOOK OF LEARNING STRATEGIES

Dedicated to Michael Kenney who has faithfully worked with these materials for a number of years and whose friendship I value

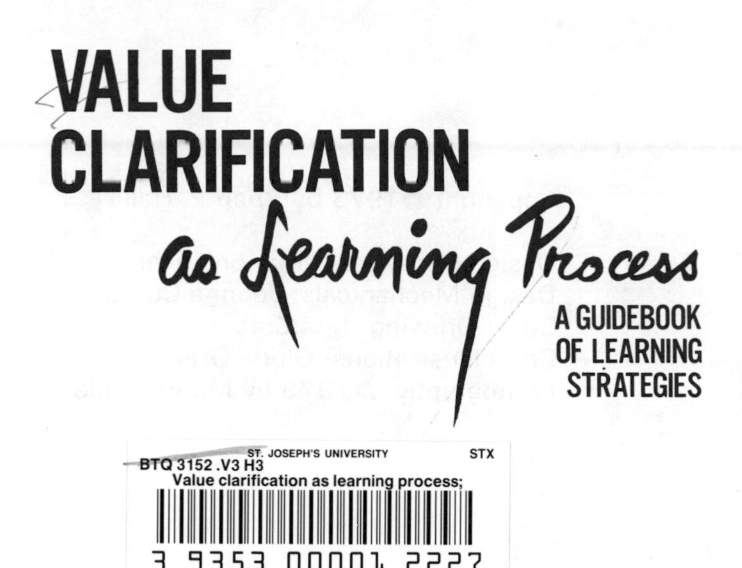

BRIAN HALL

CONSULTANT AUTHORS:
Michael J. Kenney, Maury Smith

EDUCATOR FORMATION BOOKS Director:
Richard J. Payne

PAULIST PRESS
New York, N.Y. Paramus, N.J.

Design Consultant: Marion Faller
Design Mechanicals: Joanne Cossa
Cover Drawing: Rita Corbin
Chart Illustrations: Gloria Ortiz
Photography: © 1973 by Marion Faller

Library of Congress
Catalog Card Number: 73-81108

ISBN 0-8091-1796-7

Published by Paulist Press
Editorial Office: 1865 Broadway, N.Y., N.Y. 10023
Business Office: 400 Sette Drive, Paramus, N.J. 07652

Printed and bound in the
United States of America

ACKNOWLEDGMENTS

Daniel Henninger and Nancy Esposito, "Indian Boarding Schools/Indian Jails" from *LIFE AT THE BOTTOM*, ed. by Gregory Armstrong. New York: Bantam Books. Reprinted by permission of *THE NEW REPUBLIC*, © 1969, Harrison-Blaine of New Jersey, Inc.

Editorial from *AMERICA*, February 19, 1972. Reprinted with permission. All Rights Reserved, © America Press, Inc., 106 West 56th Street, New York, N.Y., 10019.

Alfred H. Gorman. *TEACHERS AND LEARNERS: THE INTERACTIVE PROCESS OF EDUCATION*. Boston: Allyn and Bacon, 1969. Used with permission.

Warren H. Schmidt, *IS IT ALWAYS RIGHT TO BE RIGHT?* © 1970, 1971 by Wadsworth Publishing Company, Inc., Belmont, California 94002. Reprinted with permission.

Table of Contents

PART I: VALUE CLARIFICATION: INTRODUCTION 9

INTRODUCTION 10

Guidelines for the Guidebook 10
A Functional Definition of Value 11
Value-Ranking 13
Value Indicators 14
Values and Environment 15
Primary Values 16
Work and Leisure 17
Dimensions of Process 17
Psychic Effort 18
Whom the Book Is for 20
Expertise for Handling the Exercises 20
How To Use the Book 20

PART II: EXERCISES IN VALUE CLARIFICATION 23

INTRODUCTION 24

Section 1: The Nature of Value Process 29
Introduction 29
For the Student 31
For the Teacher 45
For the Professional Trainer 50

Section II: Value-Ranking 79
Introduction 79
For the Student 81
For the Teacher 84
For the Professional Trainer 86

Section III: Value Indicators 95
Introduction 95
For the Student 97
For the Teacher 101
For the Professional Trainer 105

Section IV: Values and Environment 111
Introduction 111
For the Student 113
For the Teacher 115
For the Professional Trainer 117

Section V: Primary Values 121
- Introduction 121
- For the Student 123
- For the Teacher 126
- For the Professional Trainer 129

Section VI: Work and Leisure 137
- Introduction 137
- For the Student 141
- For the Teacher 146
- For the Professional Trainer 149

PART III: CONFERENCES IN VALUE CLARIFICATION 153

INTRODUCTION 154

- Training and Evaluation Procedures 158
  - Preparation or Training for the Workshops as a New Experience 158
  - Conference Evaluations 159
- Initial Conference: 3 Days 166
  - Introduction 166
  - Time 166
  - Goals of the Conference 166
  - Schedule 166
  - Atmosphere 168
  - Number of People 170
  - Materials Needed 170
  - Conference Format 172
    - First Day 172
    - Second Day: Morning 177
    - Second Day: Afternoon 181
    - Second Day: Evening 182
    - Third Day: Morning 185
    - Third Day: Afternoon 186
- Two-Day Conference 187
  - First Day 187
  - Second Day 188
- One Day Conference 189
- One Day Workshop: Afternoon 189
- Advanced Conferences 193
  - Introduction 193
    - Participants 193
    - Facilitators 193
    - Time 193
  - Goals and Purpose 194
    - Minimal Goals 194
    - Optimal Learnings 194
    - Number of Persons Suggested 194
    - Materials Needed 194
    - Immediate Preparation 195

Conference I 198
First Day 198
Second Day: Morning 202
Second Day: Evening 206
Third Day: Morning 209
Third Day: Afternoon 211
Two Day Advanced Conference 212
One Day Advanced Conference 213
Dynamics and Suggested Outcomes 214
Suggested Outcomes from this Conference 216
Preparation of Facilitators 216
Conference Variations and Design 217
Designing Your Own Conference 218
Variations in Designing Your Own Conference 219
Exercises To Begin a Conference 219
Variations for Sessions in a Conference Which Are Neither the First Session nor Last Session 220
Exercises for Completing an Experience 221
Designing Your Own Conference 221
Conclusion and the Use of Outside Help 222

PART IV: VALUE-CLARIFICATION STRATEGIES IN THE CLASSROOM 225

INTRODUCTION 226

I. General Approach to Value Clarification in the Classroom 226
Exercises in the Book that Can Be Used in the Classroom within Any Given Subject Matter 234
II. Technique Formats 235
1. Brainstorming 235
2. Value-Ranking 236
3. A Value-Clarification Sheet 237
4. Value Continuums 240
5. Case Analysis 241
6. Role-Playing 242
A Note on Group Arrangements in the Classroom 243
The Use of Contracts 245
A Class Experience 247
III. Pedagogical Methodology 249
IV. Conclusion 253

PART I

VALUE CLARIFICATION: INTRODUCTION

Words like "value", "goal clarification", "group dynamics", "group process", "human interaction", "experiential learning" and "increased motivational skills" are found more and more frequently in educational journals, management magazines, adult education reports and sociological and religious writings. It is increasingly evident that modern man needs to seek the meaning of his life and the meaning of the institutions which involve him. These institutions can either trap him or set him free, allow him a sense of creativity or smother his initiative. This is the crisis of life and meaning today.

Value Clarification as Learning Process: A Guidebook is a companion volume to Volume I, *Value Clarification as Learning Process: A Sourcebook.*

The theory of value clarification is fully presented in the Sourcebook. A very brief summary of that theory will be given in this introductory chapter. Anyone wanting further expansion should refer to the Sourcebook.

The exercises and projects of this book are an adjunct to the Sourcebook and are designed to provide teachers and directors with the experiences and skills which will enable them to use value clarification with the people with whom they work.

The value clarification approach is neither sensitivity training nor psychotherapy, but rather provides a learning experience which leads participants to reflect on life and actions as they relate to behavior, ideas, feelings and, finally, "values". These values are basically and uniquely an individual's, at the very center of his existence, affecting his behavior, shaping his ideas, conditioning his feelings.

All of the projects and exercises in the Guidebook are designed to help participants to examine and clarify their values and to share them only to the degree that they wish. Games, tests, group dynamics, and audio-visual aids encourage participants to fantasize creatively, to decide, to celebrate a unique life.

GUIDELINES FOR THE GUIDEBOOK

The Guidebook is divided into four sections. Part I is an introduction in which we give a definition of value and value-ranking, and value indicators. Part II is a treatment of value techniques, the importance of primary values and the dimensions of the process involved in using a value education approach. Part III explains and gives several conference designs. Part IV contains simple classroom techniques that correlate with the Sourcebook. In Part II there will be exercises in six areas: Values, Value-Ranking, Value Indicators, Values and Environment, Importance of Primary Values, and Work and Leisure. In each of these six sections there will be exercises for students, for teachers and for professionals. These begin with very simple exercises for the student. They then move to more difficult exercises for the teachers and to in-depth exercises for the professionals.

In Part III there are six conferences. There are examples of conferences that can be used for one, two or three-day conferences of value clarification. Conference I is an example of an introductory conference; Conference II is for leader-teachers working with teachers. Finally, the concluding section helps gather together other resource materials and ways of using professional facilitators in value clarification.

A FUNCTIONAL DEFINITION OF VALUE

A value is something that is freely chosen from alternatives and is acted upon, that which the individual celebrates as being part of his creative integration in development as a person. The essential point here is that a value is something that is freely chosen from alternatives and is actually acted upon and lived out. The completed action or the commitment to the choice is integral to the choice itself, and, therefore, points out that one has truly chosen a value and has acted upon it. People can in their imagination "believe" that they have a value, but never act upon it. The test of a true value is whether or not it is freely chosen and acted upon, and not only acted upon, but celebrated. The person must enjoy the value in his life and participate in it. He must find, by acting on and celebrating this value, that it enhances his human development. It is granted that what enhances human development may be theoretically arguable and unclear. For different people this may well mean different things. Note also that this definition of value is in terms of the valuing process itself more than it is in terms of what a value is intrinsically, or from a philosophical point of view.

By value clarification we mean a methodology or process by which we help a person to discover values through behavior, feelings, ideas, and through important choices he has made and is continually, in fact, acting upon in and through his life. If a person is living on a set of values assimilated from his upbringing rather than chosen, then he is moving in directions and has goals that are hidden from him, of which he is not aware.

It is only as I, as an adult, clarify what choices have a major influence on my personality that I can really understand who I am and where it is that I am going. I can hardly understand what my goals are unless I am aware of the choices I have already made.

A person is continually developing his values; values can

never be static but must be continually re-chosen as the person grows in his world. As a person grows in his identity and interdependence, he is continually choosing values and fashioning his hierarchy of values.

In *Values and Teaching* by Louis E. Raths, Merrill Harmin and Sidney R. Simon, seven aspects to a true value are described. These seven aspects may be divided into three categories: (1) Choosing, (2) Prizing, (3) Acting.

In the area of choice it is stated that the value must be chosen freely. There must be no coercion; the person makes a free choice and is totally accountable for the choice he makes. Secondly, the choice must be made from alternatives. If there were not any alternatives, then there would be no free choice in the first place; one would only be able to accept what he was faced with. The third aspect of choice is the thoughtful consideration of the consequences of each of the alternatives. Therefore, choices which were made impulsively, without thought, would not constitute a valuing process.

The second category is prizing. A value that has been chosen should be prized and cherished. This means that a person who chooses a value must be happy about what he has chosen and hold it as something dear to him. A second aspect of prizing is the area of affirmation; after we have chosen something from the alternatives and are proud of it, we are then glad to be associated with it and are willing to admit so publicly.

The third category of a value is that we act upon our choice. One way in which we can see that the validity of what we say is of value to us is simply to ask the question: "Have I acted on it, or was it something I was still thinking about?" In this case, if the person has not acted upon it, it would simply not be a value. There must be commitment-in-action which would change one's behavior and which would make evident to other people that there is a value present. Finally, the value should be repeatedly acted upon. If something is really a value, it would be acted upon and acted upon repeatedly. This would then show up in several situations.

A summary of Raths, Harmin, and Simon's definition is as follows:

Choosing:

1. To choose freely.
2. To choose from alternatives.
3. To choose from alternatives after considering the consequences of each alternative.

Prizing:

4. Cherishing and being happy with the choice.
5. Willing to affirm the choice publicly.

Acting:

6. Actually doing something with the choice.
7. Acting repeatedly in some pattern of life.

The beauty of this definition is that it emphasizes the process of valuing throughout the seven aspects. It clearly expresses all the views of what a value is and what the valuing process is, as developed in current psychology and philosophy. It takes in the aspects of choice, action and prizing; moreover, it spells out what each of these means in a much more specific manner. This makes the definition of value very practical in the area of helping the person understand whether or not what he has chosen is a value. The exercises and projects in this book serve the purpose of expiating and, in a very detailed practical way, help a person to determine what his values truly are.

In Part II of this book you will find exercises that will help you understand what a value is, as to choosing, celebrating and acting.

VALUE-RANKING

Value-ranking is simply the process whereby a person examines, as comprehensively as possible, all of his values and then ranks them, prioritizes them, or puts them within a hierarchy of values, insofar as he as an individual desires. Value-ranking is a conscious, deliberate process by which a mature person arrives at a fairly well-articulated, thoughtful ranking of his chosen values. Growth and personal identity are accomplished when an individual has the opportunity to clarify his attitudes, weigh the priorities operative in the formation of these attitudes and come to chosen value-rankings which please and enhance him as a person. In this sense, value-ranking, like the valuing process, has to be chosen, prized and acted upon. It has to be something that contributes to the creative development of the personality. It is an act of celebration of a person's limitations, as he comes to grips with priorities, in time, through new behavioral patterns.

In value-ranking we are exploring the interrelationship of values within any given individual. It is important to realize that a person can have any number of value stances on an almost unlimited number of issues in his life. The issue here is not whether a person has the "right" values or the "wrong" values; it is that a person should be aware of what his hierachy of values is or his value-ranking consists of. This is important because the way a person ranks values has a great deal of influence on how he behaves in actual living. For example, Person "A" may have the values of (1) being a good student and (2) liking to be with friends. Person "A" is going through college and wants to insure his future, so he ranks studying as number one and friends as number two; therefore, he spends a great deal of time studying. Person "B" can also have the same two values, study and friends. However, Person "B" desires to have a full social life, and so he ranks friends as number one and studying as number two. The result is that Person "B" spends a great deal of time with his friends and less time studying.

In each case both values are very important, but the reverse order would change the behavior of the person, as can be simply seen in the example. Person "B" would spend more time with friends. This person might, for instance, be more of an extrovert and more social in his thinking. Person "A" would probably be more inward-thinking and more happy living in a world of ideas rather than people. Neither ranking is correct. It is only that when the rankings are reversed one is confronted with different behavior, a different world view—in fact, a different person. Values, as individually chosen elements in a person's life, are very important; however, the variety and ranking of these individually chosen elements are in the final analysis equally important.

Value-ranking between two individuals who are married becomes even more important. Very often, conflicts within marriage are the result of different value-rankings. Frequently the couple are not aware that this is the source of their difficulty. They both have very similar values, frequently. However, a difference in value-ranking can be a source of conflict and irritation within the marriage. When this is brought to their awareness and they can make accommodations and compromises with one another, the conflict can be resolved. This is merely another illustration of how important value-ranking is in our search to live a meaningful life.

Part II, Section II of the book has a number of exercises which help a person rank his values.

VALUE INDICATORS

A value indicator is simply something which falls short of fully being a value. In other words, a value indicator does not completely have all of the seven criteria that are spoken of in the discussion of values. It may be that the value indicator has five or six of the criteria that are chosen but not acted upon. Or, perhaps they are acted upon, but not really chosen. Maybe they have been celebrated once but not repeatedly. So, any value that falls short of fulfilling all seven criteria is only a value indicator and not truly a full value. In this sense a value indicator is anything which by its nature, and insofar as it does fulfill some of the criteria, is a movement toward being a full value, but at the moment is only a partially formed value.

Other value indicators are interests, feelings, beliefs, attitudes, and convictions that one may have but perhaps has not acted upon or celebrated. Or it may be that they have not been publicly acknowledged. One of the discoveries of value clarification for the individual is that he finds that many of his so-called values are not truly values but rather value indicators. This is not said in a pessimistic sense but rather in the optimistic attitude of making the individual aware of his choices and giving him the opportunity to then consciously and freely choose from alternatives in order to grow in his values.

In order to clarify whether a given thing is a value or only a value indicator, one should ask the following questions about it:

1. Was the value chosen from a range of alternatives

that I was aware of?

2. Did I consider the consequences of those alternatives I was aware of?

3. Is this value evident in my behavior? Have I acted on it recently?

4. Do I act on this value repeatedly in some fashion, through a variety of similar experiences?

5. Am I happy and pleased with the choice?

6. Am I willing to state it publicly?

7. Does the value enhance, and not impede, the development of emotional and spiritual well-being?

If the answer is not "yes" to all of the above questions, then what is spoken of is not the fully developed value but rather a value indicator. The next questions asked are: "How many chosen values, since the above is a chosen value, do we in fact live by?" "Is it possible that the majority of values that we have are part and parcel of our personality, and assimilated from our upbringing?" "Would we choose the values which we become aware of?" These questions bring to us the problem of the various types of values.

Part II, Section III of this book gives exercises and projects which help the person to become aware of what his values truly are, and to distinguish what are partially formed values. Another method of establishing value indicators is to take a close look at how we use our time, our money and our energy, as well as a look into where our imagination and fantasy carry us.

VALUES AND ENVIRONMENT

Modern psychology has pointed out rather specifically how one's environment influences a person. In value clarification we are concerned with how the environment in which we live imposes values on us. We are concerned because the environment can impose, rather than allow the person to choose freely. For example, poverty is a trapped condition—a condition where choice is a restricted possibility for the person, due to personal anxiety and the environment in which he lives. The more trapped the person is, the more he moves toward a condition of meaninglessness. Another example of environment-imposed values is the Protestant work-ethic: the attitude toward work in the United States, whereby people are forced by society to place work as a higher value in their ranking values than they might choose freely if they had alternatives to choose from. Close to the above example is the attitude of rush, rush, rush, keeping up with the Joneses, the harried middle class trying to climb up the ladder of success. People are influenced to be competitive and to be successful materially. This they might not choose if they did not have the pressures of society imposing upon them in this regard. Another example closely related to this discussion on how environment influences and imposes values on a person is the now-thing of "women's liberation". Women are fighting to overcome the values that have been imposed on them by men. Whether you agree or disagree with the women's liberation movement, the dynamics taking place between men and women today are those relating to how society and environment impose themselves on a person's value-ranking and values.

In a country where work, achievement, and material success are widely held by our society to be ranked of highest value, it is difficult for a person, for example, to choose leisure as a value and to freely *live* that value. Usually artists are the creative people who do not live regular, scheduled lives—whom most of our society looks upon as "characters" or as people with idiosyncracies. Very often society will be angered and will attack a person who chooses leisure as a value, accusing him of being lazy and of wasting his time and talent. Here again we see how environment is imposing itself on the person's value system.

Part II, Section IV of this book gives exercises that will help one to overcome the impositions of environment and to freely choose his values from alternatives.

PRIMARY VALUES

Primary values are essential to the growth of man. There are two types of authentic values—primary and chosen. By a primary value we mean a value that is chosen and acted upon, that which a person is happy with. A primary value is one which helps a human being develop to the best of his capacity and, therefore, he has a goal beyond normal functioning in society to exceptional function. This is spiritual development. Primary values are those values which are basic and necessary for development to take place. They are normal to natural development. Certainly, what is considered good as enhancing human development or helping a person grow are all controversial and arguable issues. However, there is enough research and consensus in modern psychology and theology for the authors here to postulate two basic primary values, namely, self-value and value of others.

Modern psychology has placed great emphasis on man's need to love and be loved, and on man's need to feel that he is worthwhile to himself and to others. Self-value is defined as the ability to accept that "I am of total worth to significant others". The second primary value, the worth of others, is that "Others are of total worth, as I am". In other words, briefly put, "I value myself, and I value others". These two primary values will come as no surprise to a Christian, for the Gospel of Jesus Christ is found in the love of God and the love of neighbor. Implicit in the love of neighbor is also the love of one's self; as Christ has told us, love the self as we love our neighbor: "Love your neighbor as you love yourself".

I value myself when I recognize my imagination, my ideas, my feelings, my body and what I do, as being of value.

Valuing others is when I see the good in other people, encourage them and support them in their efforts to grow in their talents and creativity. These two primary values are not possible except in relationship to each other—e.g., I will not be able to affirm others as being of total worth unless I have been affirmed myself. In order for these to be of value they must be chosen by me as being of particular importance, and they must be acted upon by me repeatedly in some form or other.

Part II, Section V of this book contains projects and exercises to help one grow in understanding, awareness and capacity for choosing the primary values of self-worth and worth of others.

WORK AND LEISURE

What is understood as work is: the way in which man modifies his environment in such a way as to enhance his creative and natural growth. Work, when it is viewed as value, has to be chosen freely, must be something a person is happy with and is willing to act on. It is also something that helps spiritual and emotional growth. Work, unlike rest or leisure, always has certain expectations, duties, and obligations attached to it. It usually has set limitations of time and space. "I work so many hours a day and expect to produce such and such a product or earn so much money".

Leisure is seen as a necessary activity for all men if they are to be in balance with the creative life forces. We need time to laugh and cry, to just be, just as we need time to rest. Leisure is understood as: an attitude of mind which permits me to be myself and allows me to free others to be themselves. It is knowing my limitations and celebrating them, rather than being ashamed of them.

Leisure differs from work in that it is those times and moments when I am free of major obligations, duties and expectations, so that I can be myself. It is timeless. Unaware of time, I have nothing I ought or must do or produce. It can be done anywhere and does not have the limits of space that work does.

The need for the balance of work and leisure in a creative way in our society is becoming more and more evident. In the value clarification process it helps persons set new life-styles and examine life direction in the context of their everyday work lives.

Work and leisure are considered in an additional section because they are so central to the American way of life as value indicators. Exercises that help a person clarify his values toward work and leisure are in Part II, Section VI of the book.

DIMENSIONS OF PROCESS

The thrust of a value education approach is toward discovery. In value clarification the effort is to create opportunity for the participant to learn by doing and to learn by discovery. The simple procedure in value clarification is not lecturing or giving answers; it is more important to ask pertinent questions. Instead of answering the student's question, it is more important to clarify what the student is asking. This creates the opportunity for him to discover his own insights, to find his own potential, to grow in his own self-worth.

Value clarification is different from the traditional method of lecture in which the primary goal is to develop the intellect of the child. It also differs in some respects from modern experiential learning which uses T-grouping in the encounter group as a learning tool. In T-groups or encounter groups, the primary goal is the development of relationships between people, understanding the self and others in relationship—and this tends to be the only goal. Value clarification accepts this goal.

In the T-group or encounter group, most often the facilitators are of a communication model-type or have a clinical therapeutical orientation. The encounter group facilitator, who is of a communication model-type, is primarily concerned with teaching communication theories and models through the experience of trying to communicate effectively in the group. Encounter group facilitators who have a clinical background have an orientation toward using therapeutic skills to help develop growth of the participants. In contrast, in value clarification we are concerned with persons and their relationships but only as a context for dealing with their values. In an encounter group very often the goal is one of growth in relationships. In value clarification we are concerned with growth in relationship in the valuing of other persons, but we are also even more concerned with the person developing his values and ranking his values.

All of the units or conferences that are designed have two basic parts. The first part consists of exercises or projects that help to build a climate of trust and warmth in which an individual has the support and encouragement of the group to examine his values. Very often in an encounter group the facilitators and groups stop short of doing this. Once a person has come to know himself better and feels more comfortable in his relationship to other people, invariably he begins to establish and to re-evaluate his values. The second part in a unit conference is that once people are free to examine their values, they are then confronted with exercises and projects which make them aware of what their values truly are and whether they are dealing with values or with only value indicators. This helps them to become aware of how they rank their values and what their values are, by the way they use their time, money and energy.

PSYCHIC EFFORT

Psychic effort on the part of the teacher is required. In the traditional inductive approach the teacher is always in a position of certainty. The model was that the teacher passed on truth to the child which the child received passively. In the inductive approach the teacher and the child act together, and thus they develop a relationship of mutual respect.

In the inductive model, the teacher creates opportunity for the student to question his own values and even the values of the teacher. The teacher sets up a climate and gives the student freedom to explore his values, as well as the values of the teacher. This then can threaten the teacher, if he has not been established and has not grown in his values. So, in this regard, the teacher who is immature in his own value-affirmation may find the inductive method a very draining experience.

A teacher who tries for the first time to use the inductive method and group process in order to be able to use value clarification will have to come to grips with his own fears about whether the method will work or not. This is the first issue the teacher must face. There will be feelings of doubt, feelings of despair, feelings of fear that things will just not work out. Here once again we see the necessity for having, as a value, trust in one's-self and the valuing of the potential that is inherent in each individual student. Whenever one begins a new group, group process starts extremely slowly. It is important for the teacher to realize that the process grows slowly; it grows at a gradual steady rate. The teacher must be prepared to move at the pace at which this particular group is capable of moving at that point.

A teacher who does not desire to be close or intimate with other people, especially a teacher who would not choose to be close to the students and to share his values with the students, will be taking the risk of self-disclosure and will be threatened by the approach that we are suggesting. However, teachers who are willing to accept the humanistic and existential values in this value clarification approach find it to be exhilarating and revitalizing. The teacher who can accept this approach can accept the intimacy that it brings, as both teacher and student strive to develop their value systems. They will find that they will be living a life of wisdom in which they are growing and discovering values in life together.

Where possible, in dealing with groups larger than 12 to 15, it is advisable to have two facilitators. This will give the group more opportunity to have present a resource person to whom they can turn for information and guidance. The exercises and projects in this book are designed so that the experience will be beneficial to the group suggested. In other words, in Section II of the book you will notice that the exercises are labeled "For Students", "For Teachers" and "For Professionals". Throughout the book at strategic points there are half pages and full pages left blank which might encourage you to begin to develop your own value clarification approach. Frequently, throughout the book you will be asked to create your own project or exercise in order to develop the values of the students you are working with and the unique situation in which they and you are.

WHOM THE BOOK IS FOR

This book is for use with both students and teachers in high schools, colleges and adult education settings. The book is designed so that the experiences in each unit can help a person gradually to grow in the clarification of his values. The book will provide exercises for teachers and leaders to actualize with their students. The book also has resources for teacher formation. There is a range of exercises and conferences, from simple experiences in one class session, all the way to an intensive three-day conference for professionals. It is hoped that this presentation will be a source book of catalytic ideas for the professional—ideas which will stimulate professionals to begin to create their own approach and their own exercises for clarifying values.

EXPERTISE FOR HANDLING THE EXERCISES

Teachers aware of the inductive method and discovery method as an approach to education will be able to adapt to this book. Examples of the inductive method or inductive approach to education are the Paulist Press "Discovery Series" or the Argus Press "Choose Life" series. Teachers who are familiar with A. S. Neill, Montessori or Rogers' Pupil-Centered Approach will understand the dynamics that are discussed in this book.

Those teachers trained in a traditional lecture approach might find the exercises difficult and should become acquainted with the group dynamics in value methods. The opportunity to attend a workshop in value clarification provides the kind of experience that would give confidence to teachers, so that they can then use the book effectively.

HOW TO USE THE BOOK

1. Get with a friend or group and experience some of the exercises yourself.
2. Do not conduct conferences unless facilitators have tested the experiences and have some awareness of the dynamics that take place.
3. Choose a theme you think you should start on from the first half of the book. If you do not know how to proceed, follow the book the first time; later on you will feel more able to design your own programs.
4. This book is not to be followed slavishly. After experimenting with the exercises with class units and class conferences, modify or create your own exercises to fit the climate of your group.

5. In each section there are three levels—for students, for teachers and for professionals. If this approach is new to you, start with the student level and experience these exercises first. Then do the teacher level and, finally, the professional level. In this way you will grow in your own value clarification.

6. Once you have become familiar with the exercises and approaches, you will feel free to arrange and rearrange units of the book to design your own program. Hopefully, you will begin to think of new and creative approaches to value clarification.

PART II

EXERCISES IN VALUE CLARIFICATION

INTRODUCTION

This chapter contains exercises in value clarification, ranging from short exercises used in the classroom to games lasting up to three hours. These exercises then can be used a number of ways, in combination, for the design of conferences. These aspects will be treated in Part III and Part IV of the book. The various exercises in this chapter fall into six categories, as follows:

1. Definition of Values.
2. Value-Ranking.
3. Value Indicators.
4. Values and Environment.
5. Primary Values.
6. Work and Leisure.

Each section is, in turn, divided into three subsections, as follows: 1. Exercises for use with students, 2. Exercises for teachers to use with their peers for training and for self-enhancement and understanding of value theory, 3. Exercises and/or suggestions for professional trainers in value clarification. The professional trainer is usually regarded as someone who has an advanced degree in counseling or educational psychology. The reader will have to evaluate whether or not he has the experience to utilize the suggestions in this section.

Under each subsection, "For Students", "For Teachers", and "For Professionals", there will be two or three exercises. The overall pattern of the chapter is as shown on the facing page.

In the accompanying diagram, note that Part II of the book is divided into six sections or chapters. Each section deals with a different part of value theory. In Part III of the book, a series of conference designs will be given, utilizing the various exercises in all these sections.

In the second column of the diagram, called "Whom the Exercise is For", we see three divisions: 1. Students, 2. Teachers, 3. Professional Trainers. If a teacher feels competent, any of the exercises in all of these three areas could be used. We have tried to give different exercises in order to provide maximum variation.

Under the division of "Students" are exercises which the teacher can use with the student in the classroom. The exercises under "Teachers" are designed so that teachers can use them with themselves, in terms of a training program for themselves, or for adults to utilize in an adult education program. We would envision these exercises being utilized, for example, by the head of a religious education program in the parish as training for the teach-

OUTLINE OF PART II

SECTION AND SUBJECT OF EXERCISE	WHOM THE EXERCISE IS FOR	NUMBER OF EXERCISES
SECTION I— THE NATURE OF VALUE PROCESS	Students	3 Exercises
	Teachers	3 Exercises
	Professional Trainers	3 Exercises
SECTION II— VALUE-RANKING (SETTING PRIORITIES)	Students	2 Exercises
	Teachers	2 Exercises
	Professional Trainers	3 Exercises
SECTION III— VALUE INDICATORS	Students	3 Exercises
	Teachers	3 Exercises
	Professional Trainers	2 Exercises
SECTION IV— VALUES AND ENVIRONMENT	Students	2 Exercises
	Teachers	3 Exercises
	Professional Trainers	3 Exercises
SECTION V— PRIMARY VALUES	Students	1 Exercise plus Variations
	Teachers	1 Exercise plus Variations
	Professional Trainers	Suggested Emphasis/Variations
SECTION VI— WORK AND LEISURE	Students	2 Exercises
	Teachers	2 Exercises
	Professional Trainers	2 Exercises

ers or as an adult religious education program. Under the section, "Professional Trainers", are exercises to be utilized by a professional teacher-educator or teacher-trainer. Some of these exercises should only be utilized with persons who have had sufficient experience to feel competent with the possible outcomes. The point is to try to give a broad range of exercises to be used by people of different experiences, as well as by a person growing in experiences. For example, a person might start by utilizing experiences with the students, then gradually be able to utilize some of the experiences under teachers and, finally, those listed under professional trainers. Generally speaking, the exercises used by professional trainers mean that the person should have had a substantial amount of training in group dynamics. In this regard, we would direct the reader to *Group Discussion as Learning Process: A Source Book* by Elizabeth Flynn and John LaFaso (Paulist Press).

Each section is divided into three parts: exercises for students, exercises for teachers and exercises for trainers. Each section will begin with an introduction giving a minimal amount of theory related to the nature of the material in that section. Section I, for example, called "The Nature of Value Process", has in the introduction a definition of a value from the book *Value Clarification as Learning Process: A Sourcebook.*

In each exercise will be the following parts:

1. Purpose and Goals.
2. Materials Needed for the Exercise.
3. Groupings: These will be suggestions as to how many people should be utilized with this exercise or what kind of group arrangements would be most suitable for the exercise.
4. Time Span.
5. Description of Exercise.
6. Possible Outcomes.
7. Applications.

At this point, let us move to Section I, "The Nature of Value Process".

Section I

The Nature of Value Process

The goal of the exercises in Section I is to help the student teacher and professional trainer develop an appreciation of the nature of the value process. You will recall that the definition of value is: something that is chosen freely from alternatives after considering the consequences of each alternative. And, that after having been chosen, they are celebrated and acted upon repeatedly.

The three primary categories of a value are: Choice, Act, and Celebration; the exercises in this section will evolve around these three categories. The exercises are geared to help the student become aware of the value process and how it consists of choice, act and celebration. For the teacher, the exercises are to help him become aware of the value process in his own life and how he may use the exercises in the teaching profession. For the professional, the exercises are designed to help the trainer become aware of the value process and its more extensive implications in the teaching process insofar as choice, act and celebration are concerned. If the teacher is not familiar with the value clarification process, instead of starting at the teacher level it would be well to do the student exercises first, to gain a familiarity with them before doing the teacher exercises in this section. It is hoped that through the experience of choosing, acting and celebrating the participants will come to an appreciation of these concepts.

PART 2—SECTION I
THE NATURE OF VALUE PROCESS

AUDIENCE	GOAL OF EXERCISE		STRATEGIES USED
STUDENT	To make the student aware of value process as consisting of:	CHOICE	1. 10 sets of 2 pictures are given to the students, each representing a choice. Questions around the interpretation of the choices lead to a discussion of the experience of choice.
		ACT	2. Questions are given on values operating in students' lives, followed by a discussion of how they acted on them.
		CELEBRATION	3. Exercises with sentence completions around prizes and value continuum on: celebration-unhappy with.
TEACHER	To make the teacher aware of value process in his/her own life and teaching as:	CHOICE	1. Value Test 1 and Value Test 2 compare choices made on continuums and in boxes. Discussion on the subject matter brings out the importance of choice.
		ACT	2. The teacher relates two major discussions in his/her life and how he/she acted on them. Discussion of the values present.
		CELEBRATION	3. Exercises in dyads on talents and limitations. The limitations are turned to potentials celebrated.
PROFESSIONAL TRAINER	To help the trainer become aware of value process and its more extensive implications in the teaching process in:	CHOICE	1. 20 sets of 2 pictures provide an exercise in choice and use of the imagination as a more in-depth look at alternatives as critical to development.
		ACT	2. Brainstorm on values. Discussion on how a value as a priority changes behavior.
		CELEBRATION	3. Exercise on talents and limitations. Emphasis on gaining skills in how limits are crucial to potential.

FOR THE STUDENT

Exercise One:

This exercise is designed to make the student aware of value processes consisting of choice.

1. INTRODUCTION: The purpose of this exercise is to give the student an opportunity to practice choosing.

2. MATERIALS NEEDED: There are several options here. One, use an overhead projector with the materials given in the book. Two, run off a stencil with a free-hand drawing of the pictures in the book.

3. NUMBERS: The students will first go through the exercise individually and then be broken up into groups of six or eight. Any number of students can do this exercise properly.

4. TIME: Use 5 minutes to show the slides, then give the students 45 minutes to discuss what their choices are and what they saw in the slides they were shown.

5. DESCRIPTION OF THE EXERCISE: The object of this exercise is to present two situations. The students are encouraged to allow their imaginations to be creative, as to what the symbolization of each picture might be. The process is as follows:

   a. Have the students sit in a circle or in groups on the floor in an arrangement where they can see the test pictures.

b. Hold each picture before them for about half a minute, and then ask them to choose Picture "A" or Picture "B", depending on which is more pleasing to them. The procedure is as follows:

Picture 1: This is a picture of a square with a circle in it on the one side, and a series of objects on Side B. (Please choose which is more pleasing to you.)

Picture 2: In this picture we see a box on one side and a circle on the other. (Please choose which is more pleasing to you.)

Picture 3: "A" is a house with people inside. "B" is a house with people walking outside. (Choose the one which is more pleasing to you.)

Picture 4: "A" represents an example of a traditional teaching situation. Picture "B" is a group situation which could be a class or discussion group. (Please choose the one that you feel more comfortable with most of the time.) While you're doing this, imagine that you are either the teacher or one of the students.

Picture 5: In these two pictures we see the floor plans of two houses. Imagine that you were exploring both of them, that you were alone, and that you had two or three hours to kill. (Choose the one you would prefer.)

Picture 6: "A" is a picture of a person standing by himself in a field. Picture "B" is of several people in a field. (Choose the one that you feel more comfortable with.)

Picture 7: In the first picture we see a person in the box. There is no way out of this box. Picture "B" is of a person who is on top of the box or on the outside of the box. (Which do you feel like most of the time? Record your answer by choosing "A" or "B".)

Picture 8: In "A" and "B" we have two pictures, each with a variation of objects. (Choose which you prefer.)

Picture 9: "A" is a person fishing in a boat. The weather is good, there is no danger, and the fisherman is having a good time. Picture "B" is of two people underwater having an extended conversation with some fish. (Which situation would you prefer to be in, and which situation do you think would offer you the most opportunities?)

Picture 10: Here again we have in "A" a square and in "B" several objects. (Choose which you prefer.)

c. Have the students get into groups of three or four. Preferably, have them in the room with persons they least know. This will help them to mix better and get to know more people.

d. Tell them that we are now going to evaluate the exercise. Point out that in all the pictures there were more choices represented in those pictures marked "B" than in those marked "A". In some of the pictures there were simply more objects in "B" than "A". In others, there were more opportunities for choice, such as the more complicated house plan or the opportunity for more questions in the classroom situation. You, as the facilitator, might make these statements: "There is no 'good' or 'bad' in how you evaluate the pictures; some of us have more ability to see, utilize and make choices than others. However, it should be pointed out that everyone has a certain amount of insecurity and, therefore, all of us need to make or be in situations where, at times, there are limited amounts of choices. Therefore, each of us should have at least some boxes marked in the "A" section".

e. Have the students now discuss what they think their ability is to make choices and to follow through with them. Have them also discuss their awareness of alternatives in given situations and in relationship to the test. If the student, for example, marked more than half of his boxes in the "A" area, this would indicate that he probably has difficulty in seeing or making choices. The student needs to be aware of this and to discuss what its implications might be in his life. If a person has all the boxes in Section "B" marked, he might want to discuss the fact that while he might not have any difficulty making choices, perhaps, at the same time, he might be a very independent person. Discuss what he thinks the implications here might be.

f. The purpose of the exercise is to give the students an opportunity to choose between alternatives. In the discussion that follows, the teacher should point out their ability to choose between alternatives and help them to become more aware that they have the opportunity for choice in their lives.

6. POSSIBLE OUTCOME: For many students this will be the first time that they will have become aware, in a significant way, of the possibilities they have for choice. It would be well in the discussion afterward to encourage them to also become aware of the implications of their choosing.

7. APPLICATION: This is a very basic exercise and can be done in a number of ways. You might well think of some very simple exercises of choice coming to mind quite readily. One of the basic approaches in the methodology of value clarification is to try to create opportunities for the student to choose.

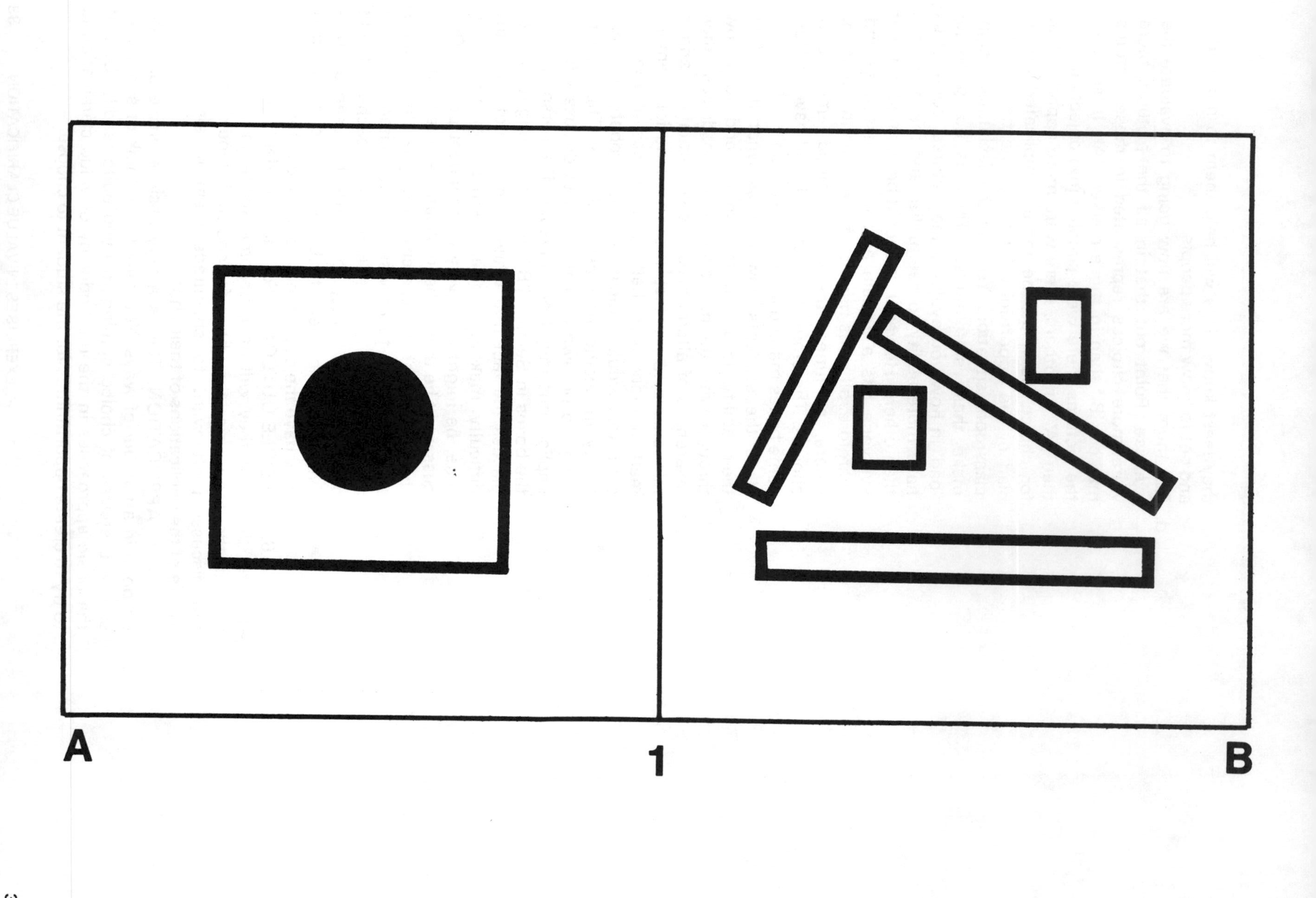
A
1
B

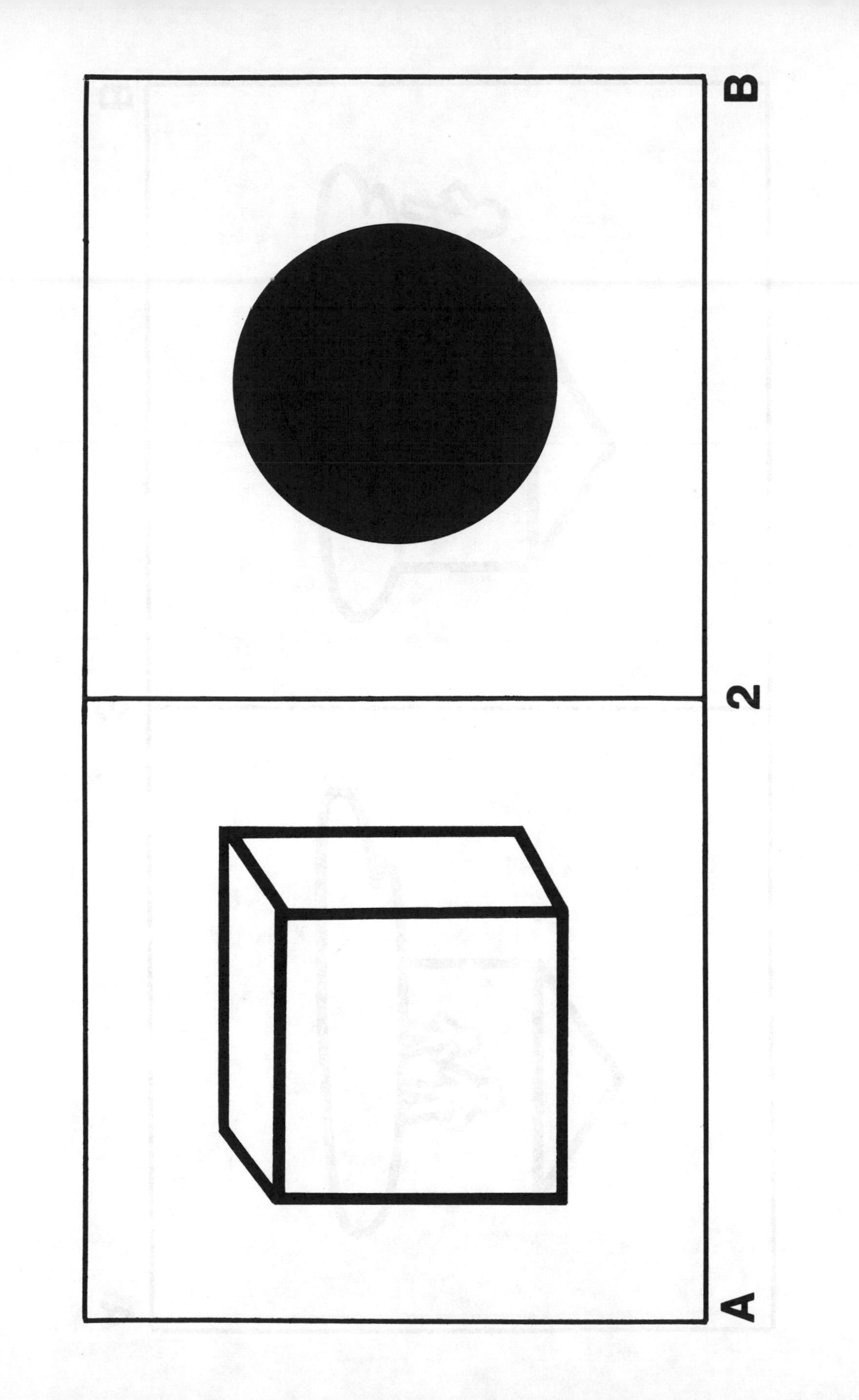
A
2
B

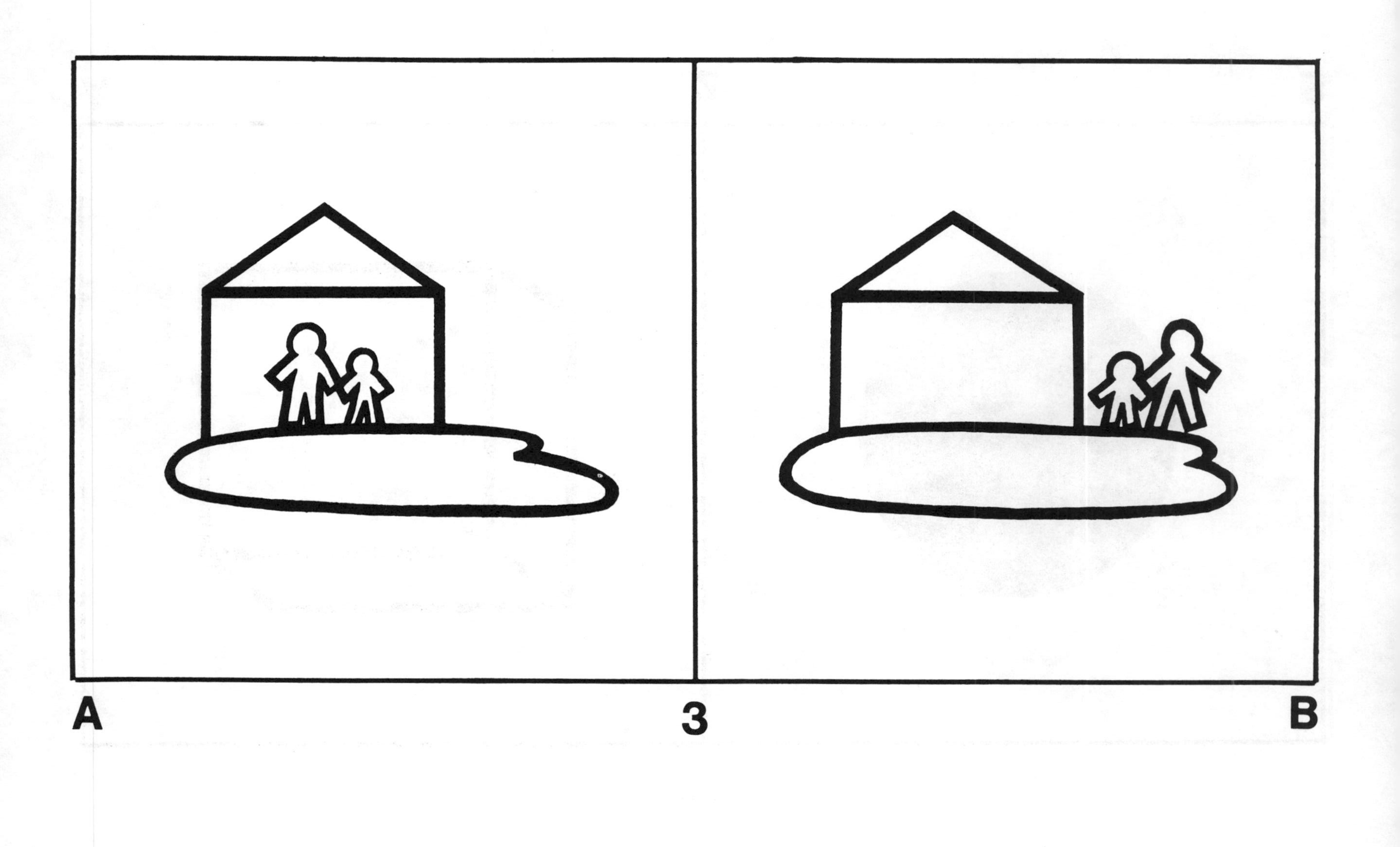
A
3
B

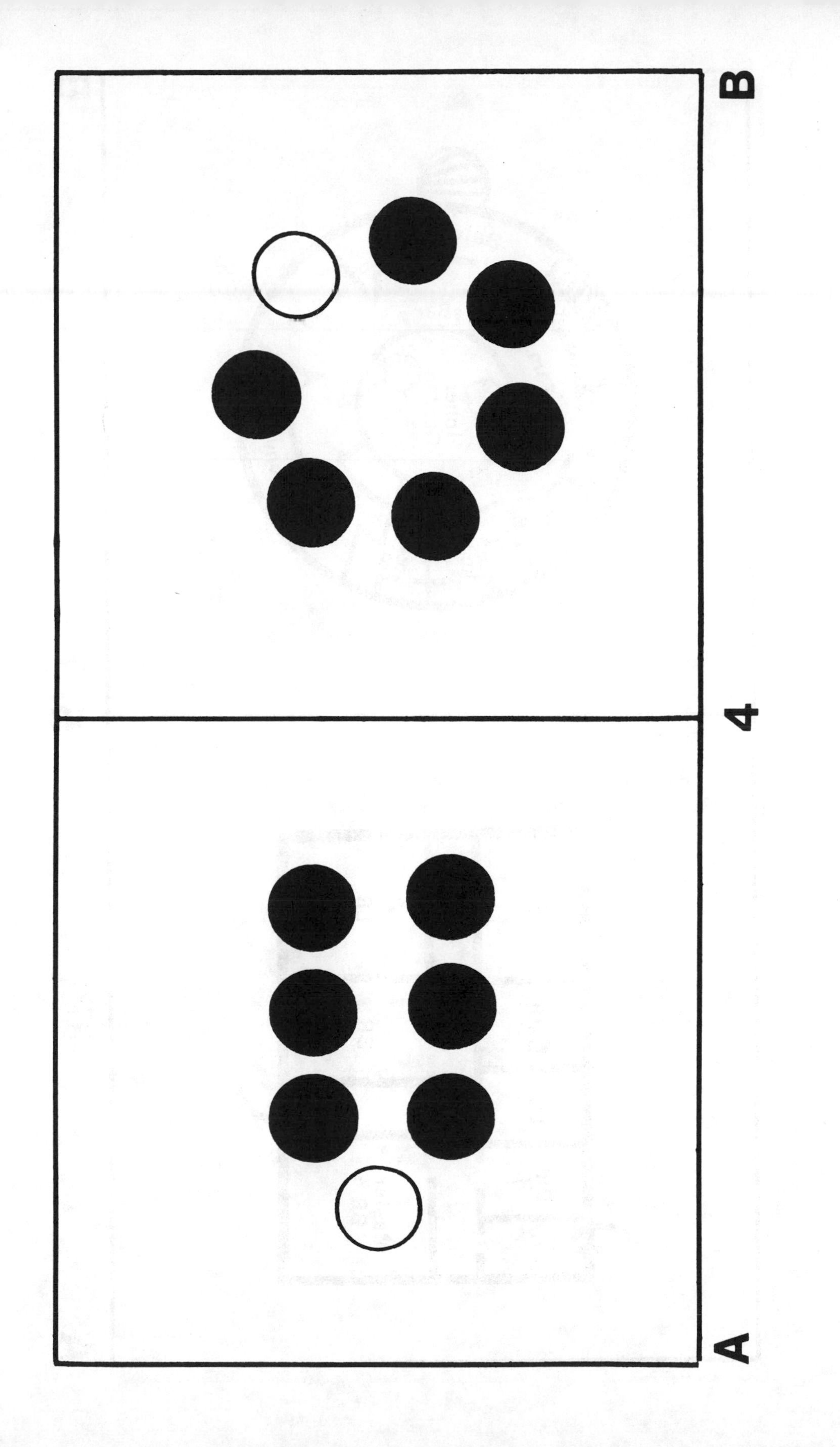
A
4
B

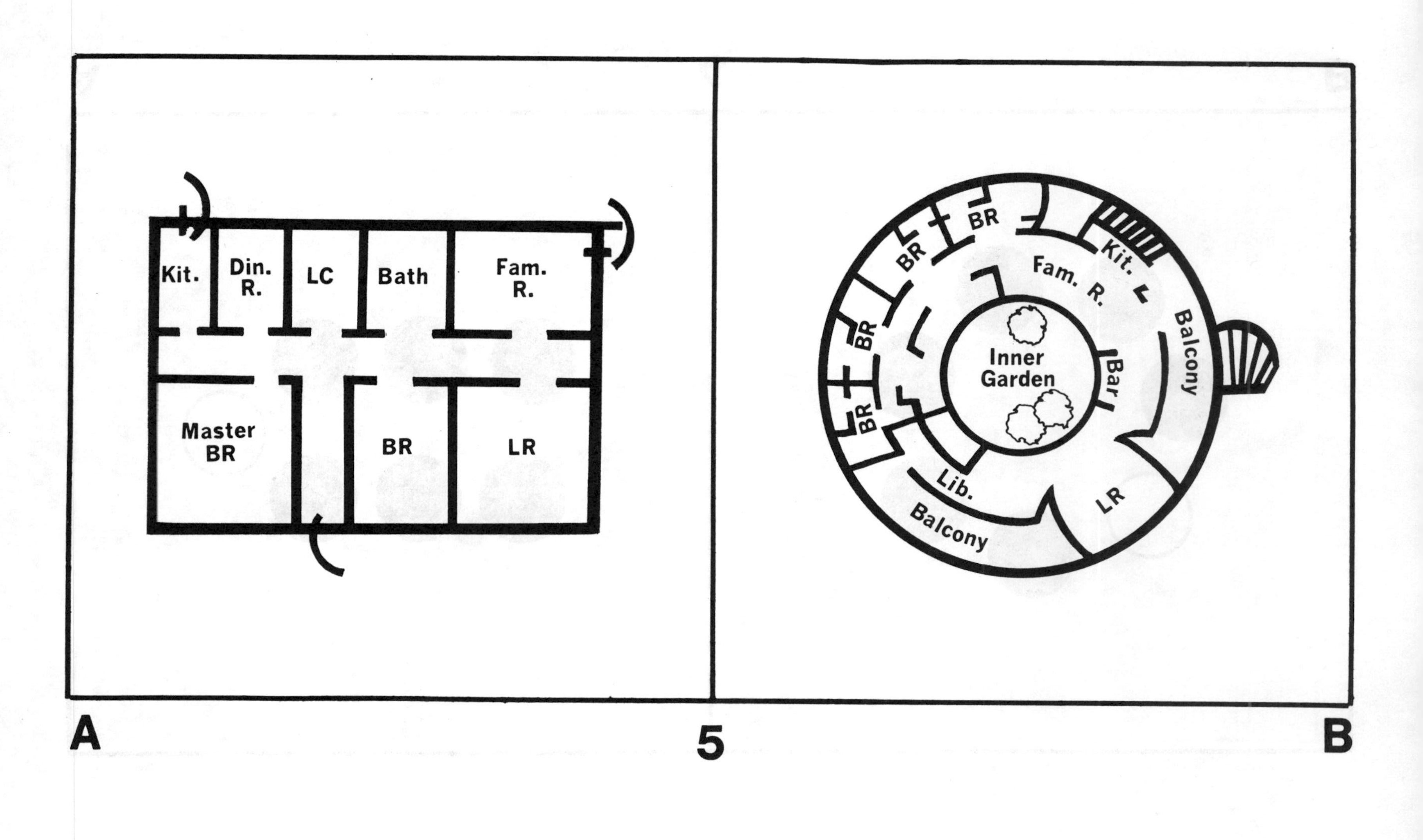
Kit.
Din. R.
LC
Bath
Fam. R.
Master BR
BR
LR
A
5
BR
BR
BR
BR
Kit.
Fam. R.
Inner Garden
Bar
Balcony
Lib.
Balcony
LR
B

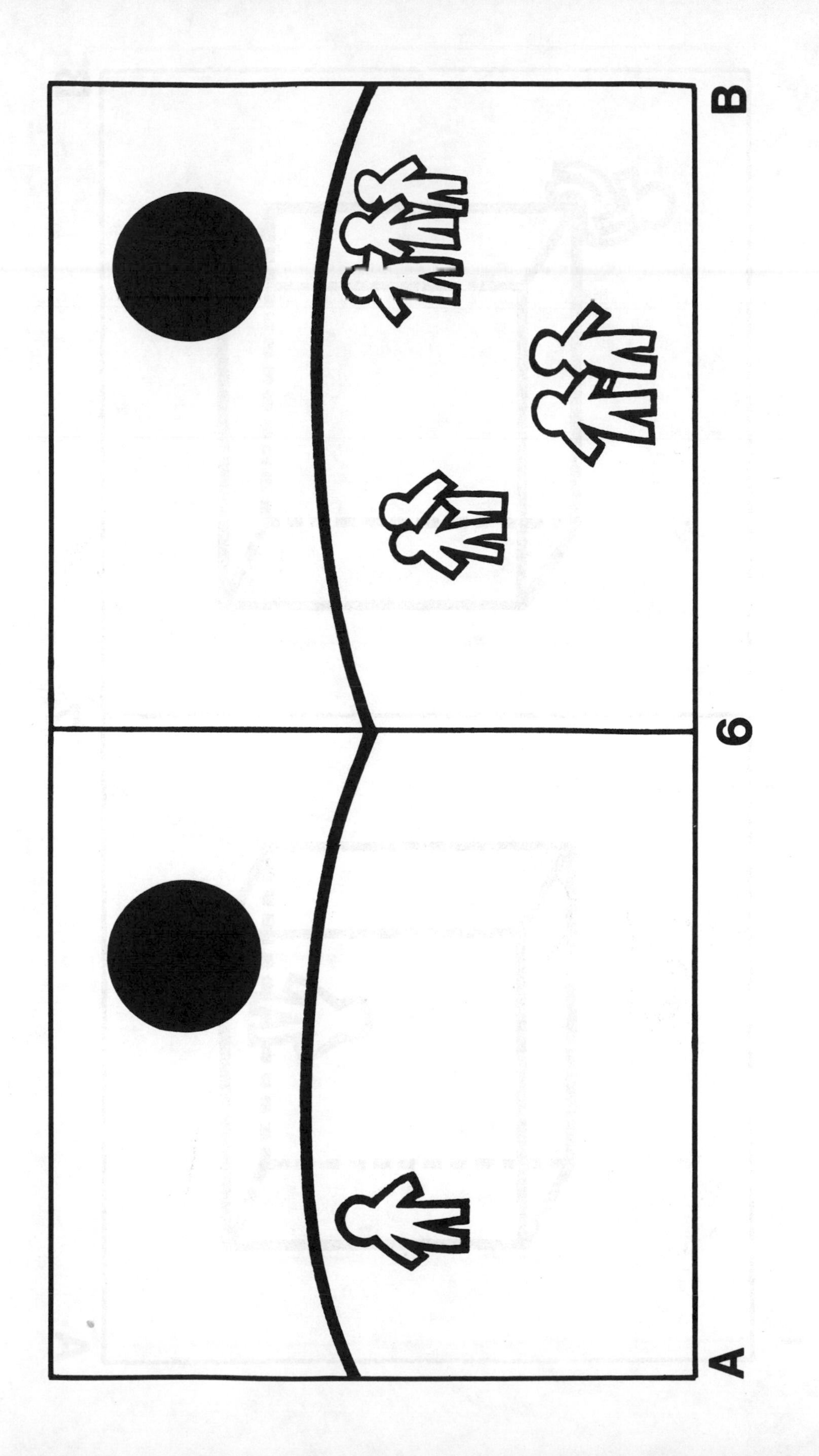
A
6
B

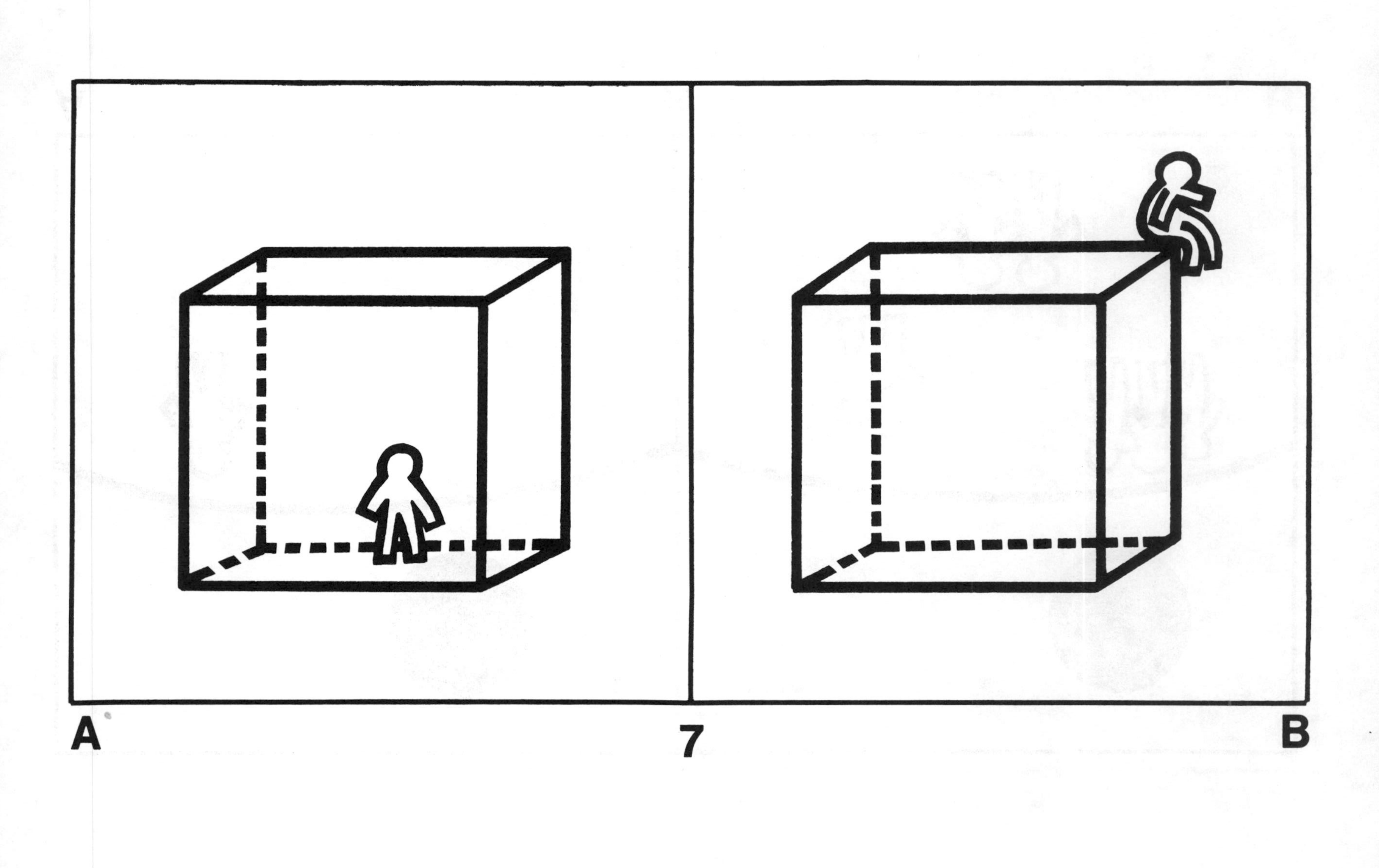
A
7
B

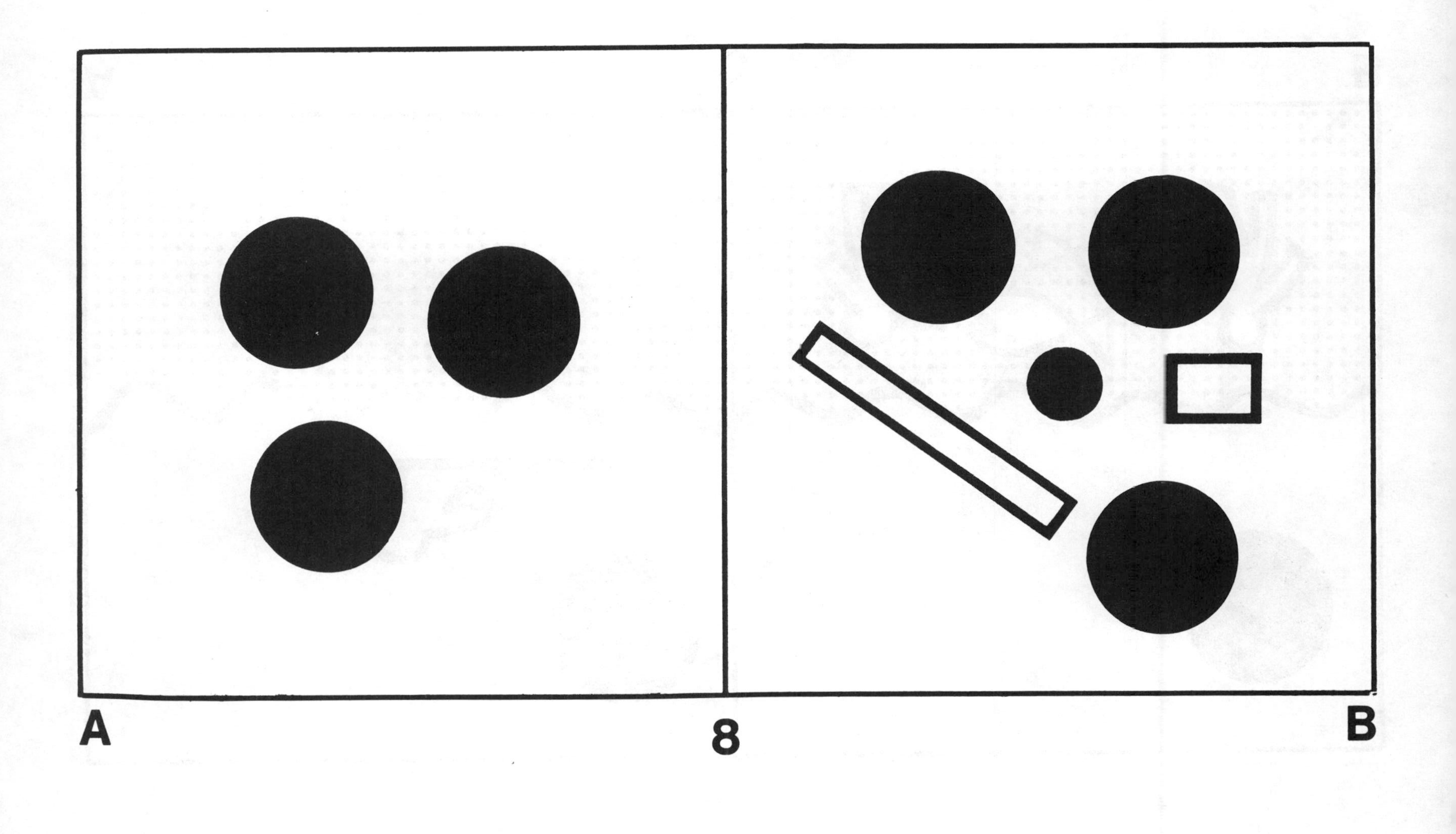
A
8
B

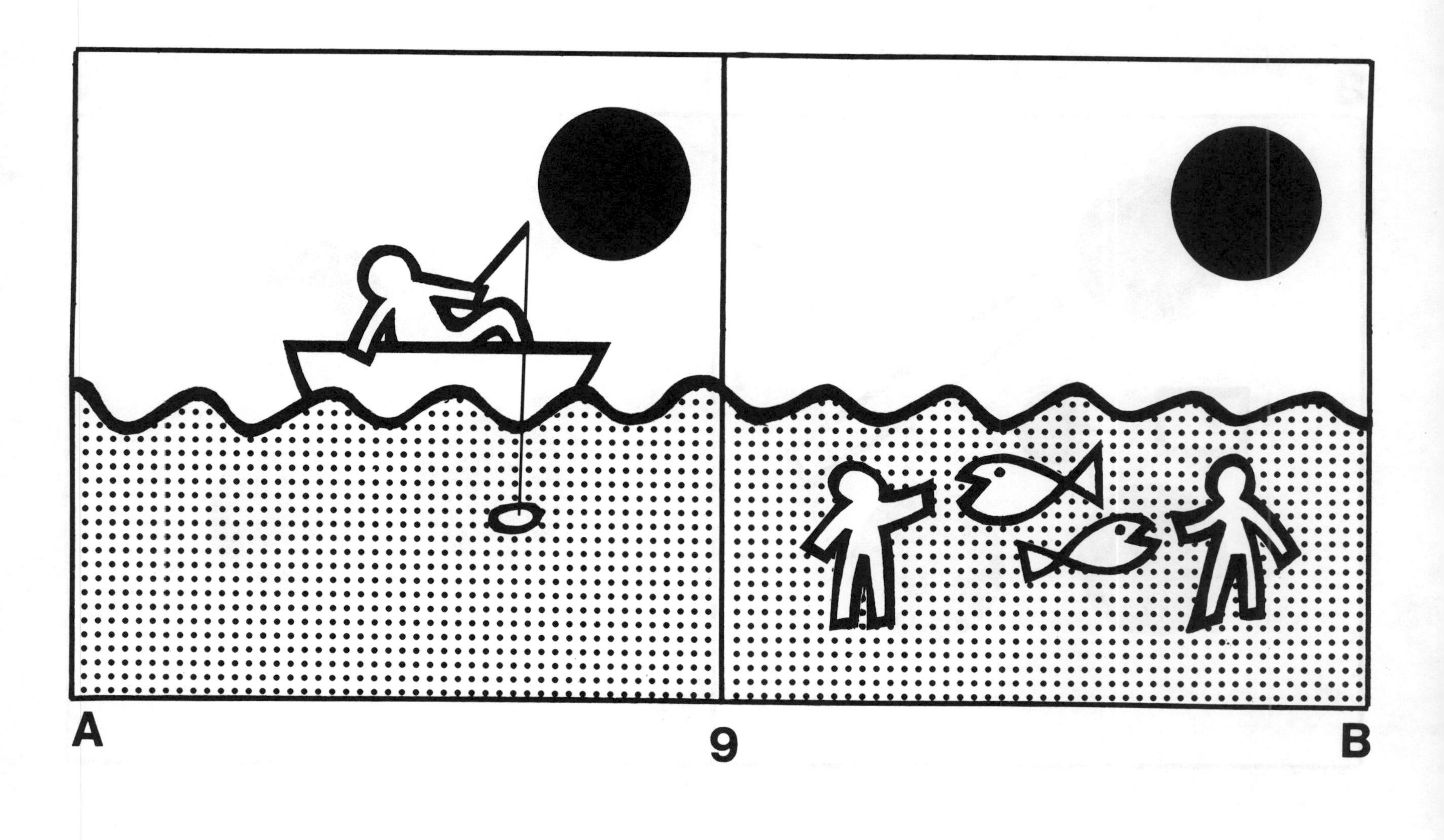
A
9
B

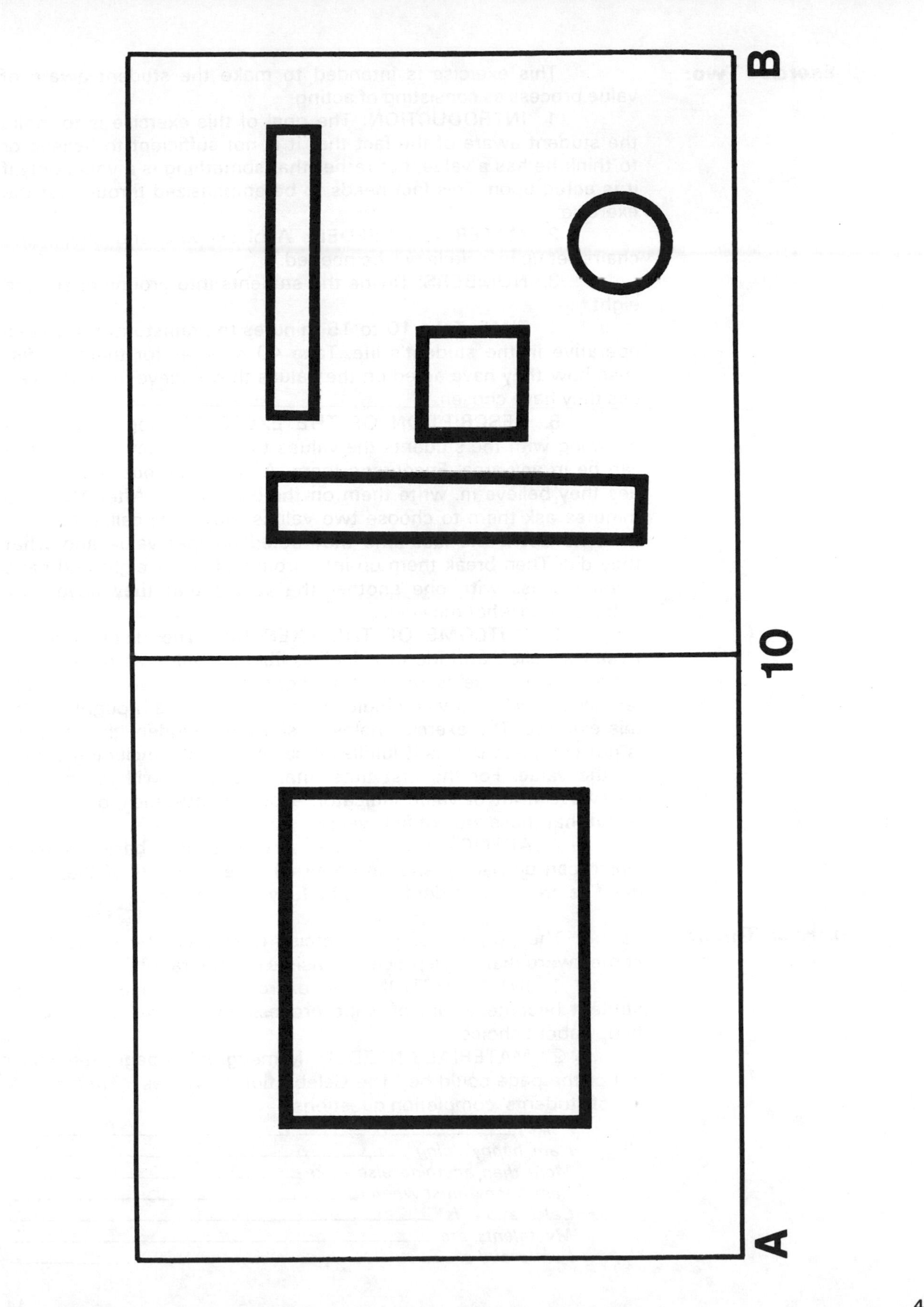
B
10
A

Exercise Two:

This exercise is intended to make the student aware of value process as consisting of acting.

1. INTRODUCTION: The goal of this exercise is to make the student aware of the fact that it is not sufficient to believe or to think he has a value, but rather that something is a value only if it is acted upon. This fact needs to be emphasized throughout the exercise.

2. MATERIALS NEEDED: A blackboard and chalk, and chairs set up in a circle will be needed.

3. NUMBERS: Divide the students into groups of six and eight.

4. TIME: Take 10 to 15 minutes to brainstorm the values operative in the student's life. Take 40 minutes for them to discuss how they have acted on the values they believe in, in the values they have chosen.

5. DESCRIPTION OF THE EXERCISE: Begin by brainstorming with the students the values they think they have. These can be in any area. Encourage them. As they call out various values they believe in, write them on the blackboard. After 10 or 15 minutes ask them to choose two values they have called out and to write down the last time they acted on that value and what they did. Then break them up into groups of six or eight and have them discuss with one another the values that they have fully acted on and what they did.

6. OUTCOME OF THE EXERCISE: The distinction between a belief, attitude or a feeling about a value as opposed to acting on a value is brought to light. In other words, the differences between a value indicator and a value are brought out by this exercise. The exercise helps to show the student that a value is not complete unless it fulfills all seven aspects, including acting on the value. For the first time, many students will realize that they have a lot of value indicators—beliefs, attitudes, or feelings—but that these are not fully values.

7. APPLICATION: This is a very simple basic exercise which can be part of showing how all seven aspects of the value must be present in order for it to be fully a value.

Exercise Three:

The purpose of this exercise is to help the student become aware that value process consists of celebration.

1. INTRODUCTION: This exercise is intended to help the student become aware of value process as celebration, as being happy about choice.

2. MATERIALS NEEDED: Mimeograph a page; the heading of the page could be "The Celebration of Values". Then give a list of students' completion questions.

I like ______________________________.
I am happy doing ________________________.
More than anything else I like ________________.
I am happy most when ____________________.
Celebration is _________________________.
My talents are _________________________.
I am proud of __________________________.

3. NUMBERS: Unlimited.

4. TIME: Give the students approximately 5 minutes to fill out the questionnaire, 45 minutes to discuss.

5. DESCRIPTION OF PROCESS: Ask the students to fill out the sentence completion form. Then have them discuss how they have filled it out, in light of an understanding of the celebration of their values. An alternative procedure, after they have selected what they would like to celebrate, is to list on the opposite side of the page what they would be unhappy about and would not like to celebrate, placing themselves on the continuum as to where they feel they are right now.

6. OUTCOME OF THE EXERCISE: Hopefully, the student will come to realize that a value is something that is enjoyed, prized and celebrated; this is an important element in an understanding of what a full value is.

7. APPLICATION: Very important in our puritanical society is for us to regain an appreciation of celebration. Use this exercise as an opportunity to see that doing the good can be fun, that virtue is not in boredom or dullness.

FOR THE TEACHER

Exercise One:

This is an exercise to make teachers aware of the value process in their own lives and teaching as choice.

1. INTRODUCTION: The goal of this exercise is to help teachers become aware of some of their values relative to young

VALUE CLARIFICATION INVENTORY NO. 1

Mark the phrase which is closest to your own inclination.

CHILDREN OR YOUNG PEOPLE SHOULD:

- ___ *Be seen and not heard*
- ___ *Be allowed to make some rules*
- ___ *Believe what their parents teach them*
- ___ *Be trusted*
- ___ *Be allowed to speak their piece*
- ___ *Follow the rules*
- ___ *Be allowed to question their parents' rules and values*
- ___ *Kept in place*

PEOPLE ARE:

- ___ *Occasions of sins*
- ___ *Inclined to evil*
- ___ *To be watched*
- ___ *Basically good*
- ___ *To be trusted*

GOD IS:

- ___ *Merciful*
- ___ *Present*
- ___ *Punisher of evil-*
- ___ *Judge*
- ___ *Remote*
- ___ *Lover of men*

people and to have them make a choice about their values.

2. MATERIALS NEEDED: It would be helpful to reproduce Value Clarification Inventory No. 1 and Value Clarification Inventory No. II.

3. NUMBERS: Groups of eight ordinarily make very good discussion groups. Frequently, a large group can be divided into groups of eight by asking individuals to choose a partner and then asking the pairs to choose another pair and the quartet to choose another quartet.

4. TIME: Give 10 minutes to finish both inventories at the same time by the individual.

5. DESCRIPTION OF THE EXERCISE:

a. Have the students arrange themselves in groups of

VALUE CLARIFICATION INVENTORY NO. II

Think of the line between the two columns as a continuum and mark where you think you would be on a scale of 1 to 10.

	1 2 3 4 5 6 7 8 9 10	
MY FUTURE:		
1. Is hopeful.	______________________	*Is fearful.*
2. Does not bear thinking about.	______________________	*Will be built by me.*
3. Depends on my actions.	______________________	*Depends on the winds of fate.*
4. Depends on external factors.	______________________	*Depends on my choices and decisions.*
STUDENTS SHOULD:		
5. Be allowed to evaluate teachers.	______________________	*Be seen and not heard.*
6. Be allowed to form their own opinions and reject the teachers.	______________________	*Listen to and believe what the experienced teacher tells them.*
7. Obey the rules.	______________________	*Help set the rules.*
8. Do as they are told.	______________________	*Have a voice in choosing programs.*
9. Speak their minds.	______________________	*Be quiet and listen.*

eight. An effective way of doing this is to ask the students to choose among themselves who they think are the more talkative ones and those who are more quiet. Then have these individuals form pairs, go off and form groups of eight by meeting or getting together with three other pairs. (People often feel awkward about admitting that they are more talkative than others. However, this is an effective method of getting people into groups, to show that the groups will be composed of quiet or talkative people. When this happens, often the quiet groups become angry or disappointed because they got nothing out of the discussion.)

b. When the groups are settled, have them sit in circles facing each other and fill out the two value inventories.

c. After they have filled out the inventories, have them compare and discuss what they have on their continuums and then their box choices. About 15 minutes of discussion would probably be a minimal time for this exercise.

d. Now have the students discuss how differently they felt between marking the continuums and marking the boxes.

e. It is very effective for the facilitator to use a voting technique at this point—which is simply posing a question and then asking the students to raise their hands to indicate those who agree or disagree with the question. In this case, ask for a show of hands of those who prefer to mark the box choices rather than the continuum choices. Next, ask for a show of hands of those who prefer to mark the continuums rather than the box choices. (Usually when this is done, about 50 percent prefer one way and 50 percent prefer the other.) After this, it is useful for the facilitator to point out that there are two types of choices in the two different inventories. On the continuum there is a greater range of choices, depending on where students put their marks. On the box choice, things tend to be placed in black or white situations. Those who prefer the boxes to the continuums are inclined to be a little more dependent, tend to prefer quick decisions and are less comfortable with process development in which there is not always a clear answer to certain problems.

f. Have the group finally discuss the implications of these two exercises, giving them about 15 minutes to come up with some of their own continuums and boxes. You may wish to suggest the following: "Brainstorm in your groups some of the issues and priorities that are important to the students you are working with and then make up your own box inventory and continuum inventory to test out with your students".

6. POSSIBLE OUTCOMES: The excitement of the discussion is in the discovery that some people have similar values and some have different values. One outcome, very frequently, is that a person learns of people he likes who have different values from his, or people he knows who are very confident but have different values than he has.

7. APPLICATION: This is a simple exercise to give teachers an opportunity to choose what their values are and to become

aware that there is a choice in the values they establish for themselves.

Exercise Two: This is an exercise to make the teachers aware of the value process in their own lives, and teaching as *action.*

1. INTRODUCTION: The goal and purpose of this exercise is to bring out to the teacher how action is an indicator of value; the goal is to show the teacher how behavior is an indication of values. As you will recall from the introduction of the book, a value must be acted upon.

2. MATERIALS NEEDED: Paper and pencil for each of the participants are needed.

3. NUMBERS: Any number may participate in this. We suggest that the groups break up into groups of six or eight.

4. TIME: The individual should be given approximately 15 to 20 minutes to write and then be given approximately 40 or 45 minutes to discuss and share what he has written. Frequently, the group is stimulated by the discussion, so the discussion might go on much longer.

5. DESCRIPTION OF THE EXERCISE: It will take the participants approximately 15 to 20 minutes to write out two major decisions that they have made in their lives and on which they have acted. Then encourage the participants to move into groups of six or eight and to share and discuss with one another what these decisions were and how making them, living them, and acting them out helped them in their lives.

6. POSSIBLE OUTCOMES: Once again this will give the teachers the opportunity to see the value of acting on values they have chosen, and the importance of behavior in relationship to and in understanding values and value clarification.

7. APPLICATION: This is a very basic and simple exercise in coming to an understanding of how action and behavior are important to values and are indicators of value.

Exercise Three: This is an exercise to make the teacher aware of value process in his own life and teaching as celebration.

1. INTRODUCTION: The goal of this exercise for the teachers is to give them an appreciation of celebration at a rather deep level. A powerful way of coming to understand and appreciate the celebration of one's choices and values is by a careful analysis of how one's limitations have positive potential. In this exercise, once the individual has turned limitations into potentials, it becomes an occasion of celebration and joy.

2. MATERIALS NEEDED: Pencil and paper.

3. NUMBERS: Unlimited.

4. TIME: Give the participants approximately 10 to 15 minutes to write out their limitations. Then announce and give them time (10 to 15 minutes) to write out the potential, the posi-

tive potential, in those limitations. Then have 30 to 45 minutes of discussion on what they have discovered.

5. DESCRIPTION OF THE PROCESS: It is important to separate the instructions here; do not give them all at once. Announce at first only that you wish them to write out their limitations. Once they have finished that, ask them to write out how they might turn their limitations into potentials. Some may have difficulty in doing this. At this point, after they have had approximately 20 to 30 minutes to write their limitations and turn them into potentials, they can move into groups of six or eight. The members of the group can become resource people who will help them to turn their limitations into positive potential.

6. POSSIBLE OUTCOMES: The possible outcomes are that people will be awakened to the fact that limitations are not merely negative influences in their lives, but rather have positive and beneficial effects. For example, you might take a person who has made a list of limitations such as: "I'm untidy in the morning". "I'm bored at school-board meetings". "I get depressed occasionally". "I fail to get dinner on time occasionally". For some people it is very difficult to take this list of limitations and turn them into the positive potential inherent in those limitations. So, it is important that the group help the person see the positive side. For example, the positive side of the limitations listed for the person who says, "I am untidy in the morning", is, quite possibly, that she waits up for her husband at night to continue to grow in that relationship. Or for the person who says, "I am bored at school-board meetings", it might well be that the positive side is that he likes more intimate relationships. Or the person who says, "I get depressed occasionally", may well be a very conscientious or creative person. A person who says, "I fail to get dinner on time", may very well be a person who works extremely hard and is very person-oriented.

6. POSSIBLE OUTCOMES: This particular exercise is a very important one. It presents opportunities for individuals in the group to overcome a one-sided view of life. It helps people begin to understand that our potential and our limitations are integrated. It is very revealing to some people to begin to see that even in their limitations there are positive potentials.

7. APPLICATION: One of the most important applications in this exercise is for the teacher to grow in the attitude of respect for the individuality of the students whom he teaches—for him to grow in the attitude of realizing that potential may even be hidden in the limitations of the student.

FOR THE PROFESSIONAL TRAINER

Exercise One:

Exercise one is to help the trainer become aware of value process in its more extensive implications in the teaching process in choice.

1. INTRODUCTION: This experience is a method of uti-

lizing and exercising imagination and ability to choose. Ultimately, what is true is that which you insightfully discover about yourself. The best way to begin this exercise is to assume a relaxed position. Try to relax all your muscles, closing your eyes and breathing deeply four or five times.

2. MATERIALS NEEDED: Again, you may either use slides or an overhead projector with the pictures in the book, or you may in free-hand style reduplicate these for passing out individually.

3. NUMBERS: Use groups of four or eight.

4. TIME: Depending on how long you wish to spend on it, this exercise can take anywhere from one hour to three hours.

5. DESCRIPTION OF THE EXERCISE: The exercise begins by trying to have everyone assume a relaxed position. Ask people to close their eyes, breathe deeply four or five times, and then begin to look at the pictures. As they go through the pictures, they make a choice. Go through the pictures slowly to give everyone a chance to really observe them closely. At the end, it would be well to break the group up into quartets or octets to discuss their experiences in this exercise.

First consider the following sets of pictures. Each set is marked "A" and "B". Place the instructions for each set of pictures on the page facing the two pictures for the first three sets. However, only one set of instructions is necessary. Allow at least 3 minutes for the exercises where the eyes are closed.

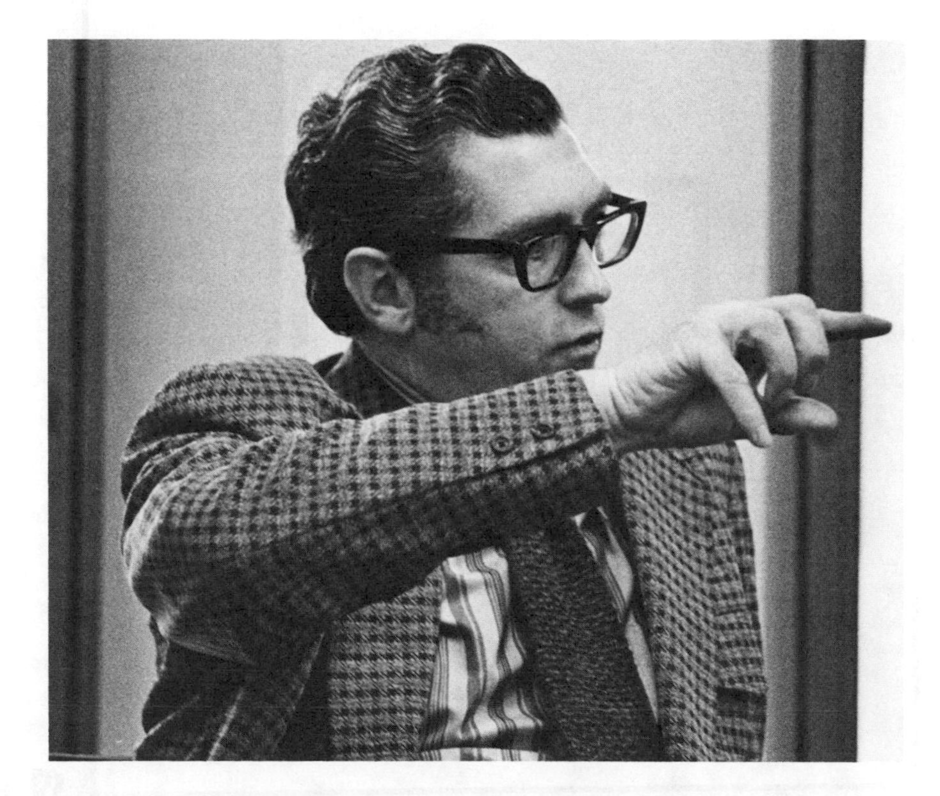

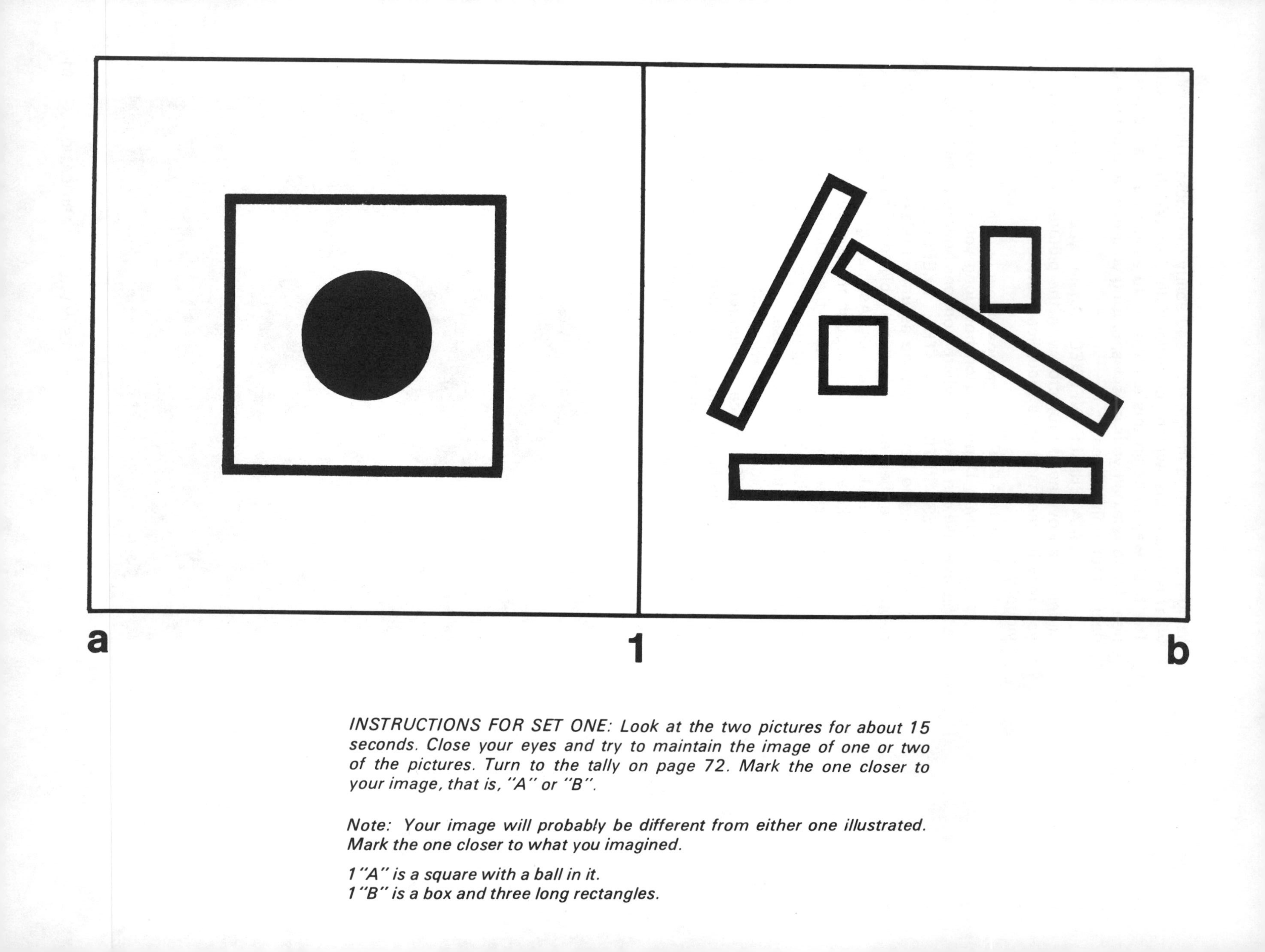

INSTRUCTIONS FOR SET ONE: Look at the two pictures for about 15 seconds. Close your eyes and try to maintain the image of one or two of the pictures. Turn to the tally on page 72. Mark the one closer to your image, that is, "A" or "B".

Note: Your image will probably be different from either one illustrated. Mark the one closer to what you imagined.

1"A" is a square with a ball in it.
1"B" is a box and three long rectangles.

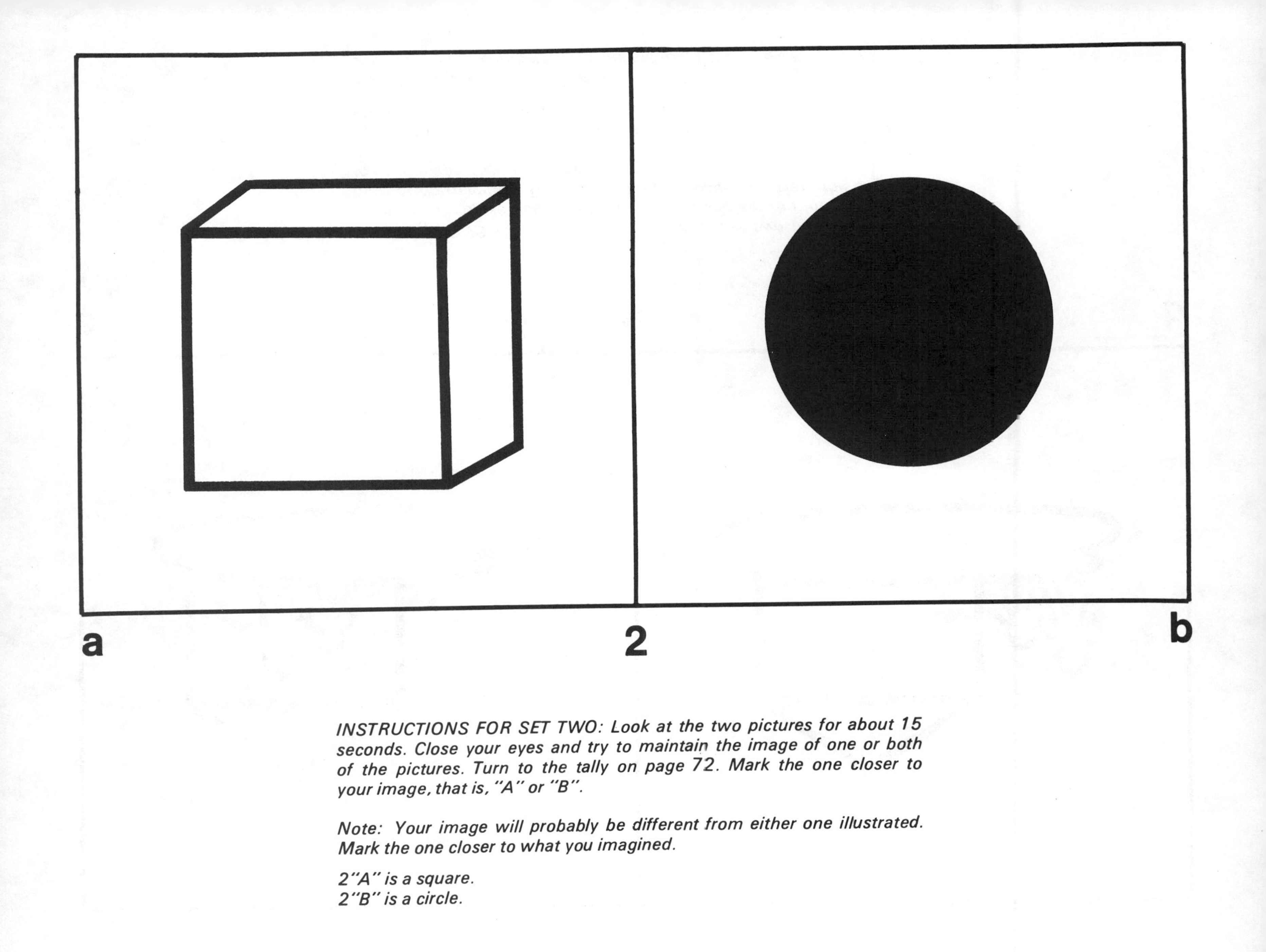

INSTRUCTIONS FOR SET TWO: Look at the two pictures for about 15 seconds. Close your eyes and try to maintain the image of one or both of the pictures. Turn to the tally on page 72. Mark the one closer to your image, that is, "A" or "B".

Note: Your image will probably be different from either one illustrated. Mark the one closer to what you imagined.

2"A" is a square.
2"B" is a circle.

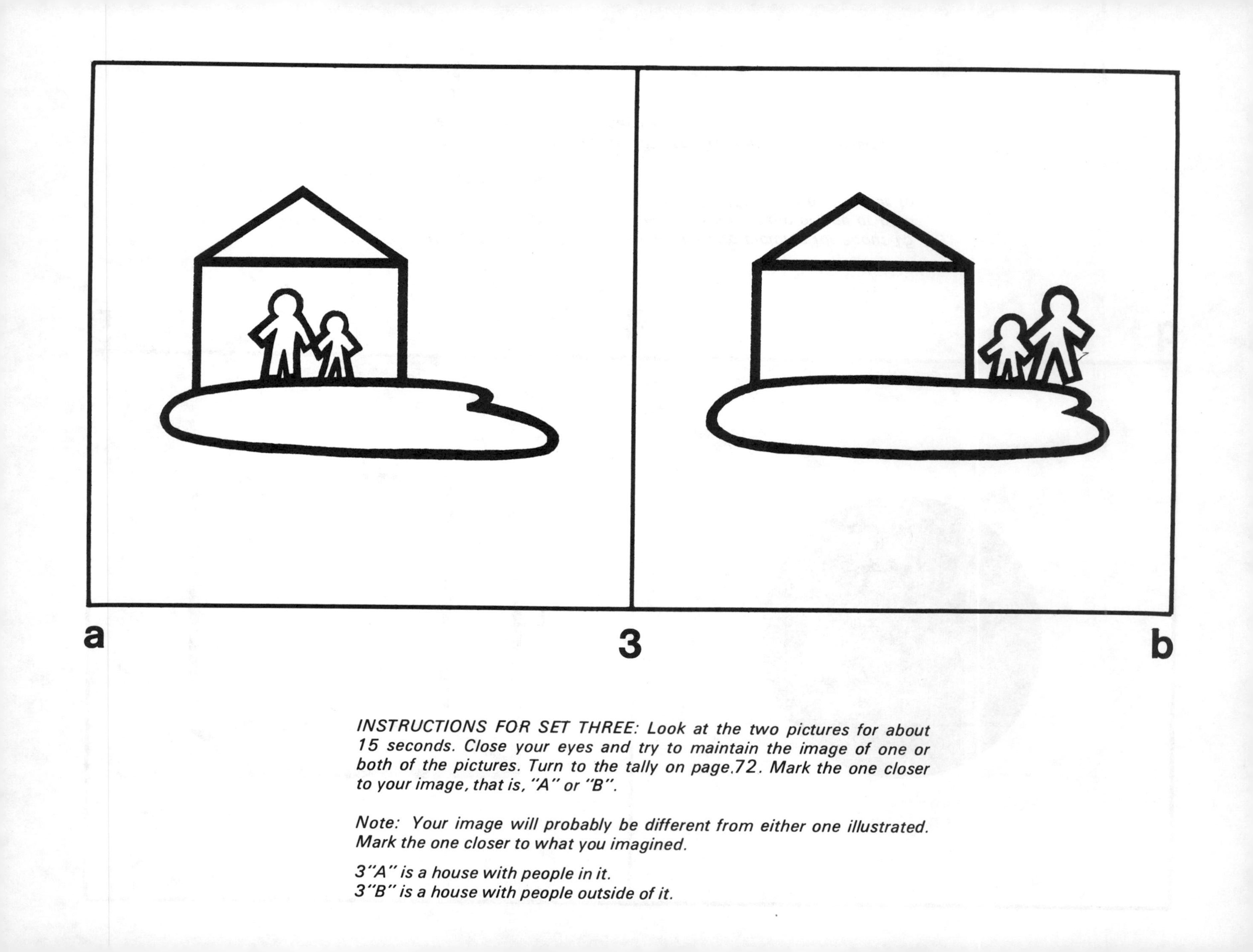

INSTRUCTIONS FOR SET THREE: Look at the two pictures for about 15 seconds. Close your eyes and try to maintain the image of one or both of the pictures. Turn to the tally on page.72. Mark the one closer to your image, that is, "A" or "B".

Note: Your image will probably be different from either one illustrated. Mark the one closer to what you imagined.

3"A" is a house with people in it.
3"B" is a house with people outside of it.

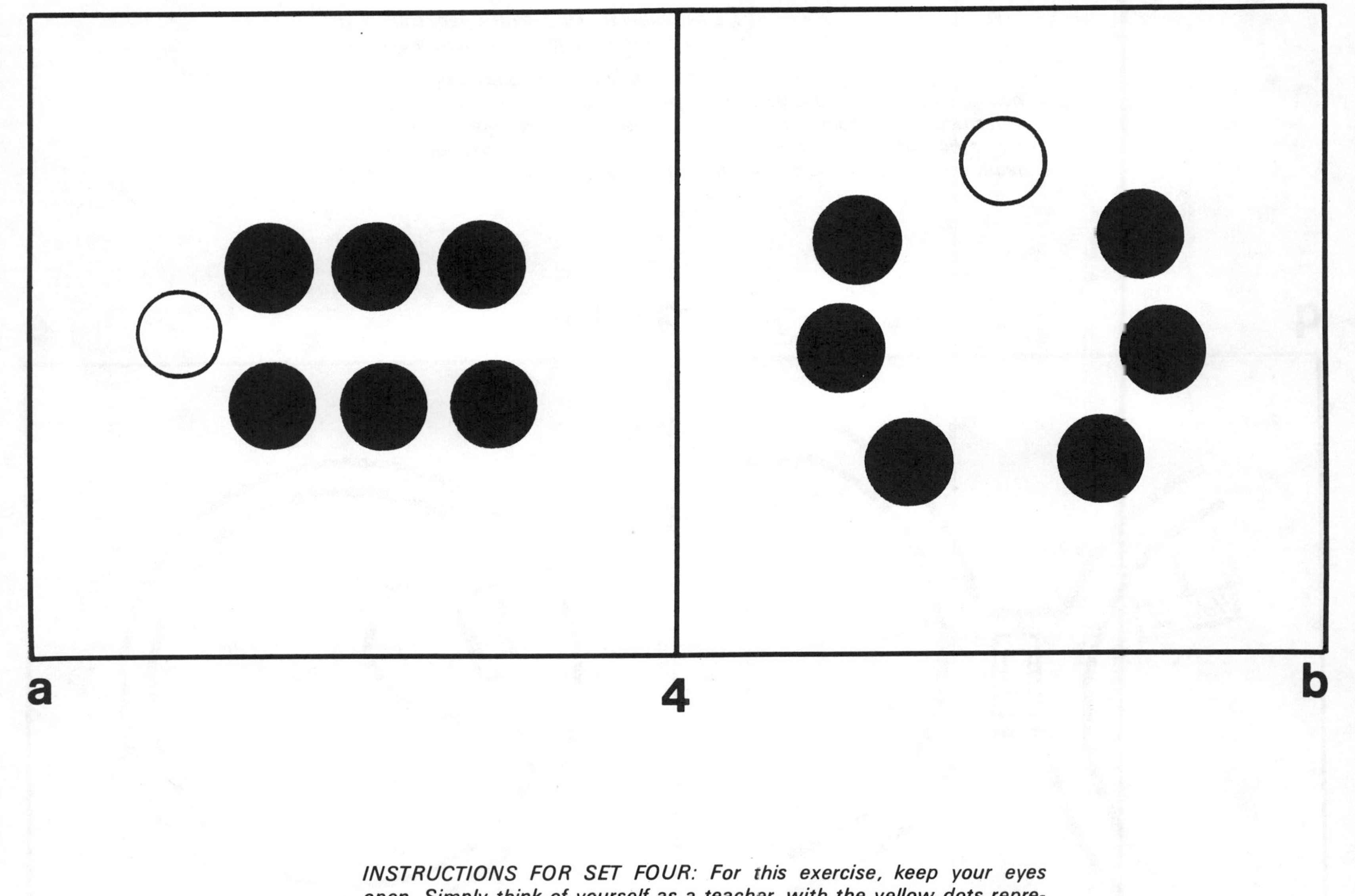

INSTRUCTIONS FOR SET FOUR: For this exercise, keep your eyes open. Simply think of yourself as a teacher, with the yellow dots representing students. Which would you choose, "A" or "B"? Mark your answer on the tally on page 72.

4"A" is seven circles with circles in rows.
4"B" is seven circles in a circle.

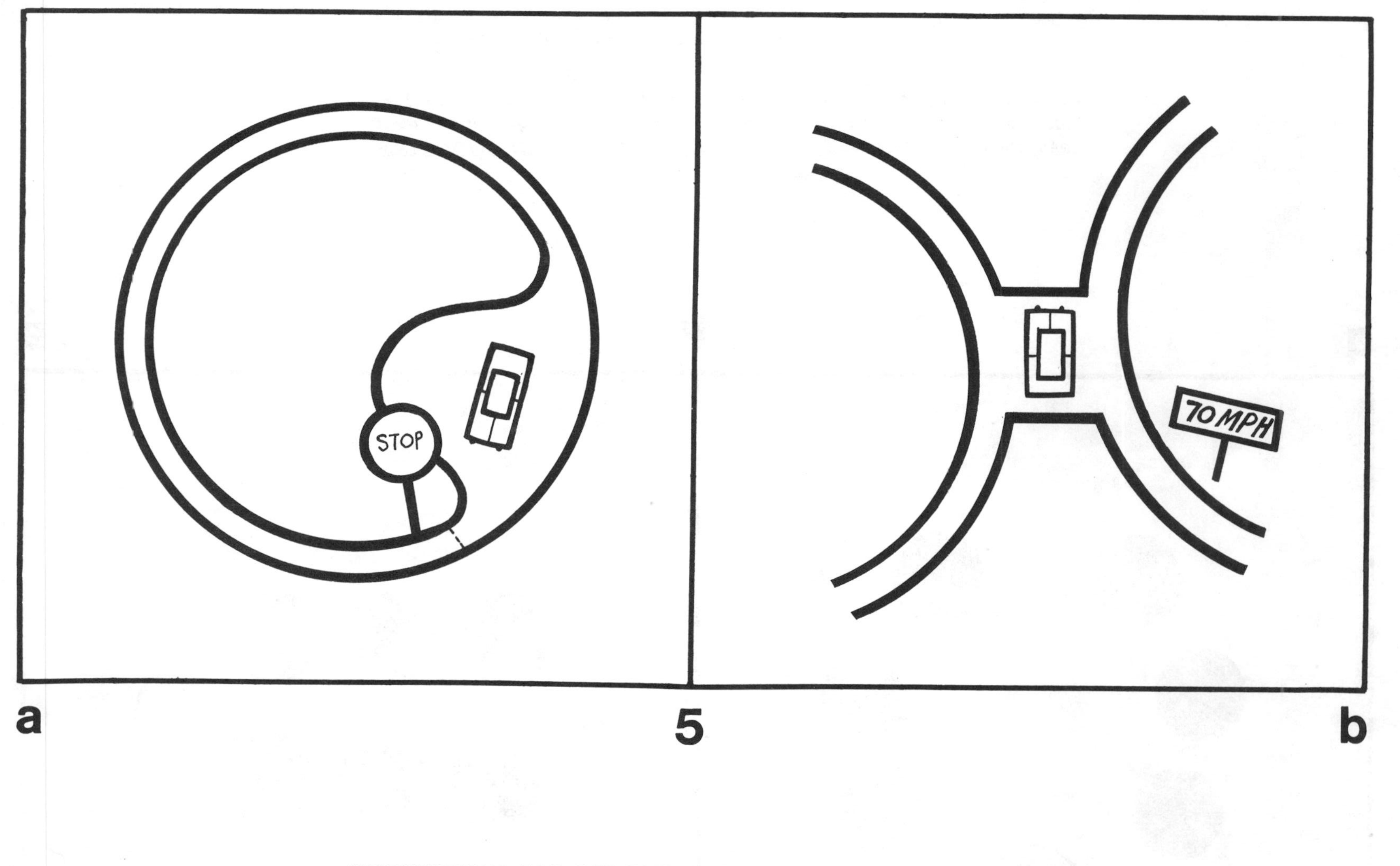

INSTRUCTIONS FOR SET FIVE: For this exercise, imagine that what you see are two road maps. The first is a circle which represents that you will be traveling in familiar territory. The second, 5"B", represents an open road system which could lead anywhere. Which would you choose? Mark your answer on the tally.

5"A" is a circle with a circle inside of it.
5"B" is a road with a V in it; it looks like a Y.

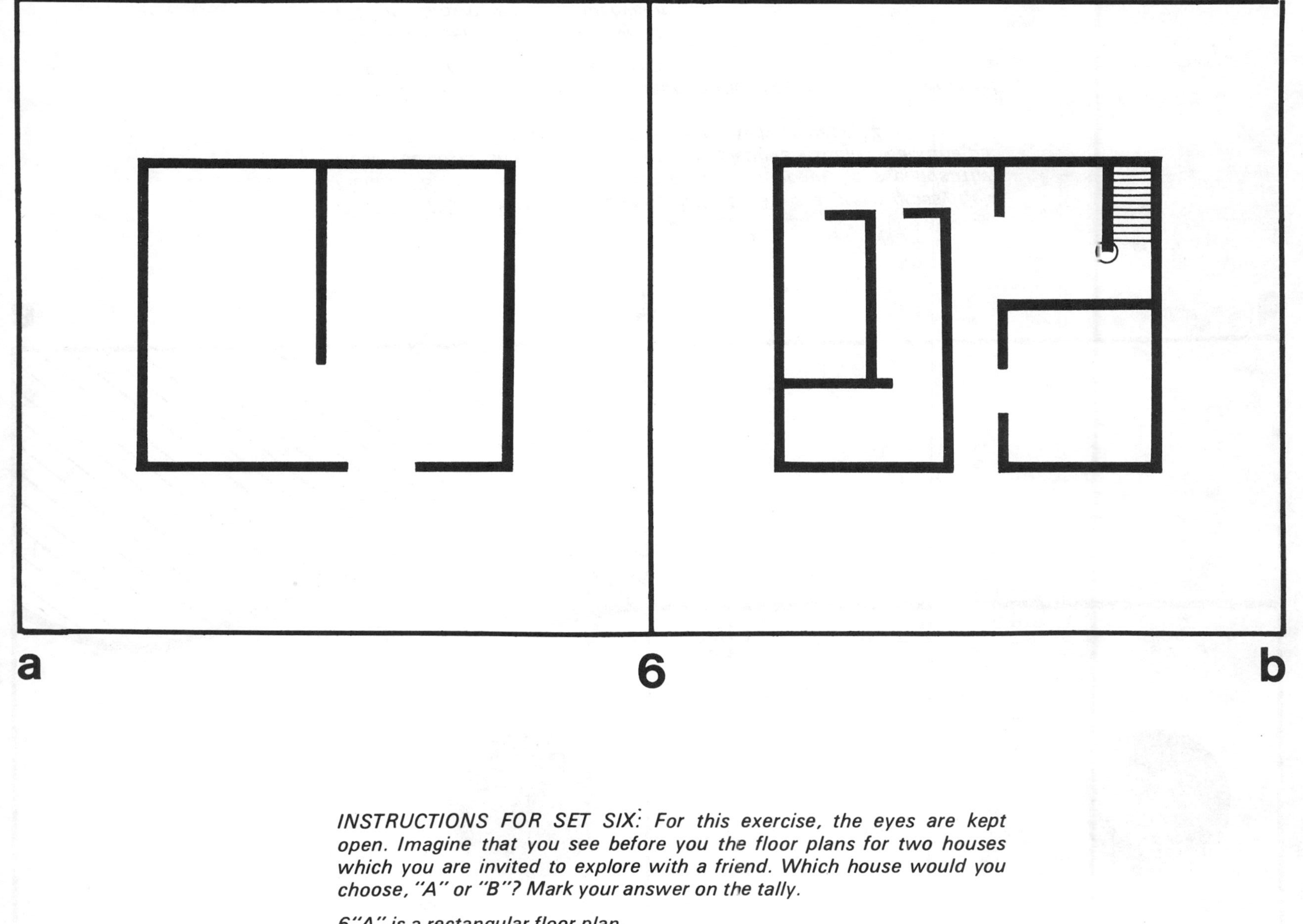

INSTRUCTIONS FOR SET SIX: For this exercise, the eyes are kept open. Imagine that you see before you the floor plans for two houses which you are invited to explore with a friend. Which house would you choose, "A" or "B"? Mark your answer on the tally.

6"A" is a rectangular floor plan.
6"B" is also a rectangular floor plan, with a chair and other articles in the house.

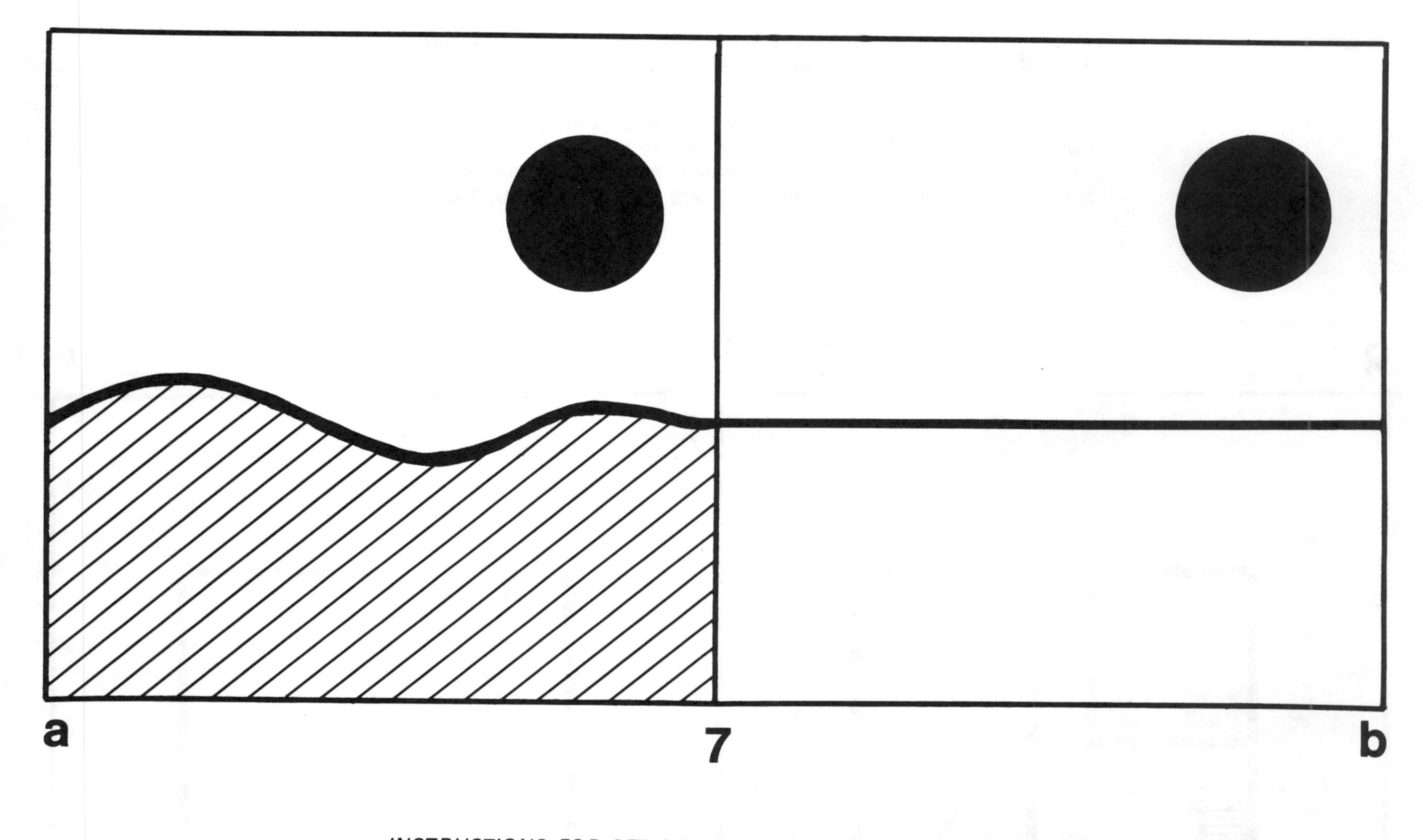

INSTRUCTIONS FOR SET SEVEN: Picture "A" is a green grassy field. Picture "B". is a dry desert. Look at both for about 15 seconds, then close your eyes and try to hold onto the pictures visually. Mark the picture closer to the image you visualize on the tally on page 72.

Note: Some people find that visualizing this way is very hard, in which case some practice will be necessary.

7"A" is a green field with sun over it.
7"B" is a brown field with sun over it.

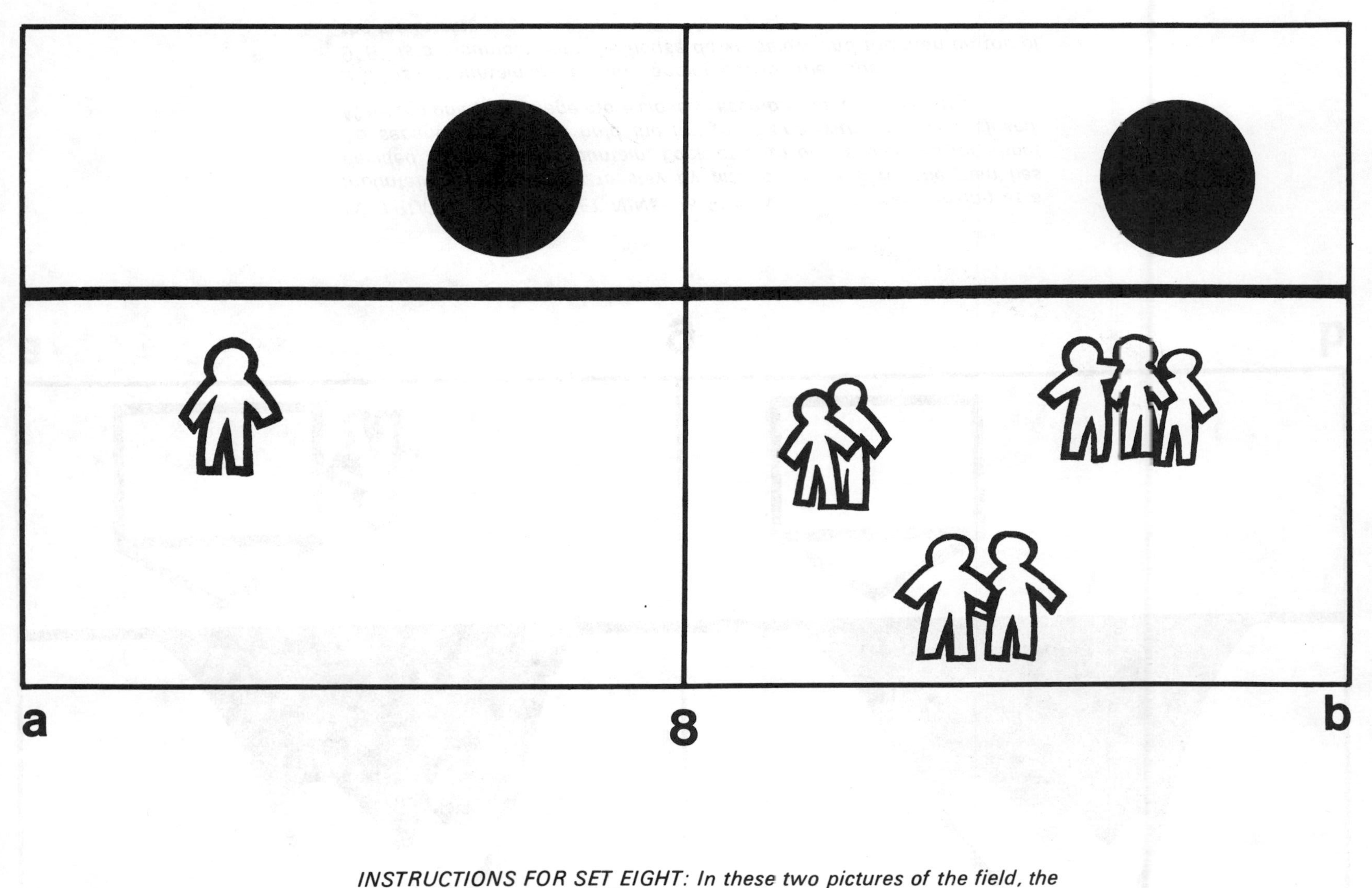

INSTRUCTIONS FOR SET EIGHT: In these two pictures of the field, the only difference is the number of people in each. Look at both the pictures for about 15 seconds and try to hold the image of one with your eyes closed. Mark the one your image more closely resembles on the tally page.

8"A" is a green field with one person in it.
8"B" is a green field with a couple of sets of people in it.

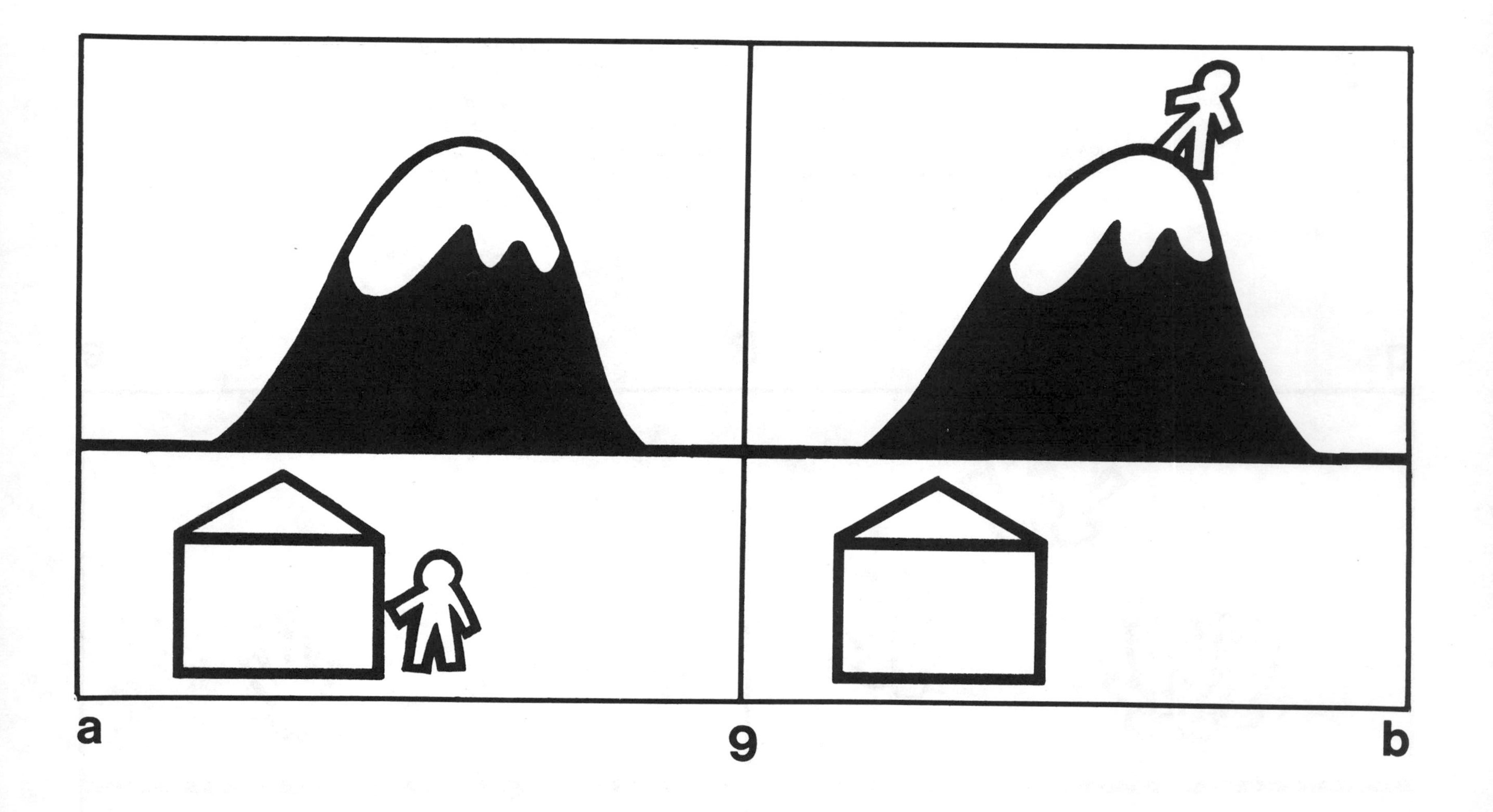

INSTRUCTIONS FOR SET NINE: In 9"A" you see a man looking at a mountain, but preferring to stay by his house; in 9"B" the man has decided to climb the mountain. Look at both of the pictures for about 15 seconds and try to hold the image of one with your eyes closed. Mark the one your image more closely resembles on the tally page.

9"A" is a mountain and a man standing outside the house.
9"B" is a mountain with the house down below and the man on top of the mountain.

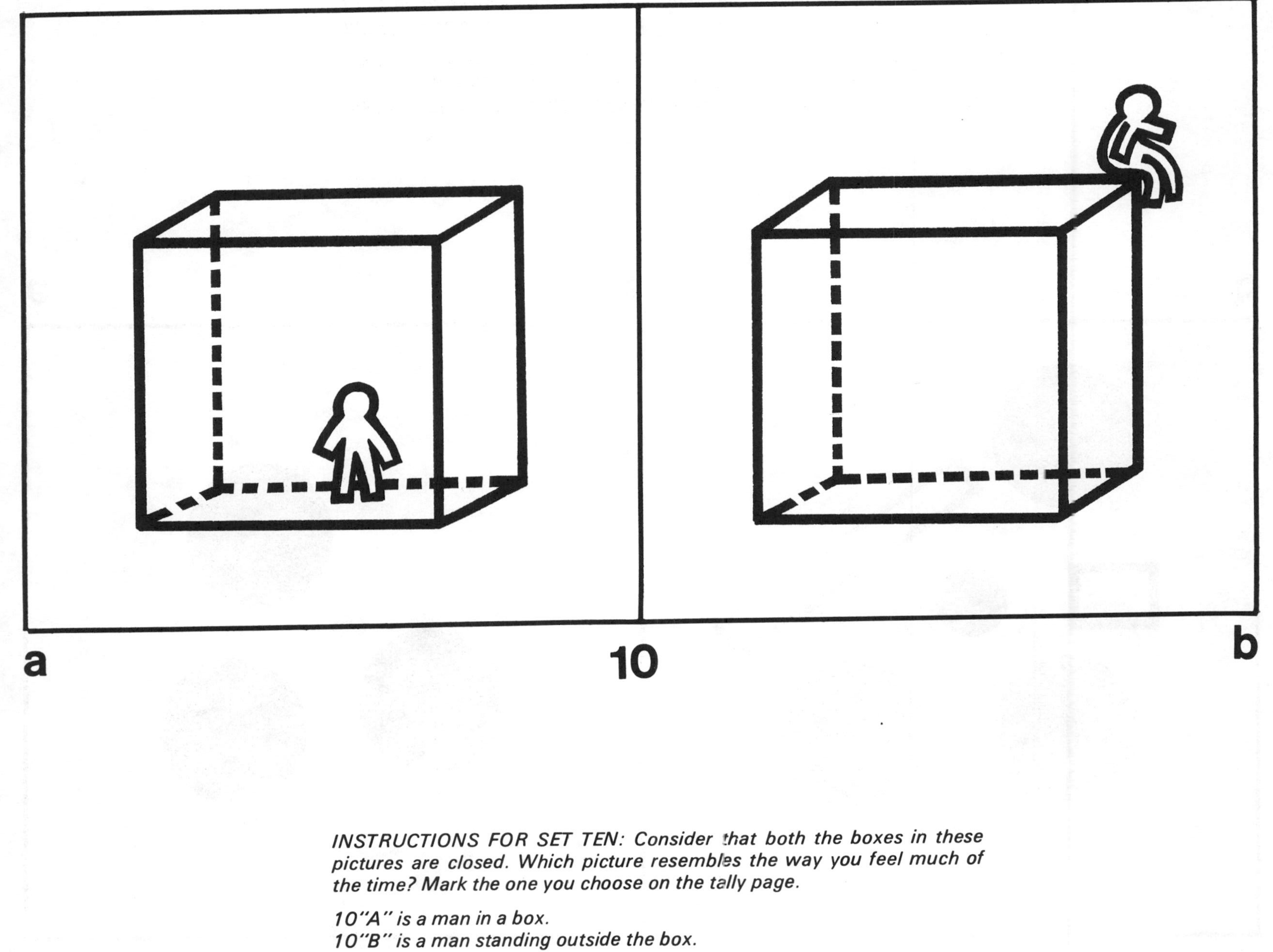

INSTRUCTIONS FOR SET TEN: Consider that both the boxes in these pictures are closed. Which picture resembles the way you feel much of the time? Mark the one you choose on the tally page.

10"A" is a man in a box.
10"B" is a man standing outside the box.

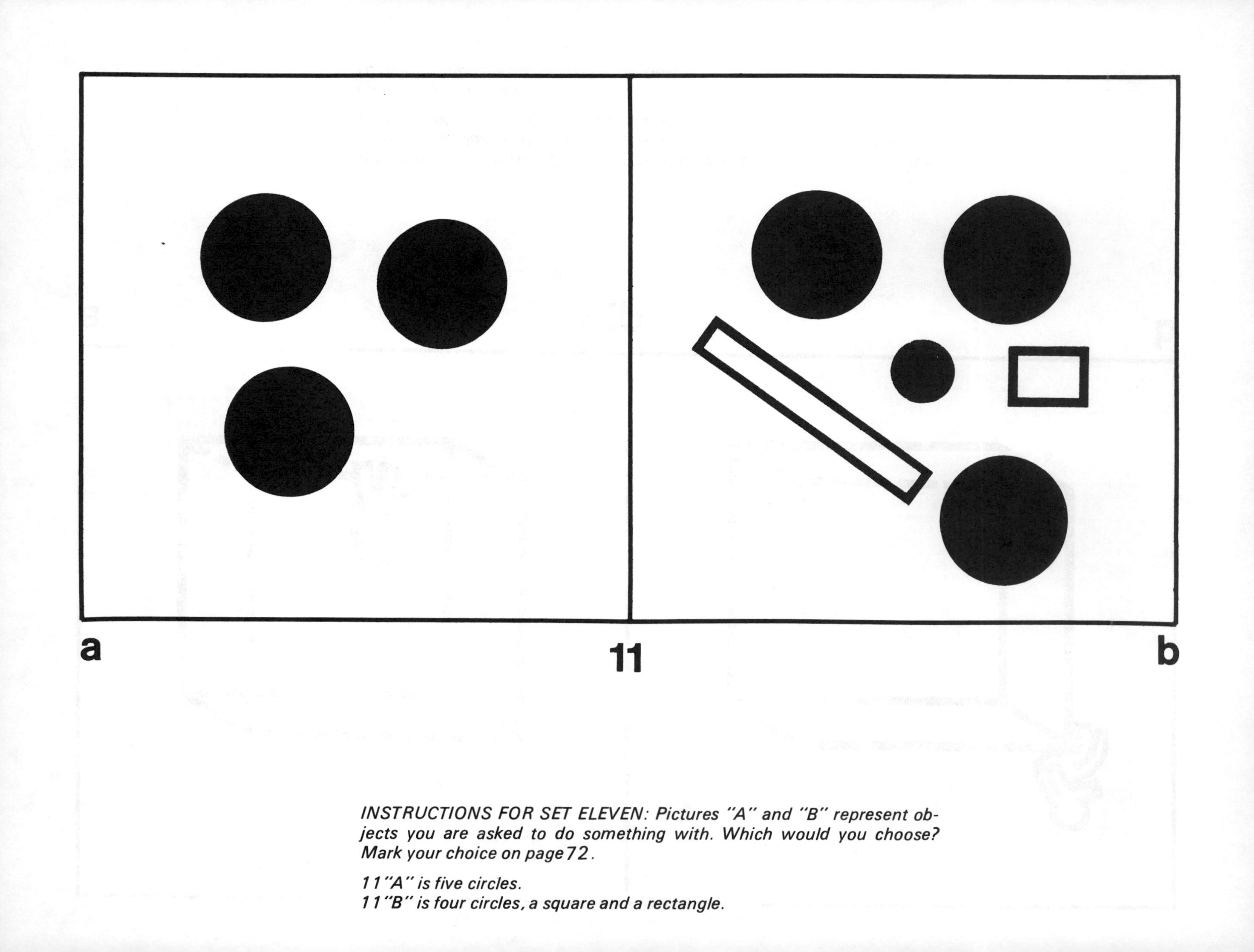

INSTRUCTIONS FOR SET ELEVEN: Pictures "A" and "B" represent objects you are asked to do something with. Which would you choose? Mark your choice on page 72.

11 "A" is five circles.
11 "B" is four circles, a square and a rectangle.

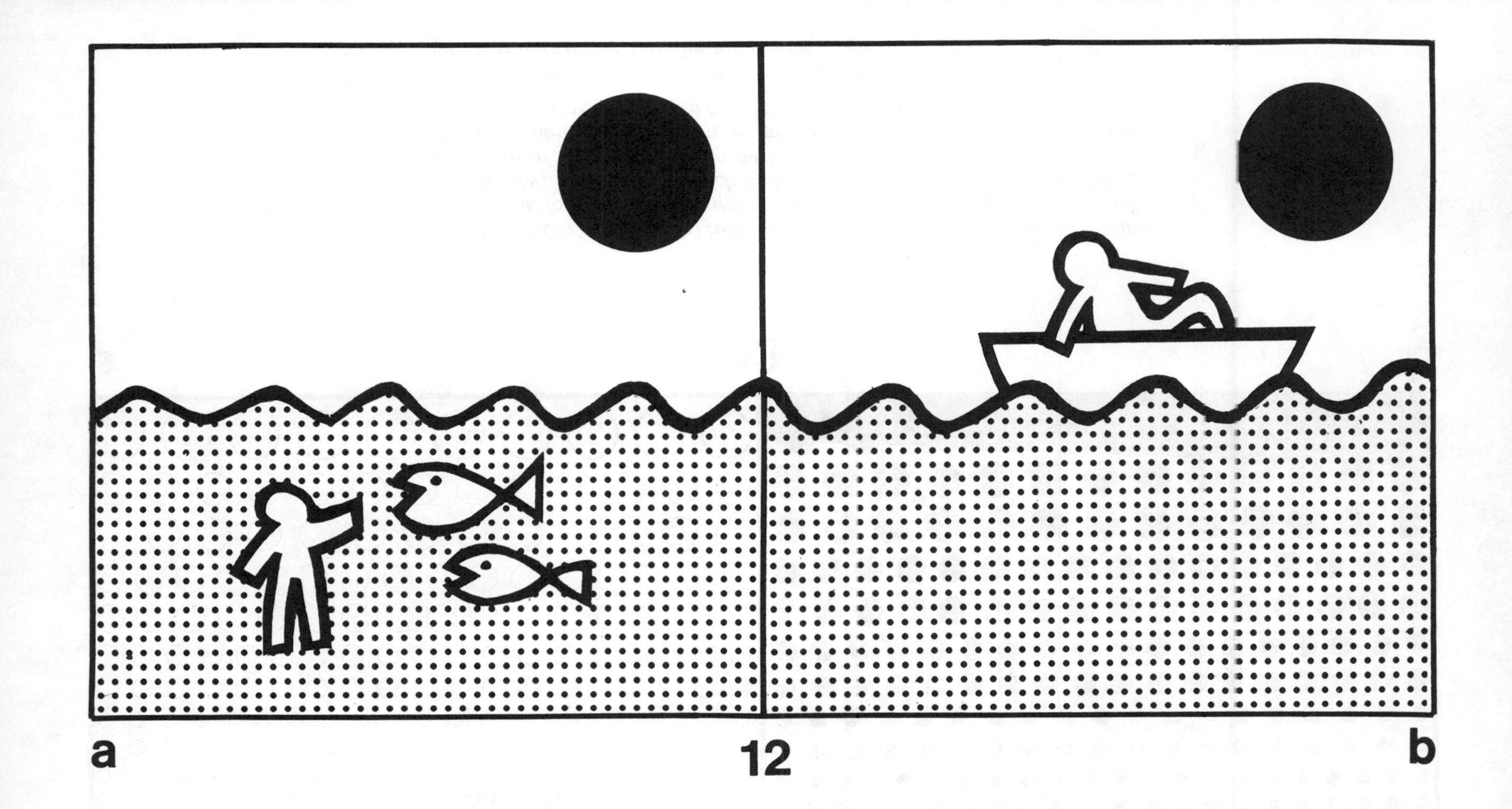

INSTRUCTIONS FOR SET TWELVE: Picture "A" is a man underwater having a conversation with the fish. "B" is a man in a boat, rowing toward the shore. Look at these for about 15 seconds, then close your eyes and allow an image to develop for a minute or so. Mark on the tally the picture your final image resembles more.

12"A" is a man in the water, talking to the fish.
12"B" is a man in the boat, rowing toward the shore.

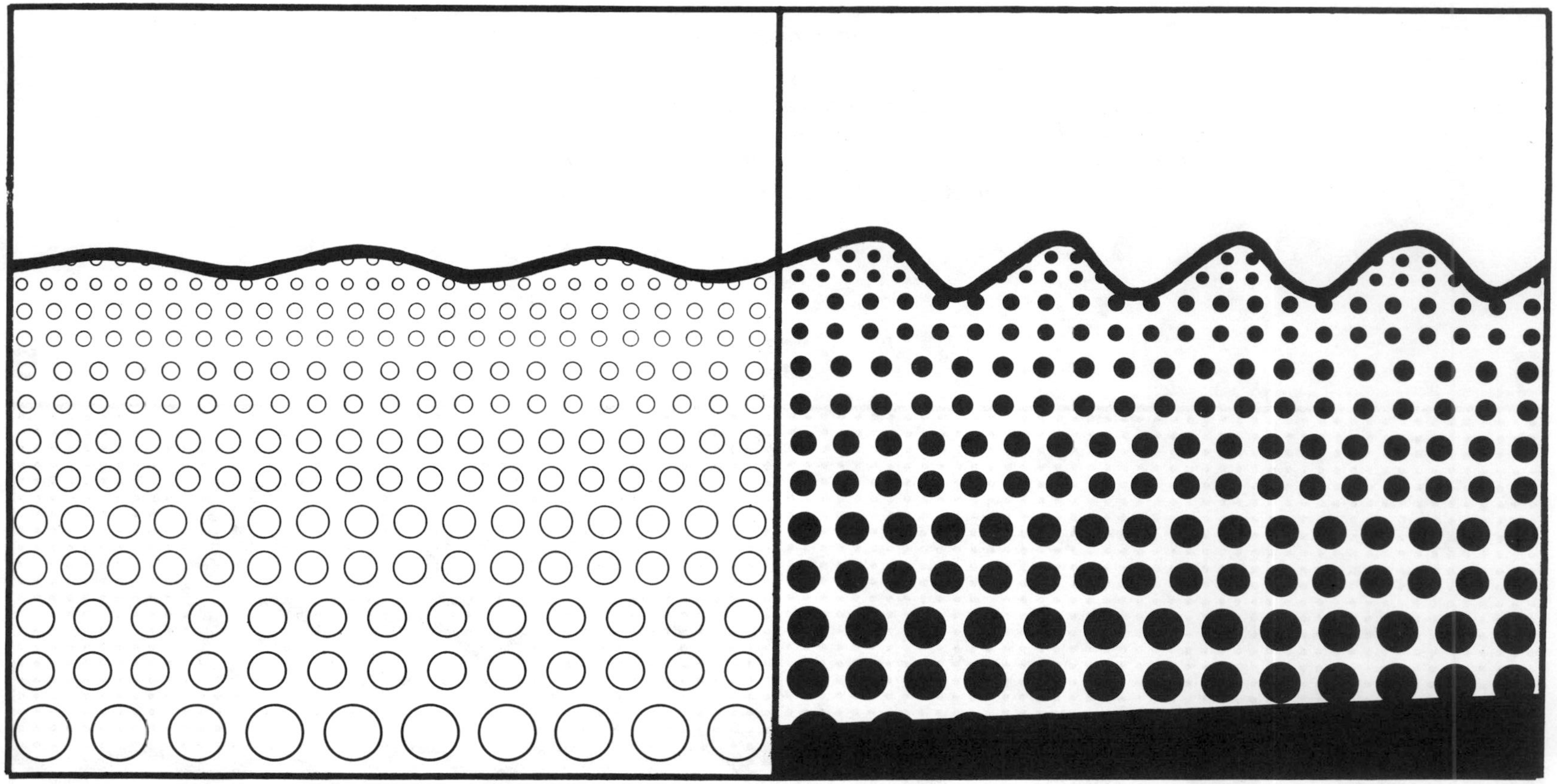

a

13

b

INSTRUCTIONS FOR SET THIRTEEN: Imagine that you are going on an underwater journey. Look at the two pictures, and close your eyes. Mark on the tally, on page 72, which picture was closer to your image. When you were in the water, was it dark and murky or blue and interesting? The blue here is not meant to be associated with the idea of "the blues", but rather will be the blueness of water, lake or ocean.

13"A" is light clear water with the sun over it.
13"B" is dark water with the sun over it.

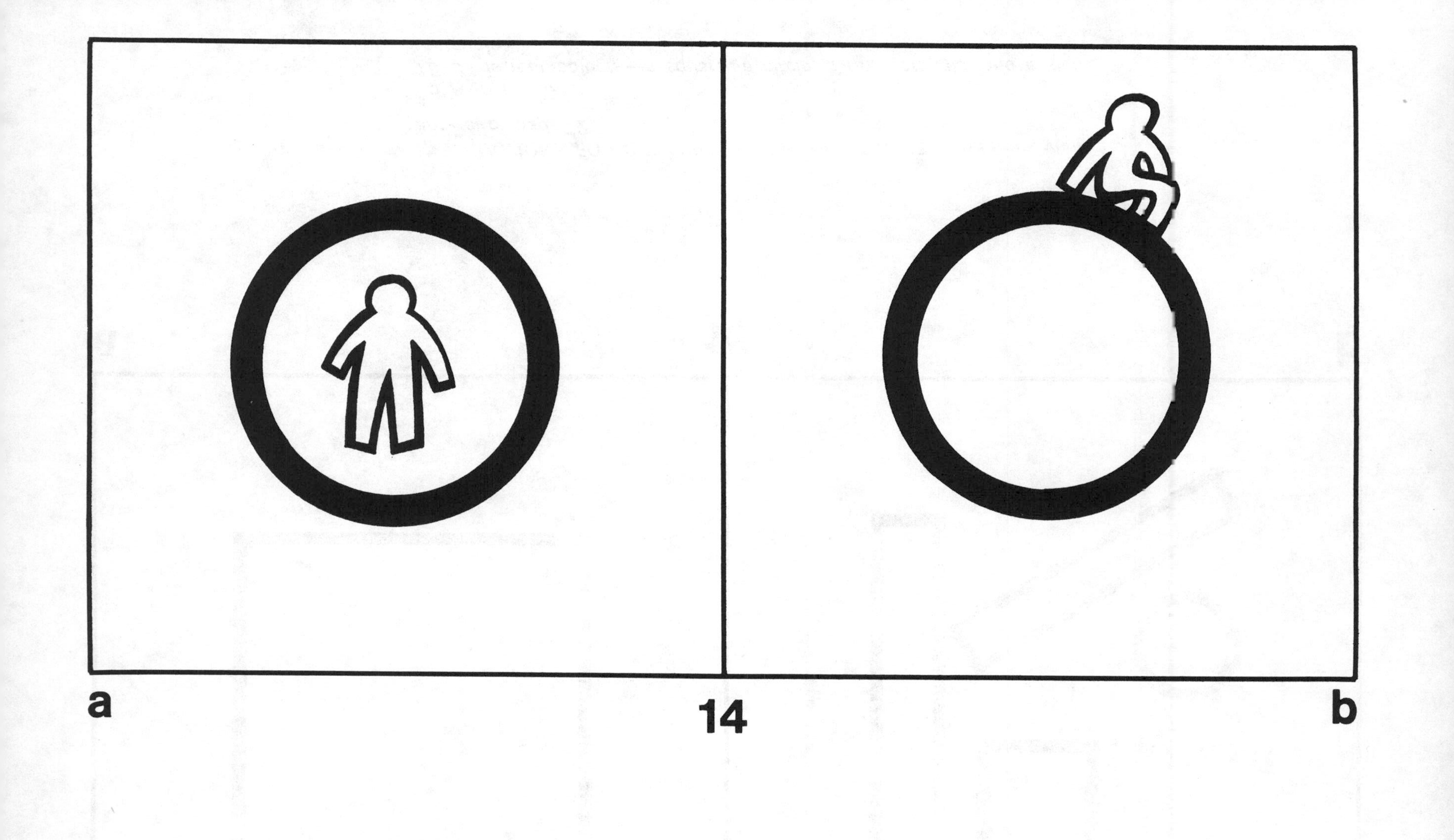

INSTRUCTIONS FOR SET FOURTEEN: The circles you see are closed circles with no way out. Which picture depicts how you feel much of the time? Mark your answer on the tally on page 72.

14"A" is a circle with a man in it.
14"B" is a circle with the man outside of it.

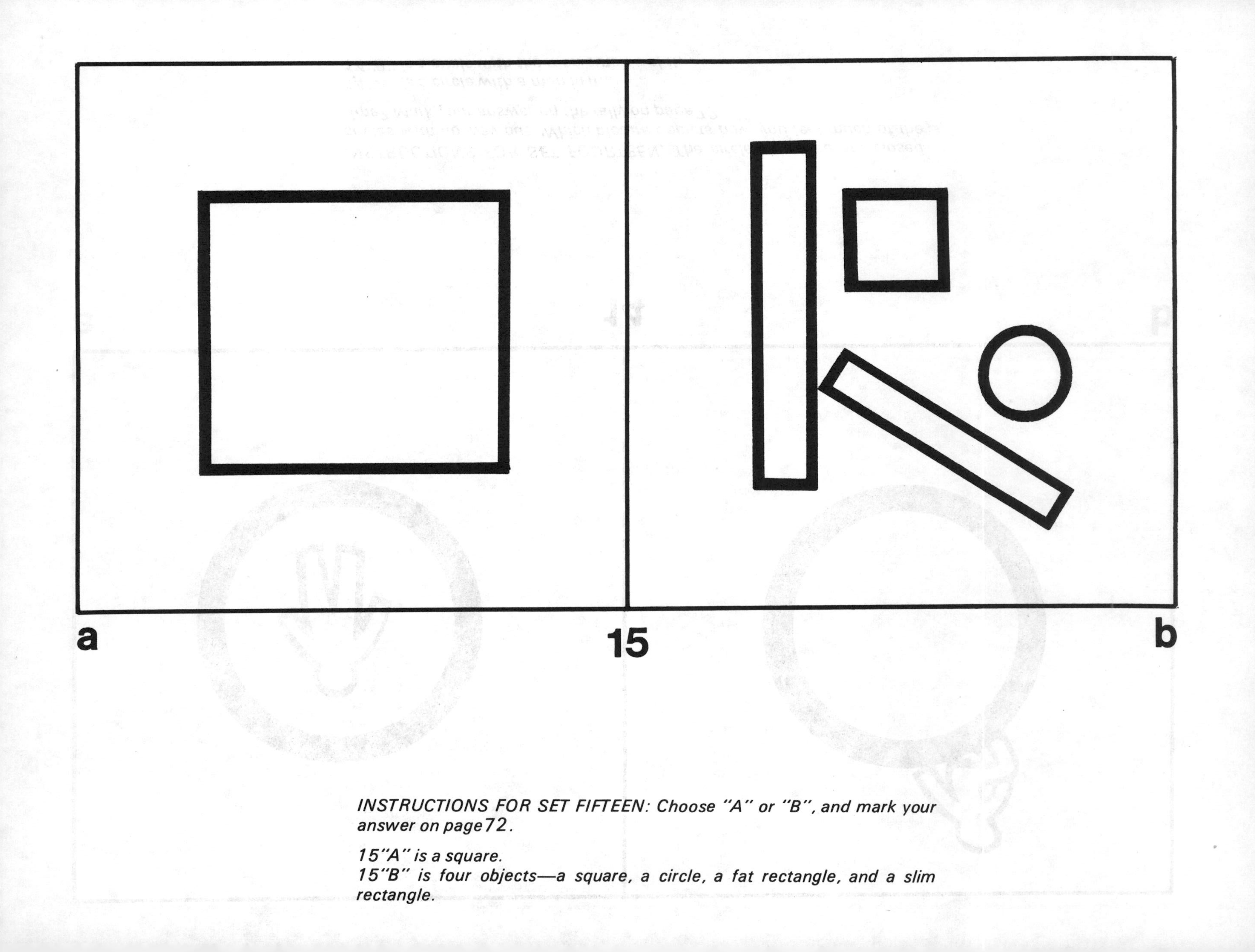

INSTRUCTIONS FOR SET FIFTEEN: Choose "A" or "B", and mark your answer on page 72.

15"A" is a square.
15"B" is four objects—a square, a circle, a fat rectangle, and a slim rectangle.

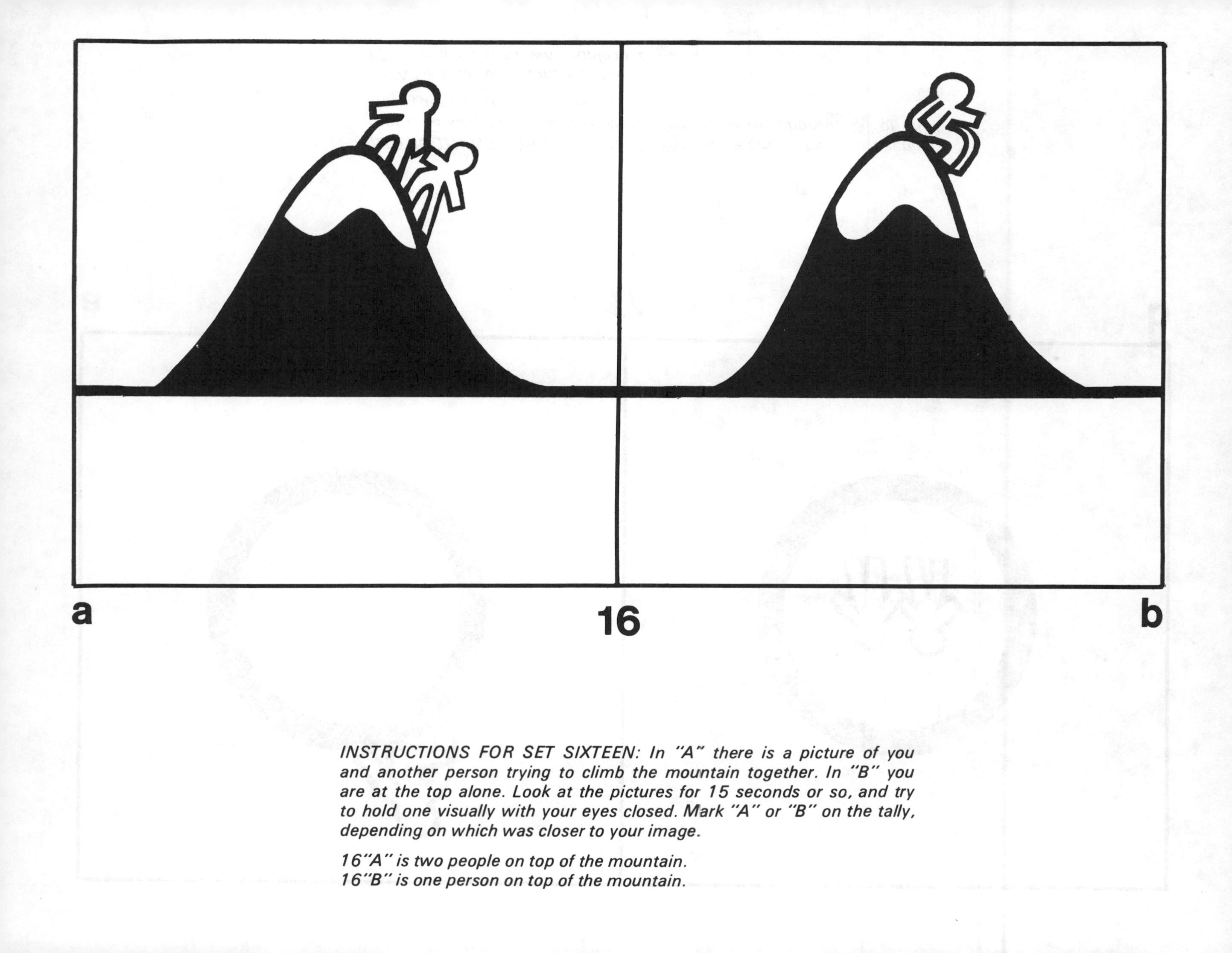

INSTRUCTIONS FOR SET SIXTEEN: In "A" there is a picture of you and another person trying to climb the mountain together. In "B" you are at the top alone. Look at the pictures for 15 seconds or so, and try to hold one visually with your eyes closed. Mark "A" or "B" on the tally, depending on which was closer to your image.

16"A" is two people on top of the mountain.
16"B" is one person on top of the mountain.

INSTRUCTIONS FOR SET SEVENTEEN: These circles have an opening. That is to say, there is a way out. Which would you choose, "A" or "B"? Mark your answer on the tally.

17"A" is a ball with a man on top of it.
17"B" is a ball with two people in it.

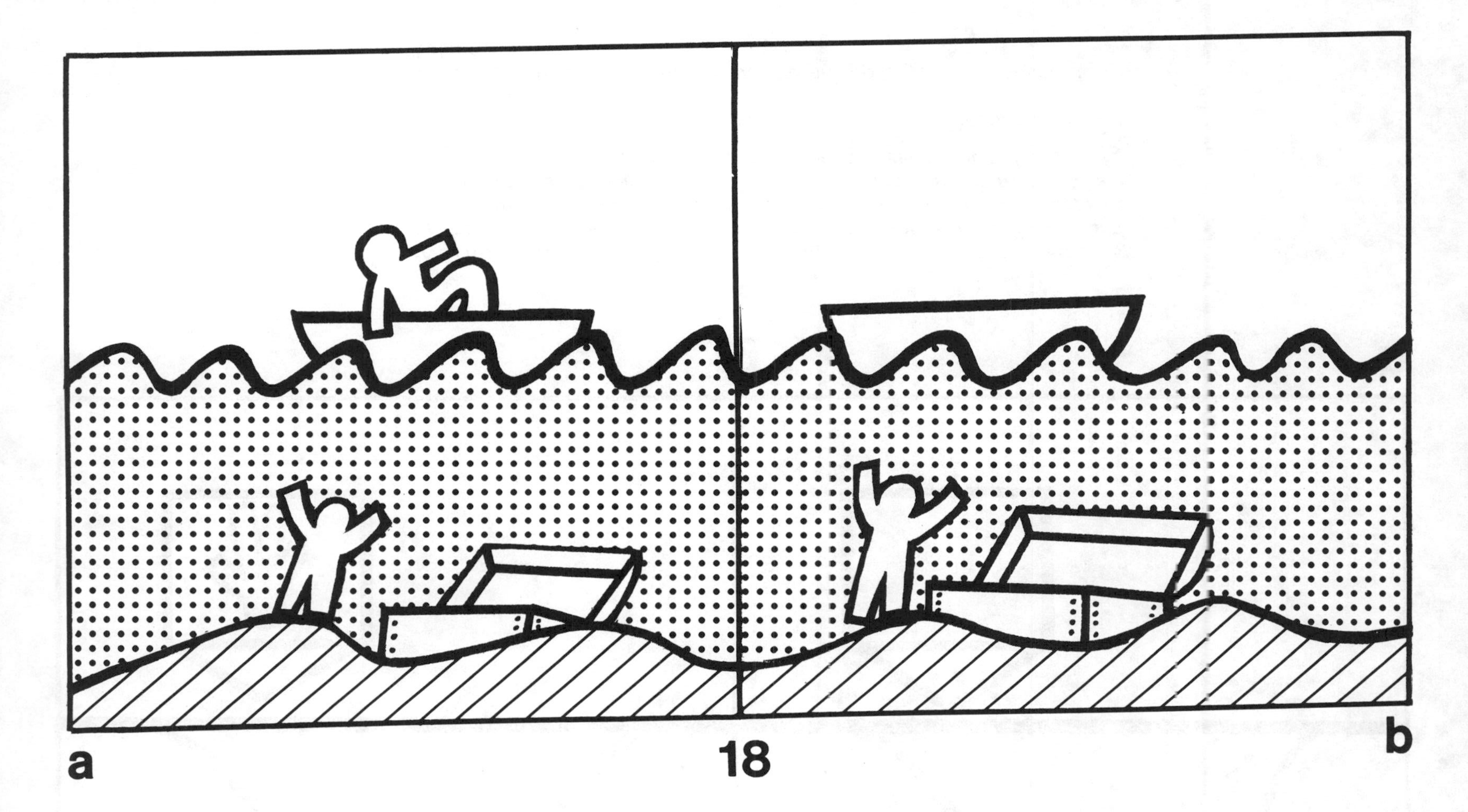

INSTRUCTIONS FOR SET EIGHTEEN: In both of these pictures, you see a person underwater, discovering a chest full of treasure from an old sunken ship. The water is calm, and there is no danger. Look at these for 15 seconds, then close your eyes and try to see one of these pictures. Which picture was your visualization closer to? Mark your answer on the tally on page 72.

18"A" is a man in a boat with another man underwater looking at a treasure chest.
18"B" is a boat without a man, and a man underwater looking at a treasure chest.

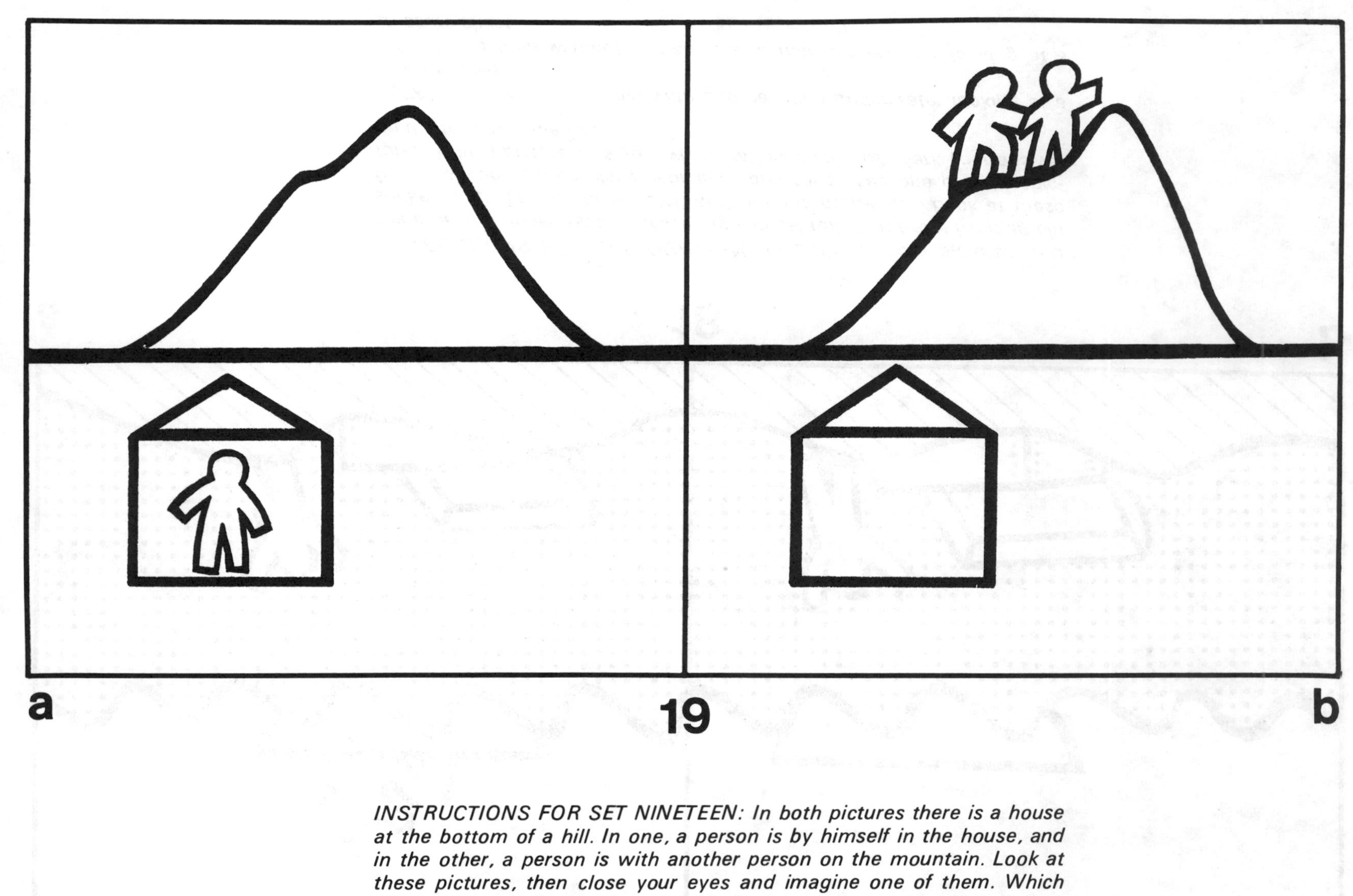

INSTRUCTIONS FOR SET NINETEEN: In both pictures there is a house at the bottom of a hill. In one, a person is by himself in the house, and in the other, a person is with another person on the mountain. Look at these pictures, then close your eyes and imagine one of them. Which picture was your image closer to? Mark your answer on the tally.

19"A" is a mountain and a home at the foot of the mountain with a person in it.
19"B" is a mountain with two people on top of it and a house down below.

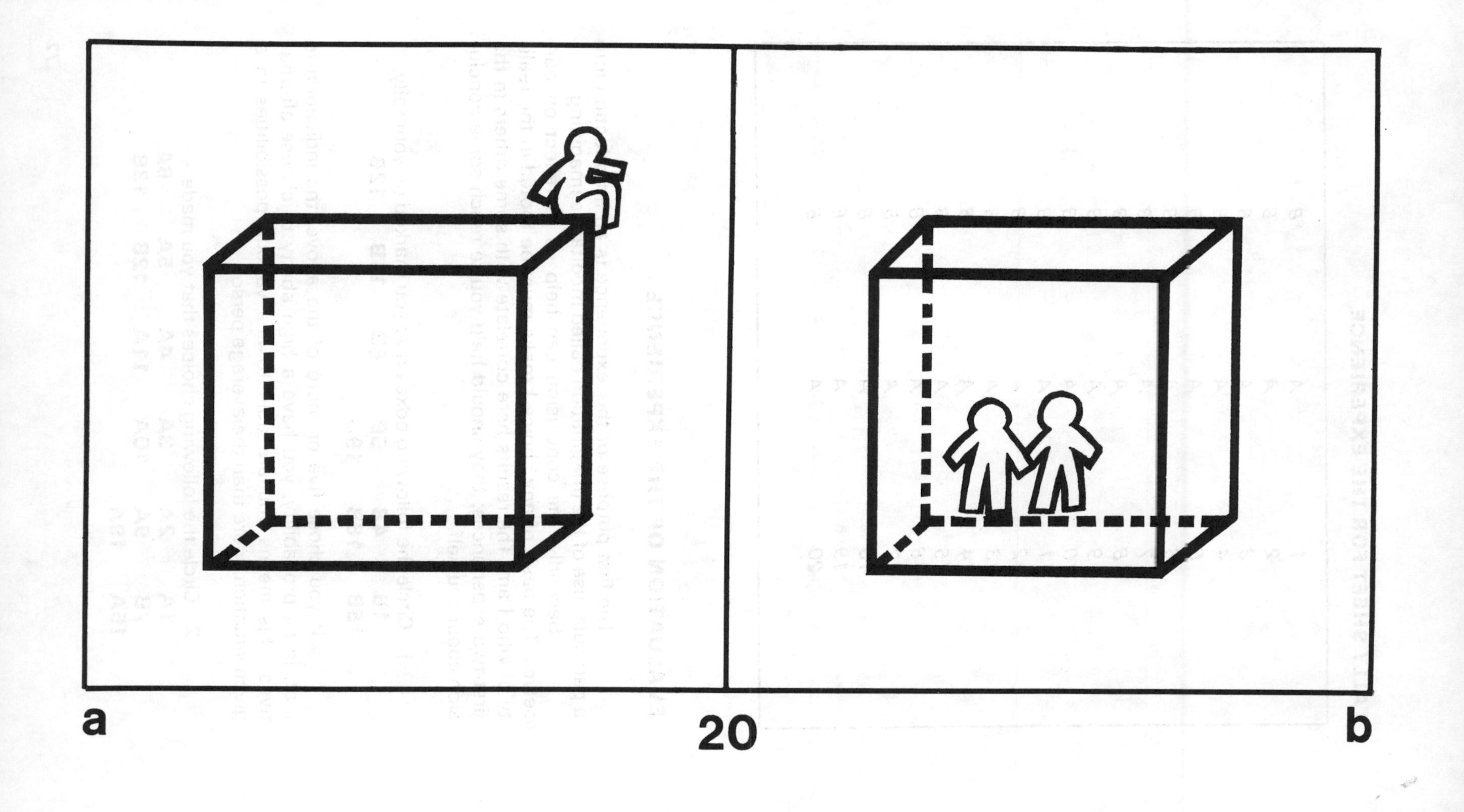

INSTRUCTIONS FOR SET TWENTY: Each of the two boxes has an opening. In other words, there is a way out if a person were to discover it. Which box would you choose, "A" or "B"? Mark your answer on the tally on the next page.

20"A" is a square with a person outside of it.
20"B" is a square with two people in it.

TALLY SHEET FOR THE EXPERIENCE

1	*A*	*B*
2	*A*	*B*
3	*A*	*B*
4	*A*	*B*
5	*A*	*B*
6	*A*	*B*
7	*A*	*B*
8	*A*	*B*
9	*A*	*B*
10	*A*	*B*
11	*A*	*B*
12	*A*	*B*
13	*A*	*B*
14	*A*	*B*
15	*A*	*B*
16	*A*	*B*
17	*A*	*B*
18	*A*	*B*
19	*A*	*B*
20	*A*	*B*

EVALUATION OF THE EXPERIENCE

The first purpose of this experience is an introduction into a particular use of the imagination called meditative imagining.

Secondly, the conclusion can help us to reflect on ourselves. The basis of any choice I make must be rooted in the reality of who I am. The results here correlate with some others in the first two experiences; they should help you to reach some conclusion about yourself.

1. Circle the following boxes that you marked on your tally:

1B 4B 6B 8B 11B 12B
15B 16B 19B

If you chose five or more of the above, the indication is that, in all probability, you have a high ability to choose alternatives. This means you are able to see various possibilities in a given situation, more than the average person.

2. Circle the following choices that you made:

1A 2A 3A 4A 5A 6A
7B 9A 10A 11A 12B 13B
15A 19A

If you marked five or less, this would indicate your need for security and permanence. Since this is a common need, you should have some of the above numbers circled.

If you circled nine or more, the indication is that you have a greater need for control. Please consider the following:

a. I find it difficult to make decisions.
b. I prefer to have choices made for me.
c. I feel nervous much of the time.
d. I need to control my surroundings.
e. I see few alternatives in my life.

3. Circle the boxes you marked on your tally:

8A 9B 10B 16B 17A 18A 20A

Marking three or four would indicate the following possibilities:

a. You have high aspirations to create and succeed.
b. You need to be a loner.
c. You do not get on well with people.
d. You may tend to put personal success before interest in other people.
e. You tend to be insensitive to people.

The point here is that although a person's creative level may be higher, it is going to be reduced, if not thwarted, unless there is an equal ability to work with people. The result would be to reduce the vista of possibilities and, therefore, alternatives. You might ask yourself the question: "Do I need to reach out more to people?"

4. Circle the boxes that you marked:

7A 8B 9B 12A 13A 16A
18A 19B 20B

If you marked four or more, this would indicate a high ability to succeed, coupled with an ability to work with others. If you scored high in this set, as well as in Set One, you would appear to have a high creative ability to avoid anxiety, and to see many possibilities in a variety of situations.

SUMMARY: Let us quickly review some of the conclusions on anxiety that would relate to our personal conclusions above:

1. The greater my anxiety, my insecurity, the less able I am to see creative alternatives for the future.
2. The more I am able to see and choose alternatives, the better am I to deal with my anxieties.
3. The better able I am to see and choose alternatives, the better able I am to overcome guilt feelings and feelings of boredom.
4. Since imagination has much to do with anxiety and guilt, the exercise and ability to see alternatives in the imagination is a first step in overcoming destructive anxiety.

The point is that those who feel themselves unable to choose or even see alternatives make their anxiety worse. The process of imagining can be a beginning to overcome this.

USE OF THE EXPERIENCE

a. The students should be in positions where they can see the pictures or slides you are showing. For each set of pictures, you should allow up to 3 minutes for reflection. On those pictures which require the use of the imagination with the eyes shut, sometimes more than 3 minutes will be needed. You can test this by asking the students whether they want longer time. Usually it takes one hour to run through the pictures themselves. As you come to each description of the picture, you might want to extend the description from the above by studying the story a little. For example, if you discuss the person talking to the fish under the sea, the students might want to spell that out a little more, but in doing so be careful not to impose any particular view or vision on them. The intention is to be as open-ended as possible.

b. Once you have finished the test, hand out mimeographed sheets of the evaluation and have the students evaluate themselves.

c. Have the students get into groups of four to discuss the evaluation. It should be noted with extreme caution that this is not a psychological test, but rather a value medium to help the students raise questions about themselves, with special reference to their ability to use their imagination to see alternatives and make choices. The valuing process means choosing freely from alternatives and is related directly to the creation of the hopeful imagination. Therefore, the ability to imagine is an ability to see various alternatives from which a choice can be made. The questions raised in the evaluation are for the student to test out with himself. By raising these questions, a person is confronted with his limitations and, as a result, can do something about his situation. The session may be completed by an evaluation whereby several groups report what they learned from the process, what they might conclude about the process of choice and how this may be increased as a method of expanding students' imagination in the classroom.

6. POSSIBLE OUTCOMES: It is hoped that this exercise will help the professionals to choose and to see alternatives without increasing their anxiety about life. It is also hoped that professionals will begin to come to a better understanding of how imagination and fantasy are an important part of a person, insofar as their choosing of values is concerned.

7. APPLICATION: It is well to point out to the professional that this kind of exercise in which the fantasy is dealt with can become very threatening to people. Many anxieties are raised when people are forced to choose between alternatives. It is well for the professional to be tuned very closely to any group with whom he would use this exercise.

Exercise Two:

This is an exercise to help the trainer become aware of value process and its more extensive implications in the teaching process in act.

1. INTRODUCTION: In this session the professionals are to discuss how a value, as a priority, influences and changes behavior.

2. MATERIALS NEEDED: Pencil and paper.

3. NUMBERS: For this exercise, we want the people to work in dyads, pairs or quartets.

4. TIME: Allow 15 to 20 minutes for the group to write out their values and to mill around among themselves, followed by 45 minutes to an hour and a half for discussion.

5. DESCRIPTION OF THE EXERCISE: Ask the participants to take a sheet of paper and to set down in large, legible writing two or three of their most cherished values. Then ask them to pin this sheet onto their chests and to mill around in the group until they find someone who has values similar to theirs but has ranked the values differently. Please note that it is important that you repeat the instructions, to make sure they understand that they are to choose someone who has values similar to their own—the same values, if possible, but ranked differently. Once they have found an individual like this, the pair then may choose

another pair who also have similar values but have ranked them differently. Then they can sit in dyads or quartets, according to the size of the group. Ask them to share and discuss with one another how their values influence their behavior.

6. POSSIBLE OUTCOMES: When participants begin to describe and explain how they use their time and money and energy because of the way they have their values ranked, and when another person who has similar values but has ranked them differently explains the same, the participants will begin to understand and appreciate how differently they behave because of their different ranking of values. This is a very powerful exercise and shows the great influence the ranking value has on a person's behavior.

7. APPLICATION: This exercise should be used only with people who have a full understanding of what a value is, with the seven aspects of a value in mind, and who are capable of beginning to understand how the ranking of values influences behavior. Another outcome of this exercise can be that people will begin to realize, by ranking values differently, that areas of conflict can arise between two people, whether they are married or whether they are striving to work together.

Exercise Three:

The following is an exercise to help the trainer to become aware of the value process and its more extensive applications in the teaching process in celebration.

1. INTRODUCTION: The purpose of this exercise is to help the professional come to a fuller understanding of how there is positive potential in one's limitations.

2. MATERIALS NEEDED: Pencil and paper.

3. NUMBERS: It is suggested that professionals work in dyads or quartets.

4. TIME: Allow 10 minutes of silence and then an hour to an hour and a half for discussion.

5. DESCRIPTION OF THE EXERCISE: Ask the professionals to list their talents and their professional limitations. Have them pair off and share their list with one another. Then let them exchange their lists, and let the other person take 10 minutes of silence to explore what the maximum possibility of the other person would be if he changed his limitations into creative potential and if he increased the talents he already has. Then allow them to share this information with one another. After 45 minutes they can move from dyads to quartets to share with other people what they have discovered. Another alternative here, instead of looking at their roles as professionals, is to look at their roles as people; instead of seeing only the maximum possibility of their profession, look at what kind of an old person they could be—a help to the community, for instance, if they were to finally create a potential in their limitations and extend the talents they have.

6. POSSIBLE OUTCOMES: This is a very interesting exercise. It helps people begin to establish their life goals. They begin to see creative possibilities—that limitations are not something to be discouraged about, but rather changed into potential as a part of a person's growth.

7. APPLICATION: It is important in this exercise for the professional to come to a deep understanding of how limitations can be changed into creative potential. This exercise can be used to help persons establish life goals; it is important here to ask them to use their imaginations and to free their fantasies so they can imagine what possibilities there are for them. Encourage them to expand themselves and to think of the greatest work that they could do. This will be an aid in coming to understand their growth process and in giving them encouragement and motivation to strive to use their talents and limitations to the fullest.

Today is the
first day of
the rest of
your life

Section II

Value-Ranking

Value-ranking is the setting of priorities. A conscious free choice of values is important, but the way we rank the many values we have is even more important. The exercises in this section endeavor to bring home the reality that behavior is changed and influenced in the way that we rank or establish our priorities in values.

One of the major goals of value clarification is to help people to become aware of what their value-rankings are and how these affect their lives and their relationships with other people. The exercises in this section also hope to give an understanding, when two people rank the same values in a different way, of how this is the area where conflict will be found. It is only by coming to understand how different rankings of the same values cause conflict that persons are able to deal with conflict situations and to resolve them.

PART 2—SECTION II
VALUE-RANKING (Setting Priorities)

AUDIENCE	GOAL FOR EXERCISES	STRATEGIES USED
STUDENT	To make the student aware of value-ranking (priorities) as being the key to understanding behavior, especially polarity, conflict and imposition.	1. Brainstorming technique. Values are then chosen from a group list by each student and marked. Discussion of how each ranking describes behavior in groups of four. 2. Brainstorming technique on "My Most Important Values". An initial list is given to which they add. Four values are chosen and ranked. Discussion on imposition, opposite rankings, conflict and polarity. 3. Attentive discussion: Values as priorities in society.
TEACHER	1. To make the teacher aware of value-ranking as the key to behavior. 2. To make the teacher aware of imposition and conflict in the educational system.	1. Brainstorming on values of students, teachers, parents. Four values in each category are chosen, ranked, and compared for conflict and imposition. 2. Function, feelings, imagination and ideas are ranked and compared to behavior. Each person tries to give examples of experiences with persons of different rankings in the educational system, to illustrate imposition and conflict.
PROFESSIONAL TRAINER	1. To make the trainer aware of value-ranking as a process of choice, act and celebration. 2. To compare the difference between growth in choice of life priorities to imposition and conflict.	1. Hallmark Card Game. 2. Suggested brainstorm on new games and goals for those games. 3. Polarity Game.

FOR THE STUDENT

These exercises are designed to make the students aware of their value-ranking priorities being the key to understanding behavior, especially polarities, conflict, and imposition.

Exercise One:

1. INTRODUCTION: This exercise is designed to help the students choose values and then rank them, to become aware of what it means to rank values.

2. MATERIALS NEEDED: Blackboard or newsprint, paper and pencil.

3. NUMBERS: This can be done with a group of any size. Break the group up into groups of six and eight for the discussion.

4. TIME: Use 15 minutes to brainstorm, 5 minutes for the students to rank their values and 40 minutes for discussion.

5. DESCRIPTION OF THE EXERCISE: Have the students brainstorm on values they have. After these have been written on the board, have them choose four values they hold. On a sheet of paper, rank the value in terms of the one most important to them, then second, third and fourth. Break the students up into groups

of six and eight and ask them to discuss with one another how they have ranked their values and what this means in terms of behavior that follows from the way they have ranked their values.

6. POSSIBLE OUTCOMES: It will become evident to the students, as they share with one another the difference of the rankings, that they use their time, money and energy differently because of the way they have ranked their values.

7. APPLICATION: This is a very simple exercise. It is meant to acquaint the students with the idea of ranking their values, with the implication this has for their lives.

Exercise Two:

1. INTRODUCTION: This is an exercise which helps the student again to practice ranking his values.

2. MATERIALS NEEDED: Reproduce the form, "My Most Important Values", as given on page 82.

3. NUMBERS: Any number.

4. TIME: Give the students time to brainstorm together, approximately 15 or 20 minutes, and then allow them 5 or 10 minutes to rank the values they chose from the brainstorm list.

5. DESCRIPTION OF THE EXERCISE: Gather the students together in a group. Once again brainstorm on values that would be important to them, using the sheet, "My Most Important Values", ranking the values from the list given to them. Tell them they may add to the list. Then allow 45 to 60 minutes for discussion. Encourage the students to discuss what their opposite rankings mean. Discuss what kind of conflicts they would get into because of the difference of their rankings, what kind of polarity this would cause in a group and whether or not they would try to impose their value-ranking on another person or group.

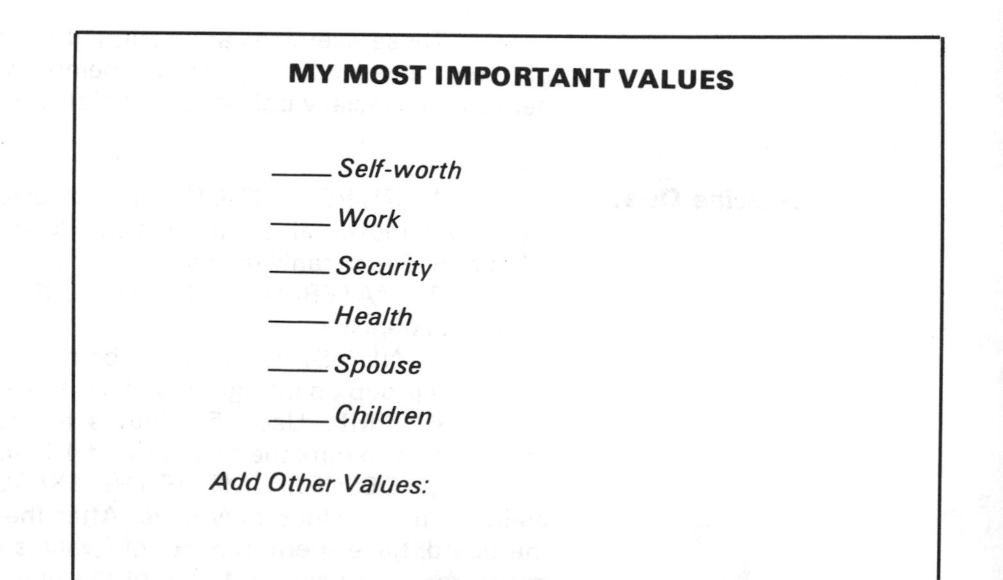

MY MOST IMPORTANT VALUES

____ *Self-worth*

____ *Work*

____ *Security*

____ *Health*

____ *Spouse*

____ *Children*

Add Other Values:

6. POSSIBLE OUTCOMES: The student should become aware of how the different rankings are the source of conflict between people and groups. They should especially begin to realize how, if one group tries to impose its rankings on another group, this is the source of much conflict between groups. They should come to a realization that when groups polarize in their rankings, they do so because of their different rankings.

7. APPLICATION: This is a very simple and basic exercise in which the student begins to realize what imposition, polarity, and conflict in regard to value-ranking can cause. This may be used with any group to begin to give them an appreciation of how value-ranking affects behavior.

Exercise Three:

An alternative possibility to number two is to encourage the students to discuss values and priorities in society. In other words, instead of dealing with individuals and how the value-ranking affects the relationship between two individuals, put the emphasis on how the value-ranking of a group affects the value-ranking of another group. This gets into a discussion on priorities in society.

FOR THE TEACHER

The purpose of these exercises is twofold: One is to make the teacher aware of value-ranking as the key to behavior; the second is to make the teacher aware of imposition and conflict in the educational system.

Exercise One:

1. INTRODUCTION: This exercise hopes to bring about an understanding of the conflict and imposition that exists between students, teachers and parents.

2. MATERIALS NEEDED: A blackboard and newsprint.

3. NUMBERS: Any number. (Preferably, break them up into groups of six or eight after the brainstorming.)

4. TIME: Give three 10-minute periods for the group to brainstorm on the values of students, of teachers and of parents. Then break them up into groups of six or eight to discuss.

5. DESCRIPTION OF THE EXERCISE: Begin this exercise with the group together and ask them to brainstorm for 10 minutes on what they feel are the values of students and how students rank these values. Do the same for teachers and then again for parents. After the group has brainstormed the values and the way they think students, teachers and parents should rank those values, let them break up into groups of six or eight to discuss how the difference in the value-ranking will cause conflict, especially when there is imposition of one group's value-ranking on the other group's value-ranking.

6. POSSIBLE OUTCOMES: This exercise will help the teachers to realize that the students, teachers and parents have different rankings and that this is a source of much of the conflict between student and teacher or teacher and parents or between students and parents.

7. APPLICATION: This exercise will give the teacher a better understanding of how he came into conflict with the student or parent. He will be able to discuss some creative ways of reconciling the conflict due to the imposition of value and also to the difference of the value-ranking.

Exercise Two:

1. INTRODUCTION: This exercise is designed to more specifically get at how the different rankings of values will create conflict and, at times, cause one person or a group of persons to impose values on others.

2. MATERIALS NEEDED: Pencil and a reproduction of the diagram sheet for each participant to use.

3. NUMBERS: It would be good for the teacher to work in teams of four or three, depending on the size of the group.

IMAGINATION *Inspirational, creativity more important search-process of developing, experimenting (or something like that).*
FUNCTION *Get the job done; operates chiefly from the point of view of use or accomplishment; emphasis on task-oriented relations (or thereabouts).*
IDEAS *Getting idea across is more important; intellectual approach, understanding entire process is basic (or somewhere in that ball park).*
FEELINGS *Feelings are more important than getting the job done, where individuals are within a program or project; persons and feelings are seen as important in how a task develops.*

4. TIME: Give the teachers 10 minutes to fill out their sheet as they see it and 50 minutes to discuss. At the end they might gather to discuss what the individual groups have done in this regard and what each group has discovered from sharing its value-ranking.

5. DESCRIPTION OF THE EXERCISE: Pass out the sheets and ask the person to rank what he feels is most important to the educational system, as to the four values of imagination, function, ideas or feelings. Allow 10 to 15 minutes to do this. Break up into groups of four, depending on the size of the group, and ask them to share their experience with persons who have ranked the four values differently, how they themselves have ranked them differently and what kind of conflict this causes in education, especially when one tries to impose value-ranking on another.

6. POSSIBLE OUTCOMES: Once again, this exercise helps to zero-in more specifically on the issue of how different value-rankings cause different behavior and, as a result, are the source of conflict and imposition between individuals and between groups.

7. APPLICATION: This exercise may be used in a number of ways to help people come to a fuller understanding of how different value-rankings affect behavior and cause conflict in groups.

FOR THE PROFESSIONAL TRAINER

The goals of the exercises in this section are to make the professional trainer aware of value-ranking as a process of choice, act and celebration, and also to improve the difference between growth in the choice of life priorities to imposition and conflict.

Exercise One:

1. INTRODUCTION: The goal of this exercise is to show how the different rankings of similar values cause conflict and polarize within a system.

2. MATERIALS NEEDED: Pencils and mimeographed copies of the following two diagrams.

DIAGRAM I—HALLMARK CARD GAME

IMAGINATION *Inspiration and creativity are more important. The person is concerned about process, developing and experimenting.*
FUNCTION *The person likes to get the job done. He operates chiefly from the point of view of something being useful. He likes to accomplish; he likes emphasis on task-orientated relationships which produce something.*
IDEAS *This person likes getting the idea across. He takes an intellectual approach. He likes to understand the whole process. He wants to comprehend things before he goes to the next stage.*
FEELINGS *This person places feelings as his top priority; these are more important than getting the job done. In a board meeting or project, he is more concerned with how people feel and what their difficulties might be than with getting the project completed.*

DIAGRAM II-HALLMARK CARD GAME-SICK CARD DIVISION

PRODUCTION
RESEARCH
MANAGEMENT
SALES

3. NUMBERS: It is suggested that a maximum of forty people be used in this exercise.

4. TIME: The session takes about 3 hours. The following schedule is suggested for an evening meeting.

5. DESCRIPTION:

a. *7:45—8:00*. Short introduction on the subject matter of value-ranking.

8:00—8:45.

1. Have the people get into groups of six.

2. Explain Diagram I. In explaining this exercise, point out that function, feelings, imagination and ideas are four equal parts of the personality. There is no right or wrong order. This is not a test. However, everybody ranks these four parts of the personality in different ways. When they do, their behavior changes. This becomes a good indication of how behavior relates to value-ranking. In addition to this, these four values present in the personality do not actually become real values unless they are considered and chosen by a person. Therefore, for most people these are value indicators. For the proper functioning of the personality all four values need to be present; a person might have emotional difficulties if any one of these four values were missing, since a part of his personality would then be missing. It is obvious also that some professions, some people or some parts of society stress some of these over the others. *Our point is that no ranking is correct.* What is important is for a person to try to rank these in order or priority and as they are manifested generally in their behavior. In crises, this ranking would change. Therefore, try to stress that, in general, we have a constant ranking. You might note that some people who are trying to change their priorities may have difficulty in ranking. The purpose of the first part of the session is to have persons rank these four words in their behavior. That is to say, they rank all four of them in the order they think is first and most important to them. Next, discussion in the group is designed to test with people who know them whether their behavior does, in fact, reflect the ranking they have designated.

b. Give each group Diagram II of the Hallmark Gift Company Sick Card Division. Then give each group the following task:

1. You are now members of the Hallmark Card Company Sick Card Division. In your company there are four divisions, as noted on the diagram sheets: Production, Research, Management, Sales.

2. The task of your group is to come up with a consensus of what you want production, research, management, and sales to mean for your company.

3. Describe what you conclude in your consensus of what production, research, etc., mean by ranking the four words "function", "feeling", "imagination", and "ideas" for each one of the divisions.

4. Each group should then have the four words ranked in order for the production, research, management and the sales departments of their Sick Card Division—four rankings of the four words on the sheet marked Diagram I.

8:45—9:00. Remind the group that they should be coming to the conclusion of their exercise. By 9:00, each person in the group should have decided which division in the Hallmark Card Company he's to move into. Each should move into the division whose ranking is most similar to the individual ranking he made at the beginning of the session.

9:00. Arrange the room so that each corner of it represents a different department of the Hallmark Card Company. For example, locate in one corner the sales division, in another the production division, and so on. At this point tell the group to break up so that each individual moves into the division he chose to be in. Tell them to move into their new groups to discuss why they have entered them and what their rankings are. Should a person find that the new group he is in has a consensus that he should be in another group, that person should find out what group and department he should be in. Once the group has decided that they all belong in the same division, then have them struggle with what different positions they could have within that group.

9:30. Have the participants move back into their original groups to discuss the following question: "In terms of what I have discovered tonight and in terms of my own ranking and what group I ended up in, in what way does this compare with the kind of work I'm doing at present? If there are discrepancies, what do I think these mean?" Tell the group to discuss the question and come up with some kind of conclusion to be presented in a general session, group-by-group, at 10:00.

6. POSSIBLE OUTCOMES: This exercise helps the participants become aware of how an organization can promote, by its very structure, various value-rankings which, in turn, become conflicts as imposition arises. A skilled facilitator can point out in this process conflicts that arise between various students or student-teachers within the process itself. Often a person will find that he is in the wrong group and will have to move; this might cause some anxiety. In order for this to happen, there must be confrontation by the groups. People might automatically feel that sales or production is more important than a research area, for example. Toward the end of the evening, it is important for the facilitator to help the group see where the differences, conflicts and priorities arose in the dynamics of the conference itself. This is a concrete way of showing how the basis of one department and its value-ranking causes conflict with one another in departments of an organization.

7. APPLICATION: This can become a very intensive exercise and should be used only with those who already have some understanding and appreciation of value clarification.

Exercise Two:

1. INTRODUCTION: It is suggested, at this point, that the students be exposed to a part of or all of the Hallmark Card Game in the last exercise. This exercise is for those who have some skill in value clarification. The aim of the class is to have the students brainstorm on sets of words, such as those used in the Hallmark Card Game: Research, Sales, Production and Management. Alternatively, the words used in the other diagram—function, feelings, imagination, and ideas—may be discussed in order to form a game illustrating value-ranking and the way in which conflict enters when opposite values are present in two or more people. Ideas for such brainstorming might be raised as follows:

"What kinds of values are necessary for a successful politician in our social system?"

"What kinds of values would a country struggling for survival need to have in order to stand up to the larger powers?"

"What kinds of values would a person in a slum or low economic area need in order to be able to become a successful businessman?"

These kinds of words could then be placed to form a game. One might also want to brainstorm on the kinds of words suitable for the ideal businessman as opposed to the kinds of words necessary for a businessman struggling for survival in a low economic area. The question might be raised, "What kinds of group structures and what kinds of games might we simulate to produce an awareness in the student of value-ranking and how it affects behavior of different persons in different situations and environments?"

Finally, it is suggested that on brainstorming on these games, the game be piloted before it is tested out on the students. The point of such an exercise is that in the brainstorming process and in struggling to try to come up with new games, the participants must become familiar with the value-ranking process even if they're not able to formulate their own simulations. It is grappling with the subject matter that is important. Note: an example of such a game is found in Part III, Advanced Conferences, Day 2, Morning.

Exercise Three:

1. INTRODUCTION: This polarity game hopes to help make the group understand how the selection of a position is a value-ranking that can cause conflict with other people who have chosen other value-rankings.

2. MATERIALS NEEDED: Reproduce on a sheet or on large cards three diagrams as follows:

a. traditional structured setting.
b. circle.
c. an experiential learning classroom having groups of people.

3. NUMBERS: Up to fifty people.

4. TIME: Allow 5 or 10 minutes for participants to choose which of the settings they want to teach in. Allow 20

POLARITY GAME

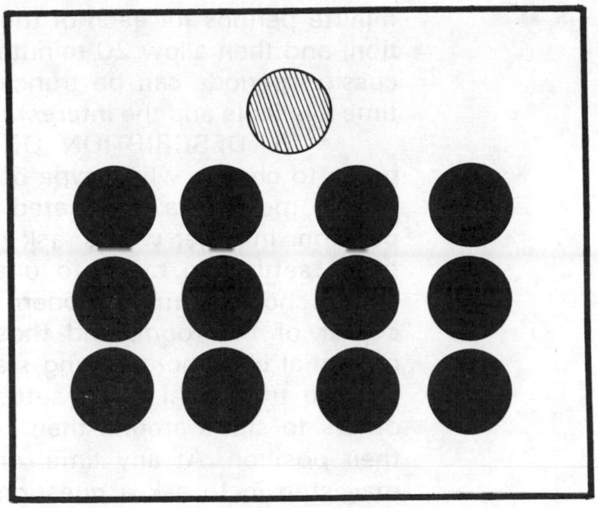

1

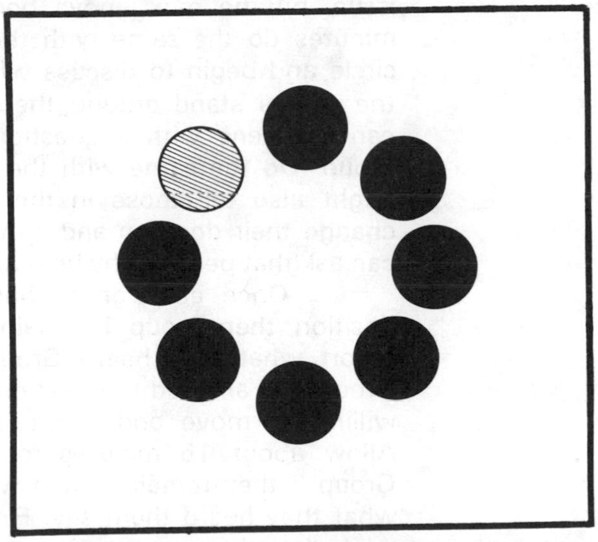

2

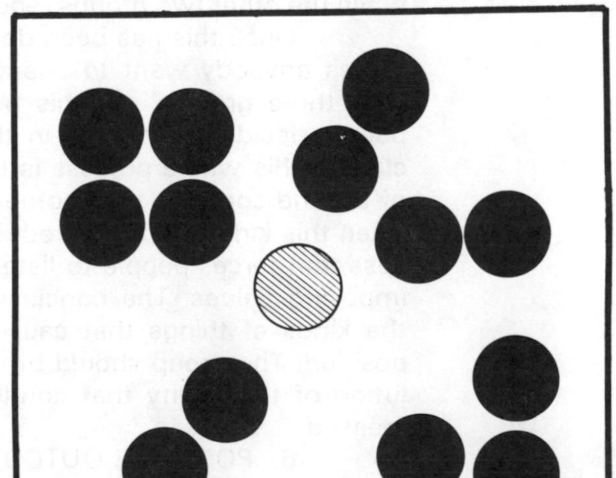

3

minute periods for each of the three groups to discuss their position, and then allow 20 minutes for general discussion. These discussion periods can be truncated or elongated, according to the time available and the interest that is shown.

5. DESCRIPTION OF THE EXERCISE: Ask the participants to choose which type of classroom they would like to be in and to move to a designated part of the room representing that position. In other words, ask those who would choose the traditional setting to move to one corner of the room. Those who would choose a more modern setting in a circle move to another corner of the room, and those who choose a free-flowing experiential classroom setting stay in the middle of the room. Then ask the traditional group-setting people to form a circle and the others to stand around them, giving them 20 minutes to discuss their position. At any time, one of the members on the outside may step in to ask a question or clarify or confront them on an issue, but he must move bodily into the group. Then after 20 minutes do the same with the modern circle classroom: form a circle and begin to discuss why they chose their setting, and let the others stand around them. The observers remain silent but can intervene with a question when they move bodily into the group. Do the same with the third group. As an alternative, you might also tell those in the group that at any time they may change their decision and move to another group. The facilitators can ask that person why he made the change.

Once each group has explained why they chose their position, then Group 1 remains silent while the other two groups report what they heard Group 1 saying. As before, no one in Group 1 is allowed to question what they say unless the person is willing to move bodily into the group and raise the question. Allow about 15 minutes for the observation period. Likewise, Group 2 then remains silent while the other two groups report on what they heard them say. Finally, the third group remains silent while the other two groups report on what they heard.

Once this has been done, the question can then be raised, "Does anybody want to change positions? If so, now re-form in your three groups." At this point you may wish to discuss why people decided to remain in their original groups. A way of concluding this whole process is to ask everybody to get into groups of six and come up with some conclusions from the process. Very often this kind of process reduces polarization, because it is a process that forces people to listen to one another rather than merely imposing values. The conclusion should be made in the area of the kinds of things that cause polarity and conflict—mainly imposition. The group should be able to move to some kind of resolution of the reality that conflict is reduced as acceptance is increased.

6. POSSIBLE OUTCOMES: This is a very graphic way of showing how the difference of value-ranking causes conflict of polarities. If it begins to happen in the group that people are trying to impose their value-ranking on others, then we have a live

example of how people who have made their value-ranking tend to impose this on other people who have different value-rankings. This is a very involved exercise and can result in a very intensive discussion on the issues. It is important, at the end, for the facilitators to help the group see the process that took place—that they don't get so involved in the task of discussing the issue of which is the best classroom that they lose track of how the process of choosing and ranking values has caused the difference, resulting in conflict in the group.

7. APPLICATION: This exercise should be used with a group that has had some experience with value clarification and can handle the intensive discussion that usually follows such an exercise.

Section III

Value Indicators

A functional definition of a value indicator is that it is anything important to me, but which falls short of fulfilling all seven aspects of what a full value is. For example, I might believe that I have a value but not act upon it. Or I may have chosen a value but not have chosen it freely or from alternatives. Or, I may have a value but do not repeat it or do not really cherish it and am not really happy with the choice of that value. In this section, we have designed exercises that will help to clarify the difference between a full value and what are only value indicators—for example, feelings, beliefs, interests, attitudes and convictions.

PART 2—SECTION III
VALUE INDICATORS

AUDIENCE	GOALS FOR EXERCISE	STRATEGIES USED
STUDENT	To help the student understand that much of what we do indicates what our values are. This should be considered helpful. It is a place of evaluation. Time and money are two excellent indicators in our society.	1. Value-versus-value indicators exercise. 2. Students are asked to use Value Indicator Sheet 1 and discuss how money relates to values. 3. Students are asked to use Value Indicator Sheet 2 and indicate on the chart what activities they put their time on. Rank the activities and discuss.
TEACHER	To help the teacher see that behavior and feelings and imagination are indicators of values. To help the teacher see the connection between behavior and time.	1. The teachers are asked to work on Value Indicator Sheet 3 on time, in small groups. 2. Fantasy shield to relate imagination to values as a value indicator. 3. Alternative: imagine the clock 100 years ago and 100 years in the future.
PROFESSIONAL TRAINER	To see the relationship between behavior, time and values as priorities. Behavior and time are seen as major value indicators.	1. Brainstorming technique to design their own value indicator sheets for different situations, using Value Indicator Sheet 5 as an example. 2. Exercise using Value Indicator Sheets 6 and 7.

FOR THE STUDENT

The exercises here are meant to help the student understand that much that we do indicates what our values are. This should be considered helpful. It is a place of evaluation. Time and money are two excellent indicators in our society.

Exercise One:

1. INTRODUCTION: The purpose of this session is to help the student distinguish between a full value and what is a value indicator.

2. MATERIALS NEEDED: Papers which reproduce the following information.

VALUE VERSUS VALUE INDICATORS

In order to clarify whether or not a given thing is a value, ask yourself the following questions about it:

1. Was the value chosen from a range of alternatives that I was sure of?

2. Did I consider the consequences of those alternatives that I was aware of?

3. Is this value evident in my behavior? That is to say, have I acted on it recently?

4. Do I act on this value repeatedly in some fashion, through a variety of similar experiences?

5. Am I happy and pleased with the choice?

6. Am I willing to state it publicly?

7. Does the value enhance, and not impede, the development of emotional and spiritual well-being?

3. NUMBERS: Any number of people.

4. TIME: Give 5 or 10 minutes for the pupils to choose three or four values. Then give them half an hour to evaluate the values they have chosen, according to the "value-versus-value indicator" sheet. Gather them into groups of six or eight to share what they learned. The discussion period can last from half an hour to an hour, according to the time available.

5. DESCRIPTION OF THE EXERCISE: Begin by asking the students to write on a piece of paper three or four values they think they have. After they've written these out, pass out the "value-versus-value indicator" sheet, and let them explore whether the three or four values they have written down are truly values or whether they are only value indicators for them.

6. POSSIBLE OUTCOMES: The purpose of this very simple exercise is to help the student distinguish between value and value indicators. This is a very important point, so it is well worth taking a session of a class to go through this process of discovering the difference between values and value indicators.

7. APPLICATION: This is a simple exercise—a basic exercise which should be used with any introductory understanding and appreciation of the value clarification process to distinguish the difference between values and value indicators.

VALUE INDICATOR 1

FINANCES			
TOTAL INCOME: $ --------			
ITEM	***% MONEY SPENT***	***RANK IN ORDER OF COST***	***RANK HOW YOU'D WANT IT TO BE***
Sustenance:			
Food			
Lodging			
Mortgage			
Rent			
Clothes			
Car			
Travel			
Other			
Other			
Development:			
Study (Books)			
Fees			
Health			
Recreation			
Equipment			
Other			
Future:			
Insurance			
Pension			
Savings			
Other			
Other			

Exercise Two:

1. INTRODUCTION: This exercise helps the student see how money is an indication of what his values may be.

2. MATERIALS NEEDED: The teacher will reproduce Value Indicator Sheet 1 on finances.

3. NUMBERS: Numbers unlimited.

4. TIME: Allow the students a half hour to fill out Value Indicator Sheet 1. Then allow half an hour to an hour for discussion. The discussion period can always be adjusted according to the time.

5. DESCRIPTION OF THE EXERCISE: Pass out Value Indicator Sheet 1 and ask the students to fill that sheet out according to how much money they spend on each of the items listed.

When the students have filled that out, point out to them how the way they spend their money is an indication of where their values are. Then let them break into groups of six or eight to discuss what they discovered about their values and to share with one another thoughts about how money is a value indicator.

6. POSSIBLE OUTCOMES: The students will often be surprised to find that money is such a forceful value indicator to them. They may well be surprised to learn how they spend their money and how this is an indication of where their values are.

7. APPLICATION: This is a very basic exercise, and it is one that would be good for any group to use to discover how money is a value indicator to them.

VALUE INDICATOR 2

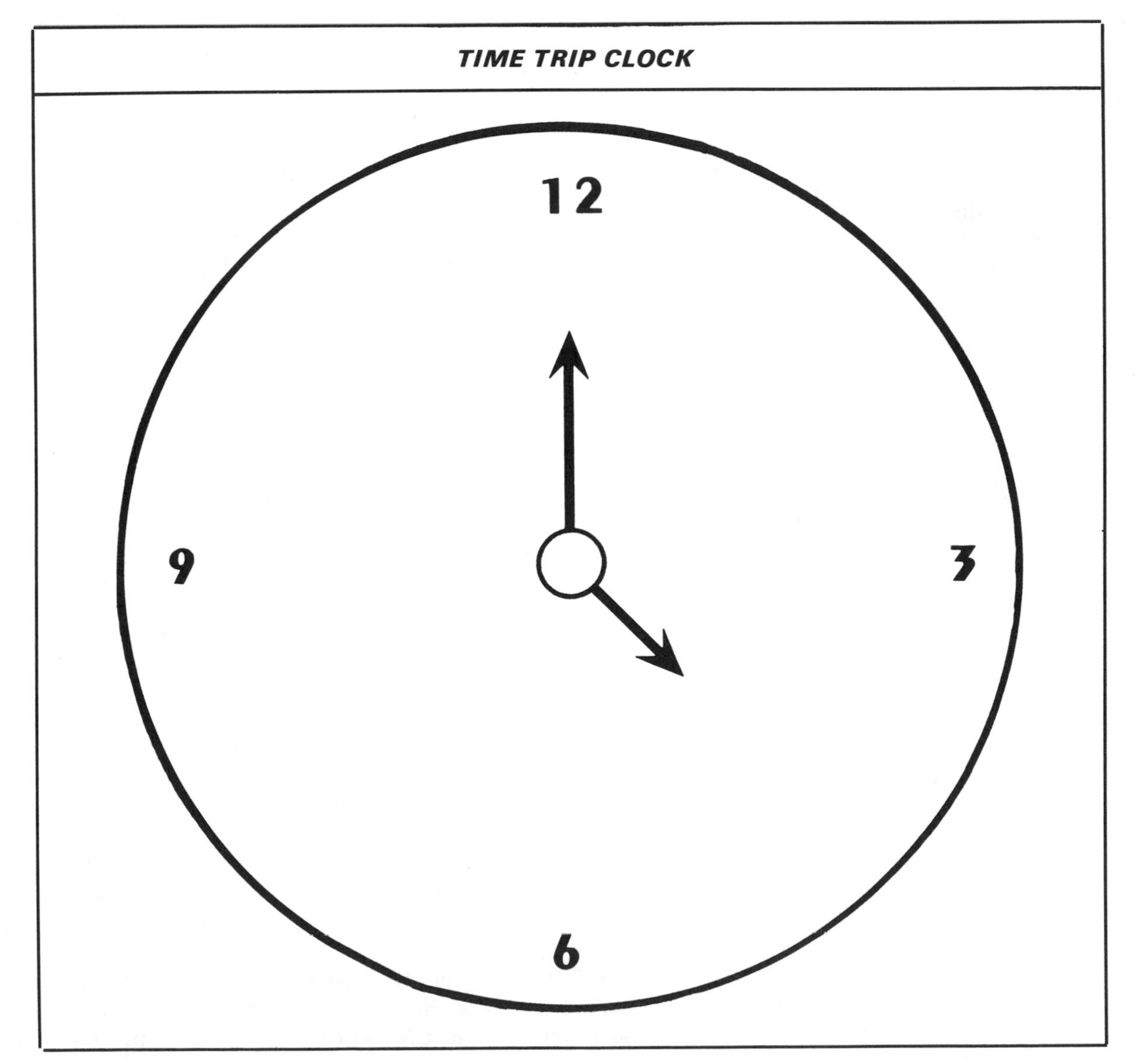

Exercise Three:

1. INTRODUCTION: The purpose of this exercise is to show the student how time is a value indicator.

2. MATERIALS NEEDED: Reproduce Value Indicator Sheet 2.

3. NUMBERS: Numbers unlimited.

4. TIME: Use approximately half an hour for the students to analyze how they use their time; then break them up into discussion groups of six or eight for a half hour to an hour to discuss their findings.

5. DESCRIPTION OF THE EXERCISE: Give the students Value Indicator Sheet 2 on the time trip, and ask them to fill out how a typical day is used time-wise. How much time do they spend during the day on the various activities they are involved in? Have them write the activities around the clock, indicating how much time was spent on each item. After they have done this, point out to them that how they use their time is a value indicator of what is important to them. Break them up into groups of six or eight to discuss what they found out about their value indicators, as concerning time.

6. POSSIBLE OUTCOMES: Once again, very often the students are surprised to learn that time is a value indicator. They may be surprised at how much time they spend on various activities. There may be a discrepancy between how they use their time and the way they would really like to use it.

7. APPLICATION: This is a very basic exercise and can be used with any group to help them understand how time is an indication of where their values are.

FOR THE TEACHER

The following exercise is to help the teacher see that behavior, feelings and imagination are indicators of values, and to help the teacher see the connection between behavior and time.

Exercise One:

1. INTRODUCTION: This exercise is designed to help the teacher understand how time is an indication of values.

2. MATERIALS NEEDED: Reproduce Value Indicator Sheet 3 for the number of participants you will have.

3. NUMBERS: Unlimited.

4. TIME: Give the teachers a half hour to complete Value Indicator Sheet 3, and then spend anywhere from a half hour to an hour discussing what they discovered about their values from Value Indicator Sheet 3.

5. DESCRIPTION OF THE EXERCISE: The facilitator passes out Value Indicator Sheet 3 and asks each person to take a half hour to fill out how he uses his time. After the half hour, point out to the group how time is an indicator of one's values. Then ask them to break into small groups of four and six or eight, depending on the size of your group, and have them discuss what

VALUE INDICATOR 3

ACTIVITIES AS TEACHER	ENERGY TIME	ACTIVITIES OUTSIDE WORK	ENERGY TIMF
Study Administration Preparation Worry Discipline Student Students Peers Other Other Other		*Study Prayer Maintenance: House Food Finances Other Other Recreation Children Friends Spouse Worry Travel Other Other*	

Ranking 1. (4 values)	*Ranking 2. (4 values)*
Rank order the top four according to the amount of ENERGY TIME that they used. These will indicate what order your values are in.	

they discovered about themselves in relation to time as a value indicator.

6. POSSIBLE OUTCOMES: An adult group which has not had a lot of experience with value clarification may be extremely surprised to discover how time is a value indicator. They may also discover discrepancies such as spending a lot of time on doing things of less value to them than they desire. In other words, they are spending more time on things that they value less than they really want to. This may call for them to re-evaluate what they do with their time and to use the opportunity to spend more time on things they really do value.

7. APPLICATION: This is a good exercise in which the teachers can learn how time is a value indicator to them.

Exercise Two:

1. INTRODUCTION: The fantasy shield is one interesting way to help a person discover some of the values that he holds.

2. MATERIALS NEEDED: Paper and pencil. (See Value Indicator 4, page 103.)

VALUE INDICATOR 4

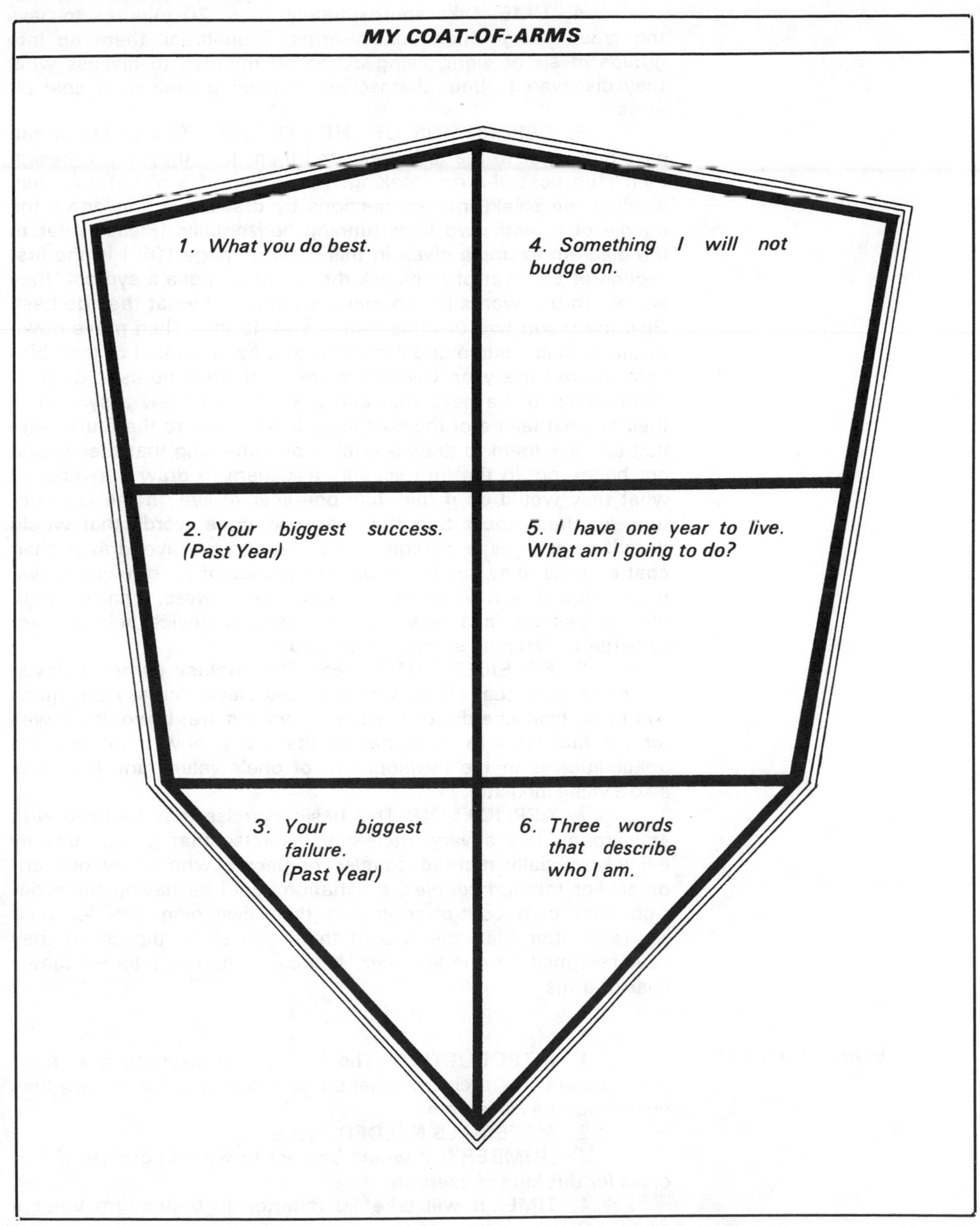
MY COAT-OF-ARMS
1. What you do best.
4. Something I will not budge on.
2. Your biggest success. (Past Year)
5. I have one year to live. What am I going to do?
3. Your biggest failure. (Past Year)
6. Three words that describe who I am.

3. NUMBERS: Unlimited.

4. TIME: Take approximately 15 to 20 minutes to have the group design their coat-of-arms. Then break them up into groups of six or eight, using 30 to 60 minutes to discuss what they discovered about themselves in making their own coat-of-arms.

5. DESCRIPTION OF THE EXERCISE: The facilitator can pass out paper to the group and tell them that they are to design their own coat-of-arms, making the outline of a shield and then dividing the shield into six sections by drawing a line down the middle of it, with two lines running horizontally. (Please refer to the diagram example given in this book on page 103.) In the first section of the coat-of-arms ask the group to make a symbol; they are not to use words but to make a symbol of what they do best. Give the group two or three minutes to do this. Then move down to the second section and ask them to draw a symbol of their biggest success this year. Give them two or three minutes to do that. Then move to the next area and ask them to draw a symbol of their biggest failure of the past year. Next, move to the fourth section and ask them to draw a symbol of something that they would not budge on. In the fifth section, ask them to draw a symbol of what they would do if they had one year to live. In the last section, let them know that they can use three words that would describe them as a person. After the group have drawn their coat-of-arms, they can break up into groups of six or eight to discover what they have found out about themselves, what some of their values are, and how this little fantasy device helped them to better understand some of their values.

6. POSSIBLE OUTCOMES: This fantasy game of devising one's own coat-of-arms shows how clever fantasy questions can be to help one discover what his values are. It would be well for the facilitator to point out to the group how important the imagination is in the development of one's values and how it is also a value indicator.

7. APPLICATION: This basic exercise may be used with any group. It is a very interesting exercise that groups usually enjoy, especially married couples or people who know one another. For married couples, a variation could be having them design their own coat-of-arms and then designing one for their spouses; after that, the two of them can share the shield they have designed for one another. They could then negotiate a family coat-of-arms.

Exercise Three:

1. INTRODUCTION: The goal of this exercise is to have the teachers use their imagination to discover what values they hold about the classroom.

2. MATERIALS NEEDED: None.

3. NUMBERS: It would be best to work in groups of four or six for this kind of exercise.

4. TIME: It will take 10 minutes to brainstorm what a

classroom was like 100 years ago and then 10 minutes to brainstorm what a classroom will be like 100 years from now. Then break the group up into sets of four and six to discuss.

5. DESCRIPTION OF THE EXERCISE: Ask the total group to brainstorm on what they imagine a classroom was like 100 years ago. Take 10 or 15 minutes to do this, and then ask the group to brainstorm on what a classroom will be like 100 years in the future. Break up into groups to discuss for half an hour a comparison of the two imaginations they have brainstormed. After about a half hour, you can ask them to take a look at how imagination influences them, as they form their values, and at the kind of values they learned of themselves when they imagined what the classroom of the future would be like.

6. POSSIBLE OUTCOMES: This is an exercise using imagination, once again, to discover what the values of the persons are. It would be well for the facilitator to point out to the group that as they project into the future what they think is the best in education, this is how imagination becomes a value indicator.

7. APPLICATION: This very simple exercise can be used in any number of situations.

FOR THE PROFESSIONAL TRAINER

The following exercises are to help the professional trainer see the relationship between behavior, time and values as priorities. Behavior and time are seen as major value indicators.

Exercise One:

1. INTRODUCTION: One of the goals of this book is to help the professional trainer become more creative in designing his own projects and exercises that will fit with his situation and students. The following exercises are designed to help the professional trainer to be creative.

2. MATERIALS NEEDED: Duplicate the Value Indicator Sheet 5.

3. NUMBERS: It is best to work in groups of four to six.

4. TIME: One to two hours, according to the time available.

5. DESCRIPTION OF THE EXERCISE: Pass out to the professional trainers Value Indicator Sheet 5, designed to help a person find his values in the situation he is in as an administrator, to learn how this situation influences values and priorities, to see how he uses time and how it influences behavior in priorities. Then on the basis of seeing Value Indicator Sheet 5, discuss it in groups of four to six for approximately half an hour. Let the group spend approximately an hour brainstorming together and working out a similar kind of value indicator sheet that would get at the situation they are in.

6. POSSIBLE OUTCOMES: Hopefully, the trainers will

VALUE INDICATOR 5

SELF 1 (Energy) As Educator	*As Administrator*
Discipline	*Inter-faculty involvement*
Class preparation and paper correction	*Class supervision*
Personal involvement with students	*Liaison with school office*
Inter-faculty involvement	*Meetings with parents*
Professional meetings	*Finance*
Professional reading	*Planning and organization meetings*
Parental involvement	*Student involvement*
Teaching	*Reports*
Add or delete your own words:	*Correction and confrontation of unhelpful behavior of other teachers*
	Add your own words, or delete any of the above:

SELF 2 Rank order educator/administrator and place on wall.

begin to see the possibilities they have for designing their own instruments, exercises and projects.

7. APPLICATION: The actual Value Indicator Sheet 5 may be used with people who are in various situations and have various roles to play. It will give them a better understanding of how their values and their roles influence their behavior.

Exercise Two:

1. INTRODUCTION: This exercise is designed again to give the professional trainer help to see how anxieties affect values and priorities and to also encourage him to begin to create his own projects and exercises.

2. MATERIALS NEEDED: Duplicate Value Indicator Sheet 6, found on page 108.

3. NUMBERS: It is suggested that trainers work in groups of four or six.

4. TIME: Give half an hour for the trainers to fill out Sheet 6. Give them half an hour to discuss what the sheet meant to them, continuing with an hour of discussion, brainstorming about creative ideas of their own for developing instruments.

5. DESCRIPTION OF THE EXERCISE: Pass out Value Indicator Sheet 6 and give the people approximately 10 minutes to fill it out. Then ask them to break up into groups of four or six, depending on the number present, and let them share the experience of what they learned about their values in doing this. After they have done this, keep them in the same group and ask them to create a new value clarification sheet that would be of help to them in their situation. The facilitator can encourage them to use one another as resource people in the development of instruments to help them in their own situation.

6. POSSIBLE OUTCOMES: The trainers will come to realize how anxiety influences the development of one's values.

7. APPLICATION: This can be a very intensive exercise and should be used only with professional groups who can handle the intensive interaction that may result from this exercise.

VALUE INDICATOR 6

Worry is a natural phenomenon and is something we all experience. This evaluation is to help you pinpoint your own areas of worry, remembering that everyone has his own particular anxieties. Mark one box for each numbered item.

I worry about . . .	*Often*	*Occasionally*	*Never*
1. Mother			
2. Father			
3. Getting old			
4. Going to church			
5. Not going to church			
6. Dying			
7. My children growing up and leaving home			
8. Retiring			
9. My job			
10. My abilities			
11. My vocation			
12. What I have done in the past			
13. My children			
14. Being ill			
15. Being alone			
16. My boss			
17. Figure or waistline			

	Often	*Occasionally*	*Never*
18. *The possibility of losing my job*			
19. *Snakes and spiders*			
20. *My friends not liking me*			
21. *Not having friends of the opposite sex*			
22. *Being robbed*			
23. *Future plans*			
24. *What my brothers and sisters think of me*			
25. *What my boss thinks of me*			
26. *About the work I am doing*			
27. *My house being robbed*			
28. *Any disaster I read or hear about on the radio or TV*			
29. *Something happening to me or my family*			
30. *Having an operation*			
31. *Growing older*			
32. *Not succeeding*			
33. *My children getting bad grades*			
34. *Failure in anything I do*			
35. *My parents*			
36. *Being blamed*			
37. *Being ignored*			

CAN

Section IV

Values and Environment

The goals of the exercises in this section are to help the student, teacher and professional trainer realize and understand how the environment we live in influences the values we form. In this section we shall begin to see how our work, our ecological environment and our culture influence our values.

PART 2—SECTION IV
VALUES AND ENVIRONMENT

AUDIENCE	GOALS FOR EXERCISE	STRATEGIES USED
STUDENT	*Work may be seen as modification of my environment. The goal here is to see how a modified environment affects a person's values or imposes values on him.*	*1. A section from "Life at the Bottom" is read. Students are grouped and asked to make a collage of the opposite environment and role-play a person's feelings in both situations.* *2. Ecological games.*
TEACHER	*To make the teacher aware of the relationship between values and space. Space here is understood as relationship between self, others and world.*	*1. Role-play of board meeting.* *2. Role-play of teacher/parent/student conflict.* *3. Fantasy role-plays of polluted environment, with discussion of feelings and values.*
PROFESSIONAL TRAINER	*To make the trainer aware of priorities in environment, through institutions, administrators and culture.*	*1. Brainstorming the priority values in two cultures. Conflict role-play designed and acted out.* *2. Brainstorm on several value priorities and design role-play environment that would impose them.* *3. Design a freeing environment.*

FOR THE STUDENT

The exercises here are designed to help the student see how work modifies his environment. The goal is to see how a modified environment affects a person's values or imposes values on him.

Exercise One:

1. INTRODUCTION: The goal of this exercise is to help the student begin to realize how an environment imposes values on him.

2. MATERIALS NEEDED: The following quote is to be read to the students:

> *"Life at a Federal boarding school is regimented and arbitrary. Seen from there, many of the schools look like military installations—complexes of one color, one-texture buildings, set in the middle of otherwise barren areas. The impression of physical isolation mirrors the cultural isolation in the classroom. The building complex usually includes dormitories, classroom buildings, and housing for the staff. Many of the buildings are in disrepair. In a number of places (two per city, in Arizona, for example) condemned buildings are still in use. The Fort Wingate Elementary School Board uses old Fort Wingate, once commanded by Douglas MacArthur's father. Forty years ago, the Brooklyn Institution Merriam report declared the site unsuitable.*
>
> *Even the new buildings are designed to reinforce the numbing sterility. Long, narrow, lifeless dormitories house row upon row of double decker iron beds in little aisles. Windows are sometimes barred. Floors are bare; the vivid personal declarations that are so much a part of so many Indian communities are discouraged. Dress, too, is strictly regulated. The system makes individualizing one's appearance or environment fairly impossible. Beneath all the regulation is the bureau's implicit concept of the children: all Indians are alike"* (Life at the Bottom, p. 146).

2. ADDITIONAL MATERIALS NEEDED: The students will need paste and pictures of slum dwellings, as well as new class dwellings.

3. NUMBERS: Break the students up into groups of three or four.

4. TIME: Use five minutes for the reading of the passage and for the students to reflect on the passage; then give them half an hour to make the collage and another half hour to discuss what they have learned from the experience.

5. DESCRIPTION OF THE EXERCISE: The facilitator reads the selection from *Life at the Bottom* and then allows the students to think about the implications of what it must be like to live as the Indians were forced to live. Then the facilitator asks them to make a collage opposite to that kind of environment. (To help the students think through the difference in the two values, take half an hour to role-play a person's feelings in both of these situations.) Then they can break up into groups of three and four

to discuss what they've learned about how the environment influences the person in his values.

6. POSSIBLE OUTCOMES: The students should learn how the environment influences one's values. In this case it may be a surprise to find how important the environment is to one's values.

7. APPLICATION: This is a very basic exercise which will help the student begin to think about how the environment affects values.

Exercise Two:

1. INTRODUCTION: There are a number of ecological games that can be discussed with the students in order to help them develop an appreciation of what the environment does to the individual's formation of values.

2. MATERIALS NEEDED: Boxes, aquarium, small animals.

3. NUMBERS: Unlimited.

4. TIME: Discussion can be arranged according to time periods available.

5. DESCRIPTION OF THE EXERCISE: One discussion is to take an animal and put it in different size boxes. Which size box

would be the best suited for the animal to live in and be a more conducive environment for it? Another possibility is to obtain an aquarium for the students to gather around and to discuss the necessary kind of environment for the fish to be in in order to exist. They can go on to discuss what kind of environment they need in order to continue to exist. Another possible discussion with the students is to have them describe and put on the blackboard what it is like to live in an inner-city neighborhood. Describe on the board what it would be like to live in an upper middle class neighborhood. Then the students will be in a position to begin to see what the influences of the environment are on an individual who comes from either of these two situations.

6. POSSIBLE OUTCOMES: The student should become very aware of how the environment influences the kind of person —the values the person has developed in his life.

7. APPLICATION: This is a very simple exercise that can be used with any group.

FOR THE TEACHER

The exercises here are designed to help the teacher become aware of the relationship between values and space. Space here is understood as the relationship between the self, others, and world. The space that we live in is our environment. It is hoped that the teachers will come to see how the environment influences the formation of their values.

Exercise One:

1. INTRODUCTION: The goal of this exercise is to give the teacher an appreciation of how the people who surround us influence our behavior and values.

2. MATERIALS NEEDED: None.

3. NUMBERS: This is best done in groups of eight.

4. TIME: Allow an hour to an hour and a half for discussion.

5. DESCRIPTION OF THE EXERCISE: This exercise is to role-play a school board meeting. Call upon the creativity of the teachers to design the roles themselves. Decide who are the various kinds of people attending a board meeting. Let them assign the roles to one another and begin to discover how the various roles influence behavior and the formation of values during the meeting. Hold the meeting for at least half an hour to give sufficient time for the influence of the roles to become manifested. After half an hour, discuss the kinds of influences the teachers saw coming from the particular roles played.

6. POSSIBLE OUTCOMES: This exercise will help the teacher become very aware of how personalities and the influences of persons in the environment and in their work are very important to their formation of values.

7. APPLICATION: This is an advanced type of exercise, demanding a group of teachers who feel flexible and free enough to role-play the various individuals that ordinarily attend a school board meeting, and who are open enough to discuss the underlying value implications of their arguments and behavior.

Exercise Two:

1. INTRODUCTION: The goal of this exercise is to see how people in the environment in which they are connected get involved in conflict.

2. MATERIALS NEEDED: None.

3. NUMBERS: This is best done in groups of eight.

4. TIME: Allow one to three hours for discussion time.

5. DESCRIPTION OF THE EXERCISE: Choose four people from each group. Assign the roles of teacher, father, mother, and student to the four members who will be participating. Let the other four members be observers, and for 15 minutes let them role-play a conflict situation between teacher, parent, and student. Then discuss for half an hour how the role that this particular environment forces each to play has an influence on their values and on the conflict they are in. Take the other four and give them the same roles, trying to act out a new set of values. Let the first four be observers and carry this process through the same way, trying to learn by role-playing how the values in that particular environment, in these roles, influence the behavior and cause conflict in the situation.

6. POSSIBLE OUTCOMES: This exercise will help the teachers become aware of the different value-rankings of parents and students and how these cause conflict in this particular environmental setting.

7. APPLICATION: This is an advanced exercise that demands people flexible enough to do role-playing.

Exercise Three:

1. INTRODUCTION: This exercise is designed to help the teachers understand how a polluted environment influences their feelings and values.

2. MATERIALS NEEDED: None.

3. NUMBERS: This exercise is best done in total group.

4. TIME: Use one or two hours for discussion.

5. DESCRIPTION OF THE EXERCISE: Begin the exercise by having the group fantasize all the elements in a polluted environment, listing all the feelings that this kind of environment would arouse in a person. Then list all of the values they think are inherent in these kinds of feelings. On the basis of this, volunteers from the audience could be asked to role-play their feelings about such an environment and what kind of values they have developed as a result of being in this kind of environment. Then the group can take time to discuss better understanding of how the environment influences their value formation.

6. POSSIBLE OUTCOMES: This exercise will help the

teachers become even more aware of the value formation process through feelings, gradually arriving at values due to the influence of the environment on the person.

7. APPLICATION: This is an advanced exercise and will only work with those who are flexible enough to role-play their imagination.

FOR THE PROFESSIONAL TRAINER

The following exercises are designed to help the trainer become aware of the priorities in environment through institutions, administration, and culture.

Exercise One:

1. INTRODUCTION: The following exercises are designed to help the person understand how the priority of two different cultures can lead to conflict.

2. MATERIALS NEEDED: Magazines, paste and scissors.

3. NUMBERS: This kind of exercise will work best in a group of ten to twelve people.

4. TIME: One to two hours.

5. DESCRIPTION OF THE EXERCISE: Have the facilitator begin the exercise by having the group brainstorm on the priority values in one culture; then choose another culture and brainstorm on the priorities of their values. Discuss what kind of conflicts would probably arise from these different value-rankings. After the group has discussed this for approximately half an hour, ask for volunteers to play roles of people from such cultures and ask them to role-play an interaction with one another. Then the group can discuss how they saw the priority values in each culture causing conflict within the situation in which the role-play was had.

A suggested procedure is to have students move to their own natural groupings to cut out pictures from magazines or collect articles from outside the classroom, in the local neighborhood, or produce photographs of situations or events and objects which point out predominant value systems in the American culture. In order to get the group initiated, some of the concepts of ideas appropriate to this might be the use of time and the whole concept of consumer orientation-production and the place of materialism in our society. Other values that may be dominant in our society but not in others are the fact of war, the amount of money being spent on the military, and so on. For a contrasting culture, you might ask the students to pick one they feel is in contrast to the American culture. This could be an African tribe which has not, for example, ever been acquainted with the materialism of our society or even the methods of transportation, matters of money, and so on. At another level it may be picking a Latin American culture or a southern Mediterranean culture which has an entirely different attitude toward time, consumption and production. Another alternative is to pick a culture that does not have a large military expenditure and whose values are differently orientated than the United States. This might be the Canadian culture or one such as that of Switzerland. As in the last exercise, it might be well to have the students make a collage by sticking pictures or collecting objects of the counter-culture. To complete the group dynamic it might be well to have a discussion of the comparison. Another alternative is to have different groups brainstorm on various cultures and then come together to make the comparison. The outcome should help people understand how different cultures pose different values and produce different orientations in persons of those cultures.

6. POSSIBLE OUTCOMES: Through this exercise, the professional trainer will begin to see how the cultural values of different cultures cause conflict between nations.

7. APPLICATION: This is a highly advanced exercise and will only work with those who feel flexible enough to role-play and to explore their values deeply.

Exercise Two:

1. INTRODUCTION: Through this exercise, the professional trainer will become aware of how the environment influences value formation of people.

2. MATERIALS NEEDED: None.

3. NUMBERS: This exercise works best with a group of twelve.

4. TIME: One to two hours.

5. DESCRIPTION OF THE EXERCISE: Have the group brainstorm on the value priorities in a closed environment, such as a hospital or prison; then have them brainstorm on the value priorities that would be held in an open environment, such as a holiday abroad or a free university. Ask for volunteers willing to play roles of people from both environments and ask them to interact with one another. Let the role-play go for at least half an hour in order for the process dynamics to begin to take place. Then the group can discuss and point out how the environment and the value priorities of different environments influence the people in their value formation.

6. POSSIBLE OUTCOMES: This exercise will help professional trainers understand how the environment influences the value formation of the person.

7. APPLICATION: This is an advanced exercise which will be successful only with people who feel flexible enough to role-play and to explore their values in depth.

Exercise Three:

1. INTRODUCTION: The purpose of this exercise is to help the professional trainer understand how an administrator establishes a particular environment in a school.

2. MATERIALS NEEDED: Pencil and paper.

3. NUMBERS: This exercise works best in groups of six to eight.

4. TIME: One to two hours.

5. DESCRIPTION OF THE EXERCISE: Ask each group, after broken up into six or eight, to design what a free environment would be for in a particular administration. Brainstorm on the priority words that would be important to such an environment. As one person writes down the priority words, another person could write the underlying value of that priority word. Help the group come to a consensus on choosing four of the priority words and their underlying value; then together design an environment that would follow the values underlining such priority words. The environment would include time schedules and job descriptions of people in that administration.

6. POSSIBLE OUTCOMES: The professional trainer would begin to have a better understanding of how an administrator sets up a particular environment.

7. APPLICATION: This is an advanced exercise which will work only with people who already have some knowledge of group dynamics and administration.

Bus to city I'll have Jesse with
Christmas so maybe he'll be
entry soon - Got
of the animals, so all
Dec 4:30 pm Jess is here with
up last night with Jack

Section V

Primary Values

The exercises in this section are designed to help the student, teacher, and professional trainer have an experience in the value of self and an experience in valuing others. In this section it will be re-emphasized that the student, teacher and professional trainer should begin to use their own creativity in designing new strategies, new projects and exercises that will help clarify their values. One of the goals of this book is to be a catalytic agent in helping those who wish to become involved in value clarification to create their own programs.

PART 2—SECTION V
PRIMARY VALUES

AUDIENCE	GOAL FOR EXERCISE	STRATEGIES USED
STUDENT	To make the student aware of the "value of self" and of "valuing others".	1. The Love Seat. 2. The Infinite Bank. 3. Students design own "self-worth and worth of others" exercise.
TEACHER	To reinforce the need to practice primary "values of self and others" in the classroom.	1. Buzz group. Stress on listening and sharing as measure of self "my abilities and limitations in showing primary values in the classroom". 2. Exercises in group evaluation of a class using primary value measures. 3. Teachers design own "self-worth and worth of others" exercises.
PROFESSIONAL TRAINER	To reinforce the awareness for the need of primary values for teachers and staff as a part of any teaching program, as well as in day-to-day life. Institutions need primary values as well as individuals.	1. Exercises in evaluation procedure to increase teacher confidence. 2. Teacher training as an experience in primary values. 3. Discussion: the problem of intimacy, trust and potential from limits.

FOR THE STUDENT

The exercises here are designed to help the student become aware of the value of self and of the value of valuing others.

Exercise One:

1. INTRODUCTION: This exercise is designed to help the student become aware of his own value as a person, to see the good qualities he has and to help others see their value.

2. MATERIALS NEEDED: Pencil and paper.

3. NUMBERS: Groups of six to eight.

4. TIME: Allow 15 minutes to write out alone and an hour to an hour and a half to carry out in round-robin fashion.

5. DESCRIPTION OF THE EXERCISE: The facilitator begins this exercise by asking the participants to take 15 minutes to make a list of all of their good qualities. It is important for the facilitator to emphasize that the good qualities should be boldly stated. There should be no qualifying statements that take away from the good quality. For example, the participants should not write, "I am patient sometimes", or "Usually I am patient, but. . . ." Rather, the participant should simply write, "I am patient". Or for example, "I am kind". Gather the participants in groups of eight; have them go around and share their list of good qualities. After the first individual has shared his good qualities, then the group is to add other good qualities they see in the person. Assign a secretary for the person so that the additional good qualities are added to the list. Have the person who is receiving the good qualities repeat the good quality and say, "I accept this good quality". Continue the same process with each individual in the group.

6. POSSIBLE OUTCOMES: Frequently, participants find this to be a difficult exercise. Many people in our society tend to believe in a false humility that says one is not to brag about himself. The goal of this exercise is for individuals to affirm in themselves the good qualities that they have and, in this way, come to understand better their own self-worth. Another important outcome of this exercise is that the participants begin to see how others are helpful in our coming to affirm ourselves, by sharing with us the good that they see in us.

7. APPLICATION: This exercise is best executed in a group which has been together for some time. It is recommended that this exercise be placed toward the end of a workshop. (Or, use after a class has had a number of sessions together, so that they have data about one another and know something of one another.)

Exercise Two:

1. INTRODUCTION: The goal of this exercise is to help the individual become aware of the good qualities that others see in him and, in this way, see his value as a person.

2. MATERIALS NEEDED: None.

3. NUMBERS: Groups of eight are best.

4. TIME: Allow an hour to an hour and a half.

5. DESCRIPTION OF THE EXERCISE: The facilitator begins this exercise by asking the group to relax, to become comfortable and begin to imagine in their minds that they have an infinite bank account—that they could buy whatever they want to give to the individuals who are present with them in their group. After a few moments of reflecting, the facilitator may encourage the group himself, by "giving" gifts that reflect their goodness and the good qualities they have. After the exercise has gone around the group and everyone has given a gift, then the facilitator can call for a general discussion on how it felt to receive these gifts and have one's good qualities pointed out.

6. POSSIBLE OUTCOMES: This exercise helps a person to become aware of the good qualities that others see in him and, thus, gives him reason for seeing his own value. It also helps the participant realize the importance of other people and the value that others have in his life, insofar as they help him to see his own value.

7. APPLICATION: This exercise will work only with those who have had some experience in groups. If the individuals have participated in a good number of the exercises in this book, they are ready for this exercise. Participants must have had some time together to know one another somewhat before this exercise can have any real benefit for them. This exercise is best used toward the end of a workshop or after there have been a number of sessions together in a classroom setting.

Exercise Three:

1. INTRODUCTION: The goal of this suggestion is to encourage the students to begin to design exercises and projects for themselves that will help them clarify their values.

2. MATERIALS NEEDED: Reproduce the "Guidelines for Creating Exercises".

3. NUMBERS: Have the group brainstorm together and then break up into groups of six or eight to work on the project.

4. TIME: This exercise takes three hours or two class sessions. Use the first session to work on designing the project and another session to execute the project.

5. DESCRIPTION OF THE EXERCISE: The facilitator or teacher is to act as a catalyst here, to encourage the group to design their own exercise. Have the group break up into groups of six to brainstorm on the area of value theory they've been through and on which they would like to begin to start creating exercises. That is to say, would they like to do something in the area of value indicators such as time or money, or would they like to start in the area of primary values to build up someone's self-worth? Or, would they like to get across the idea of how people choose or act? When each group has come upon a particular subject, they should then come to a consensus on the purpose they would like to focus on in the developing of an exercise. At this point, they

would write this purpose down under number one, using the guideline given on the preceding page. Next, the teacher should work with the groups to help them decide how large a group they want to work in; then help them work out the time schedules and description of what they want to do and what the outcome should be.

The final part of the session would probably take place in the second meeting, at which time they could then test out their exercise on other members of this class. Alternatively, they could test out their exercise with another group and then be part of the next class session. The purpose of this exercise is to help people develop their own value approaches; in so doing, they will have to exercise their imaginations and their ability to make choices, as well as to act on a given thing: to receive and experience the feelings that go along with the risk necessary in value judgment.

6. POSSIBLE OUTCOMES: This exercise will help students use their imagination and creativity in designing their own exercises in value clarification. It will also give opportunity to the teacher/facilitator to work with the group, after having worked with the group throughout the book. It will give the teacher/facilitator an opportunity to practice with the group, helping them design their project.

GUIDELINES FOR CREATING EXERCISES

1. Introduction: Give the description of the purpose of your exercise.
2. Materials Needed: Describe the materials that you will need.
3. Numbers: Decide on what size group your project will best work with.
4. Time: Schedule the exercise according to the time that you have.
5. Description of the Exercise: Describe in detail how the exercise is to flow and what is to be done.
6. Possible Outcomes: Describe briefly what you hope to accomplish through the exercise.

7. APPLICATION: This exercise will be successful only if those involved have already participated in most of the exercises in this group. In other words, this is an advanced exercise which will only be successful after the group and teacher have had some experience in value clarification.

FOR THE TEACHER

The exercises here are designed to reinforce the need to practice primary values of self and others in the classroom.

Exercise One:

1. INTRODUCTION: The goal of this exercise is to help the teachers learn of their good qualities, as others see them, and to practice helping others to see their good qualities by sharing their feelings for one another.

2. MATERIALS NEEDED: Pencil and paper.

3. NUMBERS: This works best in groups of six or eight.

4. TIME: Allow an hour to an hour and a half.

5. DESCRIPTION OF THE EXERCISE: Begin the exercise by having everyone make a list of his abilities and limitations. Give them 15 minutes to do this. Then have each individual read his list to his group of six or eight. The group then responds to the individual by pointing out to him more of his abilities that they had seen and, also, by pointing out to him how his limitations might be changed into positive assets.

6. POSSIBLE OUTCOMES: Individuals will become aware of their self-worth and how others help them in growing in their self-worth. They will also have practice in seeing the good that is in others.

7. APPLICATION: This is an advanced exercise and will work best with a group that has had some experience in value clarification.

Exercise Two:

1. INTRODUCTION: This exercise is designed to help the teachers evaluate their group in terms of the primary values. The practical application or expression of these primary values of self-worth and worth of others is manifested through the trust, openness, warmth and interdependence that is expressed in the classroom.

2. MATERIALS NEEDED: Reproduce the "Group Evaluation Sheet", found on the following page.

3. NUMBERS: Groups of eight are suggested.

4. TIME: 15 minutes to use the Group Evaluation Sheet, 45 minutes to an hour and a half to discuss.

5. DESCRIPTION OF THE EXERCISE: The facilitator will pass out the Group Evaluation Sheet and ask each person to take 15 minutes and complete the sheet. It is important for the facilitator to point out that the values of self-worth and worth of others

are manifested in a group by some practical skills of listening, accepting, being open and honest, showing warmth toward one another, respecting one another and by the interdependence of each in taking responsibility for the group. After the individuals have finished the Group Evaluation Sheet, they can move into groups of eight to share how they feel about the groups they have been in.

6. POSSIBLE OUTCOMES: At this point, the teachers will be able to begin to see how in the classroom, in a practical way, the values of self-worth and worth of others are practiced.

7. APPLICATION: This exercise will only be successful if the individuals have had experience in most of the value-clarification exercises in this book and if the facilitator helps them to deal with the correlation between the high ideals of the value of self-worth, the value of others' self-worth and the actual practicing of this through listening, accepting, being open and honest, showing warmth and exercising interdependence in the group.

Exercise Three:

1. INTRODUCTION: The goal of this session is to have the teachers begin to create their own exercises in value clarification.

2. MATERIALS NEEDED: Resource books: Elizabeth W. Flynn and John F. LaFaso, *Group Discussion as Learning Process: A Sourcebook.* Howard R. Lewis and Harold S. Streitfeld, *Growth Gains, How to Tune in Yourself, Your Family, Your Friends,* Harcourt, Brace, Jovanovich, Inc., 1970.

3. NUMBERS: Groups of four to six are best for this kind of an exercise with professional trainers.

4. TIME: Three to six hours.

5. DESCRIPTION OF THE EXERCISE: The facilitator is to act as the catalyst in helping the teachers begin to create their own exercises in value clarification for their situation back home.

GROUP EVALUATION SHEET

	YES	*NO*
People talk directly to individuals.		
People really listen to one another.		
The group gives others the opportunity to express themselves.		
The group respects ideas and feelings of individuals.		
The group feels free to express feelings.		
Anger is openly expressed by an individual without attacking anyone.		
People feel free to be humorous.		
Individuals are able to say they like or love another member.		
The group uses silence constructively.		
People accept one another.		
There is high trust in the group.		
Individuals are open and honest with each other.		
Individuals are taking their share of the responsibility for the success of the group.		
The people feel that they are a cohesive group.		
Add other criteria that you think are important to a group that is growing in the primary values of self-worth and worth of others.		

6. POSSIBLE OUTCOMES: It is hoped that the teachers will begin to see that they have the ability and talent to create value-clarification exercises that will fit the situation in which they find themselves.

7. APPLICATION: This is an advanced exercise and will only work with those who have had some experience in value clarification, either through this book or through experience in group dynamics in a group process.

FOR THE PROFESSIONAL TRAINER

The following exercises are designed to reinforce the professional trainer in his awareness of the need of the primary values for teachers and staff as a part of any teacher's program, as well as in personal life. Institutions need primary values, as well as individuals.

Exercise One:

1. INTRODUCTION: The goal of this exercise is to help individuals use one another as a helping pair in such a way that they give feedback to one another that builds up their self-worth.

2. MATERIALS NEEDED: Reproduce the Primary Values Evaluation Sheet.

GUIDELINE FOR CREATING EXERCISES

1. Introduction: Goal of the exercise.
2. Materials Needed:
3. Numbers: The size of the group that is best for the exercise.
4. Time: The suggested schedule of events.
5. Description of the Exercise:
6. Possible Outcomes: List here what you hope to achieve through the exercise.
7. Application: Describe the possible applications as to how the exercise might be used.

PRIMARY VALUES EVALUATION SHEET

Name of Partner ____________________

On the line below each question, make two marks. These marks should be in two different colors so the picture of the person in a situation of change can be easily seen. The marks should be indicative of your partner's position in relation to the two extremes given. One mark should indicate your partner's position when he entered the group; the other mark indicates his position when he left the group. You may mark anywhere along the line to visually express your impression.

1. How effective do you think this person is in contributing ideas, insights, and suggestions which help the group solve problems and achieve its goals?

He is exceptionally effective. ________|________ *He is very ineffective.*

2. How effective do you think this person is in performing functions which build the group and keep it working well?

He is exceptionally effective. ________|________ *He is very ineffective.*

3. In your opinion, how able is this person to express himself freely and comfortably in the group?

He is exceptionally free and comfortable. ________|________ *He is very restricted and tense.*

4. To what extent do you feel that this person really understands your ideas and feelings?

He has a very good understanding. ________|________ *He has very little understanding.*

5. If participation is a guide to a person's feelings of self-worth and withdrawal is an indication of lack of self-worth, how did/does your partner rank in terms of verbal feedback and body participation?

He has high self-esteem. ________|________ *He is withdrawn.*

6. *In what way do you see your partner sharing himself with the group?*

Dependent upon cooperation with others.	——I——	*Very independent of others.*

7. *To what extent does your partner give evidence of the following emotions?:*

Freedom.	——I——	*Depression.*
Enthusiasm.	——I——	*Boredom.*
Peace.	——I——	*Anger.*
Confidence.	——I——	*Fear.*

8. *To what extent is your partner able to communicate?:*

Trust.	——I——	*Mistrust.*
Listens well.	——I——	*Fails to report accurately what another person says.*
Expresses feelings.	——I——	*Expresses ideas.*
Helps others express themselves.	——I——	*Pursues point agressively.*
Shares.	——I——	*Dominates.*
Encourages others to talk.	——I——	*Withdraws.*

9. *To what extent is your partner sensitive to the group?:*

Listens to angered or upset person with good understanding.	——I——	*Little response to anger and distress of others.*
Deals directly with feelings.	——I——	*Ignores feelings or smooths them over.*

3. NUMBERS: Dyads and groups of six.

4. TIME: Allow 5 minutes to fill out the Primary Values Evaluation Sheet, half an hour to share in dyads and one hour to share in groups of six.

5. DESCRIPTION OF THE EXERCISE: The facilitator will ask the professional trainers to break up into pairs. Tell them to pick someone they feel they know and would be willing to share with and be open with. Then pass out the Primary Values Evaluation Sheet and let each partner rate the other according to that sheet. Give the dyad half an hour to share with one another their ratings. Then ask them to move into groups of six to eight, where they will share with one another what they have learned and how they might use such a sheet in teachers' training.

6. POSSIBLE OUTCOMES: The participants will receive feedback as to how effective they are in a group and so learn the good qualities they have, in order to grow in self-worth as they participate in groups. (This will also help them to realize the need for the helping-pair idea—their need for working together and giving feedback to one another so that each can grow in self-worth and feel the value of others' worth.)

7. APPLICATION: This is an advanced exercise and will only work with those who have some knowledge of one another. Normally, such an exercise will work best toward the end of a workshop or after a number of sessions have been held in a series.

Exercise Two:

1. INTRODUCTION: This session is to be spent by professional trainers in creating their own value-clarification exercise. This will give them an opportunity to share their resources with one another.

2. MATERIALS NEEDED: Course cards, 5 x 8, pencils, bulletin board for posting course cards, newsprint, format for catalog course offerings. You will also need a setting in which the group can be broken up into small rooms for sub-group meetings. Two good resource books are: J. William Pfeiffer and John E. Jones, *A Handbook of Structured Experiences for Human Relations Training,* Volumes I through III, University Associates Press, 1971. Herbert A. Otto, *Group Methods to Actualize Human Potential: A Handbook,* The Holistic Press, 1970.

3. NUMBERS: Groups of four to six people would be best for this exercise.

4. TIME: Three to six hours.

5. DESCRIPTION OF THE EXERCISE: The facilitator is to act as a catalyst to help the professional trainers create their own value-clarification exercise on the primary values. If there is a very large number of professional trainers in the workshop you are now conducting, you might want to try the idea of the "miniversity". This would give the professional trainers an opportunity to share their resources and ideas with one another in the various ways in which they have created value-clarification exercises.

MINIVERSITY COURSE OFFERINGS

Time	*Room 216*	*Room 217*	*Room 218*	*Room 219*
2:00—2:30				
2:40—3:10				
3:20—3:50				
4:00—4:30				

The goal of a miniversity is to provide for dissemination of information from participant resources during a conference, workshop or institute.

The facilitator announces that time is now available for participants to contribute their special knowledge experience to the group. This will take the form of half-hour courses offered to fellow-participants. The facilitator states that the courses will be selected by a screening committee and that a schedule will be established for offering the course. He then illustrates making course cards and posts samples to remain on display for participants to refer to when they make their own cards.

Blank cards are distributed to the participants, who fill them out if they care to present a course. Then the cards are collected. The facilitator selects a screening committee.

The screening committee meets to select courses to be offered. Courses are posted according to the format for course offering. Courses may repeat—that is, they may be offered at alternate times. Courses proceed according to the schedule, as decided by the screening committee.

6. POSSIBLE OUTCOMES: The goal of this workshop is to give an opportunity to the trainers to share the ideas and creativity they have.

7. APPLICATION: This particular session works only with people who have had a good deal of experience in group dynamics, human relations training, or value-clarification workshops.

SAMPLE COURSE DESCRIPTION CARD

ENCOUNTER GROUPS SPONSORED BY THE PSYCHOLOGICAL SERVICES CENTER
Dr. Bob Jones, Assistant Professor, *Psychology, Westfield University*
A discussion of the nature, background, and rationale of the program, with an emphasis on implication for professional training.

Exercise Three:

1. INTRODUCTION: This exercise is designed to help the professional trainers discover the issues evolving from the problems of intimacy, trust and potentials from limitations in a group.

2. MATERIALS NEEDED: Reproduce the value-clarification sheet on intimacy.

3. NUMBERS: Groups of four to six work best for this exercise.

4. TIME: Use half an hour to fill out the value-clarification sheet and an hour to an hour and a half to discuss the sheet.

5. DESCRIPTION OF THE EXERCISE: The facilitator will pass out the value-clarification sheet and give each person half an hour to fill it out. Then ask them to break up into groups of four to six, to share with one another what they have written about intimacy, trust and changing their limits into potentials.

6. POSSIBLE OUTCOMES: The goal of this exercise is to give the trainers an opportunity to discuss an issue by making use of the value-clarification sheet. It is hoped that through this experience they will learn the format of the value-clarification sheet and be able to use that in their own work.

7. APPLICATION: This is an advanced exercise and will work only with those who have had some experience either in group dynamics, human relations training or value-clarification workshops.

VALUE-CLARIFICATION SHEET

INTIMACY, TRUST AND POTENTIALS FROM LIMIT

"Intimacy" is the ability to share our deepest hopes, joys, aspirations, guilts, anxieties and problems repeatedly and recently with other people. The traditional educational system has trained people to avoid intimacy. In our large cities today, because of the high rate of crime, most people do not trust one another. In today's world it is very difficult for even a married couple to really grow in intimacy. Most people do not have anyone with whom they can share their hopes and joys, their guilts and anxieties, on an intimate level.

1. *Do you agree or disagree with the above statement? Change the statement to make it one you can agree with. Explain why you agree or disagree with the statement.*

2. *List five factors important in developing intimacy and trust between people.*

3. *List four factors that work against people growing in intimacy and trust.*

4. *Make a list of the usual limitations people have in growing in intimacy and trust.*

5. *Take the limitations in number 4 and find the positive potential inherent in them.*

Section VI

Work and Leisure

Work and leisure in our society are usually seen differently, depending on the class structure from which the person comes. That is to say, a working class man will see work differently than a middle class man. The working class man often will see work as being within the periphery of the eight-hour day and may often see it as something he does not enjoy, with leisure as that which comes at the end of the workday or shift. The middle class man has a greater opportunity to choose the kind of work he wants, and because he likes his work he often finds it difficult to know where the line is between work and leisure. For a middle class man to make arbitrary lines between work and leisure would be giving a very superficial look at these two values. However, for the purpose of study and exercise, it is necessary to separate the two words in order for people to become aware of what work and leisure can be as values.

Given that people view work differently, the point of view we are taking is that work can be a value. That is to say, work can be something chosen from alternatives, after consideration of consequences—chosen freely—that a person is happy with and acts on. In order for this to be a value it has to enhance human growth. Within this context, work has been defined as modification of the human environment for the purpose of enhancing human growth. Work viewed this way is not seen as simply something that man does in order to survive, protect himself from the elements or protect himself from other people. Rather it is seen as enhancing his personal growth. In terms of the diagram, then, work as a value does differ from leisure.

First of all work, generally speaking, is an activity by which we *do* something to *produce* something. I may work in a factory to produce cars or vacuum cleaners; as such my work is usually within a given, limited period of *time.* Generally, people can say that they work so many hours a day. A middle class person may say he works twelve hours a day. A working class man may say he works eight hours a day at a particular job; maybe he has a second job.

Secondly, work is defined in terms of *space:* a person usually works with particular people in a particular work area. As a salesman who sells books, I may see my space as working primarily with people who sell books. As such my space is restricted to those people where I work. If I work in a factory, I not only work with specific people but also in a given location or area.

Thirdly, work differs from leisure in that in work there are certain expectations placed on me as a worker. I'm expected to do certain things and produce certain things for the money I earn. It should be noted that work in this way becomes expectation, not within only the framework of the eight-hour day, but also in terms of work after work. That is to say, my wife and my children have certain expectations of me, primarily that I will provide for them; this becomes an area of work. The consequences of work are different from the consequences of leisure in that work usually is seen as providing security, shelter, education and future for myself and my family.

Leisure as a value is understood as being an attitude of mind or a stance toward life in which values can be chosen; it is a freeing environment:

1. We say that leisure is being one's self. It is a "non-activity" which is not directed toward doing or producing, but rather to *being*.

2. Leisure is a timeless activity. As such, leisure differs from work in that there are no necessarily given productive ends toward what is being done within a given period of time.

3. Leisure is a freeing environment; not only should I be able to be myself within that leisure activity, but I should become, through my attitude of leisure, the kind of person who frees other people who should also be themselves.

4. Leisure is an ability to dream and fantasize as a part of attitude. Dreaming and fantasizing are a part of the human activity, allowing a person to be able to see more and more alternatives from which he can choose. The attitude of leisure is one in which

the possibilities of values as chosen aspects of life are increased or made possible.

5. Leisure is also a celebration. "Celebration" completes the attitude of what leisure is; this is actually the root of the potential of man. It is where man faces his limitations and in that activity is able to see what his potential is. This act itself is an act of celebration.

Leisure then differs from work in that it maximizes the possibility of work by recreating man in order that he can modify his environment for the purpose of enhancing humanity generally. Leisure is an attitude rather than an activity and differs from work, which is primarily an act of doing with a given productive end. Work appears specifically in time and space, where leisure does not. Work has certain expectations on man in terms of production and modification, whereas leisure is those times in a person's life when he can be free of expectation, in order that he may be recreated. Then he can become his maximum self, both in leisure and in work.

The exercises in this section are designed to help the student, teachers and professional trainers become aware of work and leisure in their own experience and as objective values. Many people in our society place higher value on work than they do leisure. Therefore, the exercises in this section are designed to make participants aware of how they value work, and, hopefully, to create a new value for them, insofar as leisure is concerned.

We do not intend to impose the value of leisure on anyone, but rather it is a value of ours, and we wish to give opportunity to others to decide whether or not they wish to make it one of their values.

PART 2—SECTION VI
WORK AND LEISURE

AUDIENCE	GOAL FOR EXERCISE	STRATEGIES USED
STUDENT	*To help the student become aware of work and leisure in his/her own experience and as objective values.*	*1. Using Diagram 2 and 3, the student compares what work and leisure mean in society, with what they could mean.* *2. Relationship of values of work and leisure to time, utilizing Diagram 4.*
TEACHERS	*To provide the teacher with opportunities to view work and leisure as values, by examination of personal experience.*	*1. Exercise of value of work and leisure to time, utilizing Diagram 4. The teacher is then asked to design his/her own sheets reflecting on Diagram 2.* *2. Attitudes are compared in Diagram 5. Use of voting method and public interview. New list as continuum is designed.*
PROFESSIONAL TRAINERS	*To help the trainer design exercise sheets and value games to help students see work as positive value in relationship to leisure.*	*1. Continuum and juxtaposition box questions designed from Diagram 2.* *2. Role-play and public interview strategies planned around work and leisure.*

FOR THE STUDENT

The following exercises are designed to help the student become aware of work and leisure in his own experience and as objective values.

Exercise One:

1. INTRODUCTION: This exercise is designed to help the student examine what work and leisure mean in his life.

2. MATERIALS NEEDED: Reproduce Diagram 2, Work and Leisure Compared and Diagram 3, Questions on Work and Leisure.

3. NUMBERS: Groups of eight to ten students are desirable for this exercise.

4. TIME: Allow 50 minutes to evaluate Diagram 2, Work and Leisure Compared and half an hour to discuss it. Use 10 minutes to work on Diagram 3, Questions on Work and Leisure, and half an hour to an hour to share with one another, in groups of eight to ten, what they have learned.

5. DESCRIPTION OF THE EXERCISE: The facilitator will give the group Diagram 2, Work and Leisure Compared, and ask individuals to look over the concepts on work and leisure and to decide whether they agree with Diagram 2 or not. If they disagree with anything on Diagram 2, then they are to change it and make it so that they can agree with it. After they have done this, they are asked to move into groups of eight to ten and to share with one another what their concept of work and leisure is. After about

SECTION VI—DIAGRAM 2
WORK AND LEISURE COMPARED

ITEM COMPARED	*TIME*	*SPACE*	*EXPECTATION*	*CONSEQUENCES*
WORK as modification of the environment	*Usually in a limited span of time with certain expectations to produce in that time.* *Doing and Producing are the emphasis.*	*Usually in a particular place to produce a given product, e.g., factory televisions.*	*To modify environment.* *To produce something.* *To provide shelter, security, future, education, etc.*	*To maximize man's living.* *To provide securities, life, shelter, welfare, freedom.*
LEISURE as being self and freeing others to be themselves	*Majoritively timeless in nature. There is an overall limit, but no limits are placed within the span.* *Being and Becoming are the emphasis.*	*Not in any particular place. Not necessarily productive of anything.*	*Place of none.* *Expectation for self, others, family, at-work, in-school, etc.*	*Human growth, creativity, recreation, maximizes potential.* *Hoping, caring, meaning, maximizes work.*

SECTION VI—DIAGRAM 3

QUESTIONS ON WORK AND LEISURE	
	WHERE DO YOU FIT?
1. What do you see as work for poor people?	
2. What do you see as their leisure?	
3. How does working class man and woman see work?	
4. How do they view leisure?	
5. What is the middle class view of work?	
6. What is their view of leisure?	
7. What about other classes?	

half an hour of discussion, depending on how well the discussion is going, pass out Diagram 3, Questions on Work and Leisure, and give the individuals 10 to 15 minutes to answer this questionnaire. Then ask them to gather together in groups of eight to ten to share with one another what work and leisure mean to them in their lives.

6. POSSIBLE OUTCOMES: For the student this may be the first time that he really has considered leisure. It may be the first time for him because of our society's stance that work is the highest value. Frequently, people will begin to reorder their priorities on the basis of such an exercise as this. Beginning to accept leisure as a value will cause a shift in the way they rank their values.

7. APPLICATION: This is a basic exercise which may be used with any group in which the topic of work and leisure is appropriate.

Exercise Two:

1. INTRODUCTION: This exercise will use time as a value indicator to help the person better appreciate values in regard to work and leisure.

2. MATERIALS NEEDED: Reproduce for the participants Diagram 4, Assigned Priority of Values by Time Spent.

3. NUMBERS: It is best to break the group into small groups of six to eight.

4. TIME: Allow half an hour to fill out Diagram 4 and half an hour to an hour to discuss it with others in groups of six to eight.

5. DESCRIPTION OF THE EXERCISE: The facilitator will announce to the group that they are to take Diagram 4, Assigned Priority Values by Time Spent, as a means of discovering what their values are in regard to work and leisure. Give the participants 25 to 30 minutes to fill out Diagram 4. You may have to explain to them that they should first fill in the "time spent" column in the middle of the diagram. Then, on the basis of time spent, they will rank their values in the right-hand column. In other words, the more time they spend on a particular item, the higher their value as regards that item. After the participants have filled out Diagram 4, break them up into groups of six to eight to discuss what they discovered about their own values.

6. POSSIBLE OUTCOMES: By using time as a value indicator, the participants will have help in discovering what are truly their values in regard to work and leisure. This may well be the first time that they have been confronted with the value of leisure.

7. APPLICATION: This is a basic exercise which may be used with any group in which it would be appropriate to discuss work and leisure. One variation of this exercise could be that before Diagram 4 is filled out, in the left-hand column have the participants list how they would rank the various items, according to their values or what they think their values are. Then once they

SECTION VI—DIAGRAM 4
ASSIGNED PRIORITY OF VALUES BY TIME SPENT

BASIC ACTIVITY	TIME SPENT	PRIORITY ACCORDING TO TIME ALLOTTED
Work		
Sleep		
Meals		
Travel (work)		
Personal maintenance		
Leisure		
Other		

One week: 168 hours

LEISURE TIME ACTIVITY ONLY	TIME SPENT	PRIORITY ACCORDING TO TIME ALLOTTED
Friends		
Clubs		
Art		
Reading		
Sports		
Study		
Hobby		
Church		
Movies		
TV		
Theatre		
Worry		
Reflection		
Relaxation		
Other		
Other		
Other		

have finished allotting the time they spend and prioritizing or ranking the values according to the time allotted, they can compare what they thought were their value-rankings here with what, in actuality, the time indicator gives as their value in regard to work and leisure.

FOR THE TEACHER

The goal of the exercises below is to provide the teacher with the opportunity to view work and leisure as values by having them examine their own experiences of work and leisure.

Exercise One:

1. INTRODUCTION: The goal of this exercise is to help the teachers come to an understanding of their own value of work and leisure by using time as an indicator and also to encourage them to begin to design their own exercises.

2. MATERIALS NEEDED: Reproduce Diagram 2, Work and Leisure Compared, which is on page 142, and also Diagram 4, Assigned Priorities of Value by Time Spent, on page 145.

3. NUMBERS: Groups of four to six are best.

4. TIME: Take half an hour to fill out Diagram 4, an hour to an hour and a half to discuss it. Use an hour to discuss Diagram 2 as a means of developing their own description of work and leisure.

5. DESCRIPTION OF THE EXERCISE: The facilitator will begin by asking the teachers to use Diagram 4, Assigned Priorities of Values by Time Spent. He may begin by asking them to rank, on the left-hand side of the page, what they think their values are and how they would rank the items listed according to their values; they may work on the sheet for half an hour. Once they have determined their priorities by the time that they have allotted to them, they can compare what they thought were their values with what the time indicator has actually determined as to how they value the various items. Give them an hour to an hour and a half to discuss what they discovered about how they value work and leisure.

6. POSSIBLE OUTCOMES: It is hoped that the teachers will come to understand how time is a value indicator, and that the teachers themselves may come to an appreciation of what their value is in regard to work and leisure. It may well be that this will be the first time they have been confronted by the value leisure has in our work-oriented society. It is important for the teacher to have had such an experience of his own values of work and leisure before working with the students on these issues.

7. APPLICATION: These are basic exercises and may be used with any group. However, asking teachers to design their own exercise will only work with the group that has had some experience in group dynamics or has been through most of the exercises in this book.

Exercise Two:

1. INTRODUCTION: In this exercise the teacher will see that attitudes are a value indicator of how a person values work and leisure.

2. MATERIALS NEEDED: Reproduce Diagram 5, Some Common Attitudes to Work/Leisure.

3. NUMBERS: Use a total group of fifteen to twenty or break into groups of eight to twelve.

4. TIME: Allow half an hour to do Diagram 5, half an hour to an hour to discuss; spend half an hour on public interview and one hour to design a new list as a continuation.

5. DESCRIPTION OF THE EXERCISE: The facilitator will use a means of voting in the group as a way of having the group publicly affirm what their attitudes are as regards work and leisure. Ask the group to stand in a circle. If it's a rather large group, break them up into groups of twelve to fifteen. Give them the following methods of voting: tell them if an attitude that is read off is one that they highly believe in, they are to hold their *thumbs* up and to vigorously move their thumbs in a circle. If they think that the attitude is one they agree with, ask them to hold their *fist* up, with thumb up. If it is an attitude they are indifferent to, ask them merely to hold their fists *out*. If it is an attitude they disagree with, ask them to hold their *hands* out with thumb *down*. And finally, if it is an attitude they heatedly disagree with, ask them to hold their hands out, with thumb down, shaking them vigorously.

Then the facilitator will begin to read off to the group,

DIAGRAM 5—SECTION VI

SOME COMMON ATTITUDES TOWARD WORK/LEISURE

Leisure is what I do after work.

Work is a sign of how useful you are.

Work is a sign of godliness.

Leisure is laziness.

Work is what you have to do.

Looking after children isn't work.

Leisure is getting away from it all.

Leisure is a luxury I do not have time for.

Leisure is for retired or old people.

Doing nothing is laziness.

Competitive sports are leisure.

Competitive sports are work.

Watching sunsets is a waste of time.

Art and theatre are recreation.

Leisure is only for the rich.

Only oddballs have time for leisure.

Work is for slaves.

We must work to be saved.

I work best under pressure.

Going to the zoo is for kids.

Art is for students.

from Diagram 5, some of the common attitudes toward work/leisure. Give the group time to react to each attitude. This will take approximately 25 to 30 minutes; after it is completed, give the group an opportunity to discuss their reactions to voting on these attitudes and what they feel their attitudes are toward work and leisure. Then take half an hour for the group to break up into dyads and to interview one another concerning the attitudes on Diagram 5. It will be well to pass out Diagram 5, at this point, so that they will have these sheets with them. Another option here is to break the group up into groups of eight and have an observing circle. Let the first four sit in a circle and talk for 15 minutes about their attitude toward work and leisure. Then let others from the outside circle of observers come into the middle to discuss for 15 minutes what their attitudes toward work are. Then the two groups can get together to see what they've learned from one another. Allow at least an hour to an hour and a half, then gather together in groups of four to design a continuum on common attitudes toward work and leisure. They can use Diagram 5 as a help to them. For example, the teachers may use the examples in the diagram. They may take on the left-hand side, "Competitive sports are leisure", and then on a ten-point scale let the other end put that competitive sports are work. Or they may take ideas in Diagram 5 such as, "Leisure is what I do after work", on the left-hand side, and then a ten-point scale with the other side being, for example, "My work is leisure". The facilitator may have to explain what a continuum is.

6. POSSIBLE OUTCOMES: The teacher will experience a non-threatening technique that has extensive application in all sorts of limited classroom situations. She will also have the opportunity to begin to design her own exercises, as they relate to a specific group of persons only known to the teacher.

7. APPLICATION: This is one of those exercises that is particularly helpful in limited classroom situations. Those especially interested in this should refer themselves to the last chapter of the book.

FOR THE PROFESSIONAL TRAINERS

The exercises below are designed to help the trainer make up exercise sheets and value games to help students and teachers see work as a positive value in relationship to leisure.

Exercise One:

1. INTRODUCTION: The goal of this exercise is to help the trainer design materials helpful in his work with participants.

2. MATERIALS NEEDED: Reproduce Diagram 2, Work and Leisure Compared, as given on page 142.

3. NUMBERS: Groups of four to six.

4. TIME: Two to three hours.

5. DESCRIPTION OF THE EXERCISE: Give the trainers

Diagram 2, Work and Leisure Compared, and ask them to design either a continuum or a juxtaposition box question on the basis of the information that is given in Diagram 2. Or, they may use or design whatever kind of instrument they think would be helpful to come to a better understanding of their values in regard to work and leisure. A ten-point continuum might be designed with the items and issues revolving around work on the left-hand side, with the items and issues revolving around leisure on the right-hand side, using the information that is given in Diagram 2. As a person marks what his attitudes are according to items listed, the more he marks toward the left-hand side, the more he is oriented toward work. The more he marks toward the right-hand side of the continuum, the more he is oriented toward leisure. A "juxtaposition box" is simply a forced choice between two choices so that on the left-hand side of the page would be questions that would reflect, for example, "work attitudes". On the right-hand side of the page and in juxtaposition to question 1 on "Work" would be question 1 on "Leisure", which would be exploratory of attitudes toward leisure. The result would be that at the end of the questionnaire, after approximately twenty items had been marked, the participant would be able to add up columns on the left and columns on the right; the column which has the most marks is the one that would show which tendency he has, whether it be toward work or toward leisure as a higher value.

6. POSSIBLE OUTCOMES: This exercise will give the trainer, who already has experience in value clarification and who has already resolved his issues concerning work and leisure, an

opportunity to design materials which will be helpful to him. In the process of doing so, he should be able to work with colleagues in a way that will create the opportunity for them to share resources, ideas and insights.

7. APPLICATIONS: This is an advanced exercise and will work only with those who have had experience in group dynamics or value clarification. This exercise may be beneficial to a group only after they themselves have gone through an exercise to determine where their values are as to work and leisure.

Exercise Two:

1. INTRODUCTION: The goal of this exercise is to give trainers an opportunity to design strategies for dealing with the value issues of work and leisure.

2. MATERIALS NEEDED: Paper and pencil.

3. NUMBERS: Use total groups of four to six; if it is a very large group, break up into groups of twelve to fifteen.

4. TIME: Two to three hours.

5. DESCRIPTION OF THE EXERCISE: The facilitator will act as a catalyst with the professional trainers to help them design strategies helpful for them in working with their participants in regard to work and leisure. Of two strategies that may be started with, the first can be to ask the group to do a role-play: Ask for two volunteers. One volunteer will role-play a person who has a high value of work and a low value of leisure. The other volunteer will role-play a person who has a high value of leisure and a low value of work. After the two participants have carried on a role-play for 15 to 20 minutes, conduct a general discussion, in groups no larger than twelve to fifteen, of the values of work and leisure in the use of role-play in helping to understand attitudes toward work and leisure. Another strategy is to break into groups of eight. Ask one person to be an interviewer, to go around and interview each person in a group as regards his attitudes and his values as to work and leisure. Then, on the basis of these two strategies, break the group up into groups of six to eight to discuss and to design other strategies that would be helpful for them in their work with participants.

6. POSSIBLE OUTCOMES: This exercise will give the professionals an opportunity to share ideas and insights in working with participants and also to continue to help them clarify their values in regard to work and leisure.

7. APPLICATION: This is a highly advanced exercise and will only work with professionals who have had experience in group dynamics and value clarification.

PART III

CONFERENCES IN VALUE CLARIFICATION

INTRODUCTION

This part of the book contains a detailed description of six conferences which can be used for introducing and training people in the awareness and application of value clarification. These are, for the most part, teaching conferences to instruct people in the theory of value clarification. However, since value clarification is a methodology, the conferences are experiential in nature. For the most part, the cognitive input is seen as coming out of the experience of the conference or is placed at the end of the conference. Thus, the methodology is to reflect on the experience, rather than talk about the experience first.

This methodology, of course, is evidenced in all of the exercises in the book. I am simply repeating this in relationship to total conferences at this point. The application of the various value methodologies used in the book and in this conference (two teaching situations) are as follows:

1. Through the participants becoming so skilled and having such an understanding of the process that it could then be designed and made up by their own strategies.

2. By direct experimentation with some of the exercises within classroom structures.

The goal of the methodologies in this book is not to help people become skilled in the particular strategies we have presented, but rather to provide skills in strategies so that they can finally design and make up their own strategies fòr given situations. For this reason, a person who is able to participate and work through the exercises in the book, starting with the student exercises in Part II, Section I and moving through to the professional exercises in Part II, Section VI, will have finally been introduced to valuation procedures and exercises designed to help the person make up his own strategies.

The direct application of some of these strategies used in the books, such as voting and continuums will be taken up more fully in reference to the classroom in Part IV of the book. It is realized that there are two aspects in which a person might be interested: one, in teaching value theory, and two, in utilizing value theory as a teaching methodology within the context of other situations. This book is primarily dealing with teaching value theory for the purpose of helping people to design their own strategies and develop methods and ways of teaching values in the classroom.

There are basically two sets of conferences presented in this section of the book: one—a three-day conference, a two-day conference, and a one-day conference as initial conferences in value clarification; two—a three-day advance conference, a two-day advance conference, and a one-day advance conference.

The suggested format for the three-day conference is seen in the diagram marked Conference Format 1, page 156. It is felt that the three-day conference could begin in the evening of the first day, possibly a Friday night, and run through the second day completely, then end in the afternoon of the third day. We have chosen this format because it is common to many conferences.

The two-day and the one-day conferences are as in Conference Format 2, page 157. The two-day conference is seen as beginning in the evening of the first day and going to the afternoon of the second day. Finally, the one-day conference is seen as going a morning and an afternoon of one day.

It is our feeling, through our experience, that the first activity in any of the conferences should be designed to help people get to know one another, to reduce people's anxiety and generally set up a trusting atmosphere which will help the people get involved.

Similarly, the final activity should permit sufficient reflection, not ending on a note that leaves people hanging in the air. In other words, major issues should be ventilated properly. Next, you will note that we schedule no more than two activities in a day. In our opinion, material of this kind, which is often emotional in content, needs more time for the participant to assimilate, reflect and grow. To have three activities in one day would not only be too difficult for most people, it would also be very "draining" for the leadership. Another important issue here is that running through the value theory is a necessity in considering the nature of work and leisure. The main thought of the authors of this book is that leisure is necessary for human growth. Therefore, plenty of time for reflection, which will permit the conference to have an atmosphere of relaxation and ease, is necessary in the production of a successful conference. Whenever the designers of a conference become overly concerned with the amount of work and effort that people are going to do, one cannot help but reflect on the reality that there is most probably a feeling of imposition of values taking place within the structure. Values are formed by experience through human beings' growing awareness. The rate of growth of each person is different and, for this reason, we feel that plenty of time for relaxation and reflection is necessary.

The basic format for the three conferences in the initial value-clarification conferences and in the advance value-clarification conference is the same. The activities are set up in approximately three-hour units. For this reason, the units could be shifted around to suit the time needs of particular people in your conference. However, when doing this, we would suggest that you be careful to keep the same leisure and work-time rhythm. As a guideline, do not schedule more than two conferences, one following the other. Most of the activities suggested cannot be

CONFERENCE FORMAT 1
3-Day Conference

	MORNING	*AFTERNOON*	*EVENING*
DAY 1		*Registration*	*Activity 1*
DAY 2	*Activity 2*	*Activity 3 or Relaxation*	*Activity 3 or Relaxation*
DAY 3	*Activity 4*	*Final Evaluative Activity*	

rushed and, therefore, to do them in less than the time allotted might destroy the dynamic. Later on in the chapter we shall deal with the various alternatives in designing your conference: all the exercises in Section II of this book can be placed into each of the units described in these conferences. However, in doing this, there should be a continuity which will promote a reasonable dynamic for a healthy conference. Suggestions as to how this should be done and what units from Section II should be placed in these formats will be dealt with later in the book.

First, it is suggested that persons who are new to the value-clarification process start with Conference Format 1. Whether you are having the three, two or one-day conference, this will be a good beginning if you have not done much conference work or work in the area of value clarification.

The first conference is for teachers or adults working with students. Or, it can be used with teachers working with teachers. The second set of conferences is for persons who have a little more experience in value clarification and would, therefore, be designed for teachers, with teachers or directors of programs working with them. This could also be used with adults or with teachers working with students, if the students have had previous experience in value clarification. The skill of facilitators in the second conference requires higher competence than in the first.

Professional Help

If you are unsure about yourself in dealing with a conference like this, then it would be advisable to get professional help for the first. Such a person could merely act as a consultant—not actually helping with the dynamic, but just being on call or acting as an observer. This person should be skilled in group dynamics, with a knowledge of value clarification as well as group dynamics and, if possible, with a background in counseling or psychology. These qualifications are particularly necessary for the second set of conferences.

Organizations such as the National Training Laboratories,

University Associates, the American Association of Pastoral Counselors, or local colleges and universities (psychology, sociology or education departments) can probably point to people in the local area who would have these kinds of skills. It is our hope that educators will develop the necessary skills in group process and value clarification to be able to have sufficient competence to conduct most of the conferences and activities in this book. However, it is more often advisable to have a consultant who can help you during difficult sessions or periods, especially in the beginning stages. You should not use the activities from the advanced workshops or those listed on the professional section of Part II of this book unless you have had considerable experience in value clarification and group process, or have professional facilitators to aid you in the process. (These are persons who have skills in group dynamics and have a background in educational or counseling psychology.) It is to be pointed out, however, that most educators who are professional can learn most of the activities in this book. It is therefore suggested, if you are new to the process, that you start with the activities listed for the student in Section II and slowly work through to the professional activities. Work with the students' activities for all six sections in Part II, then move to the activities for the teacher and finally to the professional.

CONFERENCE FORMAT 2
THE 2- AND 1-DAY WORKSHOPS

TWO DAY			
	MORNING	*AFTERNOON*	*EVENING*
DAY 1		*Registration*	*Activity 1*
DAY 2	*Activity 2*	*Final Evaluative Activity*	

ONE DAY			
	MORNING	*AFTERNOON*	*EVENING*
DAY 1	*Activity 1 Registration*	*Activity 2 Evaluation*	

TRAINING AND EVALUATION PROCEDURES

Before you start your preparations for the conference you should ask the question, "How many people do we need as facilitators for this conference?" Most likely, there will be only two or three people available who have experience in group process. The question then of training people or preparing them to help you with the conference is an essential one which has to be considered in a conference preparation. Generally speaking, you should have one facilitator helping you for every ten to twelve participants in the conference. If running conferences is new to you, you should try not to run anything of this dimension with more than thirty people to begin with. This means you will need three people helping you in addition to the person directing the conference—four people running a conference for thirty. If you are a teacher doing a short conference with thirty students and you have no one to help you, you might consider training or giving extra preparation for three of those students to help you on the day of the conference.

Preparation or Training for the Workshops as a New Experience

What does training or preparation mean? First of all, it depends on where you are and what type of conference you're going to put on. If you are running the advanced conference or working with teacher or professional workshops, then your facilitators should have had value experience—experience in value clarification. If you are beginning and this is your first workshop and neither you nor those who are going to help you have had any experience, then turning to the workshop would be a different matter altogether.

1. First, decide the nature of the workshop in terms of design and time. It will be suggested that you take one of the initial workshops described on the conference sheets, format 3 or 4 in this section. Secondly, decide the length of the workshop. If this is the first time you've done a workshop, it might be well to

begin with a one or two-day session.

2. Try to have at least one facilitator or helper for each group of ten to twelve people. If you have not done this before, it might be better to have one person for every six people.

3. Have your facilitators involved in the planning of the workshop. Have them involved in every part of the workshop. As initial preparation you should go over very carefully together the design and the kinds of activities you plan for the workshop. Next, plan to spend half a day together in which you will help one another experience the exercises you are going to put your students through. You should have experienced the clarifications you are going to do with the students and should have some facility with them. In this way, when they ask questions you should at least be able to say, "We raised that question ourselves but didn't have the answer". The point here is that you may not have the answers to all their questions but the type of questions should be raised in your mind so that you can deal with them cooperatively, either with your facilitators or the students.

Don't forget, this is a discovery process and as such you don't always have to have the answer, but you should have had experience with the process.

4. Get together with your facilitators and go over the process once more the day before the conference or two to three hours before.

Conference Evaluations

The first question which might be raised is, "Why are we looking at conference evaluation here and not after the conference?" The reason is that the evaluation procedure should be one that you and your facilitators have experienced before you use it as an evaluation in your conference. You should at least have gone over the questions and recognized some of the points of the evaluation in your own training process as trainer facilitators or fellow-teachers. These evaluation procedures then are not only helpful for evaluation for the conference itself but are also helpful for you, together with your facilitators.

In addition to the evaluations we are going to suggest, you might devise a questionnaire sheet which you give to the participants of your conference, asking them pointed questions such as:

1. Would you rate the conference as bad, fair or good?

2. Would you care to comment on how to change anything?

3. Did you feel that the facilitators allowed you enough freedom to enjoy the process?

4. If you were to change anything, what suggestions would you make?

5. Did you have enough time for relaxation?

6. What kinds of insights or new awarenesses, if any, did you discover about yourself during the conference?

These kinds of questions will help you evaluate how you have done in terms of future preparations.

PART 3—DIAGRAM 1

INDIVIDUAL ANALYSIS OF ANOTHER MEMBER IN CHANGE

Name of Partner ______________________________

Instructions: On the line below each question, make two marks. These marks should be in two different colors so the picture of the person in a situation of change can be easily seen. The marks should be indicative of your partner's position in relation to the two extremes given. One mark should indicate your partner's position when he entered the group; the other mark indicates his position at this time. You may mark anywhere along the line to visually express your impression.

1. How effective do you think this person is in contributing ideas, insights, and suggestions which help the group solve problems and achieve its goals?

He is exceptionally effective.	______/______	*He is very ineffective.*

2. How effective do you think this person is in performing functions which build the group and keep it working well?

He is exceptionally effective.	______/______	*He is very ineffective.*

3. In your opinion, how able is this person to express himself freely and comfortably in the group?

He is exceptionally free and comfortable.	______/______	*He is very restricted and tense.*

4. To what extent do you feel that this person really understands your ideas and feelings?

He has a very good understanding.	______/______	*He has very little understanding.*

5. If participation is a guide to a person's feelings of self-worth and withdrawal is an indication of lack of self-worth, how did/does your partner rank in terms of verbal feedback and body participation?

He has high self-esteem.	______/______	*He is withdrawn.*

6. In what way do you see your partner sharing himself with the group?

Dependent upon cooperation with others.	______/______	*Very independent of others.*

7. To what extent does your partner give evidence of the following emotions?

Freedom	______/______	*Depression*
Enthusiasm	______/______	*Boredom*
Peace	______/______	*Anger*
Confidence	______/______	*Fear*

8. *To what extent is your partner able to communicate?*

Trust	______/______	*Mistrust*
Listens well	______/______	*Fails to report accurately what another person says*
Expresses feelings	______/______	*Expresses ideas*
Helps others express themselves	______/______	*Pursues point aggressively*
Shares	______/______	*Dominates*
Encourages others to talk	______/______	*Withdraws*

9. *To what extent is your partner sensitive to the group?*

Listens to angered or upset person with good understanding	______/______	*Little response to anger and distress of others*
Deals directly with feelings	______/______	*Ignores feelings or smooths them over*
Sensitive to and understanding of the emotional state of people	______/______	*Insensitive to and lacking understanding of people*

As to a more in-depth evaluation of the members of the conference for themselves, which in turn will help you evaluate your own ability to run such a conference, we offer the following three evaluative suggestions. These evaluations can be used by your trainers and trainees in their own process as they develop together in preparation and in the running of a conference. These evaluation sheets can also be used as a complete conclusive activity to any one of the conferences that will be shared in this chapter.

Please look over Diagram 1 carefully. You will note it is a very personal diagram that allows each participant to make two marks on the sheet about a partner he was working with in the conference. In many of the initial conference activities, a person discovers a partner as a part of the activity. However, if this is not the case, since you may substitute in another activity, make sure that every person has an acknowledged partner who is at least present in the group they're working in, to evaluate at the end of the conference. There is no need to have secrets, and you might point this out at the beginning of the conference. You might say something such as: "You are going to have the opportunity of evaluating each other at the end of the conference. This evaluation is not a threatening matter but simply one to help you see where you have grown and to help us discover what we have done well or what could have been improved in the way we conducted the conference". In the use of value Diagram 1, you will notice that most of the questions are personal ones and will help the participants to see how they've changed or improved in certain attitudes and feelings, expressions and behavior during the conference. You will also note that many of the types of questions relate directly to values, particularly values of self-worth and ability to reach out to other people. You might say that each of the continuums is heavily value-laden. One way of using this at the end of the conference as an activity in itself is to ask the two partners to mark each other's sheets and then discuss the sheet for half an hour. As an option, they may get back together in their group to discuss generally whether they've grown or where they think their partner needs to grow.

Diagram 2 is to be used by each person individually to mark on the continuum where or how much he thinks he has grown in each particular area. Where the sheet marks the point on the continuum called "Beginning" is considered the start of the conference. If a person felt his self-worth and feelings of adequacy to be increased through the conference, then he can mark accordingly along the line toward the mark which says "Conclusion". Similarly, he marks the column saying "Trust" and "Listen". And again on the column that says "Positive affirmation", "Expressing anger" and so on. The point is that these continuums are related directly to values and are taken off the individual analysis of another member (Diagram 1). The last two continuums in new values and renewed commitment are to help them see whether they themselves have made any particular movement in regard to values. In terms of evaluation, do not expect gigantic strides to be made since the shifting of a value or the gaining of self-worth takes a great deal of time for some people. It is another point of a valuation and will help in the awareness process.

The second way of using Diagram 2 is for the facilitators and teachers to mark this diagram as an evaluation of the individual analysis diagrams (Diagram 1). The teacher or facilitator takes Diagram 1, looks it over and thumbs it, then tries to fill out Diagram 2 as an overall evaluation. The point also of Diagram 2 is that it gives examples on which you and your facilitators may want to build to design your own sheet. (Remember, one of the major objects of this book is to help people come up with their own valuations and activities.)

Diagram 3 is for the facilitators and teacher only. This is a diagram continuum to try to help you see where your particular group, as a whole, has moved during the total conference session. One side of the diagram is marked "Beginning" and the other end is "Conclusions". Going down the continuums we see that each continuum has a center point called "zero"; the left-hand side has a "minus ten" and the right-hand side has a "plus ten". Again, these are group evaluations and should be done by the facilitators at the end of the group and are related very closely to the goals and purposes of all these groups. A minimal purpose for any such

PART 3—DIAGRAM 2

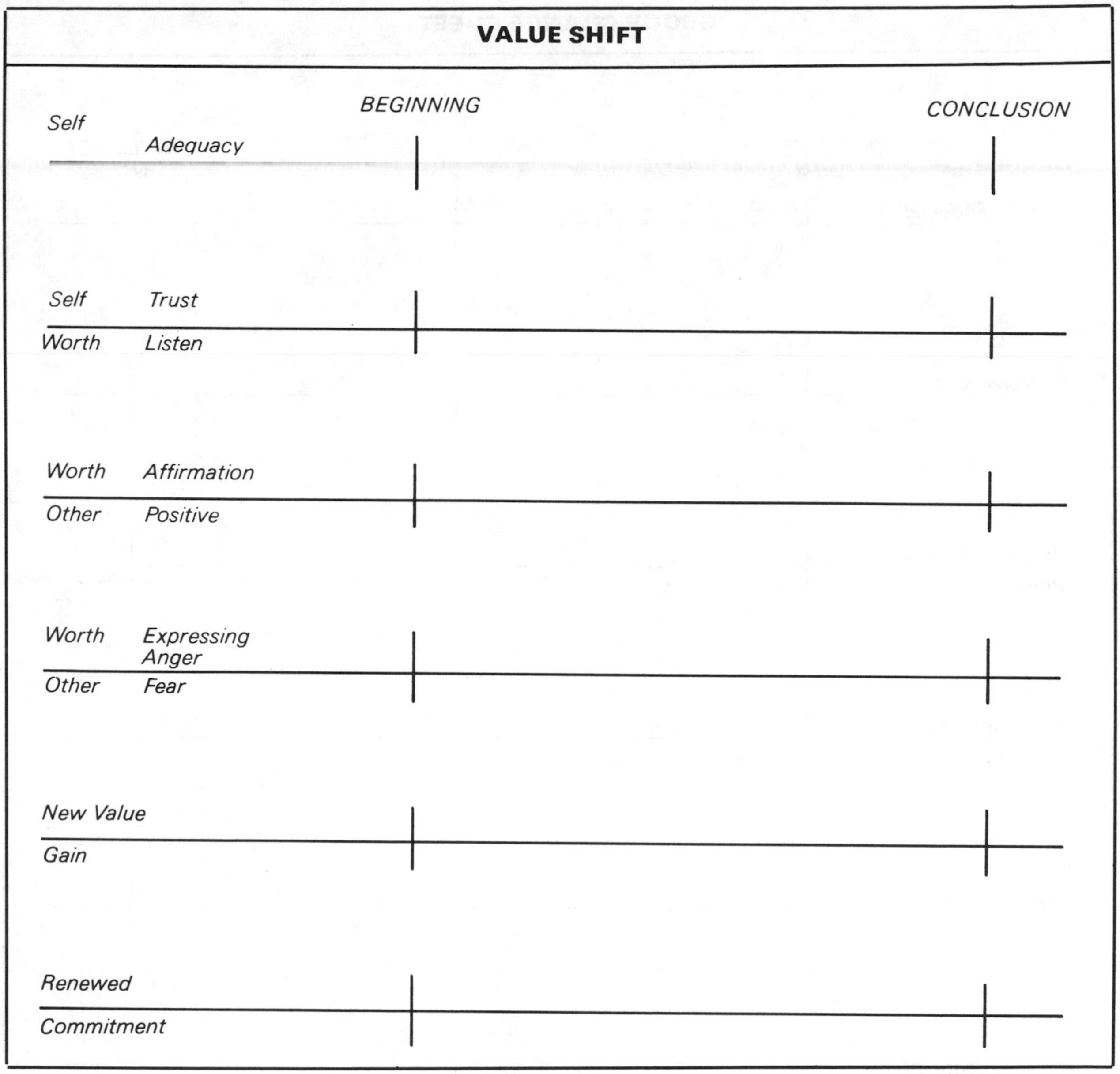

VALUE SHIFT

		BEGINNING	CONCLUSION
Self	*Adequacy*		
Self / *Worth*	*Trust* / *Listen*		
Worth / *Other*	*Affirmation* / *Positive*		
Worth / *Other*	*Expressing Anger* / *Fear*		
New Value / *Gain*			
Renewed / *Commitment*			

group is to demonstrate that some people at least will have had a measure of expansion of awareness. The sign of good group process is that members increase in their total knowledge of one another and in their ability to express openly their feelings toward one another in the spirit of trust. The key to these processes is in guidelines such as: "Do the conference members wish to continue at the end of the last session?" "Is there activity at the end of the session; do people continue to talk to each other or are they polarized or are some withdrawn, forming cliques, etc.?" The ideal

PART 3—DIAGRAM 3

GROUP CHANGE SHEET

	CONCLUSION −10	0	CONCLUSION +10
Interdependence			
Cohesiveness			
Outreach beyond small groups			
Awareness of subject matter			
Expressiveness			
Independence of leadership			
Ability to suggest new ideas			

is to have the group grow in total cohesiveness to form a much more cooperative group that can trust itself as a whole. These evaluations are guidelines to this end.

Interdependence as a continuum is intended to indicate the degree of increased cooperation between all members of the group. That is to say, when the group first came together, some members may not have known others and, perhaps, tended to talk to just one or two people. If the group was highly successful, at the end of the conference most people would have been able to talk to other people in a spirit of sharing, to one degree or another, in a spirit of inter-cooperation. Taking the "zero" at the middle of the evaluation to mean "where you were when the conference began", the question is: "Was there less interdependence at the end of the group or more interdependence?" If there was more, put a mark on the continuum toward the right-hand side of the sheet and, if there was less, put it to the left-hand side of the sheet. Cohesiveness: In this column you are to measure the increased degree of interaction and activity—"Was the group as a whole more active, more interested in itself or more ready to work as a total group, and perhaps moving more readily toward being able to make group decisions?"

Outreach beyond small groups: This is intended to measure the effect of the group on persons. How many, and to what degree, do you think people found the atmosphere in the group acceptable? Are they able to more easily reach out and be affirmative to other people? This might mean that they were more ready to express their feelings to other people in a creative manner. It could also indicate expression of anger or fear or other such negative feelings, but the point is that these feelings would be expressed creatively. We might say that the feeling should always be expressed with the condition: "What can we do about it?"

Awareness of subject matter: Evaluation here has to do with the cognitive aspect of the person. Not only are the sensitivity aspects of the personality important, but also the cognitative value aspects. This question brings out how much people increase in their understanding as awareness of the subject matter. The last three, "Expressiveness", "Independence of leadership" and "Ability to suggest new ideas", are evaluative elements more likely to occur in a long conference or after several conferences with the same number of people. A sign of real growth would be the increased expression and the ability of people to come up with their own ideas and strategies. At the first level, "Expressiveness" here means an increased creative ability to see more far-reaching alternatives in a positive manner. "Independence of leadership" means a maturing. This is not intended to mean rebellion, but rather an incorporation of the leadership as equals in the creative process. Finally, the ability to suggest new ideas, of course, is the goal of this book, and the hope of the facilitators is for people to become independent and develop their own strategies. These evaluations can be used in training facilitators as well as the students. The ultimate inter-training process would be for the facilitators to design their own programs and throw away the book.

In explanations of these conferences, we shall start with preparation, introduction and goals for the three-day conference, marked as Conference Format 3. We shall then move to the two-day conference and the one-day conference. The reason for this is that activities in the two- and one-day conferences are often repetitions of material in the three-day conference. These are suggested as initial conferences; the possibility of a number of different types of conferences can be effected by substituting activities from Section II of this book. However, in substituting, a note must be made that certain conferences are more successful in the middle, end or the beginning in terms of the dynamic. We shall deal with the alternatives for conferences later in this chapter.

INITIAL CONFERENCE: 3 DAYS

INTRODUCTION:

Participants Students or student teachers.

Facilitators Teachers or professional educators.

TIME:

Three days—understood to be late afternoon and evening of the first day, a full second day, and the morning, afternoon and evening of a third day.

GOALS OF THE CONFERENCE:

Minimal Goals To expand the students' awareness of themselves in relationship to other persons as possessing values and priorities.

Optimal Goals For the student to be aware of, and have facility with, the

CONFERENCE FORMAT 3
3 days

	MORNING	*AFTERNOON*	*EVENING*
DAY 1		*4 p.m.* *Registration* *Social hour*	*7:30 p.m.* *In and out groups* *Value game discovering the others' potential*
DAY 2	*9 a.m.* *Hallmark Card Company Game* *Exercise in value-ranking*	*Leisure period*	*7:30 p.m.* *Role-playing on conflict and polarity*
DAY 3	*9 a.m.* *Exercises in creative alternatives*	*2 p.m.* *Input* *Reflective discussion*	

clarification of his values and how he tends to order his priorities. In addition to this, the student should move toward discovering meaning with an understanding of how feelings and behavior relate to persons' underlying value systems.

SCHEDULE:

It will be noted that in the schedule labeled Conference Format 3, there is a place for a social hour and a long period of time called "Leisure period". Apart from the fact that people need meaningful reflection, each person grows at his own particular rate and at a varying speed. There is also the fact of the reality of leisure as a considered value. A relaxing period is a confrontation with behavior in a person's life-style. Whether they like this, feel it is a waste of time, or whatever, questions can be raised as to what this means in terms of their understanding of their values and life priorities. This is particularly important in a society which is competitive and production-oriented in its nature.

The social hour might be facilitated with a punch and other refreshments, possibly followed by supper. It is strongly recommended that strong drinks be avoided, since this could allow persons in the process later on to release information or become involved in a manner which they normally would not wish. It should also be noted that a relaxed atmosphere permits people to learn from one another more after the session than in the session. Consider the total conference and all the time within the limits, from beginning to end, as being a total process. This is also true of the learning that goes on after the conference. The facilitator should be aware that this is a process—that the meaning and value of his presence is to facilitate the process and not to impose values. People grow at their own rates. What you are doing is

CONFERENCE FORMAT 4
1 and 2 days

TWO DAY

	MORNING	*AFTERNOON*	*EVENING*
DAY 1		*4 p.m.* *Registration* *Social hour*	*7.30 p.m.* *Value Game*
DAY 2	*9 a.m.* *Hallmark Card Company Game*	*2 p.m.* *Creative alternatives* *Input and conclusion*	

ONE DAY

DAY 1	*9 a.m.* *Value Game* *Alternative: Hallmark Card Company Game*	*2 p.m.* *Creative alternatives* *Input and conclusion*	

facilitating this growth by affording learning material devices and strategies. It goes without saying that the relaxed attitude of a facilitator is essential; our behavior will be reflected a great deal in that of the group.

ATMOSPHERE:

The atmosphere of a conference is important. Choose a conference center which has one or more small rooms where people can arrange themselves in groups in any manner they wish. A place which has immovable chairs or large tables may not be suitable. The center should be a building with pleasant surroundings, comfortable chairs and even carpeting, so that people can sit on the floor if they wish. Either there should be blackboards or walls where brainstorming paper can be placed on the wall without harm. Although it may be true that we often place too much stress on personal comfort, these conferences can be regarded as retreat situations; enough comfort should be provided so that participants are not inhibited or inconvenienced by the environment. In addition to this, the environment can be enhanced not only by the location of the conference but by the addition of such things as posters, pictures, coffee and rolls during the day, and other little conveniences. These things require forethought; the facilitator will then want to arrive well before the conference starts. Where there is a large group in the conference (say, thirty people) the facilitator should have name tags to help people know each other's names. If it is a small group of less than twenty, you may wish to discuss whether you need to do this, since it may be better to start the session by introducing everybody at the social hour. The presence of soothing music during various parts of the conference, and especially when the conference begins, is very helpful.

Essential to the atmosphere is to get across the idea of non-imposition but at the same time to be able to move ahead so that your activities are completed. If you have 15 minutes for activity and you find the time going over, try to be flexible and make up the time at another point. If you have 15 minutes for an activity, announce to the total group, after 10 minutes, that they have 5 minutes more for their activity. Make another such announcement a minute before. Do it in a relaxed manner; it is simply a guideline to them, without imposition.

If the group is mature, they should tell you if they think you're being too imposing and may even ask for more time. If during an activity the group is enjoying the activity, learning a great deal and objects to you changing the sequence, simply point out to them what the schedule is. If the group should decide to continue without finishing the activity, then it may be much better to do so. Remember, learning is in the process. If the group is not ready to complete an activity during that time then it would be better for them to grow and learn from where they are. Always try to be flexible. When in doubt, ask the group's opinion. At the same time, you must be strong in your guidance. If you feel you cannot handle that kind of flexibility or that the group is discussing other issues, then it may be better to rule against what they are doing; it may be that the rest of the activity would answer many of the questions they are raising.

Generally speaking, a group will move through the activities you have planned for them as long as you have created an atmosphere of trust and concern and are careful to remind them, at intervals, of how much time they have. This avoids having to tell them to change groups when they're in the middle of a subject. If you give them a time warning, you place the responsibility on them rather than yourself. Do not be pressured into putting in additional activities instead of the leisure period. In our experience, more than two activities in one day become draining for most people. One or two people might "push" for extra activities because of their production-orientation, their feelings of competitiveness or the need to be useful. If this should happen, it is better to challenge them to reflect on their own values rather than to pressure the group into increased activities which may overtire some people. Always remember that the process of learning is slow and is measured by each individual. Also remember that the value of being and doing together is essential in itself.

It is continually essential that facilitators meet and evaluate all through the conference so as to understand their own self-worth in the process and not be pressured into changing activities unnecessarily. These matters can be brought out in the final reflective session.

Finally, it often happens that one or two participants will object to talking about themselves or have a problem with mistrust. These activities cannot cause harm, but often people who are emotionally ill or are rigid will be present. If you are running several three-day conferences and are using the in-depth process exercise in the professional section of the chapter, it is advisable to have a mental health consultant on call to deal with persons who may become emotionally upset. In our experiences, it has been rare that this situation has occurred, and when it does, it has little to do with the conference, but rather more to do with the nature of the kinds of persons who often seek out this type of conference. This is simply another precaution which may help to relax you and your facilitators in conducting the conference and so help improve the general atmosphere.

NUMBER OF PEOPLE:

There is generally no limit on the number of people; this kind of process-conference works well with up to forty people. If you move between forty and one hundred people, then you should have had extensive experience with the process. Otherwise, it can be a draining and defeating experience. That is to say, to attempt to handle a large number of people if you have not had the experience would not be wise. Remember, try to get at least one facilitator for each group of ten to twelve people.

MATERIALS NEEDED:

1. Name tags at the beginning of the conference.
2. Record player or tape recorder for background music.
3. Posters, materials for decorations.
4. Pencils and small pads of paper for each member of the conference.
5. Magic markers, brainstorming paper, masking tape to put the paper on the wall, cardboard, glue and magazines with pictures, pieces of wire and any kind of art materials with which people can make things.
6. Roll of white paper (the kind for picnic tables) up to fifty feet in length.
7. Overhead projector. If you wish, you may use two overhead projectors, as will be discussed later in the conference process.
8. Paints or magic markers, poster colors, etc.
9. Mimeograph copies of the following diagrams for each participant.

DIAGRAM 4

VALUE GAME	
PRIORITIES OBSERVED	*REAL VALUES (Chosen) (Celebrated) (Acted on)*
PRIORITIES ADDED	

DIAGRAM 5

IMAGINATION: *Inspirational, creativity more important, search, process of developing and experimenting (or something like that)*
FUNCTION: *Get job done; operates chiefly from the point of view of use or accomplishment, emphasis on task-oriented relations (or thereabouts)*
IDEAS: *Getting idea across is more important, intellectual approach, understanding entire process as basic (or somewhere in that ball park)*
FEELINGS: *Feelings are more important than getting job done; where individuals are within a program or project, persons and feelings are seen as important as to how a task develops*

DIAGRAM 6

HALLMARK CARD GAME – SICK CARD DIVISION
PRODUCTION
RESEARCH
MANAGEMENT
SALES

CONFERENCE FORMAT

Introduction:

This conference format is not meant to be rigid. The details of the activities, as well as the suggested times, can of course be offered; these times are suggestions. The times for lengths of parts of the activities are workable, in our experience. Therefore, if you should move the activities to another time, you should allow the same amount of time although you may want to change the actual times the conference might begin or end. Rather than stating periods of time, we thought it might be more helpful to give a model conference where we have given chosen exact times.

It is assumed that in conducting this conference, the facilitators (with the person in charge) will have amply prepared themselves, arriving one or two hours beforehand to make sure that everything is ready in terms of background music, posters, coffee and so on.

4:00 p.m.

REGISTRATION AND SOCIAL HOUR

The idea here is to have one person take registrations, giving each person a pad, pencil and name tag. At the same time, provide cheese and crackers, coffee or punch, if you wish, so that while people are being registered they can meet the facilitators in a friendly atmosphere. The social hour might be followed by supper, depending on where you are meeting. Allowing several hours for people to get to know each other, as well as getting settled in their rooms, is a wise idea; it helps reduce the anxiety and prepares people for a better conference.

While registering the people, give them a name tag with a number on it; make the numbers one through eight. When the first person comes, give him the first number, with the second person getting number two, and so on to number eight. This is a simple and arbitrary way of getting people into groups later, without too much fuss.

7:30 p.m. **INTRODUCTION**

In a small group it is best to have everybody sitting in a large circle, rather than in rows of chairs. The important thing, however, is to have everybody in the same room. First, introduce the main facilitator and the other facilitators to the group, telling them that you hope the conference will be enjoyable and relaxing for them, as well as worthwhile in terms of what they will learn. At this point, some cognizant material would be appropriate. It is our opinion that no more than a 10-minute presentation is necessary at this point.

Input *"This evening we are going to begin to discuss and try to understand what a value is. A value is something that we choose in our lives as being very important to us and which enhances the creative growth of ourselves and those around us. We would suggest the following definition of a value for your consideration and your examination during the evening".*

At this point, make sure that the definition of value is written on a board or on brainstorming paper on the walls. By "brainstorming paper" we mean newsprint, some kind of large, cheap sheets of paper which can be stuck on walls with masking tape, without harm to the walls.

Input *The definition of a value that we are about to give is really the definition of a value process or how a value comes about—the kind of process we go through in order to obtain a value. Most of the priorities we have in our lives are not, in fact, values but value indicators. That is to say, they fall short of the criteria we're about to give you for a full value, although that is not necessarily a bad thing.*

Another definition of a value indicator is that it points to a value that is not itself a value, such as aspirations, beliefs, attitudes and feelings. These are all good in themselves but are not necessarily values. A value is something that is (1) chosen, (2) celebrated, (3) acted upon. On the wall we see a definition of value as being in seven parts.

1. *it is chosen freely;*
2. *it is chosen from alternatives;*
3. *it is chosen from alternatives after considering the consequences of those alternatives;*
4. *it is something that I am happy with;*
5. *it is something manifested in my behavior that I feel is good and will ultimately enhance my growth; (It should be noted, at this point, that to be happy with something does not exclude pain. I may be very happy that I am going to college, but it may be very hard for me to determine what I have to do.)*
6. *it is something that I have acted on recently;*
7. *it is something that I have acted on repeatedly.*

At this point, the person giving this address should give one or two examples coming from the preparation period beforehand with the facilitators. Alternatively, one of the facilitators could give an example. After this, allow a few minutes for discussion and try to end the introductory period by eight o'clock.

8:00—8:30 p.m.

Ask the members of the group to stand up, walk around and find seven other people they do not know very well, to form a group of eight. They can do this by looking at the numbered name plate, so that they can find another person with a different number; each group will have eight people, with a different number one through eight. When they are in their groups of eight, tell them to form partners; stress that they will be with the same partner all evening. Then have them sit with four persons in the middle, with their four partners standing across from them as observers. The arrangement will be as it is in this picture-diagram:

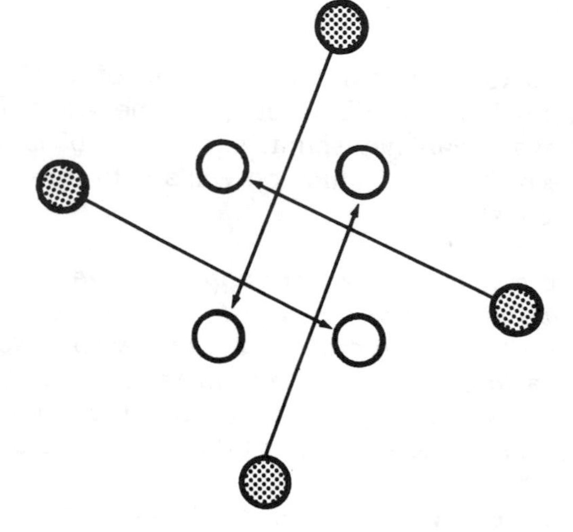

STANDING OBSERVERS

SITTING DISCUSSANTS

This grouping should take approximately 10 minutes. The instructions to the group are:

1. OBSERVERS: The following instructions should be given to the observer: *Your job is to stand across from your partner and observe, while listening carefully to what is said. Later on, you're going to report back what you heard the group say. Listening to a person is not simply listening to the words he says, but to the total person. That is to say, the manner and feelings and way he expresses himself through his body are also observed. As an observer you are not allowed to say anything except in these two circumstances:*

a. If you do not think that your partner is getting equal time;

b. If you think any person in the group is getting off the subject and not speaking about himself.

2. PERSONS DISCUSSING: *For the next 10 minutes we*

should like you to discuss the following statement, making sure that each of you has equal time to make a presentation. The statement is: "Discuss one or two significant choices you have made in your life which you are happy with and have acted on. Also mention the consequences of your acting on those choices".
Now allow the group to discuss the question for 10 minutes, with the observers silent.

3. FACILITATORS: Move around the groups; try not to interfere but make sure that each group is allowing equal time for the discussion and that the persons are discussing the subject matter.

Give a 2-minute warning before the end of the 10 minutes. At the end of the 10-minute period, ask the observers to become the discussion group in the middle and those who were discussing to now observe the partner who was observing them, by standing across from them in the same manner that they were observed. The instructions remain the same for the observers and those discussing in this group section. The discussion continues as before for 10 minutes.

8:30—8:45 p.m. Coffee break.

8:45—9:30 p.m. Give everyone in the room a copy of the value game marked Diagram 4. When everybody has a copy, give them the following instructions:

"In a few minutes we are going to ask you to go with your partner and help each other fill out the value game sheet called Diagram 4. In order to do this, one person first reports to the other what he heard him say with his 'total person' during the group discussion. Then the other person reports what he heard the other partner say. Following this, each pair then works on one person to fill out the left-hand side of the sheet. First, help each other fill in the top part of the left-hand side: 'Priorities observed'. Here you will put down the significant priorities you heard from your partner. This may not only be the one or two choices of the person talked about, but perhaps other values you heard coming through in the conversation. Secondly, you may add priorities below that which you think are important in your life, in addition to the ones mentioned. After both partners have helped each other fill out the left-hand side of the sheet, move to the right-hand side of the sheet. On the right hand we want you to ask yourself whether the values listed on the left-hand side of the sheet are, in fact, real values. That is to say, were they all chosen freely from alternatives, after considering the consequences, that you were happy with and would state publicly, that you have acted on repeatedly in your life, and that you have acted on recently? When you decide that something is a real value, then write that down on the right-hand side of the sheet".
At this point, tell the group to go with their partners to any part of the room and to work on their exercise until 9:30.

FACILITATORS: *Your job is to wander around from pair*

to pair and give them any assistance needed in doing this sheet. If people are working hard at what they're doing and have no questions, then leave them alone and allow them to work on the exercise themselves. Remember, it is not the completing of the exercise that is important, but the valuing process and the process of getting to know each other. Give them a 10- and 5-minute reminder, as you approach the 9:30 period.

9:30—10:00 p.m.

Give the group instructions to move back into their original groups of eight, sitting in a complete circle. Then give the group the following instruction: *"Each person will now reintroduce his partner. Introduce the person that you have discovered in this period of time together and the values that you see operating creatively in his life".*

ALTERNATIVE ENDING: An alternative way of ending this group is to add the following additional instruction at the end: *"By 10:00 we should like each group to have a summary statement about the evening's experience—one or two points which you think are most important and which you may have learned or re-examined in the evening".* At 10:00 then, the evening will be concluded by each group making a short summary report.

Before closing in the evening, it is well to serve some refreshments and to remind the group that they will be beginning the next morning at 9:00 sharp. It is advisable to suggest that everybody be ready the next morning by ten minutes to nine, in order to get a clean start.

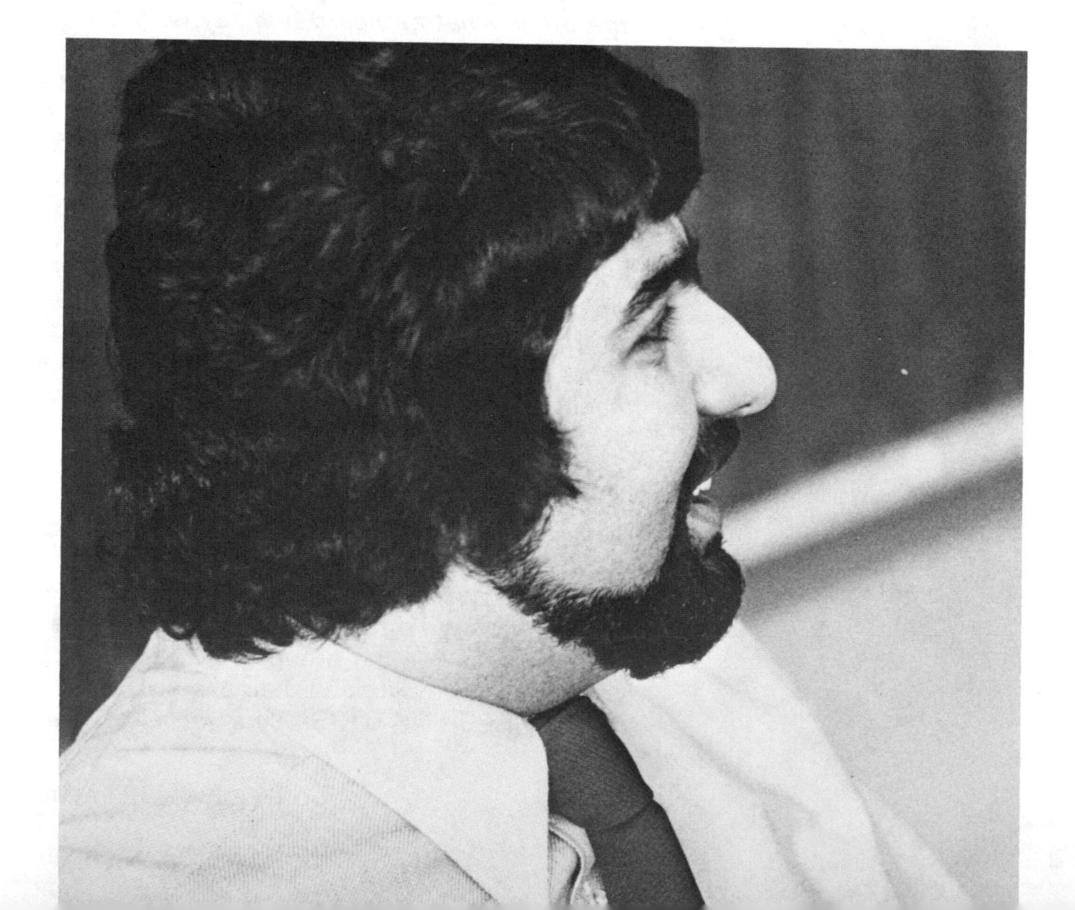

SECOND DAY: MORNING SESSION, 9:00 a.m.—12:00 midday

9:00—9:30 a.m.

INTRODUCTION: A suggested introduction is as follows: *"This morning we are going to deal with the question of value-ranking—the way in which we list the priorities in our lives, particularly when those priorities or values affect our behavior, feelings and life-style—more, even, than the particular values we might have chosen. Just think for a moment about the way you use your time: You spend so many hours at work, so many hours at this activity, or that activity, with this person or that person. If you were able to add up all those moments and then put them in the order in which you use your time most, you would probably have a strong indication of where your values lie. The way we rank or put things in priorities is very important. Many of our priorities are not actually values; they might be chosen; you might be happy with them, but you may not have acted on them. They may then just be hopes, aspirations or beliefs. Similarly, we may be doing something we're happy with and act on, but we never really chose from alternatives. It may become a value if we were to become aware of what we're doing and choose it. There are many things operating in our lives like this—often good attitudes we have picked up from our parents. This morning we are going to take four such values which we often assume to be present but often never think about, never really choose. We consider these four values to be in everyone's personality. Different words could be used, but in this game we are using these to describe the four values we are choosing: Imagination, Function, Ideas, and Feelings".*

At this point, have all facilitators pass out Diagram 5. Ask everybody to look at the definitions of the four words and reflect on them for a few moments. Tell them that these values are operating in their personalities but that none is more important than another; they are not good or bad but neuter elements existing in everybody's personality.

Next, give the following instructions: *"In a few moments we're going to ask you to get together with your partner from last evening, to work with each other for 15 minutes, ranking the four words, imagination, function, ideas, and feelings in the order in which you think they are manifested in your behavior.*

"Most of us rank these four words in a particular way. Some of you may be changing the priorities in your lives and may be finding it difficult since you may want to change what you already have. You may be able to think of a ranking you have had in the past that you want to change in the future. What we want you to do is to try to narrow down to where you are right now. You must rank all four words; one word coming first, the others second, third and fourth.

"Remember, whichever you put first is a top priority for you. For example, a good manager would probably rank function first and feeling second, then ideas and finally imagination. Why?

Because as a manager he has to get the job done but also has to be able to work well with people to get that job done. A modern artist might put ideas or imagination first and then function second since he needs order in his work. A counselor may have feelings first, imagination second, and he may have function at the end. A person running his own business might put function near the top. These are simply expressions of our personalities. We want you to rank these four areas according to where you are now and what you would like to be".

Allow a few minutes for discussion.

9:30—9:45 a.m.

Have everybody get into pairs with the same partners they had last evening. For the next 15 minutes allow them to fill out their sheets. FACILITATORS: Move around among the pairs and make sure they can do the job properly.

9:45—10:30 a.m.

Give the pairs a minute's warning that they have just a short time to finish. Then have each pair go and find two other pairs of people they do not know too well, in order to form new groups of six people. When everybody is placed in groups of six, pass out one copy of Diagram 6, "Hallmark Card Game—Sick Card Division" to each group. Now give the total group the following instructions: *"We want you to imagine, each group, that you are now members of the Hallmark Card Company—Sick Card Division. You are creating this company, which has no policies or guidelines, and it is up to you to begin the company. The way we want you to develop this company is to consider its four divisions to be as on your sheet: Production, Research, Management, Sales.*

"First, we want you to come to group consensus. We mean consensus, *not merely one or two persons' opinions on what each of those divisions means. When you have reached a consensus on the meaning of the words, you are to rank the four words, imagination, function, ideas and feelings, so as to fit your definition of each of those divisions. For example, you might decide that research should be the kind of department that goes out into different cities, visits hospitals and tries to find out from people the kinds of cards they like to receive—that comfort them the most in their situations. You might end up defining research as being feelings first, followed in order by imagination, ideas and then function. On the other hand, if you want to define research as being more production-oriented, then you must research the kinds of places most likely to buy and sell the cards—starting off by being more function-oriented. Whatever you do, come up with a definition of what you consider research to be and then rank those four words in the order you think appropriate to the definition of each word, ranking the four personality words under each. After you've done that, compare the personal ranking you've just been working on with those that you come up with in your management game and place yourself in one of the divisions. You have until 10:30 to try and do this".*

FACILITATORS: *Your job is to move around the groups and help them to do the tasks, getting them to complete the tasks by the time given. Your job is also to prevent people from dominating the group; try to get good group interaction and sharing by all persons, to come up with the definitions. If any group suggests that there might be several definitions or rankings under any one division, that's perfectly all right. In fact, this is probably the way in which it is in real life. The point is that they must try to discover this on their own. But whatever they put down, they must finally place themselves in one of those divisions. Each division should be different than its ranking. We suggest that you call time and give them 5 minutes more before the 10:30 stop-point. Should the group want to continue after 10:30, you will have to decide whether to allow this, by shortening the next session. You should allow at least 20 minutes in the next section.*

10:30—11:00 a.m.

At this point, label each corner of the room a different division; have each corner of the room marked clearly as "Production", "Management", "Sales" and "Research". Give the total group instructions for each person to move to the division he found his own personal ranking lined up with in terms of the definitions that the group arrived at. Now that each person has placed himself in a division in his group, all now move into that division in one of the corners of the room.

FACILITATORS: If you have a large group—more than ten or eleven persons in one corner of the room—split them into smaller groups of six or eight. When formed into groups, give them the following instruction: *"Discuss why you chose this group and what you understand this particular division to mean".* (If in the process some persons find that they should be in another group, they are then to leave and find the proper group. When they get to their new group, they are to argue why they are in that group and compare their rankings to see if they should be there.)

Keep these groups operating and talking on the subject and help people who might be wandering from group to group. It is well to note that people sometimes find this a traumatic experience, since it often reflects the fact that they're confused about their life direction; they may need some help in terms of what their ranking should be and what they want to do.

Once the group is under way, give them this second set of instructions: *"When you have discussed why you are in your group, try then to decide what position you would choose and what the job definition in that division would be. For example, if there are six of you in the management group, you can't all be running the show; therefore, you have to have different job definitions. Try to find out what they might be. This needs to be a group consensus".* Give the group 5 minutes' warning before the end, telling them that it is no problem if they have not finished their task. It is the process that is more important.

11:00—11:30 a.m.

Tell the groups now to disperse and go back to their original groups of six. For the next 30 minutes the group is to discuss the following question: *"In terms of the morning experience and where you ended up, compare and contrast this with your everyday life situation. As a professional or working person, are you doing a different kind of work than your ranking and description indicated, or is it the same? Are there other kinds of things you'd like to do? Make sure that everyone in the group has an opportunity to share. After you have shared your ideas with one another, allow 10 minutes at the end of the session to come up with one or two final conclusions that can be presented to the total group in a minute or two statement."*

FACILITATORS: Make sure that the groups enter a personal discussion, rather than on some extraneous issue. Also, move around the groups to make sure that during the last 10 minutes they're working on their group report. Give them a 5-minute warning to the end of the session.

11:30—11:45 a.m.

Have all the people in the groups come to one location of the room and then allow each group to make its report.

INPUT

11:45—12:00 noon

At this point in the morning, facilitators can make comments from the reports on value clarification. The kind of input that might be added at this point for 10 or 15 minutes of discussion may be as follows: *"This morning has, for the most part, been spent in an exercise in value-ranking; our behavior is affected by the way in which we rank values and priorities.*

"Further, our life-style and direction are dictated by the way in which we rank our priorities. We hope you've had a good experience this morning; perhaps you discovered some insights into yourself. However, do not think that this is necessary, since the only point of the morning session was to have some facility and exercise in the concept of value-ranking as a way of understanding a person's behavior, feelings and ideas. Another important factor we should reflect on in our next session is that when we live or work closely to a person who has opposite rankings from ourselves, this often causes conflict. I wonder how many of you know people who are very function-oriented, whereas you may put imaginational ideas first? Or, how many of you are the reverse—very function-oriented, and tending to get annoyed at people who are always feeling- or imagination-oriented? Opposite rankings in close proximity are often the origin of conflict. This means that one person is subtly (perhaps not intentionally) imposing his values on the other person. When a large group of persons imposes values on another group of persons, we call this 'polarity'. One example of polarity which is common in institutions is often evident by the simple ranking of:

"1. People

"2. Institutions

"People who have this attitude often find themselves in conflict with others who have the following value ranking:

"1. Institutions

"2. People

"Therefore, value-ranking introduces us to an understanding not only of ranking life-direction but of problems in the area of conflict and polarity".

Conclude the session by saying that the afternoon (if this is what you've decided) is free time—a "gift" of the conference to the participants. This is not a time for work, but rather for relaxing, reflecting or doing whatever they want without feeling they have an obligation to do anything productive. If anyone objects to this (as has often been our experience), point out that this is a value reality that needs to be reflected on: namely, what is the relationship of work, production and usefulness to leisure?

Remind them when their meals will be and when the next session will begin. Again, it is suggested that they be at the next session 10 minutes early so that they can start on time.

SECOND DAY: AFTERNOON

The leisure period is open but could have some program material in it, if you so wish, of a leisurely orientation, such as a cocktail party at 4:00 or a garden party in the afternoon. If you are in or near the city, you might tour some historical site, show movies, or organize some sport activity—recreation is essential to the learning process. To place another value program in at this point may be regarded as an accomplishment to some, but, on the other hand, it would present a value-orientation that might be considered questionable. Since the reader may consider this to be a value-imposition of the authors of this book, we state that we are simply making suggestions and that this point of the program has to be decided by the facilitators and the programmers. Our only note of caution is that, in our experience, when three units have been planned in one day, it is too much for some people, in terms of what they can tolerate physically and emotionally.

SECOND DAY: EVENING (7:30—10:00 p.m.)

7:30—8:00 p.m.

INPUT

Beforehand, meet with your facilitators, review the progress of the group and brainstorm examples for this unique group. It is suggested that you repeat the input of the morning session at the beginning of this session with the fresh examples brainstormed previously by your facilitators. Follow this input by a general discussion so that the facilitators with the group can clarify what value-ranking is and how it relates to conflict and polarity. As input, you might add this: *"The definition of a value that we discussed last night with its seven points more appropriately relates to the definition of how we rank values and priorities in our lives. As we rank our priorities, we choose them from alternatives which could be ranked in different ways. We rank them (if they are a value-ranking) freely and after considering the consequences of each combination of the alternatives. We should be happy with them, be able to state them publicly, and, most of all, we must be ready to act on them repeatedly"*. This could be added to the discussion and followed by more discussion.

8:00—8:30 p.m.

During this activity you will have a role-play around conflict and polarity through the development of a "body sculpture". The body sculpture is a method of role-playing which is simple to begin with and get into without too many difficulties. For the first part of the activity, you will need pencil and paper for all the participants. Instruct them: *"Please write down, in less than a paragraph, a conflict situation that happened to you in the last few years, which you will be prepared to share with the group; write down a description of the conflict, the persons in the conflict and what the situation was. We prefer a conflict with at least four or five people in it, who were actually engaged in the conflict. Try to keep your conflict situations personal. We do not want a situation that includes thirty or forty people but one limited to four to ten people. In writing out the conflict, names and places are not important. When you share this later on, we do not need intimate details in terms of persons' names but a sharing of a situation that we can use as an educational device this evening. We are going to give you about 10 or 15 minutes to write this out"*.

After they have spent 15 minutes on this, give them these instructions: *"We should now like several of you to share your conflict with us; share it by telling us a couple of things about it. Do not spend more than a minute or two to tell us. After we've had seven or eight of you share your conflicts, then we shall choose one which we think will be appropriate for the evening and concentrate on it"*.

The facilitators, at this point, can encourage people to share their conflicts, being careful not to have anyone give names, get into arguments or share conflicts between people in that group. Should someone share that kind of conflict, simply say to him that you do not think it appropriate; we're here to deal with an education situation; the conflict is for that purpose and not for dealing with a conflict presently in the group. After several people have shared their conflicts, the facilitator should then choose one that he thinks is most appropriate for an educational device. Try to choose one that has five or six people involved and in which the values are clear enough for the total group to pick out and put in their ranking order. Once you have chosen the conflict, then you will be able to give the volunteers some instructions for the body sculpture. This activity should be completed by 8:30.

8:30—9:30 p.m.

The role-play situation: First give the following instructions to the volunteers:

1. *Sculpture the original conflict situation by choosing different people from this group to represent silent figures in your original conflict. If you have five people in your original conflict, then choose five persons.*

2. *Arrange these figures so as to represent the original conflict situation. You may exaggerate the figures in order to symbolically represent the original conflict, if you wish. You do this by positioning them in relationship to each other so as to represent the conflict. Then go to each person and tell him briefly how you think he should feel in this situation and what his attitude is to others in the conflict. This whole process, apart from the short statement that you will give the person, is to be nonverbal. Then sculpture their arms and their facial expressions so as to represent their feelings in the conflict. For example, you may have "arrogance" represented by someone standing on a chair with his back to another person. Or, you may have "anger" represented by a person lying on the ground with another person standing over him with clenched fists. However the conflict is represented, all the people in it must be sculptured.*

3. The facilitators will now help the volunteer in the process by going around with him or her to sculpture each person individually, making sure that all are in relationship to each other, to represent the total conflict.

4. Once the sculpture is set up, the volunteer then fits himself into the sculpture as a part of that conflict.

5. At this point, ask all those in the sculpture, as well as all those observing, to remain absolutely silent for 2 minutes.

6. At this point, you start a discussion by having those in the sculpture tell how they felt. Give them assurance by telling them, *"I know this is a role-playing situation and, therefore, it's difficult to know how to feel and put yourself into it. You may have felt embarrassed, and those feelings will be present in the situation also. However, given all those limitations, let us try to examine what our feelings were in the situation".* After the reports on "feelings", have those observing report how they saw the situation.

7. Now try to get the group to discuss what they felt were the underlying values and what the different values each person in the conflict might have had. It is useful at this point to

have a blackboard or brainstorming paper available, so that the values and their priority rankings can be listed. Such discussion could easily take half an hour. If the discussion starts to bog down, try using the following alternatives in order to move things along:

Place the people back in the conflict situation and have them start talking so that they verbally role-play the situations; allow them to do this for about 5 minutes. Following the verbalization, have another discussion of the underlying values and then repeat the role-play by having different members who are observing replay some of the other people. That is to say, have some of the actors replaced by others who are observing.

Conclude the activity by trying to get a discussion moving in the whole group on what were the underlying values and what were the rankings. In a conflict situation, remember there is imposition of values and usually imposition of value-rankings. A question you might put to the group is, *"What values were being imposed by one or two people on each other, or what value priorities?"* If you have time, this session can be concluded by expressions and thoughts and even a continued role-play on the resolution of the conflict.

9:30—10:00 p.m.

Finish the evening by general discussion, either in original small groups or with questions from the total group. The evening should conclude at 10:00. During the conclusion, remember to

remind the group that they begin the next day at 9:00 and should be there at 8:50 a.m.

THIRD DAY: MORNING 9:00—12:00 midday

9:00 a.m.

INTRODUCTION: For this exercise you will need brainstorming paper on the walls, large sheets of paper and magic markers for facilitators. You will also need an assortment of art materials such as magic markers, paints, pieces of wire, etc. During this exercise you will also need two overhead projectors, and a roll of white paper (about fifty feet in length), such as placed on tables during parties. During the process part of the group session, tell the group something like this: *"For the last two days we've been discussing values, ranking of values, conflict and polarity. This morning we're going to try to make this more concrete, in terms of what our values are and what priorities they might be in. This will also be seen as an activity of creativity and reflection".*

At this point this question should be put to the group as a whole: *"During the last three days we've discussed many things, and you no doubt have become aware of yourselves and the value question through the different activities and exercises. What we want you to do now for a few minutes is to think of the kinds of values that are important to you and other persons, in setting life priorities. What we'd like to do is to get a list of about twenty or thirty values on the sheets on the wall".*

FACILITATORS: You should begin the process by putting up half a dozen important values, to kick the group off. A suggestion is, security, trust, work, money, freedom . . .

At this point, the leader and the facilitator should encourage everyone in the group to call out one or two values so that there is a large list of values on the board. When anybody repeats a value already there or states one that is similar, simply star that value. The activity should take approximately 30 minutes.

9:30—10:00 a.m.

Give the following instructions to the group: *"Look at all the values on the wall and consider that most people only have three or four values with which they can operate. We want you to choose four or five values on the wall, rank them in order of priority for yourself, and then find someone in the room to share these values with. We shall allow you about half an hour for this activity, and you can share your values with anybody you like. If you wish, wander around the room sharing your value list with others".*

10:00—11:30 a.m.

Give these instructions to the group: *"Please return with your original partner to the groups you were in during the first evening you were here. If you remember, at that time you were in groups of eight. Share the values you have in the group and compare them to see if they are the same values you chose on that first night. After you have done this and discussed this for awhile, we want you to decide how you might express what you've learned during this workshop, as a group. We want you to do this by using the art forms around the room: Take a long section of the fifty feet of white paper available and draw a strip of pictures or expressions which can be run on the overhead projectors and shown on the wall. Then you show these pictures, make sure they're in a straight line, so they can be pulled over the top of the overhead projectors. These pictures can be individual expressions or individual expressions within the group. Discuss in your group what kinds of expressions and learnings you want to put on the paper and then decide how you would go about doing this art form. Use any of the art forms available for this purpose, placing the expressions on the white sheet".*

FACILITATORS: Move around or even leave the building if necessary, but do not interfere with the groups; rather encourage them to do the job and ask any questions. It is our experience that in this kind of activity, the facilitators can often leave for a period of time.

11:30—12:00 noon

For the final part of the session have each group show its slide pictures on the overhead projector, explaining when they do so what it is the persons have seen. This activity will act as a complete reflective expression in itself and does not need to be added to by any comments by facilitators. You might invite the group to ask clarifying questions if they do not understand something. End by reminding everybody that the final session will be at two o'clock in the afternoon.

THIRD DAY: AFTERNOON—2:00 p.m. to end

2:00 p.m.

It is suggested that this session be used as a final reflective input session. The facilitators can, if they wish, review some of the material—cognitive material on value-ranking and values earlier used, perhaps expanding a little in order to reinforce the learning gained through the experiences of the last three days. This should be followed by a discussion.

The length of such a session can vary, depending on how tired or how stimulated the group is at this point. Often after a long conference like this, the group simply wants to be quiet, without raising more questions.

As a way of finally evaluating the group and as a valuable exercise in further clarification, have the people get together in their original pairs to work on evaluation Diagrams 1 and 2. An additional sheet which simply asks them if they have any comments or how they would improve the conference, as discussed earlier, would also be useful at this point. To conclude the session this way and to ask them to hand in their evaluations afterward is a helpful way of saying good-bye to each other and will also give you ample material to evaluate for future conferences.

CONFERENCE FORMAT 4
1 and 2 days

TWO DAY

	MORNING	*AFTERNOON*	*EVENING*
DAY 1		*4 p.m.* *Rogiotration* *Social hour*	*7:30 p.m. Value Game*
DAY 2	*9 p.m.* *Hallmark Card Company Game*	*2 p.m.* *Creative alternatives* *Input* *Conclusion*	

ONE DAY

DAY 1	*9 a.m.* *Registration* *1. Value Game* *Alternate: Hallmark Card Company Game*	*2 p.m.* *Creative alternatives* *Input* *Conclusion*	

TWO-DAY CONFERENCE

FIRST DAY

For the first afternoon and evening, the same format is suggested as in Conference 1. This value game is designed to reduce anxiety by placing emphasis on a person's potentiality, as well as being a game to help people to know and understand each other better and to get into the value question a little. As an alternative way of grouping, it is suggested that, at the registration, the numbers placed on the name tags be an arbitrary selection of numbers taken off a pre-registration list; you might have eight number ones, eight number twos and eight number threes, etc. in the room. So, when you group people in the evening, you can say, ***"Will all those with number one, number two and number three on their tabs, etc. form their groups".*** This form of numbering and grouping is easier than the one described in the last conference, but it can only be done if you have had pre-registration, so that you can arbitrarily choose the numbers beforehand. According to this format then, the first evening would be as follows:

4:00—6:00 p.m. Registration and social hour, possibly followed by supper.

7:30—10:00 p.m. Introduction on the definition of a value, followed by the in-and-out groups using Diagram 4, called the "Value Game".

SECOND DAY

9:00—12:00 midday INTRODUCTION TO VALUE GAME RANKING: Using the Hallmark Card Company Game as before, this activity follows the same format as in Conference I.

2:00 p.m. It is suggested that the afternoon session utilize the creative alternative game used in the morning of the third day in the first conference. Conclude with reflections on the comments on the people as they ran their pictures through the overhead projector. The format of this is:

2:00—2:30 p.m. Introduction and brainstorming.

2:30—3:00 p.m. Personal choice of the value-ranking and sharing with other persons.

3:00—4:30 p.m. Getting together in original groups and designing the activities for presentation at the final session.

4:30—5:00 p.m. CONCLUDING SESSION: Reflection and showing of pictures.

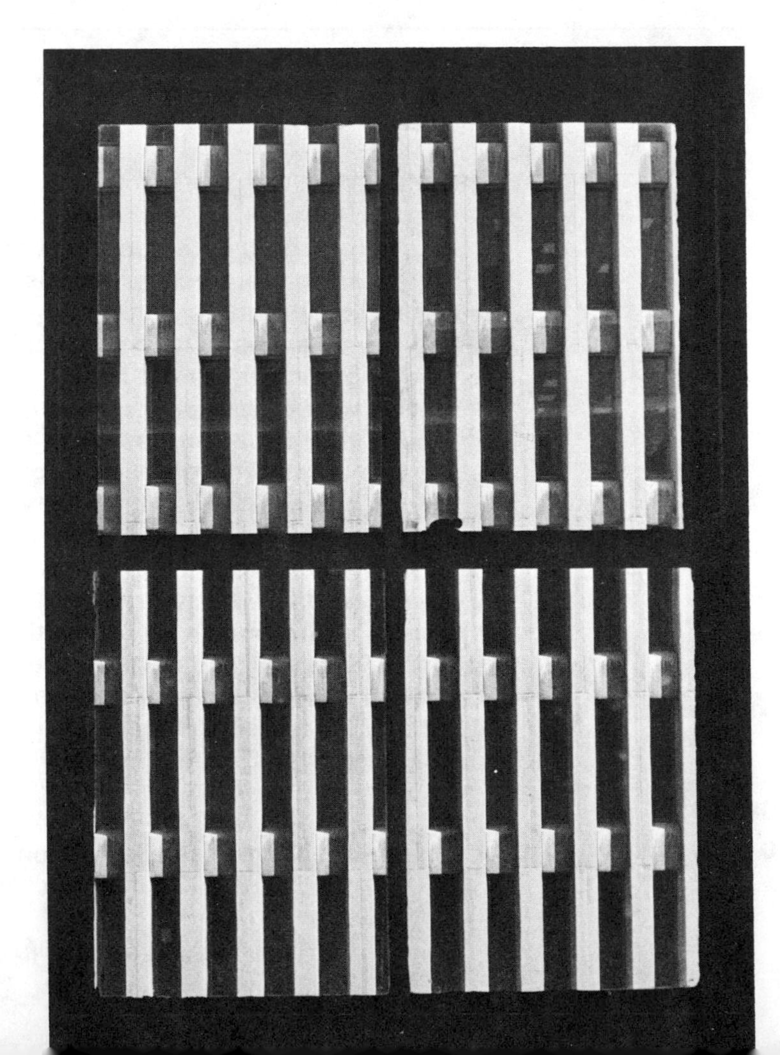

ONE-DAY CONFERENCE 9:00—5:00 p.m.

MORNING SESSION: 9:00—12:30 p.m.

9:00—9:30 a.m. Registration: The registration should include, as before, name tags with numbering for rapid grouping afterward.

9:30—12:30 p.m. It is best to choose either the value-ranking game or the value games, depending on what particular point you wanted to discuss or get across to the participants. If this activity is new to you, we suggest that you start with the value game. If you've been involved in these kinds of activities before, then the value-ranking game might be more profitable. If you are starting any new value conference with people who have no idea of values, then it's better to start with the exercises which give a definition of a value, such as the value game. Should you take the value game, the format runs like this:

9:00—9:30 a.m. Registration.

9:30—10:00 a.m. Introduction of the facilitators and input on the nature of a value, with discussion.

10:00—10:30 a.m. In this period of time, have the participants form groups of eight for observing and for sitting and discussing the value question. This will take 10 minutes for grouping and then 20 minutes for the total group discussion.

10:30—11:30 a.m. The pairs discuss and work on the value sheets.

11:30—12:00 noon Final discussion and reports.

ONE-DAY WORKSHOP AFTERNOON 2:00—5:00 p.m.

For this activity, the workshop on creative alternatives suggested in the conclusion of the two-day workshop can be used. The only difference is that instead of asking the participants to reflect only on the values they've become acquainted with in the workshop, another kind of question can be raised: *"What kinds of values and priorities do you think are essential to you and to other people in this modern world?"* The afternoon then moves to the same program as in the two-day workshop.

Note to the Facilitators: In both the one-day and two-day workshop the evaluation forms can be used. It is the opinion of the authors that the evaluation forms can work as a substitute for the creative alternative afternoon workshop in the two-day workshop, if the participants had really become involved. If they had not become deeply involved, then it will be better to stick with the plan suggested. We do not suggest using the evaluations on the one-day workshop since there has not been enough time for the participants to become involved and for those forms to be sufficiently useful.

Use of Facilitators: The use of the facilitator in these conferences was marked in the bracketed sessions throughout the conference. It is important, if you have not worked together before, that you follow these instructions. However, the main point is that as you do your first workshop or workshops together you will learn to become a team and work out these fine points. As facilitators, you need to be continually working together through the workshop and evaluating each other. It is suggested that at least once in the middle of the day and at the end of the day sessions, you get together for at least 15 minutes to half an hour (minimally) to discuss the process of workshops. In the case of the three-day workshop, you should get together for an hour at the end of the first and second evenings. To proceed in this way is advisable, especially if you are doing many workshops and have training sessions for your own facilitators between workshops. Try to develop a large enough team so that when people can't be at certain workshops, you have other people with whom you've already worked to call on.

Evaluation of Dynamics: The main evaluation of the dynamics can be derived by looking at the evaluation forms you may have used in the workshops: Diagrams 1, 2 and 3. However, in evaluating a workshop the most important is Diagram 3. When doing a workshop, it is always best to put your expectations at a minimum. Whenever I do a workshop, I never put an expectation beyond "the hope there will be an expanded awareness in the area of concern for some people in the workshop". Some trainers feel that the following statistic is useful in terms of understanding what outcomes should be: It is felt that a good workshop results in thirty percent of the participants in favor of what you did with some enthusiasm. Thirty percent might be disappointed or unfavorable to what you did and even angry at some of the things that happened. Forty percent would be moderately pleased. In other words, don't expect everybody to be entirely happy with what you're doing. It is not in the nature of people's reactions to respond entirely favorably to anything that confronts them with change. Always remember that someone who is upset may be unhappy for reasons which have nothing to do with the workshop. For this reason, evaluations of the facilitators after the workshop is important.

What kinds of things tell us that we've had a good workshop? The first is whether the group is more cohesive at the end of the session than it was at the beginning. Indications of this would be that after the workshop is ended people are still hanging around, talking to each other, asking questions and so on. A poor workshop is indicated by cliques of factions of people very happy with each other as they left, with polarities formed. However, the kind of structures and dynamics suggest that this is very unlikely to happen. The kind of maximum things you might expect from a workshop are increased outreach, awareness, explicitness and a certain amount of independence from the leadership on the part of a large percentage of the people. These are what indicate an excellent workshop. Another good indication is seen when people were able to suggest new and creative ideas helpful to you at the end. This kind of thing, of course, is a reaching out to the leadership, which is good.

How can we be sure that the workshop would not go badly? You never can be sure, and you should be aware of some of the dynamics that make for a good workshop. What causes a poor workshop is in building things up well the first night but going back to slower or secondary material the next morning. Once you build up an intimacy among the people, you must keep them interested up until the end of the workshop. Secondly, don't give them too much work; you will tire them out. A good workshop should be leisurely and recreative in its nature. Different people learn at different speeds, and you cannot cram it down their throats. Values are eternalized over a long period of time, and major value shifts should not be expected from the participants. If you push a workshop too hard or are too controlling as a facilitator, then you're suggesting a value of non-trust in people which can, in turn, make them angry. For this reason, all structures and dynamics that have been suggested have been set up in such a way that the groups for the most part move by themselves without facilitators. This is a trust in the potential of the learners. You should only be there to care for or to help the process. You are not there to impose or control persons, but rather to assist the process of learning.

Some of the things that have been programmed in are as follows: The first night is designed as a structure to enhance a person's feeling of self-worth and to reduce his anxiety. The general result of that first workshop (and we have run this workshop many hundred times) is to make people feel good about themselves, as well as to learn something about values. Does this mean giving them "the treatment" and trying to sell them on our workshop? No, of course not. It means that you are willing to give them the respect that says to them that you understand they're coming to a new workshop and that meeting new people does heighten people's anxieties. Therefore, we need to be careful on the first night to make sure that people are placed in an environment which will help them, rather than make them feel "uptight" or "flattened".

Every group goes through different phases of development. Generally speaking, these phases of development are as follows:

1. Initial feelings of anxiety and dependence on leadership.
2. Sharing of information.
3. Sharing of feelings.
4. Conflict and emotionally corrective behavior.
5. Working together in a spirit of interdependence.

Most groups go through the stages listed above, in that order, but sometimes they jump around a little. People will not share feelings until they've had a chance to share information and to have their anxiety reduced in the early stages. People are not going to get into the kind of conflict situations where they help each other correct their behavior (referred to above in stage 4) unless they've been together for some time. People may move through all these stages in the three-day workshop, but this is unlikely. They will probably move to a part of a process which will get them to stage 3 or 4. Remember this and don't worry about them becoming a close-knit group or community. It is only important that these people move through some of the processes in order to learn certain things you have programmed as your expectations at the beginning of the conference. The activities of the second day are the Hallmark Card Game or the role-playing, processes which help the people become active with one another personally but objectively. Needless to say, they are non-threatening activities which, in turn, involve personal aspects at the end of the activity. If conducted properly, these activities can intensify their feeling from the night or the morning before and provide an environment which will increase their learning behavior.

The afternoon off on the three-day conference is leisure activity we see as being absolutely essential in this kind of emotional conference and activity. For the three-day conference, the role-playing intensifies personal interaction even more and follows along the same lines of interactive and intimate process, allowing for as much expression as the participants wish. Finally, the activities at the end of the sessions, involving the art form, allow persons who are not too verbal to get involved. We can be present with each other; we can be active with each other; we can be personal with each other and, finally, we can express our thoughts about each other in a way that is not too threatening, but at the same time gets to the heart of the matter: namely, the values and priorities that we hold dear to us. The alternative form of completing the process on the two-day conference, as well as the three-day conference, is to use the evaluation test. It is a way of dealing with the grief of separation and bringing the conference to a close. Here the grief of parting and that sort of intimacy is dealt with by putting people into pairs and allowing them to part this way. Placing people in pairs, rather than in the large group, reduces the anxiety again and prepares them for leaving.

What is being said here is that the nature of these exercises moves through a process; they are not placed in any arbitrary form. There is a beginning process that helps people get to know each other, a middle process of increasing intimacy and a final process of departing participation—the creation of an environment which will maximize learning, not only at the conference, but in the reflective manner in which they leave. As we move into the next conference, you might reflect on these points and then at the end of this chapter we shall deal with some of the alternatives that could be placed in these different sections. If you make up your own conference and replace the activities from Section II of this book, keep in mind this general dynamic process. Generally speaking, we feel that the value game, or games similar to it, are excellent ways of beginning any conference.

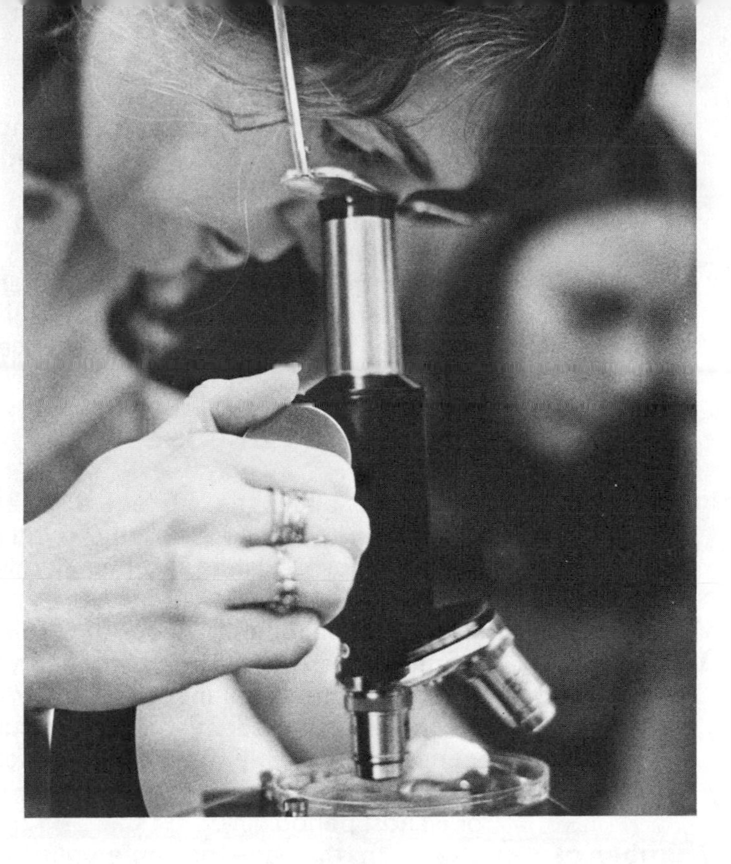

ADVANCED CONFERENCES
A THREE-DAY, TWO-DAY AND ONE-DAY CONFERENCE

The introduction to the conference format for the initial conferences still applies to this section. Therefore, the introductory material coming at this point will be only that material applying specifically to the advanced conferences. Most of the general introduction given before in regard to the leisure period or the atmosphere of the conference, and so on, all apply to this conference or these conferences also.

INTRODUCTION

Participants: The participants in this seminar are teachers in training or advanced students who have been through the initial conferences.

Facilitators: These are people who have had more advanced knowledge and training in the area of value clarification. They should have experienced the whole range of personal evaluation needed to deal with all the games in this seminar. Ideally, they should have gone through all the activities to take place, either at some time before or as a part of their training as facilitators for this conference. The leader should be extensively trained and seen as a professional in this area. If there is any doubt, it might be well to have a professional person with an advanced degree in psychology or education and who is trained in the area of group process and personal encounter.

Time: The times of the three conferences about to be listed are the same as in the initial conferences and are here illustrated under the following diagrams called Conference Format 5 and Conference Format 6.

For any further question on the timing of these conferences, please refer to the section on "Time", under the initial conferences given earlier in this chapter. As before, preparation for the conference with the facilitators is necessary, in general, and especially for this particular conference.

GOALS AND PURPOSE

Minimal Goals: To allow the student a greater awareness of his values and priorities and to see some relationship between these priorities and those existing in other people, social institutions and society.

Optimal Learnings: To become aware at a deeper level of his own values and priorities operating in his personality; to be able to see these in relationship to social institutions, conflict and polarities in society. Maximally, the student will gain enough experience through these exercises to be able to have some facility with them and use them in a classroom or situation where he might operate as a facilitator for a short period.

Number of Persons Suggested: In this kind of conference, where the dynamics are becoming more intense, smaller groups of people are advisable. It is suggested for such a conference that there be at least one facilitator for every six people. If this is the first experience with such a conference, the number should be restricted to approximately thirty people. In our experience running conferences up to fifty and sixty people, going beyond these numbers becomes difficult and very draining if there is not a large number of professional facilitators present. We mention this primarily in relationship to two- or three-day conferences. This, of course, is not true of a short classroom experience which may be run with up to thirty people, with only one or two facilitators in addition to the leader being present. However, over a long-term session such as a three-day conference, it is better to have one facilitator for each six participants present. If all the facilitators were trained in group process, then only one is needed for every ten participants.

Materials Needed:

1. Tape records or some instrument for playing background music.
2. Posters or decorations for walls.
3. Brainstorming paper and magic markers.
4. Mimeographed sheets for every participant in the conference of the following diagrams: Diagram 7, 8, 9 and 10.
5. Sheets of cardboard (white, shiny surface), approximately 2 x 3 feet in size.
6. Art materials: clay, wire, magic markers, paint, various types of paper, boxes, materials for making slides. That is to say, any art materials available for the use of the participants. There should be enough art materials for all the participants to be able

to involve themselves in some minor activity with themselves or as a group.

Immediate Preparation: Preparation for the conference is dealt with in the initial conferences. Particular emphasis for these conferences will be on special preparation, such as the in-depth preparation of the facilitators. The preparation needed here will be more extensive than in the initial conferences. This could consist of going over these activities with your facilitators, for example, on a day's retreat some weeks before the conference, then going over the conference once or twice so you know where your dynamics are and what the jobs and roles of each facilitator and the particular aspects of the conference might be. For this type of conference, team relationship is essential. Therefore, splitting the obligation is important as a part of the training of the facilitators in the process. This will be particularly true if you have professional consultants present. The way to use a professional consultant is not simply to have him "do the thing", but rather have him train the facilitators so that they can do this on their own the next time, without the need to pay for professional consultants.

DIAGRAM 7

TALENTS	*LIMITATIONS*	*POTENTIAL VALUES*
VALUE STATEMENT:		

DIAGRAM 8

EXPRESSIVENESS: *Ability to express inner feelings and fantasies. Flexibility with ideas, feeling or imagination. To create and to be are priorities.*
POWER: *Ability to lead and manage people. Puts priorities on structures. Emphasis on group movement, accomplishment and positive success. Likes to control outcomes.*
INSTRUMENTALITY: *Ability to work with bodies, manipulative and/or conjunctive skills. Priorities on ability to do, to make. Priorities in created order and its care.*
INTERDEPENDENCE: *Ability to work cooperatively with other people. Works well in teams. Priorities or feelings, as well as function.*

DIAGRAM 9 - NEW WORLD GAME

POLITICS

ARTS

MILITARY

CHURCH

SOCIAL ISSUES

Rank: Expressiveness
Power
Instrumentality
Interdependence

By group consensus

DIAGRAM 10

CONFLICT EXAMPLE

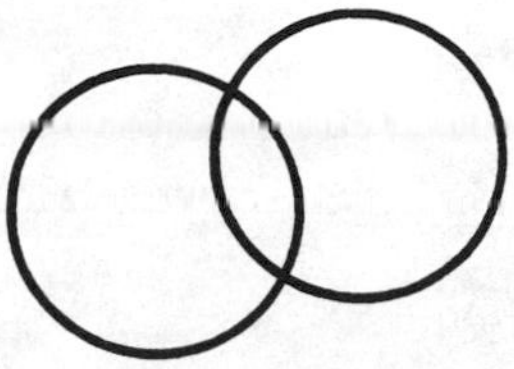

Parents 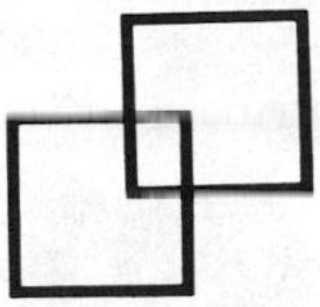 *Brothers* *One*

CONFLICT OR EVENT 1

RECENT EVENT(SIMILAR)

FUTURE GROUP SUGGESTION

CONFERENCE 1—ADVANCED THREE-DAY CONFERENCE

FIRST DAY, 4:00—10:00 p.m.

4:00 p.m.

Registration and social hour. The registration period here is suggested at 4:00 in the afternoon or later. If this is going to be a three-day conference in a given place, people need time to move in their belongings, meet other people and prepare for the evening session. As before in the initial conference, we suggest that the registration be accompanied by a social hour for this purpose, where the facilitators would act in meeting the people and making them feel at ease. It is important for the facilitators to be at the location of the conference beforehand, to set up the atmosphere with music, decorations or whatever.

During the registration period, name tags might be helpful if there are more than fifteen or twenty people; with less than fifteen people, it may not be necessary. It may be better to just have the people get to know each other by introductions. If this is the kind of conference where people are living in, it would of course be preferable to have supper together, following the social hour with the evening session beginning at 7:30.

7:30—8:00 p.m.

INTRODUCTION: This period should start with the facilitators introducing themselves and reviewing the three-day conference briefly, possibly by having them outline it on a wall. The point of this is to prevent manipulation. To do this the facilitators must be aware of what is going to happen in the processes. This should include describing what they consider to be the minimal and optimal goals of the conference. If it is a small group of less than fifteen people, it might be well to go around the group, having each person give his name and explain in a sentence or so where he is from and why he is here.

Following this, there should be a brief review of the definition of a value. A reminder of this is what was stated in the introduction to the initial meeting on the first conference on page 166. In addition to this, you might briefly give the following information: *"In addition to the review we've just been through, we'd like you to consider the idea of limitation as a value. When we use the word "limitation" this evening we will not mean something negative or bad. It is to be understood, as we use it, simply as a statement of where you are or where I am. It is, therefore, not "good" or "bad" but a* neuter word. *Minimally, we might say that it is a "good" thing since if I know my limitation I then can begin to look at what priorities, in terms of my potential, might be. We simply offer this definition of limitation for you to consider and to understand that is what we mean, as we use it in the process this evening".*

Following this might be a few questions and a brief discussion, to be completed by 8:00. It might be pointed out also that the conference is inductive—that is to say, experiential in its methodology: a learning experience. It is understood that the learning will come mainly from the participants, as they experience values through discussion and working with values in their groups. Therefore, a minimal amount of cognitive input will be placed before them with the reliance mainly on their experience and their interaction with the facilitators during the group process, as well as their interaction with fellow members of their groups. It should also be added at this point that they will be able to talk to any one of the facilitators during the conference at their leisure.

8:00—8:15 p.m.

During this period, get the participants into groups of eight, with four people sitting and four standing on the outside observing, as in the following diagram:

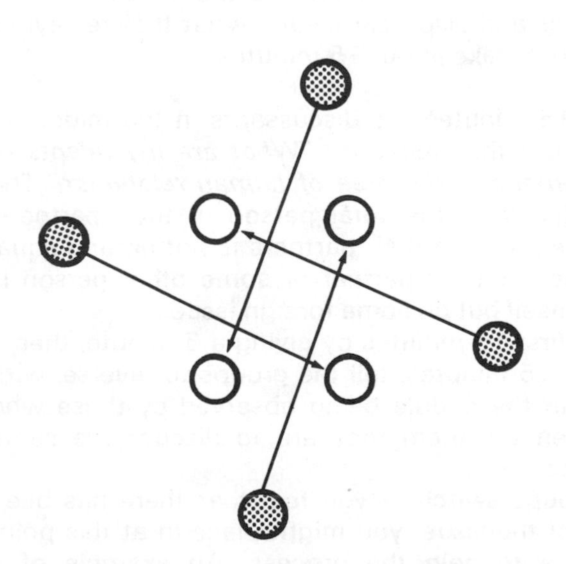

STANDING OBSERVERS

SITTING DISCUSSANTS

The method by which we suggest you group them off is stated as follows: *"We should like those of you who consider yourselves more outgoing than ingoing to raise your hands"*. Depending on the group, no one may raise his hand, or some may feel very shy about it. The point of this is to insure an arbitrary selection of partners and, at the same time, to make sure that all the quiet people, the noisy people or the more open people don't end up in one group. If this happens, some people will have a good experience and others a bad experience. Once some have raised their hands, keep probing for others to raise their hands and move to a situation where you have to say something as follows: *"All we are trying to do is get the group split in two parts to avoid having those who are more outgoing mixed up with those who are quieter in temperament. Since we need some more people to be grouped with the more outgoing ones, we'd like volunteers. Who would like to consider themselves as more outgoing people? Let's keep raising our hands until we have at least half of you in that camp"*.

Once you have the room divided equally this way, then ask those who have raised their hands to find a partner—someone they do not know too well in the other group of people. Once everybody is paired off, have the pairs find three other pairs whom they do not know too well, in order to be arranged in groups of eight. Once they are in groups of eight, direct one person of the original pair to sit and the other one to observe. The best way to manage this is for the facilitators to get on the floor and go over to each one of the groups and physically arrange the people. We have found this much more helpful; it also gets the facilitators more involved with people. Make the arrangements so that the four who are sitting are close together and comfortable for conversation between themselves and are not distracted by the observers. Have the observers stand across from their partners so that they are facing them and can observe them—so they can see their facial attitudes and also hear clearly what they're saying. This whole process should take about 15 minutes.

8:15—8:45 p.m.

For the first 15 minutes the discussants in the middle of the group are to discuss this question: *"What are my talents or abilities and my limitations in the area of human relations?"* The observers' job is to listen to the total person in their partners. They can only interfere if one of their partners is not getting equal time in the 15 minutes, if their partner or some other person is not speaking about himself but on some foreign issue.

Close off the first 15 minutes by giving a 5 minute, then a minute warning. After 15 minutes, tell the groups to reverse, with the observers sitting in the middle being observed by those who were discussants. Then tell them they are to discuss the same question for 15 minutes.

When the groups switch, if you feel that there has been too much avoidance of the issue, you might place in at this point a heightened sentence to help the process. An example of a heightened process is, *"It is difficult, when you're meeting for the first time, to talk about yourself. However, the degree to which we can talk about ourselves does say something about the way we see ourselves as being valuable people or how we trust other people. Therefore, it is important to try to keep to the subject and speak from the "I" vantage-point".*

8:45—9:30 p.m. At this point, the group moves into working in pairs. It is to be remembered, too, as you approach the 8:45 point, to try to give a few minutes' warning. At 8:45, the following instructions should be given: *"We want you now to go with your partner—the person you observed and who observed you. Take with you the talent limitation sheet marked Diagram 7 which we are giving to you. When you get into pairs, we want you to spend from now until 9:30 working on that sheet. First of all, we want you to report to each other what you heard each of us say in the group situation—not only what you heard in terms of words, but in terms of the whole person. From this interaction then, help each other fill in the talent sheets. First, you and your partner work on what talents your partner observed in you as you spoke—not only what you said, but in the way you talked and came across to the group. Secondly, work on the list of limitations you saw in your partner and heard your partner speak of. Thirdly and most importantly, we want you to take each limitation separately and try to put that limitation in positive terms. Then state what the potential value inherent in that limitation might be".* It should be noted that this exercise is quite difficult for some people and will need intimate interaction of the facilitators. Since many people are going to question how you put limitations in positive statements, a couple of examples might be given: *"One example of a positive limitation might be a person who says that he is late for work some mornings because he has trouble getting up; he might discover that the reason he gets up late is because he stays up late at night with people. The potential value then might be husband, wife or friends. Such an example does not detract from the limitation but emphasizes the potential value inherent in limitations. Another example might be a person who is somewhat withdrawn and takes time to make friends. Often such a person prefers a few deep friendships rather than many less intimate friendships. The value for such a person might be intimacy".*

Giving such an example will help to understand the nature of the process they have to do. It should be noted, at this point, that in our experience it is necessary for facilitators to be able to do this activity themselves and to move around from couple to couple to help them to whatever extent they need. It is essential to help people move from limitations to seeing the positive side of the limitation. The point here is not to avoid limitation in our lives, but to see that it is an opportunity to confront underlying values. This is a very important and essential part of the value-clarifying process—in particular, the use of value-clarifying questions. Only as the facilitator asks these appropriate clarifying questions can the potential values be discovered.

Be sure to give a 10-minute warning before the end of this activity; then give a 5 minute and perhaps a minute warning, because people are engaged more intimately at this point in the dynamic than previously. Remember, in terms of the dynamics, that it is often easier for people to speak in pairs than in a large group. Therefore, in terms of the evening dynamics, anxiety is reduced considerably by moving into pairs; some of them might feel a little apprehensive about moving back into the group again. For this reason, sufficient warning is necessary.

9:30—10:00 p.m.

Tell the partners to get back into their original groups of eight, sitting in a circle of eight and not in the in-and-out structure. Once in the group, give them the following instructions: *"Take your partner's talent limitation sheet. Look over the potential values and then make a value statement about your partner. Imagine the best kind of person your partner could become within the next year if he worked on his limitations and extended those potential values. Try to make a brief one-sentence statement on his sheet, where it says "Value Statement". Following this, each person introduces his partner to the group by explaining the value statement and why he made it. You have until ten o'clock to finish this".*

As an alternative to this exercise, you could ask the group also to make a conclusive statement about their experience of the evening. In which case, the evening would end by each group making a short statement. In our opinion, you need a little more than 30 minutes for this, and you probably should continue the group until 10:15 if you decide to do it this way. That is to say, have the group reporting to each other and then coming up with some kind of conclusion by 10:00. Then have group reports until 10:15. In our opinion, both ways are effective. As you near the end of the evening, it would be well to give the group warning. Make yourself available for questions afterward and remind them to be 10 minutes early in the morning for the morning session beginning at 9:00 a.m.

SECOND DAY 9:00—9:30

MORNING
9:00 a.m.—12:00 midday

INTRODUCTION: The facilitator should review briefly what is meant by value-ranking, pointing out that the process whereby people choose value-ranking priorities in their lives is the sevenfold definition of a value. Mainly, their value-rankings are chosen from alternatives that people are happy with and act on. Next, move directly into the exercise, first spending the rest of the introductory time to explain Diagram 8. The definitions of Expressiveness, Power, Instrumentality and Interdependence are on the diagram sheet. The facilitators should have gone over this diagram in detail before the conference in order to settle, in their own minds, what they understand of the definitions, in case conflicting thoughts arise at this point.

Following this, give the following instructions: *"In a few*

minutes we're going to ask you to go into your original pairs and rank these four words in the order of priority in which you think they exist in your behavior in life. This means that you will put one of the words first, with another second, another third and another fourth. Whichever word you put first you should consider as being a priority, behaviorally, in your life at the present. For example, if you put power first, you would consider power as a priority in the way you operate, especially at work. Perhaps you have the kind of job where you're in authority over people and words are necessary for you to be able to move people around rapidly in order to get a successful job done, as well as a method of caring for the persons themselves. That is, power is not seen here as a negative thing at all; it may be a positive thing for many of you and, as such, is to be considered as a priority for you. The person who puts instrumentality first would be one who puts a higher value on the ability of a person to work with his hands and to have cognitive and manipulative skills. Perhaps you are a mechanic, a mathematician or a chemist who has to work with numbers and have particular skills with your hands and mind. Or we might, for example, consider a person who puts power first and instrumentality second quite different from a person who puts interdependence first and power second. In other words, whatever you put as second conditions what you put as first; whatever you put as third conditions what you put first and second, and whatever you put fourth conditions what you put in the first three. What we want you to do, therefore, is to rank them in terms of your behavior".

Then allow enough time for questions so that you are sure everybody discusses these things with understanding. Should there be many questions as you near the introductory period, suggest that they start the activity and announce that the facilitators will help them directly in their pairs. Generally, we find that about twenty percent of the group has great difficulty with this, and the rest of the people have no trouble.

9:30—9:50 a.m. During this period ask the group to pair off with the partners they had the night before and for the next 20 minutes rank their Diagram 8 and discuss why they made the rankings and what they feel the implications are for themselves.

9:50—10:45 a.m. First, ask each pair to find two other pairs of their choice and to form groups of six around the room. When they have done this, hand out Diagram 9, "New World Game", to each group. Then give them the following instructions: *"We want you now as a group to consider the five major words: Politics, Arts, Military, Church, Social Issues. We want you to try to come to a common agreement on a definition for each one of those words. We want you to do this in such a way that you can rank the four words, expressiveness, power, instrumentality and interdependence, for each one of those five definitions that you come up with. We want you to define the words and then to rank expressiveness, power, instrumentality and interdependence for a person whose life work is involved in one of those five areas. For example, let us take the word arts. Once you have come to a general definition of arts, consider a person who works full time in that profession and then write down under the section "arts" what you think the value-ranking should be. For example, for the word arts you might consider that expressiveness might be the first, followed perhaps by instrumentality, interdependence and finally power. However, you may come up with a definition of arts that makes its orientation different".* Then tell the group they have until 10:45 to do this exercise. It may be necessary for the facilitator to move closely in the groups to help them do this exercise. As they work with the groups, you should remind all that one of the main issues in this exercise is to help people see that different words which indicate values, like "church" and "politics" mean something different to different people. Therefore, a part of the value-clarification process is clarifying what a value means—how different people perceive it and understand it.

Approximately 10 minutes before the end of this section, the facilitator should move around group by group and give the following instructions: *"You have another 10 minutes at this point; we want you to look at the value-ranking you did before we got into this discussion and see which of the four value-laden areas, mainly politics, arts, military, church and social issues, your ranking comes closest to. That is, for each one of these areas you have a value-ranking. Now compare it with your own value-ranking and see which one you come closest to, and then put yourself in that area".*

Approximately 2 or 3 minutes before 10:45, give the

group a warning so that they can be prepared to move to the next activity. During this kind of activity, it is appropriate to allow people to have coffee or refreshments while in the group sessions.

10:45—11:15 a.m.

At this point you should have the five parts of the room labeled as to five value-laden areas: politics, arts, military, church and social issues. Tell the group to move into the value-laden area that they have assigned themselves on their sheet. If you find there is anybody who doesn't have an area, then tell him to move into the area he thinks is closest to his value choice and find a place within that area. For example, if you have only one person who is "arts" ask him which area he would prefer to be an artist in—the church, social concerns, military or politics. If, on the other hand, you have too many people (over eleven) in one group, it might be advisable to split them into two groups so that you have groups of no more than six or seven people. The maximum size of a group should be eleven people. Once they have arrived in their groups, ask them to discuss why they are in the group and what their value-ranking is. Should any discover that they are in the wrong group according to the consensus of what kind of value-ranking should be evidence for that group, then they are to move from there and discover the group they belong in. For some people this is a traumatic experience, and you should be aware of such eventuality and move them, if necessary, to help them.

Since the instructions for this grouping are complicated, the facilitator should move in close to the groups and help people understand what it is they should do and why they are doing it. The main rationale for this activity is to help people correlate value-ranking and behavior and to correlate the reality of what is understood by a value, even though the same value would perhaps be something quite different to another person.

11:15—12:00 noon

Give sufficient warning at the end of the other group session and then at 11:15 ask the participants to move back into their original groups of six. When in the group, tell them to discuss, for the next 45 minutes, the following question: *"In terms of my morning's experience and where I ended up, what relations, comparisons, or contrasts can I make with this with my present behavior and the way I behave when I am in a work situation?"*

An alternative ending is to have the group discuss this for 30 minutes and then have each group come up with some conclusion about value clarification and value-ranking and report this at a general preliminary session from 11:45 to 12:00. (Both ways of ending the group are helpful.) If the group is sophisticated, it is better not to have a preliminary session but to allow them to come to their own conclusions. Alternatively, preliminary sessions are often helpful because people hear a greater variety of experiences, which tends to bring the total group together. If it is your goal to bring the group as a whole closer together more quickly, it may better serve your purposes to have a preliminary session at this point.

In conclusion, remind the participants to be available 10 minutes early for the evening session, with some remarks about the reality of the afternoon as a leisure period which is a gift from the self. Point out that leisure often stands in contradistinction to attitudes in our society about work and usefulness. In addition to this, the value-rankings discussed in the morning and the way people are influenced by them may say something about the way persons tend to be in this society—more functional than perhaps they need to be. Leisure, then, as an afternoon activity of relaxation can be a learning experience in confrontation with the whole problem of recreation and usefulness.

SECOND DAY—EVENING

7:30—10:00 p.m.

For this part of the session the group should be together, with the facilitators at the front and brainstorming paper on the wall. The leader should introduce the exercise by saying, *"We are going to play a polarity game in order to illustrate different points of view. Through this game, we hope to understand polarity and imposition in values".*

Then proceed by putting the following question to them, with instructions: *"We would like each of you to consider that you are being placed in an environment with a group of children who have had a different upbringing due to a war in their country. They have been placed in your hands with unlimited funds and resources with which to provide a suitable educational environment for them. "Education" is understood here to mean not only cognitive education but one which will prepare them to function in our society. We are now going to brainstorm, and we want each of you to throw out one or two words which express your ideas of things you think important in this environment as you relate to the children and as you set up this new educational system".*

At this point, encourage the whole group to throw out words; the leader and the facilitator will write them on the brainstorming paper until they have between twenty and thirty words. Having completed this, take two separate sheets of brainstorming paper and head one "Control" and the other "Freedom". Now it is the job of the facilitators to screen the words and place them under the two headings. Those words that seem to be more controlling in their nature are put under the "control" sheet. Such words might be: "discipline", "rules", "structure", "organization" and so on. On the "freedom" sheet put all those words that seem to express more of a free atmosphere, such as: "open environment", "unlimited time", "person", and so on. If you have difficulty in determining on which sheet the words should go, the facilitator should then engage all the participants in trying to separate them under "freedom" and "control", and then to add more words under each, if necessary.

The whole point of this is to play a game and characterize, to the extremes you can, aspects of freedom and aspects of

control that have appeared in the words and expressions that people have called out. Sometimes you may get a *feeling* of "control" or "freedom" that someone has verbalized, and you may wish to add new words of your own in order to capture this and put them under the "freedom" or "control" column. Remember, this is a characterization, and the purpose of this game is to polarize the group. In our experience, the group can usually be polarized into the areas of "freedom" and "control". This activity should take until 8:00.

8:00—9:30 p.m.

The facilitators now say to the group, "We want you to separate into three groups. We want you to choose, in terms of the original question, answers to this question: *'If you are setting up an ideal educational system for children of war families, where do you think the priority interests should lie in that system—in the area of control or in the area of freedom?'* " The group now moves into three sections: the freedom group on one side of the room, the control group on the other side of the room, and the "Mugwamps" in the center of the room. (This last phrase is meant to be provocative.) You should now have the group divided into three groups. Should it happen that you have only two groups, you can still utilize the process. If it happens that you have only one group (this would be very unusual in our experience) you could then separate the group arbitrarily into two groups and deal with the process in the same manner. The only difference here is that the process would probably be shorter, ending earlier in the evening. Generally speaking, there is not very much difficulty in separating a group on the issue of control and freedom.

If some people say that to separate a group or make these arbitrary decisions of freedom and control is not fair, state again that you are making a characterization. For the sake of the game you ought then to choose a priority. In our experience, there has not been too much difficulty with this. Once this situation has been set up, ask the freedom group to sit down in a circle.

Then ask the other two groups to stand on the outside of the circle. They are observers who are not allowed to say anything —only listen. If any one of them wants to say something, he must bodily pick up a chair, or if people are sitting on the floor, push his way into the group to make his statement. Having made his statement or series of statements, he is then to leave the group. The facilitators must make sure that no outsider or person in the group dominates things, so that people have equal time to speak. The people who are speaking should be given 15 minutes to say why they are in this group.

Following this, have the participants gather round as observers with the "control" group speaking for 15 minutes. Then the Mugwamps speak, with the other two groups standing on the outside observing them.

Having gone through this process 15 minutes per group, then have the first group that spoke—the "freedom" group—remain silent while the other two report what they heard the "freedom" group say. No more than 10 minutes should be allowed for this reporting. Next have the "control" group remain silent while the other two groups report for 10 minutes on what they heard the "control" group say. Thirdly, have the "mugwamps" remain silent while the other two groups report for 10 minutes on what they heard them say.

After this process, ask everybody to move back again into the three groups: "Freedom", "Control", and "Middle". This time, add the following: *"Please move back into the three areas of 'freedom', 'control' and 'mugwamps', but move to where you think you are now and not necessarily where you were at the beginning. If any of you want to shift to a different group, do it now and let us see how many changes there are".*

After this activity, have some of those who made changes briefly report on why they did so.

9:30—10:00 p.m.

The evening ends with the facilitators first making some remarks on the fact that polarity is caused by imposition of values on another group; secondly, that dissipation of polarity comes about through the process of clarification and willingness to listen to other persons. Complete the evening by a discussion on how many of these aspects the group felt they had experienced. Facilitators should try to draw out the experiences of the group in terms of what different people learned or gained insights into—points such as imposition, conflict due to different values or misunderstanding and what people meant by words, are what need to be discussed in this session. Finally, before ending the session, remind the group that they begin the next morning at 9:00 and that they should try to be 10 minutes early.

THIRD DAY
MORNING, 9:00 a.m.—12:00 midday (Diagram 10)

9:00—9:15 a.m.

INTRODUCTION: Make an introduction along the following lines: *"This morning we are going to deal a little more in depth with ourselves and, hopefully, help ourselves to see the process of development in our lives. This afternoon we shall move into the value implications of this development. Values are developed over a period of time and can be seen in our lives in perspective, from past to present and into the future".*

At this point, give the group the following instructions: *"We want you now to look at your sheet, called Diagram 10. We want you to think of a conflict or emotional event that took place in your lives somewhere between the ages of seven and thirteen or fourteen. We then want you to diagram that event. Do this by using circles and squares. The conflict example at the top of your sheet is an example of this. In this picture you're going to do,*

there are two main things to remember:

1. The size of the square or the size of the circle indicates how important that person was to you.

2. The distance between the squares and circles indicates emotional distance. Now, what is meant by importance or emotional distance is up to you to decide. For example, consider the diagram at the top of the sheet: one interpretation is that the parents are very important to each other—to me. *Their importance is seen by the fact that they are the largest circles on the picture, and they are bigger than the squares. In addition to this, the parents were very close. They were close in the same way that the brothers are quite important and close because the circles and squares interlock. The "me" on the picture is very unimportant and emotionally distant from everybody because of the distance in the picture. This then serves as an example. We now want you to take a personal conflict and draw that in conflict or event 1. When you've done that, we want you to draw another event which happened recently. We want you to do a similar event. That is to say, if your event had to do with anger or grief, then the second event should have to do with an event in which you were angry, anger was recognized or grief was recognized".*

9:15—9:30 a.m.

Give the group 15 minutes to do this exercise. The facilitator should move in the group to help people with it. You might find that some people need more time; if this is the case, going overtime will be all right since the rest of the morning is going to be spent with the group working on this together. Try to be flexible with the time and spend as long as you want with individual people, since it is quite traumatic for some people to have to do this.

9:30—11:00 a.m.

Tell the people to get into the groups of eight they were in the first evening; tell them they have one and a half hours to do the exercise and that each person in the group is now to share his two picture diagrams of a conflict or event in the past and a recent event. They are to give equal time to each person. The job of the facilitators will be to help with this process and see that people get equal time. The job of the group is to simply ask clarifying questions. That is, they are not to argue or ask any probing or intimate questions. The purpose of the exercise is to compare the two events.

It will be appropriate to put up on the board or on brainstorming paper the following ways of comparing:

1. Are there similar emotions in both events?

2. Are there opposite emotions in one event to the other?

3. Are the similar roles or opposite roles played by yourself in both events?

4. Do you find yourself in the recent event playing the role that someone else played in the first event?

5. Is the configuration and general structure of the first

event similar to the second event?

6. Is there similar or opposite behavior between the two events?

As the group moves around from one person to the other, they should become more adept at seeing the different comparisons. The facilitator should note that there are always strong comparisons in most of these diagrams; it is rare that there are no carry-overs from one to the other. It is, therefore, a matter of asking appropriate value-clarifying questions. The facilitators should not engage in this process unless they have worked through this and experienced it in their training period beforehand. *This is most essential.*

11:00—11:30 a.m.

The group should now move from person to person and try to say some positive things about the possible resolution of the behavior reflected in the first two events, by drawing a third picture which might represent the most positive potential of that person to deal with the conflict. An example of this might be to expand the size of the little "me" to equal the size of everybody else in the picture, especially the parents. This might not resolve the conflict, but it would at least show a different view of self. There might be dozens of ways of doing this. Perhaps the "me" could move closer to the brothers or in between the brothers and parents to present his view of how he feels.

11:30—11:45 a.m.

At this point, the facilitator can say, *"The whole meaning of the morning has been to help you examine yourselves in a process. We'd now like each group to come up with some conclusions as to anything they've discovered about themselves in the morning that they might find useful to tell the rest of the group".* You can then tell them that you're going to give them 15 minutes for this.

11:45—12:00 noon

Planning session. Simply have each group report its discoveries and end at midday.

THIRD DAY
AFTERNOON, 2:00 p.m.—end

2:00—3:30 p.m.

Start the group with the following instructions to the total group: *"We have here with us today a whole collection of art objects. There are things for making slides, clay, paper, paints and so on. Get into your groups of eight and work on the group project which would express utilizing poetry, music or any of the art objects here—those values you think are of major importance to the person as an individual, the person in relationship to others, and finally, the person in relationship to world, society or institution. We're going to give you until 3:30 to complete this project, at which time you will be able to share the project with other people".*

3:30—4:00 p.m.

For this part of the session, give the group instructions to discuss for half an hour the values they've come up with in terms of their art project and to discuss what they would briefly tell the total group about the major points of values, value-ranking and whatever they've learned from the total conference. Tell the group then that each presentation will be made at 4:00.

4:00—5:00 p.m.

This session should be run by each group presenting its art work and giving its content presentation, in terms of what they have learned most from the group. The job of the facilitators is to make corrective judgments or to add content and understanding to whatever is said. The total evening could end by a general discussion.

TWO-DAY ADVANCED CONFERENCE

FIRST DAY

4:00—10:00 p.m.

The pattern suggested is registration and social hour followed by supper, as in the previous conference. The evening session lasts from 7:30 through 10:00 p.m. on the exercises, using the talent limitation sheets as in the previous conference. We feel that utilizing this game is an excellent way to start a conference and get people to know each other. Alternative activities will be suggested later in the chapter.

SECOND DAY
9:00—12:00 noon

MORNING
9:00—12:00 midday

During this period the new world game could be used, or, as an alternative, the conflict-dynamic utilizing Diagram 10 could be used. The times for both of these group sessions are the same as listed for the second and third days of the three-day conference. It is suggested that if this is a new group that is not too accustomed to encounter experiences, the new world game be used rather than the circle diagrams. The circle diagram game often brings on emotional content that might be better utilized in a longer conference. However, if these persons have been involved in such conferences before, then it might be appropriate.

SECOND DAY
AFTERNOON, 2:00—5:00 p.m.

2:00—5:00 p.m.

Several alternatives might be utilized at this point:

1. To use the development of the art projects as in the advanced conference third-day conclusion.

2. To use the evaluation tests as suggested in the introduction to the initial conferences. These evaluations, of course, should be used in all these conferences.

3. To use the creative alternative exercises used to complete the two-day conference of the initial conferences.

ONE-DAY ADVANCED CONFERENCE 9:00—5:00 p.m.

MORNING, 9:00—12:30 p.m.

9:00—9:30 a.m. Registration of participants.

9:30—12:30 p.m. The talent and limitation game or the new world game. If the new world game is used, then the same time sequence would be used, placing everything half an hour in advance. The reason for this is that in this conference the registration has to take place first of all. If the talent and limitation game is used, the sequence would be as follows:

9:30—10:00 a.m. Introduction.

10:00—10:15 a.m. Arranging the participants into groups.

10:15—10:45 a.m. The group session with discussion (with observers) for 15 minutes, then reversing the group, with those discussing observing for 15 minutes.

10:45—11:30 a.m. Pairs working on talents and limitation sheets.

11:30—12:00 noon Back into the major groups with discussion and conclusion.

NOTE: Although the circle conflict game utilizing Diagram 10 could also fit into this morning session, it is not recommended unless the group has had previous and quite intense development together. To start a new group utilizing the circle game is more often than not too overwhelming for people who are not used to in-depth process.

ONE DAY CONFERENCE
AFTERNOON 2:00—5:00 p.m.

There are two alternatives we might suggest for completing an afternoon such as this:

1. The use of the art project in the completion of the three-day conference.

2. The use of creative alternative exercises as in the completion of the three-day conference—initial conference on page166 .

NOTE: It is not recommended that the evaluations be used for such a short period of time as this unless the group has been together on a continuous basis.

DYNAMICS AND SUGGESTED OUTCOMES:

2:00—5:00 p.m. The remarks here parallel those made in terms of the dynamics for the initial conference. The dynamics remarks for that conference should be read along with this. Generally, the dynamic of the conferences always begins with an activity that gets at "primary values"; that is, it gets at the issues of self-worth and valuing others. By enhancing self-worth, one reduces the anxiety of the participant in a way that allows him to talk more and get more into the subject matter with confidence. Since the nature of the advanced conference is to bring about a more in-depth relationship, the facilitator should be more aware of the possibilities that some people's emotional stability is not sufficient to undergo the degree of intimacy required in the conference. It is advisable to have a mental health consultant on call, at least. These exercises do not produce this difficulty in people, but no conference can protect itself completely from mentally unstable persons. One of the reasons for this is that many people of this nature gravitate to these kinds of conferences as a substitute for therapy, rather than facing their real problem.

The first evening, in our experience, usually does reduce people's anxiety and does start the conference off to moving toward a more in-depth understanding of one another. The grouping that evening allows people to initially meet one another; the pairing serves to reduce anxiety during the first evening, which may be high during the first group discussion with observers. As we move into the second day, the pairs remain together in order to boost one another and to keep the security factor high. At the same time, they are moved into different groups of six to increase the socialization of the total group. The idea is to build trust, intimacy and the feeling of community during this period, for the total group rather than one particular group. The leisure period is allowod and put in as a recreative period. In these conferences, more than the initial conferences, it is not *at all* recommended that you put in something extra in the afternoon. At most, you might want to run the conference in the morning and afternoon and have the evening off. The point is, never run the three units in one day, since that brings about a value imposition you might want to deal with by substituting one of the exercises on work and leisure in Section VI of this book.

It is our experience that if too many activities are scheduled in one day, the participant becomes tired, angry and ceases to learn. The recreative process, in our bias, is then necessary. However, quite apart from the bias of the authors in this area, the emotional and physical ability of the person should be considered.

The evening of the second day then capitalizes on the socializing of the total group by having an activity which involves the group as a whole. By this time, the group's anxiety should be reduced so that they can confront one another in the total group without too many difficulties. It should be pointed out that if you have a group of people who work together or have authority relationships between each other, the polarization game may become very slow if certain people have problems of expectations with other persons in the group. This often becomes a difficulty when groups who have high expectations of each other, such as groups of ministers or priests or teachers working in the same school system, are thrown together in this kind of situation. However, this activity works, but it does demand a certain amount of facility on the part of the leadership.

Having gone through this process, the group as a whole should be ready to experience the circle diagrams and conflicts on the morning of the third day. *This is an advanced activity*. The circle diagrams can be very helpful for persons at the end of this process but should not be considered as an initial activity and should not be dealt with by the facilitators unless they have had some experience with this beforehand. This will serve to deepen the process even more. It is for this reason that the collage or art project in the afternoon is essential. It is a way of dissipating the intimacy and preparing the people for the grief and reality of departure in the afternoon. By working on a project that can be largely non-verbal, they can be with each other in a leisurely activity but, at the same time, try to make self-evaluation and cognitive conclusions as to what they are doing.

Similar dynamics operate in the two-day conference, the difference being, of course, that the people are not together for such a long period and will, therefore, be engaged in less intense activity. For this reason, it is suggested that the new world game, rather than the circle game, be used on the second day, unless the group has had considerable experience with itself. However, such a decision would be up to the facilitators as they brainstorm at the beginning of the conference on what kind of project should be involved here. The main criterion for using the circle diagrams rather than the new world game is the nature of the participants.

As before, the final exercise is important as a means of departing and leaving one another in a spirit of creative learning rather than one of conflict. The one-day conference dynamics are a little different, in that you are building an atmosphere in a much shorter period of time. Since it is a short period of time, unless the group has been together long, the conflict game is not recommended. It is recommended, however, if there are people together who are professional, experienced in this kind of activity and are operating as participants. The reason for this recommendation is that the second game can cause deep emotional confrontation which doesn't have time to be dissipated over the short period of one day. However, when this is used in the three-day conference, much of the material confronted in a one-day conference has already been dealt with and, thus, works quite differently in the dynamics. Also, this kind of activity doesn't work well when people have not met one another before. Therefore, it is placed in here as a possibility, if the group knows one another and has had some kind of participation previously. If this is an initial conference, then the talent game is suggested. The new world game is a different activity related to a different value theory and works well as an initial conference, also.

Again, the afternoon is meant to be a conclusion—capitalizing, majoritively and reflectively, on the morning's experience.

SUGGESTED OUTCOMES FROM THIS CONFERENCE:

These should be in terms of the primary goals stated beforehand, minimally and optimally. One development might be (especially of the two- and three-day conference) that a community could build up, so that the people might demand further activities. The facilitators should be aware of this before they begin. This might be checked out and evaluated by handing out the evaluation sheets at the end, especially the group evaluation sheets. It is important, too, that in this kind of conference they have a mental health consultant on hand so that, if people do ask for counseling or further consultation afterward, it can be provided. Follow-up conferences should always be anticipated with this kind of intense encounter.

PREPARATION OF FACILITATORS:

As was previously recommended, facilitators should be

well prepared for this kind of conference. The best kind of recommendation we can make is that they go through their own kind of training conference previously. Since it may be totally unpractical for you to put your own facilitators through a three-day conference, it might be well to have several evenings where you cover all the experiences. Do not have your facilitators move into something like the three-day conference unless they have a clear understanding and are able to work with the groups and individuals on some of the activities. This is particularly true of the talent and limitation game and the circle diagrams. If you have doubts as to whether you can pull this off with your abilities, then we recommend you get a professional group consultant—possibly a psychologist—who has had a lot of experience with groups. If the consultant is an educator, he should have someone who has facility in handling emotional material and has no difficulty in dealing with people's feelings. Such a person's major qualifications should be clinical experience and ability. If you have doubt, you might check with organizations like National Training Laboratories, the American Association of Pastoral Counselors, or with a local psychology department, university or community mental health center.

CONFERENCE VARIATIONS AND DESIGN:

In the major part of this chapter we have tried to give you outlines for six conferences, two main conferences being the initial and the advanced three-day conference. However, in Section II of this book there are six divisions, each of which has up to ten exercises or activities within each division. Practically all the exercises and activities in Section II can be substituted as variables for different parts of the conference sections. That is, you can substitute any of those sections in a morning, afternoon or evening session. We consider that each session is to be one unit. However, it is important that you do not substitute any activity. Generally, we might consider that there are three kinds of activity you should look at when considering plans for your own conference:

1. Activities designed to begin a conference. These should be non-anxiety producing and should increase and help the socialization of the members as they begin their conference.

2. Activities that come in the center of a conference. These are activities that are neither conclusions nor initial beginners in the conference, but rather the matter in between. The sequence of such activities should always try to move beyond the depth of the initial activity in the first evening, to provide a dynamic of increased intimacy through the sessions. If one activity is much more simple than the one that preceded it, the group is likely to lose interest. It is unadvisable to start with a group session from a professional section in one of those in Part II of the book and then move to one of the activities in the teacher or student section. The reason for this is that each of the three levels is more intense than the other.

3. Finally, there should be a concluding session which again reduces anxiety and allows a sense of departing on the part of the people and time for reflection and discussion.

DESIGNING YOUR OWN CONFERENCE:

The conferences offered so far in this chapter have been tested out and generally have a continuing dynamic pattern. If conference design is new to you, we suggest that you utilize these first for experimentation. Next, you must try to design your own conference. The last word on whether you have had a good conference or not can only be tested by your own experience. The way to test your experience and to protect yourself majoritively is to make sure that you have had ample preparation time. We generally expect to spend as much time in preparation as the conference itself takes. Train your facilitators well and make sure they

go through all the experiences that they are going to put other people through. The facilitators must be much more aware and flexible than most of the participants they will be dealing with. Remember, academic qualifications or intellectual know-how are not the main qualifications in this kind of work, but rather clinical ability and flexibility. By clinical ability, we do not refer simply to psychology but to the whole process of the educator. The main issue is that a person should have ability to move with process and understand something about inductive learning and group dynamics. If these words or ideas are unknown to your facilitators, then this should be a part of their preparation.

In designing a conference, try to get the above principles involved in whatever activities you design. As you design the conference, set out the times and patterns very carefully, as they have been done in the format we have already given you. Make sure that each of your facilitators has a copy and that you have been over the details before the conference starts and that you have tested out the experiences with one another. At this point, let us move on to give some examples of the kind of activities that may be used and substituted for the three sections listed above—(1) beginning sessions, (2) interim sessions, (3) concluding sessions.

VARIATIONS IN DESIGNING YOUR OWN CONFERENCE:

First, in designing your own conference you can substitute most of the exercises from Sections I to VI in Part II of this book. In order to facilitate our discussion of this, we will repeat the six diagrams with the exercises from these chapters, as follows:

EXERCISES TO BEGIN A CONFERENCE

First of all, in each section the strategies become more intense as you move from student to teacher and to professional trainer in the above diagrams. To conduct an initial conference, there is the strategy used in the initial three-day conference earlier in this chapter. And for an advance conference there is one in the advanced conference, given earlier in this chapter. First thing, when designing a conference, is to get the facilitators together to discuss what information or goals you wish for the conference. If you want to have a conference that covers several areas like values, value-ranking, work and leisure, then, of course, you will have a selection. On the other hand, if you only want to cover one area, then you would stick to the strategies in that area. For example, if the conference was just to cover the nature of the value process, then you might only develop some of the strategies in Part II, Section I of the book. In a three-day conference, it is suggested that you try to go through several things. Therefore, for whatever conference design you make, these following suggestions are only meant as variations which will have to fit into whatever goal and purpose you have. If you are in doubt as to times and spaces, then we suggest you follow the general format indicated in the six conferences outlined. The following are suggested as beginning strategies, to help get a group started:

1. Strategies 1, 2, and 3 for students. Part II, Section I.

2. Advanced Conference: Exercise 1. Professional Trainer, Part II, Section I. This could be accompanied by a discussion of how celebration and act are related to value process.

3. Exercise 2, Teacher. Part II, Section III (The Value Shield). At this point, Exercises 1, 2, or 3, or a combination thereof. Students, Part II, Section V.

4. Exercise 1, Teacher. Part II, Section V.

VARIATIONS FOR SESSIONS IN A CONFERENCE, WHICH ARE NEITHER THE FIRST SESSION NOR LAST SESSION

Try not to conduct an exercise which is less powerful, following one that is more powerful. When this happens, the student often loses interest. For example, it would not be wise to have any of the student exercises following professional trainer or teacher exercises. It is better if the initial conference starts with student exercises, to continue with student exercises or to add exercises from the teacher section. As you go through the conference, it is better to have exercises from the teacher or professional trainer section. Remember, when giving a conference for training purposes, always make the conference deeper in its methodology than you expect the teachers to be able to accomplish themselves, for the reason that they must have a deeper experience than they will give the students. Combinations or set exercises for most of the strategies can be utilized through the rest of the conference. However, there are certain major exercises that we feel are well within conference design. These major exercises are listed above in the conferences. Variations of those exercises or other exercises which we would suggest for your first consideration as a part of a conference are:

1. Exercise 1, Student; Part II, Section I.
2. Exercises 1, 2 and 3, Part II, Section I.
3. Exercise 1, Professional Trainer; Part II, Section I.
4. Exercises 1 and 2, Teacher; Part II, Section II.
5. Exercises 1, 2 and 3, Teacher; Part II, Section III.
6. Exercises 1 and 2, Professional Trainer; Part II, Section III.
7. Exercise 2, Student; Part II, Section IV.
8. Exercises 1, 2 and 3, Teacher; Part II, Section IV.
9. Exercises 1, 2 and 3, Professional Trainer; Part II, Section IV.
10. Exercises 1 and 2, Teachers; Part II, Section VI.

11. Exercises 1 and 2, Student; Part II, Section VI.

12. Exercises 1 and 2, Professional Trainers; Part II, Section VI.

(Please note that some exercises have been left out.) Most of the exercises mentioned above can go over a period of time and can be extended between two and three hours. Other exercises which are much shorter can be combined or are much more appropriately used for examples in shorter situations such as lectures or one-hour presentations.

EXERCISES FOR COMPLETING AN EXPERIENCE:

1. We would suggest that the exercises used and given in the example conferences above (and variations which you might design) are good ways of ending conferences. In addition to these, you might consider some of the following exercises or variations thereof to finish a conference:

2. Exercise 2, Teacher; Part II, Section III. This can be concluded by a discussion of what a person or persons have learned in total conference with a sharing of the shield.

3. Exercise 2, Student; Part II, Section IV. This can be used as an exercise which involves people in a different way and with some kind of discussion and closure.

4. Exercise 3, Professional Trainer; Part II, Section IV. Such an exercise can conclude a conference with a report by each group on their conclusions.

5. Exercise 2 or 3, Teachers; Part II, Section V. Again, this should be concluded with some short evaluation of the conference.

6. Exercise 1, Professional Trainer; Part II, Section V. With concluding discussion.

DESIGNING YOUR OWN CONFERENCE

All these exercises can be used flexibly by your experimentation. There are hundreds of variations on these strategies. For example, take the talent and limitation exercise used at the advanced three-day conference; another variation is to remove the talent limitation sheet and continue the exercise by having the group report to one another what they heard, then have the final discussion on the place of listening and trust in communication and the development of values. Another variation is to go through the talent limitation sheet and have a 10-minute silence, with some music playing, while each partner fantasizes on the maximum potential of the other and reports that in the group.

Another example of a variation is in the new world game. We often find that people have a great deal of difficulty in defining the five words. A great variation here is to have the facilitators come up with a different set of words which people can define, or a smaller number of words or words around different subject matters. Another variation is to spend the whole morning on the defining of those words and their ranking, but with a final discussion on what this has meant to them in the process of value clarification.

To repeat, all of these exercises can be varied; time slots can be varied to suit the design you require for your training purposes or for your learning purposes—whatever your original goals and purposes are. The models set up here are to guide you in your initial development of conferences. If you are not sure, then start with the initial conference, design another initial conference and then move into the advanced conferences when you have more confidence or when you have a professional trainer with you. If you are used to group process then these strategies are offered as ideas for you to design your own conference. If you are in between, you might want to experiment with various strategies; we think you will find that after a period of time and a long period of experimentation, you will be able to design your own conferences. Remember, never conduct a conference on your own; always have facilitators, who are trained, to help you. We hope these experiences will be helpful and that the group experience and designs may produce new and creative ideas which will go far beyond the kind of strategies suggested in this book.

CONCLUSION AND THE USE OF OUTSIDE HELP:

In conclusion, we suggest that when in doubt you utilize professional consultants or speakers to give the input sessions or help with the conference itself. We have found, in our experience with many conferences, that professional facilitators are often badly used. The worst use of a professional facilitator is to pay him a large amount of money to come in and do the conference for you. When this happens, you are often no further trained than when he came. You are always dependent on other people. It is much better, therefore, if you're going to run a conference like this, to train yourself. First, get a group of facilitators and go through some of the rudimentary exercises, if you are not used to this kind of material. Secondly, you can employ professional consultants, psychologists, or professional educators, who have considerable experience in group process, to train your facilitators and yourself in some of these exercises. Such a person can then stand at the back as a consultant when you put on a major conference; he can be an observer of you. This way, money is well spent, you have been trained and you are preparing well for the future.

Another methodology is to have a professional psychologist, educator, or counselor present at the conferences (especially at the advanced conference) to be an observer to the process. If you are getting into national conferences or conferences that are advertised widely, then you want professional speakers and experts in the field for certain input. We suggest that you take the process seriously and have them add input for a short period of time. Then acting as consultants to the group, move around the group process as you have designed it, speaking to the participants and thus allowing them to use this professional person to his maximum. Often, highly paid speakers at a large conference come in, speak, and then leave; many participants thus lose possible benefit from such a person. Professional speakers often like to get involved in a process, rather than just speaking and leaving conference situations. There are, of course, many exceptions to this rule; you might want only a speaker, so we are commenting primarily on the kind of conference utilized above.

In conclusion, we hope that development of your conference will be a good one. We have not mentioned many of the exercises in the conference designed above; many of the short exercises can be used as experiences for short presentations to clubs or young people's groups. Many of you reading this book are often asked to give presentations of half an hour or an hour; you might consider utilizing some of these experiences in order to stimulate the evening by putting a little process into the content. In the next chapter, we shall deal more with the shorter exercises and some of the possibilities of group designs, utilization in the classroom or in small presentations such as one-time lectures.

PART IV

VALUE-CLARIFICATION STRATEGIES IN THE CLASSROOM

INTRODUCTION

The goal of this chapter is to deal with issues that will help the teacher use value clarification in the classroom. It is well to point out that a teacher may use the value-clarification approach in the classroom without giving a course in value clarification or even without explaining the basic concepts of value clarification. What is important is the process or the dynamic. These techniques help the students clarify their values even when they do not understand entirely what value indicators, ranking, primary values, or value clarification are all about as subject matter. In this chapter various techniques that can be used will be discussed as well as how curriculum may be developed from a value clarification viewpoint as a methodology.

I. GENERAL APPROACH TO VALUE CLARIFICATION IN THE CLASSROOM.

Value clarification techniques are readily adaptable to the classroom situation. It is true that the more complicated and in-depth exercises will not be able to be adequately carried out in a classroom that has only an approximately 45-to-60 minute period. However, most of the simple exercises in this book can easily be used in a classroom to help the students begin to clarify their own values.

Another resource for classroom techniques would be Raths, Harmin, and Simon's book *Values and Teaching*. The authors hope that by the time an individual has worked through the experiences in this book and has tried out various experiences with groups and in classrooms, that he will be able to capture the spirit of value clarification and begin to create his own exercises. In this regard, as you come to know your students and the particular situation that a class is in, you will be able to design exercises that actually fit your circumstances and the students with whom you are working. Exercises that you create to fit your students will be the best exercises.

Frequently, even when using one of the simpler exercises, you will find that the students will want more than one class session. It is often advisable to allow another class hour if students would like more time to work on the exercise that you have given them.

As you grow in your ability to understand the value-clarification process and have gained sufficient experience in the use of techniques, then spontaneously use them as the needs of the students manifest themselves to you. For example, a heated discussion over some social issue like race or even political elections may arise. This would be an opportunity to use a value-clarification technique, to design the exercise on the spot, and to work with the students in the resolution of this conflict. You might decide to use the value-clarification sheet, or you might role-play the situation to help clarify the values, or you might do a brainstorm ranking of all of the values that are being spoken of and then ask the students to rank and to clarify what their priorities are. The point is that once you have become comfortable with the value-clarification techniques and have experiences with them, then you will be able to be flexible in the use of them and to use these formats to help the students continue to grow. Let us review the exercises in this book by looking at the diagrams that follow.

PART 2—SECTION I
THE NATURE OF VALUE PROCESS

AUDIENCE	GOAL OF EXERCISE		STRATEGIES USED
STUDENT	To make the student aware of value process as consisting of:	CHOICE	1. 10 sets of 2 pictures are given to the students, each representing a choice. Questions around the interpretation of the choices lead to a discussion of the experience of choice.
		ACT	2. Questions are given on values operating in students' lives, followed by a discussion of how they acted on them.
		CELEBRATION	3. Exercises with sentence completions around prizes and value continuum on: celebration-unhappy with.
TEACHER	To make the teacher aware of value process in his/her own life and teaching as:	CHOICE	1. Value Test 1 and Value Test 2 compare choices made on continuums and in boxes. Discussion on the subject matter brings out the importance of choice.
		ACT	2. The teacher relates two major discussions in his/her life and how he/she acted on them. Discussion of the values present.
		CELEBRATION	3. Exercises in dyads on talents and limitations. The limitations are turned to potentials celebrated.
PROFESSIONAL TRAINER	To help the trainer become aware of value process and its more extensive implications in the teaching process in:	CHOICE	1. 20 sets of 2 pictures provide an exercise in choice and use of the imagination as a more in-depth look at alternatives as critical to development.
		ACT	2. Brainstorm on values. Discussion on how a value as a priority changes behavior.
		CELEBRATION	3. Exercise on talents and limitations. Emphasis on gaining skills in how limits are crucial to potential.

PART 2—SECTION II
VALUE-RANKING (Setting Priorities)

AUDIENCE	GOAL FOR EXERCISES	STRATEGIES USED
STUDENT	To make the student aware of value-ranking (priorities) as being the key to understanding behavior, especially polarity, conflict and imposition.	1. Brainstorming technique. Values are then chosen from a group list by each student and marked. Discussion of how each ranking describes behavior in groups of four. 2. Brainstorming technique on "My Most Important Values". An initial list is given to which they add. Four values are chosen and ranked. Discussion on imposition, opposite rankings, conflict and polarity. 3. Attentive discussion: Values as priorities in society.
TEACHER	1. To make the teacher aware of value-ranking as the key to behavior. 2. To make the teacher aware of imposition and conflict in the educational system.	1. Brainstorming on values of students, teachers, parents. Four values in each category are chosen, ranked, and compared for conflict and imposition. 2. Function, feelings, imagination and ideas are ranked and compared to behavior. Each person tries to give examples of experiences with persons of different rankings in the educational system, to illustrate imposition and conflict.
PROFESSIONAL TRAINER	1. To make the trainer aware of value-ranking as a process of choice, act and celebration. 2. To compare the difference between growth in choice of life priorities to imposition and conflict.	1. Hallmark Card Game. 2. Suggested brainstorm on new games and goals for those games. 3. Polarity Game.

PART 2—SECTION III
VALUE INDICATORS

AUDIENCE	*GOALS FOR EXERCISE*	*STRATEGUS USED*
STUDENT	*To help the student understand that much of what we do indicates what our values are. This should be considered helpful. It is a place of evaluation. Time and money are two excellent indicators in our society.*	*1. Value-versus-value indicators exercise.* *2. Students are asked to use Value Indicator Sheet 1 and discuss how money relates to values.* *3. Students are asked to use Value Indicator Sheet 2 and indicate on the chart what activities they put their time on. Rank the activities and discuss.*
TEACHER	*To help the teacher see that behavior and feelings and imagination are indicators of values. To help the teacher see the connection between behavior and time.*	*1. The teachers are asked to work on Value Indicator Sheet 3 on time, in small groups.* *2. Fantasy shield to relate imagination to values as a value indicator.* *3. Alternative: imagine the clock 100 years ago and 100 years in the future.*
PROFESSIONAL TRAINER	*To see the relationship between behavior, time and values as priorities. Behavior and time are seen as major value indicators.*	*1. Brainstorming technique to design their own value indicator sheets for different situations, using Value Indicator Sheet 5 as an example.* *2. Exercise using Value Indicator Sheets 6 and 7.*

PART 2—SECTION IV
VALUES AND ENVIRONMENT

AUDIENCE	GOALS FOR EXERCISE	STRATEGIES USED
STUDENT	*Work may be seen as modification of my environment. The goal here is to see how a modified environment affects a person's values or imposes values on him.*	*1. A section from "Life at the Bottom" is read. Students are grouped and asked to make a collage of the opposite environment and role-play a person's feelings in both situations.* *2. Ecological games.*
TEACHER	*To make the teacher aware of the relationship between values and space. Space here is understood as relationship between self, others and world.*	*1. Role-play of school board meeting.* *2. Role-play of teacher/parent/student conflict.* *3. Fantasy role-plays of polluted environment, with discussion of feelings and values.*
PROFESSIONAL TRAINER	*To make the trainer aware of priorities in environment, through institutions, administrators and culture.*	*1. Brainstorming the priority values in two cultures. Conflict role-play designed and acted out.* *2. Brainstorm on several value priorities and design role-play environment that would impose them.* *3. Design a freeing environment.*

PART 2—SECTION V
PRIMARY VALUES

AUDIENCE	GOAL FOR EXERCISE	STRATEGIES USED
STUDENT	*To make the student aware of the "value of self" and of "valuing others".*	*1. The Love Seat.* *2. The Infinite Bank.* *3. Students design own "self-worth and worth of others" exercise.*
TEACHER	*To reinforce the need to practice primary "values of self and others" in the classroom.*	*1. Buzz group. Stress on listening and sharing as measure of self "my abilities and limitations in showing primary values in the classroom".* *2. Exercises in group evaluation of a class using primary value measures.* *3. Teachers design own "self-worth and worth of others" exercises.*
PROFESSIONAL TRAINER	*To reinforce the awareness for the need of primary values for teachers and staff as a part of any teaching program, as well as in day-to-day life. Institutions need primary values as well as individuals.*	*1. Exercises in evaluation procedure to increase teacher confidence.* *2. Teacher training as an experience in primary values.* *3. Discussion: the problem of intimacy, trust and potential from limits.*

PART 2—SECTION VI
WORK AND LEISURE

AUDIENCE	*GOAL FOR EXERCISE*	*STRATEGIES USED*
STUDENT	*To help the student become aware of work and leisure in his/her own experience and as objective values.*	*1. Using Diagram 2 and 3, the student compares what work and leisure mean in society, with what they could mean.* *2. Relationship of values of work and leisure to time, utilizing Diagram 4.*
TEACHERS	*To provide the teacher with opportunities to view work and leisure as values, by examination of personal experience.*	*1. Exercise of value of work and leisure to time, utilizing Diagram 4. The teacher is then asked to design his/her own sheets reflecting on Diagram 2.* *2. Attitudes are compared in Diagram 5. Use of voting method and public interview. New list as continuum is designed.*
PROFESSIONAL TRAINERS	*To help the trainer design exercise sheets and value games to help students see work as positive value in relationship to leisure.*	*1. Continuum and juxtaposition box questions designed from Diagram 2.* *2. Role-play and public interview strategies planned around work and leisure.*

EXERCISES IN THE BOOK THAT CAN BE USED IN THE CLASSROOM WITHIN ANY GIVEN SUBJECT MATTER

In the book and through the exercises we have stressed continually the need for the teacher to develop his own exercises. That is, exercises that will apply particularly to his students rather than students in general. In this section, we are talking primarily about short exercises. Any exercises in the book, and especially those in the latter diagrams, could be used to substitute for any one class hour.

They may be used for a complete class time, for example, to bring the students closer together and increase their motivation in some given area. In such a case, it would not matter what the subject matter was. When there is better rapport between the students, they are more willing to learn. Another way of using value-clarifying techniques would be to use them at the beginning of any class for a short period of time just as a value methodology to increase the student's awareness of certain things about himself. Again, it would not be important what the subject matter of the class was. Obviously, if the class is in the area of humanities or social sciences, it would fit easier into the sequence of things. On the other hand, it should be noted that this would not necessarily be the case.

In addition to the above suggestions, there are types of exercises that can be used rapidly at the beginning of any class to increase the student's awareness of himself, to increase his ability to value—that is, to be able to see more alternatives, make choices and act on them. Such a valuing process is always necessary to the educational process. The ability to see alternatives, for example, is very important in science and mathematics.

Value techniques can be used rapidly in the classroom or even used partly at the beginning of one class and partly in another class. Examples from diagrams for you to consider for use in any class are:

1. Diagram, "The Nature of Value Process". Exercises under "Student" and "Choice". The exercise using the picture choice test. The exercise under "Choice" in the "Teacher" section. The exercise under "Act" for the "Professional Trainer" in the same diagram.

2. Diagram, "Value Ranking". Exercises 1 and 2 in the "Student" section. Shortened versions of exercises 1 and 2 in the "Teacher" section. Development of exercise 2 in the "Professional Trainer" section.

3. Diagram, "Value Indicators". Exercises 2 and 3 in the "Student" section. Exercises 1 and 2, which could be extended to the beginning of other class series or be used by having the student do them at home. This was found in the "Teacher" section. Exercise 1—the "Professional Trainer".

4. Diagram, "Values and Environment". Developments of exercises 1 and 2 under "Professional Trainer".

5. Diagram, "Primary Values". Exercises 1 and 2 in the

"Student" section. Exercise 1 cut down under "Teacher" section.

6. Diagram, "Work and Leisure". Cut down versions of exercises 1 and 2 under "Student" section. Exercise 2 for "Teacher". Development of exercises 1 and 2 for "Professional Trainer".

The above suggestions will give the teacher examples of continuums, use of voting techniques, use of time and money indicators, short group dynamic situations, brainstorming, and so on The point is that all these types of exercises can be used to enhance motivation, making students aware of their values in the classroom. The main thing is for you, the teacher, to try to utilize, test out and experiment with some of these techniques and then try to develop your own exercises. One way to do this is to ask the students to develop or experiment themselves and come up with their own games or suggestions that they could utilize in the classroom. The best way to get experience with this is first to go through some of the exercises suggested in the beginning of the book.

Next, let's look at some of the major technique formats that can be used in almost any situation.

II. TECHNIQUE FORMATS

In this section we will describe several techniques that have a general format and can readily be used in an infinite number of ways. In counter-distinction to a particular exercise that is set and can only be used for a unique and particular objective, these technique formats are universal, and they are formats that can be used in many different ways by only changing the specific content of the subject matter but keeping the same structural outlines of the format of the technique.

1. *Brainstorming:* Brainstorming is a very basic technique that can be used in many different ways in stimulating discussion, in clarifying values, and in being able to obtain data from the group. It is a creative process whereby the group tries to pool all of their resources rapidly. Brainstorming is a skill that should be learned. There are certain ingredients that are very important in order to have a successful brainstorming session.

In order to brainstorm, the teacher first must pick a topic. Let's say, for example, that the topic is "what kinds of things would you like to study when we're talking about history". The teacher now asks the students to call out words that come to their mind when the question is asked. No criticism is allowed of another person's words; no discussion is allowed. The idea of the game is simply to call out words that come to the person's mind. The idea is also to have all the students in the room participate by calling out something or other. It is also allowed for a person to call out words that other people have already mentioned. As the words are called, the teacher, or someone who is helping her, writes the words down on some brainstorming paper that may be on the walls or on a blackboard.

An innovation of brainstorming might be, once the words are on the wall, to ask students to pick out four or five of the priority words and put them in the order they think are the most important. In this way you can whittle down from many ideas what are the most important ideas in the group. In other words, brainstorming can be used in a number of ways. The words that go up are value indicators, and to help the student rank these in some order or to choose certain words puts them into a valuing process of making choices. It helps them to expose some of their thoughts and ideas to other students.

Another strategy is to write down what words they think are the most important on the board, "someone else." For example, we might have all the students put down the two words that they think are the most important to them and then to compare them and have a discussion on the different ideas, choices and interests that the students have. In order to avoid problems with brainstorming, you might consider the following points.

Begin the brainstorming session by describing brainstorming very simply.

a. The idea is for the group to pool all their resources and all of their thinking on a particular topic. This may take from 10 minutes to half an hour. For example, the first class of the year may well be entirely spent on brainstorming. What are the topics that are of interest for the students and what do they wish to learn that particular semester?

b. It must be emphasized to the students that the purpose of brainstorming is to gather as many ideas as possible. Quantity of ideas is what is asked for at first and not necessarily quality. The name of the game is that the students are not allowed to discuss an idea that has been suggested or even criticize an idea that has been offered. Both of these bog down the creative process of brainstorming.

c. Criticism will destroy the effectiveness of brainstorming. If a person disagrees he simply offers an opposite idea or word. Encourage the participants not to discuss or criticize but rather to feel completely free to suggest any idea that comes to them and also to feel free to build on the ideas expressed by others.

2. *Value-Ranking:* Ranking is a very basic and very important tool in value-clarification technique. Ranking is simply a forced choice among any number of items. For example, you might ask the students to rank the following sentences: "I use my free time to: (1) play, (2) study, (3) visit friends, (4) add another item for which you use your free time". Then ask the students to rank the four items according to the one which they like most to do. This helps the student begin to clarify which one of the items has greatest priority over the others.

A long-term approach to ranking would be to have the students keep a diary or catalog of the various value-rankings that they make throughout the semester. And then at some point in

the latter part of the year ask them to compare the rankings they have made at various times on the same subject. Ask them to describe how their behavior has changed on the basis of this change in the ranking of their values.

The opportunity may arise that when the students are in a heated discussion you can ask them to clarify what values they are talking about, what values are inherent in what they are saying, and then, for the various opinions in the group, to explicitly describe how their values are ranked in this particular area. Then it could be pointed out to the students how their difference in value-ranking is a source of conflict among them. (Please refer to the Exercises on Conflict and Value-Ranking.)

3. *A Value-Clarification Sheet:* Another beneficial format is that of a value-clarification sheet. This is simply to take a provocative statement from a book, or make up a statement that takes a very strong stand on a particular issue; then ask the students value-clarifying questions about the statement.

The format of the value-clarification sheet, as the example shows, usually begins with a paragraph or a statement made up from a book or article. The first question usually asks whether they agree or disagree with the statements and to explain why. Depending on the nature of the paragraph, the following questions may ask them to either define a particular term as they understand it or to make lists of (1) pros and cons, (2) lists of ways of doing whatever the topic is talking about, (3) questions that ask them to describe a situation they have been in that is the same or similar to the situation the quotation is talking about. (Please refer to the example given here in Volume II, Part IV, Diagram II.)

Give the value sheet to the students and let them individually spend 10-to-20 minutes filling it out, then discuss what they have decided about the issue that is being brought before them.

PART IV—DIAGRAM 2

VALUE SHEET ON WAR/PEACE
The January, 1972 issue of the Washington Newsletter of the Friends Committee on National Legislation reports on a study of the world's arms trade conducted by Stockholm's International Peace Research Institute and released in November, 1971. The study concludes that "the United States is the largest supplier of military equipment in the world, accounting for nearly half the world's total trade in weapons". We must now squarely face the fact that war is no longer tolerable for a Christian. We must speak out loudly and clearly, and repudiate war as an instrument of national policy. (From an editorial in America *2/19/72; and Bishop C. T. Dozier's Pastoral Letter, December, 1971.)*
1. Do you agree with the above statement? If not, change the statement so that you can agree. Explain why you agree or disagree.
2. Give your definition or description of a "peacemaker":
3. List 5 ways in which you have been a peacemaker:
4. List 5 living people you consider to be peacemakers:
5. List 5 new ways that you could be a peacemaker:

DIAGRAM 3

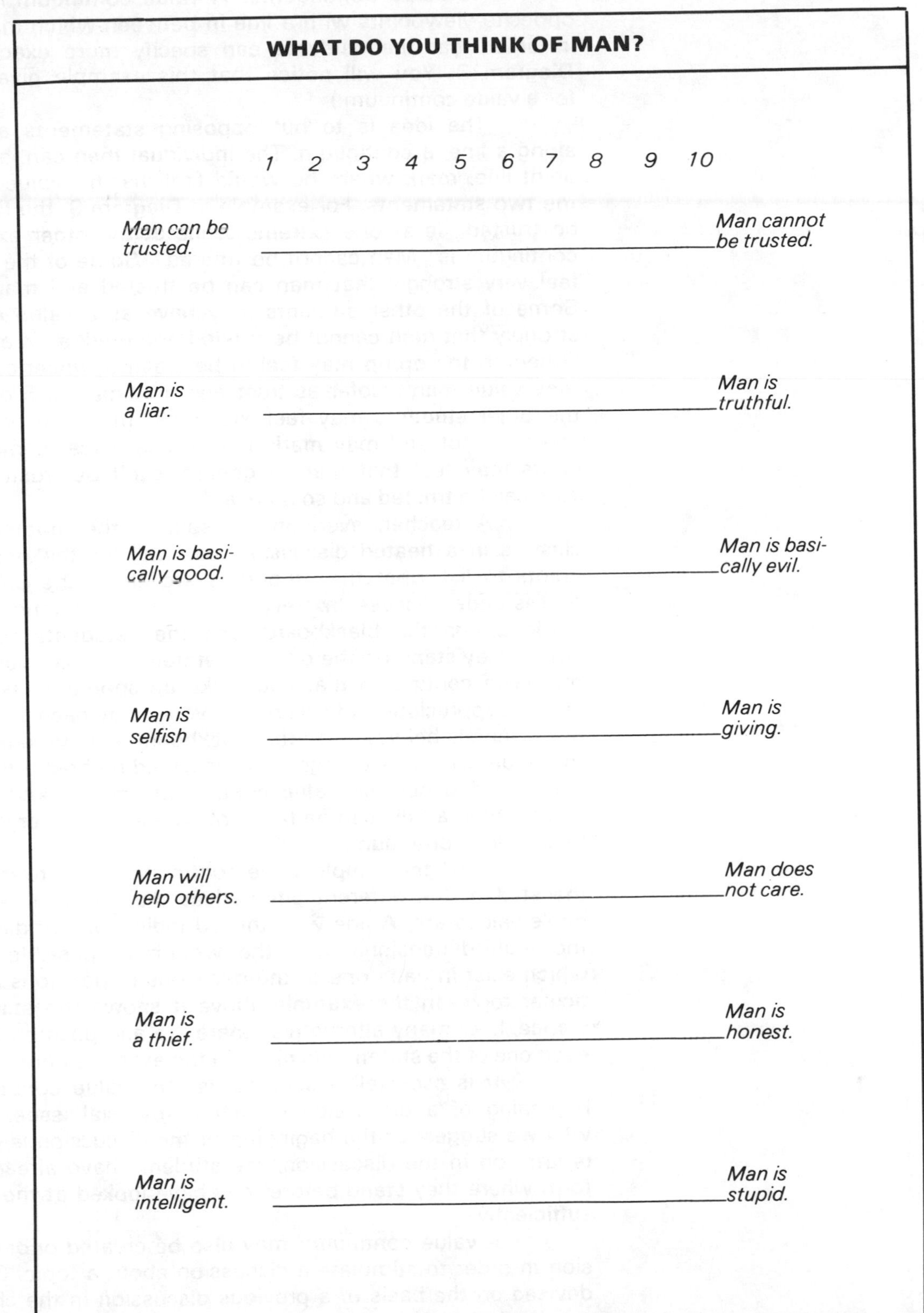

WHAT DO YOU THINK OF MAN?
1 2 3 4 5 6 7 8 9 10
Man can be trusted.
Man cannot be trusted.
Man is a liar.
Man is truthful.
Man is basically good.
Man is basically evil.
Man is selfish
Man is giving.
Man will help others.
Man does not care.
Man is a thief.
Man is honest.
Man is intelligent.
Man is stupid.

4. *Value Continuums:* A value continuum is merely two opposite viewpoints with a line in between which may be marked in order that the students can specify more exactly. (Refer to Diagram 3. You will notice that this example gives the format for a value continuum.)

The idea is to put opposing statements about a topic along a line, a continuum. The individual then can, along the ten-point line, mark where he would feel that his value lies between the two statements. For example in Diagram 3, the first "Man can be trusted" is at one extreme while at the other extreme of the continuum is "Man cannot be trusted". Some of the students will feel very strongly that man can be trusted and mark number 1. Some of the other students may have as a value and feel very strongly that man cannot be trusted and mark an X at number 10. Others in the group may feel in between or uncertain about how they value man insofar as trust and may mark a 5 or 6. Some of the other students may feel that most men can be trusted and some cannot and may mark a 3 or vice versa; some of the students may feel that man in general can't be trusted, but some men can be trusted and so mark a 7.

A teacher, even on the spur of the moment when the class is in a heated discussion, can call for the opposing viewpoints to list what their thoughts are about the particular topic that is under discussion. Very quickly a value continuum could be made up on the blackboard, and then students could call out where they stand on the different statements that were chosen for the value continuum that you make up spontaneously. The class gets an appreciation of where everyone is by each student's name or his initials being put on the blackboard as to where he stood on the issue. Or if it is a large class, it would be best if they wrote on a piece of paper the value continuum and marked it for themselves; then a tally can be taken of where most everyone is on the blackboard continuum.

What this simple value continuum helps to do is to show the student the different alternatives that exist in deciding what one's values are. A line with the 10 indications or degrees shows the multi-dimensional and the wealth of possible alternatives which exist in each one of the decisions or positions about a particular topic. In the example above it shows the student, for instance, how many alternatives there are and position of values for each one of the statements given in the example here.

It is especially useful to use the value continuum at the beginning of a discussion on a controversial issue. The reason why we suggest at the beginning of the discussion is because if it is later on in the discussion, the students have already begun to form where they stand before they have looked at the alternatives sufficiently.

A value continuum may also be created prior to a discussion in order to stimulate a discussion about a topic. Or it may be devised on the basis of a previous discussion in the class. For example, the students may well have gotten into a discussion about war and peace toward the end of the previous class, and so the teacher could come in the next class with a value continuum that would contain the various positions and values about the war and peace issue on a value continuum. The teacher then could immediately have the students, as individuals, mark where they would be on this value sheet.

5. *Case Analysis:* In the case analysis, it is important that the teacher or the students bring into the classroom some event or situation that they have either seen in the newspapers, have heard on radio or TV, or an actual event that has happened in their school or community. The role of the teacher in the case-analysis approach is to lead the discussion in a non-directive manner and also to be a resource person who asks questions and confronts the students with various points of the issue that they perhaps may overlook. The students' role is to discuss and analyze the case, to think of solutions to the situation, and hopefully in doing this to gain confidence in their ability to evaluate a situation. It is very important to have a timely situation to evaluate and, at the same time, a timely situation that is worth evaluating in order for the case-analysis approach to be successful.

The case-analysis approach will help the student to develop his own self-direction and personal commitment. As he works together with his fellow-peers and with some guidance and instruction from the teacher, he gradually learns how to think, react, and reflect upon situations in his life. In the beginning of using the case-analysis approach, the teacher may find a good deal of resistance on the part of the students who are used to receiving answers from their teachers. Some teachers fail here by being too non-directive. It is necessary for the students to be given sufficient structure so that they are able to cope with the situation.

Example of a Case Analysis:

Mark Stevens burns his draft card.

Mark Stevens, a nineteen-year-old graduate from Holmes High School, burned his draft card last night and has made the statement that he will refuse to go into the Selective Service. Mark was an honor student at Holmes High School and was also very active in the Scouts and had accomplished the honor of being an Eagle Scout. Mark's plans for the future were to become an electrician. He has spent the last two summers while in high school working as an apprentice to two electrical companies. When Mr. and Mrs. Clyde Stevens were interviewed concerning their son's decision to burn his draft card, they were shocked and did not realize that their son felt so strongly about the Selective Service system. Mark, in an interview, has said that he feels the war in Vietnam is an unjust war and one that he simply refuses to fight in. He made the statement: "If our world is going to continue to exist, then we must learn to live together in this world as brothers who are willing to help one another". (Confer Alfred H. Gorman. *Teachers and Learners, the Interactive Process of Educa-*

tion. Boston: Allyn and Bacon, Inc. 1969, pp. 109-119, on case analysis.)

6. *Role-Playing:* Role-playing is simply having the students take part in an actual situation and play out the situation as if they were acting it out on stage as a drama. When first beginning to use a role-playing situation, the teacher must structure the role-playing very carefully by focusing what the issue or event is that is to be role-played. In addition, the teacher must talk to each one of the "actors" and give them a feel for what their role is. For example, the teacher may have three students role-play a discipline problem at home concerning curfew time. One student is asked to play the role of the father and is given some directions to think over a few moments—thinking how his own father, perhaps, would respond to the situation of what the responsibilities are of a father to his son in regard to curfew and trying to really live that role and really be a father. Then the other student who is to play the mother is given similar directions with the emphasis of trying to put on the mentality of a mother in reference to a curfew. Then the student, who is given the role of playing the young son late for a curfew, is to reflect on the issues and the feelings that are involved when he is being called on the carpet by his parents. After that, the teacher may structure the situation by saying that it is 12:30—an hour and a half after curfew and you, the mother and father, are waiting now for the arrival of your son. The son comes in the door at 12:30 and the dialogue begins. Now begin the action by having the mother and father sitting, waiting for the son; the son comes through the door, approaches the parents and the dialogue begins.

Generally, students of today who have seen so much drama on TV and at the movies have no problems whatsoever in role-playing, especially once it has been done several times in the classroom and has been done well with the help of the teacher. Teachers need not feel that they must know a great deal about drama in order to have a good role-playing situation. The important point is to have a role-play on a very specific issue. This is suggested in order that there be a very definite focus to the role-playing so that the participants who are "acting" are able to live their parts. If there is not a specific issue and a definite focus, then there is too much diffusion, generality, and chaos for the role-play to be successful. Frequently, role-playing in the classroom can be a very exciting way to learn about one's self, other people and issues.

There are other formats that could be used in the classroom—for example, the voting technique or the interviewing technique, and the teacher may wish to explore these possibilities. We do not intend for our list here to be all inclusive, but these are the ones that the authors have found to be most helpful in the classroom situation. There are also many specific exercises that can be used to help bring out values. Today there are many resource books available that give games, exercises and simulations that would help bring out the values for the students. The works of Herbert Otto and the Human Potential exercises that he suggests are very helpful, insofar as the primary values of self-worth and worth of others are concerned. (Herbert A. Otto, *Group Methods To Actualize Human Potential,* Beverly Hills, California: Holistic Press, 1970, Howard R. Lewis and Dr. Harold S. Streitfeld, *Growth Games—How To Tune in Yourself, Your Family, Your Friends,* New York: Harcourt, Brace, Jovanovich, Inc., 1970, Raths, Harmin and Simon, *Values and Teaching,* Columbus, Ohio: Merrill, 1966.)

A NOTE ON GROUP ARRANGEMENTS IN THE CLASSROOM

In the inductive group process approach to value clarification it is extremely important, if at all possible, to have the group sitting in a circle instead of the traditional classroom situation. (Please confer Diagram 4, page 244.)

Notice in Diagram 4 that with the teacher in the traditional setting there may be two-way communication, but by the physical arrangement the two-way communication is between the student and the teacher only, even though the students can hear. Compare this to the other half of the diagram in which you see that in a circle there is a strong face to face two-way communication between all of the people in the group. Sitting the students in a circle is symbolic of the co-responsibility that they have in making their classroom and their education a success and is also an expression of the interdependence that hopefully has built up within the group.

Frequently throughout the book we have asked you to break a larger classroom up into smaller groups (especially when there are thirty or forty students). Break them in twos, fours, or eights, so that there is more personal contact and also so that there is sufficient "air time" for everyone to have an opportunity to express his views and to share his values as he is forming them. It is in the small groups of six and eight that the fruits of the value-clarification technique or exercise have their fullest catalytic effect.

To help a class get to know one another very quickly, it would be helpful for them to pair off in dyads and give them approximately 20 minutes to talk to one another. Then have each dyad choose another dyad and use another 20 minutes or the remainder of the class for these four people to get to know one another. The next class you might have quartets choose another quartet and give them an exercise—a simple exercise that they might get to know one another through working together on a project. Or you might simply give them time to talk to one another and to get to know one another. This is just another example of how groupings are very important to the group dynamic in value clarification.

DIAGRAM 4

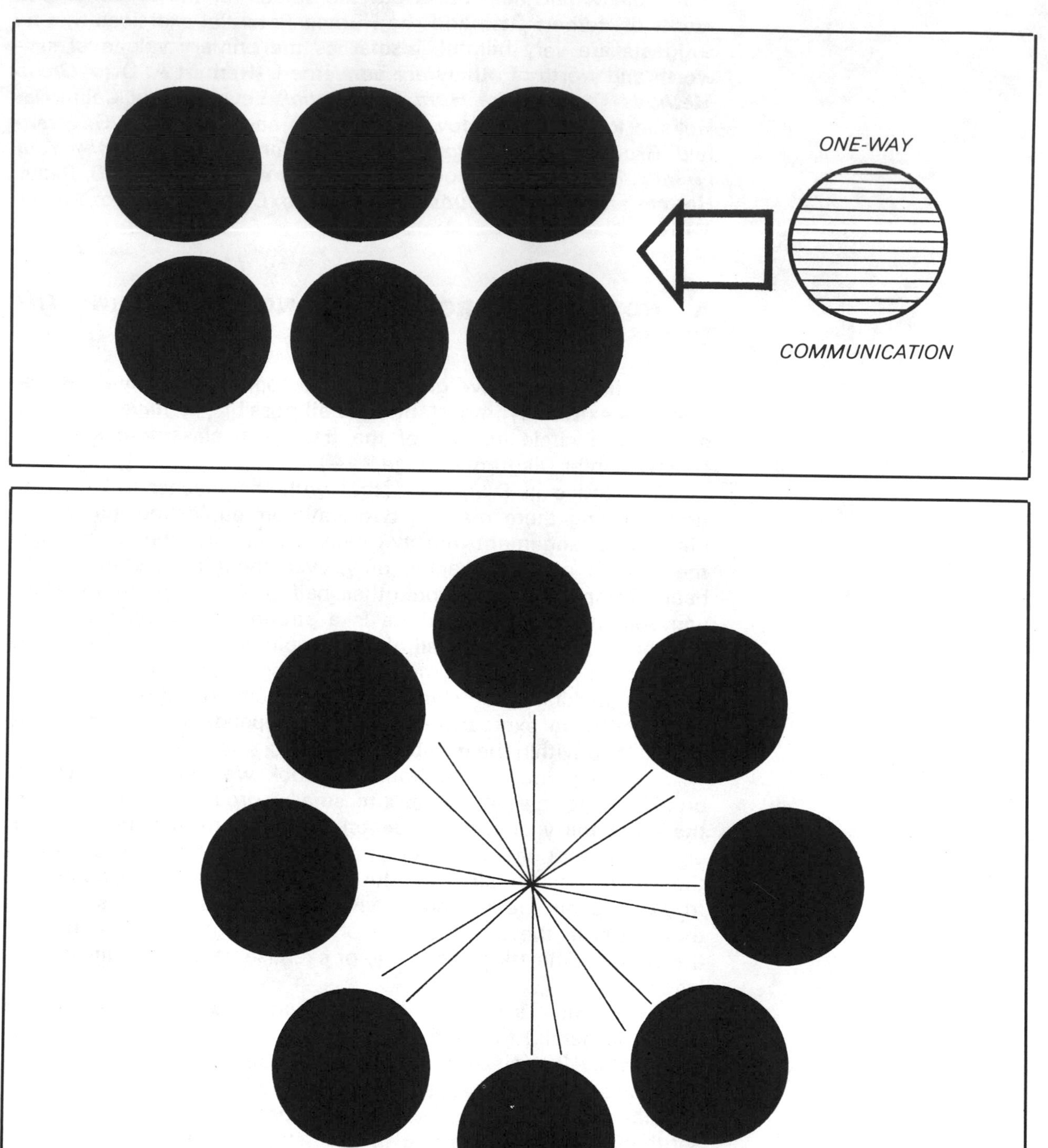
ONE-WAY
COMMUNICATION
TWO-WAY COMMUNICATION

Another helpful device in the classroom is if, for example, you have twenty-four students or thirty-two students, that you break the group up into eights and then have some group-on-groups for some of the exercises. What a group-on-group means is that one group of eight sits in a circle in the middle and the other group of eight sits on the outside of the circle as observers. This is especially very helpful when the teacher wants to work with the total group. You could have a group of eight whom you are working with in the center and then have the other two or three groups of eight sitting in the outside group as observers.

Another approach for some of the exercises is to have the students begin in small groups of four to eight and then before the class ends, using a seminar fashion, have one person from each of the groups report what is happening in his group. This helps the teacher see what are the value clarifications or learnings that the class had for that particular session.

THE USE OF CONTRACTS

The use of contracts should be mentioned at this point. The contract in teaching is an agreement that is made between the student and the teacher in regard to the student's learning. The point is that the student has the opportunity to choose subject matter, how hard he is going to work, his methodology for studying and so on. The teacher acts as a guide or consultant to the student. The point is that the student has a much greater opportunity to relate on a personal level with the teacher and as such can, if the teacher is willing, experience primary values through the love and concern of the teacher in a much more able manner. By choosing his own contract, by working out how or what he wants to learn, the student is involved very deeply in the valuing process. He makes choices from alternatives which the teacher should offer to him and give him guidance on. He should be guided so he is happy with the alternatives that he might choose and then act on them. What he acts on and the way he acts on those choices is the crux of the contractual agreement.

A contract may be made between an individual student and the teacher. The purpose of this contract would be for the student to define what his goal for learning is for that particular class. Some teachers pass out at the beginning of the semester a contract sheet that is already made up which would say, for example, that all the students who participate actively in the discussions and do their homework will receive a C. Those students who wish to obtain a B must do all of the work in C but also do two book reports in addition. Those students who wish to attain an A must do all the work of contract C and B and, in addition, also do a term paper on a topic that is listed in the contract. This particular contract is usually a very simple one and a very direct one—the teacher telling the student what is necessary to obtain a grade.

A variation of this contract is that under the listings for making a C, B or A, there are several options given by the teacher of book reports, autobiographical material, projects, exercises or term papers; the students may choose among several selections as to what they would want to do to attain the grade that they want.

Another variation on the use of the contract idea is for the student to submit a proposal of what he would like to learn and do, and to negotiate that with the teacher as to whether that would be sufficient for the grade he wishes and also would be in an area that would be considered mutually by the student and teacher to be an area worth studying.

The contract idea may also be used in relationship to a small group, as opposed to an individual. In other words, the teacher would allow the students to break up into small groups of four, six, or eight according to their choice; then the group may choose a particular topic or area that they wish to study, discuss, and write a group paper on, or perhaps do a role-play on, or make a presentation to the rest of the class on.

The teacher would meet with this group after they had formed themselves and had decided what project, or type of activity, or learning they wish to accomplish and negotiate with them why they had chosen the particular grouping that they are in and also what their reasons were for the particular topic they wished to learn about. The teacher, in negotiating with the group about a contract, would do well to make the guideline that the students do not have to tell the teacher why they came together or even why they want to work on a particular area. The point here is to give the responsibility for their learning to the students themselves. Also, this places the teacher in the rightful position of being a consultant or a resource person to the group and not the dictator of the group.

A CLASS EXPERIENCE

There are several contractual methodologies that we have experimented with in our own teaching situation. Some relate to the examples given above. One that I have found particularly effective within the structure of the classroom, rather than over the whole year in regard to grades or to study habits, is as follows: Instead of having a student working on his own on a particular subject matter—say a mathematical problom, or gathering of statistical information, I've had students group themselves within a classroom. This method works particularly well with adult students. That is to say, it should be remembered that the material in this book works for adults, college students, and the high school student in upper grades. The materials generally do not work with young people below the age of thirteen who require much more aesthetic exercises in their process.

The idea is for students to group themselves in the classroom around a particular project that may require input from several different areas. For example, in one class that I led a question was raised as to the balance of time between leisure and work within minority groups in our society. I had three experts from the community in which I was teaching visit the class. A lady came in who spoke on the attitudes of middle class compared with minority class women. Another person came in and talked about the need for success in some of the upcoming black families in our society.

The class then grouped itself in terms of projects. Generally, people were in groups of four or five. They were then asked, within the context of two or three class periods, to go to the library and research materials on the subject matter. They were to come up with two or three insightful discoveries in terms of their own experience about the balance of work and leisure in minority groups. It was suggested that the material they learned relate or tell them something about their own experience of the relationship of work to leisure. Each group then was asked to meet with the experts (those speakers mentioned earlier) and myself within a one-hour period to make a contractual agreement as to (1) what they would discuss, (2) the books that they would read, (3) the time period in which they would try to come to certain conclusions. The idea was that in the hour period, as they discussed what they were going to do, they would then come to the class leader or educational consultants who were sitting in the back of the room and just talk with them and test out whether they were in the right ball park or not.

Once the project had been decided upon they were then to come back at another class period in order to discuss their various insights. The idea was that each member of a group would study a different subject, and then they would come back and try to make some conclusions on the subject within the class period. The specific nature of the subject and how much time they would spend on that was a part of their original contractual agreement.

In the final class period we had twenty students grouped in groups of four and five who were discussing the conclusions of their material. Whenever they got stuck on their discussion or had some difficulty with it, they would then come to the faculty who were present and discuss with them some alternatives as to how they might solve the problem or what conclusions they could come up with. In other class periods that followed, each group then reported its insights. Some interesting things happened through this and might be illustrated as follows:

1. The students said they got to know the faculty at a more personal level and saw them as helpers rather than authority figures who were supposed to always have the right answer. They noted that often the faculty did not have the answer but in their experience were able to offer the students ways of finding their own answers.

2. The students, in contracting themselves for a certain amount of work, were better-motivated in their own opinion and were more enthusiastic about the subject matter. In making the choice that they were happy with, they were more willing to act on it.

3. Not in one single case did we have any student who did not complete the contract that he originally suggested. The reason was that if the contract originally seemed overburdensome then it was the role of the faculty member to reduce the contract and help the student set more realistic goals for himself. In this way frameworks of failure were avoided, and the student was able to feel his own success and to experience the value of self-worth.

The above comments are only some of the comments that were made but will perhaps help the reader see the benefits of studying the contract method as a teaching methodology that can be applied to any classroom situation. It is itself a value methodology. In addition to the contractual method, the value-clarification techniques can be introduced to the students in their small groups to help them facilitate what it is they're trying to do. If you have a group of four students who are trying to agree on what it is they should study, for example, in the area of the work and leisure aspects of minority groups, it would be very beneficial for a teacher to spend a few moments showing them a brainstorming technique. The teacher could say, "Why don't you put a piece of paper on the floor and just call out the words which cover the priorities that you think you should study and that you would be enthusiastic about looking at". The second point may be, once they have brainstormed, to take the foremost priority words and have each student research one of those areas. In this way a brainstorming technique could be used to facilitate the contractual movement as a valuing process in the group.

I'm not intending here to cover the nature of contractual teaching completely but just to suggest an additional methodology that works very well in the area of value clarification and is a clarification process in and of itself.

III. PEDAGOGICAL METHODOLOGY

What the authors have been providing in Volume I and Volume II is actually a new methodology—an education that will help students develop their value systems and enhance their personal growth by growing in the ability to choose and act according to the values that they themselves have chosen for their life. The methodology of using value clarification in conjunction with inductive group process is one that can be used within the classroom or school system and even in designing your own curriculum.

In the classroom situation a teacher who has familiarized himself with the methodology of value clarification can begin a class by exploring with the students what their learning goals are to be for that particular semester. The teacher can encourage the students to set learning goals for themselves and for their class.

In the beginning, students who are not familiar with this process might tend to resist because of their dependence; but once they have become used to the process they will readily begin to grow in maturity in regard to choosing their own life goals and their values. The teacher, in using the value-clarification approach, could begin a semester by having the students evaluate the textbook that is given for the particular course. The students themselves could choose which chapters of the book they were truly interested in, which chapters they were not interested in and wanted to throw out, and what topics they would want to include within the focus of that particular subject matter.

Within the semester the teacher could call for three or four evaluation quarters of time for the students to realign their educational and learning goals, according to what they have learned from the previous quarter. Concretely, what is meant here is that in the beginning the students, because they are not used to the process, may very well make up a rather superficial list of topics. If the teacher is true to his principles of respect for persons, responsibility to the students, and the students' taking responsibility for their own learning, then gradually the students will grow in this process. Then at a quarterly evaluation of what their learning goals are, the second list for that quarter should reflect the deeper concerns and interests of the students. In this way, the teacher is meeting the students where they are and providing the structure to help them move and grow in their learning ability as people. Today more and more teachers are aware of the inductive group process in general. This is certainly one of the skills that is necessary for the open classroom approach.

We are also suggesting that the methodology of value clarification in inductive group process may be used as a means of forming viable curriculum that is truly a help to the individual student, enhancing his personal growth and the knowledge of his life and the world he lives in. Especially is this important in reference to other cultures and to the minority groups that are in our society.

The point is that we are most normatively accustomed to certain textbooks or to utilizing curriculum that has been developed by different teams of people. More often than not, these books are very good and the curriculums are very well developed. However, any curriculum is written by people who have certain values and attitudes.

The teacher himself, in confronting a different class, is presenting them with his own values and attitudes. He may be under pressure from the system of the school to grade the students, for example. As a result, the idea of grades may become the goal of his teaching. That is, the student may pick up, "What we need to do is anything in order to get good grades". In this case grades, rather than learning, become the primary goal of the class. This, of course, is a reality that is happening in many of our schools. Criticism from people like Dr. Ivan Illich, as well as many other educators, points very strongly to the reality of how our school systems are often imposing value systems quite contrary to what we think education should be both through the teacher and the system.

As a part of this it should be clear that perhaps the teacher of the future would be a person who begins the classroom in a particular year not representing a curriculum or what he is going to teach, but rather presenting a methodology of exploration with the students, whereby they join in a venture to write and develop their own curriculum. I personally, for example, would feel as a white middle class American who was brought up majoritively in the United Kingdom, that I have no right to impose my values upon a group of black university students from a particular area, for instance, in Indianapolis. That is to say, as I teach a particular subject my methodologies, my way of doing it by its very nature imposes my values upon them. Especially if they like me, if they're dependent upon me and think I'm a good guy, then they're liable to pick up my values. What is wrong with that? Nothing, if I accept and understand teaching as a joint venture. The reality is a good teacher learns more from the students, often, than the students from the teacher.

By the choice of the very subject matter, by the choice of the text that I teach these students, I am forming values which may be good for them but, on the other hand, may not be the ones they are primarily interested in or which would be most helpful to them in their situation. Therefore, in the school of the future we may envision that the beginning of any class would be by the teacher-guide presenting his methodology and the students, with him in a joint venture, examining their values together and finding out where the areas of agreement and disagreement are. This kind of methodology, of course, would be primarily in the areas of the humanities and social sciences. This kind of methodology would not apply so much to those areas where persons go to a class to get a particular skill like mathematics or engineering, and so on, although it could apply to some degree in terms of what particular area they were going to take up.

Once they come to some agreement on their values, they might then in terms of what the subject matter was, utilizing the teacher as guide and consultant (who has had more training in this area) discover what particular areas of that subject matter would be more useful and helpful to them as students. They might research and look at certain authors and, in the process, would learn a great deal. They might discuss methodology. Finally, they might even design their own headings for curriculum which the teacher would then develop for their use.

Yes, of course, there are many problems with the kind of education suggested. It is just a dream—but a dream that maybe is already beginning to happen. For such a teacher-guide would have the skills to be able to discern when a student needed to make more mature decisions, when a student needed to work harder, when a student needed other kinds of help. In other words, such a methodology could work if teachers were trained in such a way to be able to deal with their students on a much more human level. That is, perhaps an equal stress on methodology in teaching, as well as subject matter as an area of knowledge, would be stressed. This, of course, is something that is happening so much in the training of public school teachers, but it is something almost unknown for teachers at universities and colleges, for example. Value clarification then might be a methodology, a pedagogy, or the contributor to the development of a pedagogy where teachers, as a part of their teaching, discover and design their own curriculum.

For example, we would envision that a team of experts who were well acquainted with inductive group process and the value-clarification program might well go into an area of a city and, through very careful listening to the words, the phrases, the attitudes of the people, be able to hear the underlying values that are in the language of the people. The process for the curriculum consultant would be to go into the area and listen very carefully,

to build trust with people and, in listening, to come to understand the underlying values that the people are enunciating; then, on the basis of these values, they develop a curriculum that helps these people to grow in the areas that *they* want and choose to grow in.

This is using a discovery approach to help clarify the values of the people who are to be taught and, also, to help the understanding and appreciation of the teacher for the minority groups that they are working with.

IV. CONCLUSION

It is the vision of the authors of this book that the value-clarification approach we are suggesting is a means and a structure to help bring about changes that we need in the world today, to help us learn to value and to live together, and also to help us choose conscientiously the direction that we wish our world to grow in. It has been our experience that people who have been involved in and have been exposed to such an approach have grown as persons and have often been able to learn to choose for themselves goals that give meaning to life for themselves.

There are many people today who place as a high value the human and spiritual values of the worth of the individual and of the importance of human relationship in community in our lives today. It is not a new thought to say that our world is becoming smaller and smaller and that we are living closer and closer to one another today. And so it is important that we grow in our own self-respect and self-dignity, in order that we might have respect and give due dignity to our fellowman.

It has always been the goal of education to help man use his highest qualities of intellect and will. In value clarification we hope to help the person learn to choose freely from alternatives the direction that his life is going. And we hope that, through value clarification and the inductive process, the persons will be encouraged to search out for themselves the knowledge and the abilities that they have as persons.

As the parable "Is it always right to be right?" says so well: *"They stated these beliefs in a declaration of interdependence. All men are created equal—but each develops in a unique way. All men are endowed with certain inalienable rights—but each must assume certain inalienable responsibilities. For the happiness of all depends on the commitment of each to support equality and difference, rights and responsibilities—to stop fighting long enough to listen—to learn—to try new approaches—to seek and test new relationships—and to keep at a task that never ends".* ("Is It Always Right to be Right", written by Warren H. Schmidt, King Screen Productions, 320 Aurora Avenue N., Seattle, Washington 98109.)

The Cambridge Encyclopedia of Japan is a richly illustrated introduction to Japan past and present. It charts the rise of Japan in the modern world, and analyses in non specialist language a culture and an economy that will grow still further in importance in the 21st century. Absorbing for the traveller or general reader and an essential reference source for business people, students and researchers, this book is packed with insights into a country still little understood in the West.

The Encyclopedia offers up-to-date information on every subject, from Japan's powerful banking and advertising industries to its ceramics and calligraphy, comic books and karaoke, the traditional arts of landscape gardening and the tea ceremony, and the modern love affair with gambling and golf. From Shintō shrines to capsule hotels, from traditional festivals and feudal shōguns to tattooed punks and supermarket robots, **The Cambridge Encyclopedia of Japan** provides hard information alongside a mass of vivid insights into the life of a nation.

Over fifty expert contributors explore Japan's climate and terrain, history, politics and economy, ties of family, company and society, language and literature, and arts and crafts. Full colour maps, graphics and photographs complement the text and illustrated panels are provided to highlight important issues.

Here, in a single volume for the first time, is a complete and convincing portrait of Japan–its rich inherited traditions, its modern complexities, its subtleties and vulgarities, and its central place on the world stage.

The Editors

Richard Bowring is an authority on the literature and language of Japan. He taught at Monash, Columbia and Princeton Universities before returning to Cambridge as Professor of Modern Japanese Studies in 1985. His other Cambridge books include *Murasaki Shikibu: The Tale of Genji* (1988) and *An Introduction to Modern Japanese* (1992, with Haruko Uryū Laurie).

Peter Kornicki specialises in the cultural history of Japan. He taught at the universities of Tasmania and Kyōto before coming to Cambridge in 1985 as Lecturer in Japanese. His other books include *The Reform of Fiction in Meiji Japan* (1982), *Japan* (1987) based on the Channel 4 television series of the same name, and *Early Japanese books in Cambridge University Library* (1991, with N. Hayashi).

Contributors: Helen Ballhatchet; Gina L. Barnes; Lawrence W. Beer; Frank Bennett; Carmen Blacker; Harold Bolitho; A. Boscaro; Richard Bowring; Jeffrey Broadbent; Karen L. Brock; Timothy T. Clark; William H. Coaldrake; Martin Collick; Martin Collcutt; Jenny Corbett; Gordon Daniels; Reinhard Drifte; Rupert Faulkner; Penelope Francks; Aurelia George; C. Andrew Gerstle; Roger Goodman; Ian Gow; Helen Hardacre; P. T. Harries; Joy Hendry; Irmela Hijiya-Kirschnereit; David W. Hughes; Janet Hunter; Masaru Kanbara; Sadafumi Kawato; Edward Barry Keehn; Peter Kornicki; Stephen S. Large; Sepp Linhart; Nicola Liscutin; James McMullen; Margaret Mehl; Mark Morris; Tessa Morris-Suzuki; Samuel C. Morse; I. J. Neary; Ian Nish; Gregor Paul; Brian Powell; John Pritchard; Gaye Rowley; Richard J. Samuels; Robert M. Spaulding; J. A. A. Stockwin; Bob Tadashi Wakabayashi; David Waterhouse; D. H. Whittaker; Richard Wiltshire.

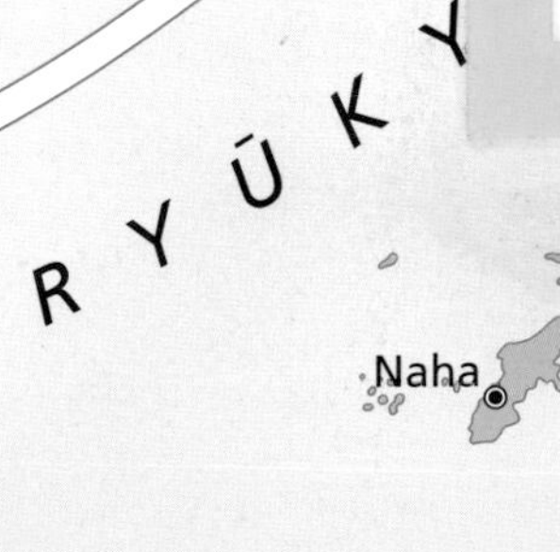

The Cambridge Encyclopedia of Japan

The Cambridge Encyclopedia of Japan

Editors Richard Bowring
PROFESSOR OF MODERN JAPANESE STUDIES
UNIVERSITY OF CAMBRIDGE

Peter Kornicki
LECTURER IN JAPANESE
UNIVERSITY OF CAMBRIDGE

CAMBRIDGE UNIVERSITY PRESS

Published by the Press Syndicate of the University of Cambridge
The Pitt Building, Trumpington Street, Cambridge CB2 1RP
40 West 20th Street, New York, NY 10011–4211, USA
10 Stamford Road, Oakleigh, Melbourne 3166, Australia

First published 1993

Printed in Italy by New Interlitho SpA, Milan
Typeset by Wyvern Typesetting, Bristol
Colour origination by Blackfriars, Norwich

A catalogue record for this book is available from the British Library

Library of Congress cataloguing in publication data available

ISBN 0 521 40352 9 hardback

Cambridge University Press acknowledges with gratitude the support of The Japan Foundation in the publication of this book

A CAMBRIDGE REFERENCE BOOK
Editor Peter Richards
Project development Christine Matthews, Susan Bowring
Design Dale Tomlinson
Maps Euromap Ltd
Illustrations Jones Sewell Associates
Picture research Paula Granados, Callie Kendall

Half-title illustration: war fan decorated with sun disc (Werner Forman Archive/L. J. Anderson Collection). Title: Nō mask on Japanese flag (Gary Gay/Image Bank). Opposite: court sword, Kazadachi; enamel and gilt, 18th century (Werner Forman Archive/Victoria and Albert Museum, London).

Pronunciation. Japanese is not difficult to pronounce: the vowels are more or less 'pure' as in Italian, the consonants more or less as in English. There is, however, a major distinction between short and long vowels: the latter have been marked with a macron, or line, over the vowel. Both ō sounds in Tōkyō are pronounced as in English 'ore' (without the final *r* sound), not as in English 'tow'.

Japanese names Japanese names are in Japanese order: family name followed by given name. In some cases you may find people being referred to by what looks like their personal name; in most of these cases this is in fact a pen-name or other sobriquet.

Contents

Geography

Physical structure *2*
Climate *7*
Vegetation and soils *13*
The sea *17*
Resources and environment *21*
People *25*
Country versus city *28*
Regions *32*

History

Early Japan *42*
The Nara period 710–94 *48*
The Heian period 794–1185 *53*
The medieval age *60*
Japan encounters the West *63*
The Tokugawa period *67*
The Meiji period *78*
From the First World War to the 1930s *88*
Japan at war *95*
Post-war Japan *106*

Language and literature

Language 114
Early literature 122
Heian literature 125
Medieval literature 130
Tokugawa literature 135
Modern literature 140

Thought and religion

Shintō and folk religion 152
Buddhism 158
Confucianism 165
Tokugawa sociopolitical thought 169
The new religions 175
Christianity 178
Modern intellectual currents 181

Arts and crafts

Pictorial art before 1600 186
Pictorial art from 1600 191
Sculpture 197
Architecture 201
Decorative arts 209
Dance 213
Music 216
Theatre 221
Film 226
The culture of tea 228
The culture of food 230

Society

The home and family 236
Minorities 241
Education 245
Working life 250
Health and welfare 255
Leisure 260
The media 265
Popular protest and citizens' movements 269
Crime and the law 273

Politics

The constitutional framework 280
How Japan is governed 284
The civil service 288
The judiciary 293
Parties and party politics 299
Elections and electioneering 305
Interest groups 309
Local government 313
Foreign policy 316
Defence 321

Economy

The post-war economy 328
Food and agriculture 333
Energy 340
Banking and finance 345
Manufacturing and services 348
Foreign trade 357
Transport and communications 363
Science and technology 369

GLOSSARY 375
FURTHER READING 377
INDEX 387

Contributors

AB Professor A. Boscaro
Università degli Studi di Venezia

AG Dr Aurelia George
University of New South Wales/Australian Defence Force Academy

BP Dr Brian Powell
University of Oxford

BTW Professor Bob Tadashi Wakabayashi
York University, Toronto

CAG Professor C. Andrew Gerstle
School of Oriental and African Studies, University of London

CB Dr Carmen Blacker
University of Cambridge

DBW Professor David Waterhouse
University of Toronto

DHW Dr D. H. Whittaker
University of Cambridge

DWH Dr David W. Hughes
School of Oriental and African Studies, University of London

EBK Edward Barry Keehn
University of Cambridge

FB Frank Bennett
School of Oriental and African Studies, University of London

GD Dr Gordon Daniels
University of Sheffield

GGR Gaye Rowley
University of Wales College of Cardiff

GLB Dr Gina L. Barnes
St John's College, Cambridge

GP Professor Dr Gregor Paul
Ōsaka City University

HB Professor Harold Bolitho
Harvard University

HH Professor Helen Hardacre
Harvard University

HJB Dr Helen Ballhatchet
Keiō University

IG Professor Ian Gow
University of Stirling

IH-K Professor Irmela Hijiya-Kirschnereit
Freie Universität, Berlin

IJM Dr James McMullen
University of Oxford

IJN Professor I. J. Neary
University of Essex

IN Professor Ian Nish
London School of Economics

JAAS Professor J. A. A. Stockwin
University of Oxford

JB Professor Jeffrey Broadbent
University of Minnesota

JC Dr Jenny Corbett
University of Oxford

JEH Dr Janet Hunter
London School of Economics

KLB Professor Karen L. Brock
Washington University, St Louis

LWB Professor Lawrence W. Beer
Lafayette College, Pennsylvania

MC Professor Martin Collcutt
Princeton University

MDM Dr Margaret Mehl
University of Cambridge

MK Professor Masaru Kanbara
Hokkaidō University

MM Dr Mark Morris
University of Cambridge

MVC Dr Martin Collick
University of Sheffield

NL Nicola Liscutin
University of Cambridge

PF Dr Penelope Francks
University of Leeds

PK Dr Peter Kornicki
University of Cambridge

PTH Dr P. T. Harries
University of Oxford

RB Professor Richard Bowring
University of Cambridge

RD Professor Reinhard Drifte
University of Newcastle upon Tyne

RFJF Dr Rupert Faulkner
Victoria and Albert Museum, London

RJG Dr Roger Goodman
University of Oxford

RJH Dr Joy Hendry
University of Stirling/Oxford Polytechnic

RJP Dr John Pritchard
King's College, University of London

RJS Professor Richard J. Samuels
Massachusetts Institute of Technology

RMS Professor Robert M. Spaulding
Oklahoma State University

RW Richard Wiltshire
School of Oriental and African Studies, University of London

SCM Professor Samuel C. Morse
Amherst College

SK Professor Sadafumi Kawato
Hokkaidō University

SL Professor Dr Sepp Linhart
Universität Wien

SSL Dr Stephen S. Large
University of Cambridge

TM-S Dr Tessa Morris-Suzuki
Australian National University

TTC Timothy T. Clark
British Museum, London

WHC Professor William H. Coaldrake
University of Melbourne

Preface

Why a whole encyclopedia devoted to Japan? Thirty years ago, the question might well have been asked in all seriousness, but today the need for more information about this country, its history and its people, must be obvious to all. The size and power of the Japanese economy is such that hardly anyone remains untouched by decisions made in Tōkyō, and there is every indication that this will continue to be the case for the foreseeable future. In a post-Soviet world, Japan has become if not a superpower then certainly the only major counter-balance to the United States and Europe, and the powerhouse of a dynamic Asian economic zone with high growth rates. Japan's presence will be increasingly felt as we move into the 21st century and in such a context it makes sense to find out as much as we can about how the Japanese think and work. For the first time in modern history, 'Westerners' in Europe and North America are being forced to come to terms with an entirely unfamiliar culture from a position of weakness. For those who assumed they were born to rule it is an unsettling prospect.

It would be a pity, however, if one were to approach Japan merely as an economic giant. Present realities can only ever be correctly understood in the light of history, which is why the reader will find here not only how Japan has managed to achieve so much in recent times but also what lies behind these achievements. This information should help to answer the question: what has Japan given to the world? Some might reply in terms of car production and high-quality electronics, but a wiser reply would include reference to literature, art, sculpture, architecture and ceramics. Without these many products of Japan's culture, the world would simply be that much poorer. The so-called 'miracle' of Japan's rise to great-power status in the late 19th century was astonishing indeed, but it was no miracle; it was based on a long tradition of impressive achievements in the past.

This encyclopedia, then, is designed to be the first port-of-call for anyone who wishes to know more about Japan and its history. It is distinguished from other works of a similar nature in that it presents information not in alphabetic or chronological form, but thematically. Topics are grouped in broad categories and in most cases the author of each topic has been allowed enough space to develop a coherent argument. The result is a series of self-contained essays on everything from early Japan to the use of robots, and each topic has been handled by an expert in the field. The reader is therefore encouraged to dip into the book at any point and to refer to the section on 'Further reading' at the end of the encyclopedia for more detail.

Care has been taken to make the encyclopedia as up-to-date as possible. Although we have tried to make allowance for all the continuing political upheavals that have changed the map of Europe and Asia in recent years, the statistical data available to us have often not reflected these changes; it has therefore been impossible to avoid reference to East Germany and the USSR, for example, in figures and charts. These names also appear, of course, in historical contexts. In order not to clutter an already busy text with too many typefaces, Japanese words have, as a rule, only been italicized if they do not occur in Chamber's *English dictionary*. A glossary contains a number of Japanese terms that are difficult to translate but also difficult to do without.

It will be seen from the list of contributors that many scholars were involved in the production of this book. We are grateful for the forbearance of all who agreed to write for us, only to find that the word limit was long enough to make one think but, by the same token, painfully short. We are also grateful to those who have spared no pains in ensuring that the visual impact of the book measures up to the exacting standards of its subject.

Richard Bowring
Peter Kornicki

Geography

Physical structure

The Japanese archipelago is located in the north-western corner of the Pacific Basin, with a latitudinal extent of 25° from Okinotori Island (20° 25'N) in the Ogasawaras to the northern tip of Russian occupied Etorofu (45° 33'N) near Hokkaidō, and a longitudinal span of 31° from Yonakuni Island (122° 56'E) in the Ryūkyūs to isolated Minamitori Island (153° 58'E), far away in the Pacific. In all it contains well over a thousand islands, with a total area (including the disputed northern islands) of around 378,000 km^2, (or half as much again as the area of the United Kingdom), more than 95% of which is made up of just the four main islands of Honshū (227,000 km^2), Hokkaidō (78,000 km^2), Kyūshū (37,000 km^2) and Shikoku (18,000 km^2).

Previous page *A river valley near Kamikōchi, high in the Japan Alps*

Tectonic structure

The origins of this archipelago can be attributed to the chance intersection of four tectonic plates: the Pacific Plate underlying the Western Pacific, the Amurian Plate beneath the Eurasian land mass and the Sea of Japan, the Sea of Okhotsk Plate to the north (sometimes described in combination with the Amurian Plate as the Eurasian Plate), and the Philippines Plate to the south. New land has been created wherever these plates collide, through warping and uplifting of the earth's crust, through granitic intrusions and, most spectacularly, through a level of volcanic activity unrivalled in scale at any other place on earth. Japan has dozens of active volcanoes, and many more remain dormant. There are countless geysers and hot springs, and up to a thousand earthquakes are experienced each year.

The tectonic plates have influenced both the shape of the archipelago and its physical structure. The lines of collision between the plates are marked by a succession of deep ocean trenches located to the east of Hokkaidō, Northern Honshū, the Ogasawaras and the Ryūkyūs. Here the ocean bed slides beneath lighter rocks, in an intermittent process revealed at the surface by earthquakes and associated tidal waves (or *tsunami*). Deep beneath the three western plates the friction of this movement melts the surrounding crust, which eventually spews forth from the volcanoes that form the backbone of Japan.

Japan and Asia

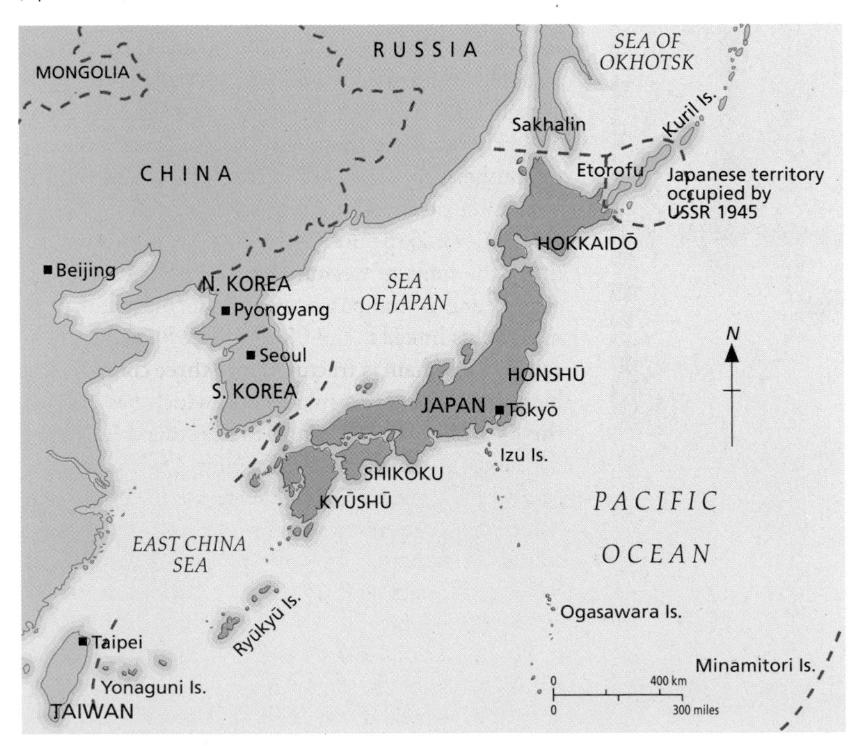

Mountains

Japan's mountains can be described in terms of six structural arcs and three nodes defined where these arcs intersect. In the centre is the Chūbu Node, where the volcanic arcs of north-eastern and south-western Honshū converge with the Bonin Arc of the Ogasawaras and Izu. The loftiest mountain ranges in the archipelago are here, including the Kantō, Hida, Kiso and Akaishi Mountains, as well as a great structural depression called the Fossa Magna, and within that depression Japan's highest mountain of all, at 3,776 m the near-perfect ash cone of Mt Fuji.

From this central node the South-western Arc leads towards Kyūshū and the North-eastern Arc through the Tōhoku District into the Ōshima Peninsula of southern Hokkaidō. These arcs divide the country into 'inner' (facing the Japan Sea) and 'outer' zones. The North-eastern Arc consists of three parallel ranges separated by a series of structural basins. The Ōu range in the centre forms the backbone of the Tōhoku District, and is capped by a chain of active and dormant volcanoes which includes (from the

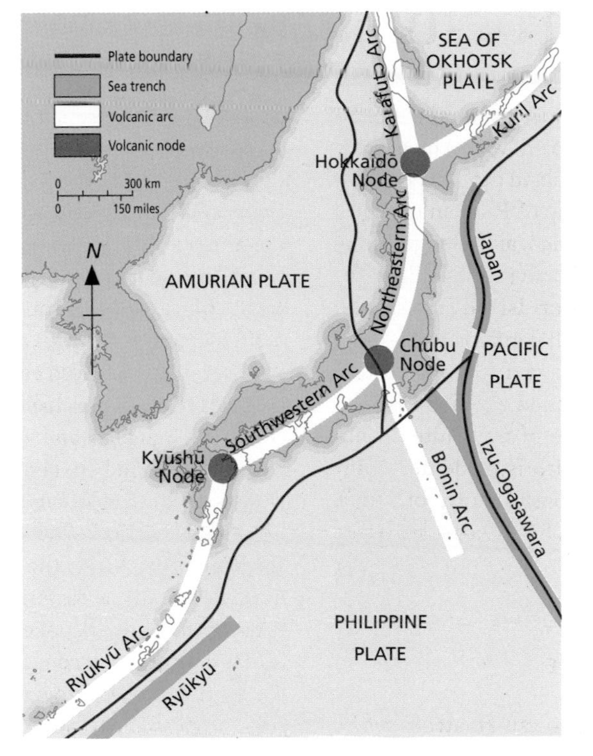

Generalized tectonic and physical structure

Below *The Hidaka range in south-eastern Hokkaidō. Spectacular ranges like these are common throughout Japan.*

south) Mts Asama, Bandai, Zaō, Iwate, Hakkōda and, on Hokkaidō's 'volcano bay', Mt Komabatake. There is also the spectacular beauty of the caldera within which Lake Towada sits, at the northern end of Honshū. To the east the mountains are split into two blocks by Sendai Bay, with the tough crystalline Abukuma Plateau to the south and the ancient sedimentary rocks of the Kitakami Highlands to the north. In the west, the Dewa mountains form a discontinuous chain sliced through by rivers which are fed by meltwaters from the Ōu range, and here too are several massive volcanoes, including Mts Iide, Gassan and Chōkai.

Hokkaidō north and east of the Ōshima Peninsula is given shape by two other structural lineaments, formed beyond the lines where the Sea of Okhotsk Plate intersects the Pacific and Amurian Plates. The Karafuto Arc runs south through Sakhalin Island to form the Kitami–Hidaka range, and meets the Chishima ranges of the Kuril Arc, which sweep in from the north-east, at the Hokkaidō Node in the Daisetsuzan range. In other latitudes these arcs would be natural stepping stones to the continental land mass, but here they lead nowhere but to an inhospitable corner of Russia.

South-west of the Chūbu Node, much of the land is formed of older sedimentary rocks and granite intrusions. The major break lies not through the middle of Honshū, but rather along a major fault system known as the Median Dislocation Line, which abruptly divides a fragmented outer zone, made up of southern Kyūshū, southern Shikoku and the Kii Peninsula of Honshū, from the inner zone of the Inland Sea and the South-western Arc of mountains down the spine of western Honshū (Chūgoku). The outer zone is composed of a chain of young fold mountains linked to the Chūbu Node by the Akaishi range. This chain is fractured into three components by local faulting and subsidence, which has created the two main lines of access to the Inland Sea from the south – the Naruto and Hōyo Straits. To the north of the Inland Sea, which is a zone of general subsidence, the mountains do not conform to particular lineaments, but are composed instead of blocks, plateaux and associated basins caused by extensive faulting.

The mountains of the South-western Arc meet the Ryūkyū Arc at the Kyūshū Node, the third great point of articulation in Japan's physical structure,

Craters of extinct volcanoes such as this one in Hokkaidō abound, but active volcanoes are also equally prevalent.

and one marked by intense volcanic activity – the Aso caldera and Mt Unzen are the best known sites. The Ryūkyū Arc lies beyond the junction between the Philippine and Amurian Plates, and gives convenient access to China and south-east Asia beyond, an important factor in the historical evolution of Japan's relationship with the outside world. The other natural route to and from Japan is across the narrow Tsushima straits, to Korea, Manchuria and northern China.

Plains and rivers

To this complex mountain framework, nature has added habitable land almost as an afterthought. Inland between the mountain ranges there are natural structural basins, some broad and continuous, such as the tectonic corridor followed by the Abukuma and Kitakami Rivers through Tōhoku, or the peculiarly rectangular basins within which Kyōto and Lake Biwa are found, others small and fragmented, such as the isolated basins between the Ōu and Dewa ranges. The continental shelf is generally quite narrow, and around much of the coast the mountains fall away abruptly to the sea. For the bulk of their habitable land the Japanese must thank climatic factors, and especially heavy rainfall which, in combination with rapid uplifting and an ample supply of unconsolidated volcanic debris, has ensured active deposition of alluvial debris wherever mountain streams disgorge themselves. The heavier materials are deposited first, creating the fans of stone, gravel and degraded alluvium (diluvium) which flank the mountains, followed in turn by the finer materials which blanket the downstream parts of the alluvial plains. The same pattern is repeated at right angles from the rivers, with the coarser materials forming natural levees which raise many of Japan's rivers above the level of the surrounding plains. This minor topographical fact has proved of major cultural significance, for it has permitted the widespread adoption of gravity-fed irrigation in rice cultivation, relegating dry field crops to the diluvial fans and terraces.

Most of Japan's flat land is located around the coast, and is broken up by local mountain barriers into isolated plains, of which the largest, and by far the most important in economic terms, is the Kantō Plain, with an area of some 13,000 km^2. The Kantō accommodates a quarter of the entire population of Japan and two of the largest cities, Tōkyō and Yokohama. Like most Japanese plains, the Kantō is ringed by a belt of diluvial terrace land, which gives way around the flanks of shallow Tōkyō Bay to finer alluvium, the continuing supply of which affords an abundance of material for extensive land reclamation works, but guarantees difficulties in keeping the main harbour waterways open. Other important plains to the west of the Kantō include the Nōbi Plain, located at the head of Ise Bay and commanded by the city of Nagoya, and the Kinki Plain at the eastern end of the Inland Sea, with Ōsaka at its seaward end. To the north the largest plains are to be found around Sendai and on Hokkaidō – particularly the Ishikari and Tokachi Plains, the latter retaining a far more rural aspect than any other major plain in Japan, thanks to its remoteness and cool climate. Note that each of these major plains is located on the Pacific Coast side of the country: by comparison, large plains are few in number along the Japan Sea Coast, the most important being the Niigata Plain.

The distribution and size of Japan's plains is a function of the debris load supplied by local rivers and streams and the peculiarities of local physiography, which determine whether the debris will accumulate

Three stages in the life of Japanese rivers: the Ginga Falls in Hokkaidō, the Azusa River in the Japan Alps, and the flood plain of the Shinano River in Niigata Prefecture.

at the seaward margin or be swept away. Physiography itself however is influenced by changes in the relative levels of land and sea, as caused both by global fluctuations in sea level, related to changes in global temperatures during and since the ice ages, by regional structural changes, including the continuing and general uplift of the land surface, and by local structural changes, especially the shifting of mountain blocks along fault lines.

As in many other parts of the world, these processes have left their mark on the landscape for the discerning eye to detect, not just in the form of obvious glacial features in the highest parts of the central mountain ranges, but also in the prevalence of wave-cut marine platforms. These are to be found not only along the present coastline, but also further inland and at higher altitudes, for the original smooth landscape may still be perceived, despite heavy subsequent incision, in the uniform heights of neighbouring peaks, other of course than where volcanoes have recently emerged.

At a more local scale, crustal movements have created a complex patchwork of submerged and emergent coastlines, with the former more common in the west, and especially around the margins of the Inland Sea, which is itself made up of five structural basins, and the latter in the north and east. There are however many exceptions to this rule, perhaps the best known being the Sanriku coast of eastern Tōhoku, where the Kitakami Highlands meet the Pacific Ocean in a picturesque sequence of drowned valleys, or rias, and tiny bayhead plains now designated as a national park. As for the effect of local faulting, a general distinction can be made between Inner Japan, where fault lines tend to run parallel to the coast, and Outer Japan, where faults tend to intersect the coast at angles. The result is a smooth coast on the Japan Sea side, with long stretches of dunes and saltwater lagoons created through a combination of longshore drift and heavy inputs of debris from local rivers, and a complicated sequence of major bays and inlets on the Pacific coast. Once again, however, there are notable exceptions, such as the relatively smooth coastline between Tōkyō Bay and the Sanriku rias, and the deeply indented coast of western Kyūshū, where a complicated fault pattern and associated subsidence have created large indentations such as Ariake Bay, as well as a plethora of offshore islands.

Overall, the combination of active mountain building and heavy precipitation has given Japan a distinctive landscape, in which few people live far either from the sea or from high mountains, and in which habitation is confined to small and isolated plains, once linked chiefly by the sea itself, but more recently joined by a sequence of notable engineering achievements: the spans which together make up the Seto Ōhashi Bridge across the Inland Sea, and the Seikan Tunnel linking Hokkaidō with Honshū being only the latest examples. Away from the coast, the plains and basins give way abruptly to ranges of forest-clad mountains which have been deeply and intricately dissected, like the veins on a leaf, and are topped in the distance by snow-clad peaks frequently hidden by clouds, Their steep slopes betray both their volcanic origin and the unconsolidated material of which they have been made. RW

The Inland Sea at dawn

Japan from space

This Landsat-C image of the Kōbe–Ōsaka–Kyōto conurbation shows very clearly the contrast between intense urbanization (blue) and steep mountainous wooded terrain (red). In the past it was usually easier to travel long distances by sea, and even today movement on land is essentially restricted to a few well-defined corridors. Pressure on cultivatable land is intense. Ōsaka lies at the centre at the head of the bay, merging imperceptibly on its western borders with Kōbe, which is squeezed in between the mountains and the sea. Kyōto lies northeast of Ōsaka, surrounded by high ground on three sides and divided off from Lake Biwa to its northeast by a narrow strip of hills. RB

Japan north to south

It often surprises visitors from northern Europe how hot Tōkyō is in the summer but, as this superimposition shows, Tōkyō lies in fact just above 35°N. Those living on the eastern seaboard of the US will be less surprised at the range of temperatures in Japan throughout the year.

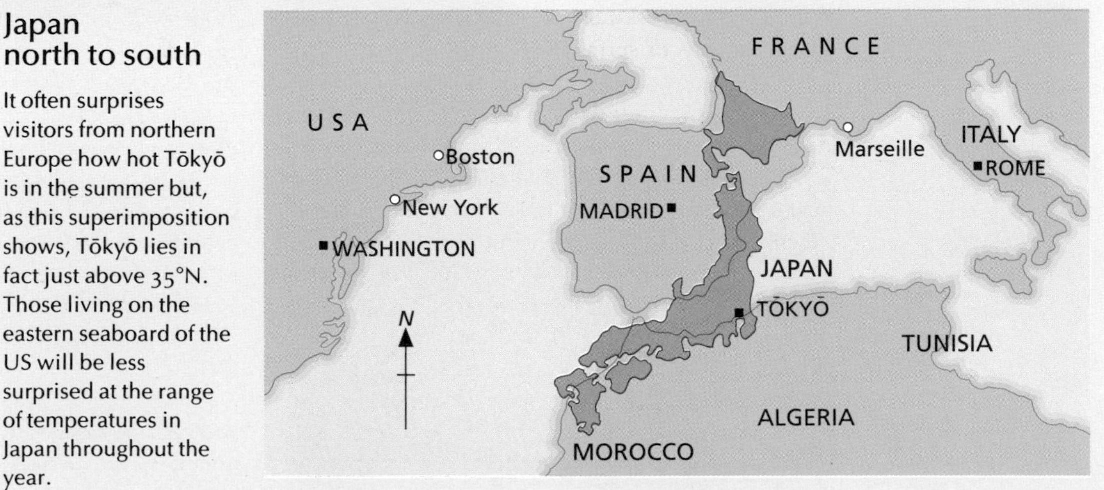

Climate

The climate of Japan is distinguished by its humidity and marked seasonal changes, both of which are consequences of the country's location along the eastern seaboard of a great land mass. The overall climatic conditions are determined by the general circulation of the atmosphere, as modified by the configuration of land and sea and associated air masses, and by latitude; while more local variations are closely related to variations in altitude and aspect, and to the distribution of currents in the waters surrounding Japan. The broad features of Japan's climate are consistent from year to year, but there can be marked variations in detail over comparatively short distances, resulting in a complex geographical distribution of rainfall and temperature patterns.

In Japan as in the rest of East Asia, a key climatic determinant is the interaction between the sea and the land, manifested in the monsoonal pattern of air streams. In winter the cold north-westerly monsoon dominates, while in summer Japan is embraced by the warm moist air of the south-easterlies. In between there are four transitional seasons; a long spring, a short autumn and, either side of midsummer, two rainy seasons, the *baiu* and *shūrin*, which mark the advance and retreat across Japan of the boundary between the dominant air masses.

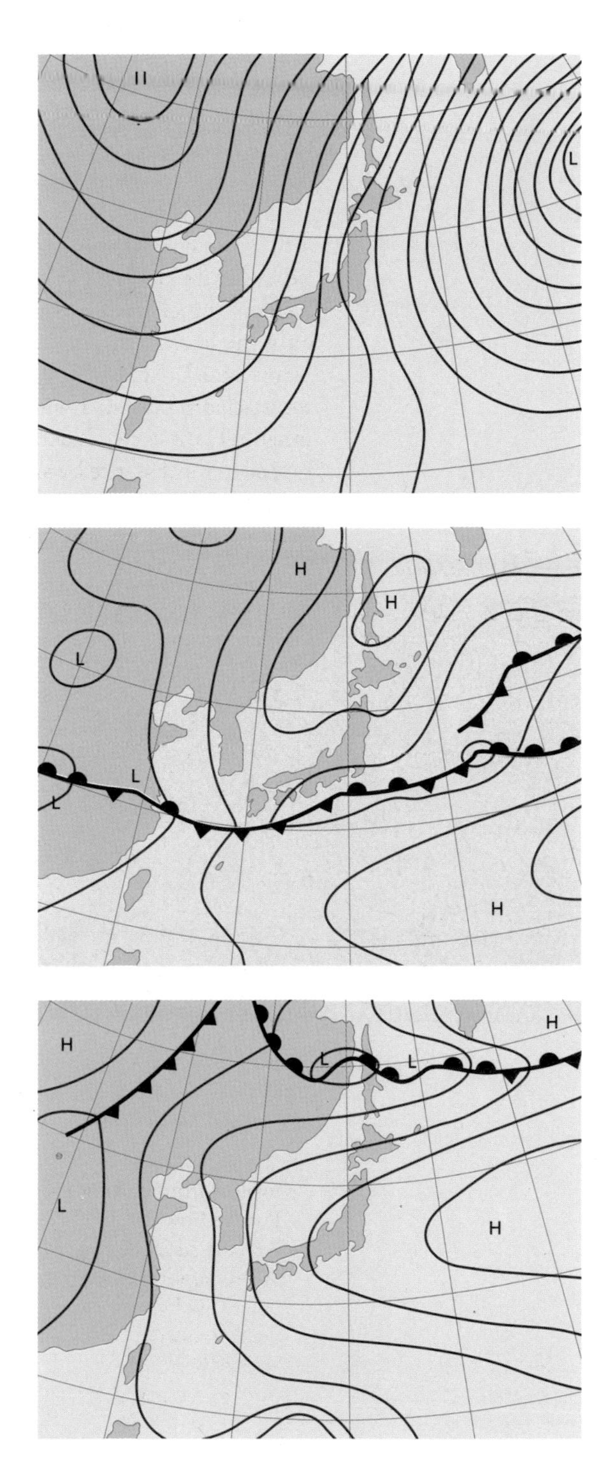

Right *Typical surface pressure patterns. In order from the top: winter monsoon,* baiu *(rainy season) and summer monsoon types.*

Winter

Winter sets in across most of Japan in late November, and gives way to spring in mid to late February, depending on latitude. During this season an intense and stable pool of cold dry air known as the Siberian High builds up across continental Asia. Part of this air seeps eastwards from the interior towards a zone of low pressure (the Aleutian Low) which covers the North Pacific. These north-westerly monsoon winds traverse the Japan Sea before reaching the islands, and in transit the air they contain is modified at lower altitudes through contact with the surface of the sea. The sea imparts both moisture and heat – not enough heat to make the winds feel other than bitter when they reach the coast of Japan, but more than enough to make the air unstable. This instability causes the formation of convection clouds, which are supplemented by the effect of the mountainous terrain to give heavy snowfall in areas exposed to the west.

Snowfall is heaviest in areas of strong relief which

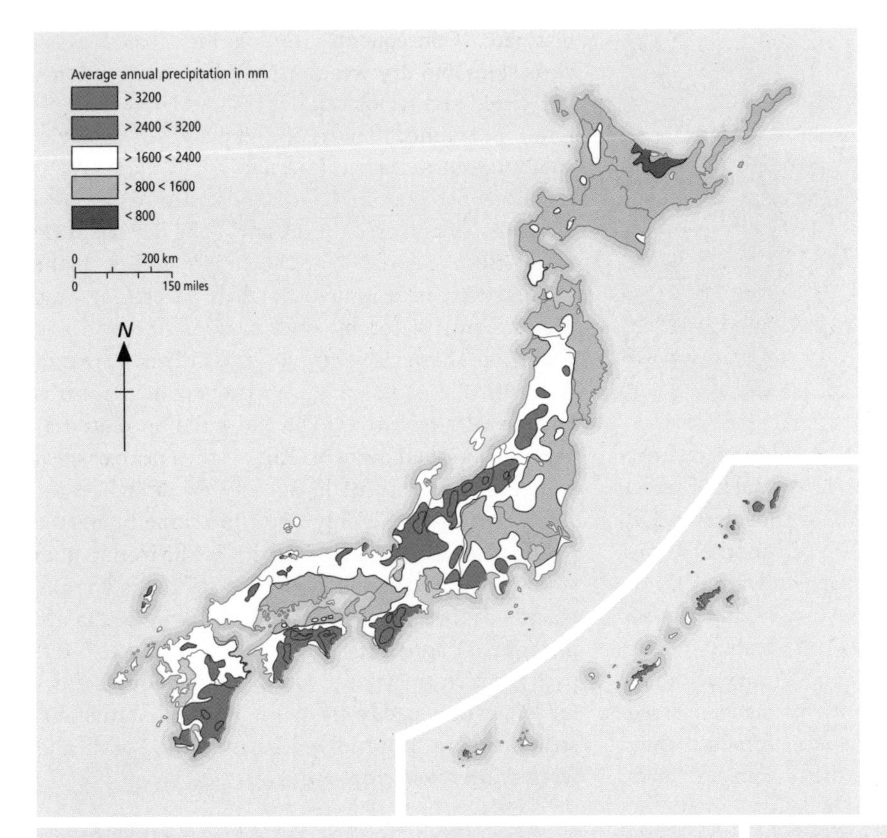

face the Japan Sea at its widest point – the coasts of Hokuriku and western Tōhoku – where several metres of snow may accumulate during the winter season even on the coastal plains. These areas enjoy most of their precipitation in winter, unlike the rest of Japan, which receives more rain in summer. The cities of Niigata and Kanazawa, for example, experience their peak monthly precipitation as snow in December, and the deepest accumulation of snow ever recorded in Japan occurred in southern Niigata Prefecture near Jōetsu – some 8.18 metres. Winters here are cold, moist and gloomy under a heavy cloud cover, with snow giving way to a higher frequency of rainy days in the more southerly coastal areas, in response to the marked latitudinal difference of temperatures during this season. This temperature pattern also gives Hokkaidō Japan's coldest winters: the mean monthly temperature in Asahikawa is −8.5 °C, and the same city holds the record for the lowest temperature ever recorded in Japan: −41.0 °C. In the more northerly parts of Honshū's 'snow country', keeping the lines of transportation open is a major challenge throughout the winter, and roofs sometimes collapse under the sheer weight of snow.

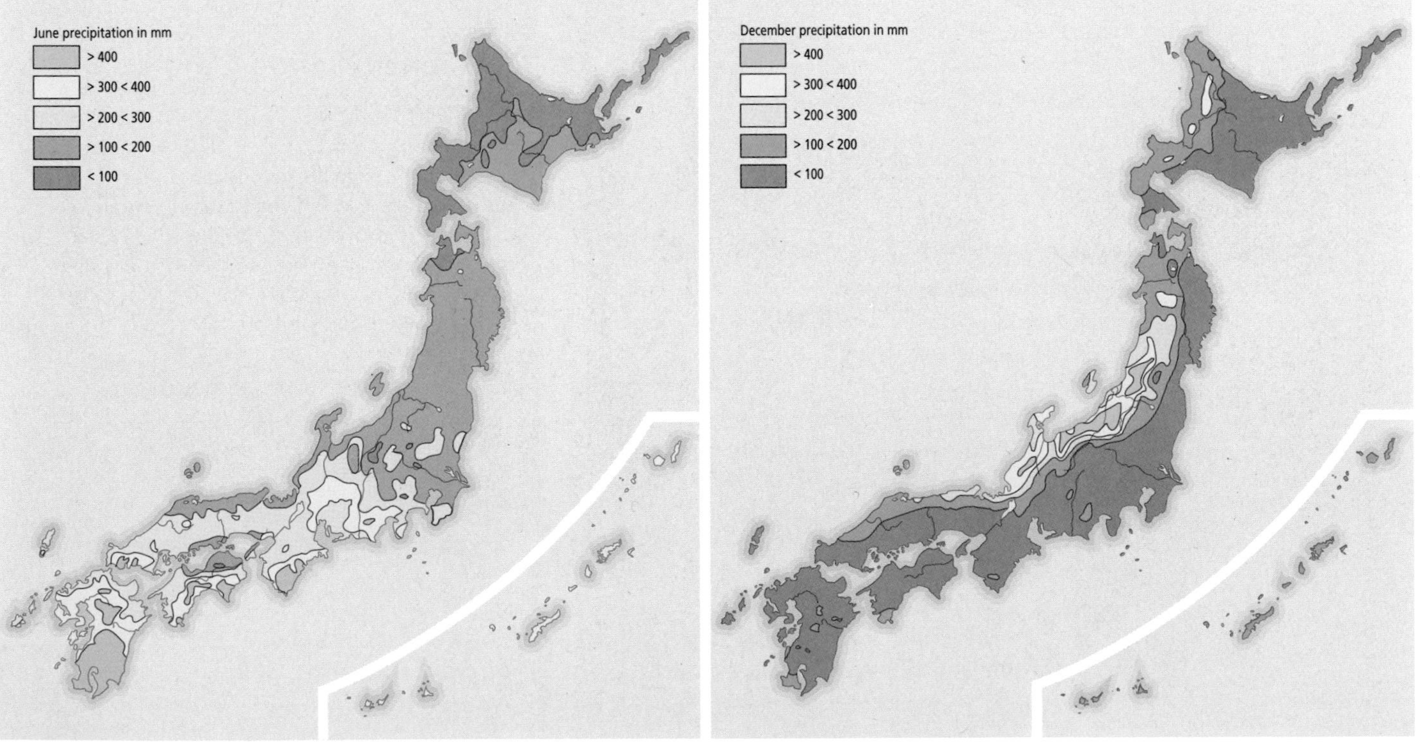

Right *Heavy snow cover in a village on the Japan Sea coast. Such conditions can last for many months and the pressing need to clear roofs often becomes a major task.*

Left *Mean precipitation in June, December and per annum*

Below *A rare view of Mt Fuji across the Kantō plain on a clear winter's day*

In the countryside most farmers abandon agriculture for the winter, and in areas where seasonal migration is common, the burden of snow removal may fall upon the frail and elderly. Here and there, the warmth of hot springs is turned to advantage, not just to please visitors at winter resorts, but also to keep streets clear of snow as naturally heated water is allowed to trickle from spouts set in the carriageway.

Once the north-westerly winds have crossed Japan's mountainous spine they are warmed as they descend to lower altitudes, and the remaining clouds dissipate. Consequently the Pacific Coast enjoys clear skies and dry weather in winter, although the air is cold and winds can be strong. Heavy precipitation is confined to parts of Shikoku, the Kii Peninsula and south-eastern Hokkaidō, where natural gaps through the mountains allow free passage to the winter monsoonal winds. In the past, long dry spells on the Pacific Coast brought the danger of fire to the major cities, fires ignited by charcoal braziers and cooking stoves, fed by constructions of wood and paper, and fanned by strong winds. This source of disaster has lost its sting, however, with the introduction of alternative fuels and building materials over the past half century. Almost the entire eastern and southern coast of Japan may experience some frost in winter, the only areas to escape being the peninsulas which jut out into the Pacific from points south of Tōkyō, together with the Ryūkyūs and the islands of the Bonin Arc. In areas where frosts are infrequent, agricultural activity continues at full pace through the winter, in vinyl greenhouses erected on vacant paddy fields or in more permanent structures. In more inland parts of the south and west, winter field crops are preferred.

How often can you see Mt Fuji from Tōkyō?

Mt Fuji (3,777 m) 100 km south-west of Tōkyō is easily visible from the capital on a clear day, but such days are few. In 1965 it was obscured for 343 days. The improvement since the 1960s has been considerable, but air pollution still hides this spectacular volcanic cone from view far more often than one would wish. RB

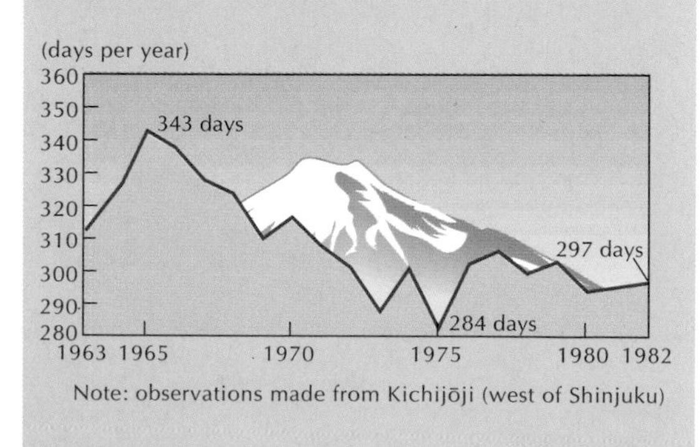

Note: observations made from Kichijōji (west of Shinjuku)

SPRING

The arrival of spring towards the end of February is punctuated by the last outbursts of cold air from the continent, and by the passage of migratory depressions, which bring changeable weather to the Pacific Coast, including some heavy snowfalls in bad years. In April and May, however, lowland Japan experiences some of the most pleasant weather of the year, with typical mean temperatures in May ranging from 12.0 °C in Sapporo to 18.4 °C in Tōkyō and to 19.2 °C in Ōsaka. By early April the zonal temperature gradient is reflected in the northward passage of the *sakura zensen* – the 'cherry-blossom front', which is widely publicized in the media and celebrated by the millions who flock to public parks from offices and factories, ostensibly to view the blossoms, but in practice to enjoy many hours of drink, song and merriment. In the first week of May, a fortuitous sequence of national holidays known as 'golden week' allows for more extended vacations across Japan.

Towards the end of spring, temperatures and humidity rise everywhere, marking the approach of the early summer rainy season, the *baiu*. The final transition is abrupt, triggered by events which take place in the upper atmosphere far from Japan. The subtropical jet stream which skirts the Tibetan Plateau on its southern side during the northern winter veers to the north of the Plateau, and splits into two arms which pass to the north and south of Japan, the gap between them maintained by a 'blocking high' which settles over the Sea of Okhotsk. The air trapped in this high pressure area meets the warm moist air of the North Pacific High, which arrives in Japan from the vicinity of the Ogasawara Islands as the south-east monsoon, along a sharp weather front known as the *baiu zensen*. This front gradually shifts northwards during the rainy season, and along it pass the ripples of small depressions which bring distinct fluctuations in temperatures and rainfall over quite short distances. The front is marked by a thick band of cloud some 300–400 km wide which obscures the sun and prevents temperatures from becoming even more uncomfortable. Rainfall is not continuous, but it can be torrential.

The cherry-blossom front

The progress north of cherries blossoming is a regular feature of weather forecasts in Japan and the vocabulary used is that of a weather 'front'. The large fluctuations in this line are due to the presence of high mountains in the interior. RB

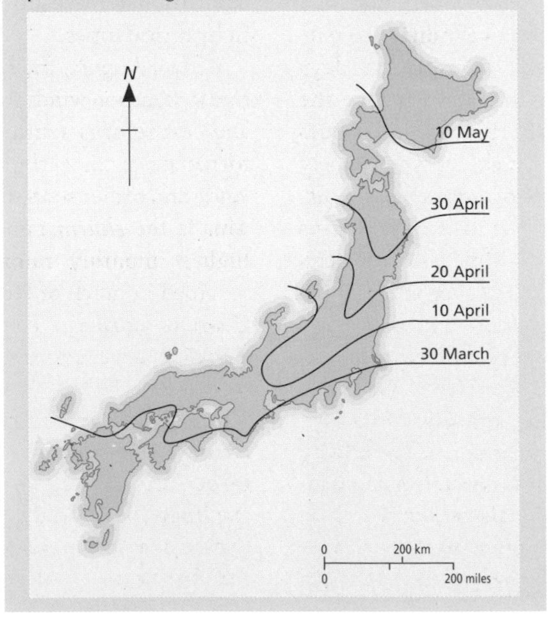

SUMMER

The *baiu* rains break in southern and western Japan in early June, spreading to the far north by the end of the month. By late June a south-westerly airstream becomes firmly established in the far south bringing heavy rain and occasionally flooding, landslides, damage to property and loss of life to exposed parts of Kyūshū. The record quantity of rainfall recorded in one day anywhere in Japan fell at a site in northern Kyūshū during a July storm which deposited over 1,100 mm of water. Rainfall shows a marked zonal distribution in this season, varying from 300–500 mm in Kyūshū to only 100 mm or so in Hokkaidō, and since the length of the season is virtually the same throughout Japan, one month, the intensity of rainfall is clearly greater in the south as well. The rain is primarily cyclonic rather than induced by mountains, which means that both the Pacific and Japan Sea coasts are affected. This produces a second rainfall maximum along the Japan Sea coast to rival the precipitation brought by the winter monsoons. In Akita, for example, the peak month for precipi-

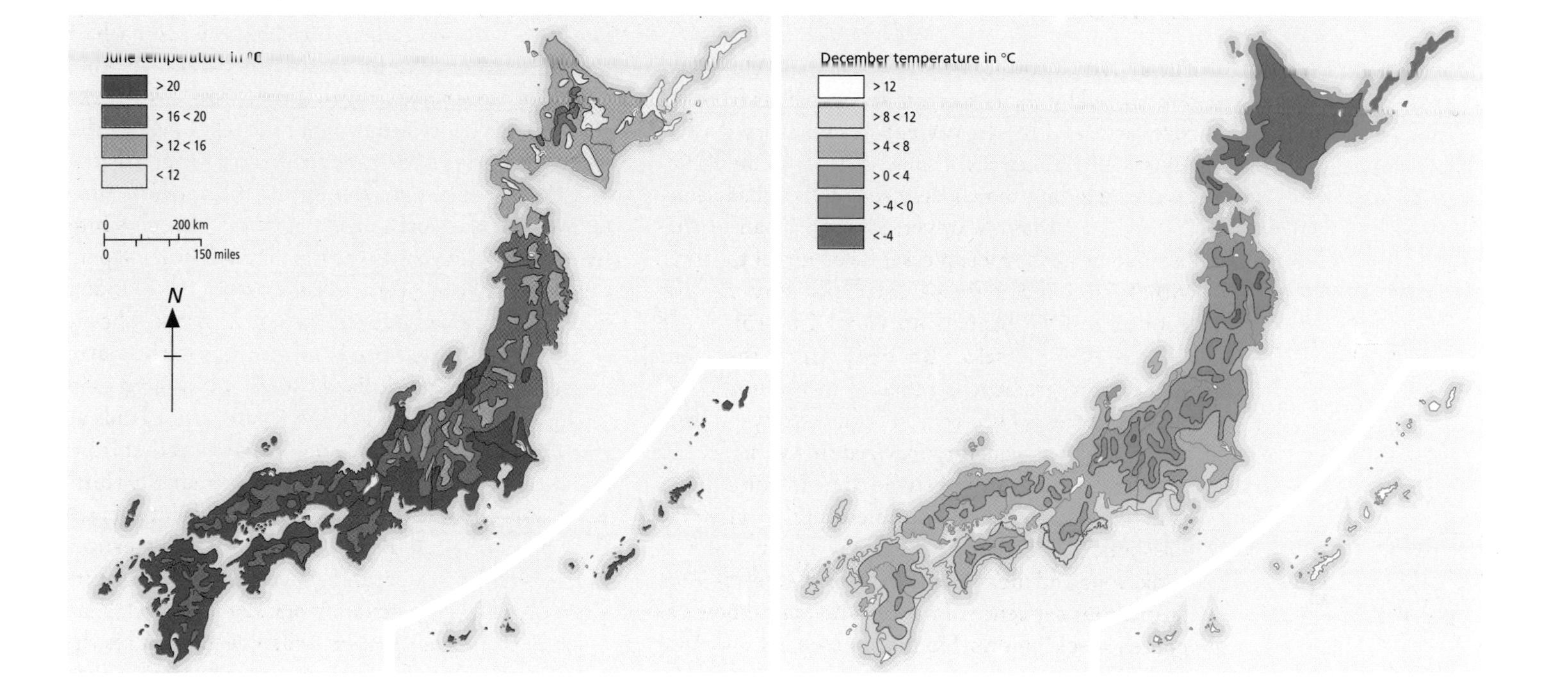

Mean temperature in June and December

tation is July, when 188 mm falls on average, with a secondary winter peak of 176 mm in November, while in Niigata the precipitation figures for July and December are 195 mm and 241 mm respectively.

As the *baiu zensen* clears northern Japan, the surface wind pattern becomes dominated by the south-easterly monsoon. This consists of hot, moist but stable air, which brings to Japan a very different pattern of weather for midsummer. There are hot days and sultry nights, with little breeze to relieve the humidity. Rainfall occurs as short heavy downpours in localized thunderstorms which are particularly frequent in the inland districts of the coastal plains. From northern Kyūshū, along the sheltered margins of the Inland Sea and across the Nōbi Plain, there can be short periods of dry weather and even droughts in this season. In the major cities the combined heat and humidity make daily life extremely uncomfortable – August temperatures average 26.7 °C in Tōkyō and 28.0 °C in Ōsaka – and those who can do so take advantage of the cooler air to be found in the nearby mountains or more generally in northern Honshū and Hokkaidō. A series of festivals held in the cities of northern Honshū during August offer a welcome excuse for millions to escape the summer heat. In some years, when the North Pacific High is less developed than usual, the high pressure area over the Sea of Okhotsk persists into midsummer, bringing a cool north-easterly wind known as the *yamase* to most of Hokkaidō and the Pacific Coast of northern Honshū. The cool cloudy and damp weather associated with this wind has long posed a risk to rice cultivation in these areas, and caused severe famines in historical times.

By late August, the front which divides the warm moist monsoon winds from the cooler air to the north and east returns south again to bring a repeat performance of the early summer rains, first to Hokkaidō and rather soon thereafter to the rest of Japan. This is the *shūrin* rainy season, during which the highest monthly rainfall totals of the year are recorded in much of Hokkaidō and along the Pacific Coast of northern Honshū: Sapporo, Sendai and Tōkyō each experience their rainfall maxima in September.

The risk of damage from typhoons is at its greatest during the *shūrin* season. These violent storms form throughout the year in the hot and humid air above the Pacific in tropical latitudes, but until this season their characteristic parabolic tracks normally swing well to the south of the Japanese archipelago. On average, however, three or four typhoons do reach

Typical typhoon tracks

Typhoons are given numbers rather than names in Japan, the number relating to the order in which they are spawned in the South Pacific in any given year. Only if they land and cause extensive damage are they given names in retrospect, names that refer either to where they made landfall or where they caused the greatest destruction. The word 'typhoon' comes from the Japanese *taifū*, which simply means 'great wind'.

The main typhoon season is autumn. The named ones on the map all hit Japan in September. The general drift of storms is towards the Chinese mainland but many are deflected northwards by high pressure, so Japan is potentially in danger at this time every year. RB

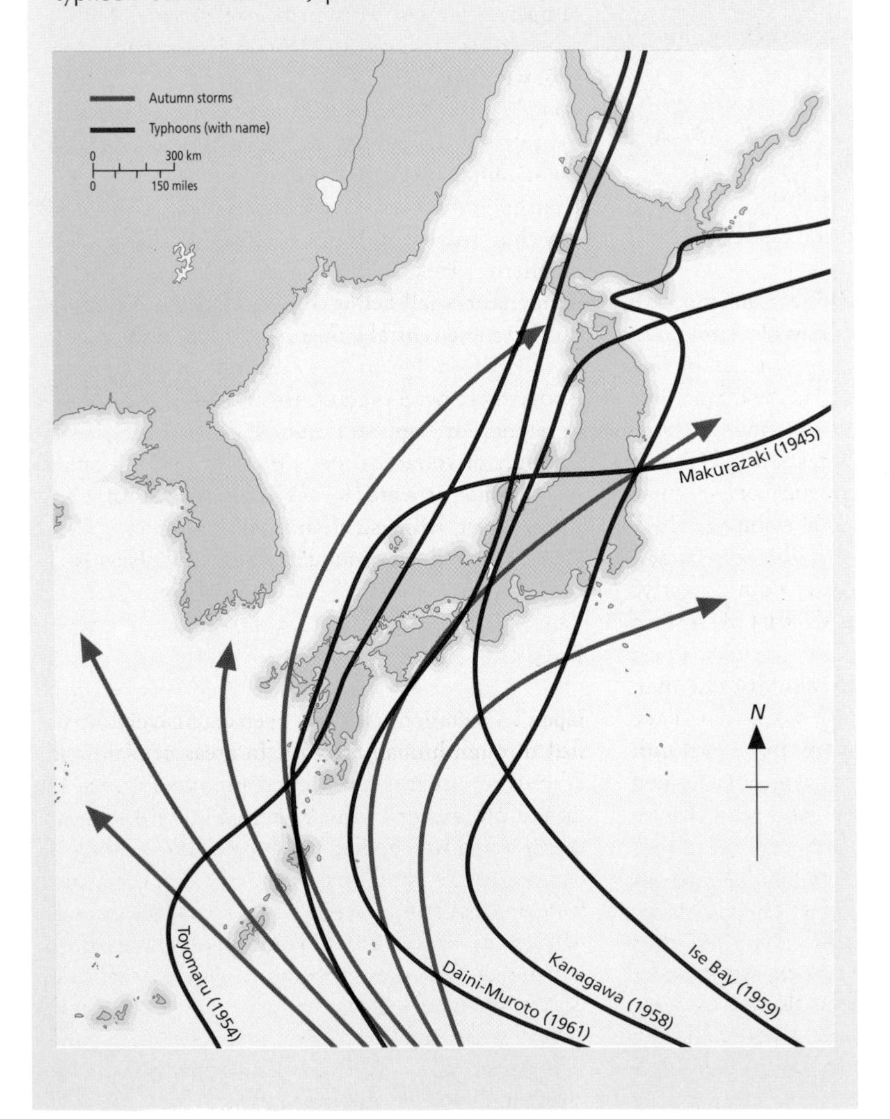

Japan each year, especially in late August and September, with the west coast of Kyūshū, the south coast of Shikoku and the southern fringes of the Kantō Plain most at risk. Occasionally a typhoon will swing so far north that it enters the Sea of Japan, before making landfall again along the western coasts of northern Honshū and Hokkaidō. The high winds and torrential downpours associated with these storms can do enormous damage whenever they strike land. The greatest danger arises when the storm track follows the line of a major coastal indentation: the effects of wind and rain are then compounded by surge tides, which threaten widespread flooding and loss of property and life to low lying areas. The Ise Bay Typhoon of 26 September 1959 was just such an event, and resulted in the deaths of over 5,000 people and the complete or partial destruction of more than 150,000 structures in and around Nagoya.

AUTUMN

By early to mid October, depending once more upon latitude, the *shūrin* rains give way to the short and transitional late autumn season, which lasts until the onset of winter in late November. Once again, the weather is dominated by migrating depressions passing eastward across Japan, bringing alternations of bright and showery days, much cooler temperatures, and welcome opportunities to view the turning of the leaves in mountain valleys and city parks. As winter approaches, the cold winds from the north-west grow more frequent, until the winter monsoon is firmly established.

The seasonal pattern within Japan's climate is compounded by the local effects of relief and altitude. In mountain areas, rainfall is boosted by uplift whenever winds blow onshore, while altitude depresses temperatures everywhere, such that Matsumoto, a city located over 600 m above sea level in the mountainous heart of central Honshū, enjoys both winter and summer temperatures similar to those experienced at the port of Akita some 3.5 degrees of latitude further north. Weather conditions can also be affected by rain shadows, which range in scale from the wholesale sheltering of the Pacific coastline during the winter to the localized shadow which Sado Island throws across the nearby coast of Honshū,

Autumn colours in the Japan Alps; a sight that can rival the displays of New England.

causing a reduction in snowfall there. Rain shadows lead not only to lower precipitation totals, but also to greater variability from year to year. One area especially prone to such variability is the Inland Sea, which is protected from rainbearing winds in summer by the mountains of central Shikoku and eastern Kyūshū and from the north-west monsoon in winter by the mountain chains of central Honshū and Chūgoku. A comparison between the cities of Tottori, Okayama and Kōchi reveals this effect quite clearly. Tottori, which is sited on the north coast of western Honshū, and is thus fully exposed to the north-west monsoon in winter, and Kōchi in southern Shikoku, which faces directly onto the Pacific Ocean, have annual rainfall totals of 2,018 mm and 2,666 mm respectively. Okayama however, which is located near to the northern coast of the Inland Sea, receives only 1,223 mm of precipitation each year.

The southernmost reaches of the archipelago in the Ryūkyū Islands enjoy a climate all their own, dominated by the greater warmth and humidity brought by a southern latitude and exposure to the surrounding seas. The subtropical climate of these islands is an important economic asset, because of the unique possibilities it creates for agriculture and tourism. RW

Vegetation and soils

The distribution of Japan's natural vegetation reflects the major climatic variables, and in particular the latitudinal and altitudinal gradients in temperature. Since there is abundant rainfall almost everywhere, there are few places where natural grassland of any description may be found. Instead, most of the country can be divided between three main forest zones: subtropical, temperate, and boreal. The boundary between the subtropical and temperate forests reaches sea level at around 38°N, the latitude of Sendai and Niigata in northern Honshū, where the mean annual temperature is approximately 12.5 °C. It extends much further south in mountain areas though, for temperate forests flank the mountain peaks of much of central and western Honshū and Shikoku, and even the higher parts of Kyūshū. The boreal forest is located in eastern and northern Hokkaidō, where average annual temperatures fall below 6 °C, and in those parts of northern and central Honshū which lie at elevations of 1,800 to 2,800 metres, depending on latitude. Above these heights there are pockets of arctic zone vegetation or even bare ground, especially near the summits of volcanic cones. Most of southern Japan was originally covered by subtropical broadleaf evergreen forest, while small areas of lush tropical vegetation are still to be found in the Ryūkyū Islands.

Forests

Japan's vegetation cover has been extensively modified through human activity. In areas of plain and diluvial terrace it is rare to find any natural vegetation at all, except in those limited areas of bog or sandy beach which have yet to be claimed for agriculture. Although forests cover two-thirds of Japan's land area, the bulk of this is either secondary growth which has been subjected to intensive use from time to time, or true forest plantation. The real 'natural' vegetation of Japan has retreated over two millennia of settlement and rice cultivation to the least accessible areas, such as the high mountain zones, the far north, and some of the smaller islands.

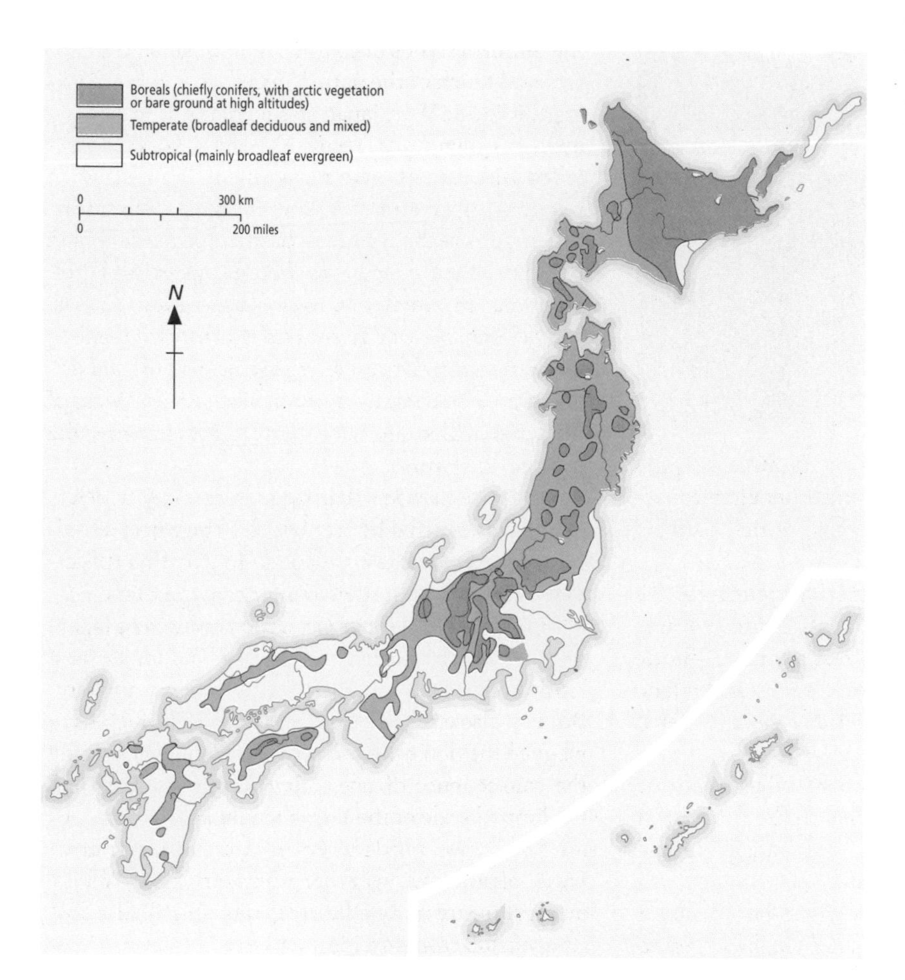

Above *Natural forest zones*

Mt Kita in the Southern Alps. A good deal of forest still remains in the high hinterland.

The original subtropical forests of Japan consisted of broadleaf evergreen hardwood species such as evergreen oak, laurel, camphor and camellia, but remnants of these forests are today confined to the more remote parts of Kyūshū and Shikoku. Elsewhere, exploitation or accidental interference by human agencies has led to the introduction of many broadleaf deciduous and coniferous species.

The temperate forests are made up of broadleaf deciduous species, intermixed in places with a variety of conifers. Common deciduous trees include the maple, birch, beech, oak, ash and chestnut, with cypress, cedar and fir as the leading coniferous species. This mixture of deciduous trees and conifers is a source of much of central and northern Japan's natural beauty, including the rich and delicate texture of the green mountainsides in spring and the fiery reds, oranges, yellows and browns of autumn.

The boreal forests of Hokkaidō and the highest parts of Honshū are dominated by conifers, especially fir and spruce, intermixed with deciduous species such as birch, aspen, willow and alder in favoured spots. Where there is flatter ground, in river valleys or natural basins, low temperatures and moist conditions sometimes cause bog vegetation to form, combining rushes, grasses and stunted trees.

While each natural vegetation zone may be described in terms of the dominant species to be found within it, this perspective overlooks the wide variety of plant life to be found within each zone, including smaller trees, shrubs and herbs filling niches in the understory and in local plant successions, as well as the beauty of many of Japan's smaller native plants. The azalea, for example, is a common inhabitant of the forest floor, and bamboos are widely distributed. Japan's forests have proved a fertile source of raw

Cleaning the moss garden in the Saihō-ji, Kyōto. Designed in the 14th century, this garden is now so popular that a high entrance fee is charged to restrict visitors.

material for the ornamental plant breeder, and thanks to the efforts of Siebold and other plant collectors, familiar Japanese species now enrich gardens the world over.

The Japanese people are themselves renowned for their love of plants and for their skills in horticulture. These qualities attain public expression in the beautiful gardens which adorn shrines, temples and public parks all over the country, in rock and moss gardens, beds of irises and avenues of flowering cherry trees. At a more intimate level, they are manifest in the art of flower arrangement or *ikebana*, in the cultivation of tiny private gardens, and in the exquisite miniaturization of nature that is *bonsai*.

The subtle design and variety to be found in Japan's gardens stands in sharp contrast, however, to the uniform stands of commercial timber which have replaced much of the natural forest vegetation. During the Pacific War, Japan was forced to draw heavily upon her own forest resources, and vast areas were felled without adequate replacement. This situation required urgent attention from the post-war authorities, to restore the resources to their former level and to ensure that the forests could continue to fulfil their functions in water and soil conservation. In the decade after the war strenuous efforts were made to assist the natural forest to regenerate and to establish plantations of commercial softwood species. Most of the latter will attain harvestable dimensions by the turn of the century.

Yet it is a paradox that Japan, a country which is two-thirds covered by trees, is also the world's leading importer of forest products. In part this reflects the sheer scale of the demand for constructional timber, for paper and for other wood products in Japan, some of which, particularly the demand for tropical hardwoods, could only be filled by imports anyway. But it is also a result of the inefficiencies which have plagued the domestic forestry sector in recent years, the consequence of poor silvicultural practices and the limited scale of the farm woodlots which account for nearly two-thirds of Japan's private forest area. Large plantations, whether under private or public ownership, are more efficiently run but still face stiff competition from foreign suppliers.

Bamboo

Bamboo is almost a miracle plant, so many and varied are its uses. The succulent shoots of some varieties can be dug up in spring and eaten as a delicacy. Indeed in Nagaoka, southwest of Kyōto, there is one famous restaurant that serves nothing but bamboo, prepared differently for each of up to ten courses. Bamboo can also serve as flexible scaffolding, and to make musical instruments, all manner of kitchen utensils, brush handles, tea whisks and vases. It is also famous for its quick growth while its underground network of roots and runners makes a bamboo grove the safest place to be during earthquakes. RB

SOILS

As for the soil endowment, this reflects Japan's climate, geology, geomorphology and topography and, in areas where settlement is possible, intense modification through millennia of human interference. The steep mountain slopes ensure that soils over most of the country are thin, stony, unstable and poorly structured. Rapid weathering causes fast replenishment of soil materials from below, but surface erosion removes these materials just as rapidly, and heavy rainfall causes marked leaching. Mountain soils cover the major part of Japan's land area, and are of limited economic value, other than as a medium to support the forest vegetation and control surface run-off.

Where shallower slopes in mountain areas permit accumulations of soil, their character varies from pure podsols, which are to be found in northern Hokkaidō and in high and wet areas in northern and central Honshū, through acidic brown forest soils, located in a belt which traverses lower altitudes in parts of southern Hokkaidō and northern and central Honshū, before merging with the heavily leached reddish and yellowish soils which are found at lower altitudes in southern Honshū, Shikoku and Kyūshū. These give way in turn to the dark red and yellow soils of the Ryūkyū Islands. The podsols are confined to areas with a cold climate, where coniferous forests provide little organic material to the soil other than a surface layer of coarse litter. These soils are acidic and inherently infertile.

Brown forest soils have a higher organic content derived from a vegetation cover which includes deciduous hardwoods, and are less heavily leached on shallower slopes. The yellow and red soils are found in some of the warmest and wettest parts of Japan, and are thus strongly leached and deficient in humus. Throughout Japan, however, the natural soil structure has been extensively modified by human agents wherever flat land is sufficient to support settlement and cultivation.

In many areas, local volcanic activity has interposed a layer of ash between the visible land surface and the underlying rocks. Ash-based soils are particularly abundant in south-eastern Hokkaidō, across the diluvial uplands of the Kantō Plain where they are a legacy of past eruptions of Mount Fuji, and in central and southern Kyūshū. The ash material is light, quickly eroded, easily leached, acidic and generally infertile, since it contains few of the mineral nutrients which make fresh volcanic soils so heavily sought after in other parts of the world. Light, sandy and infertile soils are to be found in emergent coastal areas.

In economic terms, the most important soils are those which have developed on the alluvium and adjacent, older diluvium deposited in basins, river valleys, fans and coastal plains. These soils cover less than a fifth of Japan's surface area but support the bulk of Japanese agriculture, including virtually all rice production, as well as most human settlements. The raw materials from which these soils have been made can vary widely across short distances, from coarse river gravels to sands and fine clays, but the dominant factor in determining their present structure and composition has been the impact of up to two millennia of intensive cultivation and physical modification by man, particularly where rice cultivation has been practised.

The agricultural soils with the highest natural fertility are those which have developed on finer alluvial deposits in areas with a high water table, which aids the concentration of nutrients. Conversely, much poorer soils are to be found in lowland areas with impeded drainage. The clay pan which forms in the subsoil prevents surplus water from seeping away. This is an advantage during spring, when the fields need to be flooded anyway, but it causes difficulties in other seasons, especially in winter in warmer areas, when it can hinder the cultivation of a second crop. Other problem soils are found where swamps and bogs have been reclaimed

Rice terraces on the island of Shikoku: the result of a long tradition of careful cultivation and water control over the centuries.

through artificial drainage. The peat soils are liable to shrink as they dry out, which increases the risk of flooding, and their texture must be improved through the addition of inorganic material. The latter is often obtained in the form of *kyakudo*, or 'guest soil', which is transported from surrounding hills and deposited on the rice fields. There are extensive areas in Japan which have been reclaimed from marshland through grand drainage works, such as those at Hachirōgata in Akita Prefecture, where Japan's largest lagoon has been transformed into a vast polderland of rice fields.

Agriculture

Although Japanese soils are relatively infertile, even in alluvial areas, this natural infertility has been overcome through massive capital investments in drainage and irrigation works, heavy inputs of energy to run pumps and tractors, and the application of large quantities of artificial fertilizers. Japanese agriculture is highly scientific, and in the technical sense it is also extremely productive, although it is highly inefficient in economic terms, thanks to excessive levels of subsidy and protection.

The traditional image of the paddy fields is of tiny irregular plots stacked in intricate terraces on steep hillsides or along the floors of narrow valleys, but landscapes of this kind are fast disappearing, for three reasons. First, the high labour requirements of small paddies can no longer be met in depopulated rural communities, particularly in remote mountain areas, while the small size of these fields hinders mechanization and thus the substitution of machines for absent labour. Second, government attempts to limit the area under rice cultivation have caused farmers to convert their smallest and least accessible paddies to other crops, or in extreme cases, to abandon them. And third, wherever possible, steps are being taken to increase the size of paddies to an average of 0.3 hectares each, and to convert them to a rectangular plan which simplifies irrigation, drainage and mechanization.

This drive to achieve greater technical efficiency has led to the extensive remodelling of local rural landscapes in valleys and plains into large and monotonous grids, with the bulldozer as the main implement of change. RW

The sea

The nature of the land itself, its topography, drainage, soils and vegetation, together with Japan's climate, have imposed important constraints on the development of Japanese culture and society. Another constraint can be found not on or above the land, however, but beyond it: the bays, inshore waters, and deep seas which surround Japan. The physical geography of the archipelago ensures that few people live far from salt water, or from its harvest. The sea has afforded Japan a natural insularity which has at times been transformed into a social insularity, as during the two and a half centuries of seclusion under the Tokugawa shōguns, when entry from abroad was barred to all Europeans except the Dutch who traded through the island of Deshima in Nagasaki Harbour. Centuries earlier, in the years 1274 and 1281, it was a combination of winds and waves in the waters between Kyūshū and the Korean Peninsula which saved the Japanese from invasion by the Mongols under Khubilai Khan.

But the sea is a permeable barrier, and with different attitudes it can just as easily be transformed into a convenient highway, particularly when there are island stepping stones to guide the navigator along the major sea lanes. The sea was no barrier to the importation of Buddhism, writing, and so many other elements of Chinese culture from the 6th century onwards, nor to the medieval Japanese traders who once plied the East China Sea, acquiring a notable reputation for piracy in the process. The same routes gave access from the outside, particularly to the Portuguese traders and Jesuit missionaries who arrived during the 16th century, and it was the obvious command of the sea possessed by others, the navies of Russia, the US and Britain, which finally brought seclusion to an end following the arrival of Commodore Perry in 1853, and which threatened to end the Pacific War as well, had air power and the atomic bomb not done so first.

Use for transport

In modern times, the sea has been a vital agent of cheap transportation, and the means by which Japan has surmounted the paucity of her own natural resource base. Oil, coal, ores, timber and feedgrains have flooded into the country from the world's cheapest sources of supply, in economically large tankers and bulk carriers which have also provided the basis for what was, in the first three decades after the Pacific War, one of Japan's leading growth industries, shipbuilding. In return, a never-ending stream of Japanese manufactured goods is dispatched to markets around the globe. The Pacific Basin is the most dynamic region of the world's economy, and the sea lanes to and from Japan have become the arteries of that region. The sea is also a source of vulnerability, however, for lines of supply can easily be cut, as they were during the Pacific War, or dry up, as they threatened to do during the 'oil shock' of 1973–74. The task of defending the sea lanes, and the investments which lie beyond, poses a difficult challenge to Japan's diplomatic and military position in international affairs. Strategic considerations also play a part in Japan's last territorial dispute remaining from the Pacific War, with the USSR and its successors, over the ownership of the four 'northern islands' northeast of Hokkaidō, which control access to the high seas for the former Soviet Pacific Fleet.

Major sea currents around Japan

The seas around Japan, and the currents which flow within them, play an important if modest role in ameliorating the archipelago's climate. The warm Kuroshio Current arrives from the south, skirting the east coast of Kyūshū, southern Shikoku and the Kii Peninsular, before striking east beyond the Kantō Plain and away from Japan. A branch of the Kuroshio (the Tsushima Current) snakes into the Sea of Japan through the straits between Japan and Korea, then flows northeastwards, eventually to pass by the northwestern coast of Hokkaidō, with a small branch exiting to the Pacific through the Tsugaru Straits. Meanwhile, cold water descends from the high latitudes in the northern Pacific, in currents which flow from the Sea of Okhotsk and through the Sea of Japan to the east of the Tsushima Current, as well as along the margin of the Kuril Islands and down the east coast of the Tōhoku District of Honshū as the Oyashio Current.

The warm waters of the Tsushima Current help to raise both the temperature and the humidity of the cold winds which traverse the Sea of Japan in winter, and thus contribute to the heavy snowfalls experienced along the western coast of Honshū and Hokkaidō. The effect of warm ocean currents on winter weather in Japan is far weaker, however, than the influence of the Atlantic Gulf Stream over the climate of western Europe, for example, for the reason that the Kuroshio Current, which contains most of the warmer water, skirts Japan on what is in winter the lee side of the archipelago. The other important climatic impact of ocean currents is felt in summer in northern Japan, when cool foggy air above the Oyashio Current is sometimes blown onshore in eastern Tōhoku and Hokkaidō, bringing marked reductions in temperature.

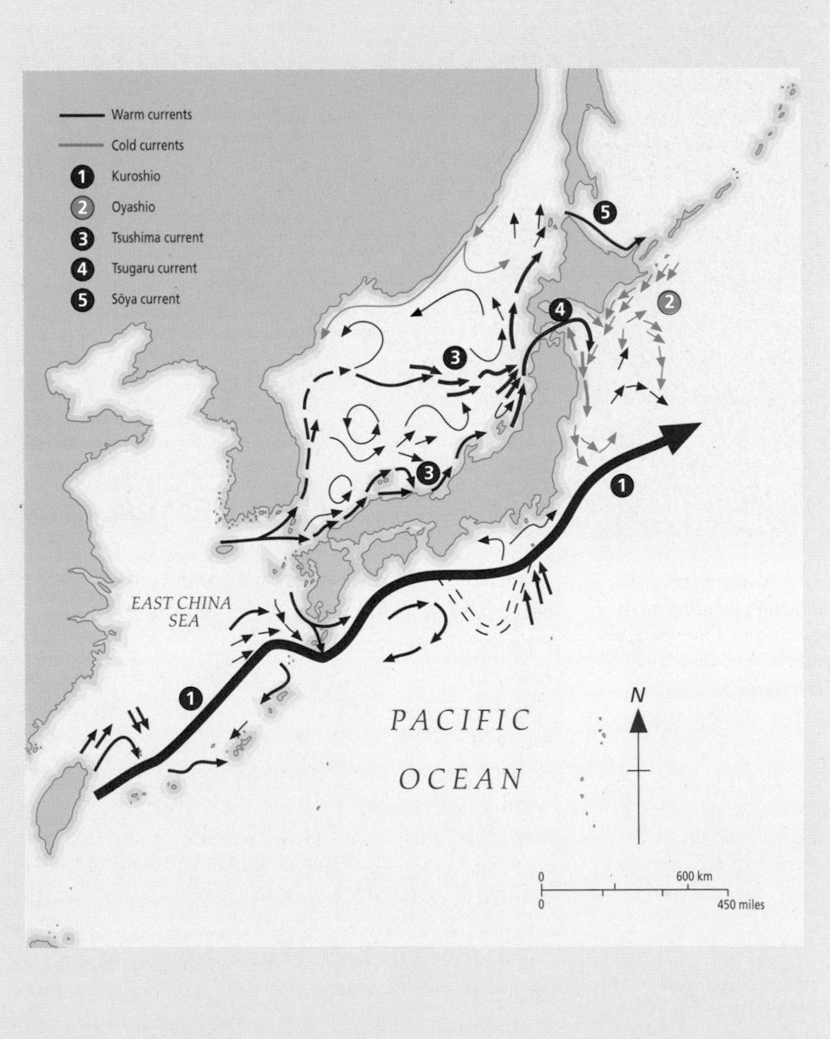

Marine resources

Above *Now under restriction, whaling has a long history. From an 18th-century woodblock print by Hokusai.*

Above right *Squid hanging out to dry in the summer sun. These will probably end up in little strips, washed down with a cool beer.*

Centre right Fugu *or blowfish. An expensive delicacy, but death follows unless the cook has been properly trained.*

The seas provide a major component of the Japanese diet, fish, which is also the leading source of animal protein. Japan's distant-water fishing fleet, which operates at least 200 nautical miles from the Japanese coast, has long roamed the oceans of the world in search of major commercial species such as salmon, pollack and tuna to satisfy the Tōkyō and Ōsaka markets, while in years past Japan also caught large numbers of whales, the meat of which remains a favoured delicacy. The distant-water fishing fleet has experienced hard times over recent years however, because of stock depletions, the introduction of 200-mile economic zones around most of the world's coastlines, and stringent controls over whaling that have reduced the catch to the minimum required for research purposes. The result within Japan has been to bring economic recession to many of the communities which are dependent on deep sea fisheries, particularly in northern Hokkaidō. A new controversy has recently added to the woes of the industry, over the use of long drift nets in deep waters, the so-called 'walls of death', which are accused of draining large areas of fish irrespective of their maturity or commercial potential.

Offshore fisheries, which are defined as those located in waters beyond 10 nautical miles but within 200 nautical miles of the coast, have been spared the negative consequences of international regulation, but have suffered from the effects of over-exploitation. The seas around Japan contain some of the world's richest natural fishing grounds, due to the fortuitous combination of ocean currents located in the vicinity. Where the Oyashio and Kuroshio Currents meet, at around latitude 36°N, and at other points where warm and cold waters mingle, microscopic marine life abounds, creating food for larger species higher up the food chain.

The main commercial species include sardines, cod and mackerel. Japanese fishermen are content to land many fish which would have little commercial value elsewhere – small sharks, the grotesques of the ocean's murky depths, and every manner of minor species, most of which can either be boiled up to extract the protein for use in reconstituted foodstuffs, or ground into fishmeal. Some of the more obscure species are considered great delicacies, including the globefish or *fugu*. This rotund little sea creature is prepared for the table by licensed chefs who are skilled in detaching the flesh from the fish without releasing the deadly toxins which lurk in the liver.

Right *Japanese pioneered the art of cultivating pearls. A 'factory' in the clear, unpolluted waters of Ise-Shima National Park.*

Japan's offshore fisheries have provided an increasing share of the total catch since the early 1970s, partly because of an expansion beyond its traditional limits by the coastal fleet, but also because international restrictions have undermined many distant-water operations. This growth has resulted in a marked shift in the composition of the overall Japanese fish catch in favour of the humble sardine, which in 1970 accounted for well under 1% of the weight of fish landed, but by 1985 had gained a share in excess of 40%. These fish are considered suitable only for fish meal, of which Japan is an exporter, since Japanese consumers are wealthy enough to indulge their taste for finer species, if not from the domestic catch then through imports of fish from other countries. As a result, the proportion of Japanese demand for fish met from imports rose from 5% in 1970 to 22% in 1985, and since the late 1970s Japan has been the world's leading importer of fish products. In effect, imports have been substituted for food which would have been caught by the distant-water fleet, had not changes in the Law of the Sea and the imposition of 200-mile zones undermined the position of the Japanese industry.

The innumerable bays and inlets around the coasts of Japan are fished by the coastal fleet, which operates within 10 nautical miles of the shore; they are also extensively farmed whenever conditions permit. Fish species including yellowtail and sea bream are raised in large cages, artificial reefs are sunk to provide suitable habitats for marine life, and the shallower bays are criss-crossed by elaborate oyster and seaweed beds. The configuration of the Japanese coastline dictates that the bulk of such marine culture (or aquaculture) activities take place along the eastern side of Japan, where bays with the requisite amount of shelter are most common. The area with the greatest natural potential is the Inland Sea, which enjoys the maximum possible protection from storms, has comparatively high water temperatures, and is studded with minor topographic features such as small islands, headlands and bays, which provide excellent site conditions for marine culture. Other important locations include the coastline of eastern Tōhoku, which is noted for its edible seaweeds, parts of Tōkyō Bay, Ise Bay with its famous pearl fisheries, and Ariake Bay in western Kyūshū.

The health of the inshore fishing industry has been threatened, however, by water pollution originating from industrial wastes and domestic sewage. The most widespread pollution occurs in the Inland Sea, which suffers the natural disadvantage that it is an enclosed water body flushed only gradually through a limited number of channels. Its waters are effectively trapped, allowing pollutants to build up. This problem became particularly acute, in this area as elsewhere in Japan, during the boom years of the 1960s, when rapid development based upon heavy industry placed new strains on the environment, without adequate safeguards to ensure proper means of waste disposal.

Over the longer term, the main threat to areas suitable for marine culture comes from the physical expansion of the land itself, partly through natural deposition in shallow water areas, but mostly as a consequence of deliberate land reclamation schemes of the type which have already claimed large slices of Tōkyō and Ise Bays and the Inland Sea for industry and settlement. Typical schemes have included the construction of massive artificial islands offshore from the Port of Kōbe, which have required the removal of large volumes of rock and debris from the flanks of Mount Rokkō. Marine reclamation is by no means a new phenomenon in Japan, and one which offers significant economic advantages, in that the new land is often sited in areas of severe congestion and high land values. It is a strategy which has its risks however, as measured not just in terms of the fisheries opportunities which may be lost, but also in the increased vulnerability to storm damage and long term inundation in the face of rising sea levels, and the chance of damage from earthquakes whenever the reclaimed land remains insufficiently consolidated.

RW

Resources and environment

A common complaint which many Japanese make about their own country concerns the supposed poverty of the resource endowment which nature has provided, especially in the context of a high population density. This grievance has deep and justifiable roots, for through most of its recorded history the Japanese economy has been dominated by agriculture, and by the need to ensure an adequate supply of foodstuffs from a limited amount of land. For much of the two and a half centuries during which Japan maintained virtual seclusion from the outside world, a fragile balance existed between population and food supply, particularly in the north-east, and periodic famines helped to ensure an extraordinarily low rate of population growth. During the subsequent rush to establish an industrial economy, mineral resources assumed greater importance, however, both as raw materials and as a new source of grievance, for Japan is also ill served in economic terms by its underlying geology.

In the early days of industrialization this mattered little, since demands upon the resource base remained comparatively small. The early history of the iron industry will serve as an example. The iron ore deposits in the mountains behind Kamaishi in Iwate Prefecture were more than adequate for the needs of Japan's earliest Western-style blast furnace, which was constructed here in 1857, and local charcoal sufficed as a source of heat and chemical carbon. When the transition came to coke firing, supplies of coal could easily be obtained by sea from the Ishikari coalfields in southern Hokkaidō. In iron and steel as in all other mineral refining industries, however, the inadequacies of the domestic resource base eventually became obvious, and Japan was obliged to look overseas for alternative sources of supply. In this respect the country has remained vulnerable throughout the 20th century, and the need to secure its mineral resource supplies was an important ingredient in the events leading to Japan's military expansion and subsequent defeat in the 1930s and 1940s. We have already noted, however, that during the period of rapid economic growth after the Pacific

Pollution

The most notorious case of inshore pollution, in Japan and perhaps the world, was caused by the contamination of the bay at Minamata in western Kyūshū by mercury wastes from a local factory. The mercury entered the food chain within the bay and accumulated in the bodies of people who ate fish caught there, unaware of the risks involved. The first sign of trouble was strange uncoordinated behaviour in the large cat population that lived off fish offal in the numerous small fishing villages that lined the bay, but by that time the damage to children in the womb had already been done.

The resulting outbreak of 'Minamata Disease' has taken the lives of several hundred victims since the early 1950s, and caused enormous suffering including painful physical disfigurements. The beautiful photograph below of a mother bathing her severely handicapped child of fourteen is a moving testimony to the continued suffering that this pollution was to cause. Minamata became a cause celèbre but it still took the affected villagers many years of legal battles and unpleasant disruption of annual general meetings of the company concerned before the causes became publically recognized and compensation arranged. Anxieties over the impact of specific industrial facilities continue, lately concerning the dangers posed to marine life by the construction of nuclear power stations on coastal sites.

The most common and widespread form of pollution, affecting large parts of the Inland Sea and the major coastal bays further north and east, is the 'red tide'. Red tides are triggered by an explosive increase in the quantity of marine algae caused by excessive accumulations of mineral nutrients in the water. The results are not only unsightly, but also render the flesh of sea creatures toxic to humans. These tides continue to occur, although a combination of heightened public awareness and concern over pollution issues, much stronger controls over industrial discharges, and a shift in Japan's industrial structure away from the older heavy industries and towards high technology manufacturing, often located at inland sites in any case, has helped to reduce the problem to more manageable proportions. RW

War, Japan benefited enormously from access to cheap overseas supplies and cheap bulk transportation, rendering the paucity of mineral endowment not so much a liability as a positive asset.

COAL

In terms of fuel minerals, Japan and Britain make an interesting contrast. The latter is sometimes described as an island of coal floating on a sea of oil. Perhaps the best that can be said of Japan is that it is an island of ash floating on a sea of lava, neither of which make very useful sources of energy. Japan does have coal, oil and natural gas, but in quantities dwarfed by the scale of its economy. The coal reserves are located in four main areas – Hokkaidō, where there were once several fields in production, including Japan's largest on the Ishikari Plain and others around Rumoi and Kushiro; the Jōban area in southern Tōhoku, the western tip of Yamaguchi Prefecture in westernmost Honshū, and the large Chikuho and associated fields in northern Kyūshū. All have been of historical significance: the Ishikari coals, for example, as one of the bases for steelmaking in Muroran and those of the Chikuho field as the source of supply for the first integrated steelworks in Japan, constructed at Yahata (now part of Kita-Kyūshū City) in 1901. Japanese coal is extremely expensive to mine, however, due to high wage rates and also basic geological difficulties, including extensive faulting within the main coal seams, which are generally thin and of poor quality. As a result the industry has been allowed to run down, despite its strategic importance and the input of substantial government subsidies, and coal is now obtained far more cheaply from the major overseas open-cast producers. Today just a few pits remain in Hokkaidō. Elsewhere the industry is dead, and local communities have had to cope with the adjustment, again with considerable help from the government.

OTHER FUEL SOURCES

Japan's small oil and natural gas fields are located in Akita and Niigata Prefectures on the Japan Sea coast, and can satisfy only a tiny proportion of the nation's needs. Nor is there much prospect of Japan finding

more oil or gas, given her geological structure. As alternatives, for electricity generation and space heating at least, Japan has looked towards hydroelectricity and, more recently, nuclear power generation, geothermal energy and solar heating. Japan's accessible hydroelectric potential has already been almost fully exploited, through developments characterized by the use of a large number of comparatively tall multipurpose dams holding back relatively small volumes of water, a situation dictated by physiographic considerations. The largest dam in Japan is the Kurobe Dam in Toyama Prefecture, which has a height of 186 metres and was completed in 1963. While dam building continues, few major projects have been commenced since the late 1960s. Nuclear power is eventually expected to provide around one half of Japan's electricity needs, if public opinion permits, but the raw material for the reactor fuel must be imported. Geothermal developments remain limited in scale, and are a natural extension of the widespread use already made of naturally heated water from geysers, particularly in hot spring resorts. As for solar heating, the past decade has seen a highly conspicuous increase in the use of rooftop solar panels. Solar heating is particularly appropriate on the Pacific Coast, which enjoys comparatively clear skies in winter.

Left *The 'Pond of Blood' in Beppu, Kyūshū. Signs of geothermal energy draw the curious and the infirm throughout Japan, but they also point to the ever-present threat of seismic activity.*

Metals

Japan has a modest endowment of several of the major metallic minerals, which formed the basis of local smelting industries in the early stages of modernization, such as the iron industry (recently closed down) at Kamaishi. Indeed, Japanese craftsmen have been famous for centuries for the quality of their metalwork, and especially for the beauty and deadly efficiency of the traditional Japanese sword. None of Japan's metallic mineral deposits has proved sufficient to meet the needs of the modern economy, however, and instead imports must fill the gap. Besides iron, the main ores to be found in Japan are those of copper, zinc and lead. The copper deposits in Akita Prefecture (in north-western Tōhoku) and Ehime Prefecture (northern Shikoku) provided the initial impetus for metallurgical industries at Akita and Niihama respectively, while the machinery and metallurgical industries in the city of Hitachi in the north-eastern corner of the Kantō Plain were initially based on local deposits of gold, silver, sulphur and copper.

Water

In theory Japan should be well endowed with water resources, given the extent of annual precipitation, but the high level of demand, when combined with the difficulties of storage, mean that water is in fact a scarce commodity. The main demands upon the nation's water resources are for power generation, irrigation, drinking water and industrial use, with additional claims from transportation and outdoor recreation. The physiography of Japan's mountain valleys ensures that dams are small and reservoir volumes limited, and the heavy debris loads carried by Japanese rivers when in flood cause storage capacities to degrade rapidly. The potential for further dam construction is also limited. Agricultural irrigation is generally conducted by means of gravity-fed canal systems, supplemented by the use of pumps when necessary. Fortunately, the period of peak demand in spring, when the fields must be flooded before the rice is transplanted, coincides with the beginning of snowmelt in the mountain areas and an associated increase in river flow volumes, which are boosted further with the onset of the *baiu* rains.

In the major urban areas, where reliability of supply throughout the year is a vital consideration, a large proportion of water for both domestic and industrial use is obtained from subterranean aquifers located within the underlying accumulations of alluvium. This source has been exploited to the limit and beyond, resulting in the widespread occurrence of subsidence in eastern Tōkyō and around Ōsaka in particular, where large areas now lie below sea level and would be at serious risk of flooding were it not for heavy investment in protective dykes. Overextraction has also caused salt water to infiltrate inland, ruining the quality of underground supplies. The availability of water has become an important consideration in industrial location decisions, and one which is compounded in the case of some high technology industries by the need for pure supplies, which can necessitate relocation from the major cities to more rural areas such as southern Tōhoku or Japan's 'silicon island', Kyūshū.

Water pollution has been a serious problem in Japan, not just in the seas and bays, but also in rivers and what limited bodies there are of surface fresh water. While individual sources of effluent discharge from factories have been easy to identify and tackle, the treatment of ordinary domestic sewage has posed much bigger problems, and the basic infrastructure for sewage treatment remains relatively underdeveloped. The consequences can be seen most clearly in the pollution of Lake Biwa, an important source of fresh water for the Keihanshin Metropolitan Area around Ōsaka as well as a noted recreational attraction. This lake has lately been subject to oxygen imbalances and algal blooms caused by heavy loads of nitrates and phosphates.

Right *Flotsam and jetsam on a Japanese beach. Unfortunately such sights are only too common along any but the most remote coastline.*

AIR

One other resource of vital importance to life is clean air. Japan experiences occasional bouts of dust pollution, which is blown across the Japan Sea from the deserts of North China, giving rise to a characteristic yellow haze. Far more important however is the air pollution derived from local sources: factories, homes, and the automobile. Concern over air pollution in the major cities reached a peak in the late 1960s, by which time more than a decade of rapid economic growth based on the development of heavy industries on sites close to large population centres had placed public health at risk. The best known case in Japan was that associated with 'Yokkaichi Asthma', a respiratory disease caused by heavy air pollution in the vicinity of the petrochemical facilities at Yokkaichi City, south-west of Nagoya. Since the early 1970s there have been marked improvements in the quality of air in urban areas, due in part to the introduction of stringent controls on factory emissions and heavy investment in pollution control equipment, but also because the recession which followed the 'oil shock' of 1973–74 saw the beginning of a major shift in the structure of the nation's economy in favour of 'knowledge intensive' high technology industries, which are generally much cleaner and create less waste.

Japan has also introduced some of the strictest controls on automobile emissions in the world, but in recent years the concentrations of exhaust gases in urban air have remained steady, despite higher standards, because of the continuing increase in the number of vehicles on Japanese roads – an important source of noise pollution as well.

As a leading industrial nation, Japan also bears considerable responsibility for air pollution of a more global kind: the release of CFCs and carbon dioxide, which together contribute to the destruction of the ozone layer and the 'greenhouse effect'. Japanese industry tends to use fuel more efficiently than its competitors, because so much of it has to be imported. Nevertheless, there is today a growing public awareness and commitment on global environmental issues in Japan, not least because as a country with little flat land, and with much of its most important real estate located at or even below sea level, Japan stands to lose a great deal from any general rise in sea level. As the leading importer of tropical hardwoods, Japan also has a special responsibility to help conserve the world's dwindling resources of tropical rainforest, a cause which has also attracted an increasing amount of public attention in recent years.

RW

Tōkyō at the end of a heavy day. Air quality is improving in many areas, but smog is not uncommon and the concentration of ozone can reach dangerous levels in the stifling heat and humidity of mid-summer.

People

Japan has a population of 123.6 millions according to the 1990 Census, or 2.5% of the world total, making it the seventh most populous nation after China, India, the former USSR, the US, Indonesia and Brazil. The population is overwhelmingly of ethnic Japanese stock, an odd fact given the enormous absolute and per capita wealth of the country, which would normally act as a powerful attraction for international migrants. Japan has strict rules on immigration and naturalization, which make it very difficult for anyone who is not Japanese by birth to assume permanent residence or to gain Japanese citizenship. The comparative homogeneity of the Japanese population is maintained in response to public concern over the threat of overcrowding, concern which has a substantial basis in fact. Ethnic homogeneity is also widely supported in its own right, however, as a safeguard against racial disharmony of the type which has afflicted other industrial nations.

There are two indigenous minorities in Japan, the Ainu and the *burakumin*. The Ainu are a residual aboriginal people of Caucasian stock (unlike the Mongoloid Japanese), numbering around 15,000, whose distribution is confined to parts of Hokkaidō. The three million or so *burakumin* are the descendants of the outcaste groups of the feudal era, and although they are racially indistinguishable from other Japanese, they have suffered (and continue to suffer) various forms of illegal discrimination within Japanese society. A third minority consists of around 700,000 Koreans, many of whom were born in Japan to parents who were forcibly removed from their homeland during the Japanese occupation in the first half of this century.

Distribution

The distribution of population within Japan is very uneven. The physiographic endowment has always necessitated a concentration of population into that very small proportion of the nation's area which can be considered habitable land – the coastal plains, inland basins, and river valleys. The development of a modern commercial and industrial economy has led to further concentration within the habitable area, however, and particularly in the three great metropolitan regions centred on Tōkyō–Yokohama, Nagoya, and Ōsaka–Kōbe–Kyōto, which together housed 45% of the Japanese population in 1990. While the mean population density in Japan was 332 persons per km^2 in 1990, the figure for Tōkyō, the most densely populated of the 47 prefectures, was 5,430 persons per km^2, and for Ōsaka 4,640, while the equivalent density for Hokkaidō, the most sparsely populated prefecture, was just 72 persons per km^2. Since the early 1950s there has been a massive redistribution of population from the more rural and remote prefectures, which peaked in the late 1960s, went into temporary reverse in the 1970s (reflecting the difficulties which the national economy experienced in that decade), and reasserted itself in the 1980s. This process drained rural areas of young people in the most productive – and most fertile – age groups, leaving behind residual populations disproportionately weighted towards the elderly. Meanwhile, the metropolitan prefectures gained not only these young people, but their offspring as well, in a cumulative process of regeneration which has now replaced intraprefectural migration as the main engine of metropolitan growth.

Migration

Although it might appear that Japan has tolerated very little immigration, a considerable number of Korean scribes and artisans arrived in pre-Nara and Nara times, and Japan has also been home to some eminent Chinese monks. More recently, Koreans were shipped over to Japan in the late 1920s and 1930s in fairly large numbers to help keep wartime industry working at full capacity. Emigration has been far more in evidence, of course, and Japan has in the past dispatched substantial numbers of emigrants to two main destinations, the west coast of the US (plus Hawaii) and the southernmost states of Brazil. Both of these overseas communities were established earlier this century, and have enjoyed considerable economic success in their adopted countries, based initially upon prowess in intensive agriculture but, in subsequent generations, upon high standards of professional competence and academic achievement. The Japanese–American and Japanese–Canadian population was subjected to discrimination and physical internment during the Pacific War, the injustice of which has since been formally recognized. Small communities of Japanese businessmen with their families are also to be found in most of the world's capitals and, with the expansion of Japanese industrial investments overseas, in many other cities as well. RW

DEMOGRAPHIC TRENDS

Paradoxically, although Japan is one of the most densely populated countries on earth, and has the highest physiographic density (population/inhabitable land) of any major nation, perhaps the greatest problem it faces in the immediate future is a shortage of population in the working age groups. In 1950 only 5% of the Japanese population was age 65 or over, but by 1975 this had risen to 8%, by the year 2000 it will rise to 16%, and by the year 2025 it may reach 23%, creating an enormous burden in pension and medical costs for future taxpayers. Population ageing is a phenomenon common to all countries which have achieved demographic maturity, with low birth rates, low death rates, and low rates of natural increase. The distinguishing characteristic of Japan, however, is the speed with which it is moving from having one of the most youthful populations amongst the leading industrial counties to one of the most top-heavy age structures. Not enough children are born in Japan to ensure the long-term stability of the population: with a net reproduction rate below one (i.e. fewer than one female child born per woman during her childbearing years), the long-term prospect is for continued decline. The population is expected to peak at 126 millions in the year 2005, before declining to some 115 millions by the year 2050.

In the short term, however, there is also much to welcome on the demographic front: Japan has the world's lowest infant mortality rate, for example, at just 5 per 1,000 live births, and the longest life expectancy at birth, currently 75.3 years for men and 81.3 years for women. The birth rate is extremely low at 10.1 per thousand, and still falling, while the death rate is stable at 6.5 per thousand. The death rate may actually increase slightly in future years, not because individuals are any less healthy, but because of the rising percentage who are elderly. When death comes it is now unlikely to be from epidemic infectious diseases such as tuberculosis or influenza, which once killed millions, but from cancer, from heart failure, or from cerebrovascular disease. The last of these three is particularly common in Japan due to the high intake of salt within the traditional diet. The other two have increased in importance with changes in diet (particularly the shift towards meat and dairy products) and lifestyles, but can be

Population density by prefecture (left) and overall (right)

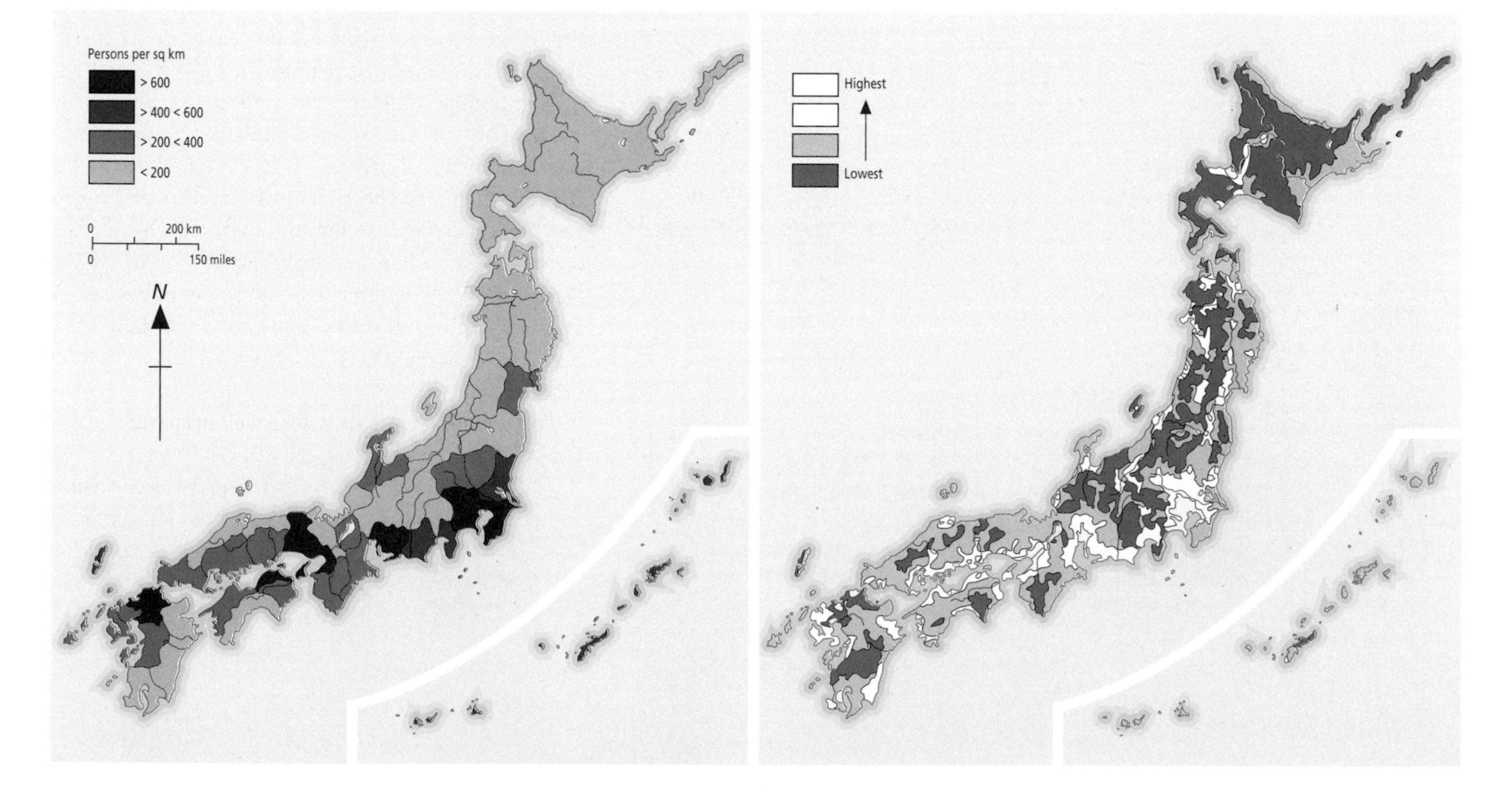

attributed in part also to the simple fact that people now live long enough not to die of something else. Overall, Japan enjoys one of the most advanced demographic régimes in the modern world.

To reach this enviable position Japan has passed through a 'demographic transition', in which high birth and death rates and a low rate of natural increase have eventually been replaced by low values for all three variables. In many countries there has been a phase in the course of this transition during which birth and death rates have diverged, triggering an explosion in the size of the population. One of the striking features of Japan's demographic transition has been the fact that, with the exception of the immediate post-war years, the rate of natural increase has hardly ever exceeded 1.5% per annum: birth rates and death rates have fallen virtually in step. Certainly the population has grown three-fold since the beginning of the modern era, from 36.3 millions in 1870 to 55.4 millions in 1920, 103.7 millions in 1970 and 123.6 millions in 1990, but this is a small increase compared with what would have happened had growth rates characteristic of many contemporary developing countries applied.

This long-term performance appears all the more striking in the context of the history of Japanese population growth during the Tokugawa period. Between 1721, when the population of Japan reached a total of around 26.1 millions, and 1846, when it is estimated to have reached 26.9 millions, the rate of natural increase averaged less than 0.03% per annum. Indeed, during several periods of famine, which were particularly severe in the Tōhoku District, the population of Japan actually decreased, with the number of deaths exceeding births. On the surface at least, these figures suggest a population that had stretched the capacity of natural resources and agricultural technology to the limit, as was often the case for poorer households. What is also distinctive about this period though is the extent to which deliberate efforts were made to limit family size, not just in periods of famine, but in good times as well.

In effect, Japan entered the modern era with a long history of successful population control to its credit. Some of the methods employed appear harsh by contemporary standards, including the practice of *mabiki* (or 'thinning out'), a euphemism for infanticide directed selectively against females. Other methods included abortion, prolonged breast feeding and late marriage. Adoption customs also helped considerably: where a family lacked a male heir it was perfectly acceptable to adopt the younger son of another family, thereby allowing each family to perpetuate its traditions without resorting to further procreation.

The Japanese were therefore well prepared to cope with the demographic consequences of modernization. They were also helped, however, by a fortuitous coincidence between entry into the demographic transition and real progress in the material economy, based on the introduction of Western industrial arts. During the transition rising incomes and increased security gave parents an incentive to reduce their childbearing aspirations, while urbanization and the associated difficulties of securing adequate housing have made life difficult both for families who choose to have more than one or two children, and for

Population statistics

Japan, with a population in excess of 122 million, leads the world in life expectancy. This very success, however, brings its own problems. In the next two or three decades Japan will experience a vast growth in the percentage of people over 60 years of age. The problem is being exacerbated by a continuing fall in the birth rate, as the accompanying charts reveal. This extraordinary demographic shift has now become the subject of much heated debate because the cost to the nation of caring for such large numbers of old people is incalculable. Brakes have already been applied to what was a burgeoning welfare system. RB

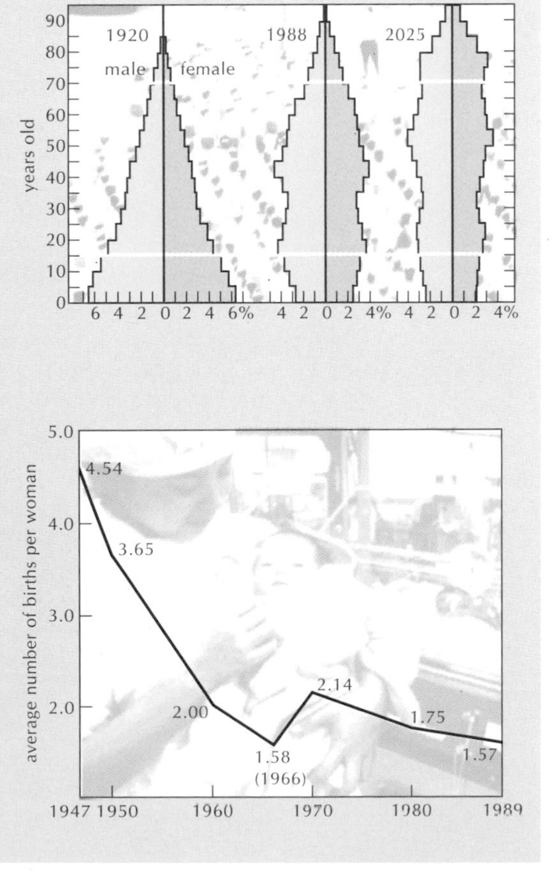

extended families who wish to stay together. Over the longer term, however, perhaps the most important factor in limiting family size has been a radical shift in the wishes of parents, and the demands of the economy, with respect to the quality as opposed to the quantity of children in a family, which requires that the family concentrate its resources on a limited number of offspring.

Two temporary aberrations in Japan's demographic transition deserve special comment. In the immediate post-war years there was a sharp increase in the population related to the repatriation of several million settlers and demobilized troops from Japan's former colonies in Korea, Manchuria and Taiwan, and to the natural 'baby boom' which occurs whenever warfare interferes with normal procreative habits. The bulge in the population pyramid related to births in the immediate post-war years replicated itself 20 to 25 years later, as the children of the baby boom themselves became parents, in a cyclical pattern that may echo through the population profile for generations to come. Second, there was a very sharp fall in the number of births recorded in the year 1966: 1.5 millions, as compared with 1.8 millions in 1965. Notwithstanding what has been said about the rationality behind Japanese family planning, this particular aberration was caused by a very ancient fear – of *hinoeuma*, the year of the fiery horse in the Chinese calendar: girls born in this year are thought likely to injure their husbands in later life. RW

EXPECTATION OF LIFE AT BIRTH

	Year or period	Male (years)	Female (years)
Japan	1970	69.31	74.66
	1980	73.35	78.76
	1990	75.86	81.81
Iceland	1987–1988	74.58	79.74
Sweden	1988	74.15	79.96
Norway	1990	73.44	79.81
Australia	1987	73.03	79.46
US	1987	71.50	78.30
France	1987	72.03	80.27
UK[a]	1986–1988	72.40	78.10
W. Germany	1986–1988	72.21	78.68
USSR	1986–1987	65.04	73.78
China	1985–1990	67.98	70.94

[a]England and Wales only.
Source: Ministry of Health and Welfare, Japan; UN, *Demographic Yearbook*.

Country versus city

Large-scale population migration from the countryside to the cities, driven by the transfer of labour between agriculture and more productive pursuits in manufacturing and commerce, has transformed Japan from a predominantly rural country when modernization began in the mid 19th century into what is today an overwhelmingly urban society. According to the 1990 Census, some 77.4% of the Japanese population live in administrative cities (or *shi*, which normally have a population in excess of 30,000), and those who remain in smaller towns or villages mostly enjoy easy access to larger settlements as and when required, thanks to an excellent railway system and the widespread diffusion of the private automobile.

Urbanization

The roots of urbanization run deep in Japanese history. The earliest cities performed administrative and ceremonial functions and were laid out according to Chinese principles of urban design, on a rectangular grid, with due attention given both to the relative sizes of cities as a reflection of their importance in the bureaucratic hierarchy, and to the need to conform to the basic rules of geomancy. The model for Japan's early imperial capital cities, including Nara (capital from 710 to 794) and its successor, Kyōto, was the great Chinese capital at Chang'an, and both of these cities have retained much of their original layout and character. Other early settlements included local administrative capitals, post towns along the main highways, and *foci* for religious observances.

With the advent of military rule from the 12th century, new elements were added to Japan's urban structure. During the Kamakura period (1185–1336) the seat of government shifted east. While Kamakura never achieved the status of a great city, the capital of the Tokugawa shōguns, who ruled Japan from 1600 to 1868, certainly did, first under the name of Edo, and, from 1868, with the name it bears today – Tōkyō. In the brief flowering of international

How Tōkyō keeps on growing

The rapid rate of expansion as Tōkyō moved out to fill more and more of the Kantō plain can be seen from this series of maps. Since 1975 the growth has been less dramatic but still appreciable. Continued increase in the suburbs has been somewhat offset by a thinning at the centre, which contains more and more non-residential buildings. This has given rise to a pronounced 'doughnut' shape with concomitant pressure on commuter transport. The photograph below shows a typical mix of mid- to high-rise apartments and offices not far from the city centre. RB

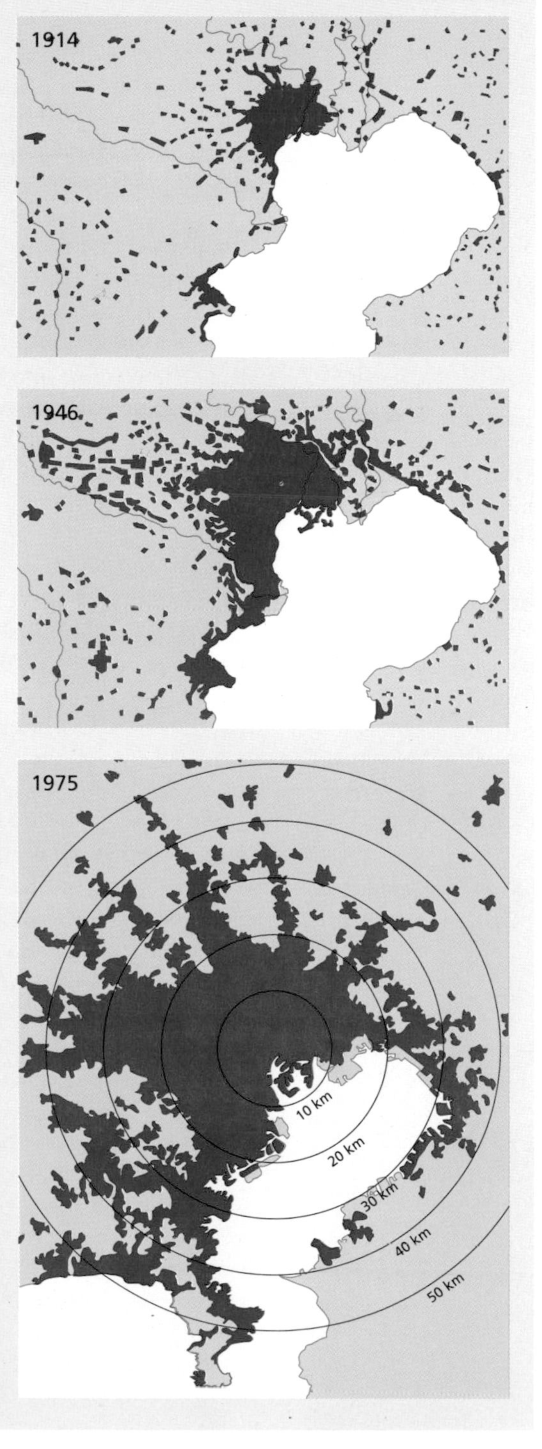

trade which took place before the Tokugawa closed Japan off from the outside world, Sakai became an important international port, along with Nagasaki, and the latter remained open to the Dutch and Chinese even during the years of seclusion, though under very strict supervision. In the centuries of periodic civil warfare which preceded the rise of the Tokugawa, castles and other defensive installations were constructed in every corner of Japan, but these were rationalized under the new régime to leave one main castle in each domain. Many of the associated castle towns (known as *jōkamachi*) have since developed into important prefectural or regional centres, such as Nagoya, Hiroshima and Sendai. Ōsaka too was originally a castle town, but during the Tokugawa era it quickly assumed a pivotal rôle in domestic commerce as the centre of inter-regional trade in rice.

The ending of Japan's seclusion and the subsequent push to industrialize and modernize the country added yet more cities to Japan's urban framework. The re-opening of general foreign trade stimulated the development of major international ports, including Yokohama and Kōbe, both of which have retained a cosmopolitan flavour to this day. Expansion into Hokkaidō required the construction of new cities from which the northern frontier could be managed, including Sapporo, Otaru and Hakodate. Sapporo, the island's capital, was set out on a rectangular grid in emulation not of the ancient Chinese model but of the contemporary American city.

The requirement of manufacturing industry for a geographically concentrated labour force stimulated the addition of industrial suburbs to existing cities and the development of entirely new urban centres alongside isolated factories. A major industrial city (Kita-Kyūshū) grew up in northern Kyūshū, for example, in response to the development of the early Japanese steel industry along the shores of Dōkai Bay. Smaller company towns dependent upon a single enterprise can be found throughout Japan, from Nobeoka in Kyūshū's Miyazaki Prefecture, the domain of Asahi Chemical, through Toyota City near Nagoya, home of the automobile manufacturer of that name, to Kamaishi in eastern Iwate Prefecture, dominated by the Nippon Steel Corporation, and Tomakomai in Hokkaidō, home of Oji Paper. The prosperity of these communities depends upon the continuing health of the economic sector in which they are specialized and the administrative decisions of their local company, both of which make them vulnerable over the long term. Other small industrial cities have developed around regionally based industries, in which the entire manufacturing process is decentralized amongst a large number of wholesalers, component suppliers and assembly firms. Typical examples include Toyooka in Hyōgo Prefecture, which manufactures bags of many types, and Tsubame in Niigata Prefecture, a centre of the Japanese tableware industry.

The development of large modern commercial cities has given rise to another form of urban settlement – the dormitory town or suburb. Old market towns, small industrial centres and farming villages on the outer fringes of cities like Tōkyō, Nagoya and Ōsaka have been transformed by the influx of commuters, often to the point where their individual identities have become submerged within that of the 'metropolitan regions' of which they form a part. The metropolitan region of Southern Kantō, centred on Tōkyō and Yokohama, is rapidly expanding beyond the confines of the four southern prefectures of the Kantō Plain (Saitama, Chiba, Tōkyō and Kanagawa), to incorporate substantial parts of Northern Kantō and the narrow coastal strip to the south and west. The four southern prefectures alone contain some 25.7% of the Japanese population, on just 3.6% of the nation's land area, and are responsible for even larger shares of the nation's universities, business organizations and government institutions. Tōkyō has emerged as one of the three great financial centres of the world, and is unrivalled within Japan in terms of population, the range of goods and services on offer, the quality of its international contacts and the control it exerts over Japan's business life. There are also two other major metropolitan regions in Japan. One is centred on Nagoya, and includes all of Aichi Prefecture as well as parts of Mie and Gifu. The other has grown up around the Ōsaka–Kōbe–Kyōto triangle within the Kinki District, and its outer suburbs are fast expanding into Shiga and Nara Prefectures to the east and south.

The Monday wash? Noodles out to dry; one of the ways in which farming households can supplement income.

THE COUNTRYSIDE

The rapid urban development which has characterized Japan during its period of modernization, and especially after the Pacific War, has been accompanied by both relative and absolute depopulation of much of the Japanese countryside. The main cause has been the underlying difference in productivity growth between agriculture and other occupations which has made factory and office work far more attractive, particularly to younger people, than work in the fields. Only a tenth of Japanese households now derive even a small part of their income from agriculture, and even this greatly overstates the residual importance of agriculture, since around two-thirds of 'farm' households actually earn more of their income off the farm than on it. Japanese agriculture has been heavily protected through a combination of input subsidies and import restrictions, which allows the government to pay producer prices to farmers for certain key products, especially rice and milk, which are many times the prevailing world prices for those products. As a result, far more households have remained on the land than might otherwise have been the case, but not as full-time farmers, for Japanese farms are much too small to yield an income equivalent to that which can be earned elsewhere, even with the assistance that the government provides. Instead most farmers work in the fields only during weekends, national holidays and the peak periods for planting and harvesting.

This system of agriculture depends upon the local availability of suitable off-farm employment opportunities. Despite high levels of migration to the metropolitan regions during the 1950s and 1960s, many urban employers found it almost impossible to obtain all the workers they needed, so a reverse flow of industrial investment began, bringing new manufacturing jobs to villages and rural areas, particularly in lowland areas with good road access to one of the metropolitan regions. In more remote districts, however, it has proved much harder to attract alternative or supplementary employment opportunities, so the rate of depopulation has been correspondingly greater. The government has implemented a number of policies designed to make life in these areas more attractive both to existing residents and to potential return migrants, but with little obvious success. Over the long term many rural communities are destined to die out entirely, for age-selective migration has left behind populations which are heavily imbalanced in favour of the elderly.

Many of those rural communities which have been able to attract factories to supplement local employment opportunities now find that these new jobs are at risk from the so-called 'hollowing out' of the Japanese economy, the relocation of investment overseas to countries with lower production costs. This process has a disproportionately severe effect on rural areas, since many of the factories which have been built there were attracted by the availability of what is, in Japanese terms at least, relatively cheap labour. These same communities must also now adjust to lower levels of agricultural protection, and to the rationalization of farm management units that may follow.

Modern urban life in Japan also has its problems. The extraordinarily high price of land in the major cities means that many ordinary salaried workers face a choice between going heavily into debt to buy a small house or apartment in a distant suburb, and accepting an expensive and exhausting journey to work on Japan's chronically congested transport system, or giving up hope of ever owning a home. The average size of new houses in Japan is rising, but it is still very small even by European standards, although Japanese domestic architecture does permit far more efficient use of the space which is available. Most entertaining is done outside the home, and every city has extensive facilities for this purpose: coffee shops, restaurants and leisure centres for the daytime, and for the night a whole section of the city known as the *sakariba*, devoted to clubs, bars, cinemas, theatres and 'adult' entertainments. Japanese cities are poorly endowed with parks and green spaces, as might be expected given the extreme scarcity of land.

Life in Japanese cities is expensive by international standards, but crime rates are low, and the shops are filled with the very latest in international fashions and goods of the highest quality. Efficient inter-regional communications and transportation systems also ensure that many of the benefits of modern urban life are available to Japanese citizens almost irrespective of where they happen to live.

RW

Land prices in the major cities

This chart shows how the increase in the price of land in the six largest cities has outstripped all other economic indicators. Recently there has in fact been a sharp fall, which is not reflected in the graph, but land for housing is still beyond even dreams for the majority. The phenomenal increase seen here was largely the result of a boom economy and a simple lack of space. In the ensuing crash many speculators and their financial backers suffered very heavy losses, which will remain to haunt the domestic economic scene for a number of years. For watchers of the economy it is important to note that the price of land and housing is not included in the official Japanese inflation figures. RB

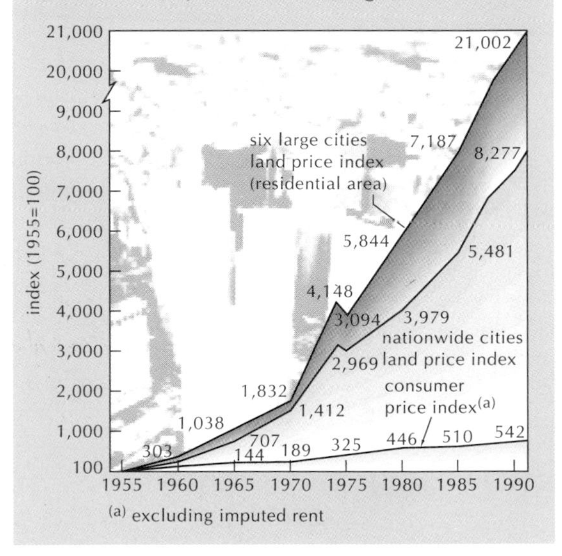

(a) excluding imputed rent

Regions

The conventional regional divisions of Japan conform closely to the major physical lineaments, not least because the ancient fiefdoms of Japan, from which today's main internal administrative divisions (the 47 prefectures) have been derived, were designed that way, in the interests of security and self-sufficiency.

An obvious regional distinction can be made between the four major islands, but this is somewhat deceptive in a country that is more often united than divided by the sea. The Inland Sea, for example, draws together the south-western coast of Honshū, the north coast of Shikoku and north-eastern Kyūshū as a functional economic region far more effectively than the weak overland links across the ranges of south-western Honshū join together its Inland Sea and Japan Sea coasts.

Japan: Prefectures and major regions.

Hokkaidō

Hokkaidō is a prefecture in its own right, the largest of the 47, and while there is some continuity in structure and climate between the Oshima Peninsula in southern Hokkaidō and the mountains of the Tsugaru Peninsula, which lie in north-eastern Honshū, in most aspects of its physical and human geographies the island is quite distinctive. It was only fully colonized by the Japanese from the late 19th century onwards, as a bulwark against the expanding Russian empire. The cultivated landscape of Hokkaidō is unique within Japan, with larger farms, pastures and barns which bespeak the influence of a cooler climate with bitter winters. Its cities reflect modern design principles, combined with special measures to cope with the winters which include extensive underground malls in the island's capital city, Sapporo. Much of Hokkaidō's mountainous interior is given over to national parks, wherein live the remnants of the indigenous Ainu population.

Hokkaidō is the only island to offer rolling 'fields' like these and a landscape generally reminiscent of northern Europe.

Tōhoku and Hokuriku

The Tsugaru Straits no longer form an effective barrier between Hokkaidō and the mainland of Honshū, for modern ferries are complemented by an undersea rail link (the Seikan Tunnel), and for most human traffic air travel has made the junction of land and sea irrelevant. The six prefectures of north-eastern Honshū together form the Tōhoku District, through which the frontier of Japanese settlement passed much earlier, between the 7th and 9th centuries. Remote from the centres of Japanese culture and political life, much of Tōhoku retained its rustic character far later into the present century than other parts of rural Japan. Today Tōhoku is the nation's ricebowl, if only for the lack of a sensible alternative crop to grow in what the winter climate dictates must be a highly seasonal agriculture.

Tōhoku can be subdivided along two main axes: north–south, along the crest of the central mountain range, and east–west, between Miyagi and Yamagata Prefectures to the south and Iwate and Akita to the north. The meridional division discriminates between the 'snow country', which faces the Japan Sea and is cut off from the main lines of communication northwards through Tōhoku, and what is in winter the more sheltered eastern belt, an area which also enjoys a much broader and more continuous endowment of inhabitable land. The main band of settlement in Tōhoku runs along the wide valley which separates the central Ōu Range from the Abukuma and Kitakami Highlands, and links the major regional capital of Sendai with Morioka to the north and Fukushima and Kōriyama to the south.

As for the east–west axis between northern and southern Tōhoku, this attains its greatest contemporary significance on the grounds of accessibility to the great centres of manufacturing activity located on the Kantō Plain. Southern Tōhoku is far more closely integrated with the national industrial economy, mainly as a component supplier, than is the north. The effective boundary line is gradually shifting northwards, however, for the Shinkansen bullet train now links Tōkyō to Morioka in just three hours, bringing the whole of southern Iwate into convenient range. Only beyond Morioka, where the Shinkansen gives way to older rolling stock, does the casual observer notice a marked difference in material prosperity.

In the south-west, the boundary between Tōhoku and the neighbouring region of Hokuriku seems arbitrary on both climatic and human grounds, for Niigata and the three prefectures further west share the cold moist winters of the Tōhoku snow country, similar remoteness from the heart of the nation's modern economy, and an important rôle in rice production. In its eastern part Hokuriku has strong links with Tōkyō and the Kantō District which have been reinforced through the construction of a Shinkansen line, much of it through mountain tunnels. The western part of Hokuriku, beyond the Noto Peninsula and the picturesque city of Kanazawa, has stronger links with the economies of the Kinki District and western Tōkai.

Kantō

To the south of Tōhoku lies the Kantō District, which takes its name from Japan's largest plain. By convention Kantō is divided into two sub-regions. Southern Kantō includes the four prefectures of Tōkyō, Kanagawa, Saitama and Chiba, the core of Japan's leading metropolitan region. During the post-war era large amounts of land have been reclaimed for industry along the shores of Tōkyō Bay, creating a ribbon of heavy industry which stretches from Yokohama round to the opposite shore in Chiba Prefecture, with a vast sprawl of factories and suburbs beyond. To the west, further development is restricted by mountainous terrain, and only a narrow and fractured coastal strip links Kantō to the neighbouring Tōkai District. To the north, however, there is considerable room for expansion across the three prefectures of Northern Kantō (Ibaraki, Tochigi and Gunma), an area that is rapidly losing its rural character.

The Kantō District marks the eastern terminus of the main zone of Japanese industrial and urban development, variously known as the 'Pacific Coast Belt' or the 'Tōkaidō Megalopolis', the latter name referring to the ancient road which linked Kyōto, the former imperial capital in the west, to Edo (modern Tōkyō), the capital of the Tokugawa shōguns. This belt consists of Southern Kantō, the adjacent Tōkai District, the inner zone of the Kinki District, a strip along the north coast of the Inland Sea (known as San'yō), and according to some definitions, Northern Kyūshū as well.

Tōkai

The Tōkai District includes Shizuoka Prefecture, within which habitable land is mostly confined to the narrow coastal plain south of Mount Fuji, plus Aichi and Mie Prefectures, which flank Ise Bay and are dominated by the city of Nagoya, and parts of Gifu Prefecture as well, although most of the latter lies within the mountainous core of Honshū. Tōkai is distinctive both for its agriculture – it is the premier tea producing region of Japan – and for its modern industries (especially automobiles), but it has always been overshadowed economically by its two larger neighbours, in part because the intervening mountains hinder effective access to what would otherwise be the region's natural hinterland, the plains of Hokuriku. Much of the Izu Peninsula, which juts into the Pacific from the south-eastern corner of Shizuoka Prefecture, is included within a National Park, and serves as a recreation zone for the nearby Keihin (Tōkyō–Yokohama) conurbation, with hot springs, beaches and golf courses to complement the wild beauty of the coastline.

Most of Japan's highest mountain ranges are contained within the prefectures of Nagano and Yamanashi, which together make up the Tōsan District. This is a thinly populated area, with settlement confined to a few deep valleys which give access to a lofty interior that is deeply snow-bound in winter. Much of the majestic scenery of this area is protected within the Southern Alps, Chūbu Sanmyaku and Jōshin'etsu Kōen National Parks.

Left *Shinjuku, looking east across the capital to Chiba. The suburbs spread as far as the eye can see.*

An aerial view of the new Kōbe, looking north to the Rokkō range behind the city. The buildings in the foreground have all recently been constructed on reclaimed land and the city continues to expand into the bay itself.

Two ways of picking green tea. The machine saves labour but the hand-picked variety will undoubtedly bring a higher price.

Kinki

The Kinki District to the west of Tōkai is the original heartland of Japanese civilization, centred around the ancient capitals of Nara and Kyōto, both of which have given their names to the surrounding prefectures and to the structural basins in which they are located. A third important basin contains Japan's largest inland fresh water body, Lake Biwa, and defines the borders of Shiga Prefecture. Kinki has traditionally been divided into two distinct zones, an industrial inner zone and a more rural outer zone, with the prefectures of Kyōto, Ōsaka and Hyōgo included in the former and Shiga, Nara and Wakayama in the latter. Unfortunately the configuration of administrative boundaries in this area does not sit well with the actual distribution of human activities on the ground, for large parts of northern Kyōto and Hyōgo are rural and have experienced rapid depopulation, while southern Shiga (around Ōtsu City) and western Nara are undergoing rapid urbanization as the outer commuting belt of the Keihanshin (Kyōto–Ōsaka–Kōbe) Metropolitan Region. Each of the three great cities of the Kinki has its own distinctive character: Ōsaka as a centre of commerce and industry, Kōbe as a major international port, and Kyōto as a repository of traditional Japanese culture. The region's economy has lagged behind that of Kantō in recent years, through the shift to Tōkyō of previously Ōsaka-based companies and the inheritance of a rather dated industrial structure. The remoter parts of the outer zone, especially the interior of the Kii Peninsula and the Pacific Coastline, are very wild and undeveloped areas which have more in common, in both physical and economic terms, with the island of Shikoku than the great metropolis to the north.

Chūgoku

The remainder of Honshū to the west of the Kinki District is known as Chūgoku. This area can also be divided into two halves: San'yō, consisting of Okayama, Hiroshima and Yamaguchi prefectures, which flanks the Inland Sea, and San'in, along the Japan Sea Coast, including the prefectures of Shimane and Tottori. Communications between the two halves of Chūgoku are poor, with the result that San'in remains one of the most backward parts of Japan in economic terms, with rapid depopulation and low per-capita incomes. The coastline of San'in is marked by some of the best developed systems of dunes and brackish lagoons to be found along the Japan Sea Coast of Honshū. San'yō has a modern industrial economy, somewhat blighted in recent years because of specialization in depressed sectors of heavy industry such as steelmaking and shipbuilding.

Shikoku

Japan's fourth largest island, Shikoku, is comparatively backwards in economic terms, due to the isolation of all but its northern coast from the main lines of communication through central Japan. Primary industry dominates on the south side of the island, while to the north, beyond the island's mountainous core, there are several locally important centres of commerce and industry, including Matsuyama, Imabari and Takamatsu. The isolation of Shikoku was at one time broken only by ferry boats, but its situation has recently been transformed by the completion of the first of three massive bridging projects, the Seto Ōhashi, which links Shikoku to Honshū via a number of islands from Okayama to Takamatsu. Flat land is in very short supply throughout the island, and larger towns such as Matsuyama completely fill the plains on which they have been constructed.

Kyūshū

Most of the inhabited area of Kyūshū lies peripheral to the central mountain core. By convention the island is divided into two regions, Northern and Southern Kyūshū, with the latter usually defined as the prefectures of Miyazaki and Kagoshima. Southern Kyūshū has long been one of the most underdeveloped regions of Japan, with a heavy dependence upon agriculture and little manufacturing activity. By contrast, Northern Kyūshū contains one of the earliest centres of heavy manufacturing industry in Japan, established on the basis of the coal resources of the Chikuho Field and the steelworks and related industries at Yahata in Kita-Kyūshū City. The narrow Kanmon Straits between Kyūshū and Honshū have been bridged and are also traversed by tunnels, one of which gives access by Shinkansen to Fukuoka City, the regional capital. Northern Kyūshū is generally considered to be the western limit of the Pacific Coast Belt. Further west still, beyond the agricultural Saga Plain, lies the rias coastline of Nagasaki Prefecture and the shipbuilding cities of Nagasaki and Sasebo.

Nagasaki retains a strong cosmopolitan flavour, derived from its long history of contact with the out-

side world, which continued through Japan's two and a half centuries of seclusion, as well as a unique Christian tradition. The latter commenced with the arrival of St Francis Xavier in Japan in 1549, and was transformed into a distinctively Japanese creed after Christianity was forced underground in the 17th century, to be preserved in secret in various remote areas.

The economy of Kumamoto Prefecture has been transformed over the past 20 years by the introduction of the semiconductor industry, which has given Kyūshū its contemporary nickname of 'silicon island'. To the east of the Kanmon Straits is Ōita Prefecture, an area once very dependent on agriculture, but which has attracted both heavy industry in the 1960s (especially steelmaking) and semiconductors in the decades since. Ōita's second city, Beppu, is one of Japan's leading hot spring resorts, noted for its steaming pools and hot mudbaths. Manifestations of active volcanism are widespread in Kyūshū, from the hot springs at Beppu through the giant caldera of Mt Aso to the cinder cone of Mt Sakurajima, which overlooks the city of Kagoshima and showers its citizens with ash from time to time. Mt Unzen in the west of the island erupted violently in 1991, killing more than 30 people.

At the southernmost end of the archipelago lies semi-tropical Okinawa. As yet, it still offers clean beaches and Pacific scenery; but for how long?

The new Seto Ōhashi bridge which now connects Shikoku to Honshū, island-hopping on the way. The ferries that used to ply the route now do just as well offering sight-seeing trips of the bridge from down below.

Okinawa

The last major region of Japan consists of the solitary prefecture of Okinawa, returned to Japanese rule in 1972 after more than a quarter of a century of American occupation. The island chain which makes up this prefecture enjoyed a separate identity as the Ryūkyū Kingdom until well into the last century, and the local culture still retains many echoes of the past. Today the islands are economically important as the sole production area within Japan for tropical crops such as sugar cane, and for a tourism industry which has grown so large that concern has been voiced over associated ecological damage, including the threat to coral reefs posed by the construction of an airport on picturesque Ishigaki Island. Okinawa is Japan's poorest prefecture in per-capita income terms, and has a rate of population increase well in excess of any found elsewhere within the archipelago.

RW

Fauna

Japan is less well known for its fauna than its flora, and one might suspect that with such dense human habitation, there would be little habitat left for other large mammals. However, substantial populations remain of bears, antelopes, deer and wild boar, in high mountain areas remote from human habitation, in national parks, and on some of the smaller and rockier offshore islands. The bear is mostly to be found in the forests of Hokkaidō, where it has long formed an important part of the folklore of the indigenous Ainu population. The Japanese antelope is well established in the mountains of central Honshū, while deer are to be found both in remote sites and in very public places indeed, such as the temple grounds of Nara and Miyajima, where they are popular tourist attractions. These and other species are the remnants of a much wider animal fauna that populated the islands during the ice ages, and which included mammoths in the north and elephants further south. Such creatures could enter Japan freely from the mainland, to which Japan was connected by a land bridge until some 12,000 years ago.

Large domesticated mammals include the horse and the Japanese cow. The Japanese cow remains important as a source of superior beef, the holstein breeds having displaced it in milk production. *Wagyū* beef is notable for its high degree of marbling, which makes it ideal for dishes such as *sukiyaki*, for which it is prepared in thin slices. The cow must be properly pampered during its life if it is to produce good beef, and this may include massaging with rice wine (*sake*).

Other large mammals inhabit the mountains and rice fields of Japan only in folklore. The *kappa*, for example, is an unlikely creature the size of a child, with a tiger-like face, a beak, and an indentation on its head which holds water and allows the *kappa* to live on land. This creature's image is used to warn children away from dangerous canals and riverbanks, where it waits to drag them under.

Smaller mammals – real ones – are also common, and many have accommodated themselves successfully to cohabitation with human beings. Besides the fox, which is an object of veneration in folklore, there are *tanuki*, racoon dogs which resemble the European badger and can occasionally be seen (and heard) in the outer suburbs of large cities. The Japanese macaque is widely distributed, and those found in northern

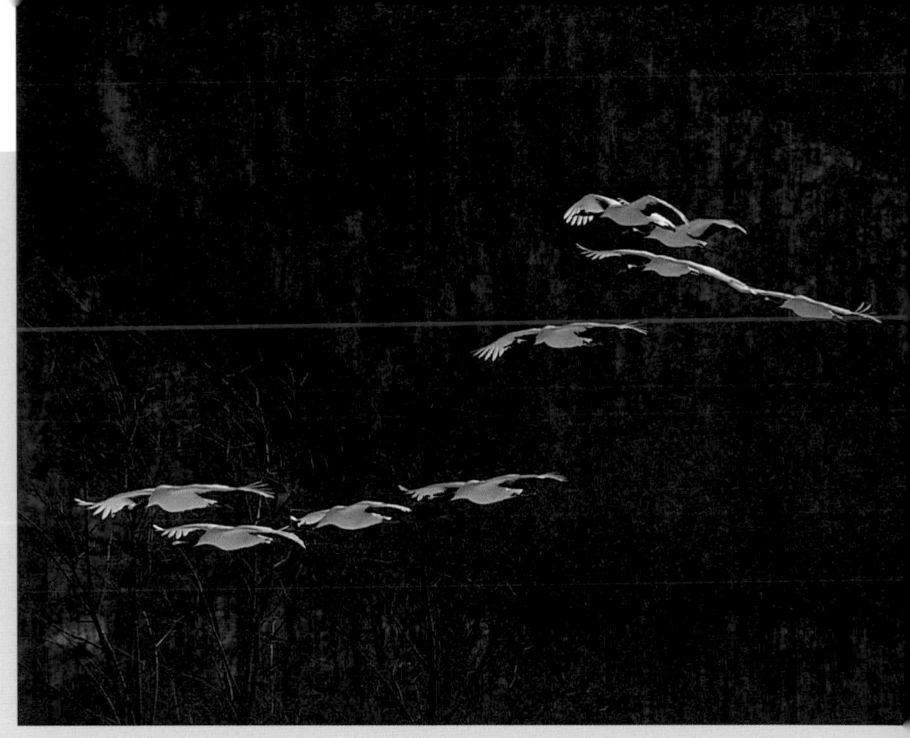

Above Grus japonensis. *The crane is a symbol of good fortune and longevity, a staple of Japanese art and poetry.*

Left *One of the sights of Nara. Tame shika deer have made their home in the Kasuga Shrine.*

Below *Adapting to their unusually cold environment in winter, macaques have discovered one of the true sybaritic delights of Japan: bathing in hot pools in sub-zero temperatures.*

Tōhoku represent the most northerly extent of the monkey's domain on earth. The fauna of urban areas includes the two main domestic species, the cat and the dog, both of which are distinctive. The Japanese domestic cat resembles the British manx cat in having no tail, while many family dogs are of a breed which has a dense coat and the face of a husky. Japan is also home to one of the largest and fiercest of all canines, the *tosa*, which takes its name from the district in southern Shikoku where it is bred. The tosa is a fighting dog of enormous stature, with a ceremonial attire modelled on that of its human equivalent, the grand champion sumō wrestler. The Tosa district is also famous for its ornate long-tailed cockerels.

The reptile population includes sea turtles and sea snakes. The giant salamanders of Kyūshū and southern Honshū can attain a length well in excess of a metre, and are the world's largest tailed amphibians. There are two poisonous snake species, including the *habu*, which is notable for causing gross disfigurations in its victims through muscle wasting in the vicinity of the bite. On one of the islands south of Tōkyō, poisonous snakes are pickled in rice wine, to produce a drink noted for its stimulative qualities. The streams and paddy fields are inhabited by frogs, toads and newts.

The seas and bays around Japan contain an abundance of marine life, but the inland fisheries have always been important too. The main fish of lakes and rivers include varieties of trout, salmon, eels, and crustaceans such as crayfish. Many other species are eaten as local delicacies in season, and may be caught in ditches and even in the paddy fields themselves. Parks and temple gardens are the home of the *koi* carp, widely bred for exhibition in a spectacular array of shapes and colour combinations. The giant carp in temple gardens have been trained to respond to the clapping of hands and gather for food when they hear the sound. Less fortunate members of the same species may end up on the dinner table in expensive restaurants.

Japan is also richly endowed with insect life, not all of it welcome to humans, such as the ubiquitous mosquitoes of summer which can bear a form of encephalitis. Midsummer nights in suburbs and villages alike are filled with the sounds of chirping crickets and the high pitched whine of the cicada. Praying mantis abound and can easily reach lengths of several inches. The grasshoppers and locusts of the rice fields are sometimes still hunted by schoolchildren, in quest of the raw materials for a tasty snack. There are many species of butterfly in Japan, and in autumn squadrons of bright yellow and red *tombo* dragonflies may be observed skimming low across gardens, fields and mountain tops.

The local variety of the Asiatic Black Bear can still be found in the mountains. Hunting is strictly regulated.

These creatures are a delightful feature of the season, for they are easily persuaded to perch on the outstretched human hand.

Finally, there is the bird life. As befits an island nation, Japan is home to a wide variety of sea birds, including gulls, auks and shearwaters, while inland waters are populated by herons, ducks, geese, swans and cranes. Birds of prey include eagles and kites, and there are many species of songbirds. The beautiful Japanese crested ibis (*toki*), once widely distributed, is now sadly diminished in numbers. The crane is the best known of all local bird species, but it is not the official 'national bird': that honour falls to the Japanese pheasant. The skills of the cormorant have been cunningly exploited by man: they are trained to catch fish at night along rivers such as the Kiso, very much for the benefit these days of the ubiquitous tourist. RW

Carp are a treasure and, occasionally, a delicacy. A handclap will bring them over, circling for food.

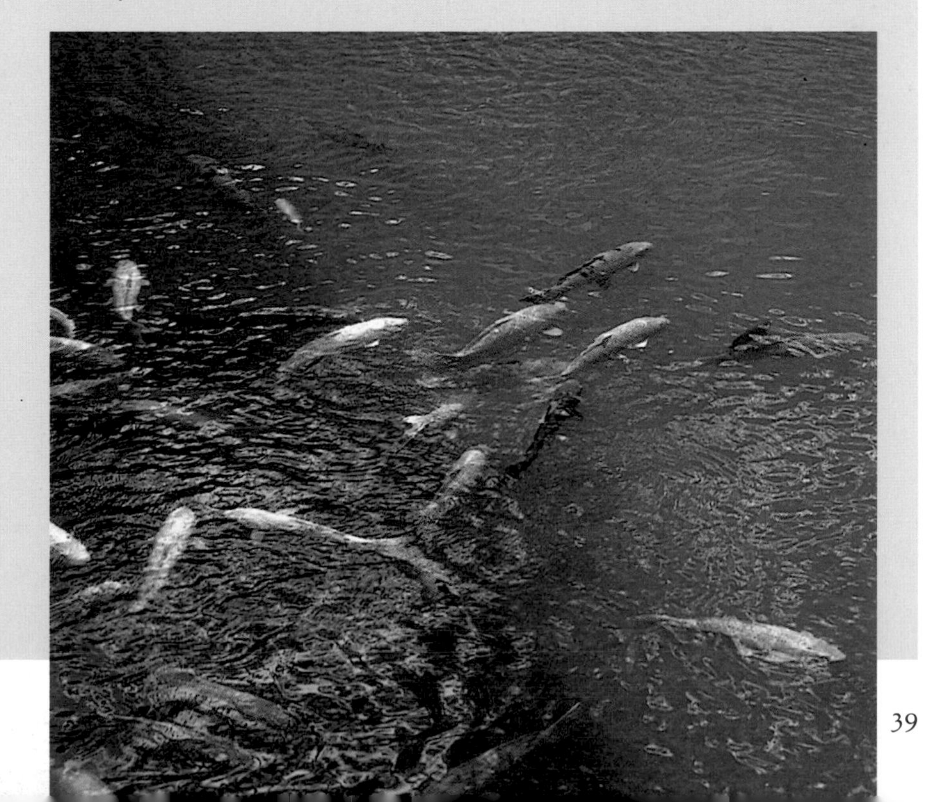

History

Early Japan

Archaeological periods

Palaeolithic (?50,000–10,000 BC)

During this period the Japanese archipelago was occupied by hunter-gatherers who used stone tools. It is assumed that they led a mobile lifestyle, but 30 sites with dwelling and hearth remains have been found.

Jōmon period (10,000–300 BC)

Previous page *Travel in 16th-century Japan: the palanquin was exclusively used by the élite but was nevertheless extremely uncomfortable.*

The Jōmon people mainly lived by hunting animals (mostly deer and boar), fishing, and collecting plant foods. Though some plants and nut trees may have been husbanded, the first agriculturalists are considered to have been those in the west who adopted rice-growing technology towards the end of the period. The archipelago was unevenly occupied, with the majority of the 30,000 or so known Jōmon sites occurring in the richer environments of the northeast. The Jōmon period is unusual in that ceramics and polished stone tools, elsewhere marks of neolithic society, existed in a hunting and gathering society without agriculture. Moreover, the Jōmon people lived in settled villages. They therefore combined a temperate-climate lifestyle with that of hunter-gatherers living in settled communities and using ceramics, and they represent a kind of society not extant in the modern world. They are used increasingly as a worldwide resource for information on this kind of socio-economic form.

The distinctive patterns of Jōmon pottery were made by impressing twisted cord on the surface. The oldest fragments so far uncovered are about 12,000 years old and are thought to be the oldest pottery yet found anywhere in the world.

Yayoi period (300 BC – AD 300)

Yayoi was the first fully agricultural society in the archipelago, with rice being grown in alluvial wetlands and millet, barley and wheat on higher ground. Both bronze and iron, having been introduced from the continent, were in widespread use for tools and ritual objects. The raw materials used for metalworking were mainly imported from the Korean peninsula, in the form either of already finished bronze objects which were melted down and recast, or of unfinished iron objects or ingots which were further forged into shape. The distribution of ceremonial bronzes such as weapons and bells parallels different burial customs, showing considerable social variability in Yayoi society. In Kyūshū, individual interment was in large urns or stone cists, sometimes occurring under dolmens and clustered in cemeteries. In the area around modern Kyōto and Nara, family burial precincts were demarcated in cemeteries with ditches. Adults were interred in wooden coffins and children in jars.

In Middle and Late Yayoi, northern Kyūshū communities were drawn into the tributary networks of the Chinese Han and Wei Dynasties. Many precious objects were obtained from the Chinese courts, and their court ethnographers recorded the customs and accoutrements of the Yayoi peoples, giving us a written record of this prehistoric period.

Kofun period (AD 300–710)

The burial of political leaders in large, richly furnished mounded tombs (*kofun*) is the hallmark of this period, during which the Yamato state was formed. International relations in this period were important, since Yamato's alliance with the state of Paekche on the Korean peninsula led to a massive influx of people, ideas, customs and material culture in the 5th and 6th centuries.

The tombs themselves are huge and symbolize class society through access to the resources, labour and goods needed for building and furnishing them. An increasing number of craft specialists became subordinate to the demands of chieftains: jade and jasper workers, ceramicists, bronze mirror manufacturers, and iron weaponry and armour producers. The élite used their products to mark their status while establishing alliances or conducting hostilities among themselves. The contents of the tombs suggest a shifting source of power, from ritual power in the 4th century to military might in the 5th. In the 6th century, tombs were built for the entire ruling-class, not just the chiefs, and their contents indicate a belief in the afterlife with offerings of food and drink. The descriptions of *yomi*, the underworld, probably derive from the structure of these family tombs and the possibility of re-entering them to see the decay of the dead.

The last 50 years of this period are known as the Asuka period (645–710) when Asuka became the capital area of the Yamato court. The year 645 is the historically transmitted date of the 'Taika reform', a process which is now understood to have occupied an entire century from Shōtoku Taishi's innovations in 604 to the Taihō Codes of 701. This period marks the shift of attention from the Korean states in the 5th century to the Chinese dynasties as a model for governmental reform.

Asuka is a very special region, rich in protohistoric remains but totally unrepresentative of general settlement patterns in Yamato or elsewhere in the archipelago. Many Paekche immigrants settled here in the 5th century, and when Buddhism was accepted at the Yamato court, after bloody confrontations in 587 between the immigrant-derived Soga clan and the native Mononobe and Nakatomi clans, the first temples were built here.

A modern reconstruction of a pit dwelling.

Ethnicity

The modern population is not a homogeneous synthesis of the Jōmon and immigrant populations of earlier times. Physical anthropological studies show tremendous variation in the distribution of particular physical traits in various parts of the archipelago. Skeletal studies suggest the indigenous populations of Okinawa and Hokkaidō (the Ainu) are more closely related to each other and to the Jōmon than to the modern population of central Japan, which shows the most affinities with modern Koreans. The protohistoric migrations of Koreans to Japan were followed by the forced immigration of Korean craftspeople in the 16th century and Korean workers in the 20th century, as well as many Chinese. Despite these inescapable facts, modern Japanese hail the Jōmon as their legitimate ancestors. This has two important ramifications in modern Japanese politics: the emphasis is shifted away from the immigrant populations in specifying the physical origins of the Japanese; and the area of Jōmon culture, which reached from Okinawa to Hokkaidō, is seen as the inalienable homeland of the Japanese, rather than the more restricted areas of the early Yayoi agriculturalists (western Japan) or the early Yamato state (the region centred on Kyōto and Nara). GLB

Populating the archipelago

It is not yet agreed when the Japanese archipelago was first populated. Datings of stone tools prior to 50,000 years ago are hotly debated, and substantial occupation remains do not appear until after 30,000 years ago. More than 2,000 sites are known for the Late Palaeolithic period (30,000–12,000 years ago), whereas only about 400 sites are known for all Palaeolithic phases on the Chinese mainland. These dates are significant not only for occupational time depth but for establishing what kind of population was first present. Remains of *Homo erectus*, the evolutionary forerunner of modern humans, have been found as close as the Liaodong Peninsula in north-eastern China. Any colonization prior to 120,000 years ago would probably have been by this species. Otherwise, it was by modern humans, *Homo sapiens*. What are now the Japanese islands formed the mountainous rim of the continent during much of the Pleistocene period (2,000,000–10,000 years ago), so it is misleading to think of this human colonization of 'Japan' as something extraordinary. People were just moving to the natural coastal limits of the existing landmass.

The Palaeolithic occupants of the Pacific rim were isolated from the continent by the post-glacial rise in sea level, which also determined the present-day shape of the islands. In the Jōmon period, dugout boats plied the waters in and around the islands, keeping the population sporadically in touch with their palaeo-asiatic neighbours on the continent. Between 1,500 and 500 BC, the Korean peninsula received new populations from north-east Asia (Tungus speakers) and the southern Chinese mainland (rice agriculturalists). Members of this augmented population then migrated into Kyūshū, mixing with the indigenous Jōmon. This hybrid population then seems to have expanded into most of western Japan at the beginning of the Yayoi period. In the Yayoi and subsequent Kofun periods, there were several more waves of immigration from the peninsula, especially in the 5th century. These various migrations are identifiable by the skeletal characteristics in excavated human burials and by documentary texts. One study has estimated that at least a million people migrated to the archipelago between 500 BC and AD 500. Accordingly it is calculated that by the 7th century AD, Jōmon genes constituted only one-ninth of the Japanese gene pool with the rest being supplied by recent continental immigrants.

Rice and fish

Rice has historically been the staple food of the Japanese islands; but rice without supplements is neither nutritious nor interesting. Moreover, there have been several periods in which many inhabitants did not eat rice for economic or social reasons. The first rice was grown by Jōmon groups of northern Kyūshū from early in the first millennium BC. Rice is not native to the islands, and it was probably introduced by a trickle of immigrants from the Korean peninsula, as assessed from the material culture accompanying it. In addition to its dietary potential, the adoption of rice agriculture had two major effects on Jōmon life: it changed the scheduling of subsistence activities throughout the year, and the ritual ceremonies that accompanied these activities invariably underwent major transformations. The resulting western Yayoi culture that was synthesized from these new elements of custom and material culture was radically different from the Jōmon way of life led by the majority of people in the north-east, who had a very successful riverine and deep-sea fishing economy along the Pacific coast.

These later Jōmon fisher-folk resisted adopting rice agriculture for a couple of centuries after it became available. Although the archaeological evidence for fishing becomes very scarce after the adoption of rice, it can hardly be thought that fishing activities were abandoned entirely. After all, fish and rice provide complementary proteins, and their combination underwrites all east and south-east Asian diets. Moreover, the importance of fish in modern Japan cannot be overemphasized.

The institution of paddy-field farming in the Yayoi period changed the lowland landscape forever. Rice requires specially constructed fields in which water can be pooled for at least three months during the growing season. Additionally, canals for supplying and draining the water must be dug. These activities modified the land surface while creating totally artificial lowland environments.

The size and shape of early paddy fields often conformed to the contours of the landscape, and fossilized field systems of different periods have been excavated from under volcanic ash deposits and flood sediments. In the 7th century AD, the Yamato state undertook large-scale land surveys and field reallocations as part of the 'Taika reform'. The grid system (*jōri*) of one-hectare square field sections established at that time is still in use in many parts of Japan today.

In the Kofun period, the rice-basket of Japan is known to have been the region centred on Nara, which supplied most of the rice for palace consumption. As rice became a political commodity, it is possible that it became more and more restricted to the élite class, with peasants growing it but not eating it. Barley, wheat and millet were also grown, perhaps with slash-and-burn technology, which survived in Japan into this century. Moreover, the gathering of wild products did not cease. Special local products, such as mushrooms or trout, were sent to the Yamato court as tribute. With the adoption of Buddhism in the 6th century, the eating of four-legged animals was prohibited. Hunting, therefore, virtually ceased. Excavations, however, have revealed that dog meat was a prime source of protein in the medieval period. Although chickens were available from the Yayoi period, they were not eaten and their eggs not consumed until the 19th century. Prior to this they seem to have been a ritual animal, associated with the sunrise.

State formation

In the Yayoi period, distinctive burials, in terms of their elaborate structure or rich contents, make their appearance at various times and places within the archipelago, suggesting that several regional communities might have been ruled by chiefs. Such socio-political regionalization increased during the Late Yayoi period, when from Kyūshū to Kantō there appeared local chiefs who were interred in a wide variety of mound-burials. This archaeological situation conforms to the accounts given in the Wei Dynasty chronicles, which describe the archipelago in the 3rd century AD as divided into more than 100 'countries', some of which were ruled by Queen Himiko of Yamatai or Yamai. Where this was located is not known, but competing hypotheses place it either in Kyūshū or in the vicinity of Nara.

At the beginning of the 4th century, the burials of chiefs changed radically, conforming to homogeneous standards of tomb size and contents. This shift signalled the incorporation of the local chiefs into a far-flung élite network in which their equivalent status became more important than their local roots. The emergence of the mounded tomb culture, as this 4th-century phenomenon is known, is interpreted as the material manifestation of the stratification of society into the two traditional classes necessary for subsequent state formation: aristocrats and commoners. It is interesting that the first state in the archipelago developed in an area that was not under heavy continental influence in the previous Yayoi period.

Exactly when the Yamato state came into being is a matter of definition. There are varying definitions of what constitutes a 'state', with Japanese scholars concentrating on the concept of 'unification'. In Western anthropological scholarship, states are defined in three different ways: the presence of class society, the legitimate monopoly of force, and specialized administration. Depending on which definition is adopted, the Yamato state came into existence at different times, each of which can clearly be correlated with different aspects of Kofun-period material culture. The homogeneous tomb structure and contents of 4th-century mounded tombs suggests that

Warfare

The Yayoi peoples have usually been looked upon by archaeologists as basically peaceful, with routine agricultural duties demanding their time and attention. This view is now changing with both textual and archaeological data showing developing competition and warfare between local groups. The Chinese dynastic histories speak of the Wa Disturbance of AD 150–190, and the archaeological evidence shows Yayoi sites developing on hilltops, fortified with surrounding ditches and possibly palisades. Stone arrowheads become larger and heavier at this time, suggesting that they were used as weapons rather than as hunting gear. The circle of conflict seems to have been widened in the Early Kofun period with increased competition for iron resources, available only on the southern Korean peninsula. The iron armour and weaponry deposited in the Middle Kofun period is mirrored in similar finds in the Kaya region of the southern Korean peninsula and attests to the development of a specialized warrior élite.

The 'horserider theory' of state formation has been proposed as one cause of Yamato state formation, with mounted warriors from the Korean peninsula conquering the central area and establishing a new state. This theory is weakly constructed and does not stand up to archaeological or textual examination. However, there is no doubt that both hostilities and alliances marked the relations between the emerging states of Yamato in Japan and Paekche, Koguryo and Silla on the Korean peninsula, while the rôle of the horse became very important in Late Kofun period politics. Horses were valued gifts from abroad, and aristocrats lavishly decorated them for court and military display. Horse trappings became a common component of élite burials.

Warfare and military alliances did play an important rôle in expanding the territory and rulership of the Yamato state. Iron swords with gold inlaid inscriptions found in Saitama and Fukuoka prefectures attest to late 5th-century alliances between the Yamato ruler and local chiefs, many of whom were integrated into the court structure as 'lords of the land'. The Iwai Rebellion of 527, involving a rebel chief ruling the north Kyūshū region, and its quick suppression by Yamato forces shows that by that date the central court was exerting strong control over these distant regions even though a local administrative system was not yet institutionalized. In the 7th century, threat of attack from Silla led to the construction of several Paekche-style mountain-top fortresses with either stone or tamped-earth walls in the Seto region. By the 8th century, central power was threatened by internal succession disputes after which trends towards centralization of government were intensified. GLB

a Yamato state came into existence through 'unification' in terms of both political ritual and social stratification. The large amounts of iron weaponry and armour in early 5th-century tombs suggests 'unification' through military conquest and the monopolization of force. The institution of the *be* system of craft goods, production and services to the court in the late 5th century suggests 'unification' through administrative means, which is documented archaeologically by the appearance of inked wooden tablets from the late 6th century.

Writing was a skill which was introduced into the Yamato Court in the 5th century by scribes from the state of Paekche on the Korean peninsula. No records survive from this early period, but the *Paekche chronicles*, which probably dated from this time and were written by Paekche scribes either in Paekche or after they arrived in Yamato, are known to have been

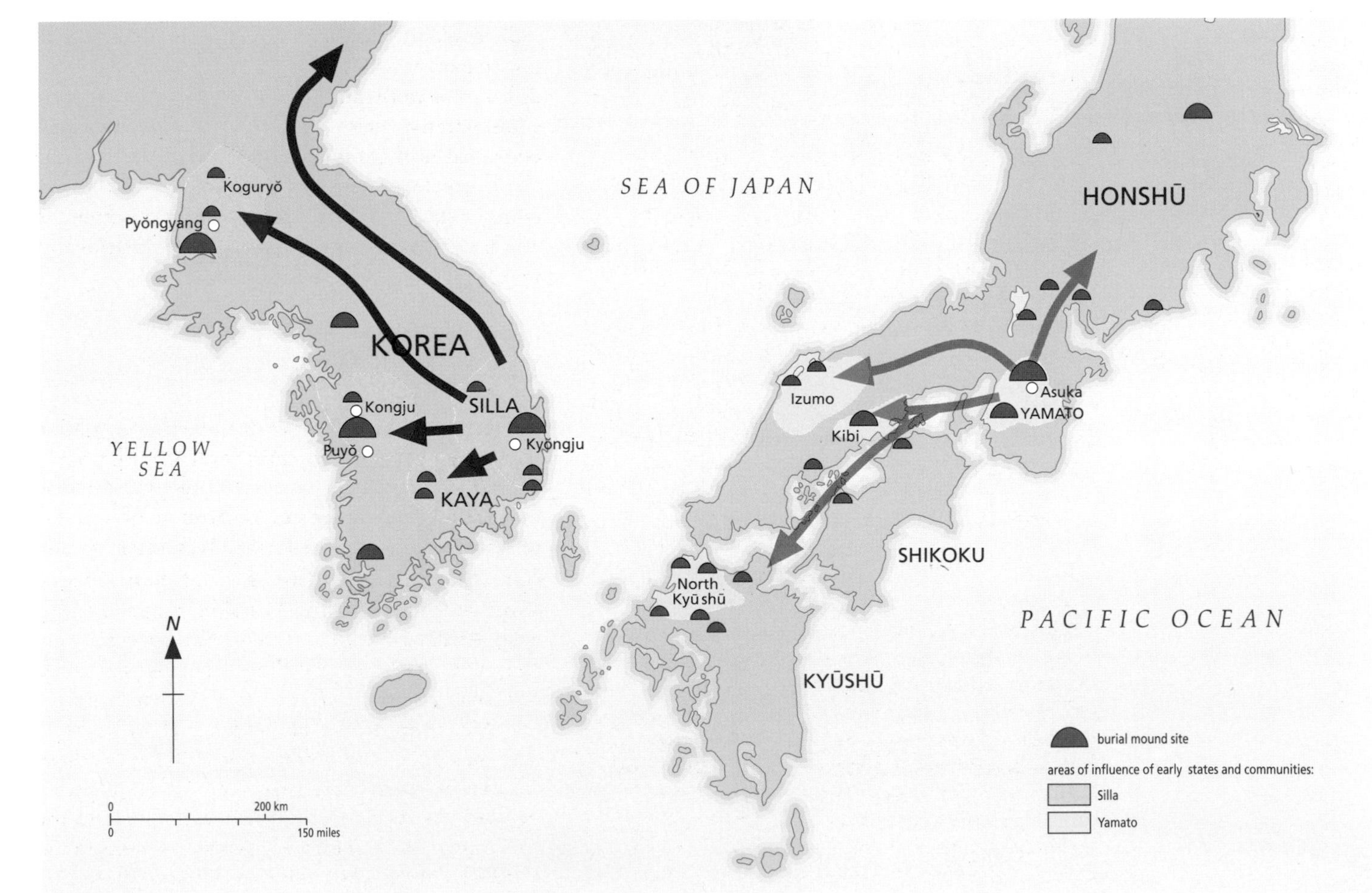

Left *The keyhole-shaped tomb of the Emperor Nintoku in Ōsaka Prefecture. Over 480 metres in length this is the largest keyhole tomb in Japan and it dates from the first half of the 5th century. It has never been excavated, but when part of it collapsed in 1872 a stone burial chamber was revealed.*

The formation of the Japanese and Korean states. Contacts between Japan and Korea were extensive in the 4th, 5th and 6th centuries and Japan gained skills, artefacts and immigrants from its more advanced neighbour. It was during this time that the nascent Yamato state was growing and spreading outwards from the Yamato district, as the spread of tomb culture clearly shows. In Korea the pressure to unify the peninsula came from the state of Silla in the south-east.

incorporated into the later Japanese court history, the *Nihon shoki*. With the accession of Keitai to the throne in 507, all the aristocratic houses were encouraged to document their own family histories, and these records were also used to compile the later *Nihon shoki* and *Kojiki*.

In the 5th century, there was a large influx of foreign craftspeople arriving from the Korean peninsula, mostly from the Paekche state. The goods newly produced for the court by these foreign craftspeople included patterned cloth and brocade, gold jewelry and ornaments, gilt bronze horse trappings, and stoneware ceramics. Their arrival stimulated the Yamato court to reorganize supervision and administration of craft production and service groups by instituting the *be* system, in which lower level aristocrats were assigned as managers for the collection of craft goods for court use. The *be* managers as well as other courtiers were given specific court ranks (*kabane*), and these individuals formed the nuclei of newly emergent clan structures (the *uji*) which were once thought to be the primeval form of Japanese social organization. The *be* system was probably the first administrative structure of Yamato, regulating the duties of subordinates beyond simple bonds of personal loyalty and allegiance.

The state infrastructure was fully overhauled in the 7th century, under the rubric of the Taika reform, as various aspects of Tang Dynasty administration were adopted from China with an eye to increasing the power and control of the central government. The *be* were dissolved and the *kabane* replaced by a different system of ranks. Among the innovations were a provincial administrative system, population censuses, the survey and government allocation to individuals of rice paddies (using the *jōri* system), taxation of individuals on their fields' produce as well as levies of cloth and labour, and the codification of administrative laws and penal codes (*ritsuryō*) embodied in the Taihō Code of 701. The resulting state structure was a fully bureaucratic system employing stipendiary officials, which continued in power until 967 when the statutes were subordinated to rule by social status and custom.

The fiction of Mimana

The *Nihon shoki* makes reference to a 'Mimana Nihonfu' (the Nihon, or Japan, headquarters in Mimana) and this has been historically understood to have been a colony of the Yamato state on the southern Korean coast between the 3rd and 7th centuries AD. Modern Koreans vehemently reject this scenario, and historians have uncovered internal textual evidence to show that the story is indeed inaccurate. The Mimana data were originally taken from a Paekche document which spoke of a Mimana Wafu (the Wa headquarters in Mimana) on the southern peninsula; the use of Nihonfu is an 8th-century anachronism, created by the *Nihon shoki* compilers. Wa is a name used in the Chinese dynastic histories for peoples living on the southern Korean coast and Japanese islands. The nature of the Wafu is now hotly debated: it has been argued that it belonged to the local aristocracy of the Wa peoples, that it was an international facility within Kaya manned by delegates from Paekche, Silla and Yamato for official communications, or that it was a Paekche outpost where Yamato troops were stationed at Paekche's request. Mimana Wafu did not survive Silla's conquest and incorporation of the south coast between 532 and 562. It was this disappearance of Mimana Wafu that the *Nihon shoki* chroniclers portrayed as Japan's 'loss'. They intended to 'revive' Mimana, despite it never having belonged to the Yamato court, in order to extract taxes from the southern peninsula. GLB

Urbanization

The Chinese court histories describe the 'capital' of Queen Himiko as having palisades and watch towers, a kind of settlement structure unknown archaeologically until the recent excavation of the site of Yoshinogari, Saga prefecture. This differs greatly from the 'shifting palace' sites of Kofun-period kings, as known from historical documents, which were newly built with each reign. These palaces were most likely elaborate dwellings which served as the residence of the king and the place of political assembly. Most Late Kofun-period kings chose to build their palaces in the Asuka region of the southern Nara basin, where most early Buddhist temples were situated. Asuka thus became the capital area of the late Yamato state albeit without dense concentration of population or significant craft production areas.

The adoption of the Chinese grid-city plan, during the 7th-century drive to emulate the Tang, was therefore a radical departure from the native settlement pattern. The first Chinese-style capital was built at Fujiwara in 694, at the mouth of the Asuka valley; it consisted of a palace, containing ministerial buildings as well as the imperial residence, at the northern edge of the city, and a street grid laid out to the south for the placement of aristocratic housing and markets, etc. The Fujiwara capital, which represented the transformation of the old Yamato state into a powerful bureaucratic structure and the fruition of the *ritsuryō* system of government, was only in use for 16 years before the move to Heijō, which marked the beginning of the Nara period. GLB

The Nara period 710–94

The Nara period commenced with the removal of the capital from Asuka to the northern Nara basin. The characters used to write the name of the new capital are now pronounced 'Heijō', but it is thought they might have been pronounced 'Nara' at that time. The Fujiwara palace buildings were dismantled and the materials transported to build the new capital, the site of which lies west of the present-day city of Nara, which is written with different characters. The city included east and west markets, aristocratic housing just south of the palace enclave, and large temples. The Tōdai-ji temple, built in 745 to the east, became an important component of the political structure. In 752, a monumental bronze statue of Buddha was dedicated at the temple, but behind the splendours lurked the more desperate face of Buddhism, for the temple and statue had been built to 'atone' for the great smallpox epidemic of 735–37.

Extending administrative control

The capital, Heijō-kyō, was linked to the southern basin and Ōsaka bay by government roads which were also laid out on a grid pattern corresponding to the land-divisioning system. These then connected to the regional trunk roads which passed through

Shōtoku Taishi

Shōtoku Taishi (574–622) was the second son of Emperor Yōmei and became regent to Empress Suiko of the Soga family in 594. He instituted reforms in 604 designed to strengthen the central government. These included the creation of 12 ranks awarded to courtiers for achievement rather than birth, and the promulgation of a 17-article 'constitution', which formalized Confucian mores of élite conduct within the court and gave it a legalist base.

He freely used his position and influence to promote Buddhism, employing imperial resources to build the first temple, the Asuka-dera in 588, and sponsoring the construction of the Shitennō-ji and Hōryū-ji. Several hundred temples are attributed to his efforts. He built his residence away from Asuka near the Hōryū-ji in the western Nara Basin, close to the exit corridor of the Yamato River into the Ōsaka plains and Inland Sea. His presence there must have facilitated control over both international and local traffic to Asuka, thereby strengthening his political position. GLB

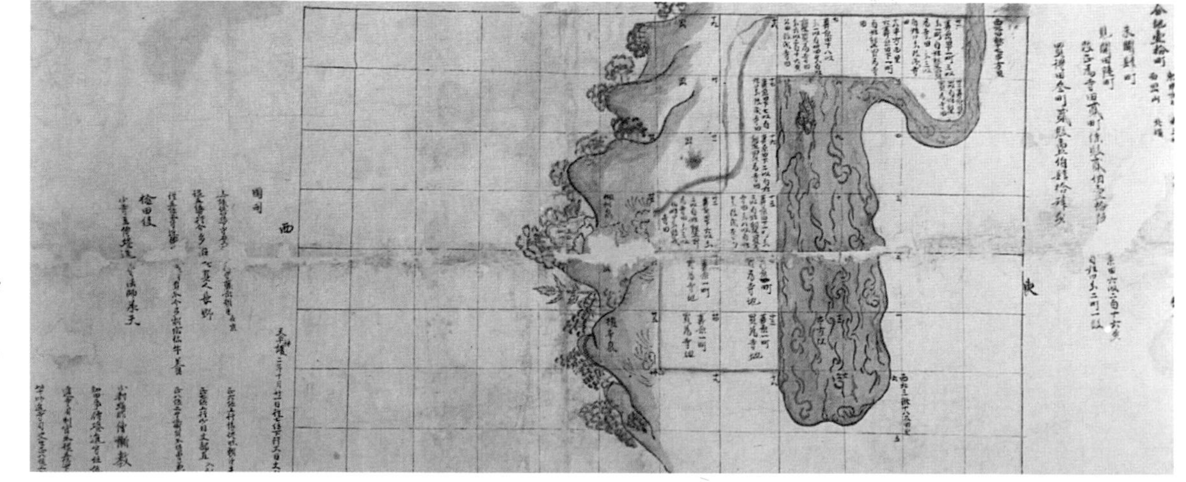

An 8th-century map of some of the provincial estates of the Tōdai-ji temple in Nara. Religious institutions owned large tracts of tax-free land and had a serious impact on the tax-gathering potential of the state.

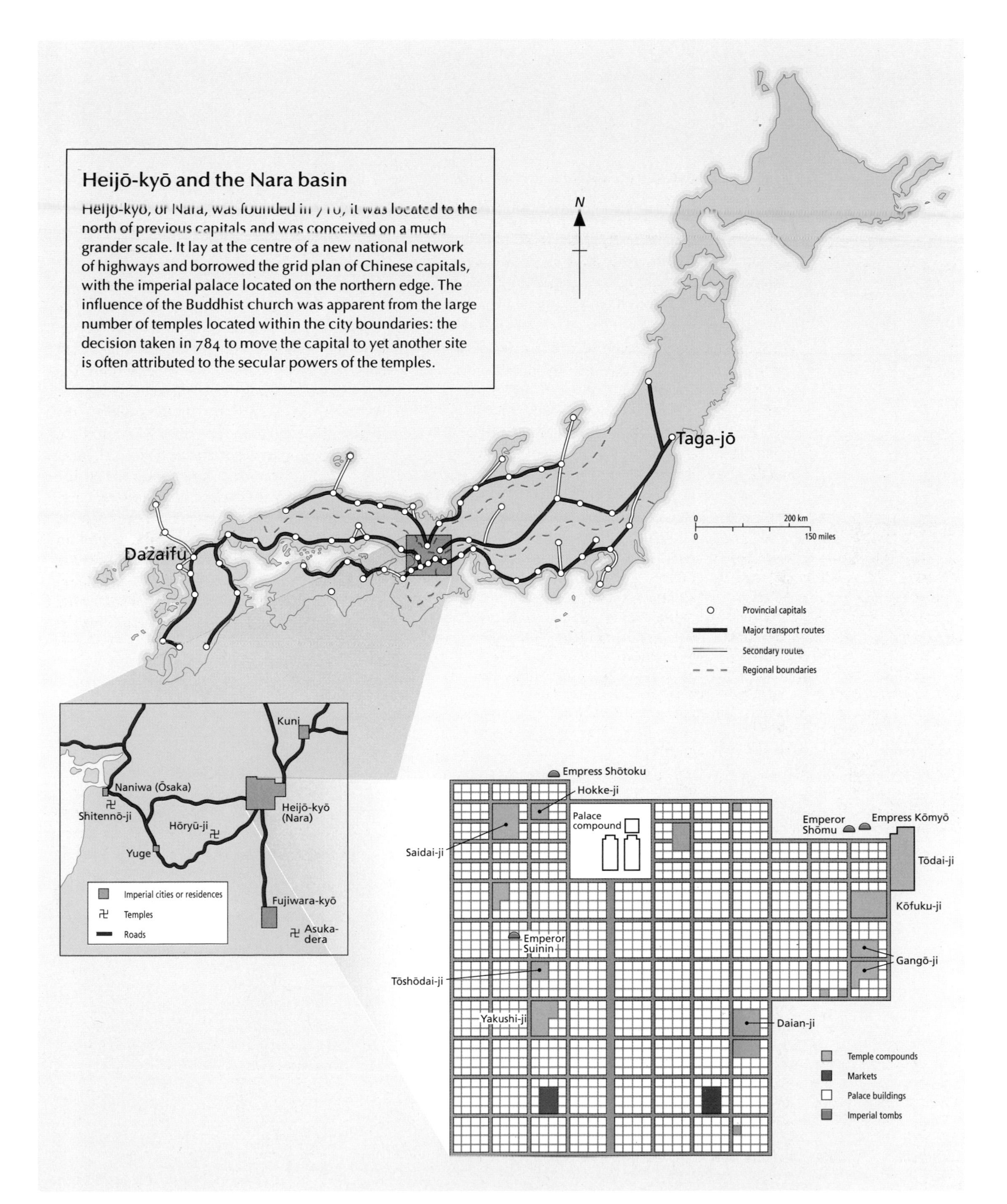

Heijō-kyō and the Nara basin

Heijō-kyō, or Nara, was founded in 710; it was located to the north of previous capitals and was conceived on a much grander scale. It lay at the centre of a new national network of highways and borrowed the grid plan of Chinese capitals, with the imperial palace located on the northern edge. The influence of the Buddhist church was apparent from the large number of temples located within the city boundaries: the decision taken in 784 to move the capital to yet another site is often attributed to the secular powers of the temples.

most provincial centres established in the reforms of the previous century. Government couriers could have their horses serviced or changed at stations along the way. The development of such communications and transport networks ensured greater control over the provinces, especially facilitating the transfer of tax goods to the capital. Two special installations, Taga-jō in the north and Dazaifu in the west, regulated relations with the communities existing beyond the reach of state administration.

The political system of the Nara period was distinguished by a dual territorial hierarchy, one comprised of the imperial court at Heijō ruling over provincial and county administrative centres along the Tang Chinese model, and one consisting of the Tōdai-ji overseeing monasteries and nunneries established in each provincial centre by the 742 decree of the emperor Shōmu (r. 724–49). The Tōdai-ji, like other temples, was granted tax-free estates to generate income for its maintenance, perhaps because the tax-paying population had been halved during the initial smallpox epidemic, with repeated losses every generation. The state could not spare direct funds from its coffers but allowed the temples to pay their own way.

Taxes were collected from the populace by county heads and sent regularly to Heijō. The excavation of tens of thousands of wooden tablets from administrative sites, including Heijō, has provided data on the tax goods and provisioning system of the capital. Fish, salt, and seaweed were collected from coastal and mountain villages; ceramics were produced for the court at specialist potting villages; and rice tended to be sent from nearby provinces. These tablets are direct evidence of the workings of the Nara-period bureaucracy, contrasting dramatically in content with the historical records produced at the time.

The first books

Soon after the establishment of Heijō, histories being compiled under imperial command were submitted to the court: the *Kojiki* in 712 and the *Nihon shoki* in 720. These are our earliest extant documents for Japan, although earlier non-surviving works were drawn on for their compilation. The two histories both begin with creation myths and continue with

Politics in the Nara period

Political machinations in this period revolved around imperial succession and attempts to gain influence over or access to the throne. Although succession rules were in place by the time of Emperor Keitai (early 6th century) stipulating succession directly from generation to generation without fraternal rotation, there was ample scope for competition and uncertainty when it came to exerting influence over a current emperor or empress or to choosing a successor. The Fujiwara family, founded by Nakatomi Kamatari around 645, increased its power and status through marrying several daughters to successive emperors. The great statesman Fujiwara Fubito (659–720), who helped draw up the Taihō Code of 701 and compiled the Yōrō Code from 718, was the father-in-law of two emperors and grandfather of another. The family was also able to drive the powerful Prince Nagaya, who was viewed as a threat to their control over the throne after Fubito's death, to suicide. A Fujiwara woman, Kōmyō, became an imperial consort soon afterwards, and her daughter became Empress Kōken in 749. In 757, Fujiwara Nakamaro managed to have his favourite accede to the throne as Emperor Junnin instead of the crown prince, and Nakamaro received the highest official court rank in 762. Later, in 770, Fujiwara members Nagate and Momokawa again engineered the accession of their chosen candidate as Emperor Kōnin.

A second powerful faction influencing imperial politics was the Buddhist priesthood. Emperor Shōmu, who wholeheartedly promoted Buddhism through the building of the Tōdai-ji and the provincial temples, was succeeded by Empress Kōken, who was his daughter by Kōmyō. Kōken also patronized Buddhism, but during her reign in 757, a plot within the priesthood to overthrow her and usurp the throne was uncovered. She went into temporary retirement, during which time she came under the influence of the monk Dōkyō, who was appointed Grand Minister on her recommendation in 764. The next year, Kōken regained the throne as Empress Shōtoku and continued to promote Dōkyō upwards in court rank until he threatened in 770 to usurp the throne. The abandonment of the Heijō capital soon thereafter was partly a strategy to distance the imperial throne from the Nara temples and influence of the priesthood. It has also been suggested that the exclusion of women from imperial succession from this time onwards was an attempt to remove the weak link which was prey to aggressive male priests. GLB accounts of the successive imperial reigns, the *Kojiki* ending with Suiko's reign (592–628), and the *Nihon shoki* ending with Jitō's reign (690–97). Much legendary material is included for the proto-historic reigns now assigned to the Kofun period, but it is thought that the chronology in the *Nihon shoki* is accurate in its descriptions from AD 500 onwards.

Both texts were written to legitimize the rule of the imperial line by documenting its long history, continuity, and ultimate derivation from the gods, and to establish the rightful position of nobles and aristocrats of the court by weaving their family origins into the imperial story. In accomplishing these objectives, much historically accurate material was misrepresented through chronological transposition or misattribution. Textual analysis has also suggested that the pre-Nara 'emperors' actually belonged to three different lineages, the Sujin (4th century), Ōjin (5th century) and Keitai (6th century onwards) lines, with the first ten 'emperors' of the series being either totally fictitious or contemporaneous personages occupying the political stage before Sujin. These would not be the only breaks in the much touted 'unbroken' imperial line of modern Japan, for discontinuities also occurred in the medieval period.

The *Nihon shoki* was followed by the *Shoku nihongi* (797), covering the events of the 8th century; these two books are the first two volumes of a series later referred to as the Six National Histories. Four more were compiled in the Heian period after which time state control over historiography declined. Two other kinds of books were compiled in the Nara period: poetry anthologies, the *Kaifūsō* in 751 and the *Man'yōshū c.* 759, and geographical treatises from the different provinces. The latter were compiled at government order as part of the drive to increase and regulate knowledge about the lands, customs and resources under court control.

THE NORTHERN FRONTIER

Heijō's administrative hold gradually weakened towards the northern Honshū frontier. As known from the early texts, the Tōhoku region was occupied by a people called Emishi. The Emishi have previously been thought to have been hunters and gatherers, perhaps the forerunners of the Ainu, the aboriginal peoples of Hokkaidō in recent times. It is clear now, however, that they must be considered to be descendants of the northern Yayoi agriculturalists. In extending the administrative reach of the state, central troops waged sporadic military campaigns against this local agricultural population in what might be termed the 'manifest destiny' of the Japanese state to control the entire archipelago. Several forts were built in Tōhoku, their founding dates showing the progress of expansion northwards. How the Emishi are related to the Ainu, who are first mentioned in documents of the 15th century, is one of the great mysteries of historic Japan; but neither can be looked upon as primitive hunter-gatherers. Curiously, there are many Ainu place-names in Tōhoku, demonstrating the once wider distribution of Ainu peoples in northern Japan. Their ancestors might have co-existed with the Emishi, occupying a different environmental niche from the lowland agriculturalists. The Emishi traded in rice and iron from the Yamato sphere, and evidence is growing that the 17th-century Ainu were also agriculturalists and forged iron implements for themselves. In 749, gold was discovered in Tōhoku, providing a source for the material previously imported from the Korean peninsula and making centralized control of Tōhoku even more important.

THE SOUTH-WESTERN GATEWAY

In northern Kyūshū, a government office was established to regulate relations with the continent. This was Dazaifu, where diplomatic and trade missions from Tang China and Silla in Korea were greeted and vetted before their travel to Heijō. Built on a plan similar to the provincial centres, it also served as a dispatching point for envoys from the capital. Official embassies travelling to China often included Buddhist monks and students bound for the great monasteries for several years' residence and study. In return, great treasures were brought from the Tang court and capital to be delivered to the emperor. Tang aristocrats partook of many fashions in music, food, and clothing from points west, especially Persia, and the Heijō élite attempted to follow suit. Many objects and goods brought in on the Silk Routes (Byzantine glass, Egyptian marquetry, Sassanian silver, Central Asian carpets, a Vietnamese

The main gate of the Tōdai-ji temple in Nara. Constructed entirely of wood in the middle of the 8th century at the behest of the Emperor Shōmu, the temple assumed the role of the protector of the nation.

rhinoceros-horn bowl), as well as Chinese products, were imported to Japan and preserved in the Shōsōin together with superb examples of Nara craftsmanship in bronze, lacquerware, painting, etc. The Shōsōin was the imperial storehouse of the Heijō court, and is located in the grounds of the Tōdai-ji temple. The present-day storehouse is only one of 50 such repositories existing at the Tōdai-ji in the 8th century; upon the death of Emperor Shōmu in 756, it received all his possessions from his widow.

Perhaps most interesting within the Shōsōin collection are the musical instruments and wooden masks, many originally derived from Persia and India, which were incorporated into the music and dance of the Tang court. These entertainments were enthusiastically adopted by the Yamato and Heijō courts. The lively masked-dance genre now known as *gigaku* soon faded away, but the *bugaku* dances and accompanying *gagaku* music survive as the court music of present-day Japan. Recent research suggests, however, that the performance of *gagaku* today has been slowed to a fraction of its former speed in acquiring a ritual rather than entertainment function. Since, as in many other aspects, all trace of these musical styles has been lost on the mainland, the Japanese survivals give scholars an invaluable window on Tang culture.

Nagaoka and other capitals

Although the construction of the Chinese-style capitals supposedly marked the end of the 'shifting capital' syndrome of the proto-historic period, in fact, several other capitals besides Heijō were temporarily designated for use during this period. Emperor Shōmu removed his court to both Kuni and Naniwa to escape clan feuds among the aristocracy. Yoshino, in the deep mountains south of Nara, was also visited by emperors in need of rest or refuge.

In 784 it was decided to move the permanent capital yet again, and a site was chosen at Nagaoka, to the south-west of present-day Kyōto. Like Fujiwara, the Nagaoka capital was destined to be short-lived; and in 794 the court moved again, this time to the site of Kyōto, and the new capital was named Heian. The *ritsuryō* system of government, based on codified laws and state ownership of land, was maintained for the first half of the Heian period, but the expansion of grants of tax-free status to aristocrats as well as temples marked the beginning of the end of *ritsuryō* rule through contraction of the tax base, the further escape of peasants to the great estates where the burdens of production were not so great, and the increase in wealthy and powerful temples and noble families who challenged the power of the court. GLB

The Heian period 794–1185

In 794 Emperor Kanmu took up residence in a new capital. The city of Heian-kyō, 'Capital of peace and tranquillity', which lends the period its name, would largely live up to its optimistic appellation for almost four centuries. It was the centre of administration, economic and political power, religious authority and cultural activity. Heian-kyō, known later as Kyōto, was *the* city of Japanese historical experience: cultural memory has always recollected and interpreted its arts and literature as Japan's classical heritage, just as political memory held on to its concrete embodiment of centralized government joined to imperial authority as a model for political organization through centuries of conflict and change.

From Nara to Heian-kyō

Heian-kyō was not Japan's first experiment in capital building and centralized authority. Throughout most of the 8th century the imperial family, aristocrats and bureaucrats had inhabited the Heijō capital, the city of Nara. Nara, with its regular grid of streets and avenues, impressive governmental buildings, temples and shrines, seemed like the physical fulfilment of all the efforts to convert competition between rival clans and imperial lineages into a stable state structure modelled along the lines of the Chinese imperial bureaucracy. Yet rivalries persisted, and in some cases grew worse. The Fujiwara family already showed signs of establishing the dual hegemony which would make them politically and socially dominant in the Heian period: they began to occupy and pass on as hereditary rights the chief positions in government; they also began the practice of regularly marrying their young women to imperial princes and emperors, a strategy calculated to produce rulers loyal to their Fujiwara fathers-in-law and grandfathers. Their success caused the hostility of other noble families and non-Fujiwara members of the imperial family. The result was a series of coups and counter-coups, leading in one instance to the near annihilation of one branch of the Fujiwara. The growth of powerful Buddhist institutions further complicated the political scene. Emperor Shōmu, and others in his family, had sponsored Buddhism as a protection for the state and, as demonstrated vividly by the scale of the Tōdai-ji temple with its massive bronze Buddha, an emblem of imperial wealth and prestige. As the temples grew larger and wealthier and as Buddhist monks began to figure prominently at court, it became apparent that members of the imperial family might use the clergy as a foil to the nobility and even that the clergy might usurp the power of both patrons and rivals. The latter possibility was almost realized when Empress Shōtoku proclaimed her confidant, the priest Dōkyō, as chief minister, with an additional title making him the equivalent of a retired emperor. Dōkyō's subsequent exile did not dispel the contentious political atmosphere of the capital. Kanmu's own ascension to the throne in 781 was engineered by a Fujiwara faction who arranged for the imprisonment and mysterious death of a rival prince and his mother.

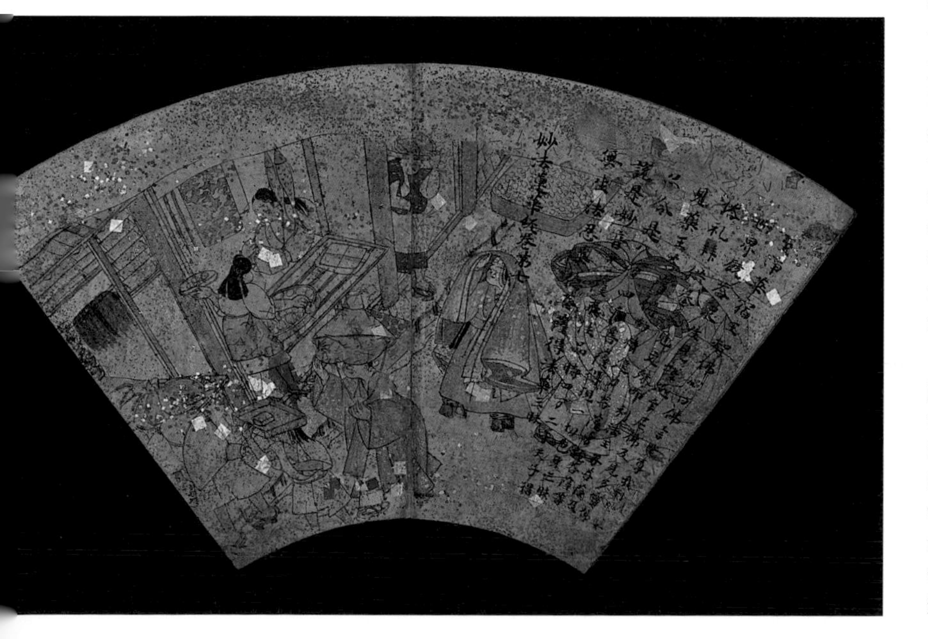

A sūtra fan dating from the end of the 12th century. The text of the Lotus Sūtra has been written over scenes of everyday life. The incongruity is still puzzling, but it is thought that objects such as this reflect a desire to extend by symbolic means the saving power of the Lotus Sūtra to ordinary life.

Kanmu's policy regarding entrenched court powers was straightforward: if you can't beat them, mobilize and move them. Concerning the Buddhist temples and monasteries it was simpler still: leave them behind in Nara. The mobilization of the vast wealth, manpower and resources required to build a new capital was an effective way to test the loyalty of the nobles, divert their in-fighting and much of their income into the project, and physically detach them

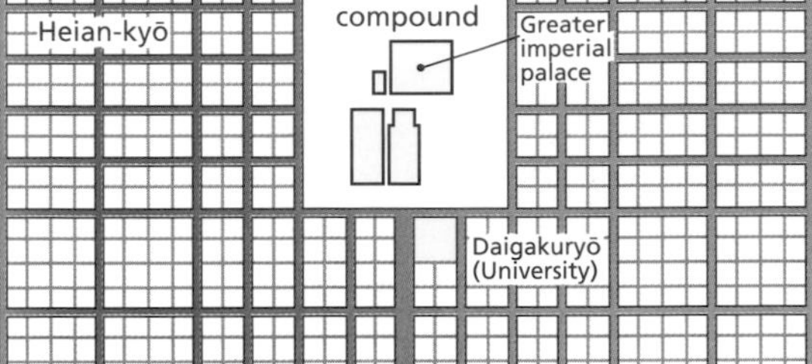

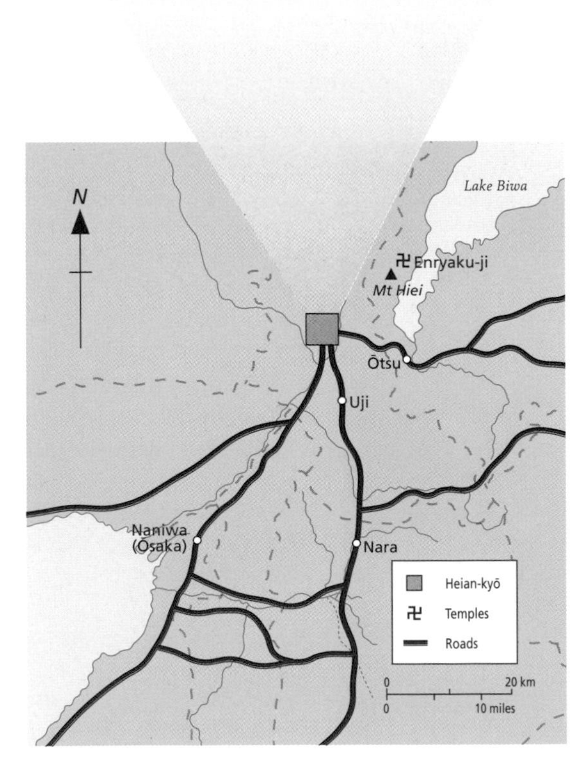

Heian-kyō, or Kyōto as it later became known, was founded in 794 and it remained the capital until 1868. Like Nara, it employed the grid pattern of Chinese capitals, but unlike Nara the presence of Buddhist temples was strictly controlled and there was only one major temple within the city boundaries. Nevertheless, in later years the soldier monks of the Enryaku-ji on Mt Hiei posed many problems for the secular government and testified to the continuing political ambitions of sections of the Buddhist church.

from their economic base in the Yamato region. The court and capital were moved in 784 to the site of Nagaoka north-east of Nara. After more plots and assassinations had claimed the lives of the Fujiwara planner of the new capital and Kanmu's younger brother, the emperor ordered the construction of yet another capital further to the north in an area settled by his mother's family of Korean immigrants and associated with his own line of the imperial family, descended from Emperor Tenji.

Capital and aristocrats

The city that Kanmu entered in 794 was taking shape in the same geometry of order and power as Nara, only on a larger scale. Its rectangular grid of avenues and streets marked out 1,200 potential units of land and extended four and a half kilometres east to west and over five kilometres north to south. The capital was divided into eastern and western halves, each containing originally a marketplace and, not surprisingly after the turmoil of the previous era, only a single temple. Bisecting the city's two halves, the broad, tree-lined Suzaku Avenue ran from the city's southern perimeter up to the central gate of the Greater Imperial Palace in the central northern sector. The moats, embankments and walls of the latter enclosed the city within the city, a 400-acre precinct of government buildings and imperial residences, storehouses and treasuries, stables and guardhouses, gardens and courtyards. During the Heian period a population that reached some 5,000,000 was governed and taxed from a capital of 100,000 people of whom perhaps 10,000 controlled and profited most from the centralized state: higher and lower titled and ranked aristocrats, lesser officials and petty functionaries.

The political élite carried with them from the old capital to the new the structure of a state apparatus uniquely reshaped from Chinese precedents to fit local realities. At the apex, an emperor whose position was sanctified by descent from Shintō deities and augmented by Chinese theories of legitimacy; implementing his rule, an elaborate bureaucracy staffed by officials minutely classified into eight basic ranks subdivided into 30 finer gradations; powering the system, aristocratic families, some like the Fujiwara descended from pre-Nara clans, whose

Court life

Sei Shōnagon served in the court of the empress as a lady-in-waiting during the closing years of the 10th century but very little is known of her life other than what she records in the jottings known as the *Pillow book*. They reveal her to have been a person for whom the court and its social hierarchies and graces were everything.

> Who pays any attention to a Palace Chaplain when he walks by? Though he may recite the scriptures in a most impressive manner and may even be quite good-looking, women despise a low-ranking priest, which is very sad for him. Yet, when this same man becomes a Bishop or Archbishop, people are overwhelmed with awe and respect, and everyone is convinced that the Buddha himself has appeared among them.
>
> If a servant girl says about someone, 'What a delightful gentleman he is!' one immediately looks down on him, whereas if she insulted the person in question it would have the opposite effect. Praise from a servant can also damage a woman's reputation. Besides, people of that class always manage to express themselves badly when they are trying to say something nice.

Sei Shōnagon refers in her *Pillow book* to many love affairs, and although her sexual life was probably not atypical of court ladies, her accounts of it have been seen to bespeak a casual promiscuity that shocked later generations of moralists.

> On one occasion a man, who invariably sent me a letter after we had spent the night together, declared that he saw no point in our relationship and that he had nothing more to say to me. There was no word from him on the next day. When dawn appeared without the usual next-morning letter, I could not help feeling rather gloomy. 'Well,' I thought as the day advanced, 'he really meant what he says.'

Lady Sarashina, on the other hand, did not relish life at court and found her first experience of it fell well short of her expectations. Torn between the sympathy of her father, who entertains no illusions about court life, and well-wishers who urge her not to pass up the opportunity, she returns once more.

> When I was summoned to the Princess's apartment for night duty, I had to lie next to women I did not know and I could not sleep a wink. Overcome with nervousness and embarrassment, I wept secretly until dawn; then I returned to my room and spent all day in loving, anxious thoughts about Father, who was growing old and feeble and depended on me completely. I also thought of my poor nieces, who had lived with me ever since they lost their mother and who even used to sleep next to me, one on each side. As I sat in my room musing vacantly, I had the impression that an eavesdropper was standing outside peeping on me, which made me most uncomfortable.

PK

noble titles gave them access and hereditary rights to suitable bureaucratic rank. The intertwining of title and rank, blood and office, had been the major inflection of the Chinese theory, if not actual practice, of a ruling meritocracy. The senior nobles occupied ranks one to three, serving as chief ministers on the Council of State. Below them were ranks four and five, one hundred or more holders of key posts. These intermediate ranks might serve as points of entry to the system for sons of senior nobles or as non-inheritable posts awarded for special service. Beneath this true aristocracy were hundreds of officials down to rank eight, and below them some 6,000 non-ranked functionaries. There were in addition some 1,000 women serving at court, from cooks to high-ranked noble daughters.

Rank meant wealth. The five aristocratic ranks received life-time grants of income from fixed areas of rice fields, guards and servants, and commodities such as silk – the most liquid form of wealth at the time. Lesser ranks received only commodities. The senior nobles received additional grants of income. Their greatest source of legal wealth were office grants: tax-exempt rice fields, hundreds of servants and guards, and taxes from as many as several thousand households. The income provided by the state for its highest noble might be one thousand times that allocated to an official in the sixth rank, below the edge of the aristocracy.

Part of the record of a 13th-century poetry competition mounted as a hanging scroll: the poets Fujiwara no Shigeie and Taira no Sadabumi are depicted below.

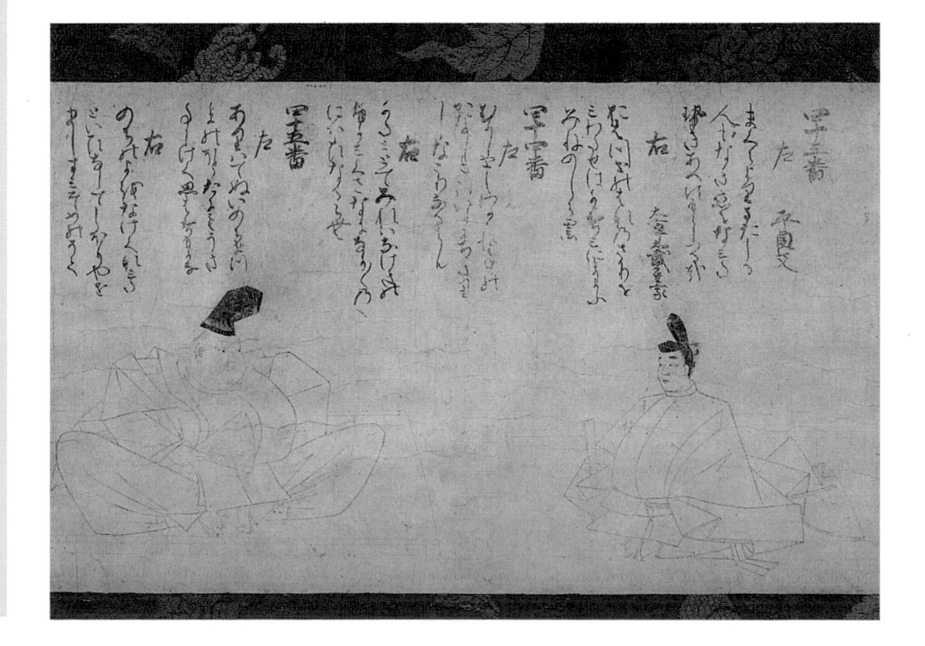

THE FUJIWARA

The vast inequalities of wealth and status built into the early aristocratic bureaucracy reflect concessions made centuries before when emperors and their allies sought to turn clan warriors into loyal courtiers. During the Heian period one branch of the proliferating Fujiwara generated a family which, in addition to wealth and power derived from rank, office and an expanding network of private rights over land, employed two tactics to secure a position well beyond anything imagined by the first state planners, including their own ancestors. One was intermarriage with the imperial family. The other was the creation of the supra-legal office of regent, from which the head of the family could directly oversee the authority and decisions of the emperor.

A sign of things to come occurred as early as 858 when Fujiwara Yoshifusa, already the highest government minister, installed his young grandson as emperor and took up the title of regent, previously reserved for members of the imperial family. His son Mototsune extended the regency to cover the reign of an adult emperor. For a century, when a non-Fujiwara emperor such as Saga, Uda or Murakami managed to attain the throne, his first task was to marshall allies and resist the imposition of a regent. The most famous victim of Fujiwara machinations, Sugawara no Michizane, was elevated from a modest background as scholar and provincial governor into the highest offices by Emperor Uda, who used the hiatus offered by the death of Mototsune to fill his Council of State with tractable nobles. In 901, within weeks of his final promotion, Michizane was dispatched into exile by the efforts of the late regent's son. From the mid 10th to mid 11th century an unbroken line of Fujiwara Regents dominated the Heian court and government.

The most spectacular of them was Fujiwara no Michinaga. In the early 11th century he and his sons were so firmly in control of official positions that Michinaga himself only served as chief minister or regent for brief periods. Not the least of his successes was the marriage of four daughters to emperors, making him grandfather to three more. In 1019, when Michinaga was in his mid fifties, ill health persuaded him to take Buddhist vows and hand over leadership of the family to his eldest son, the next regent, Yorimichi. His last thoughts before taking the tonsure were less of his sons than of what he had achieved as 'protector of many emperors' by way of his daughters.

Fujiwara marriage politics were facilitated by the marriage customs of the Heian aristocracy. Polygamy meant on the one hand that an upwardly mobile young noble could attach himself to influential families and multiply his chances of producing heirs. On the other hand, the prevalence of uxorilocal marriage – an arrangement in which a husband visits or resides in the wife's house – placed a husband and, more importantly, offspring of the union under the guidance of the wife's father or brothers. While Fujiwara empresses and consorts generally resided at the palace, their princely sons did much of their growing up inside Fujiwara mansions. When they became emperors, there attending to them at court were their Fujiwara mothers, uncles and grandfathers.

Heian marriage practices, which tightened the network of noble patriarchy, also had important results for the status of aristocratic women. The original code which had established the state structure had imposed a strict rule of male primogeniture that excluded women from inheritance rights. Later codes and general practice allowed women to inherit and transmit property. This meant that even a Michinaga might find himself living in a mansion owned by one of his wives. A woman of the senior nobility might gain rank and income from service at court, as empress or dowager empress, or by way of special

The Phoenix Hall of the Byōdō-in at Uji, south of Kyōto. The Hall was completed in 1053 by one of the sons of the celebrated Fujiwara no Michinaga.

The game of kemari *was popular among the court aristocracy in the Nara, Heian and Kamakura periods and later spread to the populace. Players formed a circle and kicked a deerskin ball around trying to prevent it from falling to the ground. The ball is at the top of the picture.*

grants. Yet even the most influential of them could not accede to the family headship, nor could they transmit their ranks downward to the next generation: increase or maintenance of wealth and status depended on male kinsmen. This is the political economy of gender which lies behind the romantically conceived anxieties and frustrations of the female characters in a work such as *The tale of Genji*. The author, Murasaki Shikibu, served at the palace in the entourage of Empress Shōshi, the daughter whose marriage and fertility cemented Michinaga's position early in the 11th century. Narrative details concerning the arts, religious and courtly ceremonies, refinements in costume and everyday etiquette reflect the material and aesthetic luxury of Fujiwara wealth; the anxiety and longing endured by female protagonists tell more about the insecurity faced by a woman on the edge of the aristocracy, such as the author herself, from a branch of the Fujiwara long superseded by the house of the regents.

The growth of shōen

The power and wealth of government and nobility were based on the control and exploitation of land and labour. During the Heian period military force extended governmental authority into northern Honshū and the southern tip of Hokkaidō, fighting or co-opting the socially, if not ethnically, distinct Ezo peoples. Throughout more densely settled provinces a wider variety of grains, trees and vegetables were being grown; double-cropping of rice alternating with wheat became common; irrigation works were improved, iron hoes and water-powered mortars introduced – all these slow developments were creating a more productive rural economy to sustain an expanding population and enrich those who dominated it. The imperial state had been founded on the principle that land and cultivators were under the administrative and fiscal control of the emperor and his officials. The latter were, by way of survey and census, to measure and redistribute land and to tax and exact corvée labour from those who worked it. This model for the extraction of peasant surplus was, however, undermined by two practical adaptations of the Nara era: one was the granting in perpetuity to title over reclaimed land; the second, the grant of tax-immune tracts of land and labourers. Before and throughout the Heian period religious institutions and noble families competed to join reclaimed land and tax-immunity to the further privilege of administrative autonomy. Realized by the labour and ingenuity of peasants and local functionaries – some of whom became in time major proprietary holders – the result was an increase in arable land and productivity, and the creation of the *shōen*. *Shōen* were aggregate areas of land held by absentee owners whose liabilities for tax and administrative authority were established by central government charter. Reclamation was the chief means of *shōen* creation through the early part of the period. Their increase in later centuries was due to the growth of a complex process of commendations. Put simply, as *shōen* holdings increased, conflict with provincial officials attempting to protect some of the state's dwindling fiscal base and with acquisitive neighbours tended to increase as well. One means by which a lesser aristocrat or regional magnate might defend his tenure was the commendation of his landholdings upward to a noble, temple or shrine with more leverage over central ratifying authority; in return he received formal title specifying rights of authority and taxation, and the share of income due to the new legal head of the chain of corporate rights. If the latter found it necessary to seek even more exemptions from taxation or government scrutiny, the chain of rights might be extended to the patronage of a senior noble or even more powerful religious institution. To manage and extend its complex rural holdings, the household office of the Fujiwara regents expanded into a large organization of household officials, many of whom continued to hold rank and office in the increasingly ceremonial state bureaucracy. As wealth circulated more and more through private channels, private administrative bodies took on many of the functions of governance. These new chains of economic interest, stretching from countryside to capital and cutting across provincial and central social hierarchies, took on a strong political coloration during the last century of the period as two new forces challenged Fujiwara dominance: the imperial family itself, reorganized around the household offices of abdicated emperors, and provincial military families, often with distant ties to the imperial family or branches of the Fujiwara.

Ex-sovereigns and warrior aristocrats

In 1068 Go-Sanjō became emperor. His mother belonged to the imperial family, not to the regent's house. He began the process continued by his heirs of controlling the imperial family's fortunes and dominating the court as ex-sovereign, elevating non-Fujiwara nobles and, eventually, leaders of provincial families into positions of influence within the court, and of manipulating the imperial succession away from Fujiwara princes. He abdicated voluntarily after only four years, the better to monitor such tactical moves free from the encumbrances of the throne. Go-Sanjō also used state machinery to curb the proliferation of *shōen*. Yet lands seized through such measures were converted into imperial family holdings, not returned to central fiscal administration. By the 12th century, the household office of the ex-emperors had taken on the structure and functions of those of the other great *shōen* managers as, abandoning its reliance on state finances or Fujiwara largesse, the imperial family joined in the accumulation of private sources of wealth and power. As a result, under subsequent abdicated sovereigns, they re-emerged as an independent political force for the first time in centuries; under such ex-sovereigns as Toba and Go-Shirakawa, they became the greatest landlords in the country.

Noble families hostile to the Fujiwara regency aided their efforts, but more significant were their provincial allies. Abdicated sovereigns promoted into their household organizations and into positions at court men drawn from the provincial governor class. They came from varied backgrounds: descendants of princes and aristocrats who had sought their fortunes on the land rather than in the capital, men from families long selected as provincial or district officials and as military leaders, men who had administered and policed *shōen* – the family of any one individual might contain elements of all such forms of provincial authority. They shared in common a tradition that was one of the most crucial gaps in the Heian system of government: the organization and use of military force.

Two years before Kanmu entered Heian-kyō his government disbanded the regional militias the early state had relied upon to protect and expand its borders. The sons of provincial notables were to command new élite troops made up of the rural gentry, although details of organization and qualification for officership were not spelled out. The government never abandoned efforts to direct law enforcement and military actions in the provinces, but they did so in piecemeal fashion. The first major challenge to central authority lasted from 935 to 940 when the regional magnate and warrior Taira no Masakado lead a rebellion stretching across several eastern provinces and proclaimed himself emperor. The government did commission a general from within the courtly Fujiwara, but the brunt of the fighting was born by a provincial Fujiwara, Hidesato, leading a private army in league with other such extra-governmental troops. Hidesato was rewarded for his service to the state with court rank and office and a generous grant of land.

As long as military leaders found their interests best served by co-operating with central authority, they might be played off against their rural competitors. By the 12th century, as ex-sovereigns and then the dominant Fujiwara family became dependent upon the descendants of these provincial warriors to enforce their claims, extend their network of commendations, and to intimidate rivals at court, the way was open to an armed conflict. The Taira and Minamoto had gained considerable influence at court just when, by the mid 12th century, major rifts had taken place within the Fujiwara and imperial families, pitting fathers against sons, emperors against ex-sovereigns. The era of peace and tranquillity was over by 1156. That year the last main figure of the regent's house, Yorinaga, died battling Taira and Minamoto troops allied to the last powerful abdicated emperor, Go-Shirakawa. The next decades witnessed the supremacy of the Taira, and even the enthronement of emperors born to Taira mothers. But the old politics of rank and marriage were over as well. The destruction of the Taira by the Minamoto in 1185 ended the political life of Heian-kyō.

MM

Dannoura and the end for the Taira

In spring 1185 the Minamoto forces brought the Taira to their knees and finally inflicted a crushing defeat on them in a naval battle at Dannoura at the extreme western end of the Inland Sea. The Minamoto were led by Yoritomo's brother, Yoshitsune, and he took advantage of local tides and currents to bring his smaller fleet to victory. It was a catastrophe for the Taira, who were also known as the Heike: once the outcome was no longer in doubt their admiral, Tomomori, threw himself into the waves, as did many of his followers. Even before that, the young Emperor Antoku, grandson of the great Taira Kiyomori and symbol of Taira ascendancy, met a similar fate, as recorded in the *Tale of the Heike*.

> 'How are things going?' the ladies asked. Tomomori uttered a sarcastic laugh. 'You will be getting acquainted with some remarkable eastern warriors [i.e. Minamoto].' 'How can you joke at a time like this?' They all began to shriek and scream. The Nun of Second Rank, who had long ago decided on a course of action, draped her two dark-gray underrobes over her head, hitched up her divided skirt of glossed silk, and took the Emperor in her arms. 'Although I am only a woman, I will not fall into enemy hands. I will go where His Majesty goes. Follow swiftly, you whose hearts are loyal to him.' She walked to the side of the ship. The Emperor had turned eight that year, but seemed very grown up for his age. His face was radiantly beautiful, and his abundant black hair reached below his waist. 'Where are you taking me, Grandmother?' he asked, with a puzzled look.

Antoku perished but his mother, who jumped in at the same time, was rescued from the waters and lived out her life as a nun in a hermitage called the Jakkōin north of Kyōto which still possesses a lock of her hair.

Dannoura was not the end of the Taira's troubles, for many of Kiyomori's followers were subsequently executed, including his son Munemori and grandson Kiyomune, as the *Tale of the Heike* records.

> Munemori at once closed his mind to distracting ideas, faced westward, folded his hands, and recited Amida Buddha's name in a loud voice. Kinnaga went around behind him from the left, a drawn sword held inconspicuously at his side, and stood poised to strike. The Minister ceased his recitations and said touchingly, 'Have you already killed Kiyomune?' Kinnaga moved in from the rear and Munemori's head fell forward in an instant. The others present could not help feeling pity, dauntless warriors though they were. Afterwards, in the same way, the holy man instructed Kiyomune and urged him to invoke the sacred name. Most touchingly, Kiyomune asked, 'How did the Minister behave at the end?' 'He was admirable. Please set your mind at ease.' Kiyomune shed tears of joy. 'There is nothing left to worry me now. Be quick about it!' Yoshitsune proceeded toward the capital with the heads. At Kinnaga's direction, the bodies of father and son were buried in a single grave. The heads of Munemori and Kiyomune entered the capital on the twenty-third. Members of the Imperial Police received them at the Sanjō riverbed, paraded them along the avenue, and hung them in the China tree to the left of the prison gate. They suffered equal shame in life and in death.

The Heian court had survived without executions until the last years when warriors came into open conflict on the streets of Kyōto. The execution of somebody with as high a rank as Munemori was not unprecedented, but the humiliation inflicted on his severed head was, and it symbolized the shift from the rule of rank to the rule of the sword.

PK

The medieval age

The medieval age spans the 12th to 16th centuries and includes the late Heian (794–1185), Kamakura (1185–1336), and Muromachi (1336–1573) periods. A time of considerable disintegration and warfare, it also saw great economic, social, and cultural changes. It began when the authority of the imperial court was undermined as warriors came to power in the provinces during the 10th and 11th centuries and ended with the wars of unification at the end of the 16th century.

The end of court domination

In the 11th century, provincial warriors became embroiled in Kyōto politics and began to seek political power. The court sought to pre-empt this by playing off one warrior clan against another, especially the powerful Taira and Minamoto. This policy worked until the mid 12th century when the Taira under their leader Kiyomori wiped out their major rivals and established a virtual hegemony over the court. Much as the Fujiwara had done, Kiyomori and the Taira monopolized court offices and tried to rule through the existing administrative framework. In his efforts to dislodge them, ex-emperor Go-Shirakawa looked to the surviving Minamoto who were regrouping in eastern Japan under the young general Yoritomo. Sweeping Minamoto victories over the Taira in the late 12th century replaced one military régime with another.

A portrait of Minamoto no Yoritomo (1147–99). It was said to have originally been placed in a Kyōto temple opposite a portrait of his foe, Taira no Kiyomori.

The Kamakura Bakufu

Yoritomo assumed the title of shōgun and established his base in Kamakura in eastern Japan. The Bakufu, or warrior government, was primarily concerned with the warrior order headed by Yoritomo and his vassals, but in time it assumed more power over landholding rights, tax payments, and legal affairs affecting the whole of society. The Hōjō regents, who dominated the Bakufu after the extinction of the Minamoto line of shōguns in the early 13th century, established a branch office of the Bakufu in Kyōto and intervened in the imperial succession. They assumed authority, too, in foreign affairs and it fell to Hōjō Tokimune to organize the defence of the country in the face of the Mongol invasions of 1274 and 1281. Unreconciled to its declining authority, the court made several attempts to recover political power. In the Jōkyū War of 1221, the forces mustered by the court were easily crushed by the Hōjō, giving them the power to confiscate more lands, to punish courtiers and members of the imperial family, and to regulate the order of the imperial succession. In the 1320s resistance to the Bakufu clustered around emperor Go-Daigo. With the support of the Ashikaga and several other powerful warrior families, Go-Daigo was able to overthrow the Bakufu in 1333 and re-establish what he called direct imperial rule. This lasted for only three years, for the court-centered policies of Go-Daigo alienated his erstwhile warrior supporters. In 1336 Go-Daigo was forced to flee Kyōto, leaving Ashikaga Takauji to take the title of shōgun and organize a new régime, the Muromachi Bakufu, under a puppet emperor. For more than three decades the country was divided in a desultory civil war between supporters of Go-Daigo and his Southern Court and the Northern Court supported by the Ashikaga.

The Muromachi Bakufu

Thus, the Muromachi Bakufu got off to an uncertain start. From the outset, the Ashikaga shōguns, who had neither extensive landed nor military power of their own, had to rely on the co-operation of their leading vassals and provincial military governors, the *shugo*. These *shugo* began to compete to enhance their local power while weak shōguns retreated from active political leadership into palace politics and cultural pursuits. A dispute over the shōgunal succession sparked the Ōnin War in 1467, a ten-year conflict between two rival leagues of *shugo* that laid waste to much of Kyōto and ushered in a century of sporadic provincial warfare.

In the confused conditions of the late 15th and early 16th centuries what counted was not an official title or the backing of an increasingly powerless shōgunate but real power in terms of loyal vassals, tightly-held lands, well-fortified castles, tactical ability, and constant readiness for attack and defence. In these circumstances many of the *shugo* were toppled by local warriors beneath them in a surge of upheaval which produced an array of small, tightly-knit domains. By the early 16th century there were some 250 of these domains throughout Japan. With the process of decentralization at an extreme, the political pendulum began to swing back in the direction of reunification under Oda Nobunaga, Toyotomi Hideyoshi, and Tokugawa Ieyasu, who in a great military victory at Sekigahara in 1600 destroyed his rivals and established a shōgunate which endured until the 19th century.

These currents of political change in the medieval period left an important legacy. On the one hand the idea of a warrior government detached from the imperial court, headed by a shōgun, had been firmly established and prevailed until the 19th century. Warrior rule was reinforced by legal codes and by the notion of a shōgun ruling under a reigning emperor. On the other hand, though weakened and financially hard-pressed, the imperial court survived. Once the idea of shōgunal authority as the military expression of imperial rule was established, the need to eliminate court and emperor was removed. Although the imperial office was enfeebled and reduced to a ritual and legitimizing role it was not stripped of sovereignty and its very weakness became something of a source of strength or, at least, of durability.

Mongol invasions

Following the unsuccessful invasion of 1274, the Mongols launched a much larger invasion of Japan in 1281 consisting of two fleets with a total of 4,400 ships and 140,000 men. They were successful in establishing a beach-head but, as in the accompanying illustration, were constantly being attacked by Japanese forces, and when a typhoon destroyed many of the ships they were forced to withdraw, losing half their men in the process. Khubilai Khan was planning a third attempt on Japan when he died in 1294. For fear of another invasion the Bakufu had to maintain a state of military preparedness for several more years.

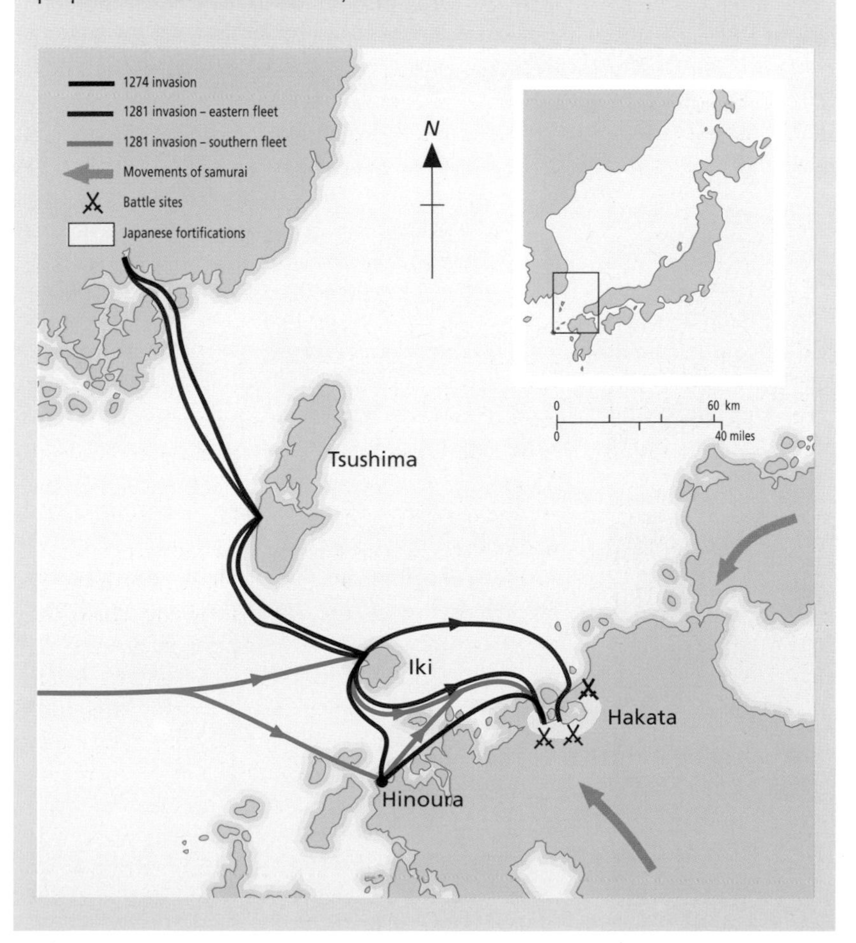

Social and economic life

The samurai were not the only newly-emergent group to make their presence felt in medieval society. Merchants, artisans, and small farmers also became more evident. In the 12th century the only local commerce was carried on by itinerant pedlars. There was little use of coinage, and hardly any market activity. Economic exchange was mostly in kind or in service, and the most common economic activity was the payment of annual taxes in rice or other products. The bulk of farmers' output was absorbed in subsistence or tax payments. There was little surplus to sell in a market or to a travelling merchant.

This rather static economic world began to change during the 13th century. One long-term economic and social transformation that was taking place was the steady dismemberment of the *shōen* estates. The control formerly exerted over *shōen* by nobles or temples was undercut or denied, by local warrior families who entrenched themselves and diverted more and more of the tax yield away from the proprietors. Nobles and temples were forced to make compromise settlements or to partition their estates. Warfare brought further dismemberment to *shōen* as *shugo*, local warriors, and daimyō all sought to exert their authority over lands in their locality held by absentee proprietors. The loosening grip of nobles and temples over *shōen* released more farmers' and artisans' labour for market-directed production.

During these centuries there were improvements in agricultural technology and farming practice. Greater use was made of draught animals and double cropping became more widespread. Markets within *shōen*, at crossroads, and temple gates became more widespread and more regular. Thrice-monthly markets were held in many areas and permanent shops began to appear. These markets in remote areas were linked with the cities by pedlars and merchants. Markets like the Horikawa lumber market in Kyōto or the Yodo fish market drew produce from far afield and became wholesale markets. Forwarding merchants established themselves in port cities around the inland sea, and specialized guilds of merchants came into existence.

Commercial and market activity continued to flourish during the Muromachi period. The location of the Bakufu in Kyōto spurred a recovery of vitality in the capital which became by the early 15th century a national market. The more active of the Ashikaga shōguns turned to foreign trade and the promotion, and taxation, of domestic commerce to make up for their lack of landed base. Ashikaga Yoshimitsu sent official trading missions to China and in the shadow of the official missions went pirates who were treated as marauders by the ruling authorities in Korea, China and Japan but who thought of themselves as freebooters and traders.

The pavilion in the Ginkaku-ji, or Temple of the Silver Pavilion, constructed by the shōgun Ashikaga Yoshimasa in 1483. The original intention was to cover the pavilion in silver foil, like the Ginkaku-ji on the other side of Kyōto, which is covered in gold foil, but Yoshimasa died before this could be done.

Cultural life

The medieval centuries witnessed far reaching changes in religious and cultural life, changes that were to lay the foundations of modern Japanese spirituality and aesthetic sensibility. From the late 12th century there was a surge of revival within Buddhism that was to carry hopes for salvation to the mass of the population. This surge was set in motion by the conviction of some young monks that all was not well with Buddhism, that it catered exclusively to the élite, that the rules of monastic life were not strictly observed, and that the age was one of spiritual decline. The reformers looked for new and easier paths to salvation, which provoked a hostile reaction from the older schools of Buddhism, but also stimulated movements for reform within the older sects.

Although the court did not lose its cultural authority, the medieval age was the age of the warrior, symbolized by fortified warrior residences and hilltop castles. Scroll paintings like the Obusama Saburō Scroll, contrasting the lives of a martially-minded warrior and his aesthetically-inclined elder brother, or the Mongol Invasion Scrolls, depicting the exploits of a Kyūshū warrior against the Mongol fleets, illustrated the details of warrior lifestyle and dress. The making of swords, armour, helmets, and horse trappings reached the highest technical and artistic levels. A developing warrior ethic of heroism, loyalty, and willingness to die for one's lord was fostered by warrior chieftains and lauded in war tales like the *Heike monogatari*. At the same time, warriors were mastering those civilian arts essential for government, for easier social intercourse with the nobility, and for cultural enjoyment. Many warriors were literate: some, including Minamoto Yoritomo, wrote poetry that was considered sufficiently accomplished to be included in major anthologies. Many other warriors participated in literary salons with nobles and monks and patronized painters, dramatists, and craftsmen. Ashikaga shōguns like Yoshimitsu, provincial warrior families like the Hosokawa and the unifiers Nobunaga and Hideyoshi were all lavish patrons and practitioners of the arts.

It was under this kind of warrior patronage that the nō theatre and the tea ceremony developed. Palaces, castles, and provincial warrior residences were decorated with screens and wall paintings by masters of the Kano and Tosa schools of painting. Warriors also became devotees and patrons of the new branches of Buddhism, especially Zen, and acquired from monks some understanding of the secular as well as the Buddhist culture of China. Buddhist monasteries were also major nodes in the medieval cultural fabric. Monks, nobles and warriors mingled on equal terms at literary salons.

No comment on the medieval age and its culture would be complete without a reference to the growing cultural visibility of the common people. Messages of Buddhist salvation and retribution and tales of military heroism were carried into the provinces by travelling priests and minstrels. The nō and kyōgen theatres had their origins in popular rural and religious entertainments and continued to be performed at village shrines throughout Japan. Tea likewise was enjoyed in villages as well as in the castles of warriors or the tea houses of wealthy merchants. On urban riverbanks, free from taxation, lived a restless urban proletariat known as the *kawaramono*. It included dropouts and outcastes who made a living slaughtering animals and tanning hides, and also poor artists, craftsmen, and popular performers. MC

Japan encounters the West

The history of Japan's encounter with the West began in 1543 with the shipwreck of three Portuguese sailors on the island of Tanegashima off the coast of Kyūshū. This event had two important consequences: the introduction of firearms in the form of the arquebus and the arrival of the Portuguese Jesuit Francis Xavier in 1549. The adoption of firearms marked a turning point in Japanese warfare and contributed to the emergence of new powers in the land. The arrival of the missionaries began what has been called Japan's 'Christian Century', during which first the Jesuits and then the Franciscans and Dominicans tried to make converts. This was to continue until the decree of 1614 expelling all missionaries, which was followed by a final edict of 1639 ending Portuguese trade with Japan and all Japanese contacts with Catholic Europe. The importance of the 'Christian Century' in the long span of Japanese history can be exaggerated, but it was through the missionaries that 16th-century Europe gained its first knowledge of Japan as they wrote home of the life and customs of the Japanese and, as excited observers and participants, of the struggles and rise to power of the three main figures Oda Nobunaga, Toyotomi Hideyoshi and Tokugawa Ieyasu.

The Jesuit mission

The arrival of the Portuguese traders and Jesuit missionaries coincided with the period in which the power of the Ashikaga shōguns was at its nadir and when anarchy had spread throughout the country. This had caused the decay of long-established power-bases and the break-up of large estates: warriors of obscure origins rose to high rank usurping the power of their lords. New names came to the fore while those of ancient families disappeared. The emperor was a shadowy figure, with no authority to draw upon. The Jesuits in their early letters sought to make sense of the situation by referring to provincial leaders as 'kings', but this gave Europeans the mistaken impression that Japan was a confederation of kingdoms.

A Portuguese merchant in Japan with attendant, servant and dog. The exotic dress and manners of the Portuguese prompted a genre of painting and a number of eccentric fads, like that whereby Japanese began addressing each other with Portuguese names.

Xavier was initially enthusiastic about the prospects for missionary work. 'The people we have met so far', he wrote, 'are the best who have yet been discovered', and he considered the Japanese 'the delight of my heart'. Subsequent events were to alter perceptions of Japan and to make the work much more arduous as all the difficulties of the cultural relationship between the missionaries and their would-be converts became apparent. Nevertheless, among them were some remarkable individuals, like Alessandro Valignano, an Italian who was chief of the Jesuit missions in the Far East. He entered upon a new programme of missionary work, founded schools and seminaries, set up the Jesuit press in Japan, wrote many works on Japan and tried a policy of adapting missionary work to its context that was too new for its time and aroused the opposition of his superiors. Of the many others, Luis Frois should be mentioned for his *History of Japan* and Rodrigues for his study of the Japanese language which was published in Portuguese in 1608.

The Jesuits operated mainly in Kyūshū, where they established their headquarters in 1571 in the port of Nagasaki, but they were also active in and around the capital, Kyōto. In 1569 the shōgun Ashikaga Yoshiteru allowed Gaspar Vilela to preach in Kyōto, Nara and the mercantile city of Sakai. Nobunaga gave Frois permission to build a church in the capital which was known as the Nanban-ji, or 'Temple of the Southern Barbarians'. Nobunaga's opposition to Buddhism, which was for political rather than religious reasons, and his affability towards the newcomers from Europe led the Jesuits to think of him as their great protector. Frois wrote in 1569 that, 'He is a man of good understanding and clear judgment, despising the Camis (Shintō gods) and Fotoques (Buddhas) and all the rest of that breed of idols and the heathen superstitions'. And it was under Nobunaga's patronage that the first official debates took place between the Buddhist clergy and the Jesuits. But come the rise to power of Hideyoshi, the Jesuits fell on hard times and their hopes were dashed. In 1587 Hideyoshi issued edicts restricting the practice of Christianity and expelling the missionaries, although these were not strictly enforced. The final blow for the Jesuits came in 1593 when Spanish Franciscans arrived: the unification of the thrones of Castile and Portugal had ended the division of the world between Spain and Portugal and hence the Jesuit monopoly in Japan.

Of the various activities of the Jesuits in Japan the establishment of a printing press with movable type was of particular importance. It was Valignano who realized the need for texts printed locally for the use of missionaries and their converts in spreading Catholic teaching, and he arranged for the necessary equipment to be brought from Europe. The Jesuit Mission Press was initially set up in Macao and then shifted to Kyūshū in 1590; once the persecutions started it was transferred to Manila and then back to Macao. The press may have had a short life in Japan but it was an active and remarkably innovative one: the missionaries were the first to print Japanese with metal rather than wooden type, the first to print a work of secular Japanese literature, the first to print the cursive script, and the first to make use of coppercuts for illustrations.

The Japanese mission to Europe of 1582–90

The first Japanese to reach Europe was probably a follower of Xavier's who travelled to Rome and Lisbon in the 1550s, but the first official visitors were four young boys aged 12 or 13 who were all students at the Jesuit seminary in Japan and who represented several daimyō families of western Japan. The mission was the idea of Alessandro Valignano, who hoped that, by demonstrating the Catholic potential in East Asia at a time when Catholicism was on the defensive in Europe, it might secure the Jesuit monopoly on missionary work in Japan and prompt the pope to offer financial support. The boys left Nagasaki with a party of Jesuit interpreters and other guides in 1582 and reached Lisbon in 1584 via Macao, Goa and the Cape of Good Hope. They were received by King Philip II of Spain and by Pope Gregory XIII, who treated them as ambassadors and was impressed enough to grant Valignano's requests, and they travelled extensively through the Italian states. In Venice, they were given a spectacular reception and Tintoretto was asked to paint them, and in many other towns, even as far away as Prague, souvenir booklets were published like the one from Milan illustrated above. In spite of the impact they had in Europe, by the time of their return to Japan in 1590 the mood had turned against Christianity. Although Hideyoshi did receive them in his castle, he had in 1587 already issued the Jesuits with an expulsion order and the experiences of the four young men had no discernible impact in Japan.

PK

AVISI
VENVTI NOVAMENTE
DA ROMA,
Dell' entrata nel publico Conciſtoro, de duoi Ambaſciatori mandati da tre Rè potenti del Giapone, conuertiti nouamente alla ſanta fede chriſtiana, à dare obedienza à ſua Santità.

Stampati in Milano, & riſtampato in Ferrara per Vittorio Baldini. 1585.

The rise of Oda Nobunaga

During the Sengoku period (1467–1568), a period of political instability, various ecclesiastical organizations greatly increased their secular power by playing on the frustrations and rebellious sentiments of the peasants in many parts of Japan. One of the leading ecclesiastical powers was the Ishiyama Hongan-ji, a temple of the True Pure Land Sect on Ōsaka Bay which had been transformed into a fortress. Within its extensive precincts a town grew up which became a commercial and cultural centre in its own right and an expression of the secular aspirations of the Sect. The Sect's principal antagonist was Nobunaga, 'the great enemy of Buddhist law'.

Oda Nobunaga (1534–82) was a minor territorial chieftain in the province of Owari who took the opportunity of the moment to defeat the army of Imagawa Yoshimoto at Okehazama in 1560. By so doing he prevented Imagawa from reaching Kyōto and gaining power, and started out on his own rise to national prominence. In fact all three of the heroes of late 16th-century Japan took part in the battle, for Toyotomi Hideyoshi, soon to be dictator, fought under Nobunaga while Tokugawa Ieyasu, the founder of the Tokugawa shōgunate, fought under Imagawa.

During the 1560s Nobunaga enjoyed the support of the emperor and of Ashikaga Yoshiaki, the pretender to the shōgunate following the assassination of the previous shōgun, and after a string of victories he finally entered Kyōto in 1568. He installed Yoshiaki as shōgun in that year, but in 1573 removed him from office for insubordination and thus put an end to the rule of the Ashikaga shōguns. In 1575 he became the first to employ firearms strategically in warfare when his 3,000 musketeers ensured victory over Takeda Katsuyori at the battle of Nagashino. His differences with the most powerful religious sects were similarly resolved in a series of bloody encounters, starting in 1571 with a massacre of the soldier monks of the Tendai Sect on Mount Hiei and ending in 1580 with a prolonged assault on the Ishiyama Hongan-ji, which was brought to its knees in spite of substantial support from Nobunaga's enemies.

By 1576 Nobunaga had established his headquarters at Azuchi on the shores of Lake Biwa where his castle stood as a symbol of his authority. He was already in total control of central Japan and was planning to complete the reunification of Japan by taking his armies further afield when in 1582 he was attacked by one of his subordinates in Kyōto and assassinated. What was new about Nobunaga was his robust assumption of political power in spite of the claims of the imperial court and the shōgunate. There is no way of knowing what kind of political order he might have introduced but it is undeniable that he had shaken the established order to its foundations and prepared the way for a new structure of authority to emerge.

Guns and warfare

The introduction of firearms to Japan by some Portuguese sailors in 1543 occasioned an immediate response. The daimyō of Tanegashima, where they landed, acknowledged their effectiveness immediately and ordered his swordsmiths to make replicas. Within two decades Japanese gunsmiths had conquered the technical problems and were producing guns in quantity. Not only did they manage to replicate the technology in a remarkably short space of time, but they also made some improvements and refinements, particularly to the spring and trigger mechanisms. They also devised a cover for the firing mechanism which made it possible to fire their muskets in the rain, or to do so at night without the fuse giving away the position of the musketeer. Gun manuals were also produced, and one, from the Inatomi School, is illustrated below.

Oda Nobunaga seems to have been one of the first to realize the potential of guns, and as early as 1549 he bought 500 for his troops. Daimyō had no choice but to begin equipping their soldiers with muskets, and in 1567 Takeda Shingen, the daimyō of Kai, declared that guns would thereafter be the most important weapons of warfare. However, the transformation of warfare by firearms did not take place overnight. It took time to prime a musket and light the fuse, and, to prevent an enemy taking advantage of this, muskets had to be discharged in sequences rather than simultaneously. The gun also involved a shift in the pattern of warfare from man-to-man combat to the tactical use of a corps of musketeers. Some musketeers were slow to realize this and failed to abandon the traditional courtesies whereby combatants first introduced themselves on the battlefield before resorting to arms.

The turning point was the battle of Nagashino on 29 June 1575, when Oda Nobunaga led a force of 40,000 men in defence of the castle there. The mounted samurai who led the assault against him were no match for his force of musketeers, 3,000 strong, waiting in a well-defended position, and they were shot to pieces. Muskets clearly determined the outcome of the battle and the lesson was not lost on the warring daimyō, who had not only to equip their troops with guns but also to improve the fortifications of their castles to cope with muskets and cannons. PK

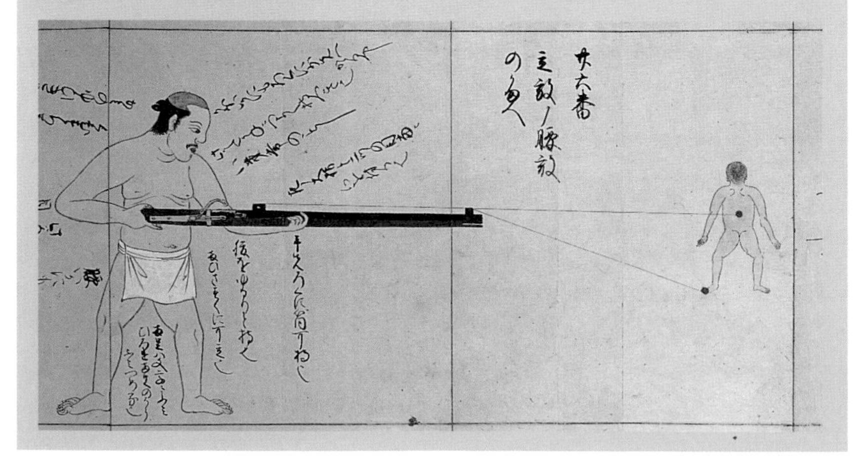

HIDEYOSHI

The reunification of Japan begun by Nobunaga was completed by Toyotomi Hideyoshi (1537–98). Hideyoshi successfully presented himself as Nobunaga's avenger: he was a brilliant strategist and made short work of his rivals. His road to mastery over all Japan was paved both with victories on the battlefield and with shrewd political alliances. His domestic campaigns ended with that in eastern Japan in 1590 which effectively brought the whole of the country under his sway, but in 1592 his armies invaded Korea in the first stage of a grandiose plan to establish a pan-Asiatic kingdom centred on China. The campaign met fierce resistance in Korea and was eventually brought to an end by Hideyoshi's death.

During his years of power Hideyoshi turned against the Christian missionaries. In 1593 Spanish Franciscans broke the Jesuit monopoly in Japan when Pedro Bautista arrived with three colleagues as an embassy from the Spanish governor of Manila and received permission to stay and preach. This brought the intense rivalry between the Jesuits and Franciscans out into the open and aroused fears of Japan becoming embroiled in European conflict or even of meeting the same fate as Mexico and Peru and becoming a colony of Spain or Portugal. The

consequences were a heightened wave of persecution in the short term and in the long term an end not only to missionary activity but also to contacts with the Catholic nations of Europe.

Hideyoshi was a commoner who rose to be undisputed leader of Japan: he was an enthusiastic amateur of all the arts and revelled in surroundings of magnificence and splendour. He also launched a land survey covering the whole country to provide a rational basis for land taxation and enforced a separation of the classes by carrying out a sword hunt to remove weapons from the farming population: by so doing he laid some of the foundations for the stable social order that developed under Tokugawa Ieyasu and his successors. AB

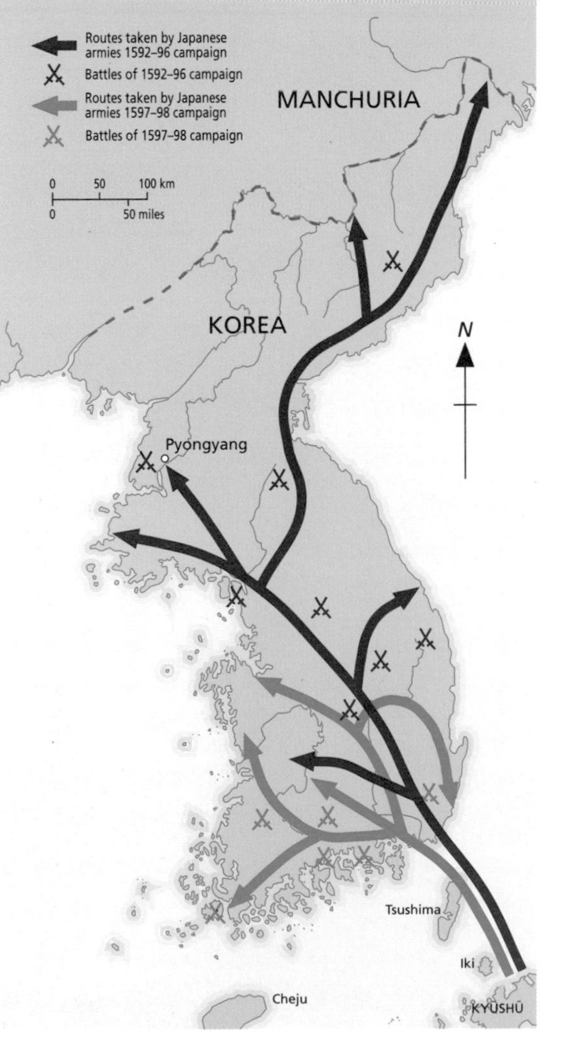

Right *The invasions of Korea.*

Below *Hideyoshi's audience chamber. This room was originally part of his castle at Fushimi, south of Kyōto, but it is now part of a temple. The raised portion was for Hideyoshi and some of the sliding doors on the right would usually have concealed armed men.*

The Tokugawa period

Tokugawa Ieyasu (1542–1616), the founder of the dynasty which presided over Japan for the better part of 300 years, had come to maturity in a country racked by civil war, a country with no central authority worthy of the name. Power was divided among, and constantly contested by, military overlords, peasant confederations, and ecclesiastical foundations. Travel was both difficult and dangerous, communications intermittent at best, and commerce precarious, hindered at every turn by private barriers, checkpoints and tariffs.

Towards the end of the 16th century a small group of warrior leaders, of whom Tokugawa Ieyasu was one, changed all this. Each of them, aiming ultimately at national ascendancy, built up his forces through conquest and diplomacy, consolidating fiscal and commercial control of increasingly larger areas. One by one the great religious foundations were brought to heel, their lands confiscated and their armies destroyed. The peasant insurrections, too, were pacified, and stability imposed upon the countryside. Above all, the warrior chieftains, whose rivalries, born as much of uncertainty and insecurity as thirst for power, had dragged Japan from one crisis to another, were brought under unified control by one or other of the overlords, using a combination of diplomacy and force. This process culminated at the battle of Sekigahara in 1600, when Tokugawa Ieyasu, at the head of 70,000 men, defeated an even larger league of opponents.

Taking the title Sei-i taishōgun, or Commander-in-chief of the Pacification of Savages, from an emperor powerless to deny it, Tokugawa Ieyasu began to lay the foundations for a form of government far more orderly and efficient than anything Japan had ever seen. In place of the instability of the 16th century, Ieyasu, together with those of his descendants who succeeded him to the office of shōgun, gave Japan an unparalleled degree of centralization. Through its administration, known as the Bakufu, the Tokugawa house quickly came to accumulate many of the functions of a national government – control of foreign affairs, of currency, of weights and measures, of religious organizations.

Above *The seige of Ōsaka castle in 1615, during which the armies of Tokugawa Ieyasu destroyed the last adherents of Hideyoshi.*

Gold coins of the 17th century.

With equal speed it claimed control of a large part of Japan's resources. Its landholdings, which ultimately spread over 47 of Japan's 68 provinces, included some of the country's most fertile areas, among them the large Kantō plain, together with the most productive gold and silver mines. To these resources it added Japan's major cities – chief among them Edo (now Tōkyō), seat of the shōgun's government, Kyōto, home of the emperor, Ōsaka, the nation's commercial hub, and Nagasaki, where Tokugawa Japan's foreign trade and diplomacy was conducted.

Controlling the daimyō

The remainder of Japan was left in the hands of the warrior chieftains, or daimyō – that is, the very class whose rivalries had kept the country in turmoil for the previous hundred years and more. But there was a difference. Each daimyō had now submitted to Tokugawa rule. Some had done so more willingly and more completely than others, but all were incorporated into an elaborate system of pledges of allegiance, acts of public homage, and in some instances dynastic marriages centred upon the shōgun and his court at Edo. Under the terms of the *Buke shohatto*, or Laws Relating to Warrior Houses, enunciated first in the summer of 1615 and issued thereafter in several different versions, many of their ancient prerogatives were taken away. The 1615 document, among other injunctions, deprived them of the right to fortify their domains any more than they were already; its 1635 successor went one step further by forbidding the construction of ships large enough to constitute a threat to the status quo. Indeed, it went two steps further, since the same document introduced a form of daimyō control which, more than any other, was to define Tokugawa superiority. This was the *sankin kōtai*, or system of alternate attendance, by which all but a tiny minority of daimyō were forced to shuttle between their domains and the shōgun's court at Edo, spending one year in one and the next in the other. Local government remained in daimyō hands, it is true, but Bakufu policy early in the 17th century seemed to indicate that failure to discharge this responsibility efficiently could lead to dismissal and disenfeoffment. To a large extent, therefore, the Tokugawa had tamed the daimyō.

Yet it was not an absolutely one-sided arrangement. By submitting to Tokugawa leadership daimyō also placed themselves under Tokugawa protection, their positions guaranteed both against each other and their own vassals. The elimination of these sources of insecurity did much to keep Tokugawa Japan peaceful. So too did the Bakufu's treatment of the imperial court; the emperor, while permitted to keep his position of nominal authority intact, was safely removed from political life, deprived of any discretionary power and denied access to all but those with official approval.

Between them, the shōgun and the daimyō (whose numbers stabilized at around 260 by the latter part of the 17th century) ruled over a population of some 30 million people, giving them the most secure and predictable form of government they had ever had. Within a very short time Japan was transformed from a country shattered by violence to one in which the rule of law prevailed. People who formerly had been tempted or compelled to take the law into their own hands were, under the Tokugawa government, obliged to turn to it for mediation. Any daimyō disputing domain boundaries or areas of jurisdiction with another had to take his case to the shōgun's tribunal in Edo. Any quarrel between temples or shrines over matters of property or precedence went automatically for the arbitration of the Bakufu official responsible for religious affairs. For individuals, too, there was machinery in place for the resolution of disputes, although custom in such cases tended to dictate settlement by informal mediation.

Government

The Japanese overseas. In the late 16th and early 17th centuries Japanese traders extended their activities over much of south-east Asia and in many towns there was a substantial number of Japanese residents engaged in international trade. In some cases, especially Siam (Thailand) they also acquired considerable political influence. All of this came to an end in the 1630s when the Bakufu placed restrictions on overseas travel and trade, but many of the communities survived until the end of the century.

The Tokugawa system of government could never have been mistaken for one established by common consent. It was established by force, underpinned by force, and preserved by force, whether actual or implicit. With its control of so much of the nation's wealth, the Tokugawa house could call on the service of some 60,000 vassals, or samurai – that is professional soldiers who staffed both standing army and bureaucracy. It could also demand military support from the daimyō, each of whom, like the shōgun, had his own army and bureaucracy staffed by samurai. At any one time during this period Japan would have been governed by as many as 300,000 samurai of various ranks, skills and occupations. This gave to Tokugawa society an unavoidably martial coloration, intensified by the ethos known as *bushidō*, or the Way of the Warrior. As it emerged in the course of the 17th century, *bushidō* emphasized the ideal of selfless service to one's lord, to be demonstrated by ostentatious self-denial, no drinking, no gambling, no extravagance, no over-eating, no visits to playhouse or brothel. It was an ethos which lent itself to hyperbole, particularly as the samurai class turned from warfare to bureaucracy. As the prospect of a battle of any kind receded into the distance, so theorists came to produce the kind of effusion found in the 18th-century devotional text, *Hagakure*. There, from a safe distance, it was asserted that, while serving one's lord in battle was all well and good, dying for him was even better. Fortunately for the samurai of the Tokugawa period this particular prospect remained comfortably remote; the peace imposed at Sekigahara and buttressed over the next two or three decades was so secure that Japan saw no battles for well over 200 years.

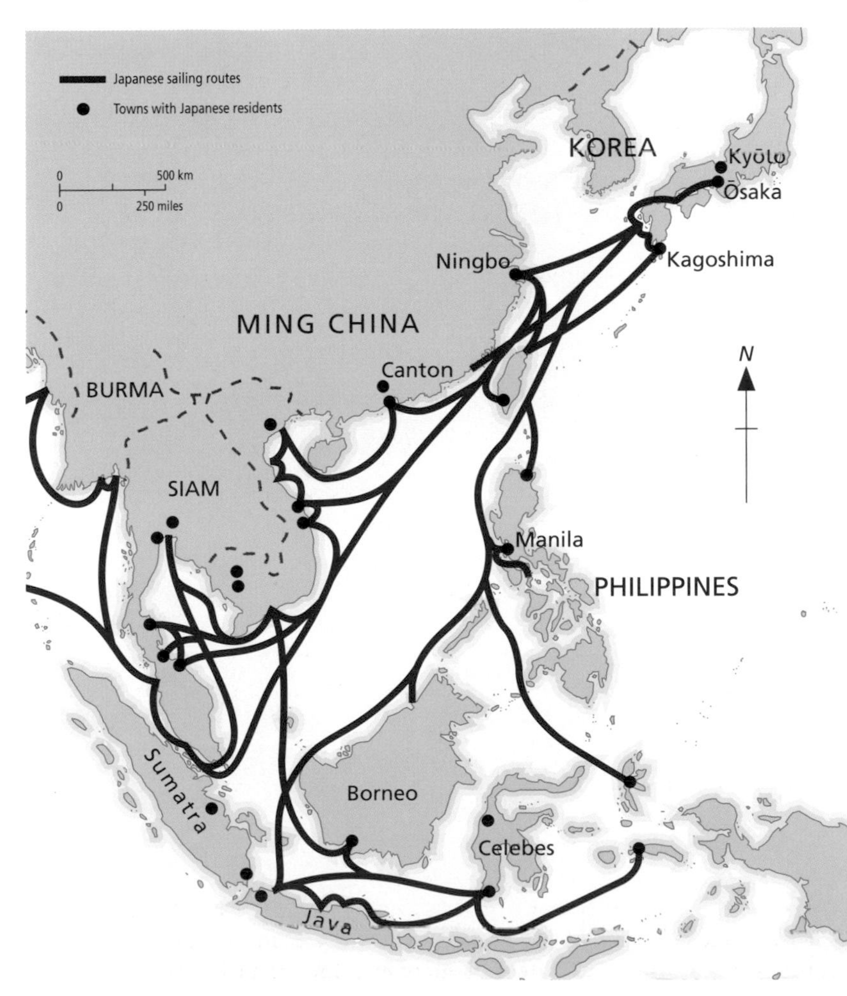

Despite its notable success in keeping the peace, however, the government of Japan during this period had its limitations. The shōgun, while having direct control of barely more than a quarter of the nation's resources, was nevertheless responsible for the well-being of the whole. The daimyō, although they owed the shōgun such military and economic assistance as he should decree, were still largely independent, and their local interests often took priority over the needs of the whole nation. Rule by the samurai class, too, whether in the Bakufu or in the governments of the daimyō domains, was far from ideal, as a great many critics were to observe. Virtually the only way to became a samurai was to be born into a samurai family; further, to be eligible for any specific position within the military-bureaucratic hierarchy one needed to be born into the particular rank from which such positions were customarily filled. This applied to the entire samurai class, from the shōgun down to the humblest foot-soldier. All too often it resulted in the appointment of unsuitable officials – shōguns like Ietsugu, who succeeded to the office at the age of 3, or like Ieshige, too sickly, and arguably too feeble-minded, to handle the responsibilities of the position. This was equally true not only of daimyō, but of their senior advisers. To the beneficiaries of this system, the samurai class, it seemed patently obvious that this was quite the best way to make government appointments; after all, had they not been fitted by nature for the duties for which they were eligible, they reasoned, then surely Heaven would not have caused them to be born into that particular station. To those who would have preferred to see responsible government positions filled by those most suited by intellect, education and character (by which they generally meant themselves and their friends), however, recruitment by heredity was a recipe for inefficiency.

Such critics were correct, although perhaps not for the reasons they advanced. The authority of the Tokugawa Bakufu had already begun to decline in the 17th century; thereafter for the most part it preserved its position by allowing daimyō domains to do as they pleased. Its financial position also worsened, as its system of taxation proved too inflexible to keep pace with economic development. Various attempts were made to rectify this, particularly in the reform movements of the Kyōhō (1716–35), Kansei (1789–1800) and Tenpō (1830–43) eras, but with little success. In the daimyō domains things were hardly any better; their own efforts at reform were largely unsuccessful. Samurai officials were simply unable to cope with the complex socio-economic forces they had unwittingly set in motion, and they paid the price in reduced standards of living, diminished prestige, and – as the events of the 19th century were to demonstrate – a military capacity which was disastrously compromised.

Nevertheless it is doubtful whether those who criticized government by a hereditary ruling class would have been any more successful. Officials and critics alike shared certain key convictions, derived from Chinese Confucianism. They all believed the ideal society to be one in which subsistence agriculture was the dominant form of activity. Commerce of any but the most basic kind was to be discouraged. The two significant respects in which critics differed from officials were, first, in their belief that the bureaucracy should be staffed by scholars, rather than samurai, and, second, in their more thoroughgoing commitment to solutions as draconian and doctrinaire as they were unworkable.

Urbanization

The truth was that, largely due to policies it had itself instigated, the samurai class had created the circumstances which destabilized it. Urbanization was one such policy. When Tokugawa Ieyasu settled in Edo in 1590, for example, it had been nothing more than a collection of fishing communities on the fringe of what is now Tōkyō Bay. Clearly it lacked all the amenities which might have been expected of the seat of one of Japan's most powerful warlords; ten years later, when Ieyasu had established himself as the

most powerful man in the country, its deficiencies were all the more noticeable. So one of his first objectives was to build for himself a seat of government more appropriate to his status and responsibilities. This he did through an ambitious building programme, draining marshland, constructing a great fortress surrounded by a network of canals, and attracting merchants and craftsmen with offers of free land and tax concessions. Within a century, thanks in part to the alternate attendance system under which large numbers of samurai were obliged to accompany their daimyō for periods of residence in Edo, the shōgun's capital had developed into the largest city in the world, with over a million residents. Half of these belonged to the samurai class, but the other half were people who provided goods and services for the entire city population – carpenters, porters, fishmongers, greengrocers, sellers of tea, cakes, medicines and fabrics, maidservants, clerks, brothel-keepers, collectors of nightsoil and a whole host of others.

Edo was Tokugawa Japan's largest city, but it was far from the only one. Other cities, too, while not developing to the same extent, nevertheless followed a comparable trajectory. Kyōto, for example, where the emperor and his court had resided for the best part of a thousand years, was also a centre for arts, crafts, and the production of luxury goods, including the silks and brocades of the Nishijin quarter. In the late 17th century the imperial capital could boast a population of 600,000, rather more than Paris at that time. Ōsaka, too, had grown to roughly the same size, turning itself from a fortress city into Tokugawa Japan's major market centre, noted particularly for its production of sake and seed oil.

Other provincial cities were also to build up substantial populations. Commonly the pattern was dictated initially by the daimyō, whose strategic and administrative needs required that his samurai administrators live in close proximity to his castle. These communities inevitably attracted merchants and craftsmen. Kanazawa, the largest of such castle towns, had built up a population of 70,000 by the end of the 17th century, making it larger than Berlin at the same time. Both Nagoya and Kagoshima came to have more than 50,000 inhabitants, while elsewhere in Japan towns with populations greater than 10,000 were not uncommon. Such numbers may not appear too singular now, but they served to make Tokugawa Japan the most highly urbanized nation in the pre-modern world.

Yet the officials were never entirely comfortable with the urban world they had created. Those who made their living there, commonly known by the term chōnin, or city-dwellers, were a perennial object of government suspicion and hostility,

A row of busy shops in Edo. In the street the samurai are identifiable by the pair of swords each carries at his side.

thought to be shiftless, cunning, and determined to enrich themselves at the expense of the common good. Much of Tokugawa Japan's urban history, therefore, is a record of attempts at suppression. The officials tried in vain to limit city growth, encouraging migrants to return to the countryside. They tried, too, with equally little success, to inhibit various commercial activities through price controls of various kinds. Nothing worked. The cities and towns grew larger, the commercial networks stronger, and those who presided over them richer. It was not long before an identifiable class of merchant princes appeared: the Mitsui, for example, who were already well-established by the end of the 17th century, both as retailers with large stores in Edo, Ōsaka, and Kyōto, and as bankers and money-changers, or the Kōnoike, who, starting off as sake brewers, moved quickly into the Ōsaka–Edo shipping business, and from there to money-lending. These and many like them were a constant irritant to samurai society. On the one hand, all levels of the samurai class depended on their services, particularly as the providers of loans: by 1800 the Kōnoike had more than 30 daimyō in their debt. On the other, the conspicuous prosperity of people considered to be at the lower extremity of polite society, particularly since it went hand in hand with the decline of samurai fortunes, made a mockery of Confucian values.

A 19th-century photograph of prostitutes displayed behind a lattice so that customers could make their choices.

The rural economy

Urbanization, together with its commercial requirements, was also responsible for equally unwelcome developments in the countryside. The farmers of the Confucian ideal were a stable and docile group, hardworking and frugal, with each man supporting himself and his family from the labours of his own hands on his own land. Further, he was scrupulously honest when it came to paying his taxes. The farmers of the Tokugawa period were not necessarily like this at all. Despite an elaborate network of joint-responsibility groups known as *goningumi,* and despite the existence of such officials as local magistrates and village headmen, farming communities soon took on lives of their own. With samurai removed from the villages and settled at a safe distance away in castle towns, farmers had every opportunity to practise tax-evasion. They also had every incentive to resist the entry of tax inspectors, which they did vociferously and not without success from the beginning of the 17th century.

More than that, the officials of Tokugawa Japan dreamed of an ideal farmer who would be content to grow the rice needed to pay his taxes, and just enough millet and vegetables to sustain himself and his family. This was not to be. Urban markets needed rice, wheat, soy beans, radishes, rape-seed, cotton and tobacco. They also needed these things to be processed into sake, bean curd, pickles, soy sauce, lamp oil and cloth. In the face of such opportunities sub-

sistence agriculture quickly turned commercial. The self-supporting yeoman farmer disappeared, to be replaced by two different figures, neither of whom was to be managed so easily. The first of these was the rural entrepreneur, a risk-taker who, provided his venture into cash-cropping was successful, was able to buy up the land of his less successful fellows, lease it, lend money, and move into small-scale processing of one kind or another. The other was the displaced landless labourer, whose attenuated roots within the village community made him much less predictable. He could remain in the village, or he could move away to find work in town or city, but whichever path he chose he took an element of instability and volatility with him.

Culture, literacy and science

Urbanization did more than destroy the tidy Tokugawa social system, however. It also provided the impetus for one of Japan's great cultural flowerings, a movement in which for the first time literature and the arts became accessible to many more than the fortunate few who had previously monopolized them. The great artistic achievements of the Japanese past had all been the property of a minority, created through the patronage of court nobles, wealthy warrior chieftains, or the abbots of the ecclesiastical foundations. Similarly the great works of literature were confined to those who were literate and had access to hand-written copies.

Itinerant basket-sellers in another 19th-century photograph.

This situation was to change in the Tokugawa period. The commercial economy created a new class of patrons, whether city businessmen commissioning works of art for their own enjoyment, or wealthy farmers entertaining itinerant artists in return for samples of their work. New patrons also meant new styles, ranging from the ornate *Kōrin* style on the one hand to the idiosyncratic understatement of the *Bunjin* movement on the other. Initially courtiers and warriors may have looked askance at the entry of arriviste taste into the charmed circle of connoisseurship, but they soon became used to it as the newly-rich also came to invade other aristocratic preserves, among them tea, gardens, flowers and incense.

At the same time urbanization created a mass market with a thirst, and with enough money to spare, for a cultural life of a new kind. City life – and, increasingly, rural life as well – called for literacy and numeracy, and soon produced institutions capable of providing training in both. Even the poorest village could ultimately boast of its *terakoya*, usually housed in the local temple, and often presided over by the local priest, where children would go to acquire the rudiments of reading, writing and arithmetic. Samurai education, too, developed as members of that class turned from warfare to administration: by the end of the Tokugawa period all but a few daimyō domains had created schools to train their bureaucrats.

Literacy, which came to be shared by an estimated 35% of the population by the end of the period, combined with the mass market to encourage an entirely new industry – commercial printing. From the second half of the 17th century, the publishers of Tokugawa Japan, aided by a growing number of professional writers, kept up a never-ending torrent of books, improving and otherwise – joke books, guide books, ghost stories, philosophical disquisitions, historical novels, devotional works, romances and works of pornography – all to keep pace with the demands of a market which never seemed satisfied. Art was as much affected by the printing industry as literature; many of the books were illustrated, and the same techniques required to print a book could also be applied to the production of large, multi-coloured woodblock prints. Much of the output, literary or artistic, was of a kind one might expect of a mass market, ephemeral and not particularly good, but there was no denying that cultural life had been delivered out of the palace and cloister forever.

The cultural flowering was by no means limited to art and literature, however. The 18th century, in particular, was to see a surge of interest in things scientific, with the appearance of scholars in fields as diverse as botany, astronomy, archaeology, geography and medicine. It produced such artifacts as the pedometer, the compass, the thermometer, and even an electrostatic generator. In medicine it was characterized by an entirely new movement in which a number of physicians turned away from the traditional Chinese model to something rather more empirical, in which the dissection of human bodies – something previously shunned – came to play an important part.

To a large extent this spirit of scientific enquiry was due to foreign influences, entering Japan by way

Printing

The art of woodblock printing reached Japan from China, but the oldest surviving examples of printing in the world, barring a single slightly earlier specimen from Korea, were produced in Japan in the 8th century. They were Buddhist invocations in Chinese, a million of them, printed not for reading but for devotional purposes between 764 and 770. The printing of texts for reading did not begin until the 11th century, but they too were Buddhist and in Chinese: the market was too small to support commercial publication, and so printing was sponsored by wealthy temples. At the end of the 16th century movable-type printing reached Japan from Europe and from Korea, where it had been developed well before the time of Gutenberg, and both emperor and shōgun sponsored the printing of secular works in Chinese and in Japanese, ending the Buddhist monopoly on printing.

Movable-type printing enjoyed only a short vogue, for the casting of metallic type proved prohibitively uneconomic, and by 1650 woodblock printing had gained the ascendancy. At this point, with a growing rate of literacy and rising mercantile prosperity, the commercial development of printing became possible for the first time and from this time onwards Japan became a print-based culture. At first, printing simply provided a means of making works that had hitherto circulated in manuscript more widely available, such as the classics of Japanese literature, but by 1650 new works were being written for commercial publication, from guidebooks and guides to etiquette and letter-writing to popular fiction aimed at the new urban market. In the 18th century, publishing spread to many regional towns and the retail book trade developed an extensive network of outlets that covered most of Japan by 1800. The early 19th century saw continued growth in the urban market for books, such that print-runs of thousands became commonplace. Contact with the West after 1853 brought the technology of the steam-driven printing press to Japan, but it was not until the 1880s that metallic movable-type printing began to overtake traditional woodblock printing.

For most of the Tokugawa period books were expensive but by the end of the 18th century commercial lending libraries had become widespread in the large towns and it is estimated that more than half of the urban population had access to books. The lending libraries also offered a means whereby books that could not be published for reasons of censorship could be circulated in manuscript, for example books exposing sexual or administrative scandals involving the daimyō or the shōgun.

There were no newspapers until the very end of the Tokugawa period, but broadsheets were produced in large numbers. They reported events of economic significance, such as flooding in rice-growing areas, and disasters such as fires and earthquakes, but never political events.

Woodblock printing served to create a literate society accustomed to seeking information in printed form to an extent that was only surpassed at the time by a few countries in western Europe. It was a society well-prepared, then, for the flood of technical, legal and other literature that reached Japan from the West from the 1860s onwards.

PK

of the trading community at Nagasaki where groups of Dutch and Chinese, although confined to ghettoes, served as a conduit for new ideas. The Tokugawa period had begun in an atmosphere in which foreigners were distrusted. This was particularly so of the Portuguese and the Spanish, given the history of conquest to which their colonial empires in Asia and Latin America attested, and given their adherence to Christianity, a religion the Tokugawa rulers found threatening. By 1640, after a rebellion in southwestern Japan in which 25,000 insurgents, many claiming allegiance to the Christian faith, resisted government forces many times more numerous, Japan had severed all ties to the Catholic world, and had restricted its foreign contacts to the more amenable Chinese and Dutch. With time, however, the Japanese became less nervous, and by the 18th century their suspicion of the outside world had abated sufficiently to allow the importing and translating of foreign books. Once this step was taken, Japanese began to learn more of the world, both the natural world in which they lived, and the world outside, towards which they maintained an attitude of reserved curiosity.

Disaster and unrest

Tokugawa Japan, then, was a far more open society than its founders had ever imagined. But this is not to say that it was a perfect society, for it was no such thing. It had its share – perhaps even more than its share – of misfortunes, among them the eruption of Mt Fuji in 1707 and of Mt Asama in 1783, and a regular progression of earthquakes, tidal waves, and landslides. Large urban populations living cheek by jowl in flimsy houses were also constantly at the mercy of fires, which were one of Japan's most abiding hazards. The most devastating of these, which struck Edo in 1657, burned for 19 days and killed an estimated 100,000. Despite the overall agricultural prosperity, too, there were always pockets of misery, and never more so than in times of famine. Untold numbers died during the three worst of these, in 1732, 1786 and 1833.

It is true, too, that among the unlooked-for results of commercialization was a degree of polarization between rich and poor, since the former were seen to benefit from the difficulties of the latter. The result was an increase in tension, both in the villages and

A view of the Dutchmen's quarters at Deshima, Nagasaki. They are in the course of eating a meal, and this picture reflects the intense curiosity about Western manners that reached a peak in the early 18th century when the Shōgun Yoshimune bade some Dutchmen prepare and eat a meal in his presence.

The Meireki fire

The most destructive fire to afflict Edo during the Tokugawa period was the Meireki fire of 1657, the third year of the Meireki era. At the time Zacharias Waganaer, the head of the Dutch mission at Nagasaki, was in Edo waiting to start the long journey back. It was only when he saw the fire from the rooftop that he recognized the danger and he left an account of the panic.

> With fear and trepidation, I realized that our lodging would soon be lost to lightning flames no less voracious than those at Troy or any great conflagration in history. The entire sun, which otherwise would have been shining brightly, was completely obscured by black smoke as though it would never be seen again. Although the fire was still about a quarter mile away, we could feel its strength and heat through the winter cold, driven on by a north wind. The rolling sea of flame was a mile wide running from east to west and it pressed forward with fire sparks falling like a strong rain. Our senior Japanese bodyguard, with a long staff in hand, led us into the street with instructions to stay together at all costs. This was indeed almost impossible because of the crowds of panic-stricken refugees, many trying to carry away their belongings in big chests on four wheels. Since nobody wished to be last, they had so congested the gateways and crossings that often hundreds of thus burdened citizens were waiting just to pass through, with the number growing with each passing moment. PK

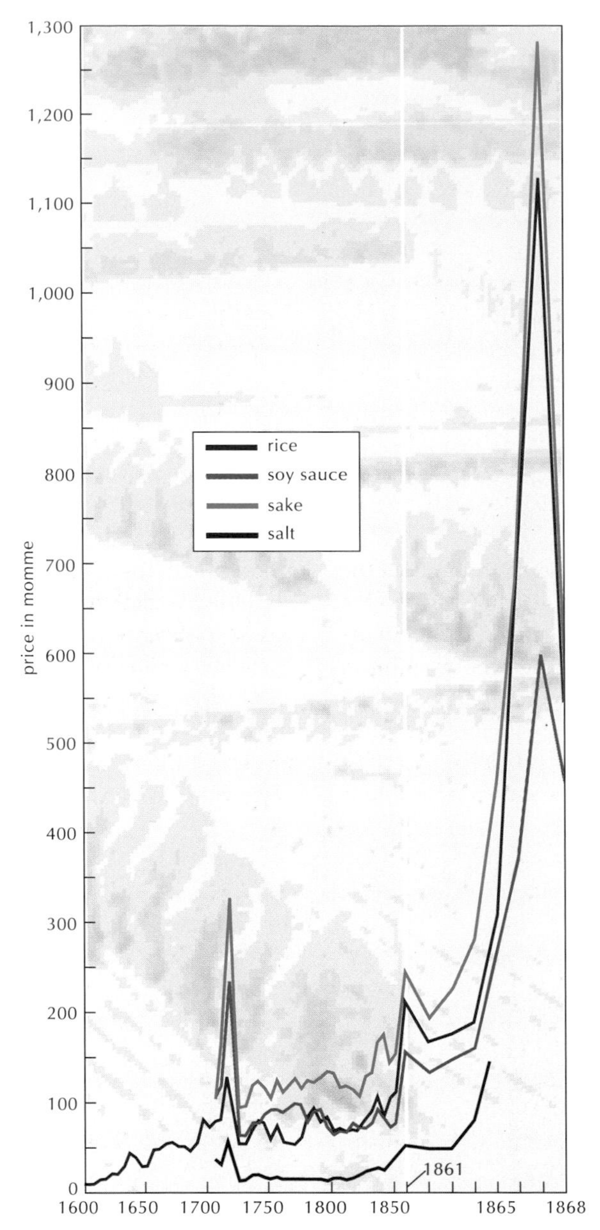

The rise in prices at the end of the Tokugawa period.

the towns, leading to rioting and violence. This never lasted too long, nor was it often on such a scale as to threaten the existing order. Nevertheless, social unrest was serious enough to cause concern among samurai officials, and that concern grew as the period progressed. For that matter, the samurai class itself was by no means immune to the prevailing social dislocation. Given rising prices, and incomes which, fixed at best, were all too often arbitrarily reduced by daimyō trying to economize, this was only to be expected. Their code of ethics did not permit outright rebellion, but there were clear signs of mounting unhappiness and instability both within and between the Tokugawa government and the daimyō domains, characterized by factionalism, purges, and political infighting of various degrees of desperation.

The 19th century was to see these tensions exacerbated. The Tenpō famine, which began in 1833 and took more than four years to run its course, did not help; it was no coincidence that more popular disturbances took place in 1836 than in any other year in the entire Tokugawa period. With these social tensions came an extraordinary uprising in Ōsaka, instigated, organized and led by Ōshio Heihachirō (1793–1837) who had himself once been a Bakufu official. The spate of reform movements triggered by these developments, as the Bakufu and the daimyō domains tried desperately and, with only a few exceptions, unsuccessfully to cope with their mounting financial problems, merely added to the confusion.

Threat from without

There was a still more ominous intimation of change, one which brought a new urgency to the task of financial reform. The rest of the world, kept at arm's length for so long, had begun to turn its attention to Japan. Already, at the end of the 18th century, there had been indications of a stirring of foreign interest. Japan's northernmost neighbour, the Russia of Catherine the Great, and her successors Paul I and Alexander I, made several attempts to establish contact, only to be rebuffed each time. Yet, as the 19th century progressed, there were unmistakeable signs that the outside world was closing in. Each succeeding year brought more sightings of foreign vessels – warships, whalers, merchantmen and survey ships from Britain, Russia, France and the US – in Japanese waters.

Whatever the intention of these movements, the Japanese government suspected the worst, and the news of the outbreak of war between Britain and China in 1839 simply served to confirm them in their fear that, if they wished to preserve their independence – and, no less a consideration, if the shōgun wished to discharge his mandate to pacify the savages from over the sea – some changes would need to be made. Specifically, they would have to make military preparations on a scale unknown for more than 200 years, and they would have to do so with a standing army now composed of bureaucrats, men not only inexperienced in warfare, but ill-equipped and demoralized.

Faced with such a dilemma, the undemanding and therefore largely amicable relationship between the Tokugawa government at the centre and the daimyō domains at the periphery began to dissolve. If Japan was to be forced to fight to defend its integrity, then the shōgun's government, already crippled, would need to call for far more aid from the daimyō than it had ever done before. Were the daimyō, themselves virtually bankrupt, to give it, they would do so at the expense of their domains, which would grow still poorer, their people, who could well be left unprotected, and their vassals, who would risk their lives in the defence of a distant shōgun in Edo.

It was a dilemma which simmered throughout the 1840s, kept bubbling by overt attempts by foreign governments to establish some kind of communication. The Dutch, from their privileged position in Nagasaki, maintained the temperature by drawing attention to the hostile intentions of other nations, and contrasting them with the benevolence of their own. The US, without a Nagasaki foothold, did so in two notable attempts, the first led by Commodore James Biddle in 1846, and the second, in 1849, by Commander James Glynn. But what caused the dilemma to boil over, finally and irrevocably, was the arrival of Commodore Matthew Perry in 1853, bringing demands that Japan establish trading and diplomatic relations with the US, and threatening to use force to bring these about.

The shōgun's government was unable to resist. Equally, however, it was unable either to force or convince the daimyō that the only way through the dangers ahead lay in the establishment of a more centralized government under Tokugawa control. The result was a decade of mistrust and paralysis, succeeded finally by open competition and defiance in which the lead was taken by the larger and more powerful domains of the south-west, Satsuma, Chōshū and Tosa. Together they made an unlikely and uneasy combination, but, aided by the general loss of confidence in the Bakufu – a sentiment shared by many senior Bakufu officials themselves – there was little resistance when, towards the end of 1867, they initiated a coup d'état which within a few weeks had brought the Bakufu down, and with it the Tokugawa period to an end. HB

Western paddle-steamers at Nagasaki, as seen in a popular print of about 1860. A few years earlier the black hulls and belching funnels of Commodore Perry's squadron had been seen as unanswerable symbols of Western technological superiority.

The Meiji period

The Meiji period (1868–1912) was an era of sweeping changes. The single most important motive for these changes was national self-preservation, which became an urgent priority when Japan was forced to confront the expansion of European and US interests in Asia and the Pacific. The Meiji leaders believed that only a powerful military capability could safeguard the nation's independence. This in turn, they argued, required a strong industrial and economic base, such as that which supported the international influence of Britain. The slogan coined to characterize this policy was *fukoku-kyōhei*, 'rich country, strong army'.

Already in the late Tokugawa period Japan's autonomy had been partially eroded by the so-called 'unequal treaties', which had granted foreigners extraterritoriality, open ports and control over Japan's import tariffs. The Japanese regarded the treaties as a national disgrace. However, they were in no position to renounce them unilaterally, and it was clear that Western nations would not agree to renegotiate them unless they could be persuaded that their own nationals and interests were adequately protected in Japan. This required institutional changes to bring Japanese practice in line with Western standards in areas such as commercial and criminal law, and policing. The desire to ensure continuing independence and freedom from European colonization, in conjunction with the imperatives of treaty revision, was thus the main focus of the government's strategy during the first half of the Meiji era and the object of its programme of economic, social and political change.

The emperor and his ministers debating a proposed invasion of Korea in 1873.

It is easy to look back on the Meiji period as an era of uninhibited 'progress', when government leaders with clear national goals successfully implemented predetermined policies. In fact, the rise to power of the new leadership in 1867–68 did not immediately usher in a new age: change in many areas of national life took decades to accomplish and institutional reform, industrialization and Western borrowing were only achieved as the result of a pragmatic, painstaking process of trial and error. One of the major concerns was how to avoid social and political anomie in an era of such rapid change, and indeed some of the features built into the new systems were to have unanticipated consequences in later years.

Political reform

The first task the new rulers faced was to consolidate their hold on power. Former supporters of the Tokugawa Bakufu offered little resistance after 1868, but opposition from dissenters in their own ranks proved more serious. A series of armed uprisings took place in the early 1870s, and in 1877 one of the main architects of the Meiji Restoration, Saigō Takamori, disillusioned by policies which he regarded as a betrayal of the aims of the Restoration, led a major anti-government rebellion in his home domain of Satsuma. The convincing defeat of Saigō and his supporters by the new conscript army, equipped with modern communications and weaponry, put an end to armed resistance.

During the first decade after the Restoration, Bakufu structures were dismantled and a new political and economic order established. By 1873 the largely independent domains had been transformed into prefectures closely supervised from Tōkyō. New structures of central and local government were introduced, and then progressively modified. The old caste-system was abolished; daimyō and samurai retainers were paid off with lump sums in government bonds and ceased to draw stipends. Landownership and land taxation were reformed into a unified national system capable of providing the state with a stable annual income. The expanding centralized bureaucracy enabled the government to become involved in a far greater range of activities than had hitherto been possible.

At this time real political power continued to be

Foreigners in Meiji Japan

The government and people of Japan were the main architects of successful modernization, but a number of fellow Asians, Europeans, and Americans made major contributions too. In the final years of the shōgunate the Tokugawa government began to employ Dutch, French and British officers to modernize its navy. Europeans were hired to teach in official language schools, and more progressive domains, such as Satsuma, appointed foreign engineers to assist in new industrial ventures. Indeed, by 1868, over 200 Westerners had served terms of employment in Japan.

After 1868 the new Meiji government not only extended the contracts of many advisers already in post but also began an even more ambitious programme of appointing 'hired foreign teachers' to promote national modernization. At first, great emphasis was placed on improved communications, and British engineers, such as Henry Brunton, were appointed to construct railways, lighthouses and a telegraph system. British advisers were again called upon to modernize the navy, but the reorganization of land forces was largely the work of French, and later German, officers. By contrast, the development of Hokkaidō was modelled on the opening of the American West, and Americans led by Horace Capron were appointed to assist the Hokkaidō Development Commission.

The selection of experts of many nationalities protected Japan from domination by any one country but it also brought serious difficulties. Europeans and Americans demanded, and got, high salaries and privileged housing, which imposed heavy burdens on the Meiji government. In addition, co-operation was often hampered by misunderstandings and racial prejudice. It was, however, Japanese organizations, public or private, that retained ultimate control of the policies, projects and conditions of service, and incompetent foreigners were briskly dismissed. Simultaneously, great efforts were made to absorb the skills of the foreign experts and, by the late 1870s, they were gradually being replaced by their Japanese pupils.

A special feature of this phase was the appointment of specialist lawyers to posts in the Ministries of Justice and Foreign Affairs. Gustave Boissonade helped shape a new legal code, Hermann Roesler influenced the drafting of the new constitution, and Henry Denison advised on the revision of the 'unequal treaties'. By the 1880s the campaign for treaty revision so dominated foreign policy that it influenced the selection of foreign employees. As the US and Germany showed increasing sympathy for Japan's position on the treaties, more of their nationals were appointed as advisers in such fields as historiography, architecture and modern medicine. Similarly, as early as 1877 an American journalist, E. H. House, was employed by a senior member of the government to launch the *Tokio times*, an English-language newspaper designed to win international sympathy for Japan. Not long afterwards an Englishman, Francis Brinkley, received financial help when he supported Japanese foreign policy in the columns of the *Japan mail*.

British, American and Canadian missionaries failed to achieve mass conversions to Christianity but their support for Western studies and women's education had a lasting impact on Japanese life. Amongst their number William Elliot Griffis taught science in Fukui and then at the embryonic Tōkyō University, Jerome Davis assisted in the establishment of Dōshisha University, now the leading private university in Kyōto, and a Canadian methodist, George Cochran, helped found Tōyō Eiwa School in Tōkyō.

Despite the seriousness of their purpose and their dedication, the missionaries also brought new forms of relaxation and leisure to Meiji Japan. American exponents of muscular Christianity encouraged the spread of baseball among students and an Englishman, Walter Weston, introduced mountaineering to large numbers of young Japanese. Less athletic missionaries developed Karuizawa as a cool summer resort which soon attracted thousands of city-dwellers.

Some of the foreign residents made remarkable progress in the study of Japanese language and culture. Even before the fall of the shōgunate, a German doctor, Philipp Franz von Siebold, had begun serious research into Japanese flora and fauna, and in the 1860s the young British diplomats Ernest Satow and W. G. Aston, who both acquired an astounding command of the language, pioneered the study of Japanese history and literature and built up superb collections of Japanese books. In the 1860s and 1870s Western diplomats believed that the study of Japanese tradition was essential for an understanding of contemporary Japan and they founded the Asiatic Society in Yokohama to this end. The Society's *Transactions* carried numerous contributions from Satow and Aston, and many others, and a parallel German-speaking Society was equally active.

These contributions to Western scholarship on Japan did far more than merely lay the foundations for future academic study. By treating Japan as a culture worthy of dedicated and disciplined study, they complemented Japan's own efforts to raise its cultural and political prestige in the world outside.

GD

wielded by a small élite. Most members of this relatively small ruling group, apart from a few court nobles, came from the old domains of Satsuma and Chōshū, which had played a leading role in the Restoration together with some members of the court nobility. The most prominent members were Ōkubo Toshimichi, Kido Takayoshi, and Iwakura Tomomi, and among the younger generation, Itō Hirobumi, Ōkuma Shigenobu, Matsukata Masayoshi, and Yamagata Aritomo. The group was not without its disagreements, and one of these had prompted Saigō to rebel in 1877, but during the 1870s it was for the most part held together by common aims.

As the ruling élite's concerns moved from mere survival towards complex matters of reform the scope for internal friction increased. One member, Itagaki Taisuke from Tosa, left the government in 1873, and soon began to campaign for more representative government, initiating what came to be known as the freedom and popular rights movement. The number of activists in the movement remained small, but the government before long felt compelled to take measures to restrict its increasingly vocal activities. Within the ruling group itself dissent increased after the assassination in 1878 of its de facto leader, Ōkubo Toshimichi. Two men, Itō Hirobumi of Chōshū and Ōkuma Shigenobu of Hizen, vied for the position of successor and the conflict came to a head in 1881 over proposals for constitutional government. The rift was never properly healed, and in a dispute over the disposal of government assets later in the year, Ōkuma was forced to resign.

Japan at the world exhibitions

International exhibitions and world fairs began with the Great Exhibition which opened at the Crystal Palace in London in 1851, but Japan was not represented: there were still a few years to go before the end of seclusion. But Japan later became one of the most enthusiastic participants in the endless round of international exhibitions, and this commitment to the ideals of the exhibition movement was recognized when Japan was awarded both an exhibition and an Olympic Games for the same year, the first Asian nation to be awarded either. The year was 1940 and both were cancelled: the Games eventually took place in Tōkyō in 1964 and the exhibition in Ōsaka in 1970.

The London Exhibition of 1862 had a Japanese section but that was contributed entirely by the first British diplomat in Japan, and it was not until the 1867 exhibition in Paris that Japan officially participated. The motives were partly political, for the shōgun's government, which was on the brink of collapse, had found a sympathetic supporter in France. In the Meiji period that followed, Japan mounted lavish displays at all the major exhibitions and many minor ones. The cost of participating was considerable, particularly given Japan's lack of foreign exchange, but there were compensations. For a nation like Japan, dedicated to technology-transfer, there was no better forum for comparing the different goods on offer as nations competed for prizes. Similarly, they furnished an ideal opportunity for finding markets for Japanese products, from tea to craft wares, and in recognition of this a series of exhibitions was launched within Japan to provide a competitive stimulus for domestic producers. A further consideration was Japan's drive to gain recognition as a civilized country, for the diplomatic rituals associated with the exhibitions gave Japan the status of an equal.

Perhaps more than anything else the Japanese displays at the great exhibitions created an enduring popular image of Japan in the West that persisted well into the 20th century. Japan had no technology to show off and the stands consisted of porcelain, lacquerware, painted fans and other craft exhibits, often adapted for Western tastes. At London in 1862, Paris in 1867, Vienna in 1873, Melbourne in 1875 and Philadelphia in 1876 these displays provoked rapture and astonishment and were amongst the most popular attractions on offer. They stimulated an enthusiasm for Japanese tastes in Western art that spread throughout Europe as 'Japonisme': many were touched by this, including Gustav Klimt in Vienna, designers such as Christopher Dresser in London, and of course the Impressionists, such as Monet. So attractive did this quaint image of Japan prove to exhibition-goers that, even when Japan had technology to exhibit, the focus of the Japanese displays remained the traditions and crafts that had excited admiration earlier and so they gave an increasingly false picture. This was true of the architecture as well: the illustration shows part of the Japanese pavilion at the St Louis World Fair of 1904. PK

Emperor Meiji and the constitution

A major result of the political upheavals of 1881 was a promise by the ruling élite to establish a Diet, or parliament, in 1890. In preparation for the enactment of a constitution, a cabinet system of rule was introduced in 1885, and in 1888 a privy council to advise on important matters, including the text of the new constitution. During the 1880s Itō spent an extended period abroad studying European systems of government. He received extensive advice from legal scholars, especially in Germany. The Imperial Japanese Constitution (Meiji Constitution) was promulgated in 1889 and put into effect the following year. This established the framework for all national political activity until the end of the Pacific War in 1945.

The cornerstone of the Meiji Constitution was the emperor of Japan. The young Emperor Meiji had acceded to the throne in 1867 and reigned until his death in 1912. Even before the Restoration he had served as a focus of loyalty and unity for the shōgun's opponents. In the post-Restoration years the imperial institution was skilfully manipulated to minimize divisions and frictions. The position allotted to the emperor by the 1889 constitution was one of immense power. The constitution itself was said to have been 'bestowed by the emperor', a statement which seemed to make any proposal for constitutional revision dangerously close to lèse-majesté. It opened by asserting the uniqueness of the Japanese imperial institution 'unbroken through ages eternal', and effectively declared the divinity of the emperor. The emperor was the repository of sovereignty. Beneath him, and responsible to him, were a series of political structures. A two-chamber Diet was established, the lower chamber elected, the upper one appointed. The main business of state was to be conducted by the cabinet, but cabinets were neither responsible to the Diet nor necessarily drawn from the majority party. The Privy Council was given substantial political power through its rôle of advising the emperor on a wide range of policy matters, while leaders of the armed forces had the right of direct access to the throne. While the Meiji emperor became a symbol of the new era, and took a close interest in the country's transformation, real political power continued to reside elsewhere even after the enactment of the constitution. How far the emperor might be willing and able to exercise the absolute power apparently assigned him by the constitution remained a matter of speculation.

A basic aim of the new constitution was to perpetuate the power of the ruling oligarchy. By providing an outlet for political opposition through the lower house of the Diet, the drafters of the constitution sought to curb the encroachment of the Diet on government decision-making by retaining an appointed rather than elected cabinet. To some degree this aim was achieved. The Satsuma–Chōshū oligarchy and its protégés remained dominant in political decision-making until well after the turn of the century. This was helped by the informal institution of the *genrō* (elder statesmen), an élite group of former prime ministers and oligarchs who until the early 1930s advised on the choice of a new prime minister and other critical issues.

Nevertheless, it soon became apparent that the constitution was not always going to function entirely as anticipated. First, the unique position allotted to the imperial institution allowed each of the various ruling élites – civil or military – to bypass the others in crucial political decisions. No single chain of responsibility between Privy Council, Diet, bureaucracy, cabinet, and the military was laid down. Moreover, non-élite or informal groups, including the *genrō*, could utilize the device of the 'imperial will' to sanction a range of actions. Second, oligarchs found themselves unable to operate totally independently of the Diet. After a period of intense antagonism in the mid 1890s, both oligarchy and Diet were compelled to move towards compromise and co-operation.

The emergence of political parties

The first major political parties, the Jiyūtō and the Kaishintō, appeared in the early 1880s, in part a revival of the popular rights movement. The parties were damaged by government suppression, lack of a focus for their campaigns and repeated incidents of violence, and so lapsed into inactivity after 1884, although they became active once more as the enactment of the constitution and the first general election approached. By manipulating their limited powers,

Tōkyō Imperial University

Often referred to as Tōdai, this is Japan's oldest and most prestigious university. Its history goes back to 1868 when the Meiji government reopened the three former Bakufu schools in Tōkyō, the Kaiseijo for Western learning, the Igakusho for medicine and the Shōheikō for Confucian studies. They were merged in 1877 under the name of the Imperial University, which was changed in 1897 to Tōkyō Imperial University to distinguish it from the newly-established Kyōto Imperial University. The Imperial University Edict of 1886 defined its purpose as to serve the needs of the state by concentrating on 'practical sciences'. In order to gain entry students had to attend a three-year course at a high school and pass a competitive exam. In the early years it was mostly Western knowledge that was taught and most of the teachers were either Europeans or North Americans teaching in their own languages, but they were gradually replaced by their students. In the 'conservative 1880s' there was felt to be a general need to counterbalance the extreme Westernization of the earlier years and to revive native traditions, and at the University a faculty of classical Chinese and Japanese studies was established in 1882 and, in 1889, a department of Japanese history. The Imperial University was modelled after German universities, but the Japanese tradition of government schools enhanced the influence of the state. This was a serious threat to academic freedom, but independence from outside interference was successfully defended in 1905. Professors at the Imperial University had considerable influence on government policies in the late Meiji period, as they were often the only experts in their fields, and graduates, especially from the Law Faculty, often became leading bureaucrats or businessmen. Even after the establishment of other imperial universities it remained the most influential. After 1945, the word 'imperial' was dropped, and, although Tōkyō University has lost much of its former influence, its graduates represent the majority of senior bureaucrats to this day. MDM

especially those relating to budget approval, lower-house members made life intensely difficult for the oligarchic cabinets in the early days of the Diet. Several dissolutions and elections took place in an atmosphere of intense bitterness. In 1898 there was a short-lived 'party' cabinet, headed by the ex-oligarch party leaders Ōkuma Shigenobu and Itagaki Taisuke. In 1900 Itō Hirobumi took the leadership of the newly formed Seiyūkai, one of the two big parties in the Diet. This marked the start of a more peaceful era, in which oligarchic cabinets, with or without formal party affiliation, sought to secure majority Diet support for their policies. At the same time, party members had a vested interest in supporting specific oligarchs, often in return for cabinet posts. More radical political parties were excluded from representation by the property qualification which restricted the franchise, and the nascent left-wing and labour movements were harshly suppressed by the state. Diet membership therefore remained strongly conservative, notwithstanding conflicts with the old establishment. These conflicts focussed not so much on ideology, as on who should hold office. Policy formulation essentially became a vehicle for political manipulation.

Religious developments and state ideology

The new Meiji leadership used Shintō religious beliefs to help establish a stable political structure centered on the emperor. In the early Meiji period religious institutions had considerable weight within the government, though their legal primacy over the secular arm of government was more a matter of form than substance. Religious institutions as such had no formal place in the 1889 constitution, but the religious aura of the imperial institution was a powerful political weapon. Old rituals relating to the emperor, formalized in what was known as State Shintō, became a fundamental part of Japanese life. Imperial rescripts and edicts had sacred connotations; the 1890 Imperial Rescript on Education, for example, was regularly read in schools and obeisance made to the text and the imperial portrait. The effectiveness of these efforts by the state to manipulate religion for political purposes was, however, restricted to selected areas of national life.

The religious rituals of everyday life continued relatively unchanged. Institutional Buddhism was severely affected by disestablishment and loss of government support, but the change did little to undermine the existing rôle of Buddhist practices. Elements of Buddhism, animism (shrine Shintō) and other religious practices continued to coexist in Japanese spiritual life, forming a syncretistic set of beliefs, from which elements were selected according to time and need. One unsurprising result of this period of dramatic upheaval was the appearance of some new religions and sects. Unlike religions such as Christianity and Islam, both the new sects and the older religious traditions were able to accommodate themselves to other beliefs.

The Neo-Confucian ideas which had underpinned the social ethic of the samurai class in the Tokugawa

Tōkyō at the turn of the century: telegraph wires, horse-drawn trams, top hats, and (on the right) an advertisement for Yebisu beer 'by appointment to the imperial household'.

period were selectively re-emphasized with a view to ensuring social stability at a time of rapid change. The hierarchical social structure built upon these concepts reinforced the emperor-centred political structure of the Meiji Constitution. The Civil Code of 1898 gave legal recognition at all levels of society to the patriarchal family system of the *ie* (house/family). Primogeniture, the dominance of the household head, and the subordinate position of women were now imposed by law. The ideology of the late Meiji period, manifest here and in other areas of society, made substantial use of pre-existing ideas, but also amounted to a major invention of tradition.

Enlightenment and Western ideas

George Bigot's caricature of a Dandy: while showing off the Western imports he owns, he has removed his trousers on account of the heat to leave just a loin-cloth.

Many measures adopted by the Meiji government posed a challenge to old beliefs and former orthodoxies. The task of spreading and promoting new, Western-influenced ideas fell to a small, self-appointed intellectual élite. These men became the main propagandists for the strategy of *bunmei–kaika* (civilization and enlightenment), which served as the intellectual background for the Meiji transformation. Many members of the group had studied Western learning either before, or in the early years after, the Restoration. Some had been taught in Japan by Westerners, while others had studied abroad. They were a diverse group, differing in perspectives and interests. What they had in common at this time was a shared belief that, without intellectual development, changes in society and the economy would either prove misguided or grind to a halt. Through institutions such as the Meirokusha (Meiji Six Society), founded in the sixth year of the Meiji period (1873), and its journal, the *Meiroku zasshi*, men such as Mori Arinori (later Minister of Education), Nishi Amane, Nakamura Masanao and Katō Hiroyuki sought to establish a new intellectual climate. Some, such as Nishimura Shigeki, felt later that Westernization had gone too far, and are remembered as conservatives. The best known member of this group is probably Fukuzawa Yukichi, the founder of Keiō Gijuku, now Keiō University.

Economic growth

The Meiji period also saw the start of industrialization along Western lines. The traditional sectors, agriculture and handicrafts, grew rapidly during these years, and in 1912 still accounted for by far the greatest proportion of economic activity. However, Western-style factories were established and mining operations were expanded and modernized, at first under state management, and later under private ownership. The production of silk, Japan's main export, underwent a technological transformation and a mechanized cotton-spinning industry grew rapidly after the 1880s. These two commodities were Japan's staple exports for the remainder of the Meiji period. New industries also appeared, manufacturing commodities such as wool, cement, beer and glass. Heavy industry lagged behind at first, but iron and steel production, engineering and shipbuilding expanded significantly after 1900.

The state played a major rôle in these developments. Reforms of the law relating to land tenure and land tax promoted greater productivity on the land, and so growth in agricultural production kept pace with population increase. The new régime ensured itself a stable income by setting tax rates as a percentage of land-value: hitherto, payments had fluctuated according to the harvest. Apart from financing a central bureaucracy, these funds went towards building a new physical, financial, legal and educational infrastructure. The government itself set up and operated factories in new and unfamiliar industries.

However, the significance of the Japanese state in the industrialization process should not obscure the importance of the private sector. Merchants, samurai and ex-farmers played a major rôle from the start in setting up new businesses. After 1880 the state sold off most of its own businesses as part of its deflationary policy, and turned to indirect intervention, encouraging the private sector through subsidies, legislation and patronage.

The old samurai contempt for business activities faded as a succession of able entrepreneurs set up new manufacturing and commercial enterprises, and established for themselves the reputation of working for the national interest. Amongst the most famous was Shibusawa Eiichi (1841–1931), founder of a string of enterprises from cotton-spinning through banking to railways. Others included the founders of the companies which later grew into the zaibatsu, huge business conglomerates often under the control of a single family, such as Mitsui, Mitsubishi, and Sumitomo. The co-operation between the state and the private sector for most of the Meiji period was of immense significance for the growth of trade and industry.

The growth in production and changes in production techniques also had negative aspects. Many rural inhabitants believed their interests were being sacrificed to those of the state, the cities and the modern industrial sector. Individuals from impoverished rural communities, hoping for something better, migrated to urban areas, where many found themselves living in slum conditions in poverty at least as great as that they had suffered in the countryside. The growing number of textile factories employed mainly girls and young women, some as young as ten; they worked long hours in unhealthy and dangerous conditions for a meagre wage. The first Factory Act was not passed until 1911, just before the end of the Meiji period, and implemented several years later. Finally, uncaring exploitation of resources and manufacturing techniques brought environmental disasters. Urban skies blackened with smoke. Mining operations and tree-felling affected water courses, devastating downstream agricultural areas dependent on a secure water supply for the production of paddy rice and other crops. Pollution from the Ashio copper mine, in Tochigi Prefecture, caused a storm of protest during the 1880s, and became a national issue in the following decade. The state's failure to impose on companies more stringent anti-pollution measures or factory legislation was a clear indication of the primacy of industrial interests in the national strategy.

A popular print of the battle of Pyongyang during the Sino-Japanese War.

DIPLOMACY AND CONFLICT

After several abortive attempts at negotiation, Japan achieved revision of the unequal treaties in 1894, although this was not to be implemented until 1899. This restored nominal equality with the Western powers, but well before this, Japan's relations with other Asian countries became problematic. Japan used the threat of force to impose a similar unequal treaty on her own nearest neighbour, Korea, in 1876. Disputes with China were frequent, and the Japanese believed that a weak, Chinese-dominated Korea made the whole area vulnerable to Western encroachments and posed a strategic danger to Japan itself. As Japan grew stronger, friction between Japan and China increased, with each seeking to dominate the Korean peninsula; from 1882 they both stationed troops there. The disagreements erupted into open conflict in the Sino-Japanese War of 1894–95. Japan,

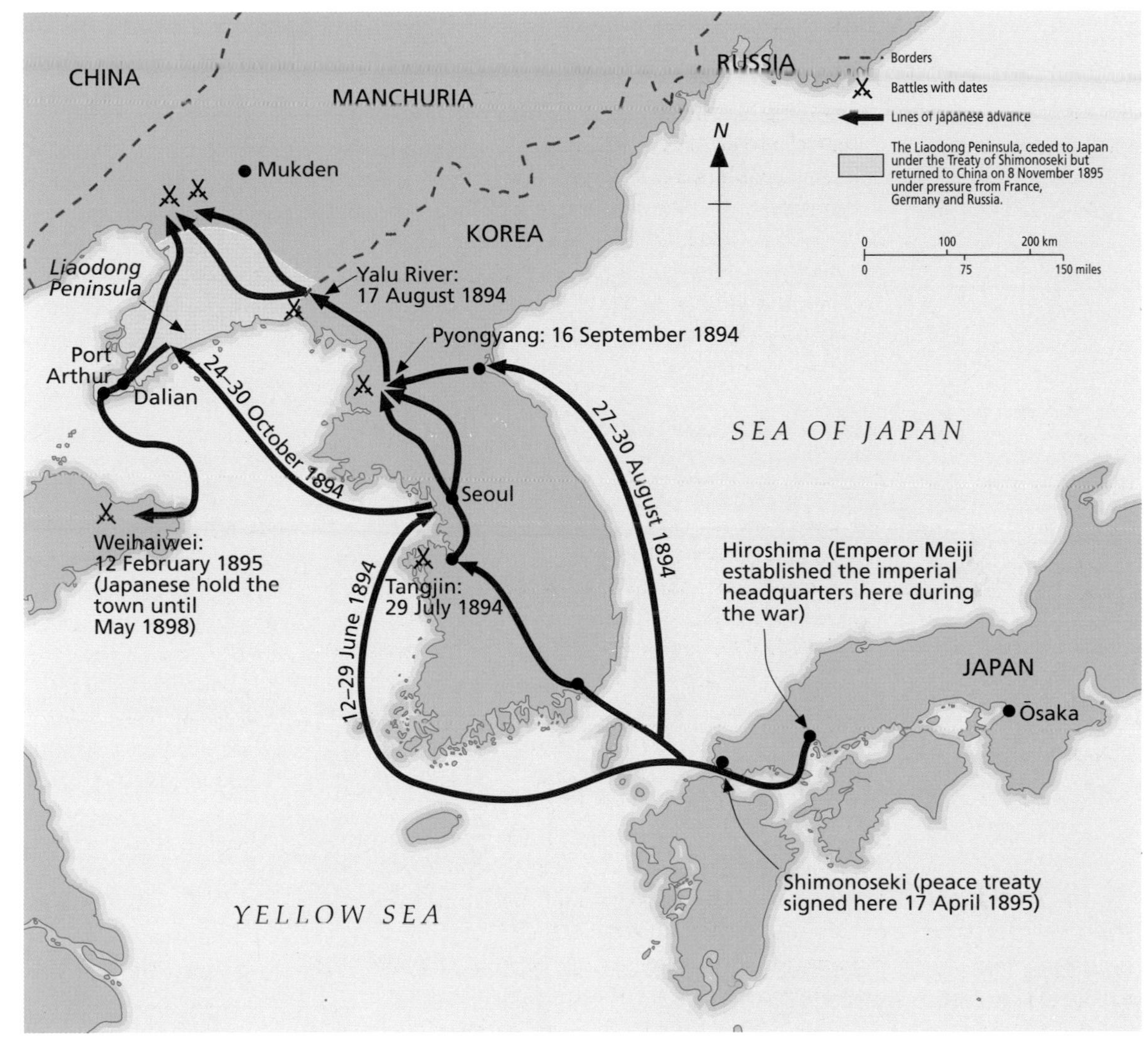

The Sino-Japanese War (1894–95) was fought over the issue of control over Korea, which the Japanese government saw as vital to Japan's national security. To the surprise of the Western powers, the military campaign went decisively in Japan's favour, but it did not resolve the issue. Instead, Russian influence replaced that of China and the prospect of a war between Japan and Russia looked increasingly likely.

faced with the vast size and manpower resources of the Chinese empire, won a resounding victory thanks to its better-equipped Western-style forces. Surprised Westerners were compelled to recognize Japan as a major force in East Asia. Under the peace settlement of the Treaty of Shimonoseki, Japan received territorial concessions, including the island of Formosa (Taiwan), marking the start of Japanese colonial power. A massive indemnity paid by China was used to put the yen on the gold standard. However, other concessions in Manchuria promised by China had to be abandoned in the face of the so-called 'Triple Intervention' by Russia, Germany and France, which compelled Japan to abandon further claims. This incident left a legacy of resentment.

The question of dominance in Korea remained unresolved, as the Chinese challenge was replaced by a Russian one. With Russia also building up her influence in Manchuria, open conflict between the two expanding empires became increasingly likely. In 1900 the Chinese 'Boxer' Rebellion brought an international expeditionary force to Beijing. Unlike the other national contingents, Russian troops failed to withdraw according to an internationally agreed schedule, and remained in occupation of large areas of Manchuria. Japan accelerated her military build-up, and in 1902 signed an alliance with Britain. One effect of the alliance was to ensure that France, Russia's ally, would be kept out of any future conflict between Japan and Russia.

The Russo-Japanese War commenced early in 1904, the immediate cause of war being Russia's occupation of Manchuria. Japanese forces made a rapid initial advance, but met increasing resistance. Victories proved costly, winter conditions were grim, and the Russian forces at Port Arthur withstood eight months of siege. Both sides incurred huge foreign debts to finance the conflict, and could ill afford the growing financial burden. Russia was also weakened by internal dissent. In May 1905 the Japanese navy defeated the Russian Baltic fleet at Tsushima in the Japan Sea, but both belligerents were under strong international and domestic pressures to reach a ceasefire. Japan had not inflicted a crushing defeat on Russia, but was able, contrary to Western expectations, to claim a victory. The US-mediated Portsmouth Treaty was signed in September 1905. The terms provoked nationwide resentment among a public which had been led to expect more of the treaty, and led to rioting in Tōkyō. There was no indemnity, though Japan did gain the southern half of Sakhalin island. However, the acquisition of

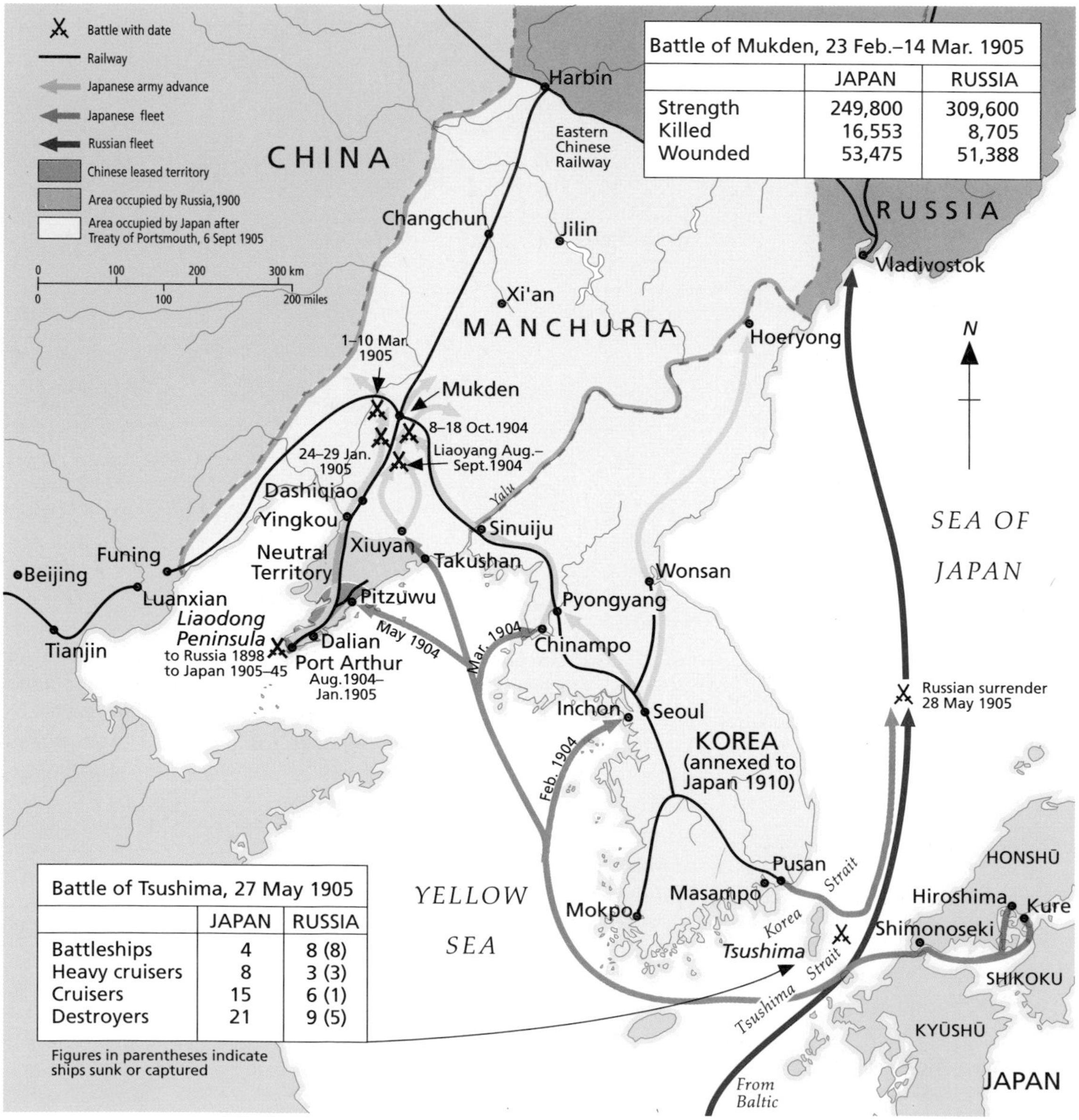

The Russo-Japanese War (1904–05) started with a surprise Japanese assault on the Russian fleet at Port Arthur, which was hailed by The Times *as an act of daring. It developed into a bloody and terrifying foretaste of the trenches and the mechanized warfare of the First World War. At the Battle of Tsushima in 1905 the Russian Baltic Fleet was annihilated, showing for the first time that a European power could be beaten by an Asian one.*

Battle of Mukden, 23 Feb.–14 Mar. 1905

	JAPAN	RUSSIA
Strength	249,800	309,600
Killed	16,553	8,705
Wounded	53,475	51,388

Battle of Tsushima, 27 May 1905

	JAPAN	RUSSIA
Battleships	4	8 (8)
Heavy cruisers	8	3 (3)
Cruisers	15	6 (1)
Destroyers	21	9 (5)

Figures in parentheses indicate ships sunk or captured

former Russian concessions in Manchuria allowed Japan to expand her interests there through the medium of the South Manchurian Railway. Also, Japan now had a free hand in Korea, which in 1905 was compelled to assume the status of a Japanese protectorate. Despite strong Korean resistance, the peninsula was annexed in 1910 and became a part of Japan. Few Western powers protested.

Two years later the Meiji period came to an end with the death of Emperor Meiji. Japan was still a predominantly agricultural economy, in which most families worked long hours for a meagre existence. Outside influences had only marginally changed traditional lifestyles, though all children by 1912 were receiving compulsory education. Externally, though, the image of Japan was transformed. In 40 years the country had adopted Western-style institutions in most areas of national life, and achieved relations of formal equality with the Western powers. Moreover, it had accumulated a substantial and proven military capability, and established itself as a regional superpower. JEH

The Russo-Japanese war

The war began with a surprise attack on the Russian fleet at Port Arthur on 8 February 1904, followed by a declaration of war two days later. Japanese troops were landed in Korea and advanced north but their attempt under General Nogi to capture Port Arthur, although ultimately successful, proved exceptionally costly and a horrifying foretaste of the trench warfare to break out in Europe 10 years later. The correspondent of the London *Daily Mail* was a witness of the heavy loss of life incurred by the Japanese troops as they tried time and time again to overcome the deeply entrenched Russian positions surrounding Port Arthur. On 28 November a force of 400 soldiers was waiting to launch an attack on 203 Metre Hill when Russian Maxim machine gunners suddenly opened fire.

> The Japanese were sitting huddled together in the narrow space, quite unconcernedly, when the avalanche of lead was poured into them. Within a few seconds the trench was turned into a veritable pandemonium, a seething mass of humanity, where men were fighting wildly to get away, trampling on the wounded, climbing over the piles of corpses which blocked the entrance, or trying to escape over the edge of the parallel down the coverless hillside. But the Maxims did their work as only Maxims can.

By the time Port Arthur, the base of the Russian Pacific Fleet, fell in January 1905, the Japanese forces had suffered more than 50,000 casualties. The battle of Mukden in March was even more costly and although the Japanese were eventually successful they were unable to inflict a decisive military defeat on the Russians. The Russian government then sent the Baltic fleet, ill-prepared and poorly equipped, half way around the world in a desperate attempt to recover Port Arthur and regain the initiative, but it met with disaster in the Tsushima Strait between Japan and Korea. On 27 May 1905 it was intercepted by Admiral Tōgō's fleet of British-built battleships and cruisers and by dawn the next day it had lost 4,830 men and 34 ships sunk or captured, including all the battleships. Novikoff-Priboy, a seaman on board the ironclad battleship *Oryol* who survived the battle, described what it was like to be on the receiving end of the Japanese fire-power, which was so accurate that many Russians were convinced they were fighting the British navy.

> The shells now seemed to be falling on and around us out of a riven sky, instead of being fired at us by an enemy. The *Oryol* was no more than a floating brazier. From the after-bridge, red tongues of flame rose, twisting upwards, almost to the level of the main-top.

He had a lucky escape when a Japanese shell struck the *Oryol* near to where he was standing.

> There was a burst of flame encircled with black smoke. A current of hot air knocked me endwise, and I felt as if I must have been shattered to bits like dust blown before the wind. Then, much to my surprise, I found that I was uninjured, verifying the fact by fingering my head, my body and my limbs. Wounded men, uttering loud cries, were running away in all directions. Two blue-jackets had been killed. A third, flung close beside me, remained motionless for a few seconds, and then clambered swiftly on to one knee as if carrying out an order. Casting terrified glances around, he seemed prepared to take to flight, though his entrails were hanging out of his torn belly like rags emerging from an open trunk.

The Battle of Tsushima cost Japan only 110 lives, but the war as a whole cost almost 90,000, and for Japan it was the bloody introduction to mechanized warfare that the First World War was to be for Europeans. Although it gained for Japan worldwide recognition as a formidable military power with the capacity to inflict a defeat on a European nation, it also brought Japan into greater competition with the Western colonial powers and thus set the stage for further conflict. By the Treaty of Portsmouth, signed in September 1905, Russia acknowledged the rights Japan claimed in Korea, and Japan acquired the Russian leases in Manchuria and control of the South Manchurian Railway. But the financial and human costs had been huge.

PK

From the First World War to the 1930s

Japan was increasingly drawn into world affairs by the First World War, during which it fought on the Allied side against Germany. For contributing to Germany's defeat, it acquired a permanent seat on the Council of the new League of Nations, established by the Treaty of Versailles. Then, over the period spanning the 1920s and mid 1930s, Japan veered from peaceful expansionism through trade and co-operative diplomacy to armed aggression against China and intensifying confrontation with the West, and from a promising, albeit qualified, democratic political evolution to authoritarian repression and domestic political violence on an unprecedented scale. These radical transformations isolated Japan and hastened the building of a garrison state in the years up to 1937 followed by the outbreak of war with China. Yet fundamentally these shifts demarcated successive and contrasting stages, prompted by dramatic changes in the international environment and in Japanese politics, along the continuum of Japan's quest, begun in the 19th century, for national wealth and power.

Central Tōkyō in the 1920s. Electric trams and cars now dominate the streets, but wooden buildings and handcarts have yet to disappear.

The First World War and its Aftermath

Citing its obligations to Britain under the Anglo–Japanese Alliance, Japan declared war on Germany on 23 August 1914, two years into the reign of the Taishō Emperor. During the conflict it seized German enclaves in the Chinese province of Shandong and German-held Pacific islands in the Marshalls, Marianas and Carolines which it later administered under League of Nations' mandates. It also used the occasion of the war to obtain economic and political concessions from China in the 'Twenty-One Demands' of 1915. Elsewhere, in 1918 Japan participated in an Allied expedition into Siberia, to rescue a contingent of Czech troops whose passage out of Russia to rejoin the war in Europe was hampered by the Russian civil war. Japan evacuated its troops from Siberia in 1922.

After Germany's defeat in 1918, Western recognition of Japan as a great power was partially compromised by the rejection of Japan's proposed racial-equality clause in the League of Nations Covenant. Nevertheless, Japan took part in the construction of a new international order designed to end the old diplomacy of imperialism that had led to the First World War. It thus supported the League and accepted the abrogation of the Anglo–Japanese alliance in agreeing to a new system of multilateral treaties, signed at the Washington Conference of 1921–22. Japan also accepted a lower level of naval armament than that set for Britain and the US and agreed to withdraw its forces from Shantung, as demanded by China.

Left *A Japanese newspaper report of the outbreak of war in Europe in 1914. The cartoonist shows European leaders pondering their options.*

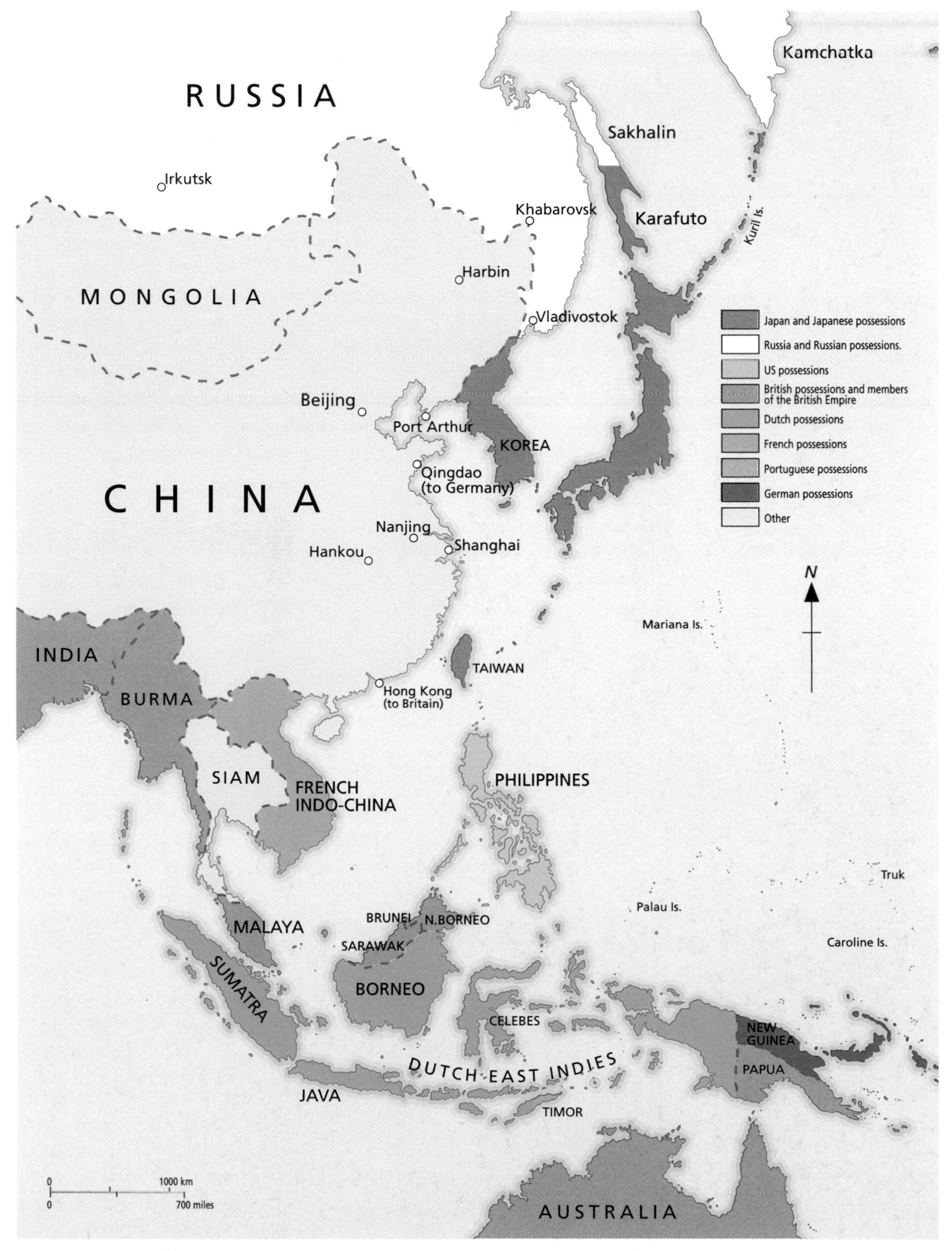

Right *Japan surrounded: the Great Powers in the Far East in 1914. By the outbreak of war in 1914 a very large part of the eastern and south-eastern parts of Asia had been taken over by the European powers. This engendered, not unnaturally, feelings of insecurity among many Japanese, who saw their country's independence of action under threat. Britons might have felt the same had Denmark, Holland, France and Germany been occupied or partially colonized by China, Japan, Vietnam and Burma.*

Significantly, the unfolding of a co-operative foreign policy was accompanied by the development of strong democratic tendencies within Japan which, although traceable to the late Meiji period, had been greatly enhanced by the impact of the First World War. For the war had quickened the pace of economic and social change which in turn produced a variety of new democratic expectations. In brief, Allied orders for munitions and other war materials triggered a wartime industrial boom, the rapid expansion of factories and of the urban work force, and widening cleavages between the salaried middle class, which had largely benefited from economic growth, and the poor, who were especially vulnerable to inflated wartime prices, including most notably the price of rice, which outstripped wages and farm income.

In consequence, Japan was swept by labour strikes and in 1918 by the nation-wide Rice Riots during which the army was called upon to restore order in some regions. Building on late-Meiji precedents, new labour unions were established to organize the workers for sustained social protest. Some were anarchist, advocating militant direct action; others advocated socialist reform of the capitalist system. A new student movement, a new women's movement and later a new tenant farmers' union movement came into being, all of which added to the social ferment of Taishō Japan. Proponents of 'liberation' were encouraged by the revolutions in Russia (1917) and Germany (1918) to believe that Japan, too, stood at the dawn of popular democracy.

The recession which hit Japan immediately after the war, and subsequent uneven economic growth, created conditions in which these social movements expanded further during the 1920s. Marxism, as popularized by the economist Kawakami Hajime of Kyōto Imperial University, gained a lasting foothold in many universities, and after the formation of the Soviet-backed Japanese Communist Party in 1922, politically-engaged Marxists resorted to Leninist strategies in striving for the revolutionary overthrow of Japanese capitalism and the 'emperor-system' (*tennōsei*). Communism supplanted anarchism on the radical left and began to compete with moderate socialism for control of the labour movement.

The devastation after the Great Kantō Earthquake of 1 September 1923. Much of the damage was caused by the fires that swept through the rows of wooden houses as cookers were overturned in the initial tremors. More than 100,000 lost their lives in Tōkyō and Yokohama. The picture here shows the main railway line into the centre of Tōkyō. The building on the right is Frank Lloyd Wright's Imperial Hotel, one of the few left intact.

Taishō democracy

The future of 'Taishō democracy' rested with the 'liberal' middle-class parties whose long-term development culminated in the appointment of the Seiyūkai party-leader, Hara Kei, as prime minister in 1918. Hara's rise signified the transfer of power from the Meiji Restoration generation of leaders, represented by Yamagata Aritomo (d. 1922), to a new generation. With the exception of several short-lived non-party cabinets in the early 1920s, from Hara's assassination in 1921 up to May 1932 Japan was governed by liberal party cabinets. Either the Seiyūkai, or its rival, the Kenseikai (renamed the Minseitō in 1926) ruled, whichever held the balance of power in the House of Representatives, as determined by national elections. To many Japanese, especially of the middle class, party cabinets and parliamentary politics represented the 'normal course of constitutional government' in line with world trends after the triumph of democracy over autocracy in the First World War.

However, once they attained power, the parties tried to retain it by striking pragmatic compromises with more conservative political élites, with the result that they did not seriously challenge the existing, intrinsically anti-democratic, structures and processes of government that had developed under

A seated nude, painted in 1920. The nude had been new to Japanese art but had become more or less accepted by this time, although only a few years were to pass before pictures such as this were again being attacked as evidence of decadent Western tastes.

the Meiji Constitution. The well-known liberal, Yoshino Sakuzō of Tōkyō Imperial University, criticized the parties for failing to base constitutional government on the will of the people.

To be sure, in 1925, the Kenseikai cabinet of prime minister Katō Takaaki, responding to popular pressure, achieved the enactment of universal manhood suffrage which, by giving all males over 25 the right to vote, expanded the electorate from 3,000,000 voters to over 12,000,000. But the effect was to co-opt the moderate left-wing socialists, now inspired to form their own parties, into the existing political order, while the state repressed the radical left-wing with all the power at its disposal. This power was immeasurably increased by the 1925 Peace Preservation Law, aimed mainly at the communists. By the mid 1930s, they were all but extinguished on the political scene.

The essential conservatism of the parties owed much to their nationalism and to their perception of themselves as guardians of property and the imperial state. But it was also due to the influence of the *zaibatsu*. Typified by Mitsui, Mitsubishi, Yasuda and Sumitomo, these self-contained industrial, banking, and trading empires dominated the modern sector of the economy in the 1920s and thereafter. Relying on a mass of smaller subcontracting firms, they spearheaded Japanese industrial growth while the agricultural sector, which had sunk into lasting depression, lagged far behind. Above all, the *zaibatsu* looked to party government to promote Japanese capitalism.

The government responded by assisting industry, by emphasizing increased trade with America, Europe and Asia and by undertaking co-operative diplomacy to facilitate the peace that international trade required. Co-operation with Britain and the US received high priority, as at the Washington Conference; Japan recognized the USSR in 1925, despite its aversion to the Comintern's sponsorship of communism in Asia; and in 1928 Japan signed the Kellogg–Briand Pact outlawing war.

Japan also reacted with restraint to the unification of China by Chiang Kai-shek's Nationalist Army and to Chinese protests against Japan's treaty interests in China. Japan similarly acknowledged Chinese sovereignty in Manchuria but insisted that its own treaty rights in South Manchuria were non-negotiable. As if to underscore this point, in June 1928, Japanese Guandong Army agents, acting independently without authorization from Tōkyō, assassinated a Chinese warlord in the Manchurian city of Mukden. This incident prefigured the Manchurian Incident.

In retrospect, many features of 'Taishō democracy' persisted after Emperor Hirohito proclaimed his reign as 'Shōwa', or 'Illustrious Peace', upon the death of his father, the Taishō Emperor, in December 1926. Yet party government lacked the strong allegiance of the people, who resented corruption involving the parties and big business. Moreover, politically, 'Taishō democracy' was primarily an urban phenomenon, in contrast to the traditional conservatism of village Japan. It thus found its strongest cultural reflection in a lively new urban popular culture epitomized by the spread of newspapers and magazines, a growing entertainment industry including bars, coffee shops, dance revues, and modern theatre, and the appeal of new fashions and life-styles imported from the West.

As in Weimar Germany, the ethos of this urban culture was international, cosmopolitan, individualistic, materialistic, and hedonistic. These characteristics were inherently vulnerable to attack by advocates of Japanese purity as decadent 'Western' intrusions. Indeed, the most salient general point about 'Taishō democracy' was its vulnerability to upheaval: nothing made this clearer than the chaos and violence following the great Kantō earthquake of 1 September 1923, which destroyed most of Tōkyō and Yokohama leaving over 100,000 dead.

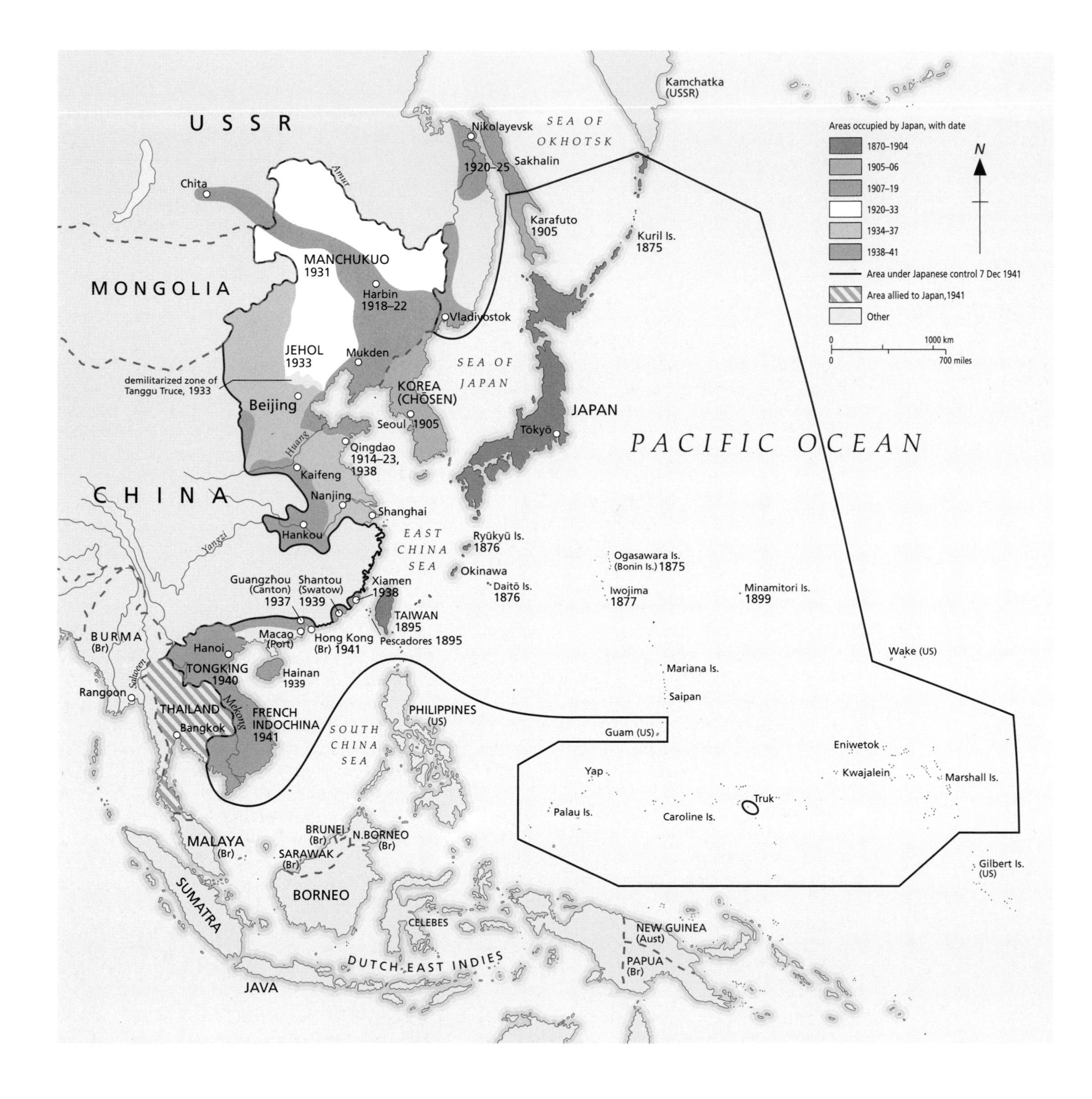

USSR
SEA OF OKHOTSK
Kamchatka (USSR)
Nikolayevsk
1920–25
Sakhalin
Karafuto 1905
Kuril Is. 1875
Chita
Amur
MANCHUKUO 1931
MONGOLIA
Harbin 1918–22
Vladivostok
JEHOL 1933
Mukden
demilitarized zone of Tanggu Truce, 1933
Beijing
SEA OF JAPAN
KOREA (CHŌSEN)
Seoul 1905
JAPAN
Tōkyō
PACIFIC OCEAN
Huang
Qingdao 1914–23, 1938
Kaifeng
CHINA
Nanjing
Shanghai
Hankou
Yangzi
EAST CHINA SEA
Ryūkyū Is. 1876
Okinawa
Daitō Is. 1876
Ogasawara Is. (Bonin Is.) 1875
Iwojima 1877
Minamitori Is. 1899
Guangzhou (Canton) 1937
Shantou (Swatow) 1939
Xiamen 1938
TAIWAN 1895
Pescadores 1895
Macao (Port)
Hong Kong (Br) 1941
BURMA (Br)
Hanoi
TONGKING 1940
Hainan 1939
Salween
Rangoon
THAILAND
Mekong
Bangkok
FRENCH INDOCHINA 1941
SOUTH CHINA SEA
PHILIPPINES (US)
Wake (US)
Mariana Is.
Saipan
Guam (US)
Eniwetok
Kwajalein
Marshall Is.
Yap
Truk
Palau Is.
Caroline Is.
Gilbert Is. (US)
MALAYA (Br)
BRUNEI (Br)
N.BORNEO (Br)
SARAWAK (Br)
BORNEO
SUMATRA
CELEBES
NEW GUINEA (Aust)
PAPUA (Br)
DUTCH EAST INDIES
JAVA
Areas occupied by Japan, with date
1870–1904
1905–06
1907–19
1920–33
1934–37
1938–41
Area under Japanese control 7 Dec 1941
Area allied to Japan, 1941
Other
N
0 1000 km
0 700 miles

The growth of the Japanese colonial empire. By the time of the attack on Pearl Harbor on 7 December 1941, Japan had acquired or occupied huge areas of the Asian mainland. Korea had been occupied and then annexed in 1910, Manchuria had been occupied and then changed into a Japanese puppet state under the name of Manchukuo in 1931, and the outbreak of war with China in 1937 had brought more and more territory under Japanese control each year.

The crisis of early Showa Japan, 1929–36

The world depression, beginning in late 1929, shattered the foundations of 'Taishō democracy'. On the one hand, by severing Japanese trade with the West and by propelling Japan into creating a self-sufficient 'Yen bloc' in East Asia to offset new Western trade barriers, it destroyed the economic framework of co-operative diplomacy and eventually led to the militarization of the Japanese economy, centred on heavy industrial growth. On the other hand, the depression also caused the immediate collapse of many factories, mass urban unemployment, an upsurge of labour strikes and widespread rural destitution. In these chaotic conditions, which betokened an apparent crisis of liberalism and capitalism, Japan was ripe for a massive political reaction which paralleled the reaction against Weimar democracy and the rise of the Nazi party.

In 1930, as the depression deepened, the Minseitō cabinet of prime minister Hamaguchi overrode the opposition of the navy general staff and committed Japan to the London Naval Treaty whereby Japan again accepted a lower ratio of naval armament vis-à-vis the US and Britain. Conservatives could now blame party government for a weak foreign policy as well as economic mismanagement. Accused of having encroached on the Emperor's prerogative of supreme command and betraying national security, Hamaguchi was shot and fatally wounded in November 1930. Japan abrogated the Treaty in 1934, thus precipitating a naval arms race with the Anglo–American powers.

In September 1931 the government completely lost control of foreign policy when the Guandong Army unilaterally precipitated the Manchurian Incident. This resulted in the Japanese seizure of Manchuria, the formation of the puppet state of Manchukuo in March 1932, and Japan's exodus from the League of Nations in February 1933 following the League's censure of Japanese aggression. The Anglo–American powers and China condemned Japan as a 'bandit nation' and refused to recognize its territorial gains. Japan, however, saw itself as the 'stabilizing' force in East Asia. Although it stood alone, it would take the first step towards a close association with Nazi Germany when it signed the Anti-Comintern Pact in 1936.

Government by assassination and terrorism

On 15 May 1932 the Seiyūkai prime minister, Inukai Tsuyoshi, was murdered because he had opposed the conquest of Manchuria. His death brought an end to party cabinets and henceforth, until defeat in 1945, Japan was governed by bureaucratic non-party cabinets increasingly responsive to army and navy requirements. Inukai's assassination was one of many such terrorist incidents against party and *zaibatsu* leaders in the depression years. The participants were young officers and civilian arch-nationalists who wanted a coup in which a senior officer would take power and carry out a 'Shōwa Restoration'. To some activists, this nebulous term connoted the elimination of 'corrupt' Western influences and sectarian political conflict associated with 'Taishō democracy', the recovery of political and social unity based on traditional Japanese values, and a better day for rural Japan, where their personal sympathies lay. Others, inspired by the national socialist thinker, Kita Ikki, emphasized the creation of a powerful military state committed to the armed liberation of Asia from Western imperialism.

This nationalistic atmosphere inspired further anti-communist crackdowns, the 'conversion' of dissidents to the emperor system, and obedient conformity to the dictates of the state. The harsh, intolerant, mood of the times was illustrated in 1935 when Minobe Tatsukichi, of Tōkyō Imperial University, was publicly vilified for having attempted to qualify the emperor's prerogatives by arguing that the emperor was but an 'organ of the state' with limited powers. Imperial absolutism now held sway, although ironically Emperor Hirohito personally regarded himself as a constitutional monarch who should not interfere with government. Disillusioned with party rule, liberalism, and the perceived bankruptcy of co-operative diplomacy, the Japanese increasingly placed their trust in the armed forces, to lead the country and revive national wealth and power.

Japan might have succumbed to a military dictatorship in the early 1930s had it not been for a virtual civil war within the army itself. This struggle for power, essentially between the 'Imperial Way Faction' (Kōdōha) and the 'Control Faction' (Tōseiha), came to a climax in the 26 February 1936

Hirohito as Crown Prince travelling in northern Japan. Note the faces in the crowd looking straight at him, rather than looking respectfully down as was expected in the harsher days of the thirties and forties. The original caption suggests that, 'the coolies who carried him count that work as one of the greatest of their lives'.

Incident when Imperial Way troops occupied central Tōkyō, assassinated several moderate government officials and proclaimed a 'Shōwa Restoration'. However, Hirohito, who opposed fascism and militarism, condemned the rebellion and within several days the Control Faction, backed by the navy, had suppressed it. Afterwards, some rebel leaders, and Kita Ikki, who had influenced them, were executed and other Imperial Way officers were purged. This left the Control Faction not only supreme in the army but also in a position to force a change of government by withdrawing the army minister if the cabinet did not comply with its policies of building a 'national defence state'. The coup had failed and the constitutional order remained intact, but the army was now able to control both domestic and foreign policy. SSL

The South Manchuria Railway

The South Manchuria Railway (SMR) came under Japanese control as a result of the Treaty of Portsmouth which ended the Russo-Japanese War and brought Russian assets and concessions in Manchuria under Japanese jurisdiction. It played a crucial rôle in facilitating Japanese domination and development of Manchuria and, recognizing its strategic importance, successive governments provided it with the necessary funds and personnel to enable it to expand. The SMR was not simply a railway, for the company had complete jurisdiction, to the exclusion of the Chinese government, over the Railway Zone, including both land adjacent to the tracks and the cities through which they passed. It had the right to levy taxes and to run civilian administration and Japanese nationals working in the zone enjoyed the privilege of extraterritoriality. Through its investments and administrative power the SMR dominated the industrial development of Manchuria, but following the Manchurian Incident of 1931 it gained a completely free hand and its profits rose accordingly. In 1933, it became the body responsible for the control of all railways in Manchuria. In 1937 its industrial interests were detached and reorganized in a new company and it concentrated thereafter on the transportation of goods and people. That year also saw the outbreak of war with China and from then on the SMR had to concentrate so much on the transportation of troops and war matériel that its profits suffered, and, as the war situation worsened, its employees were conscripted to aid the war effort. In 1945 it fell under Soviet control.

It is natural that there should be some nostalgia for the heyday of the SMR among its former employees, but it should not be forgotten that its job was to exploit Manchuria for the benefit of Japan and that the Chinese workforce suffered low wages and heavy casualties at work.

PK

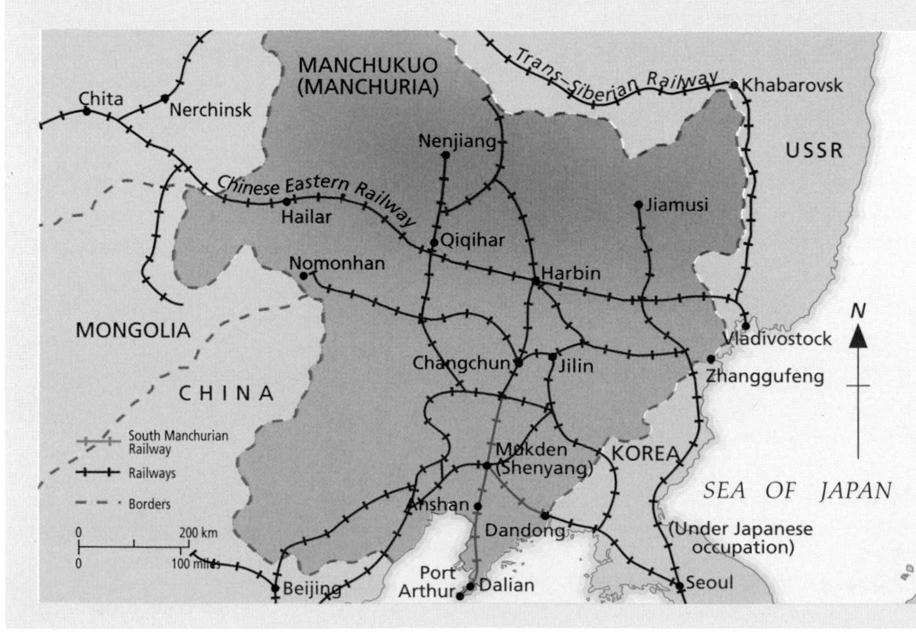

Japan at war

For the US, Britain and Australia conflict with Japan in the Second World War began in 1941 after the raid on Pearl Harbor. It is this conflict that the term 'Pacific War' refers to. But this is to distort the picture, for Japan had by then already been effectively at war for four years, not with any Western power but with China. This conflict began in 1937, two years before the outbreak of war in Europe, and is still known in Japan as the 'China Incident'.

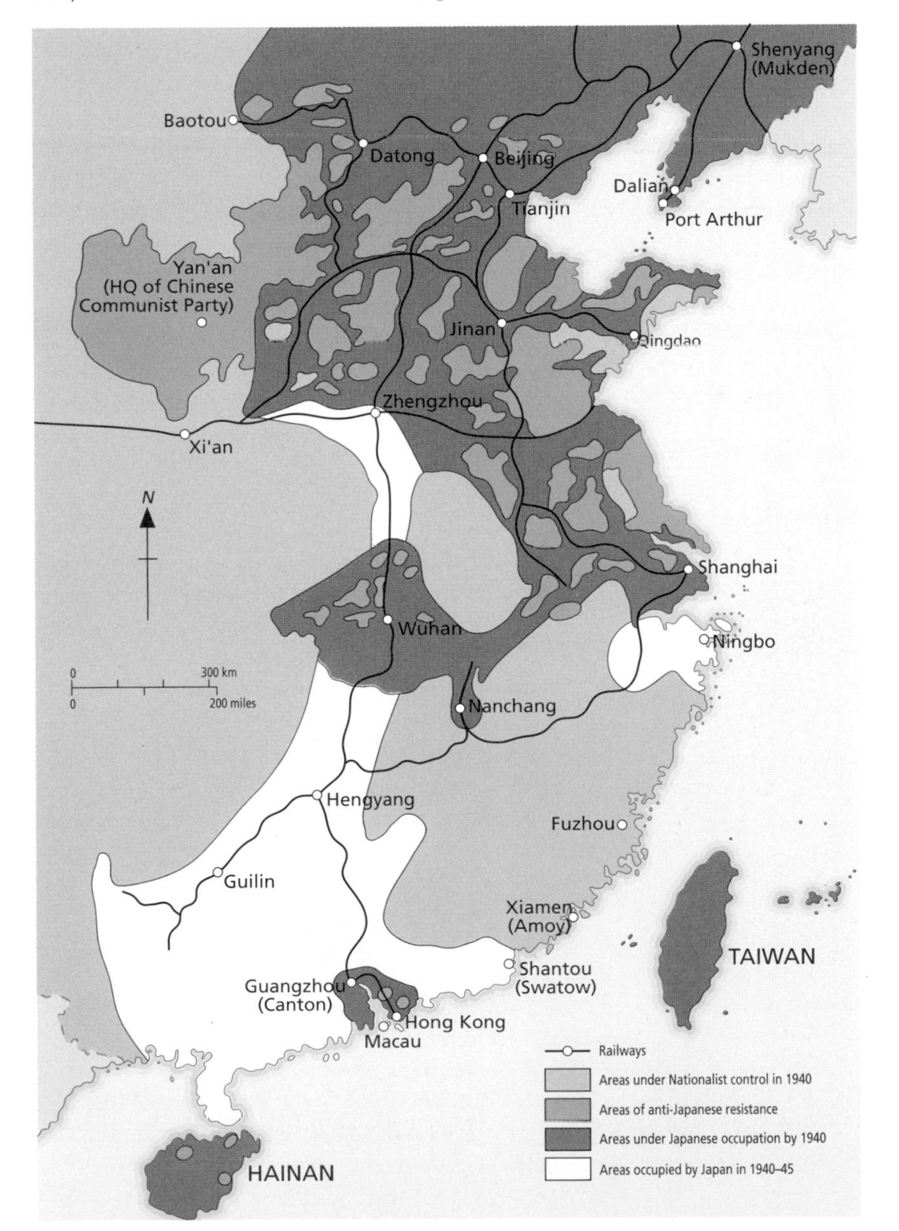

The war with China (1937–40). In 1937 Japanese troops made extensive inroads into the northern part of China and after 1941 gradually spread inland from Hong Kong. But resistance was strong and China was never fully occupied.

The outbreak of war in China

During the night of 7 July 1937 small groups of Japanese and Chinese troops exchanged fire near the Marco Polo Bridge south of Beijing. The origins of this skirmish remain unclear but it developed into a vast undeclared conflict. Local commanders arranged a truce, but powerful interests on both sides favoured warfare. The Japanese government sent three additional divisions and embarked upon full-scale hostilities. At the same time millions of patriotic Chinese attacked their government's earlier 'appeasement' policy and called for a united front against the foreign invader. In the face of these antagonisms it became impossible to negotiate a compromise.

On 9 August a Japanese naval officer was killed by Chinese troops at Shanghai, and Chinese aircraft attacked Japanese warships anchored offshore. These incidents precipitated further battles and new areas of Japanese military occupation. As the war spread many Japanese believed that only the conquest of the Chinese Nationalist capital, Nanjing, would compel Chiang Kai-shek, the leader of the Nationalists, to surrender. Yet the eventual capture of that city and the massacre of many of its citizens brought surrender no nearer. The citizens of Tōkyō celebrated the victory with lantern processions but Chinese forces simply withdrew into the interior and continued their stubborn resistance.

The home front

The campaign in China not only brought increasing casualties but also led to tighter controls on Japanese society. By late August the government had initiated a spiritual mobilization campaign and for the first time in its history Japan embarked upon total war. This required new laws controlling imports and exports and the creation of new agencies to co-ordinate decision-making and official propaganda. In October the Cabinet Planning Office was established to develop plans for a war economy while two months later the Cabinet Information Bureau began shaping propaganda policies.

Even during the first months of the war the impact of the 'China Incident' upon everyday life was clearly evident. Local ex-servicemen's associations and women's groups organized celebratory farewells for departing troops. Patriotic women made 'thousand-stitch belts' which were supposed to ward off bullets, and the ashes of the war dead were formally received back in Japan. Emotive songs such as 'A mother of our military country' were sung over the radio while newsreels, broadcasts and newspapers combined to bring news of the war to a concerned and loyal public.

Despite the public celebration of war and sacrifice, the government also sought to use more oblique and peaceful strategies in dealing with China. In November German diplomats made overtures to China on behalf of the Japanese government, but before Chiang Kai-shek could even agree to negotiations the Japanese army had stiffened its terms and a ceasefire became impossible. More successful were Japanese attempts to undermine Chinese resistance by establishing 'autonomous' régimes in conquered regions of northern China. On 27 October an autonomous government of Mongolia was established, and six weeks later the 'Provisional Government of the Republic of China' was created in Beijing.

The Sorge spy ring

Dr Richard Sorge was one of the most successful agents of the entire Second World War, although it was only in 1964 that the Soviet government finally acknowledged that he had indeed been a Soviet spy and gave him a posthumous decoration. Sorge's reputation in the German community in Tōkyō, where he worked as a foreign correspondent, was that of a reliable Nazi and he enjoyed close relations with the German ambassador and other members of the diplomatic staff. Some of his information came from these sources, but his principal informant was Ozaki Hotsumi, who was in the circle of Prime Minister Konoe's supporters and who, for a time in 1938 and 1939, enjoyed direct access to state papers as a cabinet consultant and even after that remained in touch with several of Konoe's cabinet members. He was, therefore, exceptionally well placed to provide Sorge with high-class intelligence material. Other members of the ring were an artist called Miyagi, who undertook much of the work of translating material provided by Ozaki, and Vukelic, a Yugoslav journalist who prepared the microfilm copies of documents that were then sent to Shanghai by courier and on to Moscow. The intelligence passed on to Moscow included the cabinet decision in 1941 not to join Germany in attacking the USSR but to concentrate on a move to the south. No matter how impeccable his sources, however, the value of the intelligence he supplied was not fully appreciated by Stalin.

After eight years of uninterrupted activity the members of the ring were arrested on 18 October 1941. They were secretly brought to trial in 1943 and Ozaki and Sorge were sentenced to death: they were both hanged on 7 November 1944. PK

Although 1937 had been a year of victories, the government still feared political dissidents. In mid-December Yamakawa Hitoshi and other well-known non-communist leftists were arrested and charged with planning to set up a 'popular front'. The arrests made it clear that political liberty was in decline and that official intolerance was on the rise.

Preparation for total war

By early 1938 the optimism of Japan's first victories had passed and prime minister Konoe's cabinet developed new policies for the successful conduct of the war. On 16 January he declared that he would no longer deal with Chiang's Nationalist government and prepared further legislation to centralize economic control. These new measures ranged from macroeconomic regulations to the first rationing of consumer goods. The National Mobilization Law empowered the state to control all forms of labour and material, and the unlimited powers it granted provoked remarkably outspoken criticism. One such outburst from the social democrat Nishio Suehiro led to his expulsion from the Diet. However, schemes for centralized economic planning also angered major industrialists. These far from radical figures feared that a tight network of state controls might well undermine the foundations of the private enterprise system. But plans for new government controls extended far beyond industry and trade. The Home Ministry now acted to extend and control a nation-wide network of neighbourhood associations to intensify the nation's commitment to war. Virtually the entire population was enveloped by this so-called 'popular movement', making political and social dissent even more unlikely than before.

The left wing had not yet been cowed into submission and plays inspired by 'socialist realism' were still occasionally performed in Tōkyō, but ideological and artistic conformity was enforced with increasing severity. In February 1938 more left-wing intellectuals were arrested and eight months later works by the distinguished economist Kawai Eijirō were banned, including his critique of contemporary fascism. On the other hand, Hino Ashihei's trilogy of novels on the war in China were widely read and film documentaries on China were designed to draw attention at home to the China Front.

By the autumn Japanese armies had advanced more deeply into China. In October Guangzhou (Canton) was taken and soon afterwards Wuhan was captured too. But Japanese military action on the Asian continent was not confined to action against Chinese troops nor was it uniformly successful. In late July Japanese troops attacked Soviet forces at Zhanggufeng on the border between Manchuria and the USSR near Vladivostok and both sides suffered heavy casualties. If nothing else this brief battle demonstrated that any Japanese attack on Soviet territory would meet stubborn resistance.

Events in Europe at this time did nothing to discourage the government from holding the view that military strength was the key to diplomatic success. Germany had annexed Austria without provoking any serious response from Britain or France, while in September the Munich Agreement had allowed Germany to occupy the Sudetenland. Similarly, Japanese actions in China had provoked nothing more serious than criticism at the League of Nations.

Japanese victories and advances in China were now answered by waves of guerrilla resistance. In response Konoe sought a new formula which would combine Japanese hegemony with the suspension of hostilities. In a radio address he proposed a 'New Order in East Asia' based upon an 'equal partnership' between China and Japan. Some weeks later the foreign minister, Arita, adopted a more strident tone and called for a Japan–China–Manchuria bloc to preserve Eastern civilization from the communist menace and to defend it against the discriminatory tariffs of the West.

Events in 1939 added further prestige to German and Italian styles of government. Hitler took Prague and Mussolini occupied Albania. Not surprisingly, Japanese leaders attempted to develop similar techniques of economic and political control. In January the cabinet formulated a Production Expansion Plan. In March plans were shaped to conscript all males into military or labour service. A marked emulation of Nazi methods was the new Film Law, which

Unit 731

In November 1932 a bacteriologist in the Army Medical Corps, Ishii Shirō, founded a biological experimental station in the outskirts of Harbin in Japanese-occupied Manchuria. With active support from the Japanese Kwantung Army and collaboration both from the powerful research division of the South Manchurian Railway and from scientists drawn from the Manchurian medical colleges, the Ishii unit grew rapidly. By the beginning of 1936, it had a staff of 300, of whom 50 were doctors. In that year it trebled in size and became known as the Kwantung Army Epidemic Prevention and Purified Water Supply Unit. It was not until 1941 that it was given the name by which it is known today. Well before then it was concentrating its efforts on the development and production of biological weapons in response to the army's interest in such weapons as a means of dealing with the more numerous armed forces of China, the USSR and the US. With a budget of ¥10,000,000 Unit 731 took its pick of the brightest biochemists, pathologists and epidemiologists not only from Manchuria but from the entire Japanese empire.

The research scientists experimented with a vast range of diseases, including anthrax, botulism, cholera, plague, smallpox and typhus, with mustard gas and chemical toxins, and with flamethrowers and frostbite. The 'guinea pigs' they experimented upon included more than 3,000 Chinese, White Russian and other human victims at the unit's headquarters, and an unknown number of British, US and other prisoners of war, internees and convicts at camps and research laboratories elsewhere in the Japanese empire. It operated its own air squadron for bacteriological warfare research and development and maintained its own ordnance factories, biological production facilities, and a four-storey granary to feed 8,000,000 plague-infested rats in anticipation of an offensive against the USSR planned for September 1945. The unit conducted bacteriological warfare against the Soviet–Mongolian forces at Nomonhan in 1939 and subsequently during the various campaigns against China. An attempt to bring a bacteriological warfare assault team into action against the US at Saipan failed when the ship was sunk by a US submarine. An experimental series of incendiary balloons was launched at the US to investigate the possibility of a major biological attack on the US and Canada.

By the end of the war the activities of Unit 731 were known to the Chinese, Soviet, British, Canadian and US governments. The Red Army captured some members of the unit in Manchuria and obtained confessions from them before sentencing them to terms of imprisonment. Acting on instructions from the US government, General MacArthur offered all members of Unit 731 in occupied Japan immunity from prosecution in exchange for their co-operation and for the unique human and other data their experiments had yielded. RJP intensified censorship, limited the showing of foreign films and placed controls on the production and distribution of features, news and 'cultural' films.

Austerity was the keynote of new and often minute controls imposed on the lives of Japanese civilians. Students were forbidden to wear long hair, permanent waves were banned for women, and the first day of each month was declared 'Public Service for Asia Day'. On these days the sale of alcohol ceased, neon lights were extinguished and millions of citizens performed 'labour service'. A blend of austerity and the military ethos was also apparent in junior schools where jūdō and other martial arts became part of the national curriculum.

Towards world war

Events abroad brought dilemmas as well as inspiration for Japan's leaders. Hitler's non-aggression pact with the USSR created consternation among Japanese who regarded the USSR as Japan's ideological and obvious geopolitical enemy. The difficulties of Japan's relations with the USSR were further highlighted by a second military clash with Soviet forces in May when fighting broke out at Nomonhan on the frontier between Manchuria and the Soviet satellite state of Outer Mongolia. Large-scale land and air battles continued until September when the superiority of the Soviet forces brought the fighting to an end. By this time the complexities of relations with the USSR had driven the cabinet to hand in its resignation.

Despite two years of extensive campaigning Japan had still not eliminated Chinese military resistance. Even the deployment of heavy bombers against the new Nationalist capital Chongqing failed to bring surrender. Faced with this stalemate few Japanese were prepared to acknowledge that Chinese resistance stemmed from patriotic resolve and instead they attributed it to foreign weapons and encouragement. Predictably, therefore, Japanese troops and diplomats now took new steps to harrass China's supporters and 'collaborators'. In June Japanese forces blockaded the Anglo-French Concession at Tianjin and some months later France was pressed to prevent aid reaching Chongqing through her colonies in Indo-China. In September 1939 war broke out in western Europe leaving both Britain and France unable to respond firmly to Japanese pressures. Meanwhile, the US became increasingly alarmed at Japan's economic and military power and its apparent sympathy for Germany and Italy. US demands for Japanese withdrawals brought no significant reponse and Washington retaliated by refusing to sign a new Commercial Navigation Treaty with Japan.

At the onset of war in Europe Japan was uncertain of the outcome and was apprehensive of involvement in a new conflict. But German successes in the summer of 1940 brought attractive opportunities. France's surrender left Indo-China without significant defences, Hitler's occupation of the Netherlands left the Dutch East Indies without protection and Britain's struggle for survival left it unable to reinforce Hong Kong and its south-east Asian colonies.

Events in Europe gave further encouragement to Japanese military and political leaders who wished to transform the political system into a one-party state. In July the rise of these demands led to the resignation of the cabinet and its replacement by a new administration headed once again by Konoe. During the late summer the new cabinet led formal discussions on the creation of a new political order. These talks involved political, military, bureaucratic and business leaders and generated much argument and mutual antagonism. While participants agreed on the need for political reconstruction, few could agree upon its details and ultimate purpose. Businessmen feared a loss of economic power to the army. The Home Ministry feared losing influence to a new political movement and the army favoured the creation of a 'national defence state' which it would dominate. Furthermore, there were serious obstacles in the way of forming a German-style dictatorship on account of the prestige of the imperial institution and the lack of a tradition of charismatic political leadership which might have produced a suitable 'Führer' for a new régime. Nevertheless, a loose national organization, the Imperial Rule Assistance Association, was established and in September 1940 Japan allied itself with Germany and Italy in the Tripartite Pact.

Rising tensions in 1941

In the spring of 1941 the foreign minister, Matsuoka Yōsuke, travelled to Berlin and Moscow in the hope of improving relations with the USSR to enable Japan to concentrate its attention on Asia. In Berlin he found growing hostility towards the USSR, but he was not informed of the imminent launch of Operation Barbarossa against the USSR and so in Moscow he happily concluded the Neutrality Pact, by which each party undertook not to get involved if the other became involved in conflict. On 25 June the invasion of Russia began and Matsuoka argued for solidarity with Germany and an immediate attack on the USSR in spite of the Neutrality Pact. This proposal was, however, overruled for it would have meant abandoning the proposed push southwards to gain control of the oil wells in the Dutch East Indies. Negotiations to acquire access to these oil fields without recourse to arms were not going well and in the army opinion was growing that there would have to be a military solution to the problem.

Meanwhile the Japanese ambassador to the US was trying to resolve the differences between Japan and the US. The US Secretary of State, Cordell Hull, was pressing Japan to observe the principles of territorial integrity and to renounce interference in the internal affairs of other nations. The principal sticking points were the demands that Japan withdraw from China and abrogate the Tripartite Pact; the Japanese government refused to consider these demands and insisted that normal commercial relations with the US be restored. Matsuoka favoured breaking off the negotiations, but Konoe and the new foreign minister he appointed to replace Matsuoka were determined to continue seeking a settlement.

At the end of July Japan moved troops into southern Indo-China. In response to this the US, Britain and the Netherlands froze all Japanese assets and placed an embargo on exports to Japan; the most important consequence of this was that Japan was cut off from its sources of oil, 80% of which had come from the US in 1940. Konoe, faced with growing pressure for war from the army and now the navy too, still hoped for a resolution of matters with the US and he proposed to Roosevelt that they hold a summit conference. Roosevelt, however, insisted that there would have to be some Japanese concessions on China before he would agree to a summit, and as a result Konoe resigned to be replaced by his minister of war, General Tōjō Hideki. Tōjō undertook to continue negotiations with the US while at the same time preparing for war and on 5 November Admiral Yamamoto Isoroku was ordered to plan a surprise attack on Pearl Harbor in Hawaii. The negotiations made no progress on the question of China and on 26 November a naval task force set sail in conditions of utmost secrecy for Hawaii.

The attack on Pearl Harbor caught the US Navy entirely unawares. Sailors leap into the water to escape the flames on one of the stricken ships.

The start of the Pacific War

On 7 December 1941 Japanese carrier-borne aircraft inflicted great damage on the US Pacific Fleet at anchor in Pearl Harbor. Almost simultaneously amphibious operations were launched against the Philippines, Hong Kong, Guam and Malaya, and on 10 December British naval power in the Far East was destroyed when the battleship *Prince of Wales* and the battlecruiser *Repulse* were sunk by Japanese aircraft. This new conflict was named the 'Great East Asia War', and Japanese propaganda emphasized the theme of colonial liberation and the creation of a new Asian order, led by Japan and freed from Western economic and cultural domination.

Initially Japanese forces swept all before them. Within three months Manila, Singapore, Hong Kong and Rangoon were taken and Dutch power was eliminated. Overall these victories reflected the effective training and high morale of the troops, but in Burma and Malaya local nationalists provided Japanese units with information and support. In Indonesia the Japanese forces were greeted by much of the population as emancipators and in many colonial territories they freed political prisoners. However, in the aftermath of conquest the liberators often behaved cruelly towards their new subjects, and the Chinese in South-East Asia who sympathized with Chiang Kai-shek's patriotic struggle against the invasion of China were often the victims of persecution: in Singapore some 5,000 Chinese were executed during the first three months of Japanese administration.

At home the government sought to use the euphoria of victory to tighten and consolidate its machinery of control. In the spring of 1942 it began preparations for a general election which was designed to produce a more compliant Diet and a public committed to war. To secure electoral success the government recommended and supported amenable candidates and encouraged voting as a patriotic act. As a result the April election produced a Diet of 381 'recommended' members, but the electorate's less than complete enthusiasm for the Tōjō cabinet was clear from the success of 85 'unrecommended' candidates.

The intensification of government control over its citizens was achieved by the creation of a series of officially controlled organizations. The Great Japan Imperial Rule Assistance Young Men's Corps was established to give new impetus to economic and political programmes, while the founding of the Imperial Rule Political Association and the Great Japan Women's Association further extended the scope of government power. In addition, existing patriotic, industrial, agricultural, commercial, women's and youth organizations were brought under the overall control of the Imperial Rule Assistance Association. Soon all community councils and neighbourhood associations were integrated into this nationwide body. Nowhere was government control more apparent than in publishing, where measures to control the supply of newsprint and to ensure political conformity culminated in the amalgamation of different sections of the press and the restriction of each prefecture to a single newspaper.

Despite the absence of significant domestic resistance or opposition, the government soon faced serious challenges to its military prowess. On 18 April 1942, 16 US carrier-borne B-25 bombers launched token raids on Tōkyō, Nagoya and Ōsaka. These inflicted little damage but their penetration of Japanese defences impelled the leadership to seek further conquests to give added protection to the homeland. As part of this strategy Japanese forces conquered the western Aleutian Islands, occupied new territory in China and in June launched a naval attack on the US island of Midway in the Pacific.

Midway and the troubles of 1943

The Battle of Midway on 6 June 1942 was a crucial turning point in the war for it was Japan's first and most significant military catastrophe. Like the attack on Pearl Harbor, Midway was planned as a surprise operation but US success in breaking Japanese naval codes enabled its naval commanders to anticipate much of Japan's strategy. Despite this US advantage Midway was a costly campaign for both sides, but Japan was defeated and its loss of four aircraft carriers transformed the balance of naval power in the Pacific. In the summer and autumn of 1942 Japan suffered further reverses. An overland attack on Port Moresby in New Guinea was repulsed and after months of costly land and sea battles it was decided to abandon Guadalcanal in the Solomon Islands.

The first months of 1943 were to see dramatic military reverses. At Buna in New Guinea and Attu in the Aleutians Japanese garrisons were annihilated and Japan's most distinguished admiral, Yamamoto Isoroku, was shot down over the Solomons. By

Right *John Sharpe of Leicester, photographed in 1945 after liberation from Changi Jail on Singapore. As punishment for having tried to escape from the notorious Burma Railway, he spent 3 years in a torture jail in Singapore before being transferred to the hospital at Changi.*

mid-1943 US submarines were inflicting heavy losses on Japanese merchant shipping. As a result shipyards were unable to maintain the overall strength of the merchant fleet. Losses of cargo ships interrupted the flow of food and raw materials from South-East Asia and drove General Tōjō's government to reappraise the effectiveness of Japan's war industries. Official analyses revealed that production was poorly co-ordinated, and priorities were still those of the China conflict. Weapons for a land war, not for the amphibious campaigns of the south seas, still dominated production. To resolve these difficulties the government created a Munitions Ministry to plan output, and gave a new emphasis to the construction of aircraft, tankers and cargo ships. This new sense of crisis also inspired social measures which were unprecedented: on 30 July 1943 female students were mobilized for labour service and two months later all unmarried women under 25 were mobilized for agricultural or industrial work. It was forbidden to recruit men to 17 occupations declared to be 'non-essential', and students from the élite universities were conscripted into the army and navy.

As government fears and insecurity grew, attacks on cultural and political dissidents became more and more frequent. In January jazz was banned along with approximately 1,000 British and US melodies, and in March 1943 the serialization of Tanizaki Jun'ichirō's major novel *The Makioka sisters* was suspended by government order. Later, members of the editorial staff of the distinguished monthly *Chūō kōron* were arrested on charges of left-wing activity. Even Nakano Seigo, a leader of the radical right wing, was seized and interrogated after criticizing Tōjō's authoritarian rule.

Japan's military response to growing external danger was to define a new 'Vital Defence Zone' embracing Burma, Thailand, Malaya, Indo-China, Indonesia, the Philippines, and the Caroline and Mariana Islands. However, the protection of this vast empire required the political, military and economic co-operation of south-east Asians, as well as the efforts of Japan's own forces. To inspire co-operation Japan now embarked upon a series of imaginative if hollow political gestures. On 1 August 1943 Burma was granted nominal independence and on 14 October the Philippines were recognized as an independent republic. Both régimes signed military alliances with Tōkyō, and nine days later Japan

Left *Kamikaze pilots ready to depart, one carrying a treasured doll. The first kamikaze attack took place on 25 October 1944 and proved such a success that the suicide attack programme was expanded to include manned torpedoes and other devices. Some of the young pilots received as little as 7 weeks flight training.*

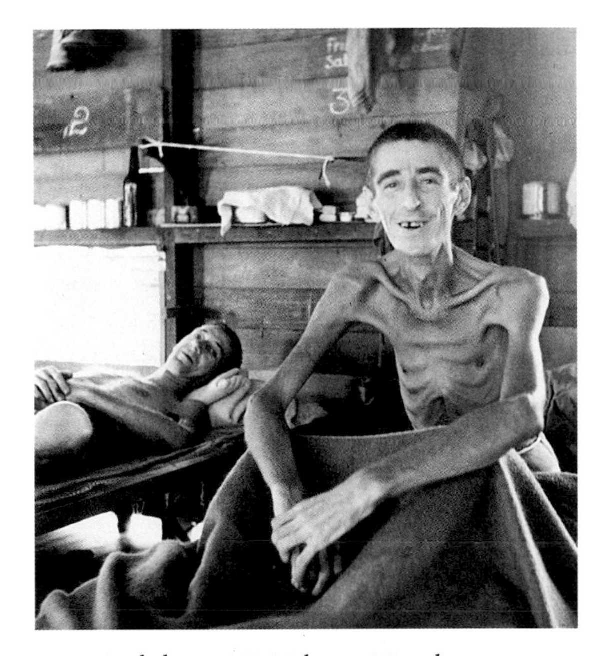

recognized the anti-British provisional government of India. As part of this new policy Japan sought to counter allied propaganda statements, such as the Atlantic Charter, with a statement of pan-Asian ideals. On 5 November a representative of Thailand and the puppet rulers of China, Burma, Manchuria, the Philippines and 'Free India' met government leaders in Tōkyō for the Great East Asia Conference. The next day they signed the Great East Asia Declaration, which attacked Western colonialism and proclaimed a new Asian order of racial equality and economic co-operation. However, it also reflected a new balance of power among Japan's leaders. Its final clause advocated world-wide trade and co-operation: this was the vision of pragmatic diplomats, such as Shigemitsu Mamoru, who had gained influence at the expense of advocates of an exclusive East Asian bloc.

Throughout 1943 defeats, retreats and news of the bombing of Germany forced the government to recognize the possibility of air attacks against Japanese cities and the Cabinet began to make preparations. Plans were drawn up for the evacuation of school children to the countryside, for the dispersal of government offices and the destruction of thousands of houses to create fire-breaks, while the administrators of Ueno Zoo in Tōkyō destroyed all the dangerous animals, fearing that bombs might free them from their cages.

THE ECONOMIC CRISIS AND THE BEGINNING OF THE END

During 1944 Japan suffered a series of calamitous defeats at the northern and southern extremities of its conquests. In March the army launched a major offensive against Imphal on the Indo-Burmese border, but after months of combat allied forces were victorious. This single campaign cost Japan 30,000 dead and 45,000 wounded. On 15 June US forces landed on Saipan in the Marianas. The battle for this small archipelago was crucial, for possession of its airfields would enable US bombers to strike at Tōkyō. The battle for Saipan lasted three weeks, cost 40,000 Japanese lives and demonstrated that the fiercest Japanese resistance was no match for US firepower.

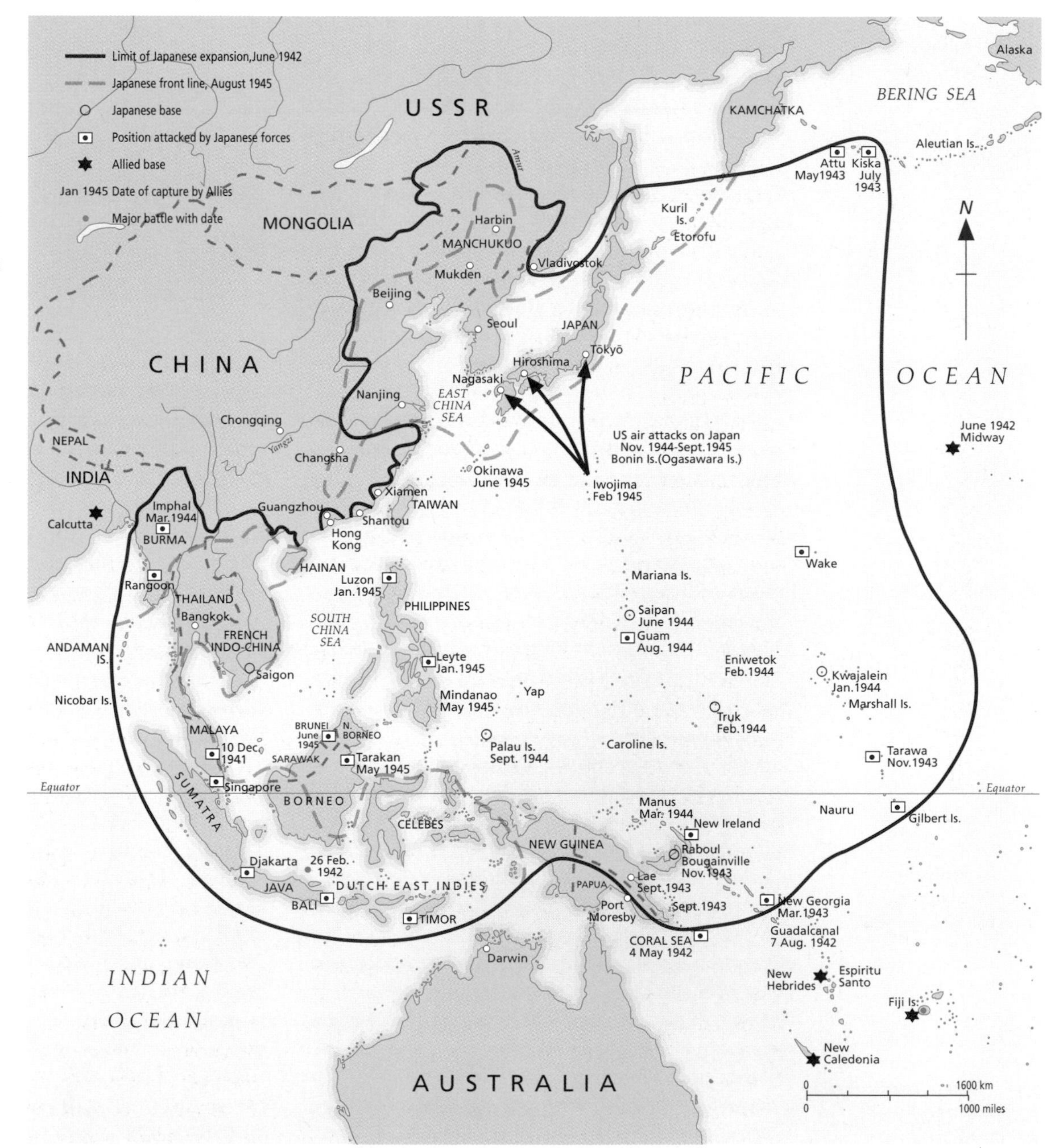

From expansion to defeat. The limits of Japanese expansion during the war stretched from the India–Burma border in the west to New Guinea in the south and the Aleutians in the north-east. Darwin in Australia suffered a number of raids, but the attempt to take the island of Midway in the Pacific in June 1942 resulted in the disastrous loss of four aircraft carriers and marked the turning point in Japan's fortunes.

Although this defeat meant the beginning of the physical destruction of Japan, its forces were still capable of gaining victories against the weaker allies of the US. In April the 'No. 1' operation was launched in China to capture territory and destroy US bomber bases. During six months eight Chinese provinces were conquered and the US base at Guilin was captured. These victories were a grievous blow to China's international prestige but they could not prevent air attacks on mainland Japan. On 25 October 100 B-29s attacked Kyūshū from the remaining US bases in China and a week later bombers from the Marianas raided Tōkyō.

The desperate military situation now had a major effect on domestic politics. Criticism of Tōjō spread among the leadership, while members of the Naval General Staff and the Cabinet Planning Staff became convinced that there could no longer be any hope of victory. Eventually, Tōjō was driven from office and on 22 July replaced by General Koiso. Koiso, however, betrayed expectations by failing to challenge the continuation of the war.

Despite acute shortages of food and raw materials, industry achieved surprising successes during 1944. Output of new ships reached an all-time record of 1.69 million tons and aircraft production reached 28,180, whereas the total in 1941 had been 5,088. Nevertheless, these levels of output could not be maintained. Workers were ill-fed and overworked, stockpiles were exhausted, and the re-cycling of scarce components had reached its limit.

Economic shortages were also apparent throughout the 'Great East Asia Co-Prosperity Sphere'. Food was requisitioned by Japanese armies, civilians were undernourished and large numbers of forced labourers were compelled to build roads, railways and fortifications. Indonesians were conscripted to work on the Asian mainland and Koreans and Chinese were transported to Japan. There they supplemented the inadequate numbers of dockers, coal and ore miners. These worsening conditions and cases of Japanese cruelty brought deep disillusionment even in territories which had originally welcomed the liberators. In 1944 and 1945 anti-Japanese resistance, often led by communists such as Ho Chi Minh, spread across Malaya, the Philippines and Indo-China.

The government now faced the immediate threat of bombing and the prospect of a future Allied invasion. Responses to the crisis were rapid but often inadequate. In July 1944 the Ministry of Education ordered the evacuation of junior school pupils from major cities and over 400,000 accompanied their teachers to live in rural inns, temples and schools. Evacuation succeeded in protecting vulnerable children from the hazards of air raids, but shelters, fire-fighting equipment and anti-aircraft batteries were inadequate to combat the large-scale attacks on the cities. Preparations to repel invasion, though ambitious, were often desperate and unreal. Tens of thousands of youths and old men were trained with inadequate weapons, and bamboo spears were distributed among women and girls. Professional commanders of distant battlefronts also resorted to increasingly wasteful and inhuman tactics. In Burma suicidal charges were commonplace and in the Philippines kamikaze raids were launched by pilots trained to crash their aircraft onto US warships.

In February 1945 some members of Japan's élite were also calling for new policies. Among proponents of peace was Konoe, who warned the emperor of the inevitability of defeat and the danger of ill-fed and disillusioned people launching a communist revolution. However, most military leaders still saw no alternative to further resistance.

In the same month US bombers launched their first incendiary raid on residential areas and its success persuaded General Le May to launch an unprecedented fire raid on the densely populated areas of northern Tōkyō. On 10 March US incendiaries killed approximately 85,000 people, and this dramatic result led to similar raids on Ōsaka, Nagoya and Kōbe. In the aftermath of these urban disasters over 8,000,000 people fled to the countryside seeking food and shelter. In this crisis the government resorted to desperate measures to protect children and augment the size of its labour and defence forces. On 18 March all school teaching, apart from the most elementary, was abandoned, for at least an entire year.

In April US forces landed on Okinawa to begin what was to be a long bloody campaign, and this led to the formation of a new cabinet. Kido, the Lord Privy Seal, believed that the new prime minister, Admiral Suzuki, would oppose the military and bring the war to an end. Initially the government hoped to gain the help of the USSR, which was still observing the Neutrality Pact signed in 1941, in negotiations with Britain and the US, but, with Germany now defeated,

No.	Town	Number of dead	Damaged or destroyed buildings	No.	Town	Number of dead	Damaged or destroyed buildings
1.	Tōkyō	95,996	755,735	16.	Hiroshima	118,661	67,860
2.	Yokohama	4,616	100,091	17.	Kure	1,939	23,589
3.	Kawasaki	768	38,514	18.	Matsuyama	251	14,300
4.	Shimizu	337	7,659	19.	Kōchi	434	12,237
5.	Numazu	318	27,444	20.	Uwajima	278	7,252
6.	Shizuoka	1,873	26,722	21.	Ube	254	6,233
7.	Shimoda	76	38	22.	Shimonoseki	324	10,168
8.	Hamamatsu	3,549	34,000	23.	Kita-Kyūshū	2,251	33,832
9.	Toyohashi	655	16,886	24.	Fukuoka	1,009	15,730
10.	Nagoya	8,625	141,951	25.	Ōita	116	2,486
11.	Ise	102	4,518	26.	Nagasaki	74,231	37,339
12.	Kōbe	8,841	154,564	27.	Nobeoka	292	3,765
13.	Ōsaka	12,620	343,613	28.	Miyazaki	132	2,397
14.	Wakayama	1,212	27,853	29.	Kagoshima	3,329	21,961
15.	Tokushima	1,451	16,300				

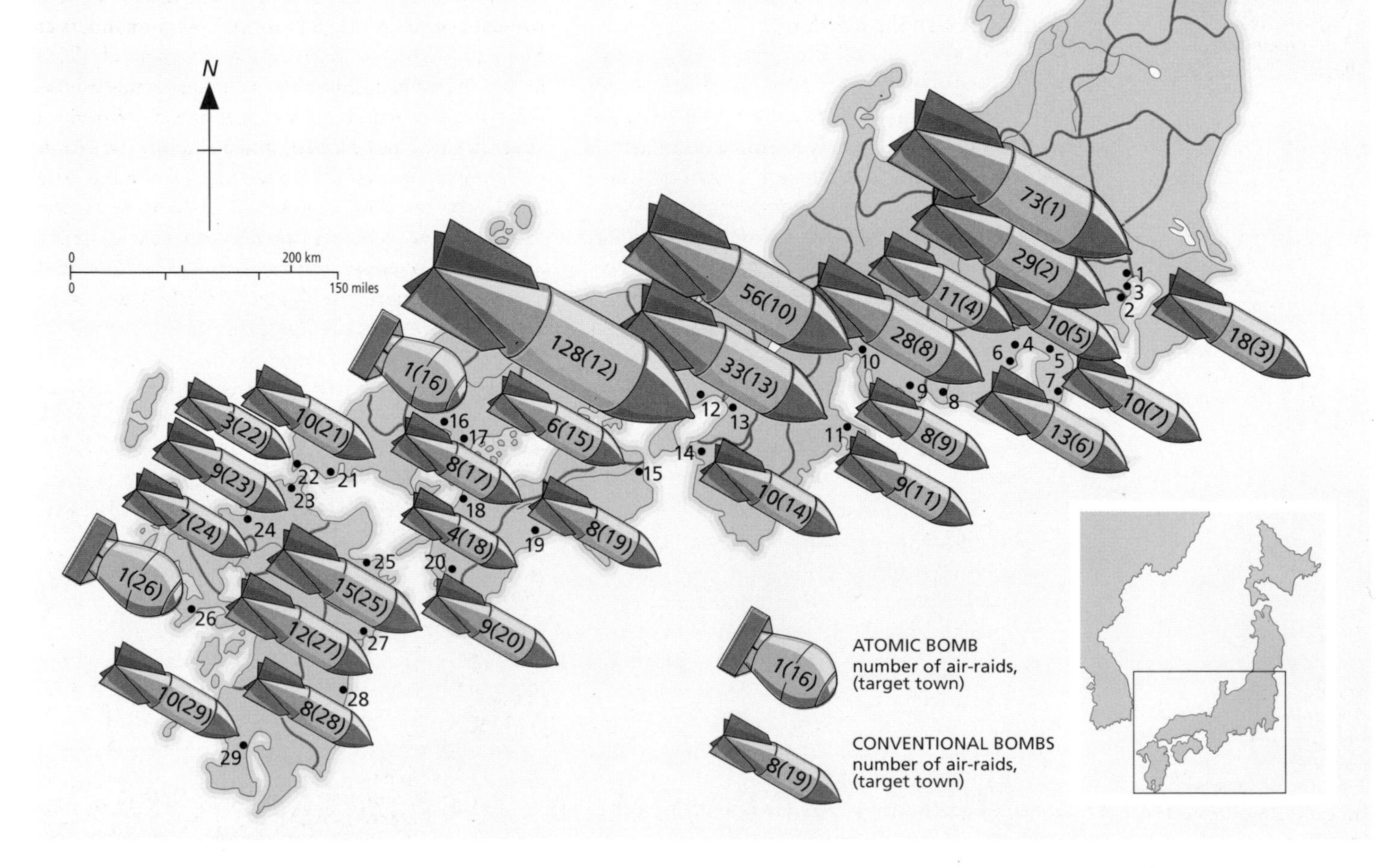

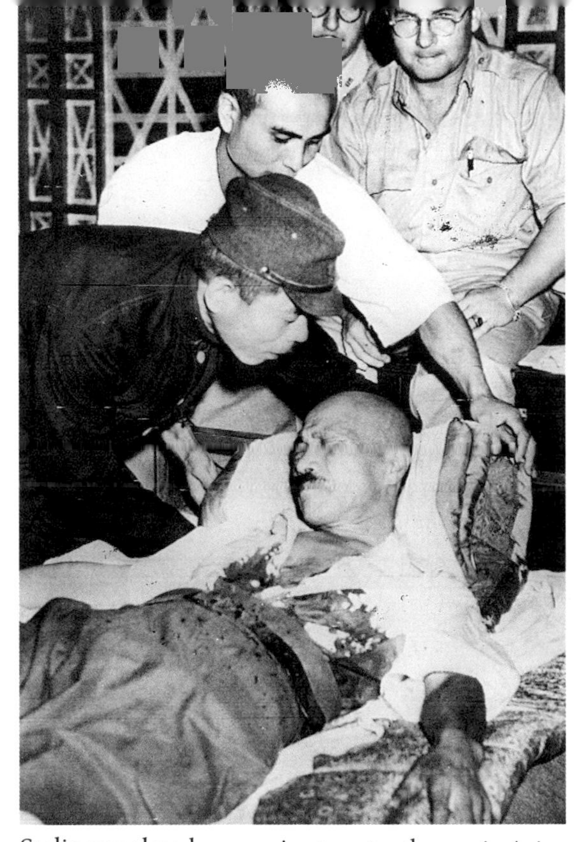

Right *Moments after a squad came to arrest him as a suspected war criminal, former Prime Minister Tōjō shot himself, but he failed to inflict a fatal wound, and he was restored to health to stand trial and later to be hanged.*

Left *The bombing of Japan. Much of the bombing was concentrated on the area to the south of Tōkyō, partly because US planes were operating from bases to the south and west. Tōkyō itself was devastated in March 1945 as a result of massive firebombing raids. Alone of the large cities, Kyōto, the old capital and the repository of many cultural treasures, escaped bomb damage, allegedly because of the representations of US politicians who had visited the city.*

Stalin was already preparing to enter the war in Asia. Not knowing this, Japan proposed that Konoe should begin talks in Moscow but Stalin rejected this suggestion out of hand.

On 26 July Britain, US and China issued the Potsdam Declaration which warned that Japan faced 'prompt and utter destruction' unless it agreed to an unconditional surrender. Although Prime Minister Suzuki favoured surrender, the Army Minister and the two Chiefs of Staff argued for continued resistance and better terms. As a result Suzuki could only make an ambiguous reply to Allied demands.

In early August three devastating blows completed the defeat of Japan. On the 6th a single B-29 destroyed Hiroshima with an atomic bomb. Two days later the USSR declared war and invaded Manchuria and the Kurile Islands; and on the 9th Nagasaki was devastated in a second nuclear attack. Now Suzuki saw acceptance of the Allied terms as the only escape from total destruction and on 14 August, at an Imperial Conference, the emperor made a decisive intervention opting for surrender. Thus the emperor's first significant contribution to policy-making during his reign brought the war to an end. The next day Emperor Hirohito made his first-ever broadcast announcing the end of the war and exhorting the whole population to avoid any act which might threaten the social order.

In spite of defeat, most members of the government still sought to preserve as much as possible of the existing political order. The Home Ministry still instructed its police to observe potential dissidents and arrest them where necessary. But of more importance were the new policies which followed the end of hostilities. Broadcasts urged people to prepare for peace, the ideal of reconstruction was promoted and over a million servicemen were demobilized and disarmed. Above all, Japanese were exhorted to avoid any acts of resistance to the Allied forces. In late August a Japanese delegation met US commanders at Manila to make arrangements for the arrival of US forces. Prince Higashikuni now became prime minister. No one was more likely to ensure the obedience of servicemen and civilians and a smooth transition to Allied occupation than a member of the imperial family. When the Supreme Commander for the Allied Powers, General Douglas McArthur, landed at Atsugi on 28 August, Japan was at peace. The formal surrender ceremony took place on 2 September on board USS *Missouri* in Tōkyō Bay.

GD

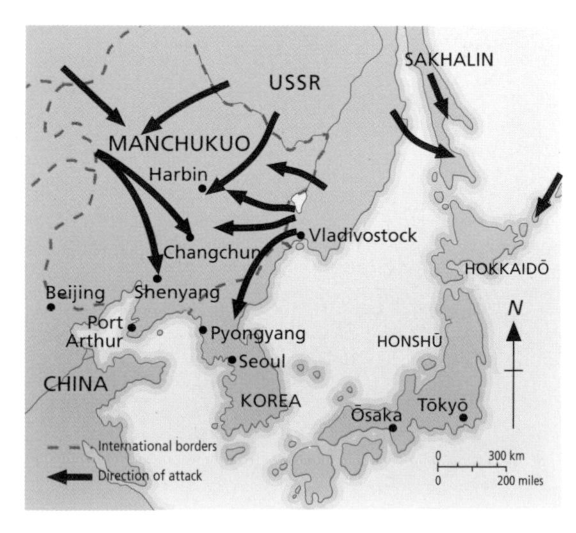

Right *The USSR attacks: August 1945.*

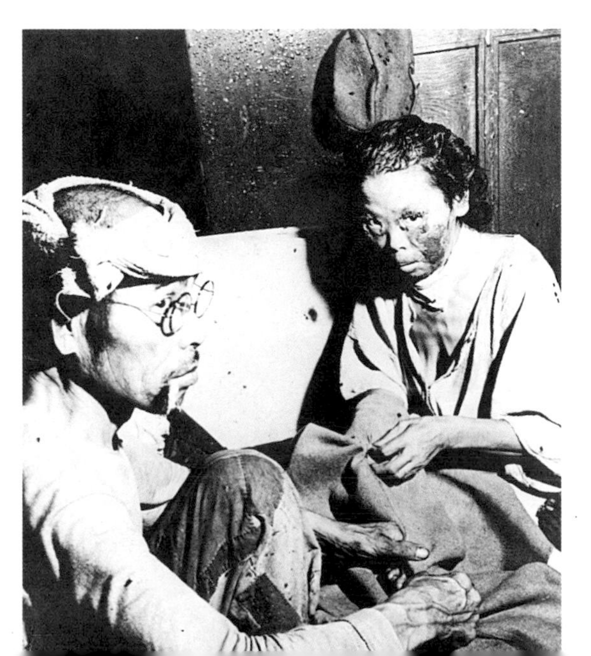

Far right *Burned survivors of the atomic blast at Hiroshima waiting for treatment in the ruins of a bank, which had been turned into a casualty clearing station.*

Post-war Japan

The Allied Occupation of Japan commenced on 28 August 1945, 13 days after the emperor had broadcast news of the surrender to the Japanese people. The first contingent of US troops landing at Atsugi, some 50 kilometres southwest of Tōkyō, found a people exhausted by war, uncertain of what the future held, and fearful of antagonizing their military rulers. Their prime aim was to secure for themselves and their families the basic necessities of life – food, clothing, shelter – against a background of economic devastation, rampant inflation and black markets. The Occupation authorities were less concerned with these humanitarian needs than with their own priorities, which were not merely to maintain order within the country, but also to transform Japan's political and economic institutions. They well understood that political, social and economic structures had played a rôle in promoting Japanese aggression in Asia and their objective was, therefore, to undertake a programme of 'demilitarization and democratization' which would prevent Japan ever again becoming a threat to peace in the world.

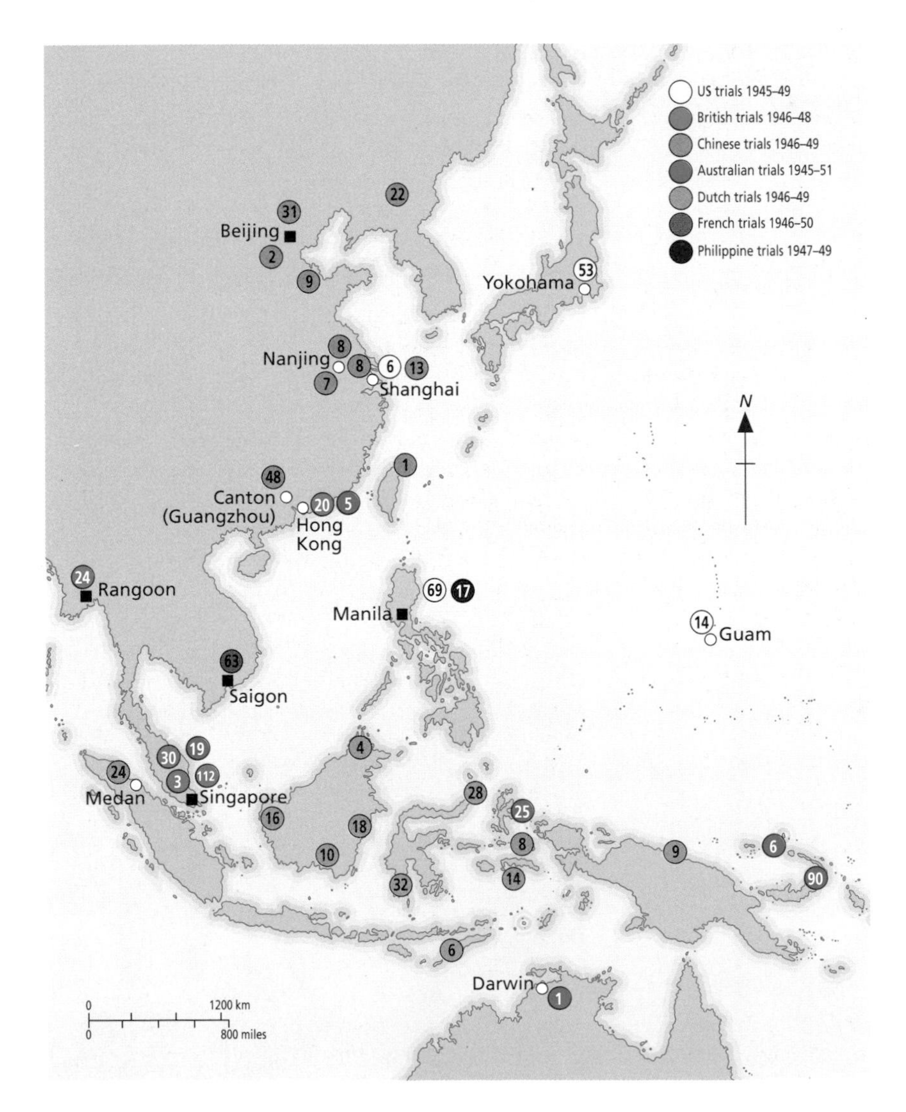

Trials of B and C class war criminals and numbers of death sentences. The Tōkyō Trials of 1946–48, which were the equivalent of the Nuremberg Trials, dealt only with a handful of the A class war criminals, such as Tōjō. Numerous other trials were held of B and C class war criminals. By 1951 more than 4,000 had been convicted.

The Occupation

Despite the presence of contingents from Britain, Australia and New Zealand, and the representation of all countries who had been at war with Japan on bodies such as the Far Eastern Commission, the Occupation was largely a US enterprise. The Occupation authorities in Japan were headed by the Supreme Commander for the Allied Powers (SCAP), General Douglas MacArthur, who received orders direct from the US president in Washington. SCAP and his headquarters (GHQ) became synonymous with US rule in Japan.

The Occupation authorities did not rule Japan directly as was done in Germany. Compelling practical reasons led them to operate through existing Japanese institutions such as the bureaucracy and the Diet, although these institutions were themselves the subject of reform.

Most areas of Japanese life were affected by the transformation led from the top by SCAP. War-crimes trials were held and thousands were purged from their posts. National political structures were transformed to produce a new constitution, the constitutional position of the emperor was altered, women were enfranchised and political parties of all shades of opinion were legalized. A new civil code removed the old *ie* (house/family) system, and promised equal rights to all, regardless of sex or origin. The separation of religion and state, a new education system, a revised judiciary and criminal code, and wholesale land reform, were accompanied by 'democratization' of the modern industrial sector through the dissolution of financial combines, anti-monopoly legislation and enhanced rights for organized labour.

War crimes trials in the Far East

On 19 January 1946 General Douglas MacArthur, Supreme Commander for the Allied Powers in Japan, promulgated the first charter for the International Military Tribunal for the Far East. On 26 April the charter was amended, so changing the Tribunals basic law and constitution only a week before the proceedings began. This was an inauspicious start to a trial which was far longer, larger and more convoluted than its counterpart at Nuremberg. The indictment was a self-conscious effort to mimic that of Nuremberg on an altogether grander scale, with the same charges of 'conspiracy', 'the preparation and waging of aggressive wars', and responsibility for 'conventional war crimes', 'crimes against peace', and 'crimes against humanity'. The Tōkyō Trial went further by seeking to establish that those who planned, prepared, initiated or waged wars of aggression were criminally responsible and guilty of mass murder. There have been no international efforts to reaffirm this doctrine in other proceedings since the Tōkyō Trial.

The International Prosecution Section, led by the American Chief Prosecutor, Joseph Keenan, contended that the defendants had been bound together by a 'common plan or conspiracy' from 1927 to the surrender of Japan in 1945. This supposed conspiracy took in virtually the whole of Japan's domestic and foreign affairs. The defence responded with a counter-interpretation of events which involved the entire history of Japan's constitutional, social, political and international history from the beginning of the 20th century. After the reading of the Indictment, the prosecution opened its case on 4 May 1946 and finished on 24 January 1947. After failing to have the charges dismissed, the defence opened its case on 3 February and continued until 12 January 1948. Further evidence was then presented by both sides, and the summations and closing arguments took until 16 April.

The court was composed of 11 members, representing Australia, Canada, China, France, Great Britain, India, the Netherlands, New Zealand, the Philippines, the USSR, and the US. Evidence relating to events in Manchuria, Mongolia, Thailand, Cambodia, Burma and Portuguese possessions in East Asia was heard by the Tribunal, but, for various political reasons, those countries were not associated with the proceedings.

There were 28 defendants, including four former prime ministers, four former foreign ministers, 12 generals, and two admirals; amongst the few civilians was Marquis Kido Kōichi, who had been Lord Keeper of the Privy Seal from 1940 and the emperor's closest political advisor. The youngest army officer named in the indictment was Colonel Hashimoto Kingorō, a firebrand and terrorist; only two naval officers were among the defendants. Emperor Hirohito was granted immunity from prosecution by General MacArthur acting in compliance with direct orders secretly issued to him by US President Truman.

Unlike the thugs and political upstarts tried at Nuremberg, the defendants at the Tōkyō Trial were by and large 'establishment' figures who had won the confidence and approbation of their fellow countrymen through their administrative competence, intellectual abilities or distinguished military service. This would have made the task of the prosecutors difficult but for the fact that the Japanese public, Western opinion and a majority of the court were happy to make the defendants sacrificial scapegoats for the sins and shortcomings of the whole nation. Each of them had at least one Japanese defence lawyer and a US associate but the strong collective defence they offered for the most part failed to convince the Tribunal.

The judgement took a week to read in November 1948. None of the defendants was found innocent. Seven were sentenced to death, 16 to life imprisonment, and the remainder to lesser terms of imprisonment. Dissenting opinions were submitted by the representatives of France and India, but the judgement and the sentences were confirmed by MacArthur on 24 November 1948. The executions were carried out shortly thereafter.

The Allied Powers also apprehended and prosecuted a number of so-called class B and C war criminals who were not involved in questions of high policy but were implicated in serious breaches of the customary and conventional laws of war. A UN War Crimes Commission based in London, and a Far East and Pacific Sub-Commission formed in Chongqing and later transferred to Nanqing were established by the Allies, excepting only the USSR, as international clearing houses for the exchange of information and those provided a mechanism for determining whether a prima facie case existed against each individual suspect. By the time the trials ended in 1951, there had been altogether 2,244 trials of 5,700 defendants, 4,405 of whom were convicted.

RJP

Towards alliance with the US

Several factors contributed to a waning of the reform impulse after the first two years of the Occupation. First, so great was the scale of the attempted transformation that the early pace could not be maintained. Second, the Japanese economy failed to recover, and threatened to be a continuing burden on the US taxpayer. Economic democratization seemed, if anything, to be undermining the country's ability to support itself, and government policy to stimulate economic activity only served to promote inflation. Trade was a fraction of its pre-war level, preventing the import of vital raw materials and energy supplies. Third, deteriorating US–Soviet relations and the Communist Party victory in China in 1949 dramatically altered US strategic considerations. Revised perceptions of Japan called for the country to be rebuilt, not as the Switzerland of East Asia, but as a US-allied capitalist bastion in the western Pacific. Finally, in Japan itself widespread labour and political unrest, in which the Communist and Socialist parties were closely involved, caused many in authority to think that change had gone too far. The result was a stilling of the momentum of reform, and even the reversal of some previous changes. Restrictions on union membership were reintroduced, and there was a purge of supposed communist supporters. A US banker, Joseph Dodge, was brought in to devise measures for stabilizing the Japanese economy, and the reconstruction of Japan as an economically strong ally of the US became the order of the day. This enthusiasm for Japanese economic revival was not shared wholeheartedly by the other allies.

This shift in policy emphasis, often known as the 'reverse course', seemed justified by subsequent events, notably the outbreak of the Korean War in June 1950. Japan was still under US control and ideally placed to act as a base for UN forces. In order to enable it to fulfil this strategic rôle, the US took steps to steer it back towards independence. The San Francisco Peace Treaty of September 1951, signed by all the Allied Powers except China and the USSR and its allies, was accompanied by a Mutual Security Treaty between Japan and the US, which permitted the US to continue stationing troops on Japanese soil and tied Japan firmly to the capitalist camp. Japan finally regained its independence on 28 April 1952.

Rehabilitation

Kishi Nobusuke was a member of Tōjō's wartime cabinet and was held as a suspected Class A war criminal: along with the other Class A prisoners, he was released on the day that Tōjō and the others in the first batch were executed, when a political decision was made not to proceed with the trials. The photograph on the left shows his younger brother, later to become prime minister as Satō Eisaku, lighting a cigarette for him just after his release. The photograph on the right shows him in 1960, now prime minister, with President Eisenhower and the US Secretary of State, John Foster Dulles, at the White House for the signing of the US-Japan Security Treaty.

The era of high-speed growth

The Korean War was also the start of Japan's real economic recovery. During and after the war, millions of dollars of 'special procurements' provided Japan with much-needed foreign currency and created a demand for a range of goods and services, from tyres and engines (Japan was still not permitted to manufacture military goods but components were possible) to recreation facilities for soldiers. In conjunction with the expanding world economy and US encouragement and assistance in such areas as technology imports and international economic relations, this economic boom made it possible for pre-war levels of production in most sectors to be achieved by the mid 1950s. New technologies, management techniques and industrial relations strategies were simultaneously helping to consolidate the steel and shipbuilding industries as world leaders. Domestic demand stimulated the growth of the next generation of products – consumer durables, cars, televisions – which in their turn achieved success in global markets. Later still, when Japanese industry

Students demonstrating in October 1967 on the way to the airport at Haneda in an attempt to stop the proposed visit of Prime Minister Satō Eisaku to Vietnam.

moved up-market into higher value-added goods, such as electronics and high technology products like computers, more basic manufacturing processes passed to the more competitive newly industrializing economies of Asia. In the late 1950s and 1960s the growth rate of the economy consistently reached double figures.

It is easy to view Japan's history since the Korean War almost exclusively as the story of a growing economy. Certainly, Japan enjoyed political stability at home and kept a low profile in international affairs. Only occasionally did the country attract international attention: the culmination of lengthy battles over foreign policy in the Anpo disturbances of 1960, when hostility to the renewal of the Mutual Security Treaty erupted in mass demonstrations and the resignation of the government; the Tōkyō Olympics of 1964; the prolonged student unrest of the late 1960s; and the suicide of novelist Mishima Yukio in 1970. Even the greater prominence of Japan on the international scene in recent years is largely the result of tension between Japan's economic might and her apparent reluctance to play a more prominent part on the world diplomatic stage.

The spectacular nature of Japan's economic expansion, however, should not be allowed to obscure the fact that growth was, if not caused, at least facilitated by the international and domestic political environment within which it occurred. In the aftermath of the Pacific War, economic recovery and growth were priorities for many Japanese. Moreover, in the rule of the conservative Liberal Democratic Party, continuously in power from its formation in 1955 onwards, the economy had a doughty patron, one closely allied to the interests of big business, and anxious to keep Japan anchored to US interests. The bureaucracy, relatively untouched by Occupation reform, remained important in strategic decision-making, thus to a degree perpetuating its old rôle as guardian of the national interest. Although there is some debate about the significance of the bureaucracy in guiding economic expansion, there is no doubt that it attempted to shape the course of economic development through formal and informal measures, including 'administrative guidance', an innocuous term which masked a powerful measure of control. Unlike the 'regulatory' states operating in some of its Western industrial counterparts, the Japanese state retained strongly 'developmental' characteristics, possessing a clear view of where it wanted things to progress, and how. More recently, Japan's increasing involvement in the international economy has constrained the Japanese state's ability to achieve its targets. Moreover, the increasing complexity of the economy has made the setting and attainment of priorities more difficult.

The oil shock

In the early 1970s a series of events appeared to foreshadow the end of the international political and economic framework which had sustained growth in the preceding two decades. Politically, the US failure to consult Japan over the question of rapprochement with the People's Republic of China (PRC) seemed to question the very standing of the US–Japan relationship. Economically, international pressure grew on Japan to liberalize her sheltered domestic market. Protectionist measures were introduced in the US against Japanese exports, while the yen was revalued and then allowed to float against the dollar. Given that Japan's manufacturing exports had grown in expanding and liberalized world markets on the back of an increasingly undervalued currency, these changes had serious implications. Then in 1973 came the oil shock. Japan had intentionally switched to massive use of cheap oil in the 1950s and 1960s, and imported over 90% of her energy needs, so the effect of the price-rise was particularly damaging. In addition, an increasing awareness of the social costs of rapid economic growth – congestion, industrial pollution, and environmental destruction – provoked many Japanese to question the priority given to such growth. In the months immediately after October 1973, inflation rocketed. Growth rates slowed, halted and in 1974 turned negative. A sense of disarray prevailed, as consumers engaged in panic-buying of basic commodities. In fact, gloom-laden predictions of the future proved ill-founded. Positive growth was resumed, and the economy showed a remarkable capacity to adjust to a steady 3–4% growth-rate from the late 1970s onwards. Energy efficiency increased dramatically. The emphasis of the economy shifted further towards less energy-intensive industries and higher value-added commodities, both of which helped to mitigate effects of the growing labour shortage. Though Japan was not unaffected by the world recession of the early 1980s, export growth had helped the economy to emerge from it by 1983.

The 1980s and 1990s

The early 1970s nevertheless promoted a shift in perceptions. People began to talk of the 'internationalization' of Japan, a term which was ambiguous in meaning but was used extensively in the 1980s. Certainly, as Japan became a more significant actor in the international economy, as more Japanese went abroad, as more visitors came to Japan, and as Japan became more affluent and cosmopolitan, it became increasingly difficult for the government to act without considering the international effects of its actions, or to remain relatively insulated from external influences, whether economic, political or cultural. A number of factors pushed Japan in the direction of becoming a more powerful actor in the international community: the dependence on external sources of energy supply, the danger of which was highlighted by the oil shock; the unavoidable need to consider the international implications of Japan's economic might; the rise of other Pacific economies; and resentment at Japan's surpluses and her 'free ride' on defence. The old low profile could no longer be maintained. Suspicions based on experience of Japanese aggression continued to colour relations with the countries of east and south-east Asia, but economic forces brought shared interests. The enthusiastic China-boom, which initially followed the resumption of relations with the PRC in the early 1970s, was soon succeeded by a more pragmatic and cautious note. This continued to mark Japanese policy towards China until after the Tienanmen incident, when Japan was the first major capitalist country to resume economic contacts. The need for labour and the increasing import of Asian manufactures have served to consolidate an Asian–Pacific economic area, and reinforce Japan's Asian identity.

At the same time close ties with the US have been a major component of Japan's post-war experience. Cultural influences remained powerful even after the Occupation ended. The security treaty has been repeatedly renewed, though its power to permit US intervention in domestic Japanese affairs has gone. However, many Japanese have campaigned against the treaty; anti-war, and in particular anti-nuclear, sentiment remains strong. Antagonisms over renewal of the treaty in 1960, the return of Okinawa to Japanese rule in May 1972, and Nixon's visit to

Left *Harajuku on a Sunday: the place to see Japanese punks in action.*

Beijing in February 1972, and more recent disputes over trade, defence expenditure and investment flows have meant that the relationship between the two countries has been far from smooth. Yet the US has remained Japan's pivotal partner. With the lessening of tension in north-east Asia, common strategic interests may have become less significant, but investment and trade flows, the strength of the yen and Japan's position as the world's leading financial market have kept Japan constantly high on the US agenda, and vice versa. Japanese attempts to develop economic and political interests within the countries of the European Community have not fundamentally shifted the balance.

In the early 1990s Japan is faced with a range of problems which cause concern for the future. Regional disparities within the country are acute; the population is ageing rapidly, and will decline if the current low birthrate continues; labour shortages are severe; consumption patterns are changing; a new generation has grown up, which has no recollection of anything other than prosperity. It is impossible to predict what these issues will mean for Japan as the country moves into the 21st century, but what is certain is that many of the factors considered significant in post-war development – recovery, hard work, ample labour, frugality – no longer have the same importance. Japan is at a critical point in its post-war development, and the early 1990s may well mark a new turning-point in its history. JEH

Emperor Akihito in traditional court robes at the ceremony to mark his accession.

Language and literature

Language

Previous page *Print from a series entitled* Writings of famous courtesans – in their own hand *by Kitao Masanobu (1761–1816). The implication is that the women have written the poems that flow above them. Masanobu was the sobriquet of the prose writer Santō Kyōden as artist.*

It might seem to the casual observer that Japanese is closely related to Chinese, but nothing could be further from the truth. Admittedly, Japanese 'looks' similar to Chinese and has absorbed a large number of Chinese words over the centuries, but these loanwords are merely a sign of cultural contact. Indeed, it would be difficult to think of two languages more dissimilar: Chinese being originally monosyllabic (now largely disyllabic), tonal, isolating, with a subject-verb-object (SVO) order; Japanese being polysyllabic, atonal, with quite complex word formation and a subject-object-verb (SOV) order. It was precisely this enormous gap between the two languages that caused so many problems when the Japanese tried to adapt the Chinese script to their own ends in the 8th and 9th centuries.

Affiliation

The whole question of where the language comes from is a highly charged subject in Japan, for the idea that Japanese is in some way unique is a potent and comfortable myth in times of self-doubt. A great many books and articles dealing with the origins and peculiarities of the language are produced for the general reading public and they sell extremely well. The roots of the language are indeed uncertain. Some scholars, perhaps the majority, argue that it is related to Korean and to the Altaic group of languages that is found throughout central Asia as far west as Turkey. Similarities in the way verbs are formed point to a common origin. Certainly, if one were to restrict oneself to syntax alone, Japanese and Korean are so similar as to appear obvious sister languages. The problem lies with the vocabulary, where it has proved extremely difficult to identify words with a common root that could not at the same time simply be loanwords from Korean into Japanese.

This relative scarcity of sets of words that are clearly connected with each other is something that plagues Altaic linguistics. Neither does it help that the sound systems of Japanese and Korean are quite distinct: Korean allows consonant clusters and makes distinctions between certain kinds of sounds that never seem to have existed in Japanese. And if it remains difficult to clarify this relationship, any hope of being able to reach further back is a forlorn one indeed. If Japanese and Korean in fact diverged from each other in the past, it may well have occurred as long as 5,000 years ago; this in itself makes the reconstruction of a possible language tree extremely difficult. It should be mentioned here, perhaps, that Ainu, which is restricted to the northern islands of Japan and which is now almost extinct, has no obvious relationship to Japanese and is usually treated as yet another isolate.

If the syntax still makes one look north or northwest to the Asian continent, certain aspects of the vocabulary and the sound system (in particular the fact that Japanese has open syllables and allows simple word reduplication for plurals) draw one south, either to the Austronesian group, or indeed as far afield as Dravidian in south India. Fairly good sound correspondences have in fact been identified here, particularly in the area of agricultural vocabulary. All that can be said at present, however, is that there is a growing consensus that Japanese may well be a hybrid, a complex mixture between Altaic in the grammar and syntax and perhaps Austronesian in the vocabulary. Whatever the truth, we know that even today the language is unusually hospitable to foreign loanwords, which can be absorbed into the structure of Japanese with surprising ease.

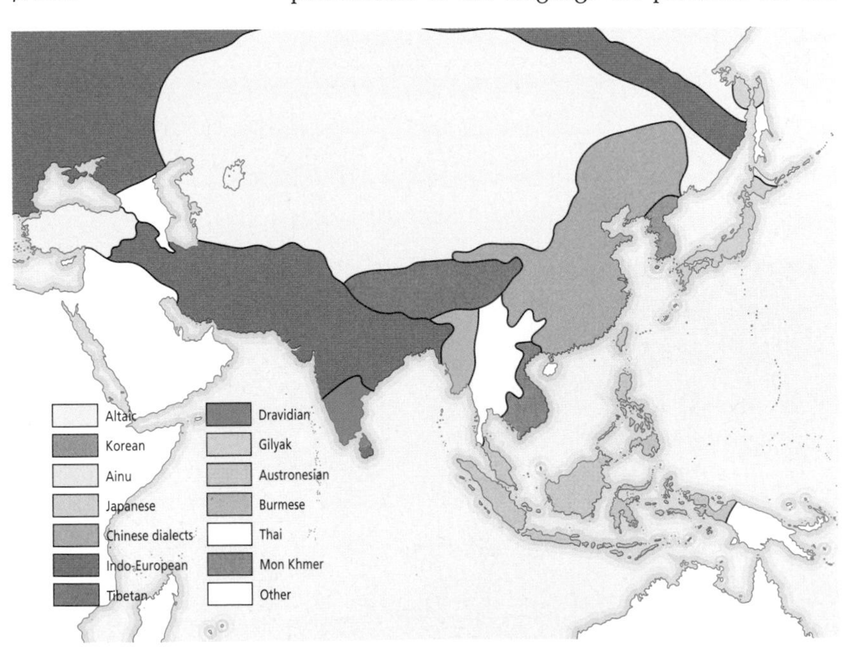

Japan's linguistic neighbours. Japanese has affinities with Korean and there is a possible link to the Altaic group. Chinese, the largest neighbour in terms of speakers, is quite unconnected, except that Japan borrowed the writing system in the 7th century. No other ties have been proved.

GRAMMAR

The rule that the Japanese verb must appear at the end of the sentence is strictly observed, except for occasional inversion for purposes of emphasis. A general and quite useful distinction can be made in the grammar between variable words, which change in one form or another, and invariable words, which never change their shape.

As one might expect, much of the grammar is concerned with the variable forms, especially the verbs. Verbs change by adding a series of suffixes for tense, aspect and mood, but they are not marked for either person or number. It is all the more surprising then that the subject of a Japanese sentence is omitted whenever possible. The reasons for this relative uninterest in marking person lie not so much with grammar as with a cultural preference for oblique reference. Context is usually enough to tell listeners what they need to know, and a major rôle is played by the highly developed system of respect language. It is perhaps this aspect of the language that causes the learner so many problems because, although the clues are always present, it sometimes demands a detailed knowledge of Japanese society and custom to interpret them correctly.

Japanese grammar

Variable	*Invariable*
True verbs, in the form root + stem + suffix(es)	Nouns, including interrogatives etc.
taberu – 'eat'	*kawa* – 'river'
tabemashita – 'ate' (polite)	*yama* – 'mountain'
tabenakatta – 'did not eat' (informal)	*nani* – 'what'
	tabemono – 'food'
Descriptive verbs, the equivalent of English adjectives	Particles, interjections, conjunctives
osoi – 'is late' (informal)	*wa* – topic marker
osokunakatta – 'was not late' (informal)	*ga* – subject marker
	shikashi – 'but'
The copula, which marks the 'is' of equivalence: a = b	Adverbs etc.
da – 'is' (informal)	*hotondo* – 'almost'
desu – 'is' (polite)	*metta ni* – 'hardly ever'
deshita – 'was' (polite)	*sukoshi* – 'a little'

RESPECT LANGUAGE

The respect language marks nouns where necessary, but the system is most highly developed in the verbs, every one of which is, or can be, marked either 'humble' or 'respectful' depending on the status of the subject of the sentence. In the commoner verbs, this can involve not just a special suffix but a completely different form altogether. Sentences are also marked either 'plain' or 'polite' with reference to the person one is addressing. Obviously, both systems interact when the subject of the sentence is in fact the addressee. No spoken Japanese sentence is without a marker that relates the speaker of the sentence to the addressee in some fashion or other. This constant presence of the so-called pragmatic aspect of language in both vocabulary and grammar is one of the distinguishing characteristics of the language.

Speech levels

Politeness operates on the level of speaker and addressee. 'What's this?' could be rendered in a number of different ways:

(a) *kore nani?* (in very informal conversation between two young male friends)
(b) *kore wa nan desu ka?* (in ordinary polite conversation)
(c) *kore wa nan de gozaimashō ne?* (middle-aged lady using ultra-polite forms)

Honorific language operates on the level of the sentence and either raises or debases the subject. Theoretically this is distinct from politeness, although they often overlap. 'Is he going to Tōkyō?' could be rendered:

(a) *Kare Tōkyō e iku no?* neutral + informal
(b) *Kare wa Tōkyō e ikimasu ka?* neutral + polite
(c) *Ano kata wa Tōkyō e irasshaimasu ka?* honorific (subject raising) + polite

This means that the word for 'going' will differ radically depending on its subject:

'Are you going too, sir?'	*Sensei mo irasshaimasu ka?* honorific (subject raising) + polite
'Yes, I'm going.'	*Hai, mairimasu.* honorific (subject debasing) + polite

What this means, of course, is that speakers of Japanese, whether native or foreign, must be constantly aware of social distinctions and appropriate ways of saying things. Not that this is not the case in other languages, but in Japanese a good deal of these concerns are overtly expressed in the choice of words and verb endings. To this extent Japanese is highly formalistic and ritualized, with such phrases as 'would you deign to' and 'could I not perhaps have the favour of your doing' being common and indeed *de rigueur* in the most ordinary of situations.

Vocabulary

The Japanese vocabulary is large, not only because of its antiquity but also because of its propensity for borrowing, first from Chinese, later from Portuguese and Dutch, and more recently from English. The majority of these loanwords have been nouns, mainly because Japanese nouns are invariable, remaining unchanged for case, gender and number; this makes their absorption a relatively simple matter in structural terms. Words of Chinese origin account for over 50% of modern Japanese vocabulary, although words of European origin are now common in all walks of life, especially advertising. Whenever a word is borrowed it is of course altered so that it will fit the fairly inflexible sound structure of Japanese. This has been true throughout history. The complex consonantal clusters and tonal variations that are typical of Chinese have all been ironed out, so contributing to an embarrassing increase in the number of homophones, and the 'difficult' sounds of western European languages have likewise been naturalized to the extent that they are not readily intelligible to the foreigner who might speak the language in question.

What is perhaps a little more disconcerting is the habit of extreme abbreviation:

English	Japanese pronunciation	Japanese abbreviation
word-processor	*wādo purosessā*	*wāpuro*
supermarket	*sūpā māketto*	*sūpā*
raise in basic salary ('base up')	*bēsu appu*	*bea*
strike	*sutoraiki*	*suto*

Words of Chinese origin

Characters	*Modern Chinese pronunciation*	*Meaning*	*Japanese pronunciation*
口腔	*kǒu-qiāng*	mouth cavity	*kōkō*
港口	*gǎng-kǒu*	harbour entrance	*kōkō*
孝行	*xiào-xíng*	filial piety	*kōkō*
航行	*háng-xíng*	navigation	*kōkō*
高校	*gāo-jiào*	high school	*kōkō*
鉱坑	*gǒng-kēng*	mine shaft	*kōkō*
煌煌	*huáng-huáng*	brilliant	*kōkō*

Words of European origin

Original	*Japanese adaptation*
volume	*boryūmu*
Cambridge	*kenburijji*
Arbeit	*arubaito*
Gelände (piste)	*gerende*
Köln	*kerun*
Champs-Elysées	*shanzerizee*

The written language

Perhaps the most unusual aspect of Japanese is its writing system. In many ways it was by an unfortunate quirk of history that Chinese was the first written language the Japanese encountered; an already difficult script had to be transformed and adapted into something even more complicated. It is true to say that Japanese as it is written today represents the most complex and cumbersome (not to say bizarre) writing system in use anywhere in the world. Not that this seems to have held back the cultural or scientific development of the nation, as this encyclopedia well testifies.

Modern Japanese is written with a combination of four different systems: romanization, the two syllabaries (*hiragana* and *katakana*), and Chinese characters (*kanji*). All four can sometimes be found together in the same sentence, although the frequency of use of any particular system will depend on the subject and the style. A rough distribution of these systems is as follows:

Romanization	Trade marks, acronyms, page numbers (arabic and roman), advertisements
Hiragana	Grammatical elements, particles, suffixes etc.
Katakana	Loanwords other than of Chinese origin, 'italics'
Kanji	Chinese loanwords, Japanese nouns and verbal roots

Romanization

Unlike the situation with Chinese, where different systems of romanization abound, there are only two systems of romanizing Japanese in common use. The differences are quickly learned. The traditional layout of the syllables is shown in the panel below.

Note that in a few cases alternates have been listed in brackets. The main system shown here is the so-called Hepburn system, after the American missionary James Curtis Hepburn (1815–1911), who devised it for his Japanese–English glossary, first published in 1867. This is in common use mainly because it allows speakers of English to produce a reasonable approximation to the Japanese sound with little effort. The alternative system, which is a more faithful rendition of the underlying sound structure of the language, is known as the *kunreishiki* or 'cabinet instruction' system, devised, as the name suggests, by the Japanese government in 1937. Both systems have their defenders, and it is fortunate that the practical differences are in fact slight.

In addition, Japanese has double consonants, *kk*, *ss*, *tt*, *pp*, etc., and an important distinction between short and long vowels (written *ō*, *ū*, etc. in this book).

The syllabaries

These syllabaries are known by the generic term *kana*. They were developed by simplifying those Chinese characters that were being used purely for their sound value rather than for their meaning, a step that was necessary if scholars were to write down Japanese sounds. This simplification took two forms. *Hiragana* emerged from the cursive form of the character taken to an extreme; it was used for the writing of personal communications, poetry, and was the main medium for the court women who dominated the writing of fiction in the late 10th and 11th centuries. *Katakana*, on the other hand, developed from the habit of taking part for whole, and first emerged in the writing of Buddhist priests. The

An example of four scripts working in two directions

A headline from the *Asahi shinbun* for 23 December 1990. In the following transcription, katakana is represented in *italic*, hiragana in roman and kanji in **bold**. The first three lines of vertical script, read right to left, are:

Shewarunaze • *so***ren gaishō**	Shevardnadze – Soviet Foreign Minister
Tōmen shokumu tsuzukeru	To continue in post for the present
START **jōyaku tantō**	In charge of START treaty (talks)

The horizontal line at the bottom is read left to right:

Hōdōkan ga **a**kasu	A spokesman reveals

シェワルナゼ・ソ連外相
当面職務続ける
START条約担当
報道官が明かす

Traditional layout of syllables

Basic										
a	ka	sa	ta	na	ha	ma	ya	ra	wa	n
i	ki	shi(si)	chi(ti)	ni	hi	mi		ri		
u	kù	su	tsu(tu)	nu	fu(hu)	mu	yu	ru		
e	ke	se	te	ne	he	me		re		
o	ko	so	to	no	ho	mo	yo	ro	[wo]	
Voiced										
	ga	za	da		ba/pa					
	gi	ji(zi)	ji(zi)		bi/pi					
	gu	zu	zu		bu/pu					
	ge	ze	de		be/pe					
	go	zo	do		bo/po					
Palatalized										
	kya	sha(sya)	cha(tya)		bya/pya					
	kyu	sha(syu)	chu(tyu)		byu/pyu					
	kyo	sho(syo)	cho(tyo)		byo/pyo					
	gya	ja(zya)		nya	hya	mya		rya		
	gyu	ju(zyu)		nyu	hyu	myu		ryu		
	gyo	jo(zyo)		nyo	hyo	myo		ryo		

Example of kana emerging from characters

Hiragana: character followed by emerging hiragana pattern

chi 知 a 安

Katakana: followed by character and emerging pattern

no ノ 乃 a ア 阿

psychological effect of choosing to write in one rather than the other syllabary differs, of course, through history; today *katakana* is largely reserved for Western loanwords and is also used to make a word stand out, much as we use italics. Any deviation from the norm can in fact be quite disturbing to read.

Note that although *kana* are used to write down sounds they are not alphabets, which represent an analysis of syllables in terms of their constituent consonants and vowels; they are syllabaries, which cannot represent single consonants. There is a *kana* sign for *ka*, for instance, but it is simply not possible to write down the consonant *k* in isolation. It should also be remembered that although either *hiragana* or *katakana* on their own would be theoretically adequate for transcribing the language, certain cultural and linguistic factors, such as the very high incidence of homophones, have conspired to make Chinese characters indispensable.

Hiragana

		k	s	t	n	h	m	y	r	w	
a	あ	か	さ	た	な	は	ま	や	ら	わ	ん
i	い	き	し	ち	に	ひ	み		り		
u	う	く	す	つ	ぬ	ふ	む	ゆ	る		
e	え	け	せ	て	ね	へ	め		れ		
o	お	こ	そ	と	の	ほ	も	よ	ろ	を	

Voicing is produced by adding a diacritical mark to the top right hand corner of the kana: か (*ka*) → が (*ga*) for example. Palatalization is shown by adding a small や *ya*, ゆ *yu*, or よ *yo* to the kana: き (*ki*) → きゃ (*kya*). Double consonants are shown by a small っ *tsu*, which precedes the sign in question: って *tte*.

Katakana

		k	s	t	n	h	m	y	r	w	
a	ア	カ	サ	タ	ナ	ハ	マ	ヤ	ラ	ワ	ン
i	イ	キ	シ	チ	ニ	ヒ	ミ		リ		
u	ウ	ク	ス	ツ	ヌ	フ	ム	ユ	ル		
e	エ	ケ	セ	テ	ネ	ヘ	メ		レ		
o	オ	コ	ソ	ト	ノ	ホ	モ	ヨ	ロ	ヲ	

For voicing and palatalization, the same rules apply as for hiragana.

Kanji

One of the commoner misconceptions is that Chinese characters are in fact ideographs, that is signs that represent ideas. This is somewhat misleading, as it can give the impression that thought can be directly written down without the medium of language and that Chinese writing is somehow more 'direct' than a phonetic system. In fact characters are more accurately described as constituting a morphemic script, in that each character represents a morpheme, which we can define here as the minimal meaningful unit in a language. In Chinese this may mean a whole word or just part of a word. The important thing to remember is that the character represents a linguistic unit rather than a disembodied idea.

Chinese characters are used in Japanese to write the large number of Chinese words that have been borrowed over the centuries; the vast majority of such words have been nouns. As we have seen, Japanese nouns are uninflected and never alter their shape, so the process of borrowing on this particular level has been fairly straightforward.

Chinese characters	Japanese word	Constituent parts	Meaning
大学	*dai-gaku*	great-learning	university
電話	*den-wa*	lightning (hence electricity)-speak	telephone
人口	*jin-kō*	people-mouth(s)	population
東京	*Tō-kyō*	east-capital	Tōkyō

In the examples shown, these words, which mean the same thing in both Chinese and Japanese, are made up of two characters, hence each character here can be said to be standing for a morpheme: part of a word rather than a whole word.

The Japanese did not stop here, however; they took the further step of using Chinese characters to write native Japanese nouns, reading them as Japanese:

Character	Japanese equivalent	Meaning
人	*hito*	person, man
口	*kuchi*	mouth

So far, so good. But now it will be seen from the two lists that the characters 人 and 口 can be read in two different ways: *hito* and *kuchi* when they occur on their own and are representing a native Japanese word, and *jin* and *kō* when they are representing a

Chinese loanword. *Hito* is what the character 人 'means' in Japanese, just as we would say that 人 means 'person' or 'man' in English. But the character 人 already had a Chinese pronunciation, the modern Japanese equivalent of which is *jin*. (It is because the sound *jin* is only a Japanese approximation rather than the original Chinese sound that this is called the Sino-Japanese reading of the character.) We have, therefore, the following complicated situation, where one character has two or more readings:

人 *JIN* (Sino-Japanese reading)
hito (Japanese reading/meaning)

As a very general rule, if the character is part of a compound then it should be pronounced with the Sino-Japanese reading; if it appears in isolation it is pronounced in its Japanese reading.

So much for nouns, which are simple in that they do not inflect. The real problem occurs when we encounter Japanese verbs, which are highly inflected. The Chinese script is not able to deal with inflections of this or any other sort and so the *hiragana* syllabary must be brought into play to write down those parts of the verb that change. Happily, Japanese verbs inflect at the end of the word rather than in the middle or at the beginning. The various forms of the verb 'speak', for example, are represented as follows, with the Chinese character standing for the uninflected root of the verb and *hiragana* being used to write down the different endings:

	ROOT ENDING	TRANSLATION
話す	*hana-su*	speaks
話した	*hana-shita*	spoke
話したい	*hana-shitai*	wants to speak
話さなかった	*hana-sanakatta*	did not speak

The dictionary entry for the character 話, which is used for both a noun and the root of a verb, will therefore look something like this:

WA (as in 電話 *denwa* 'telephone')
hana-su to speak
hanashi a talk, speech

The difficulties, as well as the fascinations, of the script should now be apparent. There are some 2,000 *kanji* in common use today: the minimum number required in order to be able to read a newspaper, and the minimum that all students in compulsory education must be taught. Novels, journals and specialist magazines are not restricted in this way however, so it is probably fair to say that the average educated Japanese can in fact passively recognize some 3,000–4,000 characters. There will also be times when the character will be recognized and understood but the reading be either not known or forgotten. In such cases, the *hiragana* syllabary is often used alongside the character in small type (known as *furigana*) to indicate the correct pronunciation. It is

Furigana

In this example from the early Meiji period, every character has been given its pronunciation down the right-hand side in small hiragana.

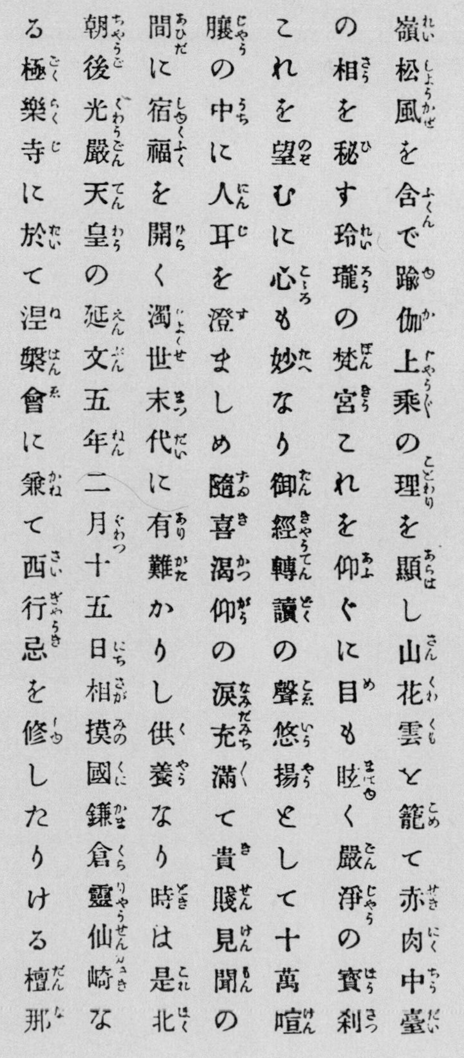

嶺松風を含で踰伽上乘の理を顯し山花雲と籠て赤肉中臺の相を秘す玲瓏の梵宮これを仰ぐに目も眩く嚴淨の寶刹これを望むに心も妙なり御經轉讀の聲悠揚として十萬喧擾の中に人耳を澄ましめ隨喜渇仰の涙充滿て貴賤見聞の間に宿福を開く濁世末代に有難かりし供養なり時は是北朝後光嚴天皇の延文五年二月十五日相摸國鎌倉靈仙崎なる極樂寺に於て涅槃會に兼て西行忌を修したりける檀那

this phenomenon that prompted the British scholar and diplomat Sir George Sansom to write: 'One hesitates for an epithet to describe a system of writing which is so complex that it needs the aid of another system to explain it.' Remembering how unfamiliar *kanji* are written can also be a problem. The unusually high rate of literacy in Japan is partly attributable to the fact that basic literacy is defined as the ability to read the syllabaries and a limited number of characters only: the syllabaries at least present none of the problems that English spelling provides.

The burden that retention of Chinese characters represents can, however, be over-emphasized. Most children manage to learn them, and dyslexia of the type that is triggered by the vagaries of English spelling is rare in Japan. In any case, such is the powerful cultural significance of *kanji*, and such is the vital rôle that they play in the task of discriminating between the many homophones in the modern language, that it now seems highly unlikely that they can ever be discarded.

Dialects

Dialect variation within Japan is as rich as in most European countries, many dialects being in fact mutually unintelligible. As elsewhere, the standard speech adopted for official, nationwide communication has always emanated from the centre of political and cultural power. From earliest times to the 18th century, this was Kyōto, but after the end of the century the centre finally shifted to Edo (now Tōkyō), where it has remained ever since. Educated Tōkyō speech is the standard for national television and radio, although regional accents often show through. Considerable social stigma is attached to those local accents from the north and the far south, the degree of opprobrium being in direct relation to the degree of comprehensibility by outsiders.

Dialect groups can be analysed along two rather different lines, depending on whether one is searching for differences in vocabulary and verb inflections on the one hand or differences in pitch accent on the other. Japanese accent is not a matter of stress, as it is in English, but rather of pitch: i.e. the difference between *ha^shi* and *ha_shi*. These differences play a major rôle in differentiating between various local accents or dialects.

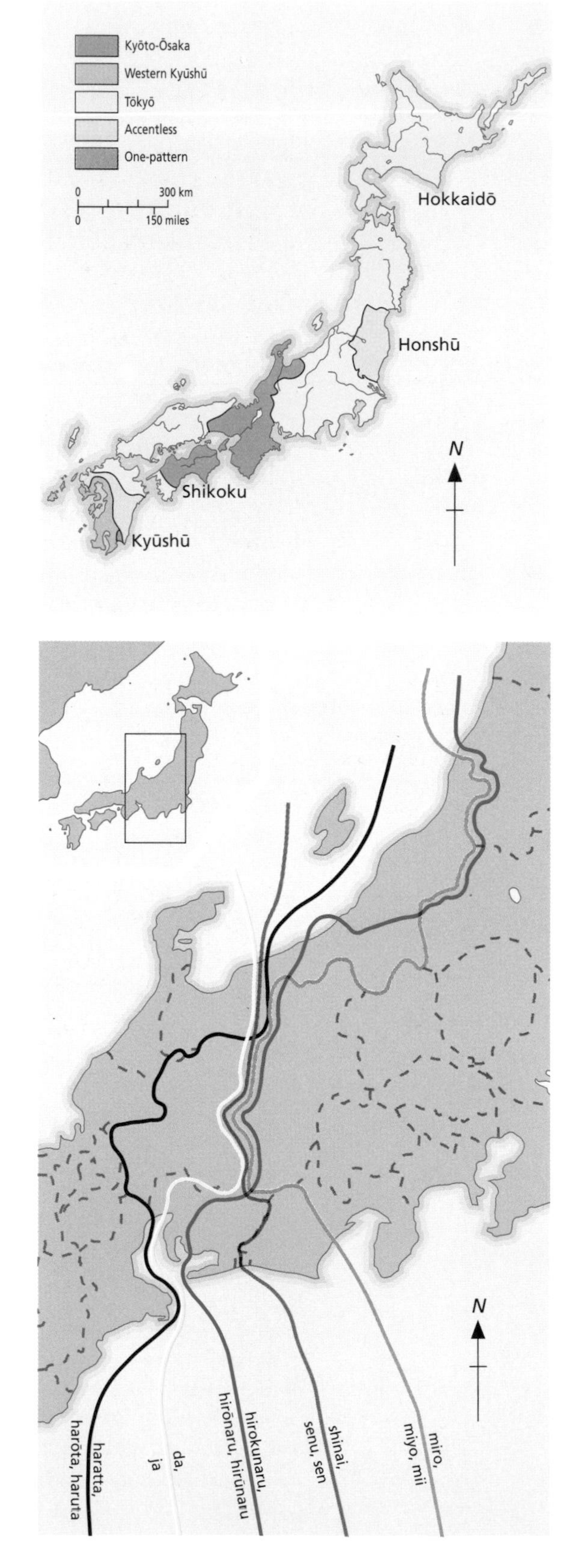

Distribution of dialects. The distribution of dialects according to broad differences in pitch accent reveals a fairly clear picture but also prompts some interesting questions. Is the Kyōto-Ōsaka accent at the centre older, the Tōkyō accent having developed out of it later? Or is in fact the Tōkyō accent older and the Kyōto-Ōsaka a new court-centred innovation? This latter theory would explain why dialects west of centre also have a Tōkyō pattern, but it goes against cultural stereotypes. The debate can become quite heated because regional pride is often at stake.

Writing styles

Partly because there are many levels at which Chinese can be absorbed into the system, Japanese has a very rich stylistic history. The use of Chinese can range from writing in classical Chinese proper, through a heavily Sinified version of Japanese, down to today's styles. In the table below 'Sino-Japanese 1' refers to those styles that make an attempt to 'look' Chinese although the underlying structure and method of reading reveal their Japanese origins. 'Sino-Japanese 2' refers to those styles which are essentially Japanese but contain a large number of loanwords and a few constructions influenced by Chinese, so making them distinct from the 'purer' forms used in Japanese poetry, for example. It is this style that has characterized much of literature apart from poetry, where there were restrictions on the use of Chinese vocabulary.

Major breaks occur, of course, in the Heian period, with the invention of the *kana* syllabaries, and at the beginning of the Meiji period (1868), when the modern styles began to emerge. All writings listed under 'Sino-Japanese 2' and ' "Pure" Japanese' that pre-date *c.* 1908 are now known as 'Classical Japanese', which is about as far from the modern styles as Chaucer's English is from present-day English. Note how recently this change has occurred. The Meiji Restoration of 1868 brought with it the need to create a new written style out of the vernacular, together with a huge increase in vocabulary to cover everything new and unfamiliar. This vocabulary was fashioned by creating new combinations of Chinese characters. The use of direct borrowings from English is essentially a post-war phenomenon. There is still, however, a considerable gap between spoken and written varieties of the language. A recent survey showed that on average words of Chinese origin comprised only 24% of a typical conversation; whereas for the written newspaper language the figure jumped to a remarkable 77%.

RB

Left *Dialect differences in vocabulary and verb inflection. The examples shown are confined to verbal forms. A map based on this kind of analysis shows a clear east-west split, which is not repeated west of Kyōto.*

Differences in written styles

Period	*Classical Chinese*	*Sino-Japanese 1*	*Sino-Japanese 2*	*'Pure' Japanese*
Nara 710–94	Official documents, Chinese poetry, Buddhist writings	Male diaries and letters		Japanese poetry
Heian 794–1192	Official histories, Chinese poetry (declining)	Official documents, male diaries	Tale collections	Emergence of kana, female writings, Japanese poetry
Medieval 1192–*c.* 1600	Chinese poetry, official documents in foreign relations	Male letters, official documents, historical events	Military romances, tales, popular religious writings, nō texts	Japanese poetry
Tokugawa *c.* 1600–1868	Chinese poetry (revival), philosophical and historical prose	Male letters, official documents	Historical romances, other 'serious fiction'	Fiction, *haikai* poetry, playscripts
Post-Restoration 1868–*c.* 1908	Male diaries, some prose	Official documents, expository prose	Modern written styles, including fiction, poetry and playscripts	
c. 1908–45		Male diaries	Modern written styles, including expository prose and official documents	
Post-war			All modern written styles	

Early literature

The earthenware *haniwa* figurines placed around prehistoric tombs present a picture of agricultural communities which had once come together to praise and bury their chieftains. Among a dead ruler's retinue of warriors and horses may also appear other figures: a seated musician playing the ancestor of the *koto*, or crudely shaped singers. Japanese literature, to the extent that it has any origin we can contact, begins here. The descendants of the musicians, singers and bards, skilled in genealogy and ritual of the tomb period, wove patterns of narrative and song brought together and written down by the centralizing Yamato clans during the late 6th and 7th centuries. Such early documents, combined with still living oral traditions, made possible the compilation of the *Record of ancient matters* (*Kojiki*) and the *Chronicles of Japan* (*Nihon shoki*) early in the 8th century.

Beginnings

The preface to the *Kojiki*, dated 712, records that the motivating force behind its creation was the powerful 7th-century emperor Tenmu. Tenmu had become emperor after a short and bloody *coup d'état* directed against the forces of a court established outside Yamato by his brother Tenji. As he and supporters carried on with the work of political and religious centralization, it was crucial to establish the divine ancestry and absolute sovereignty of the imperial family as well as the authority of its dependants and allies. Never again would the production of literature hold the social and political importance it did in this era. Disturbed that existing chronicles and legends contained errors and falsehoods, Tenmu ordered the creation of new, authorized accounts. The result was the completion after his death of the *Kojiki* and *Nihon shoki*, and the suppression of whatever rival traditions may have existed.

The *Kojiki* begins with the gods in the High Plain of Heaven, then relates the creation of the Japanese islands, the subjugation of unruly lower deities by divine ancestors of the imperial family, the miraculous birth of the legendary emperor Jinmu, his exploits and those of his successors in pacifying their earthly realm, and concludes with brief accounts of emperors down to the 7th century. The longer, more detailed *Nihon shoki* follows the same narrative trajectory, extending its scope to the late 7th century, the reigns of Tenmu and his consort Jitō. It is choice of language that most distinguishes the two works in both content and form. The *Nihon shoki* is written almost entirely in an accomplished, often ornamental style of Chinese prose. The *Kojiki* uses Chinese characters as well – there was no other writing system available to the early scribes. The latter work, however, frequently employs characters as phonetic symbols spelling out Japanese words and names, as though the fragmentary myths and legends it records had to be captured close to their oral sources. The final editor of the *Kojiki*, Ō no Yasumaro, noted in his preface a dilemma, one faced by Japanese writers even after the development of *kana* syllabaries. If one records matters succinctly in Chinese, the connotations of old native words are lost; if one writes every word out phonetically, it takes a long time. The narrative language of the *Kojiki* is a compromise; that of the *Nihon shoki* makes full use of the richness of literary Chinese in order to produce an official history fit to rank with those of China and the Korean kingdoms. This meant not merely borrowing words and phrases from Chinese texts but also a Confucian recasting of Japanese myths and tales.

In contrast, while fulfilling its political role of legitimization and patching the lineages of important clans into those of heavenly deities or early emperors, the *Kojiki* preserves a rougher, wilder version of the past. Stories about the primeval gods Izanaki and Izanami include the procreation of islands and deities, and an account of Izanaki in search of his dead wife which enacts the division of the living and the dead in a narrative of stark power. When this Japanese Orpheus gazes upon the otherworld form of his wife, he confronts a corpse erupting with thundering deities. The *Kojiki* text strains to record an ancient horror and awe on the far side of language. If a legendary emperor needs to conquer well-armed foes, the usual device is treachery. Invited to a banquet, the enemies remove their weapons and enter the hall, whereupon the emperor's men cut them down. In one of the first emperor's conquests, his men do so singing a group of bloodthirsty songs that were still performed in the

Opposite page *A haniwa figure from the Late Tomb Period, possibly meant to represent a female dancer, although the iconographic details of these figures are often unclear. They are found in and around tombs, often in large numbers, clearly designed to stand on guard or to wait upon the soul of the departed. Literature, in the sense of song and story and ritual, began in such an environment.*

Heian period. In the *Nihon shoki* Yamato Takeru, son of an emperor, is his father's filial servant. In the *Kojiki*, when his father asks him to scold his brother, he tears his brother to pieces and throws the pieces down a latrine; when dispatched east to quell barbarians, he openly laments his father's apparent desire to see him dead – not a very Confucian story.

In the *Kojiki* the ideological task of building lineages is often carried out by way of tales and songs dealing with a sexual passion shared by gods and royalty. In one tale the all-too-male deity Ōkuninushi flaunts his love affairs before his main wife Suseribime. In a witty and sexy sung riposte, she makes him an offer that he can't refuse.

Oh God of Eight Thousand Halberds,
My lord Ōkuninushi:
You, you are a man,
You have your pliant young women
On all the capes of the islands you round,
On every stony promontory you scout.
I, I am a woman, apart from you
I have no man, no husband.

A ritual prayer for pacifying fire

This text is known as a *norito*. About 30 of these incantations survive and they present some of the oldest texts in Japanese that we have. This particular *norito* was recited at the rites held in the 6th and 12th months to prevent fire breaking out in the imperial palace. Note that the account of Izanaki and Izanami given here is not quite the same as that found in the *Kojiki*.

I humbly speak by means of the heavenly ritual, the solemn ritual words entrusted
At the time that the kingdom was entrusted
By the command of the Sovereign Ancestral Gods and Goddesses,
Who divinely remain in the High Heavenly Plain,
To the Sovereign Grandchild, saying:
'Rule tranquilly the Land of the Plentiful Reed Plains and of the Fresh Ears of Grain as a peaceful land.'

The two deities Izanaki and Izanami,
Becoming wedded man and wife,
Gave birth to each of the myriad lands and each of the myriad islands,
And gave birth to the eight myriads of deities;
As their final child Izanami gave birth to Ho-musubi-no-kami,
And thereby burning her genitals,
Concealed herself within the rock and said:
'For seven nights and seven days do not look upon me, my beloved husband.'
Before the expiration of these seven days,
He thought her concealment strange and looked upon her:
He found that she was burnt in her genitals from giving birth to fire.
At that time, she said:
'Although I told my beloved husband not to look upon me,
He has rashly looked upon me.
My beloved husband shall rule the Upper Lands,
And I will rule the Lower Lands.'
Thus saying, she concealed herself in the rock.
Arriving at the pass of Yomo-tsu-hira-saka, she remembered:
'I have born and left a child of evil disposition
In the Upper Lands to be ruled by my beloved husband.'
Thus saying, she returned and gave birth to further children of four kinds:
The water deity,
The gourd dipper,
The river greens,
And the earth deity Hani-yama-hime,
And instructed and advised:
'If this child of evil disposition become wildly disposed,
Let the water deity take the gourd, and Hani-yama-hime the river greens, and pacify him!'

Because of this, I fulfil your praises,
And, in order that he do not wreak havoc in the court of the Sovereign Grandchild,
I make offerings:
Furnishing coloured cloth, radiant cloth, plain cloth, coarse cloth;
The five types of things;
As well as that which lives in the blue ocean—
The wide-finned and the narrow-finned fishes,
The sea-weeds of the deep and the sea-weeds of the shore—
And wine, raising high the soaring necks
Of the countless wine vessels, filled to the brim;
And even to the soft grain and the coarse grain—
I pile these high like a long mountain range,
And, by means of the heavenly ritual, the solemn ritual words,
Fulfil your praises. Thus I humbly speak.

RB

Beneath the billowing patterned hangings,
Beneath soft yielding bedding,
Rustling white soft bedding – come,
Embrace and hold fast
These breasts white as fresh fallen snow,
These white and pliant arms.
Stretch out your precious arms, pillow me,
Let us lay us down together.
Drink now of the sacred wine!

There are notes embedded in the narrative passages framing this and other songs about the once formidable Izumo god Ōkuninushi suggesting that they were part of full-scale performances held at the early court.

Yamato the brave

Yamato the brave (*Yamato takeru*) is a prototypical warrior-prince who subdues whole swathes of the country on behalf of his father. Both the *Nihon shoki* and the *Kojiki* record his legendary prowess and his uncompromising attitude towards his enemies, but the *Kojiki* narrative retains a distinctive raw edge. Section 79 reads as follows:

> The emperor said to him: 'why does your elder brother not come to the morning and evening meals? Take it upon yourself to teach and admonish him.' After this had been said, five days passed, but he still did not come. The emperor then asked him: 'Why has your elder brother not come for such a long time? Is it perhaps that you have not admonished him?' He replied: 'I have already entreated him.' Then he said: 'In what manner did you entreat him?' He replied: 'Early in the morning when he went into the privy, I waited and captured him, grasped him and crushed him, then pulled off his limbs, and wrapping them in a straw mat, threw them away.' At this the emperor was terrified at the fearless, wild disposition of this prince and said: 'Towards the west, there are two mighty men called the Braves of Kumaso. They are unsubmissive, disrespectful people. Therefore go and kill them.' Thus saying, he dispatched him.

RB

THE *MAN'YŌSHŪ* COLLECTION

The *Kojiki* and *Nihon shoki* preserve some 190 texts of songs and poems recorded phonetically, but the greatest collection of early verbal art is the *Collection for ten thousand generations* (*Man'yōshū*). It too grew out of the Tenmu era. Building upon a core of poems composed by or for members of Tenmu's family, later poets and editors spent 80 years adding and rearranging a wide range of material until the late 8th century; by this time the anthology contained over 4,500 poems. Generations of compilers tried out a number of schemes to organize the growing mass of texts. They learned from Chinese anthologies ways of utilizing both chronology and topic: hence the arrangement of the earliest of the *Man'yōshū*'s 20 books into ceremonial poems, poetry exchanges dealing with friendship and love, and elegies, each category moving forward through time. Later books use a variety of topics, while the final four are made up of the poems, both private and formal, of Ōtomo no Yakamochi, the most likely final shaper of the anthology. The seasons and love are key themes of the old poetry, but they are not yet the main categories they would become in the later imperial anthologies, nor are they tied to anything like the later tradition's refined diction. The use of poetry as a coded means of communicating, flirting and courting is well established, ready for later elaboration. Although some early poems are recorded in a fairly cryptic combination of phonetic characters and others are seemingly designed as semantic puzzles, the majority are written in an increasingly rationalized phonetic script. Still, this necessary use of phonetic characters produced a text which would look quite impenetrable to later poets accustomed to the simpler *kana* symbols. In the mid 10th century a group of scholar-poets was commissioned to recover the obscured pronunciations of poems long honoured more by reputation than by reading.

Judging from the *Man'yōshū*, the short poem which would dominate Japanese poetics for centuries, the 31-syllable *waka*, was already the most popular form by the late 7th century: more than 90% of *Man'yōshū* poems are *waka* (also called *tanka*, or 'short poems'). The anthology contains as well other poem forms, the most important of which is the *chōka*, literally 'long poem'. The several hundred *chōka* are made, like *waka*, of alternating phrases of five- and seven-syllable units. Where the *waka* holds to the short pattern of 5–7–5–7–7, the *chōka* links together a greater number of 5–7 phrases, finally rounding off 7–7. Some *chōka* reprise or vary their themes by means of attaching one or more companion *waka*, generally called *hanka*, 'envoys'. *Waka* represent in their ascendancy a new consciousness of language, an awareness of the pleasure and force of words, images and themes manipulated within a small rhythmic framework.

Spring passes away, summer seems come.
They give to the air white hempen robes
On Kaguyama, hill from heaven.

Empress Jitō, late 7th century

Kisayama in Yoshino,
From tips of branches in folds of the mountain
The clamour of the voices of the birds.

Yamabe no Akahito, early 8th century

Chōka are highly structured as well, but they grow out of an older ritual and ceremonial use of word-craft. Kakinomoto no Hitomaro is the most famous poet of the *Man'yōshū* and the composer of some of its finest long poems and *waka*. He wrote *chōka* about domestic tragedies such as the death of a wife or his encounter with the body of a stranger dead beside the road. Perhaps best-known are poems eulogizing members of the imperial family in which Hitomaro gave vivid poetic expression to the cult of their divine immortality. Long poems continued to be written in the 8th century, but the new capital of Nara produced a courtly society concerned with Buddhist ceremonials and political intrigues, and generations of poets composing *waka* for private enjoyment and Chinese poems for formal occasions. The religious and social context for Hitomaro's poetry of praise and death was disappearing, and with it the *chōka*. As a topic for composition, death would be excluded from the refined poetic code of the Heian period.

On the margins

The *Kojiki*, *Nihon shoki* and *Man'yōshū* assembled, organized and rewrote the Japanese past, guided but not entirely dominated by the priorities of a new centralized polity. Representing the periphery are two other kinds of text. In 713 the government ordered provincial officials to compile records detailing natural and agricultural resources of their provinces. In these formal reports they were also to provide etymologies for place-names and local legends: as usual, government and verbal craft were deemed inseparable. The best preserved of these regional surveys, known as *fudoki*, comes from Izumo; it and fragments of other *fudoki* contain tales and songs that supplement the view from the centre. Japan's first collection of Buddhist tales, the *Miracle tales of Japan* (*Nihon ryōiki*), also speaks for a regional and social periphery. With these tales of miraculous salvation and immanent damnation, the lay priest Kyōkai asserted in the face of the powerful new sects of Nara the dignity and right to salvation of the same common people whom the new state used for forced labour, while commoner and aristocrat shared famine, plagues and curses brought upon all by the violent struggle for supremacy between the great temples of Nara and an aristocratic family with old imperial connections and new ambitions, the Fujiwara. MM

Heian literature

Whether or not the move from Nara to Heian-kyō in 794 was in fact carried out to rid the court of the oppressive forces of the Buddhist clergy, the results certainly give the impression that a new era had begun. The early part of the 9th century is known almost exclusively for three anthologies of Chinese verse produced on imperial decree, and for the emergence of two outstanding practitioners of Chinese who have in many ways never been surpassed: the priest Kūkai, founder of Shingon Buddhism, who was equally at home with both poetry and expository prose, and the scholar-statesman Sugawara no Michizane. Michizane, who ended his life in exile in northern Kyūshū, wrote some of the best Chinese poetry ever produced by a Japanese. The most dramatic development, however, was the emergence during the latter part of the century of the *kana* syllabary, whereby it became possible for the first time to write the native language with ease.

Poetry

The effects of the evolution of *kana* were first felt in poetry and only a little later in prose, although the general result was an explosion of literary output. As we move into the 10th century it becomes apparent that serious efforts are being made to restore the prestige of native poetry, the chief tool being imperially-commissioned anthologies. The first one to appear was the *Collection ancient and modern* (*Kokinshū*, *c.* 905). It was to set the pattern for all subsequent collections. This is so not only in matters of content, vocabulary, and format, but also concerning the very concept of an anthology. As a statement of cultural authority, it defined correct taste; and to have a poem or poems accepted for such an anthology was later to constitute a form of immortality. In a manuscript age, it was perhaps the closest one could come to being 'published'. The concept of an anthology also meant much more than one might at first assume. The arrangement was not chronological but by theme: spring, summer, autumn, winter, love affairs etc., so the work both defined the cultural significance of the seasons and laid down the 'normal' path by which a love affair might be expected to proceed. It gave expression to the central conventions of court life.

What kind of poetry was it? Longer forms died away and we are left with an almost exclusive use of the short 31-syllable *waka* form. Poetry of this type does not lend itself well to translation, because its subject range is limited and because technical expertise dominates. There is the added problem that, in great contrast to Western and indeed Chinese poetic forms, there is a different concept of 'lines', so much so that a *waka* has been described as 'the deformation of a single sentence'. Given the nature of the Japanese language, neither rhyme nor a stress-based rhythm is possible. The grounding beat is nothing more than an alternation of 5 and 7 syllable phrases.

A *Kokinshū* manuscript

This manuscript is attributed to Emperor Fushimi (1265–1317) and is therefore a 14th-century manuscript of a 10th-century work. Read from right to left, it begins with the title '*Kokin wakashū*, vol. 2: spring poems, section 2', both lines written entirely in Chinese characters. The rest of the text is in flowing hiragana. The first poem (lines 3, 4 and 5) reads as follows:

Dai shirazu; yomibito shirazu
Harugasumi tanabiku yama no sakurabana
utsurowamu to ya iro kawariyuku.

Topic unknown; poet unknown
The cherry blossoms on the mountains where hangs spring mist:
are they, I wonder, about to fall? Their colour has begun to change.

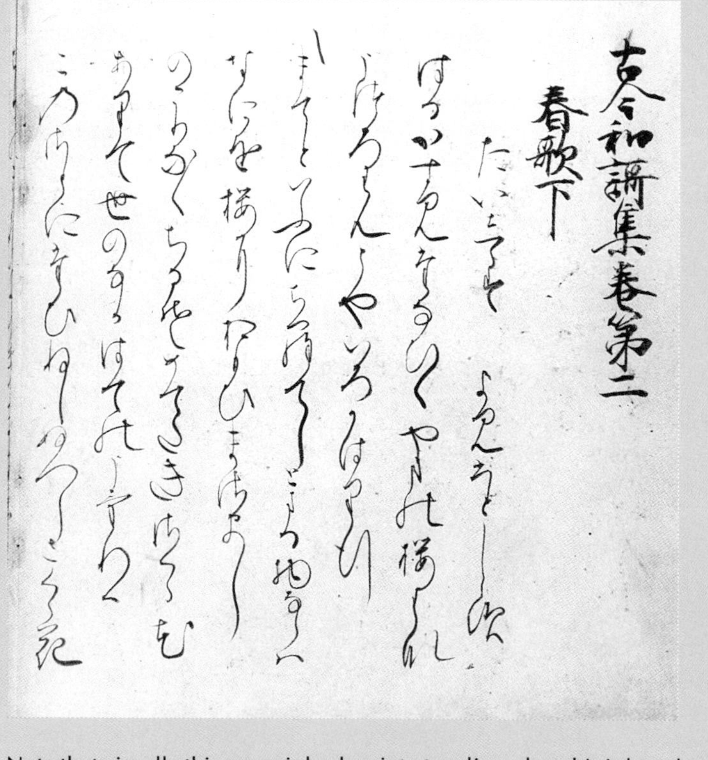

Note that visually this poem is broken into two lines, but this is largely a function of the handwriting and the page length rather than being the result of any formal requirement. RB

PROSE

The distinction of being the first piece of extended Japanese prose written in *kana* belongs to Ki no Tsurayuki's preface to the *Collection ancient and modern*. Tsurayuki was a professional court poet of low rank whose efforts to establish *kana* were socially and politically motivated. Certainly, in their official capacity men were under pressure to use Chinese and, almost by default, writing in *kana* was left to the women. Throughout the period, therefore, *kana* tended to be marked as 'female', hence 'private', and it was to be many years before men took to writing naturally in anything but a heavily Sinicized style. It was this that lay behind Tsurayuki's apparently unusual choice of a female persona when he wrote his *Tosa diary* chronicling a voyage made in 937 from the province of Tosa back to the capital.

The work that later became known as the ancestor of Japanese fiction is entitled *The tale of the bamboo cutter* (*c.* 920–60). The style, although influenced by

Chinese in certain places, is recognizably Japanese. The story itself is of interest from the point of view of folklore, for it involves a bamboo cutter who discovers a beautiful girl 7 cm high hidden inside a bamboo. She quickly grows, makes her adopted parents very rich and is wooed by the highest in the land, only to return to her home in the moon at the end.

The translation of *waka*

Japanese *waka* are notoriously difficult to render into English, partly because of their cryptic nature and partly because they make use of word play as a major poetic device. The following analysis is a simple example of what can be involved:

Romanized Japanese:
Hana no iro wa/ utsurinikeri na/ itazura ni/ waga mi yo ni furu/ nagame seshi ma ni.

Commentary
Hana no iro wa: 'the colour of the flower'; but *iro* 'colour' has connotations of face, appearance and sexuality; *hana* 'flower' seems general but may refer specifically to blossoms, either the plum or the cherry.

utsurinikeri na: 'has faded, ah!'; *utsuru* has connotations of shifting, impermanence and the motion of time; the verb ending brings with it a sigh of realization.

itazura ni: adverbial phrase 'in vain' which modifies both what has preceded and what is to follow. In a sense the poem pivots on this phrase.

waga mi yo ni furu: the meaning of this phrase on first reading is 'myself growing old in this world', but this must immediately be reinterpreted in the light of what follows: *yo ni* can mean both 'in this world' and 'very'; *furu* both 'growing old' and 'to fall (as of rain)'.

nagame seshi ma ni: *nagame seshi*: 'to do a long-gazing', contains within it the hidden word *naga-ame* 'long rains', and it is this that forces a rereading of the preceding *furu*.

Free translation
The colour of the blossoms has faded in vain, while I, getting older all the time, have passed my days to no end, doing little more than gazing at the long rains that fall so constantly. RB

A good portion of the work is taken up with descriptions of the impossible tasks that she sets five persistent suitors and with each man's come-uppance. It is, however, the structure of the tale that reveals an extraordinary degree of sophistication for such an early work. The tale is constructed in a series of sections: each section, in particular the stories that deal with each suitor, is a distinct fiction, in itself an attempt at deception, hence hollow, like a bamboo. What is more, each section ends in a knot or node that takes the form of a play on words, reinforcing the idea that language hides rather than reveals. This is in turn linked to the overt message of the tale which is strongly Buddhist: the futility of desire and attachment as, try as they may, all the forces the emperor can muster prove to be powerless to prevent the girl being returned to her magical origins.

A quite different approach to the question of structure and the nature of the relationship of language to reality is taken in the *Tales of Ise*, produced sometime in the early 10th century. This work has spawned a large number of commentaries over the centuries. It consists of a series of poems with prose contexts (125 sections). In many cases these consist of little more than scene setters, necessary because of the laconic nature of the poetic form itself. In many other cases, however, the prose approaches a small narrative.

> Section 4
>
> In the past, when the Ex-Empress is living in the eastern fifth-ward, a certain lady is occupying the west wing of the house. Quite without intending it a man falls deeply in love with the lady and begins to visit her; but around the tenth of the first month she moves away without a word and although he learns where she has gone, it is not a place where ordinary people can come and go. He can do nothing but brood over the wretchedness of life. When the plum blossoms are at their height in the next first month, poignant memories of the year before draw him back to her old apartments. He stares at the flowers from every conceivable standing and sitting position, but it is quite hopeless to recapture the past. Bursting into tears, he throws himself onto the floor of the bare room and lies there until the moon sinks low in the sky. As he thinks of the year before, he composes the poem: 'Is it not the moon? Is not the spring the spring of old? Only my own being remains unchanged.' He goes home at dawn, still weeping.

From very early times the fact that a number of the poems in this work also appear in the *Collection ancient and modern* attributed to a courtier called Ariwara no Narihira meant that the *Tales of Ise* were seen as his biography, and this reading has persisted, despite evidence that it is a compilation of a different kind. The *Tales of Ise* raises important questions about the genesis of poetry and the relationship between poetry and prose. It has proved to be an enduring classic and certain key scenes still form part of the educated Japanese vision of Heian court life.

The apparent lack of coherence is something that can be found throughout the tradition. The well-known *Pillow book* of Sei Shōnagon is a case in point. This is a miscellany, a mixture of sharp anecdote, lists of likes and dislikes, and catalogues of apposite poetic phrases. Not only does it exist in a number of radically different forms, but it is important to remember that the insistent 'I' of the translations is hardly in evidence in the original Japanese. The work is therefore far less personalized than English versions suggest and the authorial voice and the coherence that voice might bring is less distinct. The *Pillow book* stands at the beginning of a long series of such miscellanies, which are given a pride of place that may come as somewhat of a surprise.

Illustrating the *Tales of Ise*

A tradition of illustrating the *Tales of Ise* grew up during the mid Heian period and continued on into modern times. Certain sections of the work lent themselves to visual representation. These scenes were then used not only to illustrate the text but also became cultural motifs in their own right. Here are four visual references to section 9, which describes how a group of men travelling east sit down to rest in a marshy area surrounded by bridges and irises and amuse themselves by composing clever poems incorporating the word 'iris' (*kakitsubata*). Two are straightforward illustrations to the text: below, from a narrative scroll (late 16th century) and right, from a printed book (early 17th century). The other two show the image being used as a motif; one on a fan, one on a lacquer box.

RB

The tale of Genji

By far the most important prose work of this period, *The tale of Genji* (1010?), was written by a lady-in-waiting called Murasaki Shikibu. It is a vast work that chronicles political and sexual intrigue in a fictional yet recognizable court milieu. The author in fact took great care to place the story in a historical framework some 100 years before her own time. Because of its remarkable realism, it has been dubbed 'the world's first novel', an accolade that is not undeserved, provided one interprets the word 'novel' in a catholic sense.

The story-reading scene from 'The eastern cottage' chapter of The tale of Genji *narrative scroll, late Heian period, 12th century. Ukifune sits facing the viewer top left looking at pictures as the maid Ukon reads to her from the text. Nakanokimi is having her hair combed. Note the three forms of room dividers: rattan blinds on the outside, sliding doors and curtains hung from frames for the interior.*

The tale begins when an emperor conceives a passion for a woman of unsuitable rank. She bears him a son of exquisite beauty. The mother is hounded to death by her rivals, and in order to save the boy, the emperor gives him the non-imperial name of Genji. If it is known that he cannot succeed to the throne, he may survive. The emperor eventually finds a substitute for his affections, and this woman, Fujitsubo, becomes in turn an object of desire for the young Genji. The first part of the tale chronicles a succession of affairs, in the course of which Genji manages to consummate his passion for Fujitsubo just once and then find a substitute in the form of the young girl Murasaki. He then makes a political blunder and finds himself in exile. Eventually recalled to the capital, having in a sense done penance for his affair with Fujitsubo, he rises to great eminence. Murasaki becomes his one constant, but barren, companion. Gradually, however, middle age approaches and he finds himself losing control over his women, being challenged in various subtle ways by the next generation. Then Murasaki dies and soon after we are told that Genji too has gone. The last long ten chapters represent an extraordinary second departure, as we find centre stage being taken by two men who represent elements of his make-up; but the sum in this case is less than the parts. In particular the more sympathetic of the two, Kaoru, turns out to be as much a failure as Genji was a success, and so he becomes in a sense the world's first anti-hero. The tale ends on a sombre note, stressing the futility of all passion and desire.

Women's diaries

The preponderance of female authors is a marked feature of Heian prose. In addition to fictional works, a number of important diaries have come down to us, giving a vivid picture of court life. The following is an extract from Murasaki Shikibu's diary:

> That evening there was a bright moon. Assistant Master of the Household Sanenari, wanting perhaps to ask a lady-in-waiting to express his special thanks to Her Majesty, and finding that the area by the side door was wet from bath water and that no one seemed to be around, came over to Miya no Naishi's room at the eastern end of our corridor. 'Is anyone in?' he inquired. Then he moved to the middle room and pushed up the top half of the shutters that I had left unlocked. 'Anyone here?' he asked again. But I gave no reply. He was joined by the Master of Her Majesty's Household Tadanobu and, thinking it seemed a little churlish of me to continue to ignore them, I gave some noncommittal response. Neither of them seemed in the least put out. 'You ignore me, but pay great attention to the Master of the Household,' said Sanenari with a touch of sarcasm. 'It's understandable, I suppose, but nevertheless to be deplored. Why the emphasis on rank here?' And with that he started singing 'the hallowed nature of today'. His voice was rather attractive. As it was now the dead of night, the moon seemed very bright. 'Do take away the bottom of the lattice!' they insisted. Despite the nature of the situation, I felt it would be embarrassing to have these nobles demean themselves in such a manner, and while frivolous behaviour by someone younger than myself might well be overlooked and put down to inexperience, I could hardly be so reckless, so I refused.

RB

No amount of précis can do justice to this work, full of compassion and understanding of the complexities and frustrations of the human condition. The delight in life is constantly set off against the Buddhist ground note that desire is in the end a mere illusion. *The tale of Genji* is indisputably one of the world's important books and is one of the greatest gifts of Japan to world culture.

Later Heian works

The presence of the *Genji* proved to be so overwhelming that no subsequent work could entirely escape its influence. There are, however, a number of later fictions which are worthy of note in that they explore further elements of fantasy and dream. Not that these subjects were lacking in the *Genji*, but in these later works they are privileged.

One interesting example is the story known as *Torikaebaya*, which translates roughly as 'If only one were the other!' This concerns a brother–sister pair who have such strong transsexual desires that their father has no choice but to allow them to take on each other's rôles. The resulting problems give rise to a complex and somewhat confusing tale of deception and frustrated desires at court. Neither erotic nor particularly humorous, this astonishing tale questions the rôle of gender in society and the nature of sexual desire with remarkable sophistication. Tales like these have all been eclipsed by the *Genji*, but in fact they repay careful reading, for they explore quasi-Freudian themes from an interesting and entirely non-Western perspective.

Occasionally it may seem that Heian literature consists of nothing but a succession of highly-wrought poems and tales, but it would be presenting a false image not to mention a vast collection of more down-to-earth tales, the *Konjaku monogatarishū*. This is a compendium of stories from India, China and Japan which run the whole gamut from didactic to more homely, mundane and humorous stories. The collection, which seems to have been made near the end of the Heian period, bears witness to a thriving tradition of such works, probably of male rather than female provenance. Taken together, they constitute a storehouse of the historical, fictional and mythical traditions in which the Heian nobility was educated and by which it defined itself. RB

Medieval literature

The economic, political and social changes that culminated in the dominance of the provincial warrior classes after the Genpei wars of 1180–85 naturally had a far-reaching effect upon literature. Although the old court aristocracy continued to provide the pattern of civilized culture and remained the arbiters of good taste and correct form, the newly emergent classes provided a new focus and new interests. The wars themselves provided fresh subjects, while the general turmoil of the age induced a profounder consciousness of life's transcience, a keener, more serious questioning of the human place in the natural and social order and a pervasive Buddhist tone.

The new order

The importance of Buddhism in the literature of this period, while due in part to the upheavals of the time and a growing belief in the imminence of millenarian decline foretold in Buddhist scripture, was equally the result of the development of new sects during the Heian period and the spread of popular Buddhism. Rooted as it was in a long process of growth, Buddhist influence now reached its apogee and found its way into virtually every aspect of the literature, imparting a greater intellectual depth and spiritual value.

Drawing both on Buddhist ideals and on social realities, the themes of worldly renunciation, retreat to a hermit's hut and a life of travel appear insistently. At the same time, for courtiers and also for those with somewhat marginal status, self dedication and absorption in an art, particularly poetry, formed a way to retain or recreate a sense of value and of purpose in a changing world. These changes of literary milieu and theme and mood coincided with a vital change in the written language itself, the perfection of a style known as 'Japanese–Chinese mixed style' (*wakan konkōbun*), which combined the fluidity and elegance of courtly Japanese with the firmness and structural strength of Chinese to produce writing of great beauty and power, enriched with a wider range of vocabulary. It was, of course, the result of a long process of growth, but it was at this juncture that it found its most fitting use for new concerns and in new genres, which produced some of the finest writing in Japanese.

Prose

Courtly fiction had been in some sense in decline from the time of *The tale of Genji*, and in this period it all but disappears. The diary remains a constant form, a valuable recourse for those with much to lament in the changing world, and retains both its Heian configuration, often combining prose and poems to depict high points of emotion, and its essentially courtly style. The loss of husbands or lovers in battle now appears as a theme, as in *The poetic memoirs of Lady Daibu* (completed *c.* 1231), depicting the life of a court lady who was closely involved with the losing Taira faction and whose lover, a grandson of the Taira leader, died at the battle of Dannoura. The new realities of life lie behind *The diary of the waning moon* (1280) by the nun Abutsu, who tells of her journey from Heian kyō to the seat of military government at Kamakura to present a property dispute before the shōgunal courts. Rather closer to courtly concerns is *The confessions of Lady Nijō* (completed 1313), the author of which was a lady of high birth, a consort of Emperor Go-fukakusa. She embarks on a number of love affairs, and her indiscreet behaviour leads to her dismissal from court, after which she becomes a nun and spends much of her life in wandering. This work is not only distinguished for its candour and the interest of the author's escapades; it also reflects the age in the restlessness of its second half.

A sense of searching informs two major works that belong to the genre of miscellaneous essays (*zuihitsu*). *An account of my hermitage* (1212) by Kamo no Chōmei reads like a thematically unified memoir of the author's retreat from the world and his enjoyment of a hermit's existence. He stresses the impermanence of human life, especially cities and dwellings, telling of disasters that have befallen the capital, then recounts the stages by which he came to his own small hut and the pleasure he derives from this simple life, and ends by wondering if even this attachment to his hut is not an impediment to the Buddhist salvation he seeks. His flowing, limpid writing typifies the mixed style at its best.

Yoshida no Kenkō, author of *Essays in idleness* (*c.* 1330), was looking back to a classical ideal both in his style and his concerns, as he put together his collection of anecdotes and thoughts on court usage, correct behaviour and proper attitudes to life. The tone is often moral, but not without amusing touches and a tolerant grasp of the human condition. Here too can be found encapsulated many of the ideals that have been the foundation of the Japanese aesthetic from earliest times to the present, set out in a style of great purity.

At the same time, the tradition of simple, earthy stories combined with uplifting tales of Buddhist virtue continued vigorously, especially under the strengthened influence of Buddhism, and many collections, such as *Kokon chomonjū* (1254) were compiled. The origin of much of this material lay in oral forms and they led eventually to the *otogizōshi*, a type of *jongleur*'s tale that became prominent in the late medieval period and took the tradition of prose narrative into the next age.

The medieval image of the priest-poet living and travelling alone and finding salvation within nature is well expressed here in a travel scene from the Tale of Saigyō *narrative scroll, Kamakura period, 13th century. Saigyō (1118–90) left court at the age of 23 and devoted the rest of his life to poetry. His name means 'travelling towards paradise in the west'. The convention in scrolls such as these is that space equals time, hence Saigyō appears twice, moving from right to left as the scroll unfolds.*

THE MILITARY TALES

Out of this oral tradition and out of the experience of wholesale war arose a major new genre, the military tale, the greatest of which is *The tale of the Heike*. It recounts the rise and fall of the Taira clan (known also as the Heike) and is on a grand scale: it encompasses events both in the capital and in the provinces, ranges in time from the emergence of the first great warrior-courtier of the Taira line in the 1130s through the skirmishes and battles of the Genpei wars to the death of the widowed Taira empress Kenreimon'in in 1191. How the text developed is obscure, but it is likely to have grown from historical records and fragmentary early versions that were crafted over time into a form that was chanted to the accompaniment of the *biwa*, or lute, by blind priests, catering perhaps to a growing popular audience. The work probably reached something like its present form in the first quarter of the 13th century, but is likely to have undergone changes after that, and certainly exists in many different versions, reflecting the different schools of reciters. The generally accepted version consists of 12 books and an epilogue, within which there are divisions into sections or units suitable for a single recitation. The oral nature of the text is shown by the use of formulaic utterances and by the vigorous, rhythmic style, which frequently takes on a pattern of alternating seven- and five-syllable phrases, giving the language an impressive power and dignity. It is the greatest example of the new style. At the same time there are certain stock motifs, such as the description of weapons and armour, the naming of pedigrees and the ritual challenges that are common to epic in many traditions.

Despite its uncertain provenance, the work has a surprising thematic unity, which can be summed up as the lesson that all living things must perish, and the mighty will be brought low. Rather than the glory of battle, it is the tragedy and pathos of the downfall of the Taira clan that forms the main subject, and there runs through the work a strand of romantic sympathy for the losers. Buddhism informs the whole work, with its sense of justly deserved retribution and at the same time strong compassion for all human suffering. Combined with the epic deeds and the vividness of narration, it imparts a moral, spiritual and emotional weight and grandeur that are unforgettable.

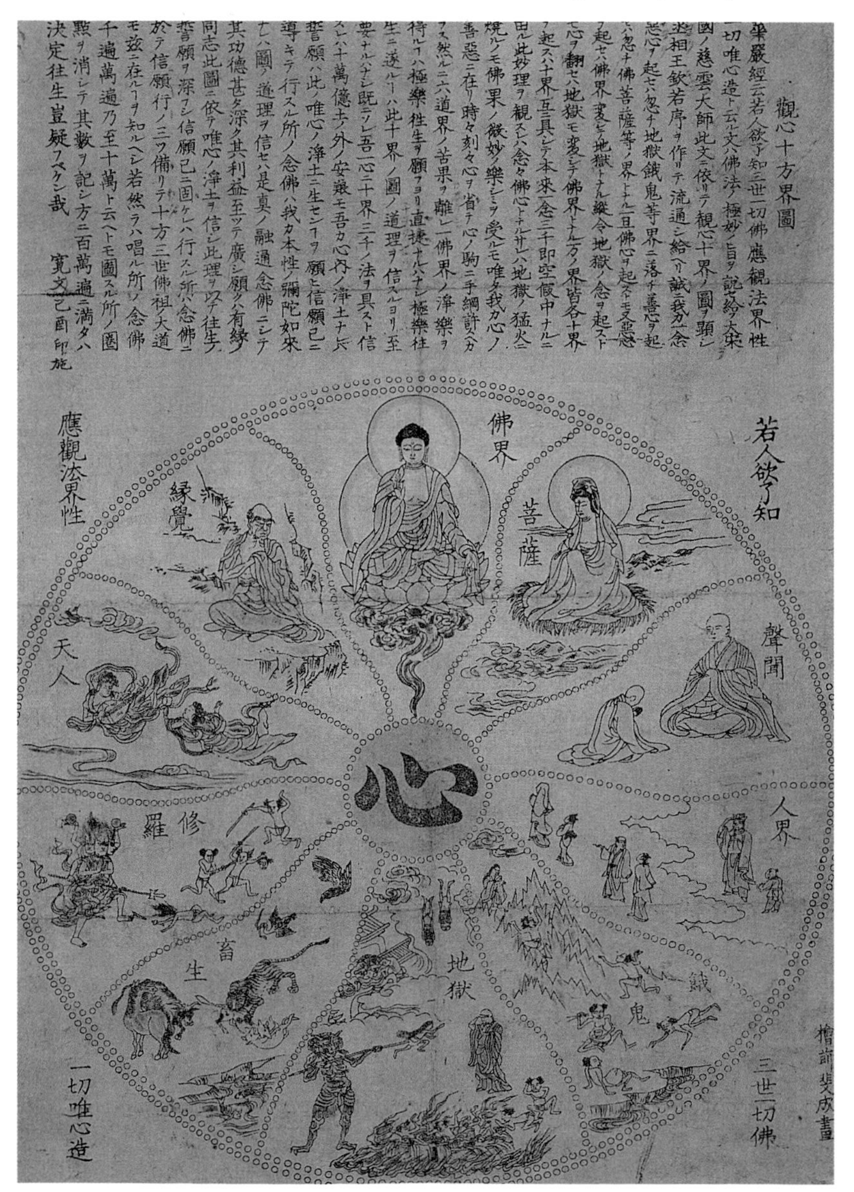

A 17th-century woodblock print of a mandala of the ten worlds, six portraying the cycle of birth and rebirth and four the worlds of the enlightened ones. It was this kind of world view that governed much of medieval thought and behaviour.

Poetry

The age opened with the appearance of the eighth imperial anthology, the *New collection ancient and modern* (*c.* 1206). As the title indicates, it was designed to rival the first anthology, which had been the pattern for those that followed, and it can well be considered the greatest of them all. It set out the styles and modes that had developed during the 12th century and which formed the dominating aesthetic for centuries to come. The rhetoric and verbal texture are complex; in many poems description comes to the fore, with a consequent receding of the poetic speaker; in love poems psychological complexity takes unexpected twists; symbolism is widely used; and over all broods the ideal of 'mystery and depth' (*yūgen*), bringing a new spiritual and metaphysical significance. As the tradition developed, description of nature and psychological probing took on an increasingly minute focus, while diction and subject matter broadened gradually under the influence of progressive poets. The age was, however, racked by disputes between innovators and conservatives, whose motives were as much political as artistic, for poetry was inextricably linked with factions and power at court. Following the compilation of the 17th imperial anthology, the *Collection of elegance* (*c.* 1349), the practice of court poetry became increasingly sterile, and true creativity moved into linked poetry (*renga*).

Linked poetry originated in an ancient practice of splitting the 31-syllable *waka* form into two sections of 17 and 14 syllables respectively. One poet would produce the first half and the second would be added by another poet. By adding yet more sections, poets could build up long chains of alternating 17 and 14 syllable stanzas. At first this sort of verse was practised as an amusement, but it gradually developed into a serious form and by the late 14th century it had become the most important sphere of poetic activity.

'Burning of the Sanjō Palace' from the narrative scroll Tale of the Heiji insurrection, *Kamakura period, 13th century. Such graphic scenes of violence and destruction were painted partly to commemorate an historical event and partly to illustrate the truth of the fact that Japan was now living in the 'Latter days of the Law'*

The aesthetic of the *New collection ancient and modern*

- The following poem by the priest Jakuren (d. 1202) gives a feel for the new aesthetic. Not only does it try to define the indefinable, first by presenting what it is not and then by providing a picture of what it might be, but it also exemplifies the monochromatic ideal that emerged much later in Japanese ink-painting based on Chinese models.

Sabishisa wa sono iro to shi mo nakarikeri
maki tatsu yama no aki no yūgure.

Loneliness: it has no definable colour;
black pines stand on a mountain at autumn dusk.

- Reference back to earlier poetry (known as *honkadori*) also became a major poetic technique during this period. The following is a good example of what is involved. The first poem comes from the *Kokinshū* of *c.* 905. The second is by a court lady, known as Shunzei's daughter, who flourished *c.* 1200. Phrases are 'borrowed' and are used in such a way as to thicken the texture and complicate the response.

Base poem

*Satsuki matsu hana***tachibana no** ka o kageba
mukashi no hito no **sode no ka zo suru**.

Catching the scent of the blossoming orange flowers that wait for the sixth month,
Brings back the scent on a sleeve of someone long ago.

New poem

Tachibana no niou atari no utatane wa
yume mo **mukashi no sode no ka zo suru**.

A brief sleep in the presence of the scent of orange flowers;
in dreams too it brings back the scent on a sleeve long ago.

RB

While it had begun among court poets, linked poetry achieved great popularity among people of humbler class both in the capital and in the provinces, and its greatest practitioner, Sōgi (1421–1502), was of quite obscure origin. No doubt the co-operative, social nature of linked poetry composition contributed largely to its popularity, while the disorder of the 15th century helped to spread its practice through all strata of society and all parts of the country. Over time, elaborate rules were evolved concerning the use of particular images and the ways in which stanzas could be linked, and establishing a standard length of either 36 or 100 stanzas. The flow from one stanza to the next and the overall effect of the complete chain were more important than the brilliance of any particular phrase. In renga a truly new poetic form, was thus created.

Nō drama

The other new form to emerge in this age was the nō drama, which had its origins in earlier, cruder dramatic entertainments, but now achieved an unsurpassed beauty of both performance and text. This achievement is attributed largely to Kan'ami (1333–84) and his son Zeami (*c.* 1364–1443), actor-authors who wrote not only plays but also treatises on performance. In contrast to linked poetry, nō rose from its popular and humble beginnings to become a pursuit of the upper classes, earning the patronage of the Ashikaga shōguns. Although as a dramatic form nō must be considered in terms of stage performance, the texts themselves constitute poetry of the highest order and are rewarding to read. The tradition of *waka* and the associative, structural techniques of linked poetry are combined with the tension of dramatic form in a dense, highly allusive language that encompasses all the concerns and images of the medieval aesthetic and conveys the pathos of the human situation with vividness and intensity. True to its age, it is strongly, overtly Buddhist, and its theme is the salvation and release of the suffering soul, a fitting symbol of its own disordered times.

PTH

A short linked-poetry sequence

A rare drawing of a renga master instructing a pupil in the art of linking verses. The sequence that follows is from the *Bunna senku daiichi hyakuin*, composed in 1355 at the mansion of Nijō Yoshimoto, a powerful courtier and the greatest exponent of linked poetry of his time. Each set of two stanzas can be viewed as a complete poem in itself, which means that each stanza except the last will have to be reinterpreted in the light of the next link in the chain. The art of the exercise lay in the ability to link to the preceding words while also opening up the possibilities for the next participant to move off in another direction. Sequences of up to 100 were common and although solo performances were possible, the norm was for four or five poets to cooperate in a session. Rulebooks were available to participants so that the anarchic flow of images could in some fashion be brought under control.

Na wa takaku koe wa ue nashi hototogisu
Famous your name, incomparable is your song, O cuckoo. BY GUSAI

The first stanza sets the season: cuckoo indicates summer. This is an auspicious image and is a tribute to Yoshimoto.

Shigeru ki nagara mina matsu no kaze
Thickly growing trees all wait – wind in the pines. BY YOSHIMOTO

Trees are associated with the cuckoo; the cuckoo's song is anxiously awaited; *matsu*, the word for 'pine tree' is homophonous with the verb 'wait for', so there is a subtle shift at this point; pine trees are auspicious.

Yamakage wa suzushiki mizu no nagare nite
Mountain shade, cool are the waters of the flowing stream. BY EIUN

Pine trees are associated with mountain shade, and wind in the pines forms a link with cool waters; the effect is to make one forget the stifling humid heat of summer.

Tsuki wa mine koso hajime narikere
Moonlight: the mountain peak is where its beauty first appears. BY SHŪA

The moonlight is suggested by the flowing waters, in which the moon often appears; the peak comes from association with mountain in the previous phrase; reference to the moon changes the season to autumn.

PTH

Tokugawa literature

The literary culture of this period is broadly characterized by a shift from manuscript to commercial woodblock printing (while still preserving the handwritten cursive element), which ended control over the production and appreciation of literature by the aristocracy or the Buddhist clergy and fostered the growth of popular culture based on literature as a commodity. As in Renaissance Europe, most works published during the first half-century of commercial printing were not new, but rather earlier products of aristocratic culture or oral storytelling. Thanks to lending libraries, commoners gained access to the hitherto closed world of the past, and by the second half of the 17th century, they themselves were producing poetry, fiction, and drama. This creative wave culminated in the Genroku age (*c.* 1680–1720), which produced the three most famous literary figures of the period: Matsuo Bashō (1644–94) in poetry, Ihara Saikaku (1642–93) in fiction, and Chikamatsu Monzaemon (1653–1725) in drama. It was, by and large, a new urban culture, the product of three great cities: Kyōto (population *c.* 350,000), Ōsaka (*c.* 350,000) and Edo (modern Tōkyō, *c.* 1,000,000).

Illustration from Young women of the world, *Ejima Kiseki (1717). This scene of everyday life, women drawing water, bathing and entertaining men, enlivens a book of light-hearted caricatures. We see here an early example of the habit of inserting snippets of dialogue into illustrations. The words above the woman washing the girl are not written on the wall behind; they are the words of the woman saying 'Now you must be a good girl'.*

The concept of the 'floating world' (*ukiyo*), inherited from medieval Japan, reveals something of Tokugawa popular aesthetics. Originally associated with Buddhism and signifying the world as suffering and existence as transitory, this pessimism was now turned on its head: if life is fleeting, then we should enjoy it while we can. The *Tales of the floating world* (1661) by Asai Ryōi (?–1691) was the first to revel in this difference. Ukiyobō, the priest-hero of the tale, renounces the world, but his route to enlightenment is through the pleasures of urban life. Ryōi satirizes the seriousness of samurai society and portrays the liveliness and varied pleasures of the townsman. Other writers, however, focussed on the frivolous or destructive aspects of human behaviour, especially eroticism and violence, in an openly escapist mode. The urban *ukiyo*, where one sought relief from social and moral strictures, was found in the pleasure quarters and the theatres, and both are therefore central to popular culture.

Nevertheless, Tokugawa Japan was dominated by an official, unsmiling Confucian ideology that took a clear position on the rôle of literature in society. Neither fiction nor drama were considered useful to state or citizen. Poetry (classical *waka* and Chinese verse, but not *haikai*) expressed human feelings in elegant language, and so was 'true'; but fiction and drama (i.e. 'invented stories') dealt too often with human weaknesses and so were both 'false'. The class system that placed merchant commoners at the bottom, even though many were wealthy and highly educated, and the official ideology that held popular fiction to be beyond the pale, created a tension, which helps explain the undercurrent of rebelliousness in so much popular writing of the time.

Haikai poetry

The extent of literacy in this period is unclear, but at least in the larger cities and castle towns, basic literacy and numeracy soon became essential for business. Contemporary fiction and drama leave the impression that by 1700, illiteracy, even among women, had become unusual in urban society. Commoners began to seek direct access to literature, and *haikai* poetry ('linked verse') became the route for anyone aspiring to enter the world of letters. *Haikai* was much freer in diction and range of topics than classical linked verse, and since each link was short, almost anyone could join in with relative ease. Amateurs usually 'apprenticed' themselves to masters who corrected their work and sometimes published their verses in edited collections.

Participation is an essential element of traditional Japanese artistic production whether poetry, fiction or drama. The separation of artist and audience, though possible with the advent of commercial publishing, was generally resisted. The Japanese preferred to participate actively by joining *haikai* circles, studying theatrical chanting and dance, and giving dramatic readings of popular fiction. *Haikai* was often an important vehicle for social intercourse. An amateur might even join a famous poet like Bashō or Buson for an evening of verse-making.

Bashō, the greatest *haikai* poet of all, led a modest existence in a hut on the bank of the Sumida River in Edo. He favoured long journeys with a single companion along the back roads of Japan, following in the tradition of wandering medieval poets like Saigyō. Bashō saw *haikai* as a spiritual Way in the Buddhist-inspired medieval tradition. For his livelihood, however, he too relied on communal linked-verse, and on his journeys he accepted the patronage of a network of amateur poets. His most famous travel diary, *The narrow road to the deep north* (published in 1702, although the journey was in 1689), has achieved the status of a classic thanks to the beauty of its individual verses and of the prose (*haibun*) that gives these verses their context. His poetry exploits the tension between the immediacy of the moment and the vastness of eternity.

Bashō's contemporary Ihara Saikaku, though himself a *haikai* poet and a traveller, represents a contrasting stream in popular literature. Saikaku was a commoner from Ōsaka who preferred the here and now of the floating world – its urban pleasure quarters and theatres, its ethic of living for the moment – without the obvious seriousness of one who situates himself, as Bashō did, within a long tradition. He headed Ōsaka's Danrin school of *haikai* poetry and was a virtuoso performer in solo linked-verse competitions. He could compose 100, 1,000, 10,000 and even more verses at a single sitting. Since Bashō left only about 1,000 verses in all, Saikaku's attitude stands in sharp contrast.

Haiku

What is now known today as 'haiku' emerged during the Tokugawa period as the result of the following process: single *waka* of 5–7–5–7–7 syllables were broken in two to produce verses of 5–7–5 and 7–7. These were then built up alternately into long chains of 36, 100 or even more links (*renga*), which were composed according to well-defined rules, either by a group of poets or by one person pretending to act as a group. This genre flourished in the 14th and 15th centuries. The light-hearted variety became known as *haikai no renga* (comic *renga*), or simply *haikai*. At first it was the ability to produce an interesting link that was prized, but gradually the first verse of a sequence, known as the *hokku*, achieved prominence as something that could stand on its own. These in turn were then gathered in collections. The present term 'haiku' came into use in the Meiji period and now refers to these stand-alone verses.

Two classic examples:

Bashō

Shizukasa ya	How still it is!
iwa ni shimiiru	Stinging into the stones
semi no koe	The locust's trill.

Buson

Yūkaze ya	The evening breezes
mizu aosagi no	The water splashes against
hagi wo utsu	A blue heron's shins.

RB

An example of Zen calligraphy, 17th century. Calligraphy was seen to reveal the state of inner mind of the artist-writer, and in turn it could be used as an aid to meditation. Here, reading from right to left, is the character for 'heart/mind' followed by a poem in Chinese. There is a deliberate contrast between the thick, heavy strokes on the right (alleviated by a flourish at the end of the diagonal) and the fluid, almost lazy, flow of the poem on the left.

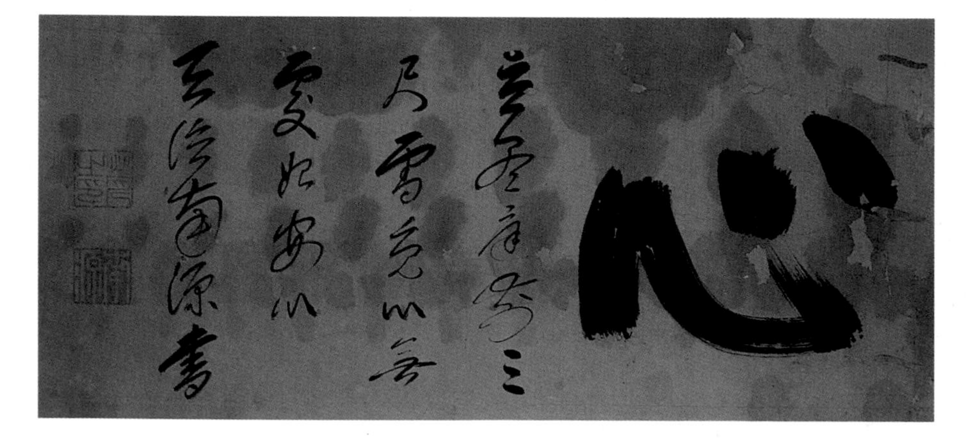

Fiction

Today, Saikaku is best known for his fiction. *The life of an amorous man* (1682) was his first work of fiction and a 'bestseller' in what became known as the genre of 'floating-world fiction' (*ukiyozōshi*). His models were *The tale of Genji* and the *Tales of Ise* with their amorous heroes, but parody, humour and a sharp focus on contemporary urban life give this and his other works a liveliness not encountered before in Japanese fiction. One sees here a parallel with the early English novel in the shape of Fielding. This work was followed by *Five women who loved love* (1686) and *The life of an amorous woman* (1686). Saikaku is a critic both of society's restrictions on human freedom and of human foolishness. Later works, such as *The eternal storehouse of Japan* (1688), focus on merchant life. He also wrote tales of homosexual love and samurai honour. An increasing trend toward introspection and pessimism is evident in his later works, as he shifts his focus from the prosperous few to the unsuccessful men and women who are crushed by the system.

Theatre

The dramatist Chikamatsu Monzaemon, who wrote over 100 plays for both the puppet theatre (*jōruri*) and kabuki in Kyōto and Ōsaka, is the third pillar of Genroku literature. Most of his works are history or period plays such as *The battles of Coxinga* (1715), but he is best known today for his contemporary-life dramas which depict current events with main characters drawn from various levels of society including the lowest. *The love suicides at Sonezaki* (1703), *Courier for hell* (1711), *Love suicides at Amijima* (1721) and *Woman-killer and the hell of oil* (1721) are among his most famous works. A major theme running through his plays is the plight of individuals caught between conflicting ethical and personal demands. In his history plays, heroes and heroines often face the ultimate demand, in the midst of a civil crisis, of sacrificing themselves or a loved one for the public welfare. Those directly involved in government, however, do not face such demands; it is almost always a lower or 'weaker' figure who must face the tragic choice. History plays, though set in

Interior of the Ichimura-za in Edo, 1744. Woodblock print by Okamura Masanobu. This gives a good impression of the depth of the stage, with all the extra perspective that this could offer. The scene is of a market with plenty of realistic props. An actor enters left through the audience along the hanamichi. *There are spectator boxes left and right in two tiers and down in the stalls people seem to be eating and drinking with only half an eye on the action. Quiet, solicitous audiences at Kabuki are only a very recent phenomenon.*

'Landscape with poet in boat'. Ink and light colour on paper. Yosa Buson (1716-84). The Chinese literati style adapted to Japanese taste. Chinese influence is directly referred to in the inscription top left, which reads 'Painted at Sankaen in the style of Jin-hong at Jin-ling'. An attempt has been made here to provide some depth by having the tree in the foreground hide part of the boat but the general impression is of flatness as the eye moves up the painting. Buson produced this work sometime in the 1760s.

the distant past, are, therefore, essentially about the current Tokugawa political system and its demands on the individual. Contemporary-life plays, though certainly critical of the social system, tend to focus on men and women whose inability to control their passion leads to tragedy. Chikamatsu's genius is to present these figures as both guilty for causing their own downfall and yet blameless in the sense that passion (*ninjō*) is the essence of the human condition.

THE SECOND CREATIVE WAVE

The second half of the 18th century saw the rise of Edo as a centre for the production of popular culture and by the end of the century it came to predominate. The 19th century is, in fact, the golden age of Edo kabuki with famous playwrights such as Tsuruya Nanboku (1755–1829) and Kawatake Mokuami (1816–93). Both men focussed primarily on low-life Edo society, including law-breakers, and drew on all aspects of earlier drama for their themes and theatrical techniques.

Significant revivals of both *haikai* and *waka* poetry took place in the mid 18th century as part of larger literati (*bunjin*) and scholarly movements, mostly in Kyōto and Ōsaka. Yosa Buson (1716–83), painter and poet, is the most famous figure of this generation. Buson's younger contemporary Ueda Akinari (1734–1809) is also a representative figure in that he faced a self-conscious conflict between the desire to produce serious art and the need to make a living. Akinari's most famous work, *Tales of moonlight and rain* (1776), shows the influence of Chinese fiction in its themes and of classical Japanese in its style. As an early example of *yomihon*, or 'book for reading', it represents a deliberate attempt to write more serious, intellectual fiction, in contrast to the earlier, more earthy style of Saikaku. The literary and aesthetic theories of this time often discuss the distinction between traditional 'high art', *ga*, and contemporary popular culture, *zoku*. All writers of poetry, prose or drama were acutely conscious of this *ga–zoku* dichotomy and of Confucian strictures on the essentially moral rôle of literature. The term *gesaku*, 'frivolous work', which encompasses most Edo popular literature of the late Tokugawa period, should be understood against this background: it is a mixture of true self-depreciation and smokescreen to avoid the pressures of censorship and included the various sub-genres of *sharebon* (pleasure-quarter fiction), *kibyōshi* (short illustrated satirical fiction), *kokkeibon* (longer humorous fiction), *gōkan* (illustrated stories of samurai adventures), and *yomihon* and *ninjōbon* (love stories set in Edo).

CAPTURING DAILY LIFE

Book illustration, even in colour, was not difficult or overly expensive because the same craftsmen carved both the blocks for the illustrations and for the text. In Tokugawa times, almost all fiction had illustrations interspersed with the text and in many cases the illustrations dominated the work. Until several decades into the 19th century, most Edo fiction was centred on city life, and since kabuki reigned supreme as the commoners' art, its influence on fiction was

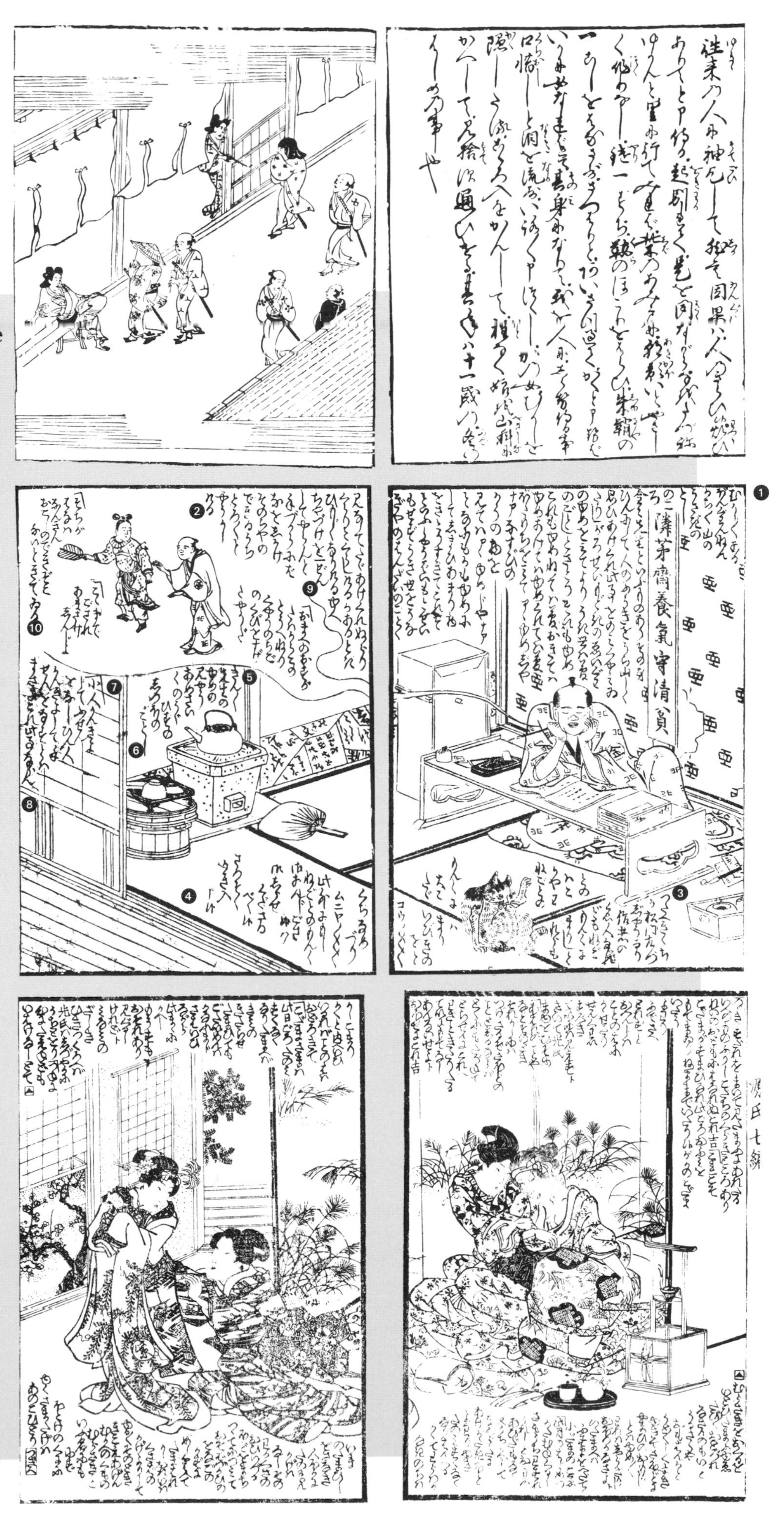

The visual excitement of the page

As one progresses through the Tokugawa period, there is increasing interaction between text and image. The first example here (top) is a straightforward illustration to a passage in Saikaku's *Life of an amorous man* (1682). The text on the right has been printed as a single block and so retains the flavour of handwriting.

By 1794, the date of this second example (centre) *Kinkin sensei zōka no yume*, full advantage is being taken of the fact that a page was cut as a single block. Indeed the whole spread is meant to be read as one. The reader is given a good deal of freedom as to the order of reading: one possible order has been marked here in numerical sequence, but it is by no means the only possible order: 1–2, 3–4, 5–6, 7–8, 9–10. The man is a chronic dreamer and this is in fact a sequel to a famous work published in 1775. 1–2 and 5–6 constitute the narrative. 7–8 and 9–10 are in the dream, despite the fact that 7–8 lies outside the 'balloon'. Section 3–4, which runs round the cat washing itself, is an authorial interjection: 'I hear say that Chikamatsu Monzaemon was a famous composer of puppet plays but suffered from complaints about his habit of talking in his sleep. I too am plagued by the problem, snoring like a pig and slobber, slobber. If you do happen to have any further complaints, I would very much like to be informed. Please excuse this hasty note.'

The third example (bottom) is from Ryūtei Tanehiko's love story *Nise Murasaki inaka Genji* (1832). Compared to the second example there is less textual complexity, but the relation between text and image is still intimate. Note the small black triangles top left and bottom right. These guide the reader around the page; they also indicate that the spread rather than the single page is the main 'unit' of reading. The small box bottom left reads: 'PTO'.

RB

all-pervasive. The language, plots, themes, characters and illustrations in the works of writers like Hiraga Gennai (1728–79), Santō Kyōden (1761–1816), Shikitei Sanba (1776–1822), Tamenaga Shunsui (1790–1843) and Ryūtei Tanehiko (1783–1842) all show this influence to a lesser or greater degree. Puppet theatre also provided a wide range of texts as models for language and stories.

Since the texts of kabuki plays were not published, commercial publishers filled the gap with critique books, actor prints and fiction. Much of this writing clearly participates in a complex discourse in which the oral element was vital. Oral storytelling and performance were an integral part of everyday Edo life. Popular texts were written for readers' ears, and readers were expected to read them aloud or at least hear them in their mind, complete with kabuki-style declamation or other storytelling techniques. Many texts indeed indicate how to stretch out the syllables in the kabuki style. Illustrations, too, portray the characters as though they were actors.

The genius of this style of writing was to capture the cadences of daily life, both in manners and language. Kyōden's many *kibyōshi*, Jippensha Ikku's (1765–1831) *Shank's mare* (1802–14), and Sanba's *Bathhouse of the floating world* (1809–13) are brilliant achievements of this style of 'performance fiction'. Shunsui's romances (*ninjōbon*) follow closely the love-story stream within the theatre and were aimed at a female readership.

Not all writers, however, sought their models in the 'floating world' of popular entertainment. A famous writer who left a wealth of writing about his life and ideas on fiction is Kyokutei Bakin (1767–1848). Bakin, like many other writers, grew up with *haikai* and puppet theatre, and then, under the tutelage of Kyōden, tried his hand at all the styles and genres of his age. His mature works, however, are long adventure stories, the best known of which is the monumental *Tale of eight dogs* (1814–42). Bakin looked to Chinese sources for inspiration and as a way to free himself from what he saw as the restricting influence of the performing arts on fiction. He maintained that fiction should exemplify Confucian morality. His 'eight dogs', for example, are metaphors for Confucian virtues such as benevolence and righteousness. Although no longer widely read, Bakin was a serious artist who reflected deeply on the rôle of literature in society. CAG

Modern literature

The beginning of the modern period is usually taken by literary historians to be the Meiji Restoration of 1868, although a true literary change can only be observed some two decades later, in the late 1880s. There is no such agreement, however, about the beginnings of 'contemporary' literature. Most historians use the end of the Pacific War in 1945 as the dividing line, and certainly the defeat brought a clear sense of a new beginning, which found its way into art and literature. Others avoid the issue by adopting the series of imperial reign names which still form the basis of the official calendar and speak of Meiji (1868–1912), Taishō (1912–26), Shōwa (1926–89), and Heisei (1989–) literature. A third variant regards the Great Kantō Earthquake of 1923, in which large parts of the old Tōkyō were destroyed, as the true break between the modern and the contemporary, yet the effects of the destruction on a number of authors then living in the Kantō region can hardly be compared with the trauma and the changes wrought in Japanese consciousness by the defeat in 1945.

Western impact

The 'modernization' of literature occurred as a result of direct contact with Western culture and with European literature in particular. At the beginning we find fictitious accounts of travels through the mysterious 'Far West' that Japanese readers were eager to learn about after the opening of the country; shortly afterwards these were followed by reports of actual travel. A growing stream of adaptations and translations of European works began to appear, so that by the late 1880s we find Japanese versions not only of Defoe's *Robinson Crusoe*, Thomas More's *Utopia*, the Bible and Rousseau's *Confessions*, but also of Schiller's *Wilhelm Tell*, and Shakespeare's *Hamlet*, *King Lear* and *The merchant of Venice*. With the whole of Western civilization to choose from, it is hardly surprising that by the turn of the century European classics were rubbing shoulders with the latest 'isms'. Mid-Meiji, between 1880 and 1890, was the heyday of the so-called 'political novel': a typical early mixture of premodern language and style wedded to material taken from the revolutionary history of Europe and America and informed by the 'message' of political education.

A basic prerequisite for a modern literature was the creation of a new form of language to bridge the gap between written and spoken styles. Inspired again by Western examples, this movement for the 'unification of speech and writing' first emerged in the writing of journalists. The changes took some time to become accepted and it was not until the early 1910s that reform of the language can be said to have taken proper root.

It was a theoretical essay by the scholar of English literature and writer Tsubouchi Shōyō (1859–1935) that marked the decisive step in the development of modern literature. In 'The essence of the novel' he argued for the autonomy and artistic integrity of fiction on the grounds that it yields insights into human behaviour and emotions by means of logically constructed plots and careful psychological characterization. This was a revolutionary concept, diametrically opposed to the moral and didactic principles that were supposed to govern popular fiction during the Tokugawa. It led in the end to a major shift by which prose fiction in the modern period moved to occupy a central position in literature, as it gradually became recognized to be an unrivalled tool for discussing and handling serious contemporary issues, something with which a young scholar could be proud to be associated.

In the field of poetry, which boasted an unbroken tradition of *waka* since the earliest imperial collections, of poetry in Chinese (*shi*), and of haiku, popular since the 17th century, attempts at a renewal start in the early 1880s. Translations from European poetry inspired a new Japanese-style free verse which produced its first highlight in the poetry collection 'Young shoots' (1897) by Shimazaki Tōson (1872–1943) as well as the works of Kanbara Ariake (1876–1952) and Kitahara Hakushū (1885–1942), whose poetry reflected the influence of European symbolism and marked the real beginning of modern-style poetry on the threshhold of the 20th century.

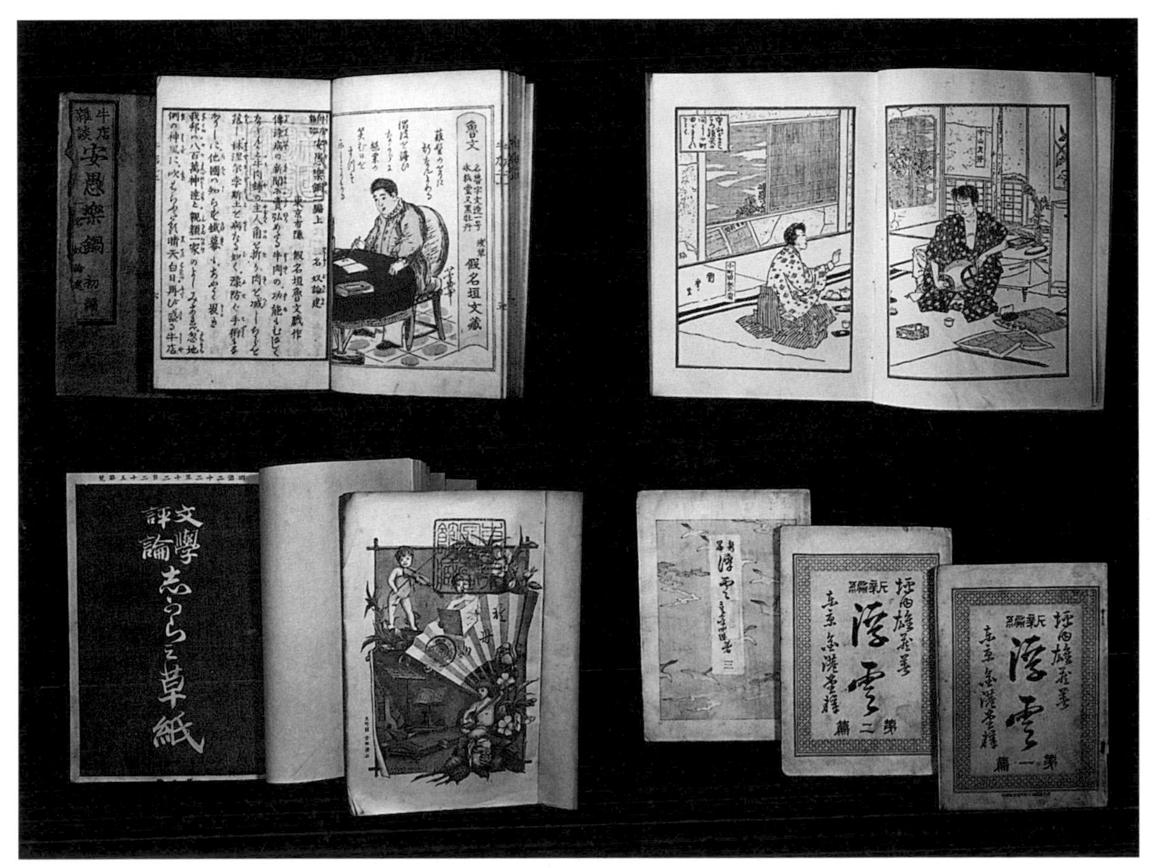

Literary products from the early Meiji period. An illustration from the satirical Aguranabe, *(The stew pot) which poked fun at the rage for everything Western (top left); a scene of students from Tsubouchi Shōyō's* Tōsei shosei katagi *(The character of modern students) (top right); covers of Mori Ōgai's collection of translated poetry* Omokage *and his journal of literary criticism* Shigaramizōshi *(bottom left); first edition of Futabatei Shimei's groundbreaking* Ukigumo *(bottom right).*

The famous illustration in Ozaki Kōyō's Konjiki yasha *(The golden demon, 1871) where the hero Hazama discards his woman for the sake of money.*

From 'realism' and 'romanticism' to 'naturalism'

The novel *The drifting clouds* (1887–88) by Futabatei Shimei (1864–1909) represents a remarkable, if somewhat precocious, achievement. It has been called Japan's first modern novel. With its new type of hero, a young Meiji intellectual disaffected with the brash modernism around him, its psychological realism and new language, this novel pointed the way forward.

To speak of 'realism' followed shortly afterwards by 'romanticism' and then 'naturalism', which flourished in the first decade of the 20th century, may provoke misunderstandings. Terms borrowed from European literary history take on different connotations in the Japanese context, and they remind us that within a few decades, Japanese writers tried a variety of styles and philosophies in their battle to understand what Western culture was and what it could offer them. Not that everyone turned their back on their own culture. The woman writer Higuchi Ichiyō (1872–96), for instance, who wrote less than two dozen stories, is famous for the way in which she succeeded in capturing this changing world within older stylistic patterns. She also stands for a revival of the feminine tradition within Japanese literature, which had almost died out since its first flowering in the Heian period.

The Romantic movement, centring on Kitamura Tōkoku (1868–94) who propagated the 'inner life' and who saw the importance of the individual in Western thought, was as influential as it was short-lived. The early novellas by Mori Ōgai (1862–1922), staged in Germany and inspired by German models, can also be classified as romantic. Ōgai, who studied medicine in Germany from 1884 to 1888, played an important rôle in introducing European literature through translations from the German, among them Naturalists such as Hauptmann, Ibsen and Strindberg, and it was he who coined the Japanese term for the 'Naturalist' movement which many historians see as marking the true beginnings of modern realist prose.

During the early years of this movement there was a desire to explore questions of heredity and social milieu and hence a nascent interest in social criticism, partly under the impact of Christian thought and socialist ideas that were absorbed by the young intellectuals. The most famous example is probably Tōson's first long novel, *The broken commandment* (1906), in which the social problem of a group of outcasts, the *burakumin*, forms the central theme. But this novel is written in the confessional mode and the narrative focus tends to shift away from social criticism *per se* to the private story and inner life of the central figure. This development was to become more and more marked in subsequent novels where the world is seen through only one pair of eyes, so giving rise to the genre known as *shishōsetsu*, a term which translates literally as 'I-story' but which is by no means limited to first-person fiction. This was to form a central narrative mode in modern and contemporary Japanese literature.

A notable exponent of the *shishōsetsu* was Shiga Naoya (1883–1971), co-founder with Mushanokōji Saneatsu (1885–1971) of the journal *White birch* and an idealistic circle propagating Tolstoyan humanism and self-perfection. Shiga's longest work, *A dark night's passing* (1921–37) depicts his hero's quest for inner harmony. The genre experienced another later peak in the stories of Dazai Osamu (1909–48) who presents a series of rebellious and self-destructive central figures.

Mori Ōgai in Germany

Mori Ōgai joined the army as a medical officer in order to be able to travel abroad. He arrived in Germany in October 1884 with a mandate to study army hygiene and worked in Leipzig, Dresden, Munich and Berlin for the next four years, returning to Japan in 1888. His real interests were more literary, however, and he spent much of his spare time absorbing European culture through the medium of German. For Meiji Japan he was to German literature what Futabatei Shimei was to Russian and Tsubouchi Shōyō was to English literature, but Ōgai ranged widest of them all. This resulted in some interesting trajectories: Byron, Hans Christian Andersen, Calderón and Shakespeare in the form of 'Macbeth' reaching Japan through the filter of a German version. Germany also brought a romantic attachment to a woman called Elise Weigert who followed Ōgai back to Japan. It took considerable pressure from his brother before she became persuaded that the family's precious eldest son was not for her. This affair lies behind Ōgai's first romantic *novelle* 'The dancing girl' (*Maihime*, 1890.)

Ōgai is shown here (right) in a studio photograph taken while he was in Munich, enjoying life to the full. The insouciant stance contrasts strongly with the more usual image of the hesitant Japanese writer abroad.

RB

Literature of social criticism and protest

The influx of Marxist and anarchist ideas stimulated a movement known as Proletarian literature (although few 'workers' were ever involved), which opened up new themes such as working conditions and the political concerns of the working class. This left-wing literary movement, based on the journal *The sowers* which was founded in 1921, only lasted a few years and was subsequently exhausted by internal conflict and increasing police pressure. The death of Kobayashi Takiji in 1933 while in police detention was a severe blow to the movement which counted among its members the poet Nakano Shigeharu (1902–79) and female authors Sata Ineko (b. 1904), Miyamoto Yuriko (1899–1951), and Hirabayashi Taiko (1905–72). The following year, 1934, saw the dissolution of the group, the majority recanting their 'mistaken', 'un-Japanese' views in public.

Women's issues were another focus of intellectual concern. The journal *Seitō* (*Bluestocking*, 1911–16), which, in spite of its title, aimed mainly at encouraging the creative talents of women, was supported, among others, by the already famous poetess Yosano Akiko (1878–1942), who from the first years of the century, had inspired traditional *waka* poetry with new life by the daring figurativeness and uncompromising passion of her lyricism.

Yosano Akiko (1878–1942) and *The tale of Genji*

Some people are one-book people; their lives and their work are dominated, usually with conscious complicity, by a single book. Yosano Akiko – hugely productive poet, essayist, educator, translator of classical Japanese literature into the modern language, and mother of 11 children – was one such person. She once said that she did not know how many times she had read *The tale of Genji* before she turned 20.

Akiko was probably the first female reader for whom a passionate attachment to the *Genji* was more than an avocation: her professional involvement with the work began early, soon developed into a significant source of income, occupied a steadily increasing amount of energy as it generated commissions on other classics, and in her latter years became the principal object of her attention. The fruits of this work include numerous articles on the life of Murasaki Shikibu; a series of lectures and poems; and a scholarly edition of the text. For 14 years between 1909 and 1923, she also worked on a commentary which, just short of completion, was totally destroyed in the fires that swept Tōkyō after the Great Kantō Earthquake of 1 September 1923.

More important, however, are two translations of the *Genji* into colloquial Japanese. The first, abbreviated version appeared in 1912–13; the second, complete version, was published in 1938–39. Like many of her contemporaries, Akiko thought of the *Genji* as Japan's greatest fiction and her translations were designed to be read from cover to cover, not pored over piecemeal.

GGR

MODERNISM AND AESTHETICISM

Among those writers who, like Ōgai, had travelled to the West the best known are perhaps Nagai Kafū (1879–1959) and Natsume Sōseki (1867–1916). Whereas Kafū's mixture of essay and fiction creates a nostalgic apotheosis for the dying culture of pre-modern Tōkyō, Sōseki, who wrote serial novels for the newspaper *Asahi shinbun*, focusses on the alienation of modern man in a world marked by the conflict between high moral aspiration and corruption. One of his protégés was Akutagawa Ryūnosuke (1892–1927), a brilliant stylist who mined medieval Japanese tale collections as a source of inspiration.

The 'Sensualist school' was a modernist movement, experimenting with new modes of expression under the influence of Western modernist currents such as futurism and surrealism. In the early work of its most famous exponent, Kawabata Yasunari (1899–1972), one finds stream of consciousness and constant overt allusions to Freud, modern medicine and science. Somewhat later, Kawabata was to turn back to the Japanese tradition for inspiration, in a pattern followed by many of his contemporaries. Tanizaki Jun'ichirō (1886–1965), who in his early years spoke much of Poe, Baudelaire, Wilde and 'art for art's sake', the critic and essayist Kobayashi Hideo (1902–83), the poet Hagiwara Sakutarō (1886–1942) and numerous others all returned to Japanese themes after a phase of intense interest in matters Western.

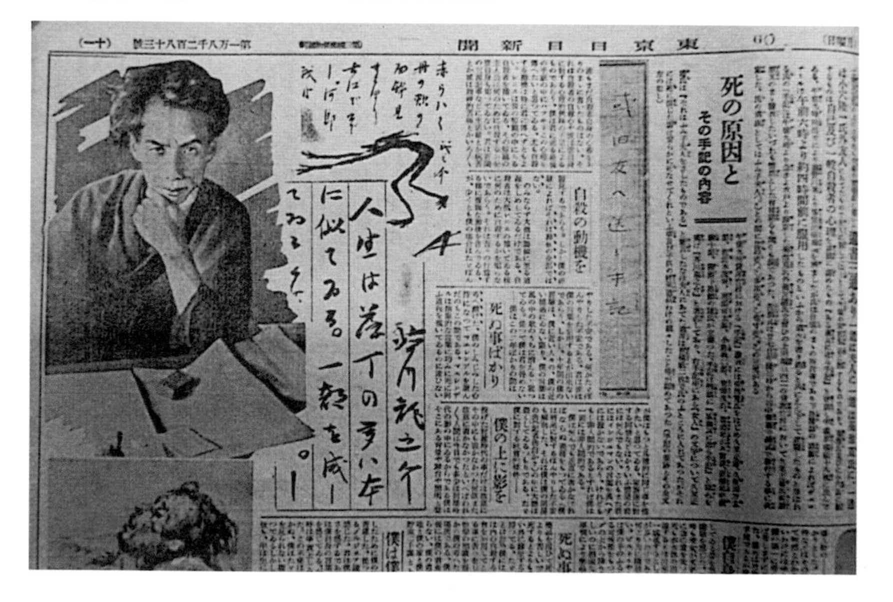
東京日日新聞

死の原因と
その手記の内容

自殺の動機を

死の事ばかり

僕の上に影を

The entry in the Tōkyō Nichi-nichi shinbun *recording the suicide of the writer Akutagawa Ryūnosuke in 1927. It reproduced his searing suicide note ('Note to a certain old friend') and a drawing of a* kappa.

Natsume Sōseki

Sōseki's novels are famous for their portrayal of haunted intellectuals. Here, near the end of *Kokoro*, in a long letter written to a young man, the central figure links his decision to die to the suicide of General Nogi, who 'followed after his lord' (*junshi*) on the death of the Emperor Meiji.

> It was two or three days later that I decided at last to commit suicide. Perhaps you will not understand clearly why I am about to die, no more than I can fully understand why General Nogi killed himself. You and I belong to different eras, and so we think differently. There is nothing we can do to bridge the gap between us. Of course, it may be more correct to say that we are different simply because we are two separate human beings. At any rate, I have done my best in the above narrative to make you understand this strange person that is myself.
>
> I am leaving my wife behind me. It is fortunate that she will have enough to live on after I am gone. I have no wish to give her a greater shock than is necessary. I intend to die in such a way that she will be spared the sight of my blood. I shall leave this world quietly while she is out of the house. I want her to think that I died suddenly, without reason. Perhaps she will think that I lost my mind: that will be all right.

RB

THE PACIFIC WAR AND AFTER

In many cases, this 'return to Japan' manifested itself in the writers' immersion in an idealized past, a move that was helped by the imposition of increasingly rigid censorship. Strict press laws and extensive 'counselling' since 1931 obliged authors to serve the state and eventually the war effort. Writers were organized into patriotic associations and sent to the front as reporters. Most of them co-operated willingly and wrote what was expected of them. Others responded either by turning to tradition for their material or to the narrow world of their private lives. Tanizaki, who had, like Yosano Akiko before him, produced a complete translation of *The tale of Genji* into modern Japanese, had to witness its suppression by censorship. Also suppressed was his novel *The Makioka sisters* in 1942, essentially because it depicted an elegant upper middle-class Ōsaka family in the

1930s and by and large ignored mention of the war effort. By August 1945, literary life was practically stifled, the more so as all of the important general and literary magazines, including those which had survived the rationing of paper since 1941, had undergone 'voluntary' liquidation.

To speak of a 'zero hour' in Japanese literature and life at the end of the war, however, would be to miss the point. There was something akin to a creative outburst in the early post-war years, when, in the midst of destruction and hunger, magazines were founded or re-established in great numbers and book production was resumed, giving the 'post-war generation' a platform for their works. Among these writers were Abe Kōbō (b. 1924) and Haniya Yutaka (b. 1910) whose abstract, experimental texts are labelled avant-garde, as well as writers who dealt directly with their wartime experience such as Ōoka Shōhei (1909–89) and Shimao Toshio (1917–86). Fiction in these early years also often dealt with the depressing reality of Japan in defeat. Poverty, hopelessness and moral disorientation form the basic mood in works of the so-called 'libertines'. One of the most popular novels of the time was Dazai Osamu's *The setting sun* (1947), which deals with the decline of an aristocratic family against the backdrop of post-war reforms.

Experiment and tradition

In retrospect, the early post-war period appears particularily prolific. Established writers like Kawabata published those works for which they are best known today – *Snow country* (1948), *A thousand cranes* (1951) and *The sound of the mountain* (1952–54) have attained the status of modern classics, as has Tanizaki's *The Makioka sisters*. In their fiction of the 1950s and 60s, these grand old men explored sexuality as a fundamental driving force of human action in the search for fulfilment, even in the face of death. In Tanizaki's sensational novels *The key* (1956) and *Diary of a mad old man* (1962), the quest for woman is directed by a subliminal longing for mother, whereas Kawabata's aestheticized ideal of a virginal young woman was raised to an extreme in the morbid contrast of youth and beauty versus age, decay and death in *Sleeping beauties* (1961). Both Tanizaki's eroticism and Kawabata's somewhat sanitized

Travelling by train at night

The following passage comes near the beginning of *Snow country* by Kawabata Yasunari. It is typical of his interest in tricks of perception and in surface textures. The story opens as Shimamura is travelling to a resort in the mountains.

> In the boredom, Shimamura stared at his left hand as the forefinger bent and unbent. Only this hand seemed to have a vital and immediate memory of the woman he was going to see. The more he tried to call up a clear picture of her, the more his memory failed him, the farther she faded away, leaving him nothing to catch and hold. In the midst of this uncertainty only the one hand, and in particular the forefinger, even now seemed damp from her touch, seemed to be pulling him back to her from afar. Taken with the strangeness of it, he brought the hand to his face, then quickly drew a line across the misted-over window. A woman's eye floated up before him. He almost called out in his astonishment. But he had been dreaming, and when he came to himself he saw that it was only the reflection in the window of the girl opposite. Outside it was growing dark, and the lights had been turned on in the train, transforming the window into a mirror. The mirror had been clouded over with steam until he drew that line across it. ...
>
> In the depths of the mirror the evening landscape moved by, the mirror and the reflected figures like motion pictures superimposed one on the other. The figures and the background were unrelated, and yet the figures, transparent and intangible, and the background, dim in the gathering darkness, melted together into a sort of symbolic world not of this world. Particularly when a light out in the mountains shone in the centre of the girl's face, Shimamura felt his chest rise at the inexpressible beauty of it.
>
> The mountain sky still carried traces of evening red. Individual shapes were clear far into the distance, but the monotonous mountain landscape, undistinguished for mile after mile, seemed all the more undistinguished for having lost its last traces of colour. There was nothing in it to catch the eye, and it seemed to flow along in a wide, unformed motion. That was of course because the girl's face was floating over it. Cut off by the face, the evening landscape moved steadily by around its outlines. The face too seemed transparent – but was it really transparent? Shimamura had the illusion that the evening landscape was actually passing over the face, and the flow did not stop to let him be sure it was not.

RB

aestheticism are seen to be the peak of an indigenous artistic sensuality and a lifestyle conscious of its roots, even though for both authors the implicit dialogue with the West is part of their intellectual and artistic identity.

Mishima Yukio (1925–70), well-known since his autobiographical *Confessions of a mask* of 1949, experimented with the adoption of European styles and forms from *fin de siècle* to Thomas Mann, from French classicism down to Radiguet and Mauriac, and attempted a synthesis of occidental and native narrative and dramatic traditions. Even though his carefully constructed and brilliantly laid-out stories and novels, which often take actual events as their material, were highly successful, the author felt increasingly dissatisfied and attempted a re-orientation which in the 1960s led him on a path of reactionary romanticism in his fiction, drama, and essays.

The first and second post-war generations were followed by writers who were less spectacular, less experimental, and who turned again to describing their private lives. They are regarded as the heirs to the *shishōsetsu* genre which they enriched thematically as well as technically. These 'third newcomers', writers such as Endō Shūsaku (b. 1923), Yoshiyuki Junnosuke (b. 1924), Kojima Nobuo (b. 1915) and others, vary widely in style and literary concern. Endō's central theme is Christianity in Japan and the resulting cultural conflict in both contemporary and historical contexts.

The general liberalization and the widening of the literary market in the post-war period opened the scene to a larger number of women writers. Enchi Fumiko (1905–86) who began as a theatre writer in the 1920s, experienced her final breakthrough with novels dealing with the difficult position of women in a patriarchal system. Uno Chiyo (b. 1897), the notorious 'new woman' of the 1920s, as well as Sata Ineko and Nogami Yaeko (1885–1985), all prolific into old age, are other *grandes dames* of Japanese fiction. In the 1960s, we have the emergence of Kurahashi Yumiko (b. 1935) who won attention for her highly abstract prose and unabashed treatment of sexual themes such as incest, while Kōno Taeko (b. 1926) with a sharp eye for detail draws a picture of frustrated wishes and daring obsessions in the uneventful life of ordinary people. Ōba Minako (b. 1930) explores female identity and a new relationship between the sexes in a dense sequence of works from 1968. She lived in Alaska for many years, so intercultural experiences form another focus of her creativity.

Prosperity and engagement

The period of high economic growth which began after the end of post-war reconstruction in the mid 1950s and ended in 1973, was also marked by a wave of politicization which originated in the public protests against the renewal of the US–Japan Security Treaty in 1960. Political themes figure prominently in the writing of Kaikō Ken (1930–89) and Oda Makoto (b. 1932) who, like the female writer Ariyoshi Sawako (1931–84), made the most of extensive experience abroad.

Three important writers of the mid twentieth century.
Left *Dazai Osamu (1909-48), who created in his pre- and post-Pacific War writings a self-destructive persona in scintillating prose. It exactly caught the mood of depression and loss in the years immediately following the surrender. Dazai managed to kill himself after numerous attempts.*
Centre *Kawabata Yasunari, who won the Nobel prize for literature in 1968. He died by gassing himself only four years later. Some have argued that if Mishima Yukio had won the prize, both Mishima and Kawabata might have survived into quiet old age.*
Right *The writer Mishima Yukio in his own carefully designed military uniformı haranguing troops from the Self-Defence Forces just prior to committing suicide by disembowelment (*seppuku*), 1970.*

Ōe Kenzaburō (b. 1935) who had entered the literary stage in the late 1950s, is considered a representative of Japanese *littérature engagée*. In his early works, his narrative interest is in outsiders. His existentialist young anti-heroes, who grow in age with their author, dream of political change but they can only act out their unfulfilled desires in aggressive and brutal sexuality. In two stories published in 1961, Ōe provided a parodistic answer to Mishima's famous 'Patriotism' of 1960, where eroticism and chauvinism are seen to be one. Mishima's carefully planned suicide by *seppuku* with members of his private student army symbolizes, as a bizarre anachronism, an extreme form of the often aesthetically motivated politicization of art at the end of the decade.

The whole subject of the dropping of the atomic bombs at the end of the Pacific War has been a topic of autobiographical writing since 1945. In the early stages this theme was censored by the Occupation authorities. In its second phase in the 1960s, 'atomic bomb literature', as it is called, was also produced by authors who were not immediate witnesses. Ōe, with his reportage *Hiroshima notes* (1965), or Ibuse Masuji with his novel *Black rain* (1965), which has since been the basis of several film versions, are good examples.

Meanwhile it was the women who took up the challenge and started writing about social problems. Ishimure Michiko's (b. 1927) account of the sufferings of the victims of mercury pollution in Minamata, for instance, is sustained by a genuinely literary amalgam of chronicle, imaginary biography, statements of figures in rhythmical dialect and reportage. Ariyoshi, who also dealt with pollution, achieved her greatest success with *The twilight years* in 1972, a novel exploring the problems of care in old age; only after her book was written did old age really become an issue of public concern.

In 1968, Kawabata was awarded the Nobel Prize, the second Asian writer after the Indian Tagore. To the Japanese this was an important milestone in winning international recognition. Writers in Japan are public figures, and they may even, like Mishima or the author of grotesque novels, Nosaka Akiyuki (b. 1930), use the media for their own narcissistic showmanship. Appearance in TV commercials is very far from being taboo for an established Japanese author.

The early 1970s, however, also saw the rise of a new 'introverted generation', a heterogeneous array of authors who have in common only a tendency to retreat to private and inner worlds. Among the leading writers are Furui Yoshikichi (b.1937) and Ogawa Kunio (b. 1927); and the genre of *shishōsetsu* continues to be important with the works of Miura Tetsuo (b. 1931) and Shimao Toshio's monumental *The thorn of death*, completed after more than 17 years in 1977. In the autobiographical works of Tsushima Yūko (b. 1947), daughter of Dazai Osamu, female life patterns, motherhood, and her own childhood with her handicapped brother form thematic clusters.

Other modern and post-modern writing

The end of the 1970s brought the 'generation of the void', a term referring to those writers born after 1950, brought up in an affluent society and articulating a new hedonism. The fact that Murakami Ryū's (b. 1952) novel *Almost transparent blue* was awarded the prestigious Akutagawa Prize in 1976 triggered a heated debate about the disappearing boundaries between so-called 'pure' literature and its popular, commercialized counterpart. It cannot be denied, however, that since the post-war period, 'pure' literature has also undergone commercialization on a large scale.

In this literature, directed solely towards the here and now and a feeling of well-being within the narrow world of the young central figure, Tanaka Yasuo's (b. 1956) best-selling *Somehow crystalline* (1981), a novel flooded with annotated brand-names, formed a first peak. Other extremely popular writers are Yamada Eimi (b. 1959) and Yoshimoto Banana (b. 1964), both female idols of a young and mainly female readership in their own age group. Among the commercially more successful writers is Murakami Haruki (b. 1949), a prolific translator of American authors such as Brautigan, Chandler and Vonnegut who prefers to live abroad. Since his first novel *Hear the wind sing* (1979), he has continued to depict the life of a young hero from the 1960s in a series of nostalgic novels reminiscent of the style of his non-Japanese models.

For many generations, the notion of Japanese literature had contained the simple equation of an

Four very different modern literary talents. Enchi Fumiko (bottom right) is now dead, but the other three are still highly productive. Kurahashi Yumiko (top left) explores sexual themes within the family with disturbing openness. Ōe Kenzaburō (top right) mixes political awareness and distrust of the right with a concern for abnormal mental states. Endō Shūsaku (bottom left) has as his main theme the extraordinary difficulty that Christianity has had in taking root in Japan.

ethnically Japanese author writing in Japanese. The notion now grows more complex, however, with the emergence of Korean writers living in Japan such as Lee Hwe-song (b. 1935), Kim Sok-pong (b. 1925) and the woman writer Lee Yang-ji (b. 1955), whose common theme is the dilemma of the dispossessed.

Contemporary Japanese culture has been termed typically post-modern, but in most authors, be it Ōba or Kurahashi, Ōe or Nakagami Kenji (b. 1946), one can also detect the rediscovery of myth and folk-traditions. There is also an astonishing degree of interest in the 'classics', not all of which can be put down to the exigencies of the education system. Modern authors have a genuine interest in all aspects of traditional writing and often write their own appreciations and commentaries.

Such an unbroken tradition is most conspicuous in the field of poetry. Traditional forms such as haiku and *tanka* are practised by a wide section of the population organized in numerous circles. For haiku alone, more than 700 periodicals and approximately 1,000 book titles appear per annum, testimony to the enormous popularity of the genre.

All these forms are limited in length, are generally rule-bound and do not allow much innovation. Nevertheless, the enormous success of Tawara Machi's (b. 1962) *tanka* collection *Salad anniversary* in 1987 demonstrates, like the custom of regular poetry columns and comment in the major newspapers, the vitality of a popular poetic practice which is understood as a playful pastime, edification and life guidance.

Modern free verse (*shi*), which resulted from the encounter with the West, is incomparably much wider in formal and thematic scope than these older forms. After the Pacific War, a circle called 'Arechi' (The Waste Land) developed an *avant-garde* style modelled after T. S. Eliot and W. H. Auden, whereas the group 'Rettō' (Archipelago), founded in 1952, was composed of professional poets who nevertheless took care to encourage a number of amateur circles. Japanese free verse, which during the 1960s assumed a more political and critical stance, gradually moved away from dependence on the group. From among the countless individual styles, mention can only be made of the female poets Shiraishi Kazuko (b. 1931), Tomioka Taeko (b. 1935), Kanai Mieko (b. 1947), and Itō Hiromi (b. 1955), who enrich the world of modern *shi* with their bold feminist imagination.

Seen from a Western perspective, contemporary Japanese fiction may appear stylistically conservative, but then this form of originality is not as important an element of literary poetics as it is in the West. On the other hand, it is precisely these traditional elements that appear most contemporary to the Western reader – a seemingly loose narrative structure which favours the fragmentary and episodic and which avoids the impression of a planned architecture and climax associated with artificiality. Another characteristic feature inherited from premodern tradition is the blurred boundary between genres such as fiction and essay. Critics and essayists such as Kobayashi Hideo or the Marxist philosopher Yoshimoto Ryūmei (b. 1924), father of the fashionable Yoshimoto Banana, are dealt with in the context of literature. On the other hand, the majority of fiction writers also produce essay-like works, and in many others, such as Yasuoka Shōtarō's (b. 1920) *My history of the Shōwa Era* (1982–88), fiction merges with essay, documentary and memoir. Japanese contemporary literature, for all its interconnectedness with the West, obviously presents another 'modern'. Among non-Western literatures, it also appears to be the one most translated into Western languages and thus it occupies a key position. Since the beginning of this century it has taken on the rôle of mediator between the West and other East Asian literatures. One gradually begins to understand its paradigmatic significance: its basic theme has been the dialogue between Orient and Occident, between the indigenous and the alien. IH-K

Salad anniversary

Traditional literary forms have proven to be remarkably resilient in Japan and perhaps none more so than the short *waka* poem. In May 1987 a 26-year old high-school teacher called Tawara Machi published a carefully crafted sequence of love poems entitled *Salad anniversary*. It immediately became a best-seller and as of early 1992 had sold over 2.6 million copies.

The appeal is partly in the bitter-sweet quality of the relationship depicted, partly in the ironic, almost world-weary, stance taken by the woman, and partly in the skill with which Tawara interweaves intensely modern words and phrases with a classical form and a classical grammar. The effect is not unlike that of the English poet John Betjeman, although in a very different context. The love affair portrayed is the age-old one of 'first love' leading to eventual sad parting, with loneliness as the main refrain.

Tawara clearly hit the right chord, for she also received over 200,000 poems written in response to her work, and a selection of these has also been published. Some might see in this commodification of poetry a typical example of how art can degenerate into bland sentiment, but there is also something heartening in such a massive spontaneous reaction to feelings expressed in a poetic form that goes back to the beginnings of literature. What follows is a short part of the opening sequence.

'Call me again' 'Wait for me'
Your love is always spoken
in commands

Glancing up at the falling rain
suddenly I want
your lips

Escape from a shower into a street stall
and drink a glass of cheap saké—
fun to be alive

The woman in the street stall
calls me your wife—
and so, for a while, I am

RB

大王窟

Thought and religion

Shintō and folk religion

Previous page *A country shrine. Holy places are often marked out with the* shimenawa, *a rope of twisted rice straw.*

Right *Offerings at a shrine. These are strings of tiny origami cranes in assorted colours. The crane is a symbol of long life and good fortune.*

Below *The* torii, *or shrine gate, of the Itsukushima Shrine near Hiroshima. The supports here are unusual, but the basic shape and colour are the same throughout Japan. This shrine was first built in the 12th century by Taira no Kiyomori. Since much of it stands in a bay, it appears to be floating in the water at high tide.*

Shintō is the name given to the religious cults which existed in Japan before the arrival of Buddhism and which have survived with remarkably little change until the present day. The single term 'Shintō' implies homogeneity, and the mythology generated in the Meiji period encouraged the belief that Shintō was the single immemorial heritage of the Japanese people. Although written sources are scanty, it is nevertheless clear from the evidence of archaeology, of surviving cult practice and of the motifs of myth and legend, that a variety of religious cults, deriving from different geographical sources, were alive in Japan in the late 6th century AD. The ideas of cosmology, of the fate of the dead and of the divinities worshipped all attest to origins in various parts of the Asian continent and in the Malayo–Polynesian areas of the south. Early Shintō, like the Japanese race and language, is thus the result of a mingling of traditions in prehistoric times. Despite this mixed origin, however, and despite the fact that it consequently lacks a single founder and a central corpus of scriptural writing, Shintō acquired a strength and persistency which has enabled it to survive to the present day with many of its ancient features unchanged.

Objects of worship: the *kami*

The principal objects of worship in Shintō from the earliest times until the present are the divinities known as *kami*. These are shadowy, formless entities, largely devoid of personality and resembling rather impersonal manifestations of power. All are considered superior to people in knowledge and powers, holding in their gift that area of life which is outside human control. The *kami* fall into several distinct types, which were probably originally distinguished by separate names, but all have the following characteristics in common.

First, they have no shape of their own. To manifest themselves they must be summoned or cajoled into a vessel of suitably inviting form. These vessels, known as *yorishiro*, are frequently long and thin: trees, wands, banners or long stones are common. The earliest dolls in Japan were not playthings, but objects in which the *kami* might find temporary residence. Certain psychically gifted people have likewise acted as mediums or vehicles for the *kami* since ancient times. Such religious specialists act as important bridges between the *kami* and the human world. Usually women, and known as *miko*, they have the added advantages as vehicles that their voices may be 'borrowed' by the *kami* for messages or answers to questions.

Second, the *kami* are inherently non-moral. They are powers who will respond either favourably or unfavourably to the human community according to the treatment they receive. Treat them well, with proper rituals, offerings and cult attention, and they can be expected to respond with blessings in the form of good rice harvests, protection from fire, famine, and disease, and flourishing progeny. Neglect them, or offend them by exposing them to the pollutions they dislike, and at once they will blast the community with *tatari*, or curses.

Third, the *kami* inhabit a 'world' of their own, but can be summoned to visit the human world at certain seasons. The principal Shintō ritual is the *matsuri*, in which the *kami* are summoned by music, dance and magic words to leave their world and descend to the village shrine. They are welcomed, entertained, asked for blessings, sometimes questioned, before being sent back to their proper realms. *Kami* are also capable of 'possessing' human beings and willy-nilly using them for their own purposes.

Ise pilgrimages

The two Shintō shrines at Ise are among the most important in Japan. The Inner Shrine, which may date from as early as the 3rd century, is dedicated to the Sun Goddess Amaterasu, the mythical progenitor of the imperial house, and the Outer Shrine, which is of later origin, is dedicated to the god who provided Amaterasu with her daily needs. In the 15th century, shrine employees began to travel the length of the land soliciting donations and promising blessings to those who undertook a pilgrimage to Ise. During the Tokugawa period pilgrimages became very popular and it was widely believed that people should visit Ise once in their lifetime. Large numbers flocked there, either singly or in family groups, or alternatively as members of *kō*, or pilgrimage associations. Pilgrims were particularly numerous in the thanksgiving years following the reconstruction of the Inner Shrine every 20 years, and in the course of the Tokugawa period there were also four mass pilgrimages, in 1650, 1705, 1771, and 1830. They were sparked off by rumours of amulets falling from heaven; the enthusiasm infected large parts of the country and millions spontaneously took to the road heading for Ise. CB

Fourth, most *kami* have in common a dislike of the pollutions of blood, dirt and death. Here their non-moral nature asserts itself. It is not moral sin that offends them any more than it is moral virtue that pleases them. It is the *kegare* or ritual pollutions which arise unavoidably in the course of human life that offend them. They are offended by blood, particularly by the internal blood generated at human birth and by women's menstruation, and by the effluvia of death. Thus no one who has suffered death in the family may approach a shrine for a stated number of days. Women are likewise debarred from visiting a shrine during their *akafujo*, or 'red pollution', and for a certain period after giving birth.

Lastly the *kami* are regarded as bestowers of external material blessings, not as revealers of interior or ultimate truth. Some *kami* can be petitioned for a wide range of favours; others specialize in one particular gift, the cure of a certain sickness, the arrangement of a happy marriage, or the gift of poetry.

Types of *kami*

For more than a millennium the divinities known as *kami* have been central to the rituals of Shintō. *Kami* appear in a number of distinct types, five of which may be usefully distinguished.

- Those which reside in natural objects, such as huge trees, oddly-shaped stones or certain mountains. The holy presence is perceived by a person with second sight, and the object thereafter given appropriate cult attention.

- Those which preside over certain crafts or skills, and bestow special excellence on the practitioner. Fishermen, mountain hunters, swordsmiths, woodworkers all have their special or patron *kami* who bring them fortune and skill. The swordsmith thus owes any flawless perfection he achieves to a supernatural gift.

- The *ujigami* on the other hand confine their protection to a certain family, or by extension, village. They are usually anonymous, but are probably the deified ancestor of the founder of the family or village.

- By contrast the *ikigami* or *hitogami* are *kami* who either are or were human beings.

  Ikigami are men and women who are worshipped as *kami* while they are still alive. Examples are religious specialists such as *miko* who by severe ascetic practices have achieved the condition of union with a particular *kami*, and are regarded as its earthly embodiment. Many founders of new religious groups in modern times are regarded as *ikigami*. The emperor used to be regarded as an *ikigami*, but he renounced this status in January 1946.

  Hitogami are people who are worshipped as *kami* after their death. Often they have died violent or untoward deaths, as a result of which their angry ghost caused a sequence of disasters. Ritual apotheosis into a *kami* of high rank is an effective means of turning the destructive powers of the ghost into a beneficial force ready to help mankind. Kitano Tenjin, who was originally the angry ghost of the learned scholar Sugawara no Michizane, and who after apotheosis is ever ready to help students pass their examinations, is an example.

- The *kami* who feature in the first book of the *Kojiki*, the ancient chronicles of Japan, and are the protagonists of the official mythology, are yet another class. These include the Sun Goddess Amaterasu, who is worshipped at the Ise shrines as the ancestor of the imperial house; the creators of the Japanese islands, Izanagi and Izanami; and the turbulent divinity Susanoo.

  Originally the deities of the Yamato people and their royal line, they were raised to prominence by the new mythology promulgated in the Meiji period. Before that time they were unknown in many parts of Japan.

CB

The spirits of the dead

Spirits of the dead are known as *tama* or *tamashii*. The *tama* resides in a host, to whom it imparts life and energy, but will detach itself in illness and leave permanently at death. It then requires nourishment by the living if it is to achieve its proper state of rest and salvation. For 33 years the surviving family of the dead spirit must therefore see that the correct *kuyō* or requiem obsequies are observed: food offerings, visits to the grave, and ritually powerful words. After 33 years the spirit is believed to lose its individual nature and to merge with the corporate ancestor in which all past forebears of the family are comprised. The ancestor and those 'newer' spirits who are properly nourished by cult attention are thus benevolent and protective. They can be expected to bless and protect their descendants. If the due offerings are neglected, however, the spirit will instantly turn malevolent, ruthlessly punishing its offending family with curses.

Discontented dead spirits, a potent source of disaster in society, are of three kinds. In addition to those who are neglected before their 33 years are up, there are those spirits who die without any surviving family. These wander the earth, starved of offerings and a source of danger to all. Most dangerous of all, however, are those spirits who die a violent or disgraceful death, with rage or resentment in their hearts. These will become angry spirits, and require for their appeasement measures stronger than ordinary obsequies. Apotheosis into a *kami* of high rank is the most effective means of pacifying them.

The relationship between *tama* and *kami* is still a matter of dispute. Yanagita Kunio, the great pioneer investigator of folk religion and folklore in Japan, believed that all *kami* originated from dead ancestral spirits. Others however believe that *tama* and *kami* were originally separate entities requiring different modes of worship.

The destination of the dead

Beliefs as to the destination of the dead in Shintō reflect the multiple origins of the early cult, for traces of more than one tradition are discernible. The myths in the first book of the *Kojiki* reflect the vertical cosmos found in north and central Asia in which

Inari

Inari is said to be the most popular *kami* in Japan, with more shrines dedicated to him than any other divinity: there are some 40,000 officially recognized Inari shrines, not including the innumerable small ones in homes and in country districts. Primarily associated with rice and the fecundity of cereals, he also appears in many other guises: as a tutelary deity in households, as a guardian of metal-workers, and as a patron of the drink and entertainment world. In the Tokugawa period he was particularly popular with the merchant class in the towns, who looked to him for commercial success. Images of foxes are a prominent feature of Inari shrines, for in medieval Japan the idea took root that the fox was the messenger of Inari, and this is the origin of the mistaken belief that he is the 'fox god'. The largest Inari shrine is at Fushimi, south of Kyōto, where pilgrim routes up the mountain behind the shrine itself are lined with red wooden *torii*, or ceremonial gateways, donated by individuals or by commercial companies in token of thanks for, or in hope of, blessings and good luck. CB

the human world stands midway between a high, bright, pure upper world, Takamagahara, and a dark polluted world known as Yomi, to which the dead were believed to go, irrespective of the quality of their lives. Traces of an older belief in a horizontal cosmos, probably deriving from a south-east Asian source, survive in certain seasonal rituals. Here the dead go to a land across the sea called Tokoyo, whence they return at certain seasons as bringers of blessings, fecundity and luck. These are the *marebito*, the supernatural visitors who were welcomed at New Year and harvest time and who, if correctly treated, would bless the harvest and the fortunes of the village. Traces of such beliefs survive in folk customs in which masked figures visit houses at harvest time, and distribute blessings in return for a feast of wine and fish.

In many parts of Japan the dead are believed to go to the tops of certain holy mountains. Such mountains are distinguished by their conical, symmetrical shape, prominent examples being Mt Fuji and Kiso Ontake. Such mountains were usually taboo until 'opened' by various Buddhist ascetic saints. A shrine at the foot of the mountain offered the dead ritual attention, and the belief that the dead return from these places at stated seasons to bless and succour their families is still widespread. New Year and Bon were the traditional seasons for welcoming back the dead, though New Year has now lost this character. At the Bon festival, in August, the ancestors are welcomed, entertained with special dances, songs and offerings of food, and at the conclusion of their visit lighted back to their world with lanterns or bonfires.

None of these beliefs about the destination of the dead embrace the ethical polarization that occurs in Buddhist eschatology, where the good go to an agreeable heaven and the wicked to some realm of a complex hell. All dead spirits seem to have been consigned indiscriminately to Yomi, Tokoyo or the holy hills, irrespective of the moral quality of their previous lives.

Ascetic practices

Ascetic practices are often attributed entirely to Buddhist influence, but it is preferable to see such practices as originating in pre-Buddhist times in the figure of the *hijiri*. The *hijiri* undertook various penances such as isolation from the world, a diet consisting of the products of trees, the cold-water

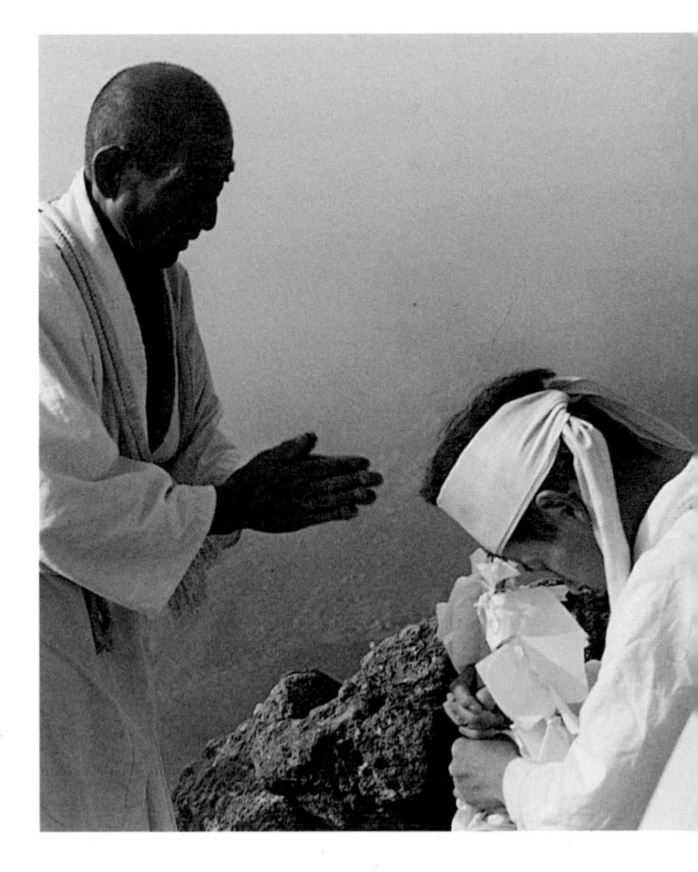

Shugendō practitioners on Mt Ontake. Having climbed all the way up on foot they then carry out rituals on the summit.

penance in winter, and repetition of holy formulae, in order to achieve union and fusion with a *kami*. In later centuries these austerities were easily assimilated with Buddhist practices of a similar kind, so that a number of mixed religious orders developed. Shugendō, whose members practise a régime of austerities in the fastnesses of holy mountains, is the most prominent and long-lived of such groups.

The later development of Shintō

From the Heian period onwards Shintō was fused into a viable syncretism with Buddhism, each religion compensating for what seemed to be the deficiencies of the other. Several systems were devised to give philosophical and doctrinal credibility to this mixed cult. Prominent among these was the *honji-suijaku* doctrine, by which all *kami* were described as temporary manifestations of 'original' buddhas or bodhisattvas. To worship a *kami* was thus no different from worshipping a bodhisattva. Buddhist icons appeared in shrines, and Shintō *kami*, both male and female, were for the first time represented in iconic form, usually in court dress. In the Ryōbu Shintō system the Buddha Dainichi, traditionally associated with the sun, was conveniently identified with the Sun Goddess Amaterasu.

During the Tokugawa period Shintō moved in the opposite direction, away from Buddhism, and a number of thinkers sought to reconcile Shintō with Neo-Confucianism, starting with Hayashi Razan early in the 17th century. Razan, who was the Confucian adviser to the shōgun Tokugawa Ieyasu and his successors, wrote several works on Shintō in which he abhorred the influence of Buddhism. Later, Yamazaki Ansai, who had turned his back on the Zen Buddhism in which he had been trained, led a revival of Shintō which emphasized its compatibility with Neo-Confucianism and associated it unequivocally with loyalty to the emperor. In the school of thought known as National Learning there was a parallel movement back to Shintō, especially in the writings of Motoori Norinaga, who argued that Japan would have been better off without the influence of Chinese culture or the religion that had accompanied it to Japan, Buddhism. In the 19th century the political implications of Norinaga's writings were spelled out by Hirata Atsutane (1776–1843) and others who favoured a return to imperial rule and to Shintō as the faith that derived from it. Atsutane was strongly nationalist in his views and his writings have a xenophobic quality.

In 1870 the new Meiji Government proclaimed the separation of *kami* and buddhas. In an attempt to purify native Japanese Shintō of the influence of foreign creeds, legislation was passed which abolished

Daijōsai – the enthronement ceremonies

Daijōsai, 'The great festival of tasting the first fruits', is the religious part of the Japanese accession ceremonies: it is a Shintō ritual performed after the official enthronement ceremony in the grounds of the imperial palace in wooden buildings erected specially for the occasion and destroyed soon afterwards. It culminates in a secret night-time ceremony during which the new emperor partakes of the first fruits of the harvest in communion with the *kami*.

The Daijōsai ceremonies were formed around 690 and so coincided with the formation of a centralized state and with the compilation of the first official state histories. Like them, the Daijōsai had political concerns: the adaptation and dramatization of a harvest ritual functioned to illustrate the relationship between the emperor and his subjects and to enforce the idea of a nation unified under the supreme rule of the emperor. The meaning of the Daijōsai changed as did the meaning of the imperial system and from 1467 to 1687 it was discontinued. The Tokugawa shōgunate sanctioned its revival, but only as a private function of the court, entirely hidden from public gaze. From the Meiji period the accession ceremonies were used to bring the emperor back into public attention and to make the populace recognize him as 'the central manifestation of Japan's unique culture and spirituality'. A new meaning was attached to the Daijōsai: the emperor was said to be imbued with an immortal, unchangeable imperial soul during the ritual, thus becoming a living god.

The enthronement of Emperor Akihito in 1990 was the first under the post-war constitution, which had stripped the emperor of his political power and divine status and stipulated the separation of religion and state. Nevertheless, the government took the controversial decision to perform the Daijōsai and even to subsidize it to the extent of £10 million, despite the fact that legislation in 1969 defined religious ceremonies performed by the emperor as 'private functions' of the court.

NL

The Sanja festival in Asakusa, Tōkyō: a portable shrine, or mikoshi, *is the usual focus of the excitement during a festival as the shrine deities are taken for a bumpy ride around their 'patch'.*

all shrines, cults and groups in which Buddhist elements were mingled with Shintō. Shugendō was proscribed as a mixed cult, and its members persecuted and imprisoned. Old shrines, such as Atagosan with its familiar 'mixed' divinity Shōgun Jizō, were destroyed, and unfamiliar 'pure' *kami* substituted. Many Buddhist temples were forcibly converted into Shintō shrines, their statues were melted down, and their monks forced to return to lay life.

In this way the familiar mixed cult of Shintō, thoroughly integrated into Japanese life through centuries of natural growth, was replaced by State Shintō, in which the government deliberately fostered certain Shintō rites and institutions with the intention of creating a national ideology in accordance with the slogan *saisei-itchi*, unity of religion and government. The cult of the emperor was given central importance. Shintō priests were made civil servants, and Shintō shrines were made instruments of state. Paramount among these were the Ise Shrines, where the Sun Goddess Amaterasu was worshipped as imperial ancestress, and the Yasukuni Shrine where the spirits of soldiers killed in the service of the emperor were enshrined. Forcible attendance at these shrines was demanded, despite the constitutional guarantee of freedom of religion, on the grounds that State Shintō was not a 'religion'. State Shintō died in December 1945, when General MacArthur, the head of the US occupation forces, issued his Shintō Directive depriving all Shintō shrines and institutions of government support.

SHINTŌ AND JAPANESE CULTURE

Certain strong and persistent traits in Japanese religious culture can only be attributed to 'Shintō'. These traits continually reassert themselves, selecting, stressing, or suppressing the forms of later cults so that despite their new disguises they are instantly recognizable as the old beliefs. These irrepressible religious and cultural traits are sometimes called the folk religion of Japan, or even folk Shintō. Their continued vitality is a remarkable feature of religion in Japan.

CB

Right *Hundreds of* ema, *or pictorial votive tablets, hung up at a shrine in Tōkyō. The practice dates from the Muromachi period, but the prayers inscribed on them these days are often for success in examinations.*

Buddhism

Buddhism is a faith wholly different from Shintō. The goal of the Buddhist disciple is interior enlightenment, as experienced and subsequently taught by the Buddha in India. The kernel of the Buddha's teaching is that the world as we ordinarily see it is unreal, insubstantial, and productive of suffering. Suffering stems from desire and desire arises through the notion of 'self'. Only extinguish this cause, realize the world and our 'selves' as they really are, and suffering will cease. The Way to extinguish our fundamental illusions is the Buddha's *dharma* or teaching.

General features

The Buddhist Way, which saw the source of ill as being within our own minds, thus stood in sharp contrast with Shintō, which looked entirely to the external world. The *kami*, or deities of Shintō, were conceived as bestowers of material blessings outside the competence of man, never as revealers of interior or ultimate truth. Most religious effort in early Shintō seems to have been directed towards divine favours in this world, such as bountiful harvests and protection from famine and disease. There was no tradition in Japan, comparable to Taoism in China, of a spiritual method directed to altering inner consciousness to comprehend an expanded mode of truth.

By the time Buddhist teachings reached Japan in the late 6th century, this original, simple but dauntingly difficult path had been overlaid by an elaborate doctrine and an iconography of saviours designed to make it easier to follow. The Mahāyāna school of Buddhism, which had made its way from India eastwards to China via the silk road through central Asia, claimed in particular to be capable of offering salvation not only to the dedicated individual but to the broad mass of humanity. To this end a pantheon of bodhisattvas had been generated who were dedicated to helping weaker sentient beings, and in addition there were other supernatural protectors such as the Four Deva Kings. From the Mahāyāna school likewise came a stream of anonymous sūtras, which not only expounded metaphysical doctrine, but also promised the disciple magical aid in every conceivable difficulty if he copied and recited the potent words.

Buddhism in Japan has always shown two different aspects which provide for two different kinds of people. For the majority, who have no real aspiration to carry out the Buddha's teachings to the letter and who are unwilling to submit themselves to a

Japanese temples exhibit great variety in the layout of buildings within the compound. The asymmetrical arrangement of the Hōryū-ji (607) is more characteristic of the earliest temples, while the symmetrical arrangement of the Yakushi-ji (681) exemplifies a later trend. In the case of the Hosshō-ji (1075), the temple compound embodies some of the characteristics of a palace garden.

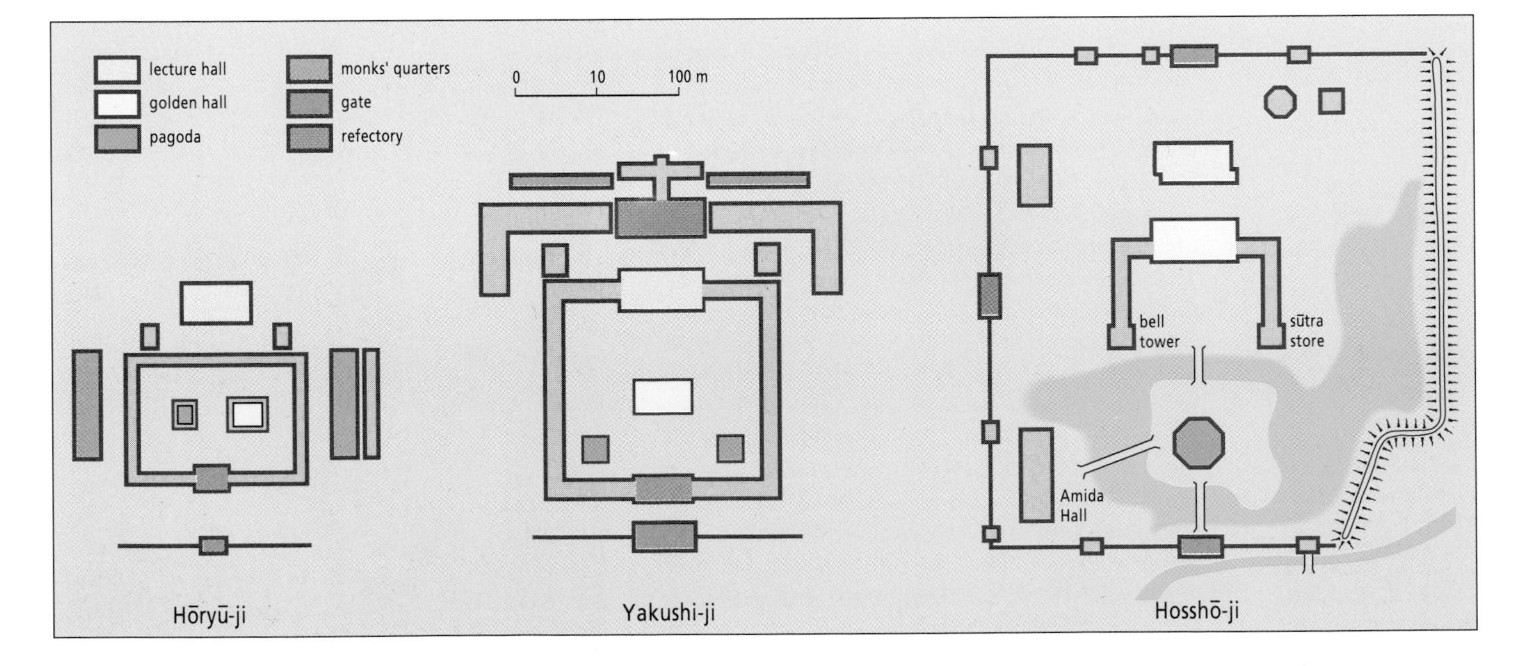

An ornate manuscript of a Buddhist sūtra, executed in gold on dark blue paper. This example dates from the 12th century.

regime of strenuous discipline, Buddhism has always provided two important services, neither of which has any connection with the original message of the Buddha. It provides familiar worldly benefits. In most sects, there are temples which derive much of their income from spells for a range of favours which include the curing of sickness, safety from traffic accidents and finding a congenial bride. Second, Buddhism takes care of the dead, in both a practical and a spiritual sense. Unhampered by the fear of pollution which always made death problematic for Shintō, Buddhism from the earliest times offered requiem obsequies, which were considered the most potent means of setting the dead to rest and obviating their curses. In this sense it filled an important gap in Japanese spiritual life, but in doing so moved further away from its doctrinal origins.

For the minority of Japanese who have experienced the call to the spiritual life, and who perceive the world to be insubstantial and full of suffering, Buddhism has supplied several viable methods of spiritual practice, whereby the disciple can hope to bring about the requisite transformation of consciousness. Notable among these are the meditative practices of the esoteric Shingon school, of Tendai, and of Zen, all of which require total commitment and taxing levels of concentration. Given this emphasis on the inner life, it is hardly surprising that Buddhism supplied for the Japanese a whole dimension of ethical concepts hitherto unknown. In Shintō there is no moral vocabulary. Buddhism gave Japanese culture the words for compassion, wisdom, mercy, kindness, all related to the spiritual end of Buddhist awakening.

One of the major strengths of Buddhism lies in its flexibility and in its recognition that there are many paths to the same final truth. There have been some notable exceptions: the Nichiren sect claimed sole and total truth for itself and denounced other versions in violent terms, and the history of Buddhism in late medieval Japan was one of constant strife. But, broadly speaking, sectarian strife is not common and Buddhism is characterized by its very variety.

Right *A Buddhist priest and his assistant praying for somebody who has died. Although most Japanese get married according to the Shintō rite, funerals are exclusively Buddhist.*

THE INTRODUCTION OF BUDDHISM TO JAPAN

When Buddhism first reached Japan from Korea it arrived in semi-magical form. It came as sūtras which promised protection for the whole land if properly recited, images of merciful bodhisattvas ready to succour and protect in any contingency, and a new, dazzling art, sculpture and architecture. It was natural therefore that for two centuries the new religion should have been understood as simply another and more potent means of producing the kind of this-worldly favours always sought after from divine beings in Shintō.

Buddhism was quickly adopted by the court as the official state religion, established to promote the welfare of the land. From Prince Shōtoku (late 6th century) to Emperor Shōmu (mid 9th century), who ordered temples to be built in all provinces and who constructed the Tōdai-ji at Nara and the huge statue

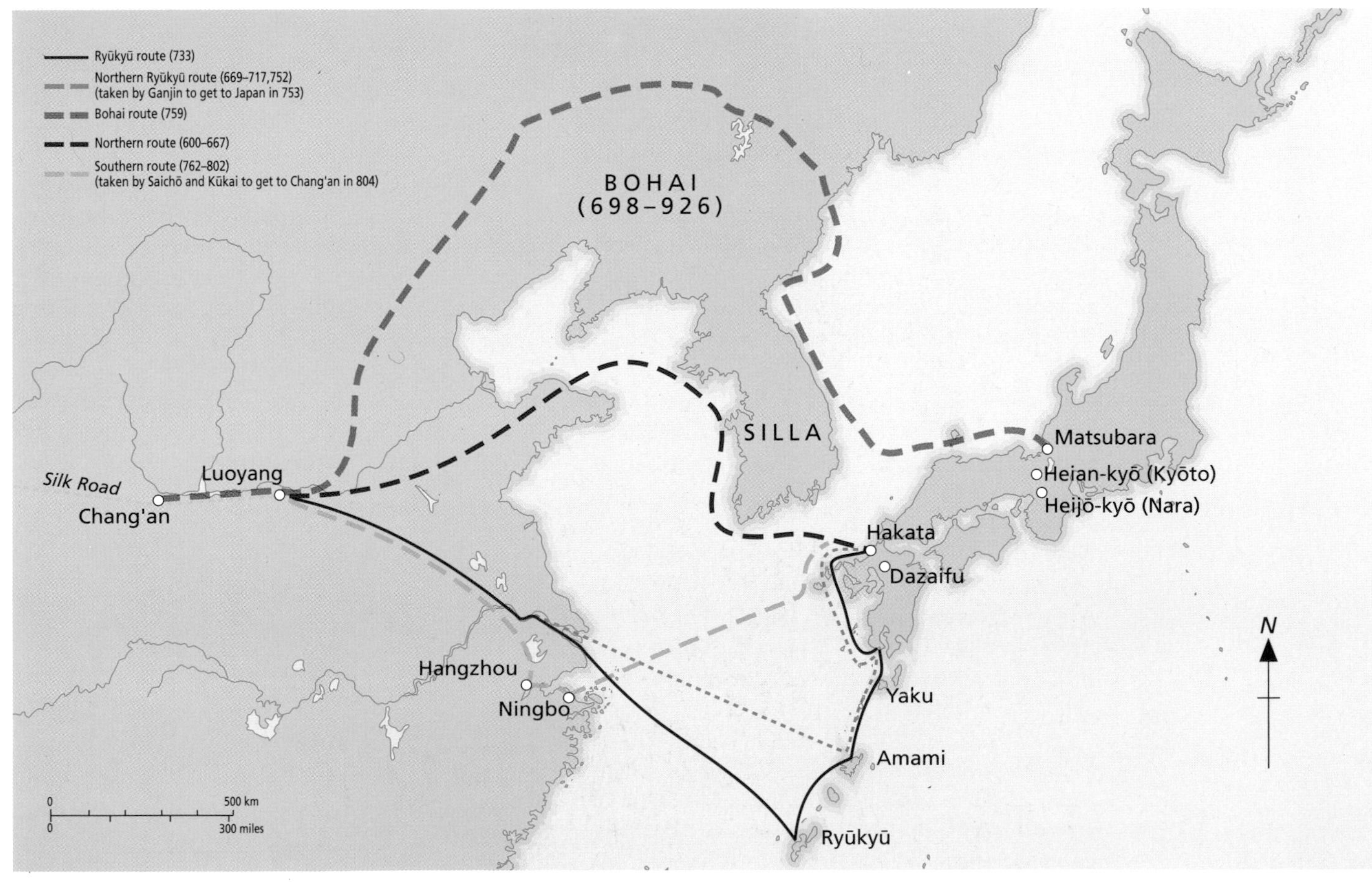

of Buddha within, the court was a devout patron, providing lavish support for the temples and the monks in return for the divine protection they afforded.

New and remarkable forms of art and architecture arose under the guidance of skilled craftsmen from Korea. Great temples were built on the Yamato plain, in and around Nara after the capital was established there in the early 8th century, and enshrined here were countless images of buddhas such as Shaka, Dainichi and Yakushi, and bodhisattvas such as Kannon, Fugen and Monju. The contrast with Shintō, a religion without icons, is marked. Within these temples were sponsored a series of seasonal rituals, based on Mahāyāna sūtras and designed to protect the state. Those texts considered especially efficacious were the *Lotus sūtra*, the *Sūtra of golden light*, and the *Sūtra of benevolent kings*. The *Lotus sūtra* was valued in particular for its extra virtue of helping the dead by annihilating their karmic sin. It became the most highly venerated scripture in Japan.

Buddhist priests in their finery at the Zōjō-ji in Tōkyō, gathering to celebrate the birthday of the Buddha.

Ganjin (688–763)

Ganjin was a Chinese Buddhist monk who spent the last 10 years of his life in Japan. For some years the court had been anxious to invite some Chinese monks to Japan to introduce formal ordination procedures and to regulate the monastic community, but not one had responded. Finally in 742 two Japanese monks persuaded Ganjin, or Jianzhen as his name was pronounced in Chinese, to leave his high and venerated position in Tang China to propagate Buddhism in Japan. Rudimentary navigation skills made the voyage a hazardous one at the time and his first five attempts (743–48) to cross the sea ended in failure when storms or pirates forced his boat back. He finally reached Japan on his sixth attempt in 753, but by this time he was totally blind. He set up an ordination platform in the Tōdai-ji in Nara, where he ordained many hundreds of monks and also gave instruction to the emperor Shōmu and other members of the imperial family. After the death of Shōmu he seems to have lost some of his influence. He lived with a few loyal followers in the Tōshōdai-ji, the principal temple of the Ritsu sect in Japan, which he founded in 759 and which is the site of his burial mound. CB

Routes from Japan to Chang'an (modern Xi'an), which was the capital of China during the Tang dynasty, the start of the Silk Road, and the goal for Japanese scholars and monks seeking secular or sacred wisdom in China.

These sūtras contained, besides spells and promises of help, passages of metaphysical doctrine, which were studied by groups of scholar priests and which in turn gave rise to what are known as the Six Schools of Nara Buddhism. Although these abstract theories themselves never reached further than the confines of the monasteries, some of the vocabulary and key concepts were eventually to percolate through to literature and culture in general.

Developments in the Heian period

From the 9th century, when the capital moved north to what is now Kyōto, Buddhism settled down in the form that was to persist for many centuries. The most notable aspect was its accommodation with Shintō. Far from branding the native beliefs as pagan or simple superstition, the *kami* were simply brought within the Buddhist fold, becoming local guardians with their special shrines in Buddhist temple precincts. More sophisticated doctrinal systems were later devised which converted *kami* into local and temporary manifestations of buddhas and bodhisattvas. Despite their differences then, both religions merged into a common system, which served as the religion of the majority of Japanese for most of their history.

It was during the Heian period that Buddhism gradually began to change from a scholastic institution supported by the élite for its own purposes into a religion with truly popular appeal. This development began with the arrival in Japan of two sects from China, Tendai and Shingon.

Tendai, introduced by Saichō (767–822), gave paramount importance to the *Lotus sūtra* but also placed great emphasis on the belief that there were many paths to truth. The aim of the Chinese founder, Zhiyi (538–97), had been to create a new synthesis of competing doctrines. So it was that Tendai incorporated a number of different practices including the study of other sūtras, Zen-like contemplation and magic and ritual. The underlying belief of Heian Buddhism was that perfection was attainable in this present life. Given its eclecticism, it is hardly surprising that it was Tendai that became the starting point for subsequent sectarian and doctrinal developments.

The other sect, Shingon ('True word') was introduced by the eminent scholar Kūkai (724–835), later known as Kōbō Daishi. Shingon placed greater emphasis on esoteric secret practices that could only be carried out by initiates; in this sense it was far more exclusive than Tendai. It made its political impact by laying claim to spells and prayers that could bring rain, cure disease and vanquish enemies, but on a more personal level it offered a viable method of spiritual practice, invoking the doctrine of 'Buddha nature': 'Buddha nature' exists within all people, perfect, original, awakened and identical with the Buddha, but is hidden and must be rediscovered by means of spiritual exercise. Shingon demanded a complex ritual, involving gestures of the hands, mantras and visualizations, whereby disciples could so transform their consciousness as to rouse their hidden oneness with the Buddha. By this method, claimed Kūkai, we may 'become Buddha in this very body'. Shingon is a manifestation of late Tantric Buddhism which now only survives in Japan and in those areas of the world where Tibetan Buddhism is still practised.

Medieval Buddhism

It was not until the 13th century that any further major developments emerged. They came as a result of the gradual spread of Buddhism throughout the population and the perceived need for less complex teachings which could offer more immediate hope of salvation to the common people. A combination of natural disasters, civil war, famine, earthquake, and a conviction that the *dharma* was already in an advanced state of decay in which people were too weak and ignorant to follow the original precepts of the Buddha, led to the emergence of new forms.

Devotion to and faith in the saving power of the Buddha Amida to rescue believers at the moment of death and personally conduct them to his paradise, the Pure Land, had been common since the 11th century at court, but it now took strong root throughout Japan. In Amidism, Buddhism came close to evolving into a monotheistic religion with paradise and salvation in the afterlife as the primary goal. It is not an exclusively Japanese phenomenon by any means, but its emergence shows just how far Buddhism could diverge from its origins. To invoke the grace of Amida, in accordance with his original Vow, all that was needed was recitation of his name in a formula known as the *nenbutsu*. Several schools based on this teaching arose during the 13th century, notably the Jōdo or Pure Land sect, founded by the monk Hōnen, and Jōdo Shinshū, founded by his disciple Shinran. Both sects are characterized as relying on *tariki*, 'force from the other', on the assumption that effort from 'self' alone is of little avail. It was also with these sects that one finds priests deciding to reject celibacy, preferring instead to partake of the lay life. Jōdo Shinshū still has huge numbers of followers in modern Japan and supports many prosperous temples.

The Nichiren sect, named after its founder Nichiren (1222–82), likewise offered an easier way to salvation. Starting from a foundation in Tendai and so preaching the primacy of the *Lotus sūtra*, Nichiren believed that everyone could be brought to salvation merely through the act of reciting with sincerity the name of the sūtra in the formula known as the *daimoku*. Nichiren was a patriot: he saw himself as the incarnation of a bodhisattva and claimed that it was owing to the efficacy of this practice that the Mongol invasions of Japan in the late 13th century had been thwarted. He was bitterly intolerant of all

Right *The Great Buddha at Kamakura, south of Tōkyō. It was built in the 13th century and has been in the open since 1495 when the structure housing it was burnt to the ground.*

Far right *Zen monks at a meditation session. The supervisor has a rod which he uses to tap the shoulders of any monks who appear to be flagging in their efforts.*

Right Pilgrims pause for photographs. The staff, white clothing, and hat to keep off the sun are all customary for serious pilgrims.

Map of the Saigoku pilgrimage route showing the order in which pilgrims must visit the 33 pilgrimage sites in western Japan.

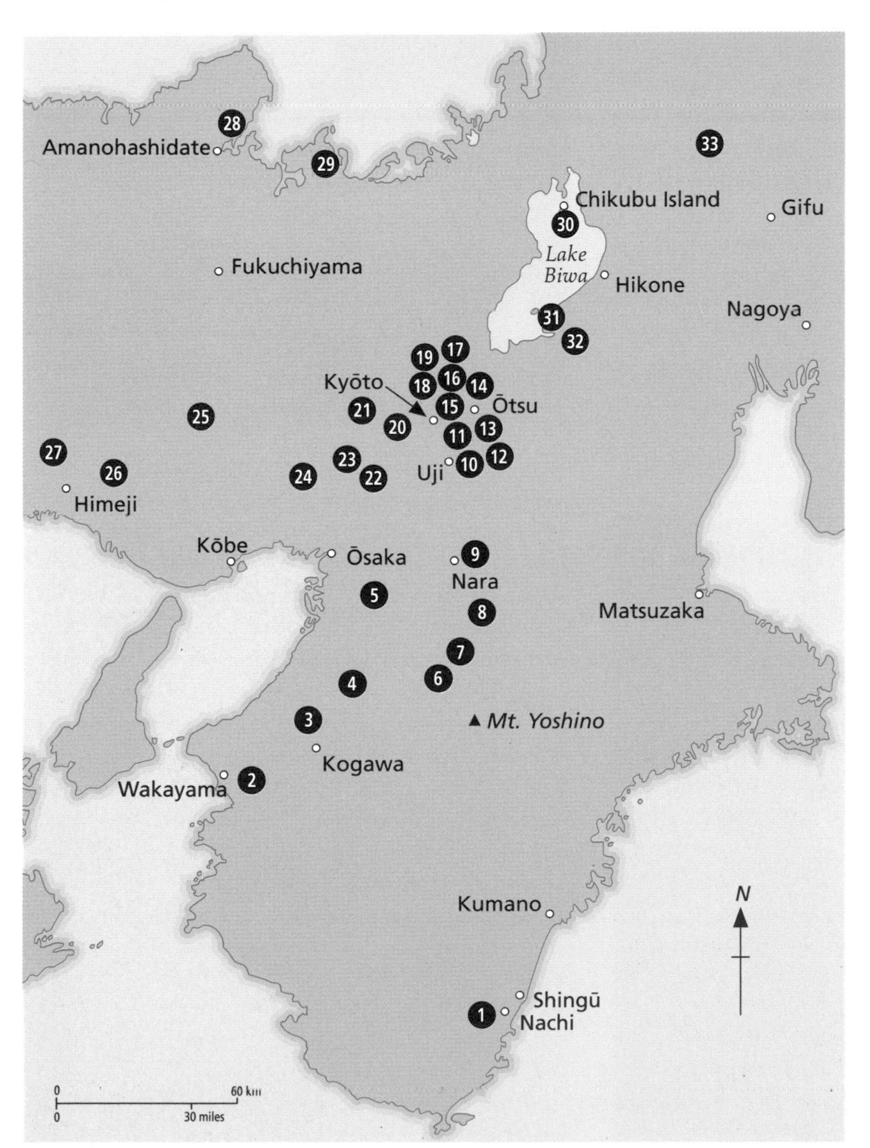

other sects which neglected the *Lotus sūtra*, particularly Jōdo Shinshū with its rival invocation to Amida, and his strong views brought him into conflict with the military authorities. The Nichiren sect continues to thrive to the present day, numerous sub-sects having hived off from the original group in recent years. Prominent among these is the aggressive Sōka Gakkai, which through propaganda and vigorous conversion techniques has managed to establish branches all over Japan and in many countries abroad.

In contrast to both Nichiren and Amidism, Zen offered another method of spiritual practice whereby disciples might recover their Buddha nature. Less complex than Shingon practice, it is no less difficult. Disciples may 'see their own nature and become a Buddha' by means of a special method of meditation, and spiritual transmission from master to pupil. This method 'points directly to the mind' without the use of words, which are recognized as ineffectual either in scripture or as means of communicating the enlightenment. Zen teachings came to Japan from China in two branches. The Rinzai sect, better known in the West, makes the *kōan* exercise central to its meditation. These riddles, not soluble by the rational mind, are set as disciplines to force the mind out of its accustomed habits. The Sōtō branch, on the other hand, founded by the celebrated master Dōgen, avoids the use of *kōan*, believing them to be counterproductive to the end they profess. The school relies instead on *shikan-taza*, 'just sitting', a method which is said to favour the advanced disciple and to be difficult for the neophyte.

FROM THE 14TH TO THE 19TH CENTURY

Although no major developments occurred during this long period, the history of Buddhism from the 14th century was hardly uneventful. Zen prospered under official patronage and spread its influence into all forms of art and culture, while those sects with a more popular appeal began not only to feud among themselves but also to come under considerable pressure in an increasingly disturbed and warlike environment. They were seen as potentially subversive and often misused their undoubtedly privileged position. The power of the Tendai sect, for example, was such that it could act at will, imposing its demands upon the capital by threatening armed force. It was only broken by the first unifier, Oda Nobunaga, who in 1580 ignored threats of divine retribution and burned their main temples to the ground for flouting his authority.

Once the Tokugawa régime was firmly established in the 17th century, this warlike behaviour of the major sects was remembered and the shōgunate decided to place Buddhism as an institution under strict government supervision. In many cases temples were reduced to little more than registration centres for all Japanese families. Although true worship undoubtedly continued, the power of Buddhism as an institution was broken forever. The history of Buddhism in this period becomes a patchwork of occasional colourful figures, some lay, some priests, who stand out as rebels, eccentrics or saintly figures.

Right *An unusual piece of Buddhist statuary of the 12th century: the subject, a famous monk, was thought to be the incarnation of a deity, and, to demonstrate this, the deity can be seen emerging from the monk's head.*

Like many outdoor Buddhist images associated with children, these statues at the Zenkō-ji temple in Nagano have been fitted with bonnets and bibs by parishioners to show that they are being looked after.

The coming of the Meiji Restoration in the late 19th century brought little comfort. Indeed the early Meiji could be seen as Buddhism's darkest hour since 1580, as the new nation state set about reviving and recreating Shintō as the state religion. The centuries-old accommodation between the two faiths was broken and in the process many temples were destroyed and much land lost. Since that time, however, Buddhism has slowly regained much of its hold on the hearts and mind of the ordinary Japanese and the old accommodation is alive again. Many new sects have emerged, older sects have retained their foothold, and the financial base of most temples is now secure. The increasing prosperity in the country has been reflected in the refurbishment of temples, and Buddhism remains the major candidate to fill the spiritual vacuum that many Japanese feel to be the legacy of their breakneck modernization.

CB

Confucianism

Confucianism is a tradition of moral, cultural and political teaching that originated in ancient China. It takes its name from its founder Kong Fuzi (551–479 BC), whose name was latinized by European missionaries as Confucius.

Confucius was a minor official who aspired to reform the violent and unstable Chinese society of his time. He considered that self-fulfilment was best achieved in a harmonious but hierarchical social context, through mastering a code of behaviour, through moral and cultural self-development, and through the exercise of administrative responsibility on the basis of merit. Confucius attached importance to familial values, particularly filial piety (the obedience of a son to his father), and to education.

The acceptance of a hierarchical order has led many to identify Confucianism as an ideology, a thought-system employed to justify a particular system of domination. Certainly, Confucius viewed society from the perspective of political authority, yet he was also a humanist who believed in the dignity, basic equality, and, within limits, the autonomy of the individual. Confucianism was a learned tradition: the early teachings of the school were recorded in scriptures that formed a canon studied by all Confucians.

Confucianism thus contained the potential both for promoting humanistic, egalitarian and meritocratic values and for legitimating the institutions of a hierarchical, bureaucratic political order. Its humanism was emphasized by one of Confucius' leading followers, Mencius (Mengzi, 371–289 BC), who developed Confucius' teaching, particularly in the area of political morality. Mencius taught that if a ruler abused his position, it was right that his people should overthrow him: a principle that was often used to justify dynastic change. The political, institutional potential of the tradition found expression in the history of the Chinese Han (206 BC – AD 220) and Tang (618–907) dynasties when Confucianism became the official learning of the imperial bureaucracy, access to which was gained on the basis of examinations on the Confucian classics. A Confucian state ritual programme was instituted, which included sacrifices to Confucius himself, conducted in the state academy.

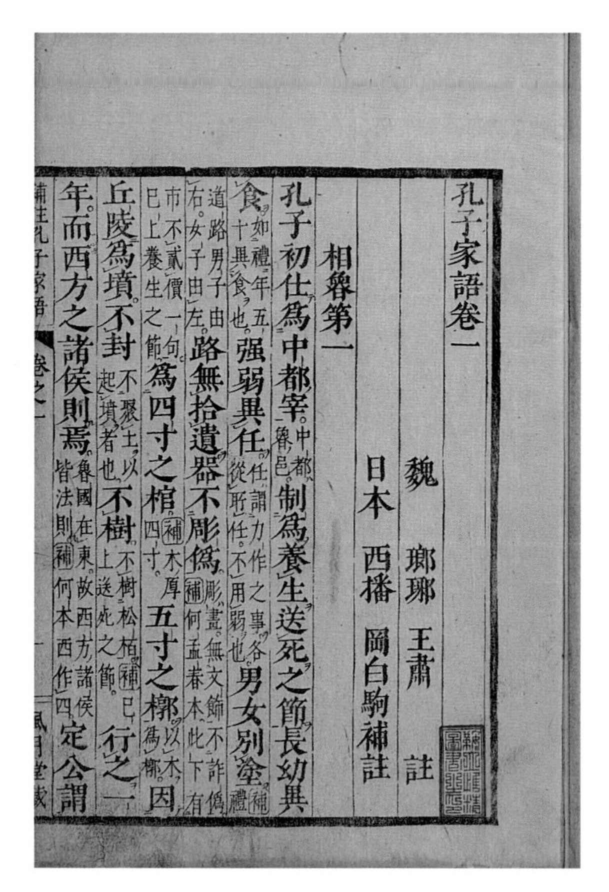
孔子家語卷一

魏 瑯琊 王肅 註

日本 西播 岡白駒補註

相魯第一

孔子初仕為中都宰中都魯邑制為養生送死之節長幼異食如禮年五十異食也強弱異任任謂力作之事各從所任不用弱也男女別塗補禮

道路男子由右女子由左路無拾遺器不彫偽彫畫無文飾不詐偽補何孟春本此下有

市不貳價一句已上養生之節為四寸之棺補木厚四寸五寸之槨以木為槨因

丘陵為墳不封不聚土以起墳者也不樹不樹松柏補上送死之節已行之一

年而西方之諸侯則焉魯國在東故西方諸侯皆法則補何本西作四定公謂

補註孔子家語 卷之一 一 風月堂藏

Right *An 18th-century Japanese edition of the* Sayings of Confucius. *The large characters constitute the text, the small signs beside them indicate how the Chinese text is to be read in Japanese, and the double columns of smaller characters are a Chinese commentary.*

Confucianism in Japan before 1600

The Confucianism of the Han and Tang dynasties was transmitted to Japan from Korea probably in the 5th century. Its influence is to be seen in the early development of the Japanese state, where Confucianism bolstered the claims to political hegemony and legitimacy of the Yamato sovereigns. The Seventeen Article Constitution of Shōtoku Taishi (574–622) makes use of Confucian texts and ideas to promote a hierarchical, incipiently bureaucratic polity under the rule of an emperor. Confucian thought seems to have been one inspiration behind the Taika coup (645) and ensuing reform. Certainly, the Confucian view of imperial sovereignty, bureaucratic administration, and egalitarian land distribution lay behind the institutions of the Chinese-style *ritsuryō* state of the 8th century. To staff these sophisticated new structures, the state instituted a metropolitan Confucian university and a system of provincial schools on the Chinese model. Here, the rites to Confucius were conducted, much as in China, though on a smaller scale. The institutions of this period, therefore, have a sinicized, meritocratic look. However, entry into the university was largely restricted to the established court aristocracy. Even within that group, hereditary rank proved more powerful than merit as a qualification for high office. Though the state education system undoubtedly supplied trained personnel for the bureaucracy, this was largely at the lower levels. There were a few exceptions: Kibi no Makibi (693–775) and Sugawara no Michizane (845–903) both rose from relatively humble social positions to very high office. On the whole, however, Confucian meritocratic and egalitarian assumptions did not overcome the tendency to aristocratic hereditary privilege in Japanese society at this time. Furthermore, Confucian education itself quickly went into a decline. The sacrifices to Confucius became not a public rite of homage to the founder of the tradition of bureaucratic learning, but more a private, aristocratic celebration. In 1177, the Confucian university burned down and was not rebuilt. Ideologically, however, the association between the Japanese imperial lineage and Confucian views of sovereignty made in the ancient period was to prove an enduring influence in Japanese history.

The medieval period of Japanese history was dominated by Buddhism. During this time in China, however, Confucianism underwent a major revival which altered its focus and restored to it something of the concern with the individual that had been lost to some extent during the Han and Tang dynasties. Neo-Confucianism, while it retained the social and political objectives of the ancient tradition, provided a more detailed methodology of self-cultivation which led to a mystical identification with the noumenal ground of the human and natural orders. While pursuing this objective, students would become morally and intellectually qualified for the exercise of administrative responsibility. There were two main branches of Neo-Confucianism. The school of Ju Xi (1130–1200) stressed study of classical texts as the main path to understanding. The autonomy of the individual was more emphasized in the idealist branch of Neo-Confucianism, whose leading thinker was Wang Yangming (1473–1529).

Neo-Confucian texts were probably transmitted to Japan in the early 13th century. Confucianism, however, did not flourish as an independent tradition in medieval Japan; rather, it was propagated by Zen monks and viewed as an 'expedient' teaching which could lead followers to a true understanding of Buddhism. However, one particular institution of Confucian learning, the Ashikaga School, prospered, largely because it devoted much of its curriculum to divination, a practice peripheral to the tradition but important in a period of chronic warfare.

Tokugawa Confucianism

The stability brought by the Tokugawa régime provided a more favourable atmosphere for Confucianism, and it was during this period that the tradition became most widely disseminated. It did not, however, achieve the status of a state orthodoxy until late in the period, and it had little influence on the structure of political institutions, although it was patronized at governmental level, both by the Bakufu and by daimyō administrations. By and large, it was the Ju Xi school that found favour with those in political authority, perhaps because it could be more readily interpreted to support a hierarchical order. The Wang Yangming school, on the other hand, was branded as subversive, and suppressed. Tokugawa Ieyasu (1542–1616), the founder of the régime, employed a Confucian adviser of the Ju Xi persuasion, Hayashi Razan (1583–1657), who was able, through his prominent position in Bakufu service, to raise the public profile of the tradition. He also built a school and a shrine to Confucius in Edo and revived the ritual to Confucius there from 1633. At the end of the 18th century, the Bakufu, in a movement that may have been inspired by the example of Korea, prohibited what were perceived as heterodox schools and established a new official college next to the Hayashi school in Edo. This school, for Bakufu retainers, produced a number of effective administrators over the remainder of the period.

Confucianism was also patronized at the domain level. Some daimyō became enthusiastic patrons of Confucianism, studied it themselves, and, in tune with its emphasis on education, established schools in their domains. There young samurai would study a syllabus of basic Confucian texts. These texts, it should be remembered, were in classical Chinese, a difficult foreign language, requiring considerable

Hayashi Razan, who entered the service of the Shōgun Tokugawa Ieyasu in 1607 and was active for the rest of his career in disseminating Neo-Confucianism.

effort to master: academic standards were probably not very high. By the end of the period, however, 73% of daimyō had schools in their domains; ceremonies to Confucius were conducted in these institutions or in specially constructed memorial halls. Many a daimyō also employed a professional Confucian adviser who would act both as tutor to his sons and as a ritualist and composer of commemorative documents in classical Chinese: in this way, his domain government, although basically military in style, would be given an aura of classical dignity.

Confucianism also attracted a following among non-samurai. Individual Confucian scholars established private schools and academies, often attended by samurai as well as commoner pupils. There were probably more than 1,500 such institutions during the period, not all of them, however, devoted to Confucian studies. These schools were often run on a more egalitarian and meritocratic basis than their official counterparts, and provided a valuable alternative to official education.

Confucianism in modern Japan

In the years following the Meiji Restoration (1868), Confucianism was temporarily discredited and neglected. However, Confucian ethical imperatives were revived as an important element in the ideological system known as *tennōsei*, the emperor system. Attempts were made to associate the rule of the Emperor Meiji with Confucian moral values, particularly loyalty and filial piety, as in the influential Imperial Rescript on Education of 1890. After the turn of the century, Confucian societies sprang up, the ritual to Confucius was revived in 1907, and Confucian moral values were consciously invoked to promote social harmony and solidarity, and to combat the perceived individualism of the West. In the 1930s and 1940s, Confucianism also became associated with Japan's expansion on the continent. The tradition was exploited as a common inheritance of East Asia that could unite Japan with occupied Korea, Manchuria and China. Because of its association with ultra-nationalism, Confucianism was once more discredited after the defeat of Japan in 1945.

The revival of self-confidence following Japan's emergence as an economic superpower, however, has encouraged Japanese in recent years to evaluate their

Confucianism for women

One of the most widely circulated texts for women's education in the Tokugawa period was *Onna daigaku*, or *The great learning for women*, which was first published in the early 18th century but remained in circulation right through to the end of the 19th century. Its title comes from one of the central texts of Confucianism, the *Great learning*. *Onna daigaku* is commonly attributed to Kaibara Ekken, a moral teacher and popularizer of Confucianism who did write a didactic work instructing fathers how to keep their daughters usefully occupied before marriage, but it was most likely compiled somewhat later with his writings as a guide. Its style was that of popular sermons, and it provided guidance for the behaviour of women in marriage. The emphasis was on subordination to husbands, chastity, the cultivation of a forgiving nature, and the fulfilment of obligations to in-laws; the fate of women, in Confucian writings of the time, was subjection – to father, then husband, and finally son. Some of its prescriptions were:

Use few words and refrain from speaking a great deal.
Do not drink a lot of tea or sake.
Have nothing to do with anything lewd like kabuki.
Until you are 40 do not frequent places like temples and shrines where lots of people gather.
Consider your husband as your master, respect him, and serve him deferentially.

In modern Japan *Onna daigaku* became notorious as a text supposedly responsible for the oppression of women, and in 1874 an updated version was published which declared that, 'it is to a woman's shame if she runs errands for men and cannot escape being his slave'. It was not until 1899 that an extensive critique of it was published, by the enlightenment pioneer Fukuzawa Yukichi. PK

Confucian heritage more positively. The Confucian shrine in Tōkyō, shabby for many years after the war, now has an air of quiet prosperity and authority. The Confucian classics continue to be widely studied and quoted, and a historical novel on Confucius has recently made the best-seller list.

Conclusions

How deeply has Japan's long exposure to Confucianism influenced her society? Would it be correct to describe Japan as Confucianized, like her neighbour Korea? Certainly the Japanese emphasis on the family, paternalism, and on harmony and hierarchy, and the use of moral vocabulary borrowed from the Confucian tradition, might suggest that Japanese society has indeed been profoundly shaped by Confucianism. A closer look, however, suggests that this is not so. The political structure of the ancient state, it is true, had a strong Chinese and Confucian colouring, but the meritocratic principle did not take root. The ancient state was superseded by the very different feudal order, based on military values, that arguably constitutes the most important influence on modern Japan. There was little common ground between the military ethos and discipline of the samurai and the civil, humanist concerns of Confucianism. Furthermore, despite the efforts of Tokugawa Confucians, the Confucian kinship system and family morality exerted rather superficial influence in Japan. In contrast to the strictly patrilineal Chinese family system, the Japanese household remained rather loosely organized, and not infrequently incorporated non-kin members. It existed not, as did the Chinese, as a kinship organization for its own sake, so much as to perform social tasks. Thus while in China filial piety had priority, in Japan it tended to be loyalty to a ruler that took first place. The Japanese, in fact, projected on to their rulers or leaders the intense dedication that in China was accorded to parents. With this went a less developed sense of the self in Japan, for the relative weakness of the family system resulted in a weaker sense of individual selfhood and autonomy than the Confucian ideal. Thus, although even now the Japanese still use Confucian vocabulary for many of their moral values, it tends to have a different meaning in practice. IJM

Tokugawa sociopolitical thought

What were the philosophical foundations on which the ruling Tokugawa shōgunal, daimyō and samurai classes built their understanding and practice of society and government? The subject is a vast one in both scope and time but can be conveniently handled from three main aspects. The first is the selective borrowing of what was known as Chinese Learning, especially Confucianism, which forged a new class ethos for Japan's military aristocracy during the 17th-century transition from civil war to peace. The next century saw a fierce Nativist reaction against the cultural dominance that Chinese Learning had come to enjoy among samurai. Lastly, we encounter the stimulation of modern nationalist sentiment, brought about by an acute crisis in foreign policy. This crisis eventually led to the restoration of power to the emperor and court in Kyōto and to the ending of eight centuries of warrior rule in Japan by 1871.

17th-century Confucianism

Confucianism may be defined as a branch of Chinese Learning whose adherents embraced two cardinal beliefs: first, that the supreme guide to life and government, 'the Way', had been revealed by semi-divine sages in classical Chinese texts that contained all necessary wisdom and morality; and second, that intimate knowledge of these classics prepared cultured men to implement the Way in society through government service, which was their proper mission in life. Such beliefs were grounded in Chinese social realities: the ruling scholar-official class in China owed its hegemony to 'talent and virtue', demonstrated by passing arduous civil service examinations based on the Confucian classics.

Such forms of Chinese Learning were in a sense foreign to the socio-cultural environment we find in early 17th-century Japan. Confucianism was in many ways as foreign as Christianity. Few members of the ruling military aristocracy could even read classical Chinese, much less dispute the finer points of Confucian doctrine. The ritual and music of the Confucian sages had no place in daily life or in the workings of government. What self-respecting samurai cried at funerals as stipulated in the *Book of rites*? Most samurai earned their keep through page service and guard duty, work despised as fit only for eunuchs in a Chinese context.

Ogyū Sorai (1666–1728)

Ogyū Sorai was one of the leading thinkers of the Tokugawa period. His family was in exile from 1679 to 1690 and as a consequence he was largely self-taught and beholden to no established school of learning. His approach to the Chinese classics was shaped by a philological rigour that drove him to seek for the original meanings and to peel away the interpretations and commentaries that seemed to him to obscure the original message of the texts. He applied himself to the study of colloquial Chinese at a time when most were content if they could simply read classical Chinese, and by the time he was 26 he had written a textbook of Chinese composition. The consequence of his studies was a rejection of the Neo-Confucian tradition, which he argued was based on a fundamental misunderstanding of the Confucian canon, and he advocated instead a return to the concern with good government which he saw as the original thrust of Confucianism. Rather than harking back to a fantasized past, however, he took a relatively pragmatic approach to problems of governance, and was consequently frequently consulted by Bakufu officials from 1716, when the shōgun Yoshimune took up office, until his death. His political recommendations were contained in two works which he submitted to the Bakufu; in these he acknowledged the severe economic difficulties besetting the daimyō and the samurai class as a whole, and proposed abolition of the system of alternate attendance by which daimyō were required to be constantly travelling between their domains and Edo, of the confinement of samurai to the towns, and of the principle of hereditary succession to office, which he saw as a barrier to bureaucratic talent. The Bakufu, however, was already committed to preservation of the status quo, and did not follow his advice. PK

Left *The Confucian shrine at Nagasaki.*

Confucianism was thus largely an alien system of beliefs and practices that had to undergo assimilation or 'naturalization' before it found a home in Japan. Unlike scholar-officials in China, Tokugawa Confucians were barred from political power and foreign meritocratic ideals of 'talent and virtue' meant little in real practice. True, the rare Confucian scholar, such as Kumazawa Banzan (1619–91) or Arai Hakuseki (1657–1725), might be asked to advise a shōgun or a daimyō. But in state or domain councils his advice was largely ignored. As Banzan's lord once said of him: 'What he says sounds reasonable, but if we really did as he tells us, it would be disastrous for the domain.'

Instead, Confucians served mainly as teachers and scholars who accommodated their foreign creed to Japanese realities. For the most part, this meant providing ethical and moral grounds for behaviour for the Tokugawa military aristocracy, who, unlike their forebears in the preceding era, no longer had to fight for a living.

The Tokugawa Bakufu ended civil war at home and precluded conquest abroad by banning foreign travel; but it upheld martial law artificially in an era of prolonged peace. Japan became a garrison state turned in upon itself; the daimyō and samurai were demilitarized but not demobilized. Battlefield heroism was now impossible, but samurai still deemed themselves fighting men whose highest honour was to die loyally, as seen in the custom of self-immolation on the death of one's lord, a practice that survived among Bakufu and daimyō retainers until the late 17th century, or in the 47 Rōnin Incident of 1702.

As time passed, this Japanese nobility of the sword felt the need to justify its self-identity and its hegemonic position in society. Daimyō and samurai as a class were in danger of seeming like parasites compared with peasants, artisans and merchants, who all did socially useful work. Almost defensively, Tokugawa warriors turned to Confucian teachers such as Yamaga Sokō (1622–85), who provided the ethical justification they craved.

Sokō likened Japanese warriors to Chinese scholar-officials; both practised moral norms in the Confucian Way, such as duty, loyalty, manly resolution and righteousness over personal gain. Influenced by such teachers, they styled themselves 'samurai of high resolve' (*shishi*), a term Confucius had used to extol 'those who destroy themselves in perfecting virtue', or they built stately gardens with names like Kōrakuen, where they reflected on the Chinese dictum: 'Be first to grieve over the realm's ills and last to enjoy its pleasure (*kōraku*)'.

Apart from a handful of professional scholars and teachers, few warriors mastered scholastic Confucianism or other branches of Chinese Learning. Instead, they selectively borrowed moral tenets from the 'Way of the sages' to fashion a class ethos which they termed the 'Way of the samurai' (*bushidō*). It held that commoners were free to pursue pleasure or personal gain, but only warriors gloried in hardship and in a willingness to die for principle; it was this that justified their hereditary privileges in Tokugawa society.

Chinese Learning came to have a profound impact on Japanese warriors. Even the intellectual snobbishness noted above marked a crucial change in samurai values, for scholarly affectation could become fashionable only after a contempt for book-learning had disappeared. By mid-Tokugawa times Confucianism and other branches of Chinese Learning had overcome their alien origins to become the core of warrior-class culture, ousting not only native poetry and prose, but also Buddhism and Shintō.

The 47 Rōnin

On 31 January 1703 a band of 46 samurai, led by Ōishi Kuranosuke, assaulted the mansion of Kira Yoshinaka and killed him. They were retainers of the daimyō Asano Naganori and their action was in revenge for a confrontation between Asano and Kira in the shōgun's palace caused by Kira's arrogance: as a result Asano had been ordered to commit suicide. Bereft of their lord, they were now *rōnin*, masterless samurai. By killing Kira they had only done what was expected of them in loyal devotion to their lord. For this they deserved admiration, but at the same time the way in which they had acted out their vendetta constituted a serious breach of the public peace and this made it difficult to condone their act. In a compromise that would enable them to preserve their honour intact, they were required to commit formal suicide and this they did in February 1703. The story of the 47 *rōnin* touched an immediate chord and they were acclaimed as heroes. It has inspired a succession of dramatizations and adaptations in books and on film: the hold that it has on the Japanese imagination shows no sign of abating. The most famous play of all on the subject is *Chūshingura*, 'Treasure house of loyal retainers', written in 1748 by Takeda Izumo and translated into English in 1971. This incident is always described as the affair of the 47 *rōnin*, although one of the 47 was in fact too elderly to take part in the raid. PK

18TH-CENTURY NATIVISM

Some Tokugawa Confucians such as Ogyu Sorai (1666–1728) were over-zealous in proselytizing their foreign creed, which, after all, presumed civilization to be synonymous with sinification. They were forced to denigrate all indigenous ways and values as barbaric. Others, such as Dazai Shundai (1680–1747), argued that Japanese in prehistoric Yamato times had lived on a par with animals, and had advanced morally and materially only after importing Chinese culture in the 4th and 5th centuries. It is hardly surprising that such views eventually provoked a backlash against seemingly excessive adulation of things Chinese.

Opposed to the Confucian sinocentric view of Japanese history, 18th-century Nativists such as Kamo no Mabuchi (1697–1769) and Motoori Norinaga (1730–1801) argued that on the contrary people in prehistoric Yamato times had been pure and good and had only been corrupted later by the pernicious influence of Chinese culture. Using rigorous philological methods, such scholars set to work decoding native classics such as the *Kojiki* and the *Man'yōshū* – works that Tokugawa sinophiles had disdained in favour of Chinese texts. These early Japanese classics had been supposedly compiled before foreign influence became strong, so the Nativist scholars reasoned that a study of them would lead to a recovery of the unsullied Yamato Spirit that made Japan different from and better than foreign lands.

Nativists harshly criticized Tokugawa Confucians on two key issues: social mores and political legitimation. First, they claimed that morality varied with time and place. What the sages of ancient China pronounced as 'evil' might be perfectly acceptable in other eras or other nations. Japanese living in the past or present should be judged by indigenous standards, not alien moral norms such as the Way, presumed to possess timeless universal validity. Actually, the existence of that Way – unwittingly glorified by Tokugawa warriors as *bushidō* – was proof of Chinese moral duplicity. The Confucian Way supposedly comprised virtues such as loyalty, righteousness and filial piety. Why? The sages had required such high-sounding precepts because the Chinese as a race had normally violated them. The sages harped on 'loyalty of subject for sovereign', but did so from a desire to forestall regicide. History showed that over 20 Chinese dynasties had suffered violent destruction, despite all Confucian good intentions.

Motoori Norinaga (1730–1801)

Norinaga was born in Matsuzaka to a family which had been running a highly successful cotton-goods business for several generations. He went to Kyōto in 1752 to study medicine and Confucianism, but soon turned to Nativism. In 1757 he returned to Matsuzaka where he made his living as a paediatrician while continuing his studies. At his death, he had over 500 disciples from some 40 provinces.

Norinaga's studies included classical language, poetry and literature, court procedures and ceremonials, and ancient history, society and folklore. Despite this diversity of topics, his scholarship centred on two beliefs: (a) that native Japanese classics contained truths which were being obfuscated by alien (= Chinese) ways and ideas; and (b) that rigorous philological study was needed to clarify the original meaning of those classics and to explain the reasons for Japanese world pre-eminence. His 38-year-long study of Japan's oldest classic, the *Kojiki*, revealed to him that Japanese spontaneously obeyed the will of the gods in revering a single imperial house, unlike foreign peoples who practised rebellion and regicide. Despite some prejudiced and irrational elements in his thought, Norinaga's erudition commanded admiration in an age when philology was considered the highest of academic endeavours. But his prime historical significance lay in refuting the claims of Confucian rationalism. Norinaga made it respectable for Japanese to proclaim uniqueness and superiority in the world based on *Kojiki* myths, which Confucians had discredited as absurd one century before. BTW

Ishida Baigan and the Shingaku movement

Shingaku was a movement dedicated to popular ethical teaching. It was founded by Ishida Baigan (1685–1744) and developed by his followers in the 18th century. It was eclectic in character, drawing on Shintō and Buddhism as well as Neo-Confucianism, and its constituency was principally the urban merchant class, though it did have some followers who were samurai or even daimyō.

Ishida Baigan was born in a farming village near Kyōto: since he was not the eldest son he could not inherit and had to look elsewhere for a livelihood. His father apprenticed him to a merchant but he rashly abandoned this and returned home. As an adult he moved to Kyōto and worked his way up as a clerk in a merchant business while in his spare time trying to preach Shintō and studying Buddhism and Neo-Confucianism. In 1729 he resigned his position and opened a hall for free lectures. He used a mixture of exposition, question-and-answer sessions, and meditation, and began to establish a following. Rather than questioning the political system of Tokugawa Japan, he concentrated on finding a moral rôle and justification for the merchant townsmen. In a society which accorded merchants the lowest status, he upheld their usefulness as circulators of wealth and distributors of goods; to those who saw them as parasites he argued that they were as entitled to their profits as samurai were to their stipends. He espoused the virtues of honesty, frugality and benevolence and took an active part in relief work, especially in times of famine.

After Baigan's death the movement was put on a sound organizational footing by Teshima Toan (1718–86), one of his followers and an accomplished preacher. He set up Shingaku study-centres, which became the main means by which Shingaku doctrines spread. At his death there were 22 of them in 14 provinces; this increased to 80 in 25 provinces by 1803 and 134 in 34 provinces by 1830.

Shingaku has been seen as a device for producing 'robots for the ruling class', or a means of preserving the social order under the Bakufu. While it is certainly true that it was in no sense a revolutionary doctrine, it did nevertheless provide a justification of economic activity that may have facilitated the transition to a capitalist economy in the late 19th century. PK

By contrast, Nativists claimed, Japanese in the Yamato era had never consciously articulated a 'Way' or elevated it to the level of moral precept because they had practised it without having to be taught. This natural goodness was revealed in their guileless reverence for native gods and their loyal submission to the dynastic line of emperors descended from Amaterasu, the Sun Goddess. Despite the baleful effects of Chinese culture, the Japanese continued to revere a single ruling house throughout their 2,400-year history. This national character, or polity as it later became known, made Japan unique and pre-eminent throughout the world.

Nativists also disputed the rationale by which Japanese Confucians justified Bakufu hegemony over the Kyōto imperial court. Both schools agreed that Japan's divine emperors descended from Amaterasu would reign forever, and that those emperors had irretrievably lost political power by medieval times. They disagreed, however, over why such a loss of power had taken place.

Confucians explained the transfer of power through a naturalized version of the 'Mandate of Heaven' theory. According to the original Chinese form of the theory, Heaven decreed that a dynasty deserved to exist only as long as it dispensed virtuous government; if it abused power, Heaven transferred the ruling mandate to a new dynastic house. Although Japanese Confucians abhorred any thought of regicide and dynastic overthrow, they argued that the emperor and court in Kyōto had ruled immorally in late-Heian and Kamakura times. So Heaven had quite rightly transferred its ruling mandate to warrior houses such as the Minamoto, Ashikaga and Tokugawa, whose shōgunal heads governed in the emperor's stead. Despite enjoying unquestioning hegemony, those shōguns still ruled as loyal ministers of their sovereign emperor.

Nativist thinkers denounced this idea, despite its emphasis on shōgunal loyalty, because it criticized divine Japanese emperors according to alien criteria. Warrior government, they argued, had replaced direct imperial rule simply because the gods had willed it so. In 1787, Norinaga refined this argument to devise a theory of imperial rather than Heavenly mandate: Amaterasu had decreed that emperors entrust the administration of the realm to Tokugawa heirs beginning with Ieyasu; and the granting of the imperial court title of 'shōgun' symbolized this investiture of power in each succeeding generation. Thus while Confucians justified Bakufu government as correct and proper by citing the incompetence and moral turpitude of past emperors, Nativists did so by recourse to divine providence. And most importantly, Norinaga politicized what had always been a purely formal and ceremonial act by the emperor: granting the court title of 'shōgun' to Tokugawa heirs. His new theory was potentially subversive of Bakufu rule; for, logically speaking, what the emperor granted he might also rescind.

But few, if any, of Norinaga's contemporaries perceived the latent danger in this theory of imperial mandate. Nativists and Confucians alike professed allegiance to the emperor, and presumed him to be irrelevant to practical government. Warrior rule had been an undisputed fact of life ever since the failed attempts at imperial restoration by emperors Gotoba in 1221 and Godaigo in 1333. Another imperial restoration was never seriously considered. Eventually it took an unprecedented crisis in foreign affairs to discredit the shōgun, his Bakufu, and the principle of warrior rule in Japan.

19TH-CENTURY NATIONALISM

According to Norinaga's idea of divine providence, everything that occurred in nature and society resulted from the will of the gods. But that idea, though convenient for affirming the status quo, lost credence after 'Western barbarians' brought the threat of semi-colonial domination. If Japanese claims to world pre-eminence were to remain cogent, certain revisions to the Nativist creed were called for. It was Hirata Atsutane (1776–1843) who provided such revision.

Norinaga had been a rigorous scholar and multifaceted thinker who tried to present textual evidence to substantiate his claim of Japanese superiority over foreign races. In addition to praising the Yamato spirit of antiquity, he valued ideals of courtly elegance and the refined gentleness of 'the poignancy of things' (*mono no aware*), as epitomized in literary classics such as *Genji monogatari* and *Shinkokinshū*. This erudite, soft side of Nativism all but disappeared under Atsutane. He disdained court poetry and discouraged his students from studying it. Instead, he espoused an uncompromising theory of racial superiority later called Japanism.

The idea of Japan as 'the land of the gods' had been but one strand of Norinaga's thought; in Atsutane's it became far more significant and assumed important political implications. Atsutane, too, argued that Japan was of divine creation, and that the emperor was a direct descendant of Amaterasu. But he went further. Within the warrior ruling class, he said, there were hierarchic lord–vassal distinctions; but 'there is only one deity-sovereign in our imperial land – the emperor'. Atsutane also stressed that all Japanese, rulers and ruled alike, were related to one another as descendants of the same national deities headed by Amaterasu. Norinaga had accepted Tokugawa supremacy and the existing sociopolitical hierarchy as divinely-willed; Atsutane hinted at egalitarianism and a family state based on kinship with the emperor.

The Western threat had grave implications for the Way of the sages as well. Up to this point, Confucianism in the form of *bushidō* had given warriors a rationale to help justify their privileged position in society: 'samurai of high resolve' deserved to rule, and eat without working, because they were ever-ready to fight and die in loyal state service. Now, for the first time in Tokugawa history, it seemed that they might be called upon to do just that. Scholars such as Aizawa Seishisai (1781–1863) urged the warrior class to rise to the occasion. Aizawa was a leader in the Mito School, which espoused a politicized and more muscular form of *bushidō*. It challenged Japan's nobility of the sword to perform in fact what they had been proclaiming all along.

The Western menace had another serious impact. All previous potential military challenges to Tokugawa supremacy had come from other daimyō, and all fighting had been limited to the samurai class; but any future war would be fought against Westerners on Japanese soil. So the shōgun would require loyal support, if not outright military service, from commoners as well as samurai. This unprecedented strategic need underscored the deficiencies of pre-modern, class-bound *bushidō*.

To overcome these deficiencies Aizawa suggested that the Tokugawa shōgun borrow religious authority from the emperor in order to instil a sense of patriotic allegiance in all Japanese classes and thereby foster national unity. By the conventional tenets of Tokugawa Confucian political thought, both the emperor in Kyōto and the mass of ordinary Japanese had been irrelevant to government and strictly excluded from politics. But now, Aizawa had no

The Dutch Consul-General, Dirk de Graeff van Polsbroek, with a fellow official in the early 1860s. A spate of attacks on foreigners by extremists caused the Bakufu to hire large numbers of trustworthy samurai to guard foreign diplomats night and day.

choice but to call on them to assist the ruling military aristocracy in Japan's hour of need.

Thus, the 19th-century Western threat produced radical changes in both Nativism and Confucianism by creating an emperor-centered nationalism, which was incompatible with the premises that underlay warrior domination. Hirata Atsutane and Aizawa Seishisai still considered the current Tokugawa state structure to be the best possible sociopolitical arrangement; but it was no longer the only conceivable one, as it had been for Norinaga.

Aizawa wrote an influential polemic called *New theses* in 1825, the very year that Bakufu leaders reaffirmed a policy of national isolation. Partly because Aizawa's tract proved so popular, upholding isolationism became the litmus test of Bakufu political legitimacy; and it became linked with 'expulsion of Western barbarians', or *jōi*, in obedience to imperial will. But Bakufu and daimyō leaders in fact did the opposite: they acceded to Western demands which were designed to reduce Japan to semi-colonial status. This totally discredited them, for they no longer seemed to be serving their sovereign in the nation's best interests. On the contrary, they appeared to be exploiting the imperial mandate and their hereditary privileges for selfish gain.

On that pretext, Chōshū and Satsuma samurai launched a rebellion in the emperor's name, and forced the Tokugawa shōgun to return his shōgunal title to the imperial court. Thus for the first time since 1333 power was restored to the emperor in 1868. Just as importantly, all daimyō domains were abolished in 1871, and samurai economic privileges were brought to an end within another five years. Taken together, the changes produced are known as the Meiji Restoration.

At first glance, the Restoration seems to be the product of historical atavism and blind xenophobia. But the new Meiji leaders, most of whom were of samurai origin, implemented radical reforms; their 'restoration' was not a return to direct imperial rule as it had supposedly existed in antiquity. At home, they abolished rule by their own class, and in its place they set up a centralized nation-state under the aegis of a European-style constitutional monarch. In foreign affairs, they abandoned isolationism and worked instead for the introduction of Western 'civilization and enlightenment'.

But these policy reversals should not really surprise us. As a prominent loyalist explained even before the Bakufu fell, he and his cohorts were pursuing national independence and autonomy – Western goals couched in Nativist terminology.

> 'Expelling the barbarians' (*jōi*) is not peculiar to our Imperial Realm; all the world's nations practise it. Americans were once subject to England; but the English king, greedy for profit, oppressed them. So Washington appealed for reduced taxes; and when the king refused to listen, he led the 13 colonies to expel the English. That was 'isolationism' (*sakoku*). That was 'expelling the barbarians'.

Thus, the 19th-century Western threat was the catalyst that helped transform existing elements in Tokugawa sociopolitical thought into two salient features of modern nationalism as it evolved in Japan: (a) a desire to forge solidarity among all classes of Japanese through allegiance to the emperor as the divine and sovereign head of a unified family-state, and (b) the need to defend that state from foreign territorial encroachment. Such ideas proved irreconcilable with Bakufu rule and the hereditary warrior-class privilege that had been justified by a form of Confucianism assimilated two centuries earlier.

BTW

The new religions

'New religions' refers to those religious associations which have been founded since 1800 and which exist outside the ecclesiastical structures of temple Buddhism and shrine Shintō. In terms of doctrine, they include Buddhist, Shintō, Christian, and completely new beliefs, and they typically incorporate elements found in more traditional forms of religious association, such as ancestor-worship, healing, and shamanistic practices. Their novelty lies not in their various practices and beliefs but in the way these are assembled into a shared perspective on human problems, a common orientation that can be described as a world view. They thus represent both historical continuity and adaptation to the modern world.

There are currently over 3,000 new religions, with a membership of betweeen 30 and 40 million. One of them alone, Sōka Gakkai, has 12 million adherents. About 15 are large and powerful, with more than 3 million members each, while the majority are much smaller. The larger ones maintain national networks of churches and proselytize widely overseas. They have been particularly concerned to address the concerns of women and have been able to provide meaningful outlets for their talents and energies.

History

The new religions were founded in three distinct waves. The first wave covered the years from 1800 to 1868 and the three most significant organizations founded during that time were Kurozumikyō (1814), Tenrikyō (1838) and Konkokyō (1858), all of which were founded in the relatively prosperous area of western Japan not, as is sometimes imagined, by the poor and oppressed, but by people from stable, even prosperous circumstances. Each founder had experienced revelations after a severe illness or a series of misfortunes. None had intended to found a Shintō sect but by the early 20th century these three religions all espoused Shintō-like doctrines as a result of pressure from the state to adopt Shintō mythology and foster ideas of loyalty and service.

The second wave came in the early 20th century when Reiyūkai Kyōdan (1921–25), Seichō no ie (1929) and Sōka Gakkai (1930) were founded.

Tenrikyō and its founder

Like many of the new religions, Tenrikyō was founded by a woman, Nakayama Miki (1798–1887), and her life illustrates some of the characteristics of the founders of new religions in general.

Nakayama was the daughter of a village headman and her son was afflicted with a chronic infection. She had him treated by a shamanic healer whose method was to induce a trance in his female assistant, to determine through her the identity of the spirits responsible for the affliction, and then to exorcize them. One day when the female medium was unavailable Nakayama took her place and then suddenly began to utter oracles. She announced that a spirit she called the 'Heavenly Shōgun' had taken up residence in her body and that she was to act as his mouthpiece henceforward and to be freed of all her social obligations as wife and mother. This possession lasted more than a week, and in spite of attempts by her family to exorcize the spirit she remained in a trance.

Ecstatic religious experiences through shamanism offered access to knowledge of the supernatural world for Nakayama and other women deprived of secular education or the religious training undergone by Buddhist and Shintō priests. They also provided women with a justification for modifying or rejecting their socially prescribed rôles. This shamanic element is common to many of the new religions in one form or another and represents a clear link with the past.

Nakayama's reputation as a woman who could ensure safe childbirth brought her a circle of female followers. Later, she came to be regarded, like many of the founders of the new religions, as a living deity: her healing and other charismatic practices were seen to be evidence of this. Her doctrine developed into a universal message according to which the universe is ruled by a single parent deity: by practising a life of service and charity with emphasis on communal labour and worship mankind can live in harmony with the will of that deity. Tenrikyō now has a membership of approximately 2,300,000 with chapters in every part of Japan and many overseas branches. Its headquarters, Tenri City, is a religious centre for pilgrims. HH

Reiyūkai and Sōka Gakkai were Buddhist, while Seichō no ie preached the unity of all creeds and incorporated such diverse elements as psychoanalysis, spiritualism and meditation. Sōka Gakkai remained relatively small until 1945, but thereafter its growth was phenomenal, as a result of massive proselytizing campaigns.

Reiyūkai's earliest adherents came from the poorest stratum, recent rural migrants to Tōkyō, among whom the founder, Kotani Kimi (1900–71), did much evangelical work. Until 1945 Reiyūkai had a strong anti-clerical streak and was also, like Seichō no ie, a strong supporter of the wartime government. Later it spawned a number of breakaway associations which have retained its doctrines and practices intact, especially its emphasis on ancestor-worship, which is regarded by most new religions as central to the religious life.

The third wave of new religions came after 1945. This was not simply a response to Japan's defeat, for many of the hundreds of religions that appeared then would undoubtedly have done so earlier had it not been for religious suppression in wartime Japan. All the same, it is probable that the decline of temple Buddhism and shrine Shintō, both of which were closely associated with the pre-war régime and suffered as a result, made it easier for the new religions to establish themselves. In addition, the post-war shift of the population to the cities undermined the rural economic base of Buddhism and Shintō, while many new religions based themselves in the cities.

Of the three major post-war new religions, Perfect Liberty Kyōdan and Sekai Kyūsei Kyō were revivals of organizations that had been severely persecuted during the war. The slogan of P. L. Kyōdan is 'religion is art' and it fosters the practice of the arts in daily life. Sekai Kyūsei Kyō encourages faith healing and farming without fertilizers. The third, Tenshōkōtai Jingūkyō, is informally known as 'the dancing religion' because of its 'dance of no ego'; it was founded in 1945 by Kitamura Sayo (1900–67) who, even before the end of the war, had castigated the emperor as a puppet and civil servants as his 'maggot beggars'.

The new headquarters in Tōkyō of the Reiyūkai, a lay religious sect that was founded in 1921–25 and now has about 3,000,000 members.

World-view

The doctrines of the new religions exhibit enormous variety, but they tend to adopt a common perspective on human problems. As they see it, the self exists in a matrix of relationships with the body, other people, society, nature and the supernatural world. When the self exists in a perfect state of virtue these relationships will be harmonious. As a means of gaining control over one's relationships, the new religions value self-cultivation in the core values of Japanese culture, sincerity, harmony, loyalty, filial piety, modesty and diligence. It is believed that illness arises when the self is not in harmony with the body or with others, and adherents are often told therefore to look into the personal relationships in their household for the origin of a sickness and are advised to repent for having been lax about self-cultivation. Belief in religious healing of this sort is widespread and remarkably persistent.

Organization and membership

The largest and most powerful new religions seek to develop organizations that can cater to all their adherents' needs. Many operate educational facilities from nursery school to high school, and Sōka Gakkai even has its own university and a newspaper with the third highest circulation in Japan. They offer social and cultural activities for both sexes and all ages.

Many followers of the new religions are people cut off from the more usual sources of prestige in Japanese society; they tend to be self-employed or employed in small businesses rather than large corporations, and they tend to be women rather than men. Unable to exercise their talents and energies to gain esteem in mainstream Japanese society, they apply themselves with great zeal to proselytization or doctrinal study. The provision of such alternative prestige structures is unquestionably one of the main reasons for the appeal of the new religions to women, whose opportunities for advancement in secular society remain limited. Since the new religions typically treat proselytization by women as an extension of the mother rôle, implying that they are the spiritual parents of the converted, there is little danger of these activities being seen to be in conflict with their domestic rôles.

The new religions and politics

In general the membership of the new religions is socially and politically conservative. They have seldom sought to influence politics, although the single greatest exception has been the Kōmeitō or 'Clean Government Party'. This political party was created by Sōka Gakkai in 1964 and has since broadened its base beyond Sōka Gakkai membership to become a party of the centre and an important force in Japanese political life. Other new religions have only involved themselves in politics by sponsoring conservative candidates for the Diet to promote their own interests. As the rural population continues to decline, some politicians look upon the new religions as important sources of urban block-votes.

In the 1980s there occurred some interesting departures from this passive political activity, particularly on the part of the Risshōkōsekai, which broke away from Reiyūkai in 1938 and now has a membership of 5 million. Until the 1980s it had routinely expressed unconditional support for conservative candidates, but it has since developed a litmus test of acceptability which has excluded some candidates it had formerly supported: it now withholds support from those found guilty of ethical impropriety, those wanting to expand the armed forces, and those who favour state support for the Yasukuni shrine, the former national shrine for the war dead. As head of the Union of New Religions, with more than 300 member organizations, Risshōkōsekai is in a position to influence the practices of many small religions and to have considerable impact on the political life of Japan. HH

Followers of one of the new religions at a prayer meeting.

Christianity

'Failure' and 'rejection' are the words most associated with Christianity in Japan. In spite of the apparent Westernization of Japanese society today, less than 1% of the population are Christians and there has been a long history of persecution and vilification of what has been seen as a foreign faith. In attempting to understand this situation, it is better to treat Christianity in Japan not as a chapter in the history of missionary work but rather as a case-study of a cross-cultural encounter in which a complex combination of factors, political as well as religious, has been involved. Above all, it is important to bear in mind, first, the obvious conceptual and sociological differences between Christianity and Japanese religion and, second, the tendency of Japanese governments to view religion as a means of social control.

Chronologically, Japan's encounter with Christianity can be divided into three periods, which coincide with important junctures in Japan's relationship with the West. Christianity has inevitably been associated with Western commercial and political interests in East Asia and this has been both a help and a hindrance to its spread in Japan. Each of these three periods started with political, economic and social disruption: Christian missionaries initially met with a positive response but their expectations of success were unfulfilled.

The early missions

The first period started with the arrival of Jesuit missionaries in 1549, at a time when Portuguese traders were also beginning to show an interest in Japan. In general the Jesuits, mainly Portuguese, favoured accommodation to Japanese culture, at least on a superficial level, rather than outright confrontation. This accorded with their strategy of starting the evangelizing process with the most powerful members of the society in which they were working. The Franciscans, who arrived in 1593 and were mainly Spanish, adopted a more confrontational approach and emphasized work among the poor.

The missionaries had limited manpower but were helped by Japanese converts. Local networks run by lay-workers performed a vital rôle during the years of persecution. In 1614, just before the persecution started in earnest, there may have been as many as 370,000 Christians in Japan, nearly 2% of the population, concentrated in Kyūshū. Some were men of learning and some were politically powerful, particularly the 'Christian daimyō' such as Takayama Ukon; but most were peasants who became Christian because that was the wish of their masters. The majority apostasized under persecution, though many did so only to remain alive and there were a great many martyrs.

The appeal of Christianity seems to have lain in its promise of salvation, for this was a period of great social upheaval, and faith in Buddhist deities such as Miroku and Kannon was also flourishing. For samurai in particular the emphasis on selflessness and moral rectitude was also appealing. On the other hand, there can be no doubt that commercial links between the missionaries and the Portuguese traders helped Christianity to gain acceptance. In the long term, however, those links worked to the detriment of the missions. Hideyoshi and Ieyasu, the de facto rulers of Japan at the end of the 16th and beginning of the 17th centuries, were both aware that Christianity had great subversive potential and were suspicious

of the links between Japanese Christians and such powerful Christian countries as Spain and Portugal. In 1612 Ieyasu issued a ban on Christianity and thereafter it became subject to greater controls and the persecution of Christians became more rigorous. After the failure of the Shimabara Rebellion of 1637–38, which was partly Christian in inspiration and was perceived as such by the authorities, Christianity went underground. In remote rural communities Christian belief was preserved for more than 200 years, but it gradually diverged from European Christianity and xenophobic anti-Christian propaganda made Christianity in general repugnant to the majority.

Japanese martyrs

The first sign that Hideyoshi, the de facto ruler of Japan, was in earnest about the persecution of Christianity came on 5 February 1597 when 26 Christians, including six Franciscans and three Jesuits, were crucified at Nagasaki. Little action was taken after this for some time, but in 1622 the 'Great martyrdom' of 51 Christians took place at Nagasaki before a crowd of more than 30,000 and thereafter persecution was relentless. Several thousand were executed in all, and many apostasized under torture, including some missionaries who then spent the remainder of their lives in Japan under house arrest.

Richard Cocks was the manager of the English Factory, or trading station, in Hirado and he has left an eyewitness account of the persecution of Japanese Christian converts.

> The emperor is a great enemy to the name of Christians, especially Japanese, so that all which are found are put to death. I saw 55 martyred at Kyōto at one time when I was there, because they would not forsake their Christian faith, and amongst them were little children of 5 or 6 years old burned in their mothers' arms, crying out, Jesus receive their souls. Also in the town of Nagasaki there were 16 more martyred for the same matter, whereof 5 were burned and the rest beheaded and cut in pieces and cast into the sea in sacks, yet the priests got them up again, and kept them secretly for relics. There is many more in prison in divers places, as also here, which look hourly when they shall die, for very few turn pagans.

These events probably took place in 1619. PK

A detail from a 17th-century screen showing two Portuguese Jesuits visiting the home of a Japanese.

From 1859 to 1945

In 1859 the first treaty ports were opened to trade. Missionaries returned to Japan but they were not permitted to evangelize openly. In 1865 a group of the so-called 'hidden' Christians made contact with Catholic missionaries: as many as 20,000 of them were discovered in the Nagasaki area alone. But this sparked off a fresh wave of persecution, which only came to an end in 1873 after intense diplomatic pressure from Western nations. A significant number of the 'hidden' Christians were unwilling to make the changes required of them to return to orthodoxy within the Catholic church and they remain separate to this day, though their numbers are declining as rural depopulation accelerates.

After 1873 there were few restrictions on Christianity in practice, though technically the bans were not lifted until the Meiji Constitution of 1889. The propaganda of earlier ages branding it an alien religion died hard, however, and Christianity continued to be vulnerable whenever nationalistic feeling ran high.

The most interesting developments in this period relate to Protestantism, which exercised considerable appeal as the possible key to the strength of nations such as Britain and the US. A small but significant number of young ex-samurai converts emerged and quickly led their churches to a position where they could be self-supporting and independent of foreign missionary control. Christianity played an influential rôle in the development of education and the growth of socialist ideas in Japan, and many writers came under Christian influence to some extent.

Once again, however, the Western associations of Christianity and the desire of the Japanese state to control religious organizations worked to its disadvantage in the long term. For most of the 1880s Christianity flourished but it suffered in the more nationalistic 1890s. In fact, the majority of Japanese Christians were highly patriotic and uneasy themselves about the non-Japanese origins of their faith. Uchimura Kanzō, probably the most well-known Christian leader in Japan, spoke out against the Russo-Japanese War of 1904–05 but also condemned the organizational structures of Western churches. He became leader of the Mukyōkai (Non-church) movement, which is modelled on the traditional Japanese teacher–pupil relationship.

Christianity and social welfare

For many Japanese today Christianity is closely associated with schools, hospitals, mental hospitals and other welfare institutions. Indeed, it is said that Buddhist churches only became extensively involved in welfare work in the 19th century because of the impact of the activities of Christian missionaries. In this century, the social consequences of Japan's rapid industrialization forged an alliance between Christian and socialist thinking that has long been influential. Many of the founding members of the Social Democratic Party in 1901 and later of early trade union organizations were Christians, although some later abandoned their Christianity for Marxism.

The most famous Christian socialist in modern Japan is Kagawa Toyohiko (1888–1960), who was baptized while still at school and subsequently spent two years at Princeton Theological Seminary in the US.

On his return to Japan he lived and worked as a pastor in the slums of Kōbe but he was also active in the embryonic labour movement, for which he spent a short time in prison in 1921. In 1922 he was the co-founder of the Japan Farmers' Union, which tackled the problem of rural poverty, but he also became prominent in the pre-war years as an evangelist and ecumenist with a mass appeal. His successors in post-war Japan have been Christian welfare workers and pastors who have worked with shell-shocked soldiers and others left destitute after the Pacific War, with children growing up in the poor quarter of Tōkyō near the municipal rubbish dumps, with old people left behind in the rush to nuclear families and smaller homes in the 1960s and 1970s, and more recently with refugees from Vietnam.

PK

Christianity in rural areas suffered both from financial difficulties and from nationalistic feelings, and mainstream Protestantism in particular became associated, as it is today, with the urban middle class. While Christians continued to be active in education and social work, the increasing tension between Japan and the West had an adverse effect on its image. The majority of Japanese Christians, with the backing of their church organizations, tried to behave as loyal citizens and tended to adapt, however reluctantly, to the increasingly militaristic mood.

Most missionaries had left Japan before the Pacific War broke out. Japanese Christians suffered during the war as much as other sections of the population, if not more so because of the suspicion with which they were regarded. The atomic bomb dropped on Nagasaki devastated the oldest centre of Christianity in Japan.

The post-war years

With the end of the Pacific War and the start of the Occupation foreign missionaries resumed their work. Christians went through a difficult time in which they tried to rebuild both the physical and spiritual damage of the war. At a time when many had lost faith in Japan and turned enthusiastically to the US, Christianity aroused much interest but the real long-term gains were made by new religious movements such as Sōka Gakkai, which were firmly based in the Japanese religious tradition.

The post-war constitution guaranteed religious freedom and the separation of religion and state. Christian groups protest about signs of government involvement with Shintō, where rites connected with the imperial family are concerned, for example, and they are also active in the peace movement. Christmas and white Christian-style weddings have become an accepted part of popular culture, and Christianity has a much more sympathetic image than it has ever had before, but this is as much a result of its Western associations as its religious message. Although they do so much to make Christianity seem attractive, these associations also make it appear remote, so that actual church membership is confined to a committed élite. It may be fated therefore to remain a marginal, if influential, part of the Japanese religious landscape.

HJB

Modern intellectual currents

Left *A church in the Amakusa islands off Kyūshū. In the foreground is a graveyard containing both Christian and Buddhist gravestones.*

Below left *The assembly house in Mita where Fukuzawa Yukichi introduced the art of public speaking to Japan in 1875.*

Below right *Fukuzawa as a young man in samurai dress with sword.*

Modern Japanese thought is characterized by a tension between the pressure to learn about the conceptual presuppositions of Western success and the perceived need to develop philosophies and ideologies that were both 'Japanese' and yet fitted the new world in which Japan found itself. Intellectual currents, even in their purest academic form, have been inextricably linked to political and historical imperatives.

During the first two decades of the Meiji era, the main interest was in positivism, pragmatism and utilitarianism, and the two most important figures in what became known as the Japanese Enlightenment were Nishi Amane (1829–97) and Fukuzawa Yukichi (1835–1901). Nishi, who had studied in Leiden, was responsible for coining much of modern Japanese intellectual vocabulary, including the word for philosophy itself: *tetsugaku*. Comte's positivist vision of the natural progress of mankind through three stages – religious, metaphysical and scientific – and J. S. Mill's liberal humanism were ideal philosophies on which to base an optimistic assessment of Japan's potential for change and growth. They explained Western success while at the same time stressing that the path of progress was universal. Like many of his contemporaries, Nishi concluded that Confucianism was largely to blame for the position in which Japan now found herself. Fukuzawa, who visited the US and Europe, held similar views, emphasizing that modernization presupposes acknowledging human equality, individual dignity and independence, and a division of power.

Partly because these liberal ideas were too optimistic and entailed a rejection of many deeply-held

values, their introduction produced a strong reaction. Traditionalists could also find within Western thought justification for a more conservative outlook, and it was not long before German philosophy, particularly in the area of social and political thought, began to make a substantial impact. The promulgation of the conservative Imperial Rescript on Education in 1890 was a major sign that these views had gained the upper hand. Hozumi Yatsuka (1860–1912), who trained in Germany, used ideas of German statism to strengthen its Japanese counterpart and Inoue Tetsujirō (1855–1944), who had also studied in Germany, returned to argue that positivism and egalitarianism neglected the life of the spirit and went counter to much that was intuitively 'Japanese'. Such correctives were only to be expected and it is fair to say that a reasonable balance between cultural pride on the one hand and modernization on the other was held until the excesses of the 1930s.

The same cannot be said for the reaction of the authorities to socialism, which emerged in the early years of the 20th century. Although liberal ideas flowered once again for a brief period in the 1920s (the so-called Taishō Democracy), both socialism and Marxism were immediately stifled as political movements, branded as being anti-emperor and hence anti-Japanese. Neither movement managed to become anything more than the preserve of middle-class intellectuals with a concern for social consequences of capitalism. Marxism itself is important mainly for the impact it had on historians, to the extent that much modern Japanese historiography can only be understood against such a theoretical background.

The use of German philosophy for the development of modern versions of traditional ideas culminated in the work of Nishida Kitarō (1870–1945), a professor of philosophy at Kyōto University, and the Kyōto School, which Nishida is credited with having established. Nishida was indebted to German idealism and mysticism, but his key notions were 'oriental nothingness' and 'oriental logic': 'oriental nothingness', he said, designated true reality as apprehended in a religious experience in accordance with 'oriental logic'. Nishida's thought is not so much a philosophy of religion as a religious philosophy, something already apparent in his early work *A study of the Good* (1911). Tanabe Hajime (1885–1962) and Nishitani Keiji (1900–90) were the most influential

Two Marxists: Katayama Sen and Kawakami Hajime

Katayama Sen (1860–1933) was the only Asian appointed to sit on the Praesidium of the Third International in Moscow and is the only Japanese buried in the Kremlin Wall.

He had a peripatetic education in Japan and the US during which he moved from Christianity to socialism and developed an interest in social work. On returning to Japan in 1897 he threw himself into the trade union movement and became the editor of its first newspaper, the bilingual *Labour world*.

Later the repression of socialist groups in Japan forced him into voluntary exile in the US, where his published writings and lectures made him internationally known. In the aftermath of the Russian Revolution of 1917 he became involved in the reorganization of the American Communist Party, but in 1921 he went to Moscow for the First Congress of Toilers of the Far East: the enthusiastic reception accorded him persuaded him to stay. Moscow became his base for the remainder of his life and he acted as the Kremlin's spokesman on Asia.

Kawakami Hajime (1879–1946), by contrast, enjoyed an élite education and a privileged position as professor of economics at Kyōto University.

A visit to Europe on the eve of the First World War gave him first-hand experience of poverty and inspired him to write his most famous work, *Binbō monogatari* (*Tales of poverty*, 1916). In 1919 he turned to Marxism and his subsequent activities as an interpreter of Marxist thought brought him into conflict with the authorities: he was compelled to resign his professorship in 1928.

As a political activist on behalf of the Labourers and Farmers Party and later as a contributor to *Red flag*, the organ of the Japan Communist Party, he was a target for the police and he was finally arrested in 1933. He was found guilty of having contravened the notorious Peace Preservation Act of 1925 and he served four years in prison. After his release in 1937 he devoted the rest of his life to an autobiographical account of his intellectual quest. PK members of the Kyōto School. They both studied with Heidegger and used Heideggerian methods to develop Nishida's thought. Members of the Kyōto School have continued spreading notions of a uniquely oriental 'nothingness' and 'logic' similar to Nishida's.

The central question that still underlies all this probing is one of cultural identity: the need to discover defining differences between Japan and the West. It is particularly clear in the work of Watsuji Tetsujirō (1889–1960) who developed a congenial theory whereby national differences were defined in terms of climate: a kind of geographical determinism that fitted well with older ideas of a divine land. Kuki Shūzō (1888–1941) located Japaneseness in the concept of *iki*, a kind of panache seen at its most typical in the life and culture of the Tokugawa townspeople. Watsuji and Kuki had also studied with Heidegger and their methods of analysis were influenced by Heideggerian phenomenology. Recourse has also been had to emphasizing the special characteristics of the Japanese language itself as a path to self-definition. The most recent trend is to see Japan as already inhabiting the future: the first truly post-modern state with rampant consumerism and a barrage of empty signifiers hiding an absence of all meaning. Comparativists like Nakamura Hajime (1921–) have emphasized cultural commonalities, such as the existence of rational traditions of thought in both Western and Japanese culture, but this perspective has proved far less popular than the seductive ideas of Japanese exclusivity. GP/RB

Problems with translation

One of the major difficulties confronting not only thinkers in the Meiji period but also reformers of all persuasions was that of the lack of Japanese terms for the concepts, technologies and artifacts being introduced from the West.

Words for 'railway', 'station', 'exhibition', 'insurance', 'economics' and 'rights' all had to be coined, and for each of them a combination of Chinese characters was put together in an attempt to represent the meaning. In the case of the first three, the problems of acceptance were non-existent once the words could be associated with visible phenomena, but the second three exemplify the difficulties faced by those who sought to educate Meiji men and women in the conceptual ways of the West.

The modern Japanese word for 'rights', *kenri*, was first used in 1869 in a translation from the French Penal Code, and had in fact been borrowed from a Chinese translation of an English work on law, but the word was not ideal for conveying the concept, for the character *ken* was generally understood at the time to connote 'might' rather than 'right'.

'Society' was another concept that posed difficulties and this is apparent from early English–Japanese dictionaries that were stuck for an equivalent and opted for words meaning 'friend', 'company' or 'social intercourse'. Some writers just used the English word written out in Japanese *kana* script, which in the 20th century became the usual way of adapting words from Western languages, but it was the combination of characters meaning 'association' and 'meet' that produced what became the standard Japanese word for 'society' *shakai*. This combination of characters was later adopted into Chinese with Chinese pronunciation as a loan word from Japanese, as in fact happened to many Meiji coinages.

The difficulty of vocabulary was at its most profound when it came to the language of logic and philosophical discourse. There was in Japanese no neutral word for philosophy itself, for existing words connoted either Buddhist or Confucian thought. It was Nishi Amane (1829–97), a government official highly enthusiastic in his espousal of Western values, who developed the terminology of modern philosophy. For some concepts, such as 'subjectivity', 'objectivity' and 'psychology', he coined new words, while for others, such as 'reason', 'reality' and 'phenomenon' he used existing words from the Chinese terminological traditions of Buddhism and Confucianism and gave them new senses.

For this reason Meiji texts presented formidable challenges to the reader: they bristled with unfamiliar words or familiar words with unfamiliar meanings, and the task of assimilating the concepts that lay behind them was a daunting one. PK

Arts and Crafts

Pictorial art before 1600

As early as the 17th century, native historians of Japanese painting conceptualized the development of this art form in terms of hereditary and stylistic lineages. This preoccupation with artistic biography, an approach paralleled in ancient Greece and Renaissance Italy, drew inspiration from Chinese convention. After 1868, the 19th-century European romantic cliché of the lone artistic genius entered Japan to reinforce existing stereotypes about artistic personality and the rôle of the artist in society.

Neither the Chinese ideal of the talented amateur scholar-painter nor European notions of genius fit the actual circumstances faced by painters in pre-Tokugawa Japan. Many members of the aristocracy, men and women, took up the brush as semi-professional calligraphers, and some painted as an avocation or as an act of religious devotion; yet painting was primarily a professional occupation. Whether they were low-ranking aristocrats in the official court painting bureau or priests and monks in shrine and temple workshops, painters were subject to the close direction of their superiors. Large-scale commissions – walls, screens, and sets of paintings in smaller formats – were usually collaborative efforts between painters, their apprentices, scribes, and mounters. In such an environment, individual signatures are rare and attributions are frequently uncertain. Not until the late 15th century, with Sinophile painters such as Sesshū (1420–1506), do a few painters self-consciously proclaim their artistic identities by seal, signature, and self-inscription. Sesshū was an exception in an age when competing workshops were busily fabricating antique lineages and vying for the business of patrons. Signatures became more common only as the work of individual painters became more highly valued, largely a Tokugawa phenomenon.

In addition to this bias towards biography, the history of Japanese painting is usually divided into periods of foreign impact alternating with periods of native synthesis and creativity. *Yamato-e*, an elusive but widely employed term, connotes the styles and subjects deemed expressive of native (*yamato*) sentiment and taste. Conversely, the terms *kara-e* (Tang painting) and *kanga* (Han painting) refer to paintings imported from China (and Korea), as well as paintings in Chinese styles or on Chinese subjects. This schema thus celebrates paintings of the 11th and 12th centuries for their 'Japaneseness'. Earlier painting is said to derive from that of Tang China and later painting to show increasing traces of contact with Song, Yuan, and Ming models. Traditional historians and modern scholars alike still argue that these opposites, native and Chinese, the vibrant and the astringent, the emotional and the intellectual, were finally synthesized in the 16th century.

Neither approach can fully tell the story of Japanese painting. Historical or political terms arbitrarily categorize developments in art, while a modernist paradigm places value only on what is new in any given period. Extant paintings of high quality or those attributed to known painters are celebrated while documentary sources and less striking works are downplayed. Closer focus on the social functions of painting is needed to elucidate the practices and beliefs that underlie its production.

Painting and religion

In AD 806, in his catalogue of objects acquired in China, the Shingon monk Kūkai asserted that painting, even more than the written word, expresses profound Buddhist truths through the representations of various deities and their relationships. Contemplation of paintings, he wrote, might enable viewers to attain Buddhahood. Although he was referring specifically to mandalas, a similar attitude towards the uses of painting and sculpture often motivated the production of religious art. The opulent beauty of many Buddhist paintings, with their lavish mineral pigments and appliquéd cut-gold patterns, demonstrates reverence for the subject depicted. But while a viewer may be captivated by this outward beauty, the complexities of Buddhist doctrine and iconography require explication, through oral preaching or sūtras and commentaries.

Depictions of buddhas preaching to assembled deities, celestial attendants, and musicians, adorned the walls, pillars, and ceilings of many Buddhist halls and pagodas. The focus of prayer, ceremony, or lecture in such buildings was the sculpted images on the altar, but the painted walls functioned both as

Previous page Egrets, irises and blossoms. *One of a pair of six-fold screens; ink and gold leaf on paper, 19th century.*

A late 17th-century example of a mandala of the matrix-world of great compassion. An object of intense contemplation, the mandala was designed by devotees of esoteric Buddhism to lead the viewer to further understanding and enlightenment.

reverent embellishment and as a device to situate the altar more fully within the spatial context of the Buddhist cosmos. Narratives, whether of the life of the historical Buddha, known in Japanese as Shaka, the parables of the *Lotus sūtra*, the transmission of Shingon secret teachings, or the Nine Stages of Rebirth in Amida's Pure Land, expanded the repertoire.

Although most such paintings have perished along with the temples, portable hanging scrolls were also hung on walls and interior partitions during lectures and ceremonies. For lectures carried out on special occasions, such as the anniversary of Shaka's attainment of nirvana, large-scale paintings were explained to the public. Paintings of individual deities from the vast Buddhist pantheon also served as the focus of private invocation, usually to alleviate illness or to ensure safe delivery in childbirth. Aristocratic devotees owned personal icons, whether in painting or sculpture, as a focus of prayer in their private rooms or chapels.

The need for correct renderings of poses, hand positions, attributes, colours, and costumes in the presentation of these deities generally constrained innovation. Iconographic compendia, sketches, tracings, and full-scale preparatory drawings provide clues to the transmission of style and iconography over time. Changes occurred with the importation of new models from abroad, or, occasionally, in response to a dream vision by monks in positions of authority. Large temples employed monk-painters to fulfil the constant demand for such paintings, a need that continued and even expanded as Buddhism spread during the medieval period beyond its aristocratic origins.

Closely related to Buddhist painting in style and appearance are renderings of Shintō deities known as *kami*. These representations depict *kami* either in native court dress or in the guise of the original Buddhist deities of whom they were believed to be native manifestations. Shintō shrines originally had neither buildings nor anthropomorphic representations, but contact with the richness of Buddhism brought about changes in all facets of native beliefs and practices. 'Shrine mandalas', especially those of the Kasuga and Kumano shrines, depict bird's-eye views of the natural settings and buildings in their shrine precincts. Such paintings initially served a

Right *Detail from a mandala devoted to the* Lotus sūtra. *Kamakura period, 13th century. In this case the central figure is Amida Buddha.*

Section from a Shintō 'deer mandala'. Portrayed here is the passage of the Kashima deity, Takemikazuchi no Mikoto, from his home in the east to the Kasuga Shrine in Nara, where he became the central object of worship. He is said to have arrived riding a white deer. Deer roam both shrine and city even today. The presence of a white deer in such a painting will always be a reference to this particular deity.

devotional function, but during the later medieval period depictions of shrine precincts and their deities metamorphosed into views of popular pilgrimage destinations filled with visitors.

Portraits generally served a religious purpose, whether to glorify a sectarian lineage or as the focus of a funeral or memorial ceremony. Depictions of the eight Shingon patriarchs adorn the walls of Shingon halls and pagodas. Within the Zen sect, students acquired self-inscribed portraits of their teachers as mementos of their training and as devotional icons. More rarely, portraits depicted imaginary visions of real people who were later revered as Shintō *kami*, as in the case of Sugawara no Michizane's (845–903) transformation into the Kitano deity. Portraits of lay benefactors were cared for in their own memorial chapels, either in private residences or within the grounds of the temples they supported. Unlike the idealized and necessarily repetitive Buddhist images, these portraits generally captured a likeness of the subject's face. Conventions of dress, pose, or attributes conveyed social status, power, and religiosity.

Painting and literature

As in China, painting in Japan has always been closely allied to poetry and calligraphy. During the Heian period, six-fold screens on Chinese and Japanese themes were created for formal and celebratory occasions. Poets composed poetic sequences incorporating the painted themes, usually the four seasons, monthly activities, or famous places. Calligraphers wrote the poems on ornamented poem-papers which were then directly affixed to the screens. Such screens were sent as diplomatic gifts, for they were included even in the 12th-century Chinese imperial collection. Although almost all such screens have been long since lost, hundreds of screen poems survive in imperial anthologies and private poetry collections. The public literary function of screen painting declined after the 11th century, but screens on poetic subjects became a mainstay of Japanese interiors, both religious and secular. The sumptuous 'golden' screens of the 15th century could be found not only among official gifts sent to Ming China but also in private houses. The poetic themes devised during the Heian period provided an eternal source of inspiration to later painters and craft designers.

If screens and their poems were created largely for celebratory occasions, a more private form of painting served literary interests within the residential quarters of the imperial palace and aristocratic mansions. Narrative picture scrolls were also derived initially from Chinese prototypes: illustrations for sūtras, the classics, or poetic narratives. In China, the horizontal scroll came to be used primarily by landscape painters, in Japan the format largely served storytelling purposes. During the Heian period, women and children formed the primary audience for illustrated tales of ancient and contemporary court life, of which *The tale of Genji* is the best-known example. Such tales were sometimes criticized for their frivolity, but these same court women commissioned lavishly ornamented copies of the *Lotus sūtra*, either for their private use or for donation to Buddhist temples. Court tales and sūtras alike utilized sumptuous materials, common motifs and pictorial styles, and elegant calligraphy for their texts.

The popular tales and songs of the late Heian and early medieval periods also inspired narrative paint-

Above *Frontispiece to the* Lotus sūtra, *Chapter 17 'Discrimination of merits'.* Heike nōkyō. *The commissioning of such work was itself an act of great merit. This particular set of illustrations, with its lavish use of gold, was dedicated to the Itsukushima Shrine by Taira no Kiyomori in 1164.*

ings. Buddhist miracles or political events were among the new subjects, along with depictions of the battles that had recently raged in the provinces and the capital. The rise of new sects and the renewal of some older sects in the 13th century led to the creation of long illustrated biographies of sectarian founders, usually commissioned and paid for by a temple or by prominent lay benefactors. These scrolls were frequently copied for deposit in branch temples, and often the pictures contained therein were recopied and reformatted into hanging scrolls for use in lectures. While the surviving picture scrolls of the 12th and 13th centuries are best known, temple and shrine histories continued to be produced throughout the medieval period, especially in connection with temple restorations. The names of their painters and scribes and the details of their production often appear on the scrolls or are known from passages in noblemen's diaries. Illustrated popular folk tales (known as *otogi zōshi* or *Nara ehon*), produced outside of official court and temple workshops, continued the earlier picture scroll tradition and spread literacy and painting to an ever-broadening audience.

Renewed contact with China and the rise of Zen in the medieval period brought new themes and techniques. In the 14th century, small-scale devotional hanging scrolls often depicted a solitary figure of Shaka, the white-robed Buddhist deity Kannon, or an eccentric monk, usually simply brushed in ink line and wash. Such paintings are often attributed to painters of uncertain origin, but the Chinese inscriptions floating in the empty space above the figure were written by prominent Chinese and Japanese Zen masters. Ashikaga Yoshimitsu (1358–1408) and his descendants actively collected Chinese imports, and, as contact with Chinese literati culture increased, Japanese ink painters expanded their repertoire to include flowers, birds, and landscapes. The poetic component flourished, and in the early 15th century narrow vertical scrolls were produced, often depicting an idyllic vision of a scholar's study in mist and trees, overpowered by the weight of multiple inscriptions above. The writers of the poems and the recipients of the paintings were Zen abbots patronized by the ruling Ashikaga and other warrior élites, with whom the abbots had frequent social and business contact. The painters are generally unrecorded; it was the content of the painting and poetry and the memory of the social occasion that were most treasured.

Right *Landscape in* haboku *('broken ink') style. Sesshū, 1495. The startling effect was produced by jabbing dark paint over a pale wash outline that was not fully dry. If shown full length, the landscape would be seen to have a series of Chinese poems in praise of the artist and a preface by Sesshū himself floating in the space above.*

Painting in architecture

The walls and sliding door panels of residences, and the screens used therein, also provided a surface for painting. As early as the 9th century, the imperial palace walls were covered with depictions of Chinese worthies and immortal landscapes, a practice still visible in the restored imperial palace in Kyōto. Since all early residences are lost and literary references to interior decor are scant, it is difficult to pinpoint when this practice became common among the aristocracy. Picture scrolls from the 12th and 13th centuries show numerous folding and stationary screens, walls and sliding door panels covered with highly coloured plants, landscapes, and figural scenes. By the late 13th century, monochrome ink landscape screens and wall-paintings appear in narrative scrolls long before they are known from other evidence. Scholars dispute whether such depictions are reliable, but it is certain that the practice of painting interior spaces began long before the 15th century, when documentary and extant evidence coincide.

After the Ōnin War (1467–77) laid waste to much of Kyōto, members of the Kano family established a successful and enduring atelier to meet the enormous demand for paintings of all subjects and formats. As their clientèle expanded to include newly wealthy warlords and merchants, Kano painters introduced colour, gold and a grand compositional scale into an artform that had previously been subdued. The incessant warfare of the 16th century brought about the development of a new architectural type, the castle, with its multi-storied towers and residential buildings. Most famous for the history of painting was Oda Nobunaga's (1534–82) Azuchi castle, its seven floors decorated by Kano Eitoku (1543–90) and assistants from 1576 to 1579. Documents from the period reveal that painting subjects (almost exclusively Chinese) and techniques (ink monochrome or heavy colours on gold) varied according to the function of the rooms. Although the castle was destroyed in 1582, the legacy of Kano Eitoku flourished in the succeeding decades.

Kano and other painting workshops also produced screens in great numbers. Contemporary genre subjects, especially views of the streets, edifices, and inhabitants of Kyōto, developed along with the newly resurgent and commercial city. Contact with Spanish and Portuguese missionaries and traders sparked curiosity about the West and the distant port of Nagasaki. Screens depicting maps and peoples of the world, European cities, and the strange appearance and customs of the foreigners known as 'Southern barbarians', now drew inspiration from a new source: Western paintings and books.

KLB

From a pair of eight-fold screens, Landscape of the four seasons. *Kaihō Yūshō (1533–1615). The combination of a prominent feature in the foreground with a receding vista of hills and rivers is typical of large-scale Muromachi-period screens.*

Pictorial art from 1600

After the death of Kano Mitsunobu in 1608, the Kano school strategy of spreading its talented members among rival political factions paid off: Naganobu (1577–1654) and, later, Tan'yū (1602–74) were sent to work for the Tokugawa in Edo and by 1617, 16-year old Tan'yū was 'painter by appointment' to the Bakufu and working on the decorative scheme for Edo castle. The vast organization of the four main Edo branches of the Kano school, and its many subsidiaries in the provinces, would dominate painting practice and patronage for the rest of the Edo period. Tan'yū's graceful and tranquil synthesis of *yamato-e* and Chinese antiquarianism was a formula guaranteed to appeal to the 'warriors turned bureaucrats' and was perpetuated in the art theories of his younger brother Yasunobu (1613–85), who championed faithful replication of the masterpieces of the past over the creative genius of any individual painter. Whilst the Kano school after 1700 continued to provide the basic model for technical facility with the brush, creativity withered and many talented painters rebelled against tradition to form unorthodox schools and styles.

New styles emerge

In the West we have become used to the notion of perpetual revolution in visual culture, the constant 'shock of the new'. Edo Japan, however, witnessed the successive birth of schools and styles of painting in opposition to the official Kano ateliers which did not replace one another but functioned *in parallel*. By the mid 19th century they numbered at least a dozen – the traditional schools of Kano, Tosa and Buddhist painting; and the new movements of Rinpa, Ōbaku, genre, ukiyo-e, Sumiyoshi, Nanga, Nagasaki, Zen, Western-style, Maruyama, and Shijō – influencing one another to be sure, but always maintaining their distinct character and base of support. Undoubtedly this reflects the official ranking of Edo society into the four classes of samurai, farmer, merchant and artisan on the broadest level; but also the kaleidoscopic fragmentation of cultural circles into proudly maintained lineages according to the ubiquitous hereditary familial system known as *iemoto*.

Even as the Kano school was establishing its hegemony, an unusual alliance was forming in Kyōto in the first decade of the 17th century between court aristocrats, craftsmen and wealthy merchants under the presiding geniuses of the painter Tawaraya Sōtatsu (d. 1643?) and the calligrapher Hon'ami

Iris screens *by Ogata Kōrin (1658–1716). Many of the themes behind such paintings were consciously rooted in the classical court culture. Irises would immediately call up a famous scene: Section 9 of the* Tales of Ise *(see panel on p. 128).*

Kōetsu (1558–1637). Motifs were plucked from medieval handscrolls and painted large and with a new bold sense of design and placing over folding screens, often with gold-leaf backgrounds. The new style had a conscious element of protest against the new military régime in its choice of nostalgic themes from the great courtly literary classics, *The tale of Genji* and *Tales of Ise*. Not formed into an hereditary lineage like other schools, the Sōtatsu style (or Rinpa [school of Kōrin] style as it came to be known) was only periodically revived: by Ogata Kōrin (1658–1716) in Kyōto and then Edo around the year 1700; by Sakai Hōitsu (1761–1828) in Edo around 1800; and finally by Kamisaka Sekka (1866–1942) in Kyōto in works such as his album *Grasses of the myriad worlds* (*Momoyogusa*) of 1909.

Genre painting and ukiyo-e

As the country reverted to peace and prosperity after more than a century of ruinous civil war, there was a demand from new military patrons for genre screens (*fūzokuga*) on a wide variety of themes to decorate their new mansions: boisterous crowds enjoying Kyōto festivals or the fairs in the dry riverbed of the Kamo river in summer; revelry beneath cherry blossom or autumn maples, or in luxuriously appointed houses of pleasure; military sports and battle scenes. These were originally done mainly by Kano masters, but as Kano painting was forced into an increasingly narrow and ideological framework at the service of the Bakufu, the burgeoning demand for genre works came to be met by anonymous 'town painters' and, from the 1670s, by artists such as Hishikawa Moronobu (d. 1694) working in the new, racy 'floating world' (ukiyo-e) style. The techniques of woodblock printing were harnessed to make these images available to a wide audience at a modest price.

The ethos of the floating world was to enjoy the pleasures of life as they came and ukiyo-e imagery was dominated by paintings and prints of courtesans of the pleasure quarters and actors of the kabuki stage, the two arenas where townsmen spent most of their money. The technology of colour woodblock printing became ever more lavish, finally breaking into full colour in 1765 with the delicate 'brocade prints' (*nishiki-e*) of Suzuki Harunobu (d. 1770), to be followed in the 1790s by the twin geniuses of Kitagawa Utamaro (1754–1806) and Tōshūsai Sharaku (worked 1794–95) designing bust portrait prints of courtesans and actors respectively. Under impetus from the tirelessly innovative Katsushika Hokusai (1760–1849) the range of subject matter of ukiyo-e was widened considerably to include new genres such as landscape, as exemplified in his series *Thirty-six views of Mt Fuji* (*Fugaku sanjū-rokkei*, c. 1830).

Right *Kitagawa Utamaro.* Portrait of Ohisa, *a famous Edo courtesan. It was prints such as this, produced in large numbers, that succeeded in transforming the world of brothels and commercialized sex on a grand scale into a vision of refinement.*

Far right *Itō Jakuchū (1716–1800).* Domestic fowl. *Jakuchū was never linked to any particular school and was often somewhat unusual in his choice of subject. The extreme attention to detail here has links to a growing interest in matters of zoology and biology at the time.*

New styles from China

Though Japan was all but isolated from the outside world by official policy, a small but steady stream of books and works of art did enter the country with Dutch and Chinese traders; particularly after the liberalizing reforms of Shōgun Yoshimune in the 1720s. Paintings and printed painting manuals imported from Qing China spawned imitators in two main styles: a small school of bird and flower painters in imitation of the meticulous, brilliantly coloured Chinese court painting, known in Japan as the Nagasaki school; and a much larger and more endur-

ing school imitating the so-called 'southern' literati painting of China, known in Japan as either Nanga (southern school) or *bunjinga* (scholar painting). Nanga painters favoured eccentric, untrammelled brushwork and a union of the sister arts of poetry, calligraphy, painting and even music. Initially their themes were highly derivative of Chinese models – plants, rocks, landscapes populated with scholar gentlemen – but in later generations Nanga painting was softened by a humorous native strain, epitomized in the work of the two later 18th-century masters Yosa Buson (1716–83) and Ikeno Taiga (1723–76).

Beginnings of Western influence

A totally novel way of organizing pictorial space was introduced to Japanese artists through popular European prints which employed perspective lines converging dramatically towards a low horizon. Taken up first by ukiyo-e print artists such as Okumura Masanobu (1686–1764) in the 1740s and later incorporated by Hokusai into his landscapes in the 19th century, 'perspective pictures' (*uki-e*) were also produced by the young Maruyama Ōkyo (1733–95) for the Owariya toyshop in Kyōto *c.* 1759. Though Ōkyo's mature screen and sliding panel paintings came to feature much more traditional subjects and brushwork, they nevertheless often have a revolutionary sense of deep space which was highly influential on all later artists, preparing them (unknowingly) for the onslaught of full-blown Western styles after the opening of the country. In addition, a small group of scholars and painters involved with foreign studies such as Hiraga Gennai (1726–79) and Shiba Kōkan (1747–1818) even experimented with copperplate prints and paintings of Western subjects in a technique imitating Western oil painting, employing the alien pictorial devices of modelling and shadow. This style was taken up by the daimyō of Akita, Satake Shōzan (1748–85) and his protégé Odano Naotake (1749–80) for a brief period in the 1770s. But perhaps because artistic contact with the West was never sustained enough and techniques were never completely mastered, Western-style painting did not enter the mainstream of artistic practice in the Edo period.

Odano Naotake, Shinobazu pond. *Colours on silk. An early attempt to adopt Western painting techniques.*

PAINTING IN KYŌTO

The last major school to evolve in the Edo period, the Shijō, was established in the 1790s by Ōkyo's pupil Matsumura Goshun (1752–1811) and named after the street in Kyōto where his studio was located. Goshun modified Ōkyo's often large-scale and generally serious style into a lighter, more genial idiom more guaranteed to appeal to the Kyōto and Ōsaka bourgeoisie. Typical Shijō works by pupils of Goshun such as Matsumura Keibun (1779–1843) and Okamoto Toyohiko (1773–1845) are hanging scrolls, handscrolls or albums showing domestic Kyōto subjects, landscapes, still-lifes, animals or plants – lightly and deftly executed in washes of colour that are allowed to resonate in the unpainted space around them. The Shijō style was taken to Edo at the end of the first decade of the 19th century, but maintained its vigour and a strong basis of support in Kyōto throughout the century – one of the reasons why the Kyōto art world was able to escape many of the vicissitudes which plagued the fragmented artistic movements of Tōkyō during the Meiji era. Thus Kyōto in the early 20th century produced the various (and generally harmonious) talents of the great Nanga practitioner Tomioka Tessai (1836–1924), the Western-style painter Umehara Ryūzaburō (1888–1986) and the Japanese-style painter Takeuchi Seiho (1868–1942).

Developments in the Meiji period

The dramatic polarization of artistic practice in Tōkyō during the Meiji era between *yōga*, as Western-style painting was known, and *nihonga*, or Japanese-style painting, should be seen in the wider context of the crisis of national identity which beset almost all spheres of culture as the country was progressively swamped by foreign influences. Even before the end of the Tokugawa period, *yōga* had been promoted for largely utilitarian ends by the Bakufu in the Bureau for Investigating Foreign Books (*Bansho shirabesho*, founded 1861) and one of its pupils, Takahashi Yuichi (1828–94), went on to be a pioneering *yōga* oil painter. In 1876, the Italian Barbizon painter Antonio Fontanesi (1818–82) was invited by the Meiji government to teach at the new Technical College Art School.

During the 1880s, however, a reaction set in led by the critic Okakura Tenshin (1862–1913) and the American educator Ernest Fenollosa (1853–1908) who championed artists of traditional schools such as Kano Hōgai (1828–88) and warned against the wholesale adoption of Western artistic practices. *Yōga* painters now found themselves barred from official exhibitions and when the Tōkyō Art School was founded in 1889, it offered no course in Western-style art. *Yōga* painters responded by founding their own Meiji Fine Arts Society and the White Horse Society led by Kuroda Seiki (1866–1924), a highly influential teacher who introduced the *pleinairism* he had studied in France.

In 1898 Okakura gathered around him a group of like-minded *nihonga* painters led by Shimomura Kanzan (1878–1930), Yokoyama Taikan (1868–1958) and others to form the Japan Fine Arts Academy whose ambition it was to revive the themes

Kuroda Seiki. Beside the lake. *This painting, done in 1897 after Kuroda's ten-year stint in Paris, is characteristic of the work of his middle period, with light airy colours and a posed model. In many ways Kuroda can be considered the father of modern Japanese painting in the Western style.*

and techniques of pre-Edo traditions of native painting, with certain concessions nevertheless to Western-style atmospheric handling of space and light; this earned them the nickname of the 'dim and hazy' school (*mōrōha*). The actual divisions between *yōga* and *nihonga* painting at this period were perhaps over-emphasized due to ideological differences and a preoccupation with technique. In fact both camps of painters often grappled with similar themes – the common vogue for history painting in the 1890s, for instance.

The artists in the Meiji era who most directly captured the turbulence of the times and the changing face of Japan were perhaps the three popular painters and printmakers in the ukiyo-e tradition: Taisō Yoshitoshi (1839–92), Kawanabe Kyōsai (1831–89) and Kobayashi Kiyochika (1847–1915). In the first decade of the new century an idealistic group of printmakers formed the so-called Creative Print movement, which aimed to be more directly involved in artistic and social movements, the artists cutting and printing their own works. Out of this movement came the great folk printmaker Munakata Shikō (1903–75) and Japan's greatest abstract printmaker Onchi Kōshirō (1891–1955). From 1907, the publisher Watanabe Shōsaburō revived the ukiyo-e collaborative print on well-worn themes such as beauties and landscapes, many of these directed at foreign buyers.

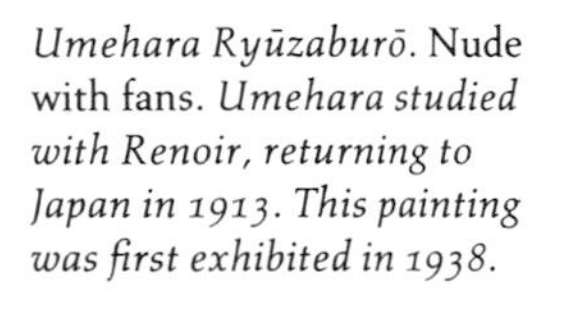

Umehara Ryūzaburō. Nude with fans. *Umehara studied with Renoir, returning to Japan in 1913. This painting was first exhibited in 1938.*

Exhibitions and government involvement

The Meiji government tried to foster some reconciliation in the divided art world by sponsoring a major new exhibition on the model of the Paris salon, the 'Bunten', inaugurated in 1907, which quickly became a major showcase for both *yōga* and *nihonga* artists. Subsequently reconstituted under a different name in 1919 and again in 1946 as the 'Nitten' (run by a private corporation since 1958), this prestigious exhibition is at the very heart of Japanese artistic practice and since the war has been shadowed by the parallel activities of numerous other private art societies.

Government paternalism was not always to be so beneficial. After the pervading liberalism and humanism of the Taishō era, the early Shōwa years saw vogues for the successive European-inspired movements of Surrealism, Futurism and Proletarian art. All this was cut short in 1935, however, by an order of the Minister of Education, Matsuda Genji, which sought to bring the art world under unified government control through a reorganized Imperial Fine Arts Academy. Art was expected to serve increasingly propagandist purposes as the Pacific War developed.

The post-war period has seen an extraordinary explosion in museum building and the sponsorship of major exhibitions of foreign art, particularly by newspaper companies. It cannot be long before the old, artificially maintained division between 'Western' and 'Japanese' will either wither away or be bypassed by younger generations. TTC

Sculpture

The earliest examples of sculpture in Japan date from the Jōmon period. Small clay figurines known as *dogū* have been excavated in considerable numbers in eastern Japan. Since most possess generalized representations of female genitalia, they are thought to have been related to fertility cults, but their exact function remains a mystery. Fully realized examples, which date from the end of the Jōmon, are characterized by large oval eyes, stiff frontal bodies, squat bowed legs and elaborately inscribed surface ornament.

Dogū disappeared by the end of the Jōmon and it was not until the Kofun period that the next sculptural tradition, *haniwa*, appears. Also distinctive to Japan, *haniwa* were low-fired cylinders of clay placed around tumuli to demarcate the sacred precinct of the deceased. Whereas the majority were simple forms, sometimes perforated, others were surmounted with representations of birds and animals, helmets, food vessels, houses and other objects of daily life; or human figures including shamanesses and armed warriors. These figural *haniwa* are distinguished by stiff foreshortened bodies and only generalized anatomical detail. Their mask-like faces rendered simply with horizontal perforations for the eyes and mouth often contrast with the detailed rendering of garments or ornament.

Right *Fired clay* dogu, *typical of many late Jōmon figures. 3rd–4th century* BC. *Why these strangely-shaped sculptures died out is unclear, but they bear witness to a vivid sense of plastic form among the early Japanese.*

Introduction of Buddhism

The Japanese encountered monumental sculpture with the transmission of Buddhism from Asia during the 6th century. The Korean kingdom of Paekche first sent Buddhist statues to Japan in 538 and dispatched the first sculptors in 577. Since Japan had no fully developed tradition of sculpture, the Japanese adopted the forms and techniques of their continental neighbours. Thus the first examples echoed the imagery of the Northern Wei dynasty as it had been reinterpreted by the kingdoms of the Korean peninsula. Most were gilt bronze, made with the lost-wax technique, while some were carved from camphor wood. The earliest record of a statue being made in Japan was a triad carved in 587 by an immigrant craftsman for the recovery of Emperor Yōmei from illness. This event set a pattern that was repeated frequently throughout the 7th and 8th centuries – the prominent rôle played by immigrant artisans and the practice of commissioning imagery for this-worldly benefits.

The earliest extant statue in Japan is the badly damaged main image of the Hōkō-ji in Nara, a gilt bronze image of Shaka, cast by Kuratsukuri no Tori, also known as Tori Busshi (fl. 600–30), a third generation immigrant from Korea. His most famous work is the *Triad of Shaka*, now the main image of the Hōryū-ji, also in Nara, commissioned in 622 to help cure an illness of Prince Shōtoku (574–622). It is distinguished by static frontal postures, rectilinear heads, and idealized facial features. While relying

Above Triad of Shaka *in the main hall of the Hōryū-ji, Nara. Gilt bronze, commissioned in 622.*

Right *Central image of the* Triad of the Healing Buddha, *Yakushi-ji, Nara. Gilt bronze, early 8th century.*

heavily on continental styles, the fluid rhythms of drapery transcend their more commonplace sources.

The sculpture of the 7th and 8th centuries is characterized by the continued adoption and reinterpretation of continental styles and techniques. Since contacts with the continent were inevitably sporadic, Chinese and Korean styles were progressively reformulated by the Japanese, yet the resulting images remained closely tied to their prototypes. Gilt bronzes were produced with considerable frequency, but other continental materials such as clay and lacquer were mastered as well.

Representative of sculpture of the late 7th century and revealing the influence of early Tang styles is the standing gilt bronze *Kannon*, known as the 'Yumetagae Kannon', in the collection of the Hōryū-ji. The stylistic transformations from the first half of the century are particularly evident in the more naturalistic treatment of the body. Some of the best-known images from the early decades of the 8th century are the statues from the clay panoramas in the base storey of the five-storey pagoda at the Hōryū-ji, which display greater realism in pose and expression. Another work of this time is the monumental gilt bronze *Triad of the Healing Buddha*, the main image of the Yakushi-ji. The natural proportions, sense of equipoise and active drapery reflect a sophisticated understanding of the High Tang styles.

The middle decades of the 8th century were dominated by the Great Buddha project first conceived by Emperor Shōmu (701–56) in 743 as a symbol of the unity of state and Buddhism. Work on the image and the temple did not begin at its present site until 745 and was not completed until 757. The statue in the Great Buddha Hall in the Tōdai-ji today is a late 17th century reconstruction; only the legs and the lotus pedestal remain from the original image. This vast project consumed the resources of the nation and resulted in the demise of the theocracy envisioned by Shōmu, yet the image has remained a lasting symbol of state Buddhism throughout Japanese history.

The growing use of wood

By the end of the 8th century the Japanese had begun to develop indigenous forms of sculptural expression that reached maturity during the Heian period. Technical changes accompanied stylistic ones as wood rapidly replaced lacquer and bronze as the preferred material and Japanese artists began to exploit this material in ways unknown on the continent. The appeal of wood seems to have been partially rooted in the indigenous Shintō tradition which conferred sanctity on monumental trees and it is probably no coincidence that the first Shintō sculptures also appeared at this time.

One of the first statues to reflect these radical changes is the standing image of the *Healing Buddha* at the Jingo-ji in Kyōto. The statue was carved from a single block of Japanese cypress and the artist emphasized the qualities inherent in his material by leaving traces of his chisel across the unpainted surface. The severe facial features and the massive body are traits derived from late Tang styles, but they attain a new intensity under the hand of the Japanese sculptor. Since the single blocks of wood utilized during the first half of the 9th century were prone to splitting, sculptors gradually devised techniques to remove the core. First, they experimented by hollowing out the back of images from the shoulders to the tops of the ankles, but by the beginning of the 10th century they had designed a method in which the wood was split before being carved. Eventually they began to use multiple blocks.

Amida Buddha *from the Phoenix Hall, Byōdōin, Uji. 1053. When the doors of the hall are open, Amida gazes out over a tranquil lotus pond. Behind him, to the left and right, are wall paintings depicting his arrival to convey the dying to the Pure Land.*

A consistent pattern of stylistic evolution can be traced from the late 9th century to the mid 11th century. Representative of what is commonly known as the native style of the mid 11th century is the seated *Amida* in the Phoenix Hall of the Byōdō-in in Uji south of Kyōto. Completed by the sculptor Jōchō in 1053, the facial expression and the body are highly idealized and the drapery folds delineate two-dimensional patterns. The image was carved from Japanese cypress in the technically demanding joined-wood block technique in which multiple blocks were first shaped and extensively hollowed before assembly. This method, perfected by Jōchō and his assistants, facilitated the rapid production of monumental images, since all the preliminary work could be done at the atelier.

The sculpture of the last century of the Heian period is dominated by the appearance throughout Japan of an unprecedented number of works that replicated the Jōchō idiom. In the capital these images were produced by artists in two competing lineages, known as the In School and the En School, who received their commissions from members of the imperial family and powerful aristocrats. By the 1150s artists outside the capital were seeking other ways to break with the dominant native style. Change first appeared in Nara with statues such as the seated *Amida triad* at the Chōgaku-ji (1151). The anonymous artist abandoned two-dimensional folds and replaced them with numerous plastic folds that set up an active surface pattern. To further enliven his images the sculptor inlaid the eyes from the inside with glass crystal and painted pupils in ink ringed with red to increase the naturalistic effect.

Reconstructing Nara

A more naturalistic treatment of form became the distinctive signature of sculptors in Nara working during the late Heian and early Kamakura periods. Foremost among them was Kōkei (active 1175–95), his son Unkei (?–1223) and his chief disciple Kaikei (active 1189–1223). The burning of the great Nara temples of Tōdai-ji and Kōfuku-ji in 1180 during the civil war between the Taira and Minamoto thrust these sculptors into the centre of artistic activity. During the 1180s and 1190s they worked to refurbish the many works that had been lost in the fire, often incorporating earlier styles in the process. In order to accommodate their innovations they had to modify the joined-wood block technique. In particular, they hollowed out less of the wood to allow for the more deeply carved folds their naturalistic styles required.

Whereas Unkei and his sons worked for a variety of patrons from eastern Japan, as well as Nara and Kyōto, Kaikei worked almost exclusively for Chōgen (1121–1206), the monk supervising the reconstruction of the Tōdai-ji. The anonymous portrait of Chōgen in the temple collection, noteworthy for its uncompromising realism, is one of the great accomplishments of Japanese sculpture of the 13th century. Unkei balanced naturalism with idealization to create works of great dynamism, intensity and inner power, evident in the portraits of *Asanga* and *Vasubandhu* at the Kōfuku-ji. In contrast, Kaikei strove to refine the naturalistic elements in his works to create images characterized by a perfection of exterior form. The popularity of Kaikei's style among the Pure Land community that formed around Chōgen is attested to by the large number of works of Amida that he produced.

Early 13th-century sculpture of Shunjō Shōnin (the priest Chōgen), from the Shujōdō, Tōdai-ji, Nara. The stark realism of these full-sized portraits of revered teachers is a marked feature of Kamakura sculpture. Having achieved enlightenment through a combination of meditation and great deeds, these men were venerated as buddhas in their own right.

After Unkei's death his sons continued working in their father's style, but by the last decades of the 13th century their work had become conventionalized. Kaikei's disciples strove to perpetuate his style, but most of their sculptures lack the deep spirituality of their master's imagery. Influence of Song styles was particularly prevalent in Kamakura where emigré Chinese monks were actively promoting the Zen sect; and under the influence of Zen Buddhism a new type of portraiture known as *chinsō*, was introduced. In these images, which served as reminders for the monastic community of the importance of direct teaching from master to disciple, the priest is usually depicted seated in a chair with his legs tucked under him. The robes are often standardized, but the sculptors lavished great attention on the physical features.

LATER DEVELOPMENTS

The sculptors of the Muromachi, Momoyama and Tokugawa periods did little more than imitate earlier styles, and the works they produced possessed little originality. Only the work of a small number of itinerant sculptors who carved as part of their religious practice shows any innovation: Enkū (?–1695), for instance, who journeyed throughout Japan producing vast quantities of roughly hewn images. Professional sculptors most frequently made architectural decorations.

As Japan gradually opened to the West during the Meiji period old patterns of patronage rapidly declined and most traditional sculptors were forced to carve *netsuke* and figures in ivory to survive. Others, such as Takamura Kōun (1852–1934), were successful in combining Western realism with indigenous traditions. In comparison to painting, however, Western sculptural idioms did not flourish during the Meiji period, since the sculptor's craft was not viewed as high art. Some of the first works to be produced in Western styles were large public images in bronze of Japanese cultural heroes important to the Meiji government. It has only been since the 1950s that Japanese sculptors have been able to assimilate Western traditions and transform them through aesthetic choices which they see as deeply rooted in their country's past. SCM

Architecture

The architecture of Japan is a manifestation of both technology and aesthetics in harmony, expressed either in the simplicity of a farmhouse or the magnificent complexity of a castle. Architecture is so important in the development of Japanese civilization that in certain periods of national consolidation, such as the Nara, Tokugawa and Meiji eras, the construction of new edifices and grand cities completely preoccupied the state and absorbed its resources. This periodic state patronage, together with the routine incidence of fire and natural disaster, combined to make the building sector one of the main pillars of the economy. For most of the Tokugawa period, for example, almost half the artisan population of the city of Edo was associated with construction, and in the 1980s stimulating domestic construction became part of government policy for dealing with the trade imbalance with the US.

Residences, palaces, retreats

The homes of the Nara élite had their origins in the raised floor structures with timber walls and thatched roofs of the 4th–6th centuries. Model houses found among the *haniwa* clay sculptures decorating the funeral mounds of rulers of this era show high gables, and ridges weighed down by cylindrical billets. The number of ridge billets and the size of the roof were indicative of power and status. Even after the introduction of Buddhism and Chinese building techniques from Korea, this form remained standard for homes of the aristocracy. With the introduction of iron tools, techniques of construction became more sophisticated. By the Heian period (794–1185) a style of residential mansion known as *shinden-zukuri* was in use. With its shingle roofs, plain removable walls, open-plan interiors and gracious disposition around a garden, this style foreshadows the harmonious forms of later Japanese architecture.

With the rise to power of the warrior class, a new style of residence more suited to the austere tastes of the samurai emerged, known as *shoin-zukuri*. Over the centuries *shoin* architecture was influenced in turn by the architecture of Zen Buddhism, by the aristocratic warrior culture of the Ashikaga courts at Kyōto in the 14th and 15th centuries, and by the restraint and contrived rusticity associated with the development of the tea ceremony which became significant in the 16th century. The end result was a set of interior features that included the *tokonoma*, or alcove for the display of objets d'art, and a marked preference for flowing interior space organized in rooms set upon a receding zigzag axis. This maximized the view of the surrounding garden and enhanced the visual isolation of each separate part of the building. It eventually evolved into the *sukiya* or 'tea-house' architecture of the Katsura Villa in Kyōto, built in stages between 1610 and 1666.

Katsura Imperial Villa. The principle behind such architecture is that the building should be as open as possible to the garden outside. In certain parts of the complex it is possible to have a garden vista as the 'wall' on three sides, as the roof itself is supported entirely by the pillars. This represents an imperative for maximum airflow in a hot sticky climate transformed into an aesthetic and philosophical ideal.

Paradoxically, at a time when *shoin* architecture was used to shape a world of retreat and contemplation for the aristocracy, it was also developing as a stage for the bombastic representation of the newly asserted power of the daimyō and national unifiers of the later 16th and 17th centuries. Edo Castle, and the palatial mansions of the great warriors and their retinues, became the sites for sumptuous architectural spectacle, as part of both the ritual and actual enactment of shōgunal government. The *shoin* residence was transformed into a complex symbol of authority, combining sculpture and painting with gilded and lacquered ornament, in order to establish distinctions in status fundamental to the Tokugawa order. The best example is now to be found in the Nijō Castle in Kyōto.

The architecture of the ordinary people, the vernacular housing, was carefully adapted to climate and environment, and to the custom and lifestyle of its agricultural inhabitants. The thatched roof and robust framing evolved naturally from the pit dwellings of the pre-Buddhist age into the style of farmhouse still visible in more isolated regions. Despite great regional variation the Japanese farmhouse is characterized in general by a large, earth-floored work area and a raised timber-floored living section.

Traditional farmhouse roof, Nagano prefecture. The thick thatching and deep eaves were necessary for insulation in both winter and summer. Snow, however, is always the greatest problem in mountain areas.

In the cities, the houses of the artisans and merchants had become well-adapted to their urban environment by the 14th century, while retaining the earth and raised-floor segregation of interior space. They were now two-storeyed, with a shop at the front and living quarters at the back and upstairs. These *machiya* were usually terraced houses, the front walls being lattice screens which opened up directly onto the narrow street. By the 16th and 17th centuries, with the development of cities like Edo, vernacular housing began to show the influence of the élite *shoin* style. The use of mats of densely packed rice straw covered with woven rush, known as *tatami*, had become common especially in the most important family or guest room of the residences of wealthier merchants. The Tokugawa shōgunate tried to restrict the spread of *tokonoma*, *tatami* and other features of *shoin* architecture to the warrior class, but inexorably the style crossed status lines, resulting in the typical Japanese residence as we recognize it today.

Shintō shrines

Unstructured at its inception, Shintō architecture became increasingly important as the setting and symbol of the Shintō *kami* with the consolidation of political power in the 5th and 6th centuries. The two major traditions in Shintō architecture dating from this era, the Grand Shrine of Ise in Mie prefecture and the Great Shrine of Izumo on the Sea of Japan coast near Matsue, were based on the granary and early élite residence respectively. Both shrine traditions retained the raised-floor structure but became increasingly abstract in form. Successive rebuildings were required by the ephemeral nature of their wood and thatch and by the need for ritual renewal.

As the tradition of Shintō architecture evolved there was some influence absorbed from Buddhist architecture, particularly in site organization, structural joinery and roof curvature. The aesthetic character of shrines also changed. The mausoleum for the deified Tokugawa shōgun Ieyasu, the Tōshōgū at Nikkō, was bedecked with black and red lacquer, gilded ornament and polychromed sculptures of virtuous sages and mythological beasts, far removed from the pristine unpainted timbers and non-iconic symbolism of Ise or Izumo.

Subsidiary building of the Inner Shrine at Ise. Note the open ridge-pole and the 'ears', characteristic of Shintō architecture.

Below *The influence of Buddhist architecture on Shintō shrines can be plainly seen here at the Tōshōgū, Nikkō, mausoleum of the first Tokugawa shōgun, Ieyasu.*

Buddhist temples

In the middle of the 6th century advanced building styles associated with Buddhist institutions on the Chinese mainland reached Japan. A series of capital cities were laid out in orderly geometric grids in the Asuka–Nara region in which impressive halls and palaces housed institutions of a centralized bureaucratic state. Great monasteries were founded in order to spread Buddhism, which became the official state religion. Today few of these grand monuments of church and state survive. The Hōryū-ji, with its five-storey pagoda and Golden Hall (*Kondō*) founded in AD 607 and rebuilt after a fire in the later 7th century, is the earliest and one of the best preserved. Its austere beauty and sophisticated design represent the fountainhead of the Chinese-inspired tradition of monumental architecture in Japan.

In the late 12th century fresh influence from southern China is evident in the rebuilding of the Tōdai-ji with a gaunt, massive timber frame, but it was the architecture of the Northern Song which

soon became a new orthodoxy favoured by the warrior governments of Kamakura and Kyōto for their Zen temples. The roofs had elegant, sweeping eaves with double tiers of radial rafters and profuse clusters of multiple bracket sets, very different in their curved gracefulness from the rectilinear severity of earlier Buddhist architecture.

Castles

The struggle for national domination in the later 16th century was focussed on the creation of vast castle complexes as the symbol and substance of power. The larger castles, Oda Nobunaga's Azuchi-jō, Hideyoshi's Ōsaka-jō, and Ieyasu's Edo-jō, were the inspired products of architectural and engineering technology harnessed to the ambitions and resources of national hegemons. Their massive stone walls gave physical protection while their soaring keeps were an eloquent testimony to authority. Himeji-jō, built between 1601 and 1609 by Ikeda Terumasa, a vassal of the Tokugawa, is the finest extant example. It is seen here in two manifestations: delicate when seen from a distance, but impenetrable when seen from the base. WHC

DESIGN AND CONSTRUCTION

Despite the obvious differences in function, scale and specialized building techniques between all these forms, they share basic structural features and have a common process of construction. The master carpenter was, like the medieval mason of Europe, both architect and builder. Building design was strongly influenced by the nature of the materials, tools and techniques of the master carpenter and the sequence and character of the construction process. For example, the use of straight-grained soft woods for pillars and beams meant that ripsaws were not in general use for longitudinal cutting until the 15th century, when Japanese cypress (*hinoki*) supplies were drastically depleted by over-use. Timber was instead split with wedges and chisels, which meant in turn that the proportions of early temples and palaces were more robustly rectilinear than later medieval buildings.

The construction process began with site selection and application of geomantic criteria to the orientation of the building. The process continued with the prefabrication of the parts of the building at the carpenter's workshop according to a comprehensive system of modules in which the dimensions, from pillars and beams to rafters and interior detailing, were determined as a proportion of the span of the post and lintel bay (*ken* or *ma*) or of *tatami* mat size (*jō*). These parts were then assembled at the building site in a well-rehearsed and rapid sequence, with erection of the timber frame to the ridge pole often taking as little as a single day in the case of ordinary houses.

The typical building is a timber-framed structure set on stone foundations. The post and lintel framing is made of resilient soft woods. *Hinoki* has long been preferred for monumental architecture but dwindling supplies forced substitution of red pine (*akamatsu*) and zelkova (*keyaki*) in the medieval period. The framing is held together by mortise and tenons and spliced joinery, often remarkable in ingenuity and execution. This joinery permits the structure to flex in order to absorb the violent shock of Japan's frequent earthquakes and to resist the buffeting of seasonal typhoon winds. Diagonal trussing or struts are not used because they would make the building rigid and prone to collapse during earthquake. The strong rectilinear geometry of the framework contributes significantly to the distinct aesthetic character of the Japanese building.

The walls themselves are non-structural, considerably varied in design and may be filled with a variety of materials, including wooden panels, screens or sliding doors, and clay and plaster daubed over split bamboo and reed lathing. Translucent mulberry paper-covered wooden frames (*shōji*) form outer walls for rooms, while opaque paper-covered frames (*fusuma*) serve as flexible interior space dividers.

The floors of early Buddhist temples, government buildings and Zen halls had stone or terracotta tiles set directly on the foundation podium. Shintō shrines and later Buddhist temples had raised wooden floors. *Tatami* mats first appeared as a floor covering in aristocratic residences in the later Heian period. *Tatami* were initially laid over wooden floorboards in areas where people sat or slept. By the 17th century they had become a complete covering for important chambers in élite residences as well as in the houses of many commoners. The dimensions of the *tatami* were standardized with a ratio of 1:2 of width to length, the space needed for one person lying down or two people sitting. *Tatami* became the module of interior space, with a prescriptive effect on the dimensions of rooms and ultimately of the structural framing.

The roof is the dominant visual element of the Japanese building. Roofs tend to be hip-gable in shape with the eaves flaring elegantly beyond the walls. The eaves of Japanese buildings are much wider than those in Chinese buildings because of the higher rainfall in the monsoon and typhoon seasons, and to protect the walls while allowing screens to remain open for good air circulation in the humid summer months. They also provide shade against the fierce summer sun. Buddhist temples and castles usually have roofs covered with terracotta tiles. Shingles of cypress bark or cypress wood were nor-

Traditional construction techniques

This illustration to the *Kasuga gongen genki* (1309) depicts the prefabrication of a building. The tōryō, or chief master builder, with measuring rod resting on his shoulder, supervises operations (right) while three carpenters and an apprentice engage in measuring and marking large timbers (centre) using a square and pluck lines (*sumitsubo*). Another team (also centre) use wedges and mallets to split large logs into pillars. Only small, leaf-shaped cross-cut saws are observable in this 14th-century scene. The introduction of the two-man frame-saw from China in the 15th century and the subsequent development of a one-man rip saw (*maebiki oga*) in Japan made it possible to cut harder, crooked wood such as *keyaki* into straight pillars and planks. Prior to this, splitting the straight-grained *hinoki* using wedges was the most efficient and universal method.

The Kasuga scroll also shows carpenters making mortise and tenon joints in a shelter at the rear of the building site, where timber is stacked in preparation for assembly. Adzes (*chōna*) and long-handled planing knives (*yariganna*) are in use for smoothing the surface of the split timbers. It is significant that planes were not introduced from China until the later 16th century.

WHC

The Marunouchi entrance to Tōkyō Central Station still offers this outstanding example of early 19th-century architecture.

mally reserved for Shintō shrines and aristocratic residences. Farmhouses predominantly used grass or reed thatch. In the 18th century, urban commoners' houses were mostly converted from shingle and thatch to tiling as a fire prevention measure.

The roof truss, which carries the rafters and purlins, is critical to both the appearance and the structural dynamics of the Japanese building. Although early Buddhist temples and 18th- and 19th-century farmhouses used rigid triangular trusses like those of European tradition, the norm was a grid system of rising parallel ties supported by vertical struts culminating in the ridge pole. The horizontal members are invariably heavy unhewn timbers retaining their natural shape while the uprights are narrow, spindly timbers dramatically different in appearance. The truss may appear top-heavy and ungainly to the Western eye but in reality its weight helps anchor the wall-framing to the foundations, especially during earthquakes and typhoon winds. The heaviness of the horizontal tie-beams also slows the shaking of a building during an earthquake, thereby avoiding resonance with the moment of the seismic waves, the cause of structural failure.

The layered truss also permits free articulation of the slope of the roof, allowing for the curvature, required by climate or the aesthetic preferences of the patron, which is a distinctive characteristic of Japanese architecture. The eaves project beyond the wall by means of cantilevers, either in the form of bracket sets with multiple arms and bearing blocks in the Buddhist temple tradition adopted from China, or with the cantilevers hidden within the framing of the roof in Shintō shrines or élite residences. This allows the eaves to project unencumbered by visual excrescences when seen from outside the building.

The modern transformation

After the fall of the Tokugawa shōgunate in 1867 the creation of new architecture in the Western style became part of national policy. Architecture in the Meiji era (1868–1912) was an exercise in national survival, an important way of demonstrating to the West that Japan had achieved a strength and sophistication that made it an equal. Construction moved from being the prerogative of master builders into the hands of government agencies and eminent European engineers and architects, who were engaged as technical consultants and university teachers to prepare a new breed of Japanese experts. Of these the British architect Josiah Conder (1852–1920) was the most influential.

Modern Japan was reflected in the handsome brick and masonry facades of the Mitsubishi buildings in Tōkyō's new commercial area at Marunouchi. In the 1870s the Ginza area was rebuilt by Thomas Waters, a British engineer, in brick and cement, offering the Japanese a physical embodiment of 'civilization and enlightenment'. It ushered in an era of red-brick construction for public and commercial buildings, many fine examples of which are still standing. It also marked the gradual demise of traditional construction in residential architecture. Rapid advances in iron and steel manufacturing in the late 19th century produced utilitarian structures such as the Shinbashi Machinery Hall belonging to Japan National Railways. The original three-storey building of the Tōkyō central railway station (completed in 1914) used brick as a lining, upholstering the steel frame construction, plaster to suggest stone, and oriels and towers merely as picturesque elements. It was the work of Tatsuno Kingo (1854–1919) one of the first and most influential of the Western-style architects trained in Japan under Josiah Conder. Another dramatic demonstration of mastery of Western architecture was the Akasaka Detached Palace, designed by Katayama Tōkuma (1853–1917).

VERNACULAR HOUSING AND MASS PRODUCTION

After the Pacific War, mass production of building components was the only solution to a chronic shortage of housing, skilled labour and materials. In the 1950s hand tools yielded to power tools and precast concrete panels, plastic and metal sheeting created a new prefabricated vernacular to rehouse the urban population. Throughout the 1960s the priority given to rapid economic growth not only caused environmental havoc in the cities; it also created a cultural climate in which the craftsmen of Japanese architectural tradition vanished, their skills dying with them.

By 1990, 15% of all new houses were factory-made with high-tech automated features such as computerized climate control, security and audio-visual equipment. These houses anticipate the rapid ageing of the Japanese population that will occur in the early part of the next century. There has been a revival of three-generation households, with nearly 50% of new homes based upon a three-storey, three-generation design which builds upon the tradition of extended families but allows greater autonomy between the generations. Even non-factory-made homes are now designed around the dimensions of standardized manufactured components, with the dimensions of aluminium window frames, prefabricated bathroom units and system kitchens forming the basis of design as modules in the way that traditional *tatami* once did. There has been a sharp decrease in the construction of timber-frame dwellings, from 86.2% of new houses nationwide in 1963 to 46.3% by 1983. In Tōkyō, Japan's biggest housing market, the figure had dropped to 27.8% by 1987, rising land costs making the dream of owning a single detached house even more remote.

Tange Kenzō's Olympic buildings of 1964. An impressive blend of modern technique and Japanese style, such an architecture achieves a degree of monumentality while at the same time avoiding a sense of gross imposition on the landscape. Compare this to one of Tange's more recent buildings (over) where the effect is very different indeed.

The architects of post-war Japan

Large-scale public and commercial architecture of the post-war decades has been dominated by Japanese architects trained internationally and influenced by Gropius and Le Corbusier. Of these, Tange Kenzō has been the most prominent. His Hiroshima Peace Park Museum, completed in 1949, used the elements of rectilinear steelframe with glass infill typical of the International Style but retained a resonance with traditional Japanese form in the measured spacing of the bays and strongly abstracted geometry. For the 1964 Tōkyō Olympics, Tange designed the Olympic Gymnasium buildings with the strong sculptural qualities favoured by Le Corbusier for the Ronchamp Chapel in France. Using cantilevered roofing panels and tensioned steel cables suspended between two huge piers in the manner of a suspension bridge, he succeeded in recreating the sweep of a temple roof. With the completion of the 62-storey Tōkyō Metropolitan Government Office complex in Shinjuku in March 1991, Tange's career reached its pinnacle as architect for the establishment. Its cathedral-like towers dominate the city as the new locus for local government, now removed from its original site near Tōkyō Station.

Meanwhile architects such as Andō Tadao and Maki Fumihiko have revived a sense of the craftsmanship of construction while maintaining their place on the cutting edge of international design and high technology with both intimate residences and large-scale projects.

By the 1980s and early 1990s Japanese architects were practising internationally while in Japan the building sector was gradually opening its doors to foreign architects such as the Frenchman Philippe Starck. His Asahi Beer Azumabashi Hall, with its great golden sculpture of a flame, is the ultimate statement of idiosyncratic self-indulgence, which typifies nouveau-riche corporate patrons in Japan today. WHC

The new Tōkyō Metropolitan Government offices at Shinjuku, designed by Tange. Imposing certainly, but some feel that the architecture has recently become overbearing.

Decorative arts

The continuing existence of diverse and sophisticated craft practices which is so striking an aspect of contemporary Japan is living testament to the richness of decorative art traditions reaching back to the earliest times. The complexity of the subject is more than can be dealt with in a brief introduction, and the overview that follows concentrates on the history of Western interaction with Japan and the nature of Western collections of Japanese decorative arts.

Commentaries by Jesuit missionaries active during the earliest period of Western contact with Japan from the middle of the 16th century made reference to the highly developed state of Japanese craft manufacture. During the 17th century an important trade in lacquerware and porcelain developed, providing wealthy Europeans with colourful and exotic products with which to furnish their mansions and palaces. If Japanese porcelain was initially sought after to make up for a temporary decline in Chinese porcelain production in the mid 17th century and was subsequently eclipsed by Chinese exports in the 18th century, it left through its decorative schemes a stylistic legacy of major significance in the history of European ceramic design. Lacquerware too, although less common an export product than porcelain, was highly regarded in Europe, where it gave rise to the development of 'japanning' as an important form of furniture decoration.

Had it not been for the policy of self-imposed isolation adopted by the Tokugawa Bakufu during the 1630s, there is no doubt that mutual stimulation between Japan and the West in fields such as the decorative arts would have developed much more quickly than it did. As it was, government proscriptions forbade Japanese merchants to travel abroad and insisted that contact with the outside world should be conducted only via Chinese merchants or members of the Dutch East India Company confined to the island of Deshima in Nagasaki Bay. The repercussions of the ending of Japan's closed door policy in 1854 were enormous, both domestically and internationally. In terms of the decorative arts, the collapse of the old feudal order and its systems of patronage together with the growth of export markets led to significant changes in the nature of production. In the West, increased access to Japanese goods was a central factor in the rise of *'japonisme'*, the craze for all things Japanese that swept Europe and the US from the 1860s onwards.

The artefacts that were exported to the West can be broadly divided into two groups. On the one hand there were traditional items, often of some antiquity, which had either become redundant as a result of changes in lifestyle brought about by the social and political upheavals of the day or, during the time of extreme adulation of Western manners and institutions characteristic of the early Meiji period, were rejected as being inappropriate to the new age. Economic factors were also involved to the extent that one of the ways that struggling samurai were able to save themselves from impoverishment was by selling off their family treasures.

On the other hand there were the items produced in response to the growth in overseas trade. Japan's new leaders were quick to seize on the possible economic gains to be made from the export of craft objects, and took a number of measures to foster the development of export-oriented manufacture. These included the setting up of special companies such as the Kiritsu Kōshō Kaisha to encourage traditional craft practices, the introduction of new technology through the employment of Western experts, and the promotion of Japanese arts and crafts through participation in international exhibitions in Europe and the US.

The most obvious examples of items no longer relevant under the changed circumstances of the Meiji period were armour, swords, sword-fittings and other symbols of the old feudal order. Lacquerware, which had been developed to extraordinary degrees of refinement during the Tokugawa period, was another category of artefact deriving primarily from former daimyō and samurai households. Dress accessories such as *inrō* and *netsuke*, which had associations both with Japan's military rulers and with wealthier members of the merchant class, became redundant as Western styles of dress were adopted.

Craft manufacture as it developed in response to the growth of export trade was extremely varied. In ivory carving, for example, the skills used in the fashioning of *netsuke* were adapted to the manufacture of decorative figurines and domestic accessories. Metal-working skills previously exercised in the making of sword-fittings were used to produce richly worked ornamental vessels. In the case of cloisonné,

Export porcelain

Porcelain was first made in Japan in the early years of the 17th century in and around the town of Arita in northern Kyūshū. Decoration involving painting in cobalt blue under the high-fired clear glaze was used to produce Blue-and-White wares. Imari type wares combine painting in underglaze blue with decoration in overglaze enamel colours fused on during a second lower temperature firing, a technique that was developed in the 1640s. The best of Kakiemon type wares are characterized by a pure white body and delicate painting executed solely in overglaze enamel colours.

Right *Square porcelain flask, Arita ware (Imari type), 1700–20, height 22.8 cm.*

Porcelain dish, Arita ware (Blue-and-White), bearing the VOC monogram of the Dutch East India Company, 1660–80, diameter 36.5 cm.

Below *Porcelain bowl, Arita ware (Kakiemon type), 1690–1710, diameter 23.5 cm.*

Meiji export crafts

These examples of work in five different media are all of the highest quality. They demonstrate the flexibility shown by Japanese craftsmen in adapting traditional skills to meet the demands of the export market that developed during the Meiji period.

Left *Metalwork vase, made at the Kiritsu Kōshō Kaisha workshops, early 1880s, height 27.2 cm.*

Left-centre *Decorated earthenware box, made at the Kinkōzan workshops, 1900s, length 14.9 cm.*

Centre *Cloisonné vase, c. 1900, height 31.0 cm.*

Right-centre *Carved ivory box, 1890s, height 16.5 cm.*

Right *Lacquerware cabinet of drawers with details in shell, ivory and horn, made at the Ōzeki workshops, c. 1900, 22.3 by 23.1 by 17.6 cm.*

Tea ceramics

The appearance of purpose-made tea wares in the 1580s represented a major breakthrough in the history of Japanese ceramics, which for many centuries had seen the domination of imported Chinese ceramics or non-ceramic artefacts such as metalwork as the models for higher quality products.

Left *Stoneware teabowl, Raku ware, by Hon'ami Kōetsu (1558–1637), early 17th century, diameter 12.7 cm.*

Centre *Stoneware vase, Mino ware (Yellow Seto type), end of the 16th century, height 19.4 cm.*

Right *Stoneware dish, Mino ware (Oribe type), early 17th century, length 12.2 cm.*

Contemporary studio crafts

The Nakagawa box, with its subtle arching of the lid to counteract the concave visual effect of the herringbone pattern, is a prime example of the continuation of superlative skills of traditional cabinet-making. The Suzuki fresh-water jar shows how the conscious exploration of sculptural interests first seen in Japanese tea ceramics of the late 16th and early 17th centuries continues to give rise to highly individualistic work. The Yokoyama glass sculpture is an example of work deriving less from Japanese craft traditions than from international movements in contemporary art and design.

Left *Fresh-water jar for the tea ceremony, stoneware, by Suzuki Osamu (b. 1934), 1989, height 20.4 cm.*

Centre *Sculpture entitled 'Candlelight', glass, by Yokoyama Naoto (b. 1937), 1988, height 59 cm.*

Right *Box, wood (ancient cryptomeria), by Nakagawa Kiyotsugu (b. 1942), 1987, 32.5 by 15.8 by 13.3 cm.*

Ivory miniature of a Dutchman hugging his money bag. Great care was lavished on these netsuke *or small toggles. As Western dress became common, the need for such accessories died away. The result is that the miniatures had far greater interest for Western art collectors than for the Japanese themselves. The 18th century* netsuke *of a grazing horse below, only 56mm in height, is now in the Victoria and Albert Museum, London.*

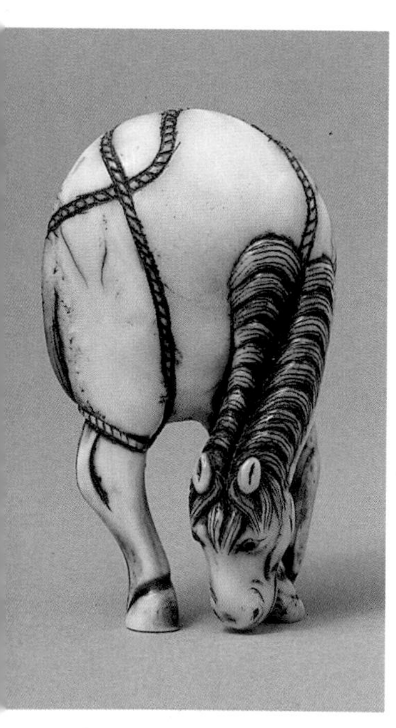

techniques that had been known about since the early 17th century but had only been employed in a limited manner were developed and improved specifically with the non-Japanese market in mind. In lacquerwork, as in other media, new shapes appeared, sometimes based directly on Western prototypes but more often newly invented to cater to foreign taste. Lacquerwork was also characterized by the use of mother-of-pearl, shell, ivory and other exotic materials that appealed to Western buyers. Exuberance of decoration was particularly striking in the case of Meiji period export ceramics, which in terms of production volumes were the most important of all export items. The best examples were executed with considerable care and sensitivity, but there was, as indeed in other media, a great deal of degenerate and poorly finished work.

Although Western exposure to and interest in Japan's decorative arts tended to be limited to rather elaborate and ornate types of work, artefacts of a more rustic or understated nature did not go unnoticed. Items such as tea ceramics whose appeal lies in their direct and spontaneous exploration of medium and technique entered Western collections in the late 19th century, and were looked upon with some interest. If early Western critique was expressed in terms of admiration for the primitive and naïve, a more informed understanding of Japanese aesthetics was promoted through the writings, published in English and other European languages, of Okakura Tenshin (1862–1913).

Okakura, together with his erstwhile teacher Ernest Fenollosa (1852–1908), played a major rôle in the re-evaluation of Japan's cultural heritage, establishing an approach to the study and collection of Japanese art that was profoundly influential both within Japan and abroad. From the point of view of the subsequent formation of Western collections of Japanese art, the legacy of this influence is most readily seen in the important holdings of painting and sculpture that were built up, particularly in the US. The decorative arts were not ignored, but on the whole there was little expansion beyond the areas of interest that had been established in the late 19th century. This situation has changed considerably in recent decades, with developments in the West accompanying a remarkable growth in technical, documentary and archaeological studies by the Japanese.

Following on from Okakura, another Japanese thinker whose ideas have been extensively disseminated in the West was Yanagi Sōetsu (1889–1961). Unlike his predecessor, who was primarily concerned with higher forms of Japanese art, Yanagi's interest lay in the preservation and promotion of the anonymous folk craft traditions which he and his associates identified in and around Japan. Yanagi played a central rôle in the establishment of the Mingei or Folk Craft movement in the late 1920s, and contributed actively to the debate about the place of the craftsman in modern society during the pre-war and post-war years. The achievement of Yanagi and his followers can be seen not only in the fostering of widespread awareness of Japan's folk craft heritage, but also in the drawing of Western attention to Japan's importance as a centre of contemporary craft practice.

While the Folk Craft movement itself is no longer the major force that it once was, aspects of Yanagi's philosophy live on in the Japanese craft world today. The aims of the Japan Craft Design Association can be regarded, for example, as a fusion of certain of Yanagi's ideas with notions about utility and good design deriving from Western modernist ideology. This association was one of a number of design-related organizations set up in the 1950s with the backing of the Ministry of International Trade and Industry. Still active today, it promotes the production of well-designed, formerly minimalist but now more playful, utilitarian goods.

A second major craft organization active in contemporary Japan is the Japan Crafts Association (Nihon Kōgeikai). This was set up in 1955 under the auspices of the Agency of Cultural Affairs with the aim of preserving and promoting traditional craft skills as part of the national heritage. Its continuing vitality lies in the fact that it encourages the development of personal artistic expression as well as that of fine craftsmanship.

Work of a more avant-garde nature constitutes the third main type of contemporary Japanese craft. Artists working in this area often exhibit at the annual Japan Arts Exhibition (Nitten), but tend to belong to small affiliations of colleagues sharing similar sets of interests. While many of these have proved to be quite short-lived, the Sōdeisha, an influential ceramicists' group founded in Kyōto in 1948, recently celebrated its 40th anniversary. RFJF

Dance

The complexity and long history of Japanese culture, the paucity of information available to the Western reader, and the range of possibilities for human body movement, can make Japanese dance appear baffling at first. A bewildering diversity of traditional dance forms has survived in performance, even if usually in altered form; and these co-exist with more recent genres, including not only ballet but also hybrids and some modern dance of striking originality.

In traditional Japanese dance, cultural constraints, including costume, have dictated a style of movement in which the feet are kept close to the ground, the knees are slightly flexed at most times, the torso is straight, and the arms make smooth, subtly differentiated gestures. The head and eyes move in concert with the arms and body; but the face is generally impassive and unsmiling.

Masked dance, with its special possibilities and limitations for expression, has helped to determine this style of movement; and, of the classical masked forms, the most influential has been nō, in which dance is a major component. Another strong influence has been puppet theatre, especially the bunraku three-man puppets. In kabuki dance a favourite effect is the *mie*, 'pose', used at climactic moments and to create variety of pace.

Outline history to 1868

The oldest mention of dance concerns an obscene performance by the goddess Ame no Uzume on an inverted tub, to entice the Sun Goddess Amaterasu out of hiding in the Rock-Cave of Heaven. The episode, described in the *Kojiki*, is taken as the origin of *kagura*, music and dance of (or for) the deities of Shintō. *Kagura* was no doubt at first the ritual dance of a shamanic priestess. Many kinds have been preserved at local Shintō shrines; and there is a special variety, *mi-kagura*, in the court music repertoire, with its own cycle of song-texts. The basic purpose of *kagura* is purification. As entertainment for festivals it has also influenced the theatrical dance, and probably been influenced by it too, especially in large urban centres.

The earliest masked form is *gigaku*, introduced in 612 by a Korean immigrant. This was a sequence of mime dances on Buddhist themes, accompanied by a flute and percussion instruments. The dancers wore masks covering the whole head and the characters portrayed were drawn from Buddhist myth. *Gigaku* was virtually extinct by the late 17th century; but a number of ancient masks have survived, together with fragments of music notation, and illustrations and descriptions of individual dances. Recently attempts have been made to recreate *gigaku*, if in a slightly sanitized form.

A kabuki dance routine. Small movements of the hands and feet, a stiff pose with bent knees and straight torso, and a pronounced preference for the side-on stance are all typical of this style.

A performance of bugaku. *Such events are still held occasionally, in the open air if at all possible. Note the fearsome mask and richly embroidered dress. Many of these dances stem from ancient Chinese ritual which, like so much else, only survives in Japan.*

In the 7th and 8th centuries other kinds of music and dance were introduced from the continent, and performed at the court or at shrines and monasteries, alongside native forms. Known by the generic term *bugaku*, such dance performance was organized initially under the Court Music Bureau, set up on Chinese lines in 702. Today, only a fraction of this repertoire has been maintained; some pieces being only performed in purely instrumental versions. The majority of dance pieces introduced during the Nara and Heian periods came from China. Some of these forms spread from the court, and interacted with local Japanese ones, particularly those used at the time of festivals. The two most important medieval dance types came to be *sarugaku*, a ritual dance-drama on mostly Buddhist themes, and *dengaku*, originally a ritual to promote good crops. They were gradually taken over by guilds of professional or semi-professional performers, who entertained at shrines and monasteries, or in the streets of the capital. Special performances might also be commissioned, or sponsored by public subscription. At certain periods *dengaku* might become a riotous communal performance in which every one joined.

It was out of dances and performances of these earlier types that nō drama emerged in the 15th century. Stylized dance-like movements are used throughout nō, but there is also a set dance section which usually occurs at an emotional climax. The pace is slow; but this partly reflects changes in style and musical structure which took place during the Tokugawa period, when nō was the 'official entertainment' (*shikigaku*) of the samurai class. Lighter relief is provided by *kyōgen* farces, which have their own dance-form, known as *komai*.

During the 17th and 18th centuries, nō was gradually superseded in popularity by the kabuki theatre, which was equally attractive to samurai and to ordinary townspeople. Kabuki borrowed themes, stage devices and even styles of movement from nō and *kyōgen*, as well as from the puppet theatre; but every effect was exaggerated, tongue-in-cheek, and calculated to appeal to the raffish taste of a new urban audience. In this theatre of spectacle, dance played a central rôle. Other kabuki dances were adapted from those of Edo street festivals, or of the Yoshiwara courtesans and the geisha; or were developed by individual actors, whose heirs in the same lineage would perpetuate and improve on them. A rich repertoire thus came into existence; and dance-pieces might be performed as separate entities, not embedded in a play.

Dance since Meiji

Dance, like every other aspect of Japanese society, has been transformed during the past 100 years. Using 20th-century lighting, kabuki has maintained many of the 19th-century plays, or parts of them, including dance pieces. In addition, a significant movement originated with the dancer Fujikage Shizue (1880–1966), who believed that women should be allowed to perform kabuki dances. In consequence, it became respectable for well-bred girls to study dance. New lineages proliferated within the old guild system; and within these lineages dance recitals are frequently given, by professional or amateur performers: the repertoire consisting partly of kabuki dance, and partly of dances from other sources. Other kinds of traditional dance flourish too; and are to be seen regularly not only at local festivals but also on national television.

A modern revival of dengaku *dance at the Gion Festival, held in Kyōto every year. Performances are now, of course, stylized and artificial, but there is historical evidence that* dengaku *was often extremely lively. The dancers and audience could become riotous with very little extra encouragement.*

Meanwhile, Western dance, of virtually every kind, has come flooding in. At the Rokumeikan, a two-storey brick building in Italian Renaissance style, which opened in 1883, society patrons, including the prime minister, gathered for lessons in ballroom dancing. There were similar opportunities to practise, and to meet foreigners socially on the dance floor, at the Grand Hotel, Yokohama. On these occasions the wearing of Western clothes went along with the new style of movement, while music would be provided by a military ensemble, playing Western instruments.

Ballet, for professional rather than amateur dancers, came later when an Italian couple named Rossi were invited to teach, and to direct the opera chorus, at the Imperial Theatre, opened in 1911. Over the next few years many performances of ballets, or of operas containing ballets, were given in Tōkyō. The Rossis eventually left for America; but in 1922 Anna Pavlova and her company were invited to perform; and this inaugurated a long period of Russian influence on Japanese ballet. The leading companies since the end of the Pacific War have been the Matsuyama (formed 1948), Maki (1963), Tōkyō Ballet (1964) and Star Dancers Ballet (1964), all based in the capital. Such companies have been aided artistically by Soviet and other foreign coaches, choreographers and visiting performers; and financially by the operation of their own ballet schools.

Modern dance was introduced not only by such visitors as Ruth St Denis and Ted Shawn (1926), Martha Graham (1955) and others, but also by Japanese dancers who trained in Germany and the US. Itō Michio (1893–1961), one such, was seen by W. B. Yeats, and later performed in his 'At the Hawk's Well' in Japan.

During the 1970s Japanese dance became less dependent on Western models. The most original movement of the period was the 'dance of darkness' (*ankoku butō*), founded by Hijikata Tatsumi (1930–86). The best-known company today is Sankai juku (artistic director Amagatsu Ushio). Rebellious, and sometimes nihilistic in conception, this is an avant-garde form which nevertheless draws on ancient Japanese symbolism, aesthetic sensibility and quality of movement. Still maturing, it is taking its place internationally as one of Japan's most notable cultural exports. DBW

Music

The early chronicles describe music and dance as having been born together, as part of the successful attempt to coax the Sun Goddess out of hiding. Practical knowledge of music-making before the 8th century, however, depends almost exclusively on archaeology, although a 7th-century Chinese history notes that in Japan 'for music there are five-string zithers and side-blown flutes' and a number of passages in the *Kojiki* and *Nihon shoki* remind us of the extensive musical interaction with the continent. The *Nihon shoki* states that for the funeral of Emperor Ingyō in the 5th century, the king of Silla on the Korean peninsula sent 80 musicians who danced, sang and played stringed instruments en route to the capital.

Information for the 8th and 9th centuries comes from the musical instruments that are miraculously preserved in the Shōsōin imperial storehouse at the Tōdai-ji. This collection, mostly gifts from the Chinese court, contains the ancestral forms of many present-day instruments.

Gagaku musicians perform at the Ise Shrine. The music and instruments are old but the superb coloured backdrop is of more recent provenance.

Early genres

The term gagaku in its broadest sense encompasses all the musics of the imperial court, although the genre now called *mi-kagura* is usually excluded. The latter descends from the court music of pre-Nara times, in which the main instrument was the *wagon* or Japanese zither. Many early *mi-kagura* song lyrics are captured in the 8th-century texts, which also refer frequently to the *wagon*'s use in ritual contexts, often played by the emperor. By the Nara period the zither had been joined by the *kagura-bue* flute, *hichiriki* oboe and *shakubyōshi* clappers.

The major genres imported from the continent during the 8th century – as reflected in the Shōsōin holdings – are today known as *tōgaku* and *komagaku*. Much of this repertoire originated in India or central Asia, was filtered through the Tang court and the Korean peninsula and organized in Japan under the Court Music Bureau (established in 702), staffed mainly by immigrants. The music survives today, each instrumental tradition passed on in family lines, although slowed down and elaborated to such an extent that the original melodies are scarcely perceptible. The primary instruments of today's ensemble are the *hichiriki*, the *ryūteki* and *komabue* side-blown flutes, the *shō* mouth organ (ancestor of the accordion), the four-string *biwa* lute, the 13-string long zither *sō* or koto, and various percussion, most notably the giant *dadaiko* dance drum. These genres are today purely instrumental, but several court vocal genres, such as *saibara* and *rōei*, also survive. Also of prime importance was Buddhist chanting (*shōmyō*), the most melodic style of which greatly influenced many subsequent Japanese vocal genres.

Medieval developments

An early popular musical offshoot of *shōmyō* was *heike biwa* (or *heikyoku*) recitation. Blind priests sang epic tales of the 12th-century battles between the Minamoto and Taira clans, accompanying themselves on a *biwa* descended from the Nara prototype. Performance was restricted to the sightless, organized under the *tōdō* guild, an arrangement that continued with governmental blessing until 1871.

The music of the nō theatre descends from both *shōmyō* and *heikyoku* – thus reflecting the strong

Courtesan with koto. The instrument is plucked somewhat like a harp and has a system of moveable bridges for tuning.

Buddhist element that permeates many of the plays. Nō musicians, all onstage, play the nō flute, the two hourglass-shaped hand-drums *ōtsuzumi* and *kotsuzumi*, and in many plays the stick drum *taiko*. A unison chorus of eight sits to the audience's right, alternating with the singing of the main characters. All performers are male, and even female rôles are sung in a deep, rumbling voice. The flute plays solo rather than accompanying vocals.

Music since 1600

The Tokugawa period saw the emergence of three important instruments: the 13-string koto, the shamisen and the shakuhachi. By the mid 17th century the koto had begun to develop its own instrumental and vocal repertoire, gaining popularity among the urban merchant classes. Early pieces such as *Rokudan* and *Midare*, attributed to the blind performer Yatsuhashi Kengyō (1614–85), are still popular today.

The shamisen is a three-string plucked long-necked lute whose sound chamber is covered with cat- or dogskin. Entering Japan in the mid 1500s from the Ryūkyūs (where snakeskin was used as in China), it quickly replaced the heavier *biwa* as instrument of choice for blind minstrels. The shamisen has evolved myriad forms, each favoured for particular genres of music with distinct performance contexts. It is the primary instrument of the kabuki and bunraku theatres, of geisha, and of the distinctive Tsugaru folk style.

The shakuhachi is a rim-blown bamboo flute with five fingerholes. Six-hole examples imported from China are in the Shōsōin, but these court instruments soon fell from use. The modern shakuhachi emerged during the 17th century in the hands of the Meian (or Myōan) Zen Buddhist sect, as an instrument for meditation and alms-gathering. It has been suggested that the government's decision to grant a monopoly on profit-making performance to this sect – whose members were mainly ex-samurai – was in return for their acting as spies during their ascetic travels. Aside from its distinctive solo repertoire, the shakuhachi now accompanies folk song and joins in ensembles known as *sankyoku*.

Japanese folk music is extremely varied. Although historical evidence is elusive, many of the ritual and festival musics of rural Japan are clearly of ancient lineage. Traditional instruments include side-blown bamboo flutes, a variety of stick-drums, cymbals and small hand-gongs, and other kinds of percussion. Only in this century have the shamisen and shakuhachi become standard accompaniments for folk singing. Folk song has now become a quasi-art music, often performed on stage and taught by professionals. Village-based 'preservation societies' also strive to keep alive the 'original' forms of many dance and work songs.

This scene, staged by young geisha for a late 19th-century photographer, shows two forms of drum (note the stiff arms of the woman on the left) and a samisen, played with a plarge plectrum. This plectrum is often used against the skin of the samisen to produce another kind of percussion.

The Ryūkyū islands have their own impressive musical culture, related to those of both Japan and China. The main instrument is the *sanshin*, ancestor of the shamisen. The music of the Ainu has interacted hardly at all with that of the rest of Japan, showing more similarities to Siberian styles.

The Meiji period brought radical changes: the end of monopoly rights for sightless performers and for the shakuhachi; the loss of élite patronage for nō; and – most crucially – the introduction of a Western-based school music education system. Traditional musics are virtually ignored in the curriculum – yet many genres are quite healthy today, with hundreds of thousands of students. The overwhelming influence of Western music has created a dilemma for would-be composers in traditional genres: the 'natural' evolution of these genres has been pre-empted. It no longer seems possible, for example, to write a convincing new nō play without sounding either super-conservative or Westernized.

Today in Japan it is possible to hear a wide range of traditional musics, virtually any type of Western music, vital hybrid forms such as the popular *enka* songs of *karaoke* fame, and even a variety of other world musics.

Characteristics of Japanese music

Despite the impressive variety of traditional genres, there are certain characteristic features or attitudes. Japanese consider themselves uniquely appreciative of *ma*, or 'space' – a concept embracing the silence between sounds as well as the elastic Japanese sense of musical timing. Similarly, correct appearance is aesthetically fundamental: it is not enough simply to produce a good sound from a drum, one must also hold the sticks exactly as taught, pick them up correctly, and so forth. Such subtle matters vary with one's 'school', and an appreciation of these differences is crucial for the connoisseur.

Musical scales and modes

Japanese music is primarily pentatonic, using five different principal pitches per octave, but the matter is not so simple. First, the scale systems are somewhat different for each major genre. Second, one or two notes often differ in ascending and descending passages (as with the European melodic minor), effectively creating heptatonic (seven-tone) scales. Japanese intervals generally correspond to Western ones, especially the fourths and fifths, but the non-nuclear pitches are often unstable, yielding non-Western intervals.

Melody and polyphony

Japanese melody lines are generally highly ornamented, and appreciation centres on this horizontal dimension of musical complexity. The vertical combination of tones – polyphony – is less exploited, and there is no system of functional, chordal harmony. Several types of polyphony do exist, however. Most common, as throughout Asia, is heterophony, in which each instrument (including voice) in an ensemble performs its own idiomatic variant of a single melody. This is perhaps clearest in *sankyoku* and least obvious, though still true, in gagaku.

Koto and shamisen genres occasionally feature a highly independent second melodic line (*kaede*), in the same metre and (usually) in the same key as the main part but otherwise vertically unrelated. The two parts converge in unison only at cadential points.

The intervals of the nō flute are quite unlike those of nō vocals, and when flute and voice overlap there is no musical connection between the two. In kabuki

Scales and modes

Most Japanese scales are built from one or more of four types of tetrachord, each consisting of a framework of two 'nuclear tones' a perfect fourth apart, with a single note infixed between them. The nuclear tones serve as competing centres and goals of tonal movement (unlike Western music with its single tonic). Combining two identical tetrachords yields four modes (nuclear tones are in capital letters):

miyako-bushi (common in Tokugawa-period urban genres): C – db – F + G – ab – C
ritsu (common in gagaku and some folk music): C – d – F + G – a – C
inaka-bushi (mostly in folk song): C – eb – F + G – bb – C
Ryūkyū (only in Okinawan music): C – e – F + G – b – C

(The *miyako-bushi* mode often uses *inaka-bushi* tetrachords in ascent, while the *Ryūkyū* mode may use *ritsu* tetrachords in descent.) The pitches shown above are only relative: except in gagaku, most pieces are performed at whatever level suits the performer(s). While the fourths and fifths separating nuclear tones hold firm, the infixed pitches are quite flexible, so that one cannot always distinguish, for example, *miyako-bushi* from *ritsu*. DWH

and folk music as well, the flute is sometimes at a different pitch level from other parts, linked only metrically. Such 'chaotic' combinations often seem suitable for symbolizing abundance, festivity or other-worldliness.

Rhythm and metre

Traditional music is largely in duple metres corresponding to Western 2/4 or 6/8, the latter being common in folk dances. (Triple metre, which dominates in Korea, is totally unknown in Japan.) The beat, however, can be quite elastic. Thus in the *tōgaku* court repertoire, where the pulse is already so slow that first-time listeners may not perceive a metre at all, the final beat of a four-beat bar sometimes lasts twice as long as the first. Often there is no beat at all. Such free metre is common in shakuhachi solos and in folk song, where durations are at the performer's discretion.

Tone colour and timbral preferences

In contrast to Western classical music's traditional emphasis on relatively 'pure' sounds, the Japanese musical aesthetic – in common with much of the world and with modern Western music – readily embraces various types of non-periodic, pitchless sounds. To Westerners these occasionally sound like mere noise, but they are the result of conscious musical choice. The plucked lutes, *biwa* and shamisen, feature a buzzing sound called *sawari*, whose quality and amount is crucial in evaluating a given instrument. A historical relation is likely with India, where a similar effect is called *jawari* or *jiwari*. The percussive striking of the large plectrum against the face of the instrument is another such feature of many genres of Japanese lute music. Koto and shamisen players often scrape a string lengthwise to create a swishing sound. Solo shakuhachi pieces may employ *muraiki*, a dramatic pitchless blast of air.

Sometimes such effects closely imitate the sounds of insects, wind, an arrow striking its target, and so forth. Other times the symbolism is highly abstract. Various conventionalized drum patterns of the offstage *geza* musicians of the kabuki theatre represent a river, the seashore, rain, snow, even a thief – but only an aficionado will recognize the connection.

Japanese vocal tone also tends to be less 'pure' (though no more artificial) than Western *bel canto*. Preference varies with each genre, and both loudness and clarity must be matched to the venue and audience. Puppet-theatre chanters, for example, once trained to develop powerful yet raspy voices by trying to 'out-sing' waterfalls. There are also the dynamic *kakegoe* or cries of the nō drummers, which often seem to overpower the vocalists. These swooping, powerful cries of *yo* and *ho* add a layer of texture to the music which is crucial in establishing both mood and timing. These calls combine with the 'out-of-tune' liquid flute and the muffled, wavering voice of the masked main actor to support the dreamlike atmosphere of most nō plays.

Shakuhachi players used to speak of 'becoming a buddha (i.e. reaching enlightenment) with a single note' (*ichion-jōbutsu*); hence we should not evaluate shakuhachi music solely on the interest of its melodies but rather on shifting timbres, subtle pitch inflections and dynamic changes on the level of the single tone or short phrase. The same is partly true of other Japanese musics as well.

Examples of Japanese musical notation

The centuries-old notation for the *hichiriki* oboe of gagaku (a) combines three columns of symbols: solid dots to the right, indicating the beat; a central column of *katakana* giving the mnemonic syllables; and a left-hand column of symbols each indicating a particular fingering. Exact pitch is not indicated, as a single fingering can yield more than one pitch. The mnemonics (*chira roruro...*) are shown below the Western notation (b), which does not capture the subtler pitch inflections and ornaments in these opening bars from 'Etenraku'. Performers stress that an ability to sing the melody using these mnemonics is essential in learning to play accurately.

(a)

(b)

The Meiji-period *bunka-fu* notation for shamisen (c) is one of several in use for different genres or schools of shamisen music. *Bunka-fu* notation is written horizontally (unlike other types) and indicates finger position with Arabic numerals, showing Western influence. The three-line staff represents the instrument's three strings. The lyrics are written below, spaced to show duration, but vocal pitch is not notated. The shamisen oral mnemonics are written above the staff. In this typical passage from the *jiuta* piece 'Yachiyo-jishi', the vocal melody (upper staff in the Western notation (d)) alternately leads or lags behind the steady pulse of the shamisen (lower staff) to create rhythmic interest. DWH

Notation and transmission

Written notation was uncommon in Japan until the Meiji period, for several reasons. First, professional performance and teaching of *heike-biwa* recitation and some types of koto and shamisen music were restricted by law to sightless people. Second, traditions such as gagaku and nō music were passed down, often from father to son, through instruction and immersion from early childhood. Third, the availability of detailed notation would have threatened the professionals' monopoly on musical knowledge and thus reduced their incomes.

Since the Tokugawa period in particular, the guild-like *iemoto* ('househead') pyramidal teaching system has ensured that the control of the musical product was firmly in the grasp of the autocratic head of each 'school'. For this reason too, each school was likely to have its own notation, incompatible with others for reasons of secrecy and exclusivity.

Such notation as existed was generally for reference – to help recall what had already been learned aurally – rather than for use in instruction or performance. Teaching has usually involved one-to-one rote imitation. Many instruments were and are taught with the aid of sophisticated systems of oral mnemonics – syllables sung to assist learning and memorization. Thus a beginning nō flute student might first – before being allowed to touch the flute – learn to sing a melody using mnemonics such as *ohyarai houhouhi...*; a student of one of the kabuki drums *ōtsuzumi* or *kotsuzumi* will learn the interlocking patterns for these two drums orally: *tsutapon tsutatsu popopon...* .

Many written notations include these mnemonics, or indeed consist of nothing else. Memorization is facilitated by the fact that much of Japanese music is constructed around a core of rhythmic or melodic units (often named) specific to each genre.

Since the Meiji period, with the loosening of restrictions on transmission and under Western influence, notations have become widely available to the amateur and are ever more detailed. Western staff notation itself, however, although taught in the schools and widely understood, is almost never used for notating traditional music except by scholars. Barriers to access have fallen in general: amateur gagaku groups and female shakuhachi players would have been unthinkable a century ago.

DWH

Theatre

Japanese theatre is meant to be seen, rather than read. The very act of reading plays and appreciating the text hardly existed in Japan until the late 19th century. For most of Japan's theatrical history performance has been paramount. There was a vigorous half-century from 1910 to 1960 when plays were written for publication as well as production, but since then performance has reasserted itself.

Japan has four classical theatre forms: nō, *kyōgen* (both from the late 14th century), bunraku (puppet theatre) and kabuki (both from the second half of the 17th century). The modern period, and in particular present-day Japan, is rich with theatrical activity of all kinds.

In many theatrical cultures the course of a genre's history has been decisively influenced by a few individuals. The same is true of Japan, but in the case of the four classical forms their history was not only influenced but almost stopped in its tracks by these individuals. As a result, Japanese theatregoers, in addition to a remarkable array of modern styles, have the benefit of being able to watch acting and production styles that have remained in many cases substantially unaltered for three centuries or more.

Scene from a Nō play. The chorus is on the far right. The green pine painted on the back wall is an obligatory feature of the stage.

Nō

In nō there were two such pioneers, a father and son, whose work spanned the second half of the 14th century and the first few decades of the 15th. The father, Kan'ami (1333–84), was an actor and playwright; the son, Zeami (*c.*1364–1443), inherited his father's rôles, and also wrote a number of theoretical treatises that give a good picture of the theatre that he and his father created.

Kan'ami and Zeami did not create nō out of nothing. As in China and many Western countries, a great variety of entertainment forms had existed from very early times. Some were pure popular entertainment, often linked to prostitution; others were patronized by the court; some fulfilled a ritualistic function of assisting in the agricultural cycle, and still others were supported by Buddhist temples, which saw the potential of drama to convey religious teaching simply and graphically.

Kan'ami was a performer of *sarugaku* ('monkey music'), which while always retaining its centuries-old character as 'variety show' had gradually been developing simple playlets in the 14th century. Kan'ami gave them form by inserting a dance known as *kusemai,* which had a strong beat and an accompanying sung narrative. Kan'ami built the central climaxes of his performances around this *kusemai* dance and the theatre which resulted came to be known simply as nō ('skill', 'accomplishment').

Kan'ami was a director in the sense that he was the head of a large troupe and would therefore have been the main actor and the source of theatrical creativity for all its members. The functions of actor and director in Japan were not separated until the 20th century, not long after the rise of the director in the West. Kan'ami's son Zeami succeeded to the headship and consciously continued and developed his father's work. He had the great advantage of the personal patronage of the shōgun Yoshimitsu, and his status as the latter's young companion gave him an entrée to the refinement of the shōgunal court that no other nō players enjoyed. Here for several decades until his fall from grace around 1429, he developed the art of nō in an environment that placed a high value on culture and was deeply imbued with Zen Buddhism. What emerged was a drama sparse in movement and text but rich in symbolism and texture.

A collection of Nō masks. Each is designed to represent a specific 'type': 'young woman', 'old man' etc. When worn, the mask only partly covers the face. An actor will spend some time studying the mask he is to wear for a particular performance. The better he knows it, the better he will know how to use light, shadow and angle to best effect.

Nō texts are short: most would take only 15 minutes to read aloud at normal speed. Zeami laid down how they were to be written: with, first, the choice of a subject, often from earlier literature and always familiar to an educated audience; second, structure, following the fundamental pattern of *jo* (introduction), *ha* (development) and *kyū* (climax); and, third, a literary style that had to be elegant and poetic. Most plays observe the following structure:

1. *jo*: entry of secondary figure (*waki*), usually a traveller, who announces the setting;
2. *ha* (i): entry of main figure (*shite*);
3. *ha* (ii): the *waki*, a stranger, asks the *shite*, apparently a local person, about the historical associations of the setting;
4. *ha* (iii): the *shite* reveals close knowledge of the place in a dance (*kuse*) which ends the first part of the play;
5. in the *kyū*, the second part, the *shite* reappears in his real identity as a historical figure linked to the setting and portrays in a dance the incident that created the link.

In performance the acting is stylized, set gestures or movements (*kata*) indicating recognized emotions. The *shite* often wears a mask. Actor training is rigorous and leads in early middle age to the 'flower' (*hana*), which allows the actor to induce a feeling of restrained beauty (*yūgen*) in his audience. The rejection of linear time in the structure of the plays, the absence of scenery, and the combination of acting, music (by four musicians who sit at the back of the stage) and chanting by the chorus created, and create (although performances are much slower now than in Zeami's time), a mood of intense contemplation.

Kyōgen

Kyōgen (literally, 'mad words') preserve the comic elements of the entertainment forms that preceded nō. The development of this genre was complementary and subordinate to nō, and *kyōgen* came to fulfil two distinct functions. First, *kyōgen* players would talk to the audience in everyday language between the two parts of a nō play, explaining and commenting on the plot. Second, they would perform independent comic pieces (also called *kyōgen*) in between performances of individual nō plays.

Like nō texts, *kyōgen* are short and built around two principal characters. The language is colloquial and often repetitive. In the largest category of play a lord's retainer (always called Tarōkaja) tricks his master to his own advantage. Other butts of *kyōgen* humour are Buddhist priests, sons-in-law, sightless people and very human devils.

Kyōgen are also performed on a bare stage with minimal or no properties. Actors are male and not masked. Most plays use no musicians or chorus and the techniques needed have more to do with timing than symbolic movement. *Kyōgen* performances are this-worldly in contrast to the invitation to something beyond actuality that is implied in nō.

Puppet theatre

Puppet theatre is now called bunraku, from the name of an early 19th-century theatre manager: *ningyō jōruri* (puppets with chanted accompaniment) is a more general term. The bunraku of today derives from a puppet theatre that developed in the mid 17th century. Puppetry in Japan had a long history, and narrative chanted to stringed accompaniment dates back to the 13th century. When puppets, a romantic narrative called 'Jōruri' (from the name of the heroine princess) and a three-stringed instrument called a shamisen introduced from the Ryūkyūs came together, a composite art of great beauty resulted.

Like nō, puppet theatre owes its establishment to two individuals: the chanter Takemoto Gidayū (1651–1714), whose name came to designate the style of chanting used to accompany the puppets, and the playwright Chikamatsu Monzaemon (1653–1724), who wrote a series of superb texts in the first two decades of the 18th century.

When Chikamatsu started writing for Gidayū in 1685, the puppets were operated from below with a single puppeteer inserting a hand into the costume. The chanter and shamisen player were not visible. Then in 1703, as a daring experiment, a celebrated and very handsome puppeteer operated the heroine in a Chikamatsu play in full view of the audience. This proved very popular and Takemoto Gidayū himself appeared before the audience in 1705, under the puppets' stage. Finally in 1728 the chanter and shamisen player acquired their present position on a special dais to the right of the stage. Meanwhile the puppets themselves developed: in 1727 being able to move their eyelids, mouths and hands; in 1734 acquiring bulk and height so that three puppeteers were now required for each, and in 1736 rolling their eyeballs and moving their eyebrows.

The plays that Chikamatsu wrote for the puppets fall into two main groups: first, *jidai-mono,* plays on historical subjects about samurai; second, *sewa-mono,* plays usually about a tragic love affair between two commoners. Later these divisions became blurred and by the 1740s, when the three most famous puppet plays were written, audiences expected to have elements of both types on the same programme. All three of these plays, which include *Kanedehon Chūshingura* (1748) on the revenge of the 47 *rōnin,* were written by a team of playwrights, but the language followed the pattern established by Chikamatsu Monzaemon, being rhythmical and full of word-play.

Puppet theatre or bunraku. The puppets have more than one operator, as can be seen on the right, but during performance it does not take long before the audience completely forgets the presence of any such human form. The chanter, who has full responsibility for the words and music, will probably be sitting on a separate, smaller stage to the audience's right.

Kabuki

Kabuki is now written with the characters for 'song, dance and action', but the word was originally derived from the verb *kabuku* 'to be unconventional'. You can read a puppet theatre text and imagine what is happening on the stage, because it contains both dialogue and narrative. This is not possible with kabuki, where so much depends on the actions that the actors themselves decide should accompany or supplement the script. Kabuki is an actors' theatre par excellence.

Important pioneers in kabuki history are: Ichikawa Danjūrō I (1660–1704), Sakata Tōjūrō I (1647–1709) and Yoshizawa Ayame I (1673–1729), all actors. Chikamatsu wrote some important plays for kabuki, and many of his plays for puppets are still performed in kabuki versions. Apart from Tsuruya Nanboku IV (1755–1829) and Kawatake Mokuami (1816–93), however, other kabuki playwrights are not generally remembered.

Early kabuki history was conditioned by external factors. The revue-type performances of travelling troupes of women entertainers (one of which was led by Okuni, credited with being the foundress of kabuki) were banned in 1629, and the young boys who took their place were banned in 1652. Other government regulations during the same period ensured that kabuki would be a dramatic form performed by adult males. Unlike Shakespearean theatre, then, kabuki could not use boys with unbroken voices for the female parts, so the distinctive art of the *onnagata* or *oyama* developed, an art distinguished by high standards of grace and stylized movement in the attempt to capture the essence of the feminine on (and even off) the stage.

Individual kabuki actors invented sequences of movements (*kata*) which were associated with certain episodes in plays and often ended in a *mie* or climactic pose. The actors decided how a play, whose outline and dialogue were suggested to them by a subservient playwright, was to be performed. The movements of the actor's body were all-important and hence dance pieces, with no dialogue, were in great demand. To the two basic categories of *jidai-mono* and *sewa-mono* was added the *shosagoto,* danced to the accompaniment of chanting and music. Music has been a significant element of kabuki performance and an accompaniment is usual for all types

Kabuki. The stage is much longer and deeper than any Western equivalent, permitting spectacular effects, which are an integral part of any performance. Kabuki playscripts are often little more than vehicles for the main business: acting and action on stage.

of traditional play. In common with the puppet theatre, continual technical innovation has also been a feature of kabuki, in particular the revolving stage, which was invented in 1758. It could hold two complete sets and made possible quick scene changes and other spectacular effects.

Kabuki acquired respectability and the status that accompanied official recognition during the early decades of the Meiji period. It was intimately linked with the first moves towards a modern Japanese theatre and in the 20th century has accepted and encouraged a large amount of new writing. In the last decade of the century kabuki is still firmly established as a major theatrical force and many of its actors have been active in other areas of theatre.

Modern theatre

The general term for modern theatre during the 20th century is *shingeki* 'new theatre', although this word is not all-inclusive. It owed its rise primarily to the influence of Shakespeare and the European Naturalists and hence has been a theatre of realism. But between representational *shingeki* and presentational kabuki there were two genres which took elements from both: *shinpa* ('new school'), which used actresses and took its themes from contemporary life, and *shinkokugeki* ('new national drama'), a form now defunct which started in 1917 and was known for period plays with set-piece sword fights. In the 1960s another modern genre emerged. At first called *angura* (a contraction of the phonetic spelling of the English 'underground'), it has since become known as the *shōgekijō* ('little theatre') movement.

Text was important to the three modern styles, but the position of the playwright has been much stronger in *shingeki* than the other two, where the playwright has usually written for a particular actor. The *shingeki* playwright has been a literary man; many of the most famous modern novelists have written plays, and many famous *shingeki* plays are counted as works of literature. The playwright was initially very important to *angura* in the 1960s, but performance has been the hallmark of the genre and the texts can only tell us so much about the totality of the playwright-director's conception.

Tsubouchi Shōyō (1859–1935) and Mori Ōgai (1862–1922) by their individual writings and a public debate in 1890–92 established the right of drama to be considered as literature. Both men also wrote plays: Tsubouchi, historical dramas for kabuki, and Mori Ōgai plays in which delicate emotional shading required modern actors and actresses. The boom in Ibsen studies in Japan after the Norwegian playwright's death in 1906 stimulated much new writing in the Naturalist mode, with social problems and the individual's relation to society being prominent themes. But there remained a gap between writing and performance due to the slow progress towards a modern acting style. The proletarian movement of the later 1920s led many young playwrights to produce revolutionary plays. Others, such as Kishida Kunio (1890–1954), rejected political themes in favour of exploring the human psyche through a new use of language, and this search for a new stage language has remained a preoccupation of many modern dramatists, notably Kinoshita Junji (b. 1914). Repression of the left-wing in the 1930s stopped overt espousal of left-wing beliefs, but several playwrights, such as Kubo Sakae (1901–58), who had begun their careers in the 1920s, did write plays of 'socialist realism' that attempted to dramatize whole social movements. New plays were also written for *shinpa*, *shinkokugeki* and kabuki, notably by Mayama Seika (1878–1948), who with trenchant dialogue and modern psychological interpretations brought alive on the modern stage some familiar characters from Edo kabuki.

Modern Japanese theatre has retained in large measure the interest in poses and strong visual impact.

For nearly two decades after the war *shingeki* continued to grapple with the problem of realism – how to define the reality of modern Japan and then show it on stage. It now seemed more natural for individuals to be uninhibited in their reactions to others and Mishima Yukio (1925–70) shocked his audiences by his liberating use of language and sexuality.

The 1960s saw the break with realism. Playwrights such as Abe Kōbō and Betsuyaku Minoru developed a distinctively Japanese type of absurd drama, while others probed the darkest recesses of the Japanese subconscious in ways that were deeply disturbing. Satō Makoto (b. 1943), Kara Jūrō (b. 1940) and Terayama Shūji (1935–83) wrote plays that ignored any conventions that did not suit them. Unexpected changes of mood and pace, jumbles of images, wit and obscenity, a parading of taboos and a contempt for inhibition of any kind – all these added up to plays that were unlike anything that had gone before. If the writing of the 1960s can be described as kaleidoscopic, the term 'Chinese-box-like' has been used about subsequent plays. Younger playwrights such as Noda Hideki (b. 1955) have a lighter approach but share the 1960s distrust of logical progression. Plays within plays within plays are characteristic of much of their work, which has the exuberant use of language pioneered in the 1960s without the compulsion to induce loathing in their audiences. Theatre in the 1990s has been criticized for relying on fantasy and sheer entertainment to attract its audiences, and the use of in-group vocabulary from television and pop songs seems to support this, but a playwright such as Watanabe Eriko will insist that fantasy can bear a serious message too.

Performance in modern theatre closely mirrors the development of drama. In 1909 and 1911 two companies usually regarded as the initiators of modern theatre in Japan mounted their first productions. The challenge was realistic acting, as the plays performed by Jiyū Gekijō and Bungei Kyōkai were by Shakespeare and Ibsen respectively. Their different solutions to the problem indicate how daunting it was: Jiyū Gekijō used kabuki actors and expected them to forget their kabuki training; Bungei Kyōkai used students without any professional experience at all. Only in 1924 did Japan acquire a theatre – the Tsukiji Little Theatre – purpose-built for *shingeki*, but even here actor-training was largely theoretical. Realism was achieved by *shingeki* actors in the decade after the war and then rejected by the *angura* movement of the 1960s. Terayama Shūji went furthest in rejecting the achievements of *shingeki* acting by bringing prostitutes and beggars off the streets and casting them in his plays. The 1960s saw the liberation of the body in acting, particularly in the work of Suzuki Tadashi, whose 'Suzuki method' emphasized the essential physicality of acting. Japanese theatre since has been noted for a richness of physical movement and it is this that has helped it to achieve international recognition. BP

Film

During the Pacific War, American director Frank Capra was asked to compile a secret report about some captured Japanese films. His verdict on one homefront melodrama was eloquently blunt: 'We can't beat this kind of thing. We make a film like that maybe once in a decade.' In the more benign climate of the post-war, similar reactions would be repeated by Western viewers, critics and makers of film once the extraordinary films of Kurosawa Akira, Mizoguchi Kenji and Ozu Yasujirō began winning international recognition.

Demonstrations of the exotic new moving pictures first captivated Japanese audiences in the late 1890s. Before the century was over, Japanese camera-men were recording well-known landscapes, geisha dances, then scenes from kabuki plays. The rapidly and unevenly developing country used both tradition and innovation in domesticating the new technology for the production of filmed narratives accessible to a growing mass audience. Initially kabuki provided a source of stories which, with changes in acting styles and borrowings from a range of popular historical legends, ensured the success of period drama. There was also a new kind of theatre presenting both modern European drama and stories set in the new Japan; this laid the groundwork for more realistic contemporary work. Between tradition and innovation was the *benshi* film narrator. Early *benshi* provided explanatory glosses for foreign settings and difficult titles. From their privileged position beside the screen and with musical accompaniment, they reshaped popular storytelling and comic narratives to become the main attraction at cinemas for decades; only the success of the sound film in the 1930s brought on their demise.

These two general categories of film provided a durable framework for the development of a wide variety of sub-genres as the industry grew through the 1920s and 1930s. They also dictated the technical and artistic specializations of producers, directors, actors, and the emerging conglomerate studios themselves which increasingly brought together film production, distribution and screening. Film companies were highly rationalized, gearing employees through training, promotion-track and a work ethic that would ultimately prove intolerable to many post-war directors. Despite competition from American films, films from which the industry learned the basics of its craft, Japan produced some 11,000 feature films between the late 1920s and the end of the war. Rapid urbanization and the growth of a consumer culture sustained this huge output and made possible new variations on conventional themes. With the Depression, filmmakers increasingly explored the fate of the threatened lower-middle and working classes, and the plight of Japanese women. Period films generated a new type of flawed hero: the masterless samurai, torn between duty and emotion, struggling against injustice alongside the common people. Censorship increased as Japan mobilized for total war; cinema was called upon to reinforce the war effort, yet what war films were made tended to be long on character and sentiment, short on jingoism and racism.

The Occupation brought new freedoms and new censors. The period film was suspect for glorifying feudalism and militarism; a new genre borrowing many of the same elements, the gangster film, was deemed safe. After the restoration of full independence, the samurai returned in force, in time to play their part in the last golden age of Japanese film-making. By 1958 there were some 8,000 cinemas; box offices recorded over one billion admissions.

Kurosawa Akira's first period films were made in the 1940s. They were suppressed by the Occupation authorities, and he turned to gangster films before making his early masterpieces, *Rashōmon* (1950), which won the Silver Lion at Venice, and *Seven samurai* (1954), a work renowned for its powerful combination of mood, ethics and sheer action.

Above *Film posters in Kōbe. The one on the left is for a very popular series entitled* Pity the male of the species!

Far right *A central scene from* Ikiru *(1952). In this film Kurosawa made much use of flashback and montage in order to give a basically simple tale a complex visual patterning.*

Kurosawa's *Ikiru* (1952), the story of a dying man desperately attempting to redeem something from an empty life against all odds, powerfully continues the realism and humanism of the pre-war contemporary drama.

Mizoguchi Kenji began making films in the 1920s. *Sisters of the Gion* (1936), voted film of the year, is a classic study of women's fate under patriarchy. He made a number of films about women during the Occupation years, and transferred their themes to the period dramas that ensured him an international reputation, the greatest of which is *Ugetsu* (1953). Mizoguchi's fluid camera movement and his characteristic one-shot one-scene tableau in depth had a strong impact on the emerging *nouvelle vague* directors in France.

Ozu Yasujirō is considered by many to be the most significant Japanese director. He spent decades refining and paring down techniques and themes to produce minimalist portrayals of the Japanese family. *I was born but...* (1932), a bitter-sweet child's-eye-view of the new salaryman, remains one of the finest silent films ever made. *Tōkyō story* (1953) is a quiet, elegiac story of the disintegration of an average family, implying the fate of the traditional core of social life itself.

In the prosperous 1960s people started buying televisions and fewer visited cinemas. Admissions plummeted to one-fifth their peak, theatres closed and studios faced bankruptcy. The expensive productions of a Kurosawa or Mizoguchi were replaced by pre-packaged commodities: gangsters, adorable teenagers, monsters, soft porn. Such tactics did little to win back a loyal audience, and made many new directors strike out into independent production. Major studios survive more through real estate investment than their output of films. It has been the independents, directors such as Ōshima Nagisa, Imamura Shōhei and more recently Itami Jūzō, who have kept Japanese cinema alive and continued its achievements throughout the world. MM

Dreams *(1990). At this most recent stage in his career Kurosawa has abandoned interest in social commentary and retreated into a world of pure fantasy. Many argue that his work has lost all force and relevance with this concentration on atmosphere and visual effect.*

The culture of tea

The custom of drinking tea was introduced to Japan from Tang dynasty China around the early 9th century. In 815 the monk Eichū, who had recently returned from a 30-year stay in China, personally served tea to Emperor Saga. For several centuries, however, tea drinking remained an aristocratic habit, or a component of Buddhist ceremonies. It was not until the late 12th century, when the monk Eisai and other Japanese monks returning from Song China brought back the teachings of Zen Buddhism and improved tea plants, that the new Song style of serving powdered tea, *matcha*, became more widespread.

Tea and Zen

Japanese monks who visited Song monasteries found that tea was commonly used as a medicine, to entertain guests, and as a stimulant to ward off sleep during long periods of meditation. After his return to Japan Eisai presented to the shōgun a treatise on tea (*The essentials of tea drinking*) in which he advocated tea as a medicament for restoring the bodily functions and prolonging life.

During the medieval period the practice of tea drinking spread from Zen monasteries to other sectors of Japanese society. In the process it was aesthetically transformed. Tea gatherings and tasting contests were held which brought together monks, emperors, nobles, the shōgun and powerful warriors and, in time, wealthy merchants from Kyōto, Sakai and Hakata. Although tea drinking was not exclusive to Zen monasteries, Zen monks formulated the more detailed rules and etiquette for the monastic style of tea drinking, known as *sarei*. Zen monks were also experts in Chinese culture and in the appreciation of the Chinese objects – utensils, calligraphic scrolls, and ink paintings – which were used during these gatherings. Moreover, Zen notions of emptiness, of the immanence of Buddha nature in all things, and of simplicity and restraint were gradually incorporated into the developing aesthetic of tea drinking and appreciation of utensils and art objects. For this reason Zen monasteries like Kennin-ji, Tōfuku-ji and Daitoku-ji tended to become centres for study of tea as well as the practice of Zen. Some monks and laymen, under the slogan 'Zen and tea are one taste', went so far as to suggest that the insights of Zen enlightenment could be attained through the practice of tea as well as through seated meditation.

Until the 15th century most tea gatherings, *chayoriai*, were lavish events held in grand chambers of temples or palaces, with pride of place given to rare Chinese utensils and art objects. In time, however, devotees began to build separate tea houses known as *chashitsu*. They also began to find greater value in native Japanese art and aesthetics. The tea houses were simple in spirit and design and were intended to recreate, in an urban environment, the rustic mountain hut of a hermit or reclusive priest. They incorporated such features of interior design as the alcove, *tokonoma*, and the use of hanging scrolls and flower arrangements.

Chanoyu, or the tea ceremony

Chanoyu as we know it today was developed to the full as an aesthetic during the 16th century by merchant tea masters from Sakai culminating in Murata Shukō (d. 1502), Takeno Jōō (1502–55) and Sen no Rikyū (1522–91).

Shukō is thought to have reduced the size of the interior of the tea room to four and a half *tatami* mats (a mat measuring approximately one by two metres) and to have actively incorporated Zen ideals. Jōō emphasized the plain, unadorned and concealed beauty of bare wood and unpainted walls and Rikyū drastically reduced the scale of the tea room even further to one and a half mats. He is also credited with the introduction of the tiny entrance through which lords as well as commoners had to crawl to enter the room. This radical reduction in space heightened the sense of separation from the mundane world, the experience of intimacy, the sense of equality between host and guests, and of utter simplicity. Rikyū incorporated a light meal, known as *kaiseki*, into *chanoyu* as a means of fuller communion between guests and host. Like the preparation of tea, the serving of *kaiseki* responded to the changing seasons, allowed the use of treasured utensils, and demonstrated generosity with frugal means. *Kaiseki* has since become the most elegant form of Japanese cuisine and has influenced the cooking and presentation of food by many contemporary Western chefs.

Tea rooms were not always built with restraint. This replica of Toyotomi Hideyoshi's tea room, covered in gold, gives some idea of the brashness of which such warrior-kings were capable.

Rikyū's greatest contribution to the culture of tea, however, may have been his emphasis on the ideal of *wabi*, an aesthetic of cultivated simplicity and poverty. *Wabi* had been developed long before, but it was Rikyū who made it the cornerstone of the tea ceremony. It had complex implications of withered beauty, of imperfection and irregularity as ideals, and of richness veiled in austerity. It was, for Rikyū, an absolute artlessness, but one that rested on carefully contrived art. He made it sound simple:

Chanoyu is nothing but this
Boil water, make tea, and drink
That is all you need to know.

A Japanese tea room, where everything has the patina of age and the aim is quiet understatement. The small square in the floor would be removed to accommodate a brazier for boiling the water. The sound of water boiling in the midst of silence is another facet of the ceremony.

Yet even the boiling of water called for mindfulness and attention to forms.

This kind of ceremony fused the everyday features of life into an artistically heightened experience. It also allowed for the development of a powerful counter-aesthetic to Chinese ideals of perfect polished beauty, elaborate ceremony, grand chambers, and rare utensils. Chinese elements were not purged from tea but through the incorporation of *wabi, chanoyu* became a distinctively Japanese aesthetic experience.

This was expressed most clearly in Rikyū's taste in tea bowls. He prized simple black tea bowls made by the former tile maker Chōjirō, founder of the Raku line of potters, as much as elegant Song Chinese ceramics.

The style of *chanoyu* and the ideals of *wabi* that Rikyū espoused have been carried down to the present by the four major tea schools that trace their lineages from him. Throughout the Tokugawa period shōguns and daimyō were expected to possess fine tea rooms, and the ceremony itself began to spread among townspeople and villagers. Along with other aspects of traditional culture, *chanoyu* suffered an eclipse in the early Meiji period but recovered in the late 19th century helped by the advocacy of Okakura Tenshin in *The book of tea* and by the revival of interest in a Japanese national identity. As a cultural pursuit, tea has now recovered much of its former popularity and schools offering instruction in the art are an integral part of what is now a highly profitable leisure industry. It also plays a central rôle in how Japan markets itself abroad. MC

The culture of food

Although Japan today imports a huge range of foods from every corner of the globe, it was not always so. The conspicuous consumption of gourmet products and the high-protein diet now enjoyed by nearly all Japanese are fairly recent phenomena. Before modern economic growth and the introduction of specialized farming methods to secure an almost year-round supply of fresh fruit, meat and vegetables, the traditional Japanese diet was sparse, based on grains such as rice and barley and supplemented with fish, vegetables in season and various pulses.

The short stature, the chronic occurrence of beriberi caused by vitamin deficiency, and the almost total lack of descriptions of food or meals in Japanese literature, all bespeak a fairly frugal and unexciting fare. And yet from such unpromising foundations, the Japanese have managed to fashion a wholly distinctive cuisine.

Food in everyday life

The symbolic use of food and drink in Japan is highly developed. Offerings are made at graves and home altars, salt is cast liberally over the *sumō* arena for ritual purification, *sake* is considered a sacred drink, and the mythical properties of rice grown on Japanese soil are a constant rallying cry for farming interest groups fighting to restrict cheaper imports. Gifts often take the form of food, particularly in mid-summer and at New Year, the two main 'giving' seasons, but also as a small token on any visit one might make. Gift-giving is highly regulated and the food industry takes full advantage of this habit. But perhaps the truly distinctive characteristic of Japanese cuisine is the concern for design and visual appeal. Many small bowls and dishes are used, almost as if the meal were entirely composed of a series of *hors d'oeuvres*. The natural result is that the food itself, its preparation and its combinations often become a major subject of conversation, as do the collections of plates and bowls in which the food is presented – usually a rich combination of porcelain, lacquerware, wood, leaves and even paper. The ideal meal, then, will be a visual as well as a gastronomic delight, an occasion where the placing of the bowls and chopsticks is itself an subject worthy of study. At times, indeed, such care borders on a fetish.

It is easy, however, to overstress this art and artifice of the Japanese meal. Fast-food restaurants and snackbars exist in such abundance in the major cities that a meal can usually be obtained at any time day or night. Be it *soba* (buckwheat noodles) or *sando* (white-bread sandwiches), 'curry rice' (a curried sauce on rice, with little or no meat) or *katsudon* (cutlet on rice), the service is usually quick and the turnover rapid. Such is the pace of life that good use is also made of the ubiquitous automatic vending machines and of the fact that many restaurants will still deliver a meal to one's home or office in response to a telephone call.

Japanese cuisine

Many of the dishes which are now considered to be quintessentially Japanese date back in their present form no further than the Tokugawa period, when the first recipe books were published: the eating of raw fish with soy sauce rather than with vinegar dates

Right *A display of dishes, complete with name and price outside a restaurant to tempt the customer. The displays are in fact carefully crafted plastic replicas.*

from this time, for example. Other elements are much older, such as *tōfu* (bean curd), which first appeared in about the 14th century, and *tenpura* (deep fried fish and vegetables), which comes from the Latin *tempora* used by the Portuguese for days when they abstained from meat and ate fried fish instead. Meat dishes, however, are no older than the 19th century, with the exception of boar, which was termed 'mountain whale' to maintain the pretence of observing the Buddhist prohibition on meat. Beef and pork were only introduced in the 19th century, and such popular dishes as *sukiyaki*, thin-sliced beef cooked at the table in a sweet sauce, are little more than 100 years old.

Japanese meals typically consist of several elements which play complementary rôles. The dishes are arranged separately for each person, sometimes on an individual tray, and are to be eaten not one by one but simultaneously. In a formal banquet they will include at least soup and three main dishes. The passing of the seasons is regularly marked by special dishes, particularly on the days of the spring and autumn equinoxes, and this is also true of other days in the calendar. On 3 March, the day of the Doll Festival, rice cakes (*mochi*) wrapped in leaves of the cherry tree are eaten, while on Boys' Day, 5 May, the rice cakes are wrapped in oak leaves. The foods served at the New Year include *o-zōni*, a soup containing some grilled *mochi* rice cakes.

The staple constituent of everyday meals is of course rice. Its importance is indicated by the fact that the words for rice, *gohan* or *meshi*, also signify simply 'meal'. The foods that complement rice are hot soup, raw or cooked fish, cooked vegetables and *tsukemono* or pickles. *Tsukemono* consist of vegetables pickled in pure salt, in a highly salted paste, or in fermented rice; they are usually served in small quantities and are the necessary and inseparable companion to the rice brought at the end of every meal. Rice is also an essential ingredient of *sushi* but it is vinegared first and rapidly cooled in order to produce a characteristic lustre. *Sushi* appears in many forms, such as cylinders of rice wrapped in dried laver seaweed and containing raw fish or vegetables known as *makizushi*, or small portions of rice topped with a slice of raw fish known as *nigirizushi*.

Japanese meals can be understood in terms of the dishes that are commonly eaten, but also in terms of the different ways of preparing the food. To make the different dishes constituting a meal a relatively small range of methods are applied to the basic ingredients, and it is the culinary process concerned, rather than the contents, that determines the generic name of a dish: grilled fish (*yakizakana*), for example, is listed on a menu as a 'something grilled' (*yakimono*) rather than as fish. The principal processes are:

A local fish store in Tōkyō. Most housewives still shop for fresh food on a daily basis.

shirumono or soups, often based on a stock derived from sea weed or dried bonito: a clear soup might contain some sliced vegetables or some shellfish, while cloudy soups consist of a stock to which *miso*, fermented bean paste, has been added.

nabemono are dishes cooked at table, of which the best known is *sukiyaki*.

yakimono are grilled or broiled foods, such as *shioyaki*, which is grilled salted fish.

agemono are deep fried foods. Sometimes a batter is used, as in *tenpura*, sometimes not, but the chef's concern is always to ensure that the food is crisp and free of oil, so the exact mixture of oils is important.

menrui are noodles, *udon* being the thickest and *sōmen* the thinnest. Both of these are made of wheat flour, while *soba* are made of buckwheat flour.

Visual display is an extremely important element in Japanese cuisine, as can be seen here in a lunch box. Colour, shape and ingredients have equal status.

Below Sashimi *or raw fish with soya sauce and stem ginger. Before use, the light wooden chopsticks will have to be split down the middle.*

The knife is very important in Japanese cuisine, particularly in the preparation of raw fish, which has to be expertly boned and cut thinly and quickly to avoid spoiling the flesh. *Sashimi* could not have emerged without a long and exact tradition of knife-making. This is especially so in the case of the notórious blowfish or *fugu*, which is so venomous that the slightest trace of the poison can cause paralysis and death. Chefs in *fugu* restaurants now have to be licensed by the authorities: a very sharp blade and a practised hand are both necessary in order to prepare the fish without puncturing the liver, and to slice it thinly enough that the pattern of the plate may show through the flesh. There is an enormous range of knives available, different in shape for the different rôles to be performed but all razor sharp. The skill of the chef is judged by the dexterity with which the knife is used, and in many restaurants the slicing of fish and raw vegetables such as radish or carrot is carried out in full view of the customers so that appreciation of the preparer's skills becomes an integral part of the eating experience.

Drink

The word *sake* is widely used in Japanese to refer to all alcoholic drinks, but in its narrower usage it refers to a transparent, slightly whitish-looking drink made from rice. It is made from a fermented mixture of rice, malted rice and water and is usually refined before bottling. The first written records referring to the manufacture of *sake* date from the 8th century, but the process is thought to be much older, dating from some time after the introduction of rice in the 3rd century BC. The centres of production were at first the imperial court and large temples, but by the 14th century it had evidently been successfully commercialized, for it appears to have become a taxable commodity about that time.

Sake has an alcoholic strength of 16–18%. Although it has recently become popular to drink it 'on the rocks', the normal practice is to heat it in a porcelain vessel called a *tokkuri* in a bath of hot water and then pour it in tiny servings into small cups known as *sakazuki*. It is then drunk warm to the accompaniment of various salted foods. The tiny servings necessitate frequent refillings, and, since the etiquette for all drinks is not to fill one's own glass,

Barrels of sake, *stacked up at a local shrine as a votive offering.* Sake *bought for the household is usually available in 1.8-litre bottles in three grades. Locally made varieties are still quite common and there is a general distinction made between 'sweet' and 'dry'.*

the drinking of *sake* inevitably involves the constant conviviality of sharing out the contents of newly warmed *tokkuri*.

In Japanese myth *sake* fulfils a purifying rôle. Offerings to the Shintō deities were and still are always accompanied by offerings of *sake*. It is not uncommon, particularly at festival time, to see outside Shintō shrines displays of large barrels of *sake* donated by local companies and residents. These are not purely decorative, for drinking the *sake* forms a part of most shrine festivals and in its origins this practice is thought to represent a way of sharing and communing with the gods. The auspicious associations of *sake* drinking survive today, for it always forms an important and ceremonial part of celebratory occasions: at Shintō weddings it is customary for bride and groom to take three sips of cold *sake* from three lacquered cups.

Drinking out in Japan now rarely involves exclusively *sake*, although the evening may well start with a few rounds. Whisky, beer and wine are all made in Japan and have become popular drinks. Whisky is commonly drunk heavily diluted with water, a drink known as *mizuwari*. Many bars have a so-called 'bottle-keep' system in operation, whereby customers buy a bottle of whisky from the bar and leave it there with their name on for subsequent visits: since the bar usually reclaims the bottle after a while this requires the customer to make frequent visits to the same establishment, which also charges the customer each time for the ice and water consumed. Japanese whisky has yet to establish an export market for itself. Beer has been brewed in Japan since the Meiji period when Europeans in Yokohama established breweries for the foreign community. There are fewer brands available now but they have been successful in finding export markets and several are now sold widely overseas. This does not apply to Japanese wines. By law Japanese wine has to contain a minimum of only 5% of grape juice produced in Japan and the bulk of what is sold as Japanese wine contains large admixtures of imported wine or grape juice. The result has a small following, but it is no match for the best European, Australian and American wines now widely available in Japanese supermarkets.

PK/RB

Society

The home and family

At first sight, Japanese families may look little different from Western families. Especially in cities, the home is usually shared by the nuclear group of parents and children who use it as a place for eating, sleeping, bathing and relaxing. It is also the place where children spend their earliest years and form their views of the world. Closer inspection, however, reveals ideas and values which are more specifically characteristic of Japan. A glance at the historical basis for the Japanese family is a good place to start.

The family in premodern Japan

In pre-industrial Japan 'continuing families' were the norm, indeed they were the primary social unit for purposes of registration, taxation and legal representation. The Japanese term for these 'continuing families', *ie*, was used both for the household at any one time and also for the continuing unit which includes both ancestors and descendants to come. Property was owned by the *ie*, although in the Tokugawa period it had to be registered under the name of the current head, and the household occupation was usually passed down from generation to generation; the *ie* had a certain status or standing in the wider community which members of the *ie* were expected to preserve.

Individual members were supposed to put the needs of the *ie* before their own personal interests and desires, contributing their labour to the household occupation, and sharing any benefits which accrued. In each generation, one child would inherit the position of head of the house, usually the eldest son, although this practice varied somewhat from region to region. Continuity was of paramount importance and other arrangements, such as adoption, would be made if necessary. The rest of the children were expected to leave on marriage, girls to other houses, younger sons either to set up branch houses or to a house with no son, as an adopted head. It was important that a bride or an adopted son fit into the existing *ie*, because if they failed to do so, they would simply be returned.

Relations within the house were based on a hierarchical pattern, with elders expecting deference from the younger members, and men likewise from women. Permanent members ranked before temporary ones, but the outsider who married in was for some time in a precarious position. The head received special privileges, such as being served first at meals, and his authority was usually unquestioned; his heir ranked second. Since other children were expected to leave, this system lent itself well to industrialization, for in each generation there would be young people available to move to the growing urban centres. These are the ones who began to create nuclear families in the cities.

The family in modern Japan

In modern Japan, the *ie* is still to be found in situations where there is substantial property or a household occupation, although in the 1947 Constitution it was abolished as a legal unit. In practice, it has been modified considerably. The absolute authority of the head of the house is over, and since children now choose their future occupations freely, less is made of an eldest son as the potential successor. Indeed, the older generation is pleased if any child stays in the family home to continue the line.

The sake *being poured for the bride at a Shintō wedding ceremony. Men rarely wear Japanese dress in public except on the day of their wedding. Behind the bride and groom stand the go-betweens, who arrange the marriage and have a more important part in the proceedings than the parents.*

In some areas families have difficulty in finding young wives for their inheriting sons, as local girls may prefer to marry a man setting up his own nuclear family. Girls who do agree to stay are treated more thoughtfully, however, since rifts between young wives and their mothers-in-law are now likely to lead to the young couple finding a new residence, rather than the return of the bride to her old home.

In cities and larger towns, nuclear families now predominate, but even here, much of the *ie* ideology remains in expectations of reciprocity between generations. First of all, ancestors must be remembered, and rites held for them at certain times. Tablets inscribed with their names are usually held in a Buddhist altar in the home of one descendant, and the wider family meets around it on special occasions. Amongst living members, there is an idea that the younger generation owes the older one care and respect in exchange for the nurture they received when they were growing up. People used to grow old and die within the comfort and familiarity of their own home; nowadays they may be left alone and move, when they can no longer manage by themselves, to the home of a child, increasingly a daughter rather than eldest son. If they do not actually share a home, the ideal is said to be that grandparents and parents live near enough to carry round a bowl of hot soup. Grandparents also provide the paraphernalia for the rites of their grandchildren as they are born.

Within the home itself, there have been subtle changes in relationships, sometimes reflected in the architecture. There is now a greater expectation of individual privacy than there used to be, symbolized by the solid walls dividing rooms which used to be separated only by sliding doors. Rooms are also set aside for individual family members who in the past would share space, even for sleeping. A newly-married couple sharing a house with their in-laws will very often move into an extension built specially for them. This they will share with their children in the early years, although the older generation may change places with the young family when they retire from active working life. This 'retirement' room (or house) was actually a feature of family life in some parts of Japan in the premodern period.

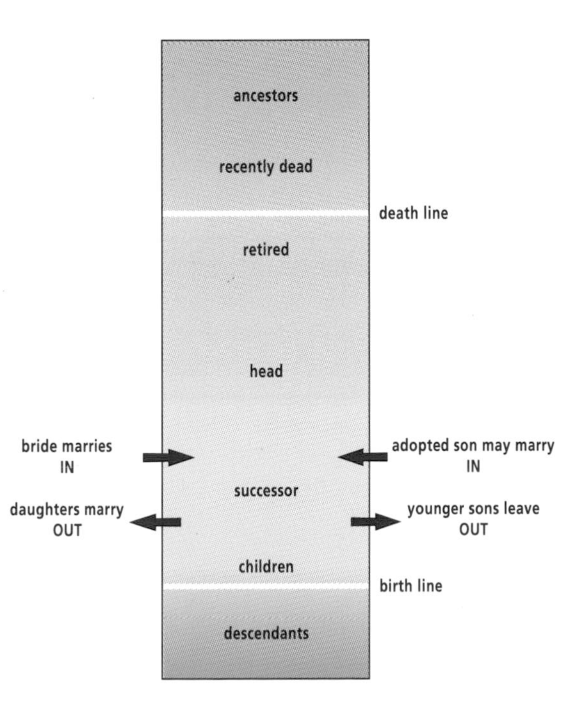

Right *The structure of the* ie. *The notion of the family in Japan characteristically includes both the ancestors and generations to come.*

Far right *In many homes there is a family Buddhist altar, or* butsudan, *usually dedicated to recently deceased members of the family.*

Child rearing

The rearing of children during the early years of life is taken very seriously in most Japanese families. It is said that the soul of a three-year-old lasts until 100, so efforts should be made to mould that soul from the very beginning. Within the home, children are socialized in a conscious and careful manner, and local authorities provide back-up facilities to help those who experience problems. This support reflects an older idea that the community had a rôle to play helping parents rear the new members of their family to become members of the wider community.

When homes were larger and there was room for grandparents to live with the next two generations, looking after the children was often a grandmother's responsibility, but increasing mobility and restricted living space make this much rarer nowadays.

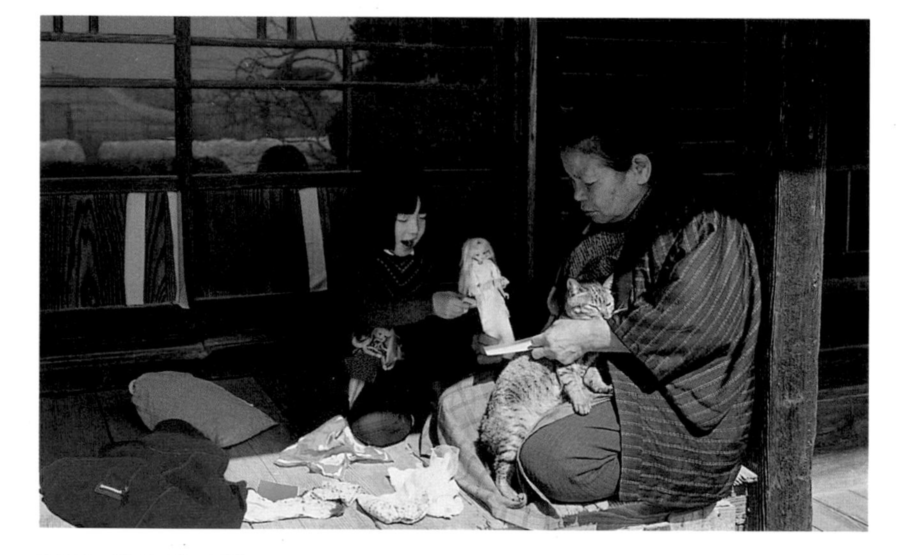

The Japanese word for child-rearing is *shitsuke*, a word also used for tacking a kimono into shape and teasing rice seedlings into an upright position. The common view is that children are basically good, so that with care and encouragement they should grow up to behave in an acceptable manner. A 'good child' is a 'straight' one, and problems can be 'mended' by appropriate training from adults. If a child misbehaves, then, the fault is thought to lie with the adults around it. An early inflexible distinction which a child learns is that between the home (*uchi*) and the outside world (*soto*). The former is associated with cleanliness and security, the latter with dirt and danger. As soon as a child can walk, it must learn to put shoes on when leaving the home, and take them off when coming back. Crossing the threshold is also accompanied by fixed phrases of departure and return, and similar distinctions are made when visiting the homes of others. This distinction between inside and outside is gradually carried through to other arenas in life: the neighbourhood, the school, and, eventually, the workplace. Behaviour within one's own group is different from behaviour for the outside world, and this difference forms a crucial component of Japanese social relations.

The distinction between *uchi* and *soto* forms part of the way in which human beings are classified, and children learn appropriate behaviour by observing the way members of their own family adjust to each situation. Language is a good index, and children find

Family planning

During the Tokugawa period the main ways of controlling family size were abortion and infanticide, but these were both banned in the Meiji period as the labour needs of the industrialized cities and the manpower needs of the growing army created political pressures for a larger population. In the early years of the 20th century, the women's movement took up the issue of birth control and several foreign advocates of family planning came to Japan to stimulate interest: some were refused permission to land and others were harassed by the police. From the late 1930s onwards, when Japan was at war with China, the birth control movement was officially suppressed and government slogans emphasized the need to increase the population.

After the Pacific War, contraceptives became available again and abortion was legalized in 1948. Both for this reason and because of the rising costs of housing and education, the birthrate went into a decline following the baby-boom of 1947–49. By far the most common method of contraception practised in Japan today is the condom, which accounts for around 80% of contraceptive users. Condoms are often sold door-to-door by public health nurses, and in recent years the high quality of Japanese condoms has brought increasing sales overseas. The second most common method is the rhythm method. The oral contraceptive pill is not licensed for contraceptive purposes in Japan although it is available for dealing with menstrual disorders: some argue that the safety of the pill has not been conclusively proved, while others point out that gynaecologists make more money from performing abortions than from prescribing the pill. At any rate, abortion is available on demand and currently well over 600,000 abortions are performed annually.

PK

that they must adopt more distant tones for outsiders, and politer ones if they are also elders. Even amongst themselves, children are always aware of their relative ages, speaking differently to those older and younger than themselves. In general, younger children defer slightly to older ones, asking them 'to do them the favour' of playing with them, and in a trivial dispute an older child is expected to give in to a younger one 'who will not yet be able to understand'.

This form of dispute-resolution among small children reflects a general idea that social relations should where possible be harmonious. In the early years parents try to create a secure atmosphere in the home by positively demonstrating ways to behave, rather than punishing their children when they do the 'wrong' thing. Small Japanese children often appear indulged to a Western observer, but their caretakers argue that in the long run this will lead to greater co-operation. Negative sanctions eventually take the form of ridicule and ostracism so that a child will be laughed at or ignored altogether for misbehaving. These sanctions continue in kindergarten where teachers encourage co-operation by simply ignoring altogether those who fail to comply.

The strategy a child gradually learns to adopt is one of adaptation to the situation. It learns that there are appropriate 'faces' for particular arenas, known in Japanese as *tatemae*, or a 'front' for the world, always to be distinguished from the *honne* or 'real feelings' which lie behind. This basic distinction very often coincides with that between *uchi* and *soto*, which makes the home an ideal place to learn it. The individual self is nurtured within the home; indeed parents urge their children to try to understand others, and think about their feelings, by projecting an understanding of themselves. Outside the home, they encourage their children to 'wrap' their needs in behaviour appropriate for each situation.

Right *Girls dressed up for the Seven–five–three Festival, so called because boys of five and girls of three or seven are taken to the local Shintō shrine to pray for their future happiness.*

THE HOME ECONOMY AND GENDER RÔLES

In nuclear families, it is usually the mother who does the child-rearing and, for many, it has become an almost full-time occupation right into the school-years. After starting their youngsters on the 'right' track in the home, such mothers help with school work for as long as they can. They also spend time investigating options for schools, perhaps even moving house to a better catchment area, for education has become the chief path to future employment, previously provided by the *ie* itself. The rôle of 'professional housewife', which involves taking complete charge of the home, and often managing the family purse as well, actually developed under Western influence along with industrialization, when men began to work away from home.

Below *Who makes the final decisions in the family? Results of a survey in 1980 on 1,054 women, aged between 20 and 75, in the Nakano Ward of Tōkyō.*

In less well-off families, however, women return at least to part-time work when their children go to school, and nearly 60% of women in the labour force are married. Women who wish to pursue full-time careers outside the home sometimes choose to avoid the conflict of having children as well, but there is an abundance of day nurseries in Japan, and conditions of maternity leave are improving: paid leave with security of employment is becoming available.

It is also common for grandparents to help out with the child-care if they live near enough, and, where day nurseries are used, a child is often delivered and collected by a grandparent. This arrangement is another example of intergenerational reciprocity creating further debt for the children to pay back by taking responsibility when their parents can no longer manage for themselves. This arrangement also replicates the way child-care used to be diffused throughout the old continuing family, more often than not being delegated to whichever grandparent was least useful to the house economically. This practice has survived wherever the *ie* system is still found, for example in agricultural and horticultural communities, in an abundance of small enterprises throughout Japan, and in occupational groups such as the medical profession, which invest in hospitals and building up a clientèle.

An apartment block by the Sumida river in Tōkyō. The futon *(bedding quilts) are hanging out in the sunshine to air.*

In continuing families, gender rôles may not be clearly divided for the economic activity of the household, and there is still an understanding that all members should pitch in as they are able. In country families, tasks may be allocated according to generation, the younger couple working with new technology, while their parents carry out more familiar tasks. Maritime communities may make clearer divisions, with men going out on long-distance fishing trips and women working closer to home, diving or collecting seaweed, but even these rôles are changing. In professional families it is increasingly common for the women to be employed in the family business as doctors, lawyers, or at least administrators, but they are often able to afford housekeepers to carry out domestic tasks. Elsewhere, it is still usually women who do the cooking, the washing and the cleaning.

Nevertheless, there are families in modern Japan where men are increasingly co-operative in helping women to pursue their own careers, and in some nuclear families men will even play an equal part in accomplishing the domestic chores. An ideal of equality is certainly heard amongst feminists in Japan, but on the whole less is still expected of marriage in terms of spending time together than in many societies. Holidays are often spent with peers of the same sex rather than with spouses, although brief family holidays have become rather fashionable recently.

With space at a premium in most modern Japanese homes, meals are usually eaten in a kitchen-diner. Ovens are still a great rarity in such households and cooking is done on gas rings. Hot water is produced, as here, from a small stand-alone unit.

Single-parent families

Divorce figures are low in Japan, but women in particular tend not to remarry. The old system required that children remain in the house of their birth, but figures show an increasing number of children remaining with their mothers. The entertainment world is also populated by women who have chosen, or sometimes been forced into, lives independent of a permanent partner. Some of these women are mistresses of men who also have a legal wife and family, but who have set them up in small businesses such as bars or restaurants.

Other women have chosen to join this world of their own accord, and have made careers as highly accomplished entertainers, epitomized by geisha. Their domestic arrangements are sometimes based on a family model whereby girls enter a house as 'younger sisters' of existing members, and several such women live and work with a 'mother' figure in the senior position. Any children they have are brought up in the house, although they may be supported financially by their natural fathers. Relations within such a domestic group are based on hierarchy, and traditional notions of 'parent–child' reciprocity sometimes still operate in these arenas more forcibly than they do in the biological families from which the model was developed.

Family rôles

Hierarchical relations of the 'parent–child' type exist between pairs of individuals in companies, in politics, in educational establishments, the arts and in the underworld. The expectation is of lifelong commitment, with benevolence from the senior being reciprocated by total loyalty from the junior. Young artists, scientists or politicians may ultimately become more successful than their teachers, but they should always show appropriate deference to them. In their turn they will attract juniors whom they must help, and relations continue down through the generations just as the *ie* would continue in family life. In the world of modern arts, heavily influenced by the outside world, splits occur as accomplishments develop, but in other fields, including big corporations, universities, and particularly that of gangs, these relations remain strong. RJH

Minorities

Discrimination against minorities has not been a prominent issue in Japan, partly because minority groups are hard to distinguish from majority Japanese and partly because the government has sought to deny the existence of a problem. In response to an enquiry from the United Nations in 1980 the Ministry of Foreign Affairs reported that there were no minorities in Japan as defined in the International Covenant on Civil and Political Rights. Nevertheless, three minority groups do exist: Burakumin, Koreans and Ainu.

Burakumin

There is evidence of prejudice and discrimination against marginal groups even in the earliest period of recorded history but the development of permanent outcaste communities is essentially the result of policies instituted during the Tokugawa period (1600–1868). Groups who did not fit into one of the four classes (samurai, peasant, artisan and merchant) were subject to customary discrimination, especially tanners and leather-workers, prison-workers and executioners. It was only in the 1720s that discrimination was enforced by law. Over the following 150 years the outcaste population increased rapidly while that of the surrounding population remained stable. As a result, the majority population became more aware of the existence of these outcaste groups while prejudice and discrimination became more deeply engrained.

These outcaste communities are referred to euphemistically as Burakumin (hamlet people) but in the Tokugawa period they used to be known by a variety of different names, including 'Eta' (filth abundant) and 'Hinin' (non-people). There was also considerable local variation in the implementation of regulations relating to them and the distribution of Burakumin across Japan has never been even.

The Emancipation Edict of 1870 freed outcastes from formal restrictions, but at the same time it removed the trade monopolies on which they had relied for economic survival; it could not of course eliminate prejudice or discrimination. In the countryside Burakumin plots of land were smaller and less

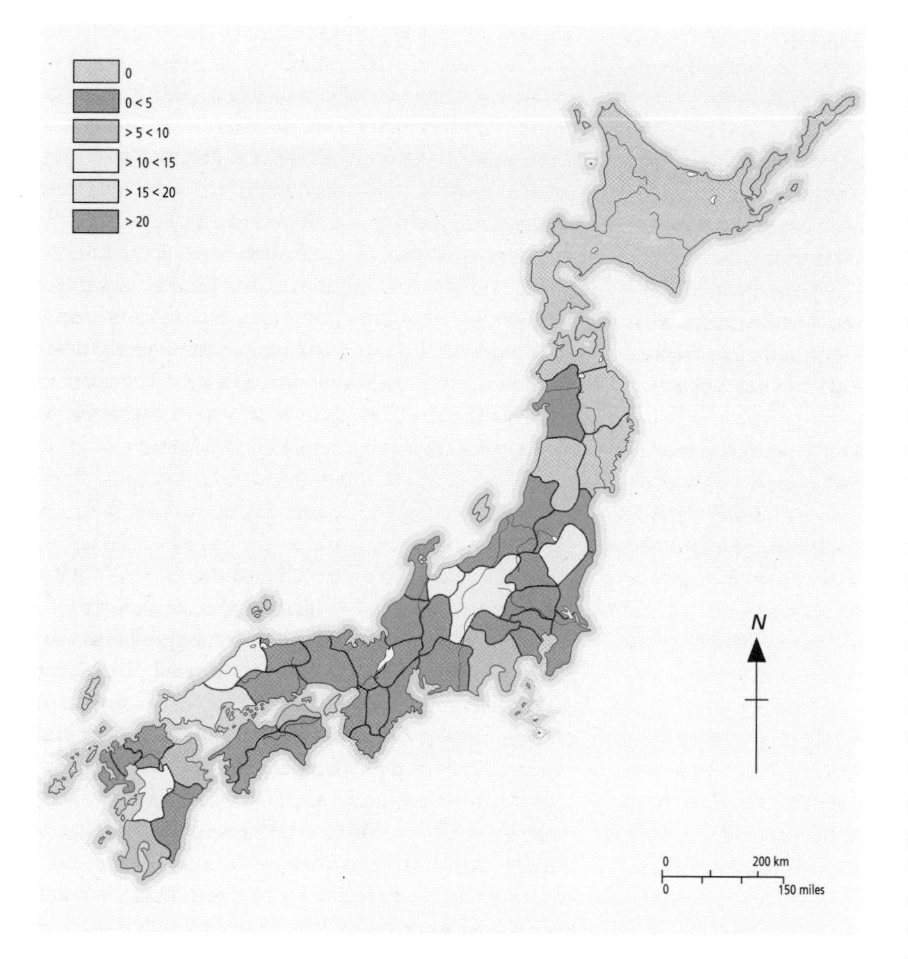

Map showing the numbers of Burakumin in each prefecture per 1,000 of the majority population in 1935. No more recent figures are available, because the fear of discrimination has prevented collection and publication of such statistics, but it is thought that the distribution has not changed markedly since then.

How many Burakumin are there?

Government figures suggest that, in 1987, there were 4,603 Buraku districts with a total population of 1,166,733. The BLL (Buraku Liberation League) suggests that there are at least 6,000 Buraku districts and 3,000,000 Burakumin. This discrepancy can be explained in two ways. First, there are some local government bodies which have refused to supply figures or whose figures are known to underestimate the numbers. Second, the government figure gives the number of people living in what are officially recognized Buraku districts eligible for assistance but does not include those Burakumin living in other districts. The BLL figure represents the total number of people subject to discrimination or concealing their Burakumin identity.

IJN

fertile than average, and in the towns they did the dirtiest work for the lowest pay: they were not able to compete on equal terms in the emergent capitalist society. Socialist and liberal ideas encouraged younger Burakumin to consider how discrimination might be eliminated and in 1922 they formed the Suiheisha (Levellers Society) 'as a new collective through which we shall emancipate ourselves'. The Suiheisha was closely related to other left-wing movements and subject to the same pressures: there were endless political debates over strategy and it was constantly harassed by the police. Nevertheless it remained a potent force well into the 1930s after most trade unions and other groups had succumbed to state control.

After the war some hoped that the democratic reforms enforced by the US occupation forces might put an end to prejudice. This was not to be. As the Japanese economy gradually recovered, the Buraku communities survived as islands of poverty in both town and countryside. Not until the 1960s was central government persuaded to do anything about this. In 1965 the Dōwa Policy Council issued a report which both set out an analysis of the problem and suggested solutions. It concluded that, despite the guarantees written into the constitution, Burakumin were being deprived of basic rights. The report described ghetto-like communities subject to flooding, with poor housing stock, often totally lacking in public services such as sewers or street lighting. Educational standards were low, the incidence of diseases such as trachoma and tuberculosis was high and many residents were dependent on public relief.

In 1969 a ten-year programme to improve the life and environment of Burakumin was launched under the Law on Special Measures for Dōwa Policy. Building projects began and a series of grant programmes came into force. Many of the projects were extended into the 1980s and the last came to an end in 1992. Most Buraku communities have been physically transformed: high-rise apartment blocks have replaced shabby shanty towns; communal facilities such as schools and clinics are as good as those elsewhere, and the number of Buraku children being educated in high school is now only just below the national average. Prejudice remains, though. The recommendation that the population at large be educated about the problem has been largely ignored. There are still examples of marriage plans being cancelled when one family learns that the prospective spouse is a Burakumin, and companies still try to identify and weed out Burakumin applicants for jobs.

The main pressure-group for the Burakumin is the Buraku Liberation League (BLL), which was formed soon after the war to carry on the work of the Suiheisha. In the Diet it has been supported by the opposition parties and the pressure it put on the government led to the creation of the Dōwa Policy Council in the early 1960s and the legislation of 1969. The BLL has however been racked by a series of internal disputes: a group affiliated to the Communist Party broke with the BLL in 1976 arguing, with the LDP, that special measures were no longer needed and that they only serve to perpetuate discrimination. The BLL continues to argue that there is a need for further special-aid programmes and for the enactment of a Fundamental Law on Buraku Liberation to protect their human rights.

Koreans

Most of the 700,000 Koreans now resident in Japan were born there and speak Japanese as their first language. Few possess Japanese citizenship and they are classed as aliens, making up 85% of the foreign resident population. Although they are tax-payers, as aliens they have restricted access to welfare benefits and they are not eligible for employment in government service. They also have difficulty finding jobs in state schools or prestigious corporations. With the exception of some individuals who have been successful in the arts, music or sport, they are confined to the lower reaches of the labour market.

Before 1900 there were few Koreans in Japan and traditionally Korean culture had been accorded considerable respect. Attitudes changed as rapid development in Meiji Japan contrasted sharply with stagnation in Korea and generated stereotypes of dynamic Japanese and lazy Koreans. In 1910 Korea was annexed by Japan and Koreans became free to move into Japan to find employment. By 1923 there were over 100,000 Koreans living and working in Japan, most as temporary or seasonal labourers. They were suspected by the authorities of being sympathetic to socialist ideas and considered to be generally unruly. These prejudices erupted into violence in the confusion which followed the Great Kantō Earthquake of 1 September 1923: vigilante groups murdered Koreans who were suspected among other things of poisoning wells, and altogether several thousand Koreans were killed. Nevertheless the flow of Koreans to Japan continued, such that by 1930 there were over 400,000 of them and by 1940 over 1,000,000. During the war Koreans were forcibly recruited to work in mines and factories, and as Japanese men were conscripted into the armed forces Korean women were compelled to provide them with 'comfort'. By 1945 there were over 2,000,000 Koreans in Japan proper and at least as many servicing the Japanese army in the field.

Both the US and Japanese authorities expected all Koreans to return home in 1945. Most did, but in spite of the difficulties involved in remaining in Japan around 500,000 preferred not to return to a peninsula torn by civil war. The division of Korea was reflected in the division of the Korean community in Japan into those supporting the communist north and those supporting the US-backed south. North Korea placed a high priority on maintaining good relations with its supporters and supplied cash and materials for a network of schools from kindergarten to university. But the lot of the Koreans in Japan was so miserable that between 1955 and 1965 over 100,000 of them, most originally from the south, voluntarily migrated to the north. It was only in the 1970s, when

Koreans resident in Japan protesting against the law requiring aliens to be fingerprinted. The balloon is supposed to represent an outstretched finger, and the slogan reads, 'No more fingerprinting!'

the South Korean economy grew rapidly while that of North Korea stagnated, that the supporters of the south began to gain confidence. Those who have South Korean citizenship now enjoy permanent residence in Japan for themselves, their children and their grandchildren, while those who support North Korea have only temporary residence permits and exist in a diplomatic limbo. But all Koreans have to re-register every five years and have their fingerprints taken. In the 1980s there was a successful campaign against the fingerprinting and in 1991 the Japanese government undertook to phase out the fingerprinting of permanent residents.

A 19th-century photograph of some Ainu fishermen. There are almost no pure-blooded Ainu left in Hokkaidō and very few fluent speakers of the language.

Ainu

Ainu have been resident in northern Japan since the beginning of recorded history. Their hunter-gatherer lifestyle was incompatible with the settled agricultural patterns of their neighbours and as a result of the ensuing conflicts the Ainu had been virtually driven out of Honshū by the end of the 9th century and were confined to Hokkaidō and adjacent islands, which together were known as Ezo. In 1604 the Matsumae clan was given control over Ezo and used force of arms to protect traders seeking to exploit Ainu resources: a rebellion in 1668 led by Shakushain prompted punitive expeditions in 1670–72, in which the Ainu arrows were no match for guns. In the 18th century Russian ships became increasingly active in the waters around Hokkaidō and, perceiving a strategic threat, the shōgunal government in Edo assumed direct control of Ezo and sought to assimilate the Ainu into Japanese culture. Neither policy was successful, but in the late 19th century the Meiji government asserted its control over Hokkaidō and in 1876 put the Ainu on the same legal basis as other Japanese subjects. Plots of land were made available to them to encourage them to adopt an agricultural lifestyle, but in 1899 they were forbidden to sell land without the permission of the governor. This law still stands in spite of the efforts of Ainu activists to have it repealed.

The Ainu population has never been large. It may have reached a peak of 80,000 in the 18th century, but Japanese traders brought with them measles and chicken pox, against which the Ainu had no resistance. By 1854 the population had dropped to just over 15,000 and it has changed little since. A survey conducted in 1986 found 24,381 Ainu in Hokkaidō, but because exogamy is common fewer than one-third can claim four Ainu grandparents, and very few are fluent in the Ainu language. The survey also found that most Ainu have a poor standard of living and a poor record of educational achievement. The Ainu are represented by the Utari Association which claims 14,000 members. It has demanded legal measures to prevent discrimination and funds to promote Ainu culture and assist the Ainu economy, but so far these demands have not been met. IJN

Education

Japan is a country with very few natural resources, but one: its people. As a result, its education system has been considered by many to be the key to economic growth and political stability. Investment in education has significance both at the national level – where the state has sought over the past hundred years to create a system which could produce an effective workforce to lead the country's drive for modernization – and at the personal level where, as individuals in Japan are nowadays ranked largely according to their educational background (*gakureki*) rather than their family standing, education is the key to social status and financial security.

History

As with the development of many other social institutions, the history of Japanese education is one of adaptation of ideas from varied external sources. A system of formal education can be dated from the introduction of writing from China in the early 5th century AD. Along with this written culture came the influence of Confucianism which, while much modified over time and between different countries, remains the distinctive basis of education systems of all Far Eastern societies. Confucianism introduced to Japan the idea of awarding social status not on the basis of birth but of merit via examination.

The idea of a meritocracy, however, was not accepted by the ruling élite for many centuries and we have to wait until the Tokugawa period (1600–1868) for the real beginnings of a system of popular education. Confucian classics then formed the main texts, and schools sought to instil ideas of morality, respect for seniors and hard work. Indeed, much of the curriculum consisted of no more than being examined on texts learned by heart: thus providing, simultaneously, education in moral behaviour and a test of effort and ability.

Without this development of education during the Tokugawa period the subsequent rapid economic and social developments of the Meiji era would not have been possible. Although not recognized as such at the time, Japan in 1868 had a better educated populace than many Western countries: 40% of males and 15% of females were receiving some form of education outside the home. Perhaps more importantly, while regional, class and gender differences did exist, there was general agreement that education, even for the lower classes, was highly desirable.

The main concern of the Meiji oligarchs was to modernize the country as quickly as possible in order to avoid colonization. Education was seen to be, in many ways, the key to this process and a new system was put in place with impressive speed by adopting the most attractive and suitable ideas from a wide range of sources in Europe and the US and building these onto the existing system. Students were sent overseas to observe and learn, and foreign experts were invited to Japan to teach those subjects in which the Japanese as yet lacked expertise. In 1873, these two programmes between them counted for 32% of the total government education budget. From this time on, the system became increasingly centralized, standardized and, for the first six years of elementary education, compulsory. By the turn of the century, over 95% of children were receiving education at the elementary level. Entrance to the middle schools that followed, however, was much more restricted and provided a sorting device for the élite few who were able to continue to the higher levels. Competition – particularly for places in the top schools – was fuelled by the realization that success could lead to rapid social advancement. The origins of what is known today as the 'examination hell' began to appear.

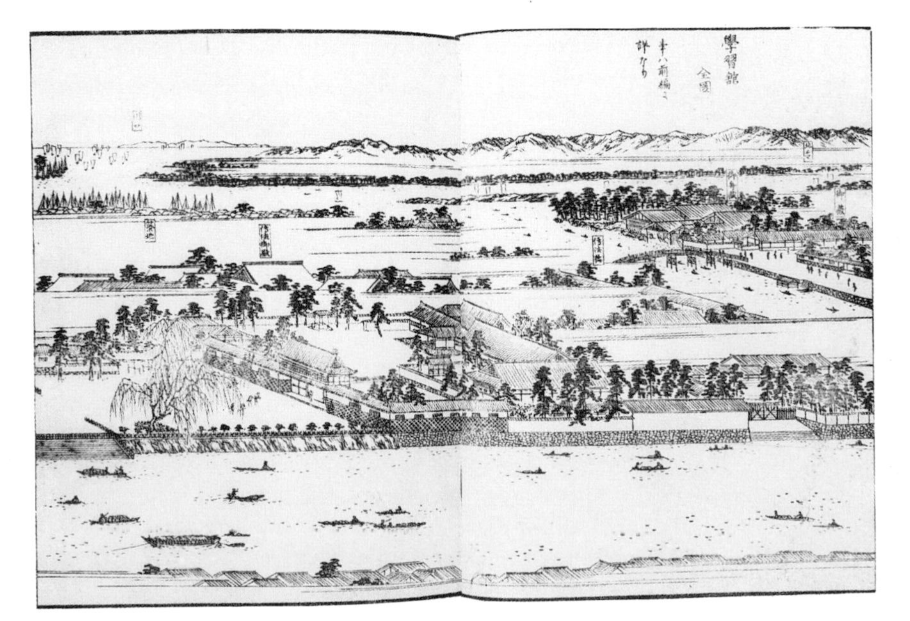

A 19th-century print of the domain school at Wakayama. Most of the feudal domains had established their own schools by this time; only samurai could enter them and the emphasis was on Chinese studies.

It is significant that the Meiji rulers decided to concentrate on developing education for the general population and not just the élite. Japanese workers were seen to play a major rôle in the modernization process and education provided the necessary skills. At the same time, it also offered a convenient vehicle for the dissemination of ideas and was increasingly used to create a sense of Japan as one nation with the emperor as its divine father.

The dangers which were thought to accrue from the pre-war system can be seen in the speed with which it was dismantled by the Allied Occupation forces at the end of the war. Teachers were purged, textbooks banned, and moral education removed altogether. The Occupation authorities introduced a comprehensive, non-élitist, co-educational system that included nine years of compulsory education for all. Educational opportunities for women were greatly expanded and there was a conscious attempt to inculcate the values of individualism. In many ways, however, the reformers were more successful in changing the structure of the system than its content. Six years at elementary school, three years each of junior high and senior high school, followed by four years at university is a replica of the US system.

Education for the state

One of the distinctive features of contemporary Japanese education is the close link that exists between school and the workplace. There is still common acceptance of the idea that one of education's main functions is to produce a workforce to drive the nation's economy. Post-war employers in Japan have demanded hardworking, conformist, literate workers who are able to adjust quickly to new ideas and technologies without questioning the basis of the employer–employee relationship, and this is exactly what the education system has been designed to produce.

As in the past, much education today consists of memorizing facts and formulae, and the basic tenet remains that success will be achieved through hard work rather than natural genius. For employers, the senior high schools sort the potential labour force into different streams so that the 'quality' of the workers can be judged in advance. All secondary and tertiary institutions rank in a clear hierarchy.

Top left *At school in the 1870s. The dress is Japanese but the pupils are now sitting on chairs, rather than on the floor as they would have been in the Tokugawa period.*

Bottom left *The first women to enroll at Tsuda College in 1900. The college was founded by Tsuda Umeko (1865–1929), who had been sent to study in the US in 1871 at the age of 6. She later became a pioneer of women's education in Japan.*

In a system where people believe that their chances will be determined by how hard they work, it is imperative that they also believe they all have an equal chance from the beginning. The notion of equality is, therefore, an important characteristic of the system. Most Japanese believe that they live in a relatively classless, homogeneous society where birth and inheritance are much less important than effort. Every year over 90% of the population declares itself 'middle-class' and while minority groups are a significant element, official policy aims to create a uni- rather than multi-cultural society.

The system is geared to the employers in one further respect: it aims to produce generalists rather than specialists. Vocational schools, for example, have considerably lower status than academic ones. Companies prefer to recruit individuals with a general education who can then be trained in company ways: this serves to tie workers to the individual company, since skills are less easily transferable, and it is also financially advantageous for the larger companies whose corporate taxation does not have to help support a large postgraduate education programme. At present, a mere 4% of undergraduates continue into postgraduate education.

Below *Uniformed Tōkyō schoolboys on the daily commute to school. Large numbers of young children cross and recross the city every day in complete safety.*

EDUCATION FOR THE INDIVIDUAL

Although there is a close correlation between the economic aims of the state and the provisions of the education system, the fact that Japan is a democracy means that Japanese are also able to ensure that they get as much as possible out of education for themselves as individuals. To obtain the best jobs, they need to progress as far as they can and, as a result, less than 4% leave school at the age of fifteen. Almost all the 96% who go on to senior high school in Japan actually finish the three-year course, although it is becoming clear from a number of surveys that many of them find the curriculum, which is geared towards passing the examinations into university, too difficult. Again, a large proportion of students stay on in education after senior high school; over 37% go to some form of tertiary institution and more would go if the places were available. Despite the fact that Japan has some 500 four-year universities and 580 two-year colleges (more than double the number that existed in 1960), in recent years up to 25% of those who have tried to get into these institutions have been unsuccessful.

As a result, there has developed in Japan a significant culture of re-take students who are known as *rōnin* – a term which refers back to the masterless samurai of the Tokugawa period – and *yobikō*, special preparatory schools designed to help students do better next time round. In many cases, however, it is not simply a question of passing into *any* institution but into the *best possible* institution. The 1,000 or so establishments of higher education form a hierarchy at the top of which stand the old imperial universities of Tōkyō and Kyōto. The power of these institutions is perpetuated largely through old-boy networks (*gakubatsu*) through which graduates can be assured employment in top jobs. Since employers in Japan still tend to be much more interested in which university recruits have attended than how they did there or even what they studied, to enter a high-ranking university is to ensure high personal status and financial security. One hears of students who gain entry to Tōkyō University at the fourth or fifth attempt. Once at university, however, students, particularly in their first two years and in non-scientific subjects, tend not to work very hard.

High school students, however, work extremely long hours. As a popular saying has it, sleep as much

as five hours a night and you can forget about going to Tōkyō University. On average, children do at least four times as much homework per day as their US counterparts, and the school year itself is one-third longer. Much of this time is spent preparing for tests which are based on memorizing 'facts' and all examinations are reduced to a multiple-choice formula where only one answer is considered correct. Essays are rarely written since there is still a feeling that their marking is too subjective and hence potentially unfair.

Could you get into Meiji University?

The following question was taken from a 1991 'World history' entrance examination for Meiji University, a highly-ranked private university in Tōkyō which was recently involved in a scandal when it was discovered that students from other universities had been paid to sit entrance examinations in place of the real candidates by wealthy parents worried that their children would not be able to pass. Such are the lengths to which people will go to secure places at good universities. About six minutes would be allowed for this question.

Read the following passage and in place of the numerals insert the letters representing what you think are the right answers.

Kuwait means 'small castle'. After the Second World War it ceased to be a protectorate of [1] and in the year [2] became independent. It has been called a tax-free paradise because of its immense underground deposits of oil. At an earlier time, however, Kuwait found itself caught up in the power struggles between Germany, Turkey and [1] and it was only through intense diplomacy that it was finally able to preserve its existence. Complacent because of its wealth, it forgot the diplomatic skills used by the wise sheikh Mubarak in the 19th century. Kuwait first began to reap the benefits of its oil in the year [3]. Because of the chaos caused by the oil nationalization policy of [4], the demand for oil from Iraq and Kuwait increased dramatically. So it was while it was achieving economic growth as a protectorate of [1] that Kuwait came to achieve independence. Yet the coming crisis for Kuwait was predictable even before this when [5], who overthrew the monarchy in the Iraqi Revolution, withdrew Iraq from [6] and proclaimed Kuwait an Iraqi possession.

a The United Nations
b The Baghdad Pact
c France
d Gaddafi
e The Arab Mutual Security Treaty
f 1955
g The Oil Redline Agreement
h 1961
i OPEC
j 1958
k Great Britain
l Russia
m Kassem
n Hussein
o Saudi Arabia
p 1951
q Libya
r 1959
s Iran
t Abu Dhabi
u Assad
v The Arab League

Answers: 1=k, 2=h, 3=p, 4=s, 5=m, 6=b

RJG

For individuals to succeed in this system, huge investments are needed not only in terms of time, but also, increasingly, money. From the age of 12 or so onwards, almost all Japanese children, but especially boys, will also start to attend 'cram school' (*juku*). These schools differ greatly in quality, and hence the financial circumstances of individual families begin to affect the chances of the student. Similarly, the rôle of private education is connected to family finances; very few children go to private institutions for compulsory education, but at senior high school level the figure is close to 30% and at university level 75%. Generally speaking, private sector education is of lower status than the public sector and yet Japanese families continue to pay in order to keep children on in the system. One reason cited for the decreasing size of the Japanese family is the enormous financial sacrifice that parents need to make in order to pay for their children's education: over 70% of the average annual expenditure of university students comes from parental contributions. Education, therefore, is not as equal as may seem at first and some surveys suggest that it is becoming increasingly unequal as the average family income of students entering Tōkyō University, for example, moves further away from the national average.

AVERAGE ANNUAL INCOME AND EXPENDITURE OF A FOUR-YEAR UNIVERSITY STUDENT (1988)

Expenditure (Unit: ¥1000)		Income (Unit: ¥1000)	
Total	1,523.2	Total	1,599.6
Educational expenses	804.5	Parental contribution	1,175.5
Living expenses	718.7	Scholarship	94.7
		Part-time job	314.2
		Full-time job	15.2

Above *Thousands of hopefuls taking university entrance examinations.*

Costs and benefits of the system

Curiously, during recent years there have been rather more supporters of Japanese education outside the country than within. Many foreign observers are convinced that the education system is the key to Japan's economic success and that other countries would do well to learn from the Japanese experience. In particular, such authors cite the high scores that Japanese children achieve in international comparative tests of mathematical and scientific skills which suggest that in these areas, at least, Japanese children are some three or more years ahead of their Western counterparts. They praise the high level of basic education and the high number of students continuing in the system, allowing a country with one of the world's most difficult writing systems to claim one of the world's highest literacy rates. They point out that education is geared not just to the interests of the individual and individual development but also to the development of the country as a whole. Among other features which have fired the imagination of Western observers – the system is not nearly so different from those of other Asian societies which share a similar cultural background – is the reluctance to label children early on in their careers as bright or dull, and the belief that they can learn anything (including music and art) if only they are taught properly and try hard enough. Most foreign observers agree that the higher up one examines the Japanese education system the less impressive it seems – there is little, for example, to learn from Japanese universities – and yet a number of important reports have made specific recommendations for lessons that can be learnt from the Japanese case.

Perhaps more important, however, are the views of the Japanese themselves, since many are far from happy with the current system. Parents and teachers complain that the pressures are intolerable for young children, and there is still much discussion about 'examination hell', violence, bullying and children with no time to play with friends or who refuse to go to school altogether. While it is important to stress that schoolchild suicide is no longer particularly high in Japan and that such problems as do occur are much less severe than in most industrialized nations, concern about such problems in Japan is widely and deeply felt. Remedies have been proposed from a number of directions. Right-wingers have demanded the removal of US-imposed elements of the education system and a return to Japanese 'traditional' values as a means of restoring correct attitudes in what they perceive to be a dissipated youth. The most visible sign of the success of this movement is the recent order from the Ministry of Education that schools should sing the national anthem and raise the national flag at school ceremonies. On the other

Right *Elementary school children in class.*

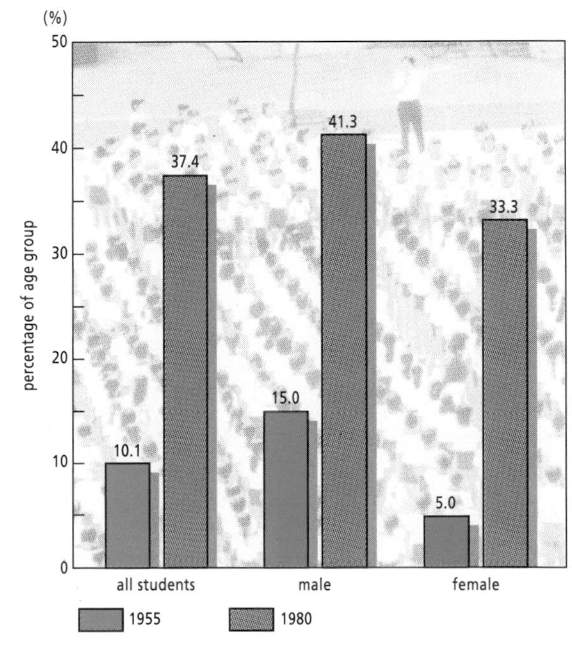

Far right *Percentages of senior high school students proceeding to university or junior college, 1955 and 1980.*

hand, those on the left wing complain that the system is already too nationalistic and believe that the system for authorizing textbooks, for example, is a process of censorship rather than quality control.

Probably the most important movement for change in the system, however, has come from the employers' organizations in Japan, who feel that while conformist workers produced by the current system have been invaluable, there is now a need for a more creative element in the workforce. Such employers are insisting on the importance of liberalizing the education system and the national curriculum and making the classes less teacher- and more pupil-centred.

Debates about directions for change continue. Areas of discussion include how to 'internationalize' the system – there are few foreign teachers or students, for example, in either schools or universities in Japan – as Japan is pulled further into the international community; how to prepare the youth of today for the changes expected in the 21st century, and how to make best use of those who missed out on higher education the first time around by instituting programmes of life-long education; how to help the disabled and minority groups and those who fail for no fault of their own in an increasingly competitive system. Put simply, these debates are encapsulated by the idea that attention should now be paid to the *quality* rather than *quantity* of education provided. The seriousness of these debates is a good example of the farsightedness and lack of complacency of planners and public alike in Japanese society. RJG

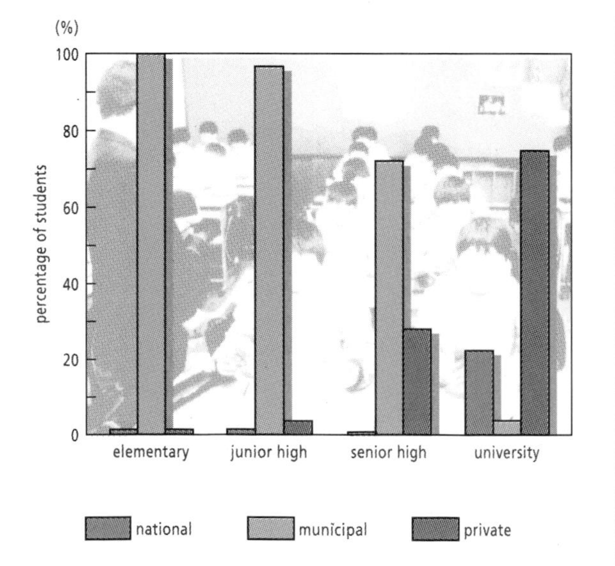

Percentages of private and state students at different school levels (1981).

Working life

The stereotypical Japanese 'company man' stays with the same company all his working life, works long hours every day, goes drinking in the evening with co-workers, stumbles from the late-night train and arrives at his 'rabbit hutch' (or more recently 'cockpit' – still small but crammed full of electronic gadgetry) in time to crawl into bed and catch not quite enough sleep for another day of more of the same. The dinner his stereotypical wife has prepared has gone cold, but she nobly helps him into bed and sees him off in the morning. She supports his 'workaholism' by taking care of the household-related tasks and looking after their children, who only get to see their 'papa' in the weekend when he is not sleeping or playing semi-obligatory golf.

These images are not without some basis, but as stereotypes they mask a wide diversity. The lifestyle of a rural farming family is quite different from that of an urban nuclear family, even though most of the income may come from non-agricultural pursuits. Outside agriculture, almost one person in five is self-employed or works for a family concern, and dislike of the 'company man' lifestyle has long provided an impetus for starting family businesses. The proportion of those employed in companies has almost doubled in the past 30 years, but even here there is considerable diversity, depending on the type of job (building versus banking, for instance), size of company (jobbing shop versus giant factory), and location.

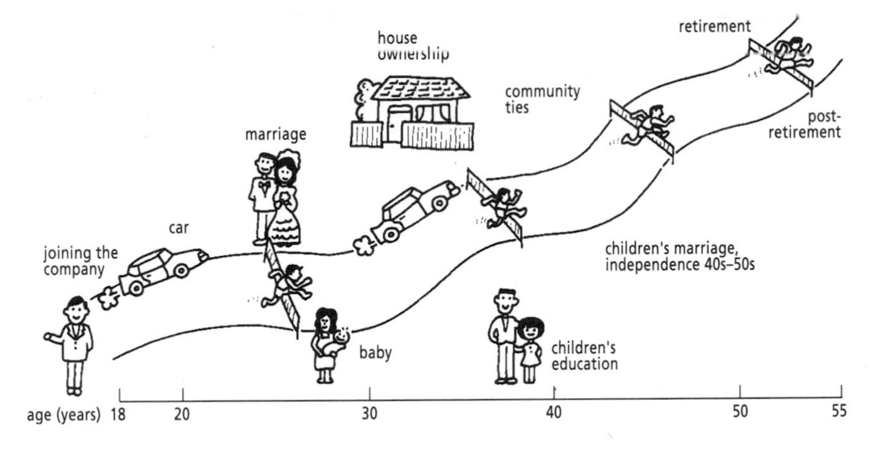

Above *Can you jump life's hurdles? This cartoon comes from a welfare handbook issued by a large enterprise union.*

Right *A cherry blossom party provides an excuse for office workers to relax and drink together outdoors.*

Below *A capsule hotel, for businessmen who have stayed in town too late, either working or socializing, to get home by the last train.*

Diversity acknowledged, work does occupy a central place in the lives of many Japanese, and to large company employees, the corporate community is often more important than the local community. Loyalty to that community in the form of time spent in it, however, does not necessarily equate with satisfaction. International comparisons of worker attitudes do not show the Japanese worker as being particularly happy. Nor is loyalty merely a cultural product. It is linked to the nature of the employment relationship, its institutional underpinnings and the choices and rewards confronting the worker.

Choosing a company

A school or college senior will weigh up a number of factors when seeking a job, such as location, type of job and company. Of these, the last has been particularly important, especially for those whose school and school records place them in the running for a job in a large, prestigious firm. In return for favourable wages, prospects, prestige and security, a worker is expected not only to be dedicated, but also flexible, and may be moved to different jobs within the company. More than choosing a job, then, one chooses a company, and students from 'top' schools tend to join 'top' companies (or government ministries). When the employment relationship is a long-term one, both sides take great care over their choices.

In joining such companies, new recruits are not signing up for a nine-to-five job in return for a wage. They are joining a 'corporate community', which an initial intense orientation period will stress. This orientation, or initiation, is followed by a period of training in different workplaces to expose them to different aspects of company operations (this is normally shortened for women), and is interspersed with visits to customer establishments to show the company in its wider community context, and get-togethers with other new recruits to strengthen social bonding. Clubs and sports are organized by the company or the enterprise union. The company is thus important for social as well as working life.

For those who find a job in a small company, the prospects are different. There is no elaborate orientation into a 'corporate community', fewer organized activities and less scope for internal careers. They may be more concerned about the location or nature of the job, which might be a stepping stone to something else, than about which company they join. The incentives for establishing companies have ensured a steady stream of entrepreneurial talent, but this course has become more difficult now, particularly in manufacturing, where entry-barriers, such as the levels of financial and technological investment needed, have been rising. An overwhelming proportion of companies are small and family-run, and often children prepare to succeed their parents by joining another firm to gain experience. But whatever their destination, almost two-thirds of junior high school leavers and a third of high school leavers give up their first job within three years, and that first job for many of them is with a smaller firm.

EMPLOYMENT SECURITY

Young workers who leave their jobs may not lose much immediately in terms of wages. Wage differentials between companies are not great for new recruits, but widen for older workers. For an older worker there is an extra disincentive to job-changing built into the employment relationship, namely the *nenkō* (seniority, or seniority plus merit) system: wages rise with age and years of service, thus the penalty for leaving rises with age, unless the worker has a much sought-after skill to offer.

Furthermore, wage differentials within companies depend both upon seniority and favourable evaluation, so there is an incentive not just to stay with the same company, but to work within it to maximize wage and promotion prospects. This is true for both blue-collar and white-collar regular workers in larger firms. It involves not just dedication to the job, but being a good 'team player' and often working long hours and socializing with co-workers. In smaller firms the age–wage curve is flatter, but employees may put in more overtime to increase their earnings.

As workers get older, too, family pressures enhance the importance of security. There may be new mouths to feed, rising education expenses, and a mortgage to pay back, which may have been arranged with company assistance. Companies take an interest in the domestic stability of their employees, believing that it encourages dedicated work. Thus a number of factors converge to promote long-term if not lifetime employment, and to a greater or lesser degree individual interests overlap with work-group responsibilities and corporate objectives.

Is 'lifetime employment' for life?

Lifetime employment means joining a company after school or university and working there until a specified retirement age of around 58–60. In some cases the 'lifetime employment sphere' has been extended from a single company to a group of companies. The proportion of such 'standard workers' in manufacturing in 1988 is shown in the table.

The proportion of 'standard workers' is higher in larger companies and has risen over the past 30 years. Nevertheless, as many as two thirds of junior high school leavers move on from their first company within three years, as do more than a third of high school leavers, and there are recent signs of increased job-changing among university graduates too. On the other hand, an increasing number of companies are 'rehiring' employees who reach the retirement age. DHW

PROPORTION OF 'STANDARD WORKERS'
(in manufacturing companies of 10+ employees, 1988)

age	male	female
25–29	56.1	60.2
30–34	48.4	36.5
35–39	54.2	21.1
40–44	44.0	9.8
45–49	40.9	5.3
50–54	25.9	3.2

Note: a 'standard worker' is an employee who meets the following criteria:

age	25–29	30–34	35–39	40–44	45–49	50–54
years in same company	5+	10+	15+	20+	25+	30+

WOMEN AT HOME AND AT WORK

Dedicated male company employees, however, sometimes have difficulty in finding a wife, particularly in companies with high proportions of male workers. They may have little time to meet women outside the company. This may undermine worker morale and make recruitment difficult for such companies. Various means are adopted to facilitate interaction with members of the opposite sex, for example by increasing the intake of female employees, which in turn may help to solve worker shortage problems. However, some women are reluctant to take up the place assigned to them by husband and system: even if they do not intend to pursue a career, they may want to enjoy the freedom to earn and spend their own wages while they can. Conventional attitudes may impede the pursuit of careers, but they also make it easier for women rather than men to take time off for leisure activities.

As family employment diminished during the high-growth period, the proportion of working women declined steadily, from 54.5% of the female population in 1960 to 45.7% in 1975, but it rose again to 50.2% in 1990. Demographic, social and economic factors are behind the recent rise, characterized by an increased proportion (more than two-thirds) who can be termed 'employed'. Women are working longer before having children, and more are re-entering employment after initial child-rearing, normally on a part-time basis, often in smaller firms, in both the manufacturing and the tertiary sectors.

In the company cafeteria all ranks eat together: the segregation that is still the norm in many Western companies is rare in Japan.

Obstacles remain for those wishing to work through childbirth and initial child-rearing, and only a small portion can re-enter their former or similar company on a regular basis.

Some (male) politicians would prefer to see women stay at home to look after elderly parents and raise more children, so to re-nurture 'traditional' values. Also, Japan's economic vitality is seen to be at risk due to the declining birth rates, which are seen to correlate with rising education levels for women. The counter-argument is that the politicians should concentrate on providing an infrastructure that will encourage compatability between women's aspirations and domestic rôles, which the present 'production-oriented' society does not. Given that educational opportunities are unlikely to be curtailed, quiet pressure for modification of gender rôles and the employment system that reinforces them is unlikely to go away.

A GREYING WORKFORCE

The average age of employees in large firms rose from 30 to almost 40 between 1970 and 1990. The government, moreover, has been prodding companies to raise their mandatory retirement ages to 60 and beyond in order to raise the pension age to 65. Greying workforces increase pressures on *nenkō* wage systems and exacerbate promotion bottlenecks. Company policies to cope with these problems may increase workers' anxiety, even among the élite: they might stay on the mainline promotion track, or be placed on a side track, or be sent to a subsidiary or affiliate before retirement on permanent 'loan'. In the last instance, the company does not technically renege on its implicit promise of security, and some workers may benefit from an extended retirement age, but it is still an upheaval.

The prospect of retirement can be traumatic, too, not just for its financial implications, but because for the 'company man' it represents a loss of community and basis of identity. Tragicomic stories abound in the media of retirees who are virtual strangers in their own homes and are regarded by their families as 'bulky rubbish'. In fact, older workers show a marked reluctance to retire, giving Japan the highest rate of working elderly in the industrialized world. Whether for financial reasons, including future welfare provision and a desire not to burden children, or a sense of purpose, roughly 73% of men and 40% of women aged 60–64, and 37% of men and 16% of women aged 65 and over were working in 1990. Many were self-employed, but in recent years as part of 'lifelong welfare' plans, large companies have started re-employing retiring workers on a part-time basis, particularly now that there is a shortage of skilled labour, or have instituted counselling and job-search mediation services for them.

Composition of the labour force. Figures for 1980 onwards include Okinawa.

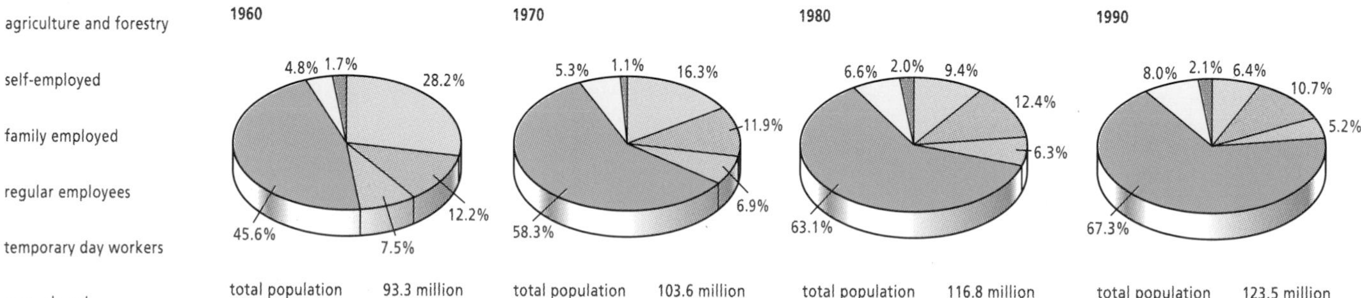

Production orientation to living orientation?

Work and the corporate community loom large in the lives of many Japanese, but there is a growing feeling that they have not shared sufficiently in the fruits of their dedication. Companies now rank among the world leaders, but improvements in living conditions lag behind. The cost of housing, for instance, rose from 4.8 times the average salary in 1983 to 8.7 times in 1988 in the greater Tōkyō area. For many the dream of owning a house has become just that, unless they wish to commute formidable distances for the privilege. Illness and even death from work-related stress, too, have been widely publicized. A national debate has been generated as to how Japan can become a giant in standard-of-living terms as well as production.

Part of this debate concerns working hours. In the early 1980s business leaders opposed attempts to reduce working hours, citing the spectre of 'advanced-nations malaise'. Subsequently they gave cautious assent to the drive to reduce the average number of annual working hours from 2,150 to 1,800 by the end of fiscal 1992.

Campaigns were launched to promote five-day working weeks, holidays and 'recharging leave', and the new labour confederation, Rengō, also pressed for more affordable housing, a reduction in domestic/foreign price differentials, improvements in maternity and child-raising leave, and a review of welfare policies for the elderly. Working hours finally dipped under 1975 levels to 2,045 hours in 1990, but the magic 1,800 hours is still a long way off. In a telling survey in the greater Tōkyō area, 85% of those interviewed thought that Japanese people work too hard ... but only 52.5% thought that applied to themselves.

DHW

CHANGING ATTITUDES TO WORK

What kind of work do you think is ideal?	1973 %	1978 %	1983 %
Short working hours	5.2	4.2	3.9
No worry about unemployment	11.0	17.6	16.3
No worry about health	28.2	21.7	21.1
Good pay	6.2	6.8	7.5
Good relations with co-workers	14.5	15.2	16.8
Responsibility	2.0	2.5	3.3
Independent work free of constraints	9.7	8.5	7.8
Use of specialist knowledge and skills	14.7	15.8	17.5
Work valued by others	0.1	0.1	0.2
Contributing to others' well-being	6.2	5.1	4.2
Other	0.1	0.1	0.1
Don't know	2.1	2.3	1.3

Source: *NHK yoron chōsa shiryō shiryōshū* (1986)

Far from the city lights

The Hamada family live far from the hustle and bustle of Tōkyō in more senses than one. Their home is in a village of 200 people on the island of Tanegashima, which lies to the south of Kyūshū. Their lives are ruled not by daily office routines or trains, but by the seasonal requirements of the crops they farm. These include sugar cane, several varieties of potato, rice, beans, corn, as well as flowers and a dozen head of cattle and calves. In all, their land totals about 4.5 hectares.

The day for their three-generation family starts at about 6:00 a.m. Mr Hamada senior, aged 63, tends to the cows before breakfast, and, with his wife, spends most of the day in the fields. In winter and spring the work involves cutting and carrying sugar cane, as well as processing it. They work seven days a week, but take time off for other activities, such as fishing, between the seasons, and feel that they are in control of their own time. The cattle auction, held every other month, is an important date on the social calendar.

Mr Hamada junior, aged 35, does shift work for a trading company exporting sugar cane between December and April, alternating every other week between the night and the day shift. He also has a part-time job with a horticultural company putting up hot houses. Otherwise he, too, works on the farm, including Sundays. Mrs Hamada grows flowers, particularly chrysanthemums, which in season she takes to the port in time to catch the evening boat north to Kagoshima. She also does most of the housework, including meal preparations. Both feel that they have too little time to relax and enjoy themselves, but would not trade their present lifestyle for one in the city.

Their two children cycle to school early in the morning, a 45 minute ride for the eldest. After getting back home, the eight year old daughter often goes out into the fields with her grandparents. She is fond of animals, and likes to help her grandfather feed the cattle. Her elder sister has lost interest in this. She prefers to spend her free time in front of the television, although she does help out in the holidays. Just how strongly the city lights will beckon this generation remains to be seen.

DHW

Health and welfare

Until 1945 state intervention in the fields of health and welfare was at a very basic level. It was restricted to specific groups, particularly those, such as war widows, whose situation was a direct result of state policies. Justification for this quite conscious policy was sought in the supportive rôle both the family and local community were expected to play in normal circumstances

The result was that much of the responsibility for the relief of the poor and the seriously ill was left in the hands of charitable institutions. At the same time employers, both public and private, increasingly provided for the needs of their own workers, either directly or by encouraging them in the ways of self-help by means of Mutual Aid Associations.

By the early 1940s systems of insurance covering both illness and financial deprivation were in existence, at least in embryo. In both cases what had developed was a patchwork of systems: schemes for employees in private industry, for the employees of central and local government, and so on, with the government providing an inadequate scheme as a safety net for some of those not covered elsewhere. Some of these schemes date back to the end of the 19th century, but their financial basis was effectively destroyed by the galloping inflation of the immediate post-war years. In effect, therefore, the development of comprehensive health and welfare provision had to await the post-war economic recovery.

Medicine

From the 6th century until the 17th, medical practice in Japan was almost exclusively based on Chinese medicine, or *kanpō*. In the 1670s, Western medicine began to make an impact through the doctors attached to the Dutch trading post at Deshima, but it was not until the late 18th century, when the first dissections of the human body were carried out, that the empirical foundations of Western medicine were fully appreciated. Thereafter many doctors based their practice on a combination of anatomy and pathology derived from Western textbooks and of herbal remedies derived from the *kanpō* traditions. In 1805 one of them, Hanaoka Seishū, was the first in the world to perform an operation using a general anaesthetic, and in doing so he successfully removed a cancerous growth from his wife's breast. The anaesthetic was a herbal one and its use antedates by several decades the first use of general anaesthetics in the West.

In the Meiji period the government looked to Germany for the development of Western medicine in Japan: German physicians came to Japan to teach and Japanese medical students were despatched to German universities, among them the famous army doctor and writer, Mori Ōgai, and Kitazato Shibasaburō, who discovered the bacillus that carries the plague. Ever since the end of the Pacific War, the influence of US medicine has gradually replaced that of Germany, but the language of Japanese medicine is still larded with loan-words from German.

Although the modern medical technologies in use in Japan would be familiar in any developed country, the patterns of disease they have to deal with are not the same: while heart disease is relatively infrequent, probably due to the low-fat diet, stomach and liver cancers are far more common than in Europe or North America. Further, alongside the familiar medical procedures there can be found a thriving set of alternatives, all derived from Chinese medical practices. In addition to herbal medicine, there are clinics for acupuncture, for moxibustion, which involves burning mixtures of herbs on the skin, and for *shiatsu* pressure therapy. These alternative therapies have enjoyed something of a boom in recent years, and many patients and even some doctors resort both to them and to 'modern' medicine. These moves towards pluralism in Japanese medical practice suggest that the days of confrontation between modern Western medicine and traditional east Asian medicine, which began in the Meiji period, may now be at an end. Certainly in the 1970s the prejudice of the health insurance systems, which paid out for the former but not for the latter, evaporated. PK

Below right *Grinding herbs and fungi to make medicines in the traditional Chinese way: Chinese pharmacology still has a strong following.*

TOWARDS A WELFARE STATE

The first system to develop was public assistance – referred to in Japan as 'livelihood protection' – which was set up by two laws enacted in 1946 and 1950. Until the end of the 1950s 'livelihood protection' was virtually the only source of financial assistance available to all citizens. Between 1947 and 1950 financial assistance of this sort accounted for some 50% of the government's social security budget, and was still accounting for over 40% in 1952. This proportion fell as economic conditions improved, so that by 1960 it stood at only about 25%. It continued to decline steadily thereafter, and in 1990 stood at less than 10%, the total number of individuals receiving public assistance standing at a level of just under 1% of the population.

In 1959–60 it became compulsory for all Japanese to be covered by insurance providing health and pension cover. For health insurance, employees in private industry were to be insured through their place of work, and all others were to join a greatly extended National Health Insurance scheme, administered through local government bodies according to the place of residence of the insured. Coverage for pensions operated in a similar way.

Little further change took place until the mid 1970s, when over a decade of rapid economic growth made it possible to upgrade the system to something approaching the levels of western Europe. There was a massive increase in the level of pension benefits in the two main insurance schemes, and it was also agreed that benefit levels should automatically rise so as to keep pace with inflation. In the field of medical care the level of cover provided by the main insurance schemes was substantially increased and a national system of free medical care for the aged was introduced.

Doctor taking a patient's pulse, c. 1868. Western medical knowledge began to reach Japan in the 17th century, but it was not until the late 19th century that it displaced traditional medical practices.

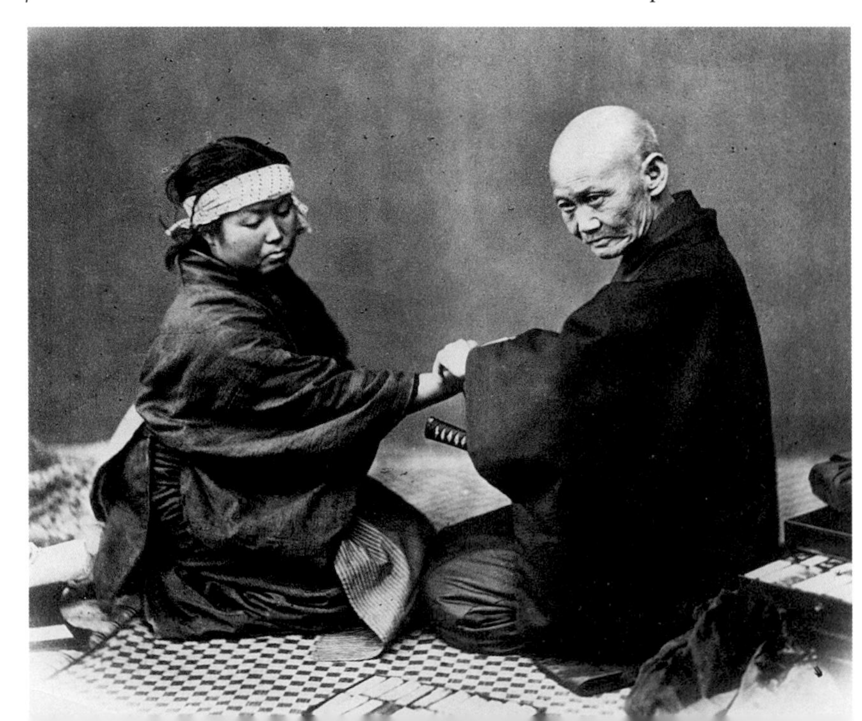

RETRENCHMENT

The next decade saw a progressive consolidation and adaptation of the system, advertised by the government as 'rationalization' and 'adjustment to changing realities' but attacked by its critics as a wholesale renunciation by the state of its responsibility for the health and welfare of the nation. On the one hand, therefore, there was a policy of amalgamating the various insurance schemes into something much nearer to a national system, removing some of the inequalities inherent in the patchwork of schemes operating hitherto, while on the other hand this rationalization involved a 'levelling downwards', with the general standards of provision being considerably lower than those provided by the most generous of the earlier schemes. Slower economic growth, pressure from business for less government intervention, and demographic changes, in particular the rapidly rising proportion of the population in the over-65 age-group, also forced a reassessment of the very generous levels of provision instituted in the 1970s.

In the general field of medical care, for example, the national scheme of free care for the aged was

SOCIAL SECURITY IN INTERNATIONAL COMPARISON

	Social security benefits as percentage of national income	Percentage population 65+
Japan	15.1	11.9
US	16.2	12.1
UK	25.5	15.3
W. Germany	29.1	15.2
France	36.3	13.1
Sweden	40.7	17.4

Note: percentages given are for 1990 in the case of Japan, and for 1986 in the case o

Source: *Kōsei hakusho* 1990 and 1991

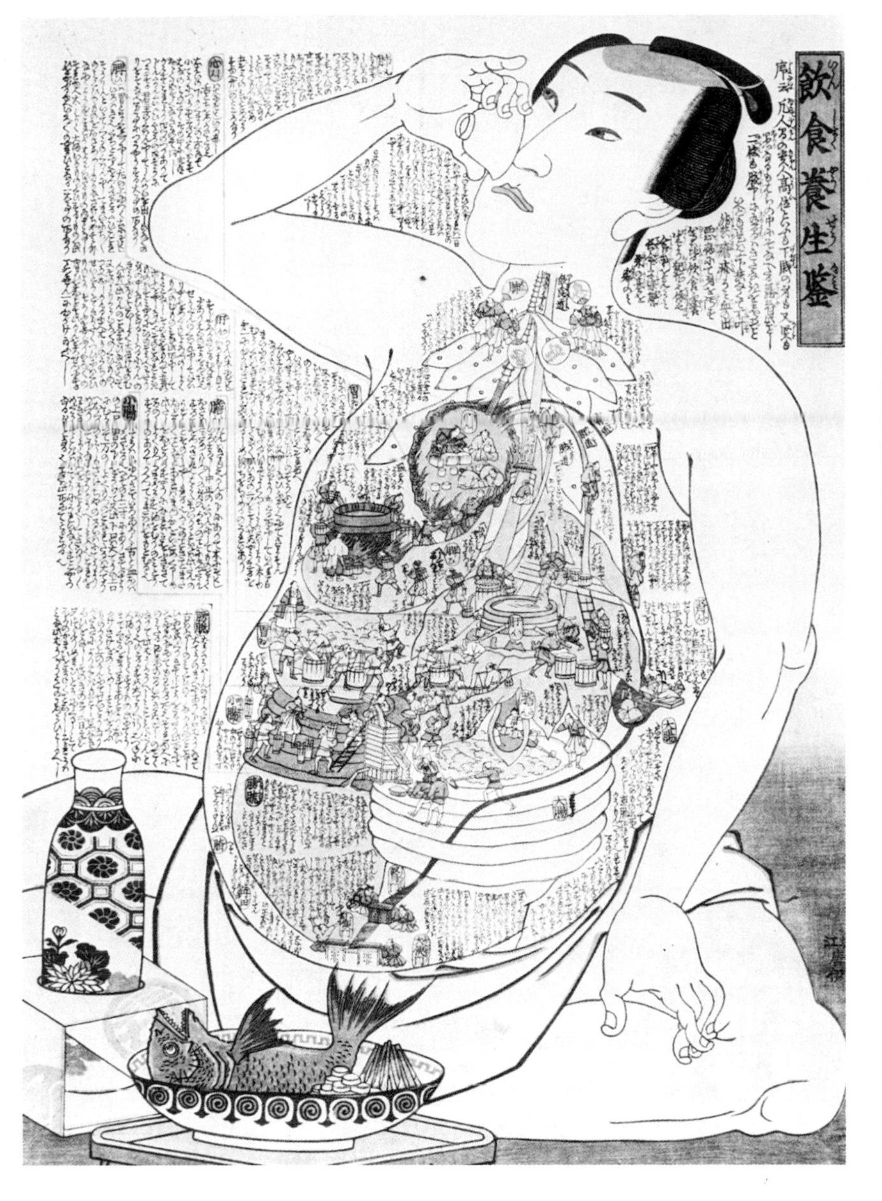

A 19th-century print showing the effects of drink and food on the body, and giving advice on a healthy diet.

Taxes and social security contributions as percentage of national income
40.1
35.5
53.9
52.2
61.5
73.3

s.

abolished in 1983, and local authorities were put under pressure to abandon their own similar schemes. The individual's contributions to treatment costs were raised, and a variety of other changes imposed. The pensions system was similarly subject to a series of rationalizing and cost-cutting changes. Legislation in 1985 established a single basic pension, with additional income-related benefits to be provided for employees by schemes administered through their place of work. Contribution levels were raised, and the level of government support for the system drastically reduced. The government also proposed to raise the age of entitlement to a pension from 60 to 65. Overall, it appeared that the declared objective of a decade earlier, of creating a welfare state on a west European or Scandinavian model, had been abandoned. The goal was now a 'Japanese-style welfare state', with a renewed emphasis on the rôle of the family and local community, and on the virtues of thrift and self-reliance.

By the end of the 1980s, however, it was clear that the nation was unwilling to accept such a dramatic reversal of course. The increasing proportion of old people in the population not only placed growing burdens on the health and welfare system, it also represented a constituency whose interests the government could not afford to ignore. By mid 1991 the government had still not succeeded in raising the age of eligibility for a pension and had felt obliged to reverse, at least partially, some of the cost-cutting measures of the mid 1980s. This has been reflected in the budget of the Ministry of Health and Welfare. This budget, which in 1975 increased by 36% over the previous year, grew at less than 3% per year for most of the 1980s. In 1989 and 1990, however, the annual rates were 5% and nearly 7% respectively.

By 1990 the Japanese welfare state bore comparison with the industrialized West, at least in terms of the main statistical indicators. There is still controversy as to the direction in which it should develop hereafter. The proportion of the population aged 65 or over is forecast to double from 12% in 1990 to a peak of about 24% by 2020, with a corresponding decrease in the proportion of working citizens on whom the costs of the system will fall. A consensus seems to be emerging, however, that comprehensive and generous provision for the sick, needy and aged is required, even at the cost of higher taxation and contribution levels. This is likely to mean that the system will remain both comprehensive and costly, and closer therefore to the European model than that of the US.

HEALTH CARE

The administration of health care in Japan is under the overall authority of the Ministry of Health and Welfare. The Ministry also controls directly a number of research institutes and national hospitals, and under it stands a pyramid of prefectural and local health departments. Another area of the Ministry's responsibility is the supervision of local health centres, which are chiefly responsible for public health and hygiene, preventive medical programmes and health education. With the shift in policy emphasis since the mid 1980s towards community care, and prevention rather than cure (as a means of cutting costs), their importance has grown rapidly.

All citizens are, at least in theory, covered by one or other of the medical insurance schemes, which cover the greater proportion of the costs of treatment. Treatment is provided by hospitals, of which the large ones are mainly public or run by charitable organizations, and clinics, which have less than 20 beds and are mostly private. Most doctors are specialists, and even small one-doctor clinics often cover a number of related specialisms instead of offering a general medical service. A patient chooses where to receive treatment, rather than being referred by a general practitioner to a specialist, though informal referrals do take place. The market-oriented nature of this system has led to a high concentration of specialists and of capital investment in popular and therefore profitable fields of specialization such as obstetrics and gynaecology. It has also meant that the availability of medical care is uneven throughout the country, with areas of high population density being at a considerable advantage. Both central and local government have made considerable efforts to redress this imbalance in recent years, putting particular emphasis on the expansion of areas where the market is likely to operate inefficiently, such as preventive medicine and the care of the aged.

Medical costs

Since 1960 all Japanese have been covered by compulsory health insurance. Historically the workplace schemes have provided higher levels of cover than the National Health Insurance Scheme: in 1990 they paid 90% of the insured person's medical costs and 70% of a dependent's, compared with the flat-rate 70% in the national scheme. Financially the workplace schemes are far more soundly based, and the main thrust of government rationalization policies during the 1980s was to reduce both the inequalities and the high level of government expenditure by setting the proportion of costs to be covered at a uniform 80%. The government has, however, so far been unable to put this measure into effect, on account of almost universal opposition from employers and employees alike, who between them form a huge and influential political constitutency.

The Old Age Health Care Law of 1983 abolished the very costly system of free medical care for the aged instituted a decade earlier and introduced in its place a system whereby patients paid a flat-rate contribution on each visit to a doctor or hospital. The main object was to reduce costs indirectly, by discouraging 'excessive' use of the system, rather than directly, by reducing the share of the burden borne by insurance. Nevertheless, medical care for the aged remains extremely costly and nearly 30% of the total cost is now carried by the Old Age Health Care system; the government has continued its attempts to reduce the burden, by increasing emphasis on community care and preventive medicine and by increasing individual contributions.

Pensions and welfare services

The structure of the pensions insurance system parallels that for medical insurance, with the whole population being covered either by schemes for employees or by the state. Problems have been posed by the rapid ageing of the population and by severe inequalities between the various systems. There are different levels of benefit and ages of eligibility ranging from 55 for miners, seamen and some state employees, to 65 for those insured under the national scheme. Government attempts to remove these disparities have only been partially successful, mainly because of resistance from private-sector employers and employees who anticipate an erosion of their own privileged position. This opposition has, for example, prevented a proposed raising of the age of eligibility for an employee's pension to 65: all that has been politically possible is the introduction by 1999 of a uniform pensionable age of 60 in all private schemes, still leaving a five-year gap. However, the government has succeeded in progressively raising the level of contributions, by almost 100% since 1975 in the case of the employees schemes, and this has made possible the provision of a minimum level of pension – for those with a full history of contributions – of over 40% of the national average wage. As a result, both contributions and benefits are comparable to those in western European countries. For public employees and those in large-scale private industry, the figure approaches 60%, which is the declared objective for the system as a whole.

It has long been argued that the support provided by the Japanese family for its members makes a thoroughgoing welfare system unnecessary. Some 70% of old people, for example, live with their children, compared with less than 25% in many Western

Pharmaceuticals

Until the 19th century, the only medicines available in Japan were herbal ones prescribed by practitioners of Chinese medicine. In the Meiji period the nascent school of Western medicine had to rely almost entirely on medicines imported from the West. Before the Pacific War a pharmaceutical industry had begun to develop in Japan, but it was destroyed during the war. After 1945, Japan again became dependent on imported pharmaceuticals, and they had a dramatic effect on deaths from tuberculosis (TB). At the time Japan had a higher rate of TB infections than any other industrialized country: in 1945 alone more than 130,000 died of TB, which was equivalent to 0.19% of the population, a rate that had changed little since 1900. A succession of antibiotics introduced from the West from 1950 onwards produced a sharp decline in TB deaths, which by 1975 had sunk to a rate of less than 0.01%.

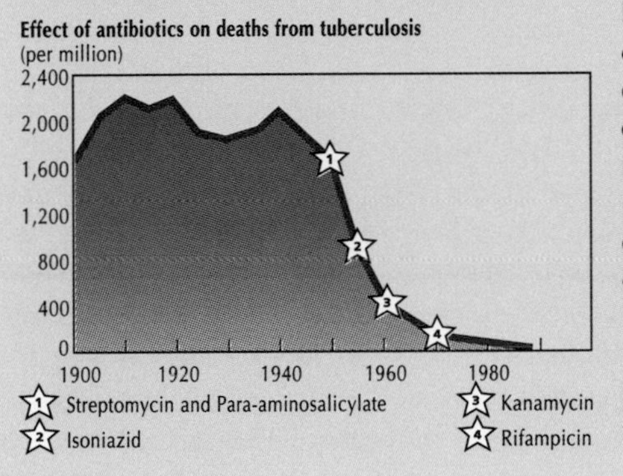

Effect of antibiotics on deaths from tuberculosis

By 1960, the pharmaceutical industry had reached its pre-war level. Now only the pharmaceutical industry of the US has a greater market value than that of Japan and all the indications are that Japan will soon overtake the US. Furthermore, although it is still true that imports of medicines account for more than exports, it is also clear that Japan is exporting more pharmaceutical technology than it imports and that before long Japan will dominate the world pharmaceutical industry. PK

World sales of pharmaceuticals

Japan 23.4%
USA 29.4%
Africa, the Middle and Near East 1.9%
Canada 2.7%
Asia 4.6%
Central and South America 4.6%
Europe 35.2%
total world sales ¥17 trillion

countries. To some extent, of course, the argument is self-fulfilling: low levels of state provision may force old people, the disabled, and single mothers to rely on their families for support. Nevertheless it does appear that this is the preferred pattern for at least a majority of old people, and is on the whole at least accepted as inevitable by many of the families themselves. One thrust of government welfare policy has therefore been to make this possible by providing the institutional framework at the local level to enable families to continue to play this rôle, rather than leaving the state to undertake it. Critics of the government of course argue, with some justification, that this is in fact an abdication of the state's social responsibilities.

Since the early 1980s there has been considerable political pressure, mainly from the government's backers in industry, for a reduced level of state intervention. This has impelled the government to place increasing emphasis on 'community care'. There has also been an increased emphasis on voluntary activity, which is seen both as economical and as representing the best Japanese traditions of community solidarity and mutual support. Although the number of social workers and other welfare professionals has grown, there has been an even larger expansion of the Local Welfare Commissioner system. These Commissioners are semi-volunteers, usually of middle-class origins and high standing within the local community, who act as social workers and advisors. Although they clearly perform an important, albeit somewhat paternalistic, rôle, their very existence has at the same time retarded the development of a fully-professionalized social welfare service.

The increased emphasis on community care has been reflected in welfare legislation, such as the major revision in 1990 of the Old People's Welfare Law, which considerably increased the provision of services and facilities for the aged, both at home and in care, but simultaneously placed the responsibility for such provision at local rather than national level. A similar pattern prevails throughout the system, exacerbating regional disparities, with wealthy municipalities providing levels of service far greater than their poorer counterparts can afford. This is not to deny, however, that there has been a genuine overall improvement in provision, particularly for the aged, and, to a lesser extent, the disabled. Nevertheless the area of the 'personal' welfare services remains the least developed sector of the Japanese welfare state. MVC

Leisure

Leisure behaviour regularly features in debate on the trade imbalances between Japan and the West. The Japanese are accused of 'social dumping' by giving too little attention to leisure, and of behaving like people living in an industrializing society rather than in a developed, post-industrial society. But leisure is by no means as unimportant for Japanese society as Western critics, and some Japanese intellectuals, would have it. Since the war Japanese journalists have coined various catchphrases to describe what they have seen as tremendous changes in values and behaviour relating to leisure and work. It started with the 'leisure boom' around 1960 and 'my-home-ism' in the 1960s; then came Japanese hippies around 1970 and the 'new family' of the 1970s, followed by 'new mankind' in the 1980s. The changes in lifestyle suggested by these catchphrases clearly did not apply to the whole society or even a whole generation, but they were far from insignificant.

Leisure in pre-industrial Japan

The concept of leisure is of course a modern one. Time in agrarian Japanese society consisted of normal working time and special time, which was either sacred (e.g. festivals) or polluted (e.g. menstruation, childbirth or death). Sacred time comes closest to our understanding of leisure, but it involved social and religious obligations and was fundamentally different from modern leisure. Even so, by around 1800 demand for more rest days and for entertainment unconnected with religious life was increasing in rural areas.

In the cities, where there were luxurious pleasure quarters, theatres, and other places of amusement, the distinction between normal and special time tended to lose its force. Since the rigid class structure of the Tokugawa period (1600–1868) offered few opportunities for social advancement, much energy was channelled into a world of pleasure-seeking and entertainment, giving rise to the culture of the 'floating world' (*ukiyo*): kabuki and bunraku theatres,

In summer, beaches near the big cities invariably get extremely crowded, but such is the heat and humidity that anything seems better than staying in the city.

Martial arts

The various Japanese martial arts which now have growing followings in the West only acquired the status of sports in the late 19th or early 20th century. In doing so they often underwent a significant change of name: jūjutsu, for example, became jūdō. The substitution of the suffix 'dō' for 'jutsu' in this and other cases indicates a transition from a perception of these martial arts as 'skills' that might be of practical use in battle to one that perceives them as having some value as an avocation or as a form of mental discipline. They are now regulated by national and international bodies which serve to accredit teachers, determine standards and rankings, and supervise competitive events.

Karate, which means 'empty hand', is a form of unarmed combat involving strikes and thrusts with the arms and kicks with the feet. It developed in the Ryūkyū islands (modern Okinawa), out of fighting styles that had been transmitted from China, from the 15th century onwards, when inhabitants of the islands were forbidden to carry weapons. It only became widely known in mainland Japan in the 1920s when an Okinawan teacher travelled around giving demonstrations. Karate clubs were subsequently formed at some universities, but it was only in the 1950s and 1960s that it became widely popular.

Jūdō is a sport of grappling and throwing that was formed by Kanō Jigorō out of unarmed self-defence techniques which had been formulated and had enjoyed some popularity in the Tokugawa period. It was first recognized when the élite Peers' School included it in its curriculum in 1883. Later, it spread in 1911 to middle schools and in 1939 to primary schools. After the Pacific War jūdō was banned by the Occupation authorities on the ground that it encouraged militarism, but it recovered in the 1950s and in 1952 the International Jūdō Federation was established which in 1956 went on to hold its first world championship in Tōkyō. It was subsequently recognized as a sport for the Tōkyō Olympics in 1964, but the gold medal on that occasion went to a Dutchman.

Kendō, a form of fencing, developed in medieval Japan and by the 14th century there were a number of different schools of practice. Like jūdō, it was banned during the Occupation and only acquired a mass following in the 1960s. It is a popular sport in schools. Practitioners use swords of split bamboo and wear face masks and body armour to prevent injury, as shown here. PK

light poetry and prose, and shamisen music. But there was a tendency for some leisure pursuits to be seen not as 'play' but as morally useful occupations and they were described as a 'way' (*dō*), as in *sadō*, the way of tea, and *kadō*, the way of flowers or *ikebana*.

Modern patterns of leisure

The process of industrialization and Westernization from the 1850s onwards introduced new leisure activities from the West. The upper classes modelled their behaviour on that of those Westerners with whom they came into contact, and started spending summer vacations in newly-developed resorts like Hakone and Karuizawa, or playing golf. Great changes also took place in the martial arts that had formerly been part of samurai training, and in sumō wrestling, formerly a sport associated with festivals, and new forms of sport were introduced through schools, a tradition that survives in the various national school sports meetings, especially the annual national high-school baseball championship.

The greatest changes in leisure behaviour occurred with the coming of mass leisure, first in the 1920s and then again after 1945. During the 1930s and 1940s, leisure served solely as a means of recovering from physical fatigue and of strengthening patriotic spirit. Similarly, many large companies today encourage employees to spend their leisure time together in facilities provided by the company, in the belief that this will promote a sense of 'company spirit'. Recently opinion polls have shown that the desire for leisure is increasing, although working hours have not been reduced to match. However, companies are now competing in a shrinking labour market and have to take some account of the desire of young people to take regular holidays. This is particularly the case with young women, who tend not to opt for a career but to leave employment on marriage or the birth of a child.

Leisure patterns today vary according to class, gender and generational differences. In kindergartens play is seen as purposeful activity and not carefree enjoyment, and teachers are under constant pressure from parents demanding that their children be taught useful things instead of wasting their time in unstructured play. School-age children tend to

Sumō

Sumō, a form of wrestling noted for the phenomenal corporal bulk of the wrestlers and the shortness and ritual of their encounters, is not properly speaking a martial art at all: its origins are more plebeian and its associations are with religious ritual. It is undoubtedly the oldest professional sport in Japan, for there were professional *rikishi*, as the wrestlers are called, in the 17th century: they were media celebrities and anti-heroes, and shared the limelight of the world of popular pin-ups with actors and courtesans. Many schools and universities now have their own sumō clubs, but sumō is principally a spectator sport: its appeal has now spread beyond Japan as it has begun to feature in sports broadcasts in the West, and in 1991 leading *rikishi* took part in the first tournament outside Japan as part of the Japan festival in Britain.

Sumō is rich with hierarchies: the *rikishi* are organized into divisions and gain or lose ranks according to their performance. Only the highest rank, that of *yokozuna*, is exempt from this rule. The objective in sumō is to force the opponent out of the ring or to make him touch the ground with some part of his body other than his foot. Since 1959 there have been six annual tournaments each lasting for 15 days, during which each *rikishi* has a bout to go through every day: his record of wins and losses will determine where he goes in the rankings. Although sumō is a contact sport, violence has little part to play, and the physical encounter is offset by the ceremonial which attends each bout and by the lengthy psychological intimidation which the *rikishi* indulge in beforehand.

Sumō is an immensely popular sport and it is rivalled only by baseball. Its popularity with foreign residents in Japan was given a boost in the 1970s when a Hawaiian reached the second highest rank and became the first foreigner to win a tournament in the highest division. PK

have little time for play since many go to private crammers (*juku*) as well as school. Their favourite leisure activities are video games, watching TV and reading comic books. Among children of this age there is a tendency to spend leisure time alone with fantasy heroes on TV or in comic books. *Shōnen janpu*, the most popular comic magazine of the many published weekly for children, has a circulation of more than 4,000,000, which shows how well the print media have managed to consolidate their position in the face of competition from electronic media.

Japanese teenagers are generally held to be overburdened with examination preparations, but this is true for at most one-third of this age group. The majority have no ambitions for higher education and participate fully in youth culture. As in the West, there is a strong tendency in both sexes to consume music, both actively and passively. The expressive creativity of girls often finds an outlet in writing diaries, novels or cartoons. Team sports like basketball and volleyball are popular with both sexes and soccer with boys, and this indicates the attraction of peer-group activities. High schools and universities have a wide range of cultural and sports clubs, which function also as means of making contact with the opposite sex. After the 'examination hell' to get into university many students see their university years as leisure time. Before embarking on a life of hard work they play hard: alcohol, sex and gambling, hitherto forbidden them, hold a special fascination and together with sports and music constitute the typical student's life-style.

Young women have various leisure possibilities including sport and accomplishments such as flower arranging, the tea ceremony and calligraphy. These activities are commonly seen as 'bridal training' but they are becoming less popular. If leisure is important for unmarried women, for young mothers there is little free time for the enjoyment of leisure, particularly if they return to work after their youngest

Above *A baseball stadium during a 'nighter'. The game is enormously popular and high school league games have a passionate following among students and businessmen alike.*

child has started school. On the other hand, housewives with children at school have time to spend with female friends from the neighbourhood or the PTA or with old school friends, or to visit the numerous 'culture centres' which have appeared since the 1970s and offer everything from handicrafts to foreign languages. The tourism industry has also been targeting this group, which it calls 'nice middies', marketing opportunites for travel with female friends rather than their husbands.

Working men come closest to our stereotype of workaholic Japanese, an image recently reinforced by reports of deaths from overwork. But not all company workers are dedicated to their companies and even those that are take measures to reduce their stress in leisure activities. Drinking, chatting and singing in bars, playing mahjong, pachinko (pinball machines), gambling and golf are the main leisure activities of adult males apart from 'family service', as spending free time with the family is significantly called. When employees are encouraged to make use of company leisure facilities with their colleagues or pressured into drinking with an office group after work, the dividing line between work and leisure is not so easy to draw. In spite of the notion that Japan is a middle-class society without noticeable class differences, the leisure behaviour of white- and blue-collar workers is different: while golf and mahjong are white-collar activities, pachinko and betting are predominantly blue-collar.

Since the 1960s old people have been turning increasingly to leisure activities. Traditionally inactive at the home, except for helping with the children or with housework, they are now less likely to be living in households with children and more likely to participate in educational and recreational activities provided by old people's clubs and other institutions. More and more companies prepare their older employees for life after retirement by teaching them to enjoy hobbies that they did not have time for during their working life.

Right *The game of gateball, which is similar to croquet, is very popular with the elderly.*

THE LEISURE MARKET IN THE 1980s

	1982 (unit: ¥ billion)	(%)	1989 (unit: ¥ billion)	(%)
Eating and drinking out	11,934	30.0	16,010	25.2
Games	5,570	14.0	14,063	22.2
Hobbies and education	7,822	19.7	10,774	17.0
Tourism and travel	6,545	16.4	10,616	16.7
Gambling	5,335	13.4	7,726	12.2
Sports	2,597	6.5	4,265	6.7
Totals	39,803	100	63,454	100

Source: *Leisure and recreational activities* (Foreign Press Centre, 1990)

Time for leisure

For many, leisure starts late in the day: male office workers have no fixed working hours and often work until late: only female office workers customarily leave work at the regulation time. Blue-collar workers usually work a fixed amount of overtime, so that their free time is also limited. The introduction of the five-day week, in response to pressures from abroad, has increased the time available for leisure, but in some industries this has yet to be fully implemented and there are many companies that have their employees work every other Saturday or ask them to participate in 'voluntary' educational programmes on Saturdays.

Vast sculptures made out of ice at the yuki matsuri, *or 'snow festival', which is held every year in Sapporo, Hokkaidō.*

Special seasonal times for leisure are New Year, when all companies and offices are closed for at least three days, Golden Week (a cluster of holidays at the end of April and beginning of May), and the Bon festival commemorating the dead in mid August. The legally guaranteed amount of paid holidays has been increased but the take-up rate is still one of the lowest in the world. The annual average has for some time been around eight days per employee, and the usual pattern is to take a few days off in combination with a weekend and make a short trip. The Western pattern of taking several weeks off and having long holidays with the family is virtually unknown. School vacations are also rather short and used for study at crammers. The government has introduced more national holidays to compensate for the reluctance to take time off work, and in 1991 Japan had the comparatively large number of 13.

SOME OF THE MAIN FESTIVALS IN JAPAN

Date	Location	Name
1st Sunday in Feb.	Sapporo	*Yuki matsuri*
12 March	Nara	*O-mizutori*
14–17 April	Takayama	*Takayama matsuri*
3–4 May	Fukuoka	*Hakata dontaku*
15 May	Kyōto	*Aoi matsuri*
14 June	Ōsaka	*Sumiyoshi o-taue*
16–17 July	Kyōto	*Gion matsuri*
24–25 July	Ōsaka	*Tenjin matsuri*
3–7 August	Aomori	*Nebuta matsuri*
6–8 August	Sendai	*Tanabata matsuri*
15–18 August	Tokushima	*Awa odori*
16 September	Kamakura	*Yabusame*
7–9 October	Nagasaki	*Nagasaki okunchi*

MODERN FESTIVALS

Japan is well known for its many colourful festivals (*matsuri*) held in every part of the country throughout the year. Most date back several hundred years but some are new, such as the Snow Festival of Sapporo. Every community holds one or two small *matsuri* every year, but since the 1950s some have become major national events attracting tourists from all over the country. A typical *matsuri* includes a colourful procession, dances and sporting events. Most have religious origins, but some older and most newer ones are purely secular, and all have some connection with local commercial interests.

In spite of the attempts to create modern *matsuri*, big sporting events and exhibitions have been the main attractions ever since the Tōkyō Olympics in 1964 and the World Exposition at Ōsaka in 1970. The late 1980s in particular saw many exhibitions and expos, all attracting large numbers of visitors. Another new trend in Japanese leisure is the development of 'leisure lands'. The first successful example was the Tōkyō Disneyland, which opened in 1983 and generated such large profits that Disneyland II opened in 1992. There are also new theme parks catering for families, such as Space World in Kita-Kyūshū: more than 60 are under construction.

Leisure patterns may be changed by the growth of resorts. The Resort Law of 1987 made investment in the development of resorts possible, and more than 200 are under construction from Hokkaidō to Okinawa. If these are to attract customers at a time when more and more are going abroad (in 1990 this number exceeded 10,000,000 for the first time), then Japanese will have to make more use of their holiday entitlement. SL

The media

Japan ranks among the top nations in the production of all forms of communication that constitute the media. Constitutional safeguards keep the gates wide open for a torrent of information, analysis, debate, opinion, ridicule and obscenity, while the public is well prepared for it by an education system that produces a high rate of literacy. The government now plans to weave homes and businesses into the ultimate mass media, an interactive national computer network: the 'information society'. The pace and breadth of Japan's torrent of information are astonishing, but at the same time domestic and foreign critics alike question how deep it really goes.

Newspapers and news magazines

During the Tokugawa period broadsheets known as *kawaraban* were the only form of printed news and it was not until 1861 that the first newspaper was published in Japan, in English, by an Englishman, A. W. Hansard. The first Japanese daily was founded in 1871 and in the 1880s the press achieved a prominent political rôle as it applied pressure on the government to establish a parliament, but until 1945 newspapers were subject to strict government censorship and many editors and journalists were imprisoned. After 1945 all pre-war controls were rescinded, new papers sprang up and 'anti-democratic' editors of established ones were dismissed. Distribution has more than doubled since then and the average size of the major dailies grew from 5.9 pages in 1951 to 26.2 by 1965. By 1985 Japan was producing more newspapers per capita than any other nation. The total circulation of daily papers has grown from 24,438,000 in 1960 to 71,457,000 in 1991.

In 1988 there were 124 dailies. Only 5 distributed to the entire nation, publishing morning and evening editions and competing fiercely for market share. In 1989 the *Yomiuri* printed 9.75 million copies of each issue, with the *Asahi* following at 8.1 million. Trailing behind with 4.1 million came the *Mainichi*, followed by the economic daily *Nihon keizai* and the *Sankei* with more than 2 million each. These newspapers differ little in the items presented, but sometimes headline different issues; each paper has regional offices which cover regional issues on local pages. The top three have many ancillary publications as well, including English-language editions, which compete with the independent *Japan times*. While not necessarily supporting the Japan Communist Party, many read its organ, *Akahata* (*Red flag*), for its critical stance since most papers are centre or centre-right. Many other papers cater to local or specialized interests, ranging from the serious to the pornographic. According to surveys by the Newspaper Association, about 70% of adults read a newspaper, for about 45 minutes per day. The most popular sections are said to be the radio and TV listings, social events and regional events, while the least popular are the editorials and foreign news.

Right *A bewildering variety of magazines and comics on display at a bookshop.*

The global information-gathering capacity of Japanese newspapers has increased rapidly. In 1871 Japan first became connected to the international telegraphic network via Shanghai and in 1893 a Japanese newsagency signed a contract with Reuters to gain direct access to foreign news. By 1986 Japan had 135 reporters in North America, 133 in Europe and 120 in Asia. The import and export of news through agencies such as Associated Press and Reuters, as well as some of the collecting of domestic news, is handled in part by Japanese service companies, of which the best known is Kyōdō News Service. These have contacts with all the major newspapers, and some prefectural newspapers derive up to 70% of their contents from them.

Getting news out of Japan is harder, however. The Japanese newspapers are often criticized by foreign reporters for keeping exclusive access to the sources of news. Reporters from the Japanese press form a club and specialize in a certain ministry or politician with whom they establish close personal relations. In return for accurate information, critics charge, reporters often suppress news unfavourable to their patron. Because of this system, the major papers rarely engage in 'investigative reporting'. They are slow to challenge established opinion, and even those that place themselves somewhat left of centre, such as the *Asahi*, are predominantly conservative. In 1972 it emerged that some Japanese news companies had agreed to publish no unfavourable comments about China in return for the right to retain their correspondents in Beijing. The media have on the whole been slow to expose corruption and in 1974 it was only the coverage in the foreign press that forced newspapers in Japan to take up the issue of the Lockheed Scandal involving Prime Minister Tanaka Kakuei. Domestic critics also charge the press with use of discriminatory language against racial and ethnic minorities.

All this may add up to a subtle system of self-imposed censorship. But formal freedoms of speech and the press are well respected, and the press does not suffer from legal restrictions such as those imposed under the Official Secrets Act and its successor in Britain. Instead of the newspapers, it is in fact often the weekly magazines that feature major scoops and scandals. Only when such stories break do the main newspapers publish information that they may well have had all along.

Television and radio

Despite the wide distribution of newspapers, since the Pacific War there has been a dramatic shift in favour of the electronic media. Radio broadcasting licences were issued to 16 privately-owned stations in 1951, opening up to the public what had until then been a monopoly of the government-owned Nihon Hōsō Kyōkai (NHK: Japan Broadcasting Corporation). In the same year NHK and one private station, Japan Television, began television broadcasting. As measured by the percentage of households owning sets, radio played a dominant rôle only during the late 1950s, and was soon surpassed by television. For black and white sets, the 1959 diffusion rate of 20% jumped to 40% in 1965. Colour sets then took over, jumping from a diffusion rate of zero in 1965 to 90% in 1975. In 1958, 51% of people derived their information from newspapers, but by 1966 this had dropped to 24%. In the same few years, the percentage drawing their information from TV rose from 0.02% to 68.3%.

Broadcasting stations have multiplied over the last 20 years: in addition to NHK , there are 137 private stations throughout Japan, including 36 using both radio and television, 34 using radio alone and 67 using only television. NHK, which runs both a news and feature channel and the educational channel, charges a viewing fee to homes, while the private stations depend upon advertising revenue. Technology has progressed rapidly, and UHF, VHF, cable television, satellite transmission and high-definition

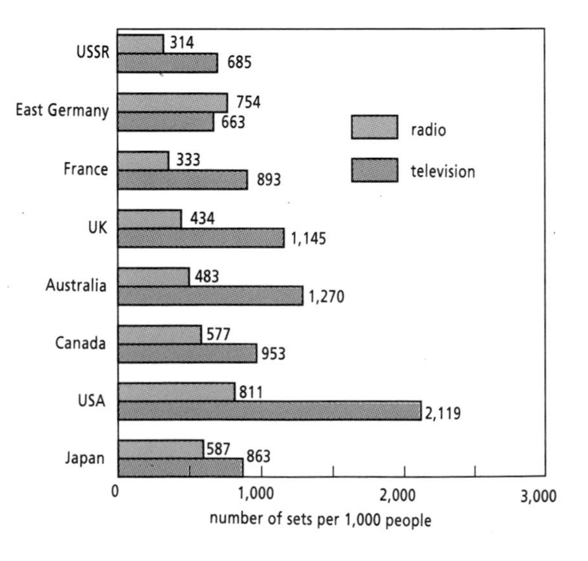

The ownership of radios and televisions in different countries in 1987.

broadcasting are all common. Transmission of foreign television programmes rose from 827 hours in 1966 to 88,616 in 1985, and now live broadcasts of foreign elections and other events are taken for granted. The University of the Air began broadcasting in 1985, and shows programmes on highly technical subjects to a wide audience. The commercial stations concentrate on soap operas, so-called 'wide-shows' (talk shows with celebrities), news and weather bulletins, and cartoons, in that order. NHK, on the other hand, is predominantly educational or cultural with news and weather bulletins.

The profile of programmes broadcast by stations in Japan is similar to that in most countries, with quiz shows and both period and domestic dramas being very popular. The soap operas and dramas from the US that were imported in large numbers in the 1960s have largely been replaced by domestic products. Programmes have a high standard of visual aesthetics, as does advertising, but dramatic plots and acting tend to follow a set pattern, with little emotional depth or subtlety. The most popular drama in recent years has been *Oshin* on NHK, which traces the life of a poor country girl married into an Ōsaka business family at the turn of the century. The second most popular drama is Mito Kōmon, in which a relative of the shōgun and his followers wander around the country incognito, despatching evil doers with artistic swordsmanship. Biting satire of society is generally conspicuous by its absence. By and large women play supporting rôles in news and talk shows, acting as a sympathetic audience, although this is beginning to change, and there are now a number of prominent women newscasters.

Advertising

The Japanese advertising industry is the second largest in the world, but it comes a distant second to the US in the amount expended and its ranking is lower still if calculated on a per capita basis. In 1985 Japan spent about US$106 per capita on advertising to make national total of $12.8 billion, compared to the US per capita figure of $397 and total of $94.7 billion. Britain, in third place for the total, spent $114 per capita. As a percentage of GNP, Japan's expenditure on advertising went from 0.61% in 1952, peaked at 1.22% in 1963 and then gradually dropped to 0.92% in 1986. The largest advertising agency in the world, measured by total sales, is the Japanese firm Dentsū, although its ranking in terms of profits was third in 1985.

Advertising first became an important part of retail trades in the Tokugawa period, when printing was used to produce handbills extolling the merits of new products, but the advent of the modern newspaper in the Meiji period brought the mass media to maturity and, from the beginning, advertising, particularly of medicines and books, had a prominent part to play. Newspapers dominated the advertising industry right through until 1974 when they were for the first time overtaken by television. Newspapers are still the second most important advertising medium, and they depend on it: the average newspaper will now devote 30–40% of its space to advertising and will rely on it for more than 50% of its revenue. Advertising agencies in Japan tend to retain close contacts with selected media institutions and to specialize in dealing with them. As a consequence, they are not constrained from accepting competing clients in the same sector of industry, unlike their counterparts in the West. JB/PK

Books and magazine publishing

In 1989 a total of 39,698 new books were published in Japan, as compared with 13,122 in 1960, 18,754 in 1970 and 27,891 in 1980. In absolute numbers this put Japan in the world league, following the USSR, US, France, England and Germany. But when calculated per capita, Japan falls to about 20th place, behind many European countries. Although selling well in the 1950s, serious novels have fallen in sales, while collected works and illustrated encyclopedias have increased. Each major publisher has its collection of representative fictional and non-fictional works in standard editions, such as the Iwanami Shinsho and Iwanami Bunko series. Paperbacks now constitute about half of all books published. Public access to books is largely through private purchase, for public libraries are used less intensively than in many other countries.

Over the post-war years, the sales of books have fallen while the sales of magazines have risen. By the 1980s magazines were the central feature of publishing, with 21,000 titles being published regularly. These include 4,600 popular magazines and 5,344 scholarly journals, the rest being for government, association, specialized group and company purposes. Some magazines, such as *Chūō kōron* and *Sekai* carry on a long tradition of serious in-depth discussion of issues of the day. *Newton* is a magazine popularizing science, *An-An* introduces fashion and romantic advice to young women, and *Prejidento* (President) discusses business affairs.

Adult and children's comics, known as *manga*, have become the largest single category of magazine. In 1987 they sold over a billion volumes, which represented an increase of 10% on the previous year. *Manga* have their roots in the cartoons of Hokusai and other artists of the Tokugawa period, but in their modern form they owe their popularity to Tezuka Osamu, who brought to the traditional picture story the techniques of the cinema. The topics of adult comics range from gory samurai and gangster adventures, to science fiction, business competition, bar life and pornography. Some comics tackle serious subjects, even mathematics, or carry condensed novels, all in easily digestible form. The most popular comic published in book-form in 1991 was *The silent service*, about espionage and secret warfare between a Soviet submarine, the Japanese Self-Defence Force and the US Seventh Fleet. JB

Bottom right *Circulation of* manga, *1965–87.*

The title page of a typical manga. *The story, 44 pages in colour, 'Xmas fantasy', is about a schoolgirl who begs a devil to procure her a 'BF', or boy friend.*

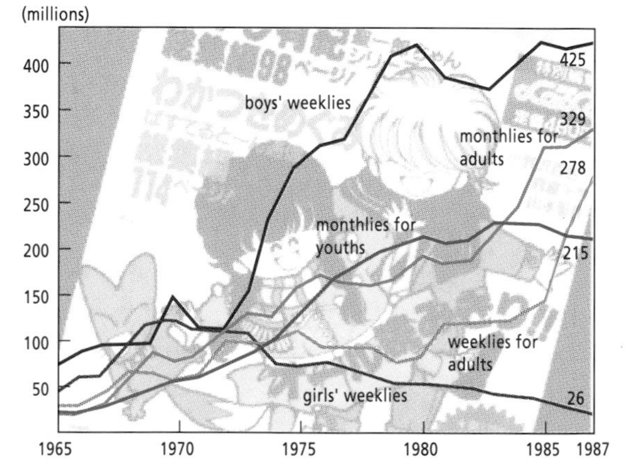

Popular protest and citizens' movements

Popular protest for or against change has been a feature of political life in Japan since the Meiji Restoration. Three overlapping types of protest can be observed. First there are those movements and activities which aim at broad political change, such as the establishment of universal manhood suffrage or opposition to the US–Japan Security Treaty. Second there is more ephemeral protest about specific issues which may have wider political implications. Third there is sustained protest about issues which are of interest mainly to those engaged in the activity. Protest of any kind was anathema to the Confucian ideology of the Tokugawa state, but peasant rebellion was surprisingly common. One author calculates that uprisings occurred at a rate of 25 per year from the 17th to the 19th centuries. Some of these were caused by the price of rice or high-handedness by the local lord; a few went further and aimed at social reform or 'renewal' (*yonaoshi*). Some involved large numbers and had precise aims. The Tenma Disturbance of 1764 involved 200,000 peasants protesting about onerous taxes to finance improvements to the road that led from Edo to Nikkō, and it forced the government to cancel the project. Uprising existed, then, in the collective consciousness of many peasants as one of a range of possible political responses.

The Meiji period

The first five years of the Meiji era witnessed a large amount of peasant violence, but once the land tax had been reformed and the new régime gained legitimacy, the target was usually landlord rather than state. Mass disturbances did, however, take place in the 1880s, by which time the protests about high interest rates and heavy tax burdens for construction projects were accompanied by demands for liberal reforms of the political system. These became linked to the freedom and popular rights movement.

In its formative period (1874–78) this movement was a small group of former samurai from Tosa who demanded the creation of a representative assembly as a panacea for all political problems. They used the language of natural rights, but at first made no attempt to spread their ideas to the mass of the population. From 1878 numerous groups sprang up in towns and cities across the country such that in 1880 a petition demanding the creation of a national assembly was signed by 135,000 people from 149 societies; there may have been as many as 600 groups in all. The Liberal Party (Jiyūtō), formed in 1881, was pledged to win popular rights and constitutional government, but it was dissolved in October 1884. The final blow came in 1887 when 600 anti-government activists were expelled from Tōkyō, but many activists who were thus forced to leave the metropolis found employment in local newspapers, which were to foster liberal ideas and this ensured fertile soil for the seeds of liberal and socialist ideas that arrived in Japan in the early 20th century.

Protest emerged again in 1905–12, when rioting occurred in Hibiya Park in September 1905 as a protest against territorial concessions following victory in the Russo–Japanese war. In the course of the rioting 17 were killed, 500 wounded and 2,000 arrested. Meanwhile socialists and anarchists tried to set up study groups and labour organizations in the face of police disruption. The end of this brief period was marked by the arrest, trial and execution of Kōtoku Shūsui and other left-wing activists on charges of plotting to assassinate the emperor.

Asanuma Inejirō, leader of the Japan Socialist Party, being stabbed to death by a right-wing student on 12 October 1960. The previous year Asanuma had aroused controversy when, during a visit to Beijing, he declared that US imperialism was the enemy of Japan and China alike.

Taishō democracy

Political protest received massive encouragement from the rising tide of interest in liberal and socialist ideas that swept the world in 1917–18, following the revolution in Russia and the apparent victory of Wilsonian idealism in the Treaty of Versailles at the end of the First World War. Japan was now familiar with the vocabulary of rights, freedom and equality, and the rice riots of 1918 had certain political consequences: the appointment of the first party politician to the post of prime minister, and a broader demonstration that in Japan, as in Russia, there existed massive peasant discontent. The task of the radical was to channel it, that of the bureaucrat to defuse it. This set the international and domestic context for the events of the 1920s which saw the rapid growth of the union movement, the creation of a communist party and the social democratic parties, as well as organizations to represent outcasts (*burakumin*), tenants and women. Demands for universal suffrage grew and mass demonstrations were held. This campaign continued into the 1920s and was in part responsible for persuading Prime Minister Katō to introduce a bill in 1925 which extended the franchise to all men over 25. However this era of political protest was brief, its demise marked by the passage of the Peace Preservation Act in 1925. Using powers which were devised to prevent the spread of Bolshevism, the police were able to harass all kinds of political activists.

Above *January 1968: students at Hōsei University clashing with the riot police. The protest was against the visit of the US nuclear-powered aircraft carrier USS* Enterprise.

Below *Students demonstrating against the new Tōkyō airport at Narita in solidarity with local farmers.*

Post-war movements

The Occupation authorities abolished most of the legislation which had inhibited protest and released political prisoners from jail. Political and social movements blossomed. Mass demonstrations were again possible: one event in Tōkyō to complain about food rationing attracted 250,000 people. Incidents of this kind and the increasing radicalism of the unions prompted the Occupation forces and the Japanese authorities to re-impose some restrictions. A general strike planned for 1947, which included anti-US demands, was banned at the last minute by the authorities. The policies of the Occupation authorities became increasingly less liberal towards the end of the 1940s, ending with a 'red purge' to eliminate

Far right *Farmers manning barricades to prevent government officials from surveying the site for the new airport at Narita in the 1970s.*

communists from positions of influence in the unions, the media and education.

When full independence was returned to the Japanese in 1952 political protest continued and took on new characteristics; defending democratic reform and opposing the close relationship with the US. Changes in the education system, for example, were opposed by the Teacher's Union with the support of the left-wing union federation Sōhyō. More successful were the mass demonstrations of late summer 1958 against measures designed to increase police power, and this resulted in the proposals being dropped. This formed the prelude to the movement against the revision of the US–Japan Security Treaty, known as Anpo. Left-wing parties, unions, and the student organization Zengakuren formed a People's Council for Preventing the Revision of the Security Treaty in spring 1959, and organized a series of demonstrations which culminated in June 1960 with an invasion of the Diet compound and confrontation with the police. So severe were these riots that Prime Minister Kishi was forced to cancel President Eisenhower's visit. Having pushed the revised treaty through the Diet, Kishi resigned and the crisis passed.

Student and other movements

Student protests, which marked the late 1960s and early 1970s, had several dimensions. There was concern about the deterioration of university facilities, especially in the private sector. There was also the international situation as protest against the treaty with Korea developed into opposition to Japan's involvement in the Vietnam War, which in turn was to lead to renewed campaigns against the revision of the Security Treaty in 1970. Demonstrations in the latter struggle involved more activists than ten years earlier but had less impact on parliamentary politics. Following the introduction of the Universities Control Act in 1969 and the agreement to provide more state cash to the private universities the campuses calmed down.

Parallel to the growth of the 'student movement' was the emergence of a 'citizens' movement' which seemed to some to be the precursor of a new democratic culture. At its core was a growing concern about industrial pollution, in particular the 'Big Four' cases of Minamata, Itai-itai (Toyama), Niigata and Yokkaichi. In the first three of these cases water polluted by industrial waste containing heavy metals led to illness and death in the neighbouring communities. Yokkaichi involved atmospheric pollution from oil refining. Protest campaigns and later demands for compensation were launched in the 1960s but met resistance from the local authorities and central government. Success in court battles for compensation in the late 1960s and early 1970s was accompanied by the introduction of legislation to reduce dangerous industrial emissions. Numerous other groups were formed to protest about local instances of pollution, actual or planned – in 1970 there were said to be 3,000 such groups with 1.5 million adult members, but only rarely did demands transcend local issues. Thus when the immediate problem was resolved, as frequently occurred, the groups ceased to be active. The long-term effect of these campaigns has been to make the government highly sensitive to parochial matters such as direct threats to human health in specific localities but less concerned about protecting the natural environment in general.

Narita airport

In 1965 the cabinet decided to construct a new international airport for Tōkyō at Tomisato near Narita City. Violent protest by farmers caused the government to change the location to Sanrizuka, also near Narita, where a large plot of land was owned by the imperial family and where less opposition from the farmers was expected. The Sanrizuka farmers' resistance was at first peaceful and ineffective, but outside support soon came from student and left-wing groups active in Tōkyō. Different groups found the struggle attractive for different reasons. For some the main issue was the betrayal of the farmers by the LDP. Others linked the need for a new airport to increased use of Japanese airspace by the US, related to imperialist aggression in Vietnam. For others it was the involvement of the emperor in the project that caused concern. There was also widespread sympathy for the campaign because it raised questions about the relationship between economic growth and the quality of the environment. By 1972 the last of the farmers had been removed from the land needed for the airport, but now the militants erected steel towers high enough to be a danger to air traffic. Battles between police and activists raged in the 1970s as final preparations were made for the opening of the airport. It finally opened in 1978, but progress on the construction of the support services was slow and the second and third stages have still not been completed. Narita airport remains protected by riot police. Here at least the struggle continues.

The decline of protest

Since the 1970s there has been a decline in political protest on all fronts. No new 'big issue' has emerged to excite the imagination of the young or the radical. Pollution is less an issue than it used to be and those groups that do exist are preoccupied with exclusively local issues; there is no sign of the emergence of a national Green movement.

The promise of a new wave of democratic culture has not been fulfilled. Urban discontent exists, of course, as was demonstrated in the street fighting in Ōsaka in autumn 1990, but it has no political dimension. All that remains are the token demonstrations occasionally to be observed in Hibiya Park as rice farmers or the disabled try to attract the attention of the media to specific demands being made at the nearby ministries.

IJN

Riot police on the left, and on the right members of a radical student faction demonstrating against the state funeral for Emperor Hirohito.

Crime and the law

Japan enjoys one of the lowest crime rates in the industrialized world, despite the social pressures of extremely rapid economic growth and urbanization. The figures on violent crime are particularly striking. Taking murder as a bench-mark category, the average number of offences committed per 100,000 inhabitants in 1986–88 was 1.3, as against 5.7 in the United Kingdom and 8.4 in the US. The corresponding figure for crimes against property is 1,135 per 100,000, as against 4,452 in West Germany, 5,634 in the United Kingdom, and 4,943 in the US.

The execution ground outside Edo (modern Tōkyō) in the 1860s, with just one severed head on the boards.

Institutions of the criminal justice system

Law enforcement and criminal justice are principally carried out by three institutions: the police, the public prosecutor's office, and the courts. The rôle of each of these institutions was substantially altered in the post-war period of sweeping constitutional change.

By the end of the Pacific War, the authority of police organizations extended deep into the social and political life of the nation. The ordinary police (*keisatsu*) were officially responsible not only for front-line law enforcement, but for a wide variety of regulatory matters affecting the conduct of business and the maintenance of public health and morals. The hierarchy of the police organization ran through local prefectural headquarters to the Interior Ministry. The police also enjoyed limited rule-making and adjudicative powers. The Special Higher Police (*Tokkō*), also under the ultimate authority of the Interior Ministry, were organized on a national basis without reference to prefectural subdivisions and were responsible for enforcement of restrictions on association, speech and political behaviour. The Military Police (*Kempei*), answerable directly to the military authorities, were also deeply involved in police activity.

After a period of radical decentralization instituted during the Occupation, the current structure of police organized on a prefectural basis was established. Finances for police operations are shared between the prefectural governments and the national government. Interprefectural matters such as training, information collection, co-ordination, and staff rotation are supervised by a national administrative body known as the National Police Agency (NPA).

A parallel structure of prefectural and national Public Safety Commissions (*Kōan iinkai*) exists, through appointment by elected officials with the approval of the relevant legislative bodies. The national-level Public Safety Commission provides indirect representation of the NPA in the cabinet. The rule-making and judicial functions of the police were eliminated during the Occupation, and have never been restored; and in accordance with the new Constitution, the authority of the police no longer extends to general restriction of political activity.

Prosecutors work under the authority of the Ministry of Justice. Post-war changes in the rôle of the prosecutor are symbolized by the fact that prosecutors no longer sit on the same level as judges, but face the judicial bench as do the defendant's counsel. But although prosecutors no longer enjoy a status equal to that of judges in the criminal process, and although the civil rights' protections of the Constitution are heavily influenced by the US Constitution, criminal procedure retains an inquisitorial (as opposed to adversarial, or common-law) character. Criminal trials are by judge, not by jury. The judge takes a more active part in proceedings than in an adversarial system of justice, and the prosecutor and the judge are not rigorously barred from raising or considering evidence that has been obtained by illegal means. Constitutional provision for security of tenure for judges and prosecutors, and the removal of the judiciary from the authority of the Ministry of Justice, together with other constitutional guarantees and the pressure of the media, help to prevent open political manipulation of the criminal process.

The kōban, *or small local police box, is a ubiquitous feature of Japanese life. They act partly as information centres and partly as a restrained form of surveillance. This modern one is in the Shinbashi district of Tōkyō.*

OPERATION AND PERFORMANCE OF THE CRIMINAL JUSTICE SYSTEM

On a review of statistics, the Japanese criminal justice system performs exceedingly well at all levels. There is a high incidence of voluntary confessions, and almost every criminal case taken to trial results in a guilty verdict. These results have been variously taken as evidence of efficient policing and judicial practice; of intrusion upon, or restriction of, civil rights; and of cultural factors peculiar to Japan which expedite police investigations. The challenge to the observer in this controversial area is to judge the extent to which each of these factors contributes to the overall result.

Although difficulties encountered in certain high-profile cases have caused the Japanese police a certain amount of embarrassment in recent years, the forces continue to achieve a high clearance rate for crime. A number of factors contribute to this result. The police as a whole have been careful to maintain good relations with the communities they serve. Uniformed officers manning a comprehensive network of non-residential police boxes (*kōban*) in urban areas, and single-family residential police boxes (*chūzaisho*) in the countryside, maintain close contact with households within their jurisdiction. Rotation of these officers, and indeed of staff throughout the police, helps prevent the onset of favouritism and graft that might arise from excessive familiarity.

The work schedule of police officers is demanding and discipline is rigorous; 'police society' is cohesive and vertically structured. Perhaps out of a desire to meet the public demand for ever more effective policing, the police have shown a particular reluctance to permit study by outsiders. As a result, there has been little field research on the Japanese police and as many studies have been conducted by foreign as by Japanese observers.

A large percentage of suspects confess to the police or the prosecutor before formal charges are filed. The police are aided in the pursuit of confessions by the Code of Criminal Procedure, which allows the detention of suspects for up to 23 days without formal indictment. During this interval, suspects do not enjoy the right of access to state-appointed lawyers, although they may hire their own legal counsel if they wish. Suspects are frequently detained in facilities operated by the police, and the police claim a

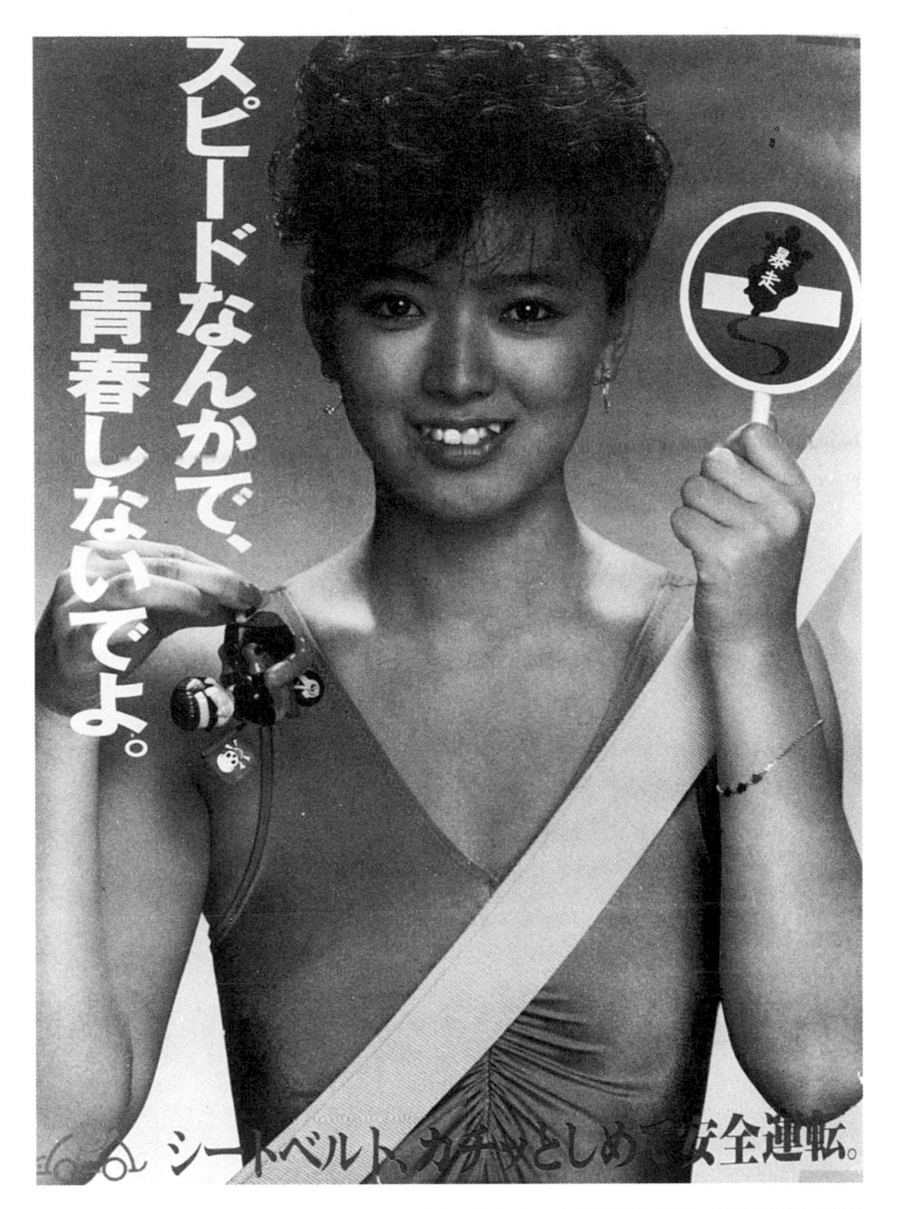

スピードなんかで、青春しないでよ。
暴走
シートベルト、カチャッとしめて安全運転。

Above *A poster warning against speeding and encouraging the use of seatbelts.*

Right *Women now have a more important rôle to play in policing society: these are the members of the 4th mobile traffic brigade in February 1992.*

right under the Code to restrict visitation (including visits by lawyers) in the interests of the investigation. These factors enable the police to proceed by developing a human relationship with the suspect, to the end of obtaining a confession or, in many cases, multiple confessions.

Cultural factors are also important. At all levels of the criminal justice system, stress is laid upon the importance of co-operation with those in authority, and of contrition by the guilty. The fact that these values are reflected in Japanese society at large is an important tool in the questioning of suspects. The high rate of confession helps in part to explain the exceptionally high rate of successful prosecutions. Although Japanese criminal procedure does not provide for a formal guilty plea, 99.9% of cases which culminated in full trial proceedings in 1988 resulted in the conviction of the accused. In the vast majority of cases, the indictment is supported by a full confession.

A second important reason for the high conviction rate is the exercise of discretion by the prosecutors. A prosecution may be dropped because of procedural difficulties or lack of evidence, or suspended for reasons unconnected with the prosecutor's capacity to prove guilt. In 1988, for example, 1,776,906 cases concerning adults were referred to the prosecutor's office. The majority of these (1,205,014) were handled by summary proceedings with the consent of the accused. Of the remaining 571,892 cases, 102,283 (17.9%) were taken to public trial, 50,709 (8.9%) were dropped, and 418,900 (73.2%) ended in suspension of prosecution.

Because suspension of prosecution terminates proceedings but leaves behind the implication that the suspect is nonetheless guilty, it has been criticized by some on the grounds that the due process of the law has not been completed. Nevertheless, when the prosecution's case is supported by a full and corroborated confession, the goal of defence lawyers is often to obtain a suspension of prosecution instead of a guilty verdict.

Japan does impose capital punishment in serious murder cases and ten death sentences were handed down in 1988. Executions are carried out by hanging in conditions of strict secrecy and usually after a lengthy process of appeals and further hearings has run its course: relatives are only informed of the execution after the event.

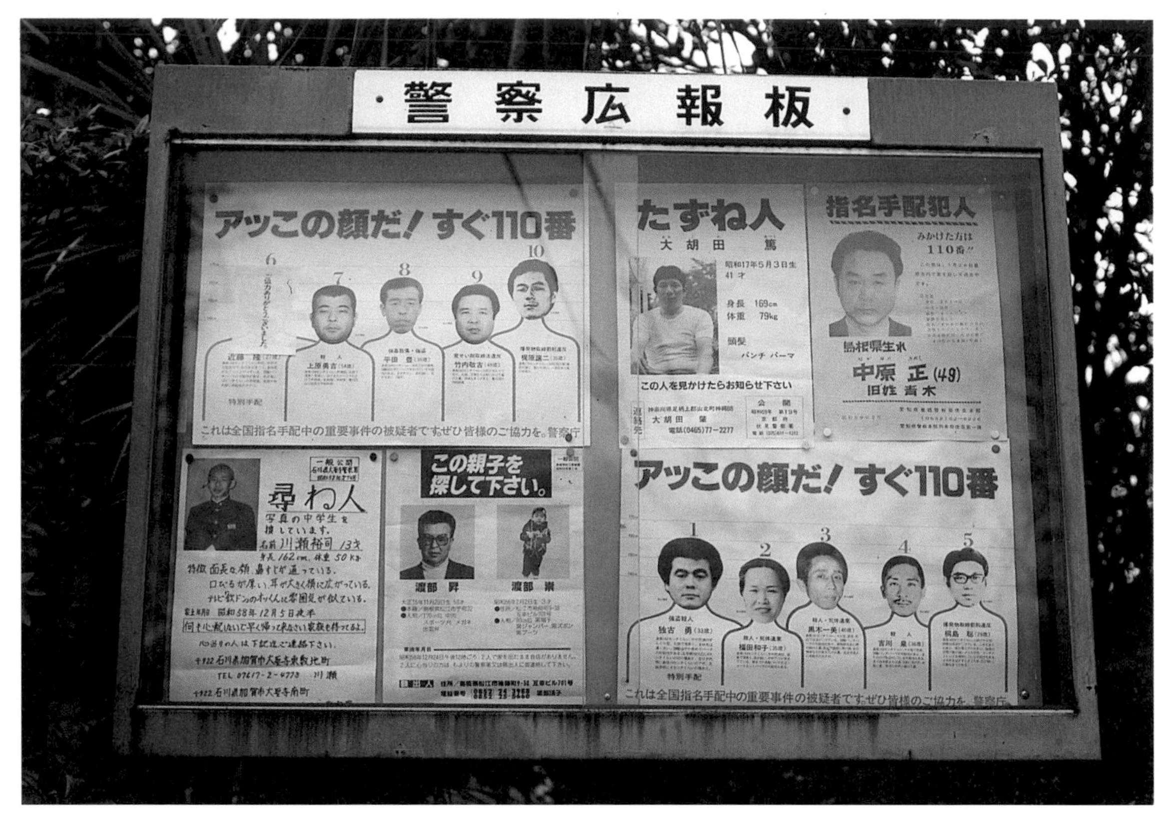

A notice board giving details of wanted criminals. 'Dial 110 for the police if you see any of these faces', the poster urges.

ORGANIZED CRIME

Members of organized crime gangs (*yakuza* or *bōryokudan*) account for approximately 30% of the prison population. Because these organizations are characterized by a rigorous internal discipline, and because their members are widely thought of as irredeemable social outcastes, suspects in such cases are unlikely to co-operate with the police, and the rate of recidivism is high.

Criminal organizations in Japan range from large-scale crime syndicates to youth motorcycle gangs. The larger organizations are involved in a wide range of activities, including the drug trade, prostitution, loan-sharking, protection rackets and fraud. Some racketeers have developed a distinctive identity, such as the *jiageya*, who specialize in driving tenants out of valuable properties, and the *sōkaiya*, who specialize in parasitic and symbiotic links with large corporations by threatening to disturb shareholders' meetings or by helping to control them.

The social organization of the *yakuza* combines elements of the business corporation and the extended family. Most organizations represent their identity in terms of a romanticized genealogy running back to the 17th and 18th centuries. Organizational identity is further reinforced by rituals of loyalty, obedience and apology. The most ostentatious of these are the large formal banquets, the body tattoos worn by many gang members, and the ritual of cutting off fingers from the left hand, which may be performed as an act of personal apology or to symbolize an agreement.

The *yakuza* are both more open in their activities and more amenable (in limited circumstances) to external control than criminal organizations in many European and American countries. On 20 November 1989, for example, gang members entered into a court-recognized settlement of claims by three citizens injured in a shoot-out at Hiroshima station. Residents of a condominium in Yokohama succeeded in appealing to the courts to evict gang members for continual and wilful refusal to respect condominium rules in 1986.

CHANGE AND REFORM

The most powerful forces working on the modern Japanese criminal justice system are social and economic changes over which the police and the courts have little or no control. The recent influx of transient foreign labour has given rise to novel forms of social tension in some areas. There are also some signs that increasing economic inequality may cause difficulties in the future. On 2 October 1989, day labourers in Ōsaka rioted after discovering that the *yakuza* who employed them had been given confidential information by a member of the local police squad.

Japan's economic success has also drawn international attention to the political difficulties of prosecuting serious white-collar crime, and to the ineffectual nature of penalties applied to it. The Recruit bribery scandals which emerged in the late 1980s have been followed by recent revelations of dealings on a large scale between criminal organizations and Japan's four largest securities firms. It remains to be seen whether the pressure of such scandals will prompt significant legislation on white-collar crime. On the other hand, Japanese defence lawyers and representatives of human rights groups have persistently criticized both the laws which allow detention of suspects for 23 days before formal indictment, and the practice of holding such suspects in police cells. There are signs that changes may be in the offing, although no concrete proposals have yet been put forward.

Finally, the economic attractions of private law practice have drawn an increasing number of those passing the National Bar Examination away from public service. The prosecutor's office has suffered worse in this respect than the judiciary. In recent years, more prosecutors have left the service than have entered it, a fact which has prompted plans to increase the number of candidates allowed to pass the National Bar Examination each year.

FB

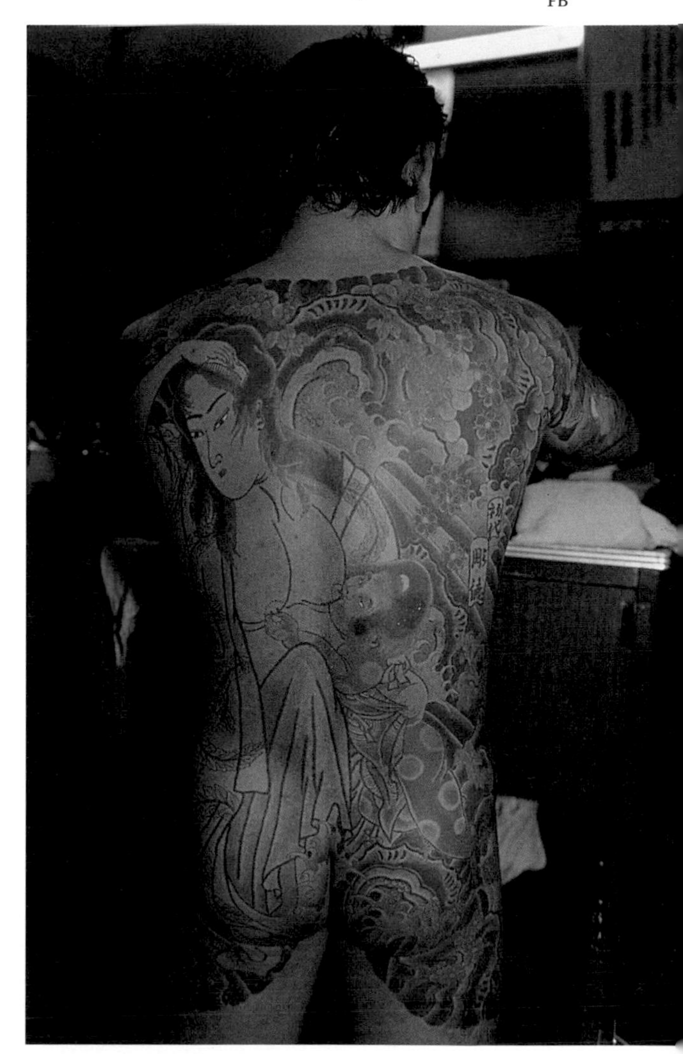

Tattoos in the Nara period were used to mark criminals, but in the Tokugawa period the tattoo became an art form while still linked to the twilight world of the demi-monde and crime. Today tattoos are still associated with gangsters, but full-body tattoos in the old style worn by this man are a rarity.

Prisons and prisoners

At the end of 1988 there were 68 main and auxiliary prisons in Japan and eight juvenile prisons. There were also 115 detention centres and 1,257 police facilities used for detention purposes. The average daily prison population of convicted offenders was 44,247, of whom 55.7% belonged to Class B of convicted offenders, which is for those considered to have an advanced tendency towards crime. Some 45% of these Class B prisoners were associated with organized crime, making up 31.7% of the total prison population. Altogether 24,605 convicted prisoners entered prison in 1988, 95.8% of whom were men and 62.3% of whom had previously served time in prison. As for their sentences, 9.8% were sentenced to 6 months imprisonment or less, 24.3% to between 6 months and 1 year, and 41.2% to between 1 year and 2 years; the remaining 24.7% included one person who received a death sentence and 47 who received life sentences, and the rest were sentenced to more than two years of imprisonment. In prison emphasis is placed on education leading to a qualification, and in 1988 prisoners gained 2,389 such qualifications, mostly as welders, electricians, drivers and beauticians. In the same year 29,601 offenders left prison, 43.7% after the completion of their sentences and 56.3% on probation.

FB

リーニング
市議候補
本店 目覚町8-16
お気軽にお問合せ下さい
西川
青木

Politics

The constitutional framework

Previous page *A politician's lot is not always a happy one. A candidate tries to attract last minute voters for the Nagasaki City Council elections.*

Far right *Promulgation of the new Meiji Constitution in the State Chamber, 14 March, 1889. Woodblock print by Adachi Ginkō.*

Modern Japan has had two constitutions. The first, known as the Imperial Japanese or Meiji Constitution, was promulgated by Emperor Meiji on 11 February 1889 and went into effect in November 1890. Combining Prussian and Japanese influences, it formed the legal basis of the emergent modern state. The second, known simply as the Constitution of Japan, was promulgated, technically as an amendment to the Meiji Constitution, on 3 November 1946 and took effect on 3 May 1947. Essentially a US creation, it became the legal keystone for the democratization of Japan during the Allied Occupation and remains the law of the land today.

The Meiji Constitution

A major catalyst for the Meiji Constitution was liberal demands for a new political system in which the Satsuma and Chōshū cliques that had dominated the government after the Restoration in 1868 would be obliged to share power. These demands came largely from the movement for 'freedom and popular rights' which was influenced by French and British democratic ideas. Equally significant, however, was the belief of the Meiji leaders that the future stability of the state depended upon a sound legal framework, as was the case in Europe and the US. The government announced in 1881 that Japan would be given a constitution providing for an elected assembly by the end of the decade. It created a peerage in 1884, a cabinet system in 1885, and in 1888 a privy council, part of whose business would be to ratify the new constitution.

Below *Itō Hirobumi, first prime minister of Japan from 1885 to 1888.*

The task of drafting the constitution was entrusted to Itō Hirobumi who visited Europe to investigate different constitutional models. He consulted several German legal specialists, including Hermann Roesler and Albert Mosse, and concluded that the Prussian constitutional system offered the most appropriate model for imperial Japan. Not surprisingly, therefore, the Meiji Constitution was a highly authoritarian document and its adoption proved to have far-reaching consequences.

Sovereignty rested with the emperor (*tennō*), the 'head of the empire', who, tracing his ancestry back to the Sun Goddess, was 'sacred and inviolable'. Having granted the constitution to his people, only he had the power to amend it. His prerogatives potentially made him an absolute monarch. To illustrate: he could convoke, open, close and prorogue the bicameral parliament, known as the Diet, and he could dissolve the elected House of Representatives. The powers of this lower house, which were checked by those of the House of Peers (which was appointed rather than elected), were in any case limited to certain budgetary controls. The emperor was also empowered to issue imperial ordinances in place of law. Furthermore, he controlled state administration and could declare war, make peace and conclude treaties. He could determine the peace-time standing of the armed forces and, above all, Article 11 of the constitution gave him 'supreme command of the army and navy'. This meant that the army and navy chiefs of staff were responsible to him alone. The cabinet was similarly responsible to the emperor, rather than to the Diet.

Altogether, the emperor's theoretical supremacy reflected his rôle as the nation's 'spiritual pivot', in Itō's words, and there soon arose a pervasive imperial cult, centred on State Shintō, which imbued the 'emperor system' (*tennōsei*) with a powerful religious mystique. Any political movement that appeared to threaten the monarchy was rigorously suppressed.

It must be emphasized, however, that Itō had not initially planned for imperial autocracy. On the contrary, he had envisaged that the emperor would use his ultimate authority to give automatic sanction to the policies of the government, as Japanese sovereigns had indeed done for centuries. Consequently, in key respects the emperor's powers were significantly qualified. For example, Article 4 stipulated that his sovereign rights were exercised 'according to the provisions of the present constitution'; Article 5, that his legislative powers were exercised 'with the consent of the Diet'; and Article 55, that all laws, imperial ordinances and rescripts were to be counter-signed by ministers of state.

The Meiji Constitution therefore contained the conflicting notions of both absolute and limited monarchy, and this led to considerable interpretative controversy over the years. Conservative theorists,

Below *Satirical sketch done for the journal* Tonchi kyōkai zasshi *by Adachi Ginkō, artist also of the woodblock above, 28 February 1889. This piece of irreverence cost the editor three years in gaol and the artist one year.*

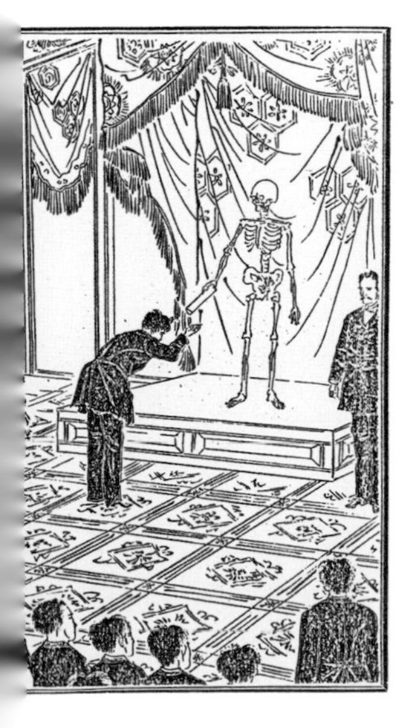

such as Hozumi Yatsuka and Uesugi Shinkichi of Tōkyō Imperial University, insisted that the constitution prescribed direct rule by a divine emperor who represented an imperial line 'unbroken for ages eternal', as Article 1 proclaimed. Others, notably Minobe Tatsukichi of the same university, endorsed the concept of imperial sovereignty but argued that the emperor was an 'organ of the state' whose prerogatives were subject to constraint by other organs, primarily the cabinet and the Diet.

These controversies were exacerbated by the fact that the Meiji Constitution had created a complex political system in which the emperor reigned but did not actually rule, and in which rival political élites, who were ostensibly responsible to him, in fact competed to legitimize their respective policies through invoking the 'imperial will'. Whoever controlled the emperor could use his sacred authority.

The authoritarian character of the Meiji Constitution ensured that the elder statesmen, such as Itō, who manipulated the emperor's prerogatives to govern from behind the throne, would hold the balance of power over the developing liberal party movement as Japan embarked upon constitutional government. Their predominance was ensured by the fact that they recommended a candidate for prime minister, typically from their own circle, whom the emperor would then appoint. However, the Meiji Constitution was not so authoritarian as to preclude the parties from making substantial political inroads: the budgetary controls of the lower house could be used to force policy concessions from the government. Indeed, when the parties later gained the strong support of an expanding electorate, the prime minister came to be appointed from their ranks for most of the period from 1918 to 1932.

From 1932 onwards, however, Japan was governed by bureaucratic, non-party cabinets increasingly dominated by the armed forces, who gradually usurped the emperor's prerogative of supreme command. This was possible because Article 11 precluded civilian control of the military and because it had always been somewhat unclear how the emperor should take responsibility for controlling the army and navy chiefs of staff in practice.

The capacity of the military to exploit the so-called 'independence of supreme command' in obtaining automatic imperial sanction for aggression and war, and to do so legally, was one of many factors which later convinced the Occupation authorities that Japan had to have a new constitution, if democracy were to prevail.

Prime ministers of Japan

	Prime minister (cabinet no. in brackets)	Dates
1	Itō Hirobumi (1)	22 Dec. 1885–30 Apr. 1888
2	Kuroda Kiyotaka	30 Apr. 1888–25 Oct. 1889
	(Sanjō Sanetomi)*	(25 Oct. 1889–24 Dec. 1889)
3	Yamagata Aritomo (1)	24 Dec. 1889–6 May 1891
4	Matsukata Masayoshi (1)	6 May 1891–8 Aug. 1892
5	Itō Hirobumi (2)	8 Aug. 1892–31 Aug. 1896
	(Kuroda Kiyotaka)*	(1 Aug. 1896–18 Sept. 1896)
6	Matsukata Masayoshi (2)	18 Sept. 1896–12 Jan. 1898
7	Itō Hirobumi (3)	12 Jan. 1898–30 June 1898
8	Ōkuma Shigenobu (1)	30 June 1898–8 Nov. 1898
9	Yamagata Aritomo (2)	8 Nov. 1898–19 Oct. 1900
10	Itō Hirobumi (4)	19 Oct. 1900–10 May 1901
	(Saionji Kinmochi)*	(10 May 1901–2 June 1901)
11	Katsura Tarō (1)	2 June 1901–7 Jan. 1906
12	Saionji Kinmochi (1)	7 Jan. 1906–14 July 1908
13	Katsura Tarō (2)	14 July 1908–30 Aug. 1911
14	Saionji Kinmochi (2)	30 Aug. 1911–21 Dec. 1912
15	Katsura Tarō (3)	21 Dec. 1912–20 Feb. 1913
16	Yamamoto Gonnohyōe (1)	20 Feb. 1913–16 Apr. 1914
17	Ōkuma Shigenobu (2)	16 Apr. 1914–9 Oct. 1916
18	Terauchi Masatake	Oct. 1916–29 Sept. 1918
19	Hara Takashi (Kei)	Sept. 1918–4 Nov. 1921
	(Uchida Kōsai)*	(4 Nov. 1921–13 Nov. 1921)
20	Takahashi Korekiyo	13 Nov. 1921–12 June 1922
21	Katō Tomosaburō	12 June 1922–24 Aug. 1923
	(Uchida Kōsai)*	(24 Aug. 1923–2 Sept. 1923)
22	Yamamoto Gonnohyōe (2)	2 Sept. 1923–7 Jan. 1924
23	Kiyoura Keigo	7 Jan. 1924–11 June 1924
24	Katō Takaaki	11 June 1924–28 Jan. 1926
	(Wakatsuki Reijirō)*	(28 Jan. 1926–30 Jan. 1926)
25	Wakatsuki Reijirō (1)	30 Jan. 1926–20 Apr. 1927
26	Tanaka Giichi	20 Apr. 1927–2 July 1929
27	Hamaguchi Osachi	2 July 1929–14 Apr. 1931
28	Wakatsuki Reijirō (2)	14 Apr. 1931–13 Dec. 1931
29	Inukai Tsuyoshi	13 Dec. 1931–16 May 1932
	(Takahashi Korekiyo)*	(16 May 1932–26 May 1932)
30	Saitō Makoto	26 May 1932–8 July 1934
31	Okada Keisuke	8 July 1934–9 Mar. 1936
32	Hirota Kōki	9 Mar. 1936–2 Feb. 1937
33	Hayashi Senjūrō	2 Feb. 1937–4 June 1937
34	Konoe Fumimaro (1)	4 June 1937–5 Jan. 1939
35	Hiranuma Kiichirō	5 Jan. 1939–30 Aug. 1939
36	Abe Nobuyuki	30 Aug. 1939–16 Jan. 1940
37	Yonai Mitsumasa	16 Jan. 1940–22 July 1940
38	Konoe Fumimaro (2)	22 July 1940–18 July 1941
39	Konoe Fumimaro (3)	18 July 1941–18 Oct. 1941
40	Tōjō Hideki	18 Oct. 1941–22 July 1944
41	Koiso Kuniaki	22 July 1944–7 Apr. 1945
42	Suzuki Kantarō	7 Apr. 1945–17 Aug. 1945
43	Higashikuni Naruhiko	17 Aug. 1945–9 Oct. 1945
44	Shidehara Kijūrō	9 Oct. 1945–22 May 1946
45	Yoshida Shigeru (1)	22 May 1946–24 May 1947
46	Katayama Tetsu	24 May 1947–10 Mar. 1948
47	Ashida Hitoshi	10 Mar. 1948–15 Oct. 1948
48	Yoshida Shigeru (2)	15 Oct. 1948–16 Feb. 1949
49	Yoshida Shigeru (3)	16 Feb. 1949–30 Oct. 1952
50	Yoshida Shigeru (4)	30 Oct. 1952–21 May 1953
51	Yoshida Shigeru (5)	21 May 1953–10 Dec. 1954
52	Hatoyama Ichirō (1)	10 Dec. 1954–19 Mar. 1955
53	Hatoyama Ichirō (2)	19 Mar. 1955–22 Nov. 1955
54	Hatoyama Ichirō (3)	22 Nov. 1955–23 Dec. 1956
55	Ishibashi Tanzan	23 Dec. 1956–25 Feb. 1957
56	Kishi Nobusuke (1)	25 Feb. 1957–12 June 1958
57	Kishi Nobusuke (2)	12 June 1958–19 July 1960
58	Ikeda Hayato (1)	19 July 1960–8 Dec. 1960
59	Ikeda Hayato (2)	8 Dec. 1960–9 Dec. 1963
60	Ikeda Hayato (3)	9 Dec. 1963–9 Nov. 1964
61	Satō Eisaku (1)	9 Nov. 1964–17 Feb. 1967
62	Satō Eisaku (2)	17 Feb. 1967–14 Jan. 1970
63	Satō Eisaku (3)	14 Jan. 1970–7 July 1972
64	Tanaka Kakuei (1)	7 July 1972–22 Dec. 1972
65	Tanaka Kakuei (2)	22 Dec. 1972–9 Dec. 1974
66	Miki Takeo	9 Dec. 1974–24 Dec. 1976
67	Fukuda Takeo	24 Dec. 1976–7 Dec. 1978
68	Ōhira Masayoshi (1)	7 Dec. 1978–9 Nov. 1979
69	Ōhira Masayoshi (2)	9 Nov. 1979–12 June 1980
	(Itō Masayoshi)*	(12 June 1980–17 July 1980)
70	Suzuki Zenkō	17 July 1980–27 Nov. 1982
71	Nakasone Yasuhiro (1)	27 Nov. 1982–27 Dec. 1983
72	Nakasone Yasuhiro (2)	27 Dec. 1983–22 July 1986
73	Nakasone Yasuhiro (3)	22 July 1986–6 Nov. 1987
74	Takeshita Noboru	6 Nov. 1987–3 June 1989
75	Uno Sōsuke	3 June 1989–9 Aug. 1989
76	Kaifu Toshiki	9 Aug. 1989–5 Nov. 1991
77	Miyazawa Kiichi	5 Nov. 1991–

*Interim caretaker cabinets not counted in official lists

Official portrait of the Emperor Meiji (1852–1912) in the new westernized imperial uniform.

The Constitution of 1946

The necessity of constitutional revision was communicated to the Japanese government in October 1945, within two months of Japan's surrender in the Pacific War. It then fell to a committee chaired by the minister of state, Matsumoto Jōji, an acknowledged expert in commercial law with considerable experience in government, to draft a new constitution. The Matsumoto Committee adopted a minimalist approach, contending that pre-war militarism, not the Meiji Constitution itself, had led to repression and disaster.

Accordingly, on 4 February 1946, after a newspaper had published the Matsumoto draft, General Douglas MacArthur, Supreme Commander of the Allied Powers, established a committee chaired by Colonel Charles L. Kades to draft a new model constitution. This work was accomplished hurriedly and on 13 February, when the Matsumoto Committee was given the US draft, it was led to understand that unless it followed the model at hand, the future of the imperial institution could not be guaranteed. This was a bluff, for the US had already decided to retain the monarchy for the sake of political stability in a period of far-reaching reform; but the Japanese complied and apart from adding provision for a bicameral legislature, the final Japanese draft closely followed the US model. After extensive deliberations, it was approved by the Privy Council and the Diet.

The present 'amended' constitution contrasts sharply with its predecessor. Written in colloquial, as opposed to literary, Japanese, it reads in places as though it has been translated from the English. It reduced the emperor to a purely ceremonial rôle as 'the symbol of the state and of the unity of the people, deriving his position from the will of the people with whom resides sovereign power' (Article 1). Reflecting the sovereignty of the people, the Diet was now made the 'highest organ of state power', 'the sole law-making organ of the state' (Article 41). Executive power rested with the cabinet, which was responsible to the Diet, as in the British system. The people, including women, who were given the right to vote for the first time in Japan, would choose their representatives.

Other major constitutional innovations included the separation of church and state as part of the elimination of State Shintō; an independent judiciary; an emphasis on human rights and the equality of the sexes under the law; and provision for amendment on the basis of two-thirds or more votes in both houses of the Diet and a majority of votes in a national referendum. An additional, and critically important, feature of the constitution was Article 9, which is unique in renouncing war and 'the right of belligerency of the state', while pledging that 'land, sea, and air forces, as well as other war potential, will never be maintained'. Whether the primary initiative for Article 9 came from MacArthur or a Japanese politician is uncertain, but it was clearly meant to guarantee that the post-war retention of the monarchy would not lead to a revival of Japanese militarism.

The new constitution eliminated the ambiguities and the authoritarianism of the Meiji Constitution and established a strong foundation for democracy in Japan. Accordingly, national polls have shown overwhelming public support for it and a deep-seated reluctance to see it changed. However, conservatives object to its foreign origins, to its demotion of the emperor, now no longer head of state, and to Article 9, which hinders full-scale rearmament. They have tried many times to amend it over the years and pressure for change will undoubtedly continue.

These attempts at revision have been successfully resisted by the opposition parties, for whom the constitution is the foremost defence of democratic principles. There is no little irony in the fact that the left-wing parties, which have generally taken an anti-US position on foreign policy issues, have been determined to preserve what is in effect Japan's US constitution, while the otherwise pro-US Liberal Democratic Party, which has governed ever since the party was founded in 1955, has been the most anxious to revise it.

Though there has been no amendment to date, there are many respects in which Japanese political practice has in fact departed from the constitution. Article 9 notwithstanding, the incremental, and highly controversial, post-war development of the 'Self-Defence Forces' (Jieitai) has made Japan a formidable regional military power in East Asia, and the state's gradual rehabilitation of the Yasukuni Shrine, which formerly received state patronage as the focal point for honouring the spirits of Japan's war dead, has to some extent compromised the separation of church and state. SSL

How Japan is governed

The way a nation is governed will depend to a large degree on its history, and in particular on formative events, such as wars and revolutions, precipitating comprehensive institutional change. In the Japanese case two such periods in the modern history of the nation may be regarded as 'heroic' in the sense that they generated wholesale reshaping of the system of government: the period of the Meiji reforms, from the Meiji Restoration of 1868 until about the end of the 19th century; and the decade or so following military defeat in 1945, which includes the Allied Occupation (1945–52) and the consolidation of conservative political forces into the Liberal Democratic Party (LDP) in 1955.

The modern political development of Japan is remarkable in that, in formal institutional terms, the political systems established in the Meiji period and in the decade after 1945 both proved remarkably stable. Neither the Meiji Constitution of 1889 nor the present constitution has ever been revised in any respect whatsoever. Moreover, despite the great differences between the two, the governance of Japan from the late 19th century until the present offers many examples of organic evolution and continuity.

Emperor Hirohito receiving an address from Prime Minister Konoe in the House of Peers during the celebration of the 50th anniversary of the establishment of the Diet, November 1944.

Even so, government under the present constitution has been much more stable than government under the Meiji system. Part of this contrast results from the enormous international and domestic pressures Japan was subjected to while creating a modern state and a modern economy. Since 1952, Japan has been protected by the US and has enjoyed greater freedom to concentrate on economic growth.

Governing Japan under the 1889 Constitution

There were clear institutional reasons for the greater instability of politics and government under the Meiji Constitution. There is irony here, because those who so carefully drew up the constitution were desperately concerned with issues of stability, and wanted to entrench executive dominance. The paradoxical result of these efforts, however, was a constitution which lacked a clear and realistic statement of where power was supposed to lie. Broadly speaking there were two reasons for this.

The first relates to the position of the emperor. The almost dormant imperial institution was picked up and recreated in radically new form by the revolutionary leaders of 1868. The fact that there was an 'unbroken' line of emperors meant that for the new leadership the emperor was a potent instrument ready for use in the tasks of nation building, motivating the people to make sacrifices for development, building effective armed forces, and suppressing dissent. A potent emperor-cult was gradually created, and graphically represented in the language of the constitution, and other documents which served as instruments of control. On the other hand no real attempt was made to give the emperor true political power, still less to make him into a dictator, though the Meiji and Shōwa emperors were not without influence. The result was a discrepancy between the language of the constitution and the reality of power distribution. In practice, the location of power was determined by a complex and shifting process of competition between various élites. Over this process the *genrō* (a self-appointed group of elder statesmen) exercised control until the 1920s, when death had removed nearly all of them from the scene.

Later the system became difficult to co-ordinate and cabinets came and went with great frequency.

The second reason was the rôle of the armed forces within the political system. Because of the priority given to military development from the early Meiji period, there was conspicuous lack of civilian control. Army and navy chiefs of staff had independent access to the emperor on matters of military concern. Within any cabinet the minister for the army had to be a general and the minister of the navy had to be an admiral, so that merely by withdrawing their minister the army or navy could bring down a cabinet.

Despite the many obstacles placed in their path, political parties were able to evolve from the purely oppositional force they were in the 1890s to occupy a central political rôle in the 1920s. The rôle of the Diet under the constitution was limited but significant. Universal male suffrage was achieved in 1925. By the 1920s the principle of party cabinets appeared to have triumphed over that of 'transcendental' cabinets (cabinets neither controlled by parties nor obliged to resign if defeated in the Diet). Events during the 1930s, however, negated this and placed more and more power into the hands of the armed forces, although until authoritarian reforms in 1940 political institutions changed little.

THE 1945 REFORMS

When the US occupying forces arrived in Japan in 1945 under General MacArthur, they were mandated to introduce radical political, as well as social and economic, reform. Their programme is often referred to as 'democratization and demilitarization'. Apart from the key reforms of reducing the status of the emperor and abolishing the armed forces, other changes included: abolition of the aristocracy, apart from immediate imperial relatives; the abolition of the Privy Council, the Imperial Household Ministry, and the *genrō* and other groups of the senior statesmen, which as extra-parliamentary bodies had diluted the power of parliament. The Diet (renamed National Diet) had its legislative power over the budget and finance guaranteed. The appointive House of Peers was replaced by an elective House of Councillors, the suffrage was broadened to cover men *and women* over 20 and civil liberties, including freedom of expression, were guaranteed.

Emperor Hirohito being received by General Douglas MacArthur in the US Embassy, Tōkyō, October, 1946; both men somewhat ill at ease.

Why General MacArthur should have preferred for Japan a British-style relationship between cabinet, parliament, the electorate and the bureaucracy, rather than a presidential system on the US model, is an intriguing question. No doubt the fact that the pre-war system was embryonically British, so that enhancing the rôle of parliament within it would combine democratization with continuity, was important. Also to retain the emperor, even as a mere symbol, and then to introduce a president, would have caused difficulties. However this may be, the 'cabinet-within-parliament' system that emerged from the Occupation ultimately proved compatible with a high level of political stability.

GOVERNING JAPAN SINCE 1945

At the risk of simplifying a complicated story, it can be argued that two powerful factors operated alongside the choice of a political system to produce stability. The first was that the government bureaucracy was able to survive the Occupation with the bulk of its powers intact. This was partly because the Occupation needed to use the existing civilian bureaucracy in order to implement its reforms, but partly also because the ministries were no longer in competition with a huge military bureaucracy, and could concentrate single-mindedly on creating the conditions for economic growth. The second factor, which was closely linked to the first, was that after its formation in 1955 out of previously competing parties, the LDP never failed to win a sufficient number of parliamentary seats to form a government. Though essentially conservative and oriented towards business and agriculture, the LDP was able to function as a broadly based 'catch-all' party, with sufficient flexibility to attract new categories of support when this provéd necessary.

This was not of course without cost in terms of policy-making capacity. It has been argued that the LDP has successively broadened its base by responding to crises with compensatory packages to affected interests. In a number of areas, this has led to considerable policy immobilism, graphically demonstrated, for instance, in the long-term failure to liberalize imports of rice and slowness in responding to international demands for action at the time of the 1990–91 Gulf crisis. At the same time, while there is

Election results 1958–86: House of Representatives

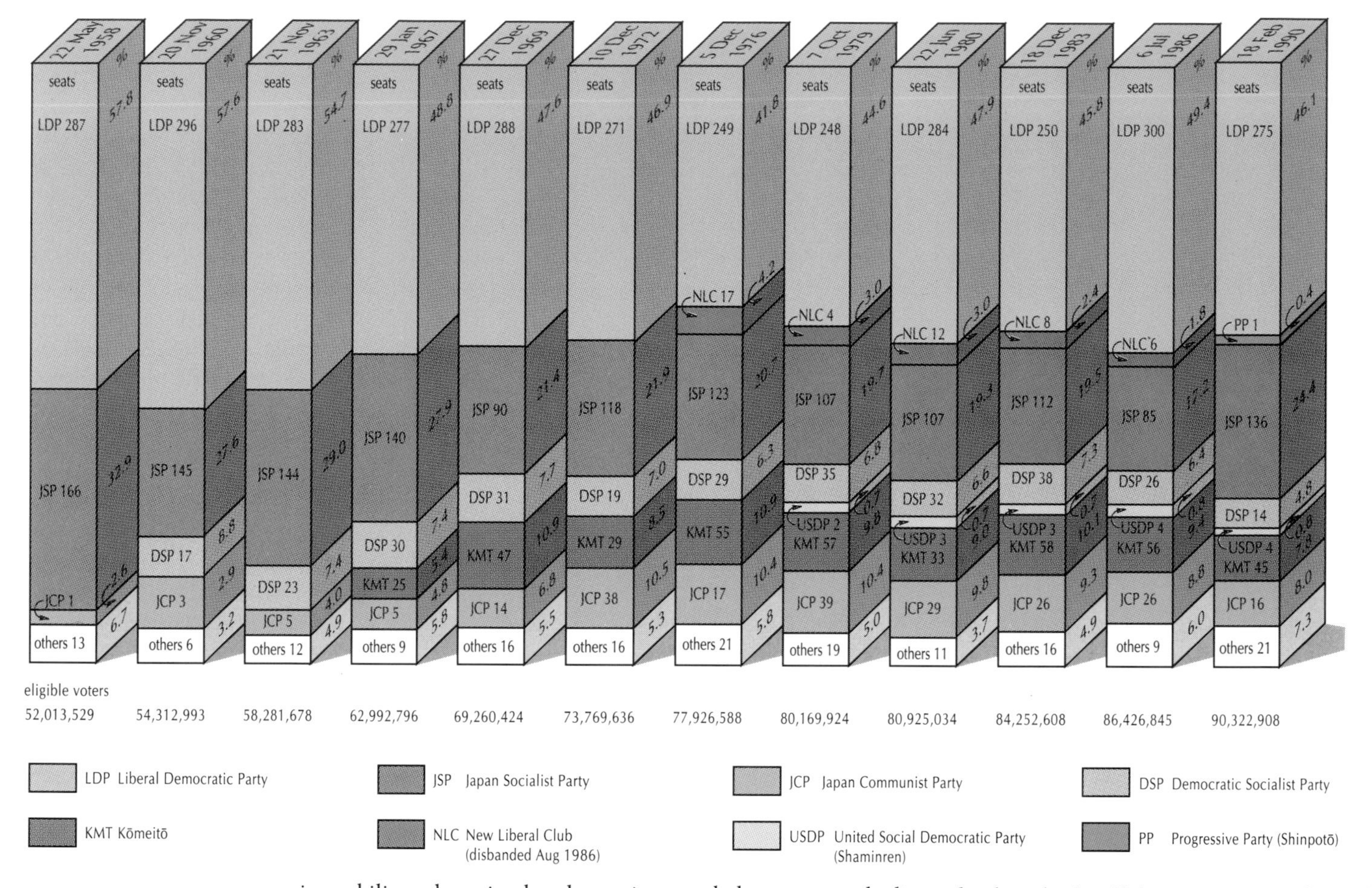

immobilism there is also dynamism, and the constant interaction between the LDP, the various government ministries and key interest groups has been compatible with effective policy-making across a range of policy areas. Indeed, perhaps the principal paradox of the way Japan is governed is that even though the system exhibits much the same tendency to distort economic 'rationality' by buying off interests as is said to have sapped the economic dynamism of several European countries, nevertheless the Japanese economy remains extraordinarily effective in its performance. Analysts differ greatly in their assessment of how far this effectiveness results from action by government and how far from the dynamics of the industrial system operating independently of government.

The maintenance of this system over such a long period is in turn bound up with three further features, the electoral system for the House of Representatives, factionalism within the LDP and the limited political rôle of labour. First, members of the House of Representatives are elected from multi-member constituencies (though there is no transferable-vote system), which tend to favour a large catch-all party such as the LDP by encouraging intra-party competition between several candidates from the same party. Apart from the intense competitiveness that this engenders, it encourages appeals based on personality, rather than party or policy, and this greatly favours the style of the LDP. (In addition, there is a seriously imbalanced apportionment of votes favouring rural constituencies, which also helps the LDP). Second, power broking and channelling of funds through LDP factions has tended broadly to separate policy struggles from struggles over cabinet and party posts, and over money. This in a negative sense has helped the cohesion of the ruling party. Third, labour unions, being based on the enterprise rather than the craft or industry, have enjoyed only limited mutual solidarity. They have,

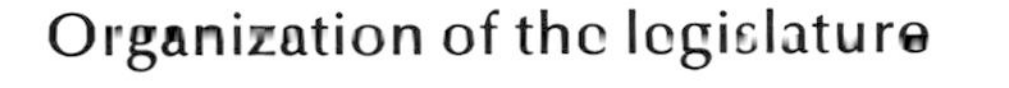

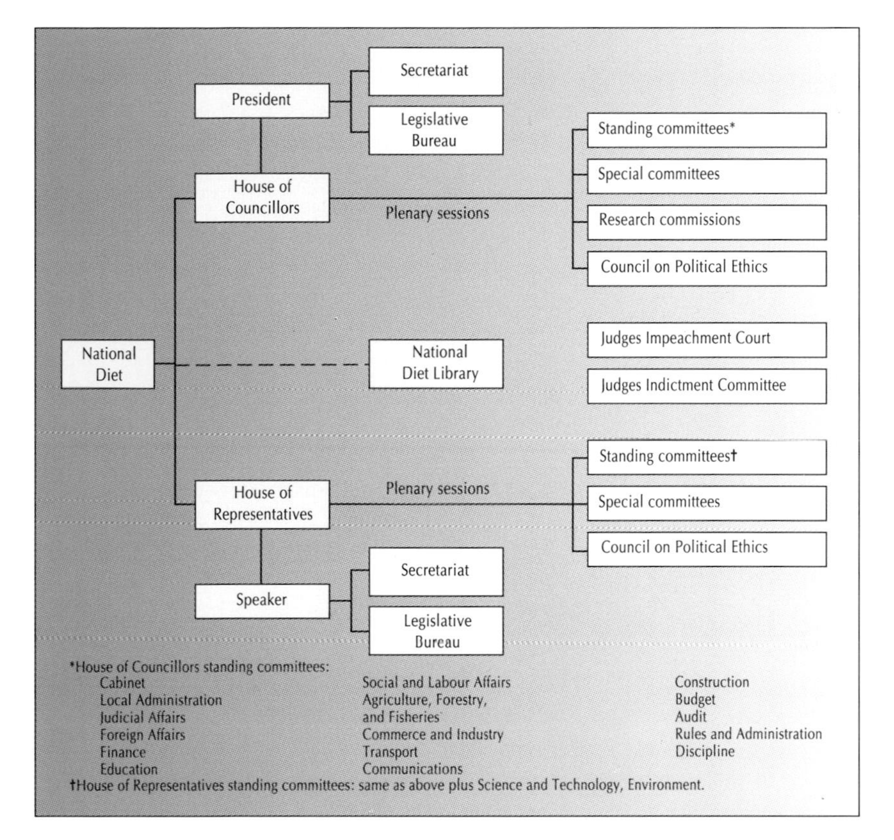

The relationship of powers under the present constitution

The accompanying diagram is a somewhat idealized version of how the system should work; in practice of course things are not so clear cut. The people may be forgiven for wondering at times in what sense sovereignty resides with them, although it is also a truism that in a country with free elections people deserve the government they get.

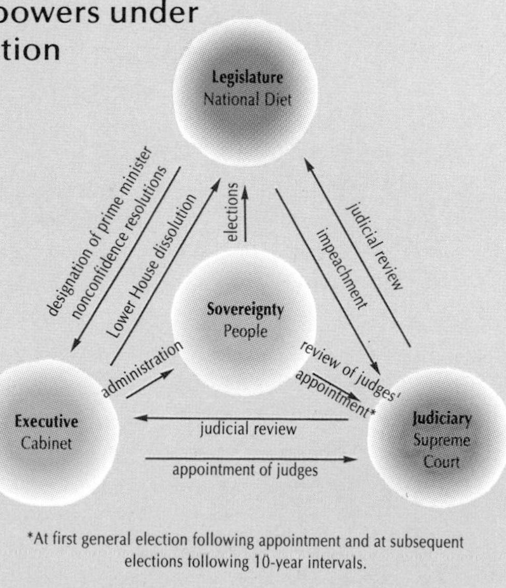

*At first general election following appointment and at subsequent elections following 10-year intervals.

moreover, supported parties without power rather than the ruling party, and this has kept them away from the centres of political impact, though they have not been entirely without influence. The Japanese decision-making system has been characterized as 'corporatism without labour', although it may be questioned whether, if labour is absent, the system ought to be designated 'corporatist'.

Perhaps a more useful way to conceptualize how Japan is governed is to regard the system as a set of interacting bureaucratic hierarchies, each having conspicuous 'Japanese' features in respect of promotion of their members, and interaction between the hierarchies. Government ministries promote their competitively selected élite officials automatically up to a certain level, when merit and ability take over as the key promotion criteria. Quite similar patterns may be observed in industrial firms and other types of organization. More surprisingly, it is also the case that the LDP operates a seniority promotion system, mediated by competition between the powerful factions of which the party is composed, whereby virtually all affiliated members of the House of Representatives have achieved one cabinet post by their sixth term in the Diet. Beyond that, however, only the conspicuously able and ambitious continue to occupy key government and party offices. Meanwhile, the various hierarchies in the system both jealously guard their areas of jurisdiction and intensively interact through a variety of channels. Movement of former bureaucrats into new business and political careers is a related feature.

Thus constant and relatively predictable tensions between promotion guaranteed and promotion struggled for, as well as between 'turf' protection and group interaction, do much to explain the mixture of dynamism and immobilism which characterizes the way Japan is governed. The system has held together over a long period at considerable costs in terms of corruption, policy rigidity and limitations on electoral choice. At the same time it has provided Japan with social and economic stability, flexibility and responsiveness in many policy areas, as well as firm and reasonably responsible government. It is arguable that systemic change is now needed, particularly to the electoral system, to permit greater openness in politics and government, and to respond better to the needs of a mature economy and society as Japan approaches the 21st century. JAAS

The civil service

'Civil service' here means officials of the executive branch of the national government, especially the cabinet ministries. The Japanese term *kōmuin* (public employees) is vastly broader in scope and includes everyone (whether appointed or elected) in the executive, legislative and judicial branches of the national government, the prefectural and municipal governments, and public enterprises.

Officials of all Japanese governments before 1868 came from a hereditary élite that was civilian until the 12th century, military thereafter. From 1600 to 1868, the samurai class was highly stratified both vertically in the form of hereditary ranks and horizontally among 250 fiefs. Even within this privileged class, only a small minority were eligible for 'national' office. The system was overthrown in 1868 by samurai from fiefs long excluded from the power structure. Many junior officials were chosen on the basis of ability, regardless of regional ties or inherited rank. By 1872 all classes had been made legally equal. By 1894 Japan had perfected a civil service appointment system based on education and merit. Despite periodic revisions, especially after the Pacific War, the salient characteristics of the 1894 system remain strong today.

Structure

To ensure that comparable positions in every ministry are held by officials of similar rank, the government has since 1869 prescribed a uniform structure of civil service ranks, each comprising numerous pay grades. The ranks have been renumbered often, most recently in 1985. Formerly they were broadly divided into 'higher officials' and 'ordinary officials'. In 1948 these terms were abolished as being undemocratic, but a sharp distinction between the two persists unofficially and by custom (not law) promotion from the lower category into the higher is extremely difficult.

Since 1894, the higher civil service has been considered a lifetime career. It carries high prestige because it is difficult to enter. Only a few very senior 'policy' positions, such as cabinet minister, are filled by 'free appointment' (*jiyū nin'yō*) from outside. Virtually all other positions are reserved for career officials who are first appointed in their early twenties and then promoted periodically over the next 30 years.

Initial appointment is based chiefly on education, verified either by written and oral examination (*shiken*), or by evaluation of credentials (*senkō*). After examinations conducted annually by the National Personnel Authority, each ministry interviews applicants and makes its own appointments. There has never been any formal educational requirement but the most prestigious examinations have an extremely high rate of failure. Nearly all who pass have a university degree and often a postgraduate qualification also. Passing establishes eligibility, but it does not guarantee appointment; ministries compete for the best applicants and applicants compete to enter the most influential ministries.

Career patterns

After initial appointment to junior rank in the higher civil service, two career patterns emerge. Both lead to periodic increases in pay and promotions in rank, but one is far more likely than the other to lead to senior managerial positions. Although officials recruited by evaluation have rewarding careers as technical specialists or national university professors, they are far less likely (in most ministries) to become senior administrators.

Officials recruited through the most prestigious examinations are considered 'administrative generalists' but are not expected to move from ministry to ministry. There is a strong tradition of career-long loyalty to a single ministry, although temporary secondment to another ministry (*kennin*) is not uncommon. Permanent transfers of higher officials out of their original ministry result chiefly from transfers of functions, or from the creation of new cabinet-level agencies whose senior staff must initially come from an existing pool.

Most administrative generalists acquire broad and diverse experience within one ministry, moving periodically from one section or bureau to another, and between the ministry proper and its regional or overseas offices. After initial appointment, such an official typically spends about 20 years moving

Organization of the executive

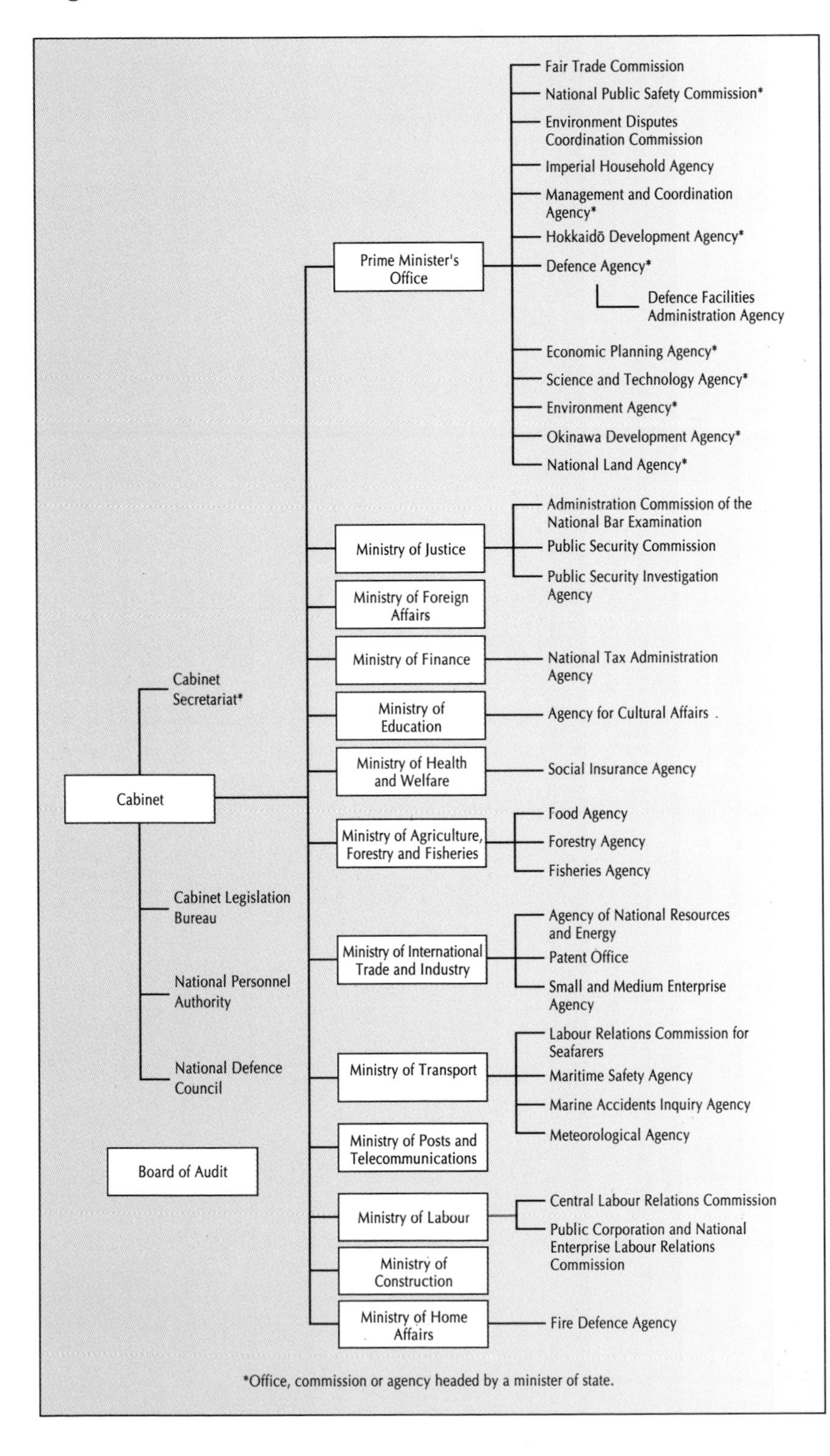

laterally as well as vertically within a ministry before becoming a section chief (*kachō*).

Lateral movement continues at the section-chief level for another five to ten years before any further promotion to a higher managerial level. Above this level, the pyramid narrows sharply through three, sometimes four, levels. Parts of some ministries have a division chief (*buchō*) level, which lies between section and bureau. Every ministry has several bureaux with deputy chiefs (*kyoku jichō*) and chiefs (*kyokuchō*), a secretariat, and one administrative vice-minister (*jimu jikan*), the highest career position.

Since the number of positions is smaller the higher one goes, only a minority can become section chiefs, and much smaller percentages become bureau chiefs or vice-ministers. Four main factors affect promotion. As already noted, one is the mode of initial entry into the service. In most ministries, managerial positions are given much more often to those who passed the élite examinations than to those recruited by evaluation of credentials. Educational background is also an important factor both in recruitment and promotion. Graduates of national universities, and especially Tōkyō University, form a disproportionately high percentage of those passing the examinations, receiving appointment, and winning promotion to senior positions.

Range and quality of civil service experience is also important. Successful performance in several section-chief positions, especially in the ministry secretariat and in more than one important bureau, improves prospects for promotion to division chief or deputy bureau chief around age 50, after about 28 years in the civil service. Promotion to bureau chief comes around age 53, if at all.

A fourth factor of pervasive importance at all levels is seniority (*nenkō*, 'the merit of years'), which correlates fairly closely with age. On the élite track, tradition requires that officials entering the service in the same year be promoted before those who entered later. When a few members of one 'year group' (*dōnenpai*) become bureau chiefs, most of the others retire. When one member becomes an administrative vice-minister, usually around age 55, all others of that year group in the same ministry who remain in office are expected to retire from the service. Many will have already retired when passed over for lower-level promotions.

Four catch-phrases about the Establishment

Kanson minpi. The 1946 constitution (Article 15) specifies that 'all public officials are servants of the whole community'– a concept alien to Japanese tradition. Before 1947, officials of all ranks took pride in being 'the emperor's officials' and the executive branch played a dominant rôle in governing the state. Critics of the system saw this as being a revival of Confucian attitudes and branded such behaviour *kanson minpi* ('officials revered, the people scorned'). Since 1947, bureaucratic arrogance has been tempered but hardly eliminated.

Tōdaibatsu. The pre-eminent position of graduates from Tōkyō University (Tōdai) in the upper echelons of the civil service is well documented. The phenomenon is known as *Tōdaibatsu* or Tōkyō University clique. As the following tables show, the overwhelming predominance has weakened somewhat in recent years, but Tōkyō University still remains a major source of recruits.

Hōka bannō. In 1882, senior Japanese leaders adopted the German notion that training in law is the best preparation for administrators as well as judges. This profoundly affected university curricula and the higher civil service examinations. By the early 1900s, law graduates were predominant in managerial levels of the higher civil service. Criticism of the 'omnipotence of law graduates' (*hōka bannō*) continues to the present. Since 1947, the percentage of senior positions held by law graduates has declined but remains significant, as does the overall position of Tōkyō University.

Amakudari. Higher officials who move from the civil service into high-level corporate positions are described as 'descending from heaven' (*amakudari*) – even when the new position carries higher pay or prestige. Although managerial experience in any ministry is a marketable asset, officials of ministries involved with the economy have the best prospects for high-level entry into a corporate bureaucracy.

RMS

SUCCESSFUL CANDIDATES IN THE ADMINISTRATIVE SECTION OF THE HIGHER CIVIL-SERVICE EXAMINATION, BY YEAR AND UNIVERSITY BACKGROUND

University	1894–1917 (%)		1918–1931 (%)		1932–1947 (%)	
Tōkyō	1,566	(76.3)	2,033	(57.8)	2,370	(59.3)
Kyōto	101	(4.9)	379	(10.8)	315	(7.9)
Other	385	(18.8)	1,107	(31.4)	1,309	(32.8)
Total	2,052	(100.0)	3,519	(100.0)	3,994	(100.0)

Source: Koh, *Japan's administrative elite*

RESULTS OF HIGHER CIVIL-SERVICE EXAMINATIONS, IN SELECTED YEARS

Year	A Number of applicants	B Number passing	C Number hired	B/A %	C/B %
1949[a]	21,438*[b]	2,355[c]	833		35.4
1952	24,392*	2,142	961	8.8	44.9
1955	23,053*	1,314	635	5.7	48.3
1958	20,228*	1,751	761	8.7	43.5
1961					
A[d]	9,152*	1,133	642	12.4	56.7
B	693*	397	183	57.3	46.1
1964					
A	12,420*	1,434	814	11.5	56.8
B	1,449*	373	146	25.7	39.1
1967					
A	21,567	1,364	667	6.3	48.9
B	3,659	148	68	4.0	45.9
1970					
A	14,550*	1,353	729	9.2	53.9
B	2,069*	143	91	6.9	63.6
1973					
A	30,129	1,410	639	4.7	45.3
B	4,855	134	58	2.8	43.3
1976					
A	44,518	1,136	567	1.3	49.9
B	5,417	100	55	1.0	55.0
1979					
A	51,896	1,265	615	2.4	48.6
B	4,814	90	54	1.9	60.0
1982					
A	36,856	1,383	618	3.8	44.7
B	3,646	95	53	2.6	58.8
1985	36,072	1,655	721	4.6	43.6
1988	28,833	1,814		6.3	

Note: The numbers in column A with asterisks refer to those applicants who actually took the examinations. During those years, between 10.5% and 22.6% of the applicants failed to show up for the exams. The mean no-show rate is 18.3%. The relevant statistics are not available for the remaining years.

[a] There were two examinations in 1949. The data reported here pertain to the one given in Nov. of that year.

[b] This number includes candidates for both grade-6 (higher-level) and grade-5 (intermediate-level) positions.

[c] Those who passed the grade-6 exam only.

[d] From 1960 to 1984 the higher civil-service examination consisted of two types: A (*kōshu*) and B (*otsushu*). In 1985, type B was abolished, and type A renamed type I.

Source: Koh, *Japan's administrative elite*.

Political power

Although subordinate to both cabinet and Diet, the higher civil service is in fact a major political force in making, as well as implementing, government policy. Only the Diet can enact laws, but most laws are drafted by career officials in the executive branch. The Diet may reject civil-service drafts, but those that it does enact usually show few major changes. Moreover, most laws delegate considerable discretion in prescribing regulations to the cabinet or to individual ministries.

Each cabinet minister (almost invariably a Diet member) is the legal head of his ministry, but he usually has little specialized knowledge and serves for only a year or two. He is in many ways dependent on the expertise of the ministry's career civil service led by the administrative vice-minister. The minister is therefore often less a leader than a spokesman for his ministry as a whole. On the other hand, when one party has a majority in the Diet, party officials actually have a major voice in each ministry's policy-making. Consultation and co-operation between the career civil service and the majority party's policy planners have become essential for both groups.

One of the oldest and strongest Japanese traditions is that respect for differences in rank should be balanced with collective or consensual decision-making. Superiors and subordinates do not have an equal voice, but decisions are normally based on wide consultation and consensus-building. In the modern civil service, this pattern is complicated both by the growing interaction between politicians and bureaucrats, and by jurisdictional rivalries between ministries and within each ministry.

In the career civil service, the chief vehicles for consensual decision-making are weekly or twice-weekly conferences and the circulation of documents called *ringisho*, usually drafted by relatively low-rank officials, such as assistant section chiefs, under general or specific guidance from superiors. Each *ringisho* is circulated for consideration and concurrence, with or without changes. Although this system of conferences and *ringisho* is very slow, diffuses responsibility, and discourages individual initiative, it builds support for a decision by giving officials of different ranks in different parts of a ministry a feeling of having been consulted.

Panoramic view of Nagata-chō, the centre of Japanese government, usually one of the more peaceful areas of downtown Tōkyō.

Left *The Japanese Diet building, severe and architecturally undistinguished.*

NATIONAL RÔLE

Co-operation, rather than hostility, between the career civil service and the business community has been a vital factor in Japan's economic success. This co-operation is facilitated by similarities between the government and corporate bureaucracies in recruitment, career patterns, and decision-making procedures. Another link is that higher officials who reach managerial positions often retire from the civil service in their mid 50s and move to high-level positions in public or private corporations.

Although corruption in the higher civil service appears to be minimal, such high-level movement from the civil service into corporations can create real or apparent conflicts of interest either before or after leaving the service. The law requires a two-year wait between retirement and employment by a profit-making enterprise 'closely connected' with the official's ministry, but the National Personnel Authority is fairly liberal in granting exemptions.

The higher civil service enjoys high prestige as a life career. It attracts able men and a growing number of women. Its career patterns and emphasis on consensus produce an impressive *esprit de corps*. Its political influence derives from its high level of competence and efficiency, within limits imposed by the national preference for consensual decision-making. These strengths appear to outweigh its faults, which include arrogance, legalism, jurisdictional rivalries, and real or apparent conflicts of interest. RMS

APPROVALS OF RE-EMPLOYMENT OF RETIRED OFFICIALS IN THE PRIVATE SECTOR, BY YEAR AND MINISTRY

	Ministry						
Year	Finance	MITI	Const.	Agric.	Trans.	Other	Total
1965	30	28	14	10	19	27	128
1968	34	18	14	17	13	40	136
1971	44	17	10	18	22	56	167
1974	59	18	21	12	15	64	189
1977	49	18	21	16	17	77	198
1980	46	25	27	17	25	88	228
1983	51	32	27	32	23	102	267
1986	54	25	29	25	20	99	252

Source: Koh, *Japan's administrative elite*

SUCCESSFUL CANDIDATES IN HIGHER CIVIL-SERVICE EXAMINATIONS, BY UNIVERSITY BACKGROUND

	Tōkyō University (%)		Kyōto University (%)		Other[a] (%)	
1936	138	(71.1)	4	(2.1)	52	(26.8)
1941–43	547	(46.7)	112	(9.6)	512	(43.7)
1947[b]	154	(81.5)	10	(5.3)	25	(13.2)
1966[c]	318	(21.1)	142	(9.4)	1,047	(69.5)
1967	350	(25.7)	174	(12.7)	840	(61.6)
1970	335	(24.8)	129	(9.5)	889	(65.7)
1971	453	(32.3)	174	(12.4)	774	(55.3)
1972[d]	266	(17.9)	146	(9.8)	1,078	(72.3)
1973	499	(35.4)	204	(14.5)	707	(50.1)
1974	435	(29.1)	191	(12.8)	870	(58.1)
1975	459	(35.2)	172	(13.2)	674	(51.6)
1976	461	(37.3)	193	(15.6)	582	(47.1)
1977	488	(38.0)	211	(16.4)	585	(45.6)
1978	535	(38.2)	211	(15.1)	655	(46.7)
1979	541	(39.9)	206	(15.2)	608	(44.9)
1980	519	(38.6)	216	(16.1)	609	(45.3)
1981	545	(37.6)	210	(14.5)	696	(47.9)
1982	563	(38.1)	191	(12.9)	724	(49.0)
1983	547	(34.9)	203	(12.9)	818	(52.2)
1984	527	(31.8)	216	(13.0)	915	(55.2)
1985	541	(32.7)	219	(13.2)	895	(54.1)
1986	548	(31.9)	231	(13.4)	939	(54.7)
1987	525	(30.9)	220	(13.0)	951	(56.1)
1988	583	(32.1)	207	(11.4)	1,024	(56.5)

[a] This category includes not only those who attended the other colleges and universities but also those without college education.
[b] The data presented in this row pertain only to the examination given in Dec. 1947. A similar examination was given in Apr. of the same year, producing a total of 173 successes.
[c] The data for 1966–71 pertain to type A only.
[d] The data for 1972–84 represent the combined totals of both types A and B. The type-B exam was abolished in 1985.
Source: Koh, *Japan's administrative elite*

The judiciary

Right *A vision of justice in former times. The Lord of Hell sits in judgement; 13th-century painting in the Chinese style.*

A seminal element in Japan's post-war constitutional revolution was the remaking of the judiciary into a separate branch of government, administratively beholden only to the Supreme Court, equal in status to the Diet and the cabinet, empowered to render final judgement on all questions of constitutionality and legality, and pre-eminently responsible for upholding in concrete cases the human rights of individuals when under challenge. This US-influenced revolution marks the only basic change in the modern system of laws and courts since Japan decided to adopt continental European legal traditions over a century ago.

Today, the constitutional powers of judges in Japan are somewhat like those of their US counterparts; but when deciding cases they must comply with great magisterial 'codes', a hallmark of Europe's civil law tradition, the world's most extensively used framework for modern law. The 'Six Codes' (*roppō*) provide the basic law governing public, private, criminal and commercial matters. All statutes, local ordinances, and administrative rules and actions must be consistent with the Constitution of Japan, the Civil Code, the Code of Civil Procedure, the Criminal Code, the Code of Criminal Procedure, and the Commercial Code. Scholarly treatment of law, the codes and the state are also on European lines. In addition, judges are guided by prior judicial decisions, though even Supreme Court precedents are binding on other courts only in the case at hand (as when a retrial is ordered).

Judges have developed a proud tradition of independence in deciding individual cases according to law. The landmark is the 1891 Ōtsu Case, when in defiance of government and popular demands that an attempted assassination of a Russian prince be punished with the death penalty, the highest tribunal followed the law and imposed instead a prison sentence. Under the 1889 Meiji Constitution, judges had authority over ordinary private law disputes and criminal cases, but the courts were within the emperor's executive branch as part of the Justice Ministry. Judicial authority to deal with allegations of official violation of a subject's limited rights was restricted to one administrative court. Since 1947, no administrative court, court-martial, or other special tribunal has been allowed by the constitution; the ordinary courts have comprehensive jurisdiction over all types of legal disputes. Under the present constitution, the judiciary has become the most widely trusted governmental institution. Its rôles in constitutional democracy are crucial and complex; its record in confirming human rights mixed, under a dynamic fusion of Japanese, European and US legal elements.

Court organization and jurisdiction

At the apex is the Supreme Court (*saikō saibansho*) with 15 justices, which renders final judgement on appeals from lower courts, makes court rules and appointments, administers all the nation's courts, and trains their personnel. Usually, it divides into three five-member Petty Benches, which decide all but the few cases transferred to the Grand Bench of all justices because they involve constitutional questions or a possible change in established legal doctrine. The Supreme Court normally relies exclusively on appellate briefs and lower court records, ably assisted by judicial research officials drawn from

Above *Law courts in session.*

the ranks of experienced lower court judges. Nine constitutes a Grand Bench quorum; decisions are by majority, and each justice not fully satisfied with the majority opinion must write either a dissenting or concurring opinion. The pre-war Court issued only one view.

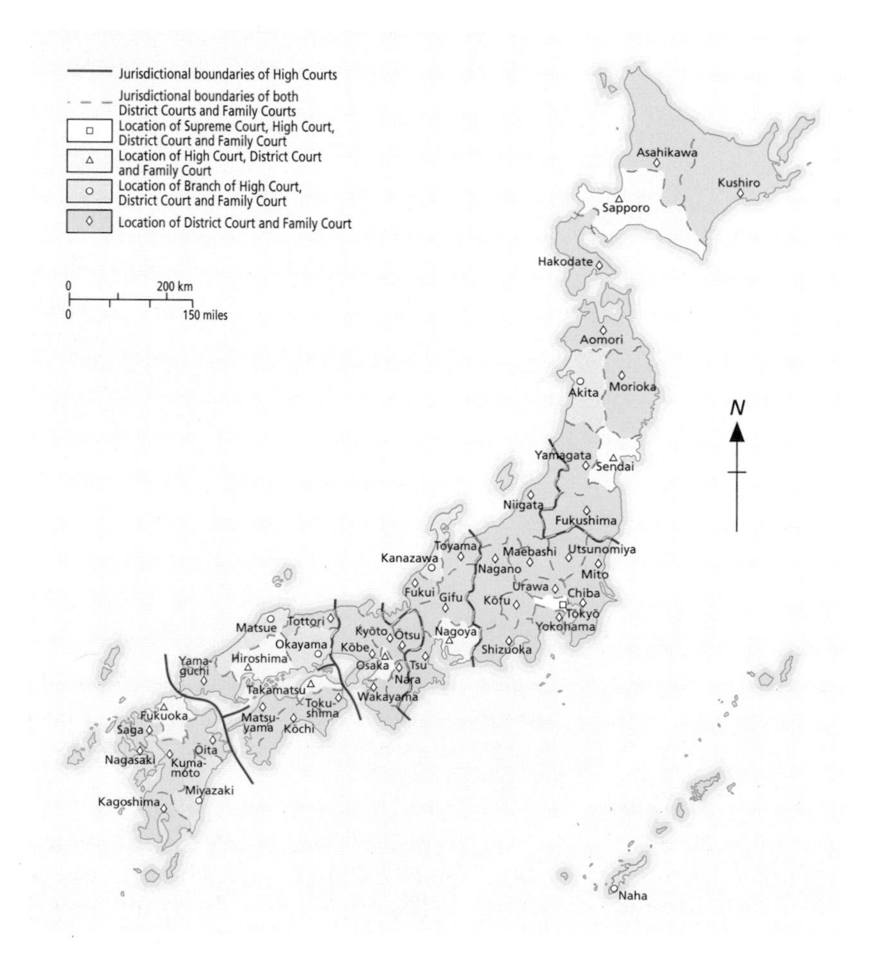

Location of courts throughout Japan.

Below the Supreme Court are eight high courts (*kōtō saibansho*), located in Tōkyō, Ōsaka, Nagoya, Hiroshima, Fukuoka, Sendai, Sapporo and Takamatsu, with six branches elsewhere. Eight presidents oversee about 280 high court judges. In a high court or district court, judges serve in either the criminal division or the civil division. Three-judge panels decide all high court cases and certain major disputes in district courts. High courts primarily hear appeals, but have original jurisdiction over election disputes and a few other matters.

At the base of the judicial hierarchy are: 50 district courts sited in the principal city of each large governmental territory with 201 branches in other cities and towns; over 300 family courts; and 452 summary courts. The latter handle minor crimes and civil disputes. In all, 910 judges and 460 assistant judges occupy the district court bench. Trials are public; there is no jury system; most district court disputes and all family court and summary court cases are decided with a single judge presiding. Family courts seek non-litigious settlement of domestic disputes and have jurisdiction over all crimes of minors (under 20) and of adults adversely affecting juveniles. Usually, youth crime is treated privately with educational remedies, dismissal of the case, or probation. Only in a rare case and where the juvenile is over 16 is a minor's case referred to a criminal court.

Family court judges (some concurrently serving as district court judges) are assisted by lay people and by 1,500 family court probation officers who prepare records and advise. A major feature of Japan's legal structure is the use in many official decision-making contexts of respected lay people with knowledge and broad experience; for example, a psychiatrist, teacher or social worker in a family court. Such

Organizational chart of the Supreme Court

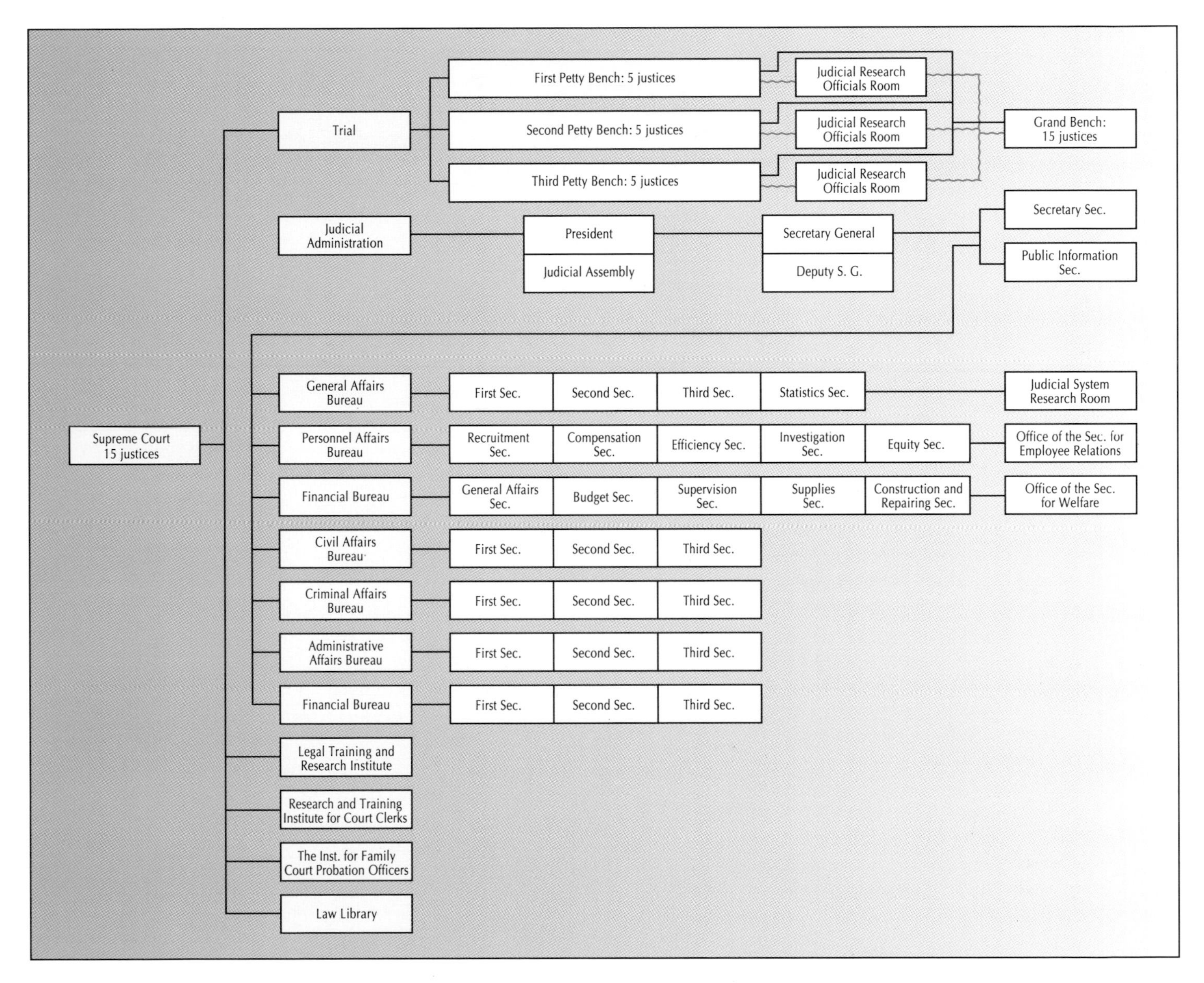

volunteers help judges and parties to devise mutually acceptable settlements without wasteful trials or neglect of rights. Moreover, court-established conciliation committees with a judge and two lay conciliation commissioners often devise voluntary compromise plans. Rooted in Tokugawa compulsory conciliation, this system continued in pre-democratic modern Japan and has flowered in the past 40 years under a democratic Conciliation Law.

Under the final authority of the justices, the General Secretariat of the Supreme Court is the most important institution servicing the court system and managing personnel matters. It oversees the operation of the Training and Research Institute for Court Clerks, the Institute for Family Court Probation Officers, and the Legal Training and Research Institute (LTRI), which trains virtually all of Japan's judges, prosecutors and attorneys.

THE RECRUITMENT AND APPOINTMENT OF JUDGES

The rigorous selection process assures Japan an exceptionally able body of jurists, but produces too few to meet needs. Any adult of any educational background may take the National Law Examination an unlimited number of times. Of over 20,000 aspirants each year roughly 500 pass (this will rise to 700 in 1993). Almost all successful examinees spend years in special cramming schools; their average age reached 30 in 1991. Legal 'apprentices' receive two years of training with the LTRI. Besides lectures and practice in preparation of briefs, all spend four months each as interns in a criminal court, a civil court, a prosecutor's office and a law office. Most become attorneys, over 50 become judges, and about 30 choose a prosecutor's career. Currently, around 14,000 lawyers serve 125 million citizens. Among major reforms discussed in the 1990s were a radical increase in the number passing the law examination and a limit on the number of times it may be taken.

Well over half of Japan's attorneys practise in Tōkyō or Ōsaka, where most large corporations are based. Medium-sized and small businesses and the general citizenry are underserviced, consulting a lawyer never or only after serious problems arise. Notaries Public (*kōshōnin*) confirm contracts in law. To some degree, this lack is compensated for by family courts, conciliation procedures, unpaid human-rights commissioners, local administrative counsellors, and other avenues of rights protection and dispute resolution. Moreover, Japan's undergraduate law programmes add substantially to national legal expertise by educating many thousands for law-related careers in government and business without need for LTRI credentials. Nevertheless, the shortage of attorneys, judges, prosecutors, and legal aid seems acute.

Besides LTRI training, a full judge has had ten years of experience as assistant judge, prosecutor or attorney; a law professor qualifies after five years of teaching. Judges serve for renewable ten-year terms and retire at 65. Justices and summary court judges must retire at 70. In 1990, judges numbered 1,400, assistant judges 610, and summary court judges 810. Able lay people, retired judges, and legal professionals with three years of experience serve as summary court judges.

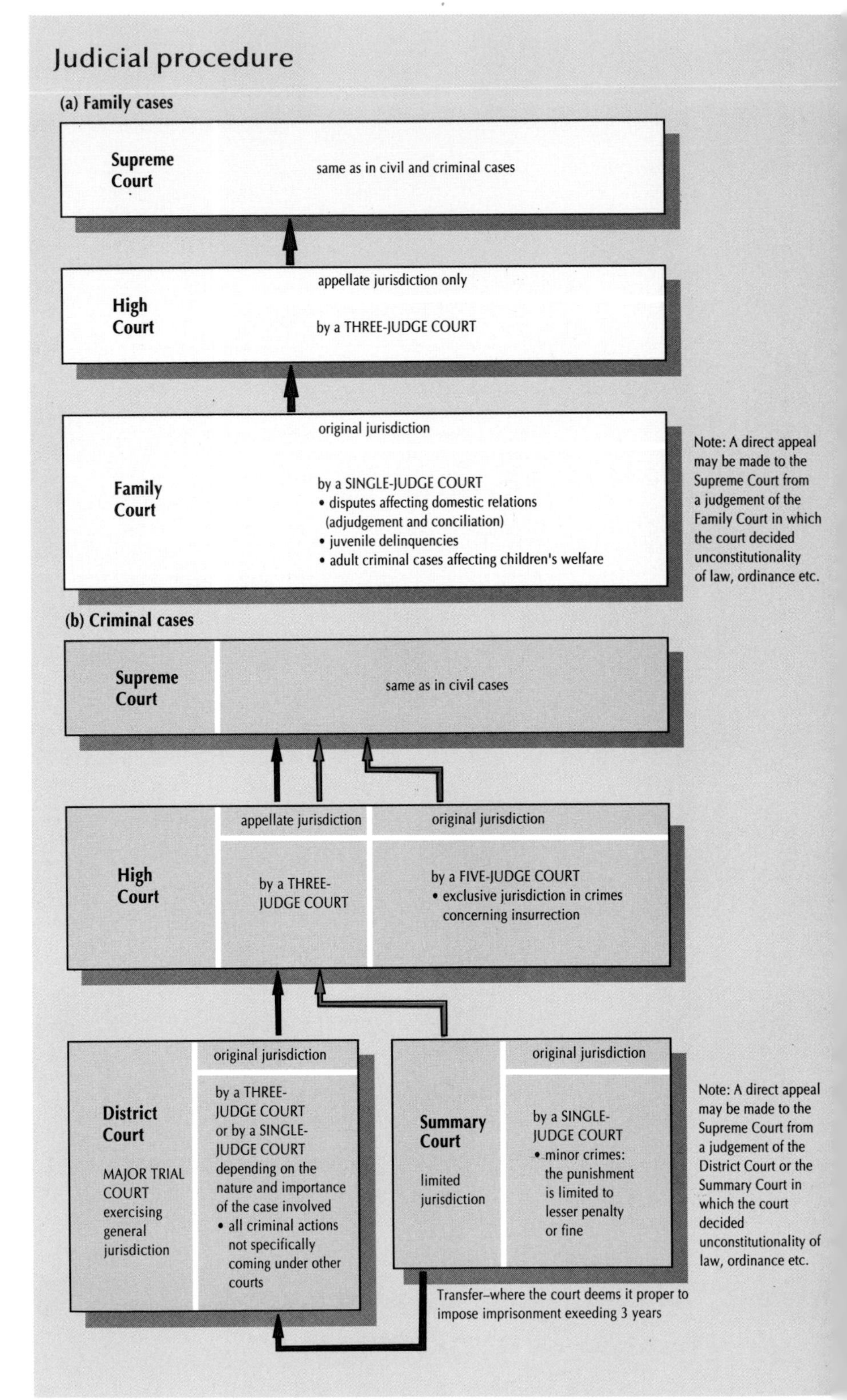

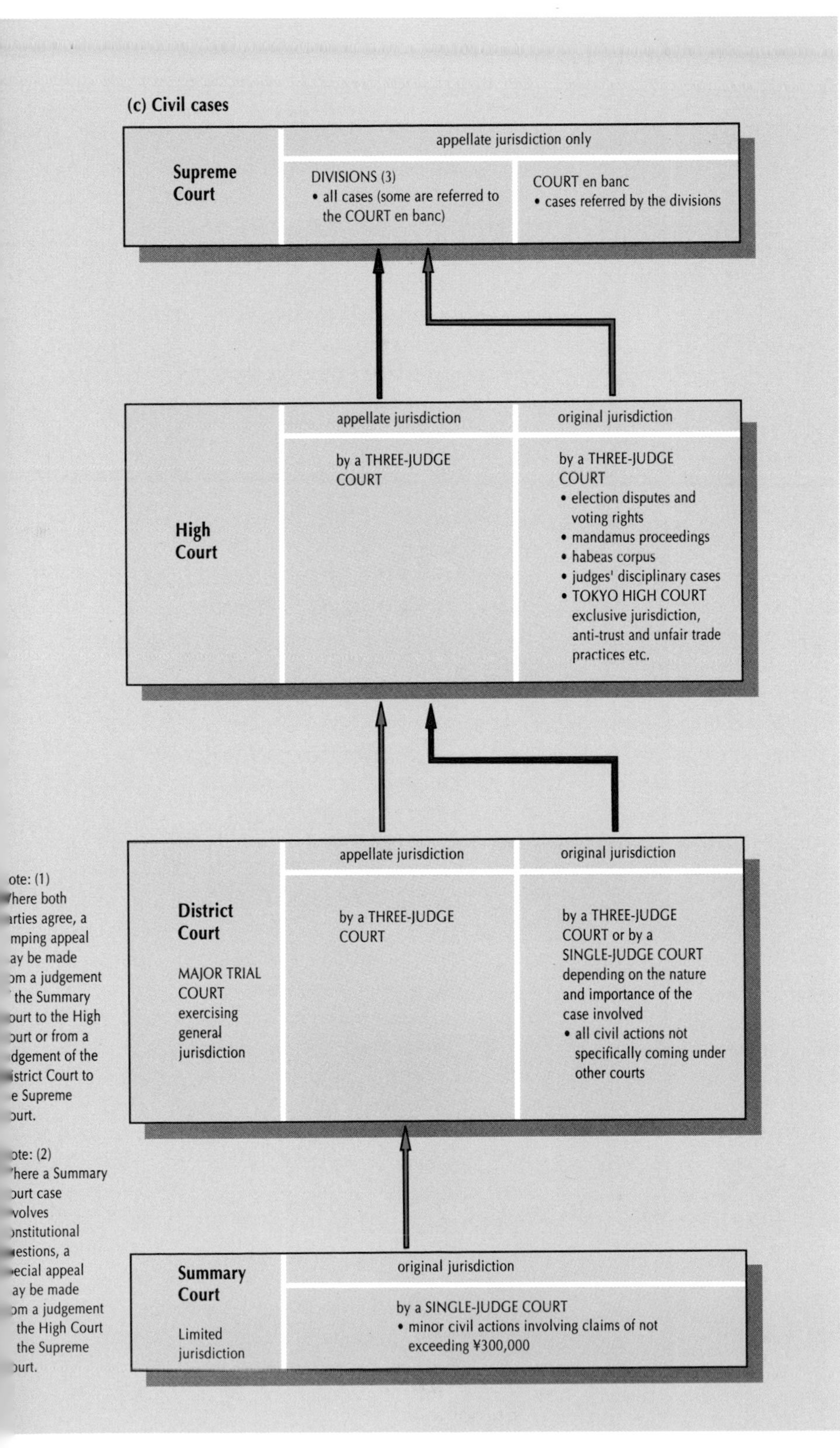

To make court rules, the annual budget, and personnel assignments to specific courts, the Supreme Court constitutes itself the 'Judicial Conference'. Although in formal law the cabinet appoints many judges, in fact almost all recommendations by the Chief Justice and Secretary General are approved with little or no discussion among incumbent justices or cabinet members. By law, justices must be appointed by the cabinet from among distinguished judges, attorneys, prosecutors, scholars and (rarely) persons of other background – for example, diplomats. In practice, the chief justice, prime minister and cabinet usually confirm choices autonomously made within the organizational centres of the various law professions. Thus, judge-members of the Supreme Court are selected by the secretary general and chief justice; prosecutor-members by the office of the procurator general; and attorney-members by bar associations, usually of Tōkyō or Ōsaka, taking turns. The under-represented legal scholars have no unified representative organ(s), but many learned societies. To avoid chaos in selecting the one or two scholar-justices, by custom an eminent professor is approached after his compulsory retirement at 60 from Tōkyō University's Faculty of Law. The current scholar-justice, Sonobe Itsuo, had prior experience at Kyōto University and in the courts. Most other justices are appointed in their mid or late 60s to allow a maximum number to enjoy this high honour before retiring at 70.

The cabinet formally legitimizes choices made by others. No political tests are imposed from beyond the judiciary, but the exceptionally long régime of the Liberal Democratic Party *cum* bureaucracy makes unlikely the appointment to the best judicial positions of those favouring rigorous human rights protection or an extreme rightist view. Very rarely, a politically aggressive prime minister (such as Nakasone Yasuhiro) may politically intrude on a judicial personnel decision.

The political rôles of the judiciary

The judiciary normally maintains an establishmentarian demeanour of high dignity above the hurly-burly, and keeps its internal politics to itself. Only in the late 1960s and 1970s did politicized courts come

Former Prime Minister Tanaka leaving the Tōkyō District Court, where for the second time he denied his involvement in the Lockheed pay-off scandal, 22 December 1981.

to centre stage. On ideological grounds, impeachments of judges (including Chief Justice Ishida Kazuto) by the Diet were demanded at both ends of the political spectrum, judicial appointments were denied, and pressures exerted on younger judges not to associate with the allegedly left-leaning Young Lawyers Association (Seihōkyō). However, settlement of legal issues in concrete cases, not general policy debate, is the main judicial mode of political participation. For example, in 1991 the Sendai High Court held local legislative funding of Shintō shrines to the war dead to be unconstitutional.

The judiciary is the nation's core institution for annually settling millions of disputes in a civilized, authoritative manner. In their work, judges are bound in law and largely in practice only by their consciences, the constitution and the codes. The independent courts generally provide consistency, integrity, stability, predictability, and attention to justice and principle to counterbalance, in the public perception of the constitutional system, the recurring disrepute of party politics and the Diet, the changeability of cabinets under amorphous group leadership, the considerable discretion of functionaries, and the hierarchy and favouritism of social dynamics.

On only six occasions has the Supreme Court held law unconstitutional, for allowing: seizure of third-party evidence in a smuggling case (1962); more severe punishment of patricide than ordinary murder (1973); restraints on a pharmacy opening near an existing pharmacy (1975); denial of the right to division of jointly owned forest land (1987); and the imbalanced apportionment of votes in election districts (1976, 1985). However, judicial decisions have also vindicated victims of industrial pollution, improper reliance on crime confessions, excessive trial delays, economic discrimination against women employees, and interference with aspects of freedom of expression. On the other hand, it has allowed laws and practices of questionable constitutionality to stand; for example, Customs Bureau censorship of obscenity, denial of reasonable access to an attorney in criminal justice, and the ban on canvassing during elections.

The Supreme Court is not a constitutional court responsible for judging the constitutionality of a law during or after a legislative process, as in some countries; rather, a court can pass judgement on constitutional validity only in the context of settling a concrete dispute brought before it according to legally prescribed procedures. In this sense, Japan's courts, like most, are inherently passive unless case-activated. The laws are generally sensitive to individual rights and freedoms; but lower courts and appellate courts defer rather often to the government's broad legislative and administrative discretion in human rights cases.

The Cabinet Legislative Bureau serves as an important screening mechanism by meticulously reviewing all bills before their formal Diet consideration lest their wording be constitutionally suspect and open to challenge in court. Another quasi-judicial agency in the court's system must be mentioned – the prosecutor. A very large proportion of Japan's relatively few criminal cases are disposed of by prosecutors without trial. Since prosecutors tend towards leniency, few indictments are brought. Although the courts almost always convict those accused, very few are sent to prison by world standards.

The courts serve as society's ultimate legitimizing authority, as a restraining presence in the background during national and local law-making and policy deliberations, and as the provider of standards and court case examples to guide behaviour under law. At its best, the judiciary sets high standards of ability, official integrity, and fairness in applying democratic law in rigorous compliance with the constitution. LWB

Parties and party politics

Since the 1870s Japan has produced a rich culture of political parties, and indeed well over 200 have existed at one time or another. Whereas under the Meiji Constitution of 1889, which strictly limited the degree of popular representation, parties needed to struggle to assert political influence, the 1946 Constitution gave them an assured rôle at the centre of the political system.

The cultural tradition of Japan's political parties is thus long and varied, both in ideological and organizational terms. There have been narrow sectarian parties of the far left and far right, broad catch-all parties with loose organization and personalized rather than ideological appeal, ephemeral parties based on temporary alliances of politicians jockeying for advantage, ideological but loosely organized parties based on labour unions and at least one party founded by a religious sect. There was also a single government-controlled party between 1940 and 1945, when all other parties were banned.

Not all types of party have been of equal importance, however, and the kind of party which has tended to predominate has been a conservative alliance of locally oriented politicians, lacking a strong base in party membership or ideological appeal, but vitally concerned with the acquisition and maintenance of power. Often there has been little to distinguish parties from factions, and some factions have actually had a longer history than the parties of which they – perhaps temporarily – form a part. Even so, where coherent party organization is needed to stay in power, it is often forthcoming, as in the case of the Seiyūkai under Hara Kei after the First World War and the Liberal Democratic Party (LDP) from the 1960s. Indeed, it can be argued that the LDP has become a different kind of political entity from all other Japanese political parties, past or present, embedded as it is quasi-permanently within the ruling structure of the state.

In seeking to understand the way Japanese parties operate, it is important to take account of the constitutional, and in particular the electoral, systems, as well as the cultural milieu enveloping party political practice.

The situation before 1945

From the 1870s political groupings resembling parties began to be formed, but often at local level only, since the Diet was not opened until 1890. The Aikokukōtō of Itagaki Taisuke, founded in 1874, is usually regarded as Japan's first political party, though it only lasted a few months. Between 1874 and 1900 the 'popular parties' were formed essentially in opposition to oligarchic government and derived many of their ideas from Western doctrines of popular participation in politics. One strand of party development was that led by Itagaki, who in 1881 formed the Jiyūtō, and another that of Ōkuma Shigenobu, founder in 1882 of the Rikken Kaishintō. These two parties existed under various names until 1898 when they briefly united. Less important than any major ideological differences was the fact that the former had backing from landlords and the latter attracted rather more support among urban commercial interests. Since in 1890 the suffrage was narrowly confined by a property franchise, the parties in general only represented the well off.

In 1900 the Seiyūkai party was founded by Itō Hirobumi with the express purpose of breaking the stalemate between the oligarchy and the parties in the Diet which had plagued the business of government throughout the 1890s. He succeeded in combining members of the oligarchy and party politicians together in the same organization, thus making compromise possible. The Seiyūkai remained intact until 1937, and greatly profited from the grass-roots organizational genius of Hara Kei, who during the mid Taishō period turned it into a party capable of challenging for a major share in national power. Opposing it was a rival lineage made up of a number of parties under the general name of Minseitō. From time to time there were also defections from one side to the other, and many smaller groups made a temporary appearance. During the 1920s and 1930s there was something approaching alternation in office between the Seiyūkai and the Minseitō lineages, but by the early 1930s the brief period of party ascendency known as 'Taishō democracy' had given way to 'transcendental' cabinets and domination of politics by the military. Among many other factors, parties in general had become discredited by their perceived corruption and intimate links with big business groups. A strand of

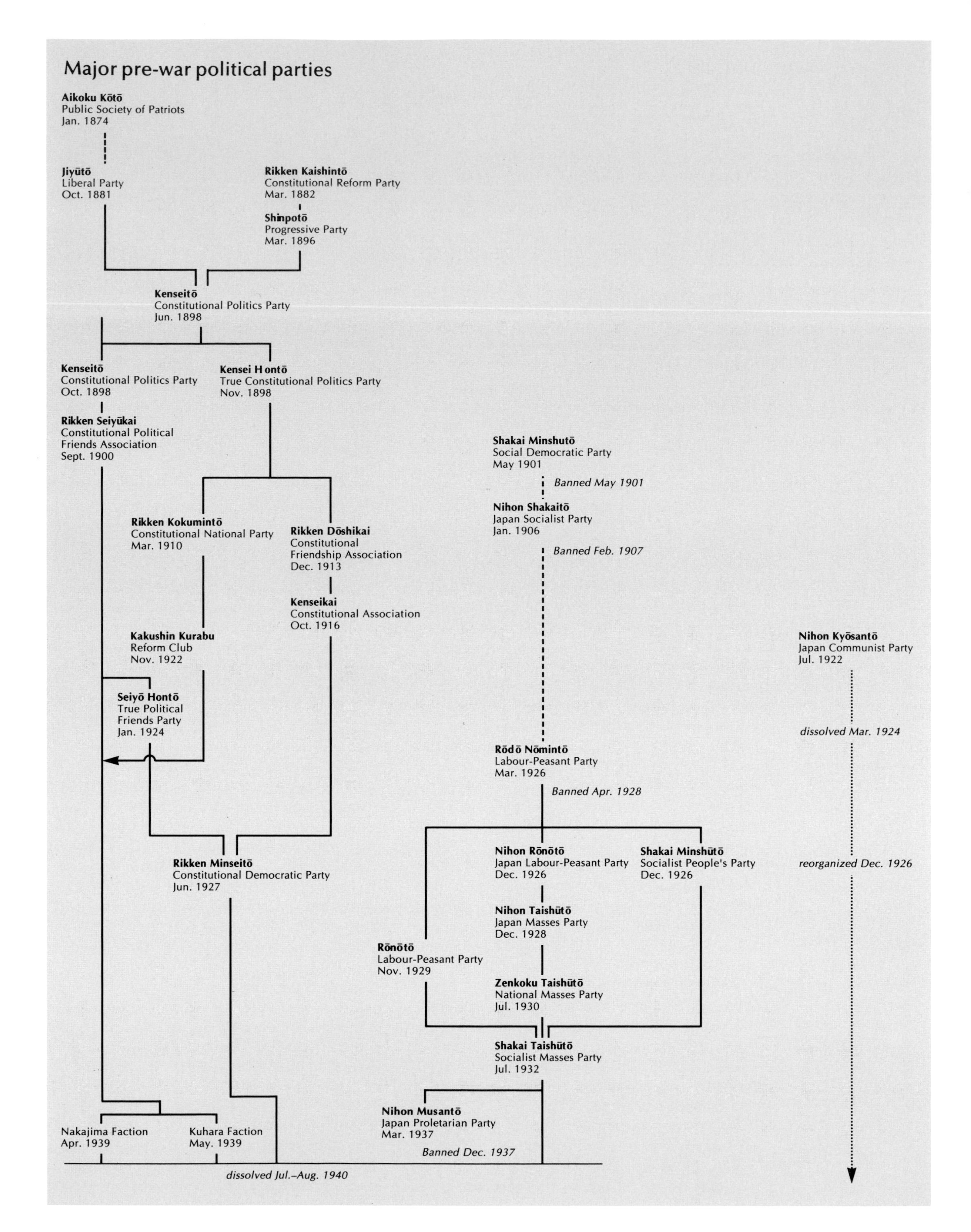
Major pre-war political parties
Aikoku Kōtō
Public Society of Patriots
Jan. 1874
Jiyūtō
Liberal Party
Oct. 1881
Rikken Kaishintō
Constitutional Reform Party
Mar. 1882
Shinpotō
Progressive Party
Mar. 1896
Kenseitō
Constitutional Politics Party
Jun. 1898
Kenseitō
Constitutional Politics Party
Oct. 1898
Kensei Hontō
True Constitutional Politics Party
Nov. 1898
Rikken Seiyūkai
Constitutional Political
Friends Association
Sept. 1900
Shakai Minshutō
Social Democratic Party
May 1901
Banned May 1901
Nihon Shakaitō
Japan Socialist Party
Jan. 1906
Banned Feb. 1907
Rikken Kokumintō
Constitutional National Party
Mar. 1910
Rikken Dōshikai
Constitutional
Friendship Association
Dec. 1913
Kenseikai
Constitutional Association
Oct. 1916
Kakushin Kurabu
Reform Club
Nov. 1922
Nihon Kyōsantō
Japan Communist Party
Jul. 1922
Seiyō Hontō
True Political
Friends Party
Jan. 1924
dissolved Mar. 1924
Rōdō Nōmintō
Labour-Peasant Party
Mar. 1926
Banned Apr. 1928
Rikken Minseitō
Constitutional Democratic Party
Jun. 1927
Nihon Rōnōtō
Japan Labour-Peasant Party
Dec. 1926
Shakai Minshūtō
Socialist People's Party
Dec. 1926
reorganized Dec. 1926
Nihon Taishūtō
Japan Masses Party
Dec. 1928
Rōnōtō
Labour-Peasant Party
Nov. 1929
Zenkoku Taishūtō
National Masses Party
Jul. 1930
Shakai Taishūtō
Socialist Masses Party
Jul. 1932
Nihon Musantō
Japan Proletarian Party
Mar. 1937
Nakajima Faction
Apr. 1939
Kuhara Faction
May. 1939
Banned Dec. 1937
dissolved Jul.–Aug. 1940

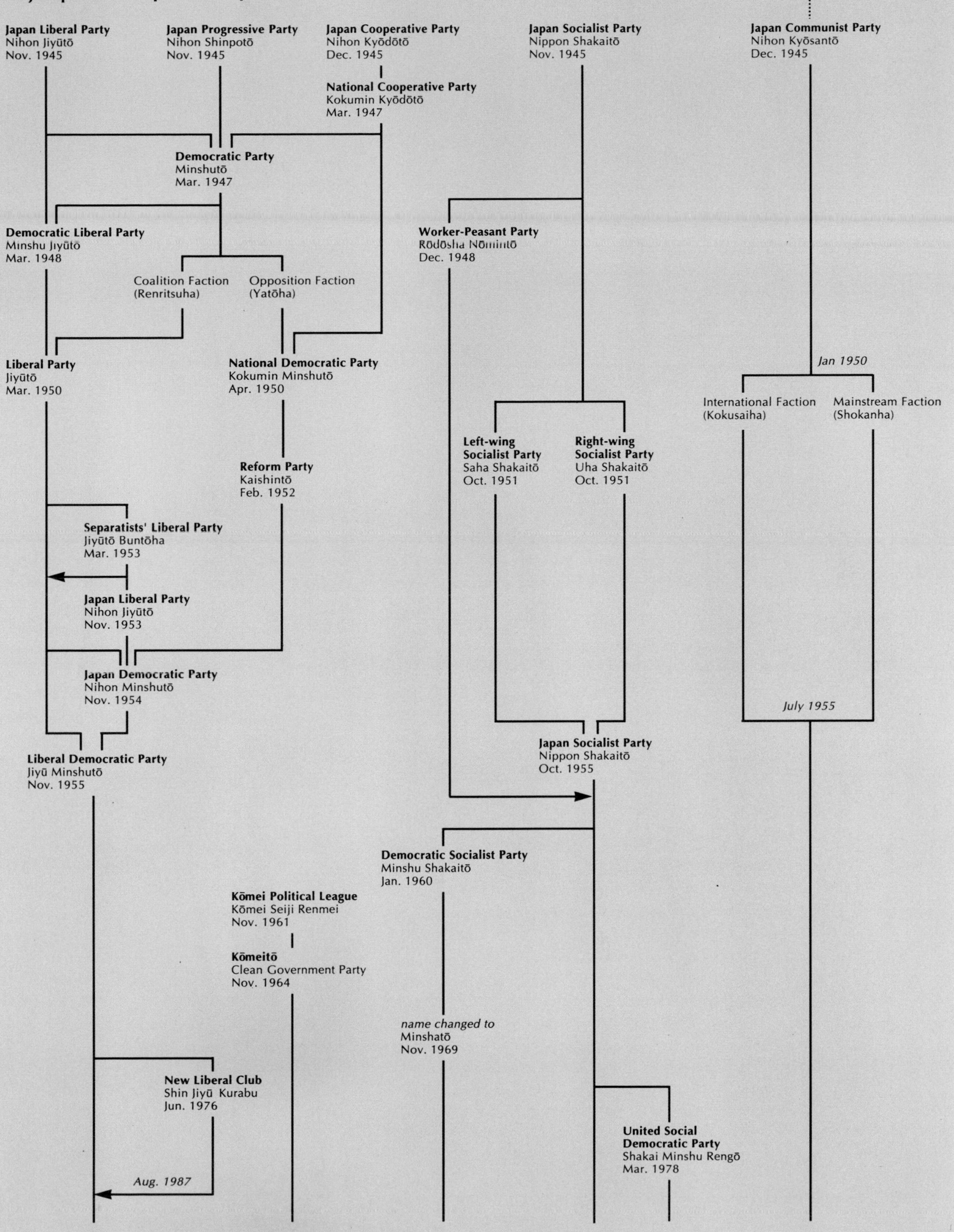

Major post-war political parties
Japan Liberal Party
Nihon Jiyūtō
Nov. 1945
Japan Progressive Party
Nihon Shinpotō
Nov. 1945
Japan Cooperative Party
Nihon Kyōdōtō
Dec. 1945
Japan Socialist Party
Nippon Shakaitō
Nov. 1945
Japan Communist Party
Nihon Kyōsantō
Dec. 1945
National Cooperative Party
Kokumin Kyōdōtō
Mar. 1947
Democratic Party
Minshutō
Mar. 1947
Democratic Liberal Party
Minshu Jiyūtō
Mar. 1948
Worker-Peasant Party
Rōdōsha Nōmintō
Dec. 1948
Coalition Faction
(Renritsuha)
Opposition Faction
(Yatōha)
Liberal Party
Jiyūtō
Mar. 1950
National Democratic Party
Kokumin Minshutō
Apr. 1950
Jan 1950
International Faction
(Kokusaiha)
Mainstream Faction
(Shokanha)
Left-wing
Socialist Party
Saha Shakaitō
Oct. 1951
Right-wing
Socialist Party
Uha Shakaitō
Oct. 1951
Reform Party
Kaishintō
Feb. 1952
Separatists' Liberal Party
Jiyūtō Buntōha
Mar. 1953
Japan Liberal Party
Nihon Jiyūtō
Nov. 1953
Japan Democratic Party
Nihon Minshutō
Nov. 1954
July 1955
Japan Socialist Party
Nippon Shakaitō
Oct. 1955
Liberal Democratic Party
Jiyū Minshutō
Nov. 1955
Democratic Socialist Party
Minshu Shakaitō
Jan. 1960
Kōmei Political League
Kōmei Seiji Renmei
Nov. 1961
Kōmeitō
Clean Government Party
Nov. 1964
name changed to
Minshatō
Nov. 1969
New Liberal Club
Shin Jiyū Kurabu
Jun. 1976
United Social
Democratic Party
Shakai Minshu Rengō
Mar. 1978
Aug. 1987

socialist parties also made its appearance in elections after 1925, culminating in the Shakai Taishūtō formed in 1932. A Japan Communist Party existed – mostly underground – from 1922. There were also some small parties on the extreme right.

THE YEARS 1945–60

After being banned during the war, parties once again proliferated after the defeat. The democratic reforms of the Allied Occupation increased the political stakes for parties and intensified competition. The period 1945–55 was a formative one in which changes were absorbed, and parties of all shades emerged and merged in kaleidoscopic fashion. On the conservative side the two main parties initially were the Nihon Jiyūtō and the Shinpotō. Several splits and amalgamations took place before virtually all conservative groups merged into the Jiyū Minshutō (LDP) in November 1955.

The political left emerged from the war far stronger and freer than it had been before. Late in 1945 the Nihon Shakaitō (usually known as the Japan Socialist Party, or JSP, in English) was formed, and became the largest single party in the House of Representatives following the 1947 general elections. Its subsequent participation, together with the Minshutō and Kokumin Kyōdōtō (both parties of the centre-right) in a coalition government, first under its own leader Katayama Tetsu, and later under the leader of the Minshutō, was hardly a success and resulted in subsequent electoral retribution. In October 1951 the JSP split over the peace settlement into right-wing and left-wing Socialist parties, which merged once again in October 1955, just a month before the formation of the LDP. The Nihon Kyōsantō (Japan Communist Party or JCP) emerged legally for the first time in 1945 and achieved some success with the electorate, before being reduced to impotence in 1950 by the Occupation's 'red purge' and its own Moscow-dictated shift to a militant line.

Throughout the 1950s the JSP was gaining ground electorally, so that the formation of what looked like a two-party system in 1955 brought expectations of alternating politics between two major parties, as in Britain. It soon became apparent, however, that Japan had in fact a 'one-and-a-half party system', with the Socialists quite unable to sustain their earlier electoral advances. Nor indeed were they long able to maintain the unity forged in 1955. During the political struggles over renegotiation of the US–Japan Security Treaty in 1959–60, a right-of-centre section of the JSP defected, to form the Minshatō (Democratic Socialist Party, or DSP). Meanwhile the LDP, faction-ridden but able to utilize its grip on government to consolidate its political position, gradually entrenched itself as the party of power.

1960 TO THE PRESENT

The period from 1960 until about 1975 saw two principal interrelated developments. First, both the the LDP and the JSP began losing support in successive elections. This trend was most marked in metropolitan electorates; the countryside retained the 'one-and-a-half party' pattern. Second, from 1960 onwards parties in opposition fragmented and proliferated. The DSP made modest electoral gains. A new party called the Kōmeitō (also known as the 'Clean Government Party' or CGP in English), created by the Nichiren Buddhist sect Sōka Gakkai was formed in 1964, and made spectacular electoral gains in the elections of the late 1960s and early 1970s. The JCP, apparently moribund, started carving out new areas of support in the early 1970s. The Kōmeitō and JCP were winning precisely those votes which the LDP and JSP were losing in Japan's overcrowded and polluted cities. By the mid 1970s the LDP was still much the biggest single party but the combined vote of the opposition came close to challenging its supremacy.

From the mid 1970s, however, things began to move in a rather different direction. Even though the LDP suffered its first minor defection with the formation of the Shin Jiyū Kurabu (New Liberal Club or NLC) in 1976, support for the ruling party was in fact again on the rise. Despite severe factional strife throughout the 1970s, the LDP won the 1980 double elections shortly after the death of Prime Minister Ōhira. During the 1980s the electorate behaved more unpredictably than before, and after a bad result in 1983, the LDP again did well under Nakasone in the general elections of 1986. Up to 1986 the JSP showed little sign of revival but the smaller parties, which had registered successes during the era of high economic growth, also failed to sustain their advance.

The House of Representatives

In both houses, senior members sit at the back, junior members in front. Membership of standing committees is decided according to the relative strength of each party. There are 252 seats in the House of Councillors and 512 in the House of Representatives.

In the photograph below, opposition members show their displeasure at the Recruit scandal by boycotting the budget committee meetings in the House of Representatives.

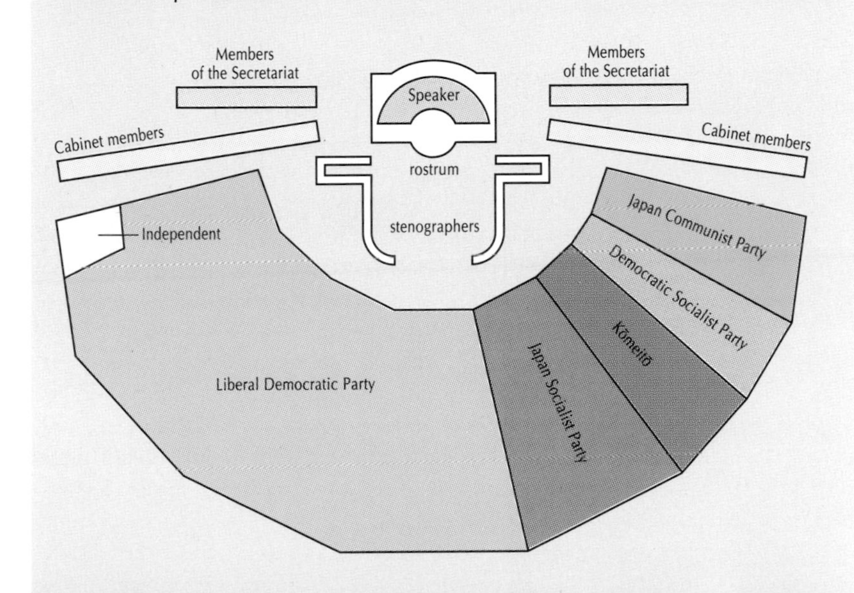

A new phase emerged after the election of Doi Takako as leader of the JSP in 1986 – the first woman ever to head a party in Japan's history. Her party gradually began to gain support, particularly from women. When the LDP became embroiled in the Recruit scandal during 1988–89, coinciding with the imposition of a new unpopular consumption tax and the liberalization of markets for certain agricultural products, support quickly surged in the direction of the JSP. At the House of Councillors elections of July 1989 the JSP, in alliance with candidates sponsored by the recently formed Rengō federation of labour, actually won more votes than the LDP, which lost its upper house majority for the first time since its formation. By the time of the House of Representatives elections the following February, the LDP, now led by the 'clean' prime minister Kaifu Toshiki, won back much of the ground it had lost the previous year, though the JSP also did much better than in any lower house election since 1967, largely at the expense of the smaller parties. In 1990 and 1991 a series of policy failures cost the JSP further support, Doi resigned, and the LDP was left once again in a strong position.

Japan since the 1950s has often been designated a 'predominant party system'. A single party has been continously in power (though since 1989 its legislative power is somewhat inhibited by its loss of control over the House of Councillors). Though it would of course be an exaggeration to compare its position with that of the former Communist Party of the Soviet Union, there is some similarity in the sense that the LDP is well entrenched in the organs of government, which respond to its will without realistic expectation that their masters will change. The present lower house electoral system, in place with modifications since the 1920s, appears to suit the political style of the LDP much better than it suits the opposition. Whereas it has allowed fragmentation and proliferation of opposition parties, it is conducive to campaigning by a party that combines internal factional competition with an ability to provide largesse to local electorates. Imbalanced apportionment of votes in favour of rural areas also benefits the LDP, but it is probably now a factor of less importance than that of multi-member electorates attracting plural LDP candidacies. A change away from the present system would probably require a drastic change in the electoral law. JAAS

Abe, Takeshita, Nakasone and Miyazawa playing stone–paper–scissors to decide who leads off a round of golf. At times it must seem as though matters of succession are decided on a similar basis.

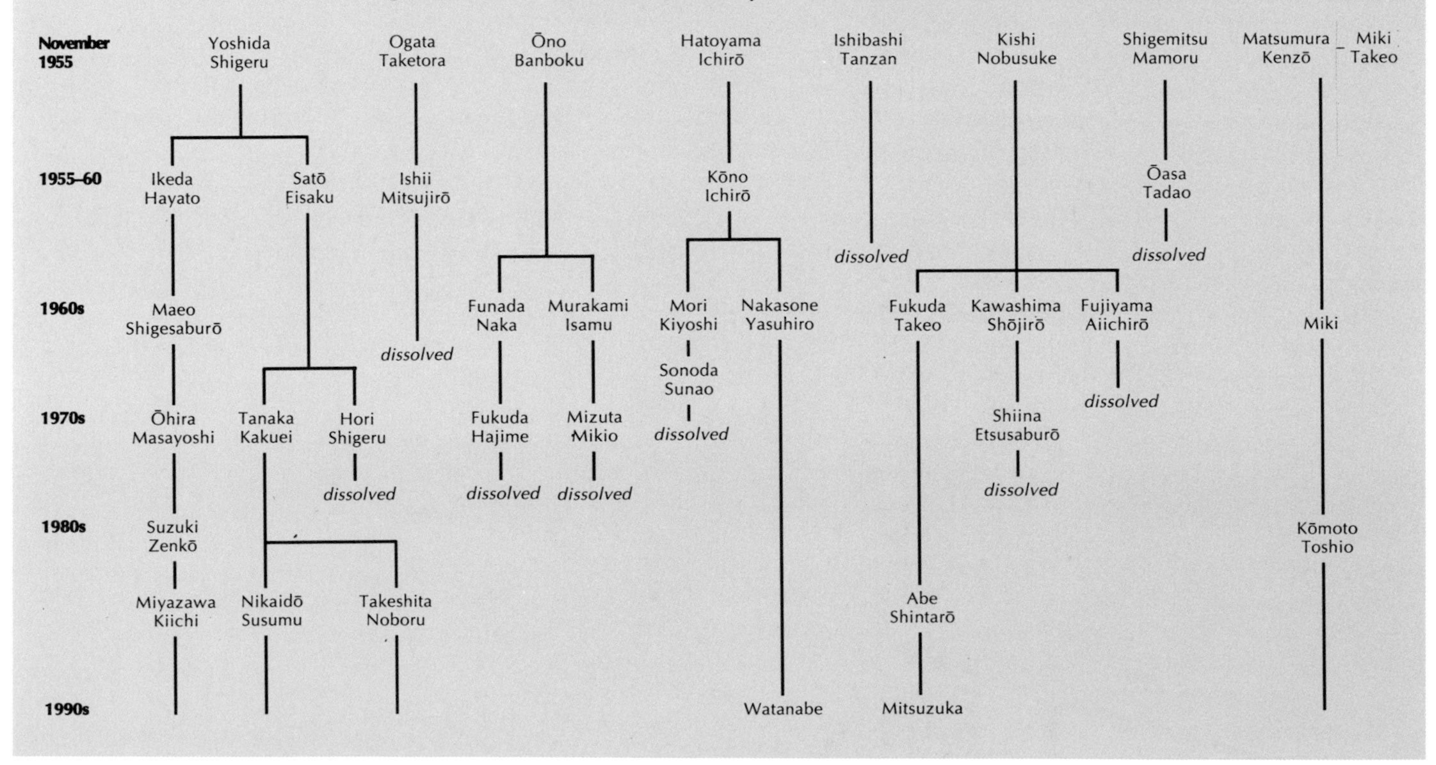

Elections and electioneering

In the summer of 1988, the mass media reported that Ezoe Hiromasa had offered and sold bargain-priced shares in his Recruit Cosmos Co. to many of Japan's leading politicians and bureaucrats. This Recruit scandal drew public attention to the chronic problem of politics and money in Japan. Because most of the Recruit-tainted politicians were senior members of the ruling Liberal Democratic Party, support for the LDP and support for the Takeshita cabinet plummeted to an unprecedented degree (in a May 1989 opinion poll 22.1% supported the LDP and only 4.4% the cabinet). Takeshita resigned and the subsequent Uno cabinet survived only two months before Kaifu Toshiki formed his cabinet in August 1989.

The eighth Election System Council was set up in June 1989 for a term of two years in order to dispel the nation's distrust in the political system. It was a prime-ministerial advisory body and was asked to make proposals for a new electoral system and for the regulation of political funds. The basic concern was that the current system had not only favoured the continuance of LDP power but had also led to corrupt practices in both political funding and electioneering. The council's proposals became a major issue of controversy in 1990 and 1991.

The current electoral system

All elections are regulated by the Law on Public Offices and Elections. Any citizen 20 years or older is automatically registered as a voter after three month's residence in his or her district. Any citizen 25 years or older can run for any electoral office except for the House of Councillors (the Upper House) and the prefectural governorship, where candidates must be at least 30 years old.

In the current system, 512 members of the House of Representatives (the lower house) are elected from 130 districts. The term of the House is four years, although it may also be dissolved before that time. The number of members per district varies from one (the Amami Islands) to six (Hokkaidō No. 1), but most districts return between three and five members. A voter casts a single, non-transferable vote. This system of electing, on average, three to five members from each area is called the 'medium' district system, to distinguish it from the 'small' district (or single-member) system in use in Britain, and from the 'large' district system, which was used in Japan from 1902–17 and again in 1946 and which involved the election of anything up to 13 members per district.

The medium district system differs from the British system and from proportional representation (PR) in three main ways. First, the percentage of votes needed for election is contingent on the competition itself. The single-member system usually has a simple first-past-the-post rule. In PR, seats are allotted in proportion to the votes won. But in Japan today, it is a question of how high one ranks in the list of candidates, so the rank of one candidate of course depends on the performance of the others. If a popular candidate earns a substantial share of the votes, other candidates may still win a seat despite having a very low percentage of the overall vote; and when such a popular candidate is absent, the situation changes radically: a small fraction of 1% may separate winners from losers.

Second, in a system that elects 512 members from 130 districts, a party has to put forward at least two candidates per district in order to win a majority in the House of Representatives. In the 1990 general election, the LDP put forward 338 candidates, while other parties put forward only one candidate per district, or fewer. The inevitable consequence of this is intense intra-party rivalry of LDP candidates within

1990 GENERAL ELECTION RESULTS

Party	Number of candidates	Number elected
Liberal Democratic Party	338	275
Japan Socialist Party	149	136
Kōmei Party	58	45
Communist Party	131	16
Democratic Socialist Party	44	14
Others	77	5
Independent	156	21
Total	953	512

a single district. They must build their own 'associations' (*kōenkai*) to secure votes. On the other hand, inter-party competition among opposition candidates makes it difficult for them to co-operate on policy or to create an anti-LDP coalition.

Third, whereas the single-member system produces the greatest distortion between votes and seats to the advantage of the largest party, and the PR system produces the least distortion, the medium system falls somewhere in between. By and large, the system is advantageous to the LDP and the JSP, but in certain districts smaller parties can get their candidates elected with very few votes.

Members of the House of Councillors are elected on a different basis. Half the 252 seats come up for election every three years for a term of six years. Of the 126 seats, 76 are elected from 47 prefectural districts and 50 are elected separately on a nationwide PR system (the d'Hondt formula). A voter casts one vote for a candidate in a prefectural district and another vote for a party via PR. Parties can present candidates for PR only if they meet one of three conditions: first, they must have at least five elected members of the Diet; second, they must have won 4% or more of the total vote in the previous national election; and third, they must present 10 or more candidates, with deposits subject to forfeit if their share of the vote is low.

All this works to the disadvantage of the smaller parties, but the LDP also has its problems. In order to get elected in this PR group, the individual candidate must be ranked high on the party list. To regulate competition within the party, the LDP employs as an index the number of party members recruited by each candidate. As it is common for candidates to pay the party membership fees of new recruits, this 'party-centered' PR election in fact turns into an expensive individual competition for party members within the LDP. The problem of politics and money raises its head here too.

VOTING INEQUALITIES

One of the most serious defects of Japan's electoral system is the growing inequalities in the value of a vote in different regions, because of the massive post-war movement of people from rural to metropolitan areas. In the schedule attached to the Law on Public Offices and Elections describing the composition of the number of seats allocated in districts a note reads: 'after this law has been enacted, this table shall be updated every five years according to the latest census results'. But there are no legal provisions for the implementation of this note. As a result, updating the schedule requires the full legislative process of revising the law. Any redrawing of district boundaries or re-allocation of seats affects the electoral fortunes of the legislators themselves, so they have naturally been extremely reluctant to promote any major revisions.

In the 1983 general election, the value of a vote in the sparsely populated rural areas was 4.4 times greater than that in the metropolitan areas. Voters in several districts brought suits claiming that the present allocation of seats was in breach of equality before the law, which is prescribed in the Constitution. In July 1985, the Supreme Court held that the present allocation was indeed unconstitutional. This made the dissolution of the House of Representatives impossible until the electoral law had been revised. The general election of 1986 was held just after the Diet had passed the revised law, which for the first time reallocated seats from the sparsely populated to the densely populated districts. But districts actually affected only amounted to 15 out of 130. The revision therefore changed very little. In an accompanying resolution it was stated that 'this revision is a provisional measure to get rid of the unconstitutional situation and a thorough revision shall be made according to the census results of 1985'. No party has yet proposed to act on this measure.

Above *Miyazawa Kiichi campaigning near Tōkyō station.*

Below *Same truck, same banners, same personalities, different location: LDP supporters out in force.*

ELECTIONEERING AND THE LAW

Another feature of Japan's system is the detailed prescriptions on electioneering. The law distinguishes between election campaigns (*senkyo undō*) and political activity (*seiji katsudō*). The former is undertaken to seek election for a particular candidate in a particular election. The latter is intended to publicize the party's policies and to extend its influence among the electorate, but not to secure votes *per se*. Electioneering is allowed only during the official campaign period, which is a mere 15 days for the House of Representatives. A candidate can use one office, one car and one set of loudspeakers. Posters, notice boards, and fliers are strictly limited in number, size and location. On the other hand, the government provides every candidate with equal space in the official bulletins, and an equal amount of time (five and a half minutes) on television, so that they can explain their political platform at public expense.

Other restrictions include: a prohibition on house-to-house canvassing; a prohibition on collecting signatures, and a ban on publication of opinion polls. Violation of these restrictions, as well as the buying of votes, entertaining voters, and interfering with election campaigns is a civil offence. These campaign restrictions operate mainly to the advantage of incumbent candidates. Every candidate drives around the district in a car with a loudspeaker repeating his name and asking people to vote, while accompanying staff bow deeply and wave. What makes the difference between incumbents and newcomers is the extent of *pre-election* activity. Incumbents have many ways of reaching constituents. One important practice is to build a *kōenkai*. This takes the form of a voluntary association of people who support a particular candidate, although in actual fact the candidate employs the staff and bears most of the association's expenses. Such an association may have tens of thousands of members and many branches throughout a district. The primary purpose is, of course, to secure supporters who will vote at a coming election, although it is considered a political activity and so does not violate the election law.

PROPOSALS FOR REFORM

The Election System Council submitted two reports in 1990 and a new districting plan in 1991. The Council agreed that the present system forces intra-party rivalry, especially within the majority party, and undermines essential inter-party competition. Candidate-centered elections also force up the expenditure needed to maintain *kōenkai*. The council suggested that the present system be replaced by one which promotes party-centered and policy oriented elections.

Based on this report, the government introduced a package of three reform bills to an extraordinary session of the Diet in August 1991. It proposed a combination of single-member districts and PR for the lower House. Each voter would have one vote in one of 300 single-member districts, and another separate PR vote in a nationwide constituency which would elect 171 members. Candidates would be allowed to stand under both lists. Canvassing would be permitted within certain limits, and the government would have to establish a council on district boundaries to adjust for population changes every ten years.

The reform bills also propose public funding for political activities. About ¥30 billion would be given in proportion to the number of Diet members and the percentage of votes. At the same time, fundraising activities would be restricted. Each politician would be limited to a maximum of two fundraising organizations, where political donations of more than ¥1,000,000 would have to be made public. Business and labour organizations would be forbidden from making donations to individuals five years after the date of the enactment of the law.

These bills were killed in early October 1991 because of strong objections from within both the LDP and opposition parties. Even Kaifu Toshiki had to abandon his attempt to be re-elected president of the party and so had to relinquish the prime ministership. Recruit-tainted politicians returned to important posts in both government and party, including Prime Minister Miyazawa Kiichi. The prospects for political reform became again doubtful.

SK

Campaign funds

The Japanese government provides finance for many aspects of a candidate's campaign, from the production and distribution of posters and handbills to radio, television, and newspaper advertising, and the amount a candidate may spend during the official campaign period is strictly controlled. This system was designed to limit the influence of money on elections, but to little effect. Even a well-established incumbent can easily spend the equivalent of US$2 million to wage a successful bid for re-election, and new candidates must often spend far more.

One reason for these high figures is that candidates spend as heavily as possible in the weeks before an election officially begins. This is termed 'political activity' and is exempt from official spending limits as long as it follows certain conventions – not mentioning the candidate's name, for example. Another reason for the high cost of political life is that candidates must establish and maintain well-oiled political machines in their districts to ensure a reliable flow of favours, finance, and electoral support.

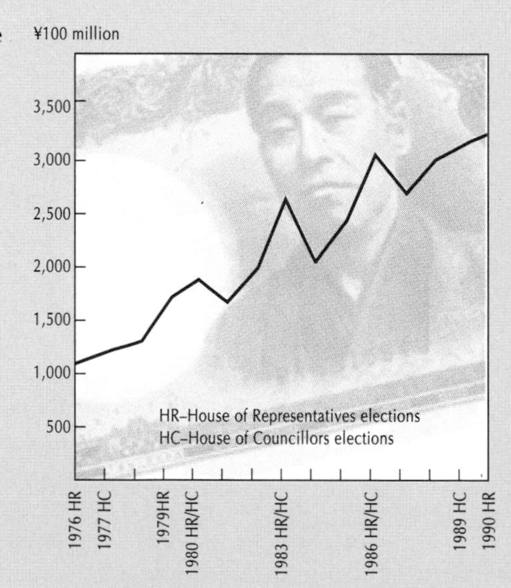

Business provides the largest percentage of reported political contributions for the LDP. The party's hierarchy sets targets each year, and organizations such as the Federation of Economic Organizations (Keidanren) then set contribution quotas for members. Diet members also collect vast amounts of money by sponsoring expensive dinner parties, tickets for which can cost anywhere from ¥20,000 to ¥1,000,000 each. Since the Ministry of Home Affairs defines this as 'payment for refreshment', contributors of these funds need not be reported. Stock tips and gifts of pre-flotation shares are an additional source of indirect political funding, although it is precisely this sort of arrangement that led to the Recruit scandal of 1989, which involved the entire LDP hierarchy. The accompanying graph, which covers not just campaigning but funds for all kinds of 'political activity', shows the continuing rise in the cost of keeping one's head above water. EBK

Interest groups

Although organizations representing farmers and businessmen were active in pre-war Japan, the emergence of interest groups on a large scale was essentially a post-war phenomenon resulting from the democratization process instituted under the Occupation. By the mid 1950s trade union organizations had begun to make their political mark, along with groups representing the interests of local politicians, large and small businesses, former landowners, farmers, medical professionals, war veterans and bereaved families. Since that time, the number of interest groups has proliferated, extending beyond the major economic sectors to all kinds of occupational categories including lawyers, postmasters, nurses and teachers, as well as numerous political, social and cultural associations. An important development in the late 1960s and early 1970s was the emergence of a host of citizens' and protest groups demanding rectification of environmental damage and compensation for its victims. The 1980s saw new impetus given to the environmental movement, along with consumer, feminist, anti-nuclear and regional interest groups. In the 1990s, 'grey power' has become a significant force.

Right *Japanese farmers dressed for the occasion protesting in front of the US Embassy about US pressure to open up the barriers on the import of cheaper foreign rice.*

Direct representation

The ways in which Japanese interest groups seek to influence government conform to the customary patterns in democratic societies. Their leaders and members lobby politicians and government officials to gain support for their demands, testify before Diet and party committees, hold mass rallies and marches, conduct various kinds of public relations activities, and press their views in more informal and private contexts. One distinctive feature of Japanese interest group politics, however, is the extent to which politicians in elected assemblies, including the national Diet, hold official positions within interest groups themselves. As a form of 'direct representation', this is a very effective way of gaining access to the political process.

For groups in the business and agricultural sectors, the practice of direct representation is a long-standing one, with roots going back to the pre-war Diet. It is not now restricted to the established sectoral and occupational groupings but involves many other types of voluntary organization. Studies have shown that approximately 25–30% of members of the House of Representatives are current or former interest group officials, while the figure is closer to 40% in the House of Councillors. Former trade union officials are the most numerous: in the 1990 Diet they comprised 14% of all members, while officials of agricultural organizations constituted 12%. Other groups directly represented in the Diet include professional, business, local government, religious, welfare, women's and consumer organizations.

Party affiliation

Another way in which interest groups seek to influence government is by forming close relationships with political parties, politicians and election candidates and by providing them with various forms of support. These activities are not only associated with the promotion of leaders to political office but are also part of a much broader range of contacts that interest groups maintain with the political world. It is not unusual for some groups to establish their own specialist electoral organizations. In fact the involvement of interest groups in elections and associated political support activities is so extensive that few politicians are without such ties. The best-known

Still going strong after some 40 years: the veteran anti-communist right-wing street protester Akao Bin and his All Japan Patriotic Party.

examples of party-group ties are, of course, those between the governing Liberal Democratic Party (LDP) and organizations representing business and agriculture, while the socialist parties have traditionally been symbiotically tied to trade union organizations. A more recent development has been the emergence of a new party, the Japanese Trade Union Confederation (Rengō), which successfully elected its own representatives to the Diet for the first time in the 1989 upper house elections. The main support group for the Kōmeitō (Clean Government Party) is the neo-Buddhist Sōka Gakkai sect, while the Japan Communist Party is associated with various trade unions, women's organizations and consumer co-operatives.

An important factor encouraging close ties between politicians and interest groups is the nature of party organization itself. Most Japanese parties are top-heavy groupings of politicians with little or no organization at grass-roots level. Lack of a mass membership base undermines their organizational and financial independence. Interest groups often fill this gap by undertaking functions such as supplying campaign workers and election funds to candidates, providing more generalized financial support to party organizations, mobilizing voting support amongst their members, recruiting candidates for political office and influencing the pre-selection of candidates. They also provide members for candidates' personal support groups (*kōenkai*).

POLITICAL GOALS

The political goals of these groups vary. For many, the chief objective is to obtain patronage in the form of subsidies from the national or local-government budgets. Associations representing local politicians and construction contractors seek allocations for public works. Other organizations such as the agricultural co-operatives and chambers of commerce and industry focus on various forms of financial assistance for their members, including subsidies, price supports and low-interest loans. For some organizations, government subsidies are the chief source of funding. So-called 'extra-departmental groups' (*gaikaku dantai*) are a good example: these are organizations established by ministries to assist in the process of policy implementation. They form an important element in the network by which the Japanese government administers various economic and social sectors. The ministries to which these 'institutionalized' interest groups are attached become, of course, a natural target for pressure.

Other groups focus on tax concessions and government regulations with income spin-offs for various occupational groupings such as doctors, farmers, shopkeepers, and small businesses. In contrast, organizations representing large enterprises tend to focus on policy issues relating to the development of the Japanese economy as a whole or to the broad interests of economic or industrial sectors. For many other groups, the main focus is not economic, but specific political or social causes. Those espousing the revival of the emperor system and Japanese militarism, or protesting against nuclear weapons or the siting of nuclear power plants are good examples.

Degrees of influence

Although almost impossible to measure, interest group influence is linked to such factors as the quality of access to politicians and government officials, the nature of party affiliation, organizational resources such as funds, members, professional staff and voting power, as well as less finite attributes such as the legitimacy of a group's participation in the political process. Organizations representing the business and financial worlds have traditionally been considered powerful because of their large political donations to the LDP and its factions. Similarly, the financial resources of the Japan Medical Association have reputedly enabled doctors to influence policy on payments for medical treatment and to prevent the importation of the birth-control pill. On the other hand, the political power of the agricultural co-operative organization (Nōkyō) is exercised through the ballot box. Almost all Japan's farm families are members of this organization, amounting to several million households throughout the country. Its strong ties to large numbers of politicians help to explain why Japan has maintained relatively high levels of agricultural protection.

Characteristic of interest group influence is the fact that it tends to be limited to the policy sector in which the group operates. Interest groups cluster around specific ministries and associated groups of policy experts (*zoku*) in the LDP, forming what are known as 'iron triangles', or regularized patterns of interaction in policy-making. Even groups considered powerful, such as those representing big business, find it difficult to extend their influence across policy sectors. In spite of open confrontation between Nōkyō and the 'peak' big business group, the Federation of Economic Organizations (Keidanren), big business interests have been unable to persuade the Japanese government to institute rapid deregulation and market opening of the farm sector.

Organizations do not always require vast political or economic resources, or close connections to the LDP, to articulate their interests successfully. Although the trade unions are affiliated with Japan's permanent opposition parties, the bureaucracy provides a channel for union input on labour policy through its system of consultative advisory councils. In addition, mass protests, publicity through the media and action through the court system can sometimes be politically effective, as in the case of the citizens' movement against mercury pollution in Minamata Bay.

Implications of the system

The political implications of this whole system of interest groups are significant in several respects. Given the extent of interest group involvement in

The Japan Medical Association

The Japan Medical Association (JMA) is one of the most successful interest groups in Japan, fitting the general pattern that the most powerful groups are representatives of the producers and providers of goods and services, not of consumer or public interest groups. The JMA's success derives from its strong links with politicians, the bureaucracy, and the pharmaceutical industry. It is a generous and regular contributor to the election campaigns of LDP politicians. The JMA has also sponsored its own successful candidates for national elected office, giving it an even more direct voice in the Diet. Close links with the Ministry of Health and Welfare, the government's main medical regulatory body, ensure that the JMA has a prominent voice in all policy decisions affecting the medical profession.

The JMA's relationship with the pharmaceutical industry is particularly close, and is encouraged indirectly by government incentives in the sense that the government bases payment to doctors partly on the amount of medication they prescribe to national health patients. Most doctors augment this income by selling medication to their patients directly from their offices. Over-prescription is in fact a chronic problem, but as a result of the JMA's political influence, it is not one that is likely to be addressed in the near future.

The JMA's ability to lobby effectively for its interests can result in other forms of questionable public-health policy. It has played a decisive rôle in persuading the government to continue restricting the availability of oral contraception for women. This is ostensibly to protect public health, but critics charge that the primary effect is to swell abortion rates to the profit of doctors. Critics also charge that the JMA has occasionally been responsible for blocking new treatments or the importation of foreign medical equipment that might lead to an eventual decrease in doctors' profits.

EBK

Nōkyō kumiai: union of agricultural co-operatives

Nōkyō is a major political force in Japan. It runs one of Japan's largest banks, the Nōrin chūgin, controls a nationwide bureaucracy of 380,000, and virtually every farmer in Japan is a member.

This union is powerful because of the unique position farmers occupy in the LDP's uninterrupted hold on post-war political power. Despite some half-hearted attempts to correct the rural–urban imbalance in the value of a vote, the massive post-war demographic shift to urban centres has left rural constituencies heavily over-represented. In some districts one rural vote can carry nearly five times the electoral weight of an urban vote, with the result that approximately 200 of the Diet's 500-plus representatives depend on the farm vote for election.

Nōkyō is closely associated with the high price of rice. Rice is a controlled commodity in Japan, with the government barring nearly all imports and paying rice growers an artificially high price for their crop. It is sold to consumers at a reduced price, yet this still means the cost of rice is up to seven times the US average. The political power of agricultural interests also extends to protection of wheat, beef, sugar, dairy, and numerous other agricultural products. External pressures and the continuing depopulation of rural areas mean that the political power of Nōkyō is likely to wane in the near future. EBK

semi-administrative rôles on behalf of government, Japan is considered to exhibit quite high levels of 'state corporatism', at least in highly regulated sectors such as agriculture and small business. Distinctions between political parties and interest groups are equally blurred by the fact that interest groups often carry out functions normally undertaken by grassroots party organizations. The other side of this coin is the important rôle played by Japanese politicians as interest intermediaries. Most of the lobbying in Japanese politics is done by politicians, acting as spokespersons on behalf of their supporting groups, rather than by lobbyists hired for that purpose. Within the Diet, politicians group together in informal policy caucuses or 'Diet members' leagues' which mobilize to promote or defend certain interests in the policy-making process. Around 40 of these operate in the agricultural policy sector alone. As a result, politicians are often viewed as being interest-driven, rather than motivated by a willingness to seek solutions based on consideration of principle, long-term comprehensive strategies, or the national interest. When, for example, the Ministry of Finance proposed taking the control of interest rates on postal savings away from the Ministry of Posts and Telecommunications in order to unify the decision-making system, they were blocked by politicians representing postmasters' associations.

Although Japanese democracy provides avenues for the expression of diverse interests, the LDP government is widely regarded as beholden to certain vested interests, with the ruling party using its monopoly powers over government policy and patronage to consolidate a broad coalition of supporting groups centring on large and small businesses, primary producers and the white-collar professions. The opposition parties find it difficult to compete in the patronage stakes. In policy terms, the interests of producers tend to predominate over the interests of consumers, who are organizationally fragmented and who concentrate their political connections on the more 'progressive' side of politics. Another consequence is the politicization of the bureaucracy in areas like construction, agriculture, and local government where the ruling party services its patronage networks through the national budget. 'Immobilism' also tends to characterize the policy-making process when vested interests are challenged and reductions in patronage are proposed.

In some cases, close associations between interest groups and the government have prompted allegations of political collusion. A fine line separates special pleading for groups that provide politicians with vital elements of support such as funding and votes, and collusion in which special favours are 'bought' from politicians at 'special' prices. A number of celebrated cases such as the Lockheed and Recruit scandals provide evidence of corruption on a large scale, entangling Japan's corporate and political worlds in a web of illegal activity.

For these reasons, the social legitimacy of groups that plead for special interests is not as strong as it might be. Groups that put their case to the Japanese public in terms that emphasize the national interest are more likely to win broad support for their cause than organizations that rely on special pleading. This principle has been applied by the agricultural co-operatives which have justified the maintenance of import protection for Japan's farmers in terms of the need to ensure food security and to preserve the cultural and environmental value of agriculture, particularly rice farming. Generally speaking, the media and public opinion are two of the most important countervailing influences to the vested interest group system. AG

Local government

Japan began its process of modernization when it abolished its feudal régime in 1868 and established a constitutional monarchy in 1890. From 1868 onward the system of local government went through a number of changes but the enactment of the governing codes for municipalities in 1888, and for prefectures and counties in 1890 secured official recognition of at least some degree of local autonomy. Out of approximately 300 feudal domains some 40 prefectures were created, comprising about 300 counties and 10,000 municipalities. The system of counties was abolished in 1918, but the broad outlines of this system continued intact until Japan's defeat in 1945.

The pre-war system of local government had no constitutional guarantees. It was based on the Prussian model, and its chief characteristic was the extreme concentration of power in the hands of the central authorities. For example, although Japan created prefectural assemblies and although candidates were elected by direct vote, the right to vote was held only by large landowners and upper-bracket taxpayers. A large group of people was thereby disenfranchised. Moreover, the authority of these assemblies was severely restricted by a system of prefectural and county governors appointed by the Ministry of Home Affairs. Only municipal assemblies were able to exercise some degree of self-government through their authority to choose mayors and village headmen.

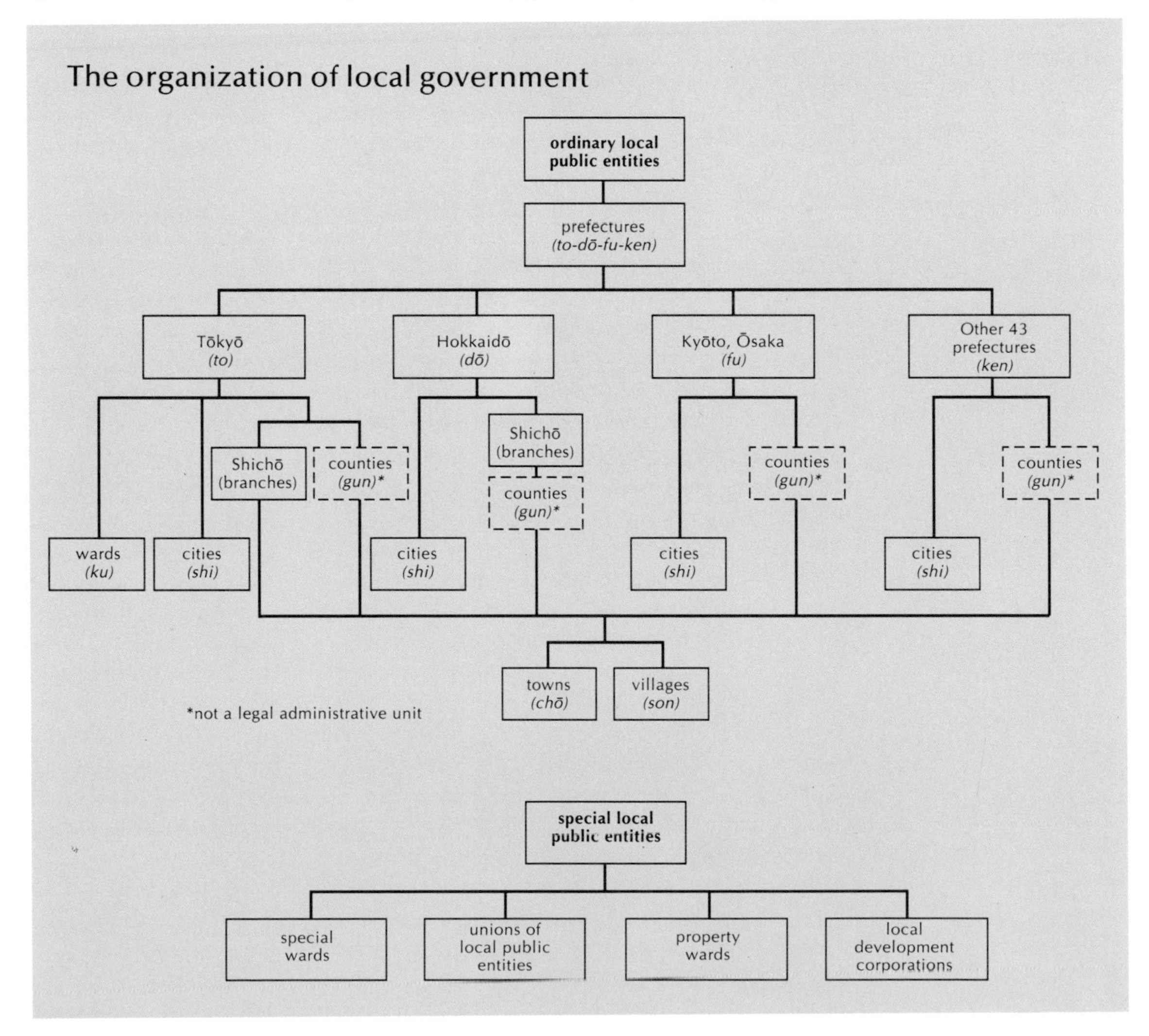

The post-war local government system

After Japan's defeat in 1945, the Allied Occupation embarked on a series of democratic reforms. A central link in these reforms was the creation of a new system of local government and the concept of local self-government was guaranteed by articles contained in the new constitution. Governors and mayors would be elected by direct vote, with universal suffrage extended to all men and women 20 years and older. A new Local Autonomy Law was also enacted. The law provided for the recall of elected officials, introduced the ballot initiative and audits, and strengthened the formal authority of local assemblies.

The old Ministry of Home Affairs was abolished by the Occupation authorities in 1947 as part of its programme of reform, reducing the degree of central control over local affairs. This established the general outlines of the post-war system of local government. From 1953 municipalities began a process of large-scale reorganization, with the total number being reduced by one third. The current governmental system is three tiered and consists of the central government, 47 urban and rural prefectures, known as *todōfuken*, and approximately 3,200 municipalities, known as *shichōson*.

However, even with these democratic reforms, the central government has continued to exercise a good deal of power over local affairs, best symbolized by the system whereby the central authorities delegate much of their work down to local level. This does not mean that local authorities have freedom of action; rather they are carrying out policies entrusted to them. Under this system, the design and implementation of policy is often decided in detail at the centre, leaving little room for discretion at local level. Although there are no exact figures on what percentage of local government business is in fact devoted to this kind of simple implementation of central policy, it is generally believed that 80% of prefectural affairs, and 40% of municipal affairs are predetermined by the central government. This system of delegated authority began to expand greatly in the 1960s, during the period of high economic growth.

Local finances, for example, are largely under firm central control. While localities accounted for 75% of all public expenditure in 1990, local revenues contributed only 36%. The central government makes up the difference through such methods as the disbursement of Treasury grants and the Local Allocation Tax. Though local authorities have steadily increased their direct influence over central government policy affecting regional affairs in some areas, control over finance remains a major problem in centre–local relations.

Description and function of local government

Japan has two levels of local government. Municipalities are at the basic level of public organization in Japan and are therefore closest to the daily lives of their citizens. They deliver a broad range of local services while at the same time also implementing central government directives. In 1990 there were 655 cities, 2,003 towns, and 587 villages. Cities have slightly more autonomy in setting their own policies than towns and villages, but there is no discernible difference as far as towns and villages are concerned. Classification schemes usually define cities as densely populated urban communities, villages as agricultural regions, with towns falling into an intermediate category. However, rapid regional change in Japan has resulted in a large number of mixed communities that do not easily fit into any of these categories.

Urban and rural prefectures represent the next level of governmental hierarchy in Japan. Administratively this includes one metropolis (Tōkyō), one district (Hokkaidō), two urban prefectures (Kyōto and Ōsaka), and 43 prefectures. With the exception of Tōkyō, all of these entities have the same level of formal authority, though variations in local conditions require them to deliver a widely divergent set of services. In addition to co-ordinating a broad range of regional affairs, prefectural governments also give administrative support to municipalities within their borders. In fact there is a good deal of duplication built in to the system. The distinctive difference between the autonomy of urban and rural prefectures on the one hand and municipalities on the other is the higher proportion of mandated affairs the prefectures implement for the central government.

In addition to the two fundamental categories of municipalities and prefectures, there are two further

Local government in the rain. Prime Minister Uno Sōsuke here campaigning for the LDP candidate during elections for the Tōkyō Metropolitan Assembly, 1989.

sub-categories. These are a nationwide system of 'designated' cities, and a system of administrative wards in Tōkyō. Cities are specially designated by the central government when their populations approximate one million. They are then given partial prefectural powers over such areas as city planning and welfare administration. Eleven cities were included in this category in 1990: Sapporo, Sendai, Kawasaki, Yokohama, Nagoya, Kyōto, Ōsaka, Kōbe, Hiroshima, Kita-Kyūshū, and Fukuoka. Unlike these 'designated' cities, Tōkyō's 23 wards have no independent authority over their water supplies, waste systems, and fire fighting services, which are all centrally administered by the Tōkyō city government.

Urbanization and increased local autonomy

In 1990, Japan's urban population was 94 million (76.9%) out of a total national population of 122 million. The remaining 28 million (23.1%) resided in villages and the countryside. In this same period the population of Japan's major cities totalled 16 million, with Tōkyō accounting for a substantial proportion. This is part of a long term historical trend. In 1920 only 18.1% of the population lived in major urban areas. By 1935 this figure was 32.9%, increasing to 56.3% in 1955, and to 68.1% in 1965. As a result of its experience with high economic growth and rapid industrialization, Japan shifted decisively from an agrarian to an urban society in the 1960s.

The socioeconomic changes that accompanied high economic growth resulted in a dramatic increase in demands for improved local government services. Rapid urbanization accelerated the need for improvements in housing, transportation, and roads, and for improvements in the social welfare of children, the elderly, and the disabled. The central government showed itself unable to keep up with this increase in demand for improved services and infrastructure. The result was a nationwide increase in citizen campaigns to force these improvements and the strategy these campaigns used was to focus their energies on local authorities as the representatives of government policy.

Although Japan's post-war constitution established a decentralized system of local government, in practice the system remains closely tied to strong central government control and lacks full autonomy. However, citizen demands on local governments for improved living conditions led local governments to play an increasingly effective political rôle in the management of regional affairs.

Reform-minded scholars provided support for this trend by developing theories of local democracy and reform that looked towards local governments to use locally mobilized groups as a means to encourage the central government to respond to local citizen demands.

This movement was further strengthened by an increase in the number of reform-minded local governments voted into office in this period. These progressive local governments challenged central government authority over local issues and worked actively both in the areas of welfare and in the regional enforcement of environmental standards. They also increased public access to government information and to policy planning processes.

By the early 1980s, with Japan's cycle of high speed economic growth clearly over, progressive local governments began to decrease in numbers and effectiveness. However, their practice of responding to local demands has been carried forward by both conservative and reformist politicians alike. As a result, local government has gradually increased its ability to challenge and alter central government policy towards localities.

It is conceptually inconsistent to expect central government control and local autonomy to expand at the same time. The more likely trend is for local autonomy to continue to advance under relatively stable conditions of central governmental authority. It is quite possible that improved policies can evolve out of this process. For example, the central government can conduct pilot projects for environmental protection and welfare at the local level in co-operation with local authorities. If successful, projects like these might later be adopted by the central government, resulting in higher national minimum standards.

As long as input into central government policy by local autonomous bodies remains dynamic, centralized authority need not be considered in an entirely negative light. MK/EBK

Foreign policy

Japan regained control of foreign relations in 1952 when the Allied Occupation ended. Its overseas embassies and consulates were reopened and the diplomatic staff reconstituted. During the Occupation, Japan's foreign policy had been conducted by the Supreme Commander Allied Powers (SCAP, a term referring both to the commander and to the organization he led). In practice, however, Japan's diplomats had played a substantial part in affairs through their rôle in the Central Liaison Office. The fact that they constituted a corps with a strong knowledge of English made them invaluable. Diplomatic procedures were gradually reformed. The Foreign Ministry became responsible to the cabinet and ultimately to the prime minister. The conduct of foreign affairs was subject to consultation with, and debate in, the Diet; and, as party politics developed, the foreign minister came to be drawn from the ranks of the party leaders. Japan's post-war foreign relations have therefore been subject to democratic controls which were relatively unknown in the pre-war period.

Inevitably the new government of independent Japan inherited many features from the Occupation, in particular a dependence on the US. Since the revival of the Japanese economy became the top priority of successive governments, there developed a sort of 'merchant diplomacy'. On political issues Tōkyō was content to follow the lead of Washington. Although the governments of Prime Minister Yoshida Shigeru (1948–54) tried to maintain a balance during the Cold War, there was a widespread perception that Japan was on the US and anti-communist side. A second characteristic resulted from the promulgation of the new constitution on 3 November 1946. Under Article 9, it was stated that 'the Japanese people forever renounce war as a sovereign right of the nation and the threat or use of force as a means of settling international disputes. In order to accomplish this, land, sea and air forces as well as other war potential will never be maintained. The right of belligerency of the state will not be recognized.' This was phrased in an extreme form and, though historical evidence suggests that it was devised by the military under General Douglas MacArthur and subsequently adopted by the

The London Summit of G7 leaders, July 1991. Unfortunately Prime Minister Kaifu was out of office only four months later.

Japanese cabinet, the fact is that the Japanese as a whole have accepted this as an article of faith ever since. In post-war diplomacy the Japanese have adopted a broadly pacifist stance. They have a low perception of military threat and have never fully shared US views; generally they have been happy to have constitutional restrictions preventing the sending of Japanese troops overseas. Japanese troop strength has consequently been much below that of its neighbours for most of the post-war years.

Consequences of the peace treaty

Japan made peace with most of the wartime allies (except for the USSR and China, among others) at the San Francisco peace conference of September 1951. A US–Japan Security Treaty was signed at that time stipulating that US forces might continue to occupy military, naval and air bases on Japanese soil. During the peace-treaty negotiations John Foster Dulles, the US secretary of state, had tried to persuade the Japanese to set up their own armed forces because it seemed anomalous that Japan, so close to the battle front in the Korean War, should have no real capacity for self-defence. A further mutual defence assistance agreement was signed on 1 May 1954 in which the US made available to Japan defence technology, equipment and materials, provided they set up their own forces. On 1 July of that year the Japanese established the so-called volunteer Self-Defence Forces (Jieitai) which have continued to this day under strict civilian control.

As a consequence of the settlement, Japan concluded a treaty in 1952 with the Republic of China (Taiwan) rather than with the People's Republic. Anxious to restore its trade with continental China as well, Japan argued for the separation of trade from politics and eventually trade restarted based on 'friendly firms arrangements', but the volume remained small compared with the 1930s.

Another aspect of the 1950s was the relationship with the USSR, which had not signed the San Francisco treaty. Certain territories in Manchuria, Korea and the islands north of Hokkaidō had been occupied by Soviet forces between 15 August and 3 September 1945. After the resignation in 1954 of Prime Minister Yoshida it was decided to try and re-establish relations with the USSR and London was chosen as a neutral capital for negotiations in 1955 and 1956. The hope was that they could negotiate the return of these disputed islands. During the negotiations the Soviets did offer back the island groups of Habomai and Shikotan but, since the Japanese insisted on all four being returned, this offer was withdrawn. Diplomatic relations between the two countries were restored, but Japan insisted that peace could not be established between the two until the Northern Territories issue was resolved.

Changes to the Security Treaty

Throughout the 1950s with the improvement of the economy Japan acquired greater confidence. The government negotiated significant amendments to the US–Japan Security Treaty and in January 1960 Prime Minister Kishi signed the revised treaty. Ratification by the Diet proved to be difficult because of Socialist opposition and a wave of demonstrations in major cities. It was eventually ratified in May; but a proposed visit by President Eisenhower had to be called off because of the unpopularity of the government's tactics. While the provision of military bases continued, the revision laid down that no nuclear weapons would be brought onto Japanese territory: 'Major changes in deployment into Japan of US armed forces and also major changes in their equipment are to be subjects of prior consultation with the government of Japan.' With the coming of the Vietnam War Japan and Okinawa became important bases, and the question of prior consultation whenever nuclear weapons were brought into Japanese ports or airports became a critical issue. In 1968 the Japanese formulated what they called their 'three nuclear principles': (1) Japan will never possess nuclear weapons; (2) Japan will not manufacture nuclear weapons; (3) Japan will not cause nuclear weapons to be brought into its territory.

Results of economic success

The 1960s like the 1950s were a time of rapid economic rehabilitation, and Japan remained content to follow a low-posture foreign policy, leaving initiatives on most issues to the US. By the start of the 1970s, however, economic success led inevitably to an estrangement between the US and Japan caused by economic tensions on the one hand and by the US initiative towards China in 1971 on the other. These two developments were called the 'Nixon shocks' because of the surprise they caused. Japan spoke of its need for a more 'diversified foreign policy', less tied to the US, and this became even more crucial with the oil crisis in the mid 1970s when the Japanese had to build up the goodwill of Middle Eastern countries at short notice. For most of the 1970s Japan was trying to remould its relationships with the People's Republic of China. After signing a number of treaties dealing with shipping (1974), air transport (1974), trade (1975), and fisheries (1975), Japan finally in August 1978 concluded a treaty of peace and friendship with China and a new era of Sino–Japanese relations emerged which has since gone from strength to strength.

As tension was relaxed on the China front, it was intensified in relations with the USSR. In response to the Sino–Japanese rapprochement, the Soviets stepped up their activities by building runways and increasing garrisons in the Northern Territories. For the Japanese the issue of these islands became a subject of great political sensitivity, and pressure of public opinion made negotiation extremely difficult. Visits were exchanged in the 1980s, but little progress was made towards a solution, even during President Gorbachev's visit to Japan in spring 1991. This deterioration of Soviet–Japanese relations tended to draw Tōkyō and Washington closer together. Thus Japan supported the US position over the invasion of Afghanistan, refusing to send any athletes to the Moscow Olympics in 1980. In 1983 came the shooting down by Soviet fighters of a Korean Airlines passenger jet with many Japanese on board, causing a further chill in relations.

Present issues

Despite Japan's support for the US in a number of areas of foreign policy throughout the world, bilateral relations during the 1980s were somewhat more problematic and steps had to be taken to arrest the deterioration in US–Japan relations. This was necessary in the face of a succession of trade disputes and Washington's frequent complaints about Japan's favourable trade balances. In the defence field, the Japanese were blamed for having a 'free ride'. When Nakasone became prime minister in 1982, he was determined to address the issue. He pledged that Japan would transfer to the US military-related technologies in which Japanese industry had reached a considerable degree of sophistication. One of the objectives was to demonstrate that the Security Treaty could be given a new lease of life on the basis of defence co-operation. First of all, the Japanese increased their contributions towards the cost of US forces in Japan. Second, they accepted the proposal to operate a naval defence perimeter at 1,000 miles from

'Decapitation' by members of the right-wing Issuikai. An effigy of the former French prime minister, Edith Cresson, who hit the headlines in July 1991 when she accused the Japanese of being 'ants' planning to conquer the world. Such outbursts and their consequences are hardly conducive to international understanding.

Japanese shores. Third, they took part in various defence exercises which in some cases took place in the south Pacific. Perhaps the most dramatic of all was the lifting in 1987 of the ceiling on national defence expenditure, which had been limited to 1% of GNP since 1976. On the whole, a relationship of cordiality was re-established between successive prime ministers and presidents, whether by personal meetings or at G7 summits. In spite of frequent protectionist calls from the US Congress, some progress was also made towards solving the trade friction issue, for example by the Trade Impediments Initiative on which a report was published in 1990.

The most important issue of 1990–91 was Japan's response to the Gulf War. Kaifu Toshiki, prime minister since August 1989, was a compromise candidate and had a weak power base, and after Iraq's invasion of Kuwait, the government's reaction was slow and indecisive. After a good deal of pressure from abroad, a package of measures was announced which was primarily financial and avoided the question of military involvement. Kaifu himself visited the Middle East to see what could be done. A special emergency session of the Diet was convened in October 1990 and the government introduced a hastily contrived measure called the United Nations Co-operation Bill. There was general support for sending non-combatants; but there was resistance from the opposition parties, the centrist and left-wing parties, and also from some factions of the LDP, to sending combatants. After a great deal of impassioned debate, the government withdrew its legislation and announced it would seek a fresh consensus.

The Gulf crisis gave rise to a great deal of heart-searching in Japan where many had been looking for a global political rôle for the country commensurate with its economic position in the world. While there were constitutional restraints on sending forces overseas, it had often been mooted that Japanese self-defence units might be able to take part in United Nations' exercises without violating the constitution. But the crisis of 1990 showed that there was no political consensus for this kind of action. This is not to say that the Japanese were not generous in their financial contributions to the war effort and to the peoples of the area who suffered. Moreover Japanese technology made a formidable, if indirect, contribution to the missile systems employed in the war. But the crisis showed that the Japanese people had no wish to see their country assume a military rôle in the world and were content to abide by a narrow interpretation of the 1946 constitution. IN

Overseas development aid (ODA)

Japan has concentrated most of its ODA on its Asian neighbours. Aid reached US$4.5 billion in 1989, investment in ASEAN and China accounting for a majority share of US$2.2 billion. Although it is difficult to quantify, Japan's ODA has undoubtedly had a positive macroeconomic impact on regional growth. It has also helped to erase wartime memories and create a favourable image of Japan in Asia. A 1988 Ministry of Foreign Affairs survey of ASEAN nations suggested majority support for Japan and its investments. Yet, a segment of public opinion in Japan and in recipient countries has been consistently critical of Japan's ODA process.

In principle, aid is given on a request-only basis from recipient countries. The intent is to avoid projects that would benefit Japanese corporate interests more than those of the recipients. In practice, most successful proposals are put together by Japanese firms who would like a stake in the project. Part of the reason for this is the considerable expertise needed in putting together proposals that can survive the vetting procedures of Japan's aid agencies. However, it is also tacitly acknowledged that those companies that become involved with an aid project at the early proposal stage stand the greatest chance of profiting from the project when it is approved.

Another reason for public criticism is that the criteria and procedures for project selection are largely shielded from outside independent analysis. Once a project is approved for funding, the feasibility studies and reviews on which the selection was based are not released for two to five years, effectively preventing taxpayer scrutiny until the project is already well under way or completed. It is therefore not surprising that the Japanese public has been particularly critical of ODA, with more attention given to charges of corporate self-interest, corruption and kickbacks than to successful contributions to international development. Nevertheless, Japan will remain committed to its ODA programme, and will continue to pressure the private sector to participate. It is also likely that Japan will increase its level of financial support to the United Nations with the eventual goal of winning a permanent seat on the Security Council. EBK

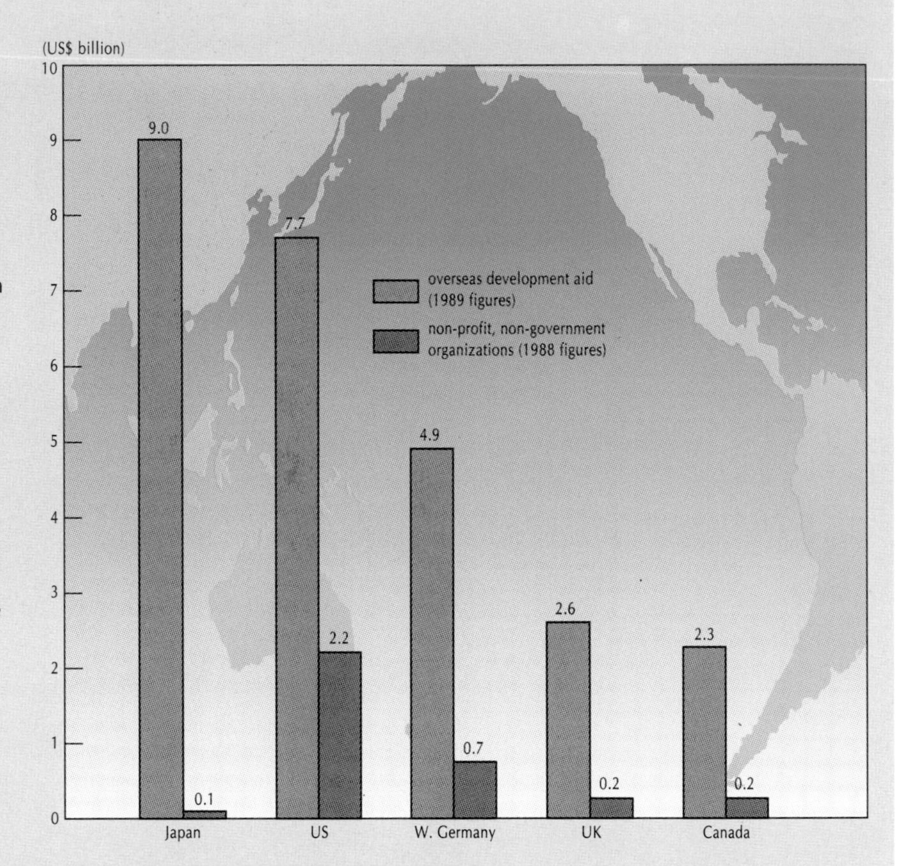

IS JAPAN A FRIENDLY NATION THAT CAN BE TRUSTED?

	YES %	NO %
Indonesia	88	7
Malaysia	76	12
Philippines	92	4
Singapore	69	13
Thailand	78	18

IS JAPANESE INVESTMENT WELCOME?

	YES %	NO %
Indonesia	93	6
Malaysia	88	5
Philippines	91	9
Singapore	93	1
Thailand	85	10

Source: Ministry of Foreign Affairs, Opinion Poll of ASEAN nations.

CONTRIBUTIONS TO THE UNITED NATIONS (1991)

	Scale of assessments (%)	Amount (US$ million)	No. of staff[a]
US	25.00	271.6	379
Japan	11.38	104.8	91
USSR	9.99	92.0	152
W. Germany	9.36	86.2	112
France	6.25	57.6	109
UK	4.86	44.8	93
Italy	3.99	36.8	52
Canada	3.09	28.5	51
Spain	1.95	18.0	33
Netherlands	1.65	15.2	32
Australia	1.57	14.5	27
China	0.79	7.3	40
160 Countries, total	100.00	962.7	2,561

[a]As of 30 June, 1990
Source: UN; Ministry of Foreign Affairs, Japan.

Defence

In 1945, in the aftermath of Japan's defeat, the Occupation authorities were determined to disarm, demilitarize and democratize Japan so that it would never again be a threat to world peace. Although the imperial army and navy were disarmed and disbanded, the truth is that some units continued in existence for a brief while after the surrender to assist the Allies in policing operations and to put down uprisings in various parts of south-east Asia. Former naval units were also used for minesweeping operations, up to and even during the Korean War.

Reform

After the surrender the Japanese armed forces started planning for a post-war existence consisting of a reorganized imperial guard to function as an army, and a coastal defence force to replace the navy. The Supreme Commander Allied Powers (SCAP) made it clear, however, that a major reform of the military system was inevitable. SCAP asked for revised proposals but the responses consisted of vague proposals for a military establishment subject to strong civilian control. These were rejected out of hand by SCAP, and work commenced on drafting a clause for the new constitution that would prohibit Japan from ever again possessing armed forces of any kind. This eventually became the famous Article 9, or Peace Clause. There is still some uncertainty about its authorship, but the original draft emerged from a discussion between MacArthur and Shidehara Kijūrō, the foreign minister. The original draft was idealistic and premised on the assumption that any future security threat to Japan would be dealt with under the protective umbrella of the United Nations. US, and subsequently Japanese, policy-makers then altered the drafts so as to leave room for an interpretation that would permit Japan to maintain military forces in the future provided that they did not constitute 'war potential'. The Allied Council, representing the several countries taking part in the Occupation, was so concerned about the oblique wording of this revised clause that it insisted on the inclusion in the constitution of a requirement that all ministers be civilians.

Article 9 forms the cornerstone of post-war defence policy, but the wording has been subject to a variety of interpretations and consequently debates on defence and security issues have been conducted in an atmosphere clouded by constitutional uncertainties as well as political tension.

As the Cold War intensified from 1947 onwards the US began pressing for a measure of Japanese rearmament in order to relieve the US of the full burden of providing for the security of Japan and of the whole region. Opinion in Japan by this time had shifted in favour of being protected by the US rather than the UN but there was resistance to the idea of substantial rearmament. There was at least one serious proposal for a Japanese military force, the Ashida Memorandum, which proposed a centralized paramilitary police force to deal with communist-fomented internal unrest, but it came to nothing. In the end, it was the outbreak of the Korean War in 1950 that provided the impetus for the creation of the post-war defence establishment.

The military establishment

Faced with the need to despatch US occupation forces based in Japan to Korea to join the UN force, MacArthur ordered the creation of a Japanese National Police Reserve with a strength of 75,000: this was the beginning of the post-war army. In 1951 came the US–Japan Security Treaty, which guaranteed nuclear protection by the US and a major conventional US presence in East Asia and the Pacific, including substantial forces stationed in Japan itself. In 1952 the National Police Reserve was reorganized into a National Safety Force, with both land and sea components, and 1954 saw the establishment of the Self-Defence Forces (SDF, or Jieitai). The SDF, consisting of Ground, Maritime and Air Forces, were placed under a civilian Defence Agency, the Bōeichō, which has the status of a junior ministry. In addition, Japan also possesses a Coastguard, which is classified as a military unit, and a force of Riot Police, the Kidōtai, some 100,000 strong. The SDF were not referred to in public as a 'military force' until Prime Minister Suzuki did so in the 1980s, but it is nevertheless clear that the SDF are not a paramilitary or parapolice force, as some have claimed, but rather a fully-fledged military organization. It can be argued,

however, that they represent a new type of military establishment in that they adhere to a policy of defensive action without an offensive capacity for military aggression.

The SDF are under the tight civilian control of the Defence Agency. From 1956 to 1986 there existed a National Defence Council, which tended to rubber-stamp the decisions of the Agency, and in 1986 this was merged with another body to form the Security Council of Japan, which remains an entirely civilian body. The Diet has, however, exerted little control over the SDF and has not established control mechanisms of its own, primarily because it has not resolved the question of whether the SDF are a military body or not. In 1980 the House of Representatives established a Committee on Security Affairs, but it is a special rather than a standing committee and its rôle is merely advisory: it does not consider or amend SDF-related legislation.

The commander-in-chief of the SDF is the prime minister and under him civilian control is exercised by the director general of the Defence Agency through its various bureaux. The uniformed head of the SDF is the Chairman of the Joint Staff Council, who chairs a council consisting of the chiefs of staff of each branch of the SDF. He can, however, only command the SDF in combined operations and is therefore much less powerful than the Chairman of the US Joint Chiefs of Staff, although the Japanese organization was originally created on the US model.

The top uniformed leaders cannot report directly to the prime minister or even to the director general of the agency, but instead they report through the civilian bureau chiefs. These have often been seconded from élite ministries and the extent of their power over the uniformed staff of the SDF is a matter of continuing debate.

Left *The Japanese Self-Defence Forces on parade; maritime forces (top) and ground forces (bottom).*

Right *The helicopter-carrying destroyer* Shirane *on naval review in 1989, the 35th anniversary of the founding of the Self-Defence Forces.*

The SDF today

Japan today has the most modern, non-nuclear conventional armed forces in the Asia–Pacific region, although the lack of experience in combat has led to some doubt about their actual combat ability. The political minefield created by debates over whether or not the SDF are constitutional has created a number of restrictions on their growth.

(1) Article 66 of the constitution, which states that all ministers must be civilians, has established civilian rather than military control over the SDF. The despatch of forces for defensive purposes is further subject to the approval of the Diet, although in an emergency this may be given retrospectively. In addition, Japan has no national emergency or security laws, for it is widely considered that they would infringe constitutional rights. This is said to inhibit effective planning for national security.

(2) It is not permissible for the SDF to be despatched overseas because this is not authorized in the relevant laws. In 1951 the House of Councillors actually passed a resolution aimed at authorizing the despatch of the SDF on UN duties in the future, but this issue has still not been resolved. It most recently surfaced in the intense debate during the Gulf War, when attempts to involve the SDF even in non-combat rôles foundered in the Diet. Article 9 is widely understood to prohibit the use of force to solve international disputes and under this interpretation even involvement in UN operations are considered unconstitutional. As a result of doubts about the constitutional propriety of collective security arrangements, exercises under Combined Military Operations with Pacific Countries (RIMPAC) still cause controversy. SDF members may, under the accepted present interpretation, be despatched abroad for embassy or peace-keeping duties.

(3) Conscription is deemed to be forbidden under Article 18, which prohibits involuntary servitude, and this has caused problems for the ground forces, which are chronically undermanned. Under Article 76 courts martial are not permitted, and SDF personnel charged with military offences therefore have access to military documentation and a full civilian defence. This has been seen to cause possible security and discipline problems, especially as SDF personnel have the right to resign their commissions at any time.

The Self-Defence Forces

The accompanying table from *Defence of Japan* (1990) gives details of the relative sizes of ground forces (GSDF), maritime forces (MSDF) and the air force (ASDF). By international standards, Japan has a relatively large military establishment. Japan is also committed to increased military production. The pace of technological innovation in the private sector, particularly in microelectronics, increasingly creates 'spin-on' applications of commercial technology to defence problems. Japan is also developing leading-edge military avionics through such projects as the FS-X fighter, a joint US–Japan project that has been seen by some observers as marking Japan's possible entry into major aircraft production. While Japan's post-war defence budget consistently hovers in the neighbourhood of 1% of GNP, the speed at which the Japanese economy continues to expand has led to nominal military spending increases of 5–7% a year, although for 1992 this dropped to 3.78%. Some idea of the relative sizes of local military forces in the region (excluding Russian and US forces) can be gained from the accompanying map. EBK

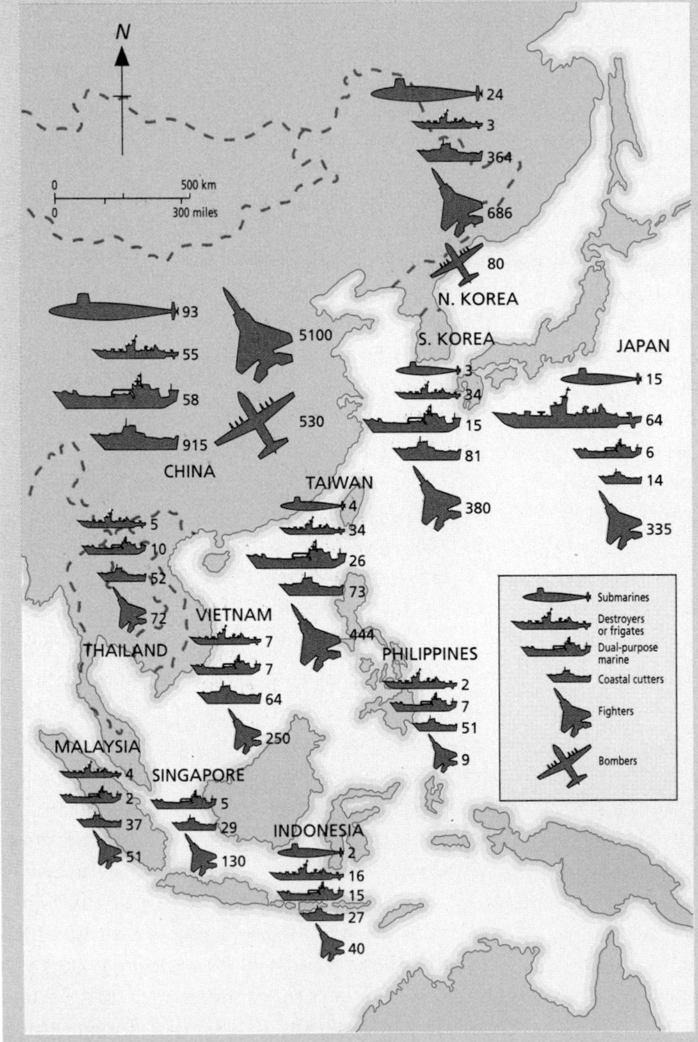

NATIONAL DEFENCE PROGRAMME OUTLINE

	Authorized number of SDF personnel	180,000 persons
GSDF	Basic units	
	Units deployed regionally in peacetime	12 divisions 2 combined brigades
	Mobile operation units	1 armoured division 1 artillery brigade 1 airborne brigade 1 training brigade 1 helicopter brigade
	Low-altitude ground-to-air missile units	8 antiaircraft artillery groups
MSDF	Basic units	
	Antisubmarine surface-ship units (for mobile operations)	4 escort flotillas
	Antisubmarine surface-ship units (regional district units)	10 divisions
	Submarine units	6 divisions
	Minesweeping units	2 flotillas
	Land-based antisubmarine aircraft units	16 squadrons
	Main equipment	
	Antisubmarine surface ships	About 60 ships
	Submarines	16 submarines
	Operational aircraft	About 220 aircraft
ASDF	Basic Units	
	Aircraft control and warning units	28 groups
	Interceptor units	10 squadrons
	Support fighter units	3 squadrons
	Air reconnaissance units	1 squadron
	Air transport units	3 squadrons
	Early warning units	1 squadron
	High-altitude ground-to-air missile units	6 groups
	Main equipment	
	Operational aircraft	About 430 aircraft

Source: *Defence of Japan*, 1990

TRENDS IN LEVEL AND SHARE OF JAPAN'S DEFENCE EXPENDITURE (FY 1955–91)

	Defence expenditure[a] (¥ billion)	Change in amount over previous year	Ratio to GNP[b]	Ratio to general account
1955	134.9	−3.3%	1.78%	13.61%
1960	156.9	0.6	1.23	9.99
1965	301.4	9.6	1.07	8.24
1970	569.5	17.7	0.79	7.16
1975	1,327.3	21.4	0.84	6.23
1980	2,230.2	6.5	0.90	5.24
1985	3,137.1	6.9	0.99	5.98
1986	3,343.5	6.6	0.99	6.18
1987	3,517.4	5.2	1.00	6.50
1988	3,700.3	5.2	1.01	6.53
1989	3,919.8	5.9	1.01	6.49
1990	4,159.3	6.1	1.00	6.28
1991	4,386.0	5.5	0.95	6.23

[a]Initial budget
[b]GNP figures are government estimates made for budget compilation purposes.
Source: Ministry of Finance, Japan.

(4) Nuclear weaponry has been unthinkable, given the experiences of Hiroshima and Nagasaki. Since 1967 a cabinet resolution has been in force banning the manufacture and possession of nuclear weapons and their carriage by foreign powers on Japanese territory, although these so-called 'three principles' have been compromised by the presence of US strategic weapons on Japanese soil or in transit. In 1970 a White Paper pronounced nuclear weapons constitutional for defence purposes, but since Article 96 states that Japan must honour its treaties and since Japan has signed the Nuclear Non-Proliferation Treaty, they are in effect still prohibited.

(5) Since the 1970s it has been cabinet policy that the SDF will not consume more than 1% of GNP, and this is thought to have limited the growth and sophistication of the forces. Under Nakasone's prime ministership this barrier was broken, but when pensions paid to former members of the Imperial Army are included the actual cost of the SDF on NATO calculations is about 2% of GNP and in real terms Japan's defence expenditure is now among the highest in the world. Continuing pressure from the US for increasing Japan's defence expenditure and encouraging Japan to play a larger rôle in national, regional and global defence has been counterbalanced by fears of resurgent Japanese military power in the region by other Asian nations.

(6) Restrictions on arms exports were introduced in 1949 and reinforced in 1967 when Prime Minister Satō prohibited the export of weapons to communist countries and to countries involved in, or about to become involved in, international disputes. In spite of these restrictions, the export of military hardware not strictly classifiable as weapons, such as helicopters suitable for military use, has been taking place on a modest scale. Nevertheless, the export of weapons systems is still subject to a ban and this has limited the growth and self-sufficiency of the Japanese defence industry.

There can be no doubt that the status of the defence establishment as a government agency rather than a full ministry has also placed limitations on its political power: efforts to promote it to a higher status have consistently failed. As a result, the director-generalship of the Defence Agency is a controversial appointment and has not been seen as a stepping stone to higher office. Nakasone, however, was an exception: he was the first former director-general of the Agency to become prime minister. This may make the position more attractive to politicians of high-calibre in the future and possibly lead to enhanced civilian control over the military establishment.

The SDF have undoubtedly become a major military force in East Asia, capable of making a considerable contribution both to the defence of Japan itself and increasingly to regional security. However, Japan's security is also assured under the US–Japan Security Treaty by which the US, through its conventional forces in Japan (now much reduced) and in the Pacific, continues to provide a nuclear umbrella and conventional support. Japanese forces are relatively well-integrated with US forces in the region and participate in joint training, intelligence-sharing, and moves towards the standardization of equipment. The SDF are likely to be restricted by both internal and external political pressures from expanding substantially. The opposition parties, having strongly and consistently opposed the SDF, seem now inclined to accept them; but they might well unite in opposition if there were to be any significant expansion in the size or rôle of the SDF or any diminution of civilian control. In all likelihood there will be little change in the position, posture and size of the SDF barring abrogation of the Security Treaty or the formation of a non-LDP government, both of which seem remote possibilities. IG

1000
VS116152C
日本銀行券
千円
日本銀行

Economy

The post-war economy

The Japanese economy is currently the wealthiest, most productive, and most technologically advanced in the world. How Japan has achieved this from a starting point of near total devastation at the end of the Pacific War is a matter of great importance for developing countries in particular. It is also a matter of controversy, both for academics seeking to explain the phenomenon and for politicians faced with the problems caused by the imbalances between Japan and its trading partners.

THE ERA OF HIGH-SPEED GROWTH

In the early years of the Occupation, the economy was plagued with inflation, shortages, and debates over Japan's post-war economic structure and its relationship to economic security. The policies that stabilized the economy in 1949–50 and set the foundation for Japan's return to international commerce are closely associated with the recommendations of a Detroit banker, Joseph Dodge. They are known as the 'Dodge line', and they engineered a deflation, stabilized the yen at ¥360 to the dollar, and allowed Japan to re-enter the world of international commerce.

The factors underlying Japan's successful post-war reconstruction are many and complex. The economy benefited from the General Agreement on Tariffs and Trade (GATT) that established a liberal trade régime throughout the world and ended colonially-based trade patterns. The prices of raw materials were either cheap or stable until the early 1970s, further favouring Japan's industrialization strategies. An unwavering state commitment to the creation of dynamic comparative advantage, increases in labour productivity and capital stock, cheap and available technology transfers, the movement of resources out of agriculture, and increasing economies of scale were also crucial factors. It is significant too that enterprise unions were promoted at the expense of early post-war trade unions, that the élite bureaucratic structure was left intact by the Occupation, and that the Liberal Democratic Party has enjoyed uninterrupted political leadership since 1955.

At both the macroeconomic and microeconomic levels the state has played a crucial rôle in Japan's economic success. Throughout the early post-war years Japan had a tightly managed economy. The Ministry of Finance (MOF) helped to ensure a high domestic savings rate and a regulated financial market in which interest rates were set by the government. Both MOF and the Ministry of International Trade and Industry (MITI) used these savings to develop a system of loans to industry that permitted a rapid expansion of the economy despite a shortage of capital. MITI was also active in organizing formal and informal production and research cartels, promoting mergers and new industries, and supplying information to the business community necessary for the further development of the

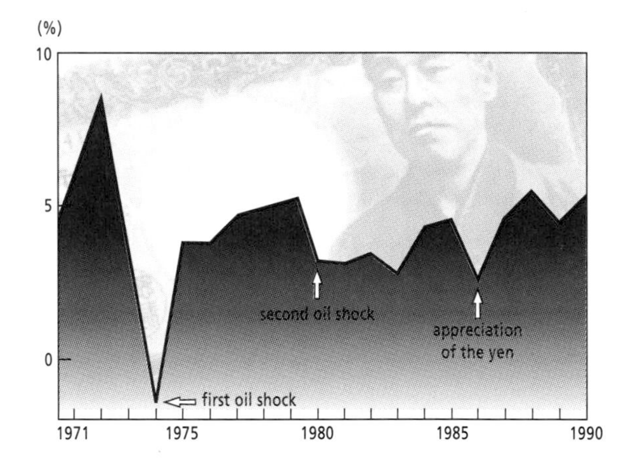

economy. It also exercised direct control over the economy through, for example, the Foreign Exchange and Foreign Trade Control Law of 1949. Entrance by highly competitive foreign firms into the Japanese market was heavily restricted or managed, with a government preference for licensing agreements that gave domestic firms access to leading-edge technologies.

By 1955 Japan had already achieved a per capita GDP higher than at any time in its pre-war history. Moreover, growth rates were gaining momentum: they averaged 8.5% in 1955–60, 9.8% in 1960–65, and 11.2% in 1965–71. The economy underwent deep structural changes in this period as resources moved out of agriculture, fishing, and mining and into manufacturing, construction, and services. The

Previous page *Working at the Tōkyō Stock Exchange, with inset of ¥1,000 banknote. The head on the note is that of the novelist Natsume Sōseki (1867–1916), a somewhat ironic choice since one of his favourite themes was the corrupting power of money.*

Central Ōsaka on a clear day. Ōsaka was the mercantile capital of Japan from the 17th century onwards, and is today Japan's second largest city with a population of more than six million. Although much of it was flattened during the Pacific War, it was the site of the World Expo in 1970 and it retains many attractions, not least among them being its cuisine. In recent years water buses have been introduced to take advantage of the network of rivers and canals to ease the congestion on commuter routes.

Left *The growth rate of Japan's GNP. The impact of the 1973–74 oil shock can be clearly seen.*

movement of labour from the rural sector into manufacturing provided a skilled and dedicated workforce for the years of rapid expansion. Labour productivity rose rapidly, with an average annual rise of 11.5% between 1963 and 1973. The government maintained a balanced budget through the mid 1960s by following tight fiscal and expansionary monetary policies. It also tailored public investment to favour further industrial expansion rather than improvements to the infrastructure.

The end of high-speed growth

The oil shock of 1973–74 was a major factor in bringing the era of high-speed growth to an end, but it was not the only factor. The 1973 oil crisis hit Japan just as it was in the last stages of a major expansion. Inflation was already gathering steam when the oil shock and US trade disputes triggered consumer panic buying of soap, toilet paper, soy sauce, and sugar. Wholesale prices rose 37% in 1974, and consumer prices by nearly 25%. A tight labour market led to substantial wage increases in this period, further fuelling inflation and forcing the government to slow the economy. An additional reason for the end of high-speed growth was the closing of the technology gap with the West, which made it no longer possible to plan for rapid industrial expansion through the introduction of imported technologies.

In the years 1974–85, Japan's economy grew at an average annual rate of 4.3%. This was less than half the growth rate of earlier periods but it was still higher than that of any other OECD country. Exports continued to play a central rôle in growth: in 1984, for example, almost 40% of growth resulted from exports. Higher energy costs, up to eight times 1970 levels by 1985, also led to slower growth, as did demands for fiscal policies aimed at pollution control and improving the infrastructure.

The high yen

As the rate of growth slowed there was an increasing imbalance in Japan's current account. The Plaza Agreement of 1985 was a largely unsuccessful attempt to correct these imbalances by allowing the yen to appreciate relative to other currencies, especially the dollar. The yen appreciated from a high of ¥260 to the dollar in 1985 to ¥130 to the dollar by 1987. Instead of weakening Japanese exports this led to increased international competitiveness and a move towards hyper-efficiency. Higher levels of productivity were achieved through further technological innovation and a shift to higher value-added products. The strong yen encouraged the production of lower value-added goods to move overseas: Japan's investment in Asia, particularly in Thailand, increased almost tenfold between 1985 and 1990, and

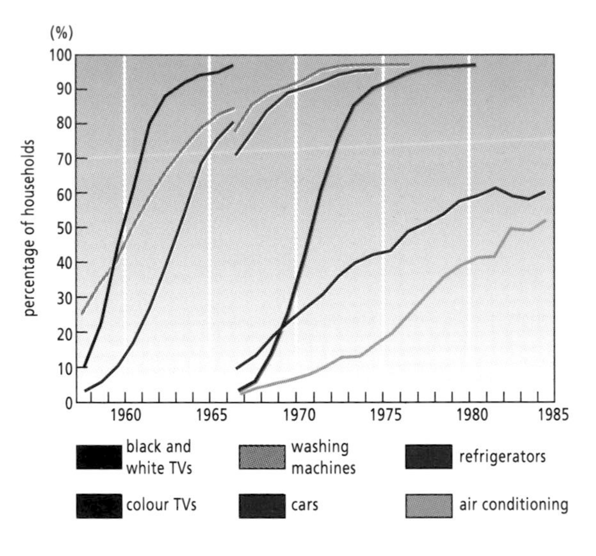

The rising ownership of consumer goods. Figures for 1957–67 are based on statistics for people living in cities of 50,000 or more, while figures for 1967–85 are for all households.

The 'bubble economy'

Much of the capital that underwrote the expansion of Japanese productive capacity in the late 1980s was made possible through a process of asset inflation in the securities, banking, and property markets that the Japanese have labelled the 'bubble economy'. This bubble was created through a combination of low interest rates, partial financial deregulation, a rising Tōkyō stock market, and rapid increases in property values; a combination which allowed Japanese businesses to raise capital for expansion on extremely favourable terms.

Fears that the bubble had expanded beyond the capacity of the real economy to sustain it prompted the Bank of Japan to institute a high interest rate policy in 1990 and early 1991. This, in turn, reduced land values and sent stock prices into a steep decline. The Nikkei average fell from a high of nearly 40,000 in late 1989 to nearer 16,000 in late 1992. Since so many outstanding loans were tied to property development and a rising stock market, the end of the bubble also meant that Japanese banks found themselves sitting on a mountain of bad debt. As a result, the government was forced to put together a rescue package.

Analysts are divided on the long term implications of the bubble economy for Japan's underlying industrial competitiveness. Western economists have tended to view the bubble as a case of unchecked speculation made possible by lax regulation and poorly informed bureaucrats. Others point out that the use of overheated equity and property markets to provide cheap capital to Japanese industry is similar in its logic to the system of overloans used by Japan's financial and industrial bureaucrats in the high growth years.

By 1992 the Japanese economy was in full recession and faced a minimum of two years of financial and industrial restructuring to work through the implications of what had occurred. EBK

has established a low-cost producer base for a number of Japanese manufacturers. The overall success of this restructuring now allows the Japanese economy to expand its volume at a rate that roughly duplicates the entire French economy every five years.

Japanese investments in the US and the EC have also greatly increased since the mid 1980s. Fear that the chronic trade disputes might encourage the US and EC to limit Japanese access to their markets prompted a flood of inward investment in manufacturing and services. Between 1985 and 1990, direct investment in the US totalled US$110 billion. If all forms of investment are calculated, the figure is approximately US$185 billion. Direct investment in the EC in this period was considerably less, at US$55 billion.

Since the late 1980s Japan has pursued policies that combine high levels of public investment with fiscal reform to control public debt. The 1989 reform package included the introduction of a 3% value added tax and income tax reforms that favour single-income households in the middle and upper income brackets while disadvantaging pensioners and low-income families with dual incomes. The controversial nature of these reforms has been mediated somewhat by a high corporate tax rate that still provides over 30% of national tax revenues.

It has been estimated that if present trends in growth and investment continue, the Japanese economy is likely to surpass that of the US and become the world's largest by the year 2005. Indeed, it has already assumed leadership in key areas. It has the world's largest per capita GNP, at US$23,472 in 1989 and steadily climbing. Japanese banks and securities firms are among the largest in the world. Japan is also the largest holder of foreign assets and debt, at US$240 billion in 1988, and it is the world's largest holder of gold, with half of global gold production going to Japan in 1988. Similarly, major Japanese firms are at the forefront in terms of innovation and efficiency.

Controversies

As a country poor in natural resources, Japan must trade to survive. Post-war strategy focussed on industrial sectors where processes, products, and markets were already well developed. An export

Right *International comparison of GNP and per capita GNP in 1989.*

orientation meant that Japan could only expand in these sectors by taking market share away from already well-established firms abroad, many already facing the difficulties that accompany the problems of a mature domestic market. Critics have labelled this an adversarial approach to trade, though few see the imitation strategy that started this process off as deliberately conspiratorial.

The consistent imbalance between savings and investment, resulting in a large current account surplus, has also been seen as a problem. Japan has attempted to address this not by promoting consumption but by expanding public sector investment: this slowed the growth of the trade surplus in the late 1980s, but the surplus is again approaching record levels. Even if Japan were to try to reduce savings by promoting household consumption, it is likely that such measures would fail since the astronomical price of land, a result of speculation in the 1980s, will continue to act as a powerful boost to household savings in the foreseeable future.

Japan's strategy of public investment in infrastructure is usually presented as an effort to reduce its international imbalances, but it also meets the test of economic rationality. For example, Japanese industry depends overwhelmingly on roads to transport goods: in 1988, 80% of all goods were moved by road, as opposed to only 8.2% by ship and 1.4% by rail. It is estimated that 40% of transportation demand could go unmet by the year 2000 unless there is massive public investment to remove transportation bottlenecks. The government intends to devote ¥430 trillion to public works in the 1990s to address this problem.

A reluctance to allow the yen to function as an international settlement and reserve currency is another potential source of instability in the years ahead. The dollar has held this rôle since 1944, but the US is no longer in a position of financial leadership. It is Japan that today sits atop the world's greatest concentration of wealth, though financial authorities in Tōkyō still resist policies that would allow large scale outflows of yen and the full development of an offshore yen market. It is true that a global rôle for the yen would somewhat reduce the government's control over domestic interest rates and the money supply, but some would argue that the gains in long-term international economic stability would more than offset this sacrifice.

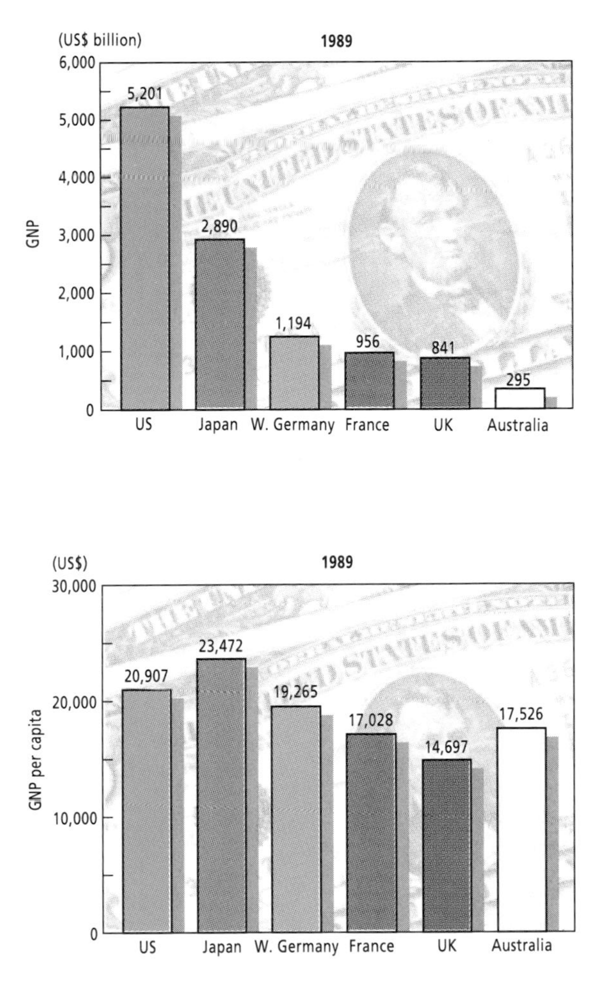

Some critics also argue that changes need to be made in the business–government relationship. Japan's Fair Trade Commission estimates that products under government regulation account for 41% of total value-added manufactures in all industries. Despite numerous liberalization packages, the number of products regulated by the state exceeds 10,000, and there are numerous laws that serve primarily to protect the interests of Japanese firms. The situation is further complicated by the problem of 'administrative guidance', by which bureaucrats make decisions on regulation and guidance through opaque proceedings that are often based more on bureaucratic fiat than on clearly worded and objectively interpreted rules and regulations.

The most controversial aspect of Japan's economic structure, and the one with the least likelihood of reform, is the large corporate groupings known as *keiretsu*. These groups dominate markets in times of

International comparison of numbers of unemployed (top) and unemployment rates (bottom).

economic expansion, drive out competition in times of downturn, and protect each other from bankruptcy and takeovers through cross-holding of shares by firms within the group. They not only allow Japanese firms to implement long-range strategies without concern for quarterly profits, hostile takeover bids, and bankruptcy, they also make penetration into the Japanese market difficult for any newly-arrived firm. *Keiretsu* distribution networks allow control over retail prices, a process complemented by highly selective enforcement of anti-monopoly legislation. The costs of this system are impressive: on average, Japanese consumers can pay 30–40% higher prices than their Western counterparts for the same products. By some estimates, this results in annual producer windfalls of approximately ¥80 trillion out of a ¥200 trillion a year domestic consumer market. *Keiretsu* are one of the most distinctive features of Japan's national economy and provide a competitive edge that other nations cannot match. Many analysts believe that they will play a fundamental rôle in shaping economic competition in the next century.

EBK

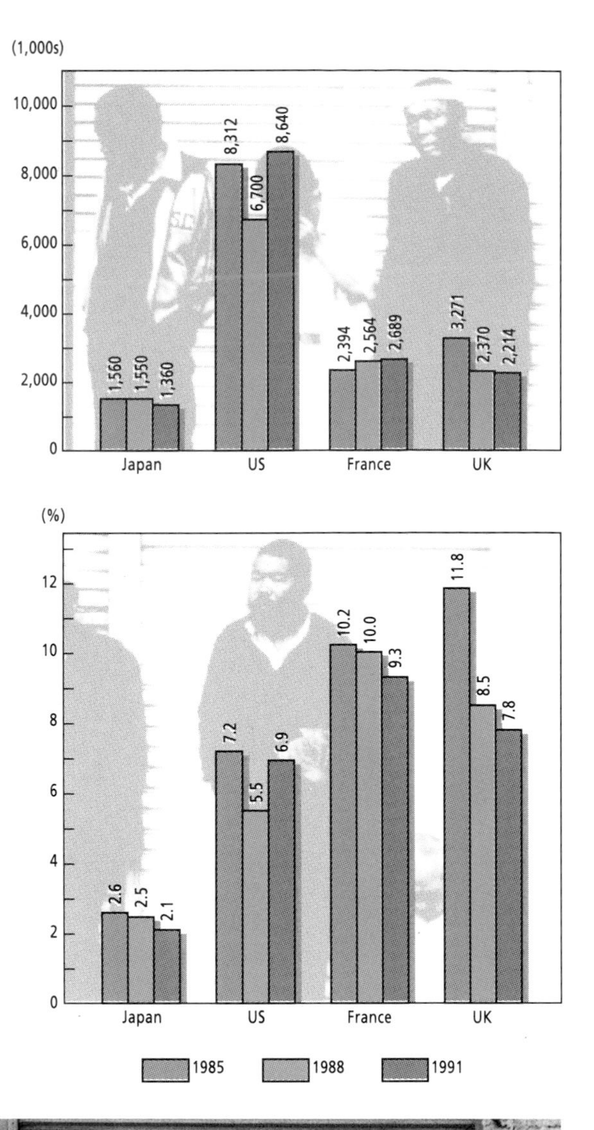

In recent years labour shortages have been a much bigger problem than unemployment in Japan, but at the unskilled end of the day-labour market queues like this one are still a common feature.

Food and agriculture

Japan is by no means an ideal country for the practice of agriculture. The steep and densely wooded mountain ranges which constitute the country's core leave only around 14% of the land area suitable for arable cultivation and it is a tribute both to the productive powers of rice as a crop and to the ingenuity and hard labour of generations of Japanese farmers that almost complete national self-sufficiency in most food crops has been maintained, despite substantial population growth, throughout most of Japan's history. With the opening up of the country to international trade in the mid 19th century, Japanese farmers became increasingly involved in production for both domestic and international markets, but nonetheless it is only in recent years that rising incomes and changing dietary patterns have significantly reduced the ability of Japan's 5 million farm households to provide for the nation's major food requirements.

Crops

Throughout the world, irrigated rice has proved to be the crop best able to support a dense population and, since its introduction into Japan around the 1st century BC, it has remained the single most important crop as well as the chief item in the Japanese diet. However, its cultivation requires both intense and careful labour on the part of farm workers and the construction and maintenance of an infrastructure of irrigation facilities to provide an adequate and controlled supply of water to each paddy field. The construction of such an infrastructure demands considerable planning and investment of time and labour. Japanese farmers entered the era of industrialization with the basis of their irrigation network already in existence, thanks to the work of previous generations, and although substantial improvements have been made in the capacity to regulate water flows, the total of approximately 3 million hectares of land adapted for paddy cultivation, constituting a little over half of the entire cultivated area, has remained relatively constant. Almost all Japanese

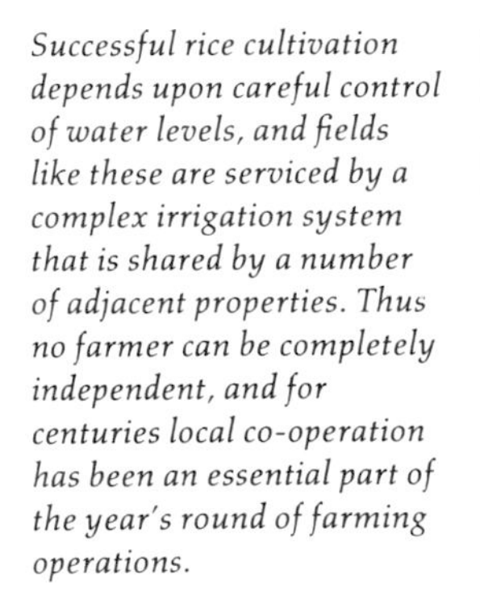

Successful rice cultivation depends upon careful control of water levels, and fields like these are serviced by a complex irrigation system that is shared by a number of adjacent properties. Thus no farmer can be completely independent, and for centuries local co-operation has been an essential part of the year's round of farming operations.

farm households have therefore always had access to one or more plots of paddy land, fitted into the irrigation network of their village community.

In addition to paddy fields, most households have also farmed some of the land that cannot be irrigated to the standards required by paddy rice. Here they have grown a wide variety of crops for their own consumption or for sale. These have included other grain crops, such as wheat, which has also been widely grown as a winter crop on paddy land where conditions permitted; fruit, vegetables and pulses, many of which are processed into the bean-based protein sources and the many different types of pickle which accompany rice in the Japanese diet, and industrial crops for use in the production of, for example, textiles. Most importantly, from the mid 19th century until the 1930s, the cultivation of mulberry orchards and the rearing of silkworms constituted a major source of income to many households in suitable areas. The use of woodlands and forests as sources of timber, fuel and natural fertilizers was also vital to the rural economy, although commercial substitutes, such as chemical fertilizer, have gradually replaced them. Livestock have never represented a very significant element in Japanese agriculture: horses and oxen were kept as draft animals and, as Western influence on the Japanese diet spread, the production of eggs and meat expanded; but, with the exception of Hokkaidō, which has continued to serve as the main source of Japan's dairy produce and beef, the Japanese islands have generally proved inhospitable territory for grazing animals.

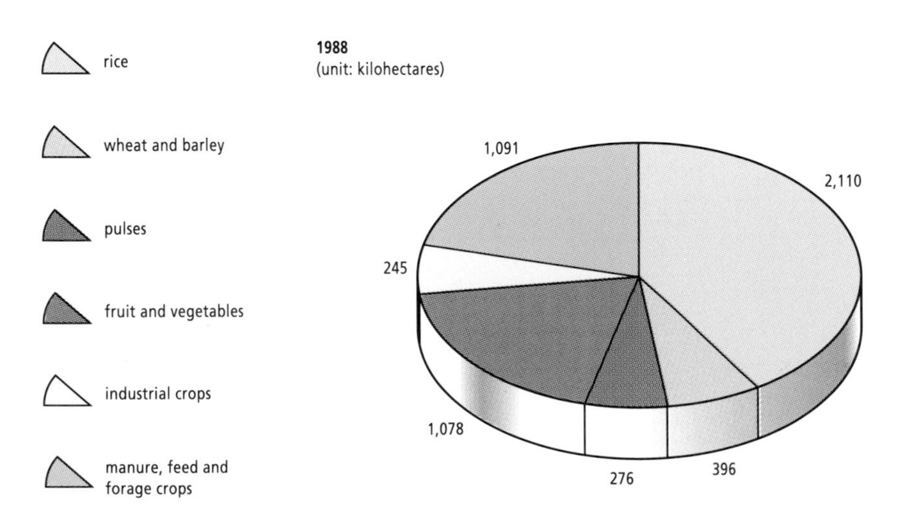

Area devoted to major crops in 1988 in kilohectares.

Agriculture in the economy

In the late 19th century, on the eve of industrialization, Japan's economy was still dominated by agriculture. For 70% of the labour force, work on the land constituted the main source of employment, and around 40% of the nation's total output consisted of agricultural products. Although estimates vary, it is probable that agricultural output had been growing steadily in many parts of the country throughout the 19th century, as improved methods spread and as the market for agricultural products grew. By the first decades of this century, rice yields on paddy land were on average substantially higher than those achieved elsewhere in Asia until relatively recently, yet, whilst continuing to meet the demand for basic grain from the growing urban population, Japanese farmers were also able to devote more time to the production of other goods, in particular silk, for sale, and to engage in non-agricultural work.

The development of urban factory industry, particularly under the boom conditions of the First World War period, offered growing numbers of rural workers full-time industrial work away from their villages and although the number of farm households remained more-or-less constant until after the Pacific War, the proportion of the labour force employed in agriculture began to decline, as the younger sons and daughters of farm families increasingly found work in the towns. By the 1910s, the growth in urban demand for food products had accelerated the steady rise in agricultural prices to the point where, in 1918, serious rioting in protest against high rice prices broke out in a number of cities. Government concern about the economic and political threat posed by such urban unrest led to plans to develop the production of rice in Japan's colonies and the impact of colonial rice imports, combined with the slow-down in the growth of demand in the depressed conditions of the inter-war economy, ushered in a period of lower prices and much slower growth. Meanwhile the shift in the economy away from agriculture continued, so that by 1940, less than half of the labour force was employed in agriculture, producing only 15% of the nation's total output.

During the Pacific War, the agricultural sector barely managed to maintain food supplies and by the winter of 1945 there were fears of starvation in

Japanese cities. After the war, however, the farm sector recovered quickly and output growth resumed at a faster rate than before. Farmers were encouraged to produce not only more rice, but also the increasing range of fruit, vegetables and meat that Japanese consumers came to demand as their incomes rose and Western influence on their food preferences intensified. The output of meat and dairy products, citrus fruits and numerous kinds of vegetable have all increased spectacularly from their low pre-war bases, as have both the scale and the sophistication of marketing and food-processing systems.

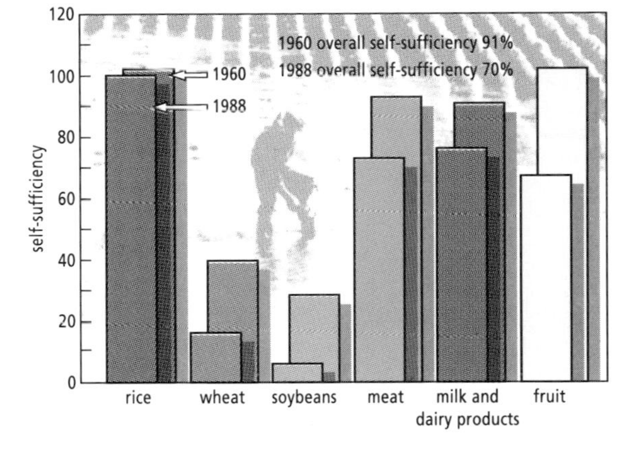

National self-sufficiency rates in major crops in 1960 and 1988.

AGRICULTURE'S SHARE IN THE ECONOMY

	Proportion of GDP (%)[1]	Proportion of employed workers (%)[2]
1885	41	71
1920	27	52
1940	14	40
1960	13	31
1985	3	8

[1]Agriculture, forestry and fishing
[2]Agriculture and forestry
Sources: 1885–1960 – Unemura *et al.*, *Chōki keizai tōkei*
1985 – *Nihon tōkei nenkan*

THE DISTRIBUTION OF FARMS BY SIZE
(1989; unit: 1,000 households; excluding Hokkaidō)

Area in hectares	Under 0.5	0.5–1	1–2	2–3	Over 3	Total
No. of farms	1,675	1,162	882	239	135	4,093

Source: *Nihon tōkei nenkan*

Nonetheless, the ability of Japan's farmers to meet the nation's food requirements at reasonable cost has continued to decline as the economy has grown to superpower status. As Japanese consumers increasingly switch from rice to bread, as sandwiches, hamburgers and Western-style breakfasts have grown in popularity, reliance on imported wheat has reached 100%. Although most of Japan's beef, pork and chicken comes from home-produced animals, the fodder they eat is almost all imported. Even the soya beans used to make so many of Japan's traditional food products are now largely of foreign origin. Overall national self-sufficiency in food products had thus declined from 90% in 1960 to around 70% by the late 1980s and Japan had become one of the world's largest importers of a number of major crops.

Meanwhile, the rapid growth of industry during the 'economic miracle' period drew workers away from the villages at a rate never experienced before. By the 1980s, less than 10% of the labour force was employed in agriculture, a dwindling proportion of whom were full-time farmers. The agricultural sector which at the beginning of the century was the nation's most important employer and producer had become by its closing decades a relatively insignificant employer and producer, yet a major political and economic burden.

Irrigation and technology

The practice of agriculture in Japan has always centred on the cultivation of irrigated rice, and the pattern of agricultural activities has long remained determined by the cycle of operations required in the planting, growing and harvesting of the *Japonica* strains of rice grown and consumed there. For maximum yields, seedlings are grown in the spring in seed-beds, preparatory to transplanting into carefully prepared and flooded fields; through the summer, the plants grow in standing water which inhibits weed growth and supplies nutrients; and in late autumn, the grain is ready for harvesting, threshing and polishing, after which it can be stored, marketed or consumed. Other activities, such as the cultivation of non-rice crops or non-agricultural work on or off the farm, have to be fitted around this cycle, and the rhythm of rural life has always revolved around the crucial points in the life of the rice plant.

Fisheries

The Japanese fisheries industry is the largest in the world: the domestic supply of, and demand for, fisheries products shows no signs of abating. In 1988, fish supplied the Japanese with more than 40% of their average daily intake of animal proteins, but satisfying this high level of demand has become increasingly difficult. In 1988, the total catch was 12,780,000 tonnes, of which 77% came from within Japanese coastal and offshore waters, 9% from foreign waters, and 14% from the high seas. The percentage of the total catch has, however, been changing ever since 1976–78 when many countries introduced 200-mile economic zones.

Japan has been deriving ever-decreasing amounts of fish from the waters of other countries, as its allocations have been reduced: its allocation in US waters has already been reduced to zero. To cope with the shortfall, imports have been rising and now some 10% of fisheries imports are air-freighted luxury seafoods such as shellfish and tuna, for which there is high domestic demand but declining domestic production. Another development has been increased use of fish-farms, particularly for shellfish. Options for the future are limited, but the government is giving high priority to the efficient exploitation of Japan's own fisheries resources, and this must include close monitoring of both pollution and the danger of overfishing.

The industry has faced a number of problems in recent years. It has coped with a declining workforce by resorting to technological aids, such as ultrasonic fishfinders and net-monitors, but it has been forced to give in to international pressures on the use of drift-nets, which have been blamed for reducing the dolphin population in the Pacific.

PK

In Japan, which does not experience a full-scale monsoon and where coastal plains and river valleys are relatively small in area, irrigation by natural flooding has long since been superseded by man-made control of the flow of river water. Sophisticated irrigation systems, involving the construction and maintenance of dams, reservoirs and feeder-channel networks, have been in existence since before 1600. Investment of labour and resources in improving and extending irrigation systems has been a continuous process ever since and although Japanese farmers can still find themselves on occasion susceptible to flood and drought, they have long had greater control over their environment than farmers in most other parts of Asia.

The organization of such interconnected systems, where the same water flows from one family's fields to another's and where many villages may depend on limited supplies of water from one source, has required the development of appropriate institutions. Within villages, the allocation of water and the organization of the maintenance of facilities has generally been carried out by a communal group to which all rice cultivators belong. This group is then represented in higher-level organizations in cases where more than one village is served by the same source. Local government authorities have always had an interest in the maintenance and improvement of irrigation systems and with the development of local government bureaucracy since the Meiji period and the increasing rôle of public funds in land improvement, local officials have become more and more involved in irrigation administration. Water rights remain nonetheless a matter of prime concern both to individual households and to villages as a whole.

The supply of labour in the right amounts at the right time has also always required a mixture of individual effort and communal organization. Since the decline of the extended family during the Tokugawa period, the day-to-day management and labour of farms has generally been provided by the members of small-scale household units. Short-term hiring of labour from other households has been practised, but in many cases the extra labour for the peak-time operations of transplanting and harvesting has been provided through exchange arrangements between households.

Although the fundamentals of rice cultivation

have remained the enduring constant in Japanese rural life, agricultural methods have nonetheless changed in many ways as farmers have adjusted to the needs of an ever more industrialized economy. The growth in agricultural output which sustained the early stages of Japanese industrialization was the result of changes which enabled each farm household to produce more with its own land and labour. These changes included the use of higher-yielding rice varieties able to respond to heavier applications of the organic, and later chemical, fertilizers which farmers were increasingly able to buy, and developments in crop rotations and cultivation practices which enabled farm workers to diversify and intensify the use of their time, both in producing other crops and in industrial work which could be combined with farming.

Only from around the 1930s did the pressures of industry's demand for labour begin to lead to moves in the direction of mechanization and it has really only been with the massive growth in industrial employment since the 1950s that machines have been widely substituted for people in Japan's agriculture. Nowadays, farms are equipped with an array of tractors, combines, transplanting machines and so on, but because of the generally small size of both fields and holdings, all such machinery has had to be designed on a small-scale. Equipment which can or must be operated on a larger scale is often communally owned by village co-operatives and the use of contractors to plant or harvest crops is also spreading. Nonetheless, Japanese farmers now own too much inefficient and duplicated capital equipment to be able to produce food crops at prices competitive with those of large-scale mechanized producers elsewhere in the world.

Landownership and agricultural organization

Visitors to the Japanese countryside always comment on the patchwork of cultivated river valleys and terraced hillsides. This patchwork arises from the generally small area of each field or plot, the result of the demands of irrigation construction in a mountainous country and the longstanding pressure to make use of every available corner of cultivatable land. The holdings of individual households have as a result generally consisted of several separate plots scattered throughout the area of irrigated and unirrigated land controlled by the village. The average size of these landholdings has always been extremely small, with a cultivated holding of around a hectare constituting a solid middle-range farm and many farm households in the past surviving on much less than this, though often supplementing their income with wages earned off the farm. Since well back into the 19th century, cultivation on a larger scale has been uneconomic (except in Hokkaidō) and those owning areas larger than could be managed and worked by the members of the household have normally found it more practical and profitable to rent out the excess.

Tenancy of agricultural land was not officially recognized during the Tokugawa period but in 1872, the new Meiji government, in its efforts to reform and stabilize the agricultural tax base on which it depended for the bulk of its revenue, gave legal title to land to those who could prove their right to it and it has been estimated that, by then, around a third of the cultivated area was in practice already farmed by tenants. As farmers struggled to cope with the ups and downs of production for the market in the industrializing economy, considerable numbers continued to mortgage and lose title to all or part of their land, so that by the inter-war years tenancy was widespread. Around a third of households then owned none of the land they cultivated and a further third owned some but not all. Nonetheless, the accumulation of large landholdings was quite rare and the majority of landlords for much of the period before the Pacific War rented out relatively small areas and supplemented their rental income with their own cultivation or income from non-agricultural sources.

However, as farmers became increasingly embedded in the commercial economy, better educated and more open to influences from beyond the village, relationships between larger and smaller landowners and cultivators changed. Where once deferential assistance towards landlord or patron households, in return for protection and help in bad times, had made sense from the point of view of poorer households, by the 1920s farmers able to reap the benefits of improved technology and to earn incomes outside agriculture increasingly challenged the rights of landlords. When the depression hit agriculture in the

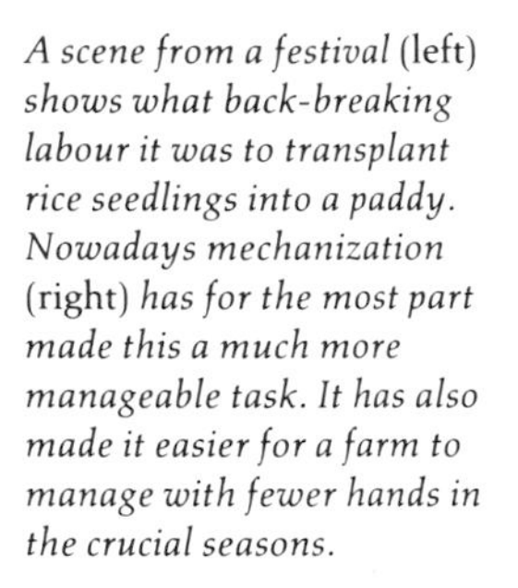

A scene from a festival (left) *shows what back-breaking labour it was to transplant rice seedlings into a paddy. Nowadays mechanization* (right) *has for the most part made this a much more manageable task. It has also made it easier for a farm to manage with fewer hands in the crucial seasons.*

1930s, disputes between landlords and tenants spread to new areas and the problem of social and economic conditions in the countryside became a significant national issue.

Thus, even before the Pacific War, landownership had begun to lose its social and economic attractions. After the war, however, the non-cultivating landowner was to disappear altogether as the Occupation authorities set about reforming the whole structure so as to create a class of landowning farmers which would act as a bastion of democracy and freedom in the countryside. Under the Land Reform legislation of 1945–46, a ceiling of 3 hectares (12 hectares in Hokkaidō) was placed on landholdings, with restrictions on how much of this could be rented out, and anything above this was transferred to the cultivator, with what turned out to be minimal compensation to the former landlord. This large-scale redistribution of land assets led to a substantial improvement in rural living standards and an upsurge in investment and output growth which undoubtedly contributed to the recovery of the economy after the war. However, the structure of small-scale owner-cultivated farms which the Land Reform legislation froze into existence has helped to preclude the emergence of larger-scale cultivation ever since.

The problems of agriculture today

Agriculture's rôle in Japan's industrialization was in many ways a more positive, or at least less problematic, one than that of the agricultural sectors of many of today's developing countries. However, the successful accommodation of a small-scale rice producing farm sector to an industrializing economy seems conversely to have bequeathed to the now highly developed Japanese economy even greater problems than those presented by the agricultural sectors of other industrialized countries. Almost all advanced countries have found cause to provide protection for their agricultural producers against cheaper imports, on the grounds of strategic needs, the survival of rural communities and the preservation of the countryside. In Japan, though, given the small scale of production into which farmers are locked and the generally unfavourable environment for agriculture, the level of protection necessary to maintain an agricultural sector of the size considered politically and strategically desirable has been extremely high. This has resulted in Japanese consumers paying a very high price for their food and in substantial friction with Japan's trading partners.

The system for controlling and restricting imports of agricultural products into Japan, and at the same time maintaining the incomes of farm households, is an elaborate and complex one, but given the centrality of rice in farm production and in the diet, it is focussed on the price of rice. Throughout the post-war period, farmers have been able to sell their rice to the state at a price calculated according to a formula designed to maintain incomes from agriculture at the level of the national average wage (although, in fact, very few farm households derive their incomes solely from agriculture), and imports of rice at the much lower prices available on the world market have been prohibited. As rice consumption has declined, as a result of changing tastes and, presumably, high prices, the incentive of this guaranteed income has led farmers to continue to produce quantities well in excess of demand and the government has been forced to accumulate growing surpluses of the grain in store. Various attempts have been made to counteract this by encouraging farmers to switch to other crops, but these moves in their turn have depended on subsidies and protected prices, so that an ever wider range of items has been subject to import controls. The cost to the consumer/tax-payer of financing agricultural support policies has therefore been consistently high and at the same time a number of bitter 'trade friction' disputes, with the US and some Third World countries, have erupted over import restrictions on some agricultural products.

Underlying the problems faced by post-war agricultural policy has been the growth in part-time farming. The guaranteed price and market for rice have enabled small-scale farmers to survive, but no more than about 15% now do so on a full-time basis and over 70% of households earn more from non-agricultural sources than they do from farming. The restrictions imposed by the Land Reform legislation on the accumulation of land have combined with the rise in the value of land as an asset to place enormous obstacles in the way of the (in any case technically difficult) consolidation of holdings into units which could generate productive full-time employment for farmers. Consequently, average costs of production and hence the prices consumers have to pay for their food remain, by international standards, very high, and the vitality of village life is draining away as the younger generations devote themselves to their off-farm careers.

If, then, as would seem to be the case, the majority of Japanese would have much to gain from a reduction in farm subsidies and protection, why has so little progress been made towards reform? The answer lies in large part in the political strength of the agricultural lobby in Japan. The nationwide organization of agricultural co-operatives is able to mobilize farmers extremely effectively and to deliver valuable backing to politicians who support its cause, which has essentially remained the protection of the small-scale rice cultivator.

The absence of any substantial redrawing of electoral boundaries since the immediate post-war period, despite large-scale movements of population to urban areas, has given added significance to farm interests by giving rural votes greater weight than urban ones, and the ruling Liberal Democratic Party depends heavily on rural support. This has enabled farmers to back up with political pressure their desire to retain control of their land (with all its concomitant financial advantages), and moves towards reducing protection and restructuring agriculture, through, for example, schemes to encourage the leasing of land to larger-scale cultivators, have had only limited effects.

The almost automatic annual increases in the guaranteed price of rice of previous years have ceased, but the scale of imports of key contentious products such as beef remains small. Agriculture thus looks set to present Japanese governments for many years to come with some extremely difficult social, political and economic problems, the solution to which will demand the skill and inventiveness which have made policy in the industrial field such a success.

PF

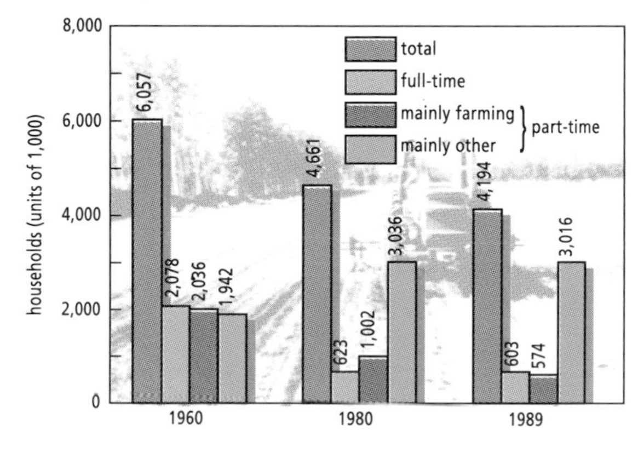

The growth of part-time farming.

Energy

Japan's economic success must be measured against its meagre resources. Japan is more dependent upon imported energy than any other industrial nation. Hydroelectric power, now accounting for under 5% of Japan's primary energy supply, was already fully installed by the 1950s; domestic coal supplies were insufficient to power the 'economic miracle' of the 1960s; and Japanese oil fields produce less than 1% of total demand. There are no domestic uranium mines, and alternative sources such as geothermal and synthetic fuels provide less than 2% of Japan's consumption. Japan imports more oil than any nation except the US, and less than one-fifth of Japan's primary energy is supplied from domestic sources.

The Japanese have lived with these vulnerabilities since their industrial revolution began. Great uncertainty in energy markets has encouraged them to pay a premium to enhance national security by acquiring stable energy resources, and by consuming energy more efficiently than others: Japan produces 15% of global wealth, but consumes just 7% of global energy.

Energy use

Patterns of energy use in post-war Japan have changed dramatically. As recently as the eve of the Pacific War, the share of oil in Japan's primary energy supply was less than the share of firewood. Early in the post-war period, Japan tried to rely upon domestic energy sources, such as coal and hydroelectricity, for its energy needs, but such supplies soon proved inadequate. Japan's post-war economic growth required that energy use increase at a dizzying rate of nearly 25% per year. Consumption grew from 41 million tonnes of oil equivalent in 1950 to 340 million in 1973.

Soaring consumption was reflected in the changing market shares for different fuels. While oil comprised only 5% of Japanese commercial energy consumption in 1950, it had increased to 75% by 1973, 90% of which came from the Middle East. Over that same period, the share of coal dropped from nearly three-quarters of total primary energy consumption to less than one-quarter. Japan's post-war economic growth was facilitated by access to cheap energy, particularly imported oil.

Japanese consumption has been dominated by large industrial consumers rather than households or the transport sector. Nowhere else in the industrial world do household and commercial consumers consume as small a portion of total primary energy as in Japan. Industry has always consumed more than half. Japanese responses to the oil crises of the 1970s were largely successful: after a short recession and

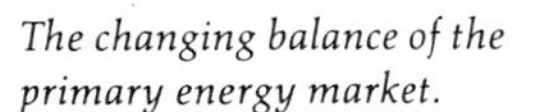

The changing balance of the primary energy market.

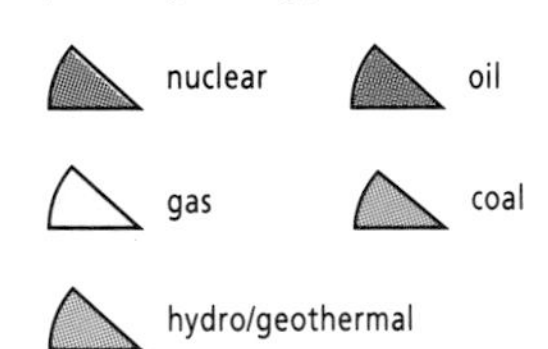

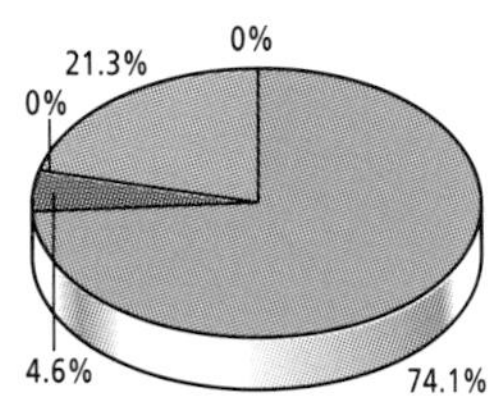

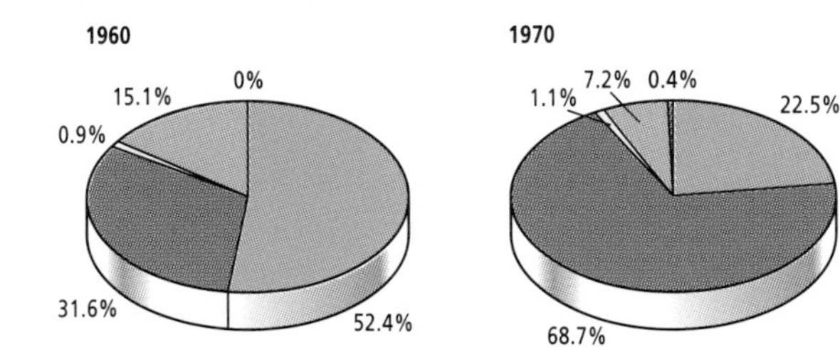

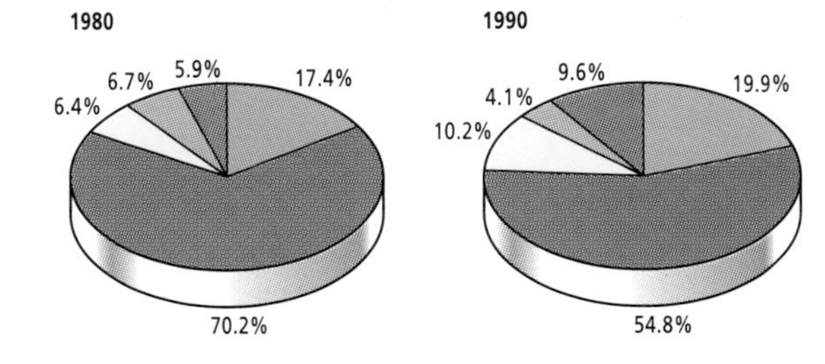

high inflation in 1974, economic growth rates returned to their previous high levels; while output more than doubled between 1973 and 1989, the energy intensity of the Japanese economy declined considerably. Fuel shares changed too, as Japan moved much of its energy intensive industrial capacity off-shore and diversified its sources. Dependence on oil was reduced from 75% in 1973 to just 58% in 1989, and the Middle Eastern share was reduced from 85% in 1970 to about 70% at the time of the 1991 Gulf War. As a proportion of primary energy supply, coal consumption increased slightly, while use of liquefied natural gas (LNG) and nuclear power both increased more than tenfold during this period. Japanese private firms and public agencies together now maintain the world's largest stockpile of petroleum (142 days). In addition, despite slack oil prices, Japan has maintained a vigorous research and development programme, and conservation measures have been far more successfully implemented than in any other industrial democracy. In 1989, Japan needed only 63% as much energy to produce the same GNP as in 1973.

Energy industry structure

Unlike in Europe, where state-owned monopolies are common, the Japanese oil, coal, and electric power industries have been kept in private hands. Government-owned entities like the Electric Power Development Corporation and the Japan National Oil Company are limited by statute to assist or subsidize private firms. Each sector has distinctive structural features.

The Japanese government has a policy of refining at the doorstep of the consumer, a strategy whereby only crude oil can be imported, so ensuring a higher added value at home. Only existing refiners are given licences to import refined products. But the Japanese oil industry has never been fully integrated from oil field to high-street pump. There is almost no domestic production and Japanese firms enjoy only limited participation abroad. Refiners are organized as the Petroleum Association of Japan and have different economic and political interests from the oil producing firms, who form the Petroleum Development Association. These two groups frequently fail

Above *Coalmining began on this island off the west coast of Kyūshū, near Nagasaki, in the late 19th century, and the population reached a peak of 5,267 in 1960. As needs and policies changed, it went into a decline and the mines closed in 1974. The island with all its buildings and houses is now totally abandoned.*

Oil storage tanks on reclaimed land. Ever since the oil shock of 1973–74 the government has sought to build up capacity for maintaining substantial oil reserves to provide energy security.

to co-ordinate their strategies. Very few refiners are involved in processing their own crude and the fact that there are 32 separate refiners in Japan makes oil the most fragmented heavy industry in the economy. There is an even split between those firms that are affiliated with foreign capital and those that are wholly domestic, although in 1991 there were only two Japanese refiners wholly foreign owned.

The coal industry was divided into large and small firms that frustrated a co-ordinated national energy policy for decades. The large mines were controlled by the pre-war *zaibatsu*, most prominently Mitsui and Mitsubishi, who used the profits from mining to fund their growing industrial empires. Their workers included convicts, women, and forced labour from Korea and China. The *zaibatsu* were confronted by small mine owners, who often succeeded in creating local political support to block bureaucratic efforts at consolidation and, in the last days of the industry, they managed to create subsidy programmes for coal as a declining sector. Long after the diversified interests of Mitsui and Mitsubishi sought to close down the industry, these small mine owners managed to slow the pace of change. Mitsubishi and Mitsui did not manage to leave the coal business until the late 1980s when the Miike and Tanegashima collieries were finally closed.

The 10 electric utilities are organized as regional monopolies. They are privately held and are among the largest utilities in the world. Their rate structure, siting decisions, and fuel choices are regulated by the Agency for Natural Resources and Energy (ANRE), which is attached to the Ministry of International Trade and Industry (MITI). Like the similar but less influential gas utilities, they do not compete with each other, except to attract industry to their particular region. Fuel choices made by the electric utilities: coal in the 1950s, oil in the 1960s and nuclear and liquefied natural gas (LNG) in the 1970s after the oil crisis, are carefully negotiated with suppliers and with the bureaucracy.

Energy policy

Energy, like the economy more generally, is seen in terms of national security. The pursuit of this security has reflected the interests of diverse constituents as well as the changing international environment. Policymakers have had to tread a fine line between the pursuit of national security and market efficiency, and between the interest of producers and consumers, large and small. In the attempt to acquire reliable supplies of energy at reasonable cost, Japanese policy has been more focussed and more sustained than that of other industrial nations in the post-war period, but energy security has remained an elusive goal.

MITI, through its agency ANRE, provides the authoritative forum for energy policy co-ordination. ANRE was established before the 1973 oil crisis in anticipation that achieving 'comprehensive security' would require careful co-ordination both within central government and among diverse industries. As the central government agency responsible for the development of Japanese industry, MITI serves both as trade gatekeeper and economic co-ordinator.

The primary forum for co-ordination within the private sector for the reconciliation of policy preferences and for the adjustment of demands among vendors, suppliers, producers, and consumers is the Federation of Economic Organizations (Keidanren). It was Keidanren that helped the government develop its original Comprehensive Energy Programme that blocked many attempts to nationalize the energy industries, and that has co-ordinated allocative decisions about supply and production ever since.

Through its formal advisory commissions (especially the Comprehensive Energy Policy Advisory Council), MITI is able to supervise all negotiations. Less formally, MITI enjoys power of administrative guidance, whereby it co-operates with regulated parties to minimize the dislocations that excessive

The changing energy balance of the electric power market.

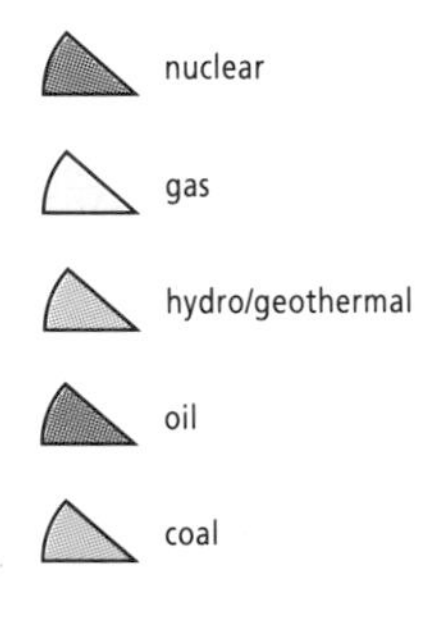

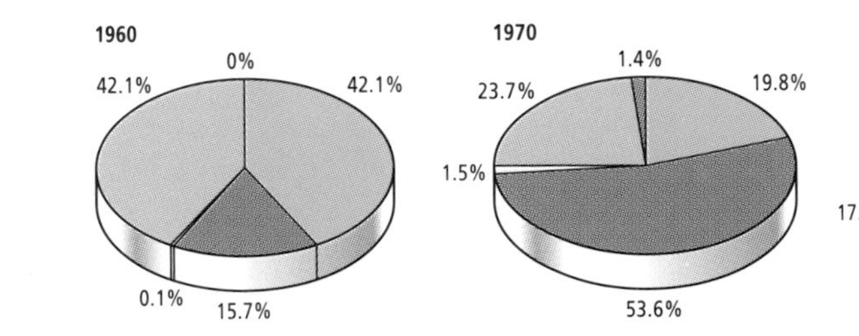

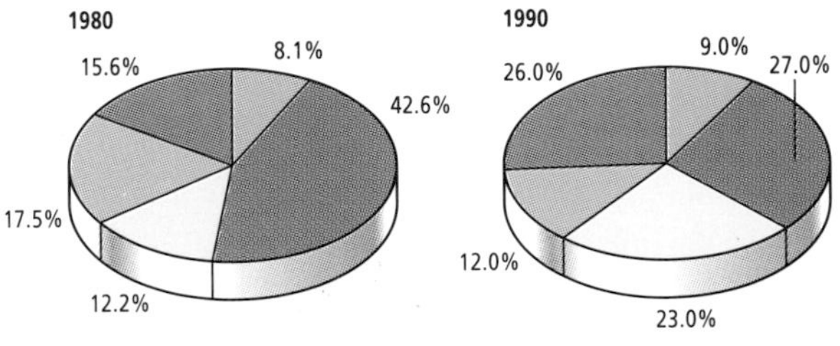

competition may cause. MITI must also co-ordinate with the Science and Technology Agency (STA) to control the agenda in nuclear power, and with the Economic Planning Agency to determine energy supply/demand forecasts. As in other matters, MITI must also negotiate with the Ministry of Finance (MOF) and the ruling Liberal Democratic Party (LDP) for budget allocations.

The attempt to achieve energy security has centred on diversification and the creation of alternative energy sources. Diversification has two objectives: diversification of suppliers and diversification of energy sources.

Diversification policies have included accommodation with foreign oil companies, oil-producing nations, direct deal and long-term supply contracts, and acquisition of foreign energy reserves. After the Arab members of OPEC initiated the 1973 oil crisis, the Japanese government immediately sought to disengage from Israel and joined the growing list of nations recognizing the Palestine Liberation Organization. Japanese firms observed the Arab blacklist of firms doing business in Israel, and investment in Middle Eastern oil-producing states by Japanese interests increased dramatically. These various efforts to diversify have been highly effective. Japan's sources of petroleum are far more numerous than they were before the first oil crisis of 1973.

The most ambitious policy to provide alternatives to petroleum has been the nuclear power programme. The government has been an aggressive advocate of nuclear power, and has authorized the construction of nearly 40 nuclear plants since the late 1960s. The intention is to ameliorate energy supply problems by developing commercially viable energy technologies that at the same time enhance Japan's international competitiveness. Only in France does nuclear power provide a greater portion of a nation's electric power supply. By contrast, the Japanese

The nuclear power station at Tōkaimura, Ibaraki Prefecture, with room for further expansion: one of the many sites scattered throughout Japan. A recent spate of small incidents has put a question mark over plans for future growth, as in many other countries.

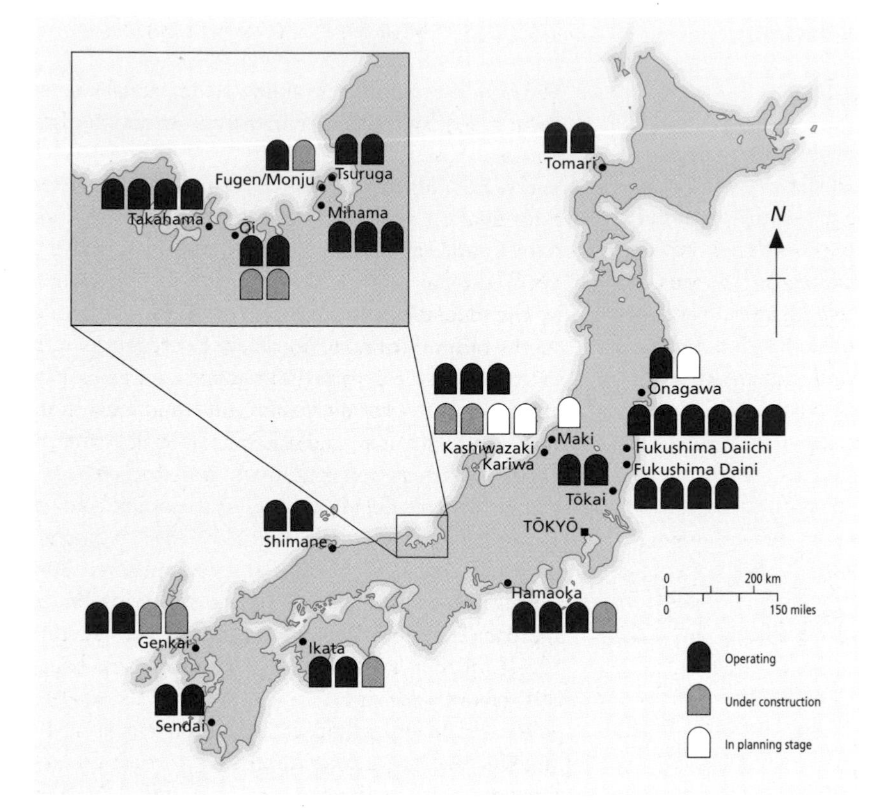

The present distribution of nuclear power plants around Japan. The plan has been to make Japan self-sufficient in energy by the early years of the next century, but it remains to be seen whether problems of safety and waste disposal can be satisfactorily solved.

vendors who build so-called 'indigenized' Japanese reactors based originally on foreign designs are part of the same industrial and financial groups that dominated the coal industry just decades earlier and that continue to dominate Japanese financial markets. With government support, they have continued to develop nuclear power technologies, such as the fast breeder reactor, that should make Japan energy self-sufficient in the 21st century.

The Japanese people, it must be noted, have been profoundly ambivalent about introducing nuclear power on a large scale. Although they recognize and accept the prevailing wisdom that nuclear power has the potential to provide Japan its elusive energy security, accidents in the US, USSR, and Japan have stimulated an influential grass-roots opposition movement. More than 90% of the Japanese now express 'unease' about nuclear power. As a result, more funds are dispersed to encourage public acceptance through the funding of unrelated projects in key localities than are actually spent designing and constructing reactors. Although the Japanese nuclear power industry boasts an admirable safety record, several accidents in the late 1980s have blemished its reputation. Japanese disposal and reprocessing capabilities also lag behind their capacity to generate such waste.

Other alternatives to fossil fuels have been slow to come on line. After the first oil price shock, the government began efforts to encourage conservation and the development of alternative fuels such as solar, geothermal, and biomass. Although these alternatives have been the target of considerable government support, to date they account for only marginal amounts of Japan's energy. After the Iranian revolution and the second oil shock in 1979 the Japanese began to take seriously the idea of alternative energy research and development. MITI plans for a new public entity, a state-owned Alternative Energy Public Corporation in 1979 were blocked by the Ministry of Finance on fiscal grounds and by Keidanren as undesirable state intervention in the economy. But in the end legislation was passed to create a New Energy Development Organization (NEDO). To placate the Ministry of Finance, new taxes to support this new institution were levied on petroleum and electricity consumption, and to satisfy business, the Chairman of Keidanren was made the Chairman of NEDO.

Conclusion

The Japanese energy system is characterized by relentless competition among bureaucratic interests and rapidly shifting market forces. This system cannot be explained without an understanding of Japanese resource dependency and without an appreciation of how the Japanese define their 'comprehensive security'. This security cannot be achieved without tolerance of higher domestic prices for goods and services by individual consumers. The Japanese invest in high cost energy projects in the belief that value added 'at the doorstep of the consumer' will enhance economic security and help technological development. The assumption of industry, government, and consumers is that these investments will contribute over the longer run to a more secure, less dependent, and more technologically sophisticated economy that serves the interests of producers and consumers alike.

RJS

Banking and finance

The biggest banks in the world are now Japanese. Over the last decade they have gradually replaced US banks in the world league tables, to the extent that the six largest ones in the world, measured by assets, and seven out of the top 10, are Japanese. This has been accompanied by such growth in their international business that some popular writers have speculated that the next wave of export dominance by Japan will be in the financial area.

WORLD'S TOP TEN BANKS 1991

	Assets in US$ billion	World ranking	Reported profits in US$ billion	World ranking
Daiichi Kangyō	426.9	1	1.5	676
Mitsubishi	412.8	2	1.3	709
Sumitomo	407.9	3	2.0	569
Mitsui Taiyō Kōbe	407.5	4	1.2	720
Sanwa	401.5	5	1.6	629
Fuji	398.3	6	1.4	679
Crédit Agricole	303.0	7	1.4	587
Banque Nationale de Paris	289.7	8	0.6	780
Industrial Bank of Japan	289.2	9	1.0	697
Crédit Lyonnais	285.2	10	1.5	523

Source: *The Banker*, July 1991

However, as in the case of Japanese manufacturing firms, the reported rates of profit in banking are low measured by international standards: when ranked by rates of profit on their assets, the six Japanese banks with the largest assets in the world do not even appear in the top 500. Some have argued that this discrepancy is due to unfair trading practices, such as low interest rates for depositors and restrictions on the activities of foreign banks in Japan. Yet the basis of competitiveness in banking is very different from that in manufacturing industry, and Japan is now in the process of trying to reform the whole financial system into a 'modern', market-oriented operation. This raises questions of how the banking and financial systems have come to be so large, how they operate, and why, if they have been so successful at home and abroad, they are felt to be in need of reform.

The system of indirect finance

The modern banking system was established and encouraged by government policy during the first decades of the 20th century but its operation was left to private interests. A financial crash in 1927 led to a consolidation of banks which greatly reduced their number and set the scene for the growing power of a small number of large institutions, many operated by the industrial conglomerates known as *zaibatsu*. As the military came to dominate the economy during the 1930s and 1940s, the government began to exert more control over the banks and close links between banks and manufacturing firms, particularly those producing munitions, were forged.

After Japan's defeat in 1945, the economic policy of the Allied Occupation forces stressed democratization and the dissolution of the *zaibatsu*. Surprisingly, the Occupation was less forceful in its approach to the banks and left much of the structure of relationships between banks and firms, and banks and government, intact. Nevertheless, Occupation policy did have an impact on capital markets. By breaking up the *zaibatsu* holding companies and forcing the wider distribution of shares, a broader base was established for the stock market than had previously existed. It was still the case, however, that the banking system handled most household savings and most company fund-raising, taking the place of direct participation in capital markets. It is this central feature of Japan's financial system, the predominance of indirect, or intermediated, finance rather than direct involvement in the capital markets by savers and borrowers, which helps to account for the rapid growth and present size of the banks.

There is disagreement about the main reasons for the development and continuation of this system of indirect finance, but it is accepted that part of the explanation lies in the high degree of regulation and control of banking and capital markets. From 1945 until the end of the 1970s the access of firms to capital markets was strictly controlled, limiting the types of firm that could raise capital, both in stock and bond markets, the amounts involved, and the terms on which capital could be raised. Since, at the same time, interest rates on bank lending were kept low by a mixture of government monetary policy and regulation, bank borrowing became the preferred method of finance.

It is less clear why savers, who ultimately provide the funds which firms can borrow, put up with the system. From their point of view, deposits in banks, while safe, provided a very poor rate of return. Deposit interest rates were kept at low levels, though at least they were exempt from tax. Investment in stocks provided a risky alternative, while access to safer markets, such as corporate or government bond markets, was difficult or impossible.

There is even more debate as to why, in the face of such poor financial returns, the Japanese have saved so much. Throughout the post-war period the rate of savings by households, and the total savings of all sectors of the economy as a share of GNP, have been very high by international standards. 'Cultural' factors are often cited as an explanation but they provide at best a partial one. Before the war the savings rate was not particularly high, so an explanation must be sought in the post-war economic environment. Several factors were at work. It was natural that people would try to rebuild their wealth after the war as soon as income growth provided a surplus. In addition, until recently there were few public pensions and only limited availability of loans for housing purchase, education and similar expenses. Many were saving, therefore, simply to provide for these needs.

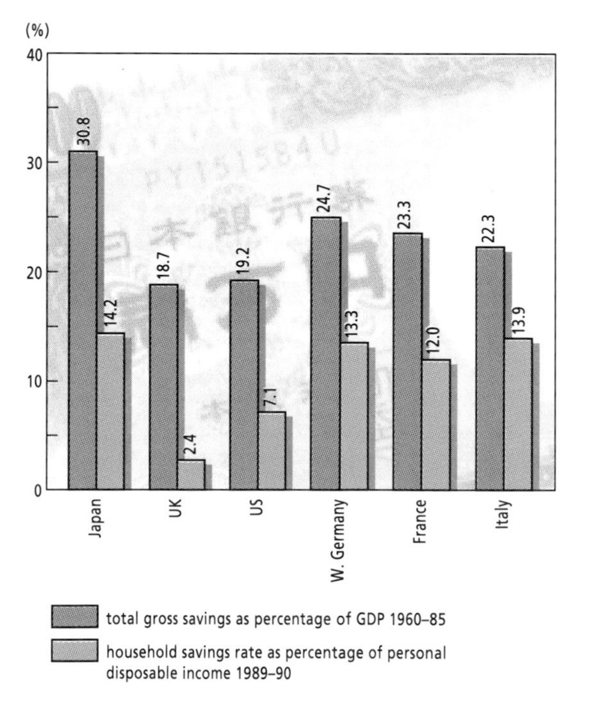

International comparison of savings rates.

Whatever the causes, the high rates of saving combined with rapid income growth during the 1960s and 1970s created large amounts of savings which were deposited in banks. At the same time firms were expanding rapidly in the growing economy and had an almost insatiable demand for capital. It is therefore no surprise that the banks grew rapidly and ultimately reached their present global stature.

Effects on the economy

The combination of the indirect finance system, with banks at its heart, and the extensive regulation of interest rates and capital markets, gave rise to one important feature of banking in Japan which marked it out from the model found in the US, and to a lesser extent in other countries. This feature, known as 'overloan', enhanced the rôle of banks in the government's macroeconomic policy. 'Overloan' referred to the situation in which banks lent more to borrowers than they took in as deposits. The difference had to be raised from other sources, usually the Bank of Japan. This meant that the banks are net borrowers from the central bank, whereas in most countries they are net depositors, being required to deposit reserves with the central bank. The Japanese system, therefore, gave the Bank of Japan an extra tool with which to control the amount of credit available in the economy and this tool was regularly used when the Bank wished to tighten policy to control inflation. By reducing the amount it lent to other banks, the Bank of Japan could restrict their lending, creating a shortage of credit and limiting firms' ability to expand. For much of the rapid-growth period this was the main policy tool of macroeconomic management.

There may have been other ways too in which the banking and financial system affected the economy. The regulatory environment encouraged, perhaps even forced, firms to rely heavily on bank borrowing and, partly as a result, firms and banks developed close relationships. These relationships are similar to those that exist in Germany. A firm's 'main bank' will have the largest share in lending to the firm and will usually own some of the firm's equity, within a legal limit of 5%. There is said to be a good deal of information-exchange between main banks and client firms, and it is usually expected that the main bank will help reorganize firms in financial difficulty

Banking is still more personal than in many Western countries, even though cash-machines have proliferated in recent years. One skill all tellers learn is how to coax large quantities of notes into a fan shape that makes counting easy.

to prevent bankruptcy. At the same time, the stock market is rarely used to carry out hostile takeovers of firms. Although there are no legal restrictions preventing such takeovers, firms try to ensure that they have a relatively small number of 'stable' shareholders, who can be relied upon not to sell the shares, and, to achieve this, firms often develop arrangements with other firms whereby each holds some shares in the other's company. It has been suggested that because of the close involvement of the banks and the low risk of takeover Japanese firms have been better able to undertake long-term planning and investment than firms elsewhere.

Recent changes

Since the mid 1970s there has been much discussion in Japan about the need for policy changes and reform. The pressure for change has come from both inside the country and outside, but the major factor has been the structural changes in the economy since the early 1970s. After the dual shocks of the breakdown in the world's currency arrangements and the huge increase in oil prices in the early 1970s, Japan's economic growth rate dropped from its previous average level of 10% per year to around 5%. This led firms to reduce their investment in new plant and equipment and hence their need to borrow. At the same time the government increased its spending above the level of its tax income and had to borrow, by issuing bonds, to finance the difference. The result was a change in the business done by banks. Banks found themselves making fewer loans to business and buying more government bonds. But these bonds were issued at regulated (below market) interest rates and a secondary (trading) market where the bonds could be sold did not exist. Gradually banks' profits began to suffer as lucrative corporate lending was replaced by low-yield government bonds and the banks, naturally, began to protest. This was the origin of the domestic pressure for liberalization of both interest rates and markets.

The story of how compromises were reached between the interests of banks and other participants in financial markets (firms, savers, and other financial institutions) is a long, though fascinating, one. There were several conflicts but the key one was that between the banks and securities companies. Under post-war legislation, banks were not, and at present are still not, permitted to engage in securities business. Article 65 of the Banking Law (1928) separates commercial banking (lending business) from investment banking (underwriting and selling securities). In the absence of an organized bond market, the banks' desire to sell their large holdings of government bonds could not be accommodated within the current law, since they would have had to engage in direct sales of bonds to third parties. The first step towards changing the regulations was the Banking Law of 1982, which permitted banks to sell government bonds 'over the counter' without going through the securities companies. Since then there have been several government advisory reports, each one edging nearer to recommending open competition between banks and securities companies, but no final formula has yet been agreed. Meanwhile the changing needs of Japanese companies for more flexible finance, and the demand by savers for better returns on their assets, has brought the steady development of new financial markets and a gradual relaxation of controls on interest rates.

It is almost certain that competition between banks and securities companies will be permitted fairly soon, ushering in a new era in which Japanese banks will engage in a wider range of activities. What is not clear is whether this will permit Japanese banks to grow even larger in the international arena or whether it will expose them to greater risks and make them more vulnerable to competition. JC

The trading floor of the Tōkyō Stock Exchange, which is now the largest in the world in terms of trading volume. The frantic pace of activity and cryptic hand-signs of the dealers have now become familiar around the world as an ever increasing segment of the world's population finds that its future is affected by what goes on here.

COMPARISON OF WORLD STOCK EXCHANGES IN 1989

	Tōkyō	New York	London
No. of member firms	114	535	409
No. of stock-listed companies			
domestic	1,597	1,633	1,955
foreign	112	77	587
Total market value (US$ billion)			
stocks	4,260	2,903	818
bonds	977	1,412	498

Source: *Japan 1992, an international comparison* (Keizai Kōhō Centre)

Manufacturing and services

Japan's rise from devastation in 1945 to the status of an economic superpower can only be understood in the context of its earlier industrialization. This helped determine both the speed of reconstruction, and the distinctive features of its industrial organization and capital and labour markets. It must be remembered too that this industrialization process was facilitated by the Tokugawa legacy of widely developed commercial practice, small-scale manufacturing and agricultural industries, and a high literacy rate. The opening of Japan in 1853 and the Occupation almost 100 years later, however, unleashed powerful currents of change, resulting in the rapid spread of modern productive techniques. The dynamic interplay between domestic receptivity and foreign influences was thus critical in bringing about industrial and economic development.

Industrialization to 1945

While the Tokugawa period may have provided a base for industrialization, traditional industries did not become modern ones overnight. Initially the two developed side by side. The Meiji government was most interested in building up transport, communications and an institutional infrastructure, as well as heavy industry and engineering for strategic reasons. The bulk of economic activity, however, continued in the traditional or semi-traditional areas, which provided the main living commodities, export revenues and employment for the growing working population: 72% of Japan's gross national expenditure in 1915 still consisted of personal consumption.

In the modern sector, the bulk of employment was outside manufacturing, in the new bureaucracies, the military, transport and communications and finance. Despite a boost for heavy industry and engineering following the Russo–Japanese War of 1905–06, modern manufacturing industry did not 'take off' in its own right until the boom caused by the First World War, when the disruption to Western exports to Asia provided substantial new market opportunities. Thereafter, it became the engine for economic

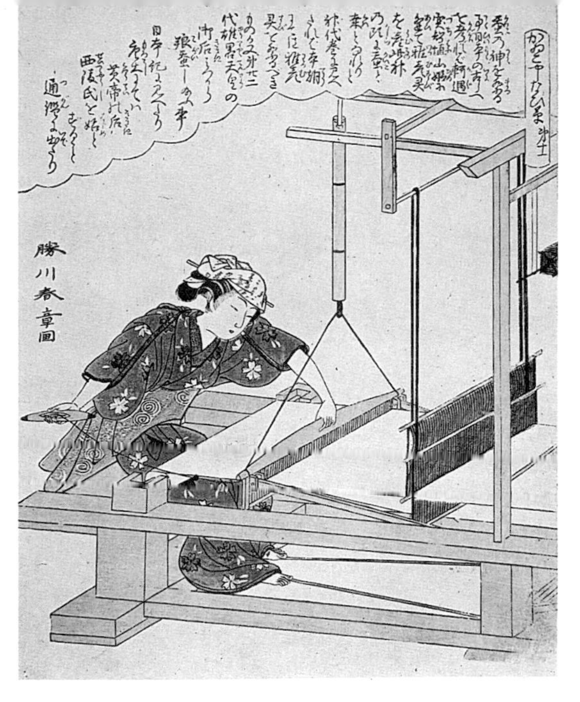

An 18th-century print of a young woman at a loom. Japan entered the modern age with extensive craft industries and before the 19th century was over had mechanized many of the processes involved. Export markets were readily procured. By 1890 a woman like this would have been working in a steam-powered factory and probably living in a company dormitory.

growth. The post-war recession and turbulent 1920s also saw a growing gap within modern manufacturing between large dominant firms and those smaller in scale with lower productivity.

Japan recovered quickly from the 1929–30 Depression with demand-led growth, including that for military supplies. Textiles remained important, but heavy industry, engineering and chemicals (including rayon and artificial fibres) grew rapidly, their share of gross output rising from 35% in 1930 to almost 60% in 1940. Large new concerns such as Nissan exploited new technologies to join the established *zaibatsu* conglomerates in industrial leadership. Japan's productive capacity was therefore advanced, but highly concentrated, and with the war in China it became increasingly devoted to military purposes.

The state was actively involved in the promotion of modern industry, which it saw as critical to Japan's continued independence. It developed a wide range of means of pursuing this policy, such as macroeconomic management, encouraging saving and discouraging consumption, channelling funds to targeted industries, direct industry supervision and 'administrative guidance'. Thus many of the tools and channels for post-war reconstruction and growth policies were developed in the pre-war period.

Until the early 1920s there was considerable direct financing of industry, spot subcontracting, high labour-turnover and skill-based market wages, together with the beginnings of wider union organization. During the 1920s and the subsequent move towards a wartime economy and wartime controls, however, other changes which were later to be features of post-war industry were also established. Banks, for example, became the main financial intermediaries. The basic pattern of industrial organization, with large *zaibatsu* firms at the top and smaller firms organized to subcontract for them, emerged at this time: so too did internalized labour markets and enterprise unions, and such familiar concepts as security of employment and age-related wages.

EMPLOYMENT BY INDUSTRY 1872–1940
(thousands of employees)

	1872	1895	1913	1920	1930	1940
Total	17,074	23,769	26,422	27,263	29,619	32,478
Agriculture and forestry	14,100	16,912	15,527	14,287	14,131	13,842
Fishing	395	473	535	561	590	559
Mining	6	96	364	448	315	597
Manufacturing	705	2,392	3,957	4,357	4,891	7,160
Construction	122	385	637	758	963	955
Transport & communications	118	288	772	952	1,159	1,364
Commerce	947	1,916	2,831	3,662	4,906	4,881
Government & professional services	502	952	1,305	1,517	1,791	2,194
Other	179	355	494	721	873	926

Source: K. Ohkawa *et al., The growth rate of the Japanese economy since 1878* (1957).

POST-WAR REFORMS, RECONSTRUCTION AND RAPID GROWTH

By 1945 much of the nation's productive capacity lay in ruins and per capita GNP was little more than half the pre-war level. Economic collapse was followed by confusion, inflation and social and industrial unrest, and reconstruction was by no means an overnight process. The Occupation authorities were initially concerned to demilitarize and democratize Japan's society and economy. Land reforms dramatically reduced the proportion of tenant farmers, establishing the basis for rural stability and productive growth. The dissolution of the *zaibatsu* and the enactment of anti-monopoly legislation reduced industrial concentration and promoted competition. Labour reforms legalized unions, changing the basis of employment and industrial relations. Some of the reforms were partial, but they had a lasting effect on the course of reconstruction.

With the deterioration of US–Soviet relations and developments on the Asian mainland, the Occupation authorities came to see Japan as a potential ally, and before long economic rehabilitation took a higher priority than reform. Procurement orders on the outbreak of the Korean War resparked industrial growth: Japan soon regained pre-war per capita GNP levels, and was poised to enter a sustained period of high growth. Small and medium-sized firms in light industry were quicker to establish themselves after the war, but before long the industrial giants had reorganized. The government drew up a priority production plan based on resurrecting the coal and iron and steel industries as the powerhouse for reconstruction. The coal plan ultimately failed, but the massive rationalization and investment programmes in iron and steel began to pay dividends, as did large-scale modernization efforts in the electric power and shipbuilding industries. Chemicals, electric machinery and automobile output grew, strengthened by innovation and technology links with foreign firms. Construction of new mass-production plants began in earnest.

Investment begat investment. Between 1955 and 1970 the economy grew at an annual rate of 10%, with productivity increasing at roughly 11% during the 1960s. Rural youth and post-war baby boomers swelled the ranks of the industrial workforce, and rising wages fuelled consumer demand. By the end of the 1960s labour shortages had become acute, and consumer prices started to edge upwards. Exports surged ahead of pre-war levels in 1959, with heavy industrial and engineering goods constituting an increasing proportion. Mushrooming exports in concentrated industries, however, began to generate trade friction. Trading partners also felt that Japan's progress towards lifting both import and capital restrictions was too slow. This perception, that Japan was a major beneficiary of, but reluctant contributor to, the post-war international trade régime was to intensify in the coming 'low growth' years, along with US government concern that Japan was enjoying a free ride in allowing the US to take care of its defence needs.

Military procurements certainly played a part in Japan's economic recovery, and the concern to catch up with the West as quickly as possible through the efficient allocation of scarce resources represented continuity from the pre-war period, but the civilian orientation of Japan's post-war growth certainly stood in contrast to the earlier pattern of industrialization. Nonetheless, during the 1960s voices were raised in criticism of 'growth at all costs' and 'GNPism', and particularly of the pollution that accompanied growth.

LOW GROWTH: MATURITY AS AN ECONOMIC SUPERPOWER

The international currency crisis and 'Nixon shocks' of 1971 brought about a belated currency revaluation. From the ¥360 = US$1 rate fixed in 1949, the yen rose to ¥308 = $1, and when floated in 1973, reached ¥280 = $1. Government spending to alleviate the feared recession added to domestic inflationary pressures, and with the 'oil shock' in the autumn of 1973 a period of spiralling price rises set in. Prices

GDP AND EMPLOYMENT PROPORTIONS BY INDUSTRY

	(a) Percentages of GDP accounted for by different sectors of industry					(b) Percentages of employees in different sectors of industry				
	1970	1975	1980	1985	1989	1970	1975	1980	1985	1990
Agriculture, forestry and fishing	6.1	5.5	3.7	3.2	2.6	19.3	13.8	10.9	9.3	7.2
Mining	0.8	0.5	0.6	0.3	0.3	0.4	0.2	0.2	0.2	0.1
Manufacturing	36.0	30.2	29.2	29.5	28.9	26.2	24.9	23.7	23.9	24.1
Construction	7.7	9.7	9.4	7.9	9.5	7.5	8.9	9.6	9.0	9.4
Electricity, gas, water	2.1	2.0	2.7	3.2	2.9	0.5	0.6	0.6	0.6	NA
Wholesale & retail	14.4	14.8	15.3	13.4	12.7	19.3	21.4	22.8	22.9	NA
Finance & insurance	4.3	5.3	5.2	5.3	5.9	2.1	2.6	2.8	3.0	NA
Real estate	8.0	8.2	9.4	10.1	11.0	0.5	0.7	0.8	0.8	NA
Transport & communications	6.9	6.4	6.2	6.6	6.6	6.2	6.3	6.3	6.0	NA
Service industries	7.6	11.0	11.7	14.5	15.3	14.6	16.4	18.4	20.5	NA
Public service	4.8	4.9	4.7	4.5	4.3	3.3	3.7	3.6	3.5	NA

Sources: *Rōdō tōkei yōran* (1986 and 1991) and *Rōdō hakusho* (1988)

Yokohama, 1987. Nissan cars await transportation to overseas markets. Those markets are now not what they were, and Japanese car manufacturers are suffering from the world-wide recession. Increasingly, Japanese cars are being manufactured overseas, where labour costs are lower, but many innovative features, such as on-board computer-controlled maps and traffic information systems are being developed in Japan itself.

were brought under control, but Japan was plunged into deep recession. It was not until 1978 that the production index for mining and manufacturing recovered its pre-1971 level.

Some industries, particularly those with high energy consumption that had been so prominent in the earlier high-growth period, were faced with long-term decline. Others, notably the automobile, machine, and consumer appliance industries, rebounded earlier with recovery in the US. Their competitiveness was enhanced by energy-saving innovations and concerted efforts to rationalize, which laid the foundations of Japan's claim to economic superpower status. Overall structural changes in the economy helped minimize the impact of the second oil shock in 1979.

The 'microelectronics revolution' progressed rapidly, both in existing industries, and in new industries producing semiconductors and computers. But this only added to trade friction. In an increasing number of high-technology industries the 'technology gap' between Japan and the West closed, and as a result companies had to devote more of their resources to research and development. According to some estimates, by the mid 1980s Japan's absolute R & D expenditure was second only to the US, and as a proportion of GNP, second to West Germany, which it surpassed in 1989 (2.91% vs 2.87%). A high proportion of expenditure takes place in the private sector, for commercial rather than military purposes.

Japanese companies have shown a remarkable ability to weather the changes from high to lower growth, business cycle fluctuations, and rises in exchange-rates. After a brief crisis caused by a 30% increase in the value of the yen in 1985–86, domestic demand-led recovery produced one of the most sustained booms in Japan's post-war history. Restructuring at all levels of the economy continues; indeed a key factor in Japan's emergence as an economic superpower is the ability to institutionalize change and innovation. This has occurred, however, along a trajectory labelled in recent years 'production orientation'. The real test of the limits of change may be whether the new national goal of increased 'living orientation', that is of improved standards of living, will modify this trajectory or whether the industrial habits of post-war Japan will prove resistant.

The rôle of government

Government concern to build up a strong, modern economy has been manifested in more direct intervention – at least at the sectoral or microeconomic level – than in most Western countries; but this should not be confused with a command economy. Private enterprise has been the main vehicle for growth; the government has sought to facilitate and guide.

In the post-war period the government channelled scarce resources into industries considered crucial for reconstruction. This involved drawing up priority areas for imports and technology-licensing, channelling post-office savings through various loan schemes, and special depreciation and tax measures. It also sought to promote economies of scale and internationally competitive units through mergers or co-operative activities. In periods of economic downturn it encouraged recession cartels, and urged companies to move out of declining industries. Collaborative research and development projects were promoted to close the 'technology gap'. Some of the policies failed or were inappropriate. Just how critical the others were in achieving growth is a subject of some debate: many observers attribute to them an influential rôle, and the least one can say is that Japan managed to avoid the kind of misallocation of resources that is associated with industrial policy in many other countries.

Policy formation involves bureaucrats, politicians and third parties, particularly business leaders, brought into the process to forge as wide a consensus as possible. This consensus can be as important as the policy itself. Bureaucrats have played an important rôle in Japan's reindustrialization, in particular those of the Ministry of International Trade and Industry (MITI). MITI's successes derive from its relative isolation from 'pork barrel' political pressures and from the close links it maintains with the business world, co-ordinating within itself the demands from different industrial sectors.

The golden days of industrial policy may have ended once industries were able to stand on their own feet, but MITI sees its rôle as an evolving one. Once seen to be the heart of 'Japan Inc.', it now tries to promote international co-operation and a greater balance between orientations for 'production' and for 'living'. Some of the large scale R & D projects run by its Industrial Science and Technology Agency have been opened to foreign participation, for instance the hypersonic transport propulsion system project to power a Mach 5 jet in the 21st century. Aerospace is considered by many to be a key industry, since it draws on a vast range of advanced technologies. Government funding is typically modest, but designed to stimulate private sector development. Space may be the final frontier, but the stakes in commercial aircraft are also very high. The 1986 Aircraft Promotion Law stipulates international collaboration as a condition for government development loans, not so much because of international friction or goodwill, but because commercial success increasingly depends on it.

LABOUR MARKETS AND LABOUR RELATIONS

Fluid labour markets gradually gave way in the 1920s to a segmented structure, which has continued in various forms to the present day. On the one hand, large companies, seeking to retain the core workers they train, offer internal careers and superior incentives to encourage loyalty. On the other hand, various groups such as temporary workers and employees in small firms do not enjoy the same security and have less favourable wages and conditions. The position of the former is enhanced by the latter, who are in a sense the 'shock-absorbers' of business fluctuations.

'Japanese-style employment' for core workers is something that has evolved. Wartime controls brought significant modifications to employment and industrial relations, as did the demands of newly-legalized unions after the war. Paternalism gave way to institutionalized 'welfare corporatism', the normative influence of which spread beyond the large firms. A significant development was the post-war elimination of status differences between blue- and white-collar workers and the harmonization of their conditions of employment. All regular employees, but not part-timers, thus became members of a corporate community.

New recruits into this corporate community undergo a period of careful socialization. Wage and promotion systems not only encourage loyalty and progressively discourage changing jobs, but encourage hard work and teamwork as well. Wages rise with age and service: a 35-year-old still earns almost twice

Is Japan's success due to imitation?

There is little doubt that Japanese companies are very efficient at scanning world markets and literature for techniques and technologies which may be creatively adapted to their own products. Research and Development (R & D) expenditures have been growing, however, especially in private industry, and while much of it remains concentrated at the 'D' end of the scale, increasing amounts are being directed towards basic research. DHW

RESEARCH AND DEVELOPMENT EXPENDITURES IN JAPAN, NATURAL SCIENCES, 1975–89

	Total expenditure (¥100 million)	Fund source (%)			Consumption (%)			Expenditure as % ratio of GNP
		Government	Private	Foreign	Government	Universities	Industry	
1975	26,218	27.5	72.4	0.1	13.3	19.7	67.0	1.95
1977	32,335	27.4	72.5	0.1	13.1	19.5	67.4	1.92
1979	40,636	27.4	72.5	0.1	13.4	19.1	67.5	2.03
	53,640	25.0	74.9	0.1	11.8	16.5	71.7	2.31
1983	65,037	22.2	77.7	0.1	10.3	15.8	73.9	2.51
	81,164	19.4	80.5	0.1	9.7	13.2	77.1	2.71
1987	90,162	19.9	80.0	0.1	10.1	13.4	76.4	2.80
1989	109,092	17.1	82.8	0.1	8.5	12.0	79.5	2.91

Source: *Trends of principal indicators on research and development activities in Japan*. Agency of Industrial Science and Technology (1991).

as much as an 18-year-old, and a 50-year-old three times as much in the larger companies, despite the claims of companies to be reducing age and service components. At the same time, wages rise more for those with favourable evaluations, so a gap emerges between the hardest-working and most co-operative and those less so. It emerges slowly, however, to encourage all to work towards the distant prizes of top pay and promotion. The result is a substantial overlap between management goals, peer pressure and self-interest.

Union structure also contributes to this orientation towards corporate community. Unions in the private sector are based on enterprise rather than occupation or class; both blue-collar and white-collar regular employees up to section-chief level belong to the same enterprise union. Given the internalized career structures, it makes sense for unions to co-operate with management in enlarging the 'pie', rather than fighting over how to divide it up. This does not mean that industrial relations have always been harmonious, however, as strike figures show. Declining strike figures do reflect declining union power, but also management acceptance of certain worker demands and a 'regularization' of relations between workers and management with improved commmunication channels.

Given the differences in security, wages and prestige according to firm size, large firms have found it easier to recruit from the top educational institutions. But small firms have not lacked competent recruits, since education levels overall tend to be high. Small firms do have to rely more on mid-term hiring, however, as well as part-time workers, a large proportion of whom are women re-entering the job market after raising their children. Still, worker shortages have persisted, especially in those industries engaged in so-called 'three-K-work': *kiken* (dangerous), *kitanai* (dirty), and *kitsui* (arduous). As a result, small firms have had to rely increasingly on illegal foreign workers despite government attempts at regulation.

How co-operative are industrial relations in Japan?

Strike figures are lower in Japan than in the UK and the US, but lower still in some northern European countries. Strikes are, however, not the only form of industrial action, nor even the most common form in Japan. The figures nonetheless reflect a steady decrease in industrial action, due to declining union strength vis-à-vis management, management acceptance of key union demands, improved communications channels, and a greater preference for co-operation and compromise rather than confrontation.

DHW

DAYS LOST IN LABOUR DISPUTES, 1965–90
(unit: 1,000 person-days)

	US	UK	Japan	W. Germany
1965	15,140	2,925	5,669	49
1970	52,761	10,980	3,915	93
1975	17,563	6,012	8,016	69
1980	20,844	11,964	1,001	128
1985	7,079	6,402	264	35
1989	16,530	4,128	220	100

Source: *Practical handbook of productivity and labour statistics '89–'90* (Japan Productivity Centre) and *Katsuyō rōdō tōkei* (1991)

INDUSTRIAL ORGANIZATION

The modern sector in the pre-war period came under the increasing domination of *zaibatsu* groups. The largest of these encompassed a wide spread of industries, and in 1937 the 'big four' (Mitsui, Mitsubishi, Sumitomo and Yasuda) alone held over 20% of the total capital in commerce and industry, with much higher concentrations in shipbuilding and shipping. The shares of the holding companies which controlled these *zaibatsu* were in most cases family-owned.

The Occupation authorities abolished the holding companies, and with them family control. Some of the large companies were split, but the banks were allowed to remain intact. After revision of the Anti-Monopoly Law in 1949 and 1953 some of the companies re-formed, as did some of the groups, with companies in the group purchasing each other's shares and thus preventing unwelcome takeovers, and with banks playing a central rôle, especially in financing. Group companies typically hold around 20% of each other's shares, with other 'safe' shareholders – companies with which the firm is closely tied – another 20–30%. While these groups are not closed, particularly in their trading practices, neither are they completely open. On the one hand there are 'horizontal' groups spanning a wide range of industries, which constitute one type of *keiretsu*, or 'linkage'; on the other, 'vertical' groups of companies in a single or narrow range of industries constitute another. Many vertical *keiretsu* also date from the pre-war period and were reconstituted in more or less the same form after the war. They are headed by large, normally manufacturing, firms, with group companies supplying parts, subassemblies or services. Relations may be further strengthened by capital and personnel links, and are multi-tiered, with the lower or peripheral tiers comprised of numerous smaller companies.

Japanese industry is characterized by a high proportion of inter-firm relations which are neither strictly markets nor hierarchies. The relations tend to be ongoing and may be mutually beneficial to both parties, but in the case of large–small firm relations, the benefits may be skewed. Many would argue that an exploitative dual structure has recently given way to greater mutuality, in which large firms now gain more from the expertise accumulated in the smaller firms than from their lower labour costs. This expertise has also given small firms a platform from which to gain greater independence from their 'parents'.

Despite the enormous sales and assets of the largest companies, in most sectors more than 98% are classified as small or medium-sized businesses (with less than 300 employees in manufacturing, 100 in wholesale and 50 in retail and services). They employ over 70% of all workers, and in manufacturing, account for more than 50% of sales and value added. Neither are they all subcontractors for bigger partners; more than 40% in manufacturing do not subcontract, a proportion that rose in the 1980s. Thus there is a great variety of small firms whose independent contribution to the Japanese economy and society should not be overlooked.

Relations between companies may be characterized by both competition and co-operation, especially when in the same industry, or when supplying the same part for the same 'parent'. In the former, co-operation is co-ordinated through industry associations; in the latter, through supplier associations. Co-operation may take the form of joint study groups, R & D projects, as well as price co-ordination (for example, recession cartels).

Industrial organization in Japan is characterized by a variety of 'networks'. Once considered backward, they are now held to be economically (though not necessarily socially) rational. They are undergoing constant modification, but will not be abandoned lightly, since they are seen to be key factors in maintaining a competitive advantage.

THE TERTIARY SECTOR

During Japan's industrialization, employment in the tertiary and secondary sectors rose, while the proportion engaged in agriculture declined. As in manufacturing, there was a duality from the beginning, with separate modern (utilities, government) and traditional (most construction, wholesale and retail businesses) spheres. Later the more productive secondary sector also drew workers from the tertiary sector, whereas recently the trend has reversed somewhat: the tertiary sector now accounts for almost 60% of employment and a similar proportion of nominal GDP.

Tertiary employment and output from the late 1960s onwards were spurred by the rise in consumption of goods and services along with rising incomes. The proportion spent on discretionary services such as education, cultural activities, travel and leisure rose noticeably. Increased employment of women

SHARE OF TERTIARY INDUSTRIES IN AGGREGATE DEMAND, 1975–85

	1975	1980	1985
Agriculture, forestry and fisheries	4.5	3.4	3.0
Mining	2.8	3.2	2.1
Manufacturing	42.4	42.6	42.8
Construction	9.7	9.3	7.8
Tertiary	38.4	39.9	43.0
utilities	1.9	2.5	3.0
retail and wholesale	8.6	8.8	8.5
finance and insurance	3.0	2.7	3.4
transportation and property	10.8	10.7	10.1
telecommunications and broadcasting	0.9	1.0	1.2
government services	2.4	2.2	2.4
education and medical	5.0	5.5	7.7
service industries	5.8	6.4	6.7

Note: aggregate demand includes corporate and household demand.
Source: *Expansion of Japan's tertiary sector: background and macro-economic implications* (Special paper No. 183), (Bank of Japan, ed.)

A team of robot workers at Nissan's Oppama plant. Computers now control almost every aspect of work. Here the robot arms are involved in welding the body of a car.

from the mid 1970s added disposable income and brought a demand for services once carried out in the home; increased tertiary sector activity in turn provided new employment opportunities. A rise in distributive activities was thus followed by a rise in services.

Even more noticeable in the recent trend of 'servicization', however, has been the growth of corporate demand for services, noticeable particularly at the level of intermediate inputs rather than final demand. In the 1980s manufacturing companies set up service subsidiaries, in part to take advantage of new business opportunities. Large tertiary sector companies did likewise, and independent corporate-service-related companies also mushroomed.

Growth in the tertiary sector is often associated with lower overall economic growth, because, for example, of lower productivity in service industries. The close inter-relationship between services and manufacturing, however, is an important factor in Japan's recent economic growth. 'Servicization' does not necessarily mean a decline in manufacturing but can be linked to its qualitative development. Furthermore, the image of the tertiary sector as a productive backwater sopping up workers in tiny firms has undergone change: establishment sizes have increased, as have investment, capital ratios and productivity.

The tertiary sector is being transformed by the revolution in information technology. Demand for information technology-related services, including leasing, has increased. The tertiary sector – especially finance and insurance, wholesale and retail, and services – purchases almost a half of all computers and is itself a major consumer of such technology. This in turn has improved the services and lowered costs in these industries, further increasing demand.

Information-related industries themselves defy easy classification into secondary and tertiary, and there are a growing number of intermediate business activities. Traditional distinctions between industries and sectors are being broken down in a new stage of development, although this is not without its problems. 'Servicization' has if anything exacerbated the concentration of economic activity in the large urban areas, particularly in and around Tōkyō, and it is by no means clear that it signals an unambiguous shift from 'production-orientation' to a greater emphasis on the quality of life.

'INTERNATIONALIZATION'

Debates about 'Japanization' are indicative of the global presence of many Japanese companies. The term refers both to the practices adopted by foreign firms in order to compete with Japanese firms, practices such as total quality control and quality control circles, team-working, and so on. It also refers to the foreign direct investment (FDI) of Japanese firms themselves.

The first major wave of FDI by Japanese companies came towards the end of the high-growth period, spurred by both rising domestic wages and worker shortages, and then by the rise of the yen. The main destinations were Asia and Latin America, and investment was concentrated particularly in textiles and electrical goods. Investors sought to maintain competitiveness by securing cheaper labour, as well as market access. Investments were modest – many were by small or medium-sized companies, and many were joint ventures – but local competitors were overwhelmed, resulting at times in friction. In 1967 investment by Japanese firms accounted for only 2% of foreign investment in ASEAN, compared with 82% by US firms; by 1975 the figures stood at 41% and 18% respectively.

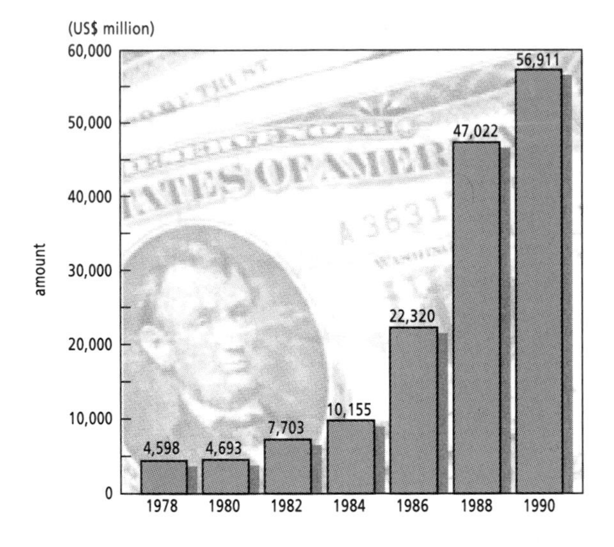

Japanese direct overseas investment, 1978–90.

The oil shock in 1973 spurred a wave of FDI aimed at securing raw and partly processed materials for import into Japan. Investments were made in the polluting industries, as pollution had become a major social and political issue. These were large in scale, and involved major manufacturers as well as trading companies. The mining of various metals, and the production of aluminium, petrochemicals, pulp and paper, etc. declined domestically but increased abroad, again mainly in Asia and Latin America.

A large portion of FDI in North America and Europe was initially in the commercial and financial industries, with steady increases in manufacturing, partly as a result of trade friction and fears of regulated trade and protectionism. The stream became a flood after the yen rise in 1985–86, with $10.2 billion, or 45.5% of the total, in 1986 going to the US, and $3.3 billion going to EC countries. Total FDI rose from $22.3 billion in 1986 to $47.0 billion in 1988 and to $56.9 billion in 1990. The automobile and consumer electronics industries were those with the highest profiles abroad. Such investments were aimed particularly at securing markets. By and large, hosts, especially local governments, have welcomed such investment because it creates employment opportunities and may stimulate local industry. The amount of local content, however, has been a cause of concern. Sometimes this has increased as a result of Japanese suppliers following manufacturers abroad. Increasingly, though, major companies have established R & D facilities in North America and Europe as part of global strategies utilizing global resources. Finance and service companies, also, which set up operations overseas partly to cater for Japanese manufacturers, have been developing regional and global operations for a world market, and retailers are now a major presence in many Asian cities.

The ultimate challenge of Japan's integration into the global economy, however, may lie in 'internal internationalization'. FDI into Japan in 1989 amounted to only $1.9 billion, despite the removal of many of the obvious barriers to inward investment. Foreign companies accounted for only 2% of the sales of all companies established in Japan, although more than 20 companies had equity-adjusted sales exceeding $1 billion. High costs and relatively long setting-up periods have acted as disincentives to would-be foreign investors. Foreign workers, on the other hand, need little convincing of opportunities in Japan. Depressed employment conditions at home, and the high yen and high wages in Japan have brought a tide of 'illegal' workers which the government has found hard to stem. Rising economic strength has confronted Japan with new challenges and responsibilities. Its achievements are tempered by a sense of fragility, but then this sense has long provided a spur to new endeavours. DHW

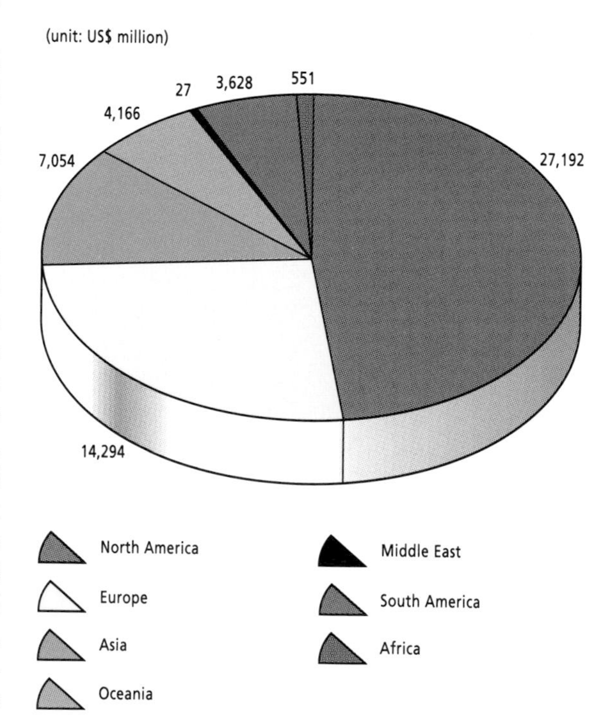

Japanese direct overseas investment by region in 1990.

Foreign trade

Yokohama. In the 1850s Yokohama grew from a fishing village into a treaty port through which most of Japan's imports and exports passed and where most of the foreign community lived. In the 1990s it is still a busy port, but it is also at the forefront of some imaginative developments which will transform communications and transport in the whole area around Tōkyō Bay.

As a predominantly agricultural country Japan had little to export in the 19th century except for tea, silk and textiles. Industrialization increased the range of manufactured goods, and in the early 20th century Japan gained both captive markets for these goods and sources of raw materials in north-east Asia and south-east Asia. During the 1930s the US became a major supplier of oil and scrap iron, and it was the US embargo on oil exports in 1941 which pushed Japan into the Pacific War. Following defeat in 1945 Japan lost its exclusive economic zones in Asia and from 1945 to 1952 was occupied by the US, its strongest military and economic competitor.

The years of export promotion

Even before the Occupation had ended, Cold War considerations prompted the US to allow Japan to re-enter its pre-war markets in south-east Asia for the sake of economic rehabilitation and political stabilization. It took Japan more than a decade to regain its pre-war share in world trade. In 1955, the year when Japan joined the General Agreement on Tariffs and Trade (GATT), its exports amounted to only 2.4% of total world exports, compared with 5.3% in 1938. The Korean War played a decisive rôle in Japan's economic rehabilitation by giving Japanese industry the opportunity to gain foreign currency by supplying the UN forces.

Initially Japan's exports were labour-intensive and

JAPAN'S MERCHANDISE TRADE BY AREA
(total trade volume including imports and exports)

	(US$ million, customs clearance basis) 1977	1985	1990
US	32,113	91,071	142,691
EC[a]	12,931	28,909	88,546
Middle East[b]	29,389	42,108	41,213
Southeast Asia	32,203	63,512	137,322
Latin America	9,357	14,728	20,131
Africa	8,771	6,435	8,606
Centrally planned economies[c]	8,229	24,670	26,819

[a]1975–1980 nine countries; 1981–1985 ten countries; 1986– twelve countries.
[b]Includes North Africa (Libya, Egypt, Sudan, Ethiopia, Djibouti, Somalia)
[c]Communist Bloc, mostly People's Republic of China
Source: *Japan 1992, an international comparison* (Keizai Kōhō Centre)

produced by a low-paid workforce on outdated equipment. High investment in heavy industry by importing mostly US technology constantly improved the range of export products. With the expansion of the steel industry, Japan became in 1956 the world's leading shipbuilder, producing 48.2% of the world's merchant vessel tonnage.

The Five-Year Plan for Economic Independence of December 1955 gave foreign trade a direction which today still dominates the thinking of industry and bureaucracy. In order to become independent of US aid and to overcome the recession resulting from the end of the Korean War, the government planned to achieve a balance-of-payments equilibrium and to put the economy on a more self-sufficient footing. A favourable international environment allowed Japan to increase its exports rapidly while limiting its imports to raw materials and energy and keeping the involvement of foreign countries in its own economy at a very low level. The open and expanding US economy provided almost unlimited access for Japan's products as well as raw materials: Japan became the US's most important security partner in East Asia and in turn enjoyed political and economic protection. This also allowed the official exchange rate of ¥360=US$1, set in 1949, to continue until 1971: such an under-valuation of the yen during the crucial period of economic rehabilitation and expansion in the 1950s and 1960s gave Japan a considerable advantage in expanding its exports.

Opening the domestic market

Later developments put pressure on Japan to open its markets more to outsiders, but this did not alter its export orientation. In the 1960s Japan became a member of the Organisation for Economic Co-operation and Development (OECD) and the International Monetary Fund (IMF) and it participated in the Kennedy Round (1964–67) on tariff reductions under GATT. The formation of the European Economic Community (EC) increased Japan's attention towards Europe because of its fear of being excluded. At the same time many European members of GATT used Article 35 (an escape clause allowing the non-application of GATT rules towards another member) to discriminate against Japanese exports, both because of their pre-war experience of floods of cheap Japanese products and because of anti-Japanese sentiments aroused by the war. In response Japan launched programmes of trade and capital liberalization. The piecemeal and selective application of these programmes showed that importing was considered to be a necessary evil to be tolerated only to the extent needed to preserve export opportunities.

The oil crisis in 1973, the collapse of the old IMF system and the end of the favourable dollar/yen exchange rate in 1971 cut deeply into the unprecedented high annual economic growth rates of over 10% and briefly led the country into a negative current account balance. These crises proved, however, a blessing in disguise because they speeded up the restructuring of an economy that consumed much raw material and energy into one which managed either to reduce the consumption of these imports

VALUE OF FOREIGN TRADE PER CAPITA AND DEGREE OF DEPENDENCY ON FOREIGN TRADE (1989) (US$)

	Value of foreign trade per capita		Degree of dependency on foreign trade (%)	
	Exports	Imports	Exports	Imports
US	1,478	2,001	7.0	9.4
W. Germany	5,578	4,408	28.4	22.4
UK	2,669	3,464	18.3	23.7
Italy	2,450	2,664	16.4	17.8
Japan	2,244	1,720	9.7	7.4
S. Korea	1,485	1,461	35.9	30.7

Source: *Comparative international statistics* (1990) (Bank of Japan)

JAPAN'S TRADE BALANCE 1980–89

Fiscal year	1980	1981	1982	1983	1984	1985	1986	1987	1988	1989
(Unit: US$ billion)	2.1	19.9	18.0	31.4	44.2	55.9	92.8	96.3	95.0	76.9

Source: *OECD economic surveys: Japan (1989–90)*

substantially or to abandon sectors which depended too much on such imports. This restructuring made exports in the end more competitive on the world market and allowed Japan to achieve commanding market shares in new product ranges.

Between 1960 and 1985 the share of metal raw materials in Japan's total imports moved from 15% to 7.6%, the share of other raw materials decreased from 17.2% to 7.6% whereas energy imports expanded from 16.5% to 46.6%. The share of textiles and clothing in total exports decreased during the same period from 38.5% to 4.5% whereas the share of machinery grew from 25.5% to 67.76%.

Two further crises, the second oil crisis in 1979 and the revaluation of the yen (Plaza Agreement) in 1985, further hastened the opening and restructuring of the economy. From a level of ¥230 to the dollar at the time of this agreement, the yen soared to ¥144 at the end of 1987 and ¥128 in January 1989. This dramatic appreciation has not so much affected the quantity of Japan's exports as their composition. The costs associated with the rise of the yen forced industry to abandon the production of certain goods, shift some production to other countries, and enhance manufacturing efficiency through automation and other means. Instead of weakening export performance these two crises led to a shakeout of Japanese industry, which made it even more competitive on the world market.

The 1970s also witnessed a shift in and a general expansion of the geographic distribution of Japan's trade. In the 1950s and 1960s the main geographic regions were North America (as a market for consumer goods, supply of raw materials and food) and south-east Asia (as a market for industrial and consumer goods, supply of raw materials). The oil crisis created a new focus for trade policy in the Middle East, while the EC gained at the same time greater importance because of its sophisticated market for high-quality goods. Since the revaluation of the yen in 1985, Japan has almost overtaken the US as a market for the member states of the Association of Southeast Asian Nations (ASEAN). In 1988 Japan's share of ASEAN's total exports (most of them from Japanese subsidiaries) amounted to 21%, compared with 15% for the EC and 23% for the US.

Japan's share of world trade in 1958 and 1987 compared with the US and EC.

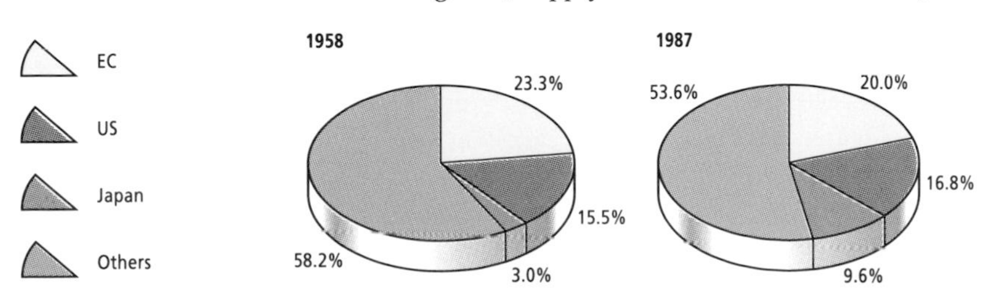

From trade friction to managed trade?

The gap between Japan's trade liberalization programmes and its growing trade surpluses has become the biggest issue in its international trade as well as in its international relations. As Japan's major trading partner, the US had already in the late 1950s started to urge Japan to accept so-called Voluntary Export Restraints (VER) on textiles and other labour-intensive light industry products. The first full-blown trade conflict occurred at the end of the 1960s over textiles but was soon followed by an unending series of other trade disputes on items such as steel, automobiles, agricultural products, machine tools, and high-technology products. In 1987, of Japan's exports to the US 39.6% were machinery, 16.3% office machines, telecommunications equipment and video recorders, and 30.2% automobiles. The trade surplus with the US grew from $7.3 billion in 1977 to $44.9 billion in 1989 while the total trade volume between the two countries increased during the same time from $32.1 billion to $141.4 billion.

The worsening trade relationship with the US has to be seen against the background of a general deterioration of US competitiveness on the world market and a weakening of its strategic position after the withdrawal from Vietnam in 1973. The US trade balance sank from a surplus of $5 billion in 1960 to a deficit of $171 billion in 1987. Up to a third of this surplus accrued in trade with Japan. Another factor was the worsening US trade balance in manufactured goods, while Japan conquered an ever-widening range of high-technology products such as computers, semiconductors and video recorders. It is therefore increasingly perceived as a threat to the

US's high-technology lead, which, in the eyes of some political and business leaders, constitutes as serious a potential security threat as did the former USSR.

There have been similar frictions with the EC, although Japan's trade with the EC is half that with the US. In 1987 Japan's exports to the EC consisted of 47.2% machinery (compared with EC exports to Japan of 15.4%), 15.6% office machines and video recorders, and 18.4% automobiles (compared with EC exports to Japan of 10.5%). The imbalance increased from US$4.5 billion in 1977 to $19.7 billion in 1989 while the overall trade volume between the two sides increased during the same period from $12.9 billion to $76.0 billion.

Avoiding trade friction

In the 1970s and early 1980s Japan's major trading partners focussed on forcing Japan to take market-opening measures in specific sectors. The US played a leading rôle through such approaches as the so-called 'market-oriented, sector-selective' (MOSS) negotiations in the mid 1980s. In response, the Japanese side presented between 1981 and 1985 seven so-called 'market-opening packages'. The immediate impact of these measures was hardly encouraging and their future effectiveness is likely to be limited.

It became apparent that more fundamental changes in Japan's foreign trade, and even in its economic and political structure, were necessary to achieve better trade balance. The US therefore began to include in its trade negotiations such topics as the yen–dollar exchange rate, Japan's macroeconomic policies, financial deregulation, internationalization of the yen, and a wide variety of Japanese government regulations and standards related to safety, health, telecommunications, etc. In the summer of 1985 the Japanese government launched a three-year action programme to promote imports. For the first time it officially declared that imports were desirable, when Prime Minister Nakasone went on TV and urged his countrymen to buy foreign products. In addition, the government stimulated domestic demand through changes in regulations and public investment programmes. In the same year Nakasone established a private advisory commission, which came to be known as the Maekawa Commission, to examine restructuring issues. The Maekawa Report, delivered in April 1987, demanded a stimulation of domestic demand, deregulation and restructuring of the industrial set-up in order to attain the goal of reducing the current-account imbalance to one 'consistent with international harmony'. It demanded a basic transformation in Japan's trade and industrial structure with orientation shifting from exports to imports.

In 1988 the so-called Structural Impediment Initiative (SII) was launched, which called on Japan to pursue structural reforms of the big industrial conglomerates, the distribution system, and the factors which account for high land prices. The US negotiators appealed successfully to the Japanese consumer who would also benefit from a more open market, and important changes have been made by the government in many areas. In addition a major public investment programme has been launched to improve the infrastructure, and this in turn should have a positive effect on imports.

Changes in the direction of a more balanced trade will, however, take much longer, for in a growing number of important industrial sectors Japan's trading partners are fighting for survival. They have therefore been relying on a variety of measures to limit certain Japanese exports, thus in effect contradicting some of their demands on Japan to end cartels and reduce government intervention in the economy. Japan has accepted a great number of Voluntary Export Restrictions (VER) agreements in order to protect the expansion of exports in other sectors. Although such agreements may look disadvantageous for Japan, in most cases they have allowed it to preserve market shares and at the same time, owing to high demand for their products, to raise prices. The various US and European agreements on VER in the automobile trade prove this point most eloquently and consumers have in the end had to pay for the protection of their domestic manufacturers. The Japan–US semiconductor agreement of 1986, which demands that the share of foreign semiconductors in Japan should increase to 20% by the end of 1992, represents the nearest to a managed-trade agreement that US negotiators have yet been able to achieve. A similar approach is attempted in the 1991 EC–Japan automobile agreement which fixes the threshold of car exports to the EC and the output of Japanese subsidiaries in the EC.

Reasons for trade friction

Various explanations have been put forward to account for the frictions that loom large in Japan's foreign trade relations, but none of them are as straightforward as they appear, as the following comments make clear.

- One explanation has it that Japan's steadily increasing share in world trade, which rose from 3.0% in 1958 to 9.6% in 1987, is to blame. The problem with this is that Germany's total trade is actually higher than Japan's and the value of its foreign trade per capita is higher too, while Japan's degree of dependency on foreign trade is lower than that of many other countries. Further, Japan has a relatively low level of integration into the world economy, as is clear from the ratio of overseas production by Japanese firms which was 4.8% in 1988, a rather low figure compared to the 16.2% for US firms.

- A second explanation points to the growth in Japan's trade surplus and current account balance: the trade balance increased from US$9.2 billion in 1981 to US$76 billion in 1987 although it has fallen slightly since then. Japan's current account balance increased similarly during the same time, then fell somewhat after 1988. On the other hand, Japan is not the only country with a considerable current account surplus: Germany's current account surplus amounted to US$50.4 billion in 1988 while most of Japan's major trading partners had a negative balance in the same year: US (−US$126.5 billion), France (−US$3.5 billion), the UK (−US$26.7 billion), and Canada (−US$8.3 billion). At the same time it is also important to notice that Japan's invisible trade account (payments for transportation, travel, investment, etc.) has been consistently negative, unlike that of its main trading partners.

- Third, even countries which do not have a substantial trade deficit with Japan suffer, it is argued, from Japan's concentration on a limited, albeit fast changing, range of products where Japan excels and can bring to bear its full potential. At the end of the 1960s and the beginning of the 1970s, this concerned textiles and steel, while today it is automobiles, electric machinery, consumer electronics, and communications equipment. However, things have now changed and, within each of these categories, Japan is fast moving from mass products or relatively simple products to the most sophisticated product ranges. In the case of automobiles, Japan is no longer solely focussing on medium range mass consumer cars, but is now using its technological and marketing power to attack the luxury range, which has so far been the preserve of European car manufacturers.

- A further argument points to the very low import ratio of manufactured goods to raw materials and energy. The ratio of Japan's manufactured imports has, however, improved considerably from 22.8% in 1980 to 50.4% in 1989 (US: 80.2%, UK: 80.0%). In 1989, the share of manufactured products in imports from the US was 58.3%, from the EC 86.1%, and from newly industrialized countries 75.5%. In 1989, the share of oil in Japan's imports was 10.2% (after a share of over 30% between 1975 and 1989); food was 14.7% and metal ore 4.4%.

- Lastly, there is the perennial 'difficulty of penetrating the Japanese market'. In terms of tariffs and quotas, however, the Japanese market is one of the most open in the world. In the sectors of manufactures and minerals the number of residual import restrictions fell from 55 in 1960 to only 5 in 1981, though they are still relatively high in the sector of agricultural and fisheries products where they fell during the same period from 67 to 22. The difficulties of foreign traders are rather caused by other circumstances, such as the high savings rate and high land prices which reduce the purchasing power of the Japanese consumer; the existence of huge industrial conglomerates with an intricate system of cross-shareholding, preferential lending and interlocking directorates which favours intra-group dealings; non-tariff barriers such as industrial standards and measurements; a very complicated, multi-layered, and thus expensive distribution system which favours established indigenous manufacturers; and government procurement policies which discriminate against foreign companies.

RD

Members of the US Congress publicly smashing a Tōshiba product on Capitol Hill in protest against violations of the embargo on the export of technology with military potential to the former USSR.

Other protectionist measures are procedures against alleged Japanese dumping of goods, which have been frequently resorted to in the EC and the US. In 1987 President Reagan imposed a $300 million tariff on certain Japanese electronics imports, and the following year the Omnibus Trade Act was passed containing a clause, popularly known as 'Super 301', which authorized the president to take retaliatory action against countries which were deemed to engage in unfair trading practices.

Japan's major reaction to these growing trade disputes has been a steep increase in investments in manufacturing industries in the US and the EC. Before the revaluation of the yen in 1985 direct foreign investment was primarily designed to secure raw materials and energy, and to reduce production costs and get closer to the markets. Since then the threat of foreign protectionism in the wake of growing trade imbalances has become the most important reason to invest abroad, encouraged by the steep rise of the yen, growing production costs at home and the need to expand aid to the Third World.

It is not clear, however, that these investments have necessarily had a beneficial effect on the trade balance of the recipients. Initially at least, investment increases the intra-firm trade of Japanese companies due to the setting up of foreign subsidiaries. In 1986 exports to Japan from overseas-based Japanese subsidiaries amounted to $27 billion, while exports from parent companies to the subsidiaries amounted to $89.9 billion. This represents 21.5% of Japan's total import of $125.4 billion, and 41.8% of its total export of $215.1 billion. Another potential risk of growing investments overseas is the development of Japanese branch economies in Europe, Asia and North America which are dependent on Japanese headquarters. The global distribution of Japanese investments is also beginning to cause friction between Japan's major trading partners who are either competing to attract Japanese investments to their own country or who are forced to accept imports from Japanese subsidiaries in countries with which they have liberalized trading régimes. Finally the use of direct foreign investment in order to counter trade imbalances creates a new, even more intractable imbalance because foreign investment in Japan is very low: in 1988 it amounted to only $12.8 billion, of which the US share was 54.7%.

CONCLUSIONS

The changes in Japan's foreign trade since 1945 have been far-reaching, as a result of its constantly developing industrial structure and of demands from its major trading partners for a more equitable trading relationship. While Japan's trade structure is becoming more balanced and more open, the economy has at the same time become even more competitive. These gains for Japan's trading partners seem, therefore, to be counterbalanced by its remaining structural advantages as well as their own economic deficiencies. Also, the rise in imports owes still more to overall economic growth in Japan rather than to any fundamental reorientation.

The international trade régime under GATT and its regulations are increasingly unable to close the slippery road to protectionism. The globalization of trade and investments by Japan and its competitors alike makes conventional concepts such as balanced bilateral trade, national economy and national products outdated, although they still prove to be politically useful.

RD

Transport and communications

Since Japan is a mountainous archipelago and habitable space is scarce and costly, communications systems are always a key issue for policymakers at national, regional and local levels. The present transportation and communications infrastructure reflects the demand for a system that can transport people, goods and information quickly and effectively, and Japan enjoys an international lead in such areas as the development of high-speed rail networks and the creation of a national optical-fibre grid. However, in other areas it lags behind its Western competitors, and it is clear that extension of the transportation network to relieve massive overloading must be a high priority, especially on the so-called Pacific Belt, stretching from Tōkyō to Kōbe.

The emergence of a national communications network

In the 17th century the Tokugawa Bakufu imposed an almost total ban on external travel and communications which lasted for 200 years but at the same time instituted a system of 'alternate attendance', whereby daimyō were required to make periodic visits to Edo (=Tōkyō) with large retinues. This gave a considerable boost to internal travel, although in the interests of the security of the shōgun's castle in Edo travellers were carefully scrutinized at checkpoints, while the building of bridges over major rivers was banned because it might facilitate the passage of armies.

In the Meiji period (1868–1912) a modern communications system developed rapidly to achieve the objectives expressed in the slogan 'rich country, strong army'. The telegraph was introduced in 1869, contact with the outside world came in 1872 with the Nagasaki–Shanghai submarine cable, and the telephone arrived in 1877. The first railway service started in 1875 and the first private line was established in 1879. Largely because railways were perceived as a major priority if the army was to function effectively as a means of ensuring domestic security, the Meiji government took a close interest in the planning of railways, and most of them were state-owned. The first major nationalization of private lines was undertaken in 1906 and laws were passed stipulating that inter-city lines were to be state-owned. A second major surge of nationalizations took place in the late 1930s as part of the mobilization for war. Meanwhile, the government had been fostering an indigenous shipbuilding industry to provide for the needs of merchant shipping and the growing navy. Japan's first automobile had been produced in 1899 and its first aircraft in 1911, but the aircraft industry only really developed in the 1920s in answer to military needs.

The 'bullet train', or Shinkansen. Introduced in 1964 for the Tōkyō Olympics, it cut the journey time between Tōkyō and Ōsaka dramatically. New rolling-stock has since been introduced and the system extended to other (but not all) parts of Japan. Although the French TGV is a faster express train, it still cannot remotely compare with the Shinkansen in terms of frequency and passengers carried per year.

The Yokohama coastal railway in the late 1870s. The first railway in Japan was completed in 1872, but the engineers and staff were almost all Europeans employed by the government. By the end of the century Japanese engineers had expanded the network to most corners of the country.

In the 1930s the railways dominated the market for passenger traffic, while freight was carried mostly by the coastal shipping fleet. Jurisdiction over the communications system at this time was shared by the Ministry of Transport and the Ministry of Communications, although the needs of the Army, the Navy and the Home Ministry exerted considerable influence on communications policies in the 1930s and 1940s. The communications system was devastated during the war, and, during the Occupation, US forces gave priority to reviving the telecommunications system to ensure more effective implementation of their policies for the disarmament and reshaping of Japanese society. Simultaneously, the shipbuilding and aircraft industries, which were trying to re-establish themselves to resuscitate Japan's international communications, were placed under a ban because of the fear that they might provide the basis for a resurgence of militarism. However, as the Cold War intensified and Japan moved closer to regaining its independence under US protection, the government began planning a new communications infrastructure which might guarantee economic prosperity in the future.

The railways

The rural rail network emerged relatively unscathed from the war but that in the cities suffered extensive damage. In 1949 the Japanese National Railways (JNR) was established by order of the Occupation authorities as a public corporation separate from the Ministry of Transport. The pre-war pattern, whereby the national system ran in parallel with a number of private rail companies but had a monopoly on the inter-city routes, was maintained. JNR was privatized in 1985 and broken up into a central company and a number of regional companies. The national system still has the largest share of passenger rail transport at 70% but it is losing ground to the highly innovative and extensively modernized private railway systems, which comprise a group of 14 large companies and nearly 60 smaller ones. The system as a whole is extremely efficient, particularly in the cities, but it remains severely congested. It is undergoing constant modernization and even extension: the completion in 1988 of the Seikan tunnel linking Honshū and Hokkaidō brought Hokkaidō into direct rail communication with the rest of Japan.

In 1964 the Shinkansen, or 'bullet train', service was opened between Ōsaka and Tōkyō. There are now 1,832 kilometres of Shinkansen tracks, but the massive expansion of the system that was first envisaged has been delayed by the huge deficits incurred by JNR since 1974, by government austerity measures in the 1980s, and by the break-up of JNR. In 1991 the government announced a ¥1,000 billion investment plan for a Shinkansen route to Nagano, where the 1998 winter olympics will be held, but other routes will probably continue to suffer from delays caused by friction between local and central government and by protests against noise pollution. Meanwhile planning is going ahead for the construction of the Maglev or magnetic levitation train. This, the successor to the Shinkansen, will relieve congestion, and, travelling at speeds in excess of 350 kilometres per hour, will cut the travel time between Tōkyō and Ōsaka to one hour. This is bound to pose a serious challenge to air traffic between the two cities, but the investment costs are enormous and many years undoubtedly lie ahead before Maglev trains start taking fare-paying passengers.

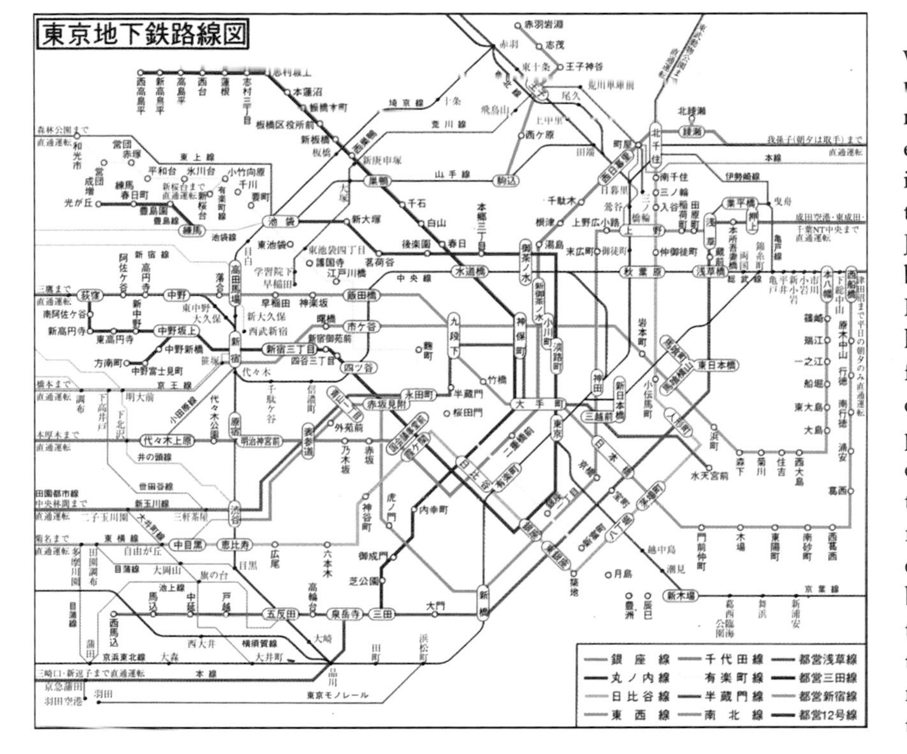

Above *A map of the Tōkyō underground railway system, with surface line extensions. The expansion is such that maps have to be regularly updated.*

Right *The Maglev linear conduction motor relies on magnetic force to raise it above the track and is expected to provide the next generation of high-speed land transport. At present it runs on experimental tracks in Kyūshū, but when introduced it will cut the journey time between Tōkyō and Ōsaka to about one hour.*

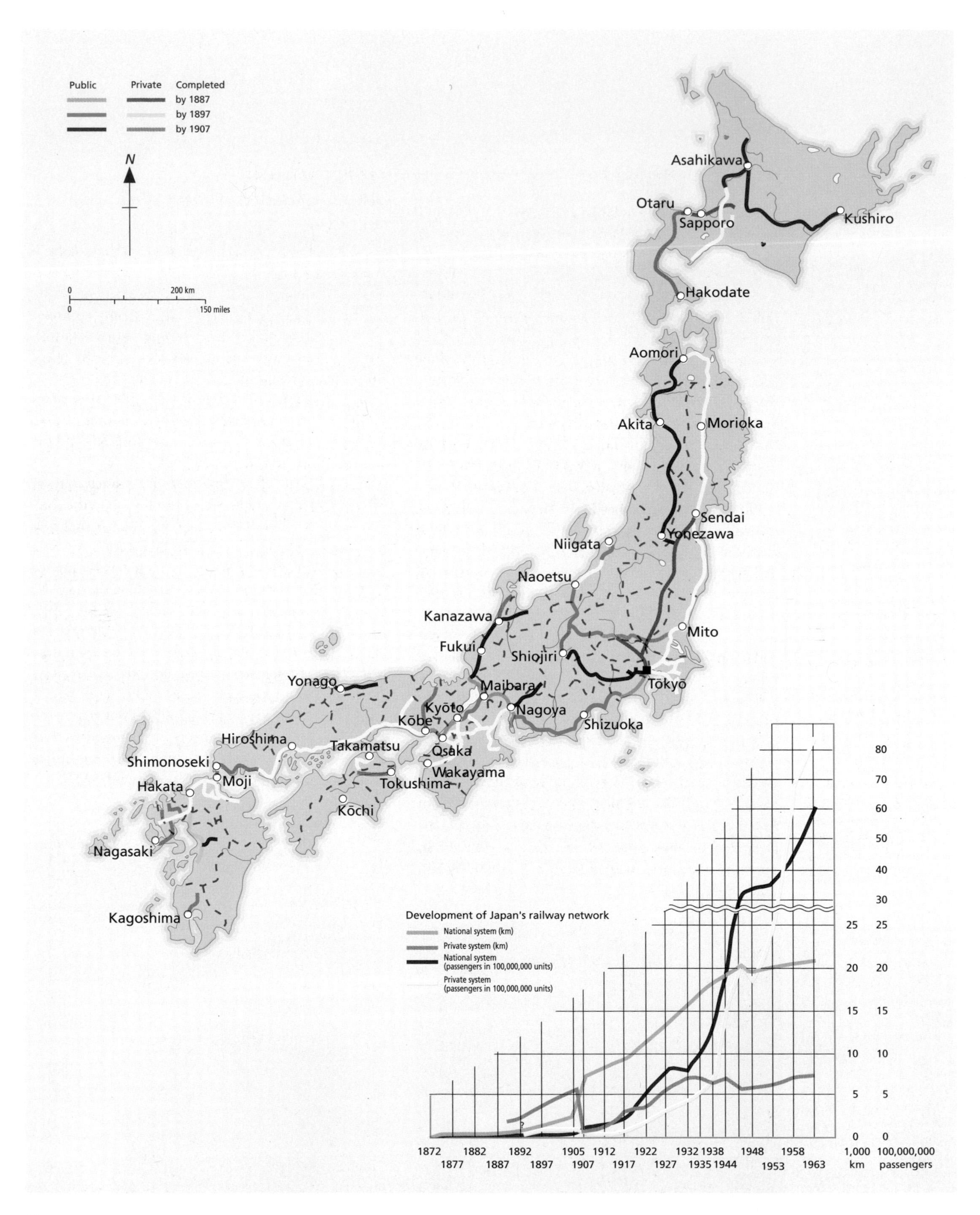

Public
Private
Completed
by 1887
by 1897
by 1907
N
0
200 km
0
150 miles
Asahikawa
Otaru
Sapporo
Kushiro
Hakodate
Aomori
Akita
Morioka
Sendai
Yonezawa
Niigata
Naoetsu
Kanazawa
Mito
Fukui
Shiojiri
Tōkyō
Yonago
Maibara
Kyōto
Nagoya
Kōbe
Shizuoka
Hiroshima
Takamatsu
Ōsaka
Shimonoseki
Wakayama
Moji
Tokushima
Hakata
Kōchi
Nagasaki
Kagoshima
Development of Japan's railway network
National system (km)
Private system (km)
National system (passengers in 100,000,000 units)
Private system (passengers in 100,000,000 units)
1872 1877 1882 1887 1892 1897 1905 1907 1912 1917 1922 1927 1932 1935 1938 1944 1948 1953 1958 1963
1,000 km
100,000,000 passengers
0 5 10 15 20 25 30 40 50 60 70 80

Left *The map shows the expansion of Japan's private and public railway networks. The graph shows the development of these networks in terms of track and numbers of passengers carried.*

Road transport

The first expressway in Japan was opened in 1965 and today there are approximately 5,000 kilometres of high-speed roads, with plans to double this by early in the next century. By comparison with its international competitors, Japan is, however, well behind in the construction of expressways, because of the scarcity of space, and the percentage of paved roads is low at 70%. Moreover, the growth of the automobile industry and vast increases in passenger traffic and road-freight traffic (now 90% of the freight market) has led to severe congestion. The worst affected are the Tōmei and Meishin expressways connecting Tōkyō with Kōbe, and a parallel expressway to remove some of the pressure is seen as essential.

Hitherto the traffic needs of the Pacific Belt have taken priority over regional development but now a vastly improved national highway network is planned which will give the regions a greater rôle. A series of major national construction projects is now linking the main islands for a Trans-Japan expressway of the future. The Seto Bridge linking Shikoku and Honshū has already been completed and two other projects linking Shikoku to the main islands are scheduled for completion in 1997. The congestion on the railways, the boost that road construction can give to a sluggish economy, and the promise to the US that Japan will vastly increase its outlay on public works have all served to promote road construction. US pressure is also behind the deregulation in 1990 of the road haulage system: the principle of open competition has been accepted and this is seen as an opportunity for the entry of foreign, particularly US, road haulage firms.

Below *For all the efficiency of the urban transport systems in Japan, the sheer number of people on the move each day calls for split-second timing and precision placement. These travellers on the surface circle line, the Yamanote, know that the next train will arrive in a few minutes and that when it does, the doors will open at exactly the right spot.*

Maritime and air communications

Although Japan has long depended on coastal and inter-island transport systems, the completion of the Seikan tunnel and the Seto bridge has considerably reduced the need for ferries and local shipping services. Maritime cargo transport, which in any case now accounts for a mere 8% of freight transportation, may well not recover from this blow. On the other hand, leisure transport by sea is enjoying a boom, including overseas cruises, and Japan's large merchant fleet remains of course a vital communications lifeline for massive imports of raw materials and for exports of manufactured products.

The growth of a domestic air transportation system was hampered by the prohibition on the construction of aircraft imposed by the Occupation authorities, which remained in force until 1953. The late start, together with the perennial problems of land scarcity and costs, have been major impediments up to the present. The national carrier, Japan Airlines (JAL), was formed in 1953 and it dominated the lucrative Tōkyō–Ōsaka route until the inauguration of the Shinkansen in 1964 severely damaged its share of the passenger traffic. JAL also had a monopoly of the international routes but that came to an end in 1986 when All Nippon Airways (ANA) began to operate international flights: ANA now has 11 international routes and competes with JAL.

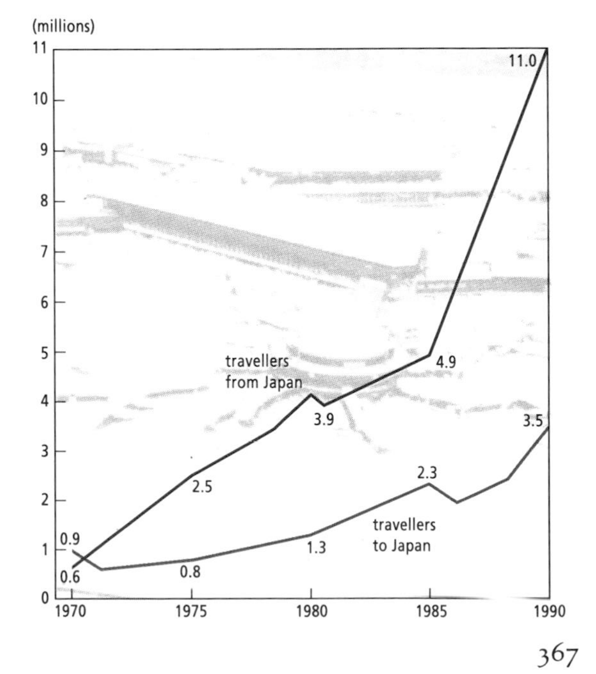

Bottom right *Travellers to and from Japan, 1970–90. The late 1980s and 1990s saw a sharp increase in the numbers of Japanese travelling abroad: a reflection of the increased strength of the yen.*

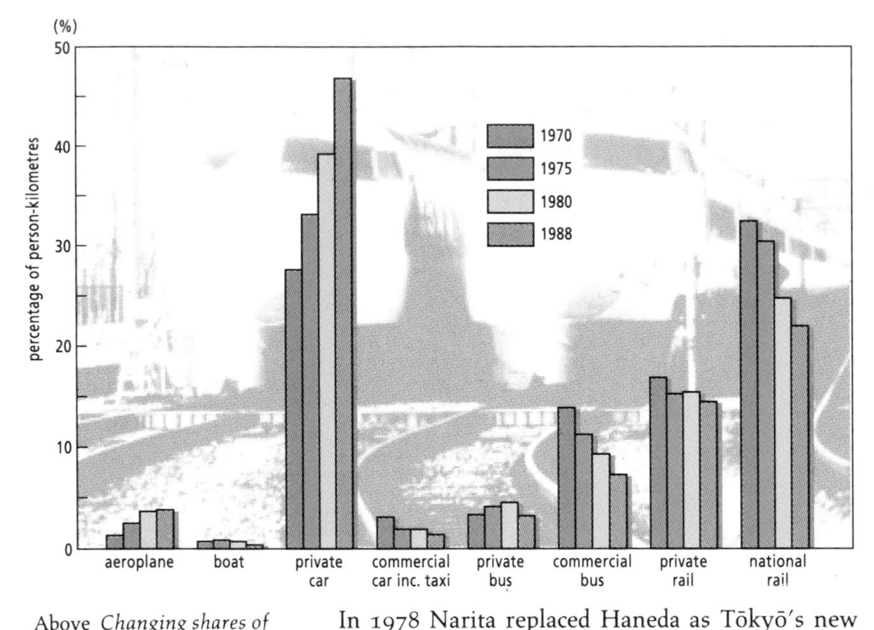

Above *Changing shares of domestic passenger travel, 1970–88: as elsewhere, the car has prospered at the expense of the railways.*

In 1978 Narita replaced Haneda as Tōkyō's new international airport, and all international airlines now land either there or at Itami Airport in Ōsaka; Haneda serves now as a hub for domestic flights, though China Airlines of Taiwan also has landing rights there. There are 24 regional airports and domestic passenger traffic has risen from 40,000,000 in 1982 to 60,000,000 in 1989, while some 28,000,000 international passengers are now landing annually at the international airports. The construction of new runways at Haneda and Narita has been held up for years by local protests, while Itami Airport is operating at capacity and the completion of the Kansai International Airport which will replace it has been pushed back to 1994. In order to deal with growing congestion, the government is now accelerating plans to expand regional airports and to create new regional hubs for international traffic. Domestic air travel is also being promoted, because it has the short-term benefit of increasing high-cost imports of aircraft to relieve the trade surplus and the long-term benefit of fostering the growth of the domestic aircraft construction industry. The three main carriers purchased new aircraft valued at one trillion yen in fiscal 1990, which was a major boost for US and European aircraft manufacturers. It is clear that the air communications systems will continue to expand dramatically in the years to come, although so far this mostly concerns passenger traffic: less than 1% of domestic freight is carried by air.

Top right *The public telephone is a ubiquitous feature of urban life. Here two card-operated telephones stand beside a telephone card dispenser. The cards are thinner than those in use in most other countries and can be personalized with one's own design; they are now used widely as presents and are traded like postage stamps. Vandalism of telephones or card dispensers is virtually unknown.*

TELECOMMUNICATIONS

Following several post-war reorganizations of the telecommunications system Nippon Telephone and Telegraph (NTT) acquired a monopoly of domestic services in 1952 and in 1953 a monopoly of international services was given to Kokusai Denshin Denwa. NTT had the responsibility for implementing a series of plans for creating a national network and by the late 1970s had achieved its targets with the help of technologies developed by a family of off-shoot firms: the network was technologically efficient and had a high density, with a high ratio of telephones per capita. In 1985 NTT was privatized and competitors were allowed to handle both domestic and international communications, using existing lines, microwaves, newly-laid lines, and satellites. These and other recent developments have brought Japan closer to realization of the idea of an 'Information Society', and the Integrated Systems Digital Network (ISDN), a national communications grid based on optical fibres, is currently setting new international standards for a dense system of communications media.

IG

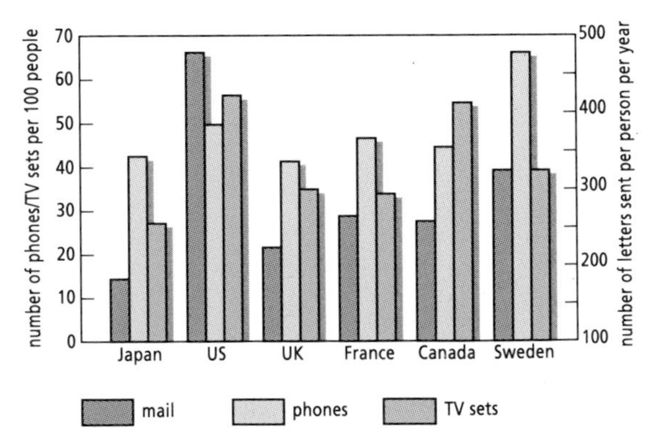

Right *International comparison of communications media: the Japanese may be poor letter-writers but they more than make up for that by their avid use of the telephone and, more recently, of the fax machine.*

Science and technology

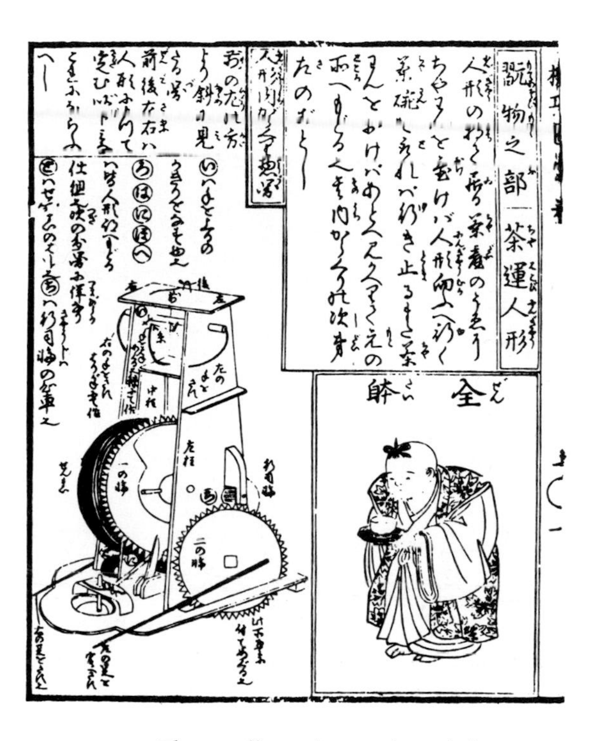

Right *The Tokugawa period was one of great fascination with mechanical objects. The diagram on the left shows the workings of the doll on the right, which moves forward to offer a cup of tea.*

Technological advances have made a particularly important contribution to Japan's economic growth. Until recently, it was common to attribute this technological development simply to the copying of foreign ideas. Now that Japan has become an important innovator in its own right, however, it has become clear that indigenous as well as imported scientific and technological advances have had a rôle to play in Japan's development.

The history of Japanese science

Like so much of Japan's cultural heritage, scientific thought in early Japan was strongly influenced by that of China. The first influx of Chinese scientific ideas occurred in the 6th and 7th centuries AD, when Japan also imported many other aspects of Chinese learning. During the Heian Period (794–1185) a University and Institutes of Divination and Medicine were established, and a number of Chinese texts on astronomy, astrology, mathematics and medicine were brought in. As a result, Japanese ideas about the physical world were profoundly influenced by Chinese concepts, including the notions of *yin* and *yang* and of the five basic elements (wood, fire, earth, metal and water).

At this stage, however, scholarship was largely restricted to members of the court nobility, and, as the University and Institutes declined in the 9th and 10th centuries, a hereditary system of house learning emerged, with a handful of noble families each dominating a particular area of study. During the next five centuries contacts with China became tenuous, but some new ideas were introduced by Japanese Buddhist priests, whose travels in China brought them into contact with scientific developments on the continent.

A second major influx of Chinese ideas resulted from the expansion of trade with China in the 15th and 16th centuries. At about the same time, the arrival of European missionaries and merchants exposed Japan to Western scientific knowledge, including firearms, navigational techniques and astronomy. The intellectual stimulus of these new ideas introduced from different sources continued to be felt long after the imposition of isolationist policies by the Tokugawa shōguns in the 1630s. The first astronomical calendar to be devised by a Japanese scholar appeared in 1685, and further calendrical reforms were carried out in the 18th and early 19th centuries. The rise of the merchant class encouraged the study of practical arithmetic, while some samurai scholars devoted themselves to the more abstract intellectual pleasures of *wasan*, or 'Japanese mathematics'. A crucial new influence on Japanese science came from the *rangakusha*, scholars of 'Dutch studies', who eagerly pursued the fragments of Western medical, astronomical, and geographical knowledge which entered Japan through the Dutch trading post at Deshima.

Unlike scientific thinkers of earlier ages, the leading intellectuals of the Tokugawa period were often private scholars without either religious or political patronage. Many came from the lower ranks of the samurai class, although some were commoners by birth. A particularly influential rôle was played by doctors, who failed to fit into any of the official strata of the Tokugawa social hierarchy. The medical profession thus became an important vehicle for both social mobility and the importation of foreign ideas.

THE INSTITUTIONAL FRAMEWORK OF MODERN SCIENCE

The introduction of Western science formed a vital part of the policies of Westernization pursued by the Japanese government after the Meiji Restoration of 1868. British, US and German scientists were brought in to teach Japanese students, and faculties of science, medicine and later also engineering were established at Tōkyō University, which came into being in 1877 and from 1886 was known as Tōkyō Imperial University. At a more popular level the introduction of science into the curricula of primary, secondary and technical schools gave a new generation of students a knowledge of the fundamental principles of Western science. As the education system developed, other imperial universities were established. By 1918 there were five (Tōkyō, Kyōto, Kyūshū, Tōhoku and Hokkaidō) with faculty members often drawn from the select band of Japanese scholars who had studied overseas.

As far as research was concerned, the government tended to favour areas which had a practical application to suit Japan's economic needs. State-funded laboratories, such as the Electrical Laboratory set up in 1891 and the Institute of Infectious Diseases, which received government support from 1893, were generally oriented towards the applied sciences. In Japan as elsewhere, the emergence of 'scientific warfare' during the First World War focussed attention on the strategic importance of science. One consequence was the establishment in 1917 of the Research Institute for Physics and Chemistry; another was the creation in 1920 of the Academic Research Council, which funded research. During the 1920s and 1930s, however, the Research Institute too concentrated to a large degree on applied research, and from the late 1920s until 1945 even operated a number of factories to commercialize the inventions of its scientists.

Country of origin of papers cited in major scientific journals, 1975–86.

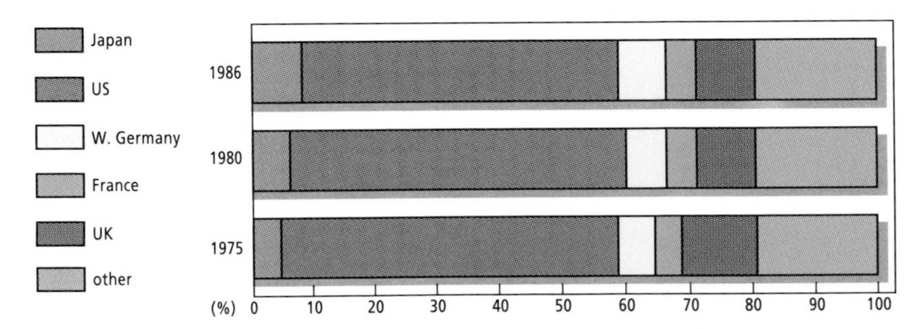

With the rise of international tensions in the 1930s, scientific research was increasingly pressed into the service of military needs. At the same time, the exemption of science students from military conscription, which remained in force until the closing stages of the Pacific War, attracted some particularly able scholars, thus paving the way for the rapid revival of Japanese science in the post-war era.

The disasters of war had convinced many people of the need for science devoted to peaceful purposes. This new emphasis was reflected in the establishment of the Science Council of Japan, a body set up in 1948 to express the views of scientists on academic, social and political issues. At a governmental level, the Science and Technology Agency (STA), created in 1956, served as the central body for the formulation of science and technology policy. In practice, however, the STA has shared its jurisdiction over technology with several other bureaucratic bodies, most notably the Ministry of International Trade and Industry (MITI), and its jurisdiction over science with the Ministry of Education, Science and Culture.

In the years which followed the Pacific War the growth of university education led to a great expansion of Japan's academic science sector. During the early 1950s new public universities were set up in major cities throughout the country, and between 1960 and 1980 the number of private universities increased from 140 to over 300. Student interest in the applied sciences was particularly strong, and by the mid 1970s Japan was producing more graduates in electrical and electronic engineering than the US. Academic scientists have sometimes been criticized for their reluctance to co-operate with private industry, and it has also been argued that the tendency of universities to appoint their own graduates to faculty positions stifles creativity and merit. These problems have become an important target of recent proposals for educational reform.

Japan was a relative latecomer to scientific research, but Japanese scholars have nevertheless made significant contributions, and five Japanese researchers have won Nobel prizes for scientific work up to 1991. On the other hand, the fact that Japan has fewer Nobel laureates than any other major industrialized country is seen by some as an indication of the weakness of basic research in Japan. Other indicators of scientific activity, however, point to the growing international influence of Japanese science.

Technology and industrialization

Nowadays the words 'science' and 'technology' are so closely associated in the Japanese mind that they are often fused into a single expression, *kagaku-gijutsu* ('science-and-technology'). When Japan embarked on industrialization in the mid 19th century, however, the productive techniques in use in Japanese factories and workshops were based on practical experience rather than on science in the modern sense of the word. Although Japan lagged far behind the West in terms of the mechanization of industry, some handicraft skills, such as those of silk-farmers, carpenters, lacquer makers and potters, had reached a high level during the Tokugawa period. Handicraft industries, indeed, became important sources of export earnings in the early stages of modernization.

The technological transformation of Japanese industry from the Meiji period to the Pacific War involved three main elements: the import of technology from the West, the application of modern science to traditional industries, and technical training and education.

There had been moves to import Western techniques even earlier. During the 1850s the Bakufu and certain daimyō established arsenals and iron-foundries based on Western models. These enterprises were later taken over by the Meiji government, which also set up its own Western-style enterprises, for example the famous Tomioka silk-reeling factory, which was built in 1872.

Although the government-run enterprises were rarely profit-making, and most were sold to wealthy businessmen in the 1880s, they served a useful purpose in introducing modern methods to Japanese entrepreneurs and workers. Most of the state-sponsored factories and mines were created with the help of Western advisers, several thousand of whom were brought to Japan in the first decades of the Meiji period. The Meiji government, however, was always anxious to avoid dependence on outside experts, and sought to ensure that foreign advisers returned home as soon as Japanese engineers and technicians were ready to take their places.

Although government-sponsored bodies like the Research Institute for Physics and Chemistry continued to play an important part in the import and development of technology during and after the First World War, the private sector was becoming increasingly active. As big Japanese firms moved into heavy industry, their managers recognized the need to upgrade technological capacity. Some, like Tōkyō Electric and Mitsubishi Shipbuilding, set up major research laboratories during or soon after the First World War, while others, such as Asahi Glass and Mitsubishi Electric, sought to import technology through links with Western firms.

Technological change in the late 19th and early 20th centuries involved not only importing sophisticated industrial processes, but also improving the techniques of traditional craft industries. The Meiji government founded a number of research centres, including the Industrial Laboratory in 1900 and the Sericulture Research Station in 1911, and similar laboratories were sponsored by local governments in many parts of Japan.

Local authorities and local business groups also played an important part in establishing technical high schools under the terms of the government's Technical School Ordinance of 1903. As the need for technicians and skilled workers increased, private industry, too, began to develop training programmes, and by the 1920s some large enterprises were introducing seniority pay rises and fringe benefits to encourage company loyalty amongst their skilled employees.

With the heightening of political tensions in the 1930s, government industrial policies placed increasing emphasis on military-related technologies, and support was given for schemes to develop alternatives to scarce raw materials such as oil. From 1942 these policies were supervised by a special Cabinet Council on Technology, but defeat in the Pacific War showed up dramatically the size of the continuing technology gap between Japan and the Western industrial powers, the US in particular.

JAPAN'S NOBEL LAUREATES IN SCIENTIFIC FIELDS

Year	Laureate	Field
1949	Yukawa Hideki (1907–81)	Physics (Meson theory)
1965	Tomonaga Shin'ichirō (1906–79)	Physics (quantum electrical dynamics)
1973	Esaki Reona (1925–)	Physics (tunnel diode effect)
1981	Fukui Ken'ichi (1918–)	Chemistry (theory of chemical reactions)
1987	Tonegawa Susumu (1939–)	Biology/Medicine (immune system)

A shopper with a robot shopping trolley at Seibu department store in Tōkyō. All systems in the store have been computerized, so that information about products on display can be obtained on a screen at the touch of a button. All members of staff, except those manning the central information desk, have been replaced by these robots, which are programmed to follow the customers at a respectful distance.

Sources of finance for research: a comparison of Japan, the US and UK.

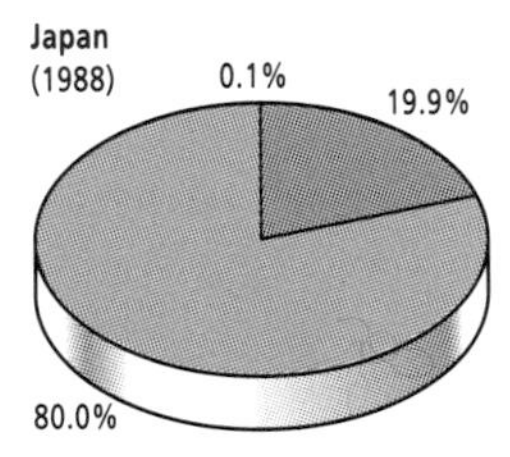

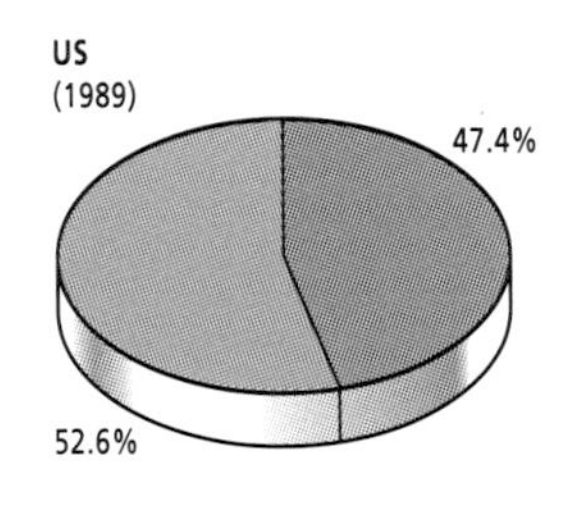

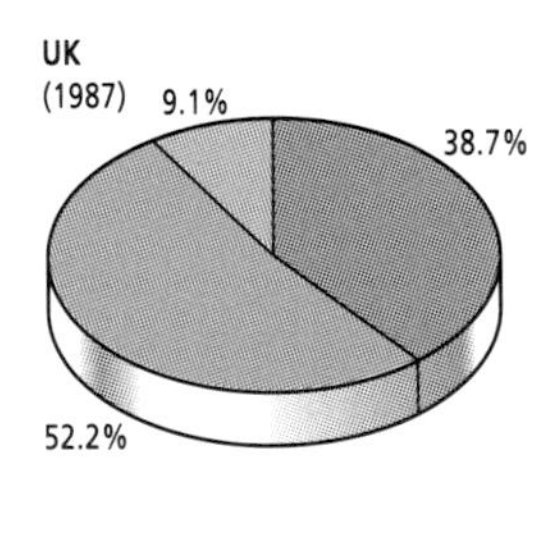

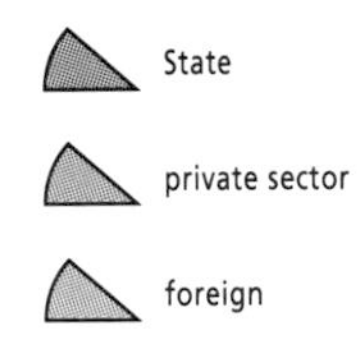

In the post-war period government policy focussed largely on creating a favourable environment for the import of advanced industrial technology. During the 1950s and 1960s MITI devised packages of financial assistance and tax relief to encourage the expansion of specific heavy industries such as steel and electrical machinery. The Japan Productivity Centre was opened in 1955 to provide private industry with up-to-date information on developments in production technology and managerial techniques, and a National Research and Development Programme (NRDP) was established in 1966 to organize co-operative research on projects of national importance. As a result of these policies and the favourable economic climate at home and abroad, technology imports grew rapidly and companies devoted much more to research and development. The key characteristic of Japan's technological research in the second half of the 20th century has been the large rôle played by the private sector: in 1989, for example, only 19.9% of Japan's research was state-funded, compared with 48.3% in the case of the US, 38.7% in the UK and 35.3% in Germany.

Until the 1960s, Japanese firms were rarely regarded as serious rivals by their Western counterparts, and access to foreign technology was easy. Technology was transferred to Japan on a large-scale, usually by means of licensing agreements with Western firms. During the 1970s and 1980s, however, Western companies became much more wary of transferring their know-how to their Japanese competitors. Meanwhile, Japan itself was emerging as a leading exporter of technology, particularly to the industrializing nations of east and south-east Asia.

Science and technology policy in contemporary Japan

With a changing international environment, rising wages and worsening environmental problems, the Japanese government has been forced to rethink its industrial strategy. From the 1970s onwards, the emphasis has been on the development of a strong independent technological capacity, particularly in 'knowledge intensive' industries such as microelectronics, computing, robotics, new materials and biotechnology.

One element of this strategy involves efforts to promote basic scientific research and to strengthen ties between academic scientists and industry. To achieve these aims in 1981 the Science and Technology Agency launched the Exploratory Research Advanced Technology (ERATO) programme, which encourages teams of scientists from various institutions to explore major new fields of research. More recently, the Agency has co-operated with MITI to set up the Human Frontiers Science Project, an international research project on human physiology and brain functions. New science-cities like Tsukuba near Tōkyō, which was developed from 1963 onwards, and Kansai Science City, designated in 1978, also aim to overcome institutional rigidities and create a suitable environment for scientific creativity.

In the promotion of high technology, the government continues to encourage co-operation between private corporations, rather than investing large sums in state-controlled programmes. Two of the major high-technology projects begun in this way during the 1980s are the Next Generation Basic

The number of industrial robots installed per 10,000 production workers: Japan's lead over its competitors stands out clearly.

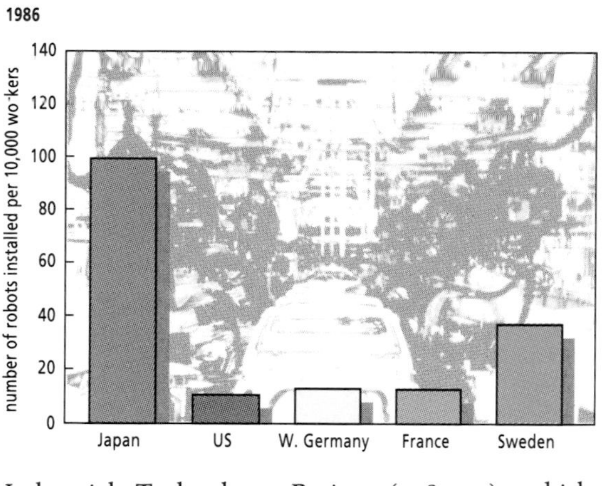

Far right *Japan's export of technology by destination in 1988.*

The hot end of a computer-controlled steel works. The solitary human figure seems redundant, for most production functions have now been taken over by computerized robots. Luddite tendencies are conspicuous by their complete absence in Japan.

Industrial Technology Project (1981-91), which created a range of co-operative research projects in new-materials technology, biotechnology and superconductivity, and the Fifth Generation Computer Project (1982-92), which aimed to develop a new form of information-processing capable of handling large quantities of symbols, images and speech. The Key Technology Centre, set up jointly by MITI and the Ministry of Posts and Telecommunications in 1985, acts as a source of venture capital for enterprises embarking on co-operative research in leading-edge technologies.

The promotion of high technology in Japan has had considerable success. Research and development spending as a percentage of national income increased from 1.96% in 1970 to 3.35% in 1988, and Japan has come to be recognized as a world leader in areas such as microelectronics and industrial automation. Although the spread of computers in schools and homes has been relatively slow, office and factory automation has advanced very rapidly, even in small and medium-sized firms, and by the 1980s Japan was the world's largest user of industrial robots. Some commentators suggest, however, that high levels of education, management skills and a generally favourable economic climate have been as important as government policy in promoting technological change. Independent projects, like the Real Operating Nucleus (TRON) computer project conceived by Sakamura Ken of Tōkyō University, have probably been as influential as government-sponsored projects in establishing Japan's place at the forefront of contemporary developments.

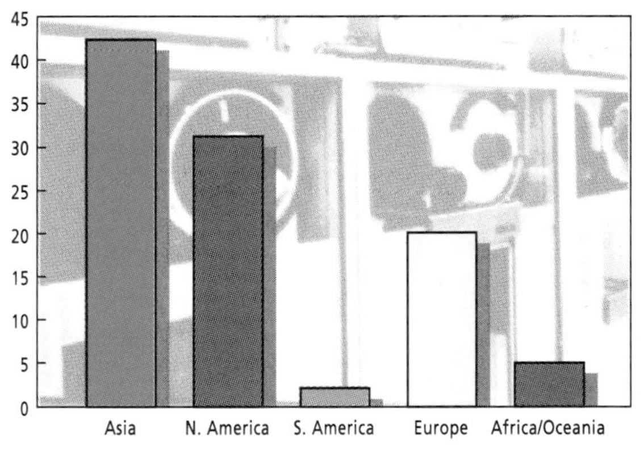

Science, technology and society

Japan's modern history, with its experiences of rapid industrialization and rising prosperity, but also of atomic bombing and of environmental pollution, draws attention to the costs as well as the benefits of scientific and technological progress. The social responsibility of the scientist has been a topic of debate ever since the interwar years, when it was discussed by the left-wing Society for the Study of Materialism, which was established in 1932 and suppressed by the government in 1938.

In the immediate post-war years organizations such as the Japan Science Council served as a forum for discussions on the social and political rôle of science. The emergence of environmental problems in the 1960s, however, led to a new and more fundamental questioning of technology by groups outside the scientific community itself. Contemporary debates focus particularly on issues such as the safety of nuclear energy and the environmental and ethical implications of biotechnology.

Concerns over the costs of technological change have resulted in the strengthening of environmental legislation and the development of technology assessment in Japan. In general, however, government and business remain committed to a strategy which defines technological advance as the key to Japan's economic future.

TM-S

Space

In 1955, two years before the USSR launched Sputnik I, the University of Tōkyō began conducting research into solid fuel rockets and this marks the start of space research in Japan, but it was not until February 1970 that the first satellite was launched. This success led in the 1970s to substantial increases in the annual budget devoted to the National Space Development Agency (NASDA), which is the Japanese equivalent of NASA and the main agency for space research in Japan.

During the 1970s and 1980s a total of 35 scientific, communications and meteorological satellites were successfully placed in orbit, with only two failures. In 1990 an observation satellite was put in orbit around the moon and for the 1990s there is a regular programme of further launches.

One of the major projects for the 1990s is the construction of Japan's contribution to the project for an international space station, which is being co-ordinated by NASA. This is the so-called Japanese Experiment Module, which will be a space laboratory equipped with advanced communications and computer facilities, and it is expected to be launched in 1997. Most of the well-known Japanese industrial firms are now involved in the NASDA and related projects, so that Mitsubishi is producing the rocket launchers, Fujitsū the satellite communications equipment, and Tōshiba the broadcasting satellites, and it comes as no surprise, therefore, that possible industrial uses of space for the manufacture of new materials and pharmaceutical research are included in the objectives of the Japanese space programme, which can be expected to attain the highest levels of space-related technology in the later 1990s.

The photographs here are of the NASDA launch site on Tanegashima, an island to the south of Kyūshū.

PK

Glossary

Amida Amitābha Buddha, in whose Pure Land paradise many hoped to be reborn. Worship involved repetition of his name.

Bakufu Designates the government during periods when samurai exercised political control. During the Tokugawa period the government was based in Edo, so it is known as the Edo Bakufu.

bodhisattva In Buddhism, name given to those enlightened beings who have not yet entered final nirvana but rather dedicate themselves to helping others reach the same state.

bushidō 'Way of the warrior'. Became synonymous with absolute loyalty and a willingness to die in the service of one's master. Translated into an effective military ethos in the modern period.

daimyō A territorial magnate or baron. The daimyō enjoyed considerable local autonomy and at times were in absolute control of their territory and answerable to nobody.

Edo Effective capital of Japan for most of the Tokugawa period (1600–1868), hence also known as the Edo period.

Genpei wars Series of battles between two clans, the Genji (also known as Minamoto) and the Heike (also known as Taira), that culminated in the destruction of the latter at Dannoura in 1185. Marked the beginning of the rise of warrior rule at the expense of the earlier court-based culture.

genrō 'Elder statesmen'. A term designating the members of the oligarchy in their capacity as advisors to the Emperor Meiji.

Heisei Era name for the reign of the present emperor (1989–).

hiragana One of the two syllabic scripts in common use (see section on Language).

ie Family as a traditional unit. Strictly hierarchical, male-dominated system, but not based exclusively on blood-ties. Adoption of males was a common practice. Still powerful in the world of art, music and crafts, where it is known as *iemoto*.

-ji Suffix attached to the names of temples.

-jō Suffix attached to the names of castles.

kabuki A theatrical tradition that originated and grew to popularity among the urban classes in the early 17th century.

kami Shintō deity or spirit (see Thought and Religion).

kamikaze 'Divine Wind'. Used to describe the typhoons that saved Japan from a full-scale Mongol invasion in the 13th century. Later applied to suicide pilots in the Pacific War.

kanji Japanese name for Chinese characters.

katakana One of the two syllabic scripts in common but restricted use (see Language).

Meiji Era name (1868–1912). From this time on, era names coincided with emperors' reigns. Hence it is also used to refer posthumously to the Emperor Meiji himself.

nō Form of slow-paced dance-drama using religious themes expressed in ornate poetic language. Emerged in the Muromachi period (see Literature and Arts and Crafts).

rōnin 'Man of the waves'. A samurai who had been dispossessed of rank, stipend and hence livelihood; a fate not always of his own making. Some made their living by writing and teaching, but many became disaffected and became a threat to public order.

samurai Formerly simply a 'servant', the word came to refer to a warrior and then to a member of the warrior class in the service of a daimyō or the ruling Tokugawa family.

Shinkansen 'New trunk line'; the term more commonly used in English is 'bullet train'.

Shintō Indigenous system of beliefs in Japan (see Thought and Religion).

shōgun A military title traditionally held by the successive heads of the Bakufu, or samurai government.

Shōwa Era name (1926–89). Now used to refer posthumously to the Emperor Shōwa (Hirohito) himself.

Taishō Era name (1912–26). Also, Emperor Taishō.

Tokugawa Name of the military clan that ruled the country from 1600–1868, hence Tokugawa period.

ukiyoe 'Pictures of the floating world'. Refers to pictures and prints of the Tokugawa period that took everyday life as their theme.

zaibatsu Industrial conglomerates combining operations in several sectors of the economy, including banking.

Abbreviations

JCP	Japan Communist Party
JSP	Japan Socialist Party (now SDPJ)
LDP	Liberal Democratic Party
MITI	Ministry of International Trade and Industry
MOF	Ministry of Finance
SCAP	Supreme Commander of the Allied Powers (Occupation forces)
SDF	Self-Defence Forces
SDPJ	Social Democratic Party of Japan (formerly JSP)

Periods in Japanese history

Nara	710–94
Heian	794–1185
Kamakura	1185–1333
Muromachi	1333–1568
Momoyama	1568–1600
Tokugawa (Edo)	1600–1868
Meiji	1868–1912
Taishō	1912–26
Shōwa	1926–89
Heisei	1989–

Periods in Chinese history from the Han

Han	202BC–AD220
Three Kingdoms	221–65
Six Dynasties	265–581
Sui	581–618
Tang	618–906
Five Dynasties	907–60
Northern Song	960–1127
Southern Song	1127–1279
Yuan	1271–1368
Ming	1368–1644
Qing	1644–1911
Republic	1911–49
People's Republic	1949–

Geography

The classic regional geography of Japan in the English language is G. T. Trewartha, *Japan: a geography* (Methuen, 1965). Trewartha's treatment of contemporary themes in human geography is now rather dated, but his coverage of Japan's physical geography remains useful, as is that contained in two shorter works: P. Dempster, *Japan advances* (Methuen, 1967), and T. Nō and D. H. Gordon, eds., *Modern Japan: land and man* (Teikoku Shoin, 1974). More recent research by Japanese geographers on their own islands is reported in detail in Association of Japanese Geographers, eds., *Geography of Japan* (Teikoku Shoin, 1980), while topics of interest to students at the secondary school level are discussed in D. MacDonald, *A geography of modern Japan* (Paul Norbury, 1985). There is also an excellent general introduction to the geography of modern Japan in its physical and historical setting in M. Collcutt *et al.*, *Cultural atlas of Japan* (Phaidon, 1988). The major aspects of Japan's economic and urban geography are covered in D. Kornhauser, *Urban Japan: its foundations and growth* (Longman, 1976), while the flavour of Japan's natural beauty is superbly captured in M. Sutherland and D. Britton, *National parks of Japan* (Kōdansha, 1980). For a well-presented atlas of modern Japan, the interested reader need look no further than Teikoku Shoin, ed., *Atlas Japan* (Teikoku Shoin, 1989).

History

EARLY JAPAN · On early Japan see C. M. Aikens and T. Higuchi, *Prehistory of Japan* (Academic Press, 1982), G. L. Barnes, *Protohistoric Yamato* (Ann Arbor: Museum of Anthropology and Center for Japanese Studies, 1988) and G. L. Barnes, ed., *Hoabinhian, Jōmon, Yayoi, early Korean states* (Oxbow Books, 1990). Art in pre-Nara Japan is treated in J. E. Kidder's *Early Japanese art: the great tombs and treasures* (Thames and Hudson, 1964) and N. Egami's *The beginnings of Japanese art* (Weatherhill, 1973).

THE NARA PERIOD 710–94 · On the archaeology of Nara, see M. Tanaka, *Unearthing Nara: the archaeology of the Japanese eighth-century capital* (UNESCO and The Centre for East Asian Cultural Studies, 1991). W. W. Farris, *Population, disease, and land in early Japan, 645–900*, (Harvard University Press, 1985) deals with demographic issues. The *Nihon shoki* has been translated by W. G. Aston as *Nihongi, chronicles of Japan from the earliest times to AD 697* (Tuttle, 1972), and D. L. Philippi has translated the *Kojiki* (Princeton University Press, 1968); T. Sakamoto 's *The six national histories of Japan* has recently appeared in a translation by J. S. Brownlee (University of British Columbia Press, 1991).

THE HEIAN PERIOD 794–1185 · Useful surveys are available in the relevant chapters of C. Totman, *Japan before Perry: a short history* (University of California Press, 1987) and J. W. Hall, *Japan from prehistory to modern times* (Dell, 1970). An important set of essays is included in J. W. Hall and J. P. Mass, eds., *Medieval Japan: essays in institutional history* (Yale University Press, 1974). Although it focusses on the final century of the period, *Insei; abdicated sovereigns in the politics of late Heian Japan, 1086–1185* (Columbia University Press, 1976) by G. C. Hurst remains the best example of research on Heian history. A wealth of detail on court life and intrigue can be found in W. H. and H. C. McCullough, trans., *A tale of flowering fortunes: annals of Japanese aristocratic life in the Heian period*, 2 vols. (Stanford University Press, 1980).

THE MEDIEVAL AGE · This period is the subject of K. Yamamura, ed., *The Cambridge history of Japan*, vol. 3 (Cambridge University Press, 1990). The shifting balance of courtly and warrior power in the Kamakura era is dealt with in essays contained in J. P. Mass, ed., *Court and Bakufu in Japan* (Yale University Press, 1982). Politics, economics and culture in the Muromachi age are discussed in J. W. Hall and T. Toyoda, eds., *Japan in the Muromachi age* (University of California Press, 1977). For more detailed studies in economic and social history in this period see J. W. Hall, K. Nagahara, and K. Yamamura, eds., *Japan before Tokugawa: political consolidation and economic growth 1500–1650* (Princeton University Press, 1981).

JAPAN ENCOUNTERS THE WEST · For accounts of the linguistic, moral and financial problems encountered by the missionaries in Japan see C. R. Boxer, *The Christian century in Japan, 1549–1650* (University of California Press, 1967) and G. Elison, *Deus destroyed: the image of Christianity in early modern Japan* (Harvard University Press, 1973). M. Cooper provides an anthology of the early writings of Europeans on Japan at this time in *They came to Japan* (University of California Press, 1965). There is no biography of Nobunaga in English but on Hideyoshi there is M. E. Berry, *Hideyoshi* (Harvard University Press, 1982), D. Elisseeff, *Hideyoshi – Bâtisseur du Japon moderne* (Paris: Fayard, 1986), and A. Boscaro, *101 Letters of Hideyoshi* (Sophia University Press, 1975). For a broader view of the period see G. Elison and L. S. Bardwell, eds., *Warlords, artists and commoners: Japan in the sixteenth century* (The University Press of Hawaii, 1981).

THE TOKUGAWA PERIOD · The organization of the Tokugawa government is treated in H. Bolitho, *Treasures among men* (Yale University Press, 1974) and C. Totman, *Politics in the Tokugawa Bakufu* (Harvard University Press, 1967), while its downfall is described in C. Totman, *The collapse of the Tokugawa Bakufu* (The University Press of Hawaii, 1980). An overview of economic development is to be found in S. B. Hanley and K. Yamamura, *Economic development and demographic change in pre-industrial Japan* (Princeton University Press, 1977). Diplomatic and intellectual relations with the outside world are treated in R. Toby, *State and diplomacy in early modern Japan* (Princeton University Press, 1984) and G. K. Goodman, *Japan: the Dutch experience* (The Athlone Press, 1988).

THE MEIJI PERIOD · Comprehensive accounts of Meiji Japan can be found in W. G. Beasley, *The rise of modern Japan* (The Athlone Press, 1989) and J. E. Hunter, *The emergence of modern Japan* (Longman, 1989). Some excellent essays can be found in M. B. Jansen, ed., *The Cambridge history of Japan*, vol. 5, and P. Duus, ed., *The Cambridge history of Japan*, vol. 6 (Cambridge University Press, 1988). J-P. Lehmann, *The roots of modern Japan* (Macmillan, 1982), is a more detailed study of the Meiji period. For a study of ideological trends, see C. Gluck, *Japan's modern myths: ideology in the late Meiji period* (Princeton University Press, 1985).

FROM THE FIRST WORLD WAR TO THE 1930S · Two overviews of Japan in this period are B. S. Silberman and H. D. Harootunian, eds., *Japan in crisis: essays on Taishō democracy* (Princeton University Press, 1974) and the relevant chapters of P. Duus, ed., *The Cambridge history of Japan*, vol. 6 (Cambridge University Press, 1988). On the Manchurian Incident and the 1936 army rebellion, see S. Ogata, *Defiance in Manchuria: the making of Japanese foreign policy, 1931–1932* (University of California Press, 1964) and B. Shillony, *Revolt in Japan: the young officers and the February 26, 1936, incident* (Princeton University Press, 1973). Concerning Hirohito, see S. S. Large, *Emperor Hirohito and Shōwa Japan: a political biography* (Routledge, 1992).

JAPAN AT WAR · The best studies of the domestic and international politics of the China incident are G. M. Berger *Parties out of power, 1931–1941* Princeton University Press, 1977) and J. H. Boyle, *China and Japan at war, 1937–1945: the politics of collaboration* (Stanford University Press, 1972). A. Iriye offers an incisive account of the origins of the Pacific War in *The origins of the Second World War in Asia and the Pacific* (Longman, 1987), while wartime Japan is covered in T. R. H. Havens, *Valley of darkness: the Japanese people and World War II* (Norton, 1978) and B-A. Shillony, *Politics and culture in wartime Japan* (Oxford University Press, 1981). Racial attitudes and the war are explored in J. W. Dower, *War without mercy: race and power in the Pacific War* (Faber, 1986), and L. Allen, *The end of the war in Asia* (MacGibbon, 1976) deals with the impact of the war on Asia. R. Guillain, *I saw Tokyo burning: an eyewitness narrative from Pearl Harbor to Hiroshima* (Murray, 1981) provides an eyewitness account of the Japanese experience of war.

POST-WAR JAPAN · The most accessible text on the post-1945 years is R. Buckley, *Japan today* (Cambridge University Press, 1990). Various textbooks on the history of modern Japan cover the post-war period to some degree, notably W. G. Beasley, *The rise of modern Japan* (The Athlone Press, 1989). On the rule of the bureaucracy see C. Johnson, *MITI and the Japanese miracle* (Stanford University Press, 1982). For the Occupation see R. Ward and Y. Sakamoto, eds., *Democratizing Japan: the Allied Occupation* (The University Press of Hawaii, 1987).

Language and literature

LANGUAGE · The first port of call should be M. Shibatani, *The languages of Japan* (Cambridge University Press, 1990), which is both up to date and lucid, if a little technical in parts. In many respects it supersedes R. A. Miller, *The Japanese language* (University of Chicago Press, 1967), although Miller is always worth reading and has written provocatively on the subject of genetic affiliation in *Japanese and the other Altaic languages* (University of Chicago Press, 1971), and on linguistic jingoism in *Japan's modern myth* (Weatherhill, 1982). G. Sampson, *Writing systems* (Hutchinson, 1985) offers an excellent treatment of the script, especially in the context of Chinese and Korean. S. E. Martin, *A reference grammar of Japanese* (Yale University Press, 1975) is over 1,000 pages long and only for the intrepid.

EARLY LITERATURE · D. L. Phillipi's translation of the *Kojiki* (Princeton University Press, 1968) is useful, despite his practice of recording names in archaic pronunciation; more dated is the only translation of the *Nihon shoki*, W. G. Aston's *Nihongi* (Tuttle, 1972). Examples of *Man'yōshū* poems are found in a number of anthologies: a good selection is in H. Sato and B. Watson, *From the country of eight islands* (University of Washington Press, 1981). For background to early poetry, see E. Miner, *Introduction to Japanese court poetry* (Stanford

University Press, 1968). G. L. Ebersole's *Ritual poetry and the politics of death in early Japan* (Princeton University Press, 1989) is the most important study yet of early literature.

HEIAN LITERATURE · Any further reading should begin with E. Seidensticker's translation of Murasaki's *The tale of Genji* (Penguin Classics, 1981). R. Bowring, *Murasaki Shikibu: the tale of Genji* (Cambridge University Press, 1988) is a short guide to both background and tale. Many translations of *waka* are available but the form remains difficult to appreciate for the general reader. I. Morris's version of *The pillow book of Sei Shōnagon* (Penguin Classics, 1971) has delighted many.

MEDIEVAL LITERATURE · The new anthology edited by H. C. McCullough, *Classical Japanese prose: an anthology* (Stanford University Press, 1991) is useful in providing partial or in some cases complete translations of several works and the same scholar has made a valiant attempt to convey the power of the original language in her translation of *The tale of the Heike* (Stanford University Press, 1988). For poetry see P. T. Harries, *The poetic memoirs of Lady Daibu* (Stanford University Press, 1980) and for linked verse S. D. Carter, *The road to Komatsubara* (Harvard University Press, 1987). Readings for nō are covered in the section on theatre.

TOKUGAWA LITERATURE · Translations of poetry, prose and plays from this period are plentiful. For straightforward literary history turn to D. Keene's *World within walls: Japanese literature of the pre-modern era 1600–1867* (Secker and Warburg, 1976). Also to be recommended on their particular subjects are *The floating world of Japanese fiction* by H. Hibbett (Oxford University Press, 1959), C. A. Gerstle's *Circles of fantasy: convention in the plays of Chikamatsu* (Harvard University Press, 1986) and E. Miner's *Japanese linked poetry* (Princeton University Press, 1979). The only useful treatment of later prose so far is R. Leutner, *Shikitei Sanba and the comic tradition in Edo fiction* (Harvard University Press, 1985).

MODERN LITERATURE · For basic information on a wide range of modern writers and poets turn to the encyclopedic work by D. Keene, *Dawn to the West: Japanese literature of the modern era* (Holt, Rinehart and Winston, 1984), but the best introductory book on a whole range of 'modern' literary matters remains M. Miyoshi, *Accomplices of silence* (University of California Press, 1974). Most of the authors mentioned in the text appear in some form of translation.

Thought and religion

SHINTŌ AND FOLK RELIGION · J. M. Kitagawa's books, *Religion in Japanese history* (Columbia University Press, 1966) and *On understanding Japanese religion* (Princeton University Press, 1987), give a general introduction to Shintō. On Shintō in modern Japan see H. Hardacre, *Shintō and the state, 1868–1988 (Princeton University Press, 1989)*, and on contemporary religious practices see C. Blacker, *The catalpa bow* (George Allen and Unwin, 1975).

BUDDHISM · For a survey of the history of Buddhism in Japan see J. M. Kitagawa, *Religion in Japanese history* (Columbia University Press, 1966). See also on specific topics Y. S. Hakeda, *Kūkai: major works* (Columbia University Press, 1972) and G. J. and W. J. Tanabe, eds., *The Lotus Sutra in Japanese culture* (The University Press of Hawaii, 1989). The best overall treatment of Japanese Zen is to be found in vol. 2 of H. Dumoulin, *Zen Buddhism: a history*, 2 vols. (Macmillan, 1988–90) and for Zen as an institution see M. Collcutt, *Five mountains: the Rinzai Zen monastic institution in medieval Japan* (Harvard University Press, 1981).

CONFUCIANISM · R. Borgen, *Sugawara no Michizane and the early Heian court* (Harvard University Press, 1986) gives a vivid sense of how Chinese Confucian bureaucratic institutions and culture developed in Japan. R. P. Dore, *Education in Tokugawa Japan* (The Athlone Press, 1984) provides a scholarly and readable account of the largely Confucian education of the Tokugawa period. W. W. Smith, *Confucianism in modern Japan: a study of conservatism in Japanese intellectual history* (The Hokuseidō Press, 1959) is a good account of Confucianism in the modern period.

TOKUGAWA SOCIOPOLITICAL THOUGHT · M. Maruyama, *Studies in the intellectual history of Tokugawa Japan* (Tōkyō University Press, 1974) and R. P. Dore, *Education in Tokugawa Japan* (The Athlone Press, 1984) are both classic studies covering the whole topic. H. Ooms, *Tokugawa ideology* (Princeton University Press, 1985) discusses early Tokugawa Confucianism and its impact on the ruling class. For an introduction to Nativism turn to S. Matsumoto, *Motoori Norinaga* (Harvard University Press, 1970) and P. Nosco, *Remembering paradise* (Harvard University Press, 1990). H. D. Harootunian, *Toward restoration* (University of California Press, 1970) and B. T. Wakabayashi, *Anti-foreignism and Western learning in early-modern Japan* (Harvard University Press, 1986) analyse the formation of 19th-century nationalism.

The new religions · W. B. Davis, *Dojo: exorcism and miracles in modern Japan* (Stanford University Press, 1980) provides a very readable account of one new religion, Sūkyō Mahikari, and H. Hardacre, *Kurozumikyō and the new religions of Japan* (Princeton University Press, 1986) considers the social significance of the new religions as a whole. For a good overall treatment see I. Reader, *Religion in contemporary Japan* (Macmillan, 1991).

Christianity · S. D. B. Picken's *Christianity and Japan: meeting, conflict, hope* (Kōdansha International, 1983) is a general survey. For a revealing autobiographical account of the difficulty of being both a Japanese and a Christian, see Uchimura Kanzō's 'How I became a Christian: out of my diary' in *The complete works of Kanzō Uchimura*, vol. 1 (Kyōbunkwan, 1971). Issues relating to the impact of Christianity in the 19th century are discussed in I. Scheiner, *Christian converts and social protest in Meiji Japan* (University of California Press, 1970) and N. R. Thelle, *Buddhism and Christianity in Japan* (The University Press of Hawaii, 1987).

Modern intellectual currents · The main survey of the period is G. K. Piovesana, *Recent Japanese philosophical thought 1862–1962* (Tōkyō: Enderle Bookstore, 1968). Meiji developments are well treated in M. Kosaka, *Japanese thought in the Meiji era* (Ōbunsha, 1958). A trenchant critique of recent trends can be found in P. N. Dale, *The myth of Japanese uniqueness* (Croom Helm, 1986)

Arts and crafts

Pictorial art before 1600 · The main general survey in English is T. Akiyama, *Japanese painting* (Skira, 1961) although for direct access to pictures the most convenient source is S. Gotō, *Nihon kaiga bijutsu zenshū*, 25 vols. (Shūeisha, 1976–80). Several popular volumes, written in the 1960s and 1970s by noted Japanese scholars appear in three English-language series: *The Heibonsha survey of Japanese art* (Heibonsha and Weatherhill, 1964–80), *The arts of Japan* (Shibundō and Weatherhill, 1973–74), and *The Japanese arts library* (Shibundō and Kōdansha, 1976–87). Exhibition catalogues incorporate more recent scholarship on individual paintings: see, in particular, J. M. Rosenfield and E. ten Grotenhuis, *Journey of the three jewels: Japanese Buddhist paintings from Western collections* (New York: Asia Society, 1979); M. Murase, *Emaki: narrative scrolls from Japan* (New York: Asia Society, 1983); and Y. Shimizu and C. Wheelwright, *Japanese ink paintings from American collections* (Princeton: The Art Museum, 1976).

Pictorial art from 1600 · For general works see above. A representative selection of important works from all schools of Edo painting is included in W. Watson et al, eds., *The great Japan exhibition: art of the Edo period 1600–1868* (London: Royal Academy of Arts, 1981), and see also J. Hillier, *Hokusai: paintings, drawings and woodcuts*, 3rd edn (Phaidon Press, 1978) and the catalogue of Tokugawa painting in the Los Angeles County Museum of Art, *Masterpieces from the Shin'enkan collection* (Thames and Hudson, 1986). A concise introduction to the complex developments in Japanese art since the Meiji Restoration is provided by M. Kawakita, *Modern currents in Japanese art* in *The Heibonsha survey of Japanese art*, vol. 24. (Heibonsha and Weatherhill, 1974). L. P. Roberts, *A dictionary of Japanese artists* (Weatherhill, 1978) is also useful.

Sculpture · Although somewhat out of date, the most complete survey remains *A guide to Japanese sculpture* by T. Kuno (Tōkyō: Mayuyama & Co., 1963). K. Nishikawa and E. J. Sano's exhibition catalogue *The great age of Japanese Buddhist sculpture – AD 600–1300* (Fort Worth: Kimball Art Gallery, 1982) is more up to date and provides an excellent survey of sculpting techniques. R. Goepper's *Shingon – Die Kunst des Geheimen Buddhismus in Japan* (Köln: Museum für Ostasiatische Kunst der Stadt, 1988) and C. G. Kanda's *Shinzō: Hachiman imagery and its development* (Harvard University Press, 1985) are distinguished introductions to more specialized topics. Information about more recent discoveries can be found in V. Harris and K. Matsushima, *Kamakura: The renaissance of Japanese sculpture 1185–1333* (British Museum, 1991).

Architecture · A useful introduction to Japanese architecture is K. Nishi and K. Hozumi, *What is Japanese architecture?*, trans. and adapted by H. M. Horton (Kōdansha, 1985). For Buddhist temples see K. Suzuki, *Early Buddhist temple architecture in Japan*, in *The Japanese arts library*, trans. and adapted by M. N. Parent and N. Shatzman (Shibundō and Kōdansha, 1980). The evolution of residential architecture is covered in F. Hashimoto, *Architecture in the shoin style*, trans. and adapted by H. M. Horton, and for castles see H. Moto'o, trans. and adapted by W. H. Coaldrake, *Japanese castles*, both in *The Japanese arts library* series. On master carpenters and their materials, tools and techniques, see Coaldrake, *The way of the carpenter: tools and Japanese architecture* (Weatherhill, 1990). For recent architecture turn to D. B. Stewart, *The making of a modern Japanese architecture: 1868 to the present* (Kōdansha International, 1987) and the quarterly issues of *The Japan architect*.

DECORATIVE ARTS · Recent publications giving broad coverage of Japanese decorative arts include: W. Watson *et al* eds., *The great Japan exhibition: art of the Edo period 1600–1868*, (London: Royal Academy of Arts, 1981); J. Earle *et al.*, *Japanese art and design* (Victoria and Albert Museum, 1986); J. Hutt, *Understanding far eastern art* (Phaidon Press, 1990); and L. Smith *et al.*, *Japanese art: masterpieces in the British Museum* (British Museum, 1990). See also the catalogue edited by Y. Shimizu, *Japan: the shaping of a daimyō culture: 1185–1868* (Washington: National Gallery of Art, 1988).

DANCE · M. Gunji's *Buyō: the classical dance* (Weatherhill and Tankōsha, 1970) offers a short survey of traditional dance. For nō dance, there is an elaborate study by M. Bethe and K. Brazell, *Dance in the nō theatre*, 3 vols. and 5 video-cassettes (Cornell University Press, 1982). There is no general book in English on Western dance in Japan, but helpful details and insights appear in T. R. H. Havens, *Artist and patron in postwar Japan: dance, music, theater, and the visual arts, 1955–1980* (Princeton University Press, 1982). There is a biography of Itō Michio by H. Caldwell, *Michio Itō* (University of California Press, 1977).

MUSIC · The most enjoyable general survey of Japanese music is still W. P. Malm's *Japanese music and musical instruments* (Tuttle, 1959). Also useful are the article 'Japan' in *The new Grove dictionary of music and musicians* (Macmillan, 1980) and the entries on Japanese instruments in *The new Grove dictionary of musical instruments* (Macmillan, 1984). E. Harich-Schneider's *A history of Japanese music* (Oxford University Press, 1973) focusses on court and Buddhist music, mostly through the study of early manuscripts; it is not for the novice. For studies of individual genres, see the excellent subject index of G. Tsuge's *Japanese music: an annotated bibliography of Western-language works* (Garland, 1986). Pre-Nara musical data are described in E. Hickmann and D. Hughes, *The archaeology of early music cultures* (Bonn: Verlag für systematische Musikwissenschaft, 1988).

THEATRE · For a general introduction to nō and bunraku, see D. Keene, *Nō and bunraku* (Columbia University Press, 1990), and for kabuki, E. Ernst, *The kabuki theatre* (The University Press of Hawaii, 1974). More detailed studies of these classical forms are T. B. Hare, *Zeami's style: the nō plays of Zeami Motokiyo* (Stanford University Press, 1986), C. A. Gerstle, *Circles of fantasy: convention in the plays of Chikamatsu* (Harvard University Press, 1986), and J. Brandon, W. Malm and D. Shively, *Studies in kabuki* (The University Press of Hawaii, 1978). J. T. Rimer covers the introduction of Western forms in *Toward a modern theatre. Kishida Kunio* (Princeton University Press, 1974) and the survival of kabuki is dealt with in B. Powell, *Kabuki in modern Japan* (Macmillan, 1990).

FILM · Indispensable are J. L. Anderson and D. Richie, *The Japanese film: art and industry*, expanded edn (Princeton University Press, 1982) and A. E. Bock, *Japanese film directors* (Kōdansha, 1978). D. Richie's most recent survey is *Japanese cinema: an introduction* (Oxford University Press, 1990). Among a growing number of studies of directors, the most important is D. Bordwell, *Ozu and the poetics of cinema* (Princeton University Press, 1988).

THE CULTURE OF TEA · The two main sources in English are Rand Castile, *The way of tea* (Weatherhill, 1971) and H. P. Varley and I. Kumakura, eds., *Tea in Japan: essays on the history of chanoyu* (The University Press of Hawaii, 1989).

THE CULTURE OF FOOD · P. and J. Martin, *Japanese cooking* (Penguin Books, 1972) and S. Tsuji, *Japanese cooking: a simple art* (Kōdansha International, 1980) are classic cook-books that also offer an introduction to the history and aesthetics of Japanese cuisine.

Society

THE HOME AND FAMILY · On the current nature of the family in urban Japan see D. Kondo, *Crafting selves* (Chicago University Press, 1990), and M. M. Hamabata, *Crested kimono* (Cornell University Press, 1990). R. P. Dore, *City life in Japan* (University of California Press, 1971) still has the best summary in English of the historical foundations of the Japanese family, and C. Nakane, *Kinship and economic organisation in rural Japan* (The Athlone Press, 1967) is a good analysis of the way the *ie* works in rural Japan. O. Moon's *From paddy field to ski slope* (Manchester University Press, 1989) reports recent changes in the country. A more detailed account of child-rearing practices is to be found in J. Hendry, *Becoming Japanese* (Manchester University Press, 1986).

MINORITIES · On Burakumin a useful introduction is G. A. DeVos and H. Wagatsuma, *Japan's invisible race* (University of California Press, 1973), while I. Neary, *Political protest and social control in pre-war Japan: the origins of Buraku liberation* (Manchester University Press, 1989) provides the historical background. Similarly, on the Koreans, see G. DeVos and C-S. Lee, eds., *Koreans in Japan* (University of California Press, 1981) for an overall assessment and M. Weiner, *The origins of the Korean community in Japan* (Manchester University Press, 1989) for the historical background. On the Ainu see F. C. C. Peng and P. Geiser, eds., *The Ainu: the past in the present* (Hiroshima: Bunka Hyōron, 1977).

Education · I. Amano's *Education and examination in modern Japan* (Tōkyō University Press, 1990) provides a good overview of the development of the modern system, while R. P. Dore's *Education in Tokugawa Japan* (The Athlone Press, 1984) covers the historical background. W. K. Cummings' *Education and equality in Japan* (Princeton University Press, 1980) gives a useful account of the younger end of the spectrum, and T. Rohlen's *Japan's high schools* (University of California Press, 1983) is the best for the higher end. For a review of English-language material consult E. R. Beauchamp and R. Rubinger's *Education in Japan: a source book* (Garland Publishing, 1989).

Working life · Classic studies of Japanese working life in the 1970s include R. Cole's *Japanese blue collar* (University of California Press, 1971), R. P. Dore's *British factory – Japanese factory* (University of California Press, 1990), T. Rohlen's *For harmony and strength* (University of California Press, 1974) and R. Clark's *The Japanese company* (Yale University Press, 1979). D. Plath, ed., *Work and lifecourse in Japan* (State University of New York Press, 1983), describes various types of working life, and J. Lincoln and A. Kalleberg's *Culture, control and commitment* (Cambridge University Press, 1990) presents comparative survey results on work attitudes and work organization.

Health and welfare · On poverty and social welfare see the concluding chapters of H. Patrick, ed., *Japanese industrialization and its social consequences* (University of California Press, 1976) and R. Rose and R. Shiratori, eds., *The welfare state East and West* (Oxford University Press, 1986). Various aspects of medical care in contemporary Japan are covered in M. M. Lock, *East Asian medicine in urban Japan* (University of California Press, 1980), E. Norbeck and M. Lock, eds., *Health, illness, and medical care in Japan* (The University Press of Hawaii, 1987), K. Sonoda, *Health and illness in changing Japanese society* (University of Tōkyō Press, 1988), and M. Powell and M. Anesaki, *Health care in Japan* (Routledge, 1990).

Leisure · For the latest data on Japanese leisure, see *Leisure and recreational activities* (Tōkyō: Foreign Press Centre, 1990). D. W. Plath, *The after hours: modern Japan and the search for enjoyment* (University of California Press, 1964), is already dated but still worth reading. On the lifestyles of blue- and white-collar workers in big companies in the 1970s see S. Linhart, *Arbeit, Freizeit und Familie in Japan* (Harrassowitz, 1976).

The media · Different aspects of the history of the mass media are treated in J. L. Huffman, *Politics of the Meiji press: the life of Fukuchi Gen'ichirō* (The University Press of Hawaii, 1980) and G. J. Kasza, *The state and the mass media in Japan, 1918–1945* (University of California Press, 1988). R. G. Powers and H. Kato, *Handbook of Japanese popular culture* (Greenwood Press, 1989), covers many forms of media, while *manga* are the subject of F. L. Schodt, *Manga! Manga! The world of Japanese comics* (Kōdansha International, 1986).

Popular protest and citizens' movements · A detailed account of the freedom and popular rights movement can be found in R. W. Bowen, *Rebellion and democracy in Meiji Japan* (University of California Press, 1980). The rice riots are dealt with at length in M. Lewis, *Rioters and citizens* (University of California Press, 1990). Citizens' movements and their participation in environmental protest are analysed in M. A. McKean, *Environmental protest and citizen politics in Japan* (University of California Press, 1981) and for an in-depth treatment of the struggle at Narita airport see D. E. Apter and N. Sawa, *Against the state* (Harvard University Press, 1984)

Crime and the law · On the police see W. Ames, *Police and community in Japan* (University of California Press, 1981), and on related issues D. Bayley, *Forces of order* (University of California Press, 1976), S. Miyazawa, *Policing in Japan: a study on making crime* (State University of New York Press, 1992) and V. Kusuda-Smick, ed., *Crime prevention and control in the United States and Japan* (Transnational Juris Publications, 1990). A good book on organized crime is D. Kaplan and A. Dubro, *Yakuza: the explosive account of Japan's criminal underworld* (Addison-Wesley, 1986).

Politics

The constitutional framework · An indispensable book on intellectual developments leading to the Meiji Constitution is J. Pittau, *Political thought in early Meiji Japan 1868–1889* (Harvard University Press, 1967). Concerning conflicting Japanese interpretations of the Meiji Constitution, see R. H. Minear, *Japanese tradition and Western law: emperor, state, and law in the thought of Hozumi Yatsuka* (Harvard University Press, 1970) and F. O. Miller, *Minobe Tatsukichi: interpreter of constitutionalism in Japan* (University of California Press, 1965). On the making of the present constitution see K. Inoue, *MacArthur's Japanese constitution: a linguistic and cultural study of its making* (University of Chicago Press, 1991). The history of immediate post-war revision is outlined in D. F. Henderson, ed., *The constitution of Japan: its first twenty years, 1947–1967* (University of Washington Press, 1968).

HOW JAPAN IS GOVERNED · For an analysis of how Japan was governed under the Meiji Constitution, see H. Wray and H. Conroy, *Japan examined* (The University Press of Hawaii, 1983). On the post-war system, see G. L. Curtis, *The Japanese way of politics* (Columbia University Press, 1988) and J. A. A. Stockwin, *et al.*, *Dynamic and immobilist politics in Japan* (Macmillan, 1988). T. J. Pempel, in *Policy and politics in Japan* (Temple University Press, 1982), analyses the system's 'creative conservatism', while K. E. Calder, in *Crisis and compensation in Japan: public policy and political stability in Japan, 1949–1986* (Princeton University Press, 1988), shows how government policy has been affected by previous concessions to various interests. How far Japan is governed democratically is examined by T. Ishida and E. S. Krauss, eds., *Democracy in Japan* (Pittsburgh University Press, 1989). Also recommended is D. I. Okimoto and T. P. Rohlen, eds., *Inside the Japanese system* (Stanford University Press, 1988)

THE CIVIL SERVICE · The best account of the present higher civil service is B. C. Koh, *Japan's administrative elite* (University of California Press, 1989). P. S. Kim, *Japan's civil service system* (Greenwood Press, 1988) is less detailed but somewhat broader and is thus a useful complement to Koh. R. M. Spaulding, *Imperial Japan's higher civil service examinations* (Princeton University Press, 1967) analyses the history (from 645 to 1945) of Japan's long journey toward accepting and perfecting a merit system.

THE JUDICIARY · On the judiciary, see L. W. Beer, *Freedom of expression in Japan* (Kōdansha, 1984); H. Itoh and L. W. Beer, *The constitutional case law of Japan: selected Supreme Court decisions, 1961–1970* (University of Washington Press, 1978); and H. Itoh, *The Japanese Supreme Court: constitutional policies* (Markus Wiener Publishing, 1989).

PARTIES AND PARTY POLITICS · For a study of parties and party politics in the first decade of the Meiji Constitution, see J. Banno, *The establishment of the Japanese constitutional system*, trans. J. A. A. Stockwin (Routledge, 1992). Other studies of pre-war parties are P. Duus, *Party rivalry and political change in Taishō Japan* (Harvard University Press, 1968) and G. Berger, *Parties out of power in Japan, 1931–1941* (Princeton University Press, 1977). On post-war parties see R. J. Hrebenar, *The Japanese party system* (Westview, 1992) and H. H. Baerwald, *Party politics in Japan* (Allen and Unwin, 1986). For a classic study of the LDP, see H. Fukui, *Party in power* (Australian National University Press, 1970).

ELECTIONS AND ELECTIONEERING · The best introductions to this subject are J. A. A. Stockwin, *Japan: divided politics in a growth economy* (Weidenfeld and Nicolson, 1982) and G. L. Curtis, *The Japanese way of politics* (Columbia University Press, 1988).

INTEREST GROUPS · A general analysis of interests groups can be found in B. Richardson and S. Flanagan, *Politics in Japan* (Little, Brown & Co., 1984). A. George, 'Japanese interest group behaviour: an institutional approach', in J.A.A. Stockwin *et al.*, *Dynamic and immobilist politics in Japan* (Macmillan, 1988) provides detailed information on Diet representation of interest groups and their relations with the bureaucracy.

LOCAL GOVERNMENT · Detailed studies on local government in Japan include: T. Gotoda, *The local politics of Kyōto* (University of California at Berkeley, Center for Japanese Studies, Japan Research Monograph 7, 1985); K. Steiner, *Local government in Japan* (Stanford University Press, 1965); K. Steiner, E. S. Krauss, and S. C. Flanagan, eds., *Political opposition and local politics in Japan* (Princeton University Press, 1980); R. J. Samuels, *The politics of regional policy in Japan* (Princeton University Press, 1983); and S. R. Reed, *Japanese prefectures and policymaking* (University of Pittsburg Press, 1986).

FOREIGN POLICY · Basic source material on Japanese foreign policy is to be found in the *Diplomatic blue book*, published annually by the Japanese Ministry of Foreign Affairs, and the *Defence of Japan*, published annually by the Defence Agency. See also R. A. Scalapino, ed., *The foreign policy of modern Japan* (University of California Press, 1977), S. Saitō, *Japan at the summit: its role in the Western alliance and in Asian Pacific cooperation* (Routledge, 1990) and R. Steven, *Japan's new imperialism* (Macmillan, 1990).

DEFENCE · On security issues and defence matters in general, see J. W. M. Chapman, R. Drifte and I. T. M. Gow, *Japan's quest for comprehensive security* (Francis Pinter, 1983) and H. H. Holland, *Managing defence: Japan's dilemma* (University Press of America, 1988). R. Drifte, *Arms production in Japan: the military applications of civilian technology* (Westview Press, 1986) deals with the technological capability of the armaments industry.

Economy

THE POST-WAR ECONOMY · The most useful recent studies of the Japanese economy are P. Francks, *Japanese economic development: theory and practice* (Routledge, 1992), L. Hollerman, *Japan, disincorporated: the economic liberalization process* (Hoover Institution, 1988) and S. Ishinomori, *Japan, Inc.* (University of California Press, 1988). For some of the international perspectives see E. J. Lincoln, *Japan's unequal trade* (The Brookings Institute, 1990) and Y. Suzuki, *Japan's economic performance and international role* (University of Tōkyō Press, 1989).

FOOD AND AGRICULTURE · R. P. Dore's *Land reform in Japan* (Oxford University Press, 1959) still provides the most straightforward and readable account of pre-war agriculture, as well as the standard account of the post-war land reform. A good feel of pre-war rural life can be obtained from Nagatsuka's novel *The soil*, trans. A. Waswo (Routledge, 1989). Policy and trade issues confronting Japanese agriculture since the war are well covered in E. N. Castle and K. Hemmi, eds., *US–Japanese agricultural trade relations* (Johns Hopkins University Press, 1982). There are a number of studies of rural communities adapting to the impact of the 'economic miracle', of which R. P. Dore, *Shinohata* (Allen Lane, 1978) is the most readable, R. J. Smith, *Kurusu* (Folkestone: Dawson, 1978) the most anthropologically thorough and G. L. Bernstein, *Haruko's world* (Stanford University Press, 1983) the most appealing.

ENERGY · More detailed studies of energy and power in Japan include: L. Hein, *Fueling growth: the energy revolution and economic policy in postwar Japan* (Harvard University Press, 1990), R. A. Morse, *Turning crisis to advantage: the politics of Japan's Gulf energy strategy* (New York: The Asia Society, 1990), and R. J. Samuels, *The business of the Japanese state: energy markets in comparative and historical perspective* (Cornell University Press, 1987).

BANKING AND FINANCE · The most useful guide to banking and finance is that compiled by the Bank of Japan: Y. Suzuki, ed., *The Japanese financial system* (Oxford University Press, 1987). F. M. Rosenbluth gives a lively discussion of the politics surrounding the changes in the Banking Law of 1982 in *Financial politics in contemporary Japan* (Cornell University Press, 1989), while comparative issues are covered in T. Cargill and S. Royama, *The transition of finance in Japan and the United States* (The Hoover Institution Press, 1988).

MANUFACTURING AND SERVICES · Recent studies of Japan's industrialization are the contributions to P. Duus, ed., *The Cambridge history of Japan*, vol. 6 (Cambridge University Press, 1988), and the critical perspectives in T. Morris-Suzuki and T. Seiyama, eds., *Japanese capitalism since 1945* (M. E. Sharpe, 1989). S. Levine and H. Kawada's *Human resources in Japanese industrial development* (Princeton University Press, 1980) and A. Gordon's *The evolution of labour relations in Japan: heavy industry, 1853–1955* (Harvard University Press, 1985) document the human resource and employment side of industrialization, and R. P. Dore's *British factory – Japanese factory* (University of California Press, 1990) combines historical perspective with a detailed account of a large manufacturing company. K. Yamamura, Y. Yasuba, T. Inoguchi and D. Okimoto, eds., *The political economy of Japan*, vols. 1 & 2 (Stanford University Press, 1987–88) are useful sources on related topics.

FOREIGN TRADE · On trade frictions, see A. M. El-Agraa, *Japan's trade frictions: realities or misconceptions?* (Macmillan, 1988). Other works covering Japan's foreign trade include R. Komiya, *The Japanese economy: trade, industry and government* (University of Tōkyō Press, 1990), M. Itoh, *The world economy crisis and Japanese capitalism* (Macmillan, 1990), and T. Inoguchi and D. J. Okimoto, eds., *The political economy of Japan*, vol. 2 (Stanford University Press, 1988).

SCIENCE AND TECHNOLOGY · On the history of Japanese science see M. Sugimoto and D. L. Swain, *Science and culture in traditional Japan* (MIT Press, 1978) and S. Nakayama, D. L. Swain and E. Yagi, eds., *Science and society in modern Japan: selected historical sources* (University of Tōkyō Press, 1974). On science in modern Japan see J. R. Bartholemew, *The formation of science in Japan* (Yale University Press, 1989); and A. M. Anderson, *Science and technology in Japan* (Longman, 1991).

Acknowledgements

Particular thanks are due to the International Society for Educational Information Inc. and to Kumiko Sekioka, Tokyo, for assistance with picture research. Every effort has been made to obtain permission for use of the photographic and textual material listed below; if any errors or omissions have occurred the publishers would welcome these being brought to their attention.

Photographs. viii, Carol Jopp/RHPL; 3, Bruce Coleman; 4, Krafft/RHPL; 5t, Bruce Coleman; 5c,b, Ardea London; 6l, JICC; 6r, Earth Satellite Corporation/Science Photo Library; 9t, Masahiro Iijima/Ardea London; 9b, International Society for Educational Information, Inc.; 13, RHPL; 14l, Kensuke Sakanizu/Ardea London; 14/15, Werner Forman Archive; 15b, National Forestry Extension Association/ISEI; 16/17, Jean-Paul Nacivet/Colorific; 19l, The Bridgeman Art Library; 19tr, Christopher G. Knight; 19br, Robert McLeod/RHPL; 20, Image Bank/G. Colliva; 21, W. Eugene Smith/Magnum; 22, RHPL; 23, J. C. Nacivet/Gamma/FSP; 24, Robin Lawrence/Photographer's Gallery; 29, Gordon/Select; 30, Sassoon/RHPL; 33, Bruce Coleman; 34, 35t, PANA-JIJI Photos; 35c/b, Mike Yamashita/Colorific; 36/37, 37t, 38l, RHPL; 38t/b, Francois Gohier/Ardea London; 39t, Masahiro Iijima/Ardea London; 39b, RHPL; 40/41, Werner Forman Archive/Kongo Nogakudo, Kyoto; 42l, Trustees of the British Museum; 42r, Dr Gina L. Barnes; 46, Geographic Photo/ISEI; 48, Ronald Sheridan/Ancient Art & Architecture Collection; 52, Werner Forman Archive; 53, Shitenno-ji Temple Museum; 55, courtesy of The Arthur M. Sackler Museum, Harvard University Art Museums. Bequest of the Hofer Collection of the Arts of Asia; 56, Geographic Photo/ISEI; 57, from *Nihon byobue shusei*, vol. 12, reproduced by permission of the Syndics of the Cambridge University Library; 60, Trustees of the British Museum; 61, scene from the *Moko shurai emaki*, reproduced by permission of the Syndics of the Cambridge University Library; 62, Werner Forman Archive; 64, Werner Forman Archive/M. H. De Young Memorial Museum, San Francisco; 65, by permission of the British Library; 66l, Spencer Collection Japanese M553, *Inatomi-ryu teppo densho*, 1612, New York Public Library; 66/67, Werner Forman Archive; 68t, Werner Forman Archive/Kuroda Collection, Japan; 68b, Ronald Sheridan/Ancient Art & Architecture Collection; 70/71, reproduced by courtesy of the Trustees of the British Museum; 72l,72/73, Ukiyo-e Books, Leiden, Holland; 74/75, The Bridgeman Art Library; 75r, from *Musashi abumi*, reproduced by permission of the Syndics of the Cambridge University Library; 77, Ronald Sheridan/Ancient Art & Architecture Collection; 78, The Bridgeman Art Library; 79, Werner Forman Archive; 80, from *The greatest of exhibitions*, St Louis, 1904, p. 64, New York Public Library; 83t, Popperfoto; 84, courtesy of the Victoria and Albert Museum, London/The Bridgeman Art Library; 88l, Popperfoto; 90, Brown Brothers, Sterling, PA 18463; 91, courtesy of the Chester Beatty Library & Gallery of Oriental Art/The Bridgeman Art Library; 94, Hulton Deutsch Collection; 99, Camera Press London; 100, Kodansha Ltd/ISEI; 101, Jack Esten/Popperfoto; 105, Hulton Deutsch Collection; 108l, Kyodo; 108r, Hulton Deutsch Collection; 109, AP; 110, Robert Wallis/JB Pictures/Colorific; 111, JICC; 112/113, courtesy of the Victoria and Albert Museum, London/The Bridgeman Art Library; 117, Asahi Shinbun; 123, Tokyo National Museum; 126, courtesy of the Arthur M. Sackler Museum, Harvard University Art Museums. Gift of Mrs Donald F. Hyde; 128tl, from *The tales of Ise* (Saga-bon version), reproduced by permission of the Syndics of the Cambridge University Library; 128tr, Hatakeyama Kinenkan; 128bl, by permission of the British Library; 128br, Tokyo National Museum; 129, Tokugawa Art Museum; 131, Manno Art Museum; 132l, Trustees of the British Museum; 132/133, Museum of Fine Arts, Boston, MA 02115; 134, from *Gunsho ruiju*, reproduced by permission of the Syndics of the Cambridge University Library; 135, *Young women of the world*, Ejima Kiseki (1717), reproduced by permission of the Syndics of the Cambridge University Library; 136, Werner Forman Archive, Private Collection, New York; 137, MOA Museum of Art, Atami; 138, The Denver Art Museum; 139t, from Saikaku: *Life of an amorous man* (1682), reproduced by permission of the Syndics of the Cambridge University Library; 139c, from *Kinkin sensei zoku no yume* (1794), reproduced by permission of the Syndics of the Cambridge University Library; 139b, Ryutei Tanehiko: *Nise Murasaki inaka Genji* (1832), reproduced by permission of the Syndics of the Cambridge University Library; 141, Kowa Slide Co. Ltd; 142, from Ozaki Koyo: *Konjiki yasha* (1871), reproduced by permission of the Syndics of the Cambridge University Library; 144, Kowa Slide Co. Ltd; 146, Camera Press London; 148, PANA-JIJI Photos; 150, RHPL; 152, Sassoon/RHPL; 153t, Watanabe Yoshio/ISEI; 153b, Image Bank/Lisl Dennis; 155, Dr Carmen Blacker; 157l, JICC; 157r, Richard Kalvar/Magnum; 159t, Ronald Sheridan/Ancient Art & Architecture Collection; 159b, Hulton Deutsch Collection; 160, Elly Beintema/RHPL; 162, Ronald Sheridan/Ancient Art & Architecture Collection; 163l, Dr Carmen Blacker; 163r, International Society for Educational Information, Inc.; 164l, Nigel Blythe/RHPL; 164r, Werner Forman Archive/National Museum, Kyoto; 165, *Sayings of Confucius*, 18th-century Japanese ed., reproduced by permission of the Syndics of the Cambridge University Library; 167, from *Sentetsu soden*, reproduced by permission of the Syndics of the Cambridge University Library; 168, Image Bank/Toyofumi Mori; 171, Motoori Norinaga Kinenkan; 174, Leiden University Bauduin Collection; 176, Tom Hanley of Bloomsbury; 177, Byron Earhart; 178/179, Werner Forman Archive/San Francisco Museum of Asiatic Art; 180, International Society for Educational Information, Inc.; 181l, Kowa Slide Co. Ltd; 181r, Fukuzawa Kenkyu Center; 184/185, courtesy of Christies, London/The Bridgeman Art Library; 187t, Trustees of the British Museum; 187b, 188, Ronald Sheridan/Ancient Art & Architecture Collection; 189l, Itsukushima Shrine/ISEI; 189r, Tokyo National Museum; 190, MOA Museum of Art, Atami; 191, courtesy of the Nezu Art Museum, Tokyo/The Bridgeman Art Library; 192, Trustees of the British Museum; 193, The Imperial Household Agency/Photographs through courtesy of the International Society for Educational Information, Inc.; 194, Akita Kenritsu Bijutsukan; 195, Tokyo Kokuritsu Bunkazai Kenkyujo; 196, Ohara Museum of Art; 197, Werner Forman Archive/Private Collection; 198l, Horyuji Temple; 198r, Ronald Sheridan/Ancient Art & Architecture Collection; 199, Byodo-in/ISEI; 200, Eisuke Ueda, Nara/Amidaji Temple; 201, Prof. William H. Coaldrake; 202, Nigel Blythe/RHPL; 203t, Prof. William H. Coaldrake; 203b, Werner Forman Archive; 204t, Prof. William H. Coaldrake; 204b, Christopher G. Knight; 205, The Imperial Household Agency/photograph through courtesy of the International Society for Educational Information, Inc.; 206, International Society for Educational Information, Inc.; 207, Prof. William H. Coaldrake; 208, RHPL; 210, 211, 212b, reproduced by permission of the Trustees of the Victoria and Albert Museum; 212t, Ronald Sheridan/Ancient Art & Architecture Collection; 213, Elliott Erwitt/Magnum; 214, Werner Forman Archive; 215, Image Bank/Toyofumi Mori; 216, Werner Forman Archive; 217, courtesy of the Chester Beatty Library & Gallery of Oriental Art, Dublin/The Bridgeman Art Library; 218, Hulton Deutsch Collection; 221, JICC; 222, Werner Forman Archive/Noh Theatre Collection, Kongo School, Kyoto; 223, JICC; 224, Image Bank/G. Colliva; 225, Robert McLeod/RHPL; 226/227, RHPL; 227tr, The Kobal Collection/National Film Archive London; 227b, The Kobal Collection; 229t, MOA Museum of Art, Atami; 229b, Nagoya Railroad Ltd/ISEI; 230/231 JICC; 231r, Image Bank/Brett Froomer; 232t, Image Bank; 232b, Paul van Riel/RHPL; 233, Mike Yamashita/Colorific; 234/235, Mike Blank; 236/237, JICC; 237r, International Society for Educational Information, Inc.; 238, JICC; 239, Jean-Paul Nacivet/Colorific; 240/241, International Society for Educational Information, Inc.; 240b, Robert McLeod/RHPL;

243, Kyodo; 244, Popperfoto; 245, by permission of the British Library; 246t, Tosho-Bunko/ISEI; 246b, Tsuda College; 247, Lewis/Network; 248/249, Murayama/FSP; 249b, Kaku Kurita/Gamma/FSP; 250/251, Lewis/Network; 251r, 253, JICC; 255, Jung-Kwan Chi/Camera Press London; 256, Hulton Deutsch Collection; 257, by permission of the British Library; 260, Jean-Paul Nacivet/Colorific; 261, Pierre Toutain-Dorbec/Sygma; 262t,c,b, Chris Cole/Allsport; 262/263, 263r, JICC; 264, Steven Kaufman/Bruce Coleman; 265, Robert Wallis/JB Pictures/Colorific; 267, Lewis/Network; 268, from *RIBON*, Dec. 1990 p. 401; 269, Popperfoto; 270/271t, AP; 270/271b, David Lomax/RHPL; 271r, Hideyuki Mihashi/Camera Press London; 272, Shigeru Tonaka/Sygma; 273, Leiden University Bauduin Collection; 274, 275b, Pierre Toutain-Dorbec/Sygma; 275t, Jung-Kwan Chi/Camera Press London; 276, John G. Ross/RHPL; 277, J. P. Laffont/Sygma; 278/279, RHPL; 280, International Society for Educational Information, Inc; 281t, The Metropolitan Museum of Art, Gift of Lincoln Kirstein, 1959 (JP3233-3235); 283,284, Hulton Deutsch Collection; 285, Popperfoto; 291, PANA-JIJI Photos; 292, RHPL; 293, Werner Forman Archive/Nara National Museum, Nara, Japan; 294, PANA-JIJI Photos; 298, AP; 303, Fukushima/PANA-JIJI Photos; 304, Sankei Shinbun; 306/307, Kyodo; 307t, PANA-JIJI Photos; 309, Kaku Kurita/Gamma/FSP; 310, Paul van Riel/RHPL; 315, Wada/Gamma/FSP; 317, Press Association/Topham; 319, Yamaguchi/Sygma; 322t, Gamma/FSP; 322b, Kaku Kurita/FSP; 323, AP; 326, Gordon/REA/Select; 326/327, Pierre Toutain-Dorbec/Sygma; 329, JICC; 332, Greg Davis/Colorific; 333, Ernst Haas/Magnum; 336, 338l, Jean-Paul Nacivet/Colorific; 338/339, Gordon/REA/Select; 340/341, PANA-JIJI Photos; 341b, Nippon Oil Co. Ltd/ISEI; 343, The Japan Atomic Power Co./ISEI; 347, The Dai-Ichi Kangyo Bank, Ltd; 348, Alex Bartel/Science Photo Library; 349, Ronald Sheridan/Ancient Art & Architecture Collection; 351, P. Perrin/Sygma; 355, Richard Kalvar/Magnum; 357, Mike Yamashita/Colorific; 362, Kyodo; 363, Lewis/Network; 364, Nippon Express Co. Ltd./ISEI; 365t, Japan Travel Bureau; 365b, JICC; 367, International Society for Educational Information, Inc.; 368, Pierre Toutain-Dorbec/Sygma; 369, from *Edo kagaku koten sosho*, vol. 3, reproduced by permission of the Syndics of the Cambridge University Library; 372, Daudier, Jerrican/Science Photo Library; 373, JICC; 374, National Space Development Agency, Tokyo, Japan.

TEXT EXTRACTS. 55, I. Morris, *The pillow book of Sei Shonagon* (Oxford University Press, 1967); 55, I. Morris, *As I crossed a bridge of dreams* (Oxford University Press, 1971); 59, H. C. McCullough (trans.), *The tale of the Heike* (Stanford University Press, 1988); 75, T. and K. Heineken, *Tansu: traditional Japanese cabinetry* (John Weatherhill, 1981); 123, D. Phillipi (trans.), *Norito* (Princeton University Press, 1991); 123, 124, D. Phillipi (trans.), *Kojiki* (Princeton University Press, 1968); 129, R. Bowring (trans.), *Murasaki Shikibu: her diary and poetic memoirs* (Princeton University Press, 1982; 136, D. Keene (trans.), *World within walls* (Secker and Warburg, 1976), reprinted by permission of Georges Borchardt, Inc. on behalf of Donald Keene. Translation copyright © 1976 by Donald Keene; 144, E. McClellan (trans.), *Kokoro* (Henry Regnery Co.); 145, from *Snow country* by Yasunari Kawabata, trans. E. Seidensticker. Copyright © 1956 by Alfred A. Knopf, Inc. Reprinted by permission of the publisher; 149, from *Salad anniversary* by Machi Tawara, published by Kodansha International Ltd. Reprinted by permission. All rights reserved.

MAPS. 2, after Collcutt, Jansen and Kumakura, *Cultural atlas of Japan* (Phaidon/Facts on File 1988), p. 15; 3, after *Japan Echo* (Winter 1987), p. 81/Collcutt (1988), p. 18; 6, after L. Frédéric, *Japon: l'empire éternel* (1985), p. 27; 7, after Association of Japanese Geographers, *Geography of Japan* (1980), p. 56; 8, after Collcutt (1988), p. 16/*Geography of Japan*, p. 74; 11, after Collcutt (1988), p. 17; 14, after G. T. Trewartha, *Japan: a geography* (1965), p. 68; 18, after *The national atlas of Japan* (1990), p. 25; 29, after W. Flüchter, *Die Bucht von Tokyo* (1985); 32, after Collcutt (1988), p. 21; 46, after *Past times: the Times atlas of archaeology* (1988), p. 197; 54, after Collcutt (1988), p. 71; 61, after Collcutt (1988), p. 105; 67, 69, after Kodama Kota, *Nihonshi chizu* (1970) p. 31; 85, after Collcutt (1988), p. 191; 86, after Collcutt (1988), p. 192; 89, after Collcutt (1988), p. 195; 92, after Collcutt (1988), p. 201; 94, after A. Coox, *Nomonhan* (1985); 95, after *Shukan Asahi hyakka Nihon no rekishi*, no. 116, p. 176; 102, after Collcutt (1988), p. 204; 104, after *Shukan Asahi hyakka Nihon no rekishi*, no. 122, pp. 16–17; 105, after *Chronicle of the Second World War* (1990), p. 654, with additions; 106, after *Shukan Asahi hyakka Nihon no rekishi*, no. 125; 120t, after M. Shibatani, *The languages of Japan* (1990), p. 211; 120b, after Shibatani (1990), p. 197; 160, after *Past times: the Times atlas of archaeology*, p. 261/Collcutt (1988), pp. 68–9; 242, after I. Neary, *Political protest and social control in pre-war Japan* (1989), p. 6; 294, Japan, Supreme Court; 324, *Military balance 1990–91*; 344, after *Look Japan*, September 1991, p. 331/Japan Agency of Natural Resources and Energy, June 1991; 366, Kodama Kota, *Nihonshi chizu* (1970), p. 49.

DIAGRAMS. 9, after *Look Japan*, June 1987, p. 23/Tokyo Metropolitan Government, Bureau of Environmental Protection; 27t, after *Japan 1992: an international comparison* (*Keizai Koho Centre*), p. 8/Japan Institute of Population Problems (photo: Nigel Blythe/RHPL); 27b, after *Look Japan*, October 1990 (photo: Kyodo); 31, after *Japan 1992*, p. 86/Japan Real Estate Institute (photo: Pierre Toutain-Dorbec/Sygma); 76, after Kodama Kota, *Nihonshi chizu* (1970) (photo: Mike Yamashita/Colorific); 158, after *Kokushi daijiten* (1983); 237, after Joy Hendry; 239, after *Shukan Asahi hyakka Nihon no rekishi*, no. 129; 249, after *Japan 1992* (photo: Nigel Blythe/RHPL); 250, after *Japan 1992* (photo: Kaku Kurita/Gamma/FSP); 251, Nippon Denso labour union; 253, *Rodo tokei yoran*, Japan Institute of Labour, 1988/91; 259l, after *Look Japan*, July 1991, p. 34/Japan Ministry of Health and Welfare; 259r, Japan Pharmaceutical Manufacturers Association; 266, after *Nihon tokei nenkan* (1991); 268, after *Look Japan*, January 1989, p. 41; 286, after *Shukan Asahi hyakka Nihon no rekishi*, no. 127; 287t, after K. Kishimoto, *Politics in modern Japan* (1988), Fig. 4.1; 287b, after Kishimoto, Fig. 3.1; 289, after Kishimoto, Fig. 5.1; 295, 296–7, Japan, Supreme Court; 300-1, after Kishimoto, Figs. 6.1/2; 303, after Kishimoto, Fig. 4.2; 304, after Kishimoto, Fig. 6.3; 308, after *Asahi shinbun*, 29 November 1991; 313, after Kishimoto, Fig. 8.1; 320, after *Look Japan*, September 1991, p. 47; 328, Japan, Economic Planning Agency; 330, after *Shukan Asahi hyakka Nihon no rekishi*, no. 127; 331, after *Japan 1992*; 332t, 332b, after *Japan 1992* (photos: Greg Davis/Colorific); 334, 335, after *Nihon tokei nenkan* (1988) (photo: Carol Jopp/RHPL); 339, after *Nihon tokei nenkan* (1988) (photo: Mike Yamashita/Colorific); 340, 342, Japan Economic Institute report on energy (1991); 346, *Historical statistics 1960–85* (OECD)/Comparative economic and financial statistics (Bank of Japan, 1991); 356, after *Japan 1992*; 359, after *EG* magazine, no. 9, September 1989; 367, after *Japan 1992* /Japan Ministry of Justice (photo: PANA-JIJI Photos); 368t, *Japan 1992* (photo: Peter Menzel/Science Photo Library); 368b, after *Japan 1992*; 370, 372, after *Kagaku gijutsu hakusho* (1990); 373l, after F. L. Schodt, *Inside the robot kingdom* (1990), p. 16 (photo: Allen Green/Science Photo Library); 373r, after *Kagaku gijutsu hakusho* (1990) (photo Luis Castaneda/Image Bank).

Index

References in bold figures denote main entries; those in italics denote illustrations (there may also be textual references on these pages).

A

Abe Kōbō 145, 225, *304*
abortion 238, 311
acupuncture 255
adoption 27, 236
advertising *226–7*, **267**; television 147, 267, 307, 308
agriculture **333–9**; Confucian ideal 70, 72; crops **333–4**; current problems **338–9**; in economy **334–5**, 350, 354; family farms 254, 336, 337; government subsidies 17, 30, 339; history (pre-Nara) 42, 44, (Heian) 57, (medieval) 62, (Tokugawa) 70, 72–3, 334, (Modern) 83–4, 87, 91, 328, 334–5; and industrialization 337, 338; LDP and 310, 312, 339; mechanization 17, 336–7, *338*; organization **337–8**; part-time farming 339; religious rituals 155, 221; self-sufficiency 333, *335*; size of farms limits efficiency *335*, 337, 338, 339; soils 16, 17; subsidies 17, 30; technology **336–7**; tenant farmers 90, 270; *see also individual crops*; fertilizers; irrigation
aid, overseas development **320**, 362
Aikoku Kōtō 299, 300
Ainu people 25, 32, **244**; and Emishi 51; ethnicity 43; folklore 38; language 79, 114, 244; music 218
air quality 9, 24
air transport 32, 37, 272, 318, 365, **367–8**
aircraft construction 101, 103, 324, 352, 363, 364, 367
Aizawa Seishisai 173–4
Akao Bin *310*
Akasaka Detached Palace 207
Akihito, Emperor *111*, 156
Akutagawa Prize for literature 147
Akutagawa Ryūnosuke *144*
alcoholic drinks **232–3**, 262, 263; *see also sake*
All Nippon Airways 367
aluminium production 356
Amaterasu (Shintō Sun Goddess) 156, 172, 173, 213, 216; Ise shrines 153, 154, 157
ancestor-worship 176, 236, 237
angura theatre 224, 225
animals *see* fauna; livestock
Anpo *see* United States (Security Treaty)
Antoku, Emperor 59
Aomori festival 264
Arai Hakuseki 170
archaeological periods 42–3
architecture **201–8**; aristocratic residences **201–2**, 206; Chinese influence 201, 203–4; design and construction **204–6**; Heian era 201; mass production **207**; Modern *88*, 206, **208**; *shoin* 201–2; tea houses 228; wall paintings, 186–7, 190; Westernization **206–7**; *see also* castles *and under* Buddhism; housing; Shintō
Arechi poetic circle 149
aristocracy: abolition 285; Meiji 280; residences **201–2**, 206; scholarship 369; tea drinking 228; women 56–7
Ariwara no Narihira 128
Ariyoshi Sawako 146, 147
armed forces **321–5**; communications 363, 364; in constitution 280, 283, 285, 316–17, 321; disbanded (1946) 261, 283, 285, 321, 364, 367; Meiji era 78, 79, 85, 87, 281, 285, 348, 363; political rôle 281, 285, 299, 345; technology 318, 319, 324, 325, 370, 371; *see also* Army, Imperial; militarism; Navy, Imperial; Self-Defence Forces; Yasukuni Shrine
arms and armour 63, 132, 209, 325
Army, Imperial: conscription 97, 101; disbanded 283, 285, 321; factions, 1930s 93–4; Meiji modernization *78*, 79, 85; and Second World War 99, 243
art, pictorial: in architecture 186–7, **190**; and calligraphy 188, 193; conformity, WWII period 96; exhibitions 196; genre painting 191, 192; government involvement 196; Heian era 188; and literature **188–9**, 193; medieval 62–3; Meiji 79, 80, **195–6**; and music 193; native and Chinese strands 186, 191; and poetry 188; printmakers 193, 196; and religion 160, **186–8**, 191; and tea culture 228; Tokugawa era 73, 192–3; Western *Japonisme* 80, 209; Western-style 191, 193, 194, 195–6; *see also individual schools*; portraiture; screen painting; scroll painting; *and under* books; Buddhism; China; *ukiyo*
arts and crafts **184–233**; *see also* architecture; art, pictorial; cinema; crafts; dance; decorative arts; drama; *japonisme*; music; sculpture
Arts Exhibition, Japan (Nitten) 196, 212
Asahi Beer Azumabashi Hall 208
Asai Ryōi 135
Asama, Mt 75
Asanuma Inejirō *269*
asceticism 154, 155–6, 159
ASEAN 320, 324, 355, 356, 359
Ashikaga shōguns 60, **61**, 65, 172; and arts 134, 201; and West 62, 63; *see also individual shōguns*
Ashikaga Takauji 60
Ashikaga Yoshiaki 65
Ashikaga Yoshimasa 62
Ashikaga Yoshimitsu 62, 63, 189, 221
Ashikaga Yoshiteru 64
Ashio copper mines 84
Asia: access to south-east 4, *69*; attitudes to Japan 320, 325; Japanese industries in 329–30, 355, 356, 362; music from central 216; trade 357, 358, 359
Asian Pacific economic area 93, 101, 110
Association of Southeast Asian Nations *see* ASEAN
Asuka period 43, *46*, 47–8, 203
Asuka-dera (temple) 48, *49*
Atagosan shrine 157
Atsugi; US landings 105, 106
automobiles: air pollution 24; exports 359, 360, 361; manufacture 34, 108, 350, *351*, 356, 363, 367; ownership 28
Azuchi castle 65, 190, 204

B

baiu rains 7, 10–11, 23
Bakin 140
Bakufu: and arts 191, 192, 195; and Confucianism 166, 169, 172–3; Kamakura 60; Muromachi *see* Ashikaga shōguns; rise 58–9, 60–1; *see also* shōguns; Tokugawa period
ballet 215
bamboo 14, 15
Bank of Japan 346
banking 312, 330, **345–8**, 349, 353
baseball 79, 261, *262–3*
Bashō 135, 136
be system 46, 47
beef 38, 231, 339
beer 83, 233
Beppu *22*, 37
beri-beri 230
Betsuyaku Minoru 225
Biddle, Commodore James, USN 77
biological warfare 97
biotechnology 372, 374
birth control 27, 28, **238**, 248
birth rate 26, 27, 28, 111
biwa (lute) 132, 216, 219
Biwa, Lake 4, 6, 23, 35, 65
blowfish (*fugu*) *19*, 232
Bōeichō 321, 322, 325
Boissonade, Gustave 79
bomb, atomic 105, 147, 180
bonsai 15
books 50–1, 73, 74, 262, **268**; illustrations 73, *128*, *135*, 138, *139*
bōryokudan (criminal gangs) 276
brewing 83, 233
bribery *see* Recruit scandal
bridge: Kyūshū-Honshū 36; *see also* Seto Ōhashi bridge
Britain and Japan: Meiji contacts 79, 80, 85; Opium War 76; and science and technology 370; and WWII 98, 99, 106
bronze working, Yayoi period 42
Buddhism **158–64**; altars 237; Amidism 162, *187*, *199*, 200; architecture 160, 186–7, **203–4**, (*see also* temples, Buddhist); art, pictorial 160, 186–7,

Buddhism *cont.*
188, 191; asceticism 155, 156, 159; Chinese connections 17, 25, 51, 63, *160*, 203–4, 369; Dainichi 156, 161; and death 155, *159*, 161; decline, WWII 176; diet regulations 44, 231; divinities 156, 161; and 'floating world' 135; Heian 52, 57, 58, 126–7, 130, 161–2; and imperial power 52, 65, 67; introduction to Japan 17, 25, 160–1; literature 121, 123, 130, 132, 161, (*see also* sūtras *and* tales *below*); magic 158, 159; Mahāyāna 158, 161; mandalas 186, *187*; medieval 62, 63, 130, 131, 132, 159, 162–3, 164, 166; Meiji disestablishment 82, 164; monasteries 50, 63, 65, 67, 161, *163*, *164*, 187, 203; Nara 50, 51, 53, 74, 123, 125, 161; Nichiren 159, 162–3; and nō 134, 216–17, 221; Pure Land (Jōdo) 65, 162, 163; rituals 159, *161*, 162, 228; sculpture 48, 53, 160–1, *162*, *164*, **197–8**, *199*; Shingon 125, 159, 161, 162, 187, 188; and Shintō 82, 156–7, 161, 164, 187, 202; sūtras 158, *159*, 160, 161, 162, 186, 187, 188, *189*; tales 125, 126–7, 131; Tendai 65, 159, 161, 162, 164; Tokugawa 64, 65, 67, 68, 164, 170, 178; *see also* temples, Buddhist; Zen
bugaku dances 52, *214*
building *see* architecture; construction; housing
Bungei Kyōkai 225
Bunjin movement 73, 138
bunjinga painting 193
bunmei-kaika ('civilization and enlightenment') 83
bunraku theatre 213, 217, 221, **222–3**, 260
Buraku Liberation League 242, 243
Burakumin 25, 142, **241–3**, 270
bureaucracy **288–92**; Chinese 43, 47, 53, 54, 55; Confucianism and 165, 166, 290; and economy 351–2; Heian 54; Meiji 78, 82, 84; Nara 50, 51, 53; 1932–45 93; post-war 106, 109, 285, 287, 328, 349
burial customs: imperial 272; Kofun 42–3, 45, *46*, 122, *123*, 197, 201; Yayoi 42, 45
Burma 97, 99, 100, 101, 103, 107
bushidō ('way of the warrior') 69, 170, 171, 173
Buson 136, *138*, 193
butsudan (Buddhist altar) *237*
Byōdō-in, Uji; Phoenix Hall *56*, *199*

C

cabinet 280, 281, 283, 288, 297, 298; 'transcendental' 281, 285, 299
calligraphy *136*, 188, 193, 228, 262
capital markets 328, 345, 346, 347; *see also* stock market
capital punishment *273*, *275*
capsule hotels *250–1*
Caroline Islands 88, 101
carp (*koi*) *39*
cars *see* automobiles
castle towns (*jōkamachi*) 29, 71
castles: medieval 29, 61, 62; 16th–17th century 65, 66, 68, 190, 191, 202, **204**
censorship 147, 226, 250, 265, 266, 298; in Pacific War 97–8, 100, 101, 144–5
censuses 47, 57
ceramics: Jōmon *42*; Meiji 212; Nara 50; porcelain 209, *210*, 230; tea utensils *211*, 212, 229; Tokugawa 371
cereals 42, 44, 155, 334; *see also* rice; wheat
chanoyu see tea, culture of
charitable institutions 255, 259
chemical industry 334, 337, 349, 350
chemical warfare 97
cherry blossom *10*, 15
Chiang Kai-shek 96
Chikamatsu Monzaemon 135, 137–8, 222–3
Chikuho coalfield 22, 36
children: leisure 261–2; school work 247–8; suicide 249; upbringing 237, **238–9**, 240, 252–3; *see also* adoption; birth-rate; education
China 17, 28, 156; architecture 201, 203–4; art, pictorial 186, 189, 191, **192–3**; 'Boxer' Rebellion (1900) 85; Buddhism 17, 25, 51, 63, *160*, 203–4, 369; bureaucracy 43, 47, 53, 54, 55; Chinese Learning 169, 369; communist victory (1949) 108; Confucianism 165–6, 169, 171; Heian contacts 54, 188, 214; histories 42, 45, 47, 216; Japanese occupation 167, 342; and Korea 84–5; language 114, 116, 118, 121, 123, 126, 183; and Manchuria 91; medicine 255, 259, 369; medieval 62, 63, 189; merchants 209; migration to Japan 43, 103; Nara contacts 51–2, 53, 214; Opium War 76; and Pacific War 100, 103; poetry 125, 141, 148–9; post-war relations 110, 317, 318, 320, 324; pre-Nara contacts 42, 43–4, 45, 47, 48, *160*; Tokugawa contacts 29, *69*, 74, 156; and 'Twenty-One Demands' (1915) 88; unification by nationalists 91; US rapprochement 109, 110–11; war (1937–40) *see* War, Chinese; in WWI 88; *see also* Taiwan
Chōshū clique, Meiji era 77, 80, 81, 174, 280
Christianity 142, **178–80**; missionaries 37, **63–4**, 65, 66–7, 74, 79, 178–9, 369; *see also* Jesuits
cinema 97–8, **226–7**
cities **28–30**; company towns 29–30; culture 73, 91, 135, (*see also under* Edo); fires 9, *75*, 143, 206; food supply 312, 334; growth 25, 29–30, 30–1, 35, 176, 207, 329, 335, 350, 355; land values 20, 31, 207, 331, 360, 361; local government 313, **315–16**; Nara 28, 35, 40, 50, 52, 53–4; pre-Nara 47–8; population 28; religions 176, 177, 180; science-cities 372; Tokugawa 68, **70–2**, 73, *75*, 135; *see also* castle towns; *and individual cities*
citizens' movements *see* protest; rights
civil service *see* bureaucracy
'civilization and enlightenment' (*bunmei-kaika*) 83
class, social *see* social order
Clean Government Party *see* Kōmeitō
climate *6*, **7–13**, 18, 183, 336; and architecture 204, 205, 206; and settlement patterns 4, 6; *see also* rainfall; snowfall; *and under individual regions*
cloisonné work 209, *210*, 212
coal: domestic resources 21, 22, 36, *340–1*, 350; imports 18, 22; patterns of use 340, 341, 342
Cocks, Richard 179
coinage *68*
colonial empire *92*, 334; *see also individual states*
comic books and magazines 262, *268*
commerce: interest groups 309, 310, 311; Meiji law 78; pre-war size 349; Tokugawa *70–1*; *see also* banking; companies; finance; industry; monopolies
common people: medieval 63, 134; Meiji 246; Tokugawa 73, 135, 138–40, 173, 269
communications **363–8**; and armed forces 363, 364; Meiji era 78, 79, 348, 363; Pacific War 99, 364; *see also* telecommunications; transport
communism 91, 93, 96, 103, 108; *see also* Japan Communist Party
community support 238, 255, 257, 259
commuting 30, *234–5*
companies: and architecture 208; banking links 345, 346–7; co-operation between 351, 354, 361, 372–3; and crime 276, 277; cross-shareholdings 308, 361; family businesses 250, 251; family relations as model 241; and government 290, 292, 308, 331, 351; *keiretsu* groupings 331–2, 354; loyalty to 251, 261, 371; and political parties 299, 308; small 352, 353, 354; taxation 330; *see also* employment; *zaibatsu*
computers 109, 265, 351, 355, 372, 373
Conder, Josiah 206, 207
Confucianism **165–8**; in modern Japan 167–8; Ju Xi school 166; meritocracy 165, 166, 245; modern philosophers and 181; Nagasaki shrine *168*; Nara court and 166; Nativist reaction 171–3; paternalism 167, 168; Wang

Yangming school 166; and women 167; Yamato 48, 165; *see also under* agriculture, Bakufu, bureaucracy; China; education; emperor; Korea; morality; samurai; Tokugawa period
constitution, Meiji **81**, **280–1**; emperor 174, 280–1, 284–5; foreign influence 79, 81; government under 284–5, 287; judiciary 293; political parties under 81–2, 299; and religion 82
constitution, post-war **106**, 280, **283**, 284; aristocracy abolished 285; cabinet 283; demilitarization 106, 285, 316–17, 321; Diet 280, 283, 285; emperor 106, 283, 285; and family 106, 236; government under **285**; judiciary 293; political system 106, 285, 299; separation of church and state 156, 157, 180, 283; suffrage 283, 285; US Constitution influences 274
construction: Meiji 201, 206, 269; modern industry 9, 328, 349, 350, 354; Nara 201; Tokugawa 201; traditional methods 9, 15, *129*, 201, **204–6**, 207
consumer co-operatives 310
consumer goods 31, 108, 330, 351, 356, 359, 361
consumer interests 309, 312, 332, 342
copper 23, 84
cosmology 122, 123, 152, 154–5
cotton spinning 83
countryside 30–1; depopulation 17, 25, 30, 31, 35, 329, 334, 350; industry 31; 1930s destitution 93; and politics 306, 312, 339; Tokugawa period **72–3**
court, imperial: arts 187; Buddhism 160–1; Heian 52, 55, **125–30**, 133, 188, 369; Music Bureau 214, 216; and nō 221; poetry 125–6, 133; Tokugawa period 221
courtesans 192, 214
courts, judicial **293–5**
crafts 161, 207, *211*, *212*; early Japan 42, 43, 46, 47, (immigrant craftsmen) 43, 44, 47, 54, 161, 197; Meiji 80, 83, 212; Tokugawa 71, 371
crime **273–7**; confessions 298; juvenile 294; organized 276, 277
criminal justice system 273–5, 293–5
cuisine 228, **230–2**, 329
culture centres 263
culture, traditional 35, 71, 157, 177, 183, 249–50; *see also* folk culture
currency 62, 67, *68*, 85, 109, 111, *327*; internationalization 331, 360; yen–dollar exchange rate 328, **329–30**, 350, 351, 356, 358, 359, 360
currents, marine *18*, 19

D

daimyō: alternate attendance 68, 71, 169, 363; castles 202; Christian 178; and Confucianism 166–7; and industry 371; local government 69, 70, 166–7, 174; Meiji demise 78, 174; and samurai 69, 70, 76; self-justification 170; and *shōen* 62; and Tokugawa shōguns 67, **68**, 69, 71, 77; warfare 66
Dainichi (Buddha) 156, 161
dairy products 30, *335*
dams 22, 23
dance 52, **213–15**, 223
Dannoura, battle of 59, 131
Dazai Osamu 142, 145, *146*
Dazaifu *49*, 50, 51
death 26: Buddhism and 155, *159*, 161; capital punishment 275; prehistoric beliefs 152; Shintō beliefs 154–5; work-related stress and 254, 263; *see also* burial customs; suicide
decorative arts **209–12**
defence *see* armed forces; Army, Imperial; munitions industry; Navy, Imperial; Self-Defence Forces; science and technology (military); *and under* United States
Defence Agency (Bōeichō) 321, 322, 325
Democratic Socialist Party *see* Minshatō
demography 25–8, 50, 111
dengaku (dance) 214, *215*
Deshima Island 17, 209, 210, 255, 369
dialects **120**
diaries 121, 129, 131
Diet (Parliament) *284*, *292*; in Allied Occupation 106; Burakumin in 243; campaign for establishment 265, 269, 280; in constitution 280, 283, 285; and defence 318, 322, 323; House of Councillors 303, 305, 306, 309; House of Representatives 303, 309, 322, (elections) 286, 305–6, 307, 308; impeachment of judges 298; interest groups 309, 312; legislation 291, 298; Meiji era 81, 82, 299; Peace Preservation Act (1925) 91, 182, 270; and US–Japan Security Treaty 318
diet **230–3**, 255, *257*, 336; bamboo 15; and health 26; noodles *30*; seaweeds 20; *see also* cuisine; meat; *and under* Buddhism; fish
diplomacy 18, 68, 80; between World Wars 88, 90, 91, 93, 96
disabled people 250, 272
disasters, natural **75–6**; *see also* earthquakes; flooding
distribution system 361
divination 166, 369
divorce 241
Dōgen 163
Doi Takako 303
Dōkyō (Grand Minister) 50, 53
dolls 152
Dōwa Policy Council 242, 243
drama 135, 136, 137–8, **221–5**, 226, 260; television 267; *see also* bunraku; kabuki; kyōgen; nō; puppet theatre
dress 209, 215, 236–7, *283*
drugs: herbal *155*; illegal trade 276; *see also* pharmaceuticals
drums 216, 217, *218*, *219*
Dulles, John Foster *108*, 317

E

early Japan *see* pre-Nara period
earthquakes 2, 15, 20, 75; and architecture 204, 206; Great Kantō (1923) *90*, 140, 143, 243
Economic Planning Agency 343
economy **327–74**; capitalism 172; controversies 330–2; education and 245, 249; export orientation 330–1; GDP 328, 330, 331, 335, 350; government policies 328, 330, 331, 347, 351–2; internationalization **355–6**; 19th century 78, **83–4**; 1914–18 boom 334; 1920s–30s crises 90, 93; in 1930s–40s 95, 97, 100, 103; post-war, (during Occupation) 106, 328, 345, 348, 349, 353, 357, (high-speed growth) 21–2, 28, 30, 105, **108–9**, 110, 167–8, 316, **328–32**, 335, 338, 350; 1970s restructuring 24, 110, 350–1, 358–9; Tokugawa period 67, **72–3**, *76*; *see also* agriculture; banking; communications; energy; finance; food production; industry; investment; productivity; science and technology; trade; transport
Edo (*now* Tōkyō) 28, 68, *70–1*, 75, 120; castle 191, 204; culture 120, 135, *137*, 138, 140, 192, 214; daimyō's alternate attendance 68, 71, 169, 363; execution ground *273*; roads 34, 269
education **245–50**; Burakumin and 242; Chinese influence 245; Christianity and 179, 180; and civil service entry 288, 289, 290; Confucianism and 165–6, 167, 245; cost 248, 346, 354; cramming schools 248, 262, 264, 296; 'examination hell' *157*, 245, *248–9*, 262; government schools 79, 82; hierarchy of institutions 246, 247, 289, 290, 292; history of 245–6; Imperial Rescript (1890) 167, 182; and industrial workforce 246; kindergarten 239, 261; music 218, 220; reforms, current 249–50, 271; scientific/technological 370, 371; tertiary 247, (*see also* universities); Tokugawa period 73, *245*; work ethic 245, 246, 247–8; *see also under* economy; employment; Meiji era; Occupation; women
Eisai 228
Eisenhower, Dwight D. *108*, 271, 318
Ejima Kiseki *135*
elderly: and childcare 237, *238*, 240; deference to 236, 239, 245;

elderly *cont.*
employment **253**; health and welfare 254, 256–7, 258, 259; leisure *263*; nuclear family and 180; pensions 256–7, 258–9, 346; population 111, 207, 256–7, 258; retirement 237, 253, 258, 263
elections and electioneering **305–8**; ban on canvassing 298, 307; House of Representatives 286; interest groups and 309–10; local government *278–9*, *315*; regional inequalities 306, 312, 339
electricity 22, 23, 340, 342, 350
electronics 109, 330, 351, 355, 356, 359, 361; *see also* computers
emigration 25
emperor and emperor system (*tennōsei*): and Buddhism 52, 65, 67; Confucian view 166, 167, 168; in constitution 106, 174, 280–1, 283, 284–5; divinity 54, 81, 125, 154, 156, 157, 172, 173, 180, 280, 284; Heian period 52, 54, (ex-emperors) 58, 59, (and Fujiwara) 53, 56–7, 58, 59; medieval era 173; Meiji ideology and rituals **81**, 82, 167, 173–4, 280; 7th–8th century legitimization 51, 54, 122; and shōguns 61, 63, 68, 172–3; succession 50, 51, 81, 284; *tennōsei* (emperor system) 167, 280, 310; 20th century 93, *94*, 310; *see also* court, imperial
employment **250–4**; career structure 292, 352, 371; company loyalty 251, 261, 352, 371; education and 239, **246–7**, 250, 353; of elderly **253**; equality *252–3*, 352; health insurance 258; hereditary occupations 236; holidays 254, 261, 264; lifestyle *250–1*, 252, 261, 263; minorities 243; old-boy networks 247; in Pacific War 101; promotion 287, 288–9, **352–3**, 371; recruitment 251, 253, 292, 353; retirement 237, 253, 258, 263; security 252; statistics 332, 350; stress 254, 263; vocational training 247, 251; welfare 255; working hours 253, 254, 261, 263–4; *see also nenkō*; pay; *and under* women
Enchi Fumiko 146, *148*
Endō Shūsaku 146, *148*
energy **340–4**; alternative sources 340, 343–4, 371; conservation 341, 344, 358–9, 361; costs 329; government policy 341, **342–4**; imports 22, 340; industry structure **341–2**; patterns of use **340–1**; security 342–4; *see also* coal; electricity; gas; geothermal energy; nuclear power
engineering 349; civil 6, *36–7*, 364, 367; electrical and electronic 370; Meiji 79, 83, 348; *see also* bridge; tunnels
Enkū 200
entertainment industry 31, 91, 223, 241; *see also* drama; geisha; television
environment **21–4**; government and 316, 374; greenhouse effect 24; Okinawa 37; timber imports and world 15, 18, 24; *see also* pollution
equality, social 228, 247, *252–3*, 352
ethnicity 43, 44, 45
European Community 111; Eurodollar 331; Japanese investment 330, 356, 362; trade 330, 358, 359, 360, 368
exhibitions **80**, 196, 264, 329
exports 18, 329, 330–1, 350, 373
Ezo 57, 244
Ezoe Hiromasa 305

F

family 168, **236–41**; ancestors 176, 236, 237; businesses 250, 251; child-rearing 28, 237, **238–9**, 240, 252–3; Confucian stress on 165, 167, 168; farming 336, 337; gender rôles **239–40**; *ie*, 'continuing family' 27–8, 106, 207, 236–7, 240, 336; *iemoto* hereditary system 106, 191, 216, 220; in law 83, 106, 236; leisure 240, 263; model for social organization 241, 276; nuclear 180, 236; obligation 237, 240; planning 27, 28, **238**, 248; single-parent **241**; and social welfare 255, 257, 258–9; three-generation households 207; *see also* adoption; marriage
famines 11, 21, 27, 75, 76
fans *53*, *128*
fauna **38–9**
Federation of Economic Organizations *see* Keidanren
feminism *see under* women
Fenollosa, Ernest 79, 195, 212
fertilizers 17, 334, 337
festivals **264**; Bon 155, 264; Boys' Day 231; Christmas 180; Doll 231; Golden Week 10, 264; harvest 155; New Year 155, 231, 264; rice *338*; Sanja *157*; Sapporo Snow *264*; Seven–five–three *239*
finance 111, **345–8**; fiscal reform (1989) 330; government policies 314, 328, 329, 345, **346–7**, 360, (agricultural)17, 30, 339; indirect **345–6**; recent changes **347–8**; size of sector 350, 354; *see also* banking
firearms 63, 65, 66, 369
fires, accidental 9, 75, 143, 206
fish: in diet *19*, 20, 21, 39, 44, 230–1, *232*, 336; *see also* fisheries
fisheries **19–20**, **336**; inland 39; size of industry 328, 349, 350; treaty with PRC 318
'floating world' see *ukiyo*
flooding 10, 12, 20
flowers 15, 73, 228, 261, 262; *see also* gardens
flutes 216, 217, 218–19
folk culture 38, 212, 217, 219
Fontanesi, Antonio 195
food: culture of **230–3**; prices *76*, 334, 338–9; production **333–9** (*see also* agriculture); supply 21, *76*, 101, 103, 312, 334; votive offerings 230, 232, *233*; *see also* cuisine; diet
foreign policy **316–20**; Meiji 79, 80, 83, **84–7**; and oil 318, 340, 341, 343, 357, 359; Tokugawa period 67, 68, *69*, 73–4, **76–7**, 78, 80, (trade, *see* Deshima; Nagasaki); 20th century 88, 90, 109, 110, 316; *see also individual countries and wars and* trade, overseas
foreign residents 79, 82; fingerprinting of *243*, 244; *see also under* Korea
forests **13–15**, 334, 350
Formosa 85; *see also* Taiwan
forty-seven rōnin *170*, 223
France 79, 80, 85, *89*, 98, 107
franchise *see* suffrage
Franciscan Order 63, 64, 66, 178, 179
fraud 276, 277; *see also* Recruit scandal
freedom of expression 298
freedom and popular rights movement, Meiji 80, 81, 269, 280
Frois, Luis 64
fruit cultivation 334, 335
fudoki (regional surveys) 125
fugu (blowfish) *19*, 232
Fuji, Mt 2, *6*, *9*, 16, 75, 155
Fujikage Shizue 214
Fujitsū corporation 374
Fujiwara family 50, 53, 54, **56–7**, 58–9, 125
Fujiwara Fubito 50
Fujiwara Mototsune 56
Fujiwara no Michinaga 56, 57
Fujiwara no Yorimichi 56
Fujiwara Yorinaga 59
Fujiwara Yoshifusa 56
fukoku-kyōhei (Meiji slogan) 78
Fukuoka 36, *104*, 264, 294, 315
Fukuzawa Yukichi 83, 167, *181*
furigana script 119–20
Furui Yoshikichi 147
Fushimi *66*, 155
Fushimi, Emperor 126
Futabatei Shimei *141*, 142, 143

G

gagaku music 52, 216, 218, 219, 220
gambling 262, 263
gangsters 226, 276, *277*
Ganjin 161
gardens *14–15*, 39, 73, 170, 201
gas industry 22, 340, 341, 342, 350
gateball *263*
GATT (General Agreement on Tariffs and Trade) 328, 357, 358, 362
GDP 328, 330, 331, 335, 350

geisha 214, 217, *218*, 241
Genji monogatari **129–30**, 137, 143, 144, 173
genrō (elder statesmen) 81, 284, 285
Genroku age; literature **135–8**
geomancy 28, 204
geothermal energy 22, 340, 341, 342, 344
Germany: advisers in Meiji Japan 79, 81, 82; Far East possessions (1914) 88, *89*; Nazi 93, 96, 97–8; philosophy 182, 183; political system 280, 290, 313; sciences 255, 370; and USSR in WWII 93, 98, 99
gesaku (popular literature) 138
gift-giving 188, 230
gigaku (dance) 52, 213
globefish (*fugu*) *19*
gold 23, 51, 68, 330
Golden Week 10, 264
golf 261, 263
Go-Sanjō, Emperor 58
Go-Shirakawa, Emperor 58, 59
Gotoba, Emperor 173
government, central **284–7**; agricultural subsidies 17, 30, 339; armed forces and 281, 285, 299, 345; and arts 196, 212; consensus 291, 292, 352; construction projects 206; under constitution of 1946 284–5, 287; Defence Agency 321, 322; and infrastructure 331, 348, 360; LDP entrenchment 109, 285–6, 299, 303, 328; legislature organization 287; and local government 314, 316; Meiji 78, 84, 284–5; Nara **48–50**, 51; 1932–45 93, 95–6, 100; 1950s–60s 109; during Occupation 284, 314; post-war operation 284, **285–7**; procurement policies 361; relationship of powers 287; and science and technology 370, **372–3**; stability 109, 284, 285, 299, 303, 328; 'state corporatism' 312; Tokugawa **69–70**; *see also* bureaucracy; cabinet; *and under* agriculture; economy; energy; environment; finance; Heian period; industry; Yamato period
government, local 312, **313–16**; central government control 314, 316; elections *278–9*, *315*; Meiji reforms 78, 313; post-war era 313, 314–15; pre-war 313; Tokugawa 69, 70, 166–7, 174
grain crops *see* cereals
Guadalcanal, Solomon Islands 100
Guam 99
guilds 62, 216, 220

H

Habomai islands 317
Hachirōgata 17
Hagiwara Sakutarō 144
haibun prose 136
haikai poetry 121, **135–6**, 138, 141, 148
Hamaguchi Osachi 93, 282
Hanaoka Seishū 255
Haneda airport 368
haniwa sculpture 122, *123*, 197, 201
Haniya Yutaka 145
Hara Kei 90, 282, 299
harvest festivals 155
Hawaii 25, 99, 262
Hayashi Razan 156, 166, *167*
health and welfare **255–9**; Buddhism and 180; Christianity and 180, 182; diet 255; elderly 254, 256–7, 258, 259; employers and 255; family and 255, 257, 258–9; insurance 255, 256–7; local government and 316; minorities 242, 243; mortality 26; mosquitos and 39; pollution threats to 271; pre-modern vitamin deficiency 230; regional disparities 259; welfare state **255–7**; work-related stress 254, 263; *see also* charitable institutions; community support
Heian period **53–9**; agriculture 57; architecture 201; dance 214; gardens 201; government 51, 52, 54, 59, 60; land holdings; *shōen* 57–8; painting 188; provincial military families 58–9, 60, 61, 130; sculpture 199–200; songs 188–9; tales 127–8, 130, 188–9; taxation 52, 55, 57–8; *see also under* aristocracy; Buddhism; China; constitution; emperor; literature
Heian-kyō (*later* Kyōto) 52, 53–4, *54*
Heijō; Nara capital 28, 35, 48, *49*, 50, 53
Heike family *see* Taira family
Heike monogatari 59, 63, 132, *133*
Heisei reign 140
Hepburn, James Curtis 117
Hideyoshi *see* Toyotomi Hideyoshi
hierarchies: Confucianism and 165, 168; educational 246, 247, 289, 290, 292; family 236, 241; government 287, 288, 291
Higashikuni, Prince Naruhiko 105
Higuchi Ichiyō 142
Hijikata Tatsumi 215
hijiri (asceticism) 155–6
Himiko 45, 47
Hino Ashihei 96
Hirabayashi Taiko 143
Hiraga Gennai 140, 193
hiragana script **117–18**, 119–20, 126
Hirata Atsutane 156, 173, 174
Hirohito, Emperor 91, 93, *94*, *284*, *285*, *272*; and Pacific War 105, 107
Hiroshima 29, *104*, 105, *152*, 208, 276, 294, *315*
Hishikawa Moronobu 192
historiography: Heian 51; Meiji 79; modern Japanese 182; Nara 47, 50–1; shrine and temple histories 189; Six National Histories 51; writing styles 121, 122–3; *see also Kojiki*; *Nihon shoki*; *and under* China
history **41–111**; *see also individual periods*
Hōjō family 60
Hōjō Tokimune 60
Hokkaidō: agriculture 337; Ainu 32, 43, 244; cities 29, 32; climate 8, 9, 10, 11, 12, 18, 32; coal 22; colonization 32, 57; communications 6, 33, 364, 367; fauna 38; fisheries 19; forests 13, 14; landscape 33; local government 314; Meiji development 79; national parks 32; population 25; university 370
Hokusai *19*, 193, 268
home life **236–41**
Hon'ami Kōetsu 191–2, 211
Hōnen 162
Hong Kong 98, 99
Honshū: Ainu 244; area 2; climate 8, 11, 12–13, 18; coal 22; communications 364, 367; forests 13, 14; regions of **32–6**
horses and horse trappings 38, 45, 63
hospitals 257, 258
hot springs 2, 9, 22, 34, 37, *38*
house/family (*ie*) *see under* family
housing: architecture *129*, *202*, 206, 207, 237, *238*; Burakumin 242; cost 31, 254, 346; restricted space 27, 180, 240–1; snow damage 8, *9*
Hozumi Yatsuka 182, 281
Hull, Cordell 99
hydroelectric power 340, 341, 342

I

Ibsen, Henrik 224, 225
Ibuse Masuji 147
Ichikawa Danjūrō I 223
identity, national 114, 173, 183, 195, 229, 245; *see also* ethnicity
ie, *iemoto* see under family
Ihara Saikaku 135, 136, 137, *139*
ikebana 15, 261
Ikeno Taiga 193
Imagawa Yoshimoto 65
Imamura Shōhei 227
Imperial Household Ministry 285
Imperial Rule Assistance Association 98, 100
Imphal campaign 102
imports **17–18**; dependence on 21–2, 330, 335, 340, 344, 371; fish 20; luxuries 31, 51–2; Nara era 51–2; oil 18, 340, 357; raw materials 15, 17–18, 21–2, 24; restrictions *see* protectionism
Impressionists 80
Inari (divinity) 155
India 107, 114, 216
Indo-China 98, 99, 101, 103
Indonesia 100, 101, 103, 320, 324
industry **348–56**; company towns 30–1; employment proportions by industry

industry *cont.*
350; energy consumption 340; expansion between wars 91; GDP by industry 350; government and 84, 91, 328, 331, 349, **351–2**, 372; heavy 348–9, 358, 372; 'internationalization' **355–6**; knowledge-intensive 24, 329, 372; Manchuria 94; Meiji expansion 78, 83, 84, 348, **371–2**; (1930s–40s) 93, 101, 103; (1970s) 351; organization **353–4**; overseas operations 31, 329–30, 341, 351, **355–6**, 359, 362; planning 332; post-war growth 106, 108–9, 236, 328–9, 335, **349–50**, 372; pre-war 348–9; quality control 355; rural 31; and technology **371–2**; tertiary sector 328–9, 350, **354–5**; Tokugawa period 371; and urban growth 30–1; and water resources 23; workforce 236, 334, **352–3**; WWI boom 90, 334, 348–9; in WWII 259, 345; *see also* companies; pollution (industrial); research and development; workforce; *individual industries and under individual places*
inflation 31, 110, 255, 328, 329, 346, 350–1
information society 265, 368
inheritance 236; *iemoto* 106, 191, 216, 220
Inland Sea 3, 5, *6*, 11, 13, 20, 32
Inoue Tetsujirō 182
inrō (dress accessories) 209
insurance, health and pensions 255, 256–7, 257–8
interest groups **309–12**; agricultural 272, *309*, 311, 312, 339; degrees of influence 309, 311, 339; *see also* protest, popular
interest rates 328, 346, 347, 348
International Monetary Fund 358
international rôle of Japan 80, 88, 285, 319, 331, 352, 355–6, 360; *see also* industry (overseas)
Inukai Tsuyoshi 93, 282
investment 331, 360; foreign, in Japan 356, 358, 362, 372
iron and steel industry 21; computer control *373*; depression, recent 36; foreign trade 361; Kamaishi 21, 29; Kyūshū 22, 29, 36, 37; Meiji 83; Nara era 51; post-war development 350, 358, 372; pre-Nara 42, 45; raw materials 21, 22, 23; San'yō area 36; Tokugawa 371; and urban development 29; Yahata works 22, 36
irrigation 4, 17, 23, *333*, **335–6**; Heian 57; pre-Nara 44
Ise, shrines at 153, 157, 202, *203*
Ishida Baigan 172
Ishii Shirō 97
Ishimure Michiko 147
Itagaki Taisuke 80, 82, 299
Itai-itai disease 271
Italy 97, 98
Itami airport, Ōsaka 368
Itami Jūzō 227
Itō Hirobumi 80, *280*, 281, 282; and constitution 81, 280; founds Seiyūkai 82, 299
Itō Hiromi 149
Itō Jakuchū *193*
ivory carving 200, 209, *210*
Iwakura Tomomi 80
Iwate 33
Izanagi and Izanami (divinities) 122, 154
Izumo region 125, 202

J

Jakkōin hermitage 59
Jakuren 133
Japan Airlines (JAL) 367
Japan Communist Party (Nihon Kyōsantō) 300, 301, 302, 303; under Allied Occupation 270–1; and Burakumin 243; creation 270; election results (1958–86) 286; publications 182, 265; Soviet influence 90, 182, 302; supporting interest groups 310
Japan Fine Arts Academy 195
Japan Medical Association 311
Japan Science Council 373–4
Japan Socialist Party (Nihon Shakaitō) *269*, 300, 301, 302, 303; election results 286, 306
japonisme 80, 209
Jesuits 17, 37, **63–4**, 65, *178–9*, 209
Jieitai *see* Self-Defence Forces
Jippensha Ikku 140
Jitō, Empress 125
Jiyū Gekijō 225
Jiyū Minshutō *see* Liberal Democratic Party
Jiyūtō *see* Liberal Party
Jōchō 199
jōi (expulsion of barbarians) 174
jōkamachi see castle towns
Jōmon period **42**, 43–4, *197*
jōruri puppet theatre 137
journalism 79, 91, 100, 101, 145, 148
judiciary 283, **293–8**
jūdō 98, 261
juku (cramming schools) 248, 262, 264, 296
justice **273–7**, 298, 323; medieval view *293*; *see also* courts; crime; judiciary; law

K

kabane rank system 47
kabuki *137*, 221, **223–4**, *224*; dance *213*, 214, 223; music 217, 218–19, 223–4; Tokugawa 138, 140, 260
Kagawa Toyohiko 180
kagura (ritual dance) 213
Kaifu Toshiki 282, 303, 305, 308, *317*, 319
Kaikei 199, 200
kaiseki (type of cuisine) 228
Kaishintō party 81, 299, 300
Kakinomoto no Hitomaro 125
Kamakura *162*, 264
Kamakura period 28, 60, 199–200, 204
kami see Shintō (divinities)
kamikaze ('typhoon'): and Mongol defeat 61; Pacific War pilots 61, *100*, 103
Kamisaka Sekka 192
Kamo no Chōmei 131
Kamo no Mabuchi 171
kana syllabary 117–18, 121, 125, 126, 183
Kan'ami 134, 221
Kanbara Ariake 141
Kano school of painting 63, 190, 191, 192, 195
kanpō (Chinese medicine) 255
Kantō Plain 4, 12, 16, 30, 34, 68; Great Earthquake (1923) *90*, 140, 143, 243
kappa (mythical creature) 38, *144*
karaoke 218
karate 261
Karuizawa 79, 261
katakana syllabary **117–18**
Katayama Sen 182
Katayama Tetsu 282, 302
Katayama Tōkuma 207
Katō Hiroyuki 83
Katō Takaaki 91, 270, 282
Kawabata Yasunari 144, 145, *146*, 147
Kawai Eijirō 96
Kawakami Hajime 90, 182
Kawanabe Kyōsai 196
Kawatake Mokuami 138, 223
Kaya state, Korea *46*, 47
Keenan, Joseph 107
Keidanren (Federation of Economic Organizations) 308, 311, 342, 344
Keihanshin Metropolitan Region 23, 25, 30, **35**
Keihin Metropolitan Region 25, 30, **34**
Keiō University 83
keiretsu (groups of companies) 331–2, 354
Kellogg–Briand Pact (1928) 91
kemari 57
kendō 261
Kennedy Round (1964–67) 358
Kennin-ji monastery 228
Kenreimon, Empress 132
Kenseikai party 90
Ki no Tsurayuki 126
Kibi no Makibi 166
Kido Kōichi 103, 107
Kido Takayoshi 80
Kidōtai (Riot Police) 321
kindergartens 239, 261
Kinki District 4, 34, **35**
Kinoshita Junji 224
Kira Yoshinaka 170
Kiritsu Kōshō Kaisha 209, *210*
Kishi Nobusuke *108*, 271, 282, 318

Kishida Kunio 224
Kita Ikki 93, 94
Kita Kyūshū City 29, 36, *104*, 264, 315
Kitahara Hakushū 141
Kitamura Sayo 176
Kitamura Tōkokū 142
Kitao Masanobu (Santō Kyōden) *112–13*
Kitazato Shibasaburō 255
Kōan iinkai (Public Safety Commissions) 273
kōban (police box) *274*
Kobayashi Hideo 144, 149
Kobayashi Kiyochika 196
Kobayashi Takiji 143
Kōbe *35, 226–7*; development 29; local government 315; in Pacific War 103, *104*; population density 25; port 20, 35
Kōbō Daishi (Kūkai) 125, 162, 186
Kōdoha faction in army 93–4
kōenkai (politicians' support associations) 306, 307, 308, 310
Kofun period **42–3**; agriculture 44; burial customs 42–3, 45, *46*, 122, 197; cities 47–8; *haniwa* sculpture 122, *123*, 197, 201; state formation 45–7; warfare 45; *see also* Yamato period
Koguryo state, Korea 45, *46*
Koiso, General Kuniaki 103
Kojiki 47, 50–1, **122–4**, 154–5, 171, 213, 216
Kokumin Kyōdōtō 301, 302
Kōmeitō (Clean Government Party) 177, 286, 301, 302, 303, 310
Konjaku monogatarishū 130
Kōno Taeko 146
Konoe Fumimaro 96, 97, 98, 99, 103, 282, *284*
Kōnoike family 72
Korea: Buddhism 160; building techniques 201; Confucianism 165, 166, 168; dance 213; defence 324; early states *46*, (*see also* Kaya; Mimana; Paekche; Silla); ethnicity 43; Hideyoshi's invasion (1592) 66, *67*; iron resources 45; Japanese occupation (1910–45) 25, 27–8, 87, 103, 167, 243, 317, 342; language 114; Meiji conflict with China over 84–5; migrants in Japan (early) 42–3, 44, 47, 54, 161, 197, (16th century) 43, (modern) 25, 148, **243–4**; music 219; pictorial art 186; prehistoric 42, 43–4, 45; printing 74; sculpture 198; Soviet shooting down of passenger jet (1983) 318; writers living in modern Japan 148; *see also* War, Korean
Kotani Kimi 176
koto (zither) 216, *217*, 218, 219, 220
Kōtoku Shūsui 269
Kubo Sakae 224
Kūkai (Kōbō Daishi) 125, 162, 186
Kuki Shūzō 183
Kumano shrine 187
Kumazawa Banzan 170
kunreishiki system of romanization **117**
Kurahashi Yumiko 146, *148*
Kuroda Seiki *195*
Kurosawa Akira 226–7
Kurozumikyō 175
Kyōdō News Service 266
kyōgen theatre 63, 214, 221, **222**
Kyokutei Bakin 140
Kyōto: architecture 204; capital city 28, 35, 120; cultural centre 35, 53–4, 71, 120; festivals 264; Ginkaku-ji *62*; Heian period *see* Heian-kyō; Horikawa lumber market 62; imperial residences 190, *201*; Jesuits 64; Kamakura period 60; local government 314, 315; under Muromachi Bakufu 62; Nijō Castle 202; Ōnin War 61; painting 190, 191–2, **194**; philosophy 182–3; Saihō-ji gardens *14–15*; temples *62*, 199; theatre, Genroku era 137; Tokugawa 68, 71, 135, 137, 138; universities 79, 90, 247, 290, 292, 370; *see also* Keihanshin
Kyūshū 2, **36–7**; climate 10, 11, 12; forests 13, 14; industry 23, 36, 37; marine culture 20; Pacific War 103; physical structure 5; pre-Nara 42, 44, 45, *46*; volcanic activity 37

L

labour force *see* workforce
labour movement 82, 106; *see also* Rengō; trade unions
lacquerware *128*, 209, *210*, 212, 230, 371
land and land holdings: agricultural 4, 333, *335*, **337–8**, 339; Ainu 244; Burakumin 241–2; Heian period 57–8, (*see also shōen*); landlords 90, 269, 270, 299, 337–8; medieval 60, 62, 67; Meiji 78, 83–4, 269, 337; Nara 48; reclamation 4, 16–17, 20, 34, 57, 58, 71, *341*; reform under Occupation 338, 339, 349; Tokugawa 68, 71; Yamato *jōri* system 44, 47; *see also under* cities
language **112–21**; affiliation **114**; dialects **120**; grammar **115**; and Japanese identity 114, 183; respect language **115–16**; Ryūkyū Islands 79; and social relations 238–9; translation problems 183; vocabulary 114, **116**, 118, 123, 126, 183; *wakan konkōbun* 130–1; Western studies, Meiji period 79; writing styles **121**, 122–3, 130–1, 141; written language **116–20**, 141; *see also under* Ainu; China
law **273–7**; *Buke shohatto* 68; bureaucrats trained in 290; Civil Code 83, 106; commercial 78, 349, 353; constitution (1889) 79, 81; courts *294*; criminal justice system **273–5**, 277; Diet and legislation 291, 298; on electioneering 298, 307; environmental 374; family in 83, 106, 236; and human rights 276; Kamakura Bakafu and.60; land tenure 83; Meiji period 79, 83; Ōtsu Case (1891) 293; Peace Preservation (1925) 91, 182, 270; post-war reform 106; public assistance scheme 256; Six Codes 293; Taihō Code (701) 47, 50; Tokugawa 68; under shōguns 61; Yamato 47; Yōrō Code 50; *see also* courts; crime; judiciary
League of Nations 88, 93, 97
legislature, organization 287
leisure 229, 240, *251*, **260–4**, 268, 354; *see also* festivals *and individual sports*
Liberal Democratic Party (Jiyū Minshutō) 301; and agriculture 310, 312, 339; and business sector 308, 310; consolidation, post-war 284; and constitution (1946) 283; elections 286, 306, 311; energy policy 343; factionalism 286, 287, 302, 304, 305–6; formation 299, 302; in government 109, 285–6, 299, 303, 328; and interest groups 311, 312; promotion system 287; Recruit scandal 303, 305
Liberal Party (Jiyūtō) 81, 269, 299, 300, 301, 302
libraries, lending 74, 135, 268
literacy 120, 135, 249, 265, 348; Tokugawa era **73**, 135
literati movement (*bunjin*) 138
literature **122–49**; aestheticism 144; and art **188–9**; Christian influence 179; commercialization 147; Confucian moral view 138; court 125–30; early Japan 51, **122–5**; government control 51, 101; Heian 51, 121, **125–30**, 188–9; Korean migrants 148; medieval 63, 121, **130–4**; Meiji 121, **140–2**, 143; modern **140–9**; Nara 51, 121, 125; oral tradition 122, 132, 140; Pacific War and 101, 140, 144–5, 147; popular 138, 148; recitation 132, 136, 216; social comment 142, 143, 147; and state formation 122; Tokugawa era 73, 121, **135–40**; traditional elements in contemporary 148, 149; of travel 136, 140; writing styles **121**
livestock 18, 62, 334, 335, 339
Lockheed scandal 266, *298*, 312
London Naval Treaty (1930) 93

M

ma (space) 218
MacArthur, General Douglas 105, *285*; and constitution 157, 283, 285, 316, 321; and war crimes 97, 107

machinery production 350, 359, 360, 361, 372
Maekawa Commission 360
magazines 262, **265–6**, **268**
Maglev train *365*
Maki ballet company 215
Maki Fumihiko 208
Malaya 97, 99, 100, 101, 103
Malaysia 320, 324
Manchuria 4, 28, 85, 91, 317; Japanese occupation, Manchukuo *92*, 93, 94, 167; Manchurian Incident 91, 94; in Pacific War 105, 107, (Unit 731) 97
mandalas *132*, 186, *187*, 188
manga (comic magazines) *268*
manners, social *74–5*, 236, 238–9, 245
Man'yōshū 51, 124–5, 171
Marco Polo Bridge Incident 95
Mariana Islands 88, 97, 101, 102, 103
marriage: Burakumin and 242–3; Christian-style 180; divorce 241; gender rôles **239–40**; Heian era 56; mistresses 241; petitions to *kami* 153; polygamy 56; Shintō ceremony 233, *236–7*; within *ie* 236, 237
Marshall Islands 88
martial arts 98, **261**
Maruyama Ōkyo 193
Marxism 90, 143, 182
masks, dance and theatrical 52, 213, *214*, *222*
mathematics 369
mats, rush see *tatami*
Matsukata Masayoshi 80
Matsumoto Jōji 283
Matsumura Goshun 194
Matsuo Bashō 135, 136
Matsuoka Yōsuke 99
matsuri (Shintō ritual) 152
Matsuyama ballet company 215
Mayama Seika 224
meat in diet 38, 231, 335
media 120, **265–8**, 312; *see also individual media*
medicine **255**; Buddhist 159; Chinese *255*, 259, 369; costs 258; diet and *257*; family planning 238; health care provision 257–8, 355; Heian era 369; Institute of Infectious Diseases 370; Japan Medical Association 311; Meiji era 79, 370; pharmaceuticals *255*, 259; and politics 311; research 370, 372; Tokugawa period 73, 369; *see also* health and welfare
medieval era **60–3**; art 62–3; Chinese contacts 62, 63, 189; common people 63, 134; cultural life **62–3**; dance 214; emperor 173; justice *293*; late Heian period 59, **60**; music 216–17; piracy 17; science 369; social and economic life **62**; trade 17; *see also under* Bakufu (Kamakura, Muromachi); Buddhism; castles; literature; provincial military families; taxation
mediums, spirit 152
Meiji, Emperor 87, 167, *283*
Meiji era **78–87**; agriculture 83–4, 87; Ainu 244; architecture 79, *80*, 206; arts 79, 80, **195–6**, 212, 218, 200; Christianity 179; communications 363; constitution *see separate entry*; economy 78, **83–4**; education 79, 82, 87, 218, 245–6, 370; exhibitions **80**; local government 78, 313; music 218; national identity 195, 245, 246; newspapers 267; popular protest 269; reform **78**, **80**; religion 82, 156–7, 164, 167, 169; satire *281*; shipbuilding 363; silk manufacture 371; trade 80; *see also under* armed forces; bureaucracy; construction; crafts; foreign policy; government, central; industry; land; literature; politics; railways; rights, human; samurai; science; social order; taxation; thought
Meiji Restoration 77, 78, 80, 174, 280
Meiroku zasshi (journal) 83
Meishin expressway 367
merchants, Tokugawa 71, 72, 155, 172, 217, 369; and arts 190, 217, 228; Dutch 17, *74–5*, 209, 210, 255, 369; guilds 62; Portuguese *64*
metal ores 18, 23
metalwork, craft 209, *210*
microelectronics 351, 372
Middle East 318, 340, 341, 343, 358, 359; *see also* War, Gulf
Midway, Battle of 100
migration: pre-Nara 42–3, 44, 47, 54, 197, 216; seasonal 9; 16th century 43; 20th century 25, 103, 148, **243–4**, 277, 353, 356, (*see also* cities (growth))
miko (spirit mediums) 152
militarism 78, 87, 93, 283, 310, 325, 345, 370
Mimana 47
Minamata Bay 21, 147, 271, 311
Minamoto family 59, 60, 172, 200, 216
Minamoto no Yoritomo *60*, 63
Minamoto no Yoshitsune 59
minerals **21–2**; *see also* coal; metal ores; mining
Mingei or Folk Craft Movement 212
mining: coal *340–1*, 342; overseas operations 356; recession and recovery, 1970s 351; size of industry 328, 349, 350, 354
Ministry of Finance 328, 343
Ministry of International Trade and Industry (MITI) 328, 342–3, 344, 352, 370, 372,373
Minobe Tatsukichi 93, 281
minorities **241–4**, 250, 266; *see also* Ainu; Burakumin; Korea (migrants)
Minseitō political grouping 90, 93, 299
Minshatō 286, 301, 302, 303
Minshutō 300, 301, 302
Mishima Yukio 109, *146*, 147, 225
Mito School 173
Mitsubishi corporation 84, 91, 342, 353, 371, 374
Mitsui corporation 72, 84, 91, 342, 353
Miura Tetsuo 147
Miyamoto Yuriko 143
Miyazawa Kiichi 282, *304*, *306–7*, 308
Mizoguchi Kenji 226, 227
Momoyama era 200
Mongol Invasion Scrolls 63
Mongol invasions 17, **61**, 162–3
Mongolia 96, 97, 107
Mononobe clan 43
monopolies legislation 349, 353
monsoons 7, 10, 336
morality: Buddhist 159; Confucian 167, 168, 170; Nativist interpretation 171; Shintō 152, 153, 155, 159
Mori Arinori 83
Mori Ōgai *141*, 142, **143**, 224, 255
Morse, Edward 79
MOSS negotiations 360
Motoori Norinaga 156, *171*, 172–3
mountains **2–4**, 13, 38; holy 155, 162; and settlement patterns 6, 25, 333
moxibustion 255
Mukden, battle of *86*, 87
Mukyōkai (Non-church) movement 179
mulberry cultivation 334
Munakata Shikō 196
Murakami, Emperor 56
Murakami Haruki 147
Murakami Ryū 147
Murasaki Shikibu 57, 129–30, 143
Murata Shukō 228
Muromachi Bakufu 60, **61**, 62, 63, 200; *see also* Ashikaga shōguns
Mushanokōji Saneatsu 142
music **216–20**; *gigaku* 52, 213; instruments 15, 52, (*see also individual instruments*); new religions and 177; Pacific War censorship 101; and pictorial art 193; popular, youth culture 262; *sarugaku* 221; *see also* gagaku *and under* kabuki; nō
mythology 122–3, 124, 148

N

Nagai Kafū 144
Nagano prefecture *202*, 365
Nagaoka 52, 53–4
Nagasaki: atomic bomb *104*, 105, 180; Christianity 37, 64, 179, 180; Confucian shrine *168*; cosmopolitan flavour 36–7; elections *278–9*; festival 264; painting 191, 192; ria coastline 36; shipbuilding 36; Tokugawa foreign trade 17, 29, 37, 68, 74–5, 190, 209
Nagashino, battle of 65, 66
Nagoya 4, 6, 34; commuters 30; development 29; high court 294; Ise

Bay Typhoon (1959) 12; local government 315; metropolitan region 30; in Pacific War 100, 103, *104*; Tokugawa development 71
Nakamura Hajime 183
Nakamura Masanao 83
Nakano Shigeharu 143
Nakasone Yasuhiro 282, 297, 302, *304*, 318, 325, 360
Nakatomi clan 43
Nakatomi Kamatari 50
Nakayama Miki 175
Nanga school of painting 191, 193, 194
Naniwa (*later* Ōsaka) *49*, 52
Nara: ancient capital 28, 35; Kasuga shrine *38*; Kofun period 44; Nara period *see separate entry*; temples *38*, *158*, 160–1, 199–200, (Chōgaku-ji) 199, (Hōkō-ji)*158*, 197, (Hōryū-ji) *48*, *49*, *158*, 197, *198*, 203, (sculpture) 48, 53, 197, *198*, 199–200, (Tōdai-ji) *48*, 50,52, 53, 160–1, 198, *200*, 203, 216, 217, (Yakushi-ji) *158*, *198*; Yayoi period 42
Nara ehon 189
Nara period **48–52**; capitals (Heijō) 28, 35, 48, *49*, 50, 53, (others) 52, 53–4; dance 214; Emishi people 51; Fujiwara family 50, 125; government control 48–50, 51; northern frontier 51; *see also under* Buddhism; bureaucracy; China; construction; land; literature; politics; roads; taxation
Narita airport *270–1*, 272, 368
National Space Development Agency (NASDA) 374
nationalism: and education system 246, 249–50; and Christianity 179; emperor-centred 173–4; 19th century 169, 172, 173–4, 195, 245, 246; Shintō and 157
Natsume Sōseki 144, *327*
Naturalism 142
Navy, Imperial 18, 79; disbanded 321; 20th century 86, 87, 88, 93, (Pacific War) 17, 18, 99
nenkō system 252, 253, 289
Neo-Confucianism 156, 166, 169
Netherlands: experts in Meiji Japan 79; Far East possessions (1914) *89*; in Second World War 98, 99–100; and Tokugawa Japan 17, 29, *74–5*, *77*, 209, 210, 255, 369
netsuke (dress accessories) 200, 209, *212*
New Liberal Club 286, 301, 302
New Year festival 155, 230, 231, 264
newspapers 196, **265–6**, 267, 269; censorship 100, 265, 266; and politics 182, 265, 269, 308; Sōka Gakkai-owned 177
NHK (Nihon Hōsō Kyōkai) 266
Nihon Shakaitō *see* Japan Socialist Party
Nihon shoki 47, 50–1, **122**, 123, 124, 216
nihonga style of painting 194, 195–6
Niigata 4, *5*, 8, 11, 34, 271
Nijō, Lady 131
Nijō Yoshimoto 134
Nikkō 202, *203*, 269
Nintoku, Emperor, tomb of *46*
Nishi Amane 83, 181, 183
Nishida Kitarō 182
Nishimura Shigeki 83
Nishitani Keiji 182–3
Nissan corporation 349, *351*, *355*
Nitten (Japan Art Exhibition) 196, 212
Nixon, Richard Milhous 110–11; 'Nixon shocks' 318, 350
nō theatre 63, **134**, **221–2**; Buddhist element 134, 216–17, 221; dance 213, 214; Meiji 218; music 216–17, 218, 219, 220, 222; origins 214, 221; writing style 121
Nobel Prizewinners *146*, 147, 370, 371
Nobunaga *see* Oda Nobunaga
Nogami Yaeko 146
Nogi, General 87, 144
Nōkyō kumiai 311, **312**
Nomonhan, USSR 98
Nōrin chūgin (bank) 312
Northern Territories 18, 317, 318
Nosaka Akiyuki 147
nuclear power 22, 310, **343–4**, 374
nuclear weapons 309, 310, 318, 321, 325

O

Ō no Yasumaro 122
Ōba Minako 146, 148
Occupation, Allied **106–8**; censorship 147, 226; Central Liaison Office 316; cinema 226; communications 364; defence 321; defence industries 364, 367; demilitarization 261, 283, 285, 321, 364, 367; economy and commerce 328, 345, 348, 349, 353, 357; education 106, 246, 249; foreign policy 316; political reforms 242, 270–1, **285**, 302, 309; popular protest facilitated 270–1, 273; religion and state separated 156, 157, 180, 283; trade unions 349; *see also* constitution (post-war); Supreme Commander; *and under* economy; government; land
Oda Makoto 146
Oda Nobunaga 61, 63, 64, **65–6**, 164; Azuchi castle 65, 190, 204
Ōe Kenzaburō 147, *148*
Ogata Kōrin *191*, 192
Ogawa Kunio 147
Ogyū Sorai 169, 171
oil, mineral: domestic resources 22; and electricity generation *342*; and foreign policy 318, 340, 341, 343, 359; imports 18, 340, 357; industry structure 341–2; patterns of use *340*, 341; pollution 271; refining 271, 341–2; shocks (1973) 18, 24, **109–10**, 318, *328*, 329, 340–1, 343, 344, 347, 350, 356, 358, 359, (1979) 340–1, 351, 359; stock-piling *341*; in WWII 99, 357, 371
Ōishi Kuranosuke 170
Okakura Tenshin 195, 212, 229
Okamoto Toyohiko 194
Okehazama, battle of 65
Okinawa (Ryūkyū Islands) **37**; agriculture 13; Ainu 43; airport plans 37; climate 9, 13; ecology 37; karate 261; language 79; music 217, 218, 219; in Pacific War 103; Ryūkyū Kingdom 37; sea routes 4; tourism 13, 37; US occupation 37, 110; vegetation 13
Ōkubo Toshimichi 80
Ōkuma Shigenobu 80, 82, 282, 299
Okumura Masanobu 193
Okuni 223
old age *see* elderly
Olympic Games: Moscow (1980) 318; Nagano (winter 1998) 365; Tōkyō (1964) 80, 109, *207*, 208, 261, 264
Onchi Kōshirō 196
Ōoka Shōhei 145
Oppama; Nissan plant *355*
optical-fibre technology 363, 368
oral tradition 122, 132, 140
Organisation for Economic Co-operation and Development 358
origami *153*
Ōsaka *329*; castle town 29, 204; climate 10, 11; commuters 30; industry and commerce 35; Itami airport 368; justice 294, 296; local government 314, 315; location 4, *6*; Nara era (Naniwa) *49*; Pacific War 100, 103, *104*; Shinkansen 365, 367; Tokugawa era 68, (commerce) 29, 71, (culture) 135, 136, 137, 138; unrest (1836), 76, (recent) 272, 277; water resources 23; World Exhibition 80, 264; *see also* Keihanshin
Oshima Nagisa 227
Ōshio Heihachirō 76
Ōtomo no Yakamochi 124
Ōtsu Case (1891) 293
outcastes *see* Burakumin
Ozaki Hotsumi 96
Ozaki Kōyō *142*
Ozu Yasujirō 226, 227

P

pachinko (pinball) 263
pacifism 316–17, 319, 370
Paekche state, Korea 42–3, 45, 47, 197
painting *see* art, pictorial
palaces 190, **201–2**, 206, 207
paper: manufacture 29, 356; origami *153*; tableware 230
parks, national 5, *20*, 32, 34, 38
Parliament *see* Diet

paternalism 167, 168, 259
pay 22, 252, 253, 329, 349, 350, 351, **352–3**, 371, 372
peace movement 180
Pearl Harbor, attack on *99*
pearls 20
peasant insurrections 65, 67, 269, 270
pensions 256–7, 258–9, 346
people **24–8**; Emishi 51; prehistoric 43–4; *see also* Ainu; demography; ethnicity; migration; minorities; population
Perfect Liberty Kyōdan 176
Perry, Commodore Matthew Galbraith, US Navy 17, 77
pharmaceuticals *255*, **259**, 311, 374
Philippines *69*, 99, 101, 103, 320, 324
philosophy *see* thought
physical structure **2–6**
pilgrimage 153, 155, 157, 162, *163*, 175, 188
piracy 17, 62, 161
planning, long-term 250, 332, 347
Plaza Agreement (1985) 329, 359
poetry: contemporary 148–9; anthologies, imperial 125, 126, 133; Chinese 125, 141, 148–9; *chōka* 124, 125; court 125–6, 133; early China 124–5; epic 132; free verse 141, 148–9; *haikai* 121, **135–6**, 138, 141, 148; Heian 125–6; *Man'yōshū* collection 124–5; medieval *55*, 63, 131; modern 141, 148–9; Nara period 51; in nō drama 134; and painting 188, 193; and popular culture 148; *renga* 133–4; screen poems 188; *shi* 141, 149; Tokugawa 135, 138; *waka* 124–5, 126, 127, 141; writing styles 117, 121
police: and Burakumin 242; and civil rights 274; confessions 298; *kōban* (police box) *274*; Meiji 78; operations and performance 274–5, 276; organization 273; and protest 143, 269, *270–1*, 272, 321; women in *275*; and *yakuza* 277
politics **278–325**; armed forces and 281, 285, 299, 345; Burakumin and 242–3; Christianity and 178–9; cost of participation 306, 307, 308; educational reform lobby 249–50; freedom and popular rights movement, Meiji 80, 81, 269, 280; labour and 286–7; Meiji period **78, 80, 81–2**, 140–1, 269; new religions and 177; Nara 50, 53; 1920s–30s 88, 91; 1930s–40s 88, 93–4, 95–6, 98, 143, 144; parties 81–2, 106, 285, 298, **299–304**, 309–10; political novels 140–1; post-war 105, 106, 108, 109, 110, 270–1, 284, **285**, 301, 302; press and 265; prime ministers **282**; stability 109, 245, 285, 299, 328; unrest (1930s) 88, 93–4, (post-war) 108; women in 303, 310; *zaibatsu* and 91; *see also* bureaucracy; constitution, Meiji; constitution, post-war; corruption; defence; elections; foreign policy; government; interest groups; judiciary; *kōenkai*; legislature; protest
pollution 260; air *9*, 24; industrial 21, 84, 110, 298, 350, 356, 372, 373, 374, (*see also* Minamata Bay); noise 24, 365; protests 271, 272, 329; water 20, *21*, 23, 336
population **24–8**; ageing 111, 207, 256–7, 258; Ainu 244; current size 24–5; distribution 21, 24, 25, 28; and food supply 21; mobility 236; post-war baby boom 28, 350; rural 17, 25, 30, 31, 35; urban 28, 71, 176, 236, 329, 350; *see also* birth control; demography; family
porcelain 209, *210*, 230
Port Arthur 86, 87
portraiture 188, 200
Portsmouth, Treaty of 86–7, 94
Portugal 74, *89*; 16th-century contacts 17, 63, *64*, 66, 178
Potsdam Declaration 105
prehistory 42, **43–4**; burial customs 122; religion 152, 154
pre-Nara era: clans 47, 54, 122; history **42–8**; literature **122–5**; music 216
press *see* newspapers
prices: agricultural 334, 337, 338–9; energy 344; housing 31, 254, 346; inter-company co-operation 332, 354; land *see under* cities; rises (C19th) *76*, (early C20th) 334, (1960s-70s) 329, 350–1
prime ministers 270, **282**, 322
printing 64, 73, **74**, 135, 192; pictorial *128*, 138, *139*, 193, 196
prisoners of war 97, *101*, 103
prisons **277**, 298, 342
Privy Council 280, 285
productivity 329; agriculture 25, 334, 337, 338, 339; labour 328, 329
professions 240, 349
Progressive Party *see* Shinpotō
Proletarian literature 143
proletarian movement, 1920s 224
propaganda: in education 246; road safety *275*; wartime 95, 96, 196, 226
prosecutor, public 273–4, 275, 276, 296, 298
prostitution 72, 221, 225, 276
protectionism 17, 30, 361; agricultural 17, 30, 230, 285, 303, 311, 312, 338–9; and FDI 356
protest, popular **269–72**, 315; agriculture *309*; over airports *270–1*, **272**, 368; anti-nuclear 310, 344; environmental 271, 272, 309, 329, 365; Korean residents' *243*, 244; student *270–1*, 272; suppression (1930s-40s) 93, 96, 101, 105; and US-Japan Security Treaty 109, 271, 318; *see also* peasant insurrections *and under* students
provincial administration 47, 50, 69, 70, 166–7, 174; *see also* government, local
provincial military families, 16th century 58–9, 60, 61, 130
Public Safety Commissions (*Kōan iinkai*) 273
publishing 100, **265–8**; *see also* books; magazines; newspapers
puppet theatre 137, 140, 213, 219, 221, **222–3**; *see also* bunraku
Pyongyang, battle of *84*

Q

quality control 355

R

railways **364–6**, 368; access to cities from countryside 28; congestion 364, *367*; Maglev *365*; map of Tōkyō network *365*; Meiji development 79, *363*, *364*; post-war era 364; Shinkansen bullet train 33, 36, *363*, 365, *367*; South Manchurian 87, 94, 97; *see also* Seikan *and under* Tōkyō
rainfall 4, 7, *8*, 11, 12–13, 15, 205; *see also baiu*; monsoons
Raku line of potters 229
rangakusha (scholars of Dutch studies) 369
raw materials: alternative 371; efficiency of use 358–9, 361; import reliance 15, 17–18, 21–2, 24, 101, 330, 335, 340, 344, 371
Reagan, Ronald 362
recessions: (1929–30) 349; (1950s) 358; (1970s) 340–1, 351; (1990s) 330
Recruit scandal 277, *303*, 305, 308, 312
regions **32–7**, 259, 265, 306, **313–16**
Reiyūkai Kyōdan 175, *176*, 177
religion **151–80**; and art **186–8**; and education 177; folk 157; and leisure 260; new religions **175–7**, 180; and social control 178; and state **82–3**, 106, (post-war separation) 156, 157, 180, 283; votive offerings 197, 230, 232, *233*; *see also* Buddhism; Christianity; Confucianism; pilgrimage; Shintō; Sōka Gakkai
renga (linked poetry) 133, *134*
Rengō (labour confederation) 254, 303, 310
research and development 341, 351, 352, 356, 370, 371, 372–3
Research Institute for Physics and Chemistry 370, 371
resources, natural **21–4**; *see also* air quality; coal; energy; gas; metals; minerals; oil, mineral; raw materials; sea; water
retail sector 350, 355, 372
Rettō (Archipelago) poetic group 149

reunification of Japan, 16th century 65, 66
rice: areas of production 16, *17*, 33, 34, 334; cuisine 231; cultivation **333–4**, 335; festivals *338*; history of cultivation 42, 44, 50, 51, 57; Inari as god of fertility 155; irrigation 4, 23, 44, *333*, 335–6; mechanization 17, *338*; price *76*, 339; productivity 57, 333, 334, 337; protectionism 30, 230, 285, 312; riots (1918) 90, 270, 334; self-sufficiency rate 335; Tokugawa era 29, *76*; *yamase* wind 11
rice wine, *see sake*
rights, human 183, 242–3, 296; in law 274, 276, 283, 293; Meiji freedom and popular rights movement 80, 81, 269, 280
RIMPAC 323
Rinpa style of painting 191, 192
riots: after Great Kantō Earthquake 243; Ōsaka, recent 272, *277*; rice (1918) 90, 270, 334
Risshōkōsekai 177
ritsuryō system 47, 48, 52, 165
rituals: agricultural, and nō 221; Buddhist 159, 161, 162, 228; *bugaku* dances 52; Confucian 165, 167; dance 214; for dead *159*; family 237; Jōmon period 44; Shintō 152, 156, 157; shugendō *155*; sumō 230, 262
roads **367**, 368; congestion 331, 367; Edo–Nikkō, Tokugawa era 269; Nara period 48, *49*, 50; public investment 331; safety campaigns *275*; Tōkaidō (ancient, Kyōto–Edo) 34
robotics *355*, *372*, *373*
Roesler, Hermann 79, 280
Romantic movement 142, 186
rōnin: forty-seven *170*, 223; re-take students 247
Roosevelt, Franklin D. 99
Russia: imperial 33, 76, 85–7, *89*; Revolution 90, 270; *see also* Union of Soviet Socialist Republics
Ryūkyū Islands *see* Okinawa
Ryūtei Tanehiko *139*, 140

S

Saga, Emperor 56, 228
Saichō 162
Saigō Takamori 78, 80
Saigyō *131*
Saipan, Mariana Islands 97, 102
Sakai 29, 64, 228
Sakai Hōitsu 192
Sakamura Ken 373
Sakata Tōjūrō I 223
sake (rice wine) 38, 71, 72, *76*, 230, **232–3**
Sakhalin Island 86
Sakurajima, Mt 37
salt 26, 50
samurai **69**; as administrators 69–70, 71, 288; and Christianity 178, 179; confinement to towns 169; Confucianism 70, 72, 82–3, 166–7, 168, 169, 170, 173; education 73, 245; ethic 62–3, 69, 82–3, 84; fiction about 138; films 226; forty-seven *rōnin 170*; hierarchies 288; loss of military competence 69, 70, 77; and Meiji Restoration 76, 78, 174, 280, (*see also* Chōshū *and* Satsuma cliques); and nō 214; residences 201; scholarship 169, 369; self-justification 170, 173; and Shingaku movement 172; suicide 170; *see also bushidō*
San Francisco Treaty (1951) 108, 302, 317
Sankai juku dance company 215
sankin kōtai (alternate attendance) 68, 71, 169, 363
Sanrizuka; planned airport 272
Sansom, Sir George 120
Santō Kyōden *112–13*, 140
Sapporo 10, 11, 29, 33, *264*, 294, 315
sarugaku music 214, 221
Sasebo 36
sashimi (fish) *232*
Sata Ineko 143, 146
Satake Shōzan 193
satellites, space 374
Satō Eisaku *108*, *109*, 282, 325
Satō Makoto 225
Satsuma clique, Meiji era 77, 78, 80, 81, 174, 280
savings, domestic 328, 331, 346, 351, 361
SCAP *see* Supreme Commander Allied Powers
science and technology **369–74**; agricultural **336–7**; arts and crafts 209; exports 373; and fisheries 336; government policies 370, **372–3**; history **369**; and industrialization **371–2**; institutional framework **370**; Meiji 79, 80, 370, 371; military 318, 319, 324, 325, *362*, 370, 371; and society **373–4**; space **374**; Tokugawa **73**, 369, 371; transfers 328; Western 209, 371, (gap) 329, 351, 352, 369, 371
Science and Technology Agency 343, 370, 372
science-cities 372
Science Council of Japan 370
screen painting *68*, *184–5*, 188, *190*, *191*, 192
scroll painting 62–3, *128*, *129*, *131*, *133*, 187, *188*, 189, 228
sculpture **197–200**; glass *211*; *haniwa 122*, *123*, 197, 201; ice *264*; *see also under* Buddhism
sea **17–21**; currents *18*; level 5, 20, 24, 43; marine life 39; ocean trenches 2; pollution 20, 21; resources 19–20; *see also* fisheries; shipping
seaweed 20, 50
securities companies 330, **347–8**
Security Council of Japan 322
security, national 342, 344
Sei Shōnagon 55, 128
Seichō no Ie 175–6
Seihōkyō (Young Lawyers Association) 298
Seikan railway tunnel 6, 33, 364, 367
Seiyūkai party 82, 90, 93, 299, 300
Sekai Kyūsei Kyō 176
Sekigahara, battle of 61, 67, 69
Self-Defence Forces (Jieitai) **321–5**; formation 283, 317, 321; organization and strength 317, 321–2, 323, 324
semiconductor industry 37, 360
Sen no Rikyū 228–9
Sendai 4, 11, 29, 264, 315; high court 294, 298
Sengoku period 65, 67
service industries 328–9, 350, **354–5**
Sesshū 186, *189*
Seto Ōhashi bridge 6, *36–7*, 367
shakuhachi (flute music) 217, 218, 219
shamanism 175, 213
Shaminren 286
shamisen 217, *218*, 219, 220, 222, 261
Shanghai Incident (1937) 95
Sharaku 192
shi (Chinese poetry) 141, 149
Shiba Kōkan 193
Shibusawa Eiichi 84
Shidehara Kijūrō 282, 321
Shiga Naoya 142
Shigemitsu Mamoru 101
Shijō school of painting 191, 194
Shikitei Sanba 140
Shikoku 2, **36**; climate 9; copper deposits 23; forests 13, 14; rice cultivation *17*; *see also* Seto Ōhashi Bridge
Shikotan island 317
Shimabara Revolt 179, *180*
Shimao Toshio 145, 147
Shimazaki Tōson 141, 142
Shimomura Kanzan 195
Shimonoseki, Treaty of 85
Shin Jiyū Kurabu 286, 301, 302
Shingaku movement 172
shingeki ('new theatre') **224–5**
Shinkansen *see under* railways
Shinpotō 286, 301, 302
Shinran 162
Shintō **152–7**; architecture 202, *203*, 205, 206; art 187–8, 199; asceticism 155–6; and Buddhism 82, 156–7, 161, 164, 187, 202; and death 154–5; divinities **152–4**, 155, 156, 158, 161, 187, *188*, (Buddhist syncretism) 156, 161, (*see also under* emperor); festivals 155, *157*; Ise shrines 153, 157; Meiji purification 164; morality 152, 153, 155, 159; and nationalism 157; new religions and 175; origins 152, 154; pilgrimage 153, 157;

Shinto *cont.*
pollution 153; rituals *111*, 152, 154, 155, 156, 157, 213, 233, *236–7*; Ryōbu system 156; samurai and 170; Shingaku and 172; shrine Shintō 82; State Shintō 54, 82, 156, (post-war disestablishment) 156, 157, 180, 283, (*see also* emperor (divinity); Yasukuni Shrine); votive offerings *153*, *157*, 230, 232, *233*; weddings 233, *236–7*; world view 158
shipbuilding: 17th century 68; 19th century 83, 363; 20th century 18, 36, 101, 103, 350, 353, 358, 364
shipping **17–18**, **367**, 368; coastal, 1930s 364; ferries 36, 367; 19th-century technology 77, 79; routes to mainland 4; Tokugawa 68, 72; *zaibatsu* control 353; *see also* fisheries; whaling
Shiraishi Kazuko 149
Shitennō-ji 48, *49*
shōen estates **57–8**, 62
shōguns 17; and emperors 61, 172–3; Minamoto 60; *see also* Ashikaga shōguns; Bakufu; Tokugawa period
Shōmu, Emperor 50, 52, 53, 160–1, 198
Shōsōin imperial storehouse 52, 216, 217
Shōtoku, Empress (Empress Kōken) 50, 53
Shōtoku Taishi 43, *48*, 160, 165, 197
Shōwa reign 93, 94, 140
Shugendō religious practices *155*, 156, *157*
shugo (provincial military governors) 61, 62
silk manufacture 334, 357; Meiji 83, 371; Tokugawa 71, 371
Silla state, Korea 45, *46*, 47, 51, 216
silver 23, 68
Singapore 99, 100, *101*, 320, 324
smallpox 48, 50
snowfall 7–8, 10, 18, 33, 34
social order 238–9, 241, 263, 276, 336; dialects and 120; Hideyoshi and 67; Meiji 78, 82, 83; respect language 116; Tokugawa 67, 68, 69, 73, **75–6**, 135, 191, 241, 260, 369; 20th century 90, 96, 100; *see also* equality; status
socialism 142, 179, 182, 269, 270, 310, 318; *see also* Japan Socialist Party; trade unions
Soga clan 43
Sōhyō trade union federation 271
Sōka Gakkai 163, 175–6, 177, 180; and Kōmeitō 177, 301, 302, 310
solar energy 22, 344
Solomon Islands 100
Sorge, Dr Richard 96
South Manchurian Railway 87, 94, 97
soya beans *335*; sauce *76*
space technology 352, **374**
Spain 64, 65, 66, 74
sports 31, *57*, 79, 261, 262, 264; *see also individual sports and* Olympic Games
Stalin, Josef 96, 105
standard of living 244, 254, 342, 351, 352, 355
state formation 45–7, 122, 165
statesmen, elder *see genrō*
status, social 177, 245, 251
steel *see* iron and steel
stock market 308, *327*, 345, *348*, 361
strikes 90, 93, 353
students: life-style 262; Pacific War conscription 101; protest 90, *109*, *270*, **271**, *272*
suffrage: current 305; local government 313, 314; Meiji 82, 299; universal male 91,.269, 270; women's 106, 283, 285
Sugawara no Michizane 56, 125, 154, 166, 188
suicide: children 249; samurai 170; writers 146
Suiheisha (Levellers Society) 242
sukiyaki (cuisine) 38, 231
Sumitomo corporation 84, 91, 353
sumō 230, 261, **262**
Supreme Commander Allied Powers 106, 316, 321; *see also* MacArthur, General Douglas; Occupation, Allied
sushi (cuisine) 231
Suzuki Harunobu 192
Suzuki Kantarō, Admiral 103, 105, 282
Suzuki Tadashi 225
Suzuki Zenkō 282, 321
swords 23, 209
syllabaries **117–18**

T

Taika reforms 43, 44, 47, 48, 165
Taira family 55, *58–9*, 60, 131, 200, 216; *see also Tale of the Heike*
Taira no Kiyomori 60, *152*
Taira no Masakado 58–9
Taira no Sadabumi *55*
Taishō reign 88, 91, 140; democracy **90–1**, 93, 182, 270, 299
Taiwan 28, 85, 317, 324, 368
Takahashi Yuichi 195
Takayama Ukon 178
Takeda Izumo 170
Takeda Katsuyori 65
Takeda Shingen 66
Takemoto Gidayū 222–3
Takeshita Noboru 282, *304*, 305
Takeuchi Seiho 194
Tale of Genji **129–30**, 137, 143, 144, 173
Tale of the Heike 59, 63, 132, *133*
Tales of Ise 127–8, *128*, 137
tama, tamashii (spirits of dead) 154
Tamenaga Shunsui 140
Tanabe Hajime 182–3
Tanaka Kakuei 266, 282, *298*
Tanaka Yasuo 147
Tanegashima 63, 66, 254, 342, *374*
Tange Kenzō *207*, *208*
Tanizaki Jun'ichirō 101, 144–5, 145–6
tanka (poetic form) 148; *see also waka*
tanuki (racoon dogs) 38
tatami (rush mats, unit of measurement) 202, 204, 205, 228
Tatsuno Kingo 207
Tawara Machi 148, 149
Tawaraya Sōtatsu 191–2
taxation: of aliens 243; company 330; consumption 303; family unit 236; Heian 52, 55, 57–8; medieval 60, 62; Meiji 78, 83–4, 269; Nara 50, 57, 58; post-war relief for heavy industry 372; protests 269, 310; reclaimed land exempt 57, 58; reforms (1989) 330; 16th century 67; South Manchurian Railway and 94; temples exempt *48*, 50, 52; Tokugawa 70, 71, 72, 269
tea, culture of: tea ceremony (*chanoyu*) 63, 73, 201, **228–9**, 261, 262; tea houses 228, *229*; utensils 15, *211*, 212, 228, *229*; and Zen **228**
tea production *35*, 357
technology *see* science and technology
telecommunications 354, 363, 364, **368**; exports of equipment 359, 361; *see also individual types*
telegraph system 79, *83*, 266, 363
telephone 363, *368*
television **266–7**; advertising 147, 267, 307, 308; children's watching of 262; dance on 214; and decline of cinema 227; drama 267; language 120; manufacture of sets 108
temples, Buddhist 159; architecture **203–4**, 205, 206; Asuka-dera 48, *49*; historiography 189; Ishiyama Hongan-ji 65; Kamakura *163*; Miyajima 38; Nara period 50; pre-Nara 43, 47, 48; and printing 74; restorations 189, 203; on Shikoku 162; and *shōen* 62; tax exemption *48*, 50, 52; Tōshōdai-ji 161; Yamato era 161; Zen 204; Zenkō-ji *164*; *see also under* Kyōto; Nara; Tōkyō
tennōsei (emperor system) 167, 280, 310
Tenpō era 70, 76
Tenri City 175
Tenrikyō 175
Tenshōkōtai Jingūkyō 176
Terayama Shūji 225
textile industry 84, 334, *349*, 355, 357, 359, 361
Tezuka Osamu 268
Thailand 101, 107, 320, 324, 329–30
theatre *see* drama
Third World 339, 362; *see also individual countries*
thought **151–83**; Meiji **82–3**, 181; Tokugawa 156, **169–74**; translation of concepts 183; 20th century **181–3**, 269, 270; writing styles 121

tidal waves 75
timber imports 15, 18, 24, 204, 334
Tōdai-ji *see under* Nara
Tōfuku-ji 228
Togo, Admiral 87
Tōhoku 33–4; climate 8, 18, 33, 34; coastline 5; industry 23; marine culture 20; mining 22, 23; Nara period 51; national park 5; physical structure 4; rice production 33; university 370
Tōjō Hideki, General 99, 103, *105*, *108*, 282
Tōkaimura nuclear power station *343*
Tokugawa Ieshige 69
Tokugawa Ietsugu 69
Tokugawa Ieyasu 61, 63, 65, 67, *68*, 204; mausoleum 202, *203*; and religion 67, 166, 178–9
Tokugawa period **67–77**; agriculture 70, 72–3, 334; Ainu 244; arts 191, 200, 217, 221, 260; Christianity 74; Confucianism 135, 138, 166–7, 168, 169–70, 171, 172, 269; countryside **72–3**; court 221; culture **73–4**; currency 67; demography 27; disasters, natural **75–6**; economy 67, 72–3, *76*; education 73, 245; emperors' rôle 68; end 77, 174; famines 11, 21, 27, 75, *76*; government **69–70**; isolation 17, 29, 63, 74, 77, 174, 192–3, 209, 348, 363; land holdings 68, 71; law 68; leisure 221, 260; literacy **73**, 135; medicine 73, 369; nationalism 169, 172, 173–4; reforms 70, 76; samurai **69–70**, 71; Shintō 153, 156; tea culture 229; theatre 135, 137–8; unrest **75–6**, 135, 269; *see also* Bakufu; daimyō; Edo; merchants; *and under* Buddhism; China; cities; foreign policy; literature; science; social order; taxation; thought; trade
Tokugawa Yoshimune 74, 169, 192
Tōkyō: air pollution *9*, *24*; airports 368; architecture *90*, *206*, *207*, 208; Asakusa *157*; capital and cultural centre 120; climate 10, 11; communications 30, 33; congestion 367; dialect 120; festivals *157*; fire 143; Ginza area 206; growth *29*; Hibiya Park protests 269, 272; housing *240*; Imperial Theatre 215; industry 35; justice 294, 296; Kantō earthquake (1923) *90*, 143; land costs 207; local government *208*, 314, *315*; Marunouchi district *206*; Olympic Games (1964) 80, 109, *207*, 208, 261, 264; in Pacific War 100, 103, *104*; physical structure 4; population density 25; railways 33, 206–7, *363*, 364, *365*, *367*; Tokugawa era *see* Edo; university 79, 82, 91, 93, 247, 289, 290, 292, 297, 370, 373, 374; Zōjō-ji *160*
Tōkyō Ballet 215
Tōkyō–Yokohama metropolitan area *see* Keihin
Tōmei expressway 367
Tomioka silk-reeling factory 371
Tomioka Tessai 194
Tosa region 77, 269
Tosa school of painting 63, 191
Tōseiha faction in army 93–4
Tōshiba corporation 374
Tōshōdai-ji 161
Tōshōgū, Nikkō 202, *203*
tourism 13, 37, 39, 79, *260*, 263, 264
Toyotomi Hideyoshi 61, 63, 65, **66–7**, 204, *229*; and Christianity 64, 66–7, 178–9; defeat of followers *68*; tea house *229*
trade, overseas **357–62**; agricultural 230, 285, 303, 311, 312, 338–9; arms 325; with China 317, 318; Confucian aversion 70, 72, 84; decorative arts 209–12; East Asian trade area 93, 101, 110; with European Community 330, 360; frictions 339, 350, 351, 356, **359–62**; medieval 17, 62; Meiji 80; 1920s–30s 88, 93; 1970s 109; in Occupation 108; with Portugal 17; prehistoric, with Korea 42; restrictions during Chinese war (1937–40) 95; 16th–17th century *69*; surplus 331, 359, 361; with Third World 339; Tokugawa 17, 28, 29, 37, 68, *69*, *72*; *see also individual commodities*; exports; imports; protectionism; *and under* United States
trade unions **352–3**; enterprise unions 328, 349, 353; establishment 90; history 182, 270, 349; political connections 309, 310, 311; post-war era 106, 108, 270, 349, 352; *see also* Rengō; Sōhyō
transport 348, 349, 350, 352, 354, **363–8**; urban *88*, 30, 31, *234–5*; *see also* air transport; railways; roads; shipping; travel
travel: expenditure on 354; external; statistics 367; literature 136, 140
treaties, unequal 78, 79, 84
Tripartite Pact (1940) 98, 99
Triple Intervention 85
Tsubouchi Shōyō *141*, 143, 224
Tsuda College *246*
Tsuda Umeko 246
Tsukuba science city 372
Tsushima Yūko 147
Tsushima, battle of *86*, 87
tuberculosis 259
tunnels 6, 33, 36, 364, 367
typhoons 11, *12*, 20, 61, 204, 206

U

Uchimura Kanzō 179
Ueda Akinari 138
Uesugi Shinkichi 281
Uji; Phoenix Hall, Byōdō in *56*, *199*
ukiyo ('floating world') 135, 136, 137, 140, 260; art 191, 192, 193, 196; fiction 137
Umehara Ryūzaburō 194, *196*
Union of Soviet Socialist Republics: and Japan Communist Party 90, 182, 302; Japan recognizes (1925) 91; Japanese forces in Siberia (1918–22) 88; Northern Territories dispute 18, 317, 318; relations with 317, 318; trade in military technology *362*; and US 108, 316; war against Japan (1938–9) 97, 98; in WWII 94, 96, 97, 98, 99, 103, 105
Unit 731 (biological warfare unit) 97
United Nations 320, 323
United Social Democratic Party 286
United States of America: and China, 1970s 109, 110–11; defence of Japan 317, 318–19, 321, 325, 350, (*see also* Security Treaty *below*); emigration to 25; Japanese dependence on, post-war 284, 316, 367, (protests at) *269*, *271*; Japanese investment in 330, 356, 362; medicine 255; and Meiji Japan 77, 78, 79, 370; 'Nixon shocks' 318, 350; nuclear weapons 318, 321, 325; occupation of Okinawa 37; oil exports embargo (1941) 357; and Pacific War 97, 98, *99*, 100, 103, 105, 106, 357; and Portsmouth Treaty (1905) 86; post-war relations 108, 109, 110–11, 318, 350; Security Treaty 109, 146, 269, 271, **317**, **318**, 321, 325; semiconductor agreement 360; space programme 374; trade 357, 358, 368, (disputes) 201, 318, 319, 329, 330, 339, 358, **359–60**, *362*; *see also* Occupation, Allied
universities: of the Air 267; and civil service entry 290, 292; Confucian 165, 166; cost to family 248; entrance examinations *248–9*; hierarchy 247, 289, 290, 292; imperial 370; Keiō 83; post-war expansion 370; Sōka Gakkai 177; student life 247, 262, (protest) 271; *see also under* Kyōto; Tōkyō
Uno Chiyo 146
Uno Sōsuke 282, 305, *315*
Unzen, Mt 4, 37
uranium 340
Utari Association 244

V

Valignano, Alessandro 64, 65
vegetables, cultivation of 334, 335
video equipment 262, 359, 360
Vietnam 324; War 271, 272, 318
village life 336, 337, 339
volcanic activity 2–3, *4*, 16, 37, 75

W

wabi (simplicity) 229
wages *see* pay

wagon (zither) 216
waka (poetic form) 124–5, 126, 127, 138, 141, 143
Wang Yangming 166
War, Chinese (1937–40) 88, 94, **95–8**, 99, 101, 342, 349
War, Cold 316, 321, 349, 357, 364
War, First World **88–9**, 90, 334, 348–9, 370
War, Gulf 285, 319, 323
War, Jōkyū 60
War, Korean 108, 321, 349–50, 357, 358
War, Ōnin 61, 190
War, Pacific *see* War, Second World
War, Russo-Japanese (1904–5) 179, 269, 348
War, Second World **95**, **97–105**; agriculture 334–5; battle of Midway 100; beginning 99–100, 357; bombing 17, *104*, 105; build-up to Japanese entry 97–9; devastation 259, 329, 364; economic crisis **102–5**; industry 259, 345; internment of Japanese in North America 25; Korean forced labour 243; and literature 101, 140, 144–5, 147; naval war 17, 18, 99, 100; oil shortage 357, 371; prisoners of war 97, *101*, 103; propaganda 196, 226; religious suppression 176, 180; science and technology 370, 371; Sorge spy ring 96; war crimes trials *106*, **107**, *108*; *see also under* censorship; communications; kamikaze; San Francisco Treaty
War, Sino-Japanese (1894–5) 84–5
War, Vietnam 271, 272, 318
warfare: biological and chemical 97; impact of firearms 66; pre-Nara *45*
warlords, 16th–17th century **63–7**, 190, 202; *see also* Oda Nobunaga; Tokugawa Ieyasu; Toyotomi Hideyoshi
warriors: culture 62–3, 69, 170, 171, 173, 201; *see also* Bakufu; provincial military families; samurai; shōguns
Washington Conference (1921–2) 88, 91
Watanabe Shōsaburō 196
water resources 23, 84; *see also under* pollution
Watsuji Tetsujirō 183
welfare, social *see* health and welfare
whaling 19
wheat 57, 334, 335
White Horse Society 195
wholesale trade 350, 355
winds 11, *12*, 20, 61, 204, 206
women: aristocracy 50, 56–7; child-rearing 241, 252–3, 254; Confucianism and 167; in constitution of 1946 283; court 188; diaries 129, 131; education 79, *246*, 253; employment 84, 241, **252–3**, 254, 267, *275*, 292, 342, 354, (discrimination legislation) 298, (and family) 240, 241, 253, 254, (pre-war) 342, (wartime) 101, (working hours) 253, 261, 263, 353; entertainers 214, 220, 223, 241, (*see also* geisha); in family **239–40**; feminism 90, 270, 309; films on plight of 226, 227; housewives 239, 263; in law 83, 283; leisure 262–3; literacy 135; literature, (Heian) 117, 126, 129, (medieval) 131, (modern) 142, 143, 146,147, 149, (writing styles) 121; and new religions 175, 177; and politics 303, 310; subordination 167, 236; suffrage 106, 283, 285; and war effort 100, 101
wool 83
work ethic 226, 245, 246, 247–8, 261, 352, 353
workforce: agricultural 329, 334, 336, 337, 349; composition 243, 252–3; education tailored to needs 246; forced labour 57, *101*, 103, 342; immigrants 277, 353, 356; industrial 329, 334, 350, **352–3**; political rôle 286–7; productivity 328, 329; shortages 329, 332, 350, 353; unskilled *332*; *see also* trade unions
World Expo (1970) 329
wrestling *see* sumō
Wright, Frank Lloyd *90*

X

Xavier, St Francis 37, 63, 64

Y

Yahata steelworks 22, 36
yakuza (organized crime gangs) 276, 277
Yamabe no Akahito 125
Yamaga Sokō 170
Yamagata Aritomo 80, 90, 282
Yamakawa Hitoshi 96
Yamamoto Isoroku, Admiral 99, 100
Yamato the brave (*Yamato takeru*) 124
Yamato period **42–3**; areas of influence *46*; aristocracy 45; beginning 45–6; Buddhism 43, 47, 48; cities 47–8; clans 122; Confucianism 48, 165; crafts 46, 47; government 45, 47, 48; and Korea 42–3, 44, 45, 47, 54, 197; land ownership 44, 47; Nativist view of 171; religion 154; rice cultivation 44; state formation 45, *46*, 47, 165; warfare 45; *see also* Kofun period; Taika reforms
Yamazaki Ansai 156
Yanagi Sōetsu 212
Yanagita Kunio 154
Yasuda corporation 91, 353
Yasukuni Shrine 157, 177, 283, 298
Yasuoka Ṣhōtarō 149
Yayoi period **42**, 44, 45, 51
Yeats, W. B. 215
yōga (Western style painting) 194, 195–6
Yokkaichi City 24, 271
Yokohama *351*; beer 233; development after end of seclusion 29; foreign contacts *357*; Kantō earthquake (1923) 91; local government 315; organized crime 276; railway *364*; Western dance lessons 215; *see also* Keihin
Yokoyama Taikan 195
Yosa Buson 136, *138*, 193
Yosano Akiko 143, 144
Yoshida no Kenkō 131
Yoshida Shigeru 282, 316, 317
Yoshimoto Banana 147, 149
Yoshimoto Ryūmei 149
Yoshino Sakuzō 91
Yoshiyuki Junnosuke 146
yūgen ('mystery and depth') 133

Z

zaibatsu (business conglomerates) 84, 91, 93, 342, 345, 349, 350, **353–4**
Zeami 134, 221
Zen: architecture 201, 204, 205; calligraphy *136*; monasteries 201, 228; music 217; pictorial art 159, 188, 189, 191; sculpture 200; and tea **228**
Zengakuren (student organization) 271
zuihitsu (miscellaneous essays) 131

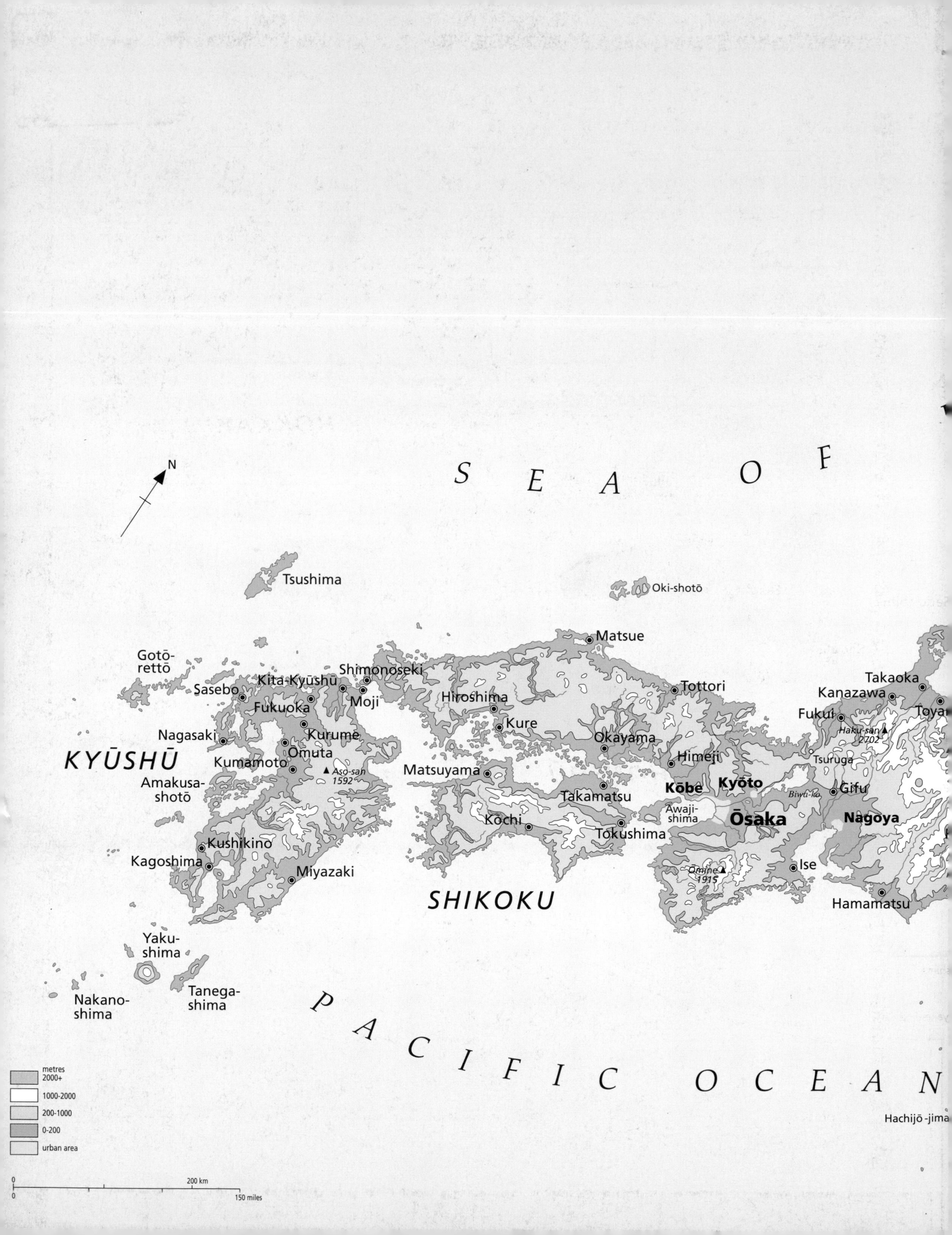
N
SEA OF
PACIFIC OCEAN
Tsushima
Oki-shotō
Matsue
Gotō-rettō
Shimonoseki
Kita-Kyūshū
Sasebo
Moji
Fukuoka
Hiroshima
Tottori
Takaoka
Kanazawa
Fukui
Nagasaki
Kurume
Kure
Okayama
Haku-san 2702
KYŪSHŪ
Ōmuta
Kumamoto
Aso-san 1592
Himeji
Tsuruga
Matsuyama
Amakusa-shotō
Kōbe
Kyōto
Gifu
Takamatsu
Biwa-ko
Awaji-shima
Ōsaka
Nagoya
Kōchi
Tokushima
Kushikino
Kagoshima
Miyazaki
Ōmine 1915
Ise
SHIKOKU
Hamamatsu
Yaku-shima
Nakano-shima
Tanega-shima
Hachijō-jima
metres
2000+
1000-2000
200-1000
0-200
urban area
0
200 km
0
150 miles